D1311676

Health Science Fundamentals

Exploring Career Pathways

Revised First Edition

Shirley A. Badasch, M.Ed, RN

Doreen S. Chesebro, B.Ed, LVN

Upper Saddle River, New Jersey 07458

Pearson Learning Solutions, 501 Boylston Street, Suite 900, Boston, MA 02116
A Pearson Education Company
www.pearsoned.com

Printed in the United States of America

9 10 11 12 13 V0UD 19 18 17 16 15

000200010270606236

MH/FC

ISBN 10: 0-558-82386-6
ISBN 13: 978-0-558-82386-3

Contents

Contents   **xi**

Procedures

CHAPTER 22 • RESPONSIBILITIES OF A DENTAL ASSISTANT

Preface

Health science educators strive to give students the skills they need to become competent and productive health care workers throughout their careers. The importance of employability skills such as Teamwork, Effective Communication, Professionalism, and Medical Ethics has led us to create *Health Science Fundamentals: Exploring Career Pathways.*

In order to emphasize these career skills, we have divided the text into two parts. The first part, Becoming a Health Care Worker, chapters one through nine, includes the basic information all health care workers must have to attain success in any department within the health care environment.

The second part, Health Care Knowledge and Skills, chapters ten through twenty-two, covers the technical concepts and clinical skills students need to gain employment in a variety of entry-level occupations.

Students can select one occupational area or several occupational areas in Part Two, giving them an opportunity to become a multiskilled health worker. This learning system also provides all areas of training required by the 1987 Omnibus Budget Reconciliation Act (OBRA), it addresses the National Standards, and allows for state differences in curriculum.

We have also created a textbook that emphasizes application of skills by providing students and teachers a number of activities in each chapter.

- Each chapter begins with a **Getting Started** activity that can serve as a "bell-ringer" activity to engage students in the topic at hand.

- **Apply It** activities help students experience real-world health care career situations.

- **Community Service** activities direct students and teachers to ideas for applying their learning within the local community.

- **Math Links**, **Science Links**, and **Language Arts Links** enable students to apply Health Science skills and concepts to their core curriculum courses.

- **Personal Wellness** features connect Health Science topics to student life.

- **Career Connections** give teachers and students ideas for ways to interact with health care workers on the job.

- **What's New?** addresses current Health Science topics, procedures and debates.

Because preventive health is a key component in twenty-first century health care, preventive health care and patient teaching are emphasized throughout *Health Science Fundamentals*. The qualities and values required to become an outstanding health care worker are also interwoven throughout the text and learning system materials. All of the information in this textbook has been carefully reviewed and updated.

The changing requirements for health care present educators and students alike with ever-changing challenges. *Health Science*

Fundamentals: Exploring Career Pathways helps meet the needs of not only the health care system, but all levels of students, from secondary and postsecondary to English as a second language (ESL) students.

New Ways to Learn

Health Science Fundamentals includes additional tools that will aid student instruction with more practice in hands-on exercises and enhanced visual learning, team building, communication, multicultural competence and familiarity with new technology. These features:

- Provide auditory learners with an **Audio Glossary** on the Companion Web site at *www.prenhall.com/badasch*.

- Increase hands-on opportunities with the **Learn by Doing** component at the end of each section.

- Help visual learners with new tables, charts and boxes and hundreds of full color photos and illustrations of concepts and **Procedures**.

- Add clarity by opening every Procedure with a **Background** paragraph that explains the rationale of the activity.

- Give enhanced documentation exposure with **Charting Examples**.

- Enhance the **Thinking Critically** segment at the end of each chapter with new kinds of activities, including those related to patient satisfaction, patient advocacy, time management, and safety.

- Strengthen student portfolios by adding a **Portfolio Tip** at the end of every chapter.

- Broaden the scope of activities away from written reports and toward group role-playing, participatory practice, and peer interactions.

- Include computer- and Web-oriented learning.

- Update content by adding new topics, such as bioterrorism in the disaster-preparedness section.

In addition, *Health Science Fundamentals* gives students and teachers the advantage of easy-to-learn features that include:

- Easy readability to meet the learning needs of all students.

- **Margin Glossary** provides immediate pronunciation and understanding of vocabulary at point of learning.

- **Student Activity Guide** provides additional reinforcement to help in the retention of content and works in tandem with the Student text to help guide students through new material.

- Skills **Check-off Sheets** in the Student Activity Guide are designed for both practice and competency assessment. These Check-Off Sheets provide step-by-step instructions to help students perform Procedures correctly and competently.

- **Portfolio Connection** helps students develop a vocational portfolio to demonstrate job or higher education readiness.

- **Case Studies** encourage students to think critically and apply unit concepts to real-life situations.

- Age-Specific Communication Skills are addressed throughout.

- Medical Math Chapter reviews the basic math concepts which students will need to succeed, such as multiplication, division, percentages, and fractions.

- Mental Illness Chapter focuses on the unique challenges faced by patients who struggle with Alzheimer's, Anxiety and Depression, and substance abuse.

- Focus on end-of-life, hospice, and geriatric care.

- Medical Terminology is addressed throughout the text and workbook, and is the focus of Chapter 10.

- Standard Precautions are highlighted throughout to safeguard the health of both students and patients.

Instructors and students alike will benefit from our complete learning package, which, like the text, has been updated and expanded with new activities and information. This package includes the following products.

Exclusive Wraparound Teacher's Edition

The exclusive Wraparound Teacher's Edition is loaded with content, teaching hints, and resources to help make your job as teacher easier. It contains:

- The complete Student Edition in conjunction with point-of-use teaching notes, strategies, and associated program resources.

- Notes to the teacher to maximize classroom presentation time.

- Customized Instruction throughout to help instruct learners at a variety of skill levels: Less Advanced, More Advanced, and Special Needs.

- Teaching notes include lesson overviews, discussion topics, teaching plans, and troubleshooting tips.

- Skills Extensions challenge students by expanding upon what they are studying.

- Quick Quizzes tap into what students are learning and help identify if students are grasping the material.

- Program resources are clearly identified throughout each lesson.

Teacher's Resource CD-ROM

The Teacher's Resource CD-ROM provides:

- PowerPoint™ presentations to add interest and facilitate learning.
- Worksheet keys for the Student Activity Guide.
- Answer keys for the Chapter Review questions.
- Rubrics for writing activities in Science, Math, and Language Arts Links.
- Transparencies to enhance and facilitate teaching each chapter.
- Transparencies of the Procedures.

Student Activity Guide

The Student Activity Guide provides students with a variety of practice activities that include worksheets, scenarios, activities, and selected check-off sheets designed for both practice and competency assessment. These check-off sheets provide step-by-step instructions to help students perform Procedures correctly and competently. All of these activities will help students successfully learn the skills required for their respective career choices.

Test Bank with Test Gen

A printed Test Bank with Test Gen software is also available as part of our complete learning package.

Lab Activity Manual

Contains check-off sheets for all the Procedures in the Student text, as well as additional Procedures for more advanced and career-specific topics such as Phlebotomist, Sub-Acute Care, Intravenous Therapy, Tracheostomy Care, Electrocardiogram Technician, Central Supply Workers, Environmental Services Technicians, and advanced Dental Assistant skills. A **Lab Activity Teacher's Manual** provides instructor support for the additional Procedures.

Companion Web Site
www.prenhall.com/badasch

The Companion Web site, tied chapter-by-chapter to the text, gives students an on-line study guide that provides immediate feedback and provides links to interesting and relevant sites on the World Wide Web. The Companion Web site shell also enables instructors to create a customized syllabus and download PowerPoint™ slides and transparency masters.

CAREER PATHWAYS FOR STUDENT SUCCESS

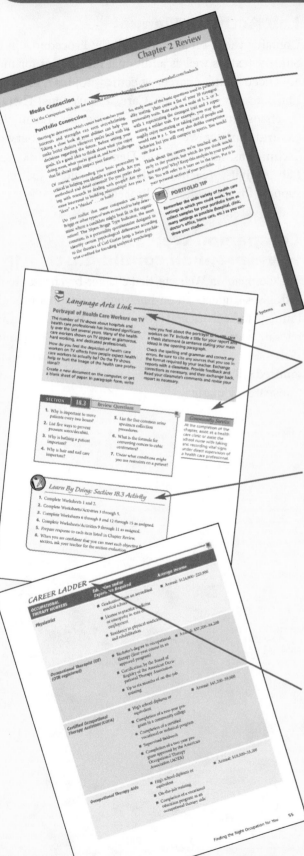

Media Connection

The Companion Web site (www.prenhall.com/badasch) serve as wonderful study companions to your textbook. Each chapter has chapter-related audio glossaries, multiple-choice questions, case studies, and other activities to help you preview and work your way successfully through the chapter. Each chapter ends with a reminder to use the Companion Web site for reviewing, reinforcing, and enriching what you have learned.

Active Learning

Every Chapter includes a multitude of activities to help you understand and apply the concepts and skills you are learning.

Learn by Doing

Every Section ends with a plan to help you effectively use your textbook and Student Activity Guide to review and to reinforce skills and concepts.

Career Ladder

What does it take to become a health care professional? The Career Ladder helps answer this question with an overview of the education/experience requirements for a variety of health careers from all four National Health Care Skill Standards career clusters. This book also covers more than 200 skills and procedures of several representative careers to give you a sense of what health care professionals do in the real world.

PROCEDURES & THE BIG WRAP-UP

Procedures

When performing procedures, it's important to do every step correctly. Brightly colored procedure boxes numbered for easy reference throughout the text clearly outline each Procedure, from beginning to end, step by step. When appropriate, procedures are supported with photos and illustrations. Procedure check-off sheets are found in the Student Activity Guide and the Lab Activity Manual.

Background

A short statement of the reason for the Procedure. The Background tells you the "why" for the "what" you will be doing in the Procedure.

Charting Examples

Gives a sample of how to chart information related to the Procedure so that you can become familiar with documentation.

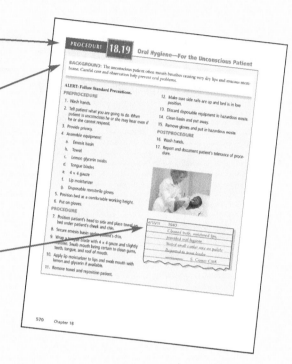

Thinking Critically

These activities will challenge you to do your best thinking and to apply chapter concepts to real-life situations in areas such as medical math, computers, law and ethics, patient education, communication, cultural competency, medical terminology, case studies, patient advocacy, patient satisfaction, time management, and safety.

Portfolio Connection

How do you plan and prepare for a career? Portfolio Connection will help you by encouraging you to create a vocational portfolio that shows your job and/or higher education readiness.

Portfolio Tip

Be sure to consider these practical hints on how you create a successful portfolio.

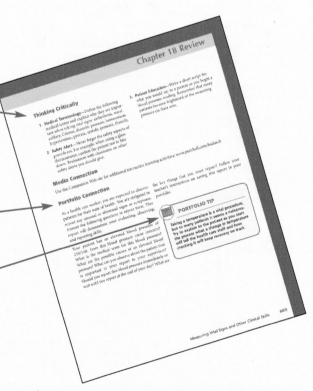

1987 Omnibus Budget Reconciliation Act (OBRA)

To ensure quality care in long-term care (Skilled Nursing) facilities new guidelines were adopted by the Federal Government. These guidelines are known as OBRA. The OBRA Act of 1987 requires that individuals employed in skilled nursing facilities receive training and be evaluated on their skills. OBRA requires a minimum of 16 hours of instruction before resident contact. These are classroom hours and are identified on the following table with an asterisk.

Omnibus Budget Reconciliation Act of 1987 Requirements Health Care Worker Subject Areas That Satisfy All OBRA Requirements

1. Communication and Interpersonal	Chapter 7	Wellness
	Section 2:	Understanding Human Needs
	Topics:	Meeting Needs of Co-Workers and Other Staff
	Section 3:	Cross-Cultural Terms and Principles
	Topics:	Culture and Behavior
		Gestures and Body Language
		Communicating Effectively with Other Cultures
		Folk Medicine
	Chapter 9:	Effective Communications
	Section 1:	Interpersonal Communication for All Ages
	Topics:	Sending a Clear Message
		Elements That Influence Your Relationships with Others
		Barriers to Communication
		Elements of Communication
		Good Listening Skills
		Assertive Communication
		Nonverbal Communication
		Verbal Communication
2. Infection Control	Chapter 17:	Controlling Infection
	Section 1:	The Nature of Microorganisms
	Topics:	Introduction to Microorganisms
		How Microorganisms Affect the Body
		How Microorganisms and Viruses Spread
		Protection from Microorganisms
		Signs and Symptoms of Infection
	Section 2:	Asepsis and Standard Precautions
	Topics:	Introduction to Asepsis
		Standard Precautions
		Controlling the Spread of Infection
	Section 3 :	Transmission-Based Precautions
	Topics:	Introduction to Standard and Transmission-Based Precautions
		Transmission-Based Precaution Rooms
	Section 4:	Bloodborne Diseases and Precautions
	Topics:	Types of Bloodborne Illnesses
		Transmission of Bloodborne Diseases
		Universal Precautions
		Testing for Bloodborne Diseases
		Ethical and Legal Issues

7. Personal Care Skills	Chapter 18:	Measuring Vital Signs and Other Clinical Skills
	Section 3:	Nursing Skills and Assistive and Therapeutic Techniques
	Topics:	Nursing Responsibilities
		Standard Precautions
		Morning and Evening Care (AM and PM Care)
		Skin Management
		Oral Hygiene
		Offering the Urinal and/or Bedpan
		Movement and Ambulation of the Patient
		Positioning and Body Alignment
		Principles of Applying Restraints
		Bathing the Patient
		Care of Hair and Nails
		Shaving the Patient
		Dressing and Undressing the Patient
		Terminal and Postmortem Care
		Prosthetic Devices
		Bedmaking
		Feeding the Patient
		Measuring Intake and Output
		Special Procedures
		Incontinent Patient
		Specimen Collection
	Chapter 19:	Therapeutic Techniques and Sports Medicine
	Section 1:	Therapeutic Techniques and Sports Medicine
	Topics:	Range of Motion
		Guarding Techniques
		Rehabilitation Equipment
8. Mental Health and Social Service Needs	Chapter 5:	Understanding Your Legal Obligations
	Section 2:	Understanding Your Legal Responsibilities
	Topics:	Understanding Your Legal Responsibilities
		Resources for Ensuring Legal Compliance
	Chapter 7:	Wellness
	Seciton 2:	Understanding Human Needs
	Topics:	Meeting Needs of Patients/Clients
		Meeting Needs of Co-Workers and Other Staff
		Defense Mechanisms
	Chapter 14:	Human Growth and Development
	Section 1:	Development and Behavior
	Topic:	Development and Behavior
	Section 2:	Aging and Role Change
	Topic:	Physical Changes in Aging
		Role Changes in People Who Are Aging
	Section 3:	Disabilities and Role Changes
	Topic:	Definition of Health
		Importance of Independence
		Physical Disabilities
		Role Changes in People Who Are Physically or Mentally Challenged

Acknowledgments

This edition is dedicated:
To our many friends and especially our families, who loved us and waited.

The authors wish to express their sincere thanks to the many people who helped develop this book from the outline to the finished product.

- To our families—a warm and loving thanks for their willingness to support us throughout this revision.

- Richmond Ramsey for advising on the Medical Math chapter.

- Sister Suzanne Sassus, Vice-President of Sponsorship, St. Joseph Health System.

- Phyllis Young-Gallagher, R.N. Neonatal and Maternity Health Specialist for Advising on Neonatal and Obstetrics/Maternal Care.

- Gloria Bizjak for reviewing the First Aid Chapter.

- Debby Ferguson, BS, REEG/EPT, RPSGT ASET Board Member & PR Committee

- Representative for the information and editing she provided for the Electroneurodiagnostic Technologist (END techs for short).

- For co-writing Chapter 9, "Effective Communications," acknowledgments go to Monica Maldonado-Puertas, Education Coordinator, Business Bristol Park Medical Group, Inc., Costa Mesa, California.

- For contributing to Chapter 22, "Responsibilities of a Dental Assistant," acknowledgments go to Vivian Muensterman, Baldy View ROP.

- For contributing to Chapters 1, 5, 8, 21 and for writing Chapter 15, "Mental Health," as well as many of the Math Links and Science Links, acknowledgments go to Mollie Ledwith, Martha Currise and the excellent writers at The Publishers Partnership.

- For contributing several new Procedures to the book, Mary Katsaropoulos RN, MSN, CNS.

- Beverly Campbell, for contributing many of the engaging new activities in the book.

- To the reviewers whose suggestions gave us fresh viewpoints on content and contributed to the overall quality of this book.

Beverly Campbell
Retired Administrator, California Department of Education; Co-Founder, National Consortium on Health Science and Technology Education
President, BECGroup Consulting
Cameron Park, CA

Mary Katsaropoulos, RN, MSN, CNS
Former Director of Nursing for the Senior Care Department
Wishard Hospital
Indianapolis, IN

Donna L. Albercht, RN, BSN
Instructor
Sollers Point Tech
Baltimore, MD

Patti Biro, B.S., M.Ed
Director of Health Care Programs
Center of Business and Community Education
Del Mar College
Corpus Christi, TX

Marilyn F. Collins, BSN, RN, PHN
Director of Health Occupations
Citrus College
Glendon, CA

Toni Decklever, RN, BSN
Career and Technical Education
Larramie County School District #1
Cheyenne, WY

Patty Fay Dimetres, RN, BSN, M.Ed, CAGS
Department of Health and Medical Sciences
Fairfax County Public Schools
Fairfax County, VA

Patty K. Leary, M.Ed
Instructor
Mecosta Osceola Career Center
Big Rapids, MI

Regina Lohre
Director of the Academy of Science and Health
Washington High School
Milwaukee, WI

Kathy S. Menezes, RN, MS
WMA Career Technical Center
Cadillac, MI

Debbie Beam, RN, BSN
CTE Instructional Coordinator/Department Chair
South Mecklenburg High School
Charlotte, NC

■ In addition, we'd like to thank members of our National Teacher's Panels:

Bonnie Barnett, Minnesota
Jan Dean, Michigan
Heather Fenton, Oklahoma
Clarice Morris, New York
Debbora Sharifi, Illinois
Kathy Thompson, California
Deb Tracy, California
Sandy Wheeler, Oklahoma
Janet Zimmerman, Indiana

About the Authors

Shirley A. Badasch, M.Ed, RN, is a graduate of California State University at Long Beach. Her career includes acute care nursing, office nursing, industrial nursing, Director of Nursing for a developmentally disabled nursing facility, and Assistant Administrator in Long Term Care. Ms. Badasch's teaching experience includes co-developing the Medical Occupations Program and teaching for nine years in a Regional Occupation Program, and part-time instructor in the Educational Psychology department, California State University at Long Beach. She also taught in the teacher certification program at Cal Poly Pomona and California State University at Sacramento. During her career she worked as a contract consultant to the California State Department of Education, presenting seminars, writing materials, developing programs, and consulting on program development. Ms. Badasch completed her career as the Director of Education for Bristol Park Medical Group. She continues to research and participate in health occupations as a volunteer in her community and as a member of the California Association of Health Career Educators.

Doreen S. Chesebro, B.Ed, LVN, is a graduate of California State University at Long Beach. Her nursing career includes ambulatory care, long-term care and acute care nursing primarily in intensive care and coronary care units. Mrs. Chesebro's teaching experience includes co-developing and teaching the Medical Occupations Program in a Regional Occupation Program. This program includes long-term care nurse assistant, advanced nurse assistant, home health aide, front and back office medical assistant, and hospital health occupations. She also served as a Program Specialist for the Long Beach Unified School District and has experience as a part-time instructor for teacher certification at California State University at Sacramento and Cal Poly Pomona. As Director of Education in the ambulatory care setting, she was responsible for development, implementation and oversight of:

- Disease prevention and management classes through patient education.
- Staff development programs ranging from new employee orientation to management/leadership preparation and mentorship.

Mrs. Chesebro is currently the Director of Mission Services for the ambulatory care setting of the St. Joseph Health System in California's Central Orange County Region. In this position, she coordinates and monitors community outreach programs and works closely with medical and business staff to promote the St. Joseph Health System Mission, Core Values and Vision.

PART I:
BECOMING A HEALTH CARE WORKER

1 Introduction to Being a Health Care Worker

Getting Started

A s you will learn in this chapter, many people have contributed to finding the causes and cures of illness, injuries, and other disabling conditions. Others have identified different body parts and their functions. Some notable discoveries include Louis Pasteur's identification of the process that makes milk safe for human consumption. This process is called pasteurization, in honor of the founder. Bartolommeo Eustachio discovered the tube leading from the ear to the throat, an important finding that was named Eustachian tube after the discoverer. Others include the Salk vaccine to prevent polio (named after Dr. Jonas Salk) and the Roentgen Ray (now called x-ray) after Wilhelm Roentgen the founder.

Assume you could find a cure for, or identify a cause of, a disease or illness such as cancer, childhood arthritis, hepatitis C, autism, or asthma. Write the condition and cure (or cause) on a 3 × 5 card, name, and share your discovery with the class. Why did you choose this particular disease or condition?

SECTION

1.1 | History of Health Care

Background

Health care has developed and changed throughout history. Knowing the history of health care helps you understand current procedures, practices, and philosophies. The experiences and discoveries of the past led to the advances of today. Today's achievements could not have occurred without the trials and errors of the past. When you understand the primitive beginnings of medicine, you appreciate the advances made during the past 5,000 years.

Objectives

When you have completed this section, you will be able to do the following:

- Match key terms with their correct meanings.

- Identify scientists and explain what they contributed to medicine.

- Choose one era in the history of health care and explain how health care technology changed.

- Discuss advances in medicine in the twentieth century.

- Research and report on possible advances in medicine for the twenty-first century.

- Explain the origin of medical ethics and the impact of medical advances on ethics.

- Compare health care in the past with health care in the twentieth and twenty-first centuries.

- Explain current trends in health care.

Early Beginnings

Primitive human beings had no electricity, few tools, and poor shelter. Their time was spent protecting themselves against **predators** and finding food. They were **superstitious** and believed that illness and disease were caused by supernatural spirits. In an attempt to heal, tribal doctors performed ceremonies to **exorcise** evil spirits. One such ceremony involved an early form of **trephining**, whereby the tribal doctor would remove part of the cranium, with a primitive tool, to exorcise demons. They also used herbs and plants as medicines. Some of the same medicines are still used today. Here are some examples:

- Digitalis comes from the foxglove plant. Today it is given in pill form, **intravenously,** or by injection to treat heart conditions. In early times, people chewed the leaves of the foxglove plant to strengthen and slow the heartbeat.

- Quinine comes from the bark of the cinchona tree. It controls fever, relieves muscle spasms, and helps prevent malaria.

- Belladonna and atropine are made from the poisonous nightshade plant. They relieve muscle spasm, especially in gastrointestinal (GI) pain.

- Morphine is made from the opium poppy. It is an effective medication for treating severe pain. It is addicting and used only when nothing else will help.

 ## Medicine in Ancient Times

The Egyptians were the earliest people to keep **accurate** health records. They were superstitious and called upon the gods to heal them. They also learned to identify certain diseases. In the Egyptian culture, the priests acted as physicians. They used medicines to heal disease, learned the art of splinting fractures, and treated disorders by bloodletting with the use of leeches. Interestingly, today, leeches are being used as a treatment to help heal skin grafts and restore blood circulation. Their primary function is to drain blood, since pooled blood around a wound can threaten the healing of tissue.

The ancient Chinese, from as early as the Stone Age, were first to use primitive acupuncture therapies. These early medical pioneers learned to treat a variety of illness and disease with stone tools. Their methods eventually developed into the advanced practice of Chinese acupuncture, still in common use today.

To the ancient Greeks, medicine was considered an art and not just a profession. Physicians had a noble and sacred mission, often housed in sacred temples of healing. They were the first to study the causes of disease and to determine that illnesses may have natural, rather than spiritual, causes. They kept records on what they observed and what they thought caused illness. The Greeks understood the importance of searching for new information about disease. This research helped eliminate superstition. In addition, Greeks further developed the use of massage and herbal therapies.

During ancient times, religious custom did not allow bodies to be dissected. The father of medicine, Hippocrates (ca. 469–377 B.C.), based his knowledge of **anatomy** and physiology on **observation** of the external body. He kept careful notes of the signs and **symptoms** of many diseases. With these records he found that disease

primitive
(PRIM i tiv)
Ancient or prehistoric.

predators
(PRED uh ter)
Organisms or beings that destroy.

superstitious
(soo per STISH uhs)
Trusting in magic or chance.

exorcise
(EK sawr sahyz)
To force out evil spirits.

trephining
(TRAY fin ing)
Surgically removing circular sections (of bone, for example).

intravenously
(in truh VEE nuhs lee)
Directly into a vein.

accurate
(AK yer it)
Exact, correct, or precise.

anatomy
(uh NAT uh mee)
The science dealing with the structure of animals and plants.

observation
(ob zur VEY shuhn)
Act of watching.

symptom
(SIMP tuhm)
A sign or indication of something.

ethics
(ETH iks)
A system of moral principles.

FIGURE 1.1

How did Hippocrates and other Greek and Roman physicians help to develop health care as we know it today?

Courtesy of National Library of Medicine.

  **Apply It**

Divide into groups, each responsible for creating a timeline and researching medical discoveries, inventions, and people of a specific era.

After researching, each group should prepare and present a paper on their findings to the class.

convents
(KON vent s)
Establishments of nuns.

monasteries
(MON uh ster ee)
Homes for men following religious standards.

custodial
(kuh STOH dee uhl)
Marked by watching and protecting rather than seeking to cure.

was not caused by supernatural forces. Hippocrates wrote the standard of **ethics** called the Oath of Hippocrates. This standard is the basis for today's medical ethics. Physicians still take this oath.

The Greeks observed and measured the effects of disease. They found that some disease was caused by lack of sanitation. The Romans learned from the Greeks and developed a sanitation system. They brought clean water into their cities by way of aqueducts (waterways). They built sewers to carry off waste. They also built public baths with filtering systems. This was the beginning of public health and sanitation.

The Romans were the first to organize medical care. They sent medical equipment and physicians with their armies to care for wounded soldiers. Roman physicians kept a room in their houses for the ill. This was the beginning of hospitals. (**Figure 1.1**) Public buildings for the care of the sick were established. Physicians were paid by the Roman government. It is interesting to note that the Roman physician wore a death mask. This mask had a spice-filled beak, which the Romans believed protected them from infection and bad odors.

The Dark Ages (A.D. 400–800) and the Middle Ages (A.D. 800–1400)

When the Roman Empire was conquered by the Huns (nomads from the north), the study of medical science stopped. For a period of 1,000 years, medicine was practiced only in **convents** and **monasteries**. Because the Church believed that life and death were in God's hands, the monks and priests had no interest in how the body functioned. The primary treatment was prayer. Medication consisted of herbal mixtures, and care was **custodial**. Monks collected and translated the writings of the Greek and Roman physicians.

🧪 *Science Link*

Lyme Disease

If not for modern day medicine and scientific research, the United States may have experienced an epidemic situation with Lyme disease.

The first case of Lyme disease was reported in Old Lyme, Connecticut in 1975. Since then, cases of Lyme disease have been reported in most parts of the United States. However, this disease can be detected by a blood test and treated with antibiotics. If caught early enough, Lyme disease may cause little or no complications.

Lyme disease is caused by a bacteria carried by ticks. The ticks contract the bacteria by biting a mouse or deer infected with Lyme disease.

Humans contract the disease if bitten by an infected tick. Initial symptoms may include a rash around the area of the bite and flu-like symptoms, including, chills, fever, fatigue, and body aches. If the infection is not treated, it can cause severe joint pain and neurological deficiencies and even heart related problems.

Meningitis (inflammation of the tissues around the brain and spinal chord), Bell's palsy (loss of muscle tone in the face), and numbness in limbs are some of the more severe effects of Lyme disease. In the most severe cases, paralysis can occur.

Why is it beneficial to study the history of health care and how it has progressed into modern day medicine and health care practices?

Terrible **epidemics** caused millions of deaths during this period. Bubonic plague (the black death) alone killed 60 million people. Other uncontrolled diseases included smallpox, diphtheria, syphilis, and tuberculosis. Today, these illnesses are not always life threatening. Scientists have discovered **vaccines** and medications to control these diseases. It is important to remember that some diseases can become epidemic if people are not vaccinated.

epidemics
(ep i DEM ik)
Diseases affecting many people at the same time.

vaccines
(VAK seen z)
A weakened bacteria or virus given to a person to build immunity against a disease.

The Renaissance (A.D. 1350–1650)

The Renaissance period saw the rebirth of learning. During this period, new scientific progress began. There were many developments during this period:

- The building of universities and medical schools for research.
- The search for new ideas about disease rather than the unquestioning acceptance of disease as the will of God.
- The acceptance of **dissection** of the body for study.
- The development of the printing press and the publishing of books, allowing greater access to knowledge from research.
- These changes influenced the future of medical science.

dissection
(di SEK shuhn)
Act or process of dividing, taking apart.

The Sixteenth and Seventeenth Centuries

The desire for learning that began during the Renaissance continued through the next two centuries. During this time, several outstanding scientists added new knowledge. Here are some examples:

- Leonardo da Vinci studied and recorded the anatomy of the body. See da Vinci's depiction of the human body in **Figure 1.2.**

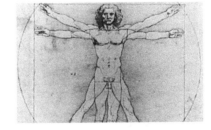

- William Harvey used this knowledge to understand **physiology**, and he was able to describe the circulation of blood and the pumping of the heart.
- Gabriele Fallopius discovered the fallopian tubes of the female anatomy.
- Bartolommeo Eustachio discovered the tube leading from the ear to the throat (Eustachian tube).
- Antonie van Leeuwenhoek (1632–1723) invented the microscope, establishing that there is life smaller than the eye can see. Van Leeuwenhoek scraped his teeth and found the bacteria that causes tooth decay. Although it was not yet realized, the germs that cause disease were now visible.
- Apothecaries, early pharmacies, started in this time. In medieval England, these apothecaries engaged in a flourishing trade in drugs and spices from the East.

Unfortunately **quackery,** mass death from childbed fever, and disease continued. The causes of infection and disease were still not understood. Interestingly, infections are, even today, one of the leading causes of death.

FIGURE 1.2
Human body as depicted by Leonardo da Vinci. (Courtesty of Galleria Dell' Accademia.) How does the figure illustrate Leonardo da Vinci's contribution to the medical field?

physiology
(fiz ee OL uh jee)
The branch of biology dealing with the functions and activities of living organisms and their parts.

quackery
(KWAK uh ree)
Practice of pretending to cure diseases.

The Eighteenth Century

Many discoveries were made in the eighteenth century that required a new way of teaching medicine. Students not only attended lectures in the classroom and laboratory, but also observed patients at the bedside. When a patient died, they dissected the body and were able to observe the disease process. This led to a better understanding of the causes of illness and death. Also, in the eighteenth century a wider range of students was studying medicine. In 1849, Elizabeth Blackwell (1821–1910) became the first female physician in the United States. The study of physiology continued, and more new discoveries were made:

- René Laënnec (1781–1826) invented the **stethoscope.** The first stethoscope was made of wood. It increased the ability to hear the heart and lungs, allowing doctors to determine if disease was present.

- Joseph Priestley discovered the element oxygen. He also observed that plants refresh air that has lost its oxygen, making it usable for **respiration.**

- Benjamin Franklin's (1706–1790) discoveries affect us in many ways. His discoveries include bifocals, and he found that colds could be passed from person to person.

- Edward Jenner (1749–1823) discovered a method of vaccination for smallpox. Smallpox killed many people in epidemics. His discovery saved millions of lives. His discovery also led to immunization and to preventive medicine in public health.

The Nineteenth and Twentieth Centuries

Medicine continued to progress rapidly, and the nineteenth century was the beginning of the organized advancement of medical science. Important events during the nineteenth and twentieth centuries include the following:

- Ignaz Semmelweis identified the cause of childbed fever (puerperal fever). Large numbers of women died from this fever after giving birth. Semmelweis noted that the patients of midwives (women who delivered babies but were not physicians) had fewer deaths. One of the differences in the care given by the physicians and the midwives was that the physicians went to the "dead room," where they dissected dead bodies. These physicians did not wash their hands or change their aprons before they delivered babies. Their hands were dirty, and they infected the women. Semmelweis realized what was happening, but other physicians laughed at him. Eventually, his studies were proved correct by others, and handwashing and cleanliness became an accepted practice. Today, handwashing is still one of the most important ways that we control the spread of infection.

- Louis Pasteur (1822–1895), known as the "Father of **Microbiology**," discovered that tiny **microorganisms** were everywhere. Through his experiments and studies, he proved that microorganisms cause disease. Before this discovery, doctors thought that microorganisms were *created by* disease. He also discovered that heating milk prevented the growth of bacteria. **Pasteurization** kills bacteria in milk. We still use this method to treat milk today. He created a vaccine for rabies in 1885.

stethoscope
(STETH uh skohp)
Instrument used to hear sound in the body (e.g., heartbeat, lung sounds, bowel sounds).

respiration
(res pu REY shuhn)
The inhalation and exhalation of air, or breathing.

microbiology
(mahy kroh bahy OL uh jee)
The branch of biology dealing with the structure, function, uses, and modes of existence of microscopic organisms.

microorganisms
(mahy kroh AWR guh niz uhms)
Organisms so small that they can only be seen through a microscope.

pasteurization
(PAS chuh rahyz)
To heat food for a period of time to destroy certain microorganisms.

- Joseph Lister (1827–1912) learned about Pasteur's discovery that microorganisms cause infection. He used carbolic acid on wounds to kill germs that cause infection. He became the first doctor to use an **antiseptic** during surgery. Using an antiseptic during surgery helped prevent infection in the incision.

- Ernst von Bergmann developed **asepsis**. He knew from Lister's and Pasteur's research that germs caused infections in wounds. He developed a method to keep an area germ-free before and during surgery. This was the beginning of asepsis.

- Robert Koch (1843–1910) discovered many disease-causing organisms. He developed the culture plate method to identify pathogens and also isolated the bacterium that causes tuberculosis. He also introduced the importance of cleanliness and sanitation in preventing the spread of disease.

- Wilhelm Roentgen (1845–1923) discovered x-rays in 1895. He took the very first picture using x-rays of his wife's hand. His discovery allowed doctors to see inside the body and helped them discover what was wrong with the patient.

- Paul Ehrlich discovered the effect of medicine on disease-causing microorganisms. His treatment was effective against some microorganisms but was not effective in killing other bacteria. His discoveries brought about the use of chemicals to fight disease. In his search to find a chemical to treat syphilis, he completed 606 experiments. On the 606th experiment, he found a treatment that worked.

antiseptic
(an tuh SEP tik)
Substance that slows or stops the growth of microorganisms.

asepsis
(uh SEP sis)
Sterile condition, free from all germs.

Before the nineteenth century, pain was a serious problem. Surgery was performed on patients without **anesthesia**. Early physicians used herbs, hashish, and alcohol to help relieve the pain of surgery. They even choked patients to cause unconsciousness to stop pain. Many patients died from shock and pain. During the nineteenth and twentieth centuries, nitrous oxide (for dental care), ether, and chloroform were discovered. These drugs have the ability to put people into a deep sleep so that they do not experience pain during surgery. The knowledge of asepsis and the ability to prevent pain during surgery are the basis of safe, painless surgery today.

anesthesia
(an uhs THEE zhuh)
Loss of feeling or sensation.

Scientists and physicians kept learning from the discoveries of the past. They continued to study and research new ways to treat diseases, illness, and injury. Some of the most important discoveries in the late 19th and 20th centuries included:

- Gerhard Domagk discovered sulfonamide compounds. These compounds were the first medications effective in killing bacteria. They changed the practice of medicine by killing deadly diseases.

- In 1892 in Russia, Dmitri Ivanovski discovered that some diseases are caused by microorganisms that cannot be seen with a microscope. They are called viruses. These viruses were not studied until the electron microscope was invented in Germany. These are some of the diseases caused by viruses:

  - Poliomyelitis.
  - Rabies.
  - Measles.
  - Influenza.
  - Chicken pox.
  - German measles.
  - Herpes zoster.
  - Mumps.

- Sigmund Freud (1836–1939) (Figure 1.3) discovered the conscious and unconscious parts of the mind. He studied the effects of the unconscious mind on the body. He determined that the mind and body work together. This led to an understanding of psychosomatic illness (physical illness caused by emotional conflict). His studies were the basis of **psychology** and **psychiatry**.

- Sir Alexander Fleming (1881–1955) found that penicillin killed life-threatening bacteria. The discovery of penicillin is considered one of the most important discoveries of the twentieth century. Before penicillin was discovered, people died of illnesses that we consider curable today, including pneumonia, gonorrhea, and blood poisoning.

- Jonas Salk (1914–1995) discovered that a dead polio virus would cause immunity to poliomyelitis. This virus paralyzed thousands of adults and children every year. It seemed to attack the most active and athletic people. It was a feared disease, and the discovery of the vaccine saved many people from death or crippling.

- In contrast to Salk's virus, Albert Sabin (1906–1993) used a live polio virus vaccine, which is more effective. This vaccine is used today to immunize babies against this dreaded disease.

- Francis Crick and James Watson discovered the molecular structure of DNA, based on its known double helix. Their model served to explain how DNA **replicates** and how hereditary information is coded on it. This set the stage for the rapid advances in molecular biology that continue to this day. In 1962, they won the Nobel Prize in Medicine for this discovery.

- Christian Barnard performed the first successful heart transplant in 1968.

- Ben Carson continues to be a pioneer in separating Siamese twins and performing hemispherectomies, surgeries on the brain to stop seizures.

The discovery of methods to control whooping cough, diphtheria, measles, tetanus, and smallpox saved many lives. These diseases kill unprotected children and adults. It is important for everyone to be immunized. Immunizations are available from doctors, clinics, hospitals, and public health services.

The Twenty-First Century

Our society is discovering new approaches to medical care every year. Patients/clients are being taught more about wellness, and they are learning more about self-care. The word healthy no longer just refers to a person's physical health. It also refers to a person's emotional, social, mental, and spiritual wellness. To help patients achieve this kind of holistic health, the medical community has become more open to alternative and complementary methods of care. People now go to ayurvedic practitioners, Chinese medicine practitioners, chiropractors, homeopaths, hypnotists, and naturopaths to help meet their medical needs. We will discuss these health care approaches and professions in greater detail in Chapter 7.

Family and friends are learning patient care skills, including how to perform detailed procedures. Nurses and technicians are visiting patients/clients at home or caring for them in an ambulatory care setting. Just a few years ago, patients were admitted to the hospital for surgery and recovered in the hospital over a period of several days. Today, many patients enter the hospital, have surgery, and are sent home the same day.

Doctors are now often practicing telemedicine. Health care providers may now e-mail, fax, or telephone important medical information to a patient or another health care provider. This has improved patient care by supplying health providers and patients with quicker access to information and greater opportunities for communication. **Telemedicine** includes consultative, diagnostic, and treatment services.

People are living longer and are usually healthier. New inventions and procedures have changed medicine as we once knew it. Here are some examples:

- The possibility of eliminating disabling disease through genetic research.
- The ability to transplant organs from a donor to a **recipient**.
- The ability to reattach severed body parts.
- The use of computers to aid in diagnosis, accurate record keeping, and research.
- The ability to use **noninvasive** techniques for diagnosis.
- The advancement in caring for the unborn fetus.
- The rediscovery and the medical profession's greater acceptance of alternative medicine and complementary medical practice including acupuncture, acupressure, herbal therapy, and healing touch.

Every day, science makes new progress. We are living in a time of great advancement and new understanding in medicine. People are living longer, creating a need to better understand **geriatric** medicine. This and OBRA—The Omnibus Budget Reconciliation Act passed in 1987 to provide a checklist for nursing home care facilities—will be covered in greater detail in Chapter 5. In addition, new types of facilities such as assisted living centers are being developed to better meet the physical, emotional, and mental needs of senior citizens. Frontiers in medical science include hope for treatment and cures for diabetes, cancer, AIDS, multiple sclerosis, arthritis, and muscular dystrophy.

telemedicine
(TEL uh med uh sin)
Using electronic communications to exchange medical information from one site to another for the health and education of the patient or health care provider.

recipient
(ri SIP ee uhnt)
One who receives.

noninvasive
(non in VEY siv)
Not involving penetration of the skin.

geriatric
(jer ee A trik)
Pertaining to old age.

 Language Arts Link

Medical Treatments: From Ancient Times through Present Day

As you read in this chapter, medical practices, beliefs, and equipment has changed significantly over time. But, some methods—such as the use of some medicinal herbs and plants—that were used thousands of years ago are still being used today.

You need to create a report highlighting major medical practices and beliefs since ancient times. The Internet is a good place to start your research, but always be careful of information you find on the Internet. Use safe Internet practices, and make sure your sources are reliable and authoritative. Another good place to do research is in a library.

Create a new document on the computer, or get a blank sheet of paper. Include a title for your

report and a thesis statement (a sentence stating your main ideas) in the opening paragraph. Be sure to include information on ancient civilizations, the dark ages, the Middle Ages, the Renaissance, and the 16th–21st Centuries.

Proofread your work to see if you can improve it by making it clearer, more concise, or more interesting to read. Check the spelling and grammar and correct any errors. Be sure to cite any sources that you use in the format required by your teacher. Exchange reports with a classmate. Provide feedback and corrections as necessary, and then exchange back. Read your classmate's comments and revise your report as necessary.

🖼 The Advancement of Nursing

In the nineteenth century, nursing became an important part of medical care. In 1860, Florence Nightingale (1820–1910) attracted well-educated, dedicated women to the Nightingale School of Nursing. (**Figure 1.4**) The graduates from this school raised the standards of nursing, and nursing became a respectable profession.

FIGURE 1.4
Florence Nightingale, founder of modern nursing. What effect did Florence Nightingale's work have on the medical field?

Before this time, nursing was considered unsuitable for a respectable lady. The people giving care to patients were among the lowest in society—"too old, too weak, too drunken, too dirty, or too bad to do anything else."

Florence Nightingale came from a cultured, middle-class family who opposed her interest in caring for the ill. However, she convinced her father to give her money to live, and she gained experience by volunteering in hospitals. During the Crimean War, she took a group of 38 women to care for soldiers dying from cholera. More soldiers were dying from cholera than from war injuries. She became a legend while she was there because of her dedication to nursing.

After the war she devoted much of her life to preparing reports on the need for better sanitation and construction and management of hospitals. Her primary goal was to gain effective training for nurses. The public established a Nightingale fund to pay for the training, protection, and living costs of nurses. This was established in recognition of her services to the military during the Crimean War.

FIGURE 1.5
Clara Barton, founder of the Red Cross. What experiences led Clara Barton to establish the American Red Cross?

She also designed a hospital ward that improved the environment and care of the patients. Prior to this time, patients were crowded into small areas that were often dirty. The ward that she designed allowed for a limited number of beds, permitted circulation of air, had windows on three sides, and was clean.

During this time, Clara Barton (1821–1912) served as a volunteer nurse in the American Civil War. (**Figure 1.5**) After the war, she established a bureau of records to help search for missing men. She also assisted in the organization of military hospitals in Europe during the Franco-Prussian War.

Barton campaigned for the United Sates to sign the Treaty of Geneva, which produced relief for sick and wounded soldiers. These experiences led her to establish the American Red Cross in 1881 and to serve as its first president.

Another step forward in the field of nursing was contributed by Lillian Wald (1867–1940). She was an American public health nurse and social reformer. She established the Henry Street Settlement in New York to bring nursing care into the homes of the poor. This led to the Visiting Nurse Service of New York. Today, visiting nurse services are found in most communities.

Patient Care Today

Nursing care has changed many times throughout the years. Patients have been cared for by teams that included a registered nurse as team leader, a licensed vocational nurse or practical nurse (LVN/LPN) as a medication nurse, and a nursing assistant who provided personal care. In primary care nursing, which followed team nursing, all patient care was provided by a registered nurse.

Today, unlicensed assistive caregivers are part of the patient caregiver team. There are many titles and new job descriptions for these positions, including clinical partner, service partner, nurse extender, health care assistant, and patient care assistant. These new positions extend the role of entry-level employees. The nurse assistant performs additional tasks, such as **phlebotomy** and recording an electrocardiogram (EKG). Employees from departments other than nursing learn patient care skills. Environmental service workers and food service workers may help with serving food and providing some routine patient care. The registered nurse delegates patient care tasks according to the training and expertise of the assistive personnel.

Because of the scientific advances in health care the role of the nurse has evolved into a more technological role. This has created a need for a complex mix of the technological nurse and the holistic caregiver. Never before has it been more important to maintain the art of nursing which includes compassion, comfort, and the ability to see the patient as an individual and a member of a family and a community.

phlebotomy
(fluh BOT uh mee)
Practice of opening a vein by incision or puncture to remove blood.

 Language Arts Link

Historical Contributions

Today we would never expect a doctor to examine us with a wooden stethoscope or for surgery to be performed without anesthesia, but, as you learned in this chapter, that wasn't always the case.

Select a medical device, procedure, or person who made an important contribution to health care. Begin your task by searching library resources or the Internet to learn more about your topic. Record the details and facts that you find. Be sure to cite any sources that you use in the format required by your teacher.

Create a new document on the computer, or get a blank sheet of paper. Write a descriptive title for your report. In paragraph form detail what you learned about your subject. Be sure to proofread your work to see if you can improve it by making it clearer, more concise, or more interesting to read. Check the spelling and grammar and correct any errors. Exchange reports with a classmate. Provide feedback and corrections as necessary, and then exchange back. Read your classmate's comments and revise your report as necessary.

If there is a Biotechnology Company in your community, ask for a group tour that focuses on the different processes necessary for inventing a new pharmaceutical product and getting it to market.

If there is no Biotechnology Company in your community, you may (1) complete an Internet search of a leading company to identify the process that is used to develop a new pharmaceutical product; or (2) assist as a guide for a museum that has a display of the evolution of medical practices, or the "Body Works" or "Body Relevant" displays that are traveling around the country.

A Look Back and an Overview of the Future

In the twentieth and twenty-first centuries, medicine has made great strides in improving health care. During these centuries, we have experienced many changes, including these:

- Antibiotics for bacterial diseases.
- Improved life expectancy.
- Organ transplants.
- Healthier hearts (reduced smoking, better diets).
- Dentistry without pain.
- Noninvasive diagnosis with computers (CAT, MRI).
- End of smallpox.
- Childhood immunizations.
- New understanding of DNA and genetics.
- Control of diabetes with the discovery of insulin.
- Decline in polio.
- Medical machines, such as those for kidney dialysis and the heart-lung machine.
- Test tube babies.
- HMOs provided an alternative to private insurance, and hospice was organized.

The future of medicine holds many promises for better health. Current and future research will provide us with many new advances, including these:

- Cure for AIDS.
- Decrease in the cases of malaria, influenza, leprosy, and African sleeping sickness.
- Cure for genetically transferred diseases (e.g., Tay-Sachs, muscular dystrophy, multiple sclerosis, cerebral palsy, Alzheimer's, lupus).
- Improved treatment for arthritis and the common cold.
- Isolation of the gene that causes depression.
- Use of electronics to allow disabled persons to walk.
- Nutritional therapy to decrease the number of cases of schizophrenia.

Medical Ethics

Advancement in medicine creates new problems. How will the recipient of an organ be chosen? Who will be allowed to receive experimental drugs? How will the creation of in vitro embryos be ethically managed? Is it ethical to provide continuing confidentiality about AIDS patients, or should they be required to report their condition? Does a terminally ill patient have the right to assisted death (euthanasia)? There are many questions now, and there will be more questions in the future as health care changes.

Summary

You have learned that the science of health care has grown and developed over the last 5,000 years. These changes increased the average life expectancy. Our standards of living improved with the progress of medical science. The dedication of the many scientists discussed in this section is responsible for the improvements in health care that we enjoy today. Their research is the foundation of the high technology that is developing in medicine.

SECTION **1.1** **Review Questions**

1. What did early human beings believe caused illness and disease?

2. Who were the first people to organize medical care?

3. Name two ways that medical progress was made during the Renaissance period.

4. Which discoveries in the nineteenth and twentieth centuries led to safer surgeries?

5. How does technology continue to improve medical care today?

6. Explain how society's view of women in medicine has changed over the years.

 # What's New?

New Vaccines

In the eighteenth century, Edward Jenner discovered a method of vaccination for smallpox that helped to end the epidemic. In the twenty-first century, doctors and scientists continue to do research to develop vaccines for diseases and illnesses.

While today's adults received only a few vaccines for illnesses such as measles, mumps, and rubella, when they were children, today's children are offered a variety of vaccines. One such vaccine is Varivax. This vaccine helps to prevent, or at least lessen, the effects of chicken pox. In previous generations, children had to suffer the uncomfortable symptoms of this virus. The vaccine gives today's children some degree of protection.

Other new vaccines now offered to children are Gardasil, a vaccine developed to protect girls from getting cervical cancer when they get older, and Menactra, a vaccine developed to prevent children from getting meningitis.

How might these new vaccines affect people's lives and the cost of health care?

Learn By Doing: Section 1.1 Activity

1. Complete Worksheet 1 from the Student Activity Guide.

2. Complete Worksheet 2 and Worksheet/Activity 3.

3. Ask your teacher for directions to complete Worksheets/Activities 4, 5, 6, and 7.

4. When you are confident that you can meet each objective listed above, ask your teacher for the section evaluation.

SECTION

1.2

Becoming a Health Care Worker

Background

A health care worker is a well-trained professional whose top concern is patient welfare. Health care workers must have a thorough knowledge of current health procedures. They must maintain a professional appearance and practice professional behavior. They must also safeguard the confidentiality of patient information. You must keep in mind all of these standards of behavior as you become a health care worker.

Objectives

When you have completed this section, you will be able to do the following:

- Match key terms with their correct meanings.

- Discuss the importance of proper health care training.

- Describe the proper appearance for a health care worker.

- Discuss standards of behavior.

- Discuss the importance of confidentiality when working with patient records.

 Health Care Education

professional
(pro FESH uh nuhl)
One who is paid for their work.

accredited
(a KRED dit ted)
Attested and approved as meeting prescribed standards.

When you have decided to become a health **professional**, it is important to choose a quality health care education program that fits your interests. Technical, community, or four-year colleges in your area may have **accredited** health care programs. These programs offer a variety of degrees, including:

- Certification, where a person is certified as being able to competently complete a job, usually by the passing of an examination. (Note: Levels of certification, licensure, and accreditation are covered in depth in Chapter 3.)

- Associates degree, usually awarded after completion of a 2-year program.

- Bachelor's degree, usually awarded after completion of a 4-year program.
- Master's degree, a post-graduate degree awarded after completion of a 1 to 6-year program.
- Doctoral degree, or doctorate, is a post-graduate degree that is the highest certificate of membership in the academic community.

Visit Web sites of schools that offer health care education to see which program appeals to you most. Visit each college and talk to students before you enroll. You may also talk to health professionals in local clinics or hospitals to find out where they received their education.

After enrolling in a health care program, be sure to work hard at your studies. Health care information can be complicated and detailed. It is important for you to learn all procedures correctly, so you can provide the best treatment to patients.

Health care procedures and knowledge change all the time. Even after you are employed as a health care professional, it is important for you to continue your education. Take any training sessions that are provided by your health care facility. Read professional journals to learn about new health breakthroughs. Discuss procedures with other health care professionals in your facility, to make sure you are all providing the most up-to-date treatment.

Continuing education credits (CEUs) are required for maintenance of certification or advancement in many positions. This is to insure that health care professionals stay current on developments in their fields to provide the best patient care.

In the health care field, there is a rise among multicompetent workers. Multicompetent workers are trained in one field or occupation and then receive additional education to work in a second field or occupation. In addition, another opportunity in health care professions is that of the **entrepreneur**. The entrepreneur organizes, manages, and assumes the risks of a business. In the health care field, entrepreneurs often work under the direction of a physician or dentist.

entrepreneur
(ahn truh pruh NUR)
A person who organizes and manages a business.

Appearance and Hygiene

A professional **appearance** makes a statement about your **commitment** to patient care. A well-groomed and well-dressed staff signals that everyone in the facility is interested in the welfare of the patient. A clean appearance reassures patients who may be anxious and sick that the staff is efficient, professional, and capable of providing necessary medical service. The following are **recommendations** for maintaining a well-groomed, professional appearance:

1. Dress according to your facility's dress code, including uniform. This usually means that clothes will be clean, neat, and in good repair. They should not be of extreme fashion. Undergarments should match the body color, so as not to "show." When wearing a skirt, wear full-length hose without runs.

2. Keep jewelry to a minimum (e.g., watch, stud earrings, and a ring). Jewelry can cause injury to the patient and the professional (if the patient grabs on to it), as well as transmit germs. Body piercings do not indicate a professional appearance, and can cause infections.

3. Wear your name badge every day, in view of patients/clients. People need to be able to relate to you, and to call you if they need you. It also helps them identify who is assisting them.

appearance
(uh PEER ents)
The way someone or something looks.

commitment
(kuh MIT ment)
A pledge or promise.

recommendations
(rek uh men DAY shuns)
Suggestions.

hygiene
(HI jean)
The practice of
keeping clean.

Community Service

Present a fashion show of what to wear (or not wear) in a professional setting. The narrator can provide information as to why the look is appropriate or inappropriate. The student models will represent each look. This can be video-taped, or you may be able to present your fashion show at a local long-term care facility or hospital.

Apply It

Working in pairs, or teams of three, role-play personal traits, such as empathy and patience, in a medical scenario. Make up 3 × 5 cards with each characteristic listed on page 19, and a variety of career choices (veterinarian, EMT, dentist, etc.), and pick an assignment. The observing students need to identify which trait is being acted out and which career is being portrayed.

4. Wear clean and appropriate shoes every day.

5. Keep your hair clean.

6. Follow rules of good **hygiene**:

    a. Brush your teeth at least twice a day.

    b. Floss daily.

    c. Use mouthwash or breath mints.

    d. Bathe daily.

    e. Use unscented deodorant. Remember that odors can be offensive to patients that are ill and nauseated and some patients may be allergic to perfumes and deodorant.

    f. Wear your hair up and off your collar. You do not want your hair to fall on a patient when working with them, nor do you want to block their view

Female

7. Keep makeup conservative (e.g., no dark, heavy makeup).

8. Do not use perfume or cologne, for the same reason as you would use unscented deodorant.

9. Keep nails short, clean, and bare or only use light-colored nail polish. Long nails can scratch a patient. Polish can cover up dirt and can chip and contaminate a patient's wound or dressing.

Male

10. Do not use cologne or strong aftershave, for the same reason as you would use unscented deodorant.

11. Keep beard or mustache neatly trimmed.

12. Shave daily. No stubble!

We will discuss the personal appearance and good health of health care professionals in greater detail in Chapter 4.

FIGURE 1.6
Health care workers should be well-groomed and professional. Why do the health care workers in the photograph appear professional?

Standards of Behavior

As a health care worker, you should always behave professionally. By practicing the following set of behaviors, you show respect for patients and your fellow health care workers:

1. Maintain a calm, **courteous** manner.
2. Listen carefully when patients or other health care workers are speaking with you.
3. Monitor patients appropriately, in order to ensure their safety.
4. Perform tasks efficiently and carefully.
5. Do not gossip about patients or other health care workers.
6. Do not use coarse or offensive language.
7. Do not practice horseplay or other dangerous behaviors.
8. Watch for hazardous situations and correct any hazards that you see.
9. Follow all safety procedures that are required by your health care facility.

 ## Personal Characteristics

In addition to professional behavior, health care workers who exhibit the following personal characteristics will be more involved and interested in the welfare of their patients and in being a critical part of the medical team:

1. Empathy—the action of understanding, being aware of, being sensitive to, and experiencing the feelings, thoughts, and experiences of another.
2. Honesty—the quality, condition, or characteristic of being fair, truthful, and morally upright.
3. Dependability—to be reliable or trustworthy.
4. Willingness to learn—the openness to admit that you don't know the answer or that you can be helped to understand a situation more fully.
5. Patience—the ability to put up with waiting, delay, or provocation without becoming annoyed or upset, or to act calmly when faced with difficulties.
6. Acceptance of criticism—the ability to deal with disapproval or a suggestion that something can be improved.
7. Enthusiasm—excited interest in or eagerness to do something.
8. Self-motivation—energetic, ambitious and able to get things done without being directed by others.
9. Tact—ability to avoid giving offense; an intuitive sense of what is right or appropriate.
10. Competence—the ability to do something well, measured against a standard, especially ability acquired through experience or training.
11. Responsibility—accountability; the state of being accountable to somebody or for something.
12. Discretion—tact; the good judgment and sensitivity needed to avoid embarrassing or upsetting others.
13. Team player—somebody who works cooperatively; a member of a group who cooperates with other people and who subordinates personal interests in order to achieve a common goal.

courteous
(KUR tee us)
Polite.

Personal Goals

Wanting or needing something can be a strong motivator, which encourages you to set goals and make decisions that will lead to your happiness and well-being. A goal is a plan to obtain something. You might set a goal to obtain a specific thing—such as a new jacket or a special phone. You might set a goal to achieve a position—such as soloist in the chorus or soccer team captain. Goals help you focus on what is really important to you and what you are willing to work for.

Long-term goals are plans that help you focus on what you want a year from now, or even 5 or 10 years from now. Short-term goals can be achieved in a shorter amount of time. For example, improving your tennis serve is a short-term goal you may be able to achieve within a few weeks or a few months. Becoming certified to work as a pharmacist is a long-term goal that will take years to achieve.

List two or three short-term goals for yourself. What steps will you need to take to achieve your goals?

Body Language

Every move that we make sends a message. Positive messages come from good eye contact, smiling, and paying close attention to the person we are interacting with. Negative messages cause the person with whom we interact to doubt the efficiency of the staff responsible for patient care.

1. Make eye contact with patients as they enter the health care facility. This will make them feel welcome.

2. **Maintain** eye contact as you **converse** with patients. This will let them know you are interested in hearing what they have to say.

3. Smile. Let people know that you're friendly.

4. Keep an open **stance**. (Crossed arms or hands indicate an unwillingness to listen or a barrier in communication.)

5. Give your full attention to one patient at a time, even when you have multiple tasks (e.g., telephone, other patients).

6. Keep your hands away from your mouth when speaking. This makes it a more "open" exchange.

7. Sit or stand at eye level with patients as you converse. Avoid standing over patients when conversing.

Maintaining Confidentiality

Maintaining the **confidentiality** of medical records is critical. Medical records contain private information that must not be shared with people who are not involved in the patient's health care. If some private information gets into the wrong hands, it may be used to damage the patient's personal reputation or financial well-being.

Each patient signs a confidentiality form before receiving treatment. This form is a legally binding document that promises that the medical facility will protect patient information. Any health care worker who does not follow procedures to ensure patient confidentiality may be **reprimanded**.

As a health care worker, you should learn your health care facility's policies and procedures related to confidentiality. Carefully follow these procedures to protect patient privacy.

Summary

In this section, you learned the professional appearance of a health care worker shows his or her commitment to patient care and the practice of professional behavior shows respect to patients. Confidentiality is an important part of staying within legal boundaries, and, as a health care worker, it is your responsibility to ensure patient confidentiality by learning your facility's policies and procedures.

Language Arts Link

Managing Your Time

Time management is a key skill in any area of study. Managing your time successfully is a matter of organizing and prioritizing what you need to get accomplished. Two handy tools for managing your time are "To Do" Lists and Planners.

"To Do" Lists: Sometimes it is helpful to write down all the things you have to do. That way you can prioritize what you have to take care of immediately and what can wait. Sometimes the process of writing your tasks down makes them seem more manageable. And, you get the satisfaction of crossing each task off as you complete them!

Weekly/Monthly Planners: Having a big picture of all your classes, appointments, and social obligations in one place is a great way to organize your time. Write down what you have to do—and where you have to be—for each day of the week. You can create a calendar page on the computer. Or, sketch it out using a ruler and paper.

Create a "To Do" list for tasks you need to complete for the next month. Sometimes it's most productive to just brainstorm all of the things you need to do and then prioritize them later. Once you've completed your draft "To Do" list, reorganize the list ranking things according to importance.

Either create a calendar page on the computer, or draw one on a paper using a ruler and pencil. (You can also find blank calendar pages on the Internet. Search on key words such as "Calendar.") Fill in all of your classes, appointments, and social commitments. If you have a paper due or a big test coming up, mark that on your calendar, too.

SECTION 1.2 Review Questions

1. How do you determine which health care education best matches your interests?

2. Why is proper health care training important?

3. List the recommendations for maintaining a well-groomed, professional appearance.

4. List five standards of behavior and list five personal characteristics for health care workers.

5. Why is it important to use positive body language?

6. As a health care worker, why is it important to learn your facility's policy and procedures related to confidentiality?

 ## Learn By Doing: Section 1.2 Activity

1. Complete Worksheets 1 through 5.

2. When you are confident that you can meet each objective for this section, ask your teacher for the section evaluation.

3. Prepare responses to each item listed in Chapter Review.

Chapter 1 Review

Chapter Review Questions

1. List three scientific discoveries that have made health care what it is today. (1.1)

2. Explain two current trends in how patients receive health care. (1.1)

3. Explain the role of the nurse in the medical field today. (1.1)

4. Explain telemedicine. (1.1)

5. Give three examples of how new inventions and procedures have changed medicine over the years. (1.1)

6. Why do you need to learn all of the complicated health care procedures? (1.2)

7. Why is a health care worker's personal appearance important? (1.2)

8. Identify the standards of behavior for health care workers. (1.2)

9. Give three examples of positive body language. (1.2)

10. Why is it important to maintain the confidentiality of medical records? (1.2)

Activities

1. Pick an era—Renaissance, sixteenth and seventeenth centuries, or the eighteenth century. What was medicine like going into that era? How did medicine change in that time period? What (or who) were the key influences? Are these advances still in use today, or have we replaced them?

2. You are working in a clinic that deals with people who have a variety of diseases that carry some "social stigma." What can you do to create an atmosphere of confidence and openness with your clients?

Case Studies

1. A patient is experiencing heart problems and GI difficulties. What would have been done for this in ancient times? What would be done today?

2. You have decided that you want to pursue a career as a health care professional. What does this entail, other than choosing a field and studying hard? What other factors will impact your success as a health care worker?

Thinking Critically

1. **History of Medicine**—Create a timeline that shows the major advancements in medicine from Ancient Times through to the twentieth century. What do you consider to be the single most important development and why?

2. **Professionalism**—If you exhibit a professional look and demeanor, your clients and colleagues will have more confidence in you. Why is this? Give specific examples of positive and negative behaviors and appearance factors.

3. **Confidentiality**—You are expected to always keep confidentiality in mind, particularly when working in areas to which clients have access. What are three specific steps that you can take that would help maintain confidentiality?

Media Connection

Use the Companion Web site for additional interactive learning activities: www.prenhall.com/badasch

Portfolio Connection

Planning and preparing for a career is a process that allows you to look back on your experiences and learn from them. You can evaluate the things in your past that worked for you and those that did not.

You now have an opportunity to create a file that reflects what you learn. This file is called a *vocational portfolio*. Your portfolio will contain documents that show what you have learned during your vocational preparation. Your work will show the abilities and skills you gain throughout your training.

You will also create a job search packet that helps you identify ways to share your portfolio with schools or potential employers. Developing your portfolio provides a chance to express the positive results of your learning experiences in a professional manner.

Think about a time when you surprised yourself by accomplishing something that you were not sure you could do. What caused you to try it when you were unsure about it? What went well in that experience? What would you do differently? Explain your answers in a short paper. Your explanation must clearly identify your self-evaluation and show how you would approach uncertain experiences in the future.

This assignment helps you review and evaluate your past experience. Some of the future assignments for your portfolio will require a similar process, with a focus on your vocational training. Turn in this assignment to your teacher. When you create your portfolio in Chapter 2 your teacher will return it to you.

PORTFOLIO TIP

As you build your portfolio, remember that you will want to show how your strengths have helped you, and how you have learned and changed from previous experiences. This will be invaluable when presenting yourself to a potential employer. It will showcase your ability to deal with new situations and to learn from your mistakes.

2 Understanding Health Care Systems

Getting Started

U se the Cognitive Mapping form from Chapter 2 in the Student Activity Guide. Put "hospital" in the center circle, and then fill in the four extending circles. Each circle will have one hospital department and the main activity that occurs in that department and what the department's responsibilities are. Share your information with the rest of the class as the teacher completes a Cognitive Mapping form including the hospital with 10 departments extending from the center circle.

2.1 Health Care Providers

Businesses

Health care providers are business organizations. Businesses provide goods and services to consumers. A business may function for profit, or not-for-profit. A health care provider may be a corporation, such as a hospital, or a sole proprietor, such as a doctor who practices alone. Some health care providers are privately-owned. Many times, however, they are public corporations, owned by shareholders and managed by a board of directors. Some health care providers are part of larger public corporations that manage many health care providers. Businesses are responsible to the communities in which they operate.

What responsibilities does a health care provider have to the community?

Background

The health of individuals in a community can have an impact on the entire community. It is the responsibility of every health care worker to help patients/clients solve their health problems. Since the health care industry has many delivery systems, it is important for future health care workers to be aware of health care agencies and facilities, their delivery systems, their organization, and some of their major services. When you understand how health care facilities and agencies serve the public, you will become a resource person for members of your community.

Objectives

When you have completed this section, you will be able to do the following:

- Match key terms with their correct meanings.
- Research a volunteer agency.
- Define managed care.
- Define ambulatory care.
- Evaluate how managed care and ambulatory care meet the needs of the changing health care system.
- Understand the role of government agencies in providing health care.
- List six types of outpatient care and the type of treatment given.
- Define wellness and preventive care.

- Contrast the current trends with health care in the twentieth century.
- Be able to use or read an organizational chart.
- Give two reasons why the organization of health care facilities is important.
- Explain a chain of command.
- List and define the major services in health care.
- Identify two departments in each major service.

Types of Health Care Providers

There are several **facilities** and agencies that provide medical care. Some are familiar, and others will be new to you. The following descriptions will help you understand the differences among the many providers of medical care. (**Figure 2.1**)

facilities
(fuh SIL i teez)
Places designed or built to serve a special function (e.g., hospital, clinic, doctor's office).

FIGURE 2.1
Types of providers and the facilities in which they provide care. Which types of facilities are represented in the pictures?

diagnostic
(dahy uhg NOS tik)
Pertaining to the determination of the nature of a disease or injury by examining (e.g., using x-ray and laboratory tests).

surgical
(SUR ji kuhl)
Repairing or removing a body part by cutting.

chronic
(KRA nik)
Continuing over many years and for a long time (e.g., chronic illness).

psychiatric
(sahy kee A trik)
Pertaining to the mind.

geriatric
(jer ee A trik)
A branch of medicine that deals with the problems and diseases of old age and aging people.

convalescence
(kon vu LES nts)
The gradual recovery of health and strength after illness.

General hospitals are facilities where patients are hospitalized for a short time, a few days to a few weeks. They do not specialize in any one type of medical treatment; rather, they provide a wide range of **diagnostic**, medical, **surgical**, and emergency care services. General hospitals are staffed by professional physicians, surgeons, nurses, and support staff to provide inpatient care to those who need close monitoring and outpatient care to those who need treatment but not constant monitoring.

Specialty hospitals provide inpatient continuity of care for clients with persistent, recurring diseases or complex medical conditions which require long-term stays (often over a month) in an acute care environment. These may include **chronic** diseases, pulmonary or physical rehabilitation, wound care, and **psychiatric** problems. Specialty hospitals are not nursing homes facilities or transitional units. One example of a specialty hospital is St. Jude's Children's hospital.

Convalescent care (e.g., nursing home, long-term care) facilities generally engage in **geriatric** care—care for elderly people needing nursing services and assistance with personal care and daily living activities. These facilities also care for physically ill or injured people of all ages who require an extended **convalescence** for recovery. Many of these facilities focus on rehabilitation, or optimizing the functional status of the client so that they may return to the community. The staff includes nurses, nursing aides and assistants, physical, occupational, and speech therapists, recreational assistants, and social workers.

ambulatory
(AM buhlu tor ee)
Serving patients who are able to walk.

specialties
(SPESH uhl teez)
Fields of study or professional work (e.g., pediatrics, orthopedics, obstetrics).

outpatients
(aout PAY shunts)
Patients/clients who do not require hospitalization but are under a physician's care.

occupational therapy
(ock you PAY shun l)
Helps to give people skills for the job of living satisfying lives, such as dealing with job-related injuries.

recreational therapy
(rek ree A shun l)
Uses play, recreation, and leisure activities to improve physical, cognitive, social, and emotional functioning; the primary goal is to develop lifetime leisure skills.

hydrotherapy
(hi dro THER a pee)
Treatment that uses water therapy for disease or injury.

prosthetics
(pros THE tiks)
Artificial parts made for the body (e.g., teeth, feet, legs, arms, hands, eyes, breasts).

immunizations
(im yuh nuh ZEY shuhns)
Substances given to make disease organisms harmless to the patient; may be given orally or by injection (e.g., tetanus, polio).

Nursing homes can differ from extended care facilities. Nursing home facilities are places of residence for people who require constant nursing care and have significant problems with activities of daily living.

Extended care facilities are designed to care for those who need assistance with activities of daily living or with medical needs. An extended care facility is needed when someone has a condition that is likely to last for a long period of time or for the rest of his or her life, like moderate Alzheimer's.

There are also independent living and *assisted living facilities*. For older individuals with an active lifestyle, independent living offers the opportunity to remain independent in a home of their own, yet close to health care professionals and facilities—people needing some assistance with activities of daily living, but who want to live as independently as possible for as long as possible. Assisted living bridges the gap between independent living and extended care or nursing homes.

Ambulatory *care/clinics* are facilities where several physicians with different **specialties** combine their practices. This allows the patient/client to have immediate care for a variety of illnesses. Ambulatory care can be delivered at a physician's office, in an area of a hospital designated for short stay care, and in urgent care centers. Patients do not spend the night in ambulatory facilities; these are outpatient services.

Physician and dental facilities provide care that promotes wellness and diagnosis of illness. Simple surgery, bone setting, counseling, and administration of drugs take place here. Diagnostic services, such as laboratory tests and x-rays, might also take place. Physicians and dentists may provide care in an ambulatory care setting.

Rehabilitation centers provide **outpatient** care for clients who require physical or **occupational therapy, recreational therapy, hydrotherapy,** and other therapies (such as speech or hearing therapy) for loss of function in mobility or the activities of daily living. They may receive **prosthetics** and learn how to use adaptive devices. Patients come from the community and will return to the community after a therapy session is completed.

Industrial Health Care Centers are located in large companies and industrial facilities. They serve to provide health care for the staff and employees of the business, including basic examinations and emergency or urgent care. In addition, many industrial health care centers teach accident prevention and safety.

School Health Services are found in educational institutions. They provide emergency care in case of accidents or sudden illnesses. School nurses also provide medication dosing, and monitor children with chronic childhood diseases and problems such as diabetes, asthma, and cognitive impairment.

Health Maintenance Organizations (HMOs) are a type of managed care organization. HMOs stress wellness (preventive health care). This avoids unnecessary major medical expenses. They provide health services that include hospitalization, basic medical services, **immunizations**, basic checkups, and education.

Home health care agencies provide care in the home for patients/clients who need health services but not hospitalization. Services include nursing, physical therapy, personal care (bathing, dressing, etc.), and homemaking (e.g., housecleaning, food shopping, and cooking). Home health care workers provide care for all ages, from infants to the elderly.

Tele-health care offers medical services through interactive audiovisual media, such as computers or close-circuit television. It is a way to provide health care, including consultations, procedures, and examinations, to remote areas or communities that do not have full time health care providers.

Senior day care provides for elderly people who are able to live at home with their families but need care when the family is away. These centers are a place where the elderly can be cared for during the day with activities, **rehabilitation**, and contact with others. The elderly are given their medications and are aided in mobility.

The *World Health Organization (WHO),* an agency funded by the United Nations, was founded in 1948. It is concerned with world health problems and publishes health information, compiles statistics, and investigates serious health problems.

Hospices are important in our health care system. Hospices provide end-of-life care to those patients expected to live six months or less. The number one diagnosis for hospice patients is cancer. Health professionals and volunteers provide medical services and psychological and spiritual support to both the patient and their family. These services are covered by Medicare, Medicaid, and commercial insurance companies. For those with no insurance coverage, Hospice offers a sliding scale based on ability to pay. The goal of hospice is to make the patient as comfortable as possible by controlling pain and providing comfort. Hospices are discussed further in Chapter 14, Section 14.4.

Government Agencies

The federal, state, and local governments provide health services. These services are funded by taxes. They are responsible for giving direct health care, safeguarding our food and water supplies, and promoting health education.

Veterans Administration hospitals are federally supported and provide care for veterans who served in the armed forces.

The *U.S. Public Health Department* is a federal agency that has six major responsibilities:

- Performing research on diseases that kill, handicap, or cripple.
- Preventing and treating alcohol and drug abuse.
- Preventing and controlling diseases that are transmitted by insects, animals, air, water, and people.
- Checking the safety of food and drugs that consumers purchase.
- Planning more effective ways to deliver health services.
- Making quality care available and affordable by encouraging health personnel to work in underserved areas.

State psychiatric hospitals serve the mentally ill.

State university medical centers provide training for health workers, give medical care, and conduct medical research.

Apply It

Form two groups. One will explore the services offered by a Genetic Counseling Center; the other will focus on an Optical Center. Create a list of these services and present the information to the class as a whole.

rehabilitation

(ree huh BIL i tey shuhn) Process that helps people who have been disabled by sickness or injury to recover as many of their original abilities for activities of daily living as possible.

Apply It

Select three partners for this team activity. One will focus on therapeutic services; one on diagnostic services; one on information services; and, one on environmental services.

Make a chart listing which types of health providers offer these services. Give two examples of how the provider supplies the service. Present your analysis to the class and compare your study with those of other teams.

Community Service

Create a chart that shows the different activities/personnel that one would likely see when entering a senior daycare center or hospice. Share the chart with your family and friends to help them prepare for such a visit.

HIV/AIDS Resources

aidsinfo.nih.gov and www.cdc.gov/HIV provide resources and information on HIV/AIDS, including treatment and prevention, along with guidelines for people living with HIV/AIDS, as well as for their families and friends and health care providers.

State public health services provide health education materials. They are responsible for water and food purity, **communicable** disease control, alcohol and drug abuse control, **maternal** health, and **licensing** of various health agencies.

The *U.S. Department of Health and Human Services (USDHHS)* protects the health of all Americans by providing vital human services, especially to those least able to help themselves. For example, WomensHealth.gov provides resources for domestic violence against women.

The *National Institute of Health (NIH)* is the world's leading agency for conducting and supporting medical research.

The *Centers for Disease Control (CDC)* monitors and prevents disease outbreaks, including bioterrorism. The CDC implements disease prevention strategies and maintains national health statistics.

The *Food and Drug Administration (FDA)* assures the safety of foods, cosmetics, pharmaceuticals, biological products, and medical devices.

The *Occupational Safety and Health Administration (OSHA)* imposes safety and health legislation to prevent injury, illness, and death in the workplace.

The *Agency for Health Care Policy and Research (AHCPR)* works to improve the quality, safety, efficiency, and effectiveness of health care for all Americans by using research and technology to promote the delivery of the best possible care.

County hospitals provide care for the ill and injured, especially those patients/clients who require financial help in order to receive care.

A *laboratory* is a facility (which may be a government or private facility) that provides controlled conditions in which scientific research, experiments, and measurements can be performed. Laboratories can be found in hospitals, dental offices, schools, universities, industry, government, and military facilities.

Local *public health departments* provide services to local communities—focusing on the reporting of communicable diseases, public health nursing, health education, **environmental sanitation**, maternal and child health services, and public health clinics.

Senior centers have clinics that provide special services for geriatric patients (e.g., **podiatry** clinic, **hypertension** clinic, general medical care).

Not-for-Profit Agencies

Volunteer, or not-for-profit, organizations receive support from donations, gifts, membership fees, fund-raisers, and **endowments**. They are not supported by the government, and many of the people who work for them are not paid. They raise funds for medical research and for public education about various health problems. Many of them focus on a particular disease or medical condition, such as:

- American Cancer Society.
- National Foundation of the March of Dimes.
- American Red Cross.
- American Heart Association.

- American Diabetes Association.
- National Association of Mental Health.
- National Association of People with AIDS
- National Coalition Against Domestic Violence
- American Respiratory Disease Association.
- There are other non-profit medical organizations, such as HOSA (Health Occupations Students of America), which is covered in Chapter 4. All of these agencies and facilities help bring good health to individuals and communities.

Managed Care: Quality Care and Managed Costs

The managed care provider's goals are to provide quality care at reasonable costs. Certain policies help ensure quality care at minimal cost. Some of these policies are discussed here.

Preventive care, such as routine physicals, well-baby care, immunizations, screenings for patients with specific risk factors, and wellness education helps keep patients healthy. Wellness education stresses the importance of good nutrition, weight control, exercise, and healthy living practices. Health education programs, wellness centers, weight-control programs, fitness centers, health food distributors, and health care organizations all promote wellness and preventive care. Being healthy helps prevent serious illness and lowers medical costs.

Primary care providers may include family and general practice physicians, internists, nurse practitioners, and physician's assistants. This is "the family doctor"—usually the first contact a patient has for an undiagnosed condition. Primary providers care for all routine medical problems. They also **refer** patients/clients to specialists.

Specialty care is care given by a provider who is trained in one special area. Specialists usually limit their practice to treating one type of problem. Specializing gives them a broad knowledge of that area. A few specialties are:

- Surgery.
- Podiatry.
- **Audiology.**
- **Obstetrics.**
- **Orthopedics.**
- **Chiropractic.**
- **Urology.**

Emergency care and *urgent care* provide different services. Emergency care is for life-threatening conditions that require hospitalization. These might include ambulance services, rescue squads, and helicopter or airplane rescue vehicles. Urgent care is for non-emergencies that require prompt treatment. Emergencies requiring hospital care are expensive. Excellent care is available in the urgent care setting, and costs are lower.

The *preadmission authorization requirement for hospitalization* allows necessary hospitalization and prevents unnecessary hospitalization. Good-quality outpatient care is encouraged when possible. Outpatient care is much less expensive, and patients/clients often prefer being in their own homes.

Apply It

Create a panel of six health care counselors. The rest of your classmates will act as clients.

Clients will create a series of questions about a specific problem; for example, perhaps they lost their job and have no health insurance or have recently returned from the National Guard duty and do not know what benefits may be available.

Each "counselor" must research three questions and respond to the client in writing, directing him/her to the appropriate agencies and explaining what services they might be able to access.

refer
(ri FER)
To send to.

audiology
(o dee A luh gee)
The study of hearing disorders.

obstetrics
(ub STE triks)
The branch of medical science concerned with childbirth.

orthopedics
(or tho PE diks)
The medical specialty concerned with correcting problems with the skeletal system.

chiropractic
(KI ruh prak tik)
The method of adjusting the segments of the spinal column.

urology
(yew RO le gee)
The study of the urine and urinary organs in health and disease.

trend
(trend)
General direction or movement.

managed care
(MAN ij d kair)
A health care plan or system that seeks to control medical costs by contracting with a network of providers and by requiring preauthorization for visits to specialists.

radiology
(rey dee OL uh jee)
The science dealing with x-rays or nuclear radiation.

 ## Ambulatory Care

The current **trend** is to develop large **managed care** organizations that provide good-quality, cost-effective health care. Ambulatory care providers are following managed care concepts. One change keeps patients/clients at home for their care whenever possible. Most patients like to be at home because it is comfortable and familiar. It also reduces health care costs. Only the very ill and severely injured are hospitalized. All other patients are cared for in facilities like these:

- Rehabilitation centers.
- Physicians' offices.
- Outpatient surgery.
- Day care.
- Outpatient medical centers/clinics.

Such facilities provide what is called ambulatory care. The patient/client goes to a facility for care and returns home. Some patients also need home health care to help with bathing, range of motion, dressing changes, intravenous therapy, and special treatments.

Ambulatory care offers opportunities for health care workers to use multidisciplinary skills. For example, a person with an EKG certificate, phlebotomy certificate, or limited **radiology** certificate is an asset to an ambulatory care organization.

 Language Arts Link

Investigate Health Care Facilities

As you learned in this chapter, there are many different types of health care facilities. Working with a partner, select two different types of health care facilities where you live. Research the two facilities using the Internet, calling the facility, or referring to any available print information. Find key information, such as the types of services the facility offers, what the facility specializes in, who is eligible to go to the health care facility, and if the facility is for outpatients or provides long-term care.

With your partner, create a brochure or a booklet on the computer with information on both facilities that can be used by local school counselors, churches, etc. Be sure to proofread your work and cite any sources that you used. Check spelling and grammar and correct any errors.

 ## Organization

An efficient health care facility must be well organized. Organization improves the performance of health care workers at a facility and ensures that the facility delivers high quality health care to patients/clients. The successful management of a health care facility is dependent on organization, as well as problem solving. Root-cause analysis is a problem-solving method that identifies the root cause of a problem or incident.

An organizational chart shows how each department of a health care facility fits into the system and identifies the line of authority. (**Figure 2.2**) When you look at an organizational chart, you can see who your immediate supervisor is. It tells you the areas of responsibility for all of the employees. The organizational chart also establishes the chain of command.

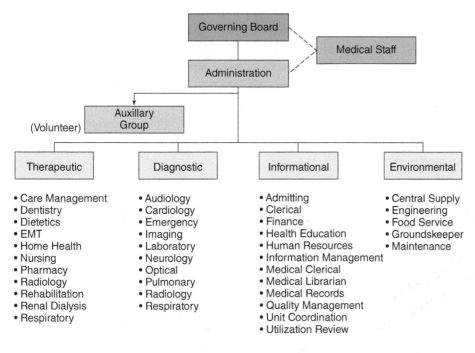

Chain of Command

The chain of command tells you to whom you take questions, reports, and problems. This is always your immediate supervisor. It is your immediate supervisor's responsibility to resolve any problem that occurs. If your immediate supervisor is unable to find a solution, he or she takes the problem to his or her immediate supervisor. This provides an efficient problem-solving structure. Bypassing a link in the chain causes misunderstanding and is unprofessional.

 ## Major Services in Health Care

As you can see in **Figure 2.2**, each service has specialized departments. These departments are determined by the type of service they give:

- Therapeutic services provide care over time.

- Diagnostic services are those used to identify a particular condition or disease, such as x-rays or blood tests.

- Informational services document and process information.

- Environmental services help to create a relaxing, healing, and supportive environment for patients.

Services can be organized in several different ways. Your facility's organizational chart is your guideline. To find titles of personnel who are employed in these agencies and facilities, refer to "Overview of Careers" in Chapter 3, Section 3.2.

 ## Health Care Regulatory Agencies

State and federal regulatory agencies for the health care industry set standards for health care, keep health care workers informed, and monitor facilities' and workers' compliance with laws that pertain to health care. As a health care worker, one of your first encounters with a health care regulatory agency will be for licensure. Based on your chosen profession, you will need to meet specific requirements set forth by the federal or state board that regulates that profession.

Quality Control

Increased public demand for high quality health care and error reduction over the past 50 years has resulted in health care providers initiating ongoing efforts to deliver excellence in care. Quality control is achieved through a process of gathering and evaluating information about the health care services provided, as well as the measurable results achieved. The gathered information and results are then compared against accepted standards, often called benchmarks. Benchmarks used for quality control may be set on a local, state, or national level.

Quality control is achieved and maintained through formal, systematic evaluations. Overall patterns of care are evaluated and compared to benchmarks. When problems, or deficiencies, are identified, the benchmarks offer a standard for improvement.

What benchmarks do you use to evaluate your work in school?

therapeutic
(ther uh PYOO tik)
Pertaining to the treatment of disease or injury (e.g., physical therapy, radiology, diet, nursing).

 ## Summary

There are many facilities that help individuals with health problems. Health care facilities offer a variety of services, including **therapeutic**, diagnostic, information, and environmental. There are also agencies—some private, some funded by federal, state, or local governments. Each agency meets a special need. All facilities and agencies have an organizational chart to help them be more efficient and to establish a chain of command. The current trend in health care is managed care, outpatient care, and ambulatory care. The emphasis is on wellness and preventive care.

 # Personal Wellness

Hospital Help

Hospitals are known for the diagnostic, medical, surgical, and emergency care services that they provide. However, many hospitals now offer classes and groups to educate patients and promote personal wellness. The instructional sessions cover a range of topics. For example, some classes help patients understand their diseases. Classes about cancer, diabetes, and arthritis can help patients anticipate symptoms and explore types of care.

Emotional support is offered in the form of support groups for bereavement, for cancer patients, and for caregivers. These groups help patients and families deal with the mental and emotional stress that often comes with disease.

Not only do hospitals help with the difficulties associated with disease, they also offer classes on topics of daily health. Classes on exercise, men's and women's health, stress management, and nutrition are available. Expectant mothers can learn about pregnancy and parenthood through weekly classes. Hospitals reach out to communities to educate people and help keep them well.

Why do you think hospitals have started to offer these types of classes?

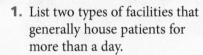

SECTION **2.1** **Review Questions**

1. List two types of facilities that generally house patients for more than a day.

2. How do volunteer agencies help the medical field?

3. What can you determine by looking at an organizational chart for a facility?

4. How does ambulatory care help to meet the needs of patients?

5. What does preventative care mean?

6. Name and describe the activities of two government agencies that provide health care-related services.

Learn By Doing: Section 2.1 Activity

1. Complete Worksheets 1 and 2 as assigned.

2. Ask your teacher for directions to complete Worksheets/Activities 3, 4, and 5.

3. Complete Worksheet 6.

4. When you are confident that you can meet each objective for this section, ask your teacher for the section evaluation.

SECTION

2.2 Health Care Systems

Background

The cost of health care has increased significantly over the years. It is important to understand the causes for the increase as well as methods providers use to help contain the costs. Every health care worker should also know the health care systems that help patients/clients afford the services they need. When patients/clients receive regular and complete care, they live healthier and happier lives.

Objectives

When you have completed this section, you will be able to do the following:

- Match key terms with their correct meanings.

- Explain how health care providers have modified their practices to provide patients quality health care at a lower cost.

- Explain the purpose of the Health Plan Employer Data and Information Set.

- Identify and differentiate the various health care systems.

- Compare and contrast health maintenance organizations and preferred provider organizations.

- Analyze and predict where and how certain factors such as cost, managed care, technology, an aging population, etc. may affect various health care delivery system models.

Quality Health Care Costs

Cost Containment

The high cost of health care has drawn much attention in recent years. Technological advances in the medical field, an aging population, and health-related **lawsuits** have all helped to drive up the price of medical care and affected health care **systems**. Advanced equipment that health care providers now use to

lawsuits
(LA soots)
A legal action started by one person against another based on a complaint that the person failed to perform a legal duty.

systems
(SIS tems)
Coordinated bodies of methods or plans of procedure.

make a more thorough diagnosis is often expensive to purchase and maintain. In addition, as the population continues to grow and age, the demand for this type of care increases.

Providing guidelines for standard care also serves to promote quality of care. When proven standards for effective care and quality outcomes are developed and encouraged for use by individual caregivers the patient will be more inclined to "get what has been proven to work."

Health care providers and the government are working to lower these costs for patients/clients. The federal government passed **legislation** in 1983, originally developed for Medicare payment systems and then modified for the general population, to regulate the price of medical care. The system ensures that the specific health care agency will have to pick up any extra costs after the government and patient have paid their part.

This legislation approved the grouping of medical conditions, the reasonable cost for each condition, and its standard treatment. These groupings are known as *diagnostic-related groupings* (DRGs). Some of the top groupings are normal newborn, heart failure, psychoses, cesarean section, angina pectoris, pneumonia, and hip/knee replacement.

DRGs help reduce unnecessary procedures and encourage self-care and home care. So, for example, a woman might wake up with a fever, sore throat and ringing in her ears. She goes to an urgent care facility where she can be seen that morning and is diagnosed with strep throat. The standard diagnosis for strep is based on a throat culture (rapid strep test) and treatment is about 10 days of antibiotics. Based on the DRG, the facility will only be reimbursed by insurance or Medicare for a fee that falls within a specific range. The facility would not, on the other hand, be reimbursed for x-rays or a CAT scan for this condition.

Health care providers also promote lower health care costs by combining services, offering outpatient services, purchasing supplies in **bulk**, and emphasizing early **intervention** and preventative care.

Health Plan Employer Data Information Set

Under the direction of the National Committee for Quality Assurance (NCQA), the Health Plan Employer Data and Information Set (HEDIS) establishes guidelines and gives a report card that:

- Measures health plan performance.
- Helps identify physicians who give high-quality medical care to their patients/clients.
- Helps identify physicians who do not meet the quality care guidelines.

These report cards are used by almost all of America's health plans to measure their performance on important aspects of care and service. Quality health care can be defined as the extent to which patients get the care they need in a manner that most effectively protects or restores their health. This means having timely access to care, getting treatment that medical evidence has found to be effective and getting appropriate preventive care.

---

legislation
(le jus LA shun)
A law or body of laws.

Systems Theory

Any kind of system has input and output, along with a feedback loop. In a system such as a health care system, the input is information, materials, and human effort or energy. The output is the services provided to patients. Both positive and negative feedback affect the input that occurs next. For a system to work, there must be goals, and feedback must govern what continues to happen within the system. Adaptability to feedback is important in achieving goals.

For more on systems theory in a health care system, go to the Companion Web site at www.prenhall.com/badasch

bulk
(bulk)
A greater amount.

intervention
(in tur VEN shun)
The act of interfering to modify an outcome.

Health Care Payments
Health Insurance: Third-Party Payers

Health care costs, including dental, are so high that most people have some type of insurance plan. These plans are called third-party payers. Insurance companies require the subscriber to pay a fee for insurance coverage and in return agree to pay for specific medical and dental care.

Each insurance company determines what it will and will not pay for and how much it will pay. For example, many third-party payers require a **co-payment**. A co-payment is a set amount the subscriber pays for each medical service. This may be from $10 to $30 that a subscriber pays to the provider on the day that he or she visits a medical office or picks up a prescription.

Most insurance companies also have a **deductible**, an amount the subscriber must pay before the insurance begins to pay. For example, a subscriber may have to pay the first $250 of medical bills in a given year. Even after a subscriber pays the co-payment and the deductible, he or she may still have to pay a **co-insurance**. For example, a subscriber may be required to pay 20 percent of every medical bill. The subscriber must pay any fees that the insurance company does not pay.

co-payment
(koh PEY muhnt)
A set amount the subscriber pays for each medical service.

deductible
(di DUHK tuh buhl)
An amount the subscriber must pay before the insurance begins to pay.

co-insurance
(koh in SHOOR uhns)
A percentage the subscriber is required to pay of every medical bill.

π *Math Link*

Finding Health Care Costs Using Percentages

When trying to figure out how much you or a patient will have to pay when dealing with a third-party payer, knowing how to work with percentages can help. A third-party payer may require the subscriber to pay a certain percentage of every medical bill. In order to figure out how much a subscriber will have to pay, follow these steps:

Step 1: Convert the percentage to a decimal. You can do this by moving the decimal point to the left two spaces. For example, 10% would be .10 and 20% would be .20.

Step 2: Multiply the decimal by the amount of the medical bill.

Example 1

Mike is having surgery on his arm. The total cost of the procedure is $982. Mike's insurance requires a 15% coinsurance.

Step 1: 15% = .15

Step 2: 982 × .15 = 147.30

Mike would have to pay $147.30 for the surgery.

Example 2

Kelly needs to have a cavity filled. The total cost of the procedure is $350. Kelly's insurance pays 30% of the cost of any dental procedure.

Step 1: In this instance, first you need to find out how much Kelly is required to pay.

```
  100%
– 30%
  70%
```

70% = .70

Step 2: 350 × .70 = 245

Kelly would have to pay $245 to have the cavity filled.

Calculate percentages to solve this example. Andrew needs to have a mole removed from his back. The total cost of the procedure is $235. Andrew's insurance pays 65% of the cost of a medical procedure. How much would Andrew have to pay?

Why is it important to know how to figure out how much money an insurance company will pay for a medical procedure?

Health Maintenance Organizations

Health maintenance organizations (HMOs) require members to pay a co-payment, or co-pay, for medical services. The member must get medical care from the physicians, labs, hospitals, etc. that agree to the fee the HMO is willing to pay. If the member gets medical care outside the HMO, he or she will have to pay for the care.

Preferred Provider Organizations

Physician groups and hospitals work together to give comprehensive health care at a reduced cost to various large companies and corporations. Employees of these companies contract with a preferred provider organization (PPO) and agree to see providers on the PPO list. If they see other providers, they pay a larger fee.

Medicaid

Health insurance is provided by the state and federal government. **Benefits** and **eligibility** are different in each state. People who are blind, disabled, or of low income are generally able to get Medicaid insurance.

Medicare

Health insurance is provided to people over the age of 65. Subscribers pay a monthly payment to the Social Security Administration. (**Figure 2.3**) Medicare consists of two parts. Part A covers in-patient care at hospitals, hospice care, and home health care. Part B helps cover medical services like doctors' services, outpatient care, and other medical services that Part A does not cover. In addition, Part B covers some **preventative** services. While most people get Part A without paying a monthly payment, Part B requires a **premium** each month. Some health care

providers accept Medicare payments, or reimbursements, as payment in full for services; others charge more than Medicare pays. To cover the extra costs, many people buy a third-party payer insurance to cover all of their medical costs. There are many programs for Medicare recipients that provide care for a small co-payment.

TRICARE

TRICARE is a health care program for active duty service members, retirees, and their families. One part of TRICARE is called TFL (TRICARE for Life). This medical care is for Medicare-eligible uniformed services retirees age 65 or older. The plan also covers family members and survivors. This health program works with Medicare to provide service members additional health benefits.

Workers' Compensation

Another example of a health care program is the workers' **compensation** program. Employees who are injured or die at work are covered by state workers' compensation laws. Workers' compensation also includes any illness that may result from the workplace. Employers are required to have workers' compensation insurance. Benefits include payment for lost wages and payment of medical bills.

---

benefits
(BEN a fits)
Payment and assistance based on an agreement.

eligibility
(e li ja BI la tee)
The quality or state of being qualified.

FIGURE 2.3
An elderly woman learns about the health care benefits she can receive from the government. What kind of health care programs are available from the government for a person over 65?

preventative
(pri VEN tuh tiv)
Intended to keep from happening.

premium
(PREE mee uhm)
The periodic payment to Medicare, an insurance company, or a health care plan for health care or prescription drug coverage.

compensation
(kom puhn SEY shuhn)
Payment.

National Health Care

Years ago the American Medical Association (AMA) was against any effort to regulate the health care system. More recently, however, even some doctors—Physicians for a National Health Program—were interested in a single "payer" health system for all Americans. They claim that eliminating private insurance bureaucracy and paperwork could save enough to provide comprehensive, high-quality coverage for all Americans.

Since Congress first debated health care reform in 1994, the cost of health insurance has doubled. Given the number of uninsured Americans, it is no surprise that health care reform is an ongoing concern in the United States. Although legislation was passed by Congress in 2010, the laws are being challenged and debated, and health care reform continues to be a work in progress.

The intent of health care reform is to provide more comprehensive care to more Americans and to focus more on preventive health care, immunizations, education, and behavior modification (i.e., encouraging people to stop smoking)—all factors that could result in lower health care costs.

 ## Summary

The price of health care has risen over the years due to technological advances, an aging population, and health-related lawsuits. However, health care providers and systems continue to help patients/clients receive affordable care. By encouraging less hospital time for the patient through outpatient services and early intervention, providers help keep costs low. In addition, health maintenance organizations and preferred provider organizations work with providers to offer patients/clients reduced costs. The federal and state governments also protect patients/clients by offering programs such as Medicaid, Medicare, TRICARE, and workers' compensation.

SECTION	2.2	Review Questions

1. List three causes of rising health care costs.

2. How are health care providers trying to reduce costs for their patients/clients?

3. What is the benefit of diagnostic-related groupings?

4. What is the difference between health maintenance organizations and preferred provider organizations?

5. Who is eligible for Medicaid?

6. When can a worker receive workers' compensation?

 ## Learn By Doing: Section 2.2 Activity

1. Complete Worksheets 1, 2, and 5 as assigned.

2. Complete Worksheets/Activities 3 and 4.

3. Prepare responses to each item listed in Chapter Review.

4. When you are confident that you can meet each objective listed above, ask your teacher for the section evaluation.

Chapter 2 Review

Chapter Review Questions

1. Under what three circumstances might ambulatory care be preferable and why? (2.1)

2. Name one health care provider and explain how they provide medical care. (2.1)

3. What are we trying to do to contain the high costs of health care? (2.2)

4. Explain several ways in which we are addressing personal wellness issues. (2.1)

5. Name three government agencies that provide health services. What does each agency do? (2.1)

6. How do the policies of managed care help to provide quality care for patients? (2.1)

7. What are the benefits of an organizational chart in a health care facility? (2.1)

8. Explain the four major services in health care. (2.1)

9. How does the Health Plan Employer Data Information Set help patients/clients? (2.2)

10. What are some of the costs that third-party payers might require a patient/client to pay? (2.2)

Activities

1. Choose a facility such as a general hospital, specialty hospital, rehabilitation center, or clinic. Visit the facility, research its Web site, or call the facility to identify the different departments in the facility and its line of authority. Then create a diagram that shows the relationship of health care professionals within that facility.

2. Choose two or three third-party payers and research the benefits they offer. Find information about deductibles, co-payments, and co-insurance. You may also research the vision and dental benefits included with each third-party payer. Create a chart that compares and contrasts the different benefits offered by each insurance company. Then determine which third-party payer you feel offers patients/clients the best services for their money.

Case Studies

1. A patient is not sure he understands his new insurance policy. He is going to have a colonoscopy procedure, which will cost $1,350. There is a co-pay of $30 and the co-insurance is 20%. The annual deductible is $1,000, of which the patient has met $325. What amount will the patient have to pay?

2. An elderly gentleman is leaving the hospital after receiving care for his broken leg. He lives with his family, but he is alone all day while family members are at work. What kind of care will the man need after he leaves the hospital? What type of facilities might you recommend to this patient so he can receive this care?

Thinking Critically

1. **Managed Care**—We hear a lot today about the benefits and difficulties of managed care. What do you think exemplifies the best of managed care? How could we further improve the system? Give examples.

2. **Health Costs**—The costs of health care continue to increase. What do you think we can do to help contain these costs? Look at the problem both from the perspective of the patient and the provider.

3. **Running the Organization**—Like any efficient corporation, each health care facility has a chain of command. Why is it important to follow this chain of command? Think of specific examples that show what might happen if you do not follow the chain of command.

Media Connection

Use the Companion Web site for additional interactive learning activities: www.prenhall.com/badasch

Portfolio Connection

Starting to determine which career best matches your interests and strengths can seen overwhelming. Taking a close look at your abilities can help you make better choices whenever you're faced with big decisions regarding the future. Before setting your goals, it's a good idea to think about what you enjoy doing most, what you're good at, and how challenges that lie ahead might impact your future.

Of course, understanding your basic personality is critical in helping you identify a career path. Are you methodical and detail oriented? Do you prefer dealing with research to dealing with people? Are you more interested in building relationships? Are you a "doer" or a "thinker" . . . or both?

Do you realize that some companies use Myers-Briggs or other types of tests as one tool to help determine where a candidate might best fit in the organization? The Myers-Briggs Type Indicator, the most common, is a personality questionnaire designed to identify certain psychological differences according to the theories of Carl Gustav Jung, a Swiss psychiatrist credited for founding analytical psychology.

So, study some of the basic questions used in personality testing. Then create a list of your 10 strongest personality traits. Rate each on a scale of 1, 2, or 3, with 1 representing the strongest trait and 3 representing a milder trait. For example, you may thoroughly enjoy nurturing or taking care of people and would rate it a 1. You may also dislike competitive behavior, but you still compete in sports. You would rate that a 2.

Think about the careers we've touched on. This is early in the process, but which do you think would best suit you? Why? Keep this analysis in your portfolio. You will refer to it later on in the term. Put it in your personal section of your portfolio.

PORTFOLIO TIP

Remember the wide variety of health care settings in which you could work. Try to collect samples for your portfolio from as many settings as possible (hospital, clinic, doctor's office, home care, etc.) as you continue your studies.

3 Finding the Right Occupation for You

Getting Started

Using the Cognitive Mapping form from Chapter 2 in the Student Activity Guide, fill in the two circles that extend from the department circles with health care professionals that work in each department. Briefly describe at least one task that each professional may perform.

Career Search

Background

When you consider an occupation in the health care field, it is important to focus on your interests, values, and abilities. When you understand yourself, it is easier to select the right occupation. There are many different career opportunities in the health care field. Researching several careers will help you choose the right career for you. Learning how to use the resources for researching occupations will make it easier for you to choose a career.

Objectives

When you have completed this section, you will be able to do the following:

- Define interests, values, and abilities.
- List five work-related values.
- Identify three resources for occupational research.
- Research three health careers.
- Explain the importance of a vocational portfolio.
- Complete an assignment addressing "What I Learned About Selecting a Career."

interests
(IN ter ists)
Something that concerns, draws the attention of, or arouses the curiosity of a person.

career
(kuh REER)
A profession; a person's life work.

occupation
(ok yuh PEY shuhn)
A person's job to earn a living.

 Interests

Your **interests** tell what you like to do and what you do not like to do. Recognizing your interests helps you make a good career choice. Do you prefer to problem solve as part of a team, or would you prefer to work on your own? For instance, if you like to work alone, a **career** in direct patient/client care probably is not right for you. Working in one of the computer areas might be better. When you know your interests early in your career search, you can identify careers that use those interests. If you discover that many of the tasks listed in an **occupation** are not interesting to you, reconsider your choice, and research careers that require your interests.

Values

A **value** is the importance that you place on various elements in your life. Money might be more important to you than leisure time. Working with people might be more important to you than what shift you work. Knowing what values you feel most strongly about helps you avoid **compromising** the things that are most important to you. Recognizing your values also helps you **prioritize** your work-related values, such as job security, **leisure** time, **wages**, recognition, creativity, advancement, working environment, home life, responsibility, and management. Ask yourself the following questions:

- **Job security.** Is it important that you find a job immediately upon the completion of your training program? How important is job availability?

- **Leisure time.** Is it important for you to have extra time for leisure activities?

- **Wages.** Is an average wage acceptable if you like your work, or is a very high wage necessary?

- **Recognition.** Is it important that the job you choose is respected by the people in your community?

- **Creativity.** Do you like to come up with new ideas to solve problems, or do you prefer a job in which there is exactly one way to do things?

- **Advancement.** Do you want a career that provides opportunities for promotion?

- **Working environment.** Do you prefer to work indoors or outdoors?

- **Home life.** Do you want to work a daytime schedule (9 to 5) with some overtime and with weekends and holidays off, or are you willing to do shift work (all hours, any day of the week)?

- **Responsibility.** Do you want a job that requires you to make a number of decisions?

- **Management.** Do you want to be responsible for supervising the work of other people or for organizing many tasks at once?

All of these factors affect your job choice. Make a list of these work values and put them in order of their importance to you. When you research an occupation, refer to your list so you do not choose a job that conflicts with many of your values.

 Abilities

An **ability** is something you do well. You have many abilities. For example, you may work well with your hands, or you may be very good at mathematics. It is much more pleasant to work in an occupation that uses your abilities. If you choose an occupation that is too far below your ability level, you will be bored. If it is too far above your ability level, you will be frustrated. It is important to evaluate your abilities during your career search. List your abilities, and use the list when researching an occupation. Match your abilities to the job description.

value
(VAL yoo)
The importance that you place on various elements in your life.

compromising
(KOM pruh mahyz)
Giving up something important.

prioritize
(prahy AWR i tahyz)
To put in order of importance.

leisure
(LEE zher)
Time free from the demands of work.

wages
(WEYJ s)
Money that is paid or received for work or services.

Apply It

Make a list of what you consider to be your five strongest abilities. Then ask someone who knows you well—a family member, friend, teacher, or clergyman—to create the same list. What have you learned about yourself?

---

ability
(uh BIL i tee)
Something a person does well.

 **Resources for Occupational Research**

There are many resources you can use in your research. Two of them are the *Dictionary of Occupational Titles* (http://www.occupationalinfo.org/), which lists job titles, tasks, and duties for 20,000 occupations, and the *Occupational Outlook Handbook* (http://www.bls.gov/oco/), which discusses the nature of the work, employment outlook, training and qualification requirements, earnings, and working conditions for a variety of occupations. *Work Briefs* by Science Research Associates, the Career Exploratory Kit, the *Encyclopedia of Careers*, and computer programs are also good resources.

In addition, check career-related pamphlets, microfilm, and videos. You can find all of these resources in libraries and career centers. Interview individuals who are already working in health care occupations, as well as looking at written materials.

job outlook
(job OUT look)
The expectation or prospect of a particular job in the future.

By conducting occupational research, you learn about the tasks performed, the **job outlook**, the education required, the working environment, and many other things. It requires time and effort to research the occupations that interest you and to prepare for a specific career. If possible, find a mentor who performs this occupation. Spend time following them on the job site. Remember, your efforts allow you to find a job that gives you satisfaction.

  *Language Arts Link*

Managing Stress

Studies have shown that job-related stress can affect your physical health. While no job is completely stress-free, these findings highlight the importance of choosing a career that works well with your interests, values, and abilities. It is important to know how to deal with this stress to protect your mental, emotional, and physical health.

One way to prevent stress is by staying organized on the job and managing your time well. In paragraph form, explain how a career that does not match your most important values can cause additional stress. Analyze why this would cause stress.

Create a new document on the computer, or get a blank sheet of paper. Include a thesis statement (a sentence stating your main ideas) in the opening paragraph. Be sure to proofread your work to see if you can improve it by making it clearer, more concise, or more interesting to read. Check the spelling and grammar and correct any errors. Exchange reports with a classmate and provide feedback and corrections as necessary. Once you've read your classmate's comments, revise your report as necessary.

 How to Do a Career Search

Choose a health career that interests you. Use the information from the resources listed in this section and the information in the following section for your research. Instructions for your research are in the Student Activity Guide.

1. Interview for information. Interview a worker in the occupation that interests you. Prepare a questionnaire before the interview.

2. Write a paper telling how the occupation you researched matches your interests, abilities, and values. Include any parts of that occupation that might not match your interests, abilities, and values. Determine if these would be a stressor for you and if so how you would manage this stress.

3. When you complete your research, you have a guideline to follow that will help you choose an occupation that you enjoy.

Developing a Vocational Portfolio

A **portfolio** is a collection of materials that show the knowledge, abilities, skills, and insights you gain in your search for a career. The purpose in developing a portfolio is to show your mastery of **vocational** requirements to an employer, a college, or a higher-level training program. You also see your own growth and accomplishments over time. Follow the directions in "Portfolio Connection" at the end of this chapter to assemble your own portfolio.

Completing this project shows your commitment to a set of values and your ability to plan, organize, and create a product. It provides an opportunity to pursue a specific interest and to meet professionals in health care occupations. This project leads you through planning, evidence of progress, final product, and oral presentations.

portfolio
(pawrt FOH lee oh)
A collection of materials that show your knowledge, abilities, skills, and insights.

vocational
(voh KA shuh nl)
Pertaining to a particular occupation, business, or profession.

Summary

In this section you learned that it is important to identify and evaluate your work interests, values, and abilities. You learned how to use this information when you choose a career, how to use many resources to research career possibilities, and the importance of developing a vocational portfolio.

SECTION	3.1	Review Questions

1. Explain the difference between interests and values.

2. List three work-related values.

3. Why is it important to choose an occupation that suits your abilities?

4. Identify two resources that could help you with occupational research.

5. What are some of the things you can learn from occupational research?

6. What are the benefits of a portfolio?

Learn By Doing: Section 3.1 Activity

1. Complete Worksheets/Activities 1 and 3 as assigned.

2. Complete Worksheet 2 as assigned.

3. Complete Worksheets/Activities 4 through 6 as assigned.

4. Read the Portfolio packet in the addendum of the Student Activity Guide and complete Worksheet/Activity 7.

5. When you are confident that you can meet each objective listed above, ask your teacher for the section evaluation.

Overview of Careers

Apply It

As a class, split up into teams of three to four students. Your teacher will give each group a pad of sticky notes; each team will receive a different color note. Your team will have five minutes to write down as many health careers as you can think of, writing each career on a separate sticky note.

The team that lists the most careers wins the competition. Each team will then post its careers to large pieces of paper the teacher has prepared for the appropriate career cluster. You can then discuss which careers are posted to the correct or incorrect career clusters, and why they are right or wrong.

Background

There are hundreds of job opportunities in the health care field. The positions in the four occupational clusters that are discussed in this section introduce you to some of the possible health care careers. These occupational clusters follow the National Health Care Skills Standards. These standards are a guide to the information you need to be a successful health care worker.

Part I of this text provides the health care core foundation skills for all health services that are covered in the national standards. Part II has entry-level occupations from each cluster in the standards. You can learn the skills from several occupations and become a multidisciplinary/unlicensed assistive personnel health care worker. Finding several areas of interest in the following occupations enhances your education and provides the skills to increase your employability. After carefully researching these careers, you can make an informed decision.

Population growth, the increase of middle-aged and elderly people, new medical technology, and the need for more rehabilitation and long-term care make a health care occupation a very good choice for the future.

Objectives

When you have completed this section, you will be able to do the following:

- Define the key terms.
- Compare and differentiate the services performed by the therapeutic, diagnostic, information, and environmental services.
- Explain the meaning of *therapeutic*, *diagnostic*, *information*, and *environmental* services.

You learned in Chapter 2 that there are four major health care service areas, each containing many occupations. On the following pages, you will study some of the possible occupations in each service and the duties that you might have as an entry-level employee. Remember that the entry-level jobs are the first step in a career ladder or lattice. The career ladder moves upward in your career. The career lattice allows you to use your transferable skills to move into other career areas. Both allow you many choices. The following information is from the *Dictionary of Occupational Titles*, the *Occupational Outlook Handbook*, and *Descriptions and Organizational Analysis for Hospitals and Related Health Services*.

Career Clusters

Health care, like other fields, will require more knowledge, better skills, and more flexible workers than ever before. Career clusters identify 16 major occupational categories, of which Health Science is one. They link what students learn in school with the knowledge and skills they will need for success in future careers or education. For more information visit, the States' Career Clusters Initiative (SCCI) Web site at http://www.careerclusters.org/.

Partnerships that involve the state, schools, educators, and industry are helping to create guidelines, technical standards, and assessment for these career clusters. The connection and relevance of school to the future helps motivate students.

The Health Science career cluster is described as "planning, managing, and providing therapeutic services, diagnostic services, health informatics, support services, and biotechnology research and development." This is one of the largest and fastest growing industries in the United States.

Therapeutic Services focus basically on the changing health status of the patient over time. Professionals here work directly with the patient; they provide care, treatment, counseling, and education. Some examples include physical therapist, respiratory therapist, athletic trainer, and dental hygienist.

The Diagnostic Services pathway addresses the tests and evaluations that help to detect, diagnosis, and treat disease, injuries, and other physical conditions. Some examples include medical lab technicians, pathologists, and radiology technicians.

Health Informatics includes many different levels of health care careers. Some of these are: health care administrators who manage health care agencies, individuals who manage patient data and information, those who handle financial information, those who work on computer applications related to health care processes and procedures, and those who develop programs to guide excellence in health care delivery. Some examples are admitting clerk, health care administrator, medical librarian, or transcriptionist.

Support Services include careers that help to provide a safe, supportive environment for the delivery of health care. These positions can start at entry level and lead to management and include technical and professional careers. Some examples include dietary technicians or hospital maintenance engineers.

Biotechnology Research and Development addresses bioscience applications to human health. These individuals may work to find new treatments for diseases, improve diagnostic testing, or create new medical devices to assist the patient. Some occupations in this field are biomedical engineer, microbiologist, pharmacist, or research assistant.

Education and Career Planning

There are many opportunities for careers in Health Care and also a variety of environments available for practice. In the mid-twentieth century, most health care was delivered at the doctor's office or in a hospital. Now, the focus has changed to include outpatient surgery, step down and short term stay units, rehab facilities, etc.

The focus on preventative medicine and health status maintenance has also promoted the use of a variety of health care workers with different educational backgrounds, skills, and licensing. The student should identify the occupation that would fit their interests, values, and abilities. They should determine the opportunities for job roles within that area. Different job roles require different educational preparation from on job training to graduate level degrees.

An example of this would be nursing. Entry level would be the Nursing Assistant. Most facilities offer on-the-job training for this position through their staff education departments. The Licensed Practical Nurse role requires one year of formal education and board certification.

The Registered Nurse will need the minimum of a two-year associate degree or up to a four-year baccalaureate degree. Successful completion of board certification would also be required for practice. Registered Nurses with graduate level degrees such as a masters degree in nursing can practice at a higher level as a nurse practitioner diagnosing, treating, and supporting the patient with simple medical problems or promoting higher standards of care for a specific population of patients, such as the geriatric client.

Registered Nurses can also complete a doctoral degree in nursing which will prepare them to participate in research and a more advanced scientific role in nursing. Most occupations offer similar levels of practice requiring varying level of educational preparation.

The student can opt to complete the most basic level of on-the-job training or educational preparation and licensing. In this case, job availability may be adequate but monetary compensation and job satisfaction may be limited. By continuing to focus on increasing educational preparation and experience the opportunities will also increase.

Often times life situations can dictate the factors used to make these decisions. Can I devote more or less years to formal education? How much does the educational preparation cost for each level? Is the monetary compensation adequate for the role I have chosen? Should I start at a lower level so I can enter the job field and begin to earn the money necessary to finance an advanced degree.

Taking the time to thoroughly investigate the job description, level of preparation necessary, and opportunity afforded by each role prior to investing time and money is time well spent.

Therapeutic Services

Therapeutic service workers observe the patient/client, instrumentation, and environment. They report results and assist the treatment team by performing procedures accurately. They also assist in reaching treatment goals.

Respiratory Therapy/Respiratory Care Workers

Every breath is the breath of life, and helping patients/clients with their breathing is a very important part of health care. Patients/clients may live without water for a few days. They may live without food for a few weeks. But without air, they will suffer brain damage within a few minutes and may die after nine minutes.

respiratory
(RES per uh tawr ee)
Pertaining to or serving for breathing.

Respiratory therapy workers and respiratory care practitioners evaluate, treat, and care for patients/clients of all ages who have breathing problems. Therapists test lung capacity and check blood for oxygen and carbon dioxide content. They give treatments and teach self-care to patients/clients with chronic respiratory problems. They also give emergency care for drowning, stroke, shock, heart failure, and other emergencies. Other duties may include keeping records and making minor repairs to equipment. (Figure 3.1)

Respiratory care workers have many career options (see Career Ladder box on page 52) and work in acute hospitals, **cardiopulmonary** laboratories, ambulatory care units, health maintenance organizations, home health agencies, and nursing homes. They work indoors and may be exposed to flammable gases and body fluids. Their jobs may require shift work and weekend work. They stand for long periods of time and carry or push equipment throughout the facility.

FIGURE 3.1
Respiratory Technician cleaning and assembling equipment. What other tasks might a respiratory therapist have to complete?

cardiopulmonary
(kahr dee oh PUHL muh ner ee)
Of, pertaining to, or affecting the heart and lungs.

Tasks—Respiratory Therapy Workers

- Spend most time taking care of equipment
- Follow tasks under the direction of a respiratory therapist
- Scrub and wash equipment, such as respirators, intermittent positive-pressure breathing machines, pulmonary function machines, and oxygen administration sets
- Inspect equipment for damage, and report problems to supervisor
- Start and test gauges, and notify supervisor of malfunction
- Deliver oxygen tanks and other equipment where needed
- Assist in administration of gas or aerosol therapy as directed
- Record amount of oxygen used by patient/client, and prepare billing forms
- Assist the respiratory technician and therapist as needed

For more information, write or go online:

American Association for Respiratory Care, www.aarc.org
9425 N. MacArthur Blvd. Suite 100
Irving, TX 75063-4706

Pharmacy Workers

Pharmacy workers prepare and **dispense** medications prescribed by physicians, podiatrists, dentists, and other health care professionals. (**Figure 3.2**) They provide information to health care professionals and to the public about medicines. Another important task is to review the medicines that patients/clients are taking. This reduces the chance that the patient/client will have a drug interaction that can cause illness or an allergic reaction. They also help in the strict control of distribution and use of government-controlled products, such as narcotics and barbiturates. Since vaccines and other drugs deteriorate, pharmacy workers are responsible for careful inventory control.

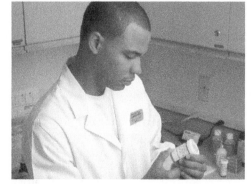

dispense
(di SPENS)
To distribute or pass out.

FIGURE 3.2
Pharmacy worker, preparing medications. How do pharmacy workers help to ensure the safety of clients?

Pharmacy workers have many career options (see Career Ladder box on page 53) and work in acute hospitals, community pharmacies, health maintenance organizations, home health agencies, and clinics. A pharmacist may also work for state and local health departments, as well as for pharmaceutical manufacturers.

CAREER LADDER

RESPIRATORY THERAPY WORKERS	Education and/or Experience Required	Average Income
Respiratory Therapist (RRT)	■ High school diploma or equivalent ■ Completion of AMA-approved respiratory therapist training program in a community college or a four-year bachelor's degree program ■ Registered respiratory therapist ■ Two years of experience in the field following training ■ Passing grade on a written examination given by the National Board of Respiratory Therapy	■ Annual: $45,300–62,570
Respiratory Therapy Technician	■ High school diploma or equivalent ■ Completion of respiratory technician training ■ Certified respiratory therapy technician (CRTT) ■ Completion of AMA-approved respiratory therapy technician program ■ One year of work experience ■ Passing grade on a written examination given by the National Board of Respiratory Therapy	■ Annual: $35,900–54,900
Respiratory Therapy Aide	■ No educational requirements ■ It is desirable to ■ Have a high school diploma or the equivalent ■ Have completed a vocational education program in respiratory therapy	■ Annual: $24,300–31,200

Pharmacy workers work indoors and may be required to work in a restricted environment, such as areas where sterile solutions are prepared. In large hospitals or community pharmacies, they may work in shifts. Their work requires lifting, carrying, pushing items, and climbing ladders in storage areas. They need good vision for close-up work. They stand for long periods of time and must take proper safety precautions when working with products that can be dangerous.

Tasks—Pharmacy Assistants

- Type labels for medication and records and transactions in the pharmacy log
- Clip typed labels to medication requests and deliver to the pharmacist
- Assign prescription numbers
- List patient/client name, physician, and prescription numbers in the log book
- Copy physician's instructions for use of medication
- Calculate charges, type billing slips for prescriptions, and enter charges on medication forms

CAREER LADDER

PHARMACY WORKERS	Education and/or Experience Required	Average Income
Pharmacist	■ Completion of five years in an accredited pharmacy program ■ One year of pharmacy internship ■ License in state of employment after passing a rigorous exam	■ Annual: $95,800–123,300
Pharmacy Technician	■ Two to twelve months of on-the-job training, completion of a high school pharmacy technician course or completion of a one- to two-year program in a community college ■ Some states offer a pharmacy technician certification upon successful completion of an examination	■ Annual: $23,000–33,800
Pharmacy Clerk/ Pharmacy Helper	■ High school diploma or equivalent ■ Good typing skills ■ Two to three months of on-the-job training or completion of a pharmacy vocational program	■ Annual: $18,000–25,000

- Compile periodic reports from log book
- Label pharmaceutical preparations by using a typewriter, printer, or computer, and maintain records and files
- Rotate stock to keep dated items current and order supplies
- Run errands and deliver orders
- Clean equipment and work areas according to department procedures
- Destroy damaged drugs according to department standards
- Use **aseptic** techniques, follow procedure for working under purification hood, and wear appropriate clothing and disposable caps

aseptic
(uh SEP tik)
Free from the living germs of disease.

For more information, write or go online:

American Association of Colleges of Pharmacy, www.aacp.org
1426 Prince Street
Alexandria, VA 22314

Occupational Therapy Workers

Occupational therapy workers treat people who are mentally, physically, developmentally, or emotionally disabled. (**Figure 3.3**) They evaluate the self-care, work, and leisure skills of their patients/clients. They plan and develop programs that help restore, develop, and maintain patients' ability to manage the activities of daily living. The goal is to optimize the patient's functional independence by helping them compensate for their limitations.

Occupational therapy workers have many career options (see Career Ladder box on page 55) and work in general hospitals, schools, nursing homes, outpatient clinics, rehabilitation centers, day care centers, mental health agencies, special workshops, health maintenance organizations, and psychiatric hospitals. They work a 40-hour week and may have to work evenings or weekends occasionally. The work environment depends on the type of facility. In a large rehabilitation center, therapists may work in a spacious room equipped with machines, hand tools, and other devices. In a psychiatric hospital, they may work on the ward. They carry and lift equipment and transfer patients from wheelchairs. Their work requires both standing and sitting. An occupational therapist needs to be creative; they have to design equipment and tools for their patient's individual needs.

FIGURE 3.3
Occupational therapy worker applying hand support to prevent contracture. What is the main goal of an occupational therapist?

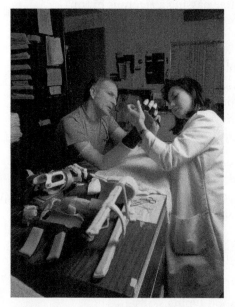

Tasks—Occupational Therapy Aides

- Transport patients, assemble equipment, and prepare and maintain work areas
- Perform **clerical** tasks, restock and order supplies, answer the phone, and schedule appointments

clerical
(KLER i kuhl)
Of or pertaining to keeping records, filing, typing, or other general office tasks.

CAREER LADDER

OCCUPATIONAL THERAPY WORKERS	Education and/or Experience Required	Average Income
Physiatrist	■ Graduation from an accredited medical school ■ License to practice medicine or osteopathy in state of employment ■ Residency in physical medicine and rehabilitation	■ Annual: $124,800–220,900
Occupational Therapist (OT) (OTR registered)	■ Bachelor's degree in occupational therapy (four-year course in an approved program) ■ Certification by the Board of Registry of the American Occupational Therapy Association ■ Up to six months of on-the-job training	■ Annual: $57,200–84,200
Certified Occupational Therapy Assistant (COTA)	■ High school diploma or equivalent ■ Completion of a two-year program in a community college ■ Completion of a certified vocational or technical program ■ Supervised fieldwork ■ Completion of a two-year program approved by the American Occupational Therapy Association (AOTA)	■ Annual: $41,200–59,900
Occupational Therapy Aide	■ High school diploma or equivalent ■ On-the-job training ■ Completion of a vocational education program as an occupational therapy aide	■ Annual: $19,500–33,200

- Teach work-related skills (e.g., use of power tools)
- Help clients with rehabilitative activities and exercises
- Teach proper method of moving from a wheelchair to bed
- Observe patient activities for progress and make reports to aid in evaluation of patient progress
- Assist in adaptation of equipment, splints, and other self-help devices
- Transport patients
- Store equipment, clean work areas, and help maintain tools and equipment
- Perform other clerical duties (e.g., filing)

For more information, write or go online:

American Occupational Therapy Association, www.aota.org
Division of Credentialing
4720 Montgomery
PO Box 31220
Bethesda, MD 20824-1220

Physical Therapy Workers

Physical therapy workers (Figure 3.4) help people with injuries or diseases of the muscles, nerves, joints, and bones to overcome their disabilities. The client may be disabled from an accident, a stroke, or a disease. Some of the conditions that require treatment are multiple sclerosis, cerebral palsy, nerve injuries, amputations, fractures, arthritis, and heart disease. Patients vary in age from newborn to aged. Physical therapy workers help the patient regain as close to normal activity as possible. A subset of this category includes sports medicine or sports therapy workers, who specialize in treating disabilities caused by sports-related injuries.

Physical therapy workers have many career options (see Career Ladder box) and work in acute care and long-term care facilities, ambulatory care units, health maintenance organizations, rehabilitation centers, schools, public health agencies, home health care agencies, and sports medicine centers. Some physical therapists are in private practice. They contract to work for health care agencies or may have an office where they provide care. They work in specially equipped physical therapy departments, in clinics, and in private homes. Their work requires lifting and carrying up to 50 pounds, stooping, pushing, and pulling patients and equipment. They stand and walk during their shifts.

FIGURE 3.4

One of the many duties of a physical therapy aide is assisting patients/clients with walking. How are the duties of a physical therapy worker and an occupational therapy worker similar?

Tasks—Physical Therapy or Sports Medicine Aides

- Prepare equipment (e.g., hydrotherapy pools, paraffin baths, and hot packs)
- Assist patients/clients to treatment area using a wheelchair or offering a shoulder to lean on

- Inform therapist or assistant if patients/clients are having difficulty with their treatment
- Change linen on beds and tables
- Clean equipment and work area
- Inventory materials and supplies
- Assist with clerical tasks

Tasks—Physical Therapy or Sports Medicine Assistants
- Apply heat, cold, and ultrasound
- Massage and perform therapeutic exercises

For more information, write or go online:

American Physical Therapy Association, www.apta.org
1111 North Fairfax Street
Alexandria, VA 22314-1488

CAREER LADDER

PHYSICAL THERAPY WORKERS	Education and/or Experience Required	Average Income
Physical Therapist	■ Four- or five-year degree in physical therapy (primarily five) ■ Supervised four-month clinical internship ■ Passing grade on a state licensure examination	■ Annual: $62,300–87,900
Physical Therapy or Sports Medicine Assistant	■ Training requirements are not uniform ■ Twenty-four states require graduation from an accredited community college ■ Students may be required to pass a written licensure examination	■ Annual: $39,100–57,800
Physical Therapy or Sports Medicine Aide	■ High school diploma or equivalent (preferred) ■ On-the-job training ■ Completion of a vocational education program as a physical therapy aide	■ Annual: $20,100–28,900

Emergency Medical Service Workers

First responders are often the first trained people to treat patients/clients. They provide emergency medical care before emergency medical technicians (EMTs) reach the scene. They may be law enforcement officers, members of the fire service, company employees, or private citizens.

FIGURE 3.5
EMTs transporting an injured or sick patient to a medical facility. What are some of the qualities that an EMT must have?

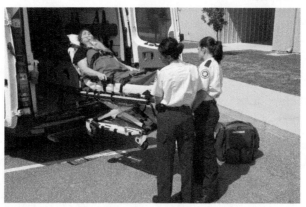

Emergency medical technicians are providers of pre-hospital medical care in an emergency. A heart attack, unscheduled birth, automobile accident, or near drowning all require immediate attention. The EMT administers basic life support and transports sick and injured people to medical facilities. (**Figure 3.5**) Paramedics, on the other hand, work within a lot of emergency room settings very closely to the role of the registered nurse. They can make independent medical emergency decisions, unlike an EMT. The difference between EMT and paramedic is the difference between basic and advanced life support.

Emergency medical service workers have many career opportunities (see Career Ladder box on page 60) and may work in rescue, police, and fire departments, ski patrols, hospital emergency departments, and private ambulance services. They must usually work shifts and weekends. They work inside and outside in all weather conditions. They may be exposed to body fluids.

Emergency medical service workers must be in good physical condition. For example, they must have good eyesight, hearing, and speech. They must also be able to lift heavy loads, reach, stoop, and climb as the job requires. Emergency medical service workers must be prepared to assess a situation quickly and to take steps for basic life saving actions.

Tasks—First Responders
- Gain access to patient, assess patient, provide appropriate care, and report assessment and care given
- Lift or move patient to a safe place if necessary

Tasks—Emergency Medical Technicians/A (Basic)
- Drive an ambulance
- Determine the nature of the victim's illness or injury
- Give appropriate care:
  - Open and maintain the airway
  - Restore breathing
  - Control bleeding
  - Treat for shock

- Immobilize fractures
- Bandage wounds
- Assist with childbirth
- Give initial care to poison and burn victims
- Use automated external defibrillators

- Use correct equipment and techniques to remove trapped victims safely

- Transport patients to hospital:
    - Place patient on stretcher
    - Constantly watch patient while in transport
    - Notify hospital of arrival

- Report to the emergency staff observations of and care given to the victim

- Maintain clean, well-equipped ambulance

- Ensure ambulance is in good running order:
    - Check gas, oil, tire pressure, siren, communication equipment

Personal Wellness

Company Wellness Plans

In today's job market, some companies now offer more than just health insurance or retirement benefits. Many employers offer personal wellness plans for their employees. These personal wellness plans benefit both the employers and the employees. Healthy workers are more productive and have a higher attendance rate. In addition, personal wellness programs help to keep the cost of insurance down.

Employees can learn to live a healthier lifestyle through a company's personal wellness plan. Companies may offer smoking cessation plans, health risk assessments, and diet counseling. Some employers also make working out more convenient by subsidizing gym programs, providing on-site workout facilities, and allowing employees to use time during the day to exercise.

While some companies offer employees ways to exercise, other companies help their employees to eat healthier. Some companies now serve healthier foods in their cafeterias or offer healthier vending machine choices. Others have created employee diet groups.

Many businesses reward their employees for participating in the wellness program. Workers may receive reduced medical co-payment costs, cash payments, gift certificates, and prizes. Employers are working hard to ensure their workforce is healthier and happier. This means that you may likely be offered these benefits, no matter which career you choose.

How might participating in a wellness program at a company help a person's career?

CAREER LADDER

EMERGENCY MEDICAL SERVICE WORKERS	Education and/or Experience Required	Average Income

Registered EMT-Paramedic	■ Completion of EMT-paramedic training in an approved program offered by one of the following:
	  ● Vocational school
	  ● State educational facility
	  ● Community college
	  ● Hospital
	  ● Medical school
	  ● University
	■ Six months of field experience as an EMT-paramedic
	■ Passing grade on a written and practical examination given by the National Registry of Emergency Medical Technicians or the state emergency medical systems board
		■ Annual: $31,000–46,200

Registered EMT-Ambulance/I (Intermediate)	■ Graduation from an approved EMT Basic program and 35–55 hours of additional instruction ■ Passing grade on a written and practical examination given by the National Registry of Emergency Medical Technicians or the state emergency medical systems board	■ Annual: $23,700–34,200
Basic EMT-Ambulance/A (Basic) (EMT)	■ At least 18 years of age ■ High school diploma or equivalent ■ Valid driver's license ■ Completion of a minimum 110-hour program offered in vocational programs ■ Passing grade on a written and practical exam given by the National Registry of Emergency Medical Technicians or the state emergency medical systems board	■ Annual: $21,300–31,800

For more information, write or go online:

National Association of Emergency Medical Technicians, www.naemt.org
PO Box 1400
Clinton, MS 39060-1400

National Registry of Emergency Medical Technicians, www.nremt.org
PO Box 29233
Columbus, OH 43229

Medical Assistants

Medical assistants are responsible for the efficient operation of a physician's office. They also work in clinics, health maintenance organizations, and ambulatory care units. Medical assistants have varied duties. Some specialize in back office procedures (Figure 3.6), while others choose to work in the front office. They work indoors in a clean environment, 40 hours a week, and some weekends. They have varied job opportunities, (see Career Ladder box on page 62) and their work requires standing on their feet most of the day (back office), lifting, reaching, and helping patients/clients. They may be exposed to body fluids. The front office worker sits at a desk for long periods.

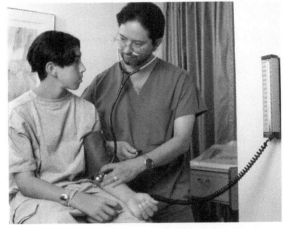

FIGURE 3.6
A back office medical assistant performing one of many duties—taking a client's blood pressure. What is the difference between a front office medical assistant and a back office medical assistant?

The current trend toward large medical groups has relocated administrative/front office responsibilities. Billing, insurance verification, medical records, appointment scheduling, and **payroll** have been relocated to departments that specialize in handling work for the increased number of patients/clients. See "Administrative Support Service Workers" later in this section for more information.

payroll
(PEY rohl)
A list of employees to be paid a specific amount.

Tasks—Administrative/Front Office Medical Assistants

- Greet patients/clients
- Answer phones
- Handle mail
- Make appointments
- Arrange hospital admissions
- Arrange for laboratory services
- Prepare insurance forms (e.g., Medicare, medical insurance, workers' compensation)
- Type medical reports
- Maintain patient files
- May handle billing and receipts
- Prepare payroll for office staff

Finding the Right Occupation for You   **61**

autoclave
(AW tuh kleyv)
A strong, pressurized, steam-heated vessel used for sterilization.

Tasks—Clinical/Back Office Medical Assistants (tasks vary according to state law)

- Sterilize instruments using an **autoclave**
- Prepare clients for examination
- Assist physician during examination
- Give injections
- Take and record temperatures, pulse, respiration, and blood pressure
- Measure height and weight
- Perform routine urinalysis
- Collect blood samples
- Perform simple blood tests
- Record electrocardiograms

CAREER LADDER

MEDICAL ASSISTANTS	Education and/or Experience Required	Average Income
Office Manager	■ Completion of administrative and clinical medical assistant program ■ Workshops ■ Seminars ■ Home study courses	■ Annual: $30,900–47,100
Clinical/Back Office Medical Assistant	■ High school diploma or equivalent ■ On-the-job training in a physician's front office ■ Completion of an administrative medical assistant program ■ Completion of an examination by the American Association of Medical Assistants, which offers a certified medical assistant (CMA) certificate (optional)	■ Annual: $27,300–32,600
Administrative/Front Office Medical Assistant	■ High school diploma or equivalent ■ On-the-job training in a physician's back office ■ Completion of an administrative medical assistant program	■ Annual: $28,500–37,000

- Assist with minor surgery
- Direct patients in preparation for x-rays and tests
- Instruct patients about medication and special diets

For more information, write or go online:

American Association of Medical Assistants, www.aama-ntl.org
20 North Wacker Drive, Suite 1575
Chicago, IL 60606-2903

Dental Workers

Dental workers (**Figure 3.7**) are responsible for maintaining oral health and repairing dental abnormalities. They emphasize treatment and prevention of problems associated with the hard and soft tissues of the mouth.

According to their level of education, dental workers have many different opportunities. They work in private practices, dental schools, hospital dental departments, private clinics, health maintenance organizations, and state and local public health departments (see Career Ladder box on page 64). Dental laboratory technicians work in a dental laboratory. Dental workers work indoors in a clean environment. They are subject to respiratory infections due to close contact with patients and may be exposed to body fluid. Their work requires standing most of the day, reaching, and handling dental instruments, equipment, and supplies.

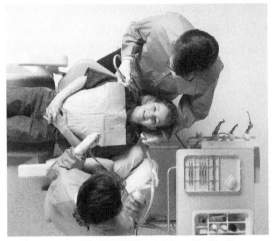

FIGURE 3.7
A dental assistant performing one of many tasks—assisting the dentist. What are some of the other tasks that a dental assistant might perform?

Tasks—Dental Assistants

- Make the patient comfortable in the dental chair
- Prepare the client for treatment
- Hand the dentist proper instruments and materials
- Suction the patient's mouth
- Prepare materials for making impressions and restorations
- Take and process dental x-rays
- Teach oral health (e.g., flossing, brushing, postoperative care)
- Prepare instruments for **sterilizing**
- Make casts of teeth and mouth from impressions taken by the dentist
- Apply medications to the teeth and oral tissue, remove cement used in the filling process, and place rubber dams on the teeth (in some states)
- May manage the office (e.g., make appointments, keep treatment records, send bills, receive payments, and order supplies and materials)

sterilizing
(STER uh lahyz ing)
The act of destroying microorganisms in or on something.

CAREER LADDER

DENTAL WORKERS	Education and/or Experience Required	Average Income
Dentist	■ Graduation from a dental school approved by the American Dental Association ■ Passing grade on written and practical examinations ■ State licensure by passing written examinations given by the National Board of Examiners	■ Annual: $119,700–155,800
Dental Hygienist	■ Graduation from an accredited dental hygienist program in a two-year community college, a four-year bachelor's degree program, or a five-year master's degree program ■ Passing grade on a written and clinical examination ■ License in the state of employment (given by the National Board of Dental Examiners)	■ Annual: $55,600–80,000
Dental Laboratory Technician	■ High school diploma or equivalent ■ Two-year vocational program ■ On-the-job training (three to four years) ■ May become certified by passing a written and practical examination given by the National Board for Certification	■ Annual: $27,000–45,100
Dental Assistant	■ High school diploma or equivalent ■ On-the-job training ■ Completion of a one- or two-year community college or vocational training program ■ Completion of an examination by the Certifying Board of the Dental Assisting National Board (CDA) (optional)	■ Annual: $27,500–39,800

For more information, write or go online:

Commission on Dental Accreditation, American Dental Association, www.ada.org
211 East Chicago Avenue, Suite 1814
Chicago, IL 60611

National Association of Health Career Schools
750 First Street NE, Suite 940
Washington, DC 20005
FAX: (202) 842-1565
E-mail: NAHCS@aol.com

American Dental Assistants Association, www.dentalassistant.org
35 East Wacker Drive, Suite 1730
Chicago, IL 60601-2211

Nursing Service Workers

Nursing service workers provide many varied and essential services. (Figure 3.8) They care for patients who are physically ill or disabled and provide preventive care (e.g., immunizations). They work in industry, community health nursing, general hospitals, long-term care facilities, government agencies, schools, educational institutions, visiting nurse associations, clinics, physicians' offices, ambulatory care units, homes, and health maintenance organizations. Nurses work indoors. They may have rotating shifts and work on weekends. Their work requires standing, walking, lifting, and pushing patients, carts, and wheelchairs. They are exposed to unpleasant odors and body fluids.

Next, we will discuss a range of nursing positions.

FIGURE 3.8

Nurse assistants (a and b) and home health aide (c) helping clients. What is the difference between a nurse assistant and a home health aid?

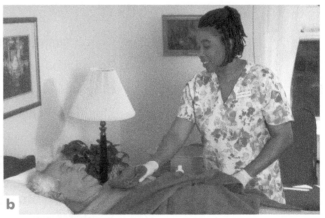

Registered Nurses

Registered nurses (RN) care for patients/clients in hospitals, clinics, doctor's offices, nursing homes, and patient's home. Registered nurses take care of sick and injured people and work directly with the patient and their families. They monitor and track vital signs and are the primary point of contact. An RN can work his/her way up the career ladder to Director of Nursing.

Tasks—Registered Nurses

- Conduct physical assessments
- Collaborate with physicians and other health care team members to develop a treatment plan for the patient
- Direct the health care team
- Coordinate delivery of care and evaluate outcome of care
- Administer treatment and medications
- Educate patients about their medical conditions
- Provide advice and emotional support to patients and their families
- Record medical histories and symptoms
- Help perform diagnostic tests and analyze results
- Operate medical equipment
- Administer treatment and medications

Tasks—Licensed Practical Nurse

- Provide technical care for the sick, injured, convalescent, and disabled under the direction of the registered nurse and physician
- Measure and record vital signs
- Prepare and give injections, dress wounds
- Assist with bathing, dressing, and personal hygiene
- Collect samples for testing
- Record food and fluid intake/output
- Clean and monitor medical equipment
- Monitor patients
- Teach family how to care for patients.

For more information, go to www.nurse.org to find a state organization for nurses.

Nurse Assistants/Home Health Aides

Home health aides care for patients/clients in their homes instead of in a health facility. They care for patients of all ages who need more care than their families can give. Their job requires them to go to different homes. Nurse assistants and home health aides stand, walk, and lift patients and may push wheelchairs. They may be exposed to body fluids.

Tasks—Nurse Assistants

- Collaborate with the licensed nurse in charge of the patient's care to establish a plan of care and goals for care
- Answer patient/client call lights

- Bathe patients
- Dress and undress clients
- Assist with personal hygiene (e.g., shaving, hair care, oral care, and dental care)
- Serve and collect food trays and feed patients who need help
- Provide between-meal nourishment and fresh drinking water
- Transport patients in wheelchair or stretcher or help patients walk
- Take and record temperature, pulse, and respiration and record blood pressure
- Record food and liquid intake and output
- May apply ice bags or heat packs
- Give back rubs, if appropriate
- Observe and report any unusual conditions
- Tidy clients' rooms, change bed linen, and collect soiled linen
- Write in patients' charts

What's New?

Technological Improvements in the Workplace

Technology has changed the duties of workers in some health careers. Advancements in computer hardware and software have helped to improve the lines of communication and streamline the tasks in careers such as administrative support services and nursing.

Medical billing software has allowed administrative support service workers to make sure that forms are filled out correctly and submitted properly. The software also cuts down the time a worker has to spend filling out tedious paperwork. Not only does the software make the medical billing process more efficient, it also makes it more flexible. Workers no longer have to be onsite to complete billing tasks. They can access information from any computer, perhaps even on their home computer.

Nurses in both acute care and long-term care facilities may now carry personal digital computers, or PDAs. These handheld computers help nurses track patient progress, access medication information, and collect data. As with the medical billing software, the computers help to lessen the amount of paperwork a nurse may be required to complete. These advances may help health providers improve the quality of client/patient care.

What other types of careers listed in this chapter may also benefit from PDAs?

CAREER LADDER

NURSING SERVICE WORKERS	Education and/or Experience Required	Average Income
Nurse Practitioner	■ All requirements for becoming a registered nurse ■ Completion of an accredited course in nurse practitioner training ■ License for the state of employment after passing a rigorous exam	■ Annual: $69,900–94,600
Registered Nurse	■ High school diploma or equivalent ■ Graduation from a two-year community college ■ Graduation from a four-year college or university ■ Graduation from an accredited school of nursing ■ Graduation from a diploma school (three-year hospital schools are being phased out) ■ License for the state of employment after passing a rigorous exam	■ Annual: $52,500–78,000 ■ $58,300–103,500 with advanced education
Licensed Vocational Nurse (LVN)/Licensed Practical Nurse (LPN)	■ High school diploma or equivalent ■ Graduation from a recognized one-year program ■ License for the state of employment after passing a rigorous exam	■ Annual: $33,900–47,200
Unlicensed Assistive Personnel	■ Additional training in specialty (e.g., EKG, phlebotomy) ■ Preservice training (40–120 hours) provided by an employing agency ■ May require certification as a nurse assistant	■ Annual: $20,200–31,200

(continued)

NURSING SERVICE WORKERS	Education and/or Experience Required	Average Income
Home Health Aide	■ High school diploma or equivalent (preferred) ■ Completion of a vocational education program as a home health aide ■ State certification may be required	■ Annual: $17,700–24,300
Nurse Assistant/Geriatric Aide	■ High school diploma or equivalent (preferred) and/or participation in a high school nursing assistant program ■ Hospital-conducted on-the-job training ■ Completion of an OBRA-approved 1987 Omnibus Budget Reconciliation Act nurse assistant program. ■ License for the state of employment after passing a rigorous exam	■ Annual: $20,500–29,000

Tasks—Home Health Aides

- Transfer patients from place to place and assist with bathing, walking, and prescribed exercises
- Assist with medication routines
- Help with braces or artificial limbs
- Check and record pulse, respiration, and blood pressure
- Change nonsterile dressings
- Provide emotional support and take client outside home as a companion
- Change bed linen, clean laundry, and clean clients' living quarters
- Shop for patients' food and prepare meals
- Report findings and observations to supervisors
- Act as a companion on shopping trips, doctor visits, and outdoor activities

For more information, write or go online:

National Association of Health Career Schools
750 First Street NE, Suite 940
Washington, DC 20002
FAX: (202) 842-1565
E-mail: NAHCS@aol.com

National Association for Home Care & Hospice, www.nahc.org
228 Seventh Street SE
Washington, DC 20003

Veterinary Workers

Veterinary assistant animal caregivers usually care for small animals such as dogs and cats. They provide basic care such as feeding, grooming, cleaning cages, exercising animals, providing companionship, and observing animals for behavioral changes that can indicate an illness or injury. Other positions in animal care include working with horses, zoo animals, and laboratory animals used for research.

Animal care workers have many career opportunities (see Career Ladder box on page 71). They may work in kennels, animal shelters, veterinary hospitals and clinics, stables, laboratories, aquariums, and zoological parks. Job titles and duties vary by employment setting. In some positions shift work may be required because the animals need 24-hour care. The work environment depends on the type of facility. Some kennels have outdoor animal runs; veterinary offices have exam and treatment rooms.

Concern for and interest in animals may cause emotional upsets due to witnessing the results of abuse or having to **euthanize** the animal. The work can be physically demanding. You may have to lift large bags of food and the work can involve kneeling, bending, crawling, and restraining of animals. There is also a chance of injury due to bites and scratches. Odors can be unpleasant.

Tasks—Animal Caretaker/Assistant
- Keep constant eye on condition of animals in their charge
- Watch animals recover from surgery
- Check dressing
- Observe animals' overall attitude
- Notify doctor of anything out of the ordinary
- Maintain sanitary conditions

Tasks—Kennel Staff
- Clean cages and dog runs
- Fill food and water dishes
- Exercise animals

euthanize
(YOO thuh nahyz)
To painlessly end the life or permit the death of a hopelessly sick or injured animal or individual for reasons of mercy.

apprenticeship
(uh PREN tis ship)
The act of learning a trade or occupation through experience.

VETERINARY WORKERS	Education and/or Experience Required	Average Income
Veterinarian (DVM or VMD)	■ Completion of three to four years of preveterinary college ■ Graduation from an accredited veterinary college and a Doctor of Veterinary Medicine degree ■ License in state of employment, after passing a rigorous exam	■ Annual: $62,800–105,200
Animal Health Technician (ATR registered)	■ Completion of certificate or associate's degree ■ Registration, certification, or licensure required in many states	■ Annual: $24,000–35,900
Veterinarian Animal Caretaker/Assistant	■ High school diploma or equivalent ■ On-the-job training ■ Home study through American Boarding Kennels Association (ABKA) ■ Passing grade on oral and written exam to become ABKA Certified Kennel Operator (CKO)	■ Annual: $18,100–26,700
Groomer	■ Completion of 6–10 weeks of informal **apprenticeship** ■ Four to 18 weeks at a state-licensed grooming school ■ Completion of National Dog Groomers Association of America written and practical skills exam	■ Annual: $24,600–37,600

Tasks—Experienced Attendants

- Provide basic animal health care
- Bathe animals
- Trim nails
- Attend to other grooming needs
- Sell pet food and supplies
- Assist in obedience training
- Help with breeding
- Prepare animals for snipping

Tasks—Groomers

- Do initial brush-out
- Clip hair with electric clippers, cobs, and grooming shears
- Cut nails
- Clean ears
- Bathe
- Blow-dry animal
- Do final clipping and styling

Tasks—Groomer/Owners

- Operate own grooming business
- Answer telephones
- Schedule appointments
- Discuss pets' grooming needs
- Collect information on pets' disposition
- Collect information on pets' veterinarian
- Inspect and report medical problems such as skin or ear infection

For more information, write or go online:

The Humane Society of the United States, www.hsus.org
2100 Street NW
Washington, DC 20037-1598

Diagnostic Services

Diagnostic service workers help with the diagnosis of illness and disease. Some diagnostic service workers have direct contact with the patient/client, whereas others do not. They plan services and prepare and perform tests accurately. They also understand quality control and report results in a timely manner.

Medical Laboratory Workers

Medical laboratory workers (**Figure 3.9**) perform many varied tests. Some of these tests are highly technical, whereas others are not as technical. In many cases, tests are performed on computerized equipment. Medical laboratory workers determine changes that have occurred in the blood, urine, lymph, and body tissues.

They identify increases or decreases in white or red blood cells, cross-match blood for transfusions, identify microscopic changes in cells, and determine the presence of parasites, viruses, or bacteria in the blood, tissue, or urine. These tests help the physician make an accurate diagnosis and correctly treat the patient.

Medical laboratory workers have many career opportunities (see Career Ladder box on page 74). They work for acute care hospitals, private laboratories, physicians' offices, clinics, ambulatory care units, health maintenance organizations, public health agencies, pharmaceutical firms, and research institutions. Their work requires a lot of walking, standing, reaching, stooping, lifting, and carrying of equipment. In addition, they need good eyesight for close work. They work indoors and may be exposed to unpleasant odors and body fluids and have frequent contact with water and cleaning solutions. Their jobs often require them to work shifts and weekends.

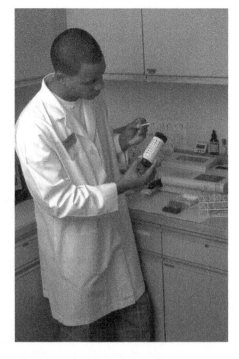

Tasks—Medical Laboratory Aides

- Clean laboratory equipment
- Prepare cleaning solutions
- Dry glassware and instruments using a cloth, hot-air dryer, or acetone bath
- Examine clean equipment for cracks or chips and store equipment properly
- Operate an autoclave to sterilize equipment
- Prepare stains, solutions, and culture media following appropriate procedures

Tasks—Phlebotomists/Venipuncture Technicians

- Draw blood from patients for testing by the technician or technologist

For more information, write or go online:

American Association of Blood Banks, www.aabb.org
8101 Glenbrook Road
Bethesda, MD 20814-2749

American Society for Clinical Laboratory Science, www.ascls.org
6701 Democracy Boulevard, Suite 300
Bethesda, MD 20817

Board of Certified Laboratory Assistants
9500 South California Avenue
Evergreen Park, IL 60642

Careers in Genetics

Career opportunities in the field of medical genetics are opening up as a result of advances in genetic technology and The Human Genome Project. Job tasks in genetics include isolation, identification, and analysis of the genes, which assists with research into the function of genes, as well as the cause of inherited diseases. There are three main areas of jobs in genetics:

- *Cytogenetics* studies chromosomes and how they are connected to disease and human body development.

- *Bioinformatics* is a discipline that focuses on managing genetics data, providing databases and computing tools for gathering, sorting, analyzing, and merging data. Computations and statistical analysis are required for sequencing projects.

- *Genetics Laboratory Research Assistants* perform genetics testing and research for a variety of purposes, including law enforcement, pharmaceutical research, and clinical medical diagnoses and treatments.

CAREER LADDER

MEDICAL LABORATORY WORKERS	Education and/or Experience Required	Average Income
Medical Pathologist	■ Graduation from a medical school approved by the Council on Medical Education and Hospitals of the American Medical Association ■ State license to practice medicine or osteopathy ■ Certification by the American Board of Pathology	■ Annual: $121,400–291,000

Medical Laboratory Supervisor, Administrator, or Chief Pathologist, Histologist, Cytologist	■ Several years of experience as a medical technologist
	
	■ Graduate education in one of the following:
	
	  ● Biological sciences
	  ● Chemistry
	  ● Management
		■ Annual: $121,400–291,000

Medical Laboratory Technologist	■ Graduate of four-year medical technology program in college or university ■ Graduate of four-year medical technology program and certification (CMT) ■ Successful completion of a written examination prepared by the Board of Registry of the American Society of Clinical Pathologists, Medical Technologists ■ Registered medical technologist (RMT) ■ Successful completion of a written examination prepared by the International Society of Clinical Laboratory Technology	■ Annual: $45,800–65,100

(continued)

MEDICAL LABORATORY WORKERS	Education and/or Experience Required	Average Income
Medical Laboratory Technician	■ Two years of training in a community college, four-year college or university, or vocational/technical school ■ Two years of training in a laboratory technician program ■ Successful completion of requirements for certification (CLT) established by the National Certification Agency for Medical Laboratory Personnel	■ Annual: $28,800–45,400
Medical Laboratory Assistant Blood and Plasma	■ High school diploma or equivalent ■ Completion of an approved 12-month medical laboratory technician certificate program in a community college, vocational school, or private program	■ Annual: $20,800–41,600
Medical Phlebotomist	■ High school graduate or equivalent ■ Ten to 20-hour certification program in a hospital, physician's office, or laboratory ■ Completion of a vocational education program as a phlebotomist	■ Annual: $26,000–32,300
Medical Laboratory Aide	■ High school diploma or equivalent ■ On-the-job training for at least two months ■ Completion of a vocational education program as a laboratory aide	■ Annual: $24,000–31,500

Radiology Workers

Radiology workers operate x-ray equipment to take pictures of the internal parts of the body. (Figure 3.10) The x-rays provide information for the diagnosis and treatment of patients. For example, x-rays of the chest help detect lung diseases, such as lung cancer and tuberculosis. Some of the diseases or injuries that x-rays help diagnose or treat are ulcers, blood clots, cancer, and fractures. The use of imaging techniques like ultrasound and magnetic resonance imaging (MRI) is growing. The term diagnostic imaging includes these procedures as well as x-ray techniques.

FIGURE 3.10
A radiologic technologist preparing to take an x-ray of a patient. What are some of the items that radiologic technologists wear to protect themselves?

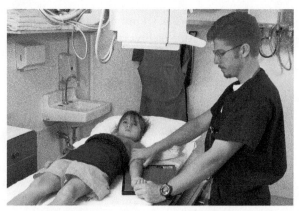

Radiology workers have a variety of job opportunities (see Career Ladder box on page 77) and may work in general hospitals, physicians' offices, trauma centers, chiropractic offices, private consulting offices, clinics federal and state agencies, health maintenance organizations, and ambulatory care facilities. They work indoors and may be in confined areas. They wear protective gloves, aprons, and film badges because the hazards of radiation are present. Shift work and evening work may be part of their schedule. Their work requires the lifting and positioning of patients, standing during most of the shift, and pushing mobile equipment. They may be exposed to body fluids.

The career ladder in the radiology field does not have an aide or assistant position. Some facilities use transport aides in radiology. Being a transport aide in a radiology department allows you to learn about the radiology department.

Diagnostic Medical Sonographers

Diagnostic medical sonographers use diagnostic ultrasound under the supervision of a physician. They are also called *ultrasound technologists.* They use equipment to transmit sound waves at high frequencies into the patient's body, resulting in an image viewed on a screen and automatically recorded on a printout strip or video. The use of ultrasound is important in prenatal care and for cardiology.

Sonographers work in acute care hospitals, in clinics, and sometimes with a group of obstetrics specialists. They work five-day weeks and generally have weekends and evenings off.

For more information, write or go online:

American Society of Radiologic Technologists, www.asrt.org
15000 Central Avenue SE
Albuquerque, NM 87123-3917

American Registry of Radiologic Technologists, www.arrt.org
1255 Northland Drive
Mendota, MN 55120

Society of Diagnostic Medical Sonographers, www.sdms.org
12770 Coit Road, Suite 708
Dallas, TX 75251

RADIOLOGY WORKERS	Education and/or Experience Required	Average Income
Radiologist	■ Graduation from an accredited medical school ■ License to practice medicine in the state of employment ■ Three years of special training in radiology recognized and approved by the board and by the Council on Medical Education and Hospitals of the ■ American Medical Association (Must take exam)	■ Annual: $93,500–329,600
Radiologic Technologist/ Sonographer/Ultrasound Radiologic Technologist Chief	■ Graduation from an accredited program ■ Bachelor's degree in radiologic technology ■ Experience in two or more radiologic disciplines (e.g., nuclear medicine, radiation therapy) ■ Should be registered as a radiologic technologist through the American Registry of Radiologic Technologies (ARRT)	■ Annual: $43,500–74,400
Diagnostic Medical Technologist	■ High school diploma or equivalent ■ One-year certificate program ■ No experience in health occupation	■ Annual: $53,300–63,600

Electrocardiography Workers
Electrocardiographic Technicians

Electrocardiography workers operate an EKG machine to record the electrical changes that occur during a heartbeat. (Figure 3.11) These recordings help physicians diagnose any irregularities or changes in the patient's heartbeat. These tests are done routinely after a certain age, before surgery, and as a diagnostic tool. EKG technicians also apply Holter monitors. EKG technicians have many job opportunities (see Career Ladder box on page 79) and work in acute care hospitals, clinics, private physicians' offices, health maintenance organizations, and ambulatory care facilities. They work indoors and may work shifts, evenings, and weekends. They spend a lot of their time standing and walking.

Tasks—Electrocardiographic Technicians

- Escort client to treatment room
- Take portable equipment to patient's room
- Explain the test procedure
- Help client remove necessary clothing

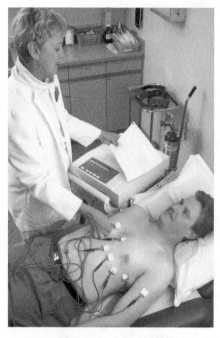

FIGURE 3.11
An EKG technician performing an electrocardiogram. Why does an EKG technician perform an electrocardiogram?

deviations
(de vee A shuns)
Departures from a standard or norm.

- Paste or attach electrodes to correct areas on patient's chest, arms, legs; connect leads from EKG machine to electrodes; and operate selector switch on EKG machine
- Reposition chest electrodes to record various positions
- Check recording for accuracy (leads placed incorrectly give an incorrect reading)
- Recognize significant **deviations** from normal heartbeat and report immediately
- Edit and mount final results
- Send copy of graph to the physician
- Maintain EKG records

- Type physician's diagnosis
- Care for equipment by cleaning electrodes and keeping all equipment well supplied with paper, etc.
- Conduct vectorcardiograms (multidimensional traces), stress testing (exercise tests), and pulse recordings
- Apply Holter monitoring (12- to 24-hour recording of an EKG)

For more information, write:

National Society for Cardiovascular Technology
120 Falcon Drive, Suite 3
Fredericksburg, VA 22408

Electroneurodiagnostic Technologists

Electroneurodiagnostic (END) technologists use computers to record electrical impulses transmitted by the brain and the nervous system. They perform several different neurological tests including electroencephalograms (EEGs), evoked potentials (EPs), nerve conduction studies (NCSs), polysomnographs (PSG/sleep studies), and surgical monitoring. EEGs assist in the diagnosis of various brain disorders such as seizures, stroke, head trauma, and brain tumors. EPs are performed on patients with possible multiple sclerosis, brainstem tumors, and spinal cord problems. NCSs evaluate peripheral nervous system problems such as carpal tunnel syndrome.

ELECTROCARDIOGRAPHY TECHNICIANS	Education and/or Experience Required	Average Income
Cardiologist	■ Graduation from an accredited school of medicine ■ One-year internship ■ One- to two-year residency in internal medicine to two years of clinical fellowship in cardiology ■ Passing grades on examinations for board certification in cardiology	■ Annual: $101,300–378,400
Cardiovascular Technologist	■ Completion of a two-year community college program in cardiovascular technology ■ Completion of a four-year college or university program	■ Annual: $33,700–63,000
EKG Technician	■ High school diploma or equivalent ■ One to six months of on-the-job training ■ Completion of a vocational education program as an EKG technician ■ One to two years of study at a community college	■ Annual: $27,200–35,500

Sleep studies are performed on patients to diagnose sleep disorders such as sleep apnea and narcolepsy. The brain, nerves and/or muscles can be monitored by END technologists during various brain and spinal cord surgeries. END technologists take medical histories, apply electrodes for the procedure beingperformed, record electrical impulses from the central and peripheral nervous systems, maintain equipment, and interact with patients to reduce anxiety during tests. END technologists have many job opportunities (see Career Ladder box on page 80). They work in hospitals, neurologist's and neurosurgeon's offices, sleep centers, and psychiatric facilities. Some positions may require on-call duty, and sleep disorder technologists usually work evenings and nights.

Tasks—Electroneurodiagnostic Technologists

- Take medical histories
- Apply electrodes to designated spots
- Record and monitor the patient's waveforms on a computer
- Interact with **neurologists** and other health care staff
- Write technical reports (possibly)
- Keep records
- Schedule appointments
- Order supplies
- Maintain equipment

neurologist
(NOO rol e jist)
A physician specializing in the nerves and nervous system.

For more information, write or go online:

Executive Office, American Society of Electroneurodiagnostic Technologists, www.aset.org
204 West Seventh Street
Carroll, IA 51401

Association of Polysomnographic Technology
2025 South Washington, Suite 300
Lansing, MI 48910-0817

Joint Review Committee on Electroneurodiagnostic Technology
Route 1, Box 63A
Genoa, WI 54632

American Board of Registration of Electroencephalographic
and Evoked Potential Technologists, www.abret.org
PO Box 916633
Longwood, FL 32791-6633

American Association of Electrodiagnostic Technologists, www.aaet.info
35 Hallett Lane
Chatham, MA 02633-2408

CAREER LADDER

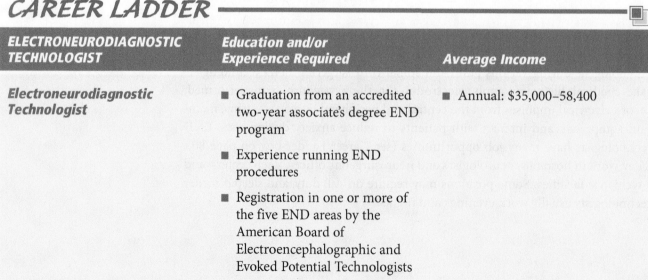

ELECTRONEURODIAGNOSTIC TECHNOLOGIST	Education and/or Experience Required	Average Income
Electroneurodiagnostic Technologist	■ Graduation from an accredited two-year associate's degree END program ■ Experience running END procedures ■ Registration in one or more of the five END areas by the American Board of Electroencephalographic and Evoked Potential Technologists	■ Annual: $35,000–58,400

Information Services

Information service workers are an important support to all other medical services. These workers analyze, **extract**, and document information using automated systems. They understand the sources, routes, and flow of information within the health care environment. They may also have special skills and advanced training in computer programming and assist in the composition of software that ensures delivery of high quality and cost effective care.

Administrative Support Service Workers

Administrative support service workers (medical clerical workers) handle complaints, interpret and explain policies or regulations, prepare payrolls, resolve billing disputes, and collect delinquent accounts. They are responsible for the everyday situations that medical organizations must deal with smoothly and efficiently to maintain business operations and good customer service. The following list of occupations is included in administrative support services:

- Claims representative
- Insurance processor or enrollment clerk
- Billing and account collector
- Clerical worker
- Computer or data processor
- Receptionist
- Appointment scheduler
- Material/supply and distribution clerk or purchasing clerk
- Payroll and timekeeping clerk
- Personnel clerk
- Secretary or word processor
- Telephone operator

Admitting Department Workers

Admitting department workers are responsible for the admitting and **discharging** of patients. They interview patients/clients for information necessary for accurate record keeping. (**Figure 3.12**) The workers in the admitting department are usually the first hospital employees that the patient sees. Employees in this department help the patient feel confident about the hospital and the care that they will receive.

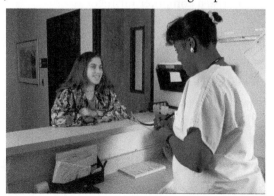

FIGURE 3.12
One of the many duties of an admitting clerk is interviewing patients/clients. What might be some questions an admitting clerk would ask when interviewing patients/clients?

Admitting workers have a variety of job opportunities (see Career Ladder box on page 82) and work in an acute care hospital and in the short stay hospital setting. They may assist with lifting patients and carrying their belongings. They may also push wheelchairs or stretchers. Their work is in an office environment and requires sitting and reaching. They may work shifts and evenings.

ADMITTING DEPARTMENT WORKERS	Education and/or Experience Required	Average Income
Admitting Officer	■ High school diploma or equivalent ■ Bachelor's degree ■ Two to three months of on-the-job training ■ One to two years of experience working in a health care facility (may be required)	■ Annual: $41,400–55,400
Admitting Clerk	■ High school diploma or equivalent ■ Computer skills ■ One to two months of on-the-job training	■ Annual: $25,300–31,800

Tasks—Admitting Clerks

- Interview incoming patients/clients and record information required for admission
- Assign rooms
- Prepare identification band
- Explain hospital rules and policies
- Store patients' valuables in hospital safe and arrange escort to room
- Send admitting forms to appropriate departments
- Prepare daily census and preadmission forms and arrange transfers
- May act as cashier and receptionist (depending on the size of the facility)
- Use a computer for records

For more information, write or go online:

American Hospital Association, www.aha.org
One North Franklin
Chicago, IL 60606-3421

Medical Records/Health Information Management Workers

Medical records/health information management workers keep permanent records that describe the patient's condition and the treatment that he or she receives.

Physicians and allied health personnel use medical records to provide care for the patients. Medical records are also legal documents that can be used in a court of law. Insurance companies use the records to determine what they will pay for the patient's care. Records are used in medical research, as well.

Medical records must be accurate and carefully filed. (Figure 3.13) Medical records/ health information management workers have many job opportunities (see Career Ladder box on page 84) and are employed by acute care hospitals, long-term care hospitals, public health departments, manufacturers of medical record systems, and insurance companies.

FIGURE 3.13
One of the many duties of a medical records/health information management files clerk is filing and pulling medical records. Why is a medical records/ health information management file clerk an important position?

Medical records/health information management specialists may have a private practice as a **consultant**. Their work requires frequent reaching and stretching for files, long periods of time at a desk, and some lifting of records.

consultant
(kuhn SUHL tnt)
A person who gives professional or expert advice.

Tasks—Medical Records/Health Information Management Clerks
- File and pull medical records
- Maintain a sign-out system for records
- Update index file of patients and check for prior records of newly admitted clients
- File cards according to established system and file medical records by numerical system
- Answer routine staff requests for information about patients
- Gather statistics for state health department
- **Transcribe** reports of operations, x-rays, and laboratory examinations

transcribe
(tran SKYRAHYB)
To make a written copy.

For more information, write or go online:

American Health Information Management Association, www.ahima.org
233 N. Michigan Avenue, 21st Floor
Chicago, IL 60601-5800

Unit Secretaries and Health Unit Coordinators

Unit secretaries and health unit coordinators are responsible for clerical, reception, and communication duties in the nursing unit. One of their main duties is to transcribe physicians' orders. Health unit coordinators are essential to the nursing units, as they relieve the nursing staff of many duties. This gives the nurses more time to devote to patient care.

MEDICAL RECORDS/HEALTH INFORMATION MANAGMENT WORKERS	Education and/or Experience Required	Average Income
Registered Medical Records Administrator (RRA)	■ Bachelor's degree from an accredited college program ■ Passing grade on the certification examination given by the American Health Information Management Association	■ Annual: $54,500–78,000
Medical Records Technician (ART registered)	■ Graduation from a program accredited by the American Health Information Management Association (AHIMA) or the AHIMA Independent Study Program and a passing grade on the AHIMA certification exam	■ Annual: $34,300–42,200
Medical Transcriptionist	■ High school diploma or equivalent ■ On-the-job training ■ Completion of a vocational education program in the area of medical transcriptionist ■ Completion of a correspondence course	■ Annual: $27,200–39,000
Medical Records/Health Information Management Clerk	■ High school diploma or equivalent ■ Typing and filing skills ■ Knowledge of office methods and medical terminology ■ Three to six months of on-the-job training ■ Completion of a vocational education program in the area of medical records clerk	■ Annual: $24,000–28,900

(continued)

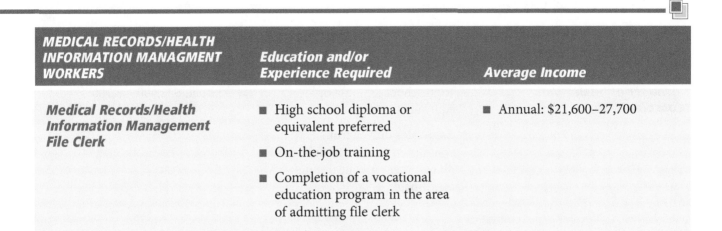

MEDICAL RECORDS/HEALTH INFORMATION MANAGMENT WORKERS	Education and/or Experience Required	Average Income
Medical Records/Health Information Management File Clerk	■ High school diploma or equivalent preferred ■ On-the-job training ■ Completion of a vocational education program in the area of admitting file clerk	■ Annual: $21,600–27,700

Health unit coordinators have various career options (see Career Ladder box on page 86) and may be employed in acute care hospitals, long-term care facilities, and clinics. Their work is indoors in a clean environment. They may work shifts and weekends. Their work requires sitting at a desk for long periods of time, frequent telephoning, and reaching for and handling charts. To function in this job, a person must have strong computer skills; they must enter diagnostic tests, diets, print charts, etc.

Tasks—Health Unit Coordinators

- Greet patients and families
- Direct patients and families as necessary
- Answer patient's and families' questions and/or locate resources as necessary
- Transcribe physicians' orders
- Prepare and compile records, including patient's name, address, and names of attending physicians
- Copy information into charts, including patients' temperature, pulse, respiration rate, and blood pressure
- Prepare **requisitions** for laboratory tests (e.g., special procedures, diagnostic tests, pharmaceutical orders)
- Order necessary supplies for the client
- Answer patients' call lights and send appropriate person for request
- Provide physicians with clients' charts, check charts for new orders, and keep charts up-to-date
- Use a computer if applicable
- File reports in patient charts
- Restock paper supplies

requisitions
(rek wuh ZISH uhns)
A formal written request for something needed.

For more information, write or go online:

National Association of Health Unit Clerks/Coordinators, www.nahuc.org
709 West Seldon Lane
Phoenix, AZ 85021

HEALTH UNIT COORDINATORS	Education and/or Experience Required	Average Income
Manager of Health Unit Coordinators	■ High school diploma or equivalent ■ Associate's degree from a community college in unit management as a health unit coordinator	■ Annual: $32,500–48,700
Unit Secretary/Health Unit Coordinator	■ High school diploma or equivalent ■ Community college ■ Hospital training program ■ Completion of a vocational education program in the area of unit secretary or health unit coordinator	■ Annual: $24,900–32,000

Environmental Services

Environmental service workers provide a therapeutic environment for the delivery of care. They repair and maintain medical and general equipment, and follow aseptic procedures.

Central Processing/Supply Workers

Central processing/supply workers supply various departments with equipment and materials. (Figure 3.14) The equipment must be in working condition. Malfunctioning equipment is life threatening. The workers keep an inventory of supplies and equipment. Supplies and equipment are properly packaged, cleaned, and sterilized. The workers in this department are key members of the health care team. Other health care workers cannot give necessary care without proper tools. Central processing/supply workers work in acute care hospitals and large outpatient clinics. The department is often in a basement or at the rear of the building. Lifting and moving articles and equipment are required. The workers stand on their feet for long periods of time and may be exposed to body fluids. See Career Ladder box on page 87 for career opportunities.

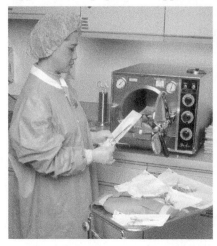

FIGURE 3.14
A central supply worker loading an autoclave. How do other health care workers depend on a central supply worker?

- Use solutions to scrub and wash surgical instruments, containers, syringes, and equipment

- Sterilize articles (e.g., instruments, equipment, linens) using the steam autoclave, gas autoclave, or antiseptic solution

- Prepare packs of supplies, instruments, dressings, and treatment trays; carefully wrap, label, and seal each pack

- Store and inventory prepared articles, supplies, and equipment

- Fill requisitions (gathering supplies and equipment as requested) and post charges

- Check expiration dates on sterilized materials

For more information, write or go online:

American Hospital Association, www.aha.org
One North Franklin
Chicago, IL 60606-3421

CAREER LADDER

CENTRAL PROCESSING/ SUPPLY WORKERS	Education and/or Experience Required	Average Income
Technician	■ High school diploma or equivalent ■ On-the-job training (six months) ■ Completion of a vocational education program as a central supply technician	■ Annual: $21,300–35,300
Chief Technician	■ On-the-job experience	■ Annual: $23,400–35,500

Hospital Cleaners (Housekeepers)/ Environmental Services Technicians

Housekeepers are responsible for the cleanliness of the environment (Figure 3.15). Cleanliness helps prevent the spread of infection and creates a more pleasant environment for patients/clients, staff, and visitors.

Hospital cleaners (housekeepers)/environmental service workers have many job opportunities (see Career Ladder box on page 89) and work in long-term care facilities, acute hospitals, and clinics. They have frequent contact with water and cleaning solutions. They walk, stand, and stoop during their shift. They also push and pull equipment, climb on ladders when necessary, and may be exposed to body fluids. Their hours may include shift work and weekend work.

Tasks—Hospital Cleaners/Housekeeping Attendants

- Load service cart
- Clean assigned areas (e.g., rooms, offices, laboratories)
- Dust, vacuum, and clean blinds, floors, furniture, and equipment
- Polish floors using a buffing machine
- Wash walls, ceilings, windows
- Empty trash
- Scour sinks, tubs, and mirrors
- Disinfect bedsprings and unit equipment
- Replenish soap and towels
- Replace cubicle curtains and soiled draperies
- Report malfunctioning equipment
- Move furniture, equipment, and supplies and turn mattresses

FIGURE 3.15
A housekeeping attendant cleaning public areas, one of housekeeping's many duties. What are some of the other common duties of a housekeeping attendant?

For more information, write or go online:

Institute of Sanitation Management
1710 Drew Street
Clearwater, FL 33515

International Executive Housekeepers Association, www.ieha.org
1001 Eastwind Drive, Suite 301
Westerville, OH 43081-3361

Food Service Department Workers

Food service workers are responsible for providing nutritional care to clients. They plan special and balanced diets. They also distribute menus, prepare food trays, and deliver food to the patients throughout the hospital. (Figure 3.16)

FIGURE 3.16
One of the many duties of a food service worker is preparing meals. What does a food service worker have to consider when preparing a meal for a patient/client?

CAREER LADDER

HOUSEKEEPING WORKERS	Education and/or Experience Required	Average Income
Director of Housekeeping Services	■ High school diploma or equivalent ■ College degree in housekeeping management or completion of courses in housekeeping and institutional management ■ Experience in the housekeeping department	■ Annual: $34,400–44,800
Housekeeping Crew Leader/Supervisor	■ High school diploma or equivalent ■ Completion of courses in hospital housekeeping and institutional management ■ One to four months of on-the-job training ■ Up to two years of experience as a housekeeping attendant ■ Completion of a vocational education program	■ Annual: $22,900–34,000
Housekeeping Aide/Attendant	■ One to three months on-the-job training ■ Completion of a vocational education program	■ Annual: $17,200–26,700

Food service workers have many career options (see Career Ladder box on page 90) and may work in acute care hospitals and in long-term care facilities. They generally work 40 hours a week and may work in shifts. The areas might be very warm, with much activity in a relatively small area. Some lifting, reaching, moving of equipment, and occasional bending are required. They walk and stand most of the shift.

Tasks—Food Service Workers

- Prepare and deliver food trays to patients/clients
- Read color-coded menu cards to determine appropriate items to place on trays
- Measure food servings according to diet list; prepare individual servings of salad, desserts, sandwiches
- Prepare foods for soft or liquid diets using a blender

Apply It

Divide into groups of three. Each group member should pick one of the following: health care facility services, medical services, or mental health and social services.

Create a brochure or Web page that details the types of job opportunities available in that field and the necessary requirements—both personal and educational—to attain those positions. Share this information with your class.

- Check trays for accuracy and completeness, push food tray carts to client floors, and serve trays to patients (according to hospital policy)
- Stock the nutrition kitchen in patient care areas
- Return food tray carts to kitchen
- Clean work area, wrap silverware, and restock condiments for tray line

Tasks—Dietitians/Nutritionists

- Plan diets for patients/clients
- Educate patients/communities about health eating habits
- Provide nutritional counseling
- Assess nutritional needs of patients/clients
- Consult with physicians to determine a patient's/client's nutritional needs and restrictions
- Develop dietary plans

CAREER LADDER

FOOD SERVICE DEPARTMENT WORKERS	Education and/or Experience Required	Average Income
Administrative Dietitian	■ Must be a registered dietitian ■ Graduate study credits in institutional or business administration	■ Annual: $41,700–67,400
Registered Dietitian	■ Bachelor's degree with a major in foods and nutrition or institutional management ■ Six to twelve month internship in a dietary department	■ Annual: $42,400–63,500
Dietetic Intern	■ Bachelor's degree with a major in foods and nutrition or institutional management	■ Annual: $28,900–38,800
Dietetic Technician	■ Completion of a dietetic technician program in a community college	■ Annual: $21,100–34,700
Food Service Worker/ Dietetic Assistant	■ On-the-job training ■ Completion of a vocational education program as a food service worker	■ Annual: $16,400–23,500

For more information, write or go online:

American **Dietetic** Association,
www.eatright.org
120 South Riverside Plaza, Suite 2000
Chicago, IL 60606-6995

American Home Economics
 Association
2010 Massachusetts Avenue NW
Washington, DC 20036

dietetic
(dahy i TET ik)
Pertaining to diet or to the
regulation of the use of
food.

Environmental Health and Medicine Careers

The health care field offers many job opportunities that are less well-known than
the more traditional careers. These involve education, disease prevention, biomedical development and research, social work and specialty assistants, among others.

Health Educator

Health educators encourage a healthy lifestyle and focus on wellness by educating
individuals and communities about health issues such as the importance of exercise and nutrition. These educators conduct lectures and classes, provide health
screenings, and distribute videos and brochures. Health educators should be good
communicators since they work with the public, have strong public speaking skills,
and be sensitive of culture differences.

Epidemiology

Epidemiologists study the occurrence and frequency of disease in large populations and determine the source and cause of infectious disease epidemics. For
example, epidemiologists might study childhood obesity, avian influenza, or AIDS.
Most epidemiologists are physicians and work in the community, universities, hospitals and government agencies such as the Centers for Disease Control.

Environmental Health Specialist

Environmental health specialists enforce regulations that protect food and water,
safeguard hazardous materials, and dispose of infectious wastes. They collect and
analyze samples, consult with physicians about environmental health hazards, prepare reports, and make suggestions on how to correct problems. Environmental
health specialists work in hospitals, health departments, and wildlife parks.

Biomedical Engineer

Biomedical engineers develop devices and procedures in order to solve medical
and health related problems. For example, biomedical engineers might develop
and evaluate prosthetics, cardiac pacemakers, or the laser system used for corrective eye surgery.

Biomedical Equipment Technician

Biomedical equipment technicians ensure that medical equipment is serviceable,
safe, and properly configured. Their responsibilities include installation, inspection, repair, calibration, maintenance of, and education about, biomedical equipment. Biomedical equipment technicians are employed by hospitals, clinics, and
the military.

Research Scientist

Research specialists plan, develop, conduct, and evaluate scientific research in the
lab, field, or teaching environment.

Career Connection

Visit a local blood bank, clinic, x-ray department, etc. to determine which health care professionals are employed at the site, their responsibilities and education preparation. You may want to arrange for a short-term job shadow to observe the work that is being done and the processes that take place.

Social Worker

Social workers help individuals and families cope with problems or situations that occur in everyday life such as relationship issues, individuals with disabilities or illnesses, unemployment or substance abuse. Social workers must be objective and sensitive to people, their cultures and their problems.

Medical Specialists

Medical specialists practice one type of medicine. For example, cardiologists study and treat the structure and function of the heart; pediatricians study and treat the care and health of babies and children; and dermatologists study and treat the makeup and pathology of skin.

Physician's Assistants

Physician's assistants, also referred to as PAs, practice medicine under the supervision of a physician or surgeon. They are trained to provide diagnostic, therapeutic, and preventive services. Physician's assistants take medical histories, examine patients, order and interpret tests, and make diagnoses. Most physician's assistants work in primary care facilities.

Chiropractor

Chiropractors are alternative health care practitioners who identify and treat problems associated with the muscular, nervous, and skeletal systems. Chiropractors treat problems with manipulation, heat/cold, exercise, and physical therapy.

Podiatrist

Podiatrists diagnose and treat diseases and injuries of the foot including corns, calluses, bunions, skin and nail infections, and deformities.

Optometrist

Optometrists provide vision care by examining the eyes for diseases such as glaucoma, nearsightedness and farsightedness, and depth and color perception. Optometrists prescribe eyeglasses and contact lenses. Optometrists do not perform surgery.

Psychologist

Psychologists study human behavior and the human mind. There are many different fields of psychology including clinical, educational, and research.

Additional Health Care Areas

There are many other positions available in the health care field. You may use the skills that you have learned in Section 3.1 to search for other career areas that interest you. Here are some suggestions for you to consider in the health-related field:

Dental Occupations

- Dental ceramist
- Orthodontist

Medical Practitioners

- Osteopath
- Physician (including specialists such as anesthesiologists, gerontologists, gynecologists, oncologists, pathologists, pediatricians, and urologists)
- Veterinarian

Vision Services

- Ophthalmologist
- Ophthalmic Technician
- Optician
- Contact lens technician
- Optometrist (OD)

Medical Technologists, Technicians, Assistants, and Aides

- Audiometrist
- Cardiopulmonary technician
- Cytotechnologist
- Dialysis technician
- Electroencephalographic (EEG) technologist
- Heart-lung machine operator/perfusionist
- Operating room technician
- Orthopedic technician
- Orthotist
- Prosthetic aide
- Surgical technician/assistant
- Transporter
- Ultrasound technologist/sonographer

Mental/Social Services Occupations

- Mental retardation assistant
- Psychiatrist
- Psychiatric aide

Nursing Occupations

- Licensed psychiatric aide
- Midwife
- Nurse anesthetist

Therapy and Rehabilitation Occupations

- Alcoholic rehabilitation center attendant
- Audiologist
- Profusionist

Apply It

Divide into groups of two or three students. Each group should select a health care occupation and research the regulatory agency or agencies that have authority over that occupation. In your research, identify the specific licensure or certification requirements for the occupation, including license or certificate renewal, and how one goes about fulfilling the requirements.

For more information on licensure and health care regulatory agencies, see page 33.

- Kinesiotherapist
- Music therapist
- Recreation therapist
- Speech pathologist
- Massage therapist
- Athletic trainer

Other Health-Related Occupations

- Clinical engineer
- Director of volunteer services
- Dispensing optician
- Funeral director/mortician
- Grounds maintenance and facilities worker
- Health service administrator/health care administrator
- Insurance clerk
- Medical illustrator
- Medical writer
- Morgue attendant/embalmist
- Nursing home administrator
- Prosthetist
- Transporter

The Future of Health Care Occupations

There is a growing shortage of health care workers in the United States. According to the Bureau of Labor and Statistics, health care generates more jobs than any other industry and will continue to do so. The continued high volume of health care jobs will be due, in large part, to a rapidly aging population. Other reasons for increased health care occupations include advances in technology and gene therapy. As medical research provides new methods of diagnosis and treatments, there are more patients to receive those diagnoses and treatment. More patients will need more health care workers of all types to care for them. The need for health care workers will exist for occupations that require all levels of education and training. Specialized clinical training, a requirement for many health care professions, is an asset for any jobseeker, even those looking for administrative jobs.

Summary

In this section, you reviewed many health occupations. You learned that each occupation has different tasks and different educational requirements. You also learned that different occupations require different traits in the worker. With this information, you can evaluate an occupation before you research it carefully. Use the information in the first section to research any occupational area.

Language Arts Link

Self Assessment

Being able to determine your likes, dislikes, and values is an important part of deciding your career path. Do you like working in a group or prefer working alone? Would you be willing to work the night shift at your local hospital or would the morning shift be better for you? No one but you can answer these questions.

Create a new document on the computer, or get a blank sheet of paper. Create a letter to your teacher describing your work-related

values and needs. Include a thesis statement (a sentence stating your main ideas) in the opening paragraph.

Be sure to incorporate information on the major factors that would influence what career path you take. Be sure to proofread your work to see if you can improve it by making it clearer, more concise, or more interesting to read. Check the spelling and grammar and correct any errors.

SECTION **3.2** 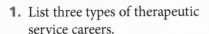 **Review Questions**

1. List three types of therapeutic service careers.

2. What are the similarities in daily tasks between an occupational therapy aid and an occupational therapy assistant? What are the differences?

3. Which type of emergency medical service worker requires the most education or experience?

4. Which organizations can you contact in order to find out more information about dental assistants?

5. Describe the schedule and physical requirements for a nursing service worker.

6. What are some of the issues that may confront a veterinary worker?

7. Name three places in which a radiology worker may work.

8. What are some of the tests an electroneurodiagnostic technologist can perform on a patient/client?

9. Name three tasks a health unit coordinator would be likely to perform.

10. What education or experience is required to become a dietetic technician?

 Learn By Doing: Section 3.2 Activity

1. Complete Worksheet 1.

2. Complete Worksheets 2 and 3 as assigned.

3. Complete Worksheets/Activities 4 and 5.

4. Prepare responses to each item listed in the Chapter Review.

5. When you are confident that you can meet each objective listed above, ask your teacher for the section evaluation.

Chapter 3 Review

Chapter Review Questions

1. What three things should you consider when choosing a career? (3.1)

2. What can you do to find out if a career is right for you? (3.1)

3. What types of information should you include in a portfolio? (3.1)

4. What does a respiratory therapy worker help a patient to do? (3.2)

5. Where might a physical therapist work? (3.2)

6. Name three daily tasks a dental assistant might perform. (3.2)

7. How does a home health aide provide more than just medical care? (3.2)

8. Name three types of diagnostic services careers. (3.2)

9. Explain what education and experience a person needs to become a medical transcriptionist. (3.2)

10. Why is the work of an environmental service technician important? (3.2)

Activities

1. Many health occupation careers require staff to be willing to work shifts covering 7 days a week, 24 hours a day. Think of your present lifestyle and the life you hope to lead in the future. Plot a chart of when you would be willing to work on a daily and weekly basis, year-round. File this in a private, personal area of your portfolio to reference when you are considering specific careers and jobs. Update this document if your thinking changes.

2. After reading this chapter, identify which major health care service area interests you the most: therapeutic services, diagnostic services, information services, or environmental services. Explain your reasons for your choice. Show how your interests, values, and abilities fit well with the major health care service area you chose.

Case Studies

1. Glenda needs to find a good job as soon as she graduates. She is uncertain as to how to find the right career. She must earn enough to pay for an apartment, a car, living expenses, and leisure activities. She wants a position that is well respected, provides a clean environment, and offers potential for professional growth. She enjoys working with people and feels really good when she is able to help others. List the steps Glenda should take to help her identify the best career options for her.

2. Sam is interested in helping people get better. He is good at encouraging people, and he is quite strong. He does not like to calculate numbers; however, he can be quite detail-oriented when it comes to activities such as cleaning or storing equipment. Sam does not want to be behind a desk all day. He prefers a job that allows him to stand or walk. Based on this information, which careers would you suggest Sam research?

Thinking Critically

1. **Understanding Yourself**—You should use your abilities, interests and values to help you choose a satisfying career. What traits will guide the choices you make?

2. **Medical**—What are the overall responsibilities and goals of therapeutic versus diagnostic service positions? Explain these goals using a specific job in each field.

3. **Career Search**—Based on the facts that different occupations require different traits in the worker—and provide different benefits—which positions would be most appropriate for you? Why?

Media Connection

Use the Companion Web site for additional interactive learning activities: www.prenhall.com/badasch

Portfolio Connection

The following provides a guideline for creating the structure of your portfolio. When you are done you can add and exchange documents as you complete them. Keeping your file current shows your organizational skills and provides you immediate access to materials that reflect the positive results of your learning. To create your portfolio, follow the instructions in the Student Activity Guide. You must acquire a three-ring notebook, three-ring pocket inserts, and tab dividers. Label each tab with the following:

Portfolio

- Title page
- Table of contents
- Letter of introduction
- Résumé
- Letter(s) of recommendation
- Advanced training or college requirements
- Certificates/licenses
- Skills check-off sheets
- Practical experience evaluation
- Evaluation of paid or unpaid time working in your vocation
- Written reports and assignments in your vocation area
- Personal tips and reminders
- Final portfolio checklist

Once your portfolio file is organized, it is ready for your work samples. Add work evaluations from current or previous jobs and keep this file in a place that is easy to access.

In the personal section of the portfolio, add any advice or insights that will help you in your career. Be sure that this section can be removed before the portfolio is given to a prospective employer.

Ask your instructor to help you seek a job shadowing opportunity in one health occupation of your choice. Complete a job sharing contract (see Student Activity Guide, Worksheet/Activity 5) after you are assigned a time, place, and person to shadow.

Write a report as described in the Vocational Portfolio in the addendum of the Student Activity Guide.

As you will observe during your job shadowing experiences, no matter what health career you choose, you will need to demonstrate step-by-step procedures for

Chapter 3 Review

problem solving. For example, nurses use a procedure called the nursing process, which, simply stated, includes the following steps:

- Assess the data or information, and state the problem. (*What is the client's health problem?*)

- Diagnose the cause(s) of the problem. (*What is causing the client's health problem?*)

- Plan the solution for the problem. (*What course of medical action can treat the client's health problem?*)

- Implement or put the plan into effect. (*Take the medical actions that are expected to successfully treat the client's health problem.*)

- Evaluate the plan's effectiveness. (*Is the client's health problem reduced or eliminated because of the plan?*)

- Demonstrate step-by-step procedures for problem solving by selecting one problem you observed during a job shadowing experience, and then writing your step-by-step plan for

solving that problem. Use the nursing process to help you. (*What problem did you see? What did you think was the cause of the problem? What plan did you create for addressing the problem? How did you put the plan into action? How effective was the plan?*) Include your written step-by-step procedures in your portfolio.

PORTFOLIO TIP

File portfolio items as soon as you complete them. If you have access to a computer, consider keeping an electronic portfolio as well as a hard copy version. You may create folders for different topics and save the portfolio to a disk if it is not your personal computer. Doing this will save space and paper and give you important practice in using a computer.

4 Employability and Leadership

Getting Started

Fashions are ever-changing and what may seem just right for one generation may not work at all for another. Additionally, what you wear to work may differ according to what you do and where you work. And the clothes you wear in your place of work may not be what you would wear when interviewing for that job.

Consider the age of the interviewer (may be about the same as your parents and friends parents or even older) and the type of clothing they would consider professional. Then, using either magazines or hand drawings, create what you believe would be the ideal outfit for job seeking. Ask your parents and teacher what they think about the outfit. With their input, make your final decision, prepare the outfit (it need not be expensive) and hang it in your closet covered by a garment bag. Wear it only for job shadow or employment interviews. After each wearing, wash the garments, press them, make sure your shoes are clean and have everything ready for the next time you will need to wear your "Job Seeking Outfit."

SECTION 4.1 Job-Seeking Skills

Background

Before you apply the skills you have learned, you must find a job and be hired as an employee. It is important to learn the skills needed to find a job and to keep a job. These skills will enable you to practice the career that you studied and trained for.

Objectives

When you have completed this section, you will be able to do the following:

- Match key terms with their correct meanings.
- List seven places to seek employment and explain the benefits of each.
- Explain four ways to contact an employer.
- Name three occasions when a cover letter is used.

- List eight items required on a résumé.
- Identify seven items generally requested on a job application form.
- Write a cover letter and a résumé.
- Complete a job application.
- List five dos and five don'ts of job interviewing.
- Write a thank-you letter to a prospective employer.

Finding a Job

Looking for and finding a job takes planning and requires the use of many skills. In this chapter, you learn the steps to follow when you are ready to find a job. These skills are tools for successful job seeking and save you a lot of time.

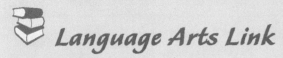

Language Arts Link

Health Care Careers

For each career in the health care profession, the paths of study and job responsibilities will vary. For some careers, you will need additional certification or degrees.

Using the Internet or a library, research the education and skills needed to go into one of the following fields: radiology, dental assistant, or medical records. If you are able to speak with professionals in these fields, interview them about how they become interested in this area of study, what the requirements were, and what their job responsibilities are.

After you've completed your research, select one of the fields and write a letter to a potential employer expressing your interest in a job in that field. Edit your letter to see if you can make it clearer, more concise, or more interesting. Check spelling and grammar and correct any errors.

Your Vocational Portfolio

As time approaches to begin your search for a job, review your portfolio notebook. Obtain a new cover and section dividers, so your finished portfolio has a clean, crisp look. Identify the items that best reflect your knowledge level, skills, and personality. When you complete your résumé and other portfolio requirements, place them in the appropriate section of your new portfolio.

Places to Seek Employment

- **Newspaper ads.** Jobs in health care careers appear in newspaper ads. When you look in the newspaper, turn to the classified ads under "Help Wanted." Some papers list all health care positions under "Medical." Others list them under a particular job. See **Figure 4.1** for examples of ads from several newspapers. You also need to become familiar with abbreviations used by newspapers.

Common Abbreviations

appl.	**applicant**	immed.	immediately
asst.	assistant	incl.	included
cert.	**certified**	lic.	licensed
exp.	experience	N.A.	nurse aide
FT	**full time**	PT	**part time**

applicant
(AP lih kent)
A person applying for a job.

certified
(SER ti fide)
A person who has received a certificate that shows he or she demonstrates understanding.

full time
(FUHL time)
Describes a job requiring between 32 and 40 hours per week.

part time
(PAHRT time)
Describes a job requiring fewer than 32 hours per week.

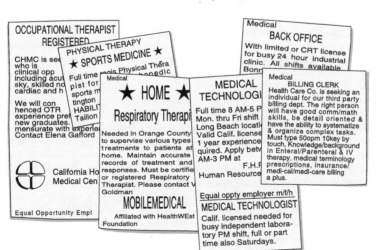

FIGURE 4.1
Examples of newspaper advertisements for health care jobs. What section of the newspaper carries job listings?

Courtesy of ShutterStock.

(a)

FIGURE 4.2
The Internet can save you time when you are searching for a job (a). Online searches may offer more job opportunities than are available in the newspaper or on a job bulletin board. You also can use the Internet to search for jobs in a different location from where you live. Some job sites list jobs for many different employers (b), while some employers have their own job sites specific to their facility or a group of affiliated facilities.

personnel
(pur suh NEL)
People who work in an establishment; a personnel office is where a worker goes to apply for a job.

agency
(EY juhn see)
An organization that helps people in a particular way.

(b)

- **Internet.** If you have access to a computer that is connected to the Internet, go to Search and type in the words "*job search*" or "*job link*" (see **Figure 4.2a**). You can find job referrals, workshops, placement activities, and tips on writing a résumé or interviewing. Many places of employment now offer a list of open positions and applications for their positions online at a job site (see **Figure 4.2b**). If you locate an appropriate position online and use this process for job application, be sure to review everything you type and enter into an online application field prior to submitting your information to the place of business.

- **Directly to the employer.** If you are looking for a position in a laboratory, you might apply directly to a medical laboratory. If you want to work in a hospital, you go to the **personnel** department. The Yellow Pages of your phone book or an Internet search are resources for possible employers to contact by telephone or in person.

- **Friends and relatives.** You may know someone in the health care field who can suggest a place to apply or who can introduce you to a possible employer.

- **School counselors.** Many schools have career counselors and/or work experience counselors. They are a good resource for the types of jobs available in your community.

- **School bulletin boards.** If you have a career center or a bulletin board where jobs are listed, be sure to check it daily.

- **Employment agencies.** There are both public and private employment **agencies**. Employers call these agencies to list the job openings that they have. A public agency does not charge a fee; however, a private agency charges either the employer or the person seeking a position. The Yellow Pages list employment agencies, and some of them specialize in health care careers. The public agencies are listed in the white pages under "Government Agencies." You may also find employment agencies online that you want to contact by telephone or by sending a cover letter and your résumé, either electronically or by regular mail.

Ways to Contact an Employer

Now that you know where to look for a job, you need to know how to make the contact and how to present yourself.

Telephone

If you have a lead on a possible job, you may choose to call for an appointment. Give your name and the job in which you are interested and ask when you may come in to apply.

E-mail

You may want to follow up on a job lead or contact an employment agency with an e-mail. If a job listing or an employment site provides an e-mail contact, write a "cover" e-mail and attach your résumé. In the text of your e-mail, rather than saying that your résumé is enclosed, state that your résumé is attached. Include your full name in the subject line of your e-mail, along with the title of a particular position in which you may be interested. If there is not a specific job available at the time you send your e-mail, you can express a general interest in working for the employer and request that your résumé be kept on file for future employment opportunities. Be sure the résumé that you attach is in a standard electronic format (see Résumé Formats on p. 104).

Cover Letter

You may be asked to send a cover letter in order to apply for a particular position. You need a **cover letter** when:

- You are applying for a job that is out of town.
- You are answering a newspaper advertisement.
- A potential employer requests a letter.

Your cover letter is a sales letter. You want to sell yourself to the employer in order to get an interview. (A sample cover letter is shown **Figure 4.3.**) Your letter should:

- Be neat.
- Have all the words spelled correctly.
- State where you heard about the job opening.
- State what you are applying for and why you are qualified for this specific position.
- Give a brief overview of your education, experience, and qualifications.
- Refer to your portfolio and/or résumé, along with work samples, skills checkoff lists, and evaluations.
- Request an interview.
- Give your address and phone number.

Résumé

In addition to your cover letter, it is helpful for a potential employer to have more details about you and your qualifications. This is accomplished by preparing a **résumé**. (See the example in **Figure 4.4.**) A résumé includes the following:

- Your name, address, phone number, e-mail address, and message number.
- Career plans.
- Details about your education.

cover letter
(KUH ver LEH tuhr)
A letter that introduces you to a potential employer.

résumé
(REZ oo mey)
A document that provides details about your work history and accomplishments.

- Your past work experience—paid or unpaid.
- What honors you have earned.
- What activities you like.
- Skills, strengths, and abilities.
- References (always ask permission to use someone as a reference).

888 Whitegate Avenue
Los Angeles, CA 90820

January 25, 2011

Mr. E. B. Burns
Director of Nurses
St. Joseph's Hospital
P.O. Box 123
Los Angeles, CA 90880

Dear Mr. Burns:

I am responding to your advertisement in <u>Nurses World</u> on January 14, 2011. I am interested in applying for the position of nurse assistant. I graduated from Medical Technologies High School on December 15, 2010. I studied nursing assisting and am well qualified for this position. My course work included communication, CPR, and a core of courses that prepared me to be employed as a nursing assistant. I also worked in a hospital setting eight hours a week for sixteen weeks. My attendance is excellent, and I am very reliable. My goal is to use my skills as a nursing assistant and to be an exemplary employee.

My résumé is enclosed. Also included is a list of skills I have mastered. I know that I am well qualified for this position. I am looking forward to an opportunity to interview for this position. I will call on Monday, February 3, at 9:00 a.m. and hope to arrange an interview at that time.

If you require additional information, or want to contact me, please call me at (123) 456-7890 after 3:00 p.m.

Sincerely,

Mark Adams, CNA

Résumé Formats. It is important to have multiple forms of your résumé. A traditional print résumé is a word processor formatted document that includes features such as bullets, italics, and underlines. Your word processing program, or an online search, will provide a selection of résumé templates that use a variety of styles and fonts. A print résumé can be mailed, faxed, hand delivered, or attached to an e-mail as a formatted electronic file.

An online résumé is an ASCII, or plain text, document with no formatting. You can copy and paste this type of résumé into online forms and databases. There are so many online sources for jobs and so many résumés posted that employers often search by **keywords** to identify potential applicants. Adding appropriate keywords for the position, such as *detail-oriented* or *bilingual*, can make the difference in attracting the attention of a potential employer. Employers put résumés in searchable databases, so it is important to have both a print and online version of your résumé.

keywords
(KEE WUHRDZ)
Significant or descriptive words.

800 E. Oak Street
Conway, AR 72032

Home: 501-666-8340
Mobile: 501-620-9180

Mary Jane Rodgers

Career Plans

Complete 2-year Associate of Science Nursing Program

Short-range: Nursing assistant

Long-range: Complete a Bachelor of Science Program as a registered nurse

Experience

2010–present Henry's Hamburger Shop Conway, AR

Sales Clerk

- Food preparation
- Counting inventory
- Customer service
- Operating a cash register and making change
- Maintaining health standards

2008–2009 June Allison Conway, AR

Babysitter

- Meal preparation
- Overnight care of two children, 8 and 10 years of age
- Planning recreation

Family Responsibilities

- Prepare dinner 2–3 times a week
- Weekly gardening
- Perform minor household tasks

Education

Diploma candidate 2010 Hoover High School Conway, AR

Interests

Dancing, classical music, reading, skiing, member of Explorer Scouts Medical Post and Health Occupation Students of America

Skills and Strengths

Fluent in oral and written Spanish communication

Proficient in Windows programs including Word, Excel, PowerPoint, and Outlook applications

FIGURE 4.4

Sample résumé. How do the different sections of the résumé organize a job applicant's information? Why is it helpful to list your interests?

Job Application

Most employers require that you fill out an application form. When you fill out a job application form, you give the employer needed information and also have an opportunity to demonstrate that you are neat and well organized. Use the information in your vocational portfolio to fill out an application. Included should be:

- Your complete address with the zip code.
- Your Social Security number, in some cases, or perhaps the last four digits.
- Your phone number or a number where you can be reached.
- A list of the schools you have attended, with dates.
- A list of any special training that you have.
- A prepared list of any past jobs, the address of the employer, the dates you worked there, and what your duties were.
- A list of people who can give you a reference. Be certain that you have their addresses and phone numbers. Also be certain that you have asked permission to use them as a reference.

There are also other ways that you can prepare. Be sure that you:

- Carry a black pen—do not use a pencil.
- Read the application form all the way through.
- Print unless you are told to write.
- Spell accurately.
- Answer every question. Put "NA" (not applicable) in the space to show that you did not overlook the question.
- Recheck for errors.

Interview

The interviewer wants to be sure that you are the best fit for the job. She is assessing your skills from the time she receives your résumé. Her focus during the interview is to determine if your explanations and behaviors match the job requirements. This evaluation occurs throughout the interview process, even when conversation is about the weather or hobbies. It is important to make a good first impression. The following guidelines tell you what to do and what not to do during an interview.

Interview Guidelines

Before you go on an interview, you should research the company. Human resource personnel suggest that you bring that research with you with specific items that you want to discuss highlighted. It shows interest in the company and the willingness to do some "upfront" work.

Follow these guidelines for a positive interview experience:

- Be well groomed.
- Dress neatly and appropriately (no jeans).
- Be on time.
- Turn off your cell phone.

- Greet the interviewer by name, and smile.
- Shake hands firmly.
- Stand until asked to sit.
- Answer questions truthfully and sincerely.
- Be enthusiastic.
- Do not chew gum.
- Do not criticize former employers or teachers.
- Look at the interviewer when you talk.
- Do not talk about personal problems.
- When the interview is over, thank the interviewer and leave quickly.

Interview Preparation

The interviewer expects you to answer a variety of questions pertinent to the job for which you are applying. Be prepared to give at least three examples of your behavior in various situations. Each experience should describe the:

- **Situation.** What exactly happened?
- **Behavior.** What did you do?
- **Outcome.** What were the results?

Read the following questions and determine how to answer them:

- Tell me about the most difficult decision you made at school or work in the last few months.
- Tell me how you get along with people at school or work.
- Tell me about the most difficult job or school task you've done. Why was it difficult? How did you get past the difficulties?
- Explain a recent situation that demonstrates your ability to be a team player.
- Describe a situation in which you had to work under pressure. What kind of pressure were you facing? How did you handle the situation? What was the outcome?
- Describe a situation where you had to be very flexible. How did your actions demonstrate your flexibility?

After the Interview

The interviewer will do a reference check to verify that your résumé and application are honest and accurate. She may also rate your responses to help her make a decision about which candidate is best for the job. The following is an example of an interview rating scale with topics.

	Excellent	Average	Not Acceptable
Appearance			
Manner			
Qualifications			
Experience			
Job fit			

Participate in a mock interview with a Human Resources Manager wearing your "Job Seeking Outfit" to determine their opinion of your outfit and your responses to questions. During the interview ask the HR Manager about the duties they perform and the education requirements for the position. It may be something you will find of interest for your future career.

Personal Wellness

Managing Stress

Job hunting can lead to concerns about where you will live, how much money you will earn, and what direction your career is taking. If these concerns cause you too much stress, they can affect your ability to present yourself well to prospective employers. Here are some tips to help manage the stress of job hunting:

- Stay organized. Keep a good supply of résumés and cover letters on hand, get good clear directions and maps to employers you are visiting. Consider locating the place of the interview during a sample run before you go to the interview. Establish the time frame necessary for the drive.

- Use a schedule. Keep a clear and up-to-date schedule of all your appointments to avoid over-scheduling yourself. Have your schedule open in front of you when you make appointments for new and follow-up meetings and interviews.

- Join a job hunter's group. Groups offer good networking opportunities and emotional support.

    Job hunting should be an exciting time. Managing the process so that you minimize stress can help you enjoy it and be successful.

    How can you help reduce the stress of a friend or family member who is job hunting? Sample answer: Be encouraging, keep phone lines clear at home, offer to shine shoes or wash the car, help brainstorm for ideas about potential employers or job opportunities.

After the interview, send a letter of thanks to the interviewer. (See the example in **Figure 4.5.**) This lets the interviewer know that you are interested in the position, and it may increase your chance of getting the job. You may also choose to send an immediate thank-you response via e-mail; follow up, however, by sending a thank-you letter in the mail, as well. Make sure you have a professional voice message on your cell phone when the perspective employer calls back.

Finding a job and then getting a job take effort on your part. Careful planning is the key to your success, and you will be glad that you took time to prepare yourself.

Summary

Finding a job requires effort on your part. When you decide to look for a job, search the Internet; check the newspaper; go to a personnel department; ask friends, relatives, and your school counselor if they know of an opening; check employment agencies and bulletin boards. After finding a possible opening, contact the employer. Call for an appointment, or send a cover letter with your résumé. You will also have to fill out a job application form.

The last step is your interview with the employer. There are some important rules to follow when you go to an interview. After your interview, send a thank-you note to the interviewer.

888 Whitegate Avenue
Los Angeles, CA 90820

February 10, 2011

Mr. E. B. Burns
Director of Nurses
St. Joseph's Hospital
P.O. Box 123
Los Angeles, CA 90880

Dear Mr. Burns:

Thank you for interviewing me yesterday afternoon. The position interests me very much, and I know that I will do a good job for you. I hope that you will give me an opportunity to work for the nursing department at St. Joseph's.

Sincerely,

Mark Adams, CNA

FIGURE 4.5
Sample thank-you letter to interviewer. What does a thank-you note do?

Community Service

Many of those living in homeless shelters or other type of location that may house individuals need to find a job.

Prepare handout materials including a drawing of your "Job Seeking Outfit" and a list of the types of questions and appropriate responses for distribution at the shelter. This information will help those who have not had the opportunity for someone to assist them with appropriate appearance and behavior as they seek employment.

SECTION 4.1 Review Questions

1. What does the term *appl.* mean?

2. Name five places to seek employment.

3. What two documents should you use to contact a potential employer that you read about in the newspaper?

4. Interviewers will ask you to describe events in your life. What three aspects of each event should you expect to describe?

5. Identify seven items generally requested on a job application form.

6. What kinds of follow up should you do after a job interview?

Learn By Doing: Section 4.1 Activity

1. Complete Worksheet 1.

2. Ask your teacher for directions to complete Worksheets/Activities 2 through 7.

3. When you are confident that you can meet each objective for this section, ask your teacher for the section evaluation.

Keeping a Job

Background

You spend a lot of time and effort learning the skills for a career in health care. You also put time and effort into finding and getting the job. Now that you have the job, you want to keep it. Employers look for specific things in an employee. The information in this section explains what these things are and how you can be a good employee.

Objectives

When you have completed this section, you will be able to do the following:

- Match key terms with their correct meanings.
- List four employer responsibilities.
- List four responsibilities of a good employee.
- Describe workplace goals.

Responsibilities

The Good Employer

An employer has responsibilities to you, and you have responsibilities to the employer. The good employer demonstrates:

dignity
(DIG nih tee)
The quality of value and worth.

excellence
(EK sell ence)
The quality of having outstanding qualities.

service
(SUHR viss)
Caring for others.

fairness
(FAYR nes)
Applying good rules equally to all people.

- **Dignity,** by respecting each employee as an important member of the health care team. Providing a safe, clean working environment is an example of treating employees and patients with dignity.
- **Excellence,** by encouraging personal and professional development, accountability, teamwork, and a commitment to quality health care. Supporting routine activities and providing the necessary materials that allow you to do the best possible job shows a dedication to excellence.
- **Service,** by establishing standards and guidelines directing appropriate, caring, compassionate health care to those dependent on the health care services. Providing clear guidelines for employees to follow gives the direction necessary to accomplish the job in a caring, compassionate manner.
- **Fairness** *and justice,* by establishing employee salaries and benefits that are fair and reliable. An employer who provides a reasonable salary for agreed-upon work and establishes a standard salary and benefit structure for all employees is striving to be a fair, equitable employer.

The Good Employee

As a good employee, you demonstrate:

- *Dignity* through communication and interpersonal effectiveness, by:
  - Being open, honest, and respectful.
  - Listening actively and seeking understanding.
  - Providing positive, helpful feedback.

- *Excellence* through teamwork and accountability, by:
  - Creating an environment of continuous improvement.
  - Trying new ways to improve performance, processes, and service.
  - Seeking growth and development opportunities for you and others.
  - Taking responsibility for individual and team actions, decisions, and results.
  - Adapting to changing needs and learning new skills, knowledge, and behaviors.
  - Asking for and being open to continuous feedback from your peers and supervisor regarding your performance.
- *Service* through being flexible and customer focused, by:
  - Responding to the needs of those served and showing concern for meeting those needs.
  - Responding quickly and effectively to problems that arise while providing service.
- *Fairness and justice:*
  - Using equipment and supplies in an appropriate manner.
  - Treating and responding to all people in the work environment with the same dignity, excellence, and service standards.

Workplace Goals

As an employee, you will have goals that you are expected to achieve. Some goals apply to all of the workers in your department, or there may be goals that are for everyone who works at the health care facility. One of your own workplace goals will be to perform the duties listed in your job description. Your job performance will be evaluated by your supervisor on a regular basis. In many work settings, you will meet with your supervisor before your performance review to set goals to help guide your work and motivate you to do your best on the job. Setting and achieving goals is a way to demonstrate that you are a good employee to your employer.

Be sure to understand all of the goals that are established for your position. In addition to your supervisor's review, you will want to monitor your own progress toward achieving these goals. Keeping notes is a helpful way to identify areas where you have been successful, as well as areas where you want to make improvements.

Teamwork and team building are essential if you and your fellow workers expect to accomplish your goals. (Figure 4.6) When you follow these guidelines, your job gives you a sense of accomplishment. Being able to keep a job until you are ready to leave builds your references for the future. Remember that each job you have becomes an important part of your professional experience, and you want it to be a positive experience.

Personal Goals in the Workplace

In addition to workplace goals that you and your supervisor set and review, think about your own goals. Consider your personal goals for having the job and what you want to, and can, accomplish and gain while you are working in the position for which you have been hired. For example, you may want to work as a nursing assistant to become familiar with health care procedures with a goal of going to school to become a registered nurse. Or you may choose to work in an assisted living facility with a goal of becoming confident in caring for older patients and clients so that you can pursue work as a home health care worker.

FIGURE 4.6
Together everyone accomplishes more. How does this saying help reinforce the benefits of teamwork?

Apply It

In teams of 4 or 5 students, prepare presentations for the class that demonstrate employability skills such as attendance, appearance, individual responsibility, professional conduct, and time management

◨ Summary

Once you acquire a job, you and your employer agree to work together to accomplish the goals of the job for which you have been hired. Your behavior reflects your attitude and values. Continually evaluate your actions using the Dignity, Excellence, Service, and Fairness/Justice criteria as a measure of your progress in the work environment. Be a team player by respecting your co-workers and encouraging them to do the best job they can do.

Personal Wellness

Self-Evaluation

Evaluating your work helps you make sure you are doing the best job you can do. Self-evaluation can be as simple as keeping a journal in which you reflect on your work or more formal questionnaires that you fill out on a regular basis. Here are some tips to help you evaluate yourself effectively:

- Be honest. Tell yourself exactly how you think you are doing.
- Be specific. Don't simply say, "I'm doing well." Say, "I like the way I handled my boss's request to itemize the request list."
- Be constructive. Identify areas in need of improvement. Find a way to help yourself do a better job of the things you are struggling with. Don't say, "I am running meetings badly." Say, "I will ask my manager how I can run meetings more efficiently."
- Evaluate how your work decisions affect the population you are serving and your peers. Remember that patient needs should be the primary driver of all caregiver actions.

If you can evaluate yourself consistently and fairly, you are more likely to avoid the small problems that may lead to bigger problems later.

Evaluation by Others

Ask your peers to notify you if they observe any problems with your practice, or any other areas in need of improvement. Letting your peers know that you value their feedback will open a communication line and help you identify things you can improve upon before they become a problem.

Review the goals and comments from your annual review. Did any of the comments in the review indicate that you should change some of your work behaviors? Determine if you have taken steps to change these behaviors.

What should you do if, while you are evaluating your work, you discover you have done something unethical?

SECTION **4.2** | Review Questions ◨

1. How do employers demonstrate that they value dignity?

2. How do employees demonstrate excellence?

3. What are four employer responsibilities?

4. Define fairness.

5. What are four responsibilities of a good employee?

6. What can an employee do to demonstrate that they are service-focused?

Learn By Doing: Section 4.2 Activity

1. Complete Worksheet 1.

2. Ask your teacher for directions to complete Worksheet/Activity 2.

3. When you are confident that you can meet each objective listed above, ask your teacher for the section evaluation.

Becoming a Professional Leader

Background

Student and professional health care organizations enhance the delivery of compassionate, high-quality care by providing knowledge, skill, and leadership development. Committed students and professionals seek opportunities provided by these organizations to keep current and to provide patients with good-quality care.

Objectives

When you have completed this section, you will be able to do the following:

- Match key terms with their correct meanings.
- Name the three main benefits of being a member of a student health vocational organization.
- Name six benefits of being a member of a professional organization.
- Identify ways to find a professional organization.
- Identify steps to becoming a leader.
- Describe the goals and role of *HOSA*.
- Summarize why you plan to participate in a student and professional organization.

Membership in an Organization

Membership in your student or professional organization gives you an opportunity to gain occupational knowledge and skills. It also provides opportunities to develop leadership skills. Some of the skills that you learn include the following:

- Professional ethics.
- Communication and interpersonal relations.
- **Leadership** skills.
- Ability to recognize and initiate change.
- How to organize activities and people.
- Time management.
- Establishing **priorities**.
- **Budgeting**.
- Fund raising.
- Current health issues.

leadership
(LEED uhr ship)
Ability to influence or lead.

priority
(pry OR it ee)
A quality of importance; tasks of high priority are more urgent than items of low priority.

budget
(BUH jet)
An amount of money allocated for a particular purpose.

HOSA (formerly Health Occupations Students of America)
The student organization for health occupation students at the secondary, postsecondary, adult, and college level.

FIGURE 4.7
Emblem of HOSA. (Reprinted with permission of the Health Occupations Students of America.) What is represented by the hands around the person in the emblem?

HOSA

HOSA is the student organization for health occupation students at the secondary, postsecondary, adult, and college level (See HOSA's emblem in **Figure 4.7**). Among HOSA's primary goals are to:

- Promote career opportunities in the health care industry.
- Enhance and promote the delivery of quality health care to all people.

- Encourage all health occupations students and instructors to be actively involved in current health care issues.

Skills Competitions

HOSA provides many opportunities for students to learn and achieve. One such opportunity is the skills competitions. Competitions are at three levels—local, state, and national—with students advancing on to the next levels by winning the previous ones. HOSA offers more than 46 different events divided into categories based on the curriculum. Competitive event categories include:

- Category I: Health Science Events:
  - Dental spelling
  - Dental terminology
  - Medical spelling
  - Medical terminology
  - Medical math
- Category II: Health Professions Events, such as:
  - Administrative assistant
  - Biotechnology
  - Clinical nursing
  - Nursing specialty
  - Dental assisting
  - Home health aid
- Category III: Emergency Preparedness Events:
  - CPR/First Aid
  - Emergency Medical Technician
  - First aid/rescue breathing
  - CERT
- Category IV: Leadership Events, such as:
  - Extemporaneous writing
  - Medical photography
  - **Extemporaneous** health poster
  - Extemporaneous writing

Extemporaneous
(ik stem puh REY nee uhs) Spoken at the spur of the moment, without preparation or notes.

- Job seeking skills
- Prepared speaking
- Interviewing skills

- Category V: Teamwork Events, such as:
  - Community awareness
  - Creative problem solving
  - HOSA Bowl participation
  - Forensic medicine
  - Medical reading
- Category VI: Recognition, such as:
  - Outstanding HOSA chapter
  - National recognition program

Competition requirements include the following:

- Student must be an active HOSA member.
- Student must be identified as either a secondary student (currently enrolled in a high school) or a postsecondary student (graduate from high school or over 18 years of age).

Students attending HOSA functions follow a strict code of conduct and official HOSA uniform and competitive event dress codes. Experiencing the challenges, structure, and competition in HOSA teaches students how to reach for and achieve their highest potential. In addition, HOSA also offers many scholarship opportunities and leadership opportunities at the local, state and national level. A complete correlation of HOSA events to the concepts and activities in this book is available on the Teacher's Resouce CD.

Professional Organizations

Professional organizations help professionals keep current in the latest technology and trends. Being aware of the advantages offered through involvement in such organizations motivates health care workers to become active in the professional group for their chosen occupation.

There are numerous professional organizations for the health care worker. Most organizations have a local chapter, state chapter, and national chapter. Each supports the other, and all work toward common goals. Belonging to a professional organization provides the following benefits:

- Updates on new technological advances.
- Communication with other geographical areas.
- Shared resources.
- Resources for employment opportunities.
- Current legislative issues.
- Interaction with other health professionals.
- Pooled money to accomplish changes for the good of the occupation/profession.

Apply It

Students can ask their teachers for guidance and directions on additional activities that will help to prepare them for the HOSA skills competition.

For example, should you want to compete in the Nursing Assistant skills competition, you will have to demonstrate skills such as handwashing, making an occupied/unoccupied bed, or transferring a patient. If you choose to compete in a teamwork event, such as Parliamentary Procedure, you will demonstrate your leadership skills and understanding of parliamentary procedure by conducting a simulated business meeting.

Apply It

Some professional organizations for health care workers are specific to a medical specialty, such as pediatrics or oncology. Other organizations are specific to types of occupations, such as nurse practitioners or medical assistants. With a partner, discuss career paths you are considering and research and identify professional organizations that will help you in your chosen professions.

- Power as a united group to encourage positive change.
- Development of new ideas that support growth.

You can find professional organizations by:

- Asking fellow employees.
- Reading the bulletin boards at work.
- Reading your professional journals.
- Reading brochures.
- Researching on the Internet.
- Attending occupationally related inservice programs.
- Checking the *Occupational Outlook Handbook*.

Leadership

The leadership role is a very important part of the health care team. Some of the skills involved in being a good leader can be learned through advanced curriculum studies. Other aspects of leadership require a desire on the part of the designated formal or informal leader to improve processes and to help others function at a higher level.

Creating and maintaining an environment that fosters excellence is an important aspect of leadership. Employees working in this type of environment are more likely to strive to do their best and to be more satisfied with their job situation.

Becoming a leader in your occupational area takes time and patience. To become a leader you must take several important steps. These include the following:

- Developing a superior skill level.
- Becoming a decision maker.
- Being a good communicator.
- Developing a balanced focus on tasks and people.

Tom Peters, author of *A Passion for Excellence,* says:

"A leader is a . . .	A leader is not a . . .
cheerleader	cop
enthusiast	referee
nurturer	devil's advocate
coach	naysayer
facilitator	pronouncer"

A true leader unites people and works toward positive outcomes.

Teamwork

All team members efforts are focused on outcomes that reflect the best possible plan of patient care. Team members respect each other and can expect the support of the team.

The team leader's responsibilities include knowing the strengths of his/her team members and facilitating the use of those strengths toward common goals. The leader is there to assist, encourage, monitor and evaluate.

Good interpersonal relationships are fostered through positive attitudes toward each other. Interpersonal competency comes from being self-aware and using that self-awareness to relate to others. Respecting and valuing the input of your team members creates an environment in which each person gives individually to make a better whole. Practicing positive interactions encourages each team member to focus on team goals and quality outcomes.

To work effectively as part of a team, it's important to assist other team members when they need help and listen carefully when another team member is sharing ideas or beliefs. You must be able to respect the opinions of others even though you may not agree with them. This will enable you to stay open-minded and willing to compromise for the benefit of the patient when needed.

Also, avoid criticizing other team members and instead, support and encourage them whenever possible. Practicing good communication skills (see Chapter 9, Effective Communications) will help you share ideas, concepts, and knowledge so that you can perform your duties to the best of your abilities.

All team members work together to identify the needs of the patient, offer their opinions on the best type of care to serve the patient, and suggest additional health care professionals who might be able to assist with specific patient needs.

To direct the input from various team members, the team leader must:

- Organize and coordinate the team's activities.
- Encourage team members to share ideas and give opinions.
- Motivate all team members to work towards established goals.
- Assist with solving problems the team encounters.
- Monitor the team's progress towards the goal.
- Provide feedback to all team members on the effectiveness of the team.

Leadership Skills

The professional leader has the basic knowledge and skills necessary to direct individuals and groups toward common goals.

The professional leader continually evaluates the individual members of the group and their goals. It is important to understand the different styles of leadership (Democratic, where all team members have a voice in decision-making; Laissez-faire, where the leader allows the team members to make decisions; and Autocratic, where the leader makes the decisions and tells team members what to do) and modifies her/his style to fit the needs of the group at any given time.

The professional leader provides guidance to individual members of the group that facilitates functioning at the highest level of performance.

The professional leader promotes an environment that facilitates excellence in the individual and the group. This includes providing the tools necessary for success and acting as an advocate for the group as it interacts with other members of the health care team. In addition, a professional leader:

- Respects the rights, dignity, opinions, and abilities of others.
- Understands his or her own strengths and weaknesses.

Leadership for Meetings

Meetings are a way for teams to communicate. Effective meetings requires specific leadership:

- **Set goals.** These goals are based on topics that need to be covered.
- **Schedule.** Set a time and location for the meeting. Be firm about attendance. Prepare an agenda to share objective(s) before, or at the start of, the meeting.
- **Maintain control.** Begin on time. Assign a note-taker. Introduce each topic, guiding the team to focus and make decisions. If something cannot be resolved, set a time to address the issue. In concluding, all attendees should be aware of resulting duties.
- **Follow up.** After the meeting, send a memo with a brief summary. List action steps and a timeline for the team to achieve required follow-up. Thank attendees for their time and attention.

For more information on meetings, see p. 209.

Apply It

In teams of 6 to 10, plan, prepare, and carry out a meeting. Determine one or more topics to discuss. Assign a leader for the meeting and follow steps to a successful meeting. After your meetings, as a class, discuss what made your meetings work well and what parts of the meetings and/or the teams' meeting behavior can be improved.

Apply It

Work in two teams to create a list of three leaders in the medical field in each of the following centuries—the nineteenth, twentieth, and twenty-first centuries. What made these people leaders?

- Displays self-confidence and willingness to take a stand.
- Communicates effectively and states ideas clearly.
- Shows self-initiative and a willingness to work.
- Completes tasks.
- Shows optimism.
- Is open-minded and can compromise.
- Praises others and gives credit to others.

Summary

Participation in HOSA is an important part of your career development and professionalism. As a member, you are introduced to various health careers, develop a responsible attitude toward your community, develop knowledge and skills for the work world, and gain self-confidence.

Membership prepares you to be a leader in your chosen occupation; it also helps you prepare to become a valuable member of your professional organization when you join the workforce.

To become a leader you must develop superior skill levels, become a decision maker, be a good communicator, and develop a balanced focus on tasks and people.

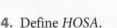

SECTION 4.3 Review Questions

1. Name the three main benefits of being a member of a student health career and technical education organization.

2. Name six benefits of being a member of a professional organization.

3. Identify the four key steps to becoming a leader.

4. Define *HOSA*.

5. Provide three examples of "What a leader is.." and three examples of "what a leader is not . . ." .

6. HOSA supports skills competitions. Name one event in each of the competitive skills categories.

Learn By Doing: Section 4.3 Activity

1. Complete Worksheet 1.

2. Ask your teacher for directions to complete Worksheet/Activity 2.

3. When you are confident that you can meet each objective for this section, ask your teacher for the section evaluation.

Background

You have to keep learning once you are in a profession. Professional development helps people grow as health science specialists, by providing opportunities to learn new skills and information from a variety of sources. Professionals also need a career plan to help them track their careers. They review this career plan periodically, and revise the plan when necessary.

Objectives

When you have completed this section, you will be able to do the following:

- Match key terms with their correct meanings.

- Explain the importance of maintaining professional competency.

- List five reasons why professionals need to learn and grow.

- Describe five resources for professional development.

- Explain how to research a health science career path,

- List the important features to research about each career.

- Explain how to revise a career plan.

- List three reasons people change careers.

 Growing as a Professional

You don't stop learning just because you graduate from school. Health science professionals need to keep learning as long as they are in their profession. Education for people who have already begun their careers is called **professional development**.

 Your Career Plan

A **career plan** is a strategy for a person's growth as a professional. Many employers require employees to create a career plan that shows how their career will change and grow over the next few years. The plan shows the responsibilities that the employee should take on and the skills he or she should learn to advance to the next stage of his or her career. Employees should review their career plan annually with a supervisor who can help adjust or revise the plan as needed.

During the annual review and evaluation conference, the employee and the employer will evaluate the employee's success at meeting the goals set up for the past term. If any problems are identified, the employee should expect the scheduling of frequent sessions until any problems identified are corrected. This is a joint effort and should reflect the goal of the organization to provide quality care and support the employee's growth in the job role.

professional development
(pro FESS shun ul dee VEL up ment)
Education for people who have already begun their careers to help them continue to grow.

career plan
(cah REER PLAN)
A strategy for a person's growth as a professional.

Apply It

Work in teams of two people. One person will be the employee; the other, the supervisor. The employee must choose an entry position and create a career plan. The supervisor must review, comment and adjust the plan.

Language Arts Link

Create a Career Plan

Once you've identified what your personal work likes, dislikes, and values are, you can begin honing in on the type of career path you'd like to follow. You will want to find out how much education the career requires, what you need to be certified, what kind of job opportunities are available, what kind of workplace environment you would likely have, and how quickly the field is growing.

The Internet is a good place to start, but always be careful of information you find on the Internet. Use safe Internet practices, and make sure your sources are reliable and authoritative.

Another good place to do research is in a library, especially a medical library. Medical libraries often have many journals and newsletters published by health care associations.

Once you've done your research, create a new document that outlines the career path that you want to follow. Write the document in paragraph form and include a thesis statement (a sentence stating your main ideas) in your opening paragraph.

Your career path document and plan will need to be revised as you continue your studies. Be sure to keep your original career plan to refer to as you grow professionally.

 Reasons to Grow as a Professional

Why should a health science professional always learn and grow? There are many reasons, such as:

- **Ethical behavior demands it.** If you are to provide the best, and most up-to-date service to your patients and clients, you need to learn the latest developments in your field. It would be unethical to offer outdated, substandard care. In fact, many licensed professionals, such as doctors, nurses, and EMTs, must participate in a specific number of hours of continuing education each year to maintain their license.

 FIGURE 4.8
Computers have dramatically changed many health science jobs. Why do you think computers have changed how hospitals store and use medical records?

- **Technology changes.** Technology in the health science industry changes rapidly. Diagnostic equipment that was unavailable a generation ago is part of routine medical care now. Computers and software programs, as seen in **Figure 4.8**, continue to be more powerful and useful in all aspects of health care, Each of these changes in technology enables professionals to provide new services and better care to patients and clients, but only if professionals learn to use the technology effectively.

- **Client needs change.** The population you serve as a health science professional is dynamic. An increase in the number of older people means you need to learn more about the health care needs of seniors. If you are a nurse, and a new disease or pathogen emerges and affects your patients, you need to learn how to treat patients with the new disease as best you can.

- **Responsibilities increase.** You probably want to advance in your career. As you advance, you will have new responsibilities at every stage. You need new skills to manage these responsibilities. For example, your position might grow and you might need you to know how to make a budget. If you have never have made a budget before, you need to learn how to make one.

- **Become more flexible.** By learning skills outside your own job, you are able to help your coworkers when they need it. You may learn that you like your new skills enough to move your career in a new direction.

Resources for Professional Development

Where can you get professional development? There are many resources available for the professional development of people working in the health sciences:

- **Associations and Organizations.** Many professional associations and organizations provide meetings, courses, workshops, and other opportunities for professional development.

- **Employer Training Courses.** Many employers offer training courses that help develop employees. Employer programs often include workshops to improve management and communication skills and courses to help employees use new equipment and software.

- **Colleges and Universities.** Many colleges and universities offer classes that can help you learn more about your profession.

- **Journals and Blogs.** Professional journals help alert people to the latest developments in their fields. You will find many online journals, blogs, on health care sites offering information and personal experiences which can provide insight into working in health care professions.

- **Mentors.** A formal or informal mentor relationship, such as the one shown in Figure 4.9, can help you in your professional development. An experienced mentor can advise you when you are unsure about what to do in a specific situation. A mentor can also advise you more broadly about how to manage your career.

Apply It

Not only will having a mentor help you, being a mentor can also benefit you. As you gain more experience, you may be asked to be someone else's mentor.

With a partner, role-play being the mentor and being mentored. What questions do you want to ask a mentor? What experiences can you share to help the person you are mentoring? Change roles at least once to experience both sides of the mentor equation.

mentor
(MEN tore)
A mentor is an experienced person who can offer advice and guidance.

FIGURE 4.9
A mentor can help you develop professionally. Do mentors always have to be older than the person they are teaching?

What's New?

Online Learning for Professional Development

Many schools, state agencies, and private companies offer distance learning courses in the health sciences. These courses are taught over the Internet. Offerings range from single classes that teach a particular skill, to entire programs, such as a Certificate of Leadership for Health Care Professionals. The programs are especially helpful to students who live in rural areas or in regions without access to a wide range options in health science education.

Before you participate in any online learning program, make sure that the program you are interested in is offered by an **accredited** organization, so that your class work will be accepted by employers. The Web site of the United States Department of Education keeps a list of accredited institutions.

What might be one benefit and one difficulty of learning leadership skills through a distance-learning class?

accredited
(ah KRED it ted)
Approved and recognized by a governing body.

 ## Revising Your Career Plan

As you grow professionally, your career plan needs to be updated annually. With a supervisor or mentor, review any professional development experiences you have had over the past year, and evaluate those experiences. Next, make a new set of learning goals for the coming year, and find concrete ways to achieve those learning goals. Discuss specific work opportunities that can help you learn and apply what you need to know.

 ## Changing Careers

When you review your career plan, you might find that you are growing in a different direction than you expected. For example, you might discover that you really enjoyed training people in a new skill, and so make training and teaching a focus of your career.

People change careers for other reasons, too. For example:

- Some people get tired, and simply need a change.
- Some careers become outdated, and replaced.
- Some people decide that they have a better chance of advancing professionally in another career area.

If you decide you would like to change careers, use the same process to investigate your new career that you used to find your first one. You can research on your own, as well as seek the help of career counselors and career centers, such as those at colleges and universities.

Summary

All health science professionals must maintain their proficiency through professional development. A career plan helps strategize how a professional develops his or her career. Professionals grow for many reasons, including ethics, technological changes, changing client needs, changing responsibilities, and improving flexibility.

Associations, employer training courses, colleges and universities, journals, and mentors are all resources for professional development. The Internet, medical libraries, and personal contacts can all help you explore a new career path. Revising a career plan can help you grow, alter your career path, or change careers entirely.

SECTION 4.4 **Review Questions**

1. Explain the importance of maintaining professional competency.

2. List five reasons why professionals need to learn and grow.

3. Describe five resources for professional development.

4. Explain how to research a health science career path.

5. Explain how to revise a career plan.

6. Name two reasons that people might decide to change careers.

Learn By Doing: Section 4.4 Activity

1. Complete Worksheets 1 and 2 as assigned.

2. Complete Worksheets/Activities 3 and 4.

3. When you are confident that you can meet each objective for this section, as your teacher for the section evaluation.

4. Prepare responses to each item listed in Chapter Review.

Chapter 4 Review

Chapter Review Questions

1. List eight items required on a résumé. (4.1)

2. Explain four ways to contact an employer. (4.1)

3. How should you greet an interviewer? (4.1)

4. What is excellence? (4.2)

5. How do employers encourage good service? (4.2)

6. What is extemporaneous speaking? (4.3)

7. Identify four ways to find a professional organization. (4.3)

8. What are six words Tom Peters uses to describe a leader? (4.3)

9. An experienced professional who can help you grow in your career is a(n)_____. (4.4)

10. A(n)_____ school is one that is approved and recognized by a governing body. (4.4)

Activities

1. Interview five employed adults about their careers. Ask them what their career is, how they found the job they are in now, and what advice they have for people trying to enter the field. Also ask for any other comments they have about their career. Fill in a table like the one below with the information you gather.

2. Using the yellow pages of your city or town, find the names of companies or organizations that you think might hire for the following occupations: medical diagnostic technician, physical therapist, medical information management specialist, and environmental scientist.

Name	Current career	How did you find the job you are in now?	Advice for people trying to enter the field	Other comments
1.				
2.				
3.				
4.				
5.				

Case Studies

1. Oscar just received a promotion and now has two people who report to him. He has never been a manager before, and would like to learn some fundamentals of managing people. What are three sources of help Oscar could use for his professional development?

2. Julie has scheduled an interview for a job as a medical records clerk. Julie wants the job, but she is nervous about the questions she might be asked during the interview. How could you help Julie reduce her stress?

Thinking Critically

1. **Relationships**—First impressions are important. Why do you think most employers refuse to read a résumé past the first spelling error?

2. **Cause and Effect**—There are many ways to be a leader, but some are more effective than others. Explain why a good leader is more likely to be a coach than a naysayer.

3. **Medical Math**—Concepts in medical math apply in calculating values when choosing a job. You make the best job choice when you take all of the benefits of a job into consideration. Some jobs pay less, but have excellent benefits. Other jobs pay a high salary and provide only minimum benefits. Calculate the full value of three different jobs by determining the

dollar value of the salary, health insurance, paid vacation time, stock or retirement benefits, and life insurance benefits. Compare your findings and evaluate which job is best for you. Your teacher can provide sources or data for you to use in this activity.

- Job 1 offers the following: Starting salary—$35,000, comprehensive health insurance plan valued at $750 per month, 2 weeks paid vacation, no retirement, no stock or life insurance.

- Job 2 offers the following: Starting salary—$32,000, comprehensive health insurance plan valued at $200 per month, 3 weeks paid vacation, employer retirement plan valued at $150 per month.

- Job 3 offers the following: Starting salary—$27,000, no health insurance, 2 weeks paid vacation, 20 shares of company stock valued at $500 each and vested (employee earns it) after 1 year on the job.

Media Connection

Use the Companion Web site for additional interactive learning activities: www.prenhall.com/badasch

Portfolio Connection

The cover letter, résumé, and thank-you letter are the primary tools for acquiring a job. There are ways to make your application packet stand out from others. Here are some of them:

- Prepare each item perfectly so that it presents you as the best possible candidate.

- Include a job objective at the top of your résumé— use key phrases that indicate your special talents and desires. Example: "I am seeking the position of a Clinical Medical Assistant in the ambulatory care setting. I am qualified for this position because it provides an opportunity to use my skills and training as a Clinical Medical Assistant."

- Add a statement to your cover letter that tells about your values concerning client-centered care and about teamwork. Example: "My school and work experience reflects a dedication to excellence through teamwork and responsibly carrying out assignments. My grades demonstrate an ability to focus on learning and to apply the learning in a clinical area."

- Add a statement to your thank-you letter that indicates your confidence in being capable of doing the job and your interest in the position. Example: "I am confident that my skill level as a Medical Assistant is appropriate for your office and that our common goals to serve patients and families through providing responsible health care will make me an asset to your team."

Rewrite your cover letter, résumé, and thank-you letter samples with these additional elements. Place them in your portfolio behind the appropriate tabs. When you complete training in a specific occupation, refer back to these documents and adapt them to focus specifically on the job you are applying for.

PORTFOLIO TIP

First impressions last: Greet everyone cheerfully and directly so that it becomes a habit.

5 | Understanding Your Legal Obligations

Getting Started

As you will learn in this chapter, the right to privacy regarding health care practices and procedures as well as a patient's condition is a legal responsibility of the entire health care workforce. There are two documents that underscore this responsibility. The Patient's Bill of Rights states "The patient has the right to every consideration of privacy. Case discussion, consultation, examination and treatment should be conducted so as to protect each patient's privacy."

In addition, the Health Information Portability and Accountability Act (HIPAA) was signed into law in 1996. On April 14, 2003 new regulations strengthening the Act went into effect. The law creates a national standard for medical privacy and gives patients greater control over their personal health information. If someone knowingly violates this law they can be fined from $50,000 to $250,000 along with imprisonment depending on the severity and intent of the offense. If you or someone in your family has been to their doctor or dentist or been in any other health care setting recently you will have been asked to sign a form declaring you have been made aware of HIPAA. This is a requirement in the law.

As you are learning more about the legal requirements relating to confidentiality you are more aware of conversations taking place in various health care settings. Imagine that you are in a small medical office and can hear the staff discussing a patient as can all others awaiting their appointment. It is a small community and several in the waiting area know the patient that is being discussed.

What would you do? Write down how you believe this situation should be handled. Be prepared to share your response with the rest of the class.

Understanding the Patient's Rights

Background

Health care team members must be aware of their legal responsibilities. This awareness protects them, the patients, their co-workers, and the facility where they work.

Objectives

When you have completed this section, you will be able to do the following:

- Explain the importance of the Patient's/Client's Bill of Rights.

- Understand the rights to which a patient is entitled.

- Measure the rights of the patient against the needs of the health care facility.

- Understand the responsibilities of the patient in the health care process.

A Patient's/Client's Bill of Rights

A Patient's Bill of Rights was first adopted by the American Hospital Association in 1973. This revision was approved by the AHA Board of Trustees on October 21, 1992.

Introduction

Effective health care requires collaboration between patients and physicians and other health care professionals. Policies and procedures are established in health care settings to facilitate this type of collaboration (see p. 134 for more about policies and procedures). Open and honest communication, respect for personal and professional values, and sensitivity to differences are integral to optimal patient care.

As the setting for the provision of health services, hospitals must provide a foundation for understanding and respecting the rights and responsibilities of patients, their families, physicians, and other caregivers. Hospitals must ensure a health care ethic that respects the role of patients in decision making about treatment choices and other aspects of their care. Hospitals must be sensitive to cultural, racial, linguistic, religious, age, gender, and other differences as well as the needs of persons with disabilities.

The American Hospital Association presents A Patient's Bill of Rights with the expectation that it will contribute to more effective patient care and be supported by the hospital on behalf of the institution, its medical staff, employees, and patients. The American Hospital Association encourages health care institutions to tailor this bill of rights to their patient community by translating and/or simplifying the language of this bill of rights as may be necessary to ensure that patients and their families understand their rights and responsibilities.

Bill of Rights

These rights can be exercised on the patient's behalf by a designated surrogate or proxy decision maker if the patient lacks decision-making capacity, is legally incompetent, or is a **minor**.

1. The patient has the right to considerate and respectful care.

2. The patient has the right to and is encouraged to obtain from physicians and other direct caregivers relevant, current, and understandable information concerning diagnosis, treatment, and prognosis.

   ■ Except in emergencies when the patient lacks decision-making capacity and the need for treatment is urgent, the patient is entitled to the opportunity to discuss and request information related to the specific procedures and/or treatments, the risks involved, the possible length of recuperation, and the medically reasonable alternatives and their accompanying risks and benefits.

   ■ Patients have the right to know the identity of physicians, nurses, and others involved in their care, as well as when those involved are students, residents, or other trainees. The patient also has the right to know the immediate and long-term financial implications of treatment choices, insofar as they are known.

law
(LAH)
A rule of conduct or procedure recognized by a community as binding or enforceable by authority.

living will
(LIV ing will)
A will in which the signer requests not to be kept alive by medical life-support systems in the event of a terminal illness.

durable power of attorney
(DYUR e bul pou r of e tur nee)
A type of advance medical directive in which legal documents provide the power of attorney (the authorization to act on someone else's behalf in a legal or business matter) to another person in the case of an incapacitating medical condition.

3. The patient has the right to make decisions about the plan of care prior to and during the course of treatment and to refuse a recommended treatment or plan of care to the extent permitted by **law** and hospital policy and to be informed of the medical consequences of this action. In case of such refusal, the patient is entitled to other appropriate care and services that the hospital provides or transfer to another hospital. The hospital should notify patients of any policy that might affect patient choice within the institution.

4. The patient has the right to have an advance directive (such as a **living will**, health care proxy, or **durable power of attorney** for health care) concerning treatment or designating a surrogate decision maker with the expectation that the hospital will honor the intent of that directive to the extent permitted by law and hospital policy.

    ■ Health care institutions must advise patients of their rights under state law and hospital policy to make informed medical choices, ask if the patient has an advance directive, and include that information in patient records. The patient has the right to timely information about hospital policy that may limit its ability to implement fully a legally valid advance directive.

5. The patient has the right to every consideration of privacy. Case discussion, consultation, examination, and treatment should be conducted so as to protect each patient's privacy.

6. The patient has the right to expect that all communications and records pertaining to his/her care will be treated as confidential by the hospital, except in cases such as suspected abuse and public health hazards when reporting is permitted or required by law. The patient has the right to expect that the hospital will emphasize the confidentiality of this information when it releases it to any other parties entitled to review information in these records.

7. The patient has the right to review the records pertaining to his/her medical care and to have the information explained or interpreted as necessary, except when restricted by law. The patient also has the right to review bills and obtain explanations for all charges.

8. The patient has the right to expect that, within its capacity and policies, a hospital will make reasonable response to the request of a patient for appropriate and medically indicated care and services. The hospital must provide evaluation, service, and/or referral as indicated by the urgency of the case. When medically appropriate and legally permissible, or when a patient has so requested, a patient may be transferred to another facility. The institution to which the patient is to be transferred must first have accepted the patient for transfer. The patient must also have the benefit of complete information and explanation concerning the need for, risks, benefits, and alternatives to such a transfer.

9. The patient has the right to ask and be informed of the existence of business relationships among the hospital, educational institutions, other health care providers, or payers that may influence the patient's treatment and care.

10. The patient has the right to consent to or decline to participate in proposed research studies or human experimentation affecting care and treatment or requiring direct patient involvement, and to have those

studies fully explained prior to consent. A patient who declines to participate in research or experimentation is entitled to the most effective care that the hospital can otherwise provide.

11. The patient has the right to expect reasonable **continuity of care** when appropriate and to be informed by physicians and other caregivers of available and realistic patient care options when hospital care is no longer appropriate. This means that

12. The patient has the right to be informed of hospital policies and practices that relate to patient care, treatment, and responsibilities. The patient has the right to be informed of available resources for resolving disputes, grievances, and conflicts, such as ethics committees, patient representatives, or other mechanisms available in the institution. The patient has the right to be informed of the hospital's charges for services and available payment methods.

The collaborative nature of health care requires that patients, or their families/surrogates, participate in their care. The effectiveness of care and patient satisfaction with the course of treatment depends, in part, on the patient fulfilling certain responsibilities.

Patients are responsible for providing information about past illnesses, hospitalizations, medications, and other matters related to health status. To participate effectively in decision making, patients must be encouraged to take responsibility for requesting additional information or clarification about their health status or treatment when they do not fully understand information and instructions.

Patients are also responsible for ensuring that the health care institution has a copy of their written advance directive if they have one. Patients are responsible for informing their physicians and other caregivers if they anticipate problems in following prescribed treatment.

Patients should also be aware of the hospital's obligation to be reasonably efficient and equitable in providing care to other patients and the community. The hospital's rules and regulations are designed to help the hospital meet this obligation. Patients are responsible for providing necessary information for insurance claims and for working with the hospital to make payment arrangements, when necessary.

A person's health depends on much more than health care services. Patients are responsible for recognizing the impact of their life-style on their personal health.

Conclusion

Hospitals have many functions to perform, including the enhancement of health status, health promotion, and the prevention and treatment of injury and disease. They also must ensure the immediate and ongoing care and rehabilitation of patients; the education of health professionals, patients, and the community; and research. All these activities must be conducted with an overriding concern for the values and dignity of patients.

All people are protected by the Patient's/Client's Bill of Rights.

continuity of care
(KON te noo it tee of kaar) Assurance that an updated, relevant "snapshot" of the patient's health information is available to any and all clinicians at time of encounter.

Community Service

Prepare a brochure or other item for distribution on the Patient's Bill of Rights and present the information to parents, faculty, and students at the high school parents' night.

Apply It

As a class, divide into teams of two or three. Each group is assigned one or two specific Patient Rights. Role play a situation in which those rights are being abused. The rest of the class identifies which Patient Right is being violated.

▣ Omnibus Budget Reconciliation Act

The Omnibus Budget Reconciliation Act (OBRA) was passed in 1987 to implement certain basic patient rights and guidelines for nursing home care facilities.

Nursing Home Reform Act

The OBRA guidelines suggest that:

1. Each resident be fully evaluated upon admission and each year after in regards to health, memory, hobbies, habits, etc.

2. A plan be created to maintain and possibly improve the resident's condition.

3. Patients have rights to a doctor and—if they can't find one on their own—the medical director of the nursing home will help them find one.

4. Patients have a right to be informed about treatment, and to refuse if desired.

5. Patients have a right to privacy and a right to complain without fear of reprisal.

OBRA also contains the Resident's Bill of Rights, which is similar to the Patient's Bill of Rights. This specifically addresses:

- Free choice of doctor, treatment, care, and participation in research.

- Freedom from abuse and chemical or physical restraints.

- Privacy and confidentiality of medical records.

- Accommodation of needs and choice regarding activities, schedules, and health care.

- The ability to voice grievances without fear.

- Organization and participation in family/resident groups and in social, religious, and community activities.

- Ability to manage their personal funds and use personal possessions.

- Unlimited access to immediate family and can share room with spouse if both are residents.

- Access to information about medical benefits medical records, things wrong with the facility, and advocacy groups including ombudsman.

- The ability to stay in the facility and not be transferred or discharged except for medical reasons, failure to pay, or if the facility cannot meet the patient's needs.

▣ Summary

In this section, you learned that the Patient's/Client's Bill of Rights is a document written by the American Hospital Association outlining expected patient/client rights while in a hospital. Health care workers are legally bound to provide care as stated in the Patient's/Client's Bill of Rights. Remember that to receive the best health, patients, or their families/surrogates, must be active participants in the process.

Language Arts Link

Patient's Bill of Rights

Hospitals and all health care facilities must treat patients and their families with the highest degree of courtesy, respect, and professionalism. A Patient's Bill of Rights is listed in the chapter. After reading the list, work with a teammate to simplify the Patient's Bill of Rights and, possibly, add any other topics that you believe should be addressed.

In your own words, create a revised Patient Bill of Rights, using simplified wording to ensure that any patient can understand it, including the elderly and those who use English as a second language. Be sure to proofread your work to see if you can improve it by making it clearer, more concise, or more interesting to read. Check the spelling and grammar and correct any errors.

Exchange your Bill of Rights with another team. Provide feedback and suggestions to each other; then revise your document as necessary.

SECTION 5.1 **Review Questions**

1. Why is the Patient's/Client's Bill of Rights important?

2. If a patient lacks decision-making capacity, or is legally incompetent or is a minor, who can exercise the Bill or Rights on the patient's behalf?

3. What happens if a patient refuses a recommended course of care?

4. What occurs if there is a conflict or dispute between the patient and the hospital?

5. What should patients, or their surrogates, provide to the medical center in order to insure proper treatment?

6. Under which, if any, circumstances is the patient NOT entitled to the opportunity to discuss and request information related to the specific procedures and/or treatments and to the medically reasonable alternatives?

 ### *Learn By Doing: Section 5.1 Activity*

1. Complete Worksheets 1–4.

2. When you are confident that you can meet each objective listed above, ask your teacher for the section evaluation.

Understanding Your Legal Responsibilities

Background

Health care workers must be aware of their legal responsibilities for the protection of patients/clients, co-workers, employers, and themselves. Policies are in place to ensure that everyone working in a hospital practices and monitors legal behavior. Maintaining confidentiality is a key factor in staying within legal boundaries.

Objectives

When you have completed this section, you will be able to do the following:

- Match key terms with their correct meanings.
- Explain why understanding legal responsibilities is important.
- Explain the importance of licensure, certification, and registration in helping improve quality health care.
- Summarize the importance of confidentiality in health care.
- Identify a law that helps ensure the confidentiality of medical information.
- Identify resources that can help you report illegal or unethical behavior.
- Understand elements of a contract.
- Explain the role of natural death guidelines and declarations.
- Describe the purpose and types of advance directives.

Apply It

Form groups of four students. Each group member should choose a health care profession. Research and list the licenses, certifications, or registrations necessary for your chosen occupation.

Find out if there are additional educational or training requirements needed to move ahead in your chosen field.

ombudsman
(OM budz muhn)
A social worker, nurse, or trained volunteer who ensures that patients are properly cared for and respected.

licensure
(LIE sen sher)
A process by which a governmental authority gives permission to a person or health care organization to operate or to work in a profession.

certification
(ser tuh fi KAY shun)
A process by which a person is made able to do a job, and recognized as such.

registration
(rej uh STRAY shun)
A list of individuals on an official record who meet the qualifications for an occupation.

Understanding Your Legal Responsibilities

It is important for health care workers to remember that patients/clients have rights that represent not only moral and ethical issues, but also rights legislated by both federal and state governments. It is each health care worker's responsibility to recognize the importance of treating patients/clients with dignity.

A list of patient/client rights is meaningless unless the person working with the patient understands and follows them. All health care workers must commit to giving the best possible care—which means complying with the professional standards of care for their particular professions. The health care worker is legally bound to provide care as it is stated in the Patient's/Client's Bill of Rights, seen in Section 5.1.

Resources for Ensuring Legal Compliance

Policies, offices, and agencies exist to ensure that everyone working in a hospital practices and monitors legal behavior. An **ombudsman** is a social worker, nurse, or trained volunteer who makes certain that the patient/client is not abused and that the person's rights are secure. Most institutions have a designated office, officer, and phone number posted for the employee to use when reporting identified problems with patients rights or institutional practice.

Other systems help ensure that health care workers are properly trained, and regulated. **Licensure**, **certification**, and **registration** tell what a health care worker may or may not do. They determine the scope of practice for the health care worker. Controls help to improve the quality of care. Although not all health occupations require licensure, certification, or registration, it is important to be aware of these controls. These are discussed further in Section 3.2, "Overview of Careers."

- *Licensure* is given by a governmental **agency** when a person meets the qualifications for a particular occupation.

- *Certification* is given for **recognition**. If specific guidelines must be met, the certification equals licensure.

- *Registration* is a list of individuals on an official record who meet the qualifications for an occupation (e.g., registered nurse, registered dental assistant). Registered nurses, such as the one seen in **Figure 5.1**, are registered with the state in which they practice.

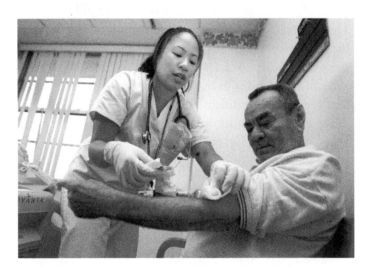

agency
(AA jen see)
An administrative division of a government or international organization.

recognition
(rek uhg NISH uhn)
The quality of being acknowledged or seen.

FIGURE 5.1
A registered nurse must be licensed to practice nursing. Why do you think states license nurses?

Confidentiality

One of the most important aspects of patient/client care is confidentiality. Patient/client information is confidential. *Confidential* means "secret." Health care workers are obligated to protect and keep <u>all</u> patient/client information confidential. A good rule is to discuss a patient/client only when the discussion affects his or her care in some way—for example:

- When you find candy with the belongings of a diabetic

- When you find alcohol or medications with the belongings of a patient/client

- When patients discuss areas of stress in their personal life, such as financial problems or relationship problems

- Even when a patient discusses information that does not pertain to his or her care, it is still subject to confidentiality. *Example:* A patient mentions that her sister is married to a local public official and has information about an upcoming ordinance that will affect property tax rates. This information is also privileged communication and should be kept in confidence.

A medical facility, a physician, or a health care worker can be fined, sued, or lose his or her job for sharing *any* information about patients/clients with others, including family members. You must report any violation of patient confidentiality.

Policies and Procedures

A policy is a principle, or rule, that guides decisions and actions in order to achieve as consistent an outcome as possible. A procedure is a series of steps also intended to achieve as consistent an outcome as possible, but for a specific task.

A health care facility develops and enacts policies and procedures to ensure patient safety and as a means of making sure that the facility is in compliance with legal requirements.

A policies and procedures manual includes descriptions of how to carry out all tasks, so workers have information to do their jobs properly. Policies and procedures are intended to provide guidance and information for workers.

relevant
(REL uh vuhnt)
Pertaining to, or having to do with, the patient/client.

written consent
(RIT en kon scent)
A person knowingly, without duress or coercion, clearly and explicitly consents to the proposed therapy in writing.

This *privileged communication* covers any personal or private information given by a patient/client to medical personnel that is **relevant** to his or her care. *Example*: A health care worker should consider all information in the chart as privileged communication.

Patients must provide **written consent** for many procedures affecting their care and for the release of medical information pertaining to their care. This includes *agreement*, usually written, given by a patient for surgery, experimental treatment, etc. after having been informed of the potential medical risks. It also includes any *legal document*, signed by the patient or his designee, stating that the patient understands any potential medical risks in surgery, experimental treatment, etc.

The Health Insurance Portability and Accountability Act (HIPAA)

The Health Insurance Portability and Accountability Act (HIPAA)
A law that includes regulations ensuring the privacy of patient information.

The medical information of a patient/client is confidential, as well. A patient's medical information is protected by the **Health Insurance Portability and Accountability Act (HIPAA).** This law regulates the sharing of medical information. Regulations in the act help ensure that a patient's medical information is kept secure and confidential. All employees of a health care system must be taught the HIPAA regulations that apply to their jobs. What kinds of information are protected by HIPPA? Here are a few examples:

- Information in medical records.
- Conversations between health care providers about patient care or treatment. (Figure 5.2)
- Health insurance information.
- Patient billing information.
- Most other information about a patient's health.

As with a confidentiality violation of a patient's personal information, a violation of confidentiality regarding a patient's medical information must be reported.

FIGURE 5.2
Information shared between physicians about a patient's care or treatment must be kept confidential. How does confidentiality show respect for the patient?

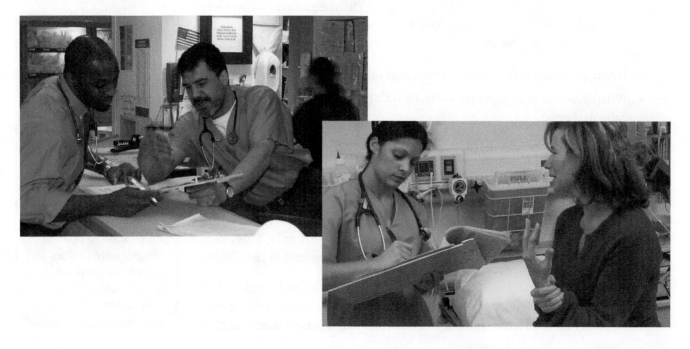

Confidential communications are protected under law against any disclosure (forced or voluntary) over the objection of the patient. The rationale behind the rule is that a level of trust must exist between a physician and the patient so that the physician can properly treat the patient. If the patient were fearful of telling the truth to the physician because he or she believed the physician would report such behavior to others, then the treatment process could be far more difficult.

However, certain information may be considered **exempt** information, such as suspected fraud, births and deaths, injuries caused by violence, including child abuse, drug abuse, communicable diseases, and sexually transmitted diseases (STDs). We know that, as the relationship between patients and health care professionals grows more complex, the definition of "privileged" or "confidential" information will be called into question.

Understanding Elements of a Contract

As an informed health care worker, it is important to understand the elements of a contract. **Contracts** are legal documents that are often used to define the terms of patient care. It is key to remember that these contracts are geared to the needs of the patient—he or she is the **principal** concern. Examples include the document patients sign declaring that they have been made aware of the terms of HIPAA regulation, as well as advance directive documents declaring their preferences in accepting or refusing medical care under certain circumstances (discussed in the following section).

Contracts are enforceable by law, and are composed of three main elements: offer, acceptance, and consideration. For a contract to be valid, one part must make an offer that the other party accepts. In many legal systems, consideration is also held to be a required component for a valid contract. Consideration means both parties bring something to the bargain specified in the agreement.

Contracts can be either implied or expressed. **Implied contracts** occur when some of the terms of the agreement are not expressed in words. An example in health care is when a patient goes to a hospital for treatment, he agrees that he will pay a fair price for the service. If he later refuses to pay for the treatment, he has breached the implied contract. **Expressed contracts** spell out the terms of the agreement in written form.

Contracts are typically made up of several parts, including boilerplate provisions and contract terms such as provisions or warranties, describing what is agreed to in the contract. Parties to a contract may only take legal action for nonfulfillment of a term. Boilerplate provisions include any standardized language used in many similar contracts to govern how the contract will be administered.

Natural Death Guidelines and Declarations

For many years people were not allowed to make decisions about death with dignity. Today, new laws allow individuals to have a say in how they want to live their last days. Each state has adopted natural death guidelines and declarations that give direction to people about how to legally tell others their desire concerning end-of-life issues.

These documents ensure the individual the right to accept or refuse medical care. In the United States, every person is encouraged to prepare this document called an "advance directive." Advance directives help ensure the right to accept or refuse

exempt
(egg ZEM p t)
To be free or released from some liability or requirement to which others are subject.

contracts
(KON trackt s)
A legally binding exchange of promises or an agreement between parties that the law will enforce.

principal
(prins si PULL)
First or among the first in importance or rank.

implied contracts
(im PLY d KON trackts)
Contracts in which some terms are not specifically stated, but are understood by the parties based on the nature of the transaction.

expressed contracts
(IK spres d KON trackts)
Contracts in which terms are written out in the document.

Apply It

As a class, create a list of medical information that might be shared between a health care professional and a patient. Then, play an in-class version of Law and Order.

In teams of four students, two students will be prosecutors who want evidence for a case; and two will be legal advocates who insist the information is covered under health care-client privilege. Present your case to the class.

medical care. Each state has slightly different laws that govern the interpretation of these documents. The advance directive is a written form providing a way for people to express how they want medical decisions made if they are unable to make decisions for themselves.

The advance directive contract is designed to help patients communicate their wishes about medical treatment at a time in which illness or injury makes them unable to make their wishes known. A formal contract will identify the agent (or health care surrogate) who makes the decisions once the patient can not do so. Then, the contract will specify the **directive**, which states the patient's wishes in terms of a terminal illness or irreversible condition. There may be additional specific requests, such as whether or not the patient wishes to be kept on life support, fed through a tube, or treated with antibiotics. The contract is then signed, witnessed by two competent adults who cannot benefit from the will, and notarized.

The advance directive takes effect when the patient is no longer able make personal decisions about medical treatment, or if they are legally disabled. A person is considered to be under a **legal disability** if they are a minor, mentally incompetent, under the influence of drugs or alcohol, semi-conscious and unconscious.

In the case of a minor, there is a legal mechanism that allows the minor to become emancipated. This means he or she is free from any authority from his or her parents or other legal guardians—they can make their own decisions. Minors can be emancipated in a variety of ways—through marriage, pregnancy, economic self-sufficiency, educational degree/diploma, and military service, for example.

If a patient lacks decision-making capacity and/or is unable to communicate their wishes, decisions regarding their health care will need to be made by someone else—their agent.

The **agent**, appointed by the patient, will have the authority to see that the patient's wishes are enforced. Since this person will be acting on the patient's behalf if they are unconscious or unable to make health care decisions, it is someone they trust thoroughly—a spouse, an adult child, a relative or an attorney/guardian.

Two common forms of advance directives are a living will and a health care (durable) power of attorney for health care.

Living Wills

A living will is a legal document prepared by a patient. This document gives instructions about the health care to be provided if the patient becomes terminally ill or falls into a permanent coma or persistent vegetative state. A living will is a way for the patient to make health care decisions before experiencing a health-care emergency.

A living will specifies whether the patient wants to be kept on life-support machines. It specifies whether the patient wants tube feedings or artificial (IV) hydration when the patient is in a coma or persistent vegetative state.

It may also contain other instructions related to health care. For example, the living will may contain a Do Not Resuscitate (DNR) order. This order instructs any health care worker not to use cardiopulmonary resuscitation if the comatose or terminally ill patient experiences a life threatening event, such as a heart attack or stroke.

directive
(de REK tiv)
Something that serves to guide or impel towards an action or goal.

legal disability
(LEE gull diss e BILL e tee)
A person has a disability for legal purposes if he has a physical or mental impairment which has a substantial and long-term adverse effect on his ability to carry out normal day-to-day activities.

agent
(EY juh nt)
A person or business authorized to act on another's behalf.

Apply It

Research the organizational policies and procedures at a health care facility in your community. Write a description of the issues and situations that the policies and procedures and address. In your description, interpret at least three of the policies and explain why you think the facility provides those policies and procedures for its employees. Discuss your interpretations with a classmate.

A living will should be on file with the patient's general health care provider. This information will be provided to any facility that is treating the patient. The physician providing treatment should add instructions from the living will to the patient's chart. Health care professionals must follow these instructions or risk legal action.

Health Care (Durable) Power of Attorney

Some patients may choose to legally appoint a health care power of attorney, or proxy. A health care proxy is a family member or close friend who is trusted to make health care decisions on behalf of the patient. A health care proxy may also be a doctor. However, a doctor who is a patient's proxy may not provide treatment and make health care decisions for the patient at the same time.

The health care proxy is asked to make decisions only when the patient can no longer think clearly or communicate. Therefore, it is important that the patient and health care proxy discuss potential medical situations and the patient's wishes for treatment before the patient becomes too ill.

The patient may also choose to write down instructions for treatment in a living will. In the event that the patient needs life support, the health care proxy works with physicians and other health care workers to carry out the patient's wishes or living will instructions.

A health care proxy becomes the patient's legal representative when the patient can no longer make decisions. In this situation, physicians and other health care workers must follow the instructions provided by the health care proxy. Other family members and friends do not have the legal right to override the decisions of the proxy.

If a patient recovers and is able to communicate, the patient then regains the right to make health care decisions. Health care workers must respect decisions made by the patient. The health care proxy cannot override these decisions.

Patient Self-Determination Act

The Patient Self-Determination Act (PSDA) was passed by Congress in November 1990 as an amendment to the Omnibus Budget Reconciliation Act of 1990. The law requires that most health care institutions (not individual doctors) inform a patient, at the time of admission or enrollment, information about their rights under state laws regarding advance directives including:

- The right to participate in and direct their own health care decisions.
- The right to accept or refuse medical or surgical treatment.
- The right to prepare an advance directive.
- Information on the provider's policies with respect to recognizing advance directives.
- Institutions to document and provide ongoing education to staff and the community on advance directives.
- Prohibits discrimination against a patient who does not have an advance directive.

It is important to remember that even without a written change, a patient's wishes stated directly to the doctor generally carry more weight than a living will, health care power of attorney, or durable power of attorney, as long as the patient can decide and communicate his or her wishes.

Summary

In this section, you learned that confidentiality is an important part of staying within legal boundaries. When health care workers perform their duties within these boundaries, they help ensure the safety and welfare of everyone around them and help prevent both medical and legal problems. There are resources at your workplace to help you report unethical or illegal incidents

You also learned about changes in the law that allow patients to have a greater say in their final care, such as Living Wills or Health Care Power of Attorneys.

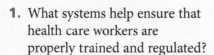

SECTION 5.2 Review Questions

1. What systems help ensure that health care workers are properly trained and regulated?

2. What is an advance directive and what are the benefits of having an advance directive?

3. Summarize the importance of confidentiality in health care.

4. Identify a law that helps ensure the confidentiality of medical information.

5. In the hospital environment, what are the responsibilities of an ombudsman?

6. Compare the differences between a living a will and the health care power of attorney.

Learn By Doing: Section 5.2 Activity

1. Complete Worksheet 1.

2. Complete Worksheet/Activity 2 and 3.

3. Complete Worksheets 4–6.

4. When you are confident that you can meet each objective listed above, ask your teacher for the section evaluation.

SECTION 5.3 Medical Liability

criminal law
(KRI me nell loh)
Body of law that defines criminal offenses; deals with the apprehension, charging, and trial of suspected persons; and sets penalties applicable to convicted offenders.

Background

Understanding legal responsibilities ensures a safe work environment and prevents lawsuits. Health care workers must perform to the best of their abilities or risk legal repercussions. These repercussions can fall under criminal or civil law. **Criminal law** is the type of law involved in punishing people for committing crimes against the state. Crimes against the state include many types of infractions of the law, such as stealing controlled substances from the hospital or stealing a patient's belongings.

Civil law, on the other hand, covers **torts**—wrongful acts that result in physical injury, property damages, or damages to a person's reputation for which the injured person is entitled to compensation. Tort law usually provides people with rights to compensation for the damages done. Torts may be categorized in two ways: intentional torts and unintentional (negligent) torts. Health care workers need to understand the law as it applies to clinical (medical) negligence. Medical malpractice, one type of tort, can result from any mistake in medical treatment. For example, a health care worker mislabels a tissue sample, resulting in a misdiagnosis of breast cancer and a mastectomy.

Objectives

When you have completed this section, you will be able to do the following:

- Match key terms with their correct meanings.
- Explain the difference between civil law and criminal law.
- Explain scope of practice.
- Explain medical liability.
- Explain medical malpractice.
- List six common categories of medical malpractice.
- Provide examples of behaviors that are infractions of medical torts.

 ## Professional Standards of Care and Scope of Practice

A professional standard of care is established on the basis of the standard that would be used by a reasonably **prudent** professional in that line of work. Professional standards of care are specific to professions. For example, a medical assistant is not held to the same standard of care as a physician. Health care workers must always remember, however, that their actions have legal consequences. To that end, there are laws that authorize the **scope of practice**—or scope of care—under which health care workers operate, or function. For example, there are tasks that are within the scope of practice for a registered nurse, such as administering medications, and there are tasks that are *not* with the registered nurse's scope of practice, such as prescribing medications.

In any health care setting, a worker must limit the methods and procedures he or she uses to the appropriate legal scope of practice for his or her health occupation. A health care facility's policies and procedures manual provides further guidelines as to the authority and responsibilities of each type of health care worker in that facility.

Emergency Care

In emergency situations, medical professionals have legal responsibilities. The first responsibility of a medical worker is a duty to act within the scope of care for his or her profession. In an emergency, health care workers are accountable to themselves, their employers, and the public for actions that are in keeping with their medical training. The second responsibility is to stay constantly ready for emergencies by understanding policies of the place of employment, and staying current with procedures and equipment. A responsibility shared by everyone who works in a health care setting is to do all that is possible to prevent emergencies.

civil law
(SI vel loh)
The body of law governing certain relationships between people, such as marriage, contracts, and torts (injuries).

tort
(TORT)
Under civil law, a wrong committed by one person against another.

Apply It

The scope of practice for a health care occupation is usually determined by a state board. Select an occupation and research your state's legal scope of practice for that occupation. Compile your findings with your classmates' and compare and contrast the scope of practice for different health care occupations.

prudent
(PRU dent)
Careful or cautious.

scope of practice
(SKOHP uv PRAK tis)
A legal set of directives developed by a state board that governs practice for a health care professional.

malpractice
(mal PRAK tis)
Failure of a professional person, such as a physician, to render proper services through ignorance or negligence or through criminal intent, especially. when injury or loss follows.

liable
(LAHY uh bul)
Legally responsible.

diagnosis
(die ug NO sis)
The identification of a medical condition.

informed consent
(in FORMD kun SENT)
The legal condition in which a person agrees to terms, after he or she understands all the facts and implications of an action or event.

Health Care Legislation

Federal and state laws regarding health care are continually updated and revised. It is the responsibility of a health care worker to stay up-to-date with legislation that affects the health care profession in which he or she works.

Information about legislation that specifically applies to health care facilities is presented in policies and procedures manuals Workers must read their manuals in order to know the laws that apply to the facilities where they work. In addition, they must pay attention to emails, memos, and other correspondence about changes to policies and procedures.

Understanding Medical Liabilities

Health care workers are obliged to do everything they can to offer high-quality care to their patients and take steps to reduce errors. If a health care worker does anything less than provide the best quality care, that professional may have committed medical **malpractice**. Malpractice means "bad practice"—care that leads to faulty practice or neglect. Malpractice is a commonly heard term, but actually refers to one type of unintentional tort. For example, suppose a patient falls on a nail and the doctor does not order a tetanus shot or check to see when the patient last had one. Then, the patient develops tetanus or lockjaw. This action would be considered malpractice. The doctor could be held legally responsible, or **liable**, for his actions.

Although these are medical issues, medical malpractice is a legal term. The legal system examines the facts of each case and determines whether or not the health care professional is guilty of malpractice. The specific facts are very important. Two very similar cases can be decided differently because of one small, but significant, difference.

What kinds of errors lead to medical malpractice lawsuits? Here are some examples:

- **Medical errors**—Any serious mistake by a caregiver may result in a lawsuit.

- **Inaccurate diagnosis**—If a medical professional makes a mistake in diagnosing a patient's/client's condition, that mistake may result in a lawsuit.

- **Failure to diagnose a condition**—If a medical professional fails to diagnose a patient's/client's condition, that mistake may result in a lawsuit.

- **Lack of informed consent**—If a medical professional does not properly explain to a patient/client his or her treatment or the likely results of that treatment, that mistake may result in a lawsuit.

- **Mistakes during surgery**—Any mistake during surgery may result in a lawsuit.

- **Medical instruments left inside patients during surgery**—If any instruments or equipment used during surgery remain inside a patient after the surgery is completed, that mistake may result in a lawsuit.

Just because a mistake was made and a lawsuit was filed, the professional who made the mistake has not necessarily committed medical malpractice. All the facts are presented to the legal system, as seen in **Figure 5.3**, and the decision is made there. Avoiding these mistakes in the first place, of course, ensures good care and helps avoid legal problems.

Other Legal Issues

Medical malpractice is just one of many legal problems that health care workers may face. Health care workers need to be aware of the whole range of possible medical-legal problems that can affect them. Read the following terms. They explain some of the other ways in which a health care worker can have a legal problem under criminal or civil law.

Language Arts Link

Tort Law

A tort is a wrongful act that results in physical injury, property damages, or damages to a person's reputation. Tort law usually provides people rights to compensation for the damages done. Torts may be categorized in two ways: negligent torts and intentional torts.

Health care workers need to understand the law as it applies to clinical (medical) negligence. Using the Internet or a library research several different kinds of tort law. Then find one medical case example of each.

Create a new document on the computer, or get a blank sheet of paper. Include a title for your report and a thesis statement (a sentence stating your main ideas) in the opening paragraph. Check the spelling and grammar and correct any errors. Be sure to cite any sources that you use in the format required by your teacher.

Exchange reports with a classmate. Provide feedback and corrections as necessary, and then exchange back. Read your classmate's comments and revise your report as necessary.

Criminal Law

- *Assault* is a threat or an attempt to injure another person. *Example*: A health care worker threatens to hit a patient/client or co-worker.

- *Battery* is the unlawful touching of another person without his or her consent, with or without **resultant** injury. Assault and battery are often charged together because of the successful attempt to injure. Both assault and battery are violations of criminal law, but they may also be subject to a civil lawsuit filed by a patient to recoup damages. *Example*: A health care worker hits a patient/client or co-worker; or a doctor operates on a patient without obtaining a signed consent form.

- *Felony* is a serious criminal offense that carries a penalty of imprisonment for more than one year and possibly the death penalty. *Example*: A health care worker withholds treatment for a terminally ill patient, which causes the patient's premature death.

- *Harassment* is any verbal or physical abuse of a person because of race, religion, age, gender, or disability. Any conduct that creates significant anguish for another person is harassment. Both state and federal criminal laws apply to harassment, but a civil lawsuit for harassment may also be filed (see sexual harassment under Civil Law on p. 144). *Example*: A health care worker makes a joke about the religion of a patient.

resultant
(ri ZUHL tunt)
Resulting from an action.

defamatory
(dee FAM uh tor ee)
Statement that causes injury to another's reputation.

misrepresentations
(mis rep ri zen TAY shuns)
Untruths; lies.

obligation
(ob li GEY shuhn)
Moral responsibility.

Civil Law

- *Libel* is writing untrue matter that is **defamatory** about an individual or group to a third party. Libel is a violation that pertains to civil law. *Example*: A newspaper writes damaging information about a local health care institution. The information is false. The paper is charged with libel. What you write in a patient record could be libel if you make a statement such as, "Mr. M. is hoarding painkillers", when—in reality—Mr. M is only requesting, and taking, the medication that has been prescribed.

- *Slander* is a spoken statement of false charges or **misrepresentations** that defame or damage another's reputation. Slander is also a violation pertaining to civil law. *Example*: A health care worker tells friends that a famous person was treated for a drug overdose when in fact he or she was treated for a serious medical problem.

- *False imprisonment* is a civil tort in which a person is held or retained against his or her will. *Example*: A physician or a health care worker refuses to allow a patient to leave the hospital.

- *Invasion of privacy* is a civil tort that unlawfully makes public knowledge of any private or personal information without the consent of the wronged person. *Example*: A health care worker gives personal information to a newspaper about a patient/client or co-worker, or a health care worker leaves the door open while bathing a patient.

- *Reportable conditions*, such as *abuse*. Abuse falls under the heading of intentional torts. There are three types of abuse: physical, verbal, and sexual. The health care worker is obligated to file a confidential report to the county health department when child or adult abuse is suspected. Reports are also required when certain diseases are diagnosed. It is important to check your facility's policy and procedures book for a current listing of reportable diseases and the procedure for reporting abuse. *Example*: A child is at the doctor for a checkup and the doctor sees bruises and burns and suspects child abuse. Or, a health care worker berates and pinches an elderly person in a nursing home.

- *Negligence* is the failure to perform in a reasonably prudent manner. The legal definition of negligence can offer more clarification of this unintentional tort: Negligence occurs when a person "does not do what a reasonable and careful person would, or does do what a reasonable and careful person would not do." *Example*: A health care worker forgets to lock the brakes on a wheelchair, and the patient/client is injured.

- *Reasonable care* is the legal **obligation** of health care workers. They must perform according to the standards of practice expected in their community for comparable workers. *Example*: Drawing blood, as seen in Figure 5.4, takes training and skill. If a laboratory aide draws blood from a patient/client after watching the procedure several times but without proper training in the procedure, then reasonable care was not exercised.

- *Sexual harassment* is defined by federal regulations as "unwelcome sexual advances, requests for sexual favors, and other verbal and physical contact of a sexual nature." Innocent remarks, inappropriate pictures, and written material can be perceived as sexual. You can guard against harassment accusations by not making personal remarks or sexual gestures and by not participating in sexually explicit discussions around co-workers. *Example:* A co-worker gets really close and frequently touches another person when talking. The closeness and physical touch could be interpreted as sexual harassment, even if it is innocent.

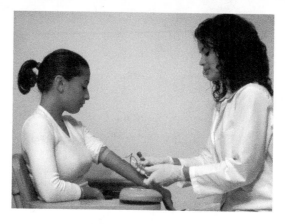

FIGURE 5.4
This health care professional was trained to draw blood. Why would it be dangerous to try to draw blood without proper training?

These definitions and examples provide the knowledge you need to avoid medical-legal problems.

 Summary

Health care workers have a responsibility to provide excellent care. A failure to provide the best care can result in lawsuits. Lawsuits are determined by the legal system based on the facts of the case. Health care workers must be aware of other legal responsibilities they face, including neglect and other unethical and illegal behavior. Avoiding illegal and unethical behavior helps promote good patient care and helps avoid legal trouble.

Career Connection

Your teacher will invite a medical ethicist or legal representative to discuss ethical and legal responsibility of working in health care. A job shadow of one of these professionals would be most valuable if you think you might be interested in one of these careers.

SECTION 5.3 **Review Questions**

1. What is a health care worker responsible for providing in order to avoid legal repercussions?

2. How can you evaluate yourself effectively?

3. What is medical malpractice?

4. Give some examples of negligence or illegal behavior that could result in legal repercussions.

5. What are six common kinds of errors that lead to lawsuits involving torts?

6. What is slander?

 Learn By Doing: Section 5.3 Activity

1. Complete Worksheets 1–3.

2. Ask your teacher for directions to complete Worksheet/Activity 4.

3. When you are confident that you can meet each objective for this section, ask your teacher for the section evaluation.

4. Prepare responses to each item listed in Chapter Review.

Chapter 5 Review

Chapter Review Questions

1. Explain the Patient's/Client's Bill of Rights. (5.1)

2. When something is _____, it is held in secret. (5.2)

3. What information is protected by HIPPA? (5.2)

4. Why are advance directives helpful? (5.2)

5. What does an ombudsman do? (5.2)

6. Who grants licensure, and when do they grant it? (5.2)

7. Give an example of slander. (5.3)

8. Give an example of libel. (5.3)

9. What are you guilty of if you hit a client or patient? (5.3)

10. A surgeon who leaves a surgical tool inside a patient is guilty of ____. (5.3)

Activities

1. Write an essay about how you would report an illegal or unethical incident at your school. Who would you tell? What would you say? Would it matter if you knew the person who did the unethical or illegal activity? In your essay, explain why it is important to report these incidents, and how reporting them helps keeps everyone in your school environment safe.

2. Use the Internet or a periodical index to research articles about legal issues and situations in the health care profession. Working in pairs, create a list of 12 medical-legal scenarios that doctors and nurses might encounter. Compare your situations with those of other students. Which ones would be considered possible malpractice and why?

Case Studies

1. A surgeon is operating on a patient's liver. While the operation is going on, the patient dies of a heart attack. The patient had a very advanced case of heart disease, but the surgeon was unaware of that problem. Do you think this is malpractice? Explain your answer.

2. A nurses' aide working in a nursing home is caring for a woman who is 95 years old and in reasonably good health. While the aide is bathing the patient, the patient has a heart attack and dies. Do you think this is malpractice? Explain your answer.

Thinking Critically

1. **Legal and Ethical**—One of your patients tells you he cannot eat because he is worried about having no will. He has no money to pay for an attorney. How would you advise this patient? What resources are available in your community for such a person? Use this as a research opportunity. Check with the country court and the local bar association. Look for current articles about similar scenarios. Let your patient know what resources are available.

2. **Patient Education**—A patient/client asks about advance directives. Describe how you will respond.

3. **Patient's Rights**—The Patient's Bill of Rights was first adopted by the American Hospital Association in 1973; then revised in 1992. What other changes do you feel need to be made in light of medical advances? Create an updated version of the Patient's Bill of Rights.

Media Connection

Use the Companion Web site for additional interactive learning activities: www.prenhall.com/badasch

Portfolio Connection

Patient Advocacy—Patient advocacy defends and promotes issues that help ensure appropriate health care.

With the many challenges that affect health care today, there is a greater awareness of the need to defend patient rights. The Patient's Bill of Rights is frequently in the news and has been presented to the House of Representatives and the Senate on several occasions. Search the newspapers, public library, and the Internet for the latest information on the struggle to protect patients' rights.

Try to identify three ways in which you can be an advocate for patient's rights. Write a short report explaining the current status of patient's rights and include your ideas on how you can be a patient advocate.

PORTFOLIO TIP

Before you file your portfolio samples, check that you have followed a step-by-step process in each document. It makes your written or recorded presentations clear and logical.

6 Medical Ethics

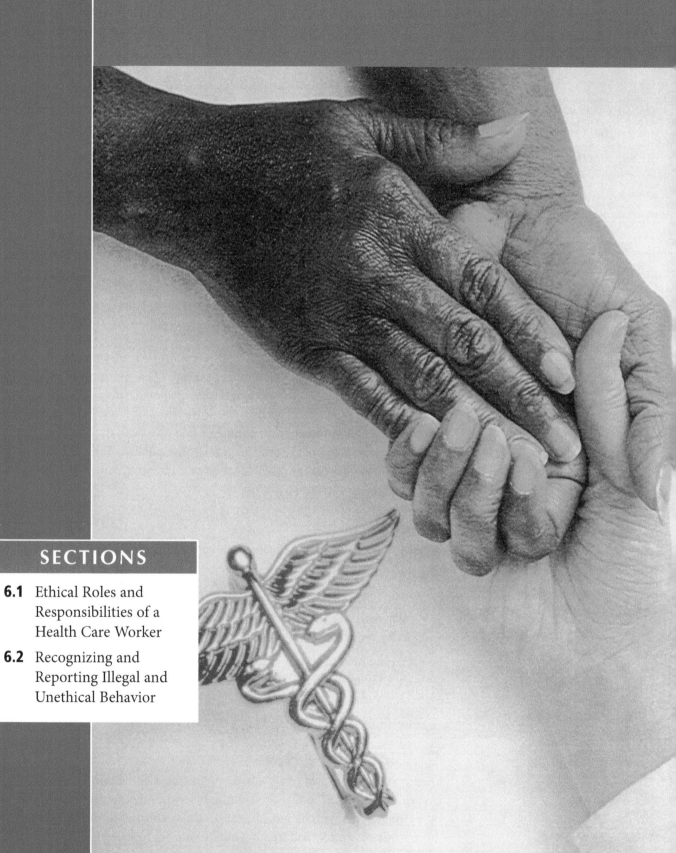

Getting Started

In addition to ethical considerations in the health care setting, school-based instruction can also help prepare students for an ethical lifestyle. One issue is the impact and importance of incorporating ethics into classes at the high school level.

Do you think this should occur? How might ethics be incorporated into your courses? Prepare an argument for and against the inclusion of ethics in your courses. You might want to discuss personal ethics such as cheating, plagiarism, or reporting unethical behavior. Or, you might choose to incorporate ethics into your actual coursework. Should your teachers bring ethics into a history course? A science course? As one of two teams created by the teacher, participate in a debate on the issue.

SECTION 6.1

Ethical Roles and Responsibilities of a Health Care Worker

Background

Members of the health care team must be aware of their ethical roles and responsibilities. This awareness protects them, the patients, their co-workers, and the facility where they work. Ethical issues differ from legal issues in health care settings. Legal issues protect patients and workers because they are based on laws, which, if not obeyed, will result in legal consequences. Ethical behavior is not based on laws, but ensures quality patient care, positive work relationships, and a well-managed workplace environment.

Objectives

When you have completed this section, you will be able to do the following:

- Match key terms with their correct meanings.
- Summarize the code of ethics that every health care worker follows.
- Explain why following a code of ethics is important.
- Use the value indicators to explain the employee's responsibilities to his or her employer.
- Explain how each health care worker affects the health care team.
- Demonstrate communication objectives that promote patient satisfaction.

Value Indicators

Quality health care workers show a commitment to certain values. Health care workers are expected to live by values that show others respect. You show respect by treating others with dignity, demonstrating a spirit of service, performing your duties with excellence, and treating others with fairness/justice.

Medical **ethics** has a long history dating back to guidelines for the practice of early physicians such as the Hippocratic Oath, widely believed to have been written by Hippocrates in the 4th century B.C. One of the earliest principles to come from this oath is to "first, do no harm." Western medical ethics has evolved to include values derived from the Muslim, Jewish, and Christian religions, including noted thinkers such as al-Razi, Maimonides, and Thomas Aquinas. In recent times, professional codes of medical ethics have incorporated legal principles to more formally spell out what conduct is expected of health care workers.

ethics
(ETH iks)
Social values; conduct; description of what is right and wrong

FIGURE 6.1
Values are reflected in your body language and your verbal responses. What kind of body language shows that you are kind?

Apply It

Research various codes of medical ethics from different historical periods, or for different health care professions. Choose two ethical codes and compare them, citing differences and similarities. Identify any legal principals addressed by the codes. Prepare a brief speech for the class, explaining what you agree with in each code, and why.

Each person determines how values are reflected in his or her day-to-day actions. An employer describes what values are important and how to reflect them while working. (**Figure 6.1**) These descriptions are usually found in an employee handbook or policy and procedure book. The values below are discussed in many parts of this text. As you read about these values in this book write your thoughts in a diary, describing other attitudes and actions that reflect parts of the four values. To understand your values and to become a values-based health care worker, see the *self-reflection exercise* in the Portfolio Connection at the end of this chapter. The following is a brief description of the values we will focus on throughout this book:

- **Dignity.** You treat people with dignity when you are honest, truthful, trustworthy, sincere, and respectful of others. Always do what is needed to the best of your abilities and ask for assistance when tasks are beyond your understanding or ability. Dignity is communicated through listening actively, being clean (**Figure 6.2**), being positive, showing understanding, and being respectful of all people.

- **Service.** Service means responding to patients/clients and co-workers with an understanding of their unique needs. You show kindness and patience, and make comments that are positive, courteous, and helpful.

- **Excellence.** Performance excellence is taking responsibility for yourself, your team's decisions, and the results. You adapt to changing needs by learning new skills, knowledge, and behaviors that encourage continuous improvement. Accepting and seeking feedback help you improve your performance excellence.

Apply It

You are conducting an orientation session for new health care employees at your hospital. Your topic is the values that you expect your employees to exhibit. In your presentation, compare and contrast the personal and professional ethics you expect in their behavior. Be clear about your organization's ethics and how that will affect your employees' work behavior. Create this speech and present it to your class. After your speech, answer questions from the audience.

appropriate
(uh PROH pree it)
Suitable, correct.

project
(pruh JEKT)
To show or reflect

confidential
(kon fi DEN shuhl)
Private; personal; restricted; secret

Apply It

Contact your local organ procurement agency to invite an agency employee or an organ recipient to talk about the legal and ethical issues pertaining to organ donation and procurement. How do these issues come into play regarding issues of death and dying?

Community Service

Prepare a chart listing the Health Care Code of Ethics for a local retirement community or senior center bulletin board. Review the information with the residents and explain how this impacts their personal rights and health care.

- **Fairness/Justice.** You treat all people with mutual respect and provide the same dignity, service, and performance excellence regardless of the patient's race, beliefs, ethnic background, or financial resources. You also use supplies and available resources effectively to provide **appropriate** care and a safe environment for everyone.

Health care workers reveal their core values and qualities in everything that they do. Tables 6.1 and 6.2 outline your responsibilities within each of the key value indicators for health care.

Patient or Customer Satisfaction

Patients and clients are more than citizens with rights. They are also customers buying goods and services. Patient and customer satisfaction is an essential element in providing effective health care. Demonstrating the values of service and excellence helps patients, their families, and their friends feel satisfied with their care. Satisfaction does not always mean that people get what they want, however. It does mean that they receive the very best care available and that the care is given with respect and with a sincere attitude. It also means that each patient/client is fully informed about the service provided by being told:

- What is needed
- Why it's needed
- Who will provide the service
- When it will be provided
- How it will be provided

Health care workers who successfully provide patient/client satisfaction practice the service guidelines outlined in Table 6.3.

When a patient's expectations are not met, there are consequences. The patient may change doctors or refuse to receive treatment from a particular health care professional in a facility. Changing caregivers can compromise a patient's care. In addition, the loss of a patient—or customer—is detrimental to a health care facility's business. Besides losing that patient's business, he or she may spread negative comments about the unsatisfactory care through word of mouth. To avoid negative consequences, focus on communicating successfully and respecting patients/clients.

Table 6.1 Code of Ethics

Ethics is a code of conduct representing ideal behavior for a group of people. A health care worker observes the following code of ethics. Often, health care facilities have special committees that develop the code of ethics for that facility. All health care workers at the facility are expected to know, understand, and abide by the facility's code of ethics.

Dignity	Service	Excellence	Fairness/Justice
Know your limitations. Know what you are trained to do and what you are capable of doing.	*Be a good citizen.* Respond to the needs of others. Demonstrate concern for meeting those needs.	*Be accountable.* Seek out and use feedback from others to learn. Take responsibility for yourself and for your team's actions, decisions, and results.	*Be loyal.* This applies to patients/clients, co-workers, and your employer. Always **project** a positive attitude toward the institution where you are employed.
Be sincere. Always be honest and trustworthy in the performance of your duties. Expect your salary in return for your work. Do not solicit gifts or additional money.	*Be caring.* Try to understand the unique needs of others. Respond quickly and effectively to problems that arise while you are working.	*Be informed.* Learn from your experiences. Seek growth and development opportunities for yourself and others.	*Respect the privacy of others.* Always keep privileged information about any personal or private matter **confidential**.
Be well groomed. Always clean your uniform, shoes, hair, nails, skin, teeth, and body to prevent the spread of disease-causing bacteria. Be sure your uniform is free of wrinkles, tears, and runs. All buttons must match. Shoes and laces must be clean and bright. Wear a name tag. This helps people you work with know you and your title. It is required in most states. Do not wear excessive jewelry. It harbors bacteria and can cause you or your patients injury. Wedding rings and watches are acceptable. Never wear perfume or aftershave lotion. They make some people who are ill feel even worse and may trigger an allergic reaction.		*Follow the rules and regulations.* Read the policy manual. Read the procedure manual. Practice Standard Precautions and the Bloodborne Pathogen Rule.	

Table 6.2 Responsibilities of an Employee

Employees are required to assume certain responsibilities. The responsibilities that are most important to employers include being dependable, honest, and well groomed; displaying a good attitude; and following the rules and regulations of the organization.

Dignity	Service	Excellence	Fairness/Justice
Communicate effectively. Express ideas, information, and viewpoints clearly. Use active listening skills, and seek to understand others. Create and maintain positive working relationships. Understand and respect differences in people. Be supportive of others' success when they do well.	*Have a good attitude.* Be willing to help your co-workers. Be aware of your body language and facial expressions, and reflect a positive outlook. Be respectful by changing your behavior when it appears to irritate others. Work effectively under pressure.	*Be dependable.* Be on time. Report in when you arrive. Report to the person taking care of your assignment prior to leaving your area. Do your job to the best of your ability. Call your supervisor ahead of time on those few occasions when you are unable to be at work.	*Be honest.* Never clock in or out for another person. Never take anything from the facility that is not yours. Never say that you have completed a task when you have not. Work with commitment and enthusiasm to improve the care patients/clients receive.

Table 6.3 Patient and Customer Satisfaction Guidelines

Communication Objective	Service/Excellence	Behavior
Demonstrate open, honest, and respectful communication. Present ideas, information, and viewpoints clearly, both verbally and in writing. Listen actively and seek to understand others.	Welcome patients, family members, and visitors in a warm, friendly manner.	Introduce yourself to the patient and his or her family. Address the patient by Mr. or Ms. unless directed otherwise. Make eye contact and smile. Explain who you are and what you do. Listen. Wear your name badge. Adhere to the dress code.
	Listen to and communicate with one another and the people you serve.	Listen attentively. Do not interrupt. Make eye contact. Clarify with more questions if necessary. Address the person's needs and take whatever action is necessary.
	Think before you speak.	Do not argue. Try to eliminate distractions when communicating with patients and families. Communicate clearly and positively. Make sure patients understand their treatment or procedures. Encourage patients to ask questions.

(continued)

Table 6.3   Patient and Customer Satisfaction Guidelines (cont.)

Communication Objective	Service/Excellence	Behavior
	Have respect for each person's privacy, comfort, and dignity.	Respect patient confidentiality in all settings. Keep noise and conversation levels low. Interview patients in private. Close curtains and doors during exams and procedures. Remember to care for the whole person—body, mind, and spirit.
Anticipate and strive to understand the unique needs of those serving as well as those served. Respond to the needs of those served and demonstrate concern for meeting those needs. Tailor each interaction to the specific needs of the person and/or situation.	Use good elevator manners.	Use the elevator as an opportunity to make a favorable impression. Be friendly. Remember confidentiality—do not discuss patients, their care, or any business on elevators. Once on an elevator, make room for others and push the door open button for them. Stand aside as others enter or exit.
	Provide a safe, clean environment.	Be alert to unsafe conditions. Correct, warn and/or report safety hazards for immediate repair. Pick up and dispose of litter. Keep all areas neat, orderly, and clutter-free.
	Anticipate the wants and needs of those served.	Be aware and sensitive to the different cultures and religious beliefs of patients. Communicate any anticipated delays. Be prepared to address special needs, such as hearing impairments, language barriers, and disabilities. Focus on education, comfort, and privacy needs at all times. Anticipate and provide appropriate comfort measures.
Seek growth and developmental opportunities for yourself and others. Adapt to changing needs by acquiring new skills, knowledge, and behaviors. Learn from your experiences.	Strive to do your best.	Identify better ways to serve patients and their families. Be a role model. Promote cooperation and teamwork. Take opportunities to improve your skills. Seek out and constructively use feedback from others. Show appreciation and thank your co-workers.

What's New?

Technology and Ethics

Sometimes technology allows scientists to study medical treatments that create ethical questions. Other times, technology helps alleviate the ethical problems. For example, scientists have known for years that stem cells might be very useful in treating many different diseases, such as Parkinson's disease. Stem cells are very basic, undeveloped cells that can develop into many different kinds of cells. Scientists hope that one day they can grow new tissues and organs using stems cells.

Until recently, however, human stem cells were only available from tissues of human embryos. This created an ethical problem: Is it acceptable to use human embryonic tissue to help fight diseases? Is it ethical *not* to treat all diseases as effectively as we can? This is a case in which technology presents an ethical problem.

Recently, scientists have discovered how to make human stem cells out of ordinary skin cells. This is helpful, because it's sometimes difficult to use one person's tissue in another person's body. Moreover, the new process eliminates the ethical problems associated with using human embryonic tissue. In this case, technology may help alleviate an ethical dilemma.

What other kinds of diseases might be treated with stem cells?

responsibility
(ri spon suh BIL i tee)
One's answerability to an employer in areas such as dependability and honesty.

Summary

As a health care worker, you are part of a very important team. You must demonstrate many qualities both in the care of your patients/clients and in your **responsibility** to your employer. Health care workers are expected to conduct themselves in an ethical manner. Ethical behavior protects you, your patients/clients, their families, the staff, and your place of employment. Dignity, service, excellence, and fairness/justice are essential for every health care worker.

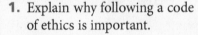

SECTION **6.1** Review Questions

1. Explain why following a code of ethics is important.

2. What values are important in health care?

3. Explain how each health care worker affects the health care team.

4. How can good communication promote patient satisfaction?

5. Identify three behaviors from the patient and customer satisfaction guidelines.

6. Quality health care workers show a commitment to certain values, including fairness/justice. Describe some actions that show fairness/justice.

Learn By Doing: Section 6.1 Activity

1. Complete Worksheets 1 and 2 as assigned.

2. Ask your teacher for directions to complete Worksheet/Activity 3.

3. Complete Worksheets 4 and 5 as assigned.

4. When you are confident that you can meet each objective listed above, ask your teacher for the section evaluation.

SECTION

6.2 Recognizing and Reporting Illegal and Unethical Behavior

Background

Health care workers must be aware of their ethical responsibilities for the protection of their patients/clients, their co-workers, their employers, and themselves. One of a health care worker's main responsibilities is to recognize and report unsafe, illegal, or unethical behaviors occurring in their work environment.

Objectives

When you have completed this section, you will be able to do the following:

- Match key terms with their correct meanings.

- Explain the importance of reporting illegal and unethical incidents.

- Identify three expectations of every employee, regarding the treatment of others.

- Identify three resources that can help you report illegal or unethical behavior.

Recognizing Reportable Incidents

Health care workers are responsible for helping to protect everyone in the work environment. If you suspect that you or another employee has been responsible for an illegal behavior or unethical conduct, that incident must be reported. How can you recognize reportable incidents? A reportable incident is any event that can adversely affect the health, safety, or welfare of students, clients, or co-workers. There are countless ways someone's behavior can negatively affect the people in the hospital. Here are a few examples:

- A nurse might administer the wrong medicine.

- A cleaning person might unplug important equipment.

- A doctor might **harass** another employee.

harass
(huh RASS)
To behave in an offensively annoying or manipulative way.

- An administrator might misuse hospital funds.
- An employee might disclose a patient's condition to a reporter.

There is no set list of reportable behaviors. Rather, it is required and expected that every employee will:

- Obey the laws of the city, state, and federal government.
- Fulfill his or her job requirements to the best of his or her ability, including following a code of ethics and respecting others.
- Treat everyone in the hospital environment with care, dignity and respect.

If you or anyone fails to fulfill these obligations, that behavior must be reported.

 ## Reporting Illegal and Unethical Behavior

Reporting an illegal or unethical incident helps ensure the health, safety, and welfare of everyone in the hospital environment. If you even suspect an incident might be illegal or unethical, report it at once. Follow your employer's policy regarding how you report illegal and unethical incidents. Here are some resources to help you report:

- Your employee manual should explain clearly how you should report illegal and unethical conduct.
- In most cases, your manager should be able to help you report illegal and unethical behavior.
- If you have any doubt about how to report an incident, contact your human resources department. They will either help you report it, or direct you to those who can.

Consequences of Illegal and Unethical Behavior

Keep in mind that there are consequences to both illegal and unethical behaviors. Both illegal and unethical behaviors may result in an employee being put on probation or fired. Illegal behavior can result in criminal charge or a civil lawsuit. In some cases, an employee who has exhibited unethical behavior will be required to take specialized training to better understand the behavior they are expected to exhibit in the workplace.

 ## Summary

In this section, you learned the importance of recognizing and reporting unethical and illegal behavior. Although illegal behavior may result in legal action, both illegal and unethical behaviors have consequences. When health care workers perform their duties within these boundaries, they help ensure the safety and welfare of everyone around them and help prevent both medical and legal problems. There are resources at your workplace to help you report unethical or illegal incidents.

Language Arts Link

Ethical and Professional Standards

As a health care worker, it's essential that you maintain a high degree of professional standards and always adhere to a code of ethics that includes acting with dignity, providing caring service, and treating people fairly and ethically.

Working with a partner brainstorm on what you feel are the some of the key qualities that will make a professional health care worker. When you've come up with enough ideas, create a document describing your principles, policies, and intentions. This type of policy is called a manifesto. Write your policy in paragraph form.

Be sure to proofread your work to see if you can improve it by making it clearer, more concise, or more interesting to read. Check the spelling and grammar and correct any errors.

Exchange your proposal with another team. Provide feedback and corrections as necessary, and then exchange back. Read your classmates' comments and revise your document as necessary.

SECTION 6.2 **Review Questions**

1. Explain the importance of reporting illegal and unethical incidents.

2. Identify three expectations of every employee regarding the treatment of others.

3. Identify three resources that can help you report illegal or unethical behavior.

4. Provide three examples of reportable behaviors.

5. What does it mean to *harass* someone?

6. How do you know that a behavior is unethical?

 Learn By Doing: Section 6.2 Activity

1. Complete Worksheets 1 and 3 as assigned.

2. Complete Worksheets/Activities 2 and 4 as assigned.

3. When you are confident that you can meet each objective listed above, ask your teacher for the section evaluation.

4. Prepare responses to each item listed in Chapter Review.

Chapter 6 Review

Chapter Review Questions

1. What four responsibilities are most important to employers? (6.1)

2. Why is the code of ethics important? (6.1)

3. What are the four key value indicators? (6.1)

4. The controversy surrounding the use of human embryonic tissue in research to help fight diseases presents a(n) _____ dilemma. (6.1)

5. How can you determine if an incident is reportable? (6.2)

6. To help you report an illegal or unethical incident, you may refer to your employee manual, your manager, or _____. (6.2)

7. Why is it important to treat everyone in the hospital environment with respect and dignity? (6.2)

8. Name three ways in which someone's behavior can negatively affect the people in the hospital. (6.2)

9. Why is reporting an illegal or unethical incident important? (6.2)

10. What is expected of every health care employee? (6.2)

Activities

1. Write an essay about how you would report an illegal or unethical incident at your school. Who would you tell? What would you say? Would it matter if you knew the person who did the unethical or illegal activity? In your essay, explain why it is important to report these incidents, and how reporting them helps keeps everyone in your school environment safe.

2. Working in pairs, create a section of an employee handbook to address illegal and unethical behavior. Explain what makes a behavior unethical or illegal and provide examples. Remember to include reporting guidelines for the employees.

Case Studies

1. While doing your rounds, you find a patient in mild distress. After checking their chart, you realize that the wrong dosage of a medication was administered. You know that this is easily corrected. What do you do?

2. A famous actress is in the hospital under an assumed name for elective surgery. The next day, a tabloid carries the story of her admission for a fatal ailment, citing an "inside" hospital source. You know who was responsible. What do you do?

3. Medical advances in biotechnology are occurring every day. Name some of these advances and describe some of the legal and ethical issues they may raise.

4. A health care worker at a hospital is found to have the HIV virus. Should patients at the hospital be informed of this?

5. An organ donor organization has determined that organs will be sold to the highest bidder. Should this be allowed to happen? Should people be allowed to sell their organs for donation?

Thinking Critically

1. **Communication**—Being an effective communicator involves active listening, honesty, and assertiveness. Think about the last time you had to tell another person something unpleasant. Were your comments constructive or destructive?

Write a skit explaining how you could change destructive comments into constructive ones; then act it out in class. Use the health care value indicators to help you decide what and how to send your message.

2. **Value Indicators**—It is particularly important to show your employer that you have a good attitude. Give 3 examples of how you would exhibit this when interacting with co-workers.

3. **Patient Satisfaction**—Patient Satisfaction is an important part of the health care worker's role. Go to Table 6.3 and select two communication objectives. Write an explanation of how behav- ior that reflects these objectives benefits patients and, their families and helps provide appropriate medical services.

4. **Technology**—Sometimes technology helps to alleviate the ethical problems; other times it can present an ethical dilemma. Can you give an example of a situation that reflects each of these scenarios?

Media Connection

Use the Companion Web site for additional interactive learning activities: www.prenhall.com/badasch

Portfolio Connection

Self-Reflection: How you express what you value causes positive or negative responses from others. Your manner encourages open and sincere or closed and guarded responses. Your values and the way you express them affect your success in your occupation. The values discussed in this chapter provide basic guidelines for working closely with others in health care. Think about your most common behaviors. List behaviors you exhibit when you are happy and when you are sad. Compare those behaviors with behaviors that reflect the health care values discussed in this chapter. Write a clear explanation of three behaviors you display. Include:

- At least one behavior that best reflects health care values. Describe why the behavior fits the value.

- At least one behavior that does not reflect health care values. Describe why the behavior does not fit the values.

Develop and describe a plan to change this behavior into a positive value-based action. Follow these guidelines when preparing your report:

- Use 8.5 × 11-inch paper.

- Type, word process, or write neatly in ink.

- Use correct spelling and grammar.

Include the following in your action plan:

- Negative behavior, with an explanation about what makes it negative or outside the health care values discussed in this chapter

- Action that changes the behavior, with an explanation about how it fits the health care values

- Evaluation plan, including a time line to determine the final outcome of the action plan

When you have completed your plan and checked format and grammar for accuracy, place it in your portfolio in the section for Written Samples.

PORTFOLIO TIP

Before you file your portfolio samples, check that you have followed a step-by-step process in each document. It makes your written or recorded presentations clear and logical.

7 Wellness

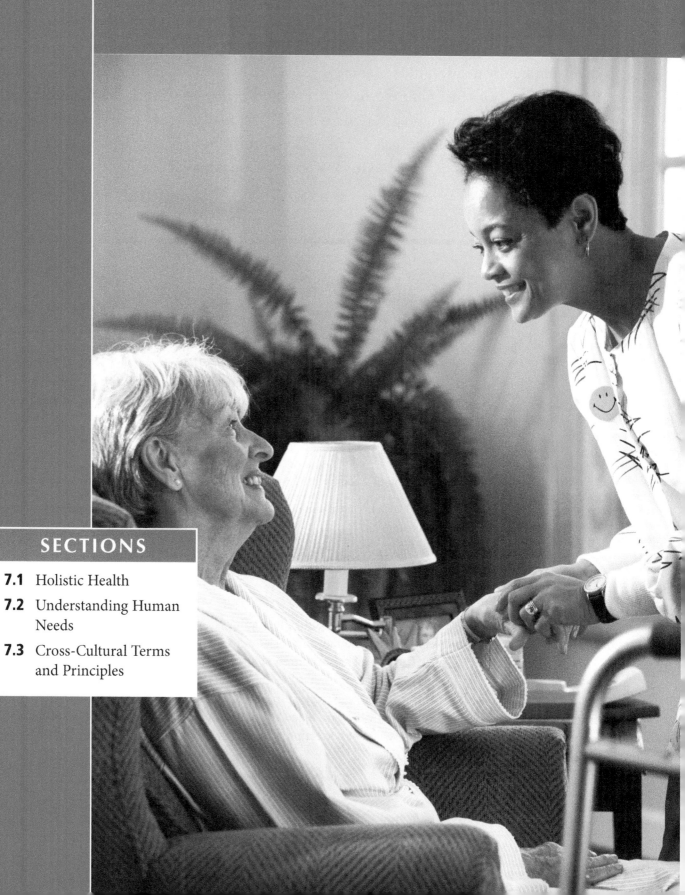

Getting Started

There are a number of basic human needs, as you will learn in this chapter. They include shelter, food and water, work that is fulfilling, safety, family relationships, and access to health care. The level of access to these needs has a direct effect on a healthy lifestyle and quality of life.

Each community is susceptible to some sort of crisis, whether it is a flood, hurricane, tornado, earthquake, or other unforeseen event. During a crisis, many of the basic needs may be jeopardized. To help with preparation for a crisis that may occur in your community, make a list of items that can be included in a "Comfort Kit"—a package that can be prepared ahead of time and delivered to those who suffer catastrophic loss.

Holistic Health

Background

Responsible health care promotes lifestyles that encourage wellness. It is important for the health care worker to understand that mind, body, spirit, and social involvement must be balanced. Understanding wellness promotes good health in the health care worker and in the patient/client.

Objectives

When you have completed this section, you will be able to do the following.

- Match key terms with their correct meaning.
- List three parts of holistic health.
- Explain wellness and preventive care.
- Compare holistic health to disease-oriented care.

infirmity
(in FIR mi tee)
Unsound or unhealthy state of being.

holistic
(hoh LIST tik)
Pertaining to the whole; considering all factors.

▣ Health and Wellness

The World Health Organization defines health as follows: "Health is a state of complete physical, mental, and social well-being and not merely the absence of disease or **infirmity**." This definition of health has been expanded with the recent growth and emphasis on **holistic** health. Today we think in terms of the body working as a unit (mental, physical, spiritual) to maintain and promote optimum wellness through daily actions. The World Health Organization definition of health gives the impression of perfection; wellness implies feeling good regardless of your infirmity or disease.

In health care, *holistic* refers to the well-being of the whole person. It is important to meet physical needs and also mental and spiritual needs when giving care. Holistic health care is a part of the wellness approach, which encourages good health and a positive self-image. Understanding these needs helps you care for yourself and for your patients/clients.

Wellness and Preventive Health Care

Wellness and preventive health care emphasize keeping patients well, not waiting until they are ill to provide treatment. Screenings are tests or examinations that are done to find a disease or condition before symptoms appear. This type of preventative care makes it easier to treat most diseases and conditions early, when treatment is often more successful. Health education is vital to helping clients maintain good health. A holistic approach includes all of the following.

Physical Fitness

Physical fitness keeps us alert and energetic in activities of daily living. It gives us enough energy to enjoy leisure time and to respond when emergencies arise. It can be achieved through:

- Routine physicals.
- Adequate rest.
- Good nutrition.
- Good posture.
- Avoiding substance abuse, including:
  - Alcohol.
  - Tobacco.
  - Excessive food intake.
- **Aerobic** exercise.
- Immunizations.
- Well-baby checks.
- Weight control.
- **Elimination** of body wastes.

aerobic
(ai ROH bik)
Requiring oxygen.

elimination
(i lim uh NEY shuhn)
Process of expelling or removing, especially of waste products from the body.

Physical fitness is good bodily health and is the result of regular exercise, proper diet and nutrition, and proper rest for physical recovery.

Physical exercise is bodily activity that develops and maintains physical fitness and overall health. This helps to strengthen muscles and the cardiovascular system, and to boost the immune system. Exercise helps prevent heart disease, cardiovascular disease, diabetes, and obesity. It also improves mental health and helps prevent depression.

Besides exercise, correct posture is a simple but very important way to keep the back and spine healthy. It is more than cosmetic—good posture and back support are critical to reducing the incidence and levels of back pain and neck pain.

A diet is all of the food consumed by a person. Dietary habits are the decisions an individual or culture makes when choosing what foods to eat. Each culture holds some food preferences and some food taboos. Individual dietary choices may be more or less healthy, but proper nutrition requires the appropriate intake and absorption of vitamins, minerals, and fuel in the form of carbohydrates, proteins, and fats. Dietary habits and choices play a significant role in health and mortality, since deficiencies, excesses, and imbalances in diet can produce negative impacts on health, which may lead to diseases such as cardiovascular disease, diabetes, scurvy, obesity, or osteoporosis.

Health Screenings

Conditions that are commonly screened for before symptoms occur include: breast cancer in women, colorectal cancer, diabetes, high blood pressure, glaucoma, high cholesterol, osteoporosis, and prostate cancer in men.

Age, gender, family history, and genetic risk factors are indications for whether a person should have particular screenings.

FIGURE 7.1

The Anatomy of MyPyramid from the United States Department of Agriculture. Why is it important to have a healthy lifestyle?

The food guide pyramid suggests optimal nutrition guidelines for each food category, per day, using a graphic of a pyramid with vertical dividing lines, to represent a suggested daily diet for each food group. The current USDA nutrition advisory program (April 2005), called "MyPyramid," (Figure 7.1) can be tailored to different groups, rather than offering a set number of servings, as in the old food pyramid guide. It indicates the need for at least three ounces of whole grain bread, cereal, rice, and pasta; more dark green and orange vegetables, peas and beans; a variety of fruit (but not many fruit juices); low fat milk, yogurt, or cheese; low fat, lean meats, poultry, and fish.

Anatomy of MyPyramid

One size doesn't fit all
USDA's new MyPyramid symbolizes a personalized approach to healthy eating and physical activity. The symbol has been designed to be simple. It has been developed to remind consumers to make healthy food choices and to be active every day. The different parts of the symbol are described below.

Activity
Activity is represented by the steps and the person climbing them, as a reminder of the importance of daily physical activity.

Moderation
Moderation is represented by the narrowing of each food group from bottom to top. The wider base stands for foods with little or no solid fats or added sugars. These should be selected more often. The narrower top area stands for foods containing more added sugars and solid fats. The more active you are, the more of these foods you can fit into your diet.

Personalization
Personalization is shown by the person on the steps, the slogan, and the URL. Find the kinds and amounts of food to eat each day at MyPyramid.gov.

Proportionality
Proportionality is shown by the different widths of the food group bands. The widths suggest how much food a person should choose from each group. The widths are just a general guide, not exact proportions. Check the website for how much is right for you.

Variety
Variety is symbolized by the 6 color bands representing the 5 food groups of the Pyramid and oils. This illustrates that foods from all groups are needed each day for good health.

Gradual Improvement
Gradual improvement is encouraged by the slogan. It suggests that individuals can benefit from taking small steps to improve their diet and lifestyle each day.

MyPyramid.gov
STEPS TO A HEALTHIER YOU

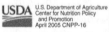

USDA U.S. Department of Agriculture Center for Nutrition Policy and Promotion April 2005 CNPP-16

USDA is an equal opportunity provider and employer.

GRAINS | VEGETABLES | FRUITS | OILS | MILK | MEAT & BEANS

The impact of substance abuse, including tobacco, alcohol, and drugs, crosses all societal boundaries, affects both genders, every ethnic group, and people in every tax bracket. Smoking tobacco particularly damages the respiratory and the circulatory systems. Regular use results in diseases that cause death or severe disability. During pregnancy, chemicals from the tobacco smoke pass through the mother's blood to the baby through the placenta and reduce the oxygen and blood flow to the baby.

Excessive alcohol use increases the risk of many harmful health conditions, such as unintentional injuries, including traffic injuries, or falls. It is associated with violence, child neglect, and risky sexual behavior. In addition, alcohol poisoning can occur, a medical emergency that results from high blood alcohol levels which suppress the central nervous system and cause loss of consciousness, low blood pressure and body temperature, coma, respiratory depression, and death. Long-term alcohol problems include chronic disease and neurological impairments. During pregnancy, miscarriage, stillbirth, and a combination of physical and mental birth defects that last throughout life can occur.

Drug abuse has a wide range of definitions related to taking a psychoactive drug or performance enhancing drug for a non-therapeutic or non-medical effect. Some of the most commonly abused drugs include alcohol, amphetamines, barbiturates, benzodiazepines, cocaine, methaqualone, and opium alkaloids. Use of these drugs may lead to criminal penalties in addition to possible physical, social, and psychological harm.

Physical and mental activities require energy and create waste products. As our energy level goes down and wastes accumulate, we experience fatigue and a need to rest. During rest, energy is restored, and the waste buildup is diminished, allowing for recovery and growth. Rest and sleep are dependent upon our ability to relax. To get a good night's rest, try to sleep in a dark, quiet, cool room.

Mental Fitness

Mental fitness allows us to interact effectively with others and to feel balanced. Mental fitness manifests in a positive self-image. Mentally healthy people:

- Self-direct (being the captain of your own ship).
- Have a sense of belonging.
- Trust their own senses and feelings.
- Accept themselves.
- Have **self-esteem**.
- Practice stress management.

Stress is what you feel when you have to handle more than you are used to. Often, your body responds in the same way as it would if you were in danger—hormones speed up your heart, make you breathe faster, and give you a burst of energy. This is sometimes known as the fight-or-flight stress response. Some stress is normal and even useful; for example, it can help you win a race or finish an important job on time. But if stress happens too often or lasts too long, it can have bad effects.

You can experience headaches, an upset stomach, back pain, or trouble sleeping. It can weaken your immune system, making it harder to fight off disease. It can make you moody, tense, or depressed. Relationships may suffer, and you may not do well at work or school.

To identify stressors, you have to know:

- What event caused the stress.
- Why you feel stress.
- How much stress you are feeling.
- If you feel negatively or positively about the situation.

"Financial Fitness"

Finances are assets in the form of money. Your personal finances include the money you earn, spend, and save.

Some people live "paycheck-to-paycheck," meaning they spend all that they earn. They may have trouble paying their bills, they may not put financial needs before wants, or they may not understand planning ahead financially. People who live this way may have stress and worries.

When you take control of your finances, you set financial goals and make healthy financial decisions for both your needs and wants. Managing your money makes you financially "fit" and contributes to your overall well-being.

For more about personal finances, go to:
www.prenhall.com/badasch

self-esteem
(SELF i STEEM)
Belief in oneself.

Apply It

Break into teams of three. Each group should identify a current or potential environmental health issue, such as gastrointestinal illnesses on cruise ships or exposure to mold in older buildings.

Create a presentation that discusses the symptoms and problems experienced by people in each specific situation as well as potential solutions for the problem. Check the CDC Web site as a resource.

As a class, divide into teams of two or three. Each group should discuss potentially stressful situations in the workplace, such as having a heavy workload, or not getting along with a coworker. Then develop a list of strategies for dealing with stressful situations in the workplace. Share your lists as a class to compare and contrast strategies and gain insight about dealing with employment stress.

Before you can get stress under control, you need to find out what is causing the it. So, you should:

- Gather information or data.
- Identify the problem.
- List possible solutions.
- Make a plan.
- Act on your solution.
- Evaluate the results.
- Change the solution.

In order to cope with stress, look for ways in which to reduce it, and learn healthy ways in which to relieve it. Some methods might include better time management, taking good care of your health, getting plenty of rest, regular exercise, not smoking, limiting alcohol intake, learning to say "no" if you are too busy, and asking for help. You can talk to family, friends, or a counselor. You can write down things that are bothering you, or find other ways to express your feelings. Finally, you can take some time to do something you enjoy or to relax yourself (with yoga, massage, aromatherapy, etc.). Also, manage the physical reaction to stress by stopping, breathing deeply, reflecting on the cause of stress, and choosing another way to react.

Personal Wellness

Time Management

Good time-management skills can help you personally and professionally. These skills help you use time effectively; they keep you in charge of what's happening. By keeping things in perspective, these skills can increase your productivity. That means you can get your work done efficiently, and have more time to relax and enjoy life.

Time management starts with setting goals. These can be short-term—stages and timeframe for getting a report done, or a long-term strategy and timeframe for running for Class President. Setting effective goals means that you state them positively, define them clearly and precisely, prioritize them, write them down, and make sure the goal is appropriate.

So, you would *not* say: "Oh, I have to write my term paper by April 15." Instead, you would create a time management plan. You would analyze and prioritize your work. And, of course, take into account your habits and preferences.

You might say: "My term paper is due on April 15. It is now April 1, so I have two weeks to finish it. Researching the topic is always the hardest part for me. "

Then, you would schedule the tasks that you must complete, make a daily "to do" list, and plan your work.

- On April 1, I will create an outline.
- On April 2, I will review it with my teacher.
- From April 3–April 8, I will research my topic and take notes.
- On April 3, I will use the school library.
- On April 4, I will go to the public library.
- On April 5, I will conduct my interview.
- On April 6 and 7, I will organize my notes.
- On April 8, I will review my outline and notes to make sure I have no gaps.
- From April 9–11, I will write the first draft.
- From April 12–14, I will review and revise.

If you avoid distractions and concentrate on following your schedule, your term paper will be done on time—and you'll be able to take credit for a job well done!

Spiritual Fitness

Spiritual fitness allows us to experience meaning and purpose in life. It provides a sense of comfort with others, creating greater acceptance of behaviors, attitudes, and beliefs. It includes:

- Enjoying companionship.
- Sharing ideas and thoughts.
- Having a sense of belonging.
- Showing enthusiasm for life.

Holistic health requires health care workers to promote physical, mental, and spiritual well-being. For example, a patient experiencing stomach pain may be referred to a psychologist if the physician suspects that the patient is under emotional stress. The psychologist may refer him to a biofeedback specialist for stress management. This process continues until the patient's/client's needs are met in all areas.

Alternative Health Care

The National Library of Medicine classifies alternative medicine as a complementary therapy. These therapeutic practices are not currently considered an integral part of conventional medical practice. They do not follow generally accepted medical methods and may not have a scientific explanation for their effectiveness; they are unconventional. However, as they become better researched some—such as physical therapy, diet, and acupuncture—become widely accepted. Others, such as humors or radium therapy, become no more than a "historical footnote." Therapies are termed as *complementary* when used in addition to conventional treatments; they are considered *alternative* when used instead of conventional treatment.

Fundamental to alternative medical practice is a strong bond between patient and doctor; the need to work as a team. These doctors do not see themselves as the source of healing; patients must take active responsibility for their health and well-being.

Initially, these therapies were used by individuals who had run out of other options—individuals with immune deficiencies, cancer, chronic back pain, arthritis, and other conditions. Today, more and more people are turning to alternative health care for wellness care. Some examples of alternative medicine include the use of herbal medicine, acupuncture, yoga, massage therapy, and spiritual healing. For example, a woman with breast cancer chooses to treat her cancer by eating a special macrobiotic diet instead of having radiation and chemotherapy, which is the standard medical practice. Or, an elderly person with arthritis uses acupuncture to treat arthritis pain instead of taking medications.

Apply It

With a partner, review the types of fitness discussed in this section. Then create a list that identifies behaviors and traits that contribute to overall fitness, or a positive self-image. In your discussion, also note the behaviors and traits that can lead to a negative self-image. Compare and contrast your list of positive behaviors and traits with the lists of your classmates.

Community Service

Review the activities offered at a local senior center or retirement community. How many of them focus on spiritual fitness? Talk to a local Yoga, Pilates, or Tai Chi instructor and ask them to put on a demonstration at the senior center (geared for that age group). What is the response of the residents?

The use of alternative medicine, of course, has its drawbacks. Many in the mainstream medical community believe that these alternative therapies, in conjunction with standard treatments, provide comfort for the patient. However, they argue that relying on these therapies alone and without doctor approval is dangerous and can even be fatal. The disease might be getting worse, even if the patient "feels" better, because it is not being adequately treated.

Using herbs that are not FDA approved may cause interactions with other medications or vitamins. It may be easier to overdose on a specific regimen that has not been adequately tested. Just because a product is natural does not mean it is safe. One example of this is foxglove which is a component of digitalis, used to treat heart conditions. Foxglove, with unsupervised use, can also be a poison.

There are minimal, if any, regulations or federal guidelines associated with alternative medicine. For example, over-the-counter herbs are not regulated and the patient cannot be sure of any standard of preparation in their formulation. This could make the patient a target for unscrupulous activity. Finally, insurance companies may not cover alternative medical treatments unless they are used in conjunction with traditional therapies.

Jobs and Professions

There are a wide variety of careers that are outside of the mainstream medical world. Of course, there are physicians and nurses who specialize in alternative medical treatments, such as homeopathy and naturopathic medicine. Others focus on breath therapy, environmental medicine and nutrition. A career in alternative health care areas will require entrepreneurship to establish a practice and bring in clients.

In addition, alternative medicine offers opportunities such as:

- **Acupuncture**—The insertion of thin, stainless steel needles into the skin at specific locations to affect the flow of energy in the body. Making sure energy is not blocked facilitates symptom relief and healing of illness.

- **Homeopathy**—Developed in Germany in the eighteenth century, homeopathic remedies are created from plant, animal, or mineral products greatly diluted in water or alcohol.

- **Massage therapy**—A wide variety of physical manipulative techniques promote relaxation and treats conditions caused by tension, such as headaches or insomnia.

- **Naturopathic medicine**—Although similar to traditional medicine, naturopathic physicians avoid drugs, major surgery, and cutting-edge technology and rely on treatment designed to strengthen the body's own healing capabilities. For example, preparations such as vitamins, nutritional supplements, and herbs might be used to treat and prevent disease.

- **Prayer and spirituality**—Often considered "alternative" by conventional medical standards, prayer and spirituality help patients maintain a sense of purpose, meaning, and hope in the face of pain, suffering, and uncertainty.

- **Chinese traditional medicine**—Utilizing methods such as herbal remedies, acupuncture, diet, meditation, and exercises such as qigong and tai chi, this therapy seeks to achieve overall balance of health in preventing as well as treating illness. Qigong is an aspect of traditional Chinese medicine which involves the coordination of different breathing patterns with various physical postures and motions of the body. Tai chi is a gentle exercise program derived from martial arts, but composed of slow, deliberate movements, meditation, and deep breathing, which enhance physical health and emotional well-being.

There are a wide range of career choices in alternative medicine. Some occupations are well known; others less so. They include:

- **Psychologist**—An expert in the systematic investigation of the human mind, including behavior, cognition, and affect. Psychologists are usually categorized under a number of different fields, the most well-known being clinical and counseling psychologists. Licensed psychologists need an academic doctoral degree, such as a Ph.D or Psy.D.

- **Social worker (rehabilitation worker)**—Concerned with social problems, their causes, their solutions and their human impacts. Social workers work with individuals, families, groups, organizations and communities. Generally, social workers need a professional degree in Social Work; and usually they must obtain a license or be professionally registered.

- **Midwife**—Practitioner who specializes in normal pregnancy, childbirth, and the postpartum. (Figure 7.2) They generally strive to help women have a healthy pregnancy and natural birth experience. Midwives are also primary care givers providing general women's health care. Direct-entry midwives learn midwifery through self-study, apprenticeship, a midwifery school, or a college- or university-based program separate from the discipline of nursing.

Apply It

Take a survey of the students in your classroom. How many of them (or their families) have used alternative medical professionals? Create a chart that shows the types of alternative care delivered—for example, chiropractic, acupuncture, aromatherapy, hypnotist, or midwife.

FIGURE 7.2
A midwife demonstrates the breech position to a pregnant woman. What are the advantages of using a midwife?

- **Biofeedback specialist**—Trained to use a form of alternative medicine that involves measuring a patient's bodily processes such as blood pressure, heart rate, skin temperature, galvanic skin response (sweating), and muscle tension and conveying such information to the patient in real time in order to raise his or her awareness and conscious control of the related physiological activities. Specialists must pass a certification exam.

- **Parish nurse specialist**—Registered nurse who commits to the healing missions of a church. They work to help fellow parishioners find support in crisis or with day-to-day struggles. They also work directly with parish staff to educate on wellness and a better quality of life. Nurses must be registered and meet the standard nursing educational requirements.

- **Acupressurist**—Uses a form of traditional Chinese medicine in which the health care provider stimulates certain pressure points to encourage the flow of vital energy (Qi) along the specific pathways called meridiens. This is often used to control chronic pain such as migraine headaches or backaches. Acupressure is generally classified as massage, and training may be offered through massage schools or independent seminars.

- **Acupuncturist**—Uses a form of traditional Chinese medicine, which treats specific health disorders with the insertion of fine needles into the body at specific points where the flow of energy is thought to be blocked. To be certified, they must attend an accredited school of acupuncture and pass a licensing exam.

- **Palliative care specialist**—Palliative care is the active total care of patients whose disease does not respond to curative treatment, including control of pain, of other symptoms, and of psychological, social, and spiritual problems. The goal is to provide the best possible quality of life for patients and their families. Palliative care specialists typically work in teams and usually are needed when the disease is advanced, life expectancy is short, and problems become complex and more urgent. Palliative care specialists are board certified physicians and must meet all of the standard requirements.

- **Ayurvedic Practitioner**—Uses a traditional system of Indian medicine, in which the basic texts analyze the human body in terms of earth, water, fire, air, and ether as well as the three bodily humours (wind, bile, and phlegm). To prevent illness, these practitioners emphasize hygiene, exercise, herbal preparations, and yoga. To cure ailments, they rely on herbal medicines, physiotherapy, and diet. Specialists must take specific courses and pass a certification exam.

- **Chiropractor**—Treats patients whose health problems are associated with the body's muscular, nervous, and skeletal systems, especially the spine. Chiropractors use manipulation and specific adjustment of body structures, such as the spinal column, to rebalance the nervous system and the body. (Figure 7.3) They must be licensed, which requires two to four years of undergraduate education and passing national and state exams.

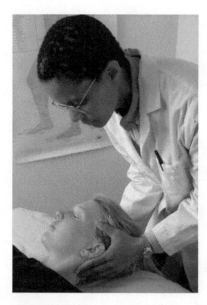

FIGURE 7.3
A chiropractor holding a patient's head performing alignment. What benefits can a chiropractor provide patients?

- **Aromatherapist**—Uses essential oils extracted from plants as therapy to promote health and well being. These can be inhaled by patients, introduced internally, or applied topically. They must pass a training course and receive a certificate.

- **Hypnotist**—Trained in inducing trance states and therapeutic suggestions to improve a wide range of medical and psychological issues, such as fears, phobias, anxiety, sleep disorders, etc. Hypnotists must take a course (about a month long) and pass a test to be certified.

Summary

The holistic approach to health is important because it includes all aspects of a person's well-being. When a person is in balance physically, mentally, and spiritually, that person can experience life in a positive way and enjoy a greater sense of well-being. (**Figure 7.4**) The trend in health care is toward wellness and preventive care. The health care worker has a responsibility to help the patient understand different care choices and the role that each of these therapies may play in seeking a goal of optimal wellness.

FIGURE 7.4
Enjoying companionship, sharing ideas, having a sense of belonging, and showing enthusiasm for life are vital to well-being. What is a way that a person might show enthusiasm for life?

SECTION **7.1** **Review Questions**

1. How does the definition of health presented by the World Health Organization go beyond physical conditions?

2. What are some habits that can help a person to stay physically fit?

3. In what ways is spiritual fitness related to a person's well being?

4. In a holistic approach to health care, a patient with neck pain might be referred to a psychologist. How might this help the person?

5. Name three professions involved in maintaining the health and wellness of others.

6. Name two conditions and explain how they might be treated using alternative therapies.

Learn By Doing: Section 7.1 Activity

1. Complete vocabulary Worksheet 1.

2. Complete Worksheets 2 and 3 as assigned.

3. When you are confident that you can meet each objective for this section, ask your teacher for the section evaluation.

7.2 Understanding Human Needs

Background

Understanding a person's physiological and psychological needs is essential for every health care worker. Each of us has needs that must be satisfied to maintain stability. Health care workers must be aware of these needs to maintain their own stability and to meet the needs of patients/clients and co-workers.

Objectives

When you have completed this section, you will be able to do the following:

- Match vocabulary terms with their correct meanings.

- Name four psychological needs that must be met to maintain stability.

- Name four physiological needs that must be met to maintain stability.

- Explain five benefits of pet-facilitated therapy.

- Match five defense mechanisms with the correct descriptions.

- Explain how you use defense mechanisms daily.

Meeting the Needs of Patients/Clients

For many years, psychologists have studied people to better determine what makes each of us act the way we do. People act and behave differently, but there are some common characteristics that were identified by Abraham Maslow over 60 years ago and explained in Maslow's Hierarchy, which focuses upon five levels of basic needs.

There are *physiological needs*, biological needs such as oxygen, food, water, and a relatively constant body temperature. After these are satisfied, there are *safety needs*, the need for security. The next class of needs is *love, affection, and belongingness*. Next, the need for *esteem* becomes dominant. When all of these needs are satisfied, then the need for *self-actualization*, a person's need to be and do what he/she think they were born to do, becomes important.

Physiological Needs

Physiological needs are divided into four categories. Biological needs are listed in Table 7.1a; safety needs in Table 7.1b; sensory needs in Table 7.1c; and motor activity needs in Table 7.1d.

Psychological Needs

Psychological needs are divided into four categories. Adequacy and security needs are listed in Table 7.2a; social approval and self-esteem needs in Table 7.2b; order and meaning in life needs in Table 7.2c; and self-growth needs in Table 7.2d.

Understanding people's **physiological** and **psychological** needs helps you be a better health care worker. You are able to recognize the reasons for certain behaviors and respond appropriately. Always report evidence of all unmet needs to your supervisor. In the next patient care meeting, your supervisor and the other caregivers will determine a plan for how best to meet the patient's/client's need.

physiological
(fiz ee uh LOJ I kuhl)
Pertaining to normal body functions.

psychological
(sahy kuh LOJ I kuhl)
Pertaining to the mind.

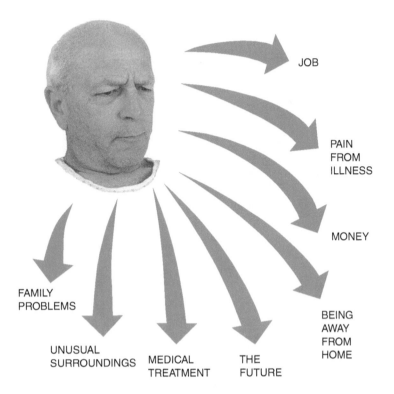

JOB

PAIN FROM ILLNESS

MONEY

FAMILY PROBLEMS

UNUSUAL SURROUNDINGS

MEDICAL TREATMENT

THE FUTURE

BEING AWAY FROM HOME

FIGURE 7.5
Clients worry about many things when hospitalized. What concerns might a person have about his or her job?

Pet-Facilitated Therapy

Recent studies have focused on the **value** of the human-pet bond, showing that petting or stroking a pet has an immediate effect on the body. Most people studied showed:

- A slowing heartbeat.
- Deeper breaths.
- Fewer abnormal heartbeats.
- Lowered blood pressure.
- An increased sense of well-being.

value
(VAL yoo)
Importance, worth.

Over 50 percent of American households have pets, primarily for the companionship that they provide. Research shows that even when people do not respond well to other people, they do respond to pets. They talk to their pets. They care for the needs of their pets. When there is a human–animal bond, people often find new meaning in life. They feel less lonely. They feel needed because their pets are totally dependent on them. They have a reason to get out of the house to buy food for their pets. The pet may be just the friend or responsibility they need to help feel better or to feel good about themselves. Research also shows that fish swimming gracefully in an aquarium with swaying plants creates a relaxing environment that reduces stress.

Table 7.1a Biological Needs—Food, Water, Sleep, and Elimination

Threatened by Illness	Communication Needs	Age-Specific and Communication Needs	Cultural Awareness	Reporting and Recording Observations
■ Food and water may be withheld before various procedures or surgery is performed. ■ Sleep may be interrupted because of the environment, noises, or anxiety. ■ Elimination is frequently affected by changes in routine, foods, or medication.	■ Be committed to reflecting the value of dignity. Use effective communication skills that demonstrate holistic care. Be alert to the biological needs and communicate how they will be met during patient care. ■ For new patients explain: 　• Physician's orders concerning activity, food, use of the bathroom, and any expected special procedures; 　• Mealtimes; 　• How to request assistance or ask questions. ■ Always ask patients if they have any special requests or questions. ■ When sleep must be interrupted, inform the patient before he or she goes to sleep.	■ Use words that the patient can understand. Ask a translator to ensure that words and thoughts are fully communicated. ■ Allow decisions concerning food and sleep to be made by the patient when possible. ■ Tell patients what to expect. ■ Reassure children and parents of times they can be together. ■ Address people by their proper names and titles, especially older people. ■ Ask coherent patients if they have any specific fears. Address their fears honestly and with sensitivity, always treating people with dignity. Ask for assistance when necessary. ■ Remember that comments like "Don't worry" are never helpful.	■ Many cultures of the world: 　• Believe that illness is caused by a supernatural power; 　• Use various herbs to treat illness and may request a specific diet; 　• Consider white bad luck. Medical personnel in white may cause an increase in fear; 　• Believe that hot and cold air currents negatively affect health. Be alert to drafts. ■ See Section 7.3 of this chapter for more information.	■ Report to your supervisor and record in the medical record: 　• Special requests; 　• Expressed fears;. 　• Your instructions about the medical routine; 　• Your observations of how the patient and family received instructions concerning the routine and potential limitations of food, water, interrupted sleep, and expected preparation for procedures that may affect elimination.

Table 7.1b   Safety Needs—Needs to Feel Secure and to Avoid Bodily Harm and Injury

Threatened by Illness	Communication Needs	Age-Specific and Communication Needs	Cultural Awareness	Reporting and Recording Observations
■ Patients needing medical procedures and treatments may feel insecure. They may be facing hospitalization for the first time and are afraid they will be hurt or die. They may be entering a long-term care facility where they will live for the rest of their lives. They may wonder: • What will happen to me? • How will I be treated? • Will I be safe? ■ Patients may also be worried about pain or accidents that could occur during procedures.	■ Be sure that the patient fully understands what you are saying. Use pictures, culturally appropriate gestures, writing and/or a translator to ensure understanding. ■ Tell patients what they can expect from you and your team. Introduce yourself and your team. Your reassuring presence and warm touch may be enough to help a patient feel safe. ■ For new hospital patients: • Tell patients how to request assistance or contact you—explain the call system and intercom. ■ Show your commitment to service and treating others with dignity by always doing what you say you're going to do. This helps create trust and builds a sense of security for patients and their families.	■ Think of the patient's age and ability to understand before speaking. Use the patient's words as much as possible. Speak at his or her level. ■ When caring for pediatric patients, ask the family if special words or objects communicate special things. For example, a child may call a special toy or blanket a "binki." ■ When possible, allow family or significant others to be present if the patient requests their presence.	■ Be alert to body language and other forms of communication that may provide clues to the patient's state of mind. ■ See Section 7.3 of this chapter for more information on various cultural beliefs that may affect the way health care is given.	■ Report to your supervisor and record in the medical record: • Special requests; • Expressed fears; • Your instructions about medical routine; • Your observations of how the patient and family received instructions.

Table 7.1c   Sensory Needs—Stimulation of the Five Senses (Hearing, Seeing, Feeling, Smelling, Tasting) as Well as Intellectual Stimulation

Threatened by Illness	Communication Needs	Age-Specific and Communication Needs	Cultural Awareness	Reporting and Recording Observations
■ When the senses are not stimulated they diminish. For example, when a patient is not able to eat, intravenous fluids may be used. Because the smell and taste sensors are not stimulated, when the patient begins to eat again it will take time for taste and smell to return to normal. ■ The senses are less responsive to stimulation as we age. Geriatric patients may have lost one or more of their senses. They may have difficulty hearing or seeing which may increase their fear and cause anxiety.	■ Communicating with people experiencing a sensory loss takes patience and imagination. Try some of the following to stimulate their senses. 　• People with hearing loss can experience music by touching a speaker while it plays music. They can feel rhythm vibrate through the speaker. 　• Patients with touch-impaired senses usually lose feeling in their hands and feet. When it is reasonable, touch their face or arms with things that they want to feel, such as a warm towel. 　• Sight-, smell-, and taste-impaired patients appreciate your description of colors, smells, or flavors in their environment. For example, you might say "Remember the smell of turkey roasting and fresh bread baking? That's what it smells like today." ■ When working with people show your commitment to excellence by being sensitive and remembering to use techniques that help people experience their senses.	■ The loss of senses during the aging process also adds to the loss of well-being. As a health care worker you can help restore a sense of well-being by being aware and using techniques that help people experience or remember the feelings of their five senses. ■ When you are aware of sensory loss, talk to the person and ask what helps him or her experience the lost sense. Try various techniques that will help stimulate the senses, always explaining what you are doing.	■ The various cultures of the world relate differently to touch, gestures, and personal space. As a health care worker it is important that you are mindful of the various cultures and the potential barriers relative to the body senses. See Section 7.3 of this chapter for details.	■ Report to your supervisor and record in the medical record: 　• Special requests; 　• Expressed fears; 　• Your instructions about medical routine; 　• Your observations of how the patient and family received instructions.

Table 7.1d Motor Activity—Movement or Exercise of the Body

Threatened by Illness	Communication Needs	Age-Specific and Communication Needs	Cultural Awareness	Reporting and Recording Observations
■ When muscles are not stimulated they atrophy (shrink) and eventually weaken and can even become frozen. The results of a lack of muscle stimulation may or may not be reversible depending on the length of time the muscle was not stimulated. For example, when a cast is removed from an arm or a leg after a long period the arm or leg is usually much smaller than the one which was not in a cast. The casted limb was not able to stimulate the muscles so they shrank and became weak. Weakened muscles can prevent free and easy movement.	■ Be sure that the patient fully understands what you are saying. Use pictures, culturally appropriate gestures, writing and/or a translator to ensure understanding. ■ People who experience difficulty moving around must be informed about how to reach you and others at all times. ■ Inform the person that you are aware of his or her condition and will take precautions to protect any special needs. ■ Explain the procedures that you will use to ensure the patient's safety as you help him or her move or as you do procedures. ■ Your commitment to difference for patients. Share expected times do the things they your patients, and always follow through.	■ Remember to ask patients if they follow a certain procedure that best accommodates their limited or painful movement. Caution: Never do anything contradictory to your training or good judgment. ■ When appropriate, encourage people to do as much as possible on their own to promote self-sufficiency.	■ Be alert to your patient's customs concerning personal space. Always tell the patient what you are going to do before you start to move or touch him or her. ■ Be aware of cultural taboos about touching the head and appropriate versus inappropriate hand gestures. ■ See Section 3 of this chapter for details.	■ Report to your supervisor and record in the medical record: • Special requests; • Expressed fears; • Your instructions about medical routine; • Your observations of how the patient and family received instructions.

Table 7.2a Adequacy and Security—Need to Feel in Control and Capable of Coping

Threatened by Illness	Communication Needs	Age-Specific and Communication Needs	Cultural Awareness	Reporting and Recording Observations
■ When a condition occurs that requires medical treatment it is easy to feel a loss of control. Medications and various procedures and disease processes can change the way the body feels and what a person is capable of doing. ■ Loss of a sense of control affects physical and emotional well-being	■ Discuss what must be done to promote good health and to treat specific conditions. Encourage the patient to comment and make decisions as much as possible. ■ Show your commitment to dignity and justice by providing opportunities for patients to be involved as much as possible in decision making.	■ When possible, provide opportunity for patients to make decisions such as what they will eat or wear.	■ Be aware of cultural customs that show respect or disrespect. For example, making direct eye contact in some cultures is disrespectful. Adapt your behavior and language to show respect for each person's dignity.	■ Report to your supervisor and record in the medical record: • Signs of insecurity; • Voiced inadequacies; • Your observations; • Special requests; • Your observations of how the patient and family received instructions.

Table 7.2b Social Approval and Self-Esteem—Recognition and Acceptance by Other People

Threatened by Illness	Communication Needs	Age-Specific and Communication Needs	Cultural Awareness	Reporting and Recording Observations
■ When illness limits what a person is able to do at work, socially and personally, depression can occur. This in turn can affect the success of treatment. The patient's ability to support his family may be taken away by an illness that causes job loss. This causes extreme stress. (Refer back to Figure 7.5.)	■ It is important to spend time with patients who feel isolated. Patients in quarantine or who have visible body changes may feel different and isolated from their friends and family. Spending time with them and learning about their life can help them feel accepted. ■ Encourage family and friends to include them in activities and events when possible. ■ Show your commitment to dignity by practicing active listening skills. Show interest in the patient's concerns and past experiences. ■ Inform the patient and family of available helpful resources (e.g., social services).	■ When caring for children use terms they can understand. ■ Be positive even when you want to say something negative. ■ As a health care worker you can help restore a sense of well-being by staying alert to your patient's preferences, moods, using resources within your facility to encourage and promote socialization with others who may be having similar experiences. ■ Use age-appropriate vocabulary. Do not use childish gestures or language to talk with an elderly person.	■ Use culturally appropriate gestures and words to show respect. Honoring a person's culture is an effective way of reinforcing self-esteem and showing social approval. ■ Be aware of dietary needs or restrictions. ■ Encourage family and friends to display pictures and articles that may bring warm and comforting memories.	■ Report to your supervisor and record in the medical record: • Signs of low self esteem; • Voiced inadequacies; • Your observations concerning any change in behavior. For example, withdrawal, passive behavior, wanting to give things away, refusing to see people; • Special requests; • Your observation of how the patient and family received instructions.

Table 7.2c Order and Meaning in Life—Understanding of What Is Going on in One's Environment

Threatened by Illness	Communication Needs	Age-Specific and Communication Needs	Cultural Awareness	Reporting and Recording Observations
■ When illness occurs it is difficult to know what to expect or how to plan for the future. ■ Meaning and purpose in life are in question if an illness changes the way we do things. ■ Order that brings a sense of control is lost, leaving a feeling of being out of control and uncertain.	■ Tell patients what to expect before, during, and after procedures to help them psychologically prepare for the experience. ■ Listen to the patient so you will have an understanding of his or her concerns. ■ Respond with understanding. For example, "We will be starting your physical therapy today and I'm bringing you the schedule so you will know when to expect the therapist."	■ Use words that the patient can understand. Ask for a translator to ensure that words and thoughts are fully communicated. ■ Write information and schedules on a paper that the patient and family can refer to. Use pictures for children, like a clock with the hands pointing to a time you will return.	■ Use culturally appropriate gestures and words to show respect. ■ Be aware of routine cultural activities that bring meaning to the patient.	■ Report to your supervisor and record in the medical record: • Signs of low self esteem; • Voiced inadequacies; • Your observations concerning any change; • Special requests.

Table 7.2d Self-Growth—Need for Fulfillment Beyond Basic Needs

Threatened by Illness	Communication Needs	Age-Specific and Communication Needs	Cultural Awareness	Reporting and Recording Observations
■ Illness often consumes our thoughts. Patients who experience a long illness or physical changes that limit their abilities may experience a loss of personal growth.	■ Use active listening skills to identify patients' special interests. Allow them to share the details of these interests. When appropriate, discuss possible options with the care team that will allow the patient to experience learning. Your service excellence and commitment to treating others with dignity are a reality when you take action in this way.	■ Use words that the patient can understand. Ask for a translator to ensure that words and thoughts are fully communicated. ■ When caring for children introduce activities at the child's level of understanding. ■ Be sure enough time is given to teach and not frustrate the patient of any age.	■ Seek culturally appropriate learning for the patient. ■ Some cultures view games as childish; being sensitive to cultural attitudes will help the patient accept new opportunities.	■ Report to your supervisor and record in the medical record: • Voiced discouragement or being bored; • Your observations concerning mood changes; • Special requests; • Involvement of any kind that promotes learning.

All of this research has alerted the medical community to promoting healthier lifestyles through the companionship of pets. People who are experiencing many changes in their lives may find a pet to be the one unchanging element. Some people may be lonely and find that a pet is a good companion, while others may just enjoy the pleasure and presence of a pet.

Pet-facilitated therapy can be used as a treatment. Animals are taken into convalescent homes and children's hospitals. Some hospitals have arranged to have a pet live on the premises. Other programs have been developed with the Humane Society, and pets are brought in to visit on a regular basis. Pet-facilitated therapy is especially effective in the home. An aging person may feel depressed and alone. A pet brings new meaning to life. Now there is something that really needs him or her and is affectionate and loving. The same kind of therapy is effective for a sick child.

Pet-facilitated therapy has become a successful form of treatment. When working with your patients, be alert to their needs. Perhaps a pet will meet a need that no other care can.

◧ Meeting the Needs of Co-Workers

Recognizing human needs in your patients/clients makes you a better health care worker. Recognizing human needs in the staff you work with helps make you a successful member of the health care team.

Physiological Needs

friction
(FRIK shuhn)
Disagreement because of a difference of opinion.

When the *biological needs* of every staff member are not met, **friction** may occur. It is important to eat properly and to get adequate sleep. Many disagreements occur when people are irritable and easily upset because they failed to meet their biological needs.

It is important that every member of the staff have their *safety needs* met. They should feel secure and know that bodily harm can be avoided. As a staff member, always follow safety regulations, such as cleaning up spills, reporting damaged equipment, and taking care to protect others. When someone needs help lifting, help the person. This establishes a sense of safety for all the staff and creates a good working environment.

As a fellow staff member, it is important to realize what the *sensory needs* are. This helps you understand fellow staff members with sensory impairments. For instance, if a co-worker's hearing or sight is impaired, you need to be aware of this impairment. Your awareness allows you to be patient and to build a good working relationship.

Psychological Needs

stability
(stuh BIL i tee)
Ability to maintain a balance, both mentally and physically.

Adequacy and *security* are important to all people and help us maintain **stability**. Your attitude toward other staff members is either cooperative or disruptive. When staff members work together, they establish a sense of a job well done.

Social approval and *self-esteem* can be met in our relationships with our fellow employees. It is important that you develop **rapport** with other staff members. As you work together to create a healthy environment for the patients/clients and the staff, everyone feels accepted and worthwhile.

Order and *meaning* needs are met by the day-to-day activities on the job. If every staff member does his or her share and comes to work when scheduled, these needs are met.

The need for *self-growth* is met as you and the other staff members are able to accomplish your jobs and look toward promotion and new learning.

Defense Mechanisms

All people use defense mechanisms to help feel more comfortable and to make their behavior seem reasonable. Defense mechanisms are mental devices that help people cope with various situations. Health care workers who are aware of defense mechanisms better understand themselves, their co-workers, their supervisors, and their patients' behavior. Following are some key defense mechanisms:

- **Rationalization:** Finding good reasons to replace the real reason for behavior in order to maintain self-esteem. *Example:* Mark did poorly on a test and explained it by saying, "I'd rather be popular than smart."

- **Compensation:** Substituting one goal for another. *Example:* Mary really wanted to be on the track team but wasn't good enough. Instead, she joined the choir and became a soloist.

- **Projection:** Placing the blame for your actions on someone or something else because you cannot accept the responsibility. *Example:* "I didn't get a good grade in my health occupations class because the teacher doesn't like me."

- **Sublimation:** Redirecting feelings toward a constructive objective. *Example:* You enjoy playing tennis and you use the game to work out **aggressiveness** and **hostility** instead of directing those feelings toward others.

- **Identification:** **Idolizing** someone you would like to be like. *Example:* Margaret especially admired her music teacher. She began to walk and dress like her.

When you are aware that everyone uses defense mechanisms, and when you know what they are, you are able to understand your behavior and the behavior of others. As a health care worker, it is important for you to realize that a defense mechanism may be involved in certain behavior. This allows you to give better care. Your knowledge of defense mechanisms also helps you understand the behavior of the people with whom you work.

rapport
(ra POHR)
Harmony; a close relationship with another.

Community Service

Prepare a report on the different religious and cultural beliefs for giving and receiving health care and present the report to a group of health care professionals. If you are bilingual, assist the staff with interpreting the requests of second language patients.

aggressiveness
(uh GRES iv ness)
Tendency to start fights and quarrels or to attack without reason.

hostility
(hos STIL i tee)
Unfriendliness; ill will toward another.

idolizing
(AHYD I ahyz ing)
Loving to excess.

 *Science Link*

Fight-or-Flight Response

You can probably recall a situation in which you felt threatened or scared. Perhaps your teacher surprised you with an unexpected test or you had an argument with a classmate. In situations like these, your heart pounds, your muscles tighten, and your mind races. You are experiencing a fight-or-flight response.

The fight-or-flight response, also known as the acute stress response, was first described by the American physiologist Walter Cannon in 1927. He described it as an inborn response that prepares the body to either deal with or flee from a perceived threat to survival. In response to the threat, changes occur in the nerve cells of the body, and hormones such as adrenaline and cortisol are released into the blood stream.

The combination of nerve cell and chemical activity causes the rate of respiration to increase. Blood is shunted away from the digestive tract and directed into muscles and limbs, which require extra energy and fuel for running or fighting. The pupils of the eyes dilate as the person's awareness of the surroundings intensifies. At the same time, the perception of pain decreases. Essentially, the fight-or-flight response bypasses your thinking mind and puts your body into an attack mode.

Long ago, the fight or flight response often saved people from physical threats, such as saber-toothed tigers and opposing warriors. Today, the threats are different. They might be found on the soccer field, in the classroom, or at the office. The response has also changed. Running and fighting are not always available options—for example, in the case of an unexpected pop quiz. Nonetheless, the response prepares your body to deal with the situation in order to protect yourself.

The natural conclusion of fight-or-flight is physical activity. Some researchers suggest that without the physical conclusion, people can suffer from the buildup of stress hormones. Some people experience symptoms such as muscle tension, headache, upset stomach, racing heartbeat, deep sighing, or shallow breathing. Others may experience anxiety, poor concentration, depression, hopelessness, frustration, anger, or fear.

Perhaps the easiest way to slow the body's activities after a fight-or-flight response is through physical exercise. Exercise helps the body break down excess stress hormones, thereby restoring both and mind to a calmer, more relaxed state.

What is a good way to slow your breathing and heart rate after a fight or flight response?

 Summary

Human beings have physiological needs, which include biological needs, safety needs, sensory needs, and motor activity needs. They also have psychological needs, which include the need to feel adequate and secure, to have social approval and self-esteem, to have order and meaning in life, and to experience self-growth. These needs must be met at all times. It is important to always be aware of these needs in our patients/clients, our co-workers, our supervisors, and ourselves. All people use defense mechanisms to help them feel comfortable inside. These include rationalization, compensation, projection, sublimation, and identification.

Personal Wellness

Depression

Everyone feels sad or blue once in a while when situations go wrong or disappointments arise. For some people, however, sadness is a constant emotion—even when there is no obvious reason for it. This disorder, known as depression, is not a passing mood or a sign of weakness. People who suffer from depression cannot simply "get over it" or assume it will go away.

The symptoms of depression go beyond mere sadness. People who suffer from depression may also experience any or all of the following symptoms:

- A change in sleeping patterns
- A change in eating habits
- An increase in fatigue
- Unexplained aches and pains
- A loss of interest in activities and friends
- Difficulty concentrating
- Feelings of hopelessness, helplessness, and worthlessness

The causes of depression vary from one person to another. Low self-esteem, pessimism, and anxiety are major contributing factors in some types of depression. Physical changes, such as a stroke, heart attack, or hormone disorders can also lead to depression. Stresses at home or school, life and relationship changes, and family history are also important factors.

If you or someone you know displays any symptoms of depression, there several steps you can take to start the healing process. Begin by identifying any problems that might be causing the symptoms. For example, consider living conditions, relationships, diet, physical fitness, and spiritual beliefs. Regain control of your life by looking for ways to fix problems and eliminate sources of sorrow. Develop a healthier diet, get regular exercise and sleep, and establish a support system of friends and family. Set realistic goals each day, and determine priorities in your life.

If symptoms persist, seek a professional counselor who can help you work through issues and refer you to a physician if medication is required. Health care workers should be aware of the signs and symptoms of depression. Basic tools used to screen the patient for depression should be available for use in the health care setting. Mental health resources for referral should be made available to the patient. This is a part of providing the patient with holistic care.

Treatment for depression can last for months or years, but a combination of psychotherapy and medication can often reduce or even eliminate symptoms of depression.

How might an increase in exercise help defeat mild depression?

1. Compare and contrast physiological and psychological needs. Give an example of each.

2. What are some physical effects on a person who strokes a pet?

3. What does it mean to say that friction develops between two people?

4. What is a common cause of friction between people?

5. Why is it important to be aware of the sensory needs of classmates and co-workers?

6. What are defense mechanisms, and why do people use them?

Learn By Doing: Section 7.2 Activity

1. Complete vocabulary Worksheet 1.

2. Complete Worksheets/Activities 2 and 3 as assigned.

3. Complete Worksheets 4 and 5.

4. Ask your teacher for directions to complete Worksheet/Activity 6.

5. When you are confident that you can meet each objective for this section, ask your teacher for the section evaluation.

SECTION 7.3 Cross-Cultural Terms and Principles

Background

Health care workers interact with people from many cultural backgrounds. It is important to know culturally acceptable and effective gestures, terms, and behaviors. This knowledge allows the health care worker to adapt his or her care and communication techniques to meet individual needs. The patient/client receives quality care, and the experience is a positive one.

Objectives

When you have completed this section, you will be able to do the following:

- Explain how culture influences behavior.

- Identify culturally acceptable and effective gestures, terms, and behaviors.

- Recognize communication techniques that create a positive exchange of information.

- Identify common folk medicine practices.

- Compare and contrast cultural differences.

- Explain how understanding cultural beliefs affects you as a health care worker.

Culture and Behavior

When caring for and working with people from different cultures, you must understand their cultural background. Understanding allows you to have positive experiences and to communicate effectively. Our understanding and opinions of other cultures develop through our life experiences. Culture includes a shared background. This means that cultural groups have shared experiences. Among those experiences common to most groups are:

- Language.
- Communication style.
- Belief system.
- Customs.
- Attitudes.
- Perceptions.
- Values.

Language and communication styles and some customs are visible to people outside of a specific cultural group. Belief systems, some customs, attitudes, perceptions, and values are less visible. Think of a tree. (Figure 7.6) The trunk, branches, and leaves are all visible—like language, communication styles, and some customs are visible in people. The roots of a tree, however, grow deep underground and nourish it to keep it strong—but they are not visible. So it is with culture: Belief systems, some customs, attitudes, perceptions, and values all come together to create a strong foundation that helps form a person.

It is important to remember that there is no right and wrong when comparing various cultures. Cultures are only different. Cultural differences do not weaken society, but in fact strengthen society if there is a sense of openness that allows understanding. This does not mean changing one culture to adopt another cultural view. It only means that there is understanding and consideration that reflect the value of dignity toward those from different cultures. Taking interest in different cultures broadens your thinking and opens doors to new adventures. Think for a moment about what life would be like if our ancestors were afraid to start a fire or go into the water. How different would your life be today without fire or an

FIGURE 7.6

Culture can be compared to a tree because some cultural characteristics are visible like the trunk, branches, and leaves of tree whereas others are less visible like the root system of a tree which is underground. What is an example of a visible characteristic of a culture?

Visible

Language
Communication style
Some customs

Less Visible

Some customs
Belief systems
Attitudes
Perceptions
Values

prejudge
(pree JUHJ)
To decide or make a decision before having the facts.

appreciation of the ocean? When we refuse to be open and do not try to understand, we can easily **prejudge** and form prejudices. Some prejudices include:

- **Age prejudice:** A person is too old or too young.
- **National prejudices:** A person comes from a foreign country.
- **Physical prejudices:** How the person looks different from you.
- **Mental prejudice:** A person judges an individual by how smart a person is, how much a person knows, how well a person thinks.
- **Religious prejudices:** A person's beliefs are different from yours.
- **Racial prejudice:** A person belongs to a different race from you.

You can overcome prejudice by learning about others. Here are some suggestions:

- Keep an open mind.
- Look for additional information. Why do people think the way they think? (For example, why does someone think people of another culture are lazy or not smart?)
- Watch documentaries, read books, magazines, and newspapers for information.
- Look at many resources before you form an opinion.
- Evaluate all the information. Ask yourself if it is true or false?

There are some basic points to keep in mind when experiencing aspects of a different culture:

- Values are an important part of every culture. Cultures have values and ideals that they believe, yet individual conduct may not always reflect those values. For example, a culture may value and honor their national flag, but not everyone in the cultural group may have a flag or display it.

- Behavior is not only the result of culture. Age, financial status, education, gender, experience, relationships, health, and many other factors influence behavior.

- It helps to look for the common characteristics of different cultures or to seek a common ground. For example, we are all part of the human race so food is common to all of us. We can explore different flavors, which are created by spices, cooking techniques, and so on. We also all have seasons of the year that have special meaning and that are celebrated through traditions.

Ethnicity, Culture, Gender, and Race

We often refer to culture, ethnicity, and race interchangeably. Culture relates to the behaviors, beliefs, and actions characteristic of a particular social, ethnic, or age group. Ethnicity refers to identity with or membership in a particular racial, national, or cultural group and observance of that group's customs, beliefs, and language. There are six main ethnicity groups: African American, Asian American, European American, Hispanic American, Middle Eastern/Arab American, and Native American. Race is a human population that is considered distinct based on physical characteristics, such as White, Black, or Latino.

In a "melting pot" country, we see a lot of cultural assimilation, the process of integration of members of an ethno-cultural group into an established, generally larger community. This can result of a loss of many characteristics of the absorbed group. So, second generation Asian American children may not be as likely to respond to the traditional; family structure.

Acculturation, on the other hand, is the exchange of cultural features that results when groups come into continuous firsthand contact. The original cultural patterns of either or both groups may be altered, but the groups remain distinct. So, for instance, we may see rap music appealing to youths of all backgrounds.

Finally, we must exhibit sensitivity—understanding the value of cultural differences and treating them with respect and dignity. For example, a traditional Muslim woman is not allowed to be examined by male members of the medical staff. It is always preferable that a female member of the medical staff is present.

Health care professionals need to be objective; they should not be predisposed in favor or against an idea. This bias can impact treatment; for instance, if you assume that all elderly patients cannot accurately describe their symptoms or make viable decisions about their care. They must also be concerned about ethnocentricity, a belief in the superiority of one ethnic group. For example, western medicine is not necessarily superior to alternative Chinese treatments. Finally, health care professionals must avoid stereotyping, expressing a simplified idea or opinion about a group of people. You cannot assume that breast cancer will only occur in women.

Apply It

Divide into groups. Each group should plan to build a health clinic in a community of a different culture. Make a presentation to convince the leaders of this community to let you build it. You must research the culture's health care beliefs so you know how to focus your oral presentations to the community leaders.

Career Connection

Invite the local Emergency Medical Services, Fire Department (80 percent of calls the fire department receives are for health care emergencies and only 20 percent for fire related emergencies), Red Cross, or Emergency Room personnel to discuss the problems they face when working in communities of different cultures and how they address these needs. Do they have specific training? How does it impact their jobs?

Being open and willing to learn about others includes choosing your words carefully so they express your desire to learn. It is best to avoid saying things like:

- "We're all alike; we're all human"—A statement like this ignores the important differences that bring depth and richness to life. A person's dignity could be diminished causing her to feel that she needs to blend in more. People may change their names to fit in or avoid traditions that may draw attention to the differences.

- "We should stay with our own culture, we are too different"—This statement may cause fear and separation. When fear causes separation, defensive attitudes and behavior often follow. Arguments or fights are often the result of such fear. Learning about other cultures is enriching and broadens our view about life. Understanding other cultures usually brings a more complete understanding of your own culture and helps you communicate better with others.

Now decide what your opinion is.

FIGURE 7.7
Motioning with a finger for someone to come. What is another gesture that you have used to communicate with family members or friends?

Our behavior sends a message to others. They receive or understand the message by the way they interpret behavior. When more than one culture is involved, the interpretation of a behavior is often different. For example, to use the motion illustrated in **Figure 7.7** to get a person to come is acceptable in the United States. In many other cultures, it is insulting and rude. Learning about communication in other cultures helps the health care worker understand the true meaning of behavior. This information allows you to respond with understanding.

Gestures and Body Language

Personal Space and Touching

Personal space and touching are defined in different societies as close-contact and more-distant contact. (**Table 7.3**) Personal space is the space needed to feel comfortable when we are with other people. **Figures 7.8** to **7.10** show examples of societies where more distant contact is expected.

People in close-contact societies are comfortable with less space between them. Close-contact societies may be more likely to touch an arm or shoulder of the person they are talking with in the United States. It is important to use caution when touching. A touch can be easily misunderstood.

Some Southeast Asian cultures believe that a person's spirit is on the head. Touching the head is often considered an insult. **Table 7.4** explains who is permitted to touch or not touch the head.

Greetings

Greeting another person is important in all cultures. The way a greeting is given and received often determines how positive or negative the meeting is. **Table 7.5** describes greetings in various cultures.

Apply It

You are a warm, outgoing pediatrician's assistant. Have four of your classmates represent a parent accompanying a small child. One is Cambodian; one is Laotian; one is African-American; one is Japanese. Conduct an initial interview with each to get the information you need. Do they respond to you? Why or why not?

Table 7.3   Close-Contact and Distant-Contact Regions

Close-Contact Regions	Distant-Contact Regions
Africa	Canada
Indonesia	Great Britain
Latin America	Northern Europe
Hispanic Americans	United States
Mediterranean	Native Americans
Southern Europe	Middle Eastern
French	Arabic Nationalities
	Asian Americans

Common Behavior:

■ Men hold hands with men and women hold hands with women.	■ People greet one another with a handshake or hand gesture.
■ Men and women greet one another by kissing on both cheeks.	■ Close friends or family members may hug each other.

Table 7.4   Guidelines Restricting Touch and Physical Closeness in Southeast Asian Cultures

Cambodian	Vietnamese	Laotian
■ Only a parent can touch the head of a child.	■ Only elderly people can touch the head of a child.	■ It is necessary to ask permission to move near another person.
■ Members of the opposite sex never touch each other in public, not even brothers and sisters.		

FIGURE 7.9
Respecting personal distance. What types of actions show that you respect another person's personal distance?

Table 7.5   Guidelines for Greeting People

Anglo-American	Latin American	Cambodian, Laotian	Vietnamese	Hmong
Shake hands if desired.	Shake hands or hug.	Do not shake hands. Instead, put hands together at different levels. 1. Equal status—hands must be at chest level. 2. Older person or stranger—hands must be at chin level. 3. Relative or teacher—hands must be at nose level.	Salute by joining both hands and moving them against the chest.	Bow head or shake hands.

FIGURE 7.10
Regions of the world showing the location of close-contact and more-distant cultures. What type of culture describes all of South America?

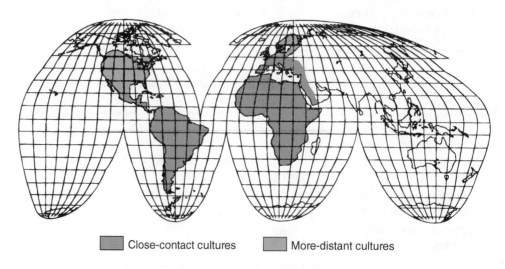

■ Close-contact cultures　　■ More-distant cultures

Hand Gestures

Hand gestures help communicate many things. It is very important to use correct gestures so that others are not offended. **Figure 7.11** illustrates gestures that are offensive in other cultures.

Eye Contact

In some cultures, eye contact may indicate that a person is listening, sincere, or honest. In other cultures, direct eye contact is considered to be hostile or disrespectful. **Table 7.6** explains some cultural views about eye contact.

Family Organization

The structure of family is important in all cultures. There are nuclear families, a term developed in western society referring to the basic family group—usually a mother, father, and children. There are also extended families—kinship groups consisting of a family nucleus and various relatives, such as grandparents, usually living in one household and functioning as a larger unit. There are also patriarchal and matriarchal family structures.

SAME GESTURE, SAME MEANING, BUT VERY DIFFERENT CONNOTATIONS

FIGURE 7.11

Hand gestures. How are the two types of pointing gestures different?

	American Culture	Asian Cultures
	OK for "Come here."	Absolutely *taboo* for calling a person, even a child. It's the way to call an animal (a dog, in particular), especially when accompanied by a whistle. Considered *very insulting.*
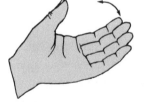	OK for "Come up here."	Never use. Only an inferior person would be summoned this way. Considered *insulting*, even to a child.
	OK to point at someone or something.	OK to point at *something* but not at *someone*. Considered too direct a reference, amounting to confrontation, which the Indo-Chinese avoid by all means.
	Slight threat (or warning) when making a point to someone.	Relatively strong threat made by a person of superior rank to an inferior (father to son, teacher to student). This is one step ahead of corporal punishment. (A parent would *never* use this gesture to a girl because it is considered too brutal.)

Table 7.6 Eye-Contact Guidelines

Anglo-American	African Americans	Navajo	Japanese, Southeast Asian, Hispanic
■ Eye contact is important; it indicates interest, honesty, and listening.	■ Eye contact may not be important. Being in the same room indicates attentiveness.	■ Direct eye contact is avoided. ■ Peripheral vision is used. ■ Direct stares are considered hostile or a way to scold children.	■ Eye contact is avoided as a form of respect.

In a patriarchal family, the actions and ideas of men and boys are dominant over those of women and girls, while in a matriarchal society, the female (especially with the mothers of a community) dominate.

For example, in the traditional patriarchal Asian culture, the family needs come before those of an individual. They often live as an extended family, including parents, children, grandparents, and families of paternal uncles. The extended family is involved in all major decisions.

Asian families view health from a variety of different perspectives, sometimes simultaneously. These perspectives may involve spiritual factors, imbalance of vital forces, and biological factors. So, Asian clients may want to combine diagnosis and treatment from different perspectives with the goal of getting maximum health benefits.

Each culture has its own set of beliefs and values that must be incorporated into any health care interaction.

Communicating Effectively with People from Other Cultures

When speaking with people from other cultures, the tone of your speaking voice is similar in importance to the gestures you use. Speaking tone includes voice quality, volume, and pitch. Voice tones cause positive or negative reactions from others. Clear pronunciations are more easily understood. When speaking to others who are learning English:

- Speak clearly; do not slur words.
- Speak so that they can hear you easily.
- Do not raise your voice or yell.
- Speak in moderate tones.
- Pronounce the entire word; do not draw it out or shorten sounds.
- Summarize often.
- Confirm their understanding.
- Clarify when necessary.
- Do not assume that they understand.

You gain greater interpersonal effectiveness when you strive to understand and respect people of a different culture and viewpoint. Making every effort to understand and to be understood is one way to treat others with dignity.

Folk Medicine

Folk medicine is a collection of **traditional** beliefs and customs for treating pain or illness. Many who practice folk medicine believe that natural materials, such as herbs, spices, and tree herbs, and spiritual prayers and rituals keep evil spirits away and allow the body to heal. The U.S., however, uses a biomedical or "Western" system which includes encouraging patients to learn about their own illness, informing patient about terminal illness, teaching self care, using medications and technology to cure or treat disease, and teaching preventive care.

traditional
(truh DISH uh nl)
Customary beliefs passed from generation to generation.

It is important to respect the beliefs of other cultures. If you insult the patient, you will be ineffective in providing care. Some caregivers work with their patients' beliefs to create positive relationships. Then they can introduce other suggestions for care.

Learn about the common practices in your clients' cultures. Read magazines and books about other cultures. Ask questions. Learn about ritual healing, folk medicine, and spiritual healing. Keep informed! Your understanding helps the patient get well faster and feel respected. The experience will be positive for both of you.

The following information is an overview of some common folk medicine practices in various cultures. Some practices that cause painful symptoms are not considered abusive because they are based on a belief of the culture.

Armenians

- Give the mother a party one week after a baby is born. The mother is served bread, which she dips into a paste of margarine, sugar, and flour. This is a celebration of the birth of the child.
- **Prohibit** a menstruating woman from attending church, taking a shower, or eating spicy foods.

prohibit
(pro HIB it)
To not allow.

Asians

- Think that health is balance of yin and yang.
- Use treatments, such as herbal remedies and acupuncture.
- Believe pain must be endured silently.

Cambodians

- Use herbs as medicine.
- Use cupping for headaches. Cupping leaves a round mark on the forehead. A cotton ball saturated in alcohol is placed in a glass and set on fire. After burning for a few seconds, the cotton is discarded. The heated glass is placed upside down over the painful area.
- Use coining for pain. Oil or ointment is applied to the skin. Then a large coin is used to rub the painful area in one direction until the blood is raised to just below the surface of the skin. This leaves red areas on the skin.
- Consider the color white to be a sign of bad luck. White indicates mourning and death. Think about a Cambodian's first visit to a caregiver. Is it possible that the white uniform might seem frightening?

Apply It

Have each student in your class come up with one traditional belief or custom about health care, reflective of their heritage. They should bring in one example from their paternal and maternal family lineage, and note them on a 3 × 5 card. Circulate the cards to other classmates. Can you determine what culture is represented by the belief or custom?

Central and South Americans

- Use herbal home remedies.
- Teach a menstruating woman not to get her head wet and to avoid eating cucumbers, oranges, lemons, pork, lard, and deer meat.

Chinese

- Use herbs as medicine.
- Practice acupuncture and use herbs over puncture sites.
- Use cupping with heated bamboo.

Europeans

- Believe that illness is caused by outside sources.
- Focus on treating with medication, surgery, diet, and exercise.

Hispanics

- Believe that health is a reward from God.
- Believe in good luck.
- Use heat and cold remedies to restore balance.
- Rely on prayers and massage.

Hmong and Mien Tribes

- Perform spiritual ceremonies to please the spirits that cause illness.
- Use herbal home remedies, including opium.

Iranians

- Believe that poor health is predetermined (fatalism).
- Use herbs, foods, rituals, and magic formulas for healing.
- Believe the "Evil Eye" (a person or animal that causes injury through a look) causes sudden illness.
- When of the Islamic faith, require washing of the face and hands before prayer.
- Require periodic baths for cleansing.

Koreans

- Practice alchemy, a medieval practice of magic and natural herbal remedies.
- Use acupuncture.
- Go to hot springs for bath rituals and massage.
- Use energy and brain stimulants.

Middle Easterners

- Believe that health is spiritual, cleanliness essential.
- Males dominate and make decisions on health care.
- Believe in spiritual causes of illness, such as the "evil eye".

Native Americans

- Use herbs and spices.
- Use modern medical practices.
- Some rely on a healer/shaman (medicine man or woman) to remove pain and evil spirits.
- Believe that health is harmony with nature.
- Believe that a tolerance of pain signifies power and strength.
- Believe that illness is caused by supernatural forces and evil spirits.

South Africans

- Believe in maintaining harmony of body, mind, and spirit.
- Believe the causes of ill health are spirits, demons or punishment from God.
- Use prayer or religious rituals as treatment.

Vietnamese

- Commonly use herbal medicine.
- Use cupping for head pain, cough, muscle pain, and motion sickness.
- Use acupuncture for musculoskeletal problems, visual problems, and other ailments.

Table 7.7 lists typical terms used by non-English-speaking Asian cultures to describe health problems.

Table 7.7 Terms That Describe Health Problems

Term	Condition
Weak heart	Palpitations, dizziness, faintness, feeling of panic
Weak kidney	Impotence, sexual dysfunction
Weak nervous system	Headache, malaise, inability to concentrate
Weak stomach or liver	Indigestion
I'm skinny.	Sickliness
Fire, hot	Dark urine, flatulence, constipation
Air/wind, cold	Illness was caused by too much air

Spiritual Beliefs

When dealing with people from other cultures, it is important to demonstrate respect for a patient's spiritual beliefs and practices. You can uncover these beliefs by talking to the patient. In helping to meet these spiritual and religious needs, the health care professional has to relate to each patient as unique and distinctive. You must be willing to listen, and to respect any symbols or books on which the patient relies. It is important to maintain hope and explore the patient's fears and doubts. Sometimes, it can help to encourage the patient's religious community or clergy involvement for support. Finally, it is very important to refrain from imposing your own beliefs on to the patient.

There are differences between spirituality and religion. Spirituality refers matters of the spirit or soul, as distinguished from material things. Religion is a belief in a supernatural power or powers regarded as the creator and governor of the universe; or beliefs based on the teachings of a spiritual leader. Some people are agnostics; they believe that it is impossible to know whether or not there is a God. You may also have patients who are atheists, who deny or do not believe in the existence of any supreme being.

Health care providers must be careful to be considerate of any patient's beliefs. They can make medical decisions that are consistent with the patient's spiritual and/or religious views. They should support the patient's use of spiritual coping during the illness, encouraging him/her to speak with their clergy or spiritual leader, or referring the patient to hospital chaplain, appropriate religious leader, or support group that addresses spiritual issues during illness.

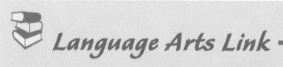

Language Arts Link

Cultural and Spiritual Beliefs

A person's cultural and spiritual beliefs may affect how they respond to different situations. Pretend that you have a pen pal in another country. Write a letter to your friend describing how your cultural and spiritual beliefs affect your attitudes towards health care. Or, write the letter based on the beliefs of another cultural. Include at least three key points on your beliefs.

Be sure to proofread your work to see if you can make it clearer, more concise, or more interesting. Check spelling and grammar and correct any errors.

When you've completed your letter, exchange it with a classmate. Provide feedback on your classmate's letter, and then exchange back. Read your classmate's comments and revise your letter as necessary.

Family Traditions

Family support is an important part of patient care. Some family traditions are unique to individual families. Other traditions are a blend of beliefs and traditions from cultures, as well as from spiritual and religious beliefs and practices. When dealing with patients and their families, their traditions, beliefs, and practices must be respected, just as you respect their culture, religion, or other beliefs. As with culture and spiritual beliefs, you will uncover family traditions while talking to the patient and observing interactions between the patient and his or her family.

As a health care provider, you must make it a priority to relate to family members in a positive and productive manner. Being aware of family traditions that can help nurture a patient will benefit everyone involved with a patient's care.

Summary

Cultural beliefs are very important to all societies. You give quality care when you take the time to understand and respect patients of other cultures. Caring about them as individuals will help them improve more quickly. If they are not ill, your caring builds mutual respect for future meetings.

SECTION 7.3 Review Questions

1. What experiences do members of a cultural group usually share?

2. In what way can culture be compared to the parts of a tree?

3. Give an example of a prejudice.

4. What are two ways of overcoming prejudice?

5. What is a customary method of greeting someone in an Anglo-American culture?

6. Why might it be considered rude to speak loudly when trying to communicate with someone who is learning English?

 ## Learn By Doing: Section 7.3 Activity

1. Complete Worksheets/Activities 1 and 2 as assigned.

2. Complete Worksheets 3 and 4 as assigned.

3. Complete Worksheet/Activity 5 and Worksheet 6.

4. Prepare responses to each item listed in Chapter Review.

5. When you are confident that you can meet each objective for this section, ask your teacher for the section evaluation.

 # What's New?

Demographics

Every ten years, the United States Census Bureau conducts a survey to learn about the demographics of the country. Demographics are statistical data summarizing the population in terms of such characteristics as age, race, marital status, language spoken at home, location, and income level. The last major census took place in 2010. At that time, the data showed that 12.5 percent of the population consisted of people born in other countries.

It also showed that more than 20 percent of the population over five years of age spoke a language other than English at home. Varying percentages of those people spoke English at different ability levels outside the home as well.

These statistics showed a continued increase in the everyday use of languages other than English since the 1990 census. In some states, the number of people not speaking English at home has risen even higher—43 percent in California, 36 percent in New Mexico, and 34 percent in Texas.

These data suggest that the American population is continuing to undergo major changes that affect the way people understand and interact with each other. Health care workers need to be especially aware of the evolving population and take cultural differences into account when providing care.

How might the language spoken at home affect a person's health care in the U.S.?

Chapter 7 Review

Chapter Review Questions

1. Name and describe three types of fitness included in a holistic approach to health. (7.1)

2. What does it mean to describe an activity as aerobic? (7.1)

3. A person needs a bandage to help a wound heal. Classify this as a physiological or a psychological need. Explain your choice. (7.2)

4. What is pet-facilitated therapy? (7.2)

5. Why is it important to establish a rapport with other staff members on a health care team? (7.2)

6. Give an example of rationalization as a defense mechanism. (7.2)

7. What does it mean to idolize someone? Why is this a negative behavior? (7.2)

8. What does it mean to exhibit age prejudice in the workplace? (7.3)

9. What is wrong with the statement, "All people are alike; they are human" in terms of cultural awareness? (7.3)

10. How does the use of eye contact vary in different cultures? (7.3)

Activities

1. Check out your physical health by measuring your pulse (which is reflective of your heart rate). Practice measuring your pulse. Count the number of beats in 10 seconds and multiply the number by 6. Record this number as beats per minute (bpm). Throughout a day, measure your pulse in different situations; for example, while rushing to get ready for school, during a test, while listening to a teacher's lecture, while stroking a pet, or resting in bed. Compare the changes throughout the day, and identify any relationship between your pulse and your mood or stress level.

2. Select an annual event, such as the beginning of a new year or a birthday. Interview five people from different cultures about how they treat this event. Prepare a chart similar to the one shown here. Fill in the information and present it to the class.

Person	Age	Country of Origin or Ancestors	Native Language	Description of Event
1				
2				
3				
4				
5				

Case Studies

1. You are assigned a patient from Iran. Her family is concerned about leaving her alone during the day, so they admit her to a long-term care facility. The patient is convinced that she is going to die because her family brought her to the hospital. Explain what basic need is not being met and develop a plan to meet that need for the patient.

2. Your co-worker is gentle and caring, but he has a loud voice and waves his hands around when he talks. You observe that some of your Cambodian patients seem to be afraid of him and tend to back away or avoid being around him. Explain why the Cambodian patients might respond to your co-worker in this way. What could you do to help your co-worker communicate his gentle, caring nature to the Cambodian patients?

Case Studies (continued)

3. You will develop a weekly menu, with a budget of $110.00 to feed a family of four. Describe the family. Is it a family with a 10 year old boy and a baby? A couple and their parents? A family with teenagers? You must pick all your food ingredients from local grocery store flyers with food items and prices on them. Menus, includ-ing breakfast, lunch, dinner, and snacks for seven full days, must meet the daily nutritional requirements identified in the Food Guide Pyramid. Menus should also meet the specific needs of individual family members (formula, baby food, etc.).

Thinking Critically

1. **Communication**—You always talk to your adult patients/clients using their title and last name as you have been trained. You cannot help noticing that many of them respond cheerfully to a co-worker who uses first names. You suspect that some of your patients/clients think you are too formal. Write a paragraph describing how you could handle this situation.

2. **Cultural Competency**—Make a list of some of the different reactions to pet therapy that you would expect from different cultures, for example, various Asian groups as well as South American and Mediterranean.

3. **Medical**—Compare and contrast the World Health Organization's definition of health with the meaning of holistic.

Media Connection

Use the Companion Web site for additional interactive learning activities: www.prenhall.com/badasch

Portfolio Connection

Mrs. Summers is an alert, ambulatory, 85-year-old patient. You observe that she argues about everything and with everyone. You cannot remember her ever agreeing to or being willing to do anything. Develop a plan to identify why Mrs. Summers is so argumentative. Your plan must clearly identify what you would do to involve other people.

In your written paper, clearly identify her behavior, what causes it, and what the positive and negative outcomes are for her. Include a proposed solution, a method of evaluation, and a time line. When you have completed your paper and checked the format and grammar for accuracy, place it in the section for written samples.

Your successful completion of this assignment shows your ability to organize, analyze, and evaluate. These skills help you work effectively with the various needs of your patients/clients.

Identify two cultural groups outside of your own culture. Research the visible and less visible characteristics of each group. Determine how health care is perceived by each group. Write your findings in a paper using the vocational portfolio guidelines for a written report. Report orally to your classmates using visual materials to help support your presentation.

PORTFOLIO TIP

Be aware of the tone and volume of your voice, especially when talking to patients from different cultures. Find a partner, role-play some situations, and tape record your voices. Critique one another. Speak clearly, not too slowly, and do not talk down to the patients.

8 Teamwork

Getting Started

Health care is provided by a team of professionals. It is essential for these team members to give and receive precise, appropriate, and accurate information to ensure quality patient care takes place.

To practice both speaking and listening skills, choose a team partner and cut out two exact copies of a variety of shapes, sizes, and colors, including rectangles, squares, diamonds, circles, and any other shapes. Each team member selects one stack of the cut outs; then, sit back to back with the shapes in front of you.

One of the team members will arrange the shapes in a selected design describing the arrangement as it is formed. The other team mate will attempt to replicate the design. Once completed the team members will look at the two and compare results. Next change roles and the listener will be the describer in the same process.

Teamwork

teamwork
(TEEM work)
Cooperative effort from a group of people working together for a common purpose.

dynamics
(di NAM ic s)
Motivating or driving forces.

conflict
(KON flikt)
A contradiction, fight, or disagreement.

cohesiveness
(koh HEE siv niss)
State of being well-integrated or unified.

Background

Health care teams have become an important part of health care today. Managed care organizations and other health care providers have formed health care teams to provide a higher level of care to the patient/client, and to meet the challenges of economic change and increased competition.

It is vital in today's medical field to know how to work with others in a team. This requires a basic knowledge of teamwork. Understanding the responsibilities of team members, learning to collaborate, and practicing conflict resolution can all help you work successfully in a health care team.

Objectives

When you have completed this section, you will be able to do the following:

- Match key terms with their correct meanings.
- Identify types of health care teams.
- Explain how a team builds cohesiveness and productivity.
- Recognize characteristics of effective teams.

- Explain the roles and responsibilities of team members.
- Recognize underlying factors and situations that may lead to conflict.
- Apply verbal and nonverbal communication skills in a team setting.
- Apply conflict resolution strategies in a team setting.

The Making of a Team

A team is a group of more than two people who work together to achieve a common goal.

Teamwork is quite helpful because an individual has only a limited amount of knowledge and experience. By bringing together different people with a variety of backgrounds, more ideas are generated, and more problems are solved.

Team **dynamics** are the motivating or driving forces that influence the actions and identity of the team. Some examples include personality styles, team roles, office layout, tools and technology, a company's culture, and procedures. A team's identity is also formed by the nature and purpose of the work to be done by the team.

Most teams develop through a series of stages. At first, members of the new team might feel nervous or uncomfortable. Individuals must interact with other members who they do not know well. They might also begin tasks that are new to them.

As teammates begin to work together, members might misunderstand or misinterpret each others' behaviors. A teammate might disagree with another's opinion.

This kind of **conflict** is natural and can actually strengthen a team as members learn to resolve their differences. Many teams will eventually achieve **cohesiveness**. The team will feel a sense of unity or team identity.

Once groups establish this unity, they are quite productive. This productive period lasts as long as the team dynamics do not change. Some teams might eventually break apart because team members move to new teams or leave a company.

 ## The Team Concept

Quality health care depends on every health care worker doing his or her part. Each member is an important part of the **interdisciplinary** team. Professionals with different backgrounds, different education, and different interests all work together to provide appropriate quality care.

The RN collaborates with the members of the interdisciplinary team and coordinates the care delivered to the patient. The RN determines the holistic plan of care and effectively delegates tasks by using the *five rights of* **delegation**:

- **Right task.** Identifying an appropriate caregiver-patient relationship.
- **Right circumstances.** Verifying that the correct patient setting and resources are available.
- **Right person.** Identifying who is trained and capable of doing the task.
- **Right direction/communication.** Providing a clear, short description of the task and clarifying limitations and the expected result.
- **Right supervision.** Providing appropriate monitoring, assistance, and **feedback**.

All departments are responsible for quality patient care, even if they are not providing hands-on care. For instance, if the medical records department fails to keep correct files of the patient/client chart, the physician will not have the test results and history needed to provide care. If housekeepers do not clean properly and bacteria are present, patients/clients might acquire additional diseases.

interdisciplinary
(in ter DIS uh pluh ner ee)
Involving two or more disciplines.

delegation
(del i gat shun)
To give another person responsibility for doing specific task.

feedback
(FEED bak)
Information received as a result of something done or said.

Career Connection

Visit the office of a dentist (or other health care professional) who runs a "one man" shop. Then visit the office of a group of doctors (for example, a group of internists, each with a different specialty). Which environment do you prefer? Think about the pros and cons of each type of operation.

discipline
(DIS uh plin)
A branch of instruction or learning, such as cardiology.

collaborate
(kuh LAB uh reyt)
To work together.

FIGURE 8.1
An interdisciplinary team works together to achieve common goals. How is an interdisciplinary team different from other types of teams?

interdependent
(in ter di PEN duh nt)
Depending on each other.

goals
(gohlz)
Aims, purposes, or intentions.

mission statement
(MISH uhn STEYT muhnt)
A summary describing the aims, values, and overall plan of an organization or individual.

Remember: It is the team effort of all health care workers that provides service to the patient/client!

Types of Health Care Teams

There are many types of health care teams today:

- Ad hoc groups are formed for a limited amount of time to address a specific problem. These may be composed of members from many departments. They may address issues such as redesigning a hospital floor or improving patient check-in procedures.

- A nominal care group includes a physician who refers a patient to different specialists. These specialists provide care independently; however, the physician may coordinate the flow of information among the specialists.

- A unidisciplinary group is organized around a single **discipline**. These are relatively permanent groups such as nursing units or hospital floors.

- A multidisciplinary team is made up of practitioners from multiple disciplines who may work with a patient/client during the same time period; however, the practitioners each have their own goals and recommendations. The practitioners do stay informed about what each other is doing.

- An interdisciplinary team consists of practitioners from two or more disciplines who work in the same setting. (Figure 8.1) Members contribute their opinions about treatment plans and then **collaborate** to implement one plan based on one set of goals.

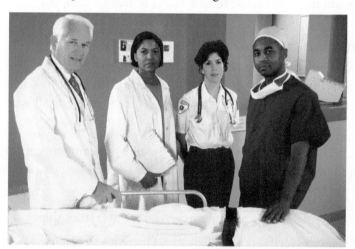

- Members of an interdisciplinary team communicate often and are **interdependent**. An interdisciplinary team is a popular type of health care team.

Team Goals

A team needs to decide early what it wants to accomplish—its **goals**. These goals may be about professional needs, patient needs, or team needs. They may include ways of exchanging information or evaluating outcomes. To develop meaningful goals, members may need to communicate clearly about individual goals so that these can be incorporated into the shared goals of the group.

Teams may want to develop a broad **mission statement** that all members can support. Goals can then be developed from this mission statement. In order to create clear, obtainable goals, a team should create goals with observable, measurable end points and objectives that help the team to achieve success. Teams may set either or both short-term and long-term goals. The definition of a short-term goal does not relate to any specific length of time. One can attain (or fail to achieve) a short-term goal in a day, week, month, year, etc. The time-frame for a short-term goal relates to the overall timeline for the mission. Long-term goals often are our most meaningful and important goals. So, for example, a long-term goal of a team may be to help an elderly patient live on his own. A short-term goal might be to help the patient learn to walk and move around steadily.

Team members may **prioritize** their goals to help members of the team stay focused and promote cohesiveness. In addition, team members may revise or add new goals based on a patient's needs.

 ## Team Roles and Tasks

An interdisciplinary team may consist of many professions, such as physicians, social workers, psychiatrists, physical therapy workers, massage therapists, medical assistants, nursing service workers, radiology workers, dieticians, and even home health care workers.

When working on a team, these workers may find some overlap in the skills of the various teammates. Several professionals, for example, have expertise in interacting with patients, forming care plans, and educating patients. Several providers can diagnosis and treat illness. Therefore, health care teams must develop **roles**.

Many teams begin by identifying the necessary **tasks** before negotiating the roles. A team's goals may help to define these tasks. Tasks may include activities such as ordering diagnostic testing, taking a patient's vital signs, contacting the patient, or writing prescriptions.

Decisions about each teammate's role may depend on availability, level of training, or member preferences. For example, a nurse's role on the health care team may be to coordinate patient care, protect the patient from illness, and teach the patient and/or family members.

Another nursing role might be assisting with mobility—a function evaluated by the physical therapist with specific activities prescribed, such as assisting the patient with transfer using a walker, carried out by the nursing staff. Assigning roles to each team member helps to eliminate conflict and establish expectations.

Commonly, one or more members of the health care team will serve as the leader(s) of the group. In the past, physicians often had the role of team leader in the health care setting. However, today many health care teams promote a more equal participation.

The leader of a team may shift depending on the nature of the problem to be solved. Emphasis on providing care for the whole person has increased the roles and responsibilities of non-physician providers.

No matter whether a team leader is a physician or another member of the health care team, a good team leader possesses all of some of the following traits; he or she is energetic, organized, reliable, charismatic, intelligent, creative, and often has a sense of humor.

prioritize
(prahy AWR itahyz)
To arrange or deal with in the order of importance.

roles
(rol s)
A position, responsibility, or duty.

tasks
(task)
A function to be performed; job.

Apply It

Regroup into the same teams you formed in the previous activity. By secret ballot, select a team leader for your team. On your ballot, identify the person you're voting for and list three qualities that would make him or her a successful leader.

In addition, a strong professional leader exhibits the following characteristics:

- Respects the rights, dignity, opinions, and abilities of others.
- Understands the principles of democracy.
- Works with a group and guides the group toward a goal.
- Understands own strengths and weaknesses.
- Displays self-confidence and willingness to take a stand.
- Communicates effectively and states ideas clearly.
- Shows self-initiative and a willingness to work.
- Completes tasks.
- Shows optimism.
- Is open minded and can compromise.
- Praises others and gives credit to others.
- Is dedicated to meeting high standards.

All strong leaders do not operate in the same type of environment. A *democratic* leader will make the final decision, but invite other members of the team to contribute to the decision-making process. This usually increases job satisfaction, because members of the team feel appreciated and respected. In addition, this leadership style can help to develop skills of team members.

Conversely, an *autocratic* leader has absolute power over the team. Members have little opportunity to offer suggestions, and often resent being treated in this manner. Sometimes this style of leadership is appropriate for routine and unskilled employees, but in many more instances, it results in high turnover and absenteeism.

A leader might take a *"laissez-faire"* approach. This French phrase means "leave it be" and is used to describe a leader who leaves team members alone to get on with their work. This style of leadership works best with an experienced staff.

Overall, skilled leaders seem able to recognize and cope with diversity, differing levels of skill, and different personalities. A successful leader has to assume responsibility for:

- Organizing and coordinating the team's activities.
- Encouraging everyone to share ideas and give opinions.
- Motivating all team members to work toward established goals.
- Assisting with problems.
- Monitoring the progress of the team.
- Providing reports and feedback to all team members on the effectiveness of the team.

While a strong leader is important to the success of a team, team members must also be committed to the group's **productivity**.

Some important qualities of a good team member include developing good interpersonal relationships, which involves:

- Working for agreement on decisions (i.e., being open minded and willing to compromise).

productivity
(proh duhk TIV i tee)
The power to reach goals and get results.

- Sharing thoughts and feelings openly and honestly (i.e., being friendly and cooperative).
- Involving others in the decision-making process.
- Trusting and supporting other team members (i.e., assisting others when they need help).
- Admitting to problems rather than blaming them on others.
- Listening carefully when another person is sharing ideas or beliefs.
- Influencing others by involving them in the issues.
- Encouraging and supporting the development of team members.
- Respecting and tolerating individual differences (i.e., respecting opinions even when you don't agree with them).
- Identifying and working through conflict openly.
- Considering and using new ideas and suggestions from others.
- Encouraging feedback on own behavior.
- Understanding and being committed to team goals and objectives.
- Maintaining a positive attitude and learning to laugh at yourself.
- Avoiding criticism of other team members.
- Learning good communication skills so you can share ideas, concepts, and knowledge.
- Performing your duties to the best of your abilities.

Team Communication

Effective interpersonal communication is vital to the smooth functioning of any team. (**Figure 8.2**) Team members should be skilled in active listening, giving and receiving feedback, and checking for comprehension.

It is also important for a team to develop an effective communication network. For example, team members should establish who relays information to whom within the team. The team must work to share relevant information in the most efficient way possible.

Some other important communication practices for a health care team include the following:

- A clear and effective record system.
- A regularly scheduled meeting for members to discuss patient's progress.
- A regularly scheduled meeting to evaluate the team's function and development.
- A procedure for communicating with other groups inside or outside the health facility.

Meetings

Meetings are important in the workplace. In a health care setting, where patient care requires teamwork, meetings are an efficient way to communicate among team members.

There are different types of meetings: a team meeting for coworkers to communicate about team duties, such as patient care; a staff meeting for supervisors and managers to communicate information to a group about topics such as policies and schedules, a status meeting for team members to report on how patients are doing, procedures, schedules, and so forth.

For more about meetings, see page 117.

FIGURE 8.2
A health care team meets to discuss a patient's progress. Why is it important for health care teams to meet regularly?

Apply It

Divide into groups of six to ten to practice having a meeting. Each group should decide on a health care topic to discuss and a goal that will be achieved through meeting as a team. Appoint a leader for your meeting. Then conduct an orderly, business-like meeting. Change leaders at least once during your meeting. At the end of your meeting, discuss how successful the team was in achieving the goal of the meeting.

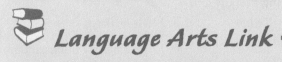

Language Arts Link

Teamwork and Mission Statements

It is vital in today's medical field to know how to work with others. To be able to work as a team, it's essential that everyone has the same end goal in mind. A mission statement, which is a brief statement of purpose, can ensure that all team members have the same intentions.

Work in a team to create a mission statement for this course. Be sure to include your teams' responsibilities, values, and main objectives. Proofread your work to see if you can improve it by making it clearer, more concise, or more interesting to read. Check the spelling and grammar and correct any errors.

Each team should prepare a presentation on their mission statement. Part of working as a team is determining who is best suited for a job. Each team member should practice delivering the mission statement; then, as a team, decide who your presenter will be.

Apply It

Create a team of four to five people. Your goal is to create a presentation on the types of teams in health care today. You will need to research the types of teams mentioned above; then find examples of each in your local community facilities. Your end product should include a brief discussion of how you determined the roles for each team member; what, if any, problems you experienced and how your resolved them.

compromise
(KOM pruh mahyz)
A settlement of differences between parties by each party agreeing to give up something that it wants.

facilitator
(fuh SIL i tey ter)
A person responsible for leading or coordinating a group.

 ## Conflict Resolution

Health care team members represent a variety of skills, professional backgrounds, and opinions. In addition, interdisciplinary collaboration can be complex. With these types of dynamics, conflict between team members is inevitable. While conflict can cause problems in a group, it can also encourage successful problem solving, trust, and understanding between team members when it is resolved effectively.

Conflict may occur because of dominating, overbearing, or even reluctant team members. It may also occur as a result of personality clashes. Sometimes a misunderstanding of roles, skills, or responsibilities of other team members leads to disagreements.

No matter what the reason, teammates need to be sure that others feel comfortable offering feedback or confronting another teammate. Just because a team may be unified does not mean that problems will not arise.

For successful resolution of a conflict, teammates must be willing to disagree. In addition, team members should approach a conflict as an individual; they should not form smaller groups within the team, especially groups that consist of the same profession. This only divides the team and breaks the cohesiveness of the group.

Members should stay focused on the overall mission of their team and the care of the patient. This helps to keep the conflict professional instead of personal.

Sometimes it may help a team to have a procedure for handling conflict in order to reach a collaborative solution or **compromise**. This may include a list of rules that teammates have to follow when resolving a conflict. These rules can be as simple as avoiding name-calling, speaking in a calm manner or focusing on putting the needs of the patient first. Sometimes a team may want a **facilitator** to help resolve the conflict.

Some of the important steps to resolving a conflict are listed below:

- Give all team members a chance to express their views and listen carefully.
- Be respectful of all team members.

- Identify the conflict or problem.

- Agree to work toward a solution.

- Deal with one problem at a time.

- Brainstorm possible solutions.

- Focus on common interests (such as patient wellness), not positions.

- Use objective criteria when possible.

- Invent new solutions where all team members gain.

- Implement the plan.

- Evaluate and review the problem-solving process after implementing the plan.

Summary

Teamwork will continue to be an important part of the future of health care. If you go into a health profession, you are likely to work on a team such as an interdisciplinary team. To be successful, you need an understanding of team dynamics. You should help to develop team goals and understand your role in achieving these goals.

You will likely experience conflict in your team at some point. However, with clear communication and effective conflict resolution, your team will grow stronger in order to better meet your needs, your team members' needs, and your patients' needs.

SECTION 8.1   **Review Questions**

1. How can working on a team be more successful than working as an individual?

2. Explain the difference between a multidisciplinary health care team and an interdisciplinary health care team.

3. What are some things a team should do in order to be one cohesive unit?

4. Name three qualities a good team member should have.

5. List two things a health care team should do to have good communication.

6. Why does conflict occur in a group? How can conflict help a group?

Learn By Doing: Section 8.1 Activity

1. Complete Worksheets 1 and 2 as assigned.

2. Ask your teacher for directions to complete Worksheets/Activities 3 and 4.

3. Complete Worksheets/Activities 5 and 6.

4. When you are confident that you can meet each objective for this section, ask your teacher for the section evaluation.

5. Prepare responses to each item listed in Chapter Review.

Chapter 8 Review

Chapter Review Questions

1. Why is teamwork important? (8.1)
2. List five examples of team dynamics. (8.1)
3. What is an interdisciplinary team? (8.1)
4. Why is assigning roles and tasks to team members so important? (8.1)
5. Describe the five rights of delegation. (8.1)
6. Compare the five types of health care teams. (8.1)
7. What is a mission statement? (8.1)
8. List five characteristics of a good team leader. (8.1)
9. What are some of the responsibilities a successful leader must assume? (8.1)
10. List five steps to resolving conflict among team members. (8.1)

Activities

1. Use a group of four people to explain the importance of team dynamics in the health profession.

2. Using the same group of four, describe at least three important communication practices for your specific group.

Case Studies

1. Your interdisciplinary team consists of a physician, social worker, psychiatrist, and medical assistant. Some of the suggested treatments appear to be independent of one another, rather than part of a cohesive treatment plan. What is the problem here and how would you resolve it?

2. You and a member of your interdisciplinary team are not getting along because you feel that he is often bossing you around. He tells you to do things that you think he should be doing. In addition, often times you are unsure about how to do the things that he asks you to do. He thinks that you are being lazy and not doing your job. Explain what you would do to help resolve this conflict.

Thinking Critically

1. **Team Dynamics**—Team dynamics are the motivating or driving forces that influence the actions and identity of the team. Use examples from a recent job to describe personality styles, team roles, and company culture.

2. **Making a Team**—Most teams go through a series of stages. Initially, members of a new team may feel nervous. Sometimes they misin-terpret others' behaviors. The situation involves new people and new tasks. Describe the process by which a team becomes a cohesive and productive unit

3. **Conflict**—Conflict may occur in any group because of misunderstandings or strong personalities. How do you resolve conflict successfully and professionally?

Media Connection

Use the Companion Web site for additional interactive learning activities: www.prenhall.com/badasch

Portfolio Connection

Health care teams are a critical part of today's health care system. Successful teams help to provide a higher level of care to the patient/client, and to meet the challenges of economic change. Therefore, every health care worker needs to do his or her part to create an effective team.

There are many resources that can help you to better understand what it takes to build a team. Go to your local library or resource center, or online, to research team building activities. These should include a variety of activities: ropes courses, minefield exercises, "Mission Impossible" or "Team Survivor" types of assignments.

Then design an activity that can be used in a health care setting to build a team. This activity can focus on turning individual strengths into team assets, learning to blend personal goals with the goals of the organization, developing team spirit and building effective communication tools within the team. Be prepared to preset this to the class. You will have to "sell" them on your idea.

What were you thinking of when you created this activity? Why do you think this is a good team building exercise? How will you measure that? What do you expect the outcome to be? What pitfalls might you encounter? Answer these questions at the end of your designed activity.

Place this assignment in Section Four, "Written Samples."

PORTFOLIO TIP

The manner in which you present your activity to your classmates is very important. Remember that you're building a team. All members of the team must feel that they are working together towards a specific goal.

9 Effective Communication

Getting Started

E ffective communications are essential to providing appropriate and accurate health care. In one study by a large health care organization, it was determined that on an average two-day stay in an acute care facility, patient information is shared among 47 different health care professionals. Clearly, if communications are not shared with care and accuracy, diagnosis and treatment can be inappropriate and even dangerous to the patient outcome.

To show how information must be shared accurately and appropriately and how very easy it is for mistakes to occur, join your classmates in a circle and with a message from your teacher whisper the information into the ear of the person next to you until the circle is completed. The last person in the circle will share what is heard. The results are then compared to the original message. A discussion led by the teacher will consider the results of treatment if the information is different than the original message. (*Example:* Mr. Johansen in room 222, bed B is lethargic and appears disoriented.)

SECTION 9.1

Interpersonal Communication for All Ages

Background

The health care worker should understand that there are many factors in communication. A knowledge of the techniques of communication will increase your skills in communicating with co-workers and patients/clients. With this knowledge, you will be able to do a better job and to make good observations about your patients.

Objectives

When you have completed this section, you will be able to do the following:

- Match key terms with their correct meanings.

- Explain why communication is important.

- Name four elements that influence our relationship with others.

- List three barriers to communication.

- Identify your communication assertiveness level.

- List four elements necessary for communication to take place.

- Describe three things that a good listener does.

- Differentiate between verbal and non-verbal communication.

Communication is essential in the exchange of ideas, feelings, and thoughts. Communication helps us to understand the needs of others and how best to meet those needs. There are several kinds of communication. These include words (either written or spoken), gestures, facial expressions (frowns, smiles), body posture, touch, and listening. The following discussion has important information to help you become a better communicator with patients, families, co-workers, and supervisors.

Effective Patient Relations

Effective patient relations are a necessity. To communicate effectively, we need to work through a process that includes engagement, understanding, education, and creating a sense of partnership.

Engagement is a connection between the health care professional and patient that sets the stage for establishing a partnership. Barriers to engagement by the health care professional might include things like not introducing yourself, pointed and critical questioning, and interrupting the patient/client.

An understanding health care professional will make patients feel accepted. To exhibit understanding of a patient's needs, you might first make introductions with the patient fully clothed, in a safe environment. You can allow the patient to share thoughts and feelings and respond by repeating them in your own words. Sharing anecdotes—without being too personal—can also help to create a positive bond between the patient and health care. (**Figure 9.1**)

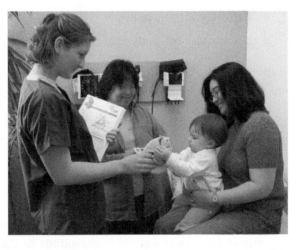

Figure 9.1
A nurse gives a toy to a baby while in an examination room. Why is it important to engage patients?

Educating the patient includes helping to increase knowledge and understanding and minimize anxiety. Health care professionals should assume that all patients share many of the same questions, including:

- What is happening to me?
- What will I have to do?
- Will it hurt?
- When will I have the results?

To have good communication, you must be certain to answer all of the patient's questions. Avoid using complicated, clinical terms and be clear. Determine if you have answered the patient's questions by using statements such as "Have I answered your questions?", "Do you have questions about anything I have not covered?", or "Is there anything you want to add to the information I have obtained about you?".

biases
(BAHY uhs ez)
Tendencies; prejudices.

prejudices
(PREJ uh dis ez)
Judgments or opinions formed before the facts are known.

inferior
(in FEER ee er)
Lower (e.g., one product is inferior in quality to another product).

impatience
(im PEY shuh ns)
Unwillingness to learn.

annoyance
(uh NOI uhns)
Irritation (e.g., to feel irritated with a co-worker or patient).

communication
(kuh myoo ni KAY shuhn)
Act of exchanging information.

Creating a partnership occurs with good communication. The health care professional and patient work together regarding the problem and the treatment plan. Many times, a patient may think he or she knows the problem. You need to make sure the patient understands the diagnosis, plan, and treatment.

Sending a Clear Message

Good communication means that you are sending a clear message—one that is understood by both your co-workers and your patients. In order to make sure you are doing so, you must:

- Use active listening skills.
- Use a positive tone.
- Watch your body language.
- Treat patients and co-workers with respect.
- Be precise and detailed about what you expect.
- Model the behavior you want others to follow.
- Explain your reasoning.
- Discuss any conflicts in a calm and rational way.

Communicating clearly is the key to creating a high functioning health care team and establishing a positive relationship with your patients.

Elements That Influence Your Relationships with Others

Prejudices

All people form opinions or **biases** as they are growing up. These **prejudices** affect how they feel about other people and how they relate to them. You may have very strong feelings about the backgrounds or the values of your patients or co-workers. Your feelings affect how you communicate. For instance, if you believe that certain people are lazy, overly emotional, or **inferior**, you need to think about your prejudices. When you understand your prejudices and feelings, you have an opportunity to overcome them.

Frustrations

When you care for and work with others, you may experience **impatience**, **annoyance**, and probably anger. Perhaps other people do not understand your directions, or they may move too slowly. You feel irritated. These feelings interfere with your ability to communicate. Take time to understand why you feel frustrated. Evaluate the situation, and then try to correct it. It is your responsibility to control your behavior and to understand that patients, families, and co-workers have problems that are the cause of their behavior.

How you act toward others and how they act toward you affect the quality of **communication**. If you are disinterested or bored, if you are in a bad mood, if you wish you were someplace else, communication breaks down. However, if you show interest and concern for others, you will experience worthwhile communication, your job will become easier, and you will be more effective.

Life Experiences

People have new experiences every day. These experiences help us know what to expect in day-to-day living and how to act in certain situations. The most effective communication is based on shared experiences. These may be experiences you went through together or experiences that you both went though individually. Perhaps you grew up in the same community, went to the same school, or even share the same language. It may be as simple as liking the same type of movies, music, or books.

You will usually have more effective communication with someone who has shared some of your experiences. Of course, the reverse is true as well; less shared experiences causes communication to be more difficult and frustrating. This is especially true in the area of slang and dialect.

To be a more effective communicator, look for things that you have in common with the other person. You can do this by listening to what they say and how they say it, looking for something familiar and then focusing a bit more on that shared experience. As you find more and more areas in common, your communication with that person will become more effective.

Aging and Communication. What happens when a younger health care professional deals with an older patient, or vice versa? There are, of course, possible physical issues that make communication with the elderly more difficult, such as hearing or vision problems. There may be mental or emotional issues, such as older people who are afraid of losing the ability to think, reason, or explain themselves. Finally, there may be certain cultural issues, such as believing the doctor is always right or being afraid to complain about aches and pains.

There are also fewer shared experiences between younger and older individuals, so it becomes even more important to work on finding some common ground that you may share.

Barriers to Communication

Recognizing barriers to communication allows you to become an understanding health care worker. The following are four major communication barriers:

- **Labeling.** Deciding the other person is mean, lazy, a complainer, or difficult causes a breakdown in communication. You do not pay attention to the message being sent. If you listen, you might find out the reason for the behavior.

- **Sensory impairment.** Deafness or blindness can be a communication barrier. Always evaluate the people you are communicating with to be certain that they do not have a sensory impairment.

- **Talking too fast.** It is especially important when you are working with elderly people to speak slowly. Communication can break down when the message is delivered too rapidly.

labeling
(LEY buhl ing)
Describing a person with a word that limits them (e.g., lazy, stupid).

- **Cognitive impairment.** Cognitive impairment includes memory, perception, problem solving, emotional reaction, and idea formulation. These types of impairments might result from autism, brain injury, Parkinson's, Alzheimer's, or old age. Be careful to make sure your patient understands what you are saying. You may want them to tell you, in their own words, what you have just explained to them. Or, you may write down suggestions for them.

Developing skills in communication helps you become a better health care worker. It is important always to be **courteous** and understanding. Take time to evaluate gestures, facial expressions, and tone of voice in order to understand what is really being said. You may feel frustrated, angry, or irritated, but as a health care worker, it is up to you to attempt to understand and to listen. Hearing accurately and then responding appropriately are essential. Remember to communicate your messages so that they can be understood easily.

Elements of Communication

For communication to take place, there are four essential **elements**:

- **A message.** There must be something that you want to convey to another person. Perhaps the purpose of the message is to give information or to acquire information. Perhaps there is something you want another person to do.

- **A sender.** Unless there is someone who wants to send a message, there cannot be communication.

- **A receiver.** Even if there is a message and a sender, there must be a receiver. If there is no one to receive the message, communication is incomplete.

- **Feedback.** Capturing feedback is of critical importance. If you are not seen to be listening and acting on what you are told, why would people tell you anything?

Interference with any of these elements can disrupt communication. Remember that in order to ensure clear communication:

- The message must be clear.
- The sender must deliver the message in a clear and concise manner.
- The receiver must be able to hear and receive the message.
- The receiver must be able to understand the message.
- Interruptions or distractions must be avoided.

How can we ensure clear communication? We have to remember that communication is a two-way street. You must listen to others to make sure they listen to you. If you're interested in what the other person has to say, that person will more likely be interested in you. Remember to smile and maintain eye contact, so that the other person knows that you are interested in him or her. Use your voice and body language to show your enthusiasm.

On the other hand, there are many elements that can disrupt communication. Don't be competitive or make it seem as if what you have to say is more important

courteous
(KUR tee uhs)
Polite; considerate toward others.

elements
(L uh ment z)
The basic assumptions or principles of a subject.

than what the other person is saying. Watch your body language. You don't want to appear bored or disinterested. Don't hunch your shoulders, fidget, tap your toes, or twiddle your hair. Finally, don't be too aggressive or pushy in your conversation.

Good Listening Skills

When you think of communication, you may not think of listening. However, listening is a very important element in all communication. If you do not receive the message that is being sent, communication has not taken place. Your understanding of how to be a good listener makes you a better health care worker.

- **Show interest.** It is important for you to show interest in the person who is sending you a message. (**Figure 9.2**) If you follow all of the other rules of being a good listener but tune out the message because you are not interested, communication will not take place.

Figure 9.2
Good eye contact, a gentle touch, and your body inflections show that you are interested in what is being said. How is showing interest an important part of listening?

- **Hear the message.** Health care workers frequently think that they understand what is being said to them when they really do not. It is important to repeat what you believe you heard to be certain you heard correctly. It is not necessary to repeat exactly what was said, but check to see that you have understood the general message. Watch the speaker closely to observe actions that may contradict what the person is saying. Evaluate how well you listen and if you are using all of the above skills during and after each conversation with patients and peers.

- **Do not interrupt.** Have you ever tried to send a message and been frustrated by the receiver's interrupting you? Allow the sender to give you the entire message without interruptions. If you need to ask a question to clarify the meaning, be patient and wait until the sender is finished. She or he may give you the information you need without your questions.

- **Pay attention.** This is critical. Eliminate distractions by moving to a quiet area for the conversations. Avoid thinking about how you are going to respond. Try to eliminate your own prejudices and see the other person's point of view.

Apply It

With a partner have a conversation about career goals. Each of you should share your thoughts and ideas for two to three minutes. As you listen to your partner, observe your listening skills. Are you showing interest? Do you find yourself interrupting, or wanting to interrupt?

After you finish with the listening exercise, take a few minutes to write down observations about your own listening skills. Note any personal barriers to listening that you notice. Review the guidelines for good listening skills on this page and make a plan for how you can improve your listening skills.

- **Maintain a positive attitude.** Keep your temper under control, even if you become irritated.

Being a good listener takes patience. You need to concentrate on being a good listener until the skills become easy for you. As a health care worker, good listening is an essential skill. Good listening skills also help you follow directions, make good observations of patients, and understand your fellow workers.

Assertive Communication

Communicating assertively is an honest and direct way to say what you feel or think. Being assertive allows you to express your feelings and thoughts. You must believe that you have the right to be heard and believed by others. You recognize that it is OK for you and for others to say no when it is appropriate—for example, when you are asked to do something you are not trained to do. It is OK to ask for something you want or need to accomplish a goal or task. This type of open, honest communication shows that you are a genuine person with self-respect and confidence. Assertiveness says that you have an awareness of and respect for others. To communicate strong health care values effectively, it is important for you to be an assertive communicator.

There are three common styles of communication:

- *Unassertive*, or *passive*, communication allows others to control the conversation.
- *Assertive* communication does not take power or authority away from others. It empowers individuals to speak up and be heard.
- *Aggressive* communication occurs when power is taken away from others and communication breaks down.

Most people communicate in all three of these styles, depending on their feelings or thoughts at the time. Health care workers are more effective when they use assertive communication skills. You can develop your skills over time. Start by rating your preferred communication style on the assertiveness inventory in the Student Activity Guide, and follow the portfolio directions at the end of this chapter.

Nonverbal Communication

Communication also takes place in nonverbal ways. It is not necessary to speak in order to send a message. You send messages with your eye contact, facial expressions, **gestures**, and touch.

- **Eye contact.** Making eye contact with the person with whom you are communicating is important. Eye contact lets others know that you are paying attention. When you do not make eye contact, you send others a message that you are not interested or that you wish to avoid them.
- **Facial expressions.** A smile sends a different message than a frown does. It is possible to say something very kind and still send a message of anger with your eyes. Try to think of an instance when you knew that what was being said was not what was meant. How did you know? The expression on the sender's face probably sent you a different message.

gestures
(JES cherz)
Motions of a part of the body to express feelings or emotions (e.g., nodding yes or no).

- **Gestures.** Shrugging your shoulders, turning your back, and leaving the room while someone is talking to you certainly convey a lack of interest in the sender's message. You need not say "I am not interested" because you have effectively sent that message through your gestures.

- **Touch.** Touch can convey great caring, warmth, concern, and tenderness. It can also convey anger, rejection, and distaste. Touch is a very important part of your communication. It is important that your nonverbal communication be supportive and positive.

 ## Science Link

Communication Differences Between Men and Women

Studies have shown that men and women vary in the way they use nonverbal communication. Differences between men and women are found in their body movements, eye contact, and use of space.

Women tend to use facial expressions to express more emotion than men. They are more likely to smile and more likely to use facial and body expressions to show friendliness. In contast, a man does not smile as much and is more likely to interrupt a person who is smiling. While women may show some friendly nonverbal cues, their posture tends to be more tense than men's posture. Men are more relaxed and more likely to use gestures.

While women do not often stare, men use staring to challenge power. This nonverbal cue for power is also seen when observing the behavior of a man during an initial gaze. Men will wait for the other person to turn away, while women are more likely to avert their eyes on initial gaze. Men also use staring to signal interest. Instead of staring, women signal interest by maintaining eye contact.

Men and women also differ in their use of personal space. Women tend to approach others more closely, while men want more personal space. However, men may also be more likely to invade another's personal space if necessary. These studied differences between men and women add to the complexity of communication.

How might these differences between men and women affect communication in the workplace?

 ## Verbal Communication

Verbal communication includes spoken and written messages.

- **Spoken messages.** When you speak to someone, you send a message. The tone of your voice, the language you use, and the message you send are interpreted by the receiver. Always speak clearly and concisely. This ensures that your message is understood.

- **Written messages.** You communicate frequently with the written word. You take messages and orders. You may write notes in the patient's/client's chart, and you may need to leave instructions for fellow workers. It is important to spell correctly, use proper grammar, and write in a clear and concise manner.

Language Arts Link

Effective Communication

Being able to communicate important information to a patient, a colleague, or your supervisor is an essential skill in any profession. Communication has many forms: written communication, oral communication, and nonverbal communication using body language.

Write a brief report on the importance of developing effective communication skills. Create a new document on the computer, or on a blank sheet of paper. Write a descriptive title for your report. In paragraph form, detail why communication skills are indispensable to anyone who

wishes to work in a health care profession. Include a thesis statement (a sentence stating your main ideas) in the opening paragraph.

Be sure to proofread your work to see if you can improve it by making it clearer, more concise, or more interesting to read. Check the spelling and grammar and correct any errors.

Exchange reports with a classmate. Provide feedback and corrections as necessary, and then exchange back. Read your classmate's comments and revise your report as necessary.

 Summary

Communication requires a sender, a receiver, and a message. The message may be verbal or nonverbal, and many factors influence the effectiveness of communication. These factors include prejudices, frustrations, attitudes, and life experiences. Good listening skills are important to ensure successful communication, and an awareness of barriers to good communication is important.

SECTION 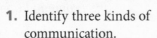 **9.1**   Review Questions

1. Identify three kinds of communication.

2. What elements might influence our relationships with others?

3. Name four barriers to communication.

4. List the four essential elements of communication.

5. Why are good listening skills so important?

6. What is assertive communication?

 Learn By Doing: Section 9.1 Activity

1. Complete Worksheet 1.

2. Ask your teacher for directions to complete Worksheet/Activity 2.

3. Complete Worksheet 3.

4. Ask your teacher for directions to complete Worksheet/Activity 4.

5. Complete Worksheets 5 and 6.

6. When you are confident that you can meet each objective listed, ask your teacher for the section evaluation.

Communication Technologies

Background

Communication between health care providers is vital to patient care. Today's technology has helped to improve the efficiency and the speed at which a message or file can be sent to another person. A worker in the health care environment needs to know how to use common software programs in order to access and record important patient information. In addition, workers need to be well-trained to work with phones, fax machines, e-mail, and the Internet in order to complete daily tasks.

Objectives

When you have completed this section, you will be able to do the following:

- Match key terms with their correct meanings.

- Demonstrate responding, transferring a caller, and taking a message.

- Apply basic listening skills.

- Use communication technology such as a fax machine, e-mail, or Internet to access and distribute data and other information.

Telephone Communication

The telephone is an important communication tool between you and those you serve. All departments in the health care setting require good telephone communication skills. You may be asked to answer the telephone, take a message, or respond to a request. Always follow good communication standards when answering an incoming or placing an outgoing call. **(Figure 9.3)**

Telephones at workstations are for communication of health care issues **pertinent** to those you serve. Personal calls and socializing must be done on your break or outside of your assignment or work time. See Table 9.1 for indicators that promote patient/client satisfaction when talking on the telephone and Table 9.2 for telephone guidelines.

> **Apply It**
>
> Play telephone. Pair up with a partner. One should be a caller to a health care professional's office; the other should be the receptionist. See how the receptionist responds, no matter how the patient acts.
>
> Is the patient angry or annoyed? Does the patient keep repeating his or her questions? Is the receptionist clear and understanding? Then switch roles.

pertinent
(PUR tn uh nt)
Relating directly to the matter at hand; relevant.

Figure 9.3
Medical professional scheduling an appointment over the phone. Why are telephone communication skills important in health care?

Table 9.1   **Indicators That Promote Patient/Client Satisfaction When Talking on the Telephone**

Communication Objective	Service/Excellence	Behavior
■ Demonstrate open, honest, and respectful communication. ■ Present ideas, information, and viewpoints clearly both verbally and in writing. ■ Listen actively and seek to understand others.	■ Use good telephone manners. ■ If the doctor asks you to screen calls at an office or clinic, answer the phone and identify the caller, or use caller ID, and then politely notify the caller that the doctor is unable to speak at the moment. Then, offer to take a message so the doctor can return the call.	■ Answer the telephone cheerfully. ■ Use a pleasant, caring, and sincere tone of voice. ■ Answer the telephone on the first ring if possible. ■ Speak clearly and courteously. ■ Remember to thank the caller when a call is returned. ■ Identify yourself and give your title (e.g., "This is Monica, nurse assistant."). ■ Identify your department or doctor's office (e.g., "Dr. Smith's office"). ■ Thank the caller for calling. ■ Allow the caller to hang up first to ensure that the caller has said everything he or she wanted to say. ■ Use appropriate words and phrases: **Appropriate:** • May I have your name, please? • Would you repeat that, please? • How may I assist you? • I'm sorry; I didn't understand. **Inappropriate:** • What's your name? • What did you say? • What do you want? • Huh?

facsimile/fax machine
(faks muh SHEEN)
A device that sends and receives printed pages or images as electronic signals over telephone lines.

cover page
(KUHV er peyj)
The first page of a fax.

 Fax Communication

If a health care employee needs to send a patient's record to another provider, the worker may use a **facsimile** or **fax machine**. A fax transmission is a way to send or receive printed pages or images over telephone lines by converting them to and from electronic signals. You may work on a computer, or have access to a printer, that is connected to a phone line so that you can send and receive faxes directly from your computer or printer. In order to send a fax, you must have a telephone number used for faxes by the person to whom you want to send the documents. There are a few things you should remember when sending a fax:

- Use a **cover page**. A cover page is the first page of a fax that gives the receiver important information about the fax. It should include your name, contact number, number of pages being sent, the name of the recipient, and any other important information.

Table 9.2 Telephone Guidelines

Being Prepared	Placing a Caller on Hold	Transferring a Caller	Writing a Message	Leaving a Message
■ Have the necessary materials • Pencil • Message pad • Telephone • Facility and public telephone directory ■ Before placing a call • Prepare questions to ask. • Gather information to share with the person you are calling. • Determine appropriate action to take. ■ Follow the patient/client satisfaction indicators in Table 9.1.	■ Ask the caller if he or she can hold and wait for the response. ■ Check every 30 seconds to see if the caller wants to continue to hold. ■ Ask if you may take a message. ■ Transfer the call as soon as possible. ■ Follow the patient/client satisfaction indicators in Table 9.1.	■ Explain where you are transferring the caller and to whom. ■ Give the caller the number you are transferring to. ■ If possible, stay on the telephone and introduce the caller to the person receiving the call. ■ Follow the patient/client satisfaction indicators in Table 9.1.	■ Record time and date. ■ Write clearly • The caller's name—verify spelling. • The telephone number—read back the number. ■ Summarize information with the caller by repeating the message. ■ Sign or initial the message. ■ Record the action you take to deliver the message. ■ Follow the patient/client satisfaction indicators in Table 9.1.	■ State • Whom you are calling for. • Your name and where you are calling from. • Your message—remembering to follow confidentiality guidelines. • The times that you will be available for a return call. ■ Document date, time, and message left. ■ Follow the patient/client satisfaction indicators in Table 9.1.

- Confirm that the intended **recipient** received the fax. Since a fax often contains important patient information, call or e-mail the recipient to ensure that he or she has received it.

- Remember that you may be dealing with confidential information. If you are sending confidential or potentially sensitive information, call ahead and let the recipient know to be ready. Using an online fax may help avoid security issues, as it lets users send and receive faxes from the privacy of their own computers.

recipient
(ri SIP ee uhnt)
A person or thing that receives.

Figure 9.4
Health care professional working online. What are the advantages of health care workers using the Internet and e-mail?

E-Mail Communication

E-mail is an important method of communication in the health care business. However, health workers sending e-mails should choose their words carefully. A person cannot hear vocal inflections in an e-mail; therefore, sarcasm and humor should not be used in a business e-mail because they may lead to miscommunication or misunderstandings.

Remember that any message you send is permanent and may be forwarded to others. Do not use a business e-mail address to send trivial or highly sensitive information.

Before you hit send, follow these guidelines to write a professional e-mail:

- Begin with a salutation.

- Include short, simple, and straight-forward information. If a message is long, discuss the topic in a short e-mail, and use an **attachment** to provide details. An attachment is a file linked to an e-mail message. You may also break up a longer e-mail that has many topics into multiple, shorter e-mails that discuss each topic separately.

- Read your e-mail aloud to check the tone of your message. Using please and thank you with requests ensures a polite tone.

- Proof the content for spelling and grammar mistakes. Remember that you should use upper and lower case when writing.

- Remember to include important contact information at the end of your e-mail. This includes your name, position, company, telephone number, e-mail address, and perhaps fax number.

- Include a subject on the subject line of the e-mail.

- Use features such as **blind carbon copy** and **carbon copy** when appropriate. Carbon copy (cc) is used to send a copy of your e-mail to another recipient. For example, you may send an e-mail to a patient, but carbon copy a doctor on the e-mail so that he or she knows what was sent to the patient. Blind carbon copy (bcc) is used when an e-mail is sent to multiple people. Blind carbon copy allows a recipient to read the message; however, the recipient cannot see the other e-mail addresses to which the message was sent. This is beneficial because it protects the recipients' e-mail addresses and eliminates clutter in the e-mail.

Respond to incoming e-mails within 24 hours. If you need more time to respond, call or e-mail that you are looking into the matter and will get back to the person as soon as possible. Also be sure to answer all questions when responding to an e-mail. When sending an e-mail with questions, allow one or two days for a response. If you need an immediate response, you may want to call the person.

In health care, **memorandums** (memos) are used as reminders, to persuade an action, to issue a directive or to provide a report. Memorandums can be delivered via e-mail. When sending a memorandum via e-mail, be sure to:

- Confirm the memorandum looks as intended in print and on the screen.
- Use fonts/graphics that are clear on all recipients' computers.
- Ensure attachments are readable by all recipients.

The Internet

Many health care positions may require a worker to find or access information. (**Figure 9.5**) In order to gain access, employees usually need to have a **username**. Usernames are names used to gain access to a computer system (**Figure 9.6**).

Once on the computer, employees may research and access information is the **Internet**. The Internet is a worldwide computer network that provides information on many subjects. When researching information, it is important to choose a **Web site** that is **credible**. Not every medical Web site is supported by research or written by experts in the medical field. Some examples of credible sources on

---

attachment
(uh TACH muhnt)
A file linked to an e-mail message.

carbon copy
(KAHR buhn KOP ee)
An e-mail feature that allows a person to send a copy of an e-mail to another person.

blind carbon copy
(blahynd KAHR buhn KOP ee)
An e-mail feature that allows a person to send an e-mail to multiple people without them seeing the other receivers' e-mail addresses.

memorandum
(mem e RAN dum)
A short note written to help a person remember something or to remind a person to do something.

username
(YOO zer naym)
A unique identifier composed of alphanumeric characters, used as a means of initial identification to gain access to a computer system or Internet Service Provider.

Internet
(IN ter net)
A worldwide computer network with information on many subjects.

Web site
(WEB sahyt)
A group of pages on the Internet developed by a person or organization about a topic.

credible
(KRED uh buhl)
Worthy of belief or confidence; trustworthy.

Figure 9.5
Many health care workers may use the Internet to find information quickly. What should you remember when searching for information on the Internet?

Please Login

Username: Username

Password: ●●●●●

☐ Remember Password

Login   Cancel

Figure 9.6
Your user name may be assigned to you, but it is usually a combination of your own name and/or initials. Do not share your password with anyone else.

reliable
(ri LAHY uh buhl)
Dependable, accurate, honest.

the Internet include organizations such as the American Cancer Society or the Leukemia and Lymphoma Society. Web sites sponsored by the government such as the Food and Drug Administration Web site are also **reliable**. Educational institutions such as John Hopkin's University are also quality sources.

A domain name is used as an Internet address to identify the location of a particular Web page. For example, the URL for the American Cancer Society is http://www.cancer.org. The domain name is cancer.

In addition, some health care providers create Web sites that provide important information to patients. These Web sites may include directions to the facility, office hours, contact phone numbers and e-mail addresses, as well as other helpful information.

 ## E-Mail and Internet Policies

With the current use of technology in the workplace, most companies have policies regarding use of the Internet and e-mail for personal business while at work. Employees may be required to read and sign a company's policy concerning Internet and e-mail use.

While some companies allow employees to use the Internet and e-mail for personal use on a limited basis, most companies' policies prohibit employees from sending disruptive or offensive e-mail. This may include forwarding jokes or pictures that have been e-mailed to an employee.

In addition, employees may not access Web sites that contain pornographic material or discriminatory messages. E-mail and Internet access should always be used in a manner that is accurate, appropriate, ethical, and lawful.

In order to ensure that workers are following these policies, many companies monitor their employees' e-mail and Internet use. Computer programs today help companies identify e-mails or Web site visits that may be inappropriate. Employees should always remember that any e-mail or file on a company computer is not confidential and may be read by someone in a company's technology department or a manager.

Community Service

Work with students in the local middle school or junior high school computer classes. Create a poster that lists the dos and don'ts of safe online communication—how to act in blogs, chat rooms, or sites such as Facebook, etc. Participate in a discussion of what students currently use the Internet for.

If an employee notices a violation of a company's policy, the company usually asks the employee to notify a supervisor. Often a company policy explains that a violation will result in disciplinary action and may even cause a person to lose his or her job.

etiquette
(ET i kit)
Professional behavior.

Summary

The telephone, e-mail, fax, and the Internet are four ways that technology helps health care workers send and receive information. Not only do you need to know how to work the technology, you also need to know proper **etiquette** when using it. In all instances, a health care employee should use technology professionally and responsibly. Telephones are helpful for a more immediate contact with another employee or patient. E-mail and fax machines can be used to send documents. The Internet can help health care worker find information on a topic or allow health care workers to present important information to their patients.

What's New?

Electronics and Health Care

For safety reasons, the health care facility where you work will probably have restrictions on use of your personal cell phone in the workplace. Cell phones can cause interference with medical equipment, including ventilators and pacemakers. Cell phones also may set off alarms on medical machines. Because of these types of problems in health care settings, cell phone use is usually restricted. You need to be aware of a facility's policy on how, where, and when patients and their families can use their phones. You may have to ask a patient or family member to turn off their phone. If so, politely explain the facility's policy.

Despite the problems associated with using cell phones in health care environments, advancing technologies offer beneficial uses for cell phones in regard to health care. Twitter, a Web site that offers social networking and microblogging services, enables doctors and other medical personnel to send and receive tweets—text-based posts of up to 140 characters—about health care issues and questions. Health care apps—applications that may be accessed on cell phones—are available, as well. You should keep in mind that patients and clients are finding access to health care information via these technological sources. Remind them that, like medical information they find on the Internet, health care information they receive in a tweet or with an app should be discussed in greater depth with their doctors.

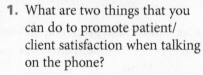

SECTION 9.2 Review Questions

1. What are two things that you can do to promote patient/client satisfaction when talking on the phone?

2. Name three things you should do when writing a telephone message.

3. What should you do if you have to send confidential or sensitive information in a fax?

4. Why should you avoid sarcasm and humor in an e-mail?

5. How is the Internet a useful tool in the health care field?

6. Why would you use blind carbon copy (bcc) rather than carbon copy (cc) on an e-mail?

Learn By Doing: Section 9.2 Activity

1. Complete Worksheets 1 and 2.

2. Ask your teacher for directions to complete Worksheet/Activity 3, 4, and 5.

3. Complete Worksheet/Activity 6.

4. When you are confident that you can meet each objective listed, ask your teacher for the section evaluation.

SECTION

9.3 Computers in Health Care

Background

Computers are essential in health care. Health care agencies use computers in most departments to help save time and improve accuracy. They are used for record keeping, diagnostic tests, education, research, and many other tasks. Health care workers must have a basic understanding of how computers work and how they are used in health care in order to be employable.

Objectives

When you have completed this section, you will be able to do the following:

- Match key terms with their correct meanings.

- List and explain how four computerized diagnostic tests help diagnose disease or illness.

- State how environmental services use computers.

- Describe ways that information services use computers.

- Discuss ethics and confidentiality as they relate to computers.

Computers in General

During the past 50 years, computer technology has grown and changed at an unbelievable rate. The early computers were made of vacuum tubes and required large, environmentally controlled rooms. They often overheated and became inoperable for many hours. Repairing them was time consuming. Large systems were very expensive, and only the largest organizations were able to afford them. Today's computer technology allows computers to be smaller, more powerful, and less expensive. Computer equipment that is used today is the result of a development process. Models and devices continue to change frequently as new technology becomes usable and marketable.

Basic Computer Components and Functions

Computers have basic components (**Figure 9.7**) and functions that you need to learn about in order to understand computer terminology. All computers allow users to input information, process information, and provide ways to output information.

Inputting

The most common device used to input data into a computer is a keyboard. In addition to alphanumeric keys, a keyboard has function keys, punctuation keys, arrow keys, and conjunction keys. Function keys have different purposes, depending on the software that is running on the computer. Arrow keys, along with a mouse, can be used to move the cursor around on the computer screen so you can control where you input information. Conjunction keys are used in combinations that are specific to the software that is running. For example, in some programs, when the Alt key is pressed in conjunction with the Shift key and the letter t, the current time is entered.

With advances in mobile-device technology, touch screens are becoming a frequently used data imput method. Touch screens, or touch pads, are common inputting devices for tablet or handheld computers. They are also used on computers in places where many people can access information, such as at a kiosk that gives directions in a medical facility. Uses for touch-screen technology in health care are growing. For example, touch screens have been developed that allow cancer patients to accurately show where their pain is and how bad the pain is at times when they may have trouble communicating with their caregivers.

For some types of computer systems used in health care facilities, tablet computers that require a stylus for inputting data may be used. A stylus looks like a pen or pencil, but using it on a tablet computer that is designed for this type of inputting allows a user to write information that can be digitally interpreted and stored. For example, some hospitals and medical offices may have patients enter their personal information directly into tablet computers; the information is digitally input into the computer system and does not need to be transcribed by a person in order to be added to the patient's medical record (see p. 249 for more on digital paperwork).

Other input devices include external hard-disk drives, floppy diskettes, CD-ROMs, DVD-ROMs, USB flash drives, optical drives, and magnetic disks. These devices are used for both inputting and storing data, or information.

Processing

A computer processes the information that is input and returns the information to the person who input it or to someone in another department. The **central processing unit** (CPU) is the working unit of the computer. The CPU consists of many electronic components and microchips. The CPU can process only the information it receives; if it receives incorrect information, it processes incorrect information. This is where the phrase "Garbage in, garbage out" comes from. You must be accurate when you enter information.

Outputting

Just as there is more than one device for inputting information into a computer, there are several devices for outputting. The two most common items used to **output** are the monitor (**Figure 9.7**) and the printer. The health care worker uses both.

input
(IN poot)
To enter data into a computer for processing.

Courtesy of ShutterStock.

Figure 9.7
Workstation computer components typically include a monitor, a keyboard, a mouse, and a hard drive, which may be placed under the desk to free up desk space. Which of these components is used for inputting?

central processing unit
(SEN truhl pros es ing yoo nit)
The part of a computer that interprets and carries out instructions.

output
(OUT poot)
To produce information; turn out.

Monitor

The monitor, or display screen, of a computer allows a user to see what is happening. Monitors may be monochrome, grayscale, or color. Monochrome monitors display one color for the background and one color for the foreground—black and white, green and black, or amber and black. Like its name suggests, a grayscale monitor is a monochrome monitor that displays in different shades of gray. Color monitors, sometimes called RGB monitors, combine the colors *red*, *green*, and *blue* to display anywhere from 16 to more than a million colors.

Printer

A printer is used to print the processed information on paper. Information printed on paper is called *hard copy* and can be filed with the patient's records. In most work environments, you will use the same printer as a group of your coworkers.

Computers in Health Care

Computers are processors of information. They process large amounts of information at incredible speeds, accurately, and consistently. Computers are used to communicate standards of care and to guide the practitioners in making patient care decisions.

Wherever your career path in the health field takes you, you will do a portion of your work on a computer. Hospitals and medical and dental offices are converting their methods of keeping medical records, as well as accounting, and purchasing functions to storage and processes that use computers. Some health care agencies have computer diagnostic services where a complete physical examination is analyzed by a computer.

Figure 9.8
Computers help monitor a patient's vital signs.

In the hospital, a computer performs many functions. The following are some of the procedures computers assist with:

- Recording physicians' notes and orders
- Creating a nursing treatment/work sheet based on physician orders and updating automatically with each additional physician order
- Creating templates for interventional protocols
- Charting at bedside
- Patient monitoring (**Figure 9.8**)
- Ordering or changing diets
- Ordering unit supplies
- Processing charges for nursing care equipment
- Ordering lab work and receiving lab results
- Recording lab results for patient records
- Scheduling x-rays, special tests, and surgeries
- Processing discharges
- Performing diagnostic testing
- Medical billing
- Emergency dispatch (**Figure 9.9**)
- Researching via the Internet

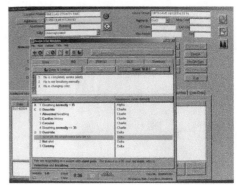

Figure 9.9
Computer software helps with instructions for emergency care.

In medical and dental offices, computers can be used to schedule appointments, set up a recall system, bill patients, schedule lab work, dial the telephone, manage the security system, and keep the inventory. Computers are an important part of the search for correct specific patient/client data that meets the **HEDIS** requirements. Electronic medical records are a necessary method of monitoring patient/client progress and quality health care; they provide data that allows physicians to provide timely disease management.

HEDIS
Health Plan Employer Data and Information Set; an organization that provides quality care guidelines

antagonist
(an TAG uh nist)
Something that works against.

homeostasis
(hoh mee uh STEY sis)
Constant balance within the body. This balance is maintained by the heartbeat, blood-making mechanisms, electrolytes, and hormone secretions.

invasive
(in VEY siv)
Entering the body.

tomography
(tuh MOG ruh fee)
X-ray technique that produces film of detailed cross sections of tissue.

transversely
(trans VURS lee)
In a cross direction.

The key benefit to electronic medical record systems is that they make information available to multiple staff at locations hundreds of miles apart at the same time. This also increases flexibility for medical professionals. Web services also play a role in providing data; for example, laboratory results are immediately sent to a Web site, allowing physicians or other professionals to access them. Medical professionals can access complete patient/client data that previously was available only in the paper medical record. There are medical environments that have a separate department dedicated to the development and use of software specific to their clients. These systems often support research and product development. Not all medical environments have the funds and training available to implement electronic medical data systems; however, the systems will gradually become more affordable and therefore more accessible over time.

Therapeutic Services

If you choose to enter an occupation in the therapeutic services, you will have opportunities to work with a computer each day. In the pharmacy, drugs are inventoried using a computer. A computer also assists the pharmacist in keeping track of medications that a person receives. The computer can alert the pharmacist when one medication acts as an **antagonist** to another medication or contains a substance that causes an allergic reaction. In physical and occupational therapy, a computer assists paralyzed patients to walk. In respiratory therapy, a computer keeps critically ill patients in **homeostasis**. In emergency services and intensive care areas, computers do direct patient/client monitoring and are programmed to warn health care workers when a potentially dangerous condition occurs.

Diagnostic Services

In diagnostic services, highly sophisticated computers are being used. In the past, surgery and other **invasive** procedures were used to reach a diagnosis. Today, computerized diagnostic equipment helps diagnose many illnesses. Using computerized equipment removes the risks of surgery and reduces the pain and discomfort of invasive tests. Computerized tests include the following:

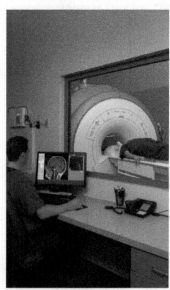

Courtesy of ShutterStock.

Figure 9.10
A technician uses the computer monitor to see what is happening with the MRI scan taking place.

- The *CAT scanner* does computerized axial **tomography**. This test allows an organ to be **transversely** dissected to help find abnormalities (such as tumors) without surgery. A photograph is taken to provide the radiologist and the physician with a permanent record for future use.

- The *Coulter counter* completes multiple examinations of many blood specimens in seconds.

- The *electrocardiogram computer* creates pictures on a computer screen. It prints out the electrical activity of the heart. This helps the physician diagnose heart disease correctly.

- The *magnetic resonance imaging* (MRI) computer scans the body (**Figure 9.10**). The scanner produces a cross-sectional image of the body. This helps the physician find tumors, see the results of medication and treatment, and diagnose the cause of an illness or disease.

- The *positron emission tomography* (PET) computer is also a scanner. It produces a three-dimensional image that shows an organ or bone from all sides.

- The *ultrasound imager* computer produces a picture of internal organs, tumors, aneurysms, and other abnormalities. It also produces pictures of the fetus developing in the uterus to help with fetal monitoring. These pictures can be seen on the monitor or can be processed on photographic film.

The latest electronic technology scans an organ and not only provides pictures, but also creates a three-dimensional object out of plastic. This object is an exact replica of the organ scanned in the patient's body. It allows the physician to practice difficult or experimental surgical procedures on the plastic replica before performing the procedure on the patient.

Environmental Services

Environmental careers also offer an opportunity to work with computers. Central supply services/central processing services are computerized for reordering inventory and for billing. Supplies are even categorized and identified by bar scanners like those you see in the grocery store.

Information Services

In information services, the computer is used in a variety of ways. Medical records workers manage and process records on computers. With diagnostic-related groupings, the computer is used to help categorize and track patients in the medical system. Health unit coordinators/unit secretaries use the computer to process many of the orders, transmitting requests to other departments.

The growing need to access medical data from patient/client files quickly requires health care providers to use computerized information systems. This means that to be employable, every health care worker must be comfortable working on computers.

Personal Wellness

Computer-Related Repetitive Strain Injury

Repetitive strain injuries happen when repeated physical movements do damage to tendons, nerves, muscles, and other soft body tissues. Nowadays, you may spend hours a day typing or clutching and dragging a mouse. An increase in the amount of time spent at the computer over the years has led to an increase in this type of injury. Some common types of repetitive strain injuries are carpal tunnel syndrome, bursitis, and tendonitis.

Typical symptoms of a repetitive strain injury include a tightness, soreness, or burning in the hands, wrists, fingers, forearms, or elbows. You may also experience tingling or numbness, coldness, or loss of strength or coordination in the hands. While most symptoms occur with the hands and arms, you may also feel pain in the upper back, shoulders, or neck.

While this type of injury can be painful, it can be prevented. You should use correct typing technique and posture, the right equipment setup, and good work habits in order to stay healthy. Be sure to sit up straight when using a computer. In addition, when you are typing, make sure that your wrists are straight and level. Your wrists should not be resting on anything, and your fingers should be in a straight line with your forearm. Also, check your work area to be sure that you do not have to stretch to reach the keys or read the computer screen. Anything that creates awkward reaches or angles in the body will create problems. Other helpful practices include using a light touch on the keyboard or mouse, keeping your arms and hands warm, and taking breaks to stretch and relax.

What other daily activities might be affected by repetitive strain injury?

contingency
(kuhn TIN juhn see)
Event that may occur but is not intended or likely to happen.

Personal Information Management (PIM)

Working in a medical setting requires management of a variety of documents and information: reports, forms (paper and digital), e-mails, instruction sheets, Web pages, and so forth. Technology can assist with the tasks of handling information, creating ease and efficiency. The goal of personal information management is for the correct and complete information to be available at the right time and in the right format. Reducing or eliminating errors and saving time with technology tools and software applications that function as personal information managers (PIMs) can make you a better employee.

Contingency Planning

Whenever human beings depend on machines, **contingency** plans need to be made just in case the machine stops functioning. When a computer is not functioning, it is said to be down. Downtime can be scheduled to allow a new program to be entered into the computer's memory or to make changes. Downtime can also be unexpected (e.g., due to a power failure or component failure). Hospitals and medical/dental offices have learned that it is important to have an alternative plan if failure occurs.

Despite modern technology, you still need to know manual methods of entering orders. The use of computers can make you more efficient in your job. With time, you will learn all of the things the computer can do, and you will learn how to do them. Practice is important in learning how to use the computer to its fullest capability.

Ethics and Confidentiality

The health care worker must remember the importance of ethics and confidentiality when using a computer. Computers contain privileged information that must be protected. Keep your identification code or password confidential to protect you and the patient.

Summary

In this section you read that computers are an essential part of health care. All health care services have gained a greater ability to treat, diagnose, and care for patients/clients through computerization. Computers do shut down occasionally, making contingency planning important.

The responsible use of computers means that all users must keep information learned about patients/clients confidential. Keeping your identification code or password a secret is also your responsibility.

SECTION	**9.3**	Review Questions

1. Name two devices used for inputting.

2. Which part of the computer processes information?

3. List three procedures in which a computer might be used.

4. Why might a physician use magnetic resonance imaging?

5. How are computers used in environmental services?

6. Why is a contingency plan important when working with computers?

 Learn By Doing: Section 9.3 Activity

1. Complete vocabulary Worksheet 1.

2. Complete Worksheets 2 and 3 as assigned.

3. When you are confident that you can meet each objective listed above, ask your teacher for the section evaluation.

Background

Observation and documentation of your observations are key components of health care. Your ability to observe patient/client behavior and symptoms will directly affect their care. Accurate documentation provides information needed to make decisions about their care. It is important that you develop sharp observation, reporting, and documentation skills.

Objectives

When you have completed this section, you will be able to do the following:

- Match key terms with their correct meanings.

- Explain the difference between subjective and objective observations.

- Explain which type of reporting allows immediate feedback and action.

- List information that must be on all health records.

- Apply five general charting guidelines.

Observation

Every health care worker is responsible for observing the patient/client. Even if you are not responsible for charting, you must report your **observations** to your supervisor. You are responsible for making good observations moment by moment. Your observation skills must be fine-tuned so that you are aware of the patient's mental and physical state. This awareness helps you and your co-workers to be more effective.

observation
(ob zur VEY shuhns)
Something that is noted or recorded.

When interacting with patients and their families, use all of your tools to evaluate the situation. Your tools are four of your five senses: sight, hearing, touch, and smell:

- *Look* for all visible signs that may indicate a reason for the client's complaint.

- *Listen* carefully. Don't put thoughts or words into others' mouths. Be sure that you understand fully what you are told.

- *Feel* for changes in the skin, body temperature, abnormal structures, and so on.

- *Smell* unusual odors, which are often the first clue to a problem (e.g., fruity breath, foul stools).

There are two types of observations:

- **Subjective** *observations* cannot be seen. They are ideas, thoughts, or opinions. If you cannot see it, feel it, hear it, or smell it, it is a subjective observation. (The patient complains of pain—you cannot see it, feel it, hear it, or smell it.)

- **Objective** *observations* can be seen. If you can see it, feel it, hear it, or smell it, it is an objective observation. (The patient has a cut—you can see it.)

The health care worker must report and document all subjective and objective observations. Any unusual event or change in a patient must be reported verbally to the supervisor and then documented on the client's legal record.

Medical Reporting. There are many kinds of medical reporting. As mentioned above, there are the reports that a health care worker might make to document observations. There are also medical billing reports, insurance reports, code analysis reports, and other administrative reporting functions.

Medical Records. A medical record is a systematic documentation of a person's medical history. It can be the actual physical folder for the patient as well as the body of information that makes up each patient's health history. Medical records are personal documents, and there are many ethical and legal issues surrounding them, such as the degree of third-party access and appropriate storage and disposal.

Reporting

Reporting unusual events or any change in behavior or condition is every health care worker's responsibility. Observation of people in a waiting area or a patient care area is important. Verbal reports to a supervisor allow immediate feedback and action when necessary. For example, you must always report changes in blood pressure, breathing, or coloring (e.g., pale, **flushed**) and any indications that a person is in **distress**.

It is also important to report anyone who acts strangely, threateningly, or weakly or appears to be in pain. Do *not* wait for others to report unusual observations. You may prevent a serious situation by reporting your observation in a timely manner.

Documentation

Documentation is required in all health care settings. **Documentation** is a record of the patient's progress throughout treatment. Many people may be responsible for documenting information on a single patient/client. This record provides the information needed to allow each health care provider to give the care that best benefits the patient (**Figure 9.11**).

All records must contain certain information:

- Client's name.
- Client's address.
- Client's age.
- Identification number.
- Diagnosis.
- Physician's orders.

---

subjective
(suhb JEK tiv)
Relating to a symptom or condition perceived by the patient and not by the examiner.

objective
(ahb JEK tiv)
Relating to a symptom or condition perceived by someone other than the person affected.

flushed
(flush d)
Showing reddening of the skin.

distress
(di STRES)
Great pain or suffering.

documentation
(dok yuh men TEY shuhn)
A record of something, such as a patient's progress.

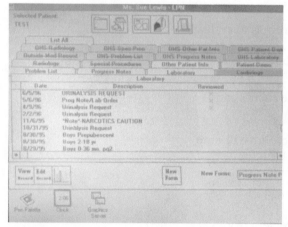

Figure 9.11
Today, health care facilities typically use computers to record a patient's information.

Depending on the department where the record is kept, other information may be required. Each health care worker who cares for the patient makes a **notation** on the chart. (Your facility policy tells you if you are required to chart. Even if you do not chart, you must always report your observations.) In the past, a health care worker's notations were always handwritten. Now, however, much patient information is entered directly into computers, including chart notations. If charts are kept electronically in the facility where you work, be sure you know how to properly record and save the notations you make (Figure 9.12). These notations should contain specific information about the client, including:

- Care or treatment given.
- Time of treatment.
- How the patient tolerated the care or treatment.
- Any observations that would be helpful to other health care workers.
- Information that the patient has given that would affect treatment.

This documentation is admissible in a court of law. This means that anything you write is considered to be true. If you do not write down something that you did for the patient, it is assumed that it was not done. As you can see, it is very important to be accurate and careful when you **chart**.

Everyone must follow these general guidelines for charting:

- Use ink for record keeping. In some facilities, different colors are used for different shifts.
- Entries must be **legible**. If your writing is hard to read, you should print.
- If you make an error, do not erase it or scratch it out or cover it up. Draw a single line through the error so that it can still be read. Write "error" next to it, and then place your initials next to the correction (e.g., "error/KG Patient tolerated procedure well.") If you are working with electronic charts, you will need to learn how to correct errors in the system your facility uses.
- Entries should be in short phrases. You do not need to write complete sentences. You do not need to use the patient's name because you are writing in the patient's chart. Your entries should be concise, clear, and meaningful.
- All entries that you make are followed by your signature. You sign with your first initial, your last name, and your title. If you are making entries in an electronic chart, you still must "sign" the entries you make.

Hospital Chart

The rules listed above apply to all charting. However, additional charting may be required. This is especially true for the nurse assistant. Each facility has its own policy and procedures for charting. Learn what these are. There are some standard types of charting that all nurse assistants are required to do:

- *Nurses' notes* may be in **narrative** or check-off form. These notes state:
  - What personal care was given.
  - What activities the client participated in.
  - The patient's skin condition.
  - General observations about the client.
  - Any unusual occurrences.

Figure 9.12
A device for electronic medical charting may be used to record patient information and observations.

notation
(noh TEY shuhn)
The act of noting, marking, or setting down in writing.

chart
(CHART)
To write observations or records of patient care.

legible
(LEJ uh buhl)
Capable of being read easily.

narrative
(NAR uh tiv)
A story or account of events.

- Any complaints that the client has.
- What treatments were given.
- Any information that is important to the patient's well-being.

During your career, you may be asked to document in many different styles. To avoid confusion in this book, we will use the following style:

- Date.
- Military time.
- A description of the care or treatment given, complaints and problems, all written as ordinary sentences.
- Signature (first initial, full last name) and certification.

Many facilities provide flow sheets with charting examples and when employed you will follow those examples.

- The **graphic chart** is a record of the patient's vital signs. All graphic charts have time blocks and numbers that relate to temperature, pulse, and respiration. On some graphic charts there is also space for blood pressure, intake and output, bowel movements, and weight. (**Figure 9.13**) Graphic charts are useful because they contain like measurements over time. When placed together, the nurse can quickly scan and determine the patient's baseline and any alterations from baseline.

graphic chart
(GRAF ik charct)
A visual record of data in graphic or tabular form.

Figure 9.13
Graphic chart with intake and output section. What types of things are included on a graphic chart?

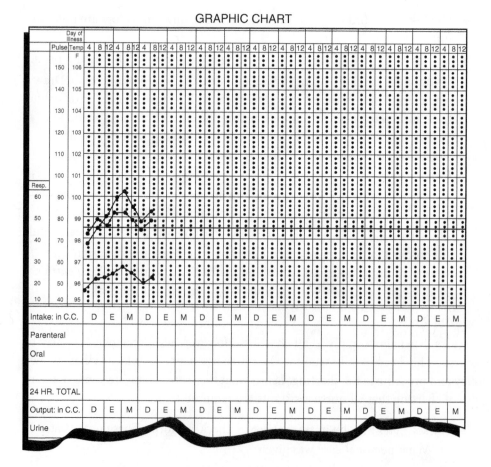

GRAPHIC CHART

Other parts of the chart include:

- A front sheet with personal information, such as name, address, marital status, place of employment, and admission diagnosis.
- A physical examination and a medical history.
- The daily progress report written by the physician.
- There may be:
  - A discharge plan.
  - A social worker's report.
  - Treatment records from other departments or from specialists.

Documentation is a very important responsibility. Learn how to write good records, and always be responsible and careful when you chart.

 ## Confidentiality

When communicating any information concerning the client, remember that it is confidential and is not discussed unless it affects the treatment. The physician and patient will decide if family members or others will share the information.

Summary

In the health care field, you will need to record both subjective and objective observations. It is your responsibility to report any unusual events or change in behavior. In addition, you will be required to maintain documentation of a client/patient's care. Accuracy is important in order for health care workers to provide the best care for a client/patient. Always remember that the information in a client/patient's chart is **confidential**.

confidential
(kon fi DEN shuhl)
Limited to persons authorized to use information or documents

---

SECTION 2.2 Review Questions

1. Explain the difference between subjective observations and objective observations.

2. Name three things that should be included on a patient record.

3. List three things you should do when charting.

4. Why is it important to chart carefully?

5. What is the benefit of verbal reporting?

6. What additional items may a nurse's assistant be required to include as part of a chart?

7. What is a graphic chart?

 Learn By Doing: Section 9.4 Activity

1. Complete Worksheets 1 and 2 as assigned.

2. When you are confident that you can meet each objective listed, ask your teacher for the section evaluation.

Scheduling and Filing

Background

As a health information technician, you will provide essential support for the medical staff and for patients. You will often be the first person the patient/client meets, either on the phone or in person. You may be in charge of gathering important health information from patients and keeping records up to date. You may also schedule office visits and work in bookkeeping and billing. The health information technician works to ensure that health providers have the information they need to provide appropriate care and that the office runs smoothly.

Objectives

When you have completed this section, you will be able to do the following:

- Match key terms with their correct meanings.
- List the guidelines for scheduling clients/patients for appointments.
- Describe a tickler file.
- List five filing systems.
- List two kinds of registration forms.

- Demonstrate how to schedule appointments.
- Demonstrate how to schedule a new client/patient: first time visit.
- Demonstrate how to schedule an outpatient diagnostic test.

(a)

(b)

Figure 9.14
Appointments may be scheduled in an appointment book (a) or a computer system (b).

Scheduling

For a smooth-running day it is important to know how to schedule clients/patients for office visits, procedures, and surgeries. Scheduling is done in one of two ways: appointments are written manually in an appointment book, or a computer system maintains appointment schedules (**Figure 9.14**).

Scheduling Office Visits

When scheduling visits, follow these guidelines:

1. A patient/client visit is scheduled every 15 minutes, 30 minutes, or hourly, depending on your provider's specialty. (**Figures 9.15** and **9.16**)

2. Learn to recognize the patients/clients who require more time with the provider.

3. Always ask the purpose of the appointment (for example, checkup, cold) to allocate enough time for the visit.

4. Ask the patient/client what would be the most convenient time for an appointment.

5. If you are not able to schedule the patient/client at the time and date requested, express regret and ask for a second choice.

6. Ask for a phone number where the patient/client can be reached during the day in case a cancellation is necessary.

7. Offer to call the client/patient as cancellations occur if the patient/client desires an earlier appointment. Use a tickler file as a reminder. (See page 245 for a description of a tickler file.)

8. Always repeat the appointment time and date to the patient/client to avoid confusion.

9. When a patient/client cancels an appointment, note the date, time, and reason for the cancellation in the chart.

10. Give all patients/clients appointment cards when scheduling a follow-up visit. Put the following information on the appointment card:
   - Provider's name.
   - Provider's address and phone number.
   - Patient's/client's name.
   - Date and time of next appointment.

Date 1-8-11				
7	30	IAN GALLAGHER		
	45	DEE ANN SHERMAN		
	00	///////////////		
8	15	MARY KELHI		
	30			
	45			
9	00			
	15			
	30			
	45			
	00			

Figure 9.15
Standard appointment sheet. What problems might result if you do not recognize when a particular patient's visit will take longer than that of some other patients?

	Dr. Smith	Dr. Jones	Ultrasound Machine
	Month _____ Date _____ Day _____		
8:00			
8:15		GREEN, LOIS 412-6190	
8:30		BACK PAIN	DR. JONES: MRS. GREEN
8:45			
9:00			
9:15			
9:30			
9:45			

Figure 9.16
Medical appointment schedule for more than one service at a time. One of Dr. Smith's patients is also having back problems that day. She will probably need an ultrasound. What time should you schedule her appointment with Dr. Smith?

BACKGROUND: Careful scheduling is essential for a well-run office. Appointments must be scheduled to prevent long waits for patients while also keeping the staff working at top efficiency. Accommodating the patient as much as possible tells the patient that you are concerned about him or her.

PREPROCEDURE

1. Assemble materials.

   a. Pen or pencil

   b. Appointment book

   c. Appointment reminder cards for tickler file

   d. Appointment cards

   e. Calendar

   f. Procedure list with approximate time allotments for each procedure

   g. Written instructions for patient/client preparation prior to visit

2. Prepare provider schedules for at least three months.

   a. Mark out vacation or holiday times.

   b. Schedule monthly, weekly, or daily meetings.

   c. Mark schedule to identify hours for patient/client appointments.

3. Follow the correct procedure for the type of appointment system in your office.

4. Write clearly and neatly so that names and procedures are easy to read.

PROCEDURE

5. Schedule appointments.

   a. By phone:

      (1) Clarify reason for appointment.

      (2) Discuss most convenient time for client/patient (e.g., a.m., p.m.).

      (3) Offer various times.

      (4) Ask for proper spelling of first and last names once a time is chosen.

      (5) Ask for information, such as birthday or Social Security number, if name is common (e.g., Smith, Jones).

      (6) Write patient's/client's telephone number and where he or she can be reached during the day of appointment.

      (7) Allocate **sufficient** time for the visit when scheduling a procedure.

   b. In person:

      (1) Follow steps 1 to 5 of procedure above.

      (2) Give patient/client an appointment card with date and time of appointment.

   c. For appointments more than three months in the future:

      (1) Ask patient/client to address an appointment reminder card.

      (2) Fill in month patient is to return.

      (3) Instruct patient/client that a card will be sent as a reminder to call and make an appointment.

   d. Place appointment reminder card in tickler file so that it is sent at the correct time.

Scheduling Surgeries/Procedures

Learn how your provider wants to schedule surgery and procedures in the hospital or office. Use the following guidelines to help you with this scheduling:

- Determine how long each procedure takes.
- Learn how to schedule patients/clients around these procedures.
- Establish what days and times your provider prefers to do surgeries (for example, Monday, Tuesday, all day, just in the morning).
- Learn the admitting procedure for the hospital where your provider performs surgery.
- Provide the patient/client with the following information:
  - Surgery time.
  - Time patient/client needs to arrive at the office or hospital.
  - Registration instructions (admitting forms) if going to the hospital.
  - The hospital's address, telephone, and directions.
  - Written instructions to follow prior to surgery (for example, *NPO after midnight*).
- Give the client/patient verbal and written instruction because the person may be nervous or apprehensive and forget what you said.
- Maintain good lines of communication with the office personnel of all referring providers and assisting providers.

Learning how your office functions allows you to schedule a smooth-running day.

sufficient
(suh FISH suhnt)
Enough.

Scheduling Diagnostic Tests

Diagnostic procedures are frequently scheduled to be performed in other facilities. The following is basic information necessary to schedule an appointment:

- Patient's/Client's name.
- Age or date of birth.
- Reason for the diagnostic test.

Give the client/patient the appointment information and instructions to prepare for the test. When scheduled for a test like an upper gastrointestinal series (UGI) give written guidelines that explain how to prepare for the test.

Figure 9.17
A tickler file may use full sized files in a drawer or index cards in a file box.

Tickler File

A **tickler file** reminds you of tasks that need to be done at a certain time (for example, by day, week, or month). When you create a tickler file, arrange 12 file dividers in a file (**Figure 9.17**). You need 1 divider for each month and 1 for each day of the month (1 through 31). When a client/patient needs to be seen at a later date:

1. Fill out a reminder card with the patient's/client's name and address.
2. Fill in the blank space with the date of the patient's/client's last visit.
3. Place the card in the file the month prior to the next required visit.
4. Each month, take cards from that month's folder, and mail them to the client/patient.

tickler file
(TIK ler fayhl)
Special file kept to remind you of tasks that need to be done at a certain time.

Scheduling a New Patient/Client: First-Time Visit

BACKGROUND: Gathering essential information from each new patient provides the information needed for patient care and timely billing for services rendered. The patient feels secure when everything is taken care of efficiently.

PREPROCEDURE

1. Assemble materials.
   a. Appointment book
   b. Scheduling guidelines
   c. Telephone
   d. Pencil

PROCEDURE

2. Ask patient/client for the following:
   a. First, last, and middle names
   b. Birth date
   c. Home address
   d. Telephone number

3. Ask patient/client if this is a referral. If yes:
   a. Determine information you need from the referring provider.
   b. Add this information to the medical chart. (Your provider needs to send a consultation report to the referring provider.)

4. Ask what the chief complaint is and when it started.

5. Find the first appointment that allows the appropriate amount of time.

6. Offer a choice of days and times.

7. Enter the following:
   a. Patient's/client's name NP next to name indicating new patient)
   b. Time and date of appointment
   c. Patient's/Client's day telephone number

8. Explain payment procedure (e.g., patient/client must pay for visit, your office will bill).

9. Give directions to the office.

10. Explain parking arrangements.

POSTPROCEDURE

11. Repeat day, date, and time the appointment is scheduled.

As you requested, Dr. R. C. Smith is reminding you that it has been _____ since your last visit.

Please call (000) 888-0000 to schedule an appointment.

R. C. Smith, M.D.
11372 City Drive
Scottsdale, WA 88888

Figure 9.18
Appointment reminder card to be placed in a tickler file. When should you look through the file to remind yourself to send the reminder card?

Check the tickler file routinely because this file tells you what to do and when to do it. The card that is in the file reminds you to notify the client/patient to make an appointment. (**Figure 9.18**) There are also tickler file software programs that automatically "pop up" reminders on the screen of your computer monitor without you having to check a file. Even with an electronic tickler file, however, the reminder information must be entered carefully and completely.

9.3 Scheduling Outpatient Diagnostic Tests

BACKGROUND: Patients are often fearful about diagnostic tests. Scheduling the diagnostic tests as soon as possible and when it is most convenient for the patients gives them confidence that they are cared for in a timely and caring way.

PREPOCEDURE

1. Assemble materials.

    a. Written order from provider

    b. Patient's chart

    c. Test preparation instructions for client/patient

    d. Name, address, and phone number of laboratory

    e. Telephone

PROCEDURE

2. Read provider's order.

3. Ask patient/client when he or she is available.

4. Call test lab.

5. Order test

    a. Set up time and date

    b. Give name, age, address, and telephone number of patient/client

    c. Ask if there are special instructions for patient/client prior to the test

6. Provide patient/client with the following:

    a. Name, address, and telephone number of laboratory

    b. Date and time

    c. Instructions (in writing) for preparation prior to test

7. Verify instructions with patient/client.

8. Record test time in patient's/client's chart.

POSTPROCEDURE

9. Put a reminder in the tickler file or on a calendar to check for results.

 Registration

New patients/clients must complete two basic forms when registering:

1. Client/patient information forms.
2. Medical history forms.

Client/Patient Information Forms

The client/patient information form gives the following information:

- Patient's/client's name, address, and phone number.
- Birth date, sex, marital status, and Social Security number.
- Patient's/client's employer name, address, and phone number.
- Insurance company's name, address, and phone number.
- Insured's employer name, address, and phone number.
- If the patient/client is a minor, name of the responsible party.

Personal Wellness

Health Risks

As a health information technician, your contact with patients will be casual. You will be talking to them, getting and giving information, but you will have little if any more physical contact. Nonetheless, anyone working in a health care environment is at some risk of infection. So, how much at risk of infection are you and what can you do to reduce your risk?

Hepatitis B Virus (HBV) is one of the most serious infections. It is typically spread through sexual contact, by sharing needles among drug users, and by accidental needle sticks, which represent the greatest risk to health care workers. HBV cannot be contracted by casual contact with infected patients. Check with your supervisor. You may be entitled to an inoculation against HBV at no cost.

Human immunodeficiency virus (HIV) is primarily transmitted by sexual contact and intravenous drug use. It is not transmitted by casual contact, through contaminated food or water, or through the air.

Influenza is a common illness that often brings patients into the medical facility. To protect yourself from infection and to avoid spreading the flu to other patients, you should consider getting an annual flu vaccination. Check with your supervisor about the provider's policy.

The health information technician may be exposed to other microorganisms that can be spread through casual contact in the medical facility. The best precaution against infection is to regularly and frequently wash your hands. Keep your hands away from your mouth. If you develop any signs or symptoms of illness, report them immediately.

How does your health affect the health of patients? How can you protect them?

Figure 9.19
A patient must complete a handwritten or electronic medical history form.

Medical History Forms

The medical history form gives the provider the necessary information to evaluate the patient's/client's physical condition. The patient/client must give you the following information (**Figure 9.19** and **Figure 9.20**):

- Previous surgeries.
- Allergies.
- Chronic illness.
- Medications taken.
- General medical history.
- Childhood diseases.

Both forms must be completed accurately to serve the needs of both the client/patient and the provider.

GREEN VALLEY MEDICAL GROUP, INC.
MEDICAL HISTORY

NAME _____   DATE OF BIRTH _____

OCCUPATION _____   MARITAL STATUS: S   M   D   W

ALLERGIES:

Are you allergic to:

Penicillin	Yes _____	No _____
Sulfa	Yes _____	No _____
Aspirin	Yes _____	No _____
Codeine	Yes _____	No _____
Tetanus Injections	Yes _____	No _____
Iodine	Yes _____	No _____
Foods	Yes _____	No _____
Tape	Yes _____	No _____

Other _____

_____

MEDICATIONS:

List all medications, including over the counter, you
are currently taking:

_____

_____

_____

_____

HABITS:

Do you:

Smoke?	Yes _____	No _____	How Much _____
Drink Alcohol?	Yes _____	No _____	How Much _____

Drink Beverages That Contain Caffeine?

	Yes _____	No _____	How Much _____
Limit Cholesterol	Yes _____	No _____	
Use Other Substances	Yes _____	No _____	
What? _____			

EXERCISE:

Do you on a regular basis:

Walk	Yes _____	No _____
Run	Yes _____	No _____
Bike	Yes _____	No _____
Swim	Yes _____	No _____
Aerobic Exercise	Yes _____	No _____
Other	Yes _____	No _____

MENSTRUAL HISTORY (FEMALES):

Date of last PAP & results _____

Date of last normal period _____

Date of last mammogram & results _____

Length of cycle (days) _____

Usual duration (days) _____

Number of pregnancies _____

Number of children _____

PRESENT COMPLAINTS:

Do you have:

Headaches	Yes _____	No _____
Fever	Yes _____	No _____
Cough	Yes _____	No _____
Chest Pains	Yes _____	No _____
Nausea	Yes _____	No _____
Vomiting	Yes _____	No _____
Diarrhea	Yes _____	No _____
Constipation	Yes _____	No _____
Black Stools	Yes _____	No _____
Bloody Stools	Yes _____	No _____
Painful Urination	Yes _____	No _____
Recent Weight Gain or Loss	Yes _____	No _____

Other Complaints _____

_____

PAST ILLNESS:

Have you ever had:

High Blood Pressure	Yes _____	No _____
Heart Trouble	Yes _____	No _____
Pneumonia	Yes _____	No _____
Hepatitis	Yes _____	No _____
Cancer	Yes _____	No _____
Diabetes	Yes _____	No _____
Tuberculosis	Yes _____	No _____
Asthma	Yes _____	No _____
Ulcers	Yes _____	No _____
Seizures	Yes _____	No _____
Sexually Transmitted Disease	Yes _____	No _____
Blood Disorder	Yes _____	No _____

Other _____

_____

OPERATIONS:

Have you had any surgery:

Appendix	Yes _____	No _____
Tonsils	Yes _____	No _____
Gallbladder	Yes _____	No _____
Stomach	Yes _____	No _____
Hemorrhoids	Yes _____	No _____
Female Organs	Yes _____	No _____
Thyroid	Yes _____	No _____
Hernia	Yes _____	No _____
Heart	Yes _____	No _____

Other _____

_____

_____

Figure 9.20

*Medical history form. Under Marital Status,
what do the initials S M D W stand for?*

What's New?

Digital Paperwork

Health care providers rely upon information from admittance forms, patient histories, lab forms, insurance forms, and much more to make the medical and business parts of the organization successful. Currently most of these forms are completed by using a paper form and pen. Information on paper forms has limited usefulness, however, so, in many cases, someone transcribes, or copies, the written information to a computer.

Periodically, new forms are completed on patients, and that information must also be entered into the computer system. Transcribing all this information represents an enormous amount of staff time that might be better spent on patient care. It also increases the possibility of errors being introduced as the information is copied.

New digitalized systems are emerging to simplify and streamline the process. Some of it is already being seen in many facilities.

Tablet PCs, for example, have special light-weight and portable slate display screens. The forms appear on the screens and can be written on with a special pen, or stylus. Handwriting recognition software reads the handwriting. Information is instantly digitalized and can be transferred to the computer system without the need for separate transcribing (Figure 9.21).

Another new technology even eliminates the display screen with special paper and digital pens. Patients simply fill out the medical forms as they normally do. The digital pens record the information as patients write. Again, the laborious manual transcription from paper forms to computer is eliminated.

How can a digitalized system like one of these improve the quality of patient care?

Figure 9.21
Handwriting recognition software reads what is written on the screen of a tablet computer.

Courtesy of ShutterStock.

Filing

Filing Systems

Proper filing helps ensure you can find information when you need it (Figure 9.22). The filing system serves to:

- Store information and records safely.
- Keep related materials together.
- Retrieve files quickly when needed.

The following are the five most common systems:

1. Alphabetical.
2. Numerical.
3. Color coding.
4. Chronological.
5. Geographic.

Each filing system involves the same basic procedures:

- Sorting.
- Coding.
- Indexing.
- Storing or filing.

Courtesy of ShutterStock.
(b)

Courtesy of ShutterStock.
(a)

Figure 9.22
A filing system must be followed carefully so that the correct files can be retrieved when needed (a). Barcodes can help make retrieval more efficient (b).

Sorting is the placement of each item according to the particular filing system you are using. Alphabetical sorting requires placing all items with the same letters together. Numerical sorting requires placing all items with the same numbers together. Color sorting requires placing all items with the same colors together. Chronological sorting requires placing all items with the same dates together. Geographical sorting requires placing all items from the same region together.

Coding identifies items that belong to a certain category. For example, surgical files may be assigned a number or letter to identify them as separate from laboratory files.

Indexing organizes items in the order in which they are filed. The American Medical Records Management Association has established rules that provide guidelines for indexing items.

Alphabetical System

The alphabetical system is simple and economical, and it is the most common method for filing records. This system follows the order of the alphabet. If you have not used the alphabet for a long time, take time to review it.

Sorting

To set up an alphabetical filing system, place all charts with the same first letter of the last name together (all *A*s, all *B*s, and so on).

sorting
(SAWR ting)
Separating items to be filed according to the filing system being used, such as alphabetical, numerical, color, chronological, and geographical.

coding
(KOH ding)
Identifying items to be filed according to particular categories, such as surgical or laboratory.

indexing
(in desk sing)
Organizing items in the order they are to be filed.

Samuelsen

Samuelson

Masters

Mendoza

Puertas

Putnam

Cruz

Culver

When there is more than one chart that begins with the same letter, alphabetize by the second, third, fourth letters (or as many as necessary). The boldface letters in the following list determine the files' placement in an alphabetical listing:

Cruz

Culver

Masters

Mendoza

Puertas

Putnam

Samuelsen

Samuelson

Coding

If your files are separated by a code, place all *A*s with the same code together, all *B*s with the same code together, and so on. Some systems do not separate coded files. In files that are not separated, the codes identify specific things. For example, an office may have several doctors, and each doctor may be identified by a different color. All charts can be filed together, or they can be separated, depending on the office procedure.

Indexing

Make three columns on a page and label the columns 1, 2, and 3. When filing by name, place the last name in the column labeled 1, the first name in the column labeled 2, and the middle name or initial in the column labeled 3. For example, if the name is Alec Monroe Goldman, it is indexed as

1	2	3
Goldman	Alec	Monroe

It is important to label charts by this indexing method. This makes placing them in order a simple task.

Charts with initials instead of a first name are placed before spelled-out names. C. Todd Sherman is indexed as

1	2	3
Sherman	C.	Todd

Names that are hyphenated are considered one name, as if the hyphen were not there. For example, Kellie Bell-White is indexed as

1	2	3
Bell-White	Kellie	

Apostrophes are ignored when indexing, so Timothy Gallagher O'Bannon is indexed as

1	2	3
OBannon	Timothy	Gallagher

Last names with prefixes are joined as one name, so Carlos A. De Leon is indexed as

1	2	3
DeLeon	Carlos	A.

Abbreviated names are indexed as if they were spelled out in full. For example, St. Gustov Edward is indexed as Gustov Saint Edward, or

1	2	3
Edward	Gustov	(Saint)

If a title precedes one name or a given name and a middle name, the title is the first indexing number. Father Gerald Rahn, Queen Erin, and Princess Monica are indexed as

1	2	3
Gerald	Rahn	(Father)
Erin	(Queen)	
Monica	(Princess)	

Titles and degrees before or after a complete name are placed in parentheses after the name for identification. For example, Dr. DeeAnn Marie Sherman or DeeAnn Marie Sherman, M.D., is indexed as

1	2	3
Sherman	DeeAnn	Marie (Dr.)
Sherman	DeeAnn	Marie (M.D.)

Store or File

Place files in alphabetical order for easy retrieval. Place the names in order by looking for the first letter that is different, indicating the sequence. For example, Gallagher, Kevin DeWayne, is filed before Gallagher, Shaun Patrick Michael, because the *K* in Kevin comes before the *S* in Shaun.

Follow the instructions in your Student Activity Guide to practice sorting, coding, indexing, and filing.

Numerical System

The numerical system is another simple way of maintaining client/patient charts. Use a notebook or computer to record the number assigned to each client/patient.

This allows you to find the client/patient name by the assigned number. The assigned number is often referred to as a medical record number or patient/client number.

- Assigned numbers are placed in numerical order.
- Assign each new patient/client a number (for example, 001, 002, 003).

Keep a log in a notebook or computer of the client/patient name and number as you assign them. This record must be **accessible** to all staff. For example, assign numbers as follows:

accessible
(ak SES uh buhl)
Available to obtain.

File Number	Client/Patient Name
001	Mendoza
002	Samuelsen
003	Putnam
004	Puertas
005	Masters
006	Culver
007	Cruz
008	Samuelson

Terminal Digits

terminal
(TUR muh nl)
Last or ending.

Numbers can indicate many different things. Grouping by **terminal** digits means that you group items according to the last few digits of their assigned number (for example, 432.80, 321.80 or 879.90, 320.90). The terminal digits in these examples are 80 and 90, so all the 80s are filed in order by the first three digits, and all the 90s are filed in the same fashion (for example, 321.80, 432.80 and 320.90, 879.90). Let's pretend that you have items that need to be filed according to their assigned number. First sort these items by grouping all the same number of digits together (for example, all two-digit numbers together, all three-digit numbers together). These are basic rules to follow:

- When zeros precede numbers, ignore them. Zeros are often added to numbers because computers call for a specific number of digits in a space. For example, the sequence 0001, 0935, 0087 is filed 0001, 0087, 0935. Because you ignore zeros before numbers when filing, you sort 0001 as a one-digit number, 0087 as having two digits, and 0935 as having three digits.
- Coding is often done by the terminal-digit method. Take the last digits of the assigned numbers and group together all those that are the same. File in ascending order within these groupings. For example, 546.10, 386.30, 957.10, and 752.30 are grouped with all numbers ending with 10 together and all numbers ending with 30 together (546.10, 957.10, 386.30, 752.30).
- Indexing places items in ascending numerical order within their groups. (For example, 546.10 and 957.10 are in one group, and 386.30 and 752.30 form another group.)
- Place files according to their numerical order.

Follow the instructions in your Student Activity Guide for sorting, coding, indexing, and filing numerically.

Color-Coding System

Color coding helps reduce the chance of filing errors. The following are guidelines for using this method.

1. Assign a color sticker to each letter of the alphabet (for example, blue is *A*, yellow is *B*, green is *C*).

2. Determine how many stickers to apply on a patient's/client's chart (depending on chart size). *Example:* If you use three colors on the chart and the client's/patient's name is Mr. Gates, place the stickers in the order that corresponds to the first three letters of the patient's/client's last name (for example, *G* is yellow, *A* is blue, and *T* is purple).

3. Place the color stickers on the side of the chart that faces out when filed.

Chronological System

Chronological filing arranges files in the order of their occurrence, usually by day. This method is most often used in storing research items. Because each day, month, and year can be referred to by number, it is easy to follow the basic numerical system.

1. Sort by placing all items of the same year together.

2. Code each item as in any filing system.

3. Index by placing all files of the same month and year together.

4. File each item by date within the appropriate month and year grouping.

Geographical System

Geographical filing is done according to location. This method is often used for storing records of research studies in specific geographical areas. File alphabetically according to the name of the state, then alphabetically according to the city. File in the following manner:

- Alphabetically according to the state name.
- Alphabetically according to the city name.
- Alphabetically according to the names of companies.

Whichever filing method you use, follow the basic rules for filing under the appropriate system. The following is an example of filing by company name:

Company Name	City	State
A.G. Corporation	Mills	Illinois
Blosson Inc.	Lakewood	California
Gamble Corporation	Reno	Nevada
General Corporation	Redlands	California
K.G. Inc.	Lakes	Utah
K.M.B. Corp.	Mills	Illinois
M.M. General	Lakewood	California
M.W.G. Corporation	Great Lakes	Florida
Water Inc.	Silverton	Illinois

The following items are alphabetized by state and city:

State	City	Company Name
California	Lakewood	Blosson Inc.
California	Lakewood	M.M. General
California	Redlands	General Corp.
Florida	Great Lakes	M.W.G. Corp.
Illinois	Mills	A.G. Corp.
Illinois	Mills	K.M.B. Corp.
Illinois	Silverton	Water Inc.
Nevada	Reno	Gamble Corp.
Utah	Lakes	K.G. Inc.

 ## Summary

Scheduling patients is an important part of a well-run medical facility. Appointments for office visits, and procedures, and diagnostic tests may be scheduled manually in an appointment book, or on a computer system. When a patient arrives for an appointment, information must be gathered and recorded on client/patient information forms and medical history forms. Follow up appointments by scheduling future appointments and placing appropriate information in a tickler file for further follow-up. Medical records are kept according to a specific filing systems that may be alphabetic, numerical, color coding, chronological, or geographic. Proper filing ensures that patient information can be found when it is needed.

SECTION 9.5 — **Review Questions**

1. List the ten guidelines for scheduling office visits.

2. Explain what a tickler file is and how it is used.

3. Name the two forms that new patients/clients must complete upon registering.

4. What are the five most common filing systems?

5. List the guidelines for scheduling surgeries/procedures.

6. What are the functions of a filing system?

 ## Learn By Doing: Section 9.5 Activity

1. Complete Worksheets 1 and 2 as directed by your teacher.

2. Complete Worksheet/Activity 3.

3. Complete Worksheets 4 and 5.

4. Prepare responses to each item listed in Chapter Review.

5. When you are confident that you can meet each objective listed, ask your teacher for the section evaluation.

Chapter Review Questions

1. Why is it important to recognize prejudices and biases? (9.1)
2. What are some things that you can do to show good listening skills? (9.1)
3. Name three communication objectives you should have when talking on the telephone with a client. (9.2)
4. List three things you should do to write a professional e-mail. (9.2)
5. How might a computer be used in a medical or dental office? (9.3)
6. How can you protect you and your patient when working with computers? (9.3)
7. Name the senses you should use when observing a patient. (9.4)
8. Explain why documentation of a client's/patient's care is needed. (9.4)
9. What information should be included on a medical history form? (9.5)
10. What are the four basic procedures common to each filing system? (9.5)

Activities

1. How would you explain to a new employee the legal importance of clear and complete documentation? Create a bulleted list of points to be made.
2. Choose a health care profession. Write an e-mail that the health care worker might write to another employee. Remember to follow the guidelines for writing a professional e-mail.

Case Studies

1. The licensed nurse you are working with has been waiting all morning for a physician to call her back about a patient. Ten minutes after the nurse leaves the facility for a late lunch, you answer the telephone and it is the physician calling her back. Explain in writing what you will say and do.
2. There are many ways in which technology helps health care workers send and receive information. You are describing the functions of the telephone, fax, email system and the Internet to a new employee. How would you illustrate the proper use and appropriate etiquette of each of these tools?

Thinking Critically

1. **Communication**—Describe a recent event in which you or someone else did not use good listening skills. Explain what you or the person you observed could have done differently to demonstrate good listening skills in that situation.
2. **Time Management**—Have you ever thought of good communication as a time saver? Write down the pluses and minuses of taking time to communicate properly. Describe in writing some problems that are caused by failure to communicate properly. Put this list in the personal section of your portfolio to remind you why you should speak with care.
3. **Patient Education**—Explain how you know when patients/clients understand and can do what you have instructed them to do.

Chapter 9 Review

Media Connection

Use the Companion Web site for additional interactive learning activities: www.prenhall.com/badasch

Portfolio Connection

The ability to communicate effectively is essential to successful interactions with others. Your decision to develop effective communication skills directly affects your success or failure in the work world. Your experience in a health occupations program is the perfect place to focus on developing assertive communication skills.

There are many easy-to-read books on assertiveness training that are helpful in learning about and practicing assertiveness. Go to your local library or resource center, and select and read a book that teaches assertive communication skills.

Identify your most common and least common communication type (unassertive, assertive, aggressive). Think of three recent experiences that demonstrate your use of unassertive or aggressive communication. What caused you to respond the way you did? What could you have done or said that would have made your responses assertive? What was the outcome of the unassertive or aggressive communication?

Explain your answer for all three experiences by writing a short paper. Your explanation must clearly identify the unassertive or aggressive statements or actions, indicate what you would change to create an assertive, effective communication, and compare the expected results with those of the unassertive or aggressive communication.

This assignment helps you evaluate the effectiveness of your most frequently used communication skill and allows you to express it in writing. Assertive written communication skills reflect your ability to communicate effectively in the health care environment. Your ability to demonstrate this skill in your portfolio presents you as an appropriate candidate for higher education or job opportunities. Place this assignment in Section Four, "Written Samples."

PORTFOLIO TIP

How you deliver your message in both words and body language may be more important than the message itself: it may decide whether your audience is willing to listen. Think before you speak.

Values are reflected in your body language and your verbal responses. What kind of body language shows that you are kind?

PART II: HEALTH CARE KNOWLEDGE AND SKILLS

10 Medical and Dental Terminology

Courtesy of ShutterStock.

Getting Started

Health care practices and procedures require a special vocabulary that could be considered a second language. Using a list of common medical terms provided by the teacher, watch a health care related television program and circle all of the words that are used by the actors. Define the words that you circled and share with the class in a discussion following the activity. Also discuss whether the medical terms in the program were used accurately.

10.1 Pronunciation, Word Elements, and Terms

Background

Health care workers use medical terminology in their work every day. It is the professional language that helps them communicate effectively and quickly. All care-givers use medical terminology to record orders, write instructions, take notes, and to chart. Health care workers are unable to perform their job if they cannot use and understand medical terminology.

Objectives

When you have completed this section, you will be able to do the following:

- Match key terms with their correct meanings.

- Define roots, prefixes, and suffixes.

- Define the word elements listed.

- Match medical terms with their correct meanings.

- Divide medical terms into elements.

- Combine word elements to form medical terms.

terminology
(ter muh NOL uh jee)
Specialized terms used in any occupation.

 ### Introduction to Medical Terminology

Medical **terminology** can be fun, interesting, and challenging. At first medical terminology may seem hard to learn. However, with practice it becomes easier and easier. You need to learn how to build a medical term, how to pronounce it, and what it means. This section gives you the tools that you need to learn and understand medical terms.

 ### Pronunciation

If you have never heard medical terms pronounced, they may seem very difficult. To make it easier for you, the following are some hints to help you pronounce the terms correctly:

- **ch** sounds like *k*

  Examples: chyme (kīm), cholecystectomy (kō-lə-sis-tek′-tō-mē), chronic (kro-nic), chondroid (kon′-droyd)

- **ps** sounds like *s*

  Examples: psychiatric (sī-kē-a′-trik), pseudomonas (sū-dō-mō′-nas), psychology (sī-kol′-ō-ji), psoriasis (sō-rī′-a-sis)

- **pn** sounds like *n*

  Examples: pneumonia (nū-mō′-ni-a), pneumatic (nū-mat′-ik)

- **c** sounds like a soft *s* when it comes before *e, i,* and *y*

  Examples: cycle (sī-kl), cytoplasm (sī′-tō-plazm), cisternal (sis-ter′-nal), centrifuge (sen′-tri-fūj)

- **g** sounds like *j* when it comes before *e,* i, and *y*

  Examples: giant (jī′-ent), gestation (jes-tā′-shun), generic (jen-er′-ik), gyration (jī-rā′-shun)

- **i** sounds like *eye* when added to the end of the word to form a plural

  Examples: glomeruli (glō-mer′-ū-lī), villi (vil′-lī), alveoli (al-vē′-ō-lī), bacilli (ba-sil′-lī)

Forming Medical Terms from Word Elements

Medical terms are words that consist of several parts. All medical terms have a word root. Most medical terms have the root word and a prefix, a combining vowel, and a suffix. In some cases, the word has only a prefix or suffix added to the root. When you add different prefixes and suffixes to the word root, you change the meaning of the medical term. The combining vowel makes the word easier to pronounce. You build a large medical term vocabulary when you learn the meanings of word parts and how to combine them. (**Figure 10.1**)

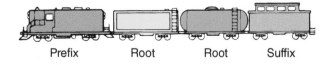

Prefix   Root   Root   Suffix

Figure 10.1
Prefix–Root–Root–Suffix. How is a prefix different from a suffix?

- The *word root* is the main part of the word and tells what the word is about. For instance, *cardio* is the root word that means "heart." This is the subject of the word you are going to build.

- The *prefix* is a word element added to the beginning of a word root. The prefix is added to the root to change the meaning or to make it more specific. The prefix *electro* means "pertaining to electricity."

- The *suffix* is an element added to the end of the word root that changes or adds to the meaning of the root. The suffix *gram* means "record."

- The *combining vowel* makes it possible to combine several word roots. It also makes the word easier to pronounce. (**Figure 10.2**)

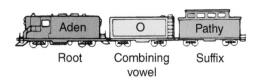

Root   Combining vowel   Suffix

Figure 10.2
Root–Combining vowel–Suffix. What is the role of the combining vowel in the word shown?

When all the previous word elements are combined, the word is *electrocardiogram* (electr/o/cardi/o/gram). It means "an electrical record of the heart."

The following are some examples of (common) English words (**Figure 10.3**):

Combining Word Elements

Prefix	Root	Suffix	Word
pre	heat	ing	preheating
	gentle	ness	gentleness
	speed	o/meter	speedometer

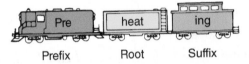

Figure 10.3
Prefix–Root–Suffix. What is the prefix and suffix in the word "Preheating"?

Prefix   Root   Suffix

Rules for Combining Word Elements

Rules help make medical terminology easier to learn. When everyone uses the rules, there are fewer mistakes. A mistake in combining a word can change its meaning and cause confusion.

Combining Vowels

- The combining vowel is usually an *o*, for example, *oste/o*. Oste means "bone," and the *o* is the combining vowel. The *o* can be added to join a word root with another word root or a suffix. Sometimes an *i*, *y*, or *u* is used. Combining vowels make it easier to pronounce the term. For example, *osteomyelitis* is easier to pronounce than *ostemyelitis*.

- When the suffix begins with one of the vowels (*a, e, i, o, u*), the *o* on the root word is not used. Since *oste/o* ends in *o* and the suffix *-itis* begins with a vowel, the *o* is dropped. The word is *osteitis*, which means "inflammation of the bone."

- The combining vowel is placed between root words, for example, *osteoporosis* (oste/o/por/osis). Pronounce the word with the combining vowel, and you can tell that it is easier to say than *osteporosis*.

The following words are examples of word elements that have been combined to form a medical term:

aden/o/pathy	disease of the glands
hepat/o/rrhagia	hemorrhage of the liver
poly/arthr/it is	inflammation of many joints
hyster/ectomy	surgical removal of the uterus
hyster/o/salping/ectomy	surgical removal of the uterus and fallopian tubes
oste/o/por/osis	condition of pores in the bone

After you learn the roots, prefixes, and suffixes, you can combine many word parts to form medical terminology. There is always at least one root word, and there may be more than one root word. When you add a prefix or a suffix you create a new word.

Changing Words from Singular to Plural

- Use the rule for changing words from singular to plural that applies to the language the word comes from; for example, the English word *wavelength* adds an *-s* to become *wavelengths*. Since many medical terms come from Greek or Latin, use the following rules for Greek or Latin words.

- Add an *-e* to a word ending in *-a*—for example, *axilla* to *axillae*.

- Drop the *-ax* at the end of a word and add *-aces*—for example, *thorax* to *thoraces*.

- Change the *-x* to *-g* in a word that ends in *-nx* and add *-es*—for example, *phalanx* to *phalanges*.

- Drop *-ix* or *-ex* at the end of the word and add *-ices*—for example, *appendix* to *appendices*.

- Drop the *-y* at the end of a word and add *-ies*—for example, *myringotomy* to *myringotomies*.

- Drop the *-us* at the end of a word and add an *-i*—for example, *alveolus* to *alveoli*.

- Drop the *-on* at the end of a word and add an *-a*—for example, *ganglion* to *ganglia*.

- Drop the *-is* at the end of a word and add *-es*—for example, *metastasis* to *metastases*.

- Drop the *-um* at the end of a word and add *-a*—for example, *ischium* to *ischia*.

- Drop the *-ma* at the end of the word and add *-mata*—for example, *stoma* to *stomata*.

Common Prefixes, Roots, and Suffixes

When you learn the word elements shown on the following two pages, you have the tools to combine hundreds of medical terms. Learn which words are prefixes, which are roots, and which are suffixes. When you know the terms, it is easy to learn the specialized language of a health care worker.

Understanding Medical Terminology

Knowing prefixes, roots, and suffixes makes it possible to write and decipher common medical and dental terms. For example, if you come across the term *tendonitis*, you can identify the root as *tendon* and the suffix *-itis*. Because this suffix means inflammation, *tendonitis* must describe an inflammation of a tendon.

Now consider the term *arthroscope*. The root is *arthro*, meaning "joint" and the suffix is *-scope*, meaning "picture." An arthroscope is a diagnostic tool that gives physicians a way to take a picture, or form an image, of a structure inside the body, such as a knee.

A related term, *osteoarthritis*, can be interpreted in a similar way. To break this term into parts, find the prefix, root, and suffix. The root is *arthro*, meaning "joint." The prefix is *osteo-*, meaning "bone," and the suffix is *-itis*, meaning "inflammation." By putting the parts of the term together, you can figure out that *osteoarthritis* is an inflammation of the bone's joint.

Apply It

Your teacher will set up two or four teams in class. Organize a word game in which one team creates a medical term, using a prefix, root and suffix. The other team has to guess what the word means, identify the prefix and suffix, and determine if it is a real medical term. Then reverse roles.

Prefix	Meaning
a, an	without
ab	away from
acr, acro	extremities (arms & legs)
ad	toward
ambi	both, both sides
ante	before
anti	against
aut	self
bi	both, two
brady	slow
circum	around
con	with
contra	against
di	two
diplo	double
dors	back
dys	painful, difficult

Prefix	Meaning
ecto	outside
endo	inside, within
epi	upper, above
ex	out from
hemi	half
hyper	excessive, above, more than
hypo	deficient, below, less than
inter	between
intra	inside, within
macro	large
mal	bad
mega	large
meta	between
micro	small
mono	one, single
neo	new

Prefix	Meaning
ortho	straight
pan	all
para	beside, beyond
peri	around
poly	many
post	behind, after
pre	before, in front of
pro	forward
pseudo	false
retro	backward
semi	half
sub	below
super	above
supra	above
tachy	rapid
tele	distant, far
trans	across
ultra	beyond, excess

Root	Meaning
Albino	white
acro	extremities
aden	gland
angio	vessel (blood)
ankyl	crooked, looped
arterio	artery
arthro	joint
aud, aur	ear, hearing
bio	life
blepharo	eyelid
brachi	arm
bronchi	bronchial
bucca	cheek
carcin	cancer
cardio	heart
caud	tail
cephal	head
cerebro	brain
cervic	neck
cheil	lip
chem.	chemistry, drug
chole	bile
cholecyst	gallbladder
(c)hondro	cartilage

Root	Meaning
chrom	color
coccus	round
col/colo	colon
colp	vagina
costo	ribs
cranio	skull
cut	skin
cyan	blue
cysto	bladder, sac
cyt, cyte	cell
dacry	Tear duct
dactyl	fingers, toes
dent	tooth
derma	skin
dextr	right
duoden	duodenum
echo	sound
edema	swelling
electr	electric
embry	fertilized ovum/ embryo
emesis	vomit
enter	intestine
epidemic	among the people

Root	Meaning
erythro	red
esophag	esophagus
esthesi	feeling
faci	face
fascia	band, fibrous
gastro	stomach
genit	related to birth
gingiva	gum
gloss	tongue
gyne	woman
hemo	blood
hepat	liver
holo	all
hom	same, alike
hydro	water
hygien	healthful
hystero	uterus, womb
iri	iris (eye)
kerat	cornea, scaly
labia	lip
lacrim	tear
lacto	milk
lapar	abdomen
laryng	larynx

Root	Meaning	Root	Meaning	Root	Meaning
leuko	white	oo	egg	pyo	pus
lingua	tongue	oophoro	ovary	ren	kidney
lip	fat	ophthal	eye	rhin	nose
lith	stone	orchis	testes	salpingo	tube
lymph	fluid	osteo	bone	semin	seed
mamm, mast	breast	oto	ear, hearing	sept	infection
melan	black	ovario	ovary	soma	body
mening	membrane (pertaining to the covering of the brain or spinal cord)	ovi	egg	splen	spleen
		part	birth, labor	spondyl	spine
		ped, pod	foot	squam	scaly
		ped	child	stoma	mouth
meno, mens	menstruate	phagia	swallow	stric	narrowing
myelo	bone marrow	pharyng	pharynx	therm	heat
myo	muscle	phasia	speak	thorac	thorax
nares	nose, nostrils	phleb	vein	thrombo	clot
necr	death	pleur	pleura of the lung	trachi	trachea
nephro/ren	kidney	pneumo	lung	vas	vessel
neuro	nerve	procto	rectum	vesic	bladder, sac
ocul	eye	psycho	mind, soul	viscera	organ
odont	tooth	pulm	lung	vit	life
onc	tumor	pyelo	pelvis of the kidney		

Suffix	Meaning	Suffix	Meaning	Root	Meaning
a, ac	pertaining to	iasis	abnormal condition	penia	deficiency
able	capable of			pexy	fixation
al	like, similar, pertaining to	ic, ical, is	pertaining to	phobia	fear
		ism	state of	plasty	surgical repair
algia	pain	itis	inflammation	plegia	paralysis
ase	enzyme	lysis	destruction	ptosis	drooping down
cele	hernia	malacia	softening	rhagia	bursting forth
cente	puncture	megaly	enlarged	sarcoma	tumor, cancer
cide	causing death	oid	like, similar	sclerosis	hardening
crine	secrete	ologist	person who studies	scope	picture, inspection
desis	surgical fixation			spasm	contraction
ectomy	surgical removal	ology	study of	stasis	stoppage
emesis	vomit	oma	tumor	trophy	development growth
emia	blood	orrhagia	hemorrhage		
esthesis	sensation	orrhaphy	suture	um	pertaining to
genesis, genic	source, origin	orrhea	flow	uria	urine
gram, graph	pictures	osis	condition of	y	the act of or result of an action
ia	a disease; an unhealthy state or condition	ostomy	surgical opening		
		otomy	incision into		
		pathy	disease		

π *Math Link*

Metric Prefixes

In the United States, most everyday measurements are made using standard units such as ounces, pounds, and feet. In the medical industry, however, many measurements are made in metric units. The meter (m), gram (g), and liter (L) are basic metric units. The metric system is a system of measurement that is based on 10, which greatly simplifies calculations. By multiplying or dividing by 10, a new metric unit can be reached.

Different metric units can be identified by their prefixes. The basic metric prefixes are listed in the next column.

If you recognize the prefix, you immediately know information about the given measurement. For example, 1 *kilo*meter equals 1,000 meters, while 1 *milli*meter equals one thousandth of a meter.

You may often need to convert from one unit to another. Converting between units is accomplished by moving the decimal point. Look at the decimal

Prefix	Symbol	Exponent Form	Decimal Equivalent
kilo-	k	10^3	1000
hecto-	h	10^2	100
deka-	da	10	10
—	—	—	—
deci-	d	10^{-1}	0.1
centi-	c	10^{-2}	0.01
milli-	m	10^{-3}	0.001

relationships in the chart. For example, suppose you are given a measurement of 1.5 kilograms, but you need the measurement in grams. To convert from kilograms to grams, move the decimal three places to the right (see exponent form above). So 1.5 kilograms is equal to 1,500 grams.

How many milliliters are in 25 liters?

Look at the following terms, their parts, and their meanings.

Term	Prefix	Root	Suffix	Meaning
arteriosclerosis		*arterio*, meaning artery	*-sclerosis*, meaning hardening	Condition in which deposits on the artery walls cause them to harden
bicuspid	*bi-*, meaning two	*cuspid*, meaning sharp point		Having two points or cusps
bronchitis		*bronchi*, meaning bronchial tubes leading into the lungs	*-itis*, meaning inflammation	Inflammation of the bronchial tubes
fibromyalgia	*fibro-*, meaning fiber	*myo*, meaning muscle	*-algia*, meaning pain	A condition involving pain in the muscle fibers
hyperventilation	*hyper-*, meaning excessive or above	*ventilation*, meaning breathing		An excessive rate of breathing
hypothyroidism	*hypo-*, meaning below or less than	*thyroid*, relating to the thyroid gland	*-ism*, meaning pertaining to	Pertaining to an underactive thyroid gland
mammogram		*mamm*, meaning breast	*-gram*, meaning picture	Image formed to examine breast tissue
ophthalmology		*opthal*, meaning eye	*-ology*, meaning study of	Study of the eye
otosclerosis	*oto-*, meaning ear or hearing		*-sclerosis*, meaning hardening	A progressive condition that can result in hearing loss
postpartum	*post-*, meaning after	*part*, meaning birth or labor	*-um*, meaning pertaining to	Pertaining to the period after giving birth

How to Use Medical Terminology

Medical terminology provides a system for health workers to communicate with each other. When a patient complains to the doctor about a "pain in the stomach," it can mean many different things. Often the patient is referring to pain in the lower abdominal cavity and not the stomach. For instance, the patient may be assuming that "the stomach" is the entire area between the ribs and the pelvis.

The doctor must ask exactly where the pain is, how it feels, how long it has been a problem, and other questions. After making a diagnosis the primary case provider must be able to tell the health care workers exactly what the problem is. When the entire health care team understands the problem they can treat the patient in the most effective way.

The patient in the above situation could have any of the following or any number of other problems:

- Gastritis.
- Gastralgia.
- Hepatitis.
- Ileitis.
- Appendicitis.
- Colitis.
- Pancreatitis.
- Diverticulitis.

Language Arts Link

Health Terms Dictionary

Sometimes a step towards learning a new vocabulary term is to actually write it out yourself, rather than just reading it in a textbook or looking it up in the dictionary. As you work through this course, it may be beneficial to create your own dictionary of terms and definitions.

If you have access to a computer, you can sort the terms alphabetically as you enter them. This will make looking up terms easier. If you do not have computer access, you can use a small notebook to make your dictionary.

Go back through the first nine chapters in this text and enter the key terms and definitions in your dictionary. Continue making entries as you complete the course. After you've completed your dictionary, you will have that as a reference tool as you continue your health care studies.

 ## Summary

Medical terminology is formed by using three components: prefixes, roots, and suffixes. To make the words easier to pronounce, a combining vowel such as *i, o, y,* or *u* may be used. In this section, you memorized many word elements to help you be a better prepared health care worker.

What's New?

Over-the-Counter Drug Labels

Many drugs are available without a prescription. Labels on these drugs, known as over-the-counter drugs (OTCs), are regulated by the U.S. Food and Drug Administration. Their goal is to make sure that the information on the label clearly states the directions so that a person can choose the right medication to treat symptoms and use the medication correctly.

At one time, labels varied greatly among manufacturers and medications, and label information was often difficult to understand for people not in the medical profession. In 1999, a new regulation required OTC drug manufacturers to use a new, standardized label on all products.

Along with a standardized format, the new drug label uses common terms instead of confusing medical terminology to describe each OTC drug. The new label also requires a type size that is large enough to be easily read, along with added spacing between lines and clearly marked sections to make the label clearer.

Thanks to this law, Drug Facts labels must now list information in the same order, as outlined below. A person should always read every section carefully before taking, or giving, a medicine as each section contains valuable information.

Active Ingredients—This section lists the ingredient or ingredients that make the product work. It is especially important for people taking more than one medicine to make sure that they are not taking too much of the same active ingredient.

Purpose—This section describes the type, or category, of medicine. For example, it might be an antacid or antihistamine.

Uses—This section outlines the symptoms or illnesses for which the product should be used.

Warnings—This section points out situations in which the medicine should not be used. It also indicates when a doctor or other health care professional needs to be consulted, any possible side effects, and when to stop using the product.

Directions—This section describes exactly how and when to use the product. It might also provide amounts to be taken depending on weight or age.

Other Information—This section contains information about how to store the product along with additional information about certain ingredients. This information includes the amount of calcium, potassium, or sodium the product contains.

Inactive Ingredients—This section lists ingredients that are in the product but do not treat the symptoms. This information is particularly important to people with known allergies.

The label of an OTC drug should be checked each time the drug is purchased and used, as manufacturers sometimes change their products and/or labeling. If there is change in a product, a flag or banner is often placed on the front of the package to alert you.

What section of a drug label should you read if you want to know how often to take a medicine?

1. What does it mean to pronounce a medical term?

2. How are prefixes and suffixes used to build medical terms?

3. What is the *o* called in the word adenopathy? Why is it used?

4. How can you change a term ending in *-a* to make it plural?

5. What root word relates to the brain?

6. What is the suffix in the term *endocrinology*? What does it mean?

Learn By Doing: Section 10.1 Activity

1. Complete Worksheet/Activity 1 as assigned.

2. Complete Worksheet 2 and Worksheet/Activity 3 as assigned.

3. Complete Worksheet 4.

4. When you are confident that you can meet each objective listed above, ask your teacher for the section evaluation.

SECTION

10.2 Abbreviations

Background

Health care workers use abbreviations to convey information about their patients/clients. Abbreviations help save time and save space on medical documents.

Objectives

When you have completed this section, you will be able to do the following:

- Match key terms with their correct meanings.

- Replace terms with abbreviations.

- Recognize and define abbreviations that are commonly used by health care workers.

Apply It

Play a medical version of charades. List some of the following abbreviations on a 3 × 5 card. A student selects a card and has to act out the abbreviation, while the rest of the class will guess the meaning.

Vocabulary Sidebar

abbreviations
(uh bree vee AY shun)
Words that have been shortened.

concisely
(kuhn SICE lee)
In a brief manner; to express in a few words.

 # Introduction to Abbreviations

Abbreviations are the shortened form of words. They are an efficient way of communicating quickly and **concisely** with other health care workers. You must be very careful when you use abbreviations.

Always use standard abbreviations. Never make up an abbreviation. Doing so is confusing and will be a problem if a record is used in a legal action, because no one will understand what you wrote. Never use an abbreviation if you are unsure about its meaning. It is better to write out the word so that it is easily understood.

Be considerate about when you use an abbreviation. Your patients/clients do not know what the abbreviations mean. For instance, *NPO* posted over the bed means "nothing by mouth." You know what it means, but you should always explain it to your patient/client. The following abbreviations are the most common abbreviations that health care workers use.

Abbreviation	Meaning
@	at
abd.	Abdomen
ABG	Arterial Blood Gas
a.c.	before meals
ADL	activities of daily living
ad lib	as desired
adm	admission
am/AM	morning (midnight to noon)
amb	ambulate/walk
amt.	amount
approx.	approximately
AIDS	acquired immune deficiency syndrome
ASA	aspirin
ASAP	as soon as possible
ASHD	Arteriosclerotic Heart Disease
AU	both ears
ax	axillary, armpit
BE	barium enema
bid/BID	twice a day
bm/BM	bowel movement
B/P/BP	blood pressure
BR, br	bed rest
BRP	bathroom privileges
BS	blood sugar
bx	biopsy
°C	Celsius degree, centigrade
c̄	with

Abbreviation	Meaning
CA	cancer
Ca	calcium
CAT	Computerized Axial Tomography
cath.	catheter
CBC	complete blood count
CC	chief complaint
cc	cubic centimeters
CCU	coronary care unit
CHF	Congestive Heart Failure
Cl	chloride
cl liq	clear liquids
cm	centimeters
c/o	complains of
CO₂	carbon dioxide
COPD	Chronic Obstructive Pulmonary Disease
CPR	cardiopulmonary resuscitation
CS	central supply
CVA	cerebrovascular accident/stroke
D&C	dilatation and curettage
dc, d/c	discontinue
Del. Rm.	delivery room
Diff	differential white count
DNR	do not resuscitate
DOA	dead on arrival
DOB	date of birth
DON	director of nursing

Abbreviation	Meaning
Dr.	doctor
dsg	dressing
dx	diagnosis
D/W	dextrose in water
ECG/EKG	electrocardiogram
EEG	electroencephalogram
EENT	eye, ear, nose, and throat
ER	emergency room
Exc	excision
Exp	exploratory
°F	Fahrenheit degree
FBS	fasting blood sugar
Fe	iron
FF	force fluid
Fl or fl	fluid
ft	foot
FUO	fever of unknown origin
fx	fracture
GB	gallbladder
Gm	gram
g	gram
GI	gastrointestinal
gr	grain
gtt	drop
GU	genitourinary
Gyn	gynecology
H	Hydrogen
H_2O	water, aqua
HA	headache
HBV	hepatitis B virus
Hct	hematocrit
Hg	mercury
Hgb	hemoglobin
HOB	head of bed
hr	hour
hs	bedtime, hour of sleep
ht	height
hyper	above, high
hypo	below, low
ICU	intensive care unit

Abbreviation	Meaning
I & D	incision and drainage
I & O	intake and output
IM	intramuscular
inj	injection
int	internal, interior
irrig	irrigation
IV	intravenous
IVP	intravenous pyelogram
K	potassium
KCL	potassium chloride
Kg or kg	kilogram
KUB	kidney, ureter and bladder x-ray
L & D	labor and delivery
Ⓛ	left
L	left/liter
lab	laboratory
Lap	laparotomy
lb	pound
liq.	Liquid
LLQ	left lower quadrant
LP	lumbar puncture
LPN	licensed practical nurse
LUQ	left upper quadrant
LVN	licensed vocational nurse
M	minim
M.D.	medical doctor
med.	Medicine
mEq	millequivalent
mg	milligram
MI	Myocardial Infarction
ML	milliliter
mm	millimeter
MRI	magnetic resonance Imaging
min.	minute
Na	sodium
NA	nurse aide/nursing assistant
NaCl	sodium chloride
ng	nasogastric tube
noct, noc.	night
NPO	nothing by mouth

Abbreviation	Meaning
N/S	normal saline
N&V	nausea and vomiting
O_2	oxygen
O&P	ova and parasites
Ob	obstetrics
Od	overdose
OD	right eye
OOB/oob	out of bed
OPD	outpatient department
OR	operating room
OS	left eye
ord.	orderly
ORTH	orthopedics
O.T.	occupational therapy
OU	both eyes
oz	ounce
PAP	Papanicolaou smear
Path	pathology
pc	after meals
PDR	Physician's Desk Reference
PEDS	pediatrics
per	by, through
pH	measure of acidity/alkalinity
PID	pelvic inflammatory disease
pm/PM	afternoon (noon to midnight)
po	by mouth
post	after
postop, PostOp	postoperative
pre	before
preop, PreOp	before surgery
prn	whenever necessary, when required
Pt, pt	patient
P.T.	physical therapy
$\bar{q}$	every
qd	every day
qh	every hour
q2h	every 2 hours
q3h	every 3 hours
q4h	every 4 hours
qhs	every night at bedtime
qid, QID	four times a day

Abbreviation	Meaning
qod/QOD	every other day
qs	quantity sufficient
qt	quart
R	respiration or rectal
r	rectal
®	right
RBC	red blood cell
RLQ	right lower quadrant
RN	registered nurse
R/O	rule out
ROM	range of motion
R.R.	recovery room
RT	respiratory therapy
RUQ	right upper quadrant
R_x	prescription or treatment ordered by a physician
$\bar{s}$	without
SIDS	sudden infant death syndrome
sob	short of breath
spec.	specimen
sp gr	specific gravity
$\overline{ss}$	one half
SSE	soap solution enema
stat	at once, immediately
surg.	surgery
T&A	tonsils and adenoids
TB	tuberculosis
tbsp	tablespoon
TIA	transient ischemic attack
TID/tid	three times a day
TLC	tender loving care
TPR	temperature, pulse, and respiration
tsp	teaspoon
tx	traction
UA or U/A	urinalysis
URI	upper respiratory infection
UTI	urinary tract infection
VS	vital signs
WBC	white blood count
w/c	wheelchair
wt	weight

Abbreviation	Meaning	Abbreviation	Meaning
x	times (2x is 2 times)	I	one
x-match	cross match	V	five
>	greater than	X	ten
<	less than	L	fifty
□	increase, elevate, higher	C	one hundred
↓	decrease, lower	D	five hundred
#	number or pound sign	M	one thousand

 ## Summary

Health care workers use abbreviations to help communicate quickly and effectively. Abbreviations are the shortened form of words and help reduce the time needed to chart important information. You have learned the most commonly used abbreviations; however, in your work experience you may find other abbreviations that are not listed here. Never assume that any of the above abbreviations are acceptable in your place of employment. A list of acceptable abbreviations for the organization will be provided for you during the job orientation process.

Community Service

Plan an afternoon at a local pharmacy. See how the pharmacist or pharmacist's assistant explains prescription instructions to people picking them up. Offer to hand out a patient-friendly form that explains the meaning of the abbreviations used on the prescription label.

SECTION 10.2 Review Questions

1. What is an abbreviation?

2. Why are abbreviations used in medical professions?

3. A doctor writes the following order for a patient: BR. What should the patient do?

4. What abbreviation might indicate that a patient should take in liquids only?

5. If a patient is in the R.R., in what part of the hospital is the patient located?

6. What does TID/tid stand for on a prescription bottle?

 ### Learn By Doing: Section 10.2 Activity

1. Complete Worksheet/Activity 1 as assigned.

2. Complete Worksheets 2 through 4.

3. Prepare responses to each item listed in Chapter Review.

4. When you are confident that you can meet each objective listed above, ask your teacher for the section evaluation.

Personal Wellness

Understanding Medical Prescriptions

As part of medical treatment, a health care provider may need to write a prescription for a patient. A prescription is a physician's order for the preparation and administration of a drug or device for a patient.

The word *prescription* comes from the Latin *praescriptus*, which is made up of the prefix *prae-*, meaning "before," and the root *scribere*, meaning "to write." A prescription must be written before certain drugs can be prepared and administered to patients.

Some health care providers write prescriptions on paper. Others input information into a computer template. Regardless of the format, all prescriptions have several basic parts:

- The *superscription* (or heading) with the symbol R or Rx, which stands for the Latin word *recipe*, meaning "to take"

- The *inscription*, which contains the names and quantities of the substances to be taken

- The *subscription*, which gives directions for compounding the drug

- The *signature*, which is often preceded by the letter *s*

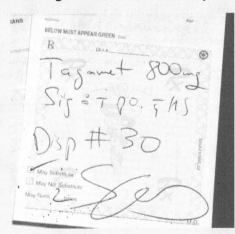

Health care providers use many abbreviations when writing prescriptions. These abbreviations are translated into common English by pharmacists when the prescription is filled.

However, it is important to understand the prescription as it is written in order to confirm that it has been filled correctly and that the directions have been translated properly. In some cases, it could mean the difference between life and death.

In addition to the abbreviations listed in this section, several additional common abbreviations found on prescriptions and their meanings are listed below:

caps = capsules

da or daw = dispense as written

g (or gm or GM) = gram

gtt. = drops (from "guttae," drops)

h. = hour

mg = milligram

ml = milliliter

tabs = tablets

ut dict. = as directed (from "ut dictum," as directed)

What does it mean if a prescription says 2 tabs q.4h?

Chapter 10 Review

Chapter Review Questions

1. What is medical terminology? (10.1)

2. Identify the combining vowel in the term *osteoporosis*. (10.1)

3. Write a word with the prefix *anti-*. (10.1)

4. To what part of a root word is the suffix added? (10.1)

5. Which letters can be used as combining vowels? Which letter is most commonly used? (10.1)

6. What is *osteoporosis*? (10.1)

7. How do you make the word *ganglion* plural? (10.1)

8. What is the meaning of the root *dent*? (10.1)

9. What abbreviation might you use when telling time? (10.2)

10. What does the abbreviation *bid* mean when written on a prescription? (10.2)

Activities

1. Use research materials to find five medical terms not presented in this chapter. Write each term and identify any prefixes, roots, and suffixes. Give the meaning of each part of the word and combine the parts to define the term. Fill in a table like the one below with the information you gather.

Term	Prefix	Root	Suffix	Meaning
1.				
2.				
3.				
4.				
5.				

2. As you go through a day, pay attention to any abbreviations you encounter. Keep a record of as many as you can. Define each abbreviation and think about how using the abbreviation is useful.

3. Rewrite the words to a favorite song or poem, such as the camp song Dry Bones or Hokey Pokey, using medical terminology.

Case Studies

1. It has been a long day and your shift is almost over. You are in a hurry to finish your charting and cannot remember some of the abbreviations you are expected to use. You can think of several ways to shorten words that you are using. Is it a good idea to use abbreviations that you make up? Explain what you should do and why.

2. You have several co-workers who have English as their second language. They are having problems learning and understanding medical terminology. They cannot interpret certain terms and are unfamiliar with some common abbreviations. How should you go about helping your coworkers to be more productive?

Chapter 10 Review

Thinking Critically

1. **Communication**—You have a patient who is complaining of multiple symptoms. Write a description of these symptoms using medical terminology so that your supervisor understands what the patient is experiencing. The symptoms include headache, vomiting, stomach pain, and excessive perspiration.

2. **Computers**—Be aware that clients may research their diagnosis on the Internet. Make a list of both the helpful and challenging outcomes of this possibility. Think of some examples of how this could affect a health occupation aide and write them down for your portfolio.

3. **Patient Education**—Take a medical condition, such as osteoporosis or polyarthritis, and write an explanation of the disease assuming that the client you are helping has a limited understanding of English.

Media Connection

Use the Companion Web site for additional interactive learning activities: www.prenhall.com/badasch

Portfolio Connections

Imagine that you are the instructor of a medical occupation class. You want your students to learn to communicate effectively in the health care environment. Create five assignments for your students to complete. Use the information in the medical terminology and abbreviation sections. Look at the objectives in your textbook to guide you in developing what you want your students to accomplish in the assignment. Develop worksheets and evaluations. Provide clear directions for the student. An employer is interested in your ability to use in a meaningful way the new information you have learned. This exercise for your portfolio develops your skills in organizing what you are learning.

PORTFOLIO TIP

Remember that your clients are not experts in medical terminology and may not understand the abbreviations that you and your colleagues use. Try to use everyday language when talking to clients and getting feedback from them. If you are giving an important instruction or explanation, check to be sure they have understood your comments.

11 Medical Math

Getting Started

Measure the length or width of a variety of different items in and around the classroom. You can include the height of the desk, the width of a chair, the height of a doorway, the length of the chalkboard, the width of a textbook, etc. Then convert these measurements to the metric system.

Next, identify items by their metric measurements; for example, find something that is 32 cm long or find something that is 1m high. Then, convert these measurements to the customary U.S. units.

SECTION

11.1 Math Review

Background

Health care workers are required to perform simple math calculations when doing various tasks. Knowing basic math concepts and knowing when to apply them are essential skills for all health care workers. To be a successful health care worker, you should know how to add, subtract, convert standard figures into metric figures, calculate percentages, and manipulate fractions.

Because math skills are critical to success in all health care jobs, this chapter begins with a math skills review. Even if you are confident about your basic math skills, it is worthwhile to take the math pretest in the Student Activity Guide as a skills check. This can help pinpoint areas you may need to review.

Objectives

When you have completed this section, you will be able to do the following:

- Match key terms with their correct meanings.
- Add and subtract whole numbers, decimals, and percentages.
- Multiply and divide whole numbers, fractions, mixed numbers, decimals, and percentages.
- Convert decimals to percentages and percentages to decimals.

Introduction to the Math Review

Some students have not used math for a long time. This section will help you accurately apply basic math concepts and skills necessary to your success as a health care worker. Take the pretest in the Student Activity Guide (Worksheet 1). If you pass it with 100 percent, skip this section. If you do not get 100 percent, read through this section and complete all Student Activity Guide assignments.

Learn By Doing: Section 11.1 Activity

1. Read the following information on numbers.
2. Complete Worksheet 2.

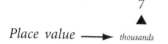 Numbers

Numbers are expressed in different forms:

- Whole numbers.
- Mixed numbers.
- Nonwhole numbers.
- Percentages.

Numbers that have more than one digit are defined by their place value. For example, the number 7777 is given the following values:

Place value ⟶   7 thousands   7 hundreds   7 tens   7 ones

This number is described by saying "seven thousand, seven hundred seventy-seven." Numbers are written with a comma placed to the left of every third digit. The number 7777 is properly written "7,777." The number 22222 is given the following place values:

Place value ⟶   2 ten thousands   2, thousands   2 hundreds   2 tens   2 ones

It is written "22,222" and described as "twenty-two thousand, two hundred twenty-two."

Numbers indicating less than a whole number are placed to the right of a decimal. The number 7,777.255 is given the following place values:

It is written "7,777.255" and described as "seven thousand, seven hundred seventy-seven and two hundred and fifty-five thousandths."

Place value ⟶   7, thousands   7 hundreds   7 tens   7. ones   2 tenths   5 hundredths   5 thousandths

Whole Numbers

Whole numbers are the counting numbers and zero. Whole numbers do not contain decimals or fractions. *Examples*: 1, 2, 3, 10, 15, 18, 0. Ignore zeros before whole numbers. *Example*: 025 → Ø25 and is written "25."

Nonwhole Numbers

Nonwhole numbers are numbers that have decimals. *Examples*: 7,777.255, 12.25, 5.9.

Mixed Numbers

Mixed numbers are whole numbers and a fraction. Examples: $12^1/_4$ or $45^3/_4$.

whole numbers
(HOHL NUHM bers)
Numbers that do not contain decimals or fractions (e.g., 1, 2, 3).

nonwhole numbers
(non HOHL NUHM bers)
Numbers with decimals (e.g., 6.25, 9.85).

mixed numbers
(mikst NUHM bers)
Numbers with whole numbers and a fraction (e.g., $6^1/_4$, $7^2/_3$).

percentages
(per SEN tij es)
Portions in relation to a whole (e.g., 65%, 22%).

Percentages

The word *percent* means "by the hundred"; 100 percent = the whole or all of something. The symbol for percent is %. (**Figure 11.1**) *Example:* Four turtles = 100% or all of the turtles present. When one turtle is sold, ¹/₄ (one-fourth) or 25% of them are gone and ³/₄ (three-fourths) or 75% are left.

FIGURE 11.1

Percentages. If there were five turtles in the figure, what percentage would one turtle represent?

Four turtles = 100%.

One turtle or 25% of the turtles are sold.

Three turtles or 75% of the turtles are left.

Learn By Doing: Section 11.1 Activity

1. Read the following information on addition and subtraction.

2. Complete Worksheet 3.

Addition

Addition is the totaling of two or more numbers. For example, 2 computers in the reception area + 3 computers in accounting = a total of 5 computers in the office. To add, place numbers in columns. Put a line under the last number in the column. Add all the numbers above the line and write the total or sum of the numbers below the line.

Examples:

```
           2      34
         + 3     + 4
Total      5      38
```

When adding more than one column of numbers, always keep the numbers in each column in a line under each other. This helps you add the correct numbers together. Always start adding numbers in the right column first.

Example:

11 + 234 + 10 + 4 is written like this:

```
   11
  234
   10
 +  4
 259
```

When figuring numbers that total more than 10 in a column, it is necessary to carry numbers to the left of the column being added. In the next example, the first column of 1 + 4 + 0 + 9 = 14. In the total, the number to the left of the 4 is 1. Move or carry the 1 to the column at the left and add it to the top number of that column (8), then add the remaining numbers in the column, $1 + 8 + 8 + 1 = 18$. The number to the left of the 8 is 1. Move or carry the 1 to the column at the left and add it to the top number of that column (3), then add the remaining numbers in the column, $1 + 3 = 4$. The total is 484. (See the examples that follow.)

Example 1:

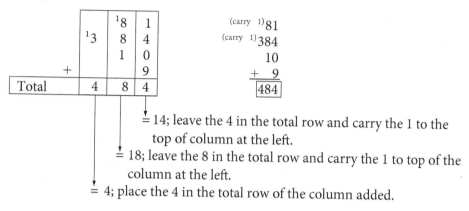

= 14; leave the 4 in the total row and carry the 1 to the top of column at the left.

= 18; leave the 8 in the total row and carry the 1 to top of the column at the left.

= 4; place the 4 in the total row of the column added.

Example 2:

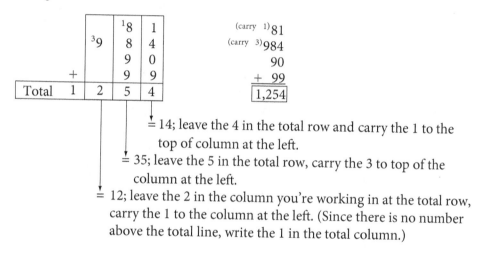

= 14; leave the 4 in the total row and carry the 1 to the top of column at the left.

= 35; leave the 5 in the total row, carry the 3 to top of the column at the left.

= 12; leave the 2 in the column you're working in at the total row, carry the 1 to the column at the left. (Since there is no number above the total line, write the 1 in the total column.)

Subtraction

Subtraction is the opposite of addition. Subtracting numbers means taking a number away from another number. Simple subtraction problems are written in the following way:

subtraction
(suhb TRAK shuhn)
Taking a number away from another number; the operation opposite of addition.

$$\begin{array}{r} 84 \\ -\ 23 \\ \hline \boxed{61} \end{array} \quad \text{or} \quad 84 - 23 = \boxed{61} \qquad \begin{array}{r} 136 \\ -\ 12 \\ \hline \boxed{124} \end{array} \quad \text{or} \quad 136 - 12 = \boxed{124}$$

Check your answer by adding the answer to the number subtracted. If your answer is correct, your total will equal the number at the top of your problem.

Examples:

$$\begin{array}{r} 84 \\ -\ \boxed{23} \\ \hline \boxed{+61} \end{array} \xrightarrow{\text{check}} = \bigcirc{84} \qquad \text{or } 23 + 61 = \bigcirc{84} \qquad \begin{array}{r} 136 \\ -\ \boxed{12} \\ \hline \boxed{+124} \end{array} \xrightarrow{\text{check}} = \bigcirc{136} \qquad \text{or } 12 + 124 = \bigcirc{136}$$

Subtracting by Borrowing Numbers

Borrow a number from the column to the left. This allows a larger number, such as 8, to be subtracted from 5. See the following examples to help you understand.

Examples:

$$\begin{array}{r} {}^2\cancel{3}\,{}^1 5 \\ -\ 1\ \ 8 \\ \hline \boxed{1\ \ 7} \end{array}$$ 5 becomes 15 when 1 is borrowed from the 3
3 becomes 2

$$\begin{array}{r} {}^1\cancel{2}\,{}^{16}7\,{}^1\cancel{2} \\ -\ 1\ \ 9\ \ 5 \\ \hline \boxed{\cancel{0}\ \ 7\ \ 7} \end{array}$$ 2 becomes 12 when 1 is borrowed from the 7
7 becomes 6 because you borrowed 1; 6 becomes 16
when 1 is borrowed from the 2; 2 becomes 1

Learn By Doing: Section 11.1 Activity

1. Read the following information on multiplication.

2. Complete Worksheet/Activity 4.

Multiplication

multiplication
(muhl tuh pli KEY shuhn)
Finding the product of two numbers.

Multiplication is a quick, easy way to add. For example, 9 + 9 + 9 = 27, but an easier process is 3 × 9 = 27. Adding large numbers is bulky and takes a lot of time. Multiplication is much easier.

To multiply numbers easily, memorize the multiplication table. (Table 11.1) Memorizing this table allows you to calculate numbers quickly and without difficulty. You probably already know the basics of multiplication. Review the table below and test yourself by completing Worksheet 1, pretest in your Student Activity Guide. For instructions on how to read a multiplication table see Worksheet 4 in your Student Activity Guide.

The following symbols are used to indicate multiplication: ×, ()(), ·, or *. These symbols are used in writing problems. *Examples:*

$$\begin{array}{r} 8 \\ \times 9 \\ \hline 72 \end{array}$$ or 8 × 9 = 72 or 8 · 9 = 72 or (8) (9) = 72 or 8 * 9 = 72

Using calculators is helpful when figuring complicated calculations; however, you are responsible for knowing how to calculate numbers without a calculator. Most of the calculations in your work are simple and easy to figure without the use of a calculator. Do not use a calculator to work through your worksheets.

π Math Link

Adding and Subtracting Decimals and Fractions

Decimals

For decimals, the process of adding and subtracting numbers is similar to the process for adding and subtracting whole numbers. The only difference is how the numbers are aligned in the column. Numbers should be aligned by the decimal point as in the following examples:

```
  12.136
+ 10.246
  22.382
```

```
  23.453
- 10.37
  13.083
```

Fractions

A fraction is made up of two parts: a numerator, which is the number on top, and a denominator, or the number on the bottom. To add or subtract a fraction, the denominator must be the same. Consider the following examples:

Example 1:

$$\frac{1}{4} + \frac{3}{4} = \frac{1+3}{4} = \frac{4}{4} = \frac{1}{1} = 1$$

Example 2:

$$\frac{1}{5} + \frac{2}{5} + 12\frac{4}{5} = \frac{1}{5} + \frac{2}{5} + \frac{64}{5} = \frac{1+2+64}{5} = \frac{67}{5} = 13\frac{3}{5}$$

Example 3:

$$\frac{2}{3} - \frac{1}{3} = \frac{2-1}{3} = \frac{1}{3}$$

Note that Example 1 shows a simplified fraction, or a fraction that does not have any common factors (other than 1) for the numerator and denominator. Example 2 shows a mixed number, which is converted to a fraction to be added or subtracted.

In some cases, fractions will need to be converted so each fraction being added has a common denominator. Consider the following example:

$$\frac{1}{3} + \frac{1}{2} = ?$$

Step 1: Convert each fraction so they have a common denominator.

The denominators, 2 and 3, are factors of 6, so multiply both the nominator and the denominator of each fraction by the number that makes the denominator equal to 6.

$$\frac{1}{3} \times \frac{2}{2} = \frac{2}{6}$$

$$\frac{1}{2} \times \frac{3}{3} = \frac{3}{6}$$

Step 2: Add fractions.

$$\frac{2}{6} + \frac{3}{6} = \frac{5}{6}$$

For subtraction, follow the same process to make fractions that have the same denominator. Simplify fractions after adding and subtracting as needed.

Step 1: Convert each fraction so they have a common denominator.

$$\frac{3}{4} \times \frac{1}{3} = \frac{3}{12}$$

$$\frac{1}{4} \times \frac{1}{3} = \frac{1}{12}$$

Step 2: Subtract fractions.

$$\frac{3}{12} - \frac{1}{12} = \frac{2}{12}$$

Add or subtract the following:

3.45 + 2.34 + 5.6

$$3\frac{3}{4} + \frac{2}{3} + \frac{4}{5}$$

3.4 − 1.28

$$2\frac{3}{4} - 1\frac{1}{3}$$

What will happen if you don't convert fractions to a common denominator before adding or subtracting them?

Table 11.1   Multiplication Table

	1	2	3	4	5	6	7	8	9	10
1	1	2	3	4	5	6	7	8	9	10
2	2	4	6	8	10	12	14	16	18	20
3	3	6	9	12	15	18	21	24	27	30
4	4	8	12	16	20	24	28	32	36	40
5	5	10	15	20	25	30	35	40	45	50
6	6	12	18	24	30	36	42	48	54	60
7	7	14	21	28	35	42	49	56	63	70
8	8	16	24	32	40	48	56	64	72	80
9	9	18	27	36	45	54	63	72	81	90
10	10	20	30	40	50	60	70	80	90	100

numerators
(NOO muh rey ters)
The top numbers of
fractions.

denominators
(di NOM uh ney ters)
The bottom numbers of
fractions.

Multiplying Fractions

Like a whole or nonwhole number, fractions can be multiplied. The **numerators**, or top numbers of the fractions, are multiplied; and the **denominators**, or bottom numbers of the fractions, are multiplied. For example:

$$\frac{3}{4} \times \frac{12}{15} = \frac{3 \times 12}{4 \times 15} = \frac{36}{60} = \frac{3}{5}$$

To reduce the fraction

$$\frac{36}{60} \text{ to } \frac{3}{5}$$

you must divide the numerator and denominator by the largest number that goes into both—in this case, 12.

Note that the final answer for the example above is simplified. For mixed numbers, convert the number to a fraction for multiplication. For example:

$$1\frac{3}{4} \times 2\frac{2}{3} = \frac{7}{4} \times \frac{8}{3} = \frac{56}{12} = 4\frac{8}{12} = 4\frac{2}{3}$$

Long Multiplication

When you are multiplying numbers that have more than one digit, it is sometimes necessary to carry and add. See the following examples to review these steps.

The next problem does not require carrying numbers. It does require multiplying and adding.

A.

$$\begin{array}{r} 5\ 2 \\ \times\ 3\ 2 \\ \hline 1\ 0\ 4 \end{array}$$

$2 \times 2 = 4$; place 4 in the first column, below 2 and 2.
$2 \times 5 = 10$; place 0 in column under the 5 and 3 and place 1 in column at left.

B.

$$\begin{array}{r} 5\ 2 \\ \times\ 3\ 2 \\ \hline 1\ 0\ 4 \\ +\ 1\ 5\ 6 \end{array}$$

$3 \times 2 = 6$; place 6 in column under the 5, 3, and 0.
$3 \times 5 = 15$; place 5 in column under 1 and place 1 in column at left.

C.

$$\begin{array}{r} 5\ 2 \\ \times\ 3\ 2 \\ \hline 1\ 0\ 4 \\ +\ 1\ 5\ 6 \\ \hline 1\ 6\ 6\ 4 \end{array}$$

} Add together, keeping each number in the correct column.

Answer

This problem requires carrying, adding, and multiplying:

A.

$$\begin{array}{r} {}^{1}8\ {}^{1}9\ 8 \\ \times\ 5\ 6\ 2 \\ \hline 1\ 7\ 9\ 6 \end{array}$$

$2 \times 8 = 16$; place 6 in first column and carry 1 to top of column at left.
$2 \times 9 = 18 + 1$ [that was carried] $= 19$; place 9 in column under 9 and 6 and carry 1 to top of column at left. $2 \times 8 = 16 + 1$ [that was carried] $= 17$; place 7 in column under 8 and 5 and place 1 in column at left of 7.

B.

$$\begin{array}{r} {}^{5}8\ {}^{4}9\ 8 \\ \times\ 5\ 6\ 2 \\ \hline 1\ 7\ 9\ 6 \\ 5\ 3\ 8\ 8 \end{array}$$

$6 \times 8 = 48$; place 8 in column under 9, 6, and 9 and carry 4 to the top of column at left. $6 \times 9 = 54 + 4$ [that was carried] $= 58$; place 8 in column under 8, 5, 7 and carry 5 to top of column at left. $6 \times 8 = 48 + 5$ [that was carried] $= 53$; place 3 in column under 1 and place 5 in column at left next to 3.

C.

$$\begin{array}{r} {}^{4}8\ {}^{4}9\ 8 \\ \times\ 5\ 6\ 2 \\ \hline 1\ 7\ 9\ 6 \\ 5\ 3\ 8\ 8 \\ 4\ 4\ 9\ 0 \end{array}$$

$5 \times 8 = 40$; place 0 in column under 8, 5, 7 and 8 and carry 4 to the top of column at left. $5 \times 9 = 45 + 4$ [that was carried] $= 49$; place 9 below 1 and 3. Carry 4 to top of column at left. $5 \times 8 = 40 + 4$ [that was carried] $= 44$; place 4 below 5 and place 4 next to 4 in column at left.

D.

$$\begin{array}{r} 8\ 9\ 8 \\ \times\ 5\ 6\ 2 \\ \hline {}^{1}1\ {}^{1}7\ 9\ 6 \\ {}^{1}5\ 3\ 8\ 8 \\ +\ {}^{1}4\ 4\ 9\ 0 \\ \hline 5\ 0\ 4\ 6\ 7\ 6 \end{array}$$

} Add together, keeping each number in the correct column.

Answer

Learn By Doing: Section 11.1 Activity

1. Read the following information on division

2. Complete Worksheet 5.

division

(di VIZH uhn)

The process of separating into parts; the operation opposite of multiplication.

 # Division

Division is the opposite of multiplication. Knowing the multiplication table is essential when dividing. As a health care worker, you may divide to determine costs per item or to determine the amount of items used daily. Here is a simple example: A medical office budget allows $600 a year for magazines. You are responsible for selecting and ordering the magazines. As you survey appropriate magazine subscriptions, you determine that the average annual cost is $35 per magazine. To determine how many subscriptions you can purchase, you divide $35 into $600. This problem is written as follows:

$600 \div 35$, or $35\overline{)600}$

$$\frac{17}{35\overline{)600}} \text{ magazine subscriptions}$$

To understand how 17 magazine subscriptions can be purchased for $600, review the following division skills:

Dividing three-digit numbers by one-digit numbers:

$812 \div 4$

Divide hundreds

$$\begin{array}{r} \boxed{2} \\ 4\overline{)812} \\ \underline{8} \\ 0 \end{array}$$

Divide tens

$$\begin{array}{r} \boxed{20} \\ 4\overline{)812} \\ \underline{8{\downarrow}} \\ 01 \\ \underline{00} \\ 1 \end{array}$$ } 4 does not divide into 1. Place a 0 next to the 2 in the answer.

Divide ones

$$\begin{array}{r} \boxed{203} \\ 4\overline{)812} \\ \underline{8} \\ 01 \\ \underline{00{\downarrow}} \\ 12 \\ \underline{12} \end{array}$$ } Divide 4 into 12.

Dividing four-digit numbers by one-digit numbers:

$7,216 \div 9$

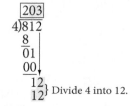

$$\begin{array}{r} \boxed{8} \\ 9\overline{)7,216} \\ \underline{7\,2} \end{array}$$

$$\begin{array}{r} \boxed{80} \\ 9\overline{)7,216} \\ \underline{7\,2{\downarrow}} \\ 1 \\ \underline{0} \\ 1 \end{array}$$

$$\begin{array}{r} \boxed{801} \\ 9\overline{)7,216} \\ \underline{7\,2{\downarrow}} \\ 16 \\ \underline{9} \\ 7 \end{array}$$

$$\begin{array}{r} \boxed{801 \text{ R or } \frac{7}{9} \text{ or } 0.8} \\ 9\overline{)7,216.0} \quad \text{Add 0s to carry answer.} \\ \underline{7\,2} \\ 16 \\ \underline{9{\downarrow}} \\ 70 \\ \underline{63} \\ 7 \end{array}$$

Answer is $801\frac{7}{9}$ or 801.8

remainder

(ri MEYN der)

The amount left over after division that is less than a whole number.

As shown in the example, "R" stands for **remainder**. The remainder is what is left over that is less than a whole number. A remainder is usually expressed as a fraction or a decimal.

Dividing Fractions

To divide fractions, you will need to invert, or turn over, the divisor (dividing number) in the calculation. So, the denominator will be on top and the numerator will be on bottom. Then, you multiply the fractions to find the answer. For example:

Step 1: Invert the divisor.

$$\frac{7}{10} \div \frac{2}{9}$$

So, $^2/_9$ is converted to $^9/_2$.

Step 2: Multiply the fractions.

$$\frac{7}{10} \times \frac{9}{2} = \frac{7 \times 9}{10 \times 2} = \frac{63}{20} = 3\frac{3}{20}$$

Note that the answer was converted from a fraction to a mixed number. When dividing mixed numbers, you will need to convert them to fractions first.

So, for example:

$$3\frac{7}{8} \div 2\frac{1}{4}$$

would convert to

$$\frac{31}{8} \div \frac{9}{4}$$

before you can divide the numbers.

 Language Arts Link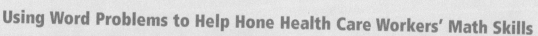

Using Word Problems to Help Hone Health Care Workers' Math Skills

As a health care worker, you must be comfortable with basic mathematical calculations. Math requires a strong foundation. Work in teams of three or four students to create a series of word problems—from simple to more difficult—that will help your classmates become more comfortable. For example:

- A weight measurement is taken for a mother and baby at 147 pounds. The mother weighs 133 pounds. How much does the baby weigh? (Answer: 14 pounds)

- A patient is allowed 2.5 quarts of fluid intake each day. There are 32 ounces in a quart. How many ounces of fluid will the patient receive at each of 3 meals? (Answer 26.7 ounces).

- There are 10 3" × 3" triple-layer gauze pads in a box, and your department uses an average of 5 boxes each week for general wound care. There are 25 2" × 2" specially treated pressure ulcer gauze pads in a box, and an average of 3 boxes are used each week. To monitor expenses, your supervisor wants to know what percentage of the total gauze pads used are 2" × 2" pads. (Answer: 60%)

Using these examples, create a workbook for the class. Be sure to proofread your work to see if you can improve it by making it clearer, more concise, or more interesting to read.

Check the spelling and grammar and correct any errors. Exchange your workbook with another team. Provide feedback and corrections as necessary, and then exchange back. Read your classmates' comments and revise your document as necessary.

Learn By Doing: Section 11.1 Activity

1. Read the following information on decimals, percentages, and fractions.

2. Complete Worksheet 6.

◼ Decimals, Percentages, and Fractions

Numbers to the left of a decimal are whole numbers. Numbers to the right of a decimal are less than one.

Dividing *decimals* by whole numbers:

$$24.5 \div 4 = 4\overline{)24.5}$$ Place the decimal point in the answer directly above the decimal point in the dividend.

$$
\begin{array}{r}
6. \\
4\overline{)24.5} \\
\underline{24}
\end{array}
\qquad
\begin{array}{r}
6.1 \\
4\overline{)24.5} \\
\underline{24} \\
5 \\
\underline{4} \\
1
\end{array}
\qquad
\begin{array}{r}
6.125 \\
4\overline{)24.500} \\
\underline{24} \\
5 \\
\underline{4} \\
10 \\
\underline{8} \\
20 \\
\underline{20}
\end{array}
$$ Add 0s to carry answer.

Numbers to the right of a decimal point indicate less than one whole. For example, 1.5 is the same as $1^1/2$.

Examples:

Decimal		Percentage		Fraction(s)
0.10	=	10%	=	$^{10}/_{100}$ or $^1/_{10}$
0.25	=	25%	=	$^{25}/_{100}$ or $^1/_4$
6.25	=	625%	=	$6^{25}/_{100}$ or $6^1/_4$

Change a decimal number into a percentage by moving the decimal two places to the right.

Examples:

0.5 = 0.5 0. = 50%

30.0 = 30.0 0. = 3000%

0.04 = .0 4. = 4%

To change a percentage into a decimal number, replace the percent sign with a decimal and move the decimal two spaces to the left.

To find the percentage of a number, first change the percentage to a decimal. Then multiply that decimal by the number.

Examples:

15% of 63 change 15% to 0.15 then multiply 0.15 × 63 = 9.45

9.45 is 15% of 63

20% of 100 change 20% to 0.20 then multiply 0.20 × 100 = 20

20 is 20% of 100

 ## Summary

In this section, you reviewed the skills for adding, subtracting, multiplying, and dividing whole numbers, nonwhole numbers, mixed numbers, fractions, and percentages. You also practiced converting percentages, decimals, and fractions.

SECTION 11.1 — **Review Questions**

1. For each of the following pairs of numbers, add and subtract the numbers:

   a. 178, 23

   b. 56.78, 12.2

   c. 56%, 34%

2. Find the answer for each of the following:

   a. 2×9

   b. $\frac{1}{4} \times \frac{15}{16}$

   c. $13\frac{3}{4} \times 7\frac{8}{9}$

   d. 45.67×3.45

   e. 33% of 60

3. Find the answer to each of the following:

   a. $56 \div 8$

   b. $\frac{5}{6} \div \frac{1}{3}$

   c. $12\frac{1}{2} \div 5\frac{2}{3}$

   d. $23.43 \div 2.3$

e. Identify the number for which 27 is 60% of the number.

4. Convert the following decimals to percentages:

   a. 0.0033

   b. 0.789

   c. 1.001

5. Convert the following percentages to decimals:

   a. 45%

   b. 23.5%

   c. 0.45%

6. For each of the following pairs of decimals, add and subtract the numbers:

   a. 2.567, 1.382

   b. 0.789, 0.294

   c. 1.934, 0.536

 ## Learn By Doing: Section 11.1 Activity

1. Review Worksheets 2 through 6.

2. When you are confident that you can meet each objective for this section, ask your teacher for the section evaluation.

The Metric System

Background

The health care worker is expected to measure and calculate weights, heights, and volume in metric units of measure. Understanding how to convert standard and metric units of measure helps you work in a variety of health care settings.

Objectives

When you have completed this section, you will be able to do the following:

- Match key terms with their correct meanings.

- State the metric unit of measure used to determine length, distance, weight, and volume.

- Use metric terms to express 100 and 1,000 units of measure.

- Use metric terms to express 0.1, 0.01, and 0.001 units of measure.

- List four basic rules to follow when using the metric system.

- Identify metric measures of length and volume.

- Convert ounces to cubic centimeters/milliliters, pounds to kilograms, and ounces to grams.

 Using the Metric System

The health care industry uses the metric system for measuring. The metric system is used by 90 percent of the world and is known as the International System of Units. Table 11.2 will help you learn the metric terms, their abbreviations, and what they measure. Each metric unit in this table is a single unit of measure. Table 11.3 explains terms used when *more than one* unit of measure (meter, gram, liter) is being measured. Following are examples of more than one unit:

- Measures of weight

    1 hectogram = 100 grams

    1.5 hectograms = 150 grams

    1 kilogram = 1,000 grams

    1.5 kilograms = 1,500 grams

- Measures of **length**

    1 hectometer = 100 meters

    1.5 hectometers = 150 meters

    1 kilometer = 1,000 meters

    1.5 kilometers = 1,500 meters

length
(LENGTH)
The measure of something from end to end.

Table 11.4 explains terms used when *less than one unit* of measure is being measured. Following are examples of less than one unit:

- Measures of length

  1 decimeter (dm) = $^1/_{10}$ or 0.1 of a meter

  1 centimeter (cm) = $^1/_{100}$ or 0.01 of a meter

  1 millimeter (mm) = $^1/_{1000}$ or 0.001 of a meter

- Measures of volume

  1 deciliter (dL) = $^1/_{10}$ or 0.1 of a liter

  1 milliliter (mL) = $^1/_{1000}$ or 0.001 of a liter

Table 11.2   Metric Terms, Their Abbreviations, and What They Measure

Term	Abbreviation	Measures	In Place of
meter	m	Length	inch, foot, yard, mile
gram	g	Weight	ounce, pound
liter	L*	Volume	fluid ounce, cup, pint, quart, gallon

*Capital *L* is commonly used to prevent confusion of lowercase letter *l* and the number *1*.

Table 11.3   Metric Terms, Their Abbreviations, and What They Measure

Term	Abbreviation	What It Measures
kilo	k	1,000 units
hecto	h	100 units

Table 11.4   Metric Terms, Their Abbreviations, and What They Measure

Term	Abbreviation	What It Measures
deci	d	$^1/_{10}$ or 0.1 unit
centi	c	$^1/_{100}$ or 0.01 unit
milli	m	$^1/_{1000}$ or 0.001 unit

There are four basic rules to follow when using the metric system:

- Numbers indicating less than one unit are always written in **decimal** form, *not* as fractions. *Example:* $^1/_{10}$ = 0.1 or $^1/_{100}$ = 0.01 or $^1/_{1000}$ = 0.001.

- When writing decimals, if there is no number before the decimal, always write a 0. *Example:* .1 is 0.1, .5 is 0.5, .75 is 0.75.

- Abbreviations for metric terms are never plural; they are always written in singular form. *Examples:* grams is *g*, not *gs*, and liters is *L*, not *Ls*. Always capitalize the abbreviation L for liter to reduce confusing the lowercase l with the number 1.

decimal
(DEH sim uhl)
A number containing a decimal point.

- Leave a space between the number and the abbreviation, as shown in the following examples: 8 g or 0.1 dm.

Using the Metric System to Measure

Meters, Centimeters, and Millimeters

A **meterstick** can be used to measure length in the following units:

- Centimeters (cm). (Figure 11.2)
- Millimeters (mm).
- Meters (m).

One meter is slightly more than 3 feet.

meterstick
(MEE ter STIK)
A measuring stick one meter long that is marked off in centimeters and usually millimeters.

FIGURE 11.2
Comparison of standard and metric units of length. About how many centimeters are in one inch?

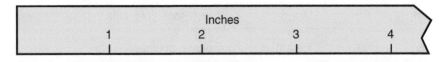

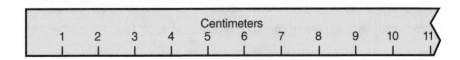

Liters, Milliliters, and Cubic Centimeters

- A liter (L) is slightly larger than a quart.
- A milliliter (mL) is $1/1000$ of a liter.
- Cubic centimeters (cc) are interchangeable with mL.

Scales can be used to measure weight in grams, hectograms, and kilograms.

Celsius (C) and Centigrade

The metric measure of heat is Celsius or centigrade, which are the same. More information can be found in the section explaining vital signs.

scales
(SKEYLZ)
Instruments with marks that help to determine weight or mass.

Changing Standard Measures to Metric Measures

It is easy to change liquid or volume measurement by multiplying 30 cc/mL times the number of ounces. (Table 11.5)

Table 11.5 Changing Ounces to Milliliters and Cubic Centimeters

1 oz medicine	1 oz × 30 cc/mL = 30 cc = 30 mL
8 oz water	8 oz × 30 cc/mL = 240 cc = 240 mL
6 oz soup	6 oz × 30 cc/mL = 180 cc = 180 mL
4 oz juice	4 oz × 30 cc/mL = 120 cc = 120 mL
12 oz soda	12 oz × 30 cc/mL = 360 cc = 360 mL

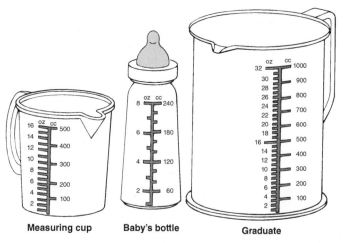

Measuring cup   Baby's bottle   Graduate

- They are all calibrated.
- They are made of metal, glass, or plastic.
- They are used for measuring liquids in cubic centimeters (cc).
- They are used for measuring liquids in ounces (oz).
- The measuring cup is used to measure liquids in the home.
- The baby's bottle is used to measure liquids in the home.
- The calibrated graduate is used to measure fluid in the health care institution.

FIGURE 11.3

Various measuring devices for fluid ounces and cubic centimeters. Give an example of a situation in which each measuring device might be used.

Apply It

Use the chart created in the Apply It earlier in this chapter. Take the same 10 and convert all of the measurements to metric units. If you did not do that exercise, then select 10 items in your refrigerator or kitchen cabinet, such as cereal, juice, or household cleaners. Create a chart and convert all of the ingredient measurements on the label to the metric scale.

Health care workers use various types of measuring devices to measure liquid. (Figure 11.3)

To change measurements of **mass** or weight, compare pounds with kilograms and grams with ounces. One pound equals 0.45 kg; 1 kilogram equals 2.2 lb. (Table 11.6)

mass
(MASS)
The amount of matter.

Table 11.6   **Changing Pounds to Kilograms and Kilograms to Pounds**

110 lb changed to kilograms: 110 lb × 0.45 kg/lb = 49.5 kg
200 lb changed to kg: 200 lb × 0.45 kg/lb = 91 kg
50 kg changed to lb: 50 kg × 2.2 lb/kg = 110 lb
91 kg changed to lb: 91 kg × 2.2 lb/kg = 200 lb

- To change pounds to kilograms, multiply the number of pounds by 0.45 lb/kg.
- To change kilograms to pounds, multiply the number of kilograms by 2.2 lb/kg.

One ounce (oz) equals 30 grams (g). To change ounces to grams, multiply 30 g/oz by the number of ounces. To change grams to ounces, divide 30 g/oz into the number of grams. (Table 11.7)

There are practice questions in your Student Activity Guide to help you learn the metric system.

Career Connection

Complete a job shadow experience at a hospital or retail pharmacy. List the various mathematical calculations that are used in the processing/filling of prescriptions. Determine the different careers represented by those that are working in the pharmacy and the education preparation required for each.

Table 11.7   **Changing Ounces to Grams**

1 oz changed to grams: 1 oz × 30 g/oz = 30 g
8 oz changed to grams: 8 oz × 30 g/oz = 240 g

 Summary

We have discussed the basic units of measure in the metric system. These include meters, grams, and liters. When the prefix *kilo* is used before a basic unit of measure, it multiplies the unit 1,000 times. When *hecto* is used, it increases the basic unit by 100 times. We have also discussed how less than one unit is expressed by using prefixes of *deci*, $1/10$ of a unit; *centi*, $1/100$ of a unit; and *milli*, $1/1000$ of a unit. You have learned four basic rules to follow when using the metric system, methods of converting standard units to metric units, and various ways to measure.

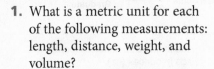

SECTION 11.2 — Review Questions

1. What is a metric unit for each of the following measurements: length, distance, weight, and volume?

2. For a metric unit, what prefixes denote 100 units, 1000 units, $1/10$ unit, $1/100$ unit, and $1/1000$ unit?

3. List four basic rules to follow when using the metric system.

4. What is the relationship between ounces, cubic centimeters, and milliliters?

5. Convert the following values as indicated:

   a. 3 lb to kg

   b. 50 oz to g

   c. 5 kg to lb

   d. 100 g to oz

6. How do you change pounds to kilograms?

Learn By Doing: Section 11.2 Activity

1. Complete Worksheet 1.

2. Complete Worksheet/Activity 2

3. Complete Worksheets 3 and 4.

4. Ask your teacher for directions to complete Worksheet/Activity 5.

5. When you are confident that you can meet each objective for this section, ask your teacher the section evaluation.

11.3 The 24-Hour Clock/Military Time

Background

Medical facilities frequently use the 24-hour clock system. The 24-hour clock clearly states time and eliminates confusion when documenting information. A health care worker is required to understand and interpret time in every health care setting.

Objectives

When you have completed this section, you will be able to do the following:

- Match key terms with their correct meanings.
- Recognize time on a 24-hour clock.
- Express 24-hour time/military time verbally and in writing.
- Convert Greenwich time to 24-hour time.

 ### Introduction to the 24-Hour Clock/ Military Time

In the health care setting, it is important that time be stated in a clear, concise manner. All medical records are legal documents. Time indicates when treatment, medication, and other activities are done and how long procedures or incidents last. A 24-hour clock eliminates the confusion between A.M. (12 midnight to 12 noon) and P.M. (12 noon to 12 midnight) hours. It provides a clear, concise record for recording medical services. The military services were the first to use a 24-hour clock; therefore, the 24-hour system is often referred to as **24-hour time/military time.** Table 11.8 shows you the difference in expressing **Greenwich and military time.** (Figure 11.4)

Military time is always expressed in four digits, and no colons are used to separate hours and minutes. Always use a 0 to complete the four-digit number (for example, for 1:00 A.M., use 0100 instead of 100). When expressing military time, remember to state it in hundreds: for example, zero one hundred hours (0100) is 1:00 A.M.; eleven hundred hours (1100) is 11:00 A.M.; twenty-three hundred hours (2300) is 11:00 P.M.

It is easy to remember that morning hours are 0100 to 1200 hours. The afternoon and nighttime hours can be added to the 1200 hours of noon. For example:

- To determine how 5:00 P.M. is expressed in military time, add 1200 and 0500 (1200 + 0500 = 1700 hours).
- To determine how 12 midnight is expressed in military time, add 1200 and 1200 = 2400 hours.

Table 11.8 will help you understand the relationship between Greenwich time and military time.

24-hour time/military time
(MIL i ter ee TIEM)
Method of telling time by counting each hour consecutively for 24 hours (i.e., . . . 11, 12, 13, . . .).

Greenwich time
(GREN ich TIEM)
Standard time, a 12-hour clock.

Apply It

Create a poster board comparing Greenwich Time and 24-Hour/Military Time. Research who uses each type of time and why we use two different accountings for time.

Present this information to 4th and 5th grade classes. Then create a short 20 question flash card game for the class. Hold up a card with a question on it, such as "What time do you start school?" or "What time do you eat dinner?" and ask who can tell you what that is in Military time.

Table 11.8 Comparison of Greenwich and 24-Hour/Military Time

Greenwich	Military	Greenwich	Military
1:00 A.M.	0100	1:00 P.M.	1300
2:00 A.M.	0200	2:00 P.M.	1400
3:00 A.M.	0300	3:00 P.M.	1500
4:00 A.M.	0400	4:00 P.M.	1600
5:00 A.M.	0500	5:00 P.M.	1700
6:00 A.M.	0600	6:00 P.M.	1800
7:00 A.M.	0700	7:00 P.M.	1900
8:00 A.M.	0800	8:00 P.M.	2000
9:00 A.M.	0900	9:00 P.M.	2100
10:00 A.M.	1000	10:00 P.M.	2200
11:00 A.M.	1100	11:00 P.M.	2300
12:00 noon	1200	12:00 P.M./midnight	2400/0000

FIGURE 11.4

24-hour clock: military time. What is the military time for the following: 8:30 A.M., 7:45 P.M., 3:15 P.M., and 12:10 A.M.?

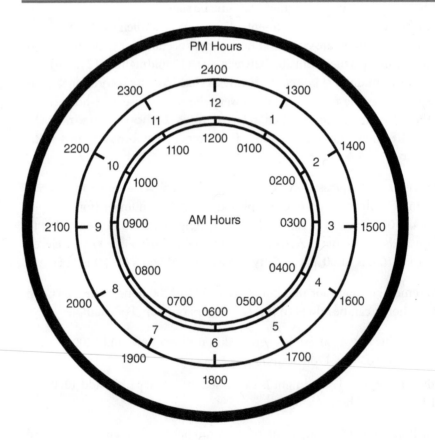

Summary

In this section, you learned the relationship between Greenwich time and military time and how to determine the time of day using a 24-hour clock. You also learned that the 24-hour clock eliminates confusion between A.M. and P.M. hours.

SECTION 11.3 | **Review Questions**

1. Describe the 24-hour clock.

2. Why should you use the 24-hour clock to record time?

3. Express the following times numerically in military time: 11:00 A.M., 4:50 P.M., and 11:45 P.M.

4. Express the following times verbally in military time: 3:20 A.M., noon, and 6:15 P.M.

5. Convert the following Greenwich times to 24-hour time: midnight, 5:35 A.M., 8:56 P.M., and 9:34 P.M.

6. What is Greenwich time?

 Learn By Doing: Section 11.3 Activity

1. Complete Worksheet 1.

2. Complete Worksheet/Activity 2.

3. Prepare responses to each item listed in Chapter Review.

4. When you are confident that you can meet each objective listed above, ask your teacher for the section evaluation.

Chapter 11 Review

Chapter Review Questions

1. Multiply and divide the following pair of numbers: $13^4/5$ and $7^1/3$. (11.1)

2. Convert the following percentages to decimals: 128.3%, 0.46%, and 32%. (11.1)

3. Identify the characteristic that each of the following units is used to measure: m, mL, cm, kg, and cc. (11.2)

4. What do deci, centi, and milli measure? (11.2)

5. Convert the following ounce measurements to mL: 4 oz, 10 oz, and 32 oz. (11.2)

6. Convert the following kilograms to pounds: 1 kg, 50 kg, and 75 kg? (11.2)

7. What is the formula for changing pounds to kilograms? (11.2)

8. Describe the 24-hour time system. (11.3)

9. Express the following time in military time numerically and verbally: 1:00 P.M. (11.3)

10. A woman goes into labor at 1400. She waits two hours before she goes to the hospital. At what time does she arrive at the hospital?

Activities

1. You have been given a list of duties and times, but the times are in minutes and fractions: updating records—1 hour; cleaning—2 $^1/3$ hours; working with patients—4 hours and 10 minutes; lunch—one-half hour. Assume your scheduled shift starts at 8:00 A.M. Set up a schedule for your day, using Standard Greenwich Time, showing when you are performing each duty. Then redo the calendar using 24-Hour Military Time.

2. Your teacher will set up a Medical Math Obstacle course. Bring in a favorite recipe. Convert the measurements from household to metric. Use the following basic measurements to start:

   3 teaspoons = 1 tablespoon
   4 tablespoons = $^1/4$ cup
   $5^1/3$ tablespoons = $^1/3$ cup
   8 tablespoons = $^1/2$ cup
   $10^2/3$ tablespoons = $^2/3$ cup
   12 tablespoons = $^3/4$ cup
   16 tablespoons = 1 cup
   1 tablespoon = $^1/2$ fluid oz.
   1 cup = 8 fluid oz.
   1 cup = $^1/2$ pint
   2 cups = 1 pint
   4 cups = 1 quart
   2 pints = 1 quart
   4 quarts = 1 gallon

Case Studies

1. A new mother arrives for the baby's first well-baby checkup at 1:00 P.M. You know that she should be taken to an examination room within 5 minutes. Your employer uses military time. Explain how 1:05 P.M. is written in military time. You call the patient's name and ask her to follow you to the scales. You weigh the baby and find she weighs 3.84 kilograms. What will you tell the mother her baby's weight is in pounds and ounces?

2. Health care workers are expected to communicate effectively with co-workers, patients, and their families. In the United States, standard units of measure are common, and metric units of measure are less common. Patients or their families may be expected to measure their medicine and fluid intake and convert these measurements to metric units. It is essential to explain how to do this in terms a patient will understand. Write instructions to a 75-year-old patient explaining the difference between ounces and cubic centimeters. Your instructions must describe how to measure and calculate the patient's 24-hour fluid intake.

Thinkng Critically

1. **Safety Alert**—Describe two scenarios in which instructions given to patients using a 12-hour clock may be confusing and put patients at risk. Explain how instructions given using a 24-hour clock can prevent problems.

2. **Medical Math**—A mother gets a prescription for her child. The instructions say to give the child 15mL of antibiotic tid. The mother only has teaspoons at home and does not know how much medicine to give her child. Can you help her?

3. **Math Facts**—Use filling prescriptions as the example for determining accurate measures. In a team of three, complete the following exercise. Fill four simulated prescriptions. Each prescription will require mathematical calculations.

   Medication A is a liquid to be taken as 2 fl. oz., four times a day, until gone. The bottle has 96 oz. How long will it last? (12 days)

Give Medication B as 10mg/kg body weight, 2 times per day for 10 days. The patient weighs 79 lbs. Each pill cannot contain more than 200 mg. of Medication B. How many mg. per day would the patient require, and how many pills per day would that be? What would be the mg. dosage of each pill? (720 mg per day = 2 pills of 180 mg. each given twice per day)

The patient requires 50 mg. of medication C every morning, via teaspoon. The medication solution contains 25 mg. /teaspoon. How many teaspoons must your patient take per day? (2)

The patient requires 1.25 mg. of Medication D. Medication D comes in a solution of 5 mg. per 5 ml. How many ml of Medication D will the patient receive? (1.25 ml)

Teams report on their conclusions and their process for finding the answers.

Chapter 11 Review

Media Connection

Use the Companion Web site for additional interactive learning activities: www.prenhall.com/badasch

Portfolio Connection

It is time to review your vocational choices once again. This assignment leads you through a cost analysis of schools and associations that can help develop your knowledge and skills.

Review the outcome of your career search from Chapter 2. Write down any new vocational areas of interest you have identified since completing your original career search. Answer the questions in Chapter 2, Section 1 Worksheets 3 and 4 in your Student Activity Guide concerning any new areas of vocational interest. Compare your answers to these questions with your values on Worksheet 1 and satisfaction on Worksheet 2 in Chapter 2. Review the vocations that seem best for you at this time.

This assignment shows your ability to organize data into an easy-to-read, usable document. Use this process to guide future research and cost comparisons. Repeat this assignment as you approach the time for finalizing your decision concerning your professional development.

PORTFOLIO TIP

Be sure to visit several facilities of the type in which you hope to work. Remember that one facility alone may not be typical. Keep a dated record of each visit with your reactions noted. This will be a private part of your portfolio. This is an important step in your career planning: deciding where you will be happiest working.

12 | Measurement and the Scientific Process

Getting Started

Using the Body Mass Index Chart provided by your teacher, determine your own personal Body Mass Index. Are you in the normal range? If not, consider a nutrition and exercise program that will help you reach a normal range. You will learn more about nutrition in Chapter 16.

12.1 The Scientific Process

Background

Scientists, including medical professionals, often perform experiments to answer the questions they have about the world around them. A health care worker should have a basic understanding of scientific methods. This understanding can help health care workers communicate with patients and their families. Understanding and using the scientific process also promotes the use of proven and effective methods of health care and the promotion of higher standards of care for all patients.

Objectives

When you have completed this section, you will be able to do the following:

- Match key terms with their correct meanings.
- List eight basic steps of scientific methods.

- Describe a controlled experiment.
- Explain the importance of communication in scientific methods.

scientific methods
(SIE uhn tif ik METH uhds)
Processes scientists use to answer questions.

 **Scientific Methods**

Scientists, including scientists working in health care, are always asking questions: What medicine will work best to treat this disease? Is the medicine safe? How does the medicine affect people? To answer these questions, scientists use **scientific methods**. The basic steps of scientific methods, which are described later in this section, include the following:

- Make observations.
- Ask a question.
- Develop a hypothesis.
- Make a prediction.

- Test the hypothesis.
- Analyze the results.
- Draw conclusions.
- Communicate results.

 Making Observations and Asking Questions

How scientists use scientific methods varies depending on what they are trying to find out and what happens during their research. However, all scientific processes start with **observations**.

Observations

To make observations, a scientist gathers information. He or she may watch, listen, touch, or even smell to gather information. Based on what the scientist observes, he or she asks a question. For example, a scientist observes that some people don't get sick when exposed to a disease, so the scientist might ask why this is happening. He or she might also ask how this information can be used to benefit other people.

Questions

There are many scientific questions that have yet to be answered. Most of those questions are quite big, and it is rarely possible for one scientist, or even one team of scientists, to find answers to big questions. Groups of scientists may work together, or separately, on smaller questions related to the big question and eventually their results provide answers to the big question. A scientific question often begins with the word "why." A why question usually stems from creatively wondering why something is the way it is, or why it isn't another way. Why questions tend to be "big" questions and, as such, are often untestable. Rephrasing a question so that it describes something specific, or asks about a cause breaks big questions down into testable questions. For example, instead of asking "Why do microorganisms multiply?" the scientist can ask, "Do microorganisms multiply when the temperature is below freezing?" or "Do warm, moist conditions cause microorganisms to multiply." The creativity that sparked the question about why microorganisms multiply is channeled into testable questions.

Hypotheses

After a testable question has been determined, the scientist will make more observations based on the question. After further observation, the scientist develops one or more hypotheses. A **hypothesis** can be tested. For example, a hypothesis might be that people who run two to three miles daily will not catch bronchitis if exposed to it. Not just an educated guess, a hypothesis is intended to answer the scientific question that was asked. A hypothesis is about causes that lead to effects.

Predicting Results and Testing Predictions

After a scientist has a hypothesis, he or she will design an experiment to test the hypothesis. (**Figure 12.1**) The scientist makes a prediction about what will happen during the experiment. All of the experiments that the scientist performs must be recorded and well documented. Accurate record keeping helps the scientist draw conclusions, identify possible errors, and develop new ideas. It also helps other scientists repeat the experiment.

Figure 12.1
A scientist tests her hypothesis. Why do scientists perform controlled experiments?

It is important for any scientist to use **controlled experiments**. In these experiments, all variables except the one being tested are the same and do not change. If more than one variable is changed, it is hard to identify what caused the results of the experiment.

Drawing Conclusions and Communicating Results

After a scientist finishes an experiment, he or she analyzes the results to see if the hypothesis is supported. If it is, the scientist will communicate the results. He or she may perform additional research. Sometimes the hypothesis is not supported. This is not a bad thing—the scientist can still use the information. Based on the data, the scientist might run the experiment again to see if there was an error. He or she can use the information to come up with a new hypothesis to test. The scientist can communicates the results so other scientists can develop their own hypotheses.

After the scientist has analyzed the results and drawn a conclusion, he or she needs to communicate the results to other scientists. This is often done by publishing reports in scientific and medical journals. These reports should clearly describe the experimental process so other scientists can perform the same experiment.

The ability to replicate an experiment and duplicate the results supports the validity of the hypotheses. Communication also helps scientists compare hypotheses and verify the accuracy of experiments. Finally, clear communication helps scientists trust each other.

 # Personal Wellness

Lab Safety

Laboratories pose many safety risks. When working in a lab, you need to consider the following:

1. **Follow all safety rules. Your teacher or facility has rules about how you should dress and behave in a lab. Follow all of these rules to avoid injury.**

2. **Know your safety symbols. Labs have standard symbols that indicate safety hazards. For example, a bottle of chemicals may have a warning symbol that indicates it is flammable. Work with your teacher or facility to recognize these symbols.**

3. **Read and follow directions. Anytime you work in a lab, carefully read through the procedure instructions. If you don't understand a step, be sure to clear up any confusion before you start.**

4. **Use safety equipment. Goggles, gloves, and aprons protect you from injury. Use them anytime you are directed to do so. If you are uncertain whether you need the equipment, ask your supervisor.**

5. **Keep your workspace clean and neat. Avoid clutter, and clean up your workspace according to your teacher's or facility's instructions.**

6. **Know emergency procedures. Work with your teacher or facility to understand what you need to do if you are injured or if another person is injured. Certain emergencies, such as eye injuries, need special equipment. Make sure you know where this equipment is located and how it is used.**

7. **Report all accidents immediately. Even if an accident is minor, tell your teacher or supervisor.**

A bottle has a symbol showing goggles on it. What should you do?

 ## Summary

Scientific methods start with observations. Then, scientists ask questions about their observations. They develop a hypothesis, which they test. After analyzing the results, scientists draw conclusions about their experiments and communicate the results to other scientists.

 **Science Link**

Using the Scientific Method

As a health care worker, understanding the scientific method can help you when communicating with patients about their treatments, potential medicine interactions, and possible side effects.

Work in teams of two students to conduct a simple in-class experiment. Begin with four "unknown" powders. Then, ascertain information from a chart that shows how the four kinds of powder react when mixed with water, iodine, rubbing alcohol and vinegar.

Hypothesize the identity of each mystery powder. Then, test how each powder reacts with water, iodine, rubbing alcohol and vinegar. Compare your results with the chart and draw a conclusion about each powder. Then you will know whether your hypothesis was correct.

Remember that the scientific method has six steps, described below. They will help you solve all kinds of problems, in and out of school.

Step 1: State a problem or ask a question.

Step 2: Gather background information.

Step 3: Form a hypothesis.

Step 4: Design and perform an experiment.

Step 5: Draw a conclusion.

Step 6: Report the results.

It is critical to document all of the steps in the scientific method. Be sure to proofread your work to ensure that it is clear. Check the spelling and grammar and correct any errors. Remember, others may have to duplicate your findings. Exchange your document with that of another team after the experiment has concluded. How are they different? How are they the same?

SECTION **12.1** **Review Questions**

1. Define the terms scientific methods and observations.

2. What are the eight steps of the scientific method?

3. During which step of the scientific method do scientists propose a possible explanation of their observations?

4. Why is it important to use controlled experiments?

5. Why should scientists communicate their results even if the results don't support their hypotheses?

6. What is a hypothesis?

 Learn By Doing: Section 12.1 Activity

1. Complete Worksheets 1 and 2.

2. Complete Worksheet/Activity 3 as assigned.

3. Complete Worksheet 4.

4. When you are confident that you can meet each objective listed above, ask your teacher for the section evaluation.

Background

Health care workers often need to make measurements. They may need to record temperature, the size of a wound, or the weight of a patient. Health care workers must understand what devices and units are used to make each of these measurements. They also need to understand the importance of estimating, accuracy, and precision in making measurements.

Objectives

When you have completed this section, you will be able to do the following:

- Match the key terms with their correct meanings

- Identify tools used to measure length, time, temperature, volume, and mass/weight.

- Identify units used to measure length, time, temperature, volume, and mass/weight.

- Describe the process of estimating.

- Round various numbers.

- Relate accuracy and precision to the validity of results.

- Explain how estimating may affect accuracy and precision.

 Tools for Making Measurements

Scientists use many different tools to make measurements. As a health care worker, you may need to use some of these tools. It is important to understand which tool is used to make a measurement.

Length

The standard units for length are inches (in), feet (f), and miles (mi). The metric units for length include the millimeter (mm), centimeter (cm), meter (m), and kilometer (km). For most of the measurements you will need to make, you will likely use a ruler or meterstick. Sometimes, you may use a flexible measuring tape.

The basic unit of length measurement is the meter. A meter is close to a yard in length (1 meter = 1.093 yard). In addition, there are:

- 2.54 centimeters in 1 inch.
- About 1.6 kilometers in 1 mile.
- 1,000 meters in 1 kilometer.
- 1,000 millimeters in 1 meter.

Temperature

Two scales that are used to measure temperature are the Celsius (°C) scale and the Fahrenheit scale (°F). You will most likely use the Fahrenheit scale. You will likely use electronic thermometers to measure temperature. The following formula can be used to covert between °C and °F:

$$°C = \frac{5}{9} \times (°F - 32)$$

$$°F = \frac{9}{5} \times (°C + 32)$$

Time

Time is measured in minutes and seconds. A stopwatch is used to measure time. You may need to record fractions of a second.

Volume

Volume measures the amount of space that something takes up. For solid objects that have measurable sides, volume is calculated by multiplying width by length by height. For liquids, instruments such as graduates and measuring cups are used to measure volume. The metric units used to measure volume include cubic centimeters (cc), milliliters (mL), and liters (L). Section 2 describes conversions between these units. The standard measurements include teaspoons (tsp), tablespoons (T), cups (C), pints (pt), quarts (Qt) and gallons (G). Some standard conversions are:

- $^1/_5$ teaspoon = 1 milliliter
- 1 teaspoon = 5 milliliters
- 1 tablespoon = 15 milliliters; 1 fluid ounce = 30 milliliters
- $^1/_5$ cup = 50 milliliters
- 1 cup = 240 milliliters
- 2 cups (1 pint) = 470 milliliters
- 4 cups (1 quart) = .95 liter
- 4 quarts (1 gallon) = 3.8 liters

Mass and Weight

Everything around you, including air, is made up of matter. **Mass** measures the amount of matter in an object. Mass is something that everything has no matter where it is. So something's mass will be the same wherever it is located–on Earth or on the moon. The metric measurement units for mass are grams (g) and kilograms (kg). We use a balance (a special kind of weighing machine) to measure mass. (**Figure 12.2a**)

In physical science, mass differs from **weight**. Weight measures the force of gravity on an object. So, your weight is different on the Earth than it would be on the moon, because there is more gravity on the Earth than on the moon. The standard units for weight include pounds (lb) and ounces (oz). Scales, including electronic scales, are used to determine weight. (**Figure 12.2b**)

In the health care setting, the term you will use is *weight*, but it sometimes describes mass rather than weight. That is because the two are connected. Something with a bigger mass will weigh more than something with a smaller mass (assuming they're in the same place.)

volume
(VAHWL yoom)
The amount of space that an object or liquid takes up.

Apply It

Divide into small groups. Each group will start at one of four measuring stations. Each station will have a specific measuring tool (either a ruler or a cylinder) and an item which can be measured with that tool, as appropriate.

To record accurate measurements, find the smallest division on the instrument. Measure the items and record the length or volume you feel is accurate (with no direction from the teacher). Then move to the next station. After all your classmates have been to all stations, compare findings and discuss correct or incorrect answers.

mass
(MAS)
The amount of matter in an object.

weight
(WAIT)
Measures the force of gravity on an object; varies due to distance between objects and mass.

π Math Link

Converting Between Units of Volume in the Metric System

All health care workers need a basic understanding of the metric system in order to complete daily duties. For example, a dental assistant may be asked to measure and mix materials when completing such tasks as creating study models. In order to measure volume, a dental assistant may use units such as milliliters, cubic centimeters, liters, and cubic liters.

Volume is the amount of space in a three-dimensional object. Volume can be measured with things such as beakers, measuring cups, measuring spoons, and graduated cylinders.

The following lists conversion information to change to different units of volume:

- 1,000 milliliters (mL) = 1 liter (L)
- 1 cubic centimeter (cm^3) = 1 milliliter (mL)
- 1,000 liters (1 L) = 1 cubic meter (m^3)

Example 1: Convert 3000 milliliters to liters.

1,000 mL = 1 L

1,000 × 3 = 1 L × 3

3,000 mL = 3 L

Example 2: Convert 500 cubic centimeters into liters.

Since 1 cm^3 = 1 mL then 500 cm^3 = 500 mL

You can use this information to help you figure out the answer.

1,000 mL = 1 L

1,000 / 2 = 1 / 2

500 mL = .5 L

If 500 mL equal .5 L then 500 cm^3 also equals .5 L.

a. Convert 10 cubic centimeters to milliliters.

b. Convert 2 cubic meters to liters.

c. Convert .25 liter to cubic centimeters.

What types of things might be measured in volume in a dental office?

FIGURE 12.2

(a) A balance measures mass. (b) Scales measure weight. (c) An electronic, or digital, scale provides precise weight measurement. There are many different kinds of scales, such as the spring scale and digital scale shown here (b), or the common bathroom scale. If you wanted to find out how many ounces of food a person is going to eat, which tool would you use?

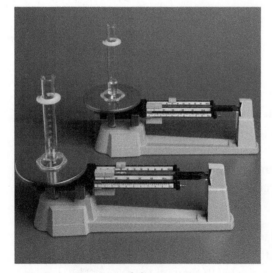

(a)

(b)

(c)

Courtesy of Fundamental Photographs NYC.

What's New?

Metric Units in the United States

Most nations around the world use metric units every day. In these countries, distances are measured in kilometers, lengths are measured in centimeters and millimeters, and volumes are measured in liters and milliliters. In the United States, we use standard units, such as miles, feet, inches, and ounces. If the metric system is so widely used, why doesn't the U.S. use it?

In fact, in the 1970s, there was a large push in the U.S. to use metric measurements. The government sponsored research studies that indicated the U.S. would eventually join the rest of the world in using metric measurements. However, this change still hasn't occurred, and fewer people are interested in making it happen. The metric system is only regularly used by people in science and medicine, mathematics, industry, and the military.

Part of the reason the U.S. has not converted to the metric system is that the public simply doesn't use these measurements regularly. Also, the transition would be expensive. For example, any sign indicating distance in miles along a highway would need to be replaced.

Because the U.S. has not converted to the metric system, we have occasionally run into problems. For example, the Mars Climate Orbiter project failed because one of the contractors on the project used standard measurements. Everyone else working on the project used metric measurements. Because of the error, the orbiter burned up in the atmosphere of Mars.

Even though metric measurements are not always used in the U.S., they can still be found on everyday items such as food labels. Many cosmetics, drinks, and nutritional supplements rely on the metric system. Several sports events, such as track and field, are measured in kilometers and meters rather than miles and feet.

Some organizations are still lobbying for the U.S. to use the metric system. It remains to be seen if we will ever make the transition.

What is a benefit of using the metric system?

Estimating

When making measurements or recording numerical data, you may need to **estimate**. Estimates can be used to quickly find approximate values. Estimating may involve rounding numbers.

estimate
(EH stuh muhnt)
Determine approximate value of a number.

To round, identify the place value that will be rounded. Then, identify the digit to the right of it. If the digit to the right is less than five, drop the digit and all numbers to the right of it. For example, the value 6.743 would be rounded to 6.74 in the hundredths place, 6.4 in the tenths place, and 7 in the ones place. If the digit is equal to or greater than five, round the place value up to the next number and drop the digits. For example, the value 23.565 would be rounded to 23.57 in the hundredths place, 23.6 in the tenths place, and 24 in the ones place.

Sometimes estimating involves identifying numbers in the tens, hundreds, or thousands place. In this case, the value 2,345 would be rounded to 2,350, 2,300, or 2,000. Notice that the rounded numbers in these cases differ more greatly from the actual value, so the estimate may cause errors.

Accuracy and Precision

When making measurements, it is important to maintain both **accuracy** and **precision**. Accurate measurements are close to the actual value of the thing being measured. Measurements are often repeated to ensure accuracy.

You may be asked to make a measurement three times. If the measurements are precise, they will not differ much from each other. Then you will average the measurements. Doing so increases the likelihood that your final value is accurate, especially if the three measurements are precise, or near each other in value.

For data to be valid, they must be both accurate and precise. Otherwise, there is an error in the data. Estimating can decrease the accuracy and precision of measurements, so it should be used carefully.

Summary

Many tools are used to make measurements—rulers, metersticks, stopwatches, thermometers, graduates, balances, and scales to name a few. The tool used depends on the characteristic being measured. Some tools measure length; other tools measure temperature. To be valid, measurements must be both accurate and precise. Estimating is a useful tool to identify approximate values, but it can introduce errors because it reduces accuracy and/or precision.

accuracy
(AK yuhr uh see)
How close a measurement is to the actual value.

precision
(PREE si shuhn)
For multiple measurements of the same thing, how close the values of the measurements are to each other.

Apply It

Practice estimating quantities and then taking the precise measurements. Set up a box filled with soil, a beaker filled with water, a jar filled with M&Ms, etc. Estimate the weight of each sample and note it on a card. Take the actual weight and see who is closest.

SECTION **12.2** | Review Questions

1. If you wanted to measure the volume of liquid a patient drinks, what tool would you use?

2. What metric units are used to measure length, volume, and mass?

3. You and your friend are stacking the supply cabinet in the school nurse's office. You pick up a container that weighs 12 pounds, and he picks up one that weighs 4.54 kilograms. Who is carrying the heavier container?

4. As part of your health class, you are told to walk 3.22 (rounded) kilometers three times a week. Your sister claims to walk 3 miles three times a week. Who is walking farther?

5. What is the relationship between accuracy and precision?

6. How does estimating the number 3,456 to the nearest thousand affect accuracy?

Learn By Doing: Section 12.2 Activity

1. Complete Worksheet 1 as assigned.

2. Complete Worksheet 2 and Worksheet/Activity 3 as assigned.

3. Complete Worksheets 4 and 5.

4. When you are confident that you can meet each objective listed above, ask your teacher for the section evaluation.

SECTION

12.3 Tables, Graphs, and Charts

Background

A health care worker will need to keep careful records in the course of care for a patient. Sometimes, the information recorded will need to be organized into a table, graph, or chart. A health care worker will need to know how to read data in a table, graph or chart. Sometimes, a caregiver will need to organize data in such ways.

Objectives

When you have completed this section, you will be able to do the following:

- Match key terms with their correct meanings.

- Describe three types of graphs.

- Explain what kind of data is represented by tables and each type of graph.

- Draw three types of graphs.

 Data Tables

As a health care worker, you are going to need to read or make tables. Tables are used to organize **data** and to help record information. For example, a patient's temperature needs to be recorded every hour for a 24-hour period. A table can be used to organize this data. Tables can also be used to record observations and other verbal data.

The first feature of a table is column labels, located at the top of each column in the table. In the example described above, the column labels would most likely be "Time of Day" and "Patient's Temperature." The column labels should be clear and concise. The columns of a table often show the relationship between **variables.** In the example, time and temperature are the variables. Table 12.1 shows part of a sample table based on the example.

data
(DA tuh)
Information.

variables
(VAR ee uh buhls)
Any factor that can change or be present in varying amounts.

Table 12.1   Sample Table—Temperature Change over Time

Time of Day	Patient's Temperature
0800	102.3°F
0900	103.1°F
1000	103.0°F
1100	102.9°F
1200	102.3°F
1300	101.0°F
1400	99.5°F
1500	98.9°F

axes
(AKS ees)
Reference lines that mark the borders of a graph; graphs may have two or more axes (singular, axis).

proportions
(pruh POR shuhns)
Parts of a whole.

 ## Graphs and Charts

Several types of graphs and charts are used to visually organize data. Usually, they show numerical data. A health care worker may not need to create these graphs and charts, but he or she will need to understand how to read them. There are several types of graphs and charts, but the most common are the following:

- **Bar graph:** Uses vertical or horizontal bars to represent numerical data. Bar graphs have vertical and horizontal **axes**. Bars are proportional to the numerical value they represent. (See **Figure 12.3a** for an example of a bar graph.)

- **Line graph:** Uses a line drawn through plotted points to show how one variable is affected by another. These graphs are often used to show time relationships and trends. Like bar graphs, line graphs have axes. (**Figure 12.3b** is an example of a line graph.)

- **Circle graph:** Also called a pie chart, circle graphs are circles that are divided into sections, similar to the way a pie might be sliced. However, the "pieces" in a circle graph are not usually even. Circle graphs are used to show **proportions** and percentages. (**Figure 12.3c** is an example of a pie graph.)

Summary

Tables, graphs, and charts are important tools for organizing data. Data are often numerical, but can also be verbal. Tables are used to record both numerical and verbal data. Graphs and charts are used for numerical data. Three types of graphs and charts include bar graphs, line graphs, and circle graphs.

(a)

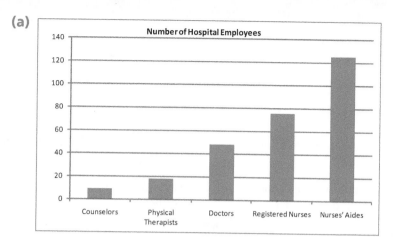

FIGURE 12.3
(a) Bar graph; (b) Line graph; (c) Circle graph.
If you wanted to compare the number of people in a hospital who are nurses' aides, registered nurses, physical therapists, counselors, and doctors, what kind of graph would you use?

(b)

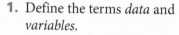

(c)

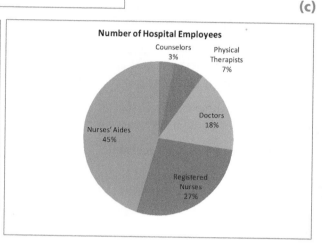

1. Define the terms *data* and *variables*.

2. How do tables differ from graphs and charts?

3. List and describe three types of graphs.

4. Should a bar graph be used to show temperature changes over time? Explain your reasoning.

5. If you wanted to show percentages from a survey, which type of graph would you use? Why?

6. What type of chart best shows time relationships and trends?

Learn By Doing: Section 12.3 Activity

1. Complete Worksheet 1 as assigned.

2. Complete Worksheet/Activity 2 through 4 as assigned.

3. Prepare responses to each item listed in Chapter Review.

4. When you are confident that you can meet each objective listed above, ask your teacher for the section evaluation.

Chapter 12 Review

Chapter Review Questions

1. What are the eight steps of scientific methods? (12.1)

2. Before starting an experiment, scientists make _____, which help them ask questions. (12.1)

3. Give an example of a controlled experiment. (12.1)

4. In measurements, _____ describes how close a measurement is to the actual value of the thing being measured. (12.2)

5. Give three examples that show when health care workers might take measurements. (12.2)

6. How is volume calculated? (12.2)

7. Why is precision and accuracy important when making measurements? (12.2)

8. Give examples of when a bar, line, and circle graph would be used in health care. (13.3)

9. Sheila wants to show proportions in a graph. She should use a _____ graph. (12.3)

10. Why would a health care worker need to create a table? (12.3)

11. Mr. Smith, who was raised in Europe, has come in for a consultation before his physical. He is told that he has 19 quarts of salt water in his body. He wants to know how many liters that is. What is your response (rounded to two decimals)? (12.2)

12. At your school physical, you are told that you weigh 49.9 kilograms. You get concerned until your friend explains that you actually weigh _____ pounds (rounded to the nearest pound). (12.2)

Activities

1. Draw a circle graph to show the percentage of the day a worker spends on each of his or her duties. Remember that a circle graph, also known as a pie chart, is a circular chart divided into triangular areas proportional to the percentages of the whole pie. Think about an apple pie. If someone eats half of it and someone else eats a third, each of those pie sizes will be different.

   You have been given a list of duties and times, but the times are in minutes and fractions. Convert the following into percentages: updating records—$1\frac{1}{2}$ hours; cleaning—$3\frac{3}{4}$ hours; working with patients—5 hours and 15 minutes; lunch—25 minutes. Then, use the percentages to draw and label a circle graph that shows how a worker spends an 8-hour shift.

2. Use the data in the table below to draw a line graph. Remember that a line graph is a graph in which line segments join points representing different values. Describe any trends that are shown in the graph. Are there other types of graphs that you can use to show the data? Explain your reasoning.

Time of Day	Heart Rate (beats per minute)	Time of Day	Heart Rate (beats per minute)	Time of Day	Heart Rate (beats per minute)
0100	46 bpm	0900	63 bpm	1700	66 bpm
0200	45 bpm	1000	64 bpm	1800	65 bpm
0300	47 bpm	1100	65 bpm	1900	64 bpm
0400	47 bpm	1200	65 bpm	2000	63 bpm
0500	48 bpm	1300	66 bpm	2100	63 bpm
0600	47 bpm	1400	65 bpm	2200	60 bpm
0700	50 bpm	1500	65 bpm	2300	56 bpm
0800	60 bpm	1600	67 bpm	2400	50 bpm

Case Studies

1. Health care researchers are tracking the early development of children who show definitive signs of allergies by age 5. They need to take 25 subjects and track their development by charting their weight, height, and instances of illness. How would they do this? Would they start with a table? What type of graphs might they use? Create a data set and set up a test model.

2. Create a hypothesis based on your work in this course or another science class, such as biology. Design an experiment that will test the hypothesis. What kind of documentation will you need to develop?

Thinking Critically

1. **Presenting Data**—Describe two scenarios, based on your present classes, in which it would be better to present data in tables or graphically. How would you present the information?

2. **Medical Math**—There are two scales that are used to measure temperature—Celsius (°C) scale and the Fahrenheit scale (°F). You will most likely use the Fahrenheit scale, but in many other areas of the world, Celsius is more common. Why is this?

3. **Scientific Processes**—During an experiment, a scientist gets results that do not support her hypothesis. She communicates her results to other scientists. What else can she do?

Media Connection

Use the Companion Web site for additional interactive learning activities: www.prenhall.com/badasch

Portfolio Connection

Research private and public schools for higher education in your vocational choice. Create a spreadsheet that clearly compares costs for each school, using the following criteria:

- Entrance requirements
- Tuition (costs must be compared equally, that is, semester to semester, quarter to quarter, or hours to hours)
- Books (number of books and the cost for new and used books)
- Supplies and materials (list and compare like items)
- Uniforms (identify all required uniform parts, e.g., shoes, name tag)
- Housing
- Transportation (type of transportation, round-trip miles)
- Miscellaneous
- Financial aid resources (eligibility criteria, amount of dollars available, repayment requirements, and interest rates)

PORTFOLIO TIP

Be sure to visit several facilities of the type in which you hope to work. Remember that one facility alone may not be typical. Keep a dated record of each visit with your reactions noted. This will be a private part of your portfolio. This is an important step in your career planning: deciding where you will be happiest working.

13 Your Body and How It Functions

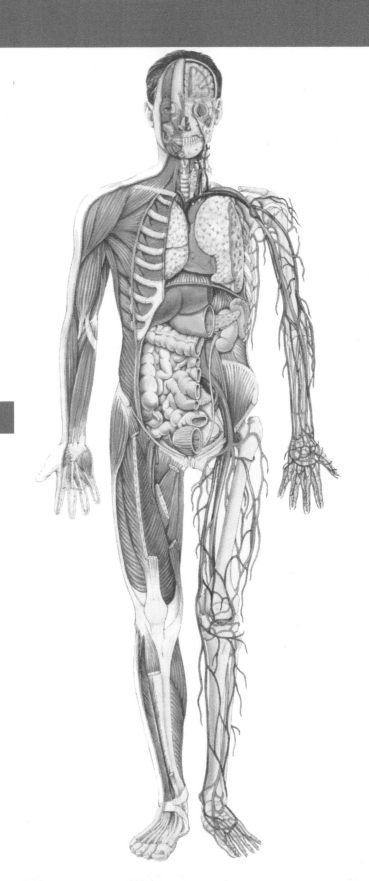

Getting Started

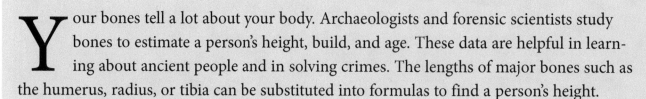

Your bones tell a lot about your body. Archaeologists and forensic scientists study bones to estimate a person's height, build, and age. These data are helpful in learning about ancient people and in solving crimes. The lengths of major bones such as the humerus, radius, or tibia can be substituted into formulas to find a person's height.

Measure the length of your radius (r), tibia (t), and humerus (h) bones to the nearest half-inch. Using the following formulas, approximate your height (H) in inches. Are the calculated heights close to your actual height?

Male

$H = 32.2 + 2.4t$
$H = 29.0 + 3.0h$
$H = 31.7 + 3.7r$

Female

$H = 28.6 + 2.5t$
$H = 25.6 + 3.1h$
$H = 28.9 + 3.9r$

Imagine that an archaeologist found an 18-inch tibia on the site of an American colonial farm. Do you think it belonged to a man or a woman? Why?

SECTION

13.1 Overview of the Body

cell
(SELL)
Smallest structural section in the body that is capable of independent functioning.

microscopic
(mahy kruh SKOP ik)
Too small to be seen by the eye but large enough to be seen through a microscope.

function
(FUHNGK shuhn)
Action or work of tissues, organs, or body parts (e.g., the heart's function is to pump blood).

Background

The health care worker assists people who are ill, injured, or seeking a healthy lifestyle. Understanding the body's structure and functions provides the health care worker with the basic knowledge necessary to help each person reach his or her goal. When you understand normal body functions you will recognize disease processes.

Objectives

When you have completed this section, you will be able to do the following:

- Match key terms with their correct meanings.
- List seven cell functions.
- Identify three main parts of the cell and explain their functions.
- Describe the relationship between cells, tissues, organs, and systems of the body.

- Identify terms relating to the body.
- Label a diagram of the body cavities.
- Explain why health care workers must have a basic knowledge of body structures and how they function.

Introduction to The Body

The Cell

The **cell** is the building block of the body. Cells are **microscopic**. This means that they are so small they can be seen only with the aid of a microscope. The body is made up of millions of cells, each programmed to do a specific job that allows the body to **function**. Each cell reproduces, grows, uses oxygen and **nutrients**, digests food for energy, eliminates waste, produces heat and energy, and is able to move. Many cells can repair themselves. The structure of the cell includes (**Figure 13.1**):

- The **nucleus**, which regulates the activity of the cell and has an important role in the **reproduction** of the cell.
- The **cytoplasm**, a jellylike liquid where the activities of the cell occur.
- The **cell membrane**, which is the outer covering of the cell that keeps the cytoplasm contained. The cell membrane also allows matter to flow in and out of the cell.

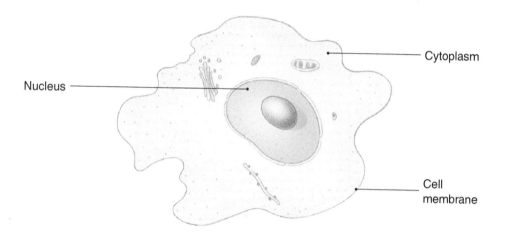

Nucleus

Cytoplasm

Cell membrane

Tissues

The body is made up of specialized groups of cells. These groups of cells form tissues. These **tissues** have a specific job. There are four primary kinds of tissue in the body: nerve, **epithelial**, connective, and muscle. (**Figure 13.2**) **Table 13.1** describes the locations and functions of each type of tissue.

Organs

Organs are made up of specialized tissues that allow each part of an organ to perform its own specific function. Several different types of tissues make up an entire organ. For example, the heart is an organ made up of **connective tissue,** cardiac tissue, and nerve tissue. These three types of tissue work together, causing the heart to beat and pump blood throughout the body. The tissues of the body combine to form organs such as the heart, skin, stomach, and all other organs of the body. **Figures 13.3a** and **13.3b** show the organs of the body and their locations.

Disease

A change in the normal structure or function of the body is disease. A characteristic set of signs and symptoms is the indication that the normal structure or function has been interrupted. Reasons for such changes in the structure or function of a cell, tissue, organ, or system in the body may or may not be known. *For more on disease, go to the Companion Web site at www.prenhall.com/badasch.*

nutrients
(NOO tree ent)
Substances that the cell needs in order to function.

reproduction
(ree pruh DUHK shuhn)
Process that takes place to create new cells or offspring.

nucleus
(NEW klee iss)
The part of a cell that is vital for its growth, metabolism, reproduction, and transmitted characteristics.

FIGURE 13.1
Basic cell. Where is the nucleus located in a cell?

cytoplasm
(SIGH toe plaz um)
The liquid within the cell that surrounds the nucleus and other parts of the cell.

cell membrane
(SELL MEM brain)
Thin, soft layer that surrounds the cell and holds it together.

tissues
(TISH yews)
Groups of cells of the same type that act together to perform a specific function.

epithelial
(e pi THEE lee uhl)
Pertaining to tissue that covers the internal and external organs of the body.

connective tissue
(cuh NEK tiv TISH yew)
Tissue specialized to bind together and support other tissues.

disease
(dih ZEEZ)
Any change in the normal structure or function of the body.

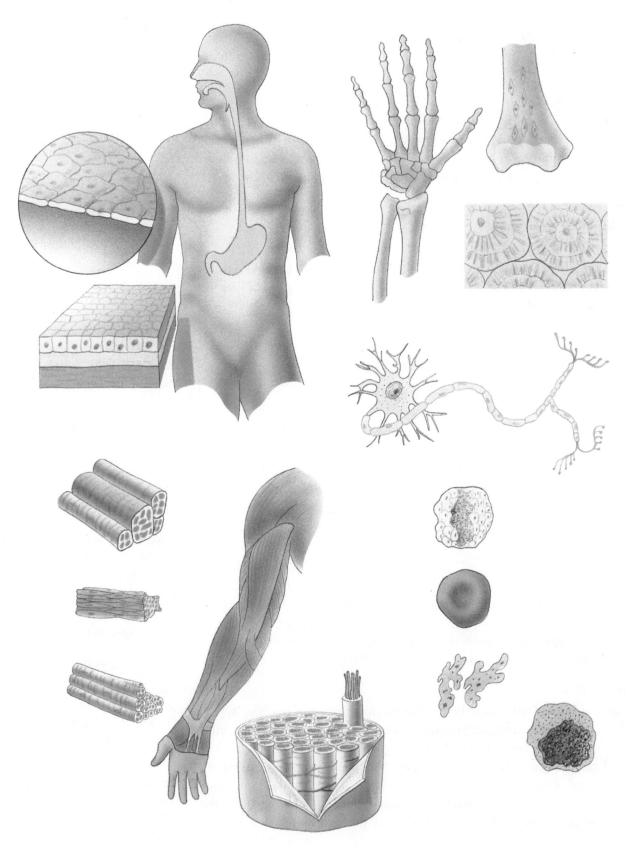

FIGURE 13.2
Types of body tissues. What are the three types of muscle tissue?

Table 13.1   Tissues of the Body

Type of Tissue	Location in the Body	Function
Nerve tissue	Throughout the body	Sends impulses to/from the central nervous system and to/from the body systems
Epithelial tissue	Forms the outer skin and lines body cavities and passages to the outside of the body	Protects, secretes, absorbs, and receives sensations (e.g., hot, cold, pressure)
Connective tissue	Bones, tendons, fat tissue	Binds, supports, and connects body tissues
Muscle tissue: 1. Cardiac 2. Smooth 3. Striated	1. Heart muscle 2. Internal organs (e.g., stomach, diaphragm) 3. Throughout the body for movement	1. Contracts heart 2. Contracts internal organs 3. Contracts and flexes to allow movement

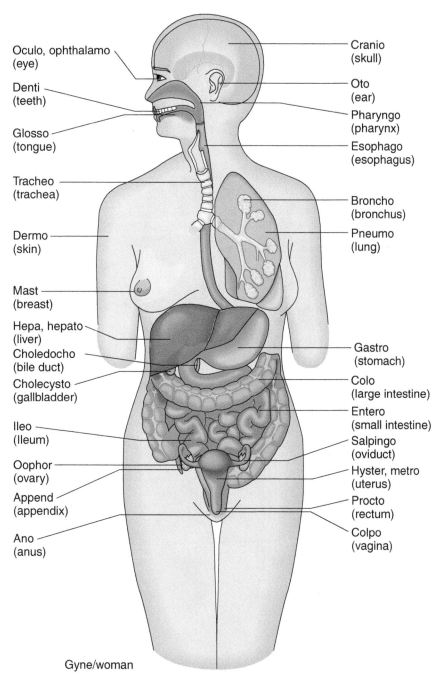

Oculo, ophthalamo (eye)
Denti (teeth)
Glosso (tongue)
Tracheo (trachea)
Dermo (skin)
Mast (breast)
Hepa, hepato (liver)
Choledocho (bile duct)
Cholecysto (gallbladder)
Ileo (ileum)
Oophor (ovary)
Append (appendix)
Ano (anus)
Gyne/woman

Cranio (skull)
Oto (ear)
Pharyngo (pharynx)
Esophago (esophagus)
Broncho (bronchus)
Pneumo (lung)
Gastro (stomach)
Colo (large intestine)
Entero (small intestine)
Salpingo (oviduct)
Hyster, metro (uterus)
Procto (rectum)
Colpo (vagina)

FIGURE 13.3a
Organs of the body. Which organ would hepatitis affect?

FIGURE 13.3b

Organs of the body. What organ would rhinitis affect?

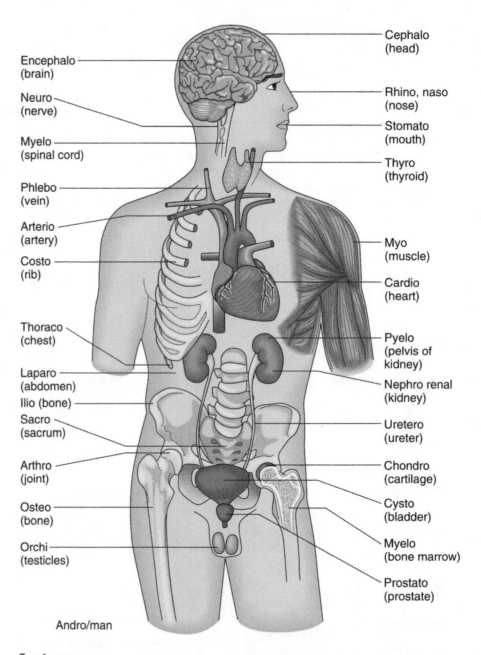

Encephalo (brain)

Neuro (nerve)

Myelo (spinal cord)

Phlebo (vein)

Arterio (artery)

Costo (rib)

Thoraco (chest)

Laparo (abdomen)

Ilio (bone)

Sacro (sacrum)

Arthro (joint)

Osteo (bone)

Orchi (testicles)

Andro/man

Cephalo (head)

Rhino, naso (nose)

Stomato (mouth)

Thyro (thyroid)

Myo (muscle)

Cardio (heart)

Pyelo (pelvis of kidney)

Nephro renal (kidney)

Uretero (ureter)

Chondro (cartilage)

Cysto (bladder)

Myelo (bone marrow)

Prostato (prostate)

composed

(kuhm POHZD)

Formed by putting many parts together.

Systems

A system is a group of organs working together to perform a certain function. The body is **composed** of several systems. In the next sections of this chapter, we discuss the following:

- Skeletal system.
- Muscular system.
- Circulatory system.
- Lymphatic system.
- Respiratory system.
- Digestive system.
- Urinary system.
- Endocrine system.

- Nervous system.
- Reproductive system.
- Integumentary system.

It is important to understand the unique **structure** and functioning of the body. You need to learn that *cells* combine to form tissues, *tissues* combine to form organs, *organs* combine to form systems, and *systems* combine to form the human body. (**Figure 13.4**)

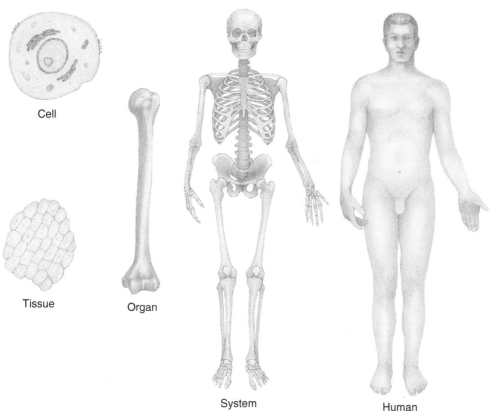

Cell

Tissue

Organ

System

Human

Directions of the Body

To document information about patients, use terms that specify regions or directions of the body; for example, to identify locations of pain or injury, write: 1 cm laceration on the right **anterior** forearm, **distal** to the elbow. (**Figure 13.5**) We normally identify these locations based on the **anatomical position**. The anatomical position is of importance in anatomy because it is the position of reference for anatomical nomenclature. Anatomic terms such as anterior and posterior, medial and lateral, abduction and adduction, and so on apply to the body when it is in the anatomical position.

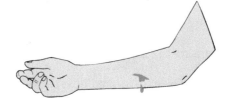

plane
(PLAYN)
A flat surface determined by the position of three points in space.

The body directions are shown in **Figure 13.6**. Medical professionals often refer to sections of the body in terms of anatomical **planes** (flat surfaces). These planes are imaginary lines—vertical or horizontal—drawn through the upright body. The terms are used to describe a specific body part. Planes include:

- Axial plane.
- Base plane.
- Coronal planes.
- Frankfort horizontal plane.
- Frontal planes.
- Horizontal plane.
- Median plane.
- Nuchal plane.

- Occipital plane.
- Orbital plane.
- Sagittal planes.
- Temporal plane.
- Transverse plane.
- Vertical plane.
- Visual plane.

FIGURE 13.6
Directions of the human body. If an injury were described as a "posterior cranial laceration," where would the injury be?

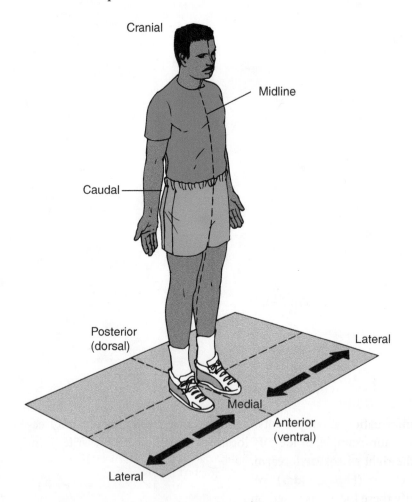

Here are the most common body directions:

- **Cranial:** located near the head.
- **Superior:** above or in a higher position. The head is superior to the torso.
- **Inferior:** below, lower. The knee is inferior to the thigh.
- **Ventral** or **anterior:** located near the surface or in front of coronal (frontal) plane.

- **Dorsal** or **posterior:** located to the back of the coronal plane.
- **Medial:** near the center or midline of the saggital plane. Think of the midline as dividing the body in half with a left and a right side.
- **Lateral:** away from the midline of the saggital plane.
- **Proximal:** nearest the point of attachment.
- **Distal:** farthest from the point of attachment or the midline.
- **Caudal:** located near the **sacral region**.

Cavities of the Body

The cavities of the body (**Figure 13.7**) are another way to identify location of pain or injury. (**Table 13.2**)

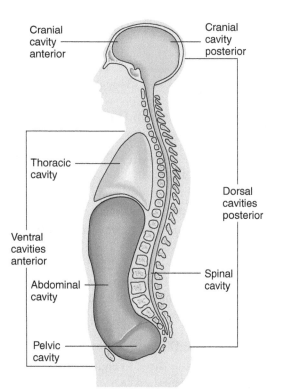

Cranial cavity anterior

Cranial cavity posterior

Thoracic cavity

Dorsal cavities posterior

Ventral cavities anterior

Spinal cavity

Abdominal cavity

Pelvic cavity

FIGURE 13.7
Body cavities. What is the chest cavity called?

Apply It

Bring in supplies and create an anatomy man, which has to stand up. Then, label the cavities, directions, planes, and abdominal regions. Make organs and then put them in the correct cavity.

Table 13.2   Cavities of the Body (see Figure 13.7)

Dorsal Cavities Located Toward the Back of the Body	Ventral Cavity Located Toward the Front of the Body
Cranial cavity—houses the brain	Thoracic cavity—houses the heart, lungs, large blood **vessels**
Spinal cavity—houses the spinal cord	Abdominal cavity—houses the stomach, most of intestines, kidney, liver, gallbladder, pancreas, spleen
	Pelvic Cavity—houses the urinary bladder, part of intestine, rectum, parts of the reproductive system

Medical Terminology

aplasia:	failure of any part of the body to develop naturally	**intralobar:**	within a lobe
endogenous:	anything occurring within the body	**necrosis:**	condition of dead or decaying tissue
exogenous:	anything occurring outside the body	**peristalsis:**	progressive wavelike movement that occurs in some of the tubes of the body (e.g., intestines, esophagus)
induration:	hardened tissue		
infarct:	tissue that has lost blood supply and died	**plasma:**	liquid part of the blood and lymph
		symptom:	any noticeable change in the body or its function
interlobar:	between lobes		
intervisceral:	between two organs	**visceratonic:**	lack of normal **tone** in an organ

tone
(TOHN)
Firmness or tightness.

 ## Jobs and Professions

Medical Doctor (M.D.)

A medical doctor (M.D.) is a licensed physician who is responsible for comprehensive patient care. An M.D. promotes and maintains health, and treats both injuries and disease. Duties include, but are not limited to: examining patients; obtaining medical histories; ordering, performing, and interpreting diagnostic tests; counseling patients on health-related issues; and prescribing medicines. Many physicians with an M.D. go on to specialize in other areas.

It is not uncommon for an M.D. to work 60 or more hours a week. Most M.D.s work in small, private offices or clinics. Some practice in large health-care organizations, an arrangement that allows for a less demanding work schedule. The education and training for an M.D. are among the most strenuous of any profession.

In general, M.D.s complete four years of undergraduate school, four years of medical school, and three to eight years of internship and residency, depending upon the specialty pursued. All candidates must also pass a licensing exam, and they must continue to study throughout their careers to keep up with advances in medical technology.

Microbiologist

A microbiologist is a scientist who studies microbes, or living organisms and infectious agents that are too small to be seen with the naked eye. Because there are so many different species of microbes, microbiologists usually select one type of microbe to study. They focus their research and build their careers in that area.

A small sampling of specialties includes: bacteriologists, who study bacteria; virologists, who study viruses; and immunologists, who study the human body and how it defends itself against disease.

Microbiologists work in almost every industry, and careers in this field are quite varied. At the lowest level are laboratory assistants, who generally have a two-year technical training degree. Those with a four-year degree in biology or microbiology work as research assistants and medical technologists.

A master's degree is required for supervisory, technical support, and teaching positions. And microbiologists who perform independent research, teach at the university level, or hold executive-level positions have doctoral degrees.

Pathologist

A pathologist is a medical doctor who examines tissue specimens, cells, and bodily fluids through laboratory tests and then interprets the results to gain an accurate diagnosis. An accurate diagnosis is necessary if the patient is to receive proper treatment. Currently, more than 2,000 different tests can be performed on blood and bodily fluids.

Many times, a pathologist helps a patient's team of doctors select the most appropriate test to gain a complete diagnosis. A pathologist is a critical member of a patient's core medical team.

To become a pathologist, one must complete medical school, a residency program, and an approved residency in pathology. Medical school generally takes four years. Residency training for pathologists lasts anywhere from three to six years, depending upon the specialty. Pathologists work in hospitals, clinics and independent laboratories.

Registered Nurse

Registered nurses (RNs) are involved in every aspect of patient care. Some RNs treat patients. They perform diagnostic tests and analyze the results. They give treatment and medication, and they closely observe patients and record their progress as well as any reactions. Other medical professionals use this detailed record as a basis for proper patient care. RNs also help with patient follow-up and rehabilitation.

Some RNs work with the public rather than individual patients. They educate the public on warning signs and symptoms of various conditions and tell them where to get help. Some RNs run immunization clinics and blood drives. Some are trained in grief counseling. RNs account for the largest health-care occupation. Although they may work in a variety of settings, roughly three out of every five RNs works in a hospital.

To become an RN, one must graduate from an approved nursing program and pass a national licensing exam. There are three main ways to become an RN. One option is to get a bachelor's of science degree in nursing (BSN) through a four-year program at a college or university.

A second option is an associate degree in nursing (ADN) through a two- or three-year program at a community or junior college.

The third option is to go through a three-year diploma program at a hospital. Advancement opportunities are usually broader for those who complete a BSN program. A master's degree is required to work in administration, teaching or any nursing specialty.

Nurse Practitioner

A nurse practitioner (NP) is a registered nurse who has received additional education and clinical training in the diagnosis and treatment of illness. Most NPs have completed a two- or three-year master's degree program. Some have a doctorate degree in their specialty. These specialties include acute care; adult or family health; gerontology health; neonatal health; oncology; pediatric/child health; psychiatric/mental health; and women's health. NPs may further specialize in everything from allergy and immunology to urology.

Nurse practitioners work in a variety of settings. They can be found everywhere from clinics, hospitals, and private practices to nursing homes, schools, and public health departments. On the job, they order, perform, and interpret diagnostic tests, diagnose and treat common acute illnesses and injuries, prescribe medications and therapies, perform procedures, and educate patients and their families on living a healthy lifestyle.

Licensed Practical and Licensed Vocational Nurse

A licensed practical nurse (LPN), or licensed vocational nurse (LVN) as they are called in Texas and California, provides basic bedside care for patients. Responsibilities are limited as all duties are conducted under the direct supervision of a physician or registered nurse.

A common task for an LPN/LVN is to take a patient's vital signs, which includes temperature, blood pressure, pulse, and respiration. LPN/LVNs also give injections and enemas, monitor catheters, collect samples, and conduct routine laboratory tests. LPN/LVNs also apply dressings, treat bedsores, and give alcohol rubs and massages. They observe patients and report any adverse reactions to medications or treatment. They also help patients with personal hygiene and ensure that patients are comfortable.

People wishing to become a LPN/LVN can attend a one-year program at a vocational or technical school. They then must pass a licensing examination. Many LPN/LVNs work in hospitals and nursing-care facilities. Others work in physicians' offices, outpatient-care facilities, or for pubic health care agencies.

Nursing Assistant

Nursing assistants (NAs) work under the direct supervision of a nurse. They have extensive daily contact with patients and are the caregivers who help patients perform day-to-day tasks, such as bathing, feeding, and dressing. They help patients walk and go to the bathroom. They transport patients, take vital signs, make beds, and set up equipment. NAs assist patients with activities of daily living and works as part of a collaborative team in the delivery of health care. Because of the physical requirements of the jobs, good physical conditioning is a plus.

NAs work in hospitals, physicians' offices, home health agencies, nursing homes, private homes, and mental health institutions. To become a NA, you need at least a high school diploma followed by 120 hours of training. Some employers offer on-site training. Courses are also offered through high school health science programs, community and state colleges Once training is complete, the NA may have the opportunity to be certified as a nursing assistant.

Summary

In the human body, cells form tissues and tissues form organs. Organs form the organ systems that are part of every individual. As a health care professional, it is important to understand how organs work together within organ systems. A good understanding of these systems can help you to correctly treat disease. It is also important to understand the language that is used to describe the positions of structures within the human body. This will help you to accurately report injury or discomfort in a patient.

SECTION	**13.1**	**Review Questions**

1. What is connective tissue?

2. What organs does the abdominal cavity contain?

3. What organ would arteriosclerosis mainly affect?

4. How would you describe a wound that is on the left front chest, close to the shoulder socket?

5. Which cavities are located in the dorsal region of the body?

6. Which type of tissue protects the outer body and the organs and also receives sensations?

7. Name the three major parts of the cell and describe their functions.

8. A _____ is a scientist who studies living organisms and infectious agents that are too small to be seen with the naked eye.

9. Name two differences between a registered nurse (RN) and a licensed practical nurse/ licensed vocational nurse (LPN/LVN).

 Learn By Doing: Section 13.1 Activity

1. Complete Worksheets 1 and 2.

2. Ask your teacher for directions to complete Worksheet/Activity 3.

3. Complete Worksheets 4 through 6.

4. When you are confident that you can meet each objective for this section, ask your teacher for the section evaluation.

The Skeletal System

Background

The skeletal system is made of tough bone tissue that supports the body and allows it to move. Some bones cover and protect vital organs, such as the heart and brain. Marrow within bones produces white and red blood cells. As a health care professional, it is important to know the parts of the skeleton, as well as diseases that may affect bone.

Objectives

When you have completed this section, you will be able to do the following:

- Match key terms with their correct meanings.
- Label a diagram of major bones in the body.
- Select from a list the functions of bones.
- Name the long, short, flat, and irregular bones of the body.
- Identify immovable, slightly movable, and freely movable joints of the body.
- Identify common disorders of the skeletal system.
- Label a diagram of four types of bone fractures.
- Explain why a health care worker must have a basic knowledge of the skeletal system and how it functions.

Introduction to the Skeletal System

Structure of the Bone

The skeletal system (Figure 13.8) is made up of bone and other connective tissues, such as ligaments and cartilage. Bones have their own system of blood vessels and nerves which allows **circulation** to occur within the bone.

The **components** of bone change from conception to old age. In the first month after **conception**, an **embryo's** skeletal framework is made up of **cartilage**. In the second and third months after conception, you can see calcium deposits in the bone.

Throughout life, calcium continues to form in the bone structure, causing the bone to become hard. This is called ossification. For example, a small child's bone is more **flexible** than the bone of a 30-year-old. The added calcium makes the bones of the 30-year-old harder, less flexible, and more **brittle**. A 60-year-old may lose calcium from the bone. This makes the bone **porous** so that it breaks easily.

circulation
(sur kyuh LEY shuhn)
Continuous one-way movement of blood through the heart and blood vessels to all parts of the body.

components
(kom PO nent s)
Parts or elements of a whole; an ingredient.

conception
(kuhn SEP shuhn)
Occurs when the male sperm fertilizes the female ovum and a new organism begins to develop.

embryo
(EM bree oh)
Living human being during the first eight weeks of development in the uterus.

cartilage
(CAR tuh lij)
Tough connective tissue; forms pads at end of bones, is found in the nasal septum and external ear, and forms the major portion of the embryonic skeleton.

flexible
(FLEK suh buhl)
Able to bend easily.

brittle
(BRIT uhl)
Fragile, easy to break.

porous
(POUR iss)
Filled with tiny holes.

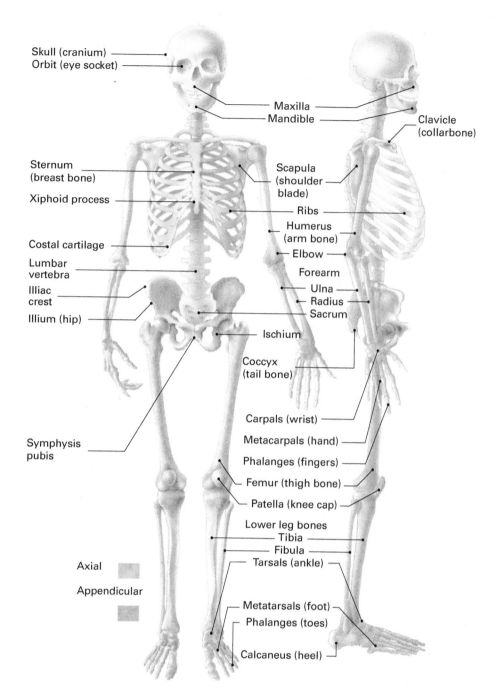

Skull (cranium)
Orbit (eye socket)
Maxilla
Mandible
Clavicle (collarbone)
Sternum (breast bone)
Scapula (shoulder blade)
Xiphoid process
Ribs
Humerus (arm bone)
Costal cartilage
Elbow
Lumbar vertebra
Forearm
Illiac crest
Ulna
Radius
Illium (hip)
Sacrum
Ischium
Coccyx (tail bone)
Symphysis pubis
Carpals (wrist)
Metacarpals (hand)
Phalanges (fingers)
Femur (thigh bone)
Patella (knee cap)
Lower leg bones
Tibia
Axial
Fibula
Appendicular
Tarsals (ankle)
Metatarsals (foot)
Phalanges (toes)
Calcaneus (heel)

Functions of the Bone

Bones perform many functions. Some of these are:

- To serve as a framework for the body, giving the body structure and support.

- To protect internal structures, such as the brain and spinal cord.

- To act as a storage area for calcium. This calcium is used in the blood if the diet does not provide enough calcium.

- To produce blood cells. The red bone marrow produces most of the red blood cells.

- To allow flexibility when muscles move them.

Types of Bones

There are four types of bones (**Figure 13.9**):

- *Long bones* (bones that are longer than their width):
  - Humerus.
  - Tibia.
  - Radius.
  - Fibula.
  - Ulna.

- *Short bones* (length and width are nearly equal):
  - Wrist and hand.
  - Ankle and feet.

- *Flat bones* (two layers of bone divided by a narrow span):
  - Skull.
  - Ribs.
  - Sternum.
  - Shoulder blade.

- *Irregular bones* (bones that do not fit into the shapes of the other three groups):
  - Face.
  - Hip.
  - Spin.

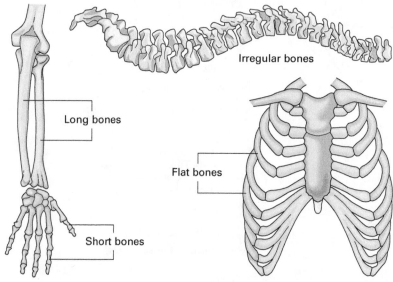

Irregular bones

Long bones

Flat bones

Short bones

FIGURE 13.9
Types of bones. What type of bones does the spine contain?

Groups of Bones

The human skeleton is divided into two groups of bones. The **axial** skeleton includes 80 bones. (**Figure 13.8**) These are found in the:

- Skull.
- Vertebrae.
- Ribs and sternum.

The **appendicular** skeleton involves the appendages and includes 126 bones. (**Figure 13.8**) These bones are found in the:

- Arms.
- Feet.
- Hands.
- Pelvis.
- Legs.

axial
(AX ee uhl)
Pertaining to the central structures of the body (e.g., vertebrae, skull, ribs, and sternum).

appendicular
(ap pen DIK you ler)
Pertaining to any body part added to the axis (e.g., arms and legs are attached to the axis of the body).

Joints

The point where two bones meet is a joint. Joints are divided into three main groups, depending on the amount of movement permitted. (Figure 13.10) These groups are:

- *Immovable joints:*
  - Cranium (suture joints).
- *Slightly movable joints:*
  - Vertebral discs.
  - Symphysis pubis.
  - Sacroiliac joints.
- *Freely movable joints:*
  - Shoulder joint.
  - Knee and ankle joints.
  - Elbow, wrist, and finger joints.

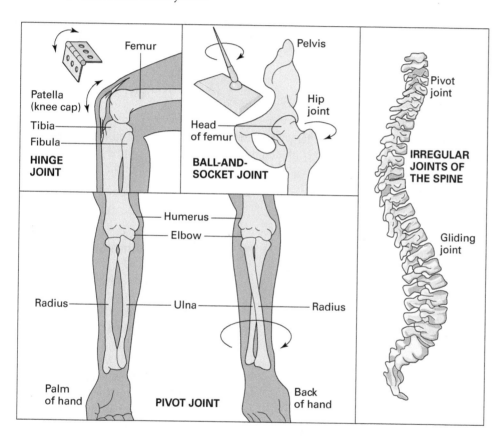

FIGURE 13.10
Types of joints. What kind of joint is at the elbow?

penetrates
(PEN i trayts)
Enters or passes through (e.g., a fractured bone passes through the skin).

calcify
(CAL si fy)
To harden by forming calcium deposits.

sedentary
(SED n ter ee)
Immobilized; does not move around very much.

spontaneous
(spon TEY nee uhs)
Occurring naturally without apparent cause.

Ligaments

Ligaments connect to bone and hold bones together. Joints are formed where the bones meet.

Common Disorders of the Skeletal System

Table 13.3 Common Disorders, Symptoms, and Preventive Measures/Treatment of the Skeletal System

Condition	Disorder	Symptoms	Preventive Measures/ Treatment
Arthritis	Inflammation of the joints. Can be caused when a joint is damaged, causing the edges of bones in the joint to rub against each other and become irritated.	Pain and swelling in the joints. (Figure 13.11)	Preventing damaging joints by using good body mechanics and limiting continuous repetitive movements that overuse specific joints. Treatments include: pain and anti-inflammatory medications; injections of steroids or gel-like substances to supplement the viscous properties of synovial fluid directly into the joint; non-traditional treatments, such as acupuncture; and, as a last resort, surgery.
Degenerative joint diseases—osteoarthritis	Inflammation of the membrane of the joint. Cause unknown, but changes in the structure of joints occur due to the inflammatory process.	Pain, stiffness, tenderness to the touch, deformity of joint regions.	Treating with anti-inflammatory medication. Surgery is sometimes indicated.
Fracture: ■ Simple ■ Compound ■ Comminuted ■ Greenstick	Broken bone: ■ The bone is broken, but the skin remains intact. ■ The bone is broken and **penetrates** the skin. ■ The bone breaks into many pieces and there are bone fragments in the tissue. ■ The bone is bent and splits, causing an incomplete fracture. (This is most common in children.)	Pain, swelling, and abnormal shape. (Figure 13.12)	Avoiding falls and situations that may put abnormal stress on bones. Treatments include: initially splinting, elevation, and ice; immobilization to help pain; then treatment by reduction (manipulation) to align the broken ends of the bone with or without some form of traction; or open reduction, an internal fixation to surgically repair a fractured bone, usually involving either the use of plates and screws or an intra-medullary (IM) rod to stabilize the bone.
Kyphosis	Abnormal outward curvature of the thoracic vertebrae (hunchback). This condition can be caused from a variety of conditions.	Appearance is the main symptom. In advanced conditions, pain may occur. Early medical care can identify the cause of this condition and early treatment may prevent progression.	Spine-stretching exercises and sleeping without a pillow. Sleeping on a firm mattress that keeps the back as straight as possible may be helpful.

(continued)

Table 13.3   Common Disorders, Symptoms, and Preventive Measures/Treatment of the Skeletal System (continued)

Condition	Disorder	Symptoms	Preventive Measures/ Treatment
Lordosis	An inward curvature of the lumbar spine (swayback). This condition can be caused from a variety of conditions.	Appearance is the main symptom; patients have an exaggerated posture. In advanced conditions, pain may occur. Early medical treatment can prevent progression.	Medication (if pain), physical therapy, and use of a brace. In severe cases, with pain and limited range of motion, surgery may be an option.
Osteoarthritis	Also known as degenerative arthritis, a condition in which low-grade inflammation results in pain in the joints, caused by abnormal wearing of the cartilage that covers and acts as a cushion inside joints, and destruction or decrease of synovial fluid that lubricates those joints.	Pain, inflammation, limiting of range of motion. Symptoms may occur in any joint, most commonly knees, hips, hands, and spine.	Relieve pain. Preserve or improve joint function. Reduce physical disability. Treatment can include pain medications, localized steroid injections, topical creams, and—as a last resort—joint surgery.
Osteomalacia	The bones do not **calcify** sufficiently, remaining soft. This is the milder, adult form of the disease. In children, this is called rickets. (See further down on chart.) Related to a lack of vitamin D.	Aches and pains in the lumbar (lower back) region and thighs, spreading later to the arms and ribs. Pain accompanied by tenderness in the involved bones. Difficulty in climbing up stairs and getting up from a squatting position.	Administration of heavy doses of vitamin D. Eating a balanced diet, especially foods with calcium, phosphorus, and vitamin D. Increased exposure to sunshine will result in the production of more vitamin D in the skin.
Osteomyelitis	Infection of the bone that is usually caused by bacteria (often staphylococci) that infects the bone and/or the bone marrow, usually introduced by trauma, or surgery. Number one complication of compound fractures.	Persistent, increasing bone pain with tenderness spreading into muscles, along with a fever.	See a physician early for treatment of infections and avoid accidents that may allow the introduction of bacteria into the body. Treatment includes strong IV antibiotics and, on occasion—in adults—surgery.
Osteoporosis	The bone becomes porous, causing it to break easily. Occurs more frequently in women after menopause, or in people who are **sedentary** or on steroid therapy for a long time.	Pain, especially in the lower back. Fractures that occur easily or with little trauma associated. Often it is the cause of **spontaneous** fractures in elderly women.	Following a proper diet, doing routine moderate exercise, and employing balanced hormone therapy as aging occurs.
Rickets	The bones do not **calcify** sufficiently, remaining soft. Related to a lack of vitamin D.	Bowlegs and knock-knees enlarged. Knoblike enlargement at ends and sides of bones. Muscle pain, enlarged skull, chest deformities, spinal curvature, enlargement of the liver and spleen, increased sweating, and general body tenderness.	Eating a balanced diet, especially foods with calcium, phosphorus, and vitamin D. Increased exposure to sunshine will result in the production of more vitamin D in the skin.

(continued)

Table 13.3   Common Disorders, Symptoms, and Preventive Measures/Treatment of the Skeletal System (continued)

Condition	Disorder	Symptoms	Preventive Measures/Treatment
Rheumatoid arthritis	An autoimmune disease that causes chronic inflammation of arthritis the joints	Fatigue, lack of appetite, low-grade fever, muscle and joint aches, and stiffness. Arthritis is common. Joints frequently become red, swollen, painful, and tender. Multiple joints are usually inflamed in a symmetrical pattern (both sides of the body affected).	No cure. Work to reduce joint inflammation and pain, maximize joint function, and prevent joint destruction and deformity. Use a combination of medications, rest, joint strengthening exercises, joint protection, and patient (and family) education.
Scoliosis	A **lateral** (to the side) curvature of the spine. (Figure 13.13)	Congenital malformation of the spine, poliomyelitis, unequal length of legs, and other physical conditions.	Seeking early recognition and treatment may prevent progression of the curvature. Treatments include: exercise, using a brace, and possibly surgically implanting rods.

FIGURE 13.11
Arthritis joint changes. What are the characteristics of an arthritic joint?

lateral
(LAT ur uhl)
Relating to the sides or side of.

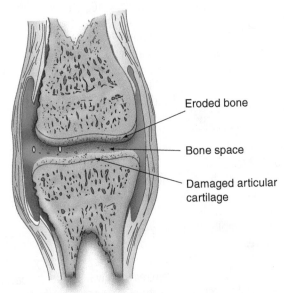

Eroded bone

Bone space

Damaged articular cartilage

Arthritis: joint changes

Apply It

Survey all of your classmates. Ask if they have ever broken a bone and if so, which one.

Create a graph—the x-axis should be labeled with the different bones that students broke; the y-axis should be labeled "number of people who have broken this bone".

Analyze the graph. Which bones were broken most? Why might that have happened?

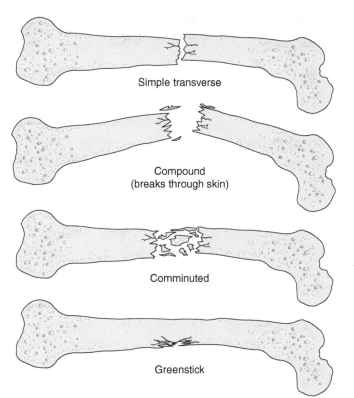

FIGURE 13.12
Common types of bone fractures. Which type of fracture produces many bone fragments?

Simple transverse

Compound (breaks through skin)

Comminuted

Greenstick

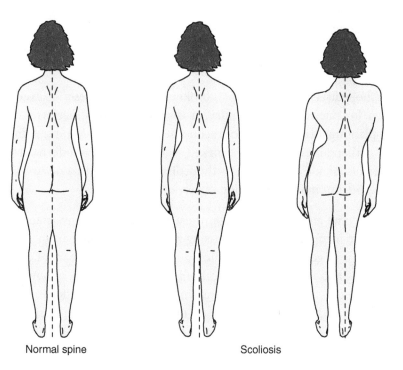

FIGURE 13.13
Comparison of normal and scoliosis spines. How is the spine of a person with scoliosis different from a normal spine?

Normal spine

Scoliosis

arthrodesis:	surgical **fixation** of a joint	**dactylus:**	toe or finger
caudocephalad:	from tail or coccyx to head	**ilio:**	pertaining to the ilium and femur
cephalalgia:	pain in the head, headache	**lumbosacral:**	pertaining to the lumbar vertebrae and the sacrum
cephalocentesis:	surgical puncture of the head		
cerebrotomy:	incision into the brain	**myelitis:**	inflammation of the spinal cord
chondroma:	tumor consisting of cartilage	**osteomalacia:**	softening of the bone
costochondral:	pertaining to a rib and its cartilage	**osteoplasty:**	plastic repair of the bone
craniomalacia:	softening of the skull bones	**osteosarcoma:**	malignant tumor of the bone
craniosclerosis:	thickening of the skull bones	**osteotomy:**	incision into a bone
dactyledema:	excess fluid in the fingers and toes	**phalanx:**	finger or toe bone
dactylology:	representing words by signs made with the fingers (sign language)	**prosthesis:**	artificial organ or part of the body

fixation
(fik SEY shuhn)
Repair or fix.

 ## Jobs and Professions

Orthopedist

An orthopedist, also called an orthopedic surgeon, is a physician who specializes in treating disorders of the musculoskeletal system. The musculoskeletal system is comprised of bones, joints, muscles, tendons, ligaments, nerves, skin, and any of the structures related to these body parts.

Orthopedists use casts to repair broken bones; they prescribe exercise and medication for musculoskeletal injury or disease; and they perform surgeries such as implanting artificial joints or reconstructing damaged limbs. Although historically orthopedists primarily worked with children, modern orthopedists have patients of all ages. Some orthopedists specialize in one area, such as sports injuries, but most treat a wide variety of conditions.

To become an orthopedist, you must first become a physician. That means four years of medical school and passing a medical licensing exam. You then complete one year of general surgery training followed by four years of orthopedic surgery training and two years in clinical practice. At this point, you must take an certification exam. Another year of training is needed to practice in a subspecialty area such as pediatric orthopedics or orthopedic sports medicine. Once certified, orthopedic surgeons must continue to take courses to keep their skills up to date.

Orthopedic Technician

An orthopedic technician, also known as an orthopedic technologist or cast technician, helps physicians and orthopedic surgeons care for and treat patients with orthopedic needs. This work is generally done in a hospital, clinic, or private practice.

The duties of an orthopedic technician are three-fold. First, there is work directly related to patient care. Orthopedic technicians help with such things as the application, adjustment, and removal of casts, splints, and braces. They also help set up, adjust, and maintain traction devices. Another aspect to the job is organizational. Orthopedic technicians are responsible for maintaining the cast room as well as orthopedic equipment and devices. The third prong is clerical. Orthopedic technicians manage insurance, medical billing, and coding for orthopedic procedures.

There are three different career levels for orthopedic technicians. Level I, or entry-level positions, requires a high school diploma and at least one year of full-time, on-the-job experience working with orthopedic patients. Level II requires certification from the National Board of Certification for Orthopaedic Technologists (NBCOT) plus either two years of experience, completion of an orthopedic technology training program, or completion of a related program and one year of full-time experience. Level III requires certification, completion of a training program, and up to eight years of experience.

Prosthetist

A prosthetist is a medical professional who evaluates, designs, and creates artificial limbs, or prostheses, for patients who have lost all or part of a limb due to disease or injury.

A prosthetist works with a team comprised of physicians, nurses, and physical and occupational therapists. Once the prosthesis is created, the prosthetist periodically evaluates the device and makes adjustments as needed.

To become a prosthetist, you must earn a B.S. degree and then complete a certificate program in prosthetics. It typically takes four years to earn a B.S. Certificate programs, which include both coursework and clinical experience, take between six months and one year to complete.

Summary

The axial and appendicular skeletons, joints, ligaments, and associated blood vessels and nerves make up the skeletal system. Skeletal system disease or fracture can make movement painful or difficult. In this section, you have learned to recognize and treat skeletal system disorders. You have also learned preventative measures to recommend to patients, so they can avoid skeletal system disorders. A strong and healthy skeletal system is essential to good overall health.

SECTION **13.2** Review Questions

1. How can a person treat rickets?

2. Which type of bone fracture results in a broken bone that penetrates the skin?

3. What are the three main groups of joints?

4. Contrast the axial skeleton with the appendicular skeleton.

5. Where are the long bones in the body found?

6. Are the maxilla and mandible found in the axial or appendicular skeleton?

7. What is arthritis and what are the symptoms?

8. Identify three duties of an orthopedic technician.

Learn By Doing: Section 13.2 Activity

1. Complete Worksheets 1 through 6 as assigned.

2. Ask your teacher for directions to complete Worksheets/Activities 7 and 8.

3. When you are confident that you can meet each objective for this section, ask your teacher for the section evaluation.

SECTION

13.3 The Muscular System

Background

The muscles in your body help you to move your arms and legs. They also help to move food, blood, and other materials around your body. In this section, you will learn about types of muscle, their functions, and their movements. You will review the different muscles of the muscular system and learn disorders related to muscles.

Objectives

When you have completed this section, you will be able to do the following:

- Match key terms with their correct meanings.

- Explain the difference between muscle and bone functions.

- List three major functions of the muscles.

- Match common disorders of the muscular system with their descriptions.

- Match basic muscle movements to their correct names.

- Label a diagram of the muscular system.

- Describe how muscles provide support and movement.

- Explain why the health care worker's understanding of the muscular system is important.

 Introduction to The Muscular System

The muscles of the body make all movement possible. Muscles move body parts, allowing for proper functioning, such as heartbeat, breathing, **digestion** of food, and movement of the body from place to place. The next sections help you understand how muscles work.

digestion
(dye JES chun)
Process of breaking down food mechanically and chemically.

Muscle Function

Skeletal muscles comprise about 40% of the mass of the average human body. Muscles are the "engine" that your body uses to propel itself. They turn energy into motion. They are efficient at turning fuel into motion; they are long-lasting, self-healing and can grow stronger with practice.

Muscles are made up of **elastic** fibers. These fibers are like a rubber band that lengthens and shortens. The thick and thin filaments do the actual work of a muscle. Thick filaments are made of a protein called **myosin**. Thin filaments are made of another protein called **actin**.

A muscle **contraction** occurs when these fibers generate tension through the action of actin and myosin cross-bridging—the process that describes the sliding of myosin and actin filaments (a sliding filament mechanism) over each other.

Muscles cannot push; they can only pull. Even when you push against a wall, each muscle in your body is working by pulling. When the muscles relax they stop pulling. your arm and another straightens it.

The main functions of muscles are to:

- Produce heat.
- Produce movement.
- Maintain posture.

Types of Muscle

There are two classifications of muscle:

- **Voluntary** *muscles* that you **contract** when you want to move (e.g., skeletal muscles; Figure13.14). You control these muscles; the movement is not automatic.
- **Involuntary** *muscles,* which contract automatically (e.g., stomach, intestine, and heart). The heart pumps blood automatically. The stomach digests food automatically. You cannot tell the heart or stomach to start or stop.

Tendons

Tendons connect muscles to bones. When the muscle moves, it moves the tendon and bone. The longest tendon is called the Achilles tendon. This is a tendon of the posterior leg; it attaches the calf muscle to the heel bone.

Types of Muscle Tissue

Muscle tissue is classified into three categories:

- *Skeletal muscles* or *striated muscles* are voluntary muscles. (Figure 13.2) These muscles provide movement of the body.
- *Visceral muscles* or *smooth muscles* form the walls of the internal organs of the body (e.g., digestive tract, respiratory passage, and walls of blood vessels). They are involuntary muscles. (Figure 13.2)
- The *cardiac muscle* forms the wall of the heart. This muscle circulates the blood. (Figure 13.2)

elastic
(ee LAS tik)
Easily stretched.

myosin
(MI essin)
A protein in muscles that helps them contract.

actin
(AK tin)
A protein present in all cells and in muscle tissue; plays a role in contraction.

contraction
(ken TRAK shun)
A tightening or narrowing of a muscle, organ, or other body part.

voluntary
(VOL en tar ee)
Under the control of the person (e.g., you voluntarily raise your arm; it does not rise automatically).

contract
(con TRAKT)
To shorten, to draw together; muscles shorten when you flex a body part.

involuntary
(IN vol en tar ee)
Not under control (e.g., muscle twitching).

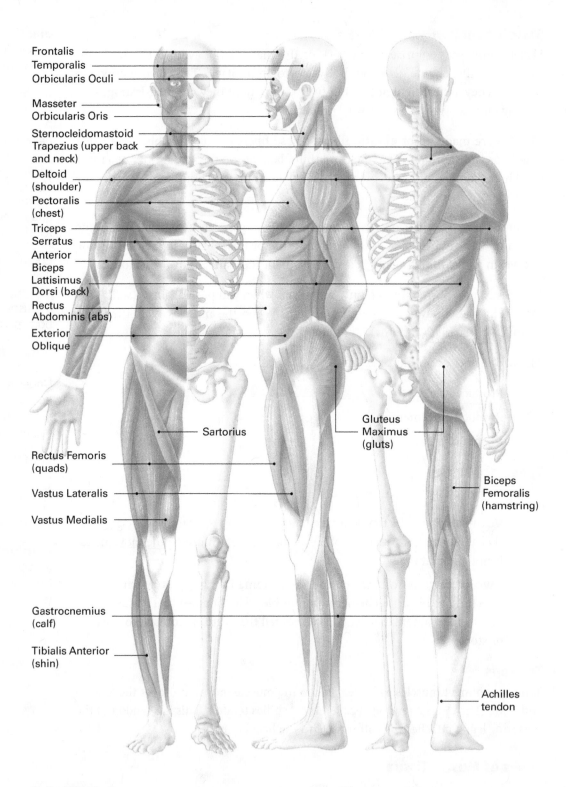

Frontalis
Temporalis
Orbicularis Oculi
Masseter
Orbicularis Oris
Sternocleidomastoid
Trapezius (upper back and neck)
Deltoid (shoulder)
Pectoralis (chest)
Triceps
Serratus Anterior
Biceps
Lattisimus Dorsi (back)
Rectus Abdominis (abs)
Exterior Oblique
Sartorius
Rectus Femoris (quads)
Vastus Lateralis
Vastus Medialis
Gastrocnemius (calf)
Tibialis Anterior (shin)
Gluteus Maximus (gluts)
Biceps Femoralis (hamstring)
Achilles tendon

FIGURE 13.14
Skeletal muscular system. Where is the lattisimus dorsi muscle?

Basic Movements of the Skeletal Muscle

There are six basic movements of skeletal muscles:

- **Adduct:** moving a body part toward the midline. (**Figure 13.15a**)

- **Abduct:** moving a body part away from the midline. (**Figure 13.15b**)

- **Extend:** increases the angle of the muscle. (**Figure 13.16**)

- **Flex:** decreases the angle of the muscle. (**Figure 13.16**)

- **Rotate:** turning a body part on its **axis**.

- **Supination and pronation:** a rotation movement. For example, supination is when the ankle appears to be "tipped" to the outside so you are standing on the outside border of the foot; conversely, pronation is the flattening out of the arch when the foot strikes the ground.

axis
(AX iss)
A center point that can be rotated around.

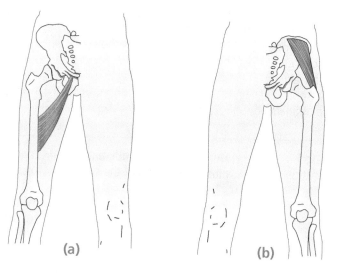

FIGURE 13.15
(a) Adduction; *(b)* abduction. How is adduction different from abduction?

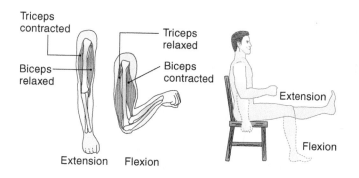

FIGURE 13.16
Extension and flexion. Which muscles contract during arm extension?

Common Disorders of the Muscular System

**Table 13.4   Common Disorders, Symptoms, and Preventive Measures/
Treatment of the Muscular System**

Condition	Disorder	Symptoms	Preventive Measures/Treatment
Atrophy	The wasting or loss of muscle tissue resulting from disease or lack of use.	Loss of mass and strength; some loss of mobility.	Application of moist heat, whirlpool baths and resistive exercises; more active exercises as mobility increases.
Fibromyalgia	Inflammation of the muscle tissues and the fibrous connective tissues.	A chronic stiffness and joint or muscle pain in eight or more specific muscle sites.	Using rest, heat, massage, and medication to relieve inflammation and swelling.
Hypertrophy	Abnormal growth and increase of the size of muscle cells caused by strength training, high-intensity anaerobic exercises, and use of anabolic steroids.	Enlarged muscles, as shown by bodybuilders.	Use lower intensity, longer duration aerobic exercise for health benefits without hypertrophy.
Muscle strain (Also called a torn muscle)	A muscle tear caused by a violent contraction.	Pain, swelling, warmth, and muscle weakness at the site.	Warming up muscles prior to exercise or strenuous activity. Not overextending muscles by trying to lift or pull objects that are beyond your capacity. Treatment includes rest and ice; then, as the pain decreases, use heat, stretch and light exercise to bring blood to the injured area.
Muscular dystrophy	A group of genetically transmitted diseases that progressively **deteriorate** muscle tissue.	Loss of strength with increased disability and deformity.	Using supportive treatment such as physical therapy and orthopedic procedures to minimize deformity. Genetic screening recommended for all family members who might be carriers.
Myalgia	Muscle pain.	Muscle pain and malaise; occurs in many infectious diseases.	Resting, taking medication, and identifying the original cause.
Tendonitis	A painful inflammation of a tendon.	Pain, swelling, stiffness in the local area of the tendon to burning sensation around the whole joint. Slow to heal and rarely regain original strength. Recurrence of injury is common.	Use of anti-inflammatory drugs (not steroids), rest and gradual return to exercise

myasthenia:	muscle weakness	***myomelanosis:***	abnormal darkening of muscle tissue
myocardium:	heart muscle or cardiac muscle	***myoparesis:***	weakness or partial paralysis of a muscle
myocele:	muscular protrusion (bulging or sticking out through a muscle)	***myosclerosis:***	hardening of a muscle
myocelialgia:	pain of the abdominal muscle	***myothermic:***	pertaining to a rise in muscle temperature
myogenic:	beginning in the muscle		
myography:	record of muscle contractions	***tenorrhaphy:***	suturing of a tendon
myoid:	resembling muscle	***tenositis:***	inflammation of a tendon
myoma:	tumor containing muscle tissue		

 ## Jobs and Professions

deteriorate
(dee TEER ee or ate)
Break down.

Myologist

An orofacial myologist diagnoses and treats abnormal patterns of the mouth and face caused by things such as thumb sucking, tongue thrusting, nail biting, and jaw clenching. Left untreated, these habits lead to problems with teeth alignment, speech, chewing, swallowing, and breathing.

The myologist works in conjunction with physicians and dentists to help patients develop new habits that lead to the proper usage and placement of the tongue, lips, and jaw. Myologists consist of professionals such as speech pathologists, physicians, dentists, and dental hygienists who have sought further training in this area.

To become certified by the International Association of Orofacial Myology, candidates, who are already practicing professionals in another area, must complete an approved 28-hour introductory course or internship, be a member in good standing for one year, and pass a take-home proficiency exam and an on-site evaluation.

Physical Therapist

Physical therapists (PTs) work with accident victims and people who suffer from disabling conditions such as lower back pain, fractures, heart disease, and cerebral palsy. They help these patients restore function, improve mobility, relieve pain, and prevent or limit permanent physical disabilities.

PTs test and measure everything from a patient's strength and range of motion to their balance and coordination. They develop individualized treatment plans that may include things such as electrical stimulation, hot packs and cold compresses, ultrasound, traction, or deep-tissue massage.

Physical therapists typically work a 40-hour week. Most PTs work in hospitals, clinics, and private offices. To become a physical therapist, you must graduate from an accredited physical therapy program. The minimum requirement is a B.S. degree. Many have a master's or doctoral degree.

Sports Medicine Assistant

Working directly under the supervision of a physician, a sports medicine assistant works specifically with athletes. Duties include helping diagnose, treat, and prevent injuries, as well as assisting athletes with their nutrition, training, and conditioning. Specifically, a sports medicine assistant might recommend protective gear, supervise trainers, or develop training or rehabilitation programs.

Sports medicine assistants can be found in school athletic departments, community recreation programs, health and fitness clubs, sports centers, resorts, clinics specializing in sports medicine, or even in a private practice. To become a sports medicine assistant, you need a four-year degree. This is a growing profession, and the qualifications required are rapidly evolving.

Tenotomist

A tenotomist is surgeon who specializes in tenotomies, or procedures in which tendons are cut. A tenotomy is performed when a muscle has developed improperly, as in the case of a club foot. It is also performed if a muscle becomes shortened and is unable to stretch to its full range of motion. The tenotomist who performs the surgery is a licensed orthopedic surgeon (see orthopedist).

Summary

Muscle tissue is made of elastic fibers that lengthen and shorten, helping the body to move, produce heat, and maintain posture. Skeletal muscles allow you to flex and extend your arms and legs. Smooth muscles move food, air, and blood throughout your body. The cardiac muscle pumps blood through your body. In this section, you have learned how muscle disorders can cause pain and inhibit movement. You have also learned that muscle disorders such as muscle strain and torn muscle can be avoided by stretching and avoiding strenuous activity.

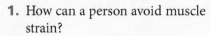

SECTION **13.3** Review Questions

1. How can a person avoid muscle strain?

2. What position is the leg in when you are sitting normally in a chair?

3. Describe the three types of muscle tissue and what they do.

4. What are the three functions of muscles?

5. What does *contract* mean?

6. What is tendonitis and how do you treat it?

7. Describe the different roles of a physical therapist and a sports medicine assistant.

Learn By Doing: Section 13.3 Activity

1. Complete Worksheets 1 through 5 as assigned.

2. When you are confident that you can meet each objective for this section, ask your teacher for the section evaluation.

13.4 The Circulatory System

Background

Arteries, veins, and the heart are the main organs of the circulatory system. Blood in the circulatory system delivers oxygen and nutrients to cells and removes waste materials. In this section, you will learn that the circulatory system is one of the most important systems of the body. Any disorder that disrupts the flow of blood can cause brain damage or death. For this reason, health care workers should be familiar with the treatment and prevention of circulatory system disorders.

Objectives

When you have completed this section, you will be able to do the following:

- Match key terms with their correct meanings.

- Name the major organs of the circulatory system.

- Label a diagram of the heart and blood vessels.

- Recognize functions of the circulatory system.

- Identify the common disorders of the circulatory system.

- List the parts of the circulatory system through which blood flows.

- Describe how the circulatory system supports life.

- Explain why the health care worker's understanding of the circulatory system is important.

oxygen
(OX uh jin)
Element in the atmosphere that is essential for maintaining life in most organisms.

waste products
(WAYST praw dukts)
Elements that are unfit for the body's use and are eliminated from the body.

adequate
(AD uh kwit)
Enough, sufficient.

oxygenated
(OX uh jin ate ed)
Containing oxygen.

unoxygenated
(UN ox uh jin ate ed)
Lacking oxygen.

carbon dioxide
(car buhn die OX eyed)
A gas, heavier than air; a waste product from the body.

Introduction to the Circulatory System

Circulation is the continuous one-way movement of blood throughout the body. All of the systems and organs depend on the circulatory system. Arteries carry blood with **oxygen** and nutrients to each cell, and veins carry away the cell's **waste products**. If the circulation is not **adequate**, cells die. When the cells die, tissues begin to die, and the organs stop working properly. This may cause an entire system to stop functioning.

Kinds of Blood Vessels

- *Arteries* carry blood from the lower chambers of the heart (ventricles) to all parts of the body. Arteries carry **oxygenated** blood, with the exception of the pulmonary artery. The *pulmonary artery* carries **unoxygenated** blood.

- *Arterioles* are small arteries that connect arteries with capillaries.

- *Capillaries* have very thin walls that allow nutrients, oxygen, and **carbon dioxide** to move in and out of the blood. (Figure 13.17)

- *Venules* are small veins that connect veins with capillaries.

- *Veins* carry blood from all the different parts of the body and return it to the heart. Veins carry unoxygenated blood, with the exception of the pulmonary vein. The pulmonary vein carries oxygenated blood. Veins have valves that aid in returning blood to the heart.

FIGURE 13.17
Blood vessels and capillary bed of the body. How are gases and other substances exchanged in the capillary bed?

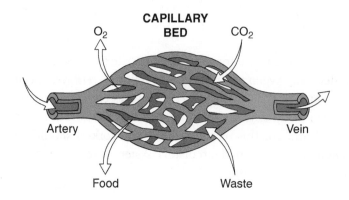

The Heart

The heart is the pump that forces blood throughout the body. (Table 13.5) The outside of the heart is made **primarily** of muscle, and the inside is divided into four hollow chambers. (Figure 13.18)

primarily
(pry MARE uh lee)
For the most part; chiefly.

FIGURE 13.18
Cross section of the heart. What structure separates the two ventricles from each other?

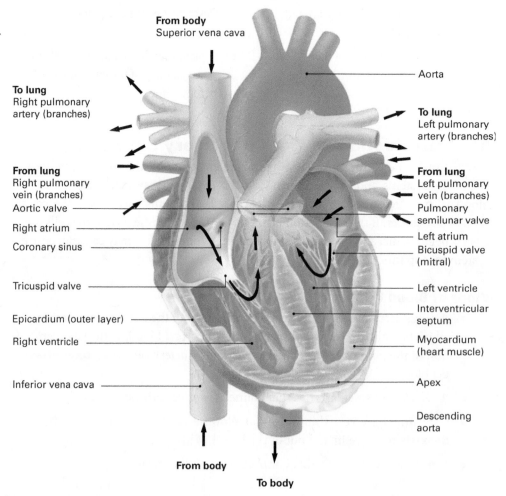

Table 13.5   Flow of Blood Through the Body

Starts in the right atrium
↓
Through the tricuspid valve
↓
Right ventricle
↓
Through the pulmonary valve
↓
Pulmonary artery
↓
Lungs (oxygen and carbon dioxide exchange)
↓
Pulmonary veins
↓
Left atrium
↓
Mitral valve
↓
Left ventricle
↓
Aortic valve
↓
Aorta
("out to the body")
↓
Arteries
↓
Arterioles
↓
Capillaries
(oxygen and carbon dioxide exchange)
↓
Venules
↓
Veins
↓
Superior or inferior vena cava
↓
Right atrium

The heart wall is made of three different layers of tissue:

- *Endocardium* is the smooth inside lining of the heart.

- *Myocardium* is the thickest layer and is made up of muscle.

- *Pericardium* is a double membrane that lines the outside of the heart.

The inside of the heart is divided into four parts or chambers:

Apply It

Construct a matching game. Create a series of cards naming circulatory disorders or other related medical terminology. Then create a set of cards with the definition/description of each term. Divide in small groups and play the matching game.

- The *right atrium* receives unoxygenated blood from the veins.
- The *right ventricle* receives blood from the right atrium and pumps it to the lungs through the pulmonary artery.
- The *left atrium* receives oxygenated blood from the lungs and pumps it into the left ventricle.
- The *left ventricle* pumps blood into the aorta, which is the largest artery in the body. The aorta delivers the blood throughout the body.

Valves separate the chambers in the heart from the vessels leaving the heart:

- The *tricuspid* valve is between the right atrium and right ventricle. It closes when the right ventricle pumps blood out of the heart. This keeps the blood from flowing back into the right atrium.
- The *pulmonary semilunar* valve lies between the right ventricle and the pulmonary artery. It closes after all the blood from the right ventricle has been pushed into the pulmonary artery. When the valve closes, it stops blood from flowing back into the ventricle.
- The *mitral* (bicuspid) valve is found between the left atrium and the left ventricle. It closes to prevent blood from flowing back into the left atrium when the left ventricle contracts.
- The *aortic semilunar* valve is located between the left ventricle and the aorta. It stops blood from returning to the left ventricle after it has been forced into the aorta.

Medical Terminology

angiocele:	hernia of a blood vessel	**endocarditis:**	inflammation of the inside of the heart
bradycardia:	abnormally slow heart rate		
cardiogenic:	beginning within the heart	**erythrocytosis:**	disease of red blood cells
cardiopulmonary:	pertaining to the heart and lungs	**hemostasis:**	stoppage of blood flow
		hyperemia:	excess of blood in any part of the body
cardioscope:	instrument used to examine the inside of the heart		
		hypertension:	high blood pressure
cardiovascular:	pertaining to the heart and blood vessels	**hypotension:**	unusually low blood pressure
		intravenous:	IV, within a vein
carditis:	inflammation of the heart muscle	**leukocyte:**	white blood cell
cyanosis:	bluish discoloration of the skin	**leukopenia:**	deficiency of white blood cells
ecchymosis:	bruised condition	**tachycardia:**	excessively rapid heart rate
electrocardiogram:	ECG/EKG, a tracing of heart activity	**thrombus:**	stationary blood clot that obstructs circulation
embolus:	a mass, most commonly a blood clot, that becomes lodged in a blood vessel and obstructs it		

Common Disorders of the Circulatory System

Table 13.6 Common Disorders, Symptoms, and Preventive Measures/Treatment of the Circulatory System

Condition	Disorder	Symptoms	Preventive Measures/Treatment
Aneurysm	An aneurysm is present when the wall of a blood vessel is weakened. Aneurysms may be found in any part of the circulatory system. Among the most serious are those that occur in the head, heart, and aorta. An aortic aneurysm that ruptures usually causes immediate death. A ruptured cerebral aneurysm can cause paralysis, speech and vision disturbances, and death.	Pulsating swelling that produces a blowing sound through a stethoscope. Pain may or may not be present.	Maintaining healthy living can be helpful in keeping blood pressure within normal range. Exercise and diet may also be a factor, but will not ensure the prevention of aneurysms. Treatment depends on where they are located and how big they are; surgery would be used to prevent rupture or to stop bleeding (if rupture has occurred).
Arteriosclerosis	Arteriosclerosis is present when the walls of the arteries become thick and harden, causing vessels to be less elastic. Less blood is able to flow through the arteries because the arteries are narrowed.	Changes in skin temperature and color, changes in peripheral pulses, headache, dizziness, and memory changes. Common in geriatric patients.	Continuing activity throughout aging, getting adequate rest, and avoiding stress.
Endocarditis	An inflammation of the inside lining of the heart that may affect the heart valves. This condition can be caused by a variety of diseases. Survival rate is 65 to 85%.	Chest pain, shortness of breath, and elevated body temperature.	Maintaining good health habits, including good dental care, may help resist this condition. Early diagnosis helps promote successful treatment, which consists of rest and IV antibiotics
Heart murmur	The valve does not close completely, allowing blood to flow back into the chamber it just left. It is most often present in the tricuspid and mitral valves.	Heart sounds that create a blowing sound between heartbeats, which indicate faulty heart valves.	Maintaining a healthy lifestyle may be helpful in preventing murmurs in later life. Some murmurs are present at birth.
Hypertension (also called the "silent killer")	A blood pressure greater than 140/90 places increased strain on the entire circulatory system. Risk of hypertension is increased due to obesity, hereditary factors race (African Americans run greater risk), gender (men run greater risk) and older age. Other factors associated with higher risk include heavy alcohol consumption, diabetes, use of oral contraceptives and lack of exercise.	In some cases, there are no symptoms. In others, we see anxiety, heart palpitations, profuse sweating, pallor, nausea, and in some cases the lungs collect fluid. May also experience headaches and blurred vision.	Maintaining good health habits may help resist this condition. Early diagnosis helps promote successful treatment. Treatment includes lifestyle changes to minimize risk factors (such as exercise and diet), monitoring blood pressure regularly and taking antihypertensive medication, if necessary.

(continued)

Table 13.6   Common Disorders, Symptoms, and Preventive Measures/Treatment of the Circulatory System (continued)

Condition	Disorder	Symptoms	Preventive Measures/Treatment
Myocardial infarction (MI) or heart attack	Occurs when the coronary arteries (the muscular blood vessels that carry blood away from the heart) are blocked. This blockage can be due to atherosclerosis, or a blood clot, which is called coronary thrombosis.	Crushing chest pain that may radiate to the left arm, neck, or stomach. The patient may complain of severe heartburn or a gallbladder attack. The patient may look ashen in color and skin may feel clammy. May experience shortness of breath, may feel faint and anxious, and may fear that they are going to die.	Not smoking, maintaining a healthy body weight, eating a balanced diet low in saturated fats, and exercising regularly. Controlling stress is also helpful. Treatment includes opening the blocked artery and restoring blood flow to the affected area of heart muscle (surgery). Treatment is also aimed at preventing further damage and the chance of repeat heart attacks in the future (changes in diet, not smoking, exercise and medication).
Myocarditis	An inflammation of the heart muscle caused by viral, bacterial, or fungal infection, serum sickness, rheumatic fever, chemical agents, or complications from a collagen disease.	Chest pain, shortness of breath, and elevated body temperature.	Maintaining good health habits may help resist this condition. Early diagnosis helps promote successful treatment.
Pericarditis	An inflammation of the outer lining of the heart caused by trauma, malignancy, infection, uremia, myocardial infarction, collagen disease, and other nonspecific conditions.	Chest pain, shortness of breath, nonproductive cough, and rapid pulse. A friction rub can be heard over the heart with a stethoscope.	Maintaining good health habits may help resist this condition. Early diagnosis helps promote successful treatment.
Varicose veins	Enlarged veins that are not efficient in returning blood to the heart. They can occur anywhere in the body but are most often found in the lower **extremities**.	Pain and muscle cramps with a feeling of fullness and heaviness in the legs. Some veins near the skin may look enlarged. May be caused by congenital defects of the veins or by congestion and increased pressure.	Minimizing prolonged times of standing and maintaining good posture can reduce the risk of varicose veins in people without congenital defects.

extremities
(ex TREM uh tees)
Arms, legs, hands, and feet.

 Jobs and Professions

Internist

An internist is a physician who may provide either primary or long-term comprehensive care. They also may specialize in fields such as cardiology, critical care, infectious disease, or pulmonology.

Internists, as the name implies, focus on the health of internal organs. They generally treat illnesses such as high blood pressure or diabetes, which do not require surgery. The majority of an internist's patients are adults.

Internists must complete medical school followed by a three-year residency in which they receive training focused on internal medicine. In order to specialize in a particular area, internists must complete another one to three years of training. Between 20 and 25 percent of all physicians are internists.

Cardiologist

Cardiologists are medical doctors who diagnose, treat, and try to prevent problems in the cardiovascular system. The cardiovascular system includes the heart and blood vessels.

Patients are usually referred to a cardiologist by their primary care physicians. If a problem is suspected, the cardiologist checks the medical records, discusses signs and symptoms, conducts tests, and recommends a course of treatment. This may involve medication, lifestyle changes, or surgery. In the case of surgery, patients are sent to a cardiovascular surgeon.

Cardiologists typically work in clinics and hospitals. Some choose to specialize their practice, such as pediatric or adult cardiology. To become a cardiologist, you must graduate from college and then medical school. You must complete a residency and become certified in internal medicine. Then, you must complete another residency and become certified in cardiology. Further specialization requires another residency and certification.

Cardiopulmonary Technician

A cardiopulmonary technician, also called a perfusionist, is someone who operates a heart-and-lung machine. This life-supporting equipment replaces the function of the heart and lungs when they must be temporarily stopped, such as during cardiac surgery.

Cardiopulmonary technicians must pay extremely close attention to detail. They must notice even the slightest change in heart or lung function during surgery as any change could indicate a problem.

Cardiopulmonary technicians may work for hospitals, surgeons, or in a group practice. Some are independent contractors who work for one or more different employers. There are several different routes to this profession.

In general, though, you must have a four-year college degree with an emphasis on medical terminology, respiratory therapy, or nursing. You must then complete a training program that can last anywhere from one to four years. This will result in either a certificate or a master's degree, depending upon the type of program completed. Finally, you pass a test to become certified by the American Board of Cardiovascular Perfusion.

ECG/EKG Technician

ECG/EKG technicians perform tests such as electrocardiograms (EKGs) and stress tests, which help physicians diagnose and treat problems with the heart and blood vessels. These tests record and monitor the electrical impulses transmitted by the heart. Tracking these impulses can identify any irregularities and potential problems.

ECG/EKG technicians work in hospitals and physicians' offices. Community colleges and vocational/technical schools offer training in this area, but most ECG/EKG technicians are trained on the job by an EKG supervisor or a cardiologist. Not all ECG/EGK technicians are certified, but there is a growing trend in that direction.

Echocardiogram Technician

Echocardiogram technicians use ultrasound equipment to perform specialized tests called echocardiograms. During these tests, high-frequency sounds waves are transmitted into the heart chambers, valves, and blood vessels to create an image. The technician checks the image on screen for any abnormalities, photographs or videotapes the image, and sends the images and a report to the patient's physician for evaluation.

Nearly three-fourths of all echocardiogram technicians work in cardiology departments in hospitals. Others are employed in physicians' offices or diagnostic laboratories. Although some are trained on the job, most have completed a two- or four-year program in this specialty. Professional certification is available.

 Summary

In this section, you have learned that diseases of the circulatory system affect blood vessels or the heart. Heart disease may weaken the muscles of the heart, causing it to pump less effectively. Diseases of the blood vessels may slow or block the delivery of oxygen to cells, causing organs to fail. You have learned the signs of and some treatments for circulatory diseases. You have also learned some ways to prevent circulatory diseases. This knowledge can help you to suggest lifestyle changes to patients to help them avoid circulatory diseases.

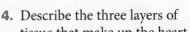

SECTION **13.4** **Review Questions**

1. What are the major organs of the circulatory system?

2. What is the function of the capillaries?

3. Describe the path that blood takes as it moves from the lungs through the heart and out to the rest of the body.

4. Describe the three layers of tissue that make up the heart.

5. What is an aneurysm?

6. What are actions that people can take to prevent myocardial infarction?

7. What are the differences between an ECG/EKG technician and an echocardiogram technician?

 Learn By Doing: Section 13.4 Activity

1. Complete Worksheets 1 through 6 as assigned.

2. When you are confident that you can meet each objective for this section, ask your teacher for the section evaluation.

13.5 The Lymphatic System

Background

The lymphatic system allows the body to maintain homeostasis. This system helps the body to fight disease and build immunity. It also prevents the buildup of fluids in tissues. In this section, you will study the structure and functions of the lymphatic system. You will also learn about disorders that affect this system. Disorders that affect the lymphatic system can weaken the body's immune response. Patients who have weakened immunity are less able to fight off disease.

Objectives

When you have completed this section, you will be able to do the following:

- Match key terms with their correct meanings.

- Describe the general functions of the lymphatic system.

- Describe what lymph is.

- Match lymph vessels and organs to their function.

- Explain the difference between an antigen and an antibody.

- Identify common disorders of the lymphatic system.

- Describe how the lymphatic system helps provide immunity.

Homeostasis

Maintaining good health depends on maintaining homeostasis. The body must constantly receive feedback from the body's regulatory mechanisms. For example, when the body's temperature rises, sweating provides feedback. There is a delicate balance between fluid, electrolytes, and pH—illness almost always threatens that balance. Medical interventions, such as intravenous fluids, can also cause imbalances.

Introduction to the Lymphatic System

The lymphatic system is an important part of the body's defense against disease. It filters out organisms that cause disease, produces white blood cells, and makes antibodies. It also drains excess fluids and protein so that tissues do not swell up.

The lymphatic system and the circulatory system have structures that are joined together by a capillary system. The lymphatic system is made up of the lymph capillaries, lymph vessels, lymph nodes, spleen, tonsils, thymus, lacteals, thoracic duct, right lymphatic duct, and the cisterna chyli.

Kinds of Lymphatic System Vessels and Organs

- *Lymph capillaries* are tubes that reach into the **interstitial** spaces of most body tissues. The capillaries have very thin walls that allow tissue fluids to move into them. When the fluid moves into the capillary, it is called lymph. The lymph contains waste products and foreign bodies from the cells. The lymph passes from the capillaries to the lymph vessels.

- *Lymph vessels* are similar to veins. Muscle contractions help move the lymph from the tissues to the lymphatic trunks. Valves prevent backflow of the lymph. The lymphatic trunks receive the lymph from the body. The lymph from the lymphatic trunks empties into the veins and becomes part of the blood **plasma**.

interstitial
(in tur STISH uhl)
Space between tissues.

plasma
(PLAZ muh)
Watery, colorless fluid containing leukocytes, erythrocytes, and platelets.

lymphocyte
(LIM fo sites)
Type of white blood cell.

monocytes
(MAWN o sites)
Large single-nucleus white blood cells.

Apply It

Create a wound somewhere on your body, using vaseline, cocoa, and tissues. Using yarn, trace the lymphatic path an infection would follow and to determine which lymph nodes would swell. Trace the path from the wound until it empties into the thoracic duct or right lymphatic duct. Determine which it would empty into based on wound location.

---

antigen
(ANN tuh jin)
Foreign matter that causes the body to produce antibodies.

antibodies
(ANN tuh bah dees)
Substances made by the body to produce immunity to an antigen.

phagocytes
(FAY go sites)
Cells that surround, ingest, and digest microorganisms and cellular waste.

- *Lymph nodes* lie along the lymph vessels. They are located in the neck, armpit, chest, abdomen, elbows, groin, and knees. (**Figure 13.19**) They filter out bacteria and other waste products from the lymph as it moves toward the lymphatic trunks. They also produce **lymphocytes**, which help the body defend itself against microorganisms.

- *Tonsils* are masses of lymph tissue that are exposed to the outside. They filter tissue fluid, not lymph. They may filter so many bacteria that the pathogens overwhelm the tonsil. The tonsils then become infected.

- The *spleen* is behind the stomach. It filters microorganisms and waste products from the blood. The spleen makes lymphocytes and **monocytes** to help the body defend itself against microorganisms. The spleen also stores red blood cells and destroys worn-out red blood cells.

- The *thymus* is in front of the aorta and behind the upper part of the sternum. It is lymphatic tissue that stores lymphocytes that work with the lymphatic system to defend the body. Most of this work is done during childhood; later, it is replaced by fat. The *lacteals* pick up digested fats from the small intestine.

- The *cisterna chyli* stores purified lymph before it empties into the bloodstream.

- *Thoracic duct* is the common trunk of all lymphatic vessels in the body except those on the upper right side of the body.

- *Right lymphatic* duct is the vessel that carries lymph from the right side of the head, neck, thorax, lung, upper right limb, right side of the heart, and the diaphragmatic surface of the liver.

The Lymphatic System and Immunity

The lymphatic system helps the body remove substances that are harmful. These substances may be microorganisms or other foreign bodies. The foreign body is called an **antigen**. Examples of antigens are poisons, splinters, and microorganisms. When these enter the body, the body responds by producing **antibodies**. The antibodies attack the antigen. This process is called the *immune response*.

Immune Response

The immune system has many specialized cells. Two types of white blood cells are lymphocytes and **phagocytes**. Phagocytes circulate through the body and ingest diseased and dead cells. Other types of white cells surround foreign bodies and destroy them. All of the white blood cells are important in protecting the body. Some things that tell you that the immune system is working are fever, inflammation, and pus. When these are present, you know that the immune system is responding to protect the body.

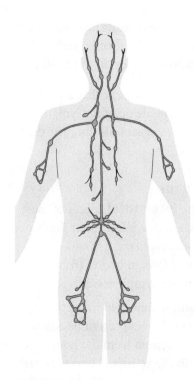

FIGURE 13.19
Lymph nodes in torso. What do lymph nodes do?

Types of Immunity

Nonspecific immunity protects the body, in general, against antigens that can cause infection. The body's nonspecific defenses include intact skin, moist mucous membranes, cilia, saliva, tears, and stomach acids. These defenses work to protect the body against a range of antigens. Specific immunity, however, protects the body against specifically identified antigens, including bacteria, fungi, and viruses.

There are two types of immunity: active and passive. When the body produces its own antibodies, **active immunity** occurs. The first time there is contact with an antigen, the slow process of antibody formation begins. Then, when exposure to the antigen happens again, the combination of antibodies and memory cells specific to that antibody quickly produce even more antibodies. This is natural active immunity. Vaccinations are an artificial means of producing active immunity. When the body receives antibodies from a source outside of itself, **passive immunity** occurs. Antibodies that a baby receives from its mother's breast milk is an example of passive immunity.

active immunity
(AK tiv im YOO ni tee)
Protection that occurs when a body produces its own antibodies.

passive immunity
(PASS iv im YOO ni tee)
Protection that occurs when a body receives antibodies from another source.

 ## Common Disorders of the Lymphatic System

Table 13.7   Common Disorders, Symptoms, and Preventive Measures/ Treatment of the Lymphatic System

Condition	Disorder	Symptoms	Preventive Measures/ Treatment
AIDS (Acquired Immune Deficiency Syndrome)	A collection of symptoms and infections resulting from specific damage to the immune system caused by the human immunodeficiency virus (HIV).	Conditions that do not normally develop in individuals with healthy immune systems, such as infections caused by bacteria, viruses, fungi and parasites. Includes infections, fevers, swollen glands, weakness, chills and weight loss. Affects nearly every organ.	No vaccine or cure for AIDS or HIV. Prevention based on avoiding exposure to the virus. Highly active antiretroviral therapy (HAART) can minimize some symptoms for a while.
Allergies	A misguided reaction by the immune system in response to bodily contact with certain foreign substances, called allergens. These substances are usually harmless and remain so to nonallergic people.	Depending on what the allergy is, symptoms can be irritation of the eyes or nose (hayfever), rash, sneezing, redness, or abdominal pain, diarrehea or vomiting (food allergies). Can be as severe as asthma. Insect stings, antibiotics and certain medicines produce a systemic allergic response that is also called anaphylaxis, a system wide reaction. (See more below.)	Allergy testing helps to identify allergens. Avoidance or reducing exposure to allergen. Desensitization treatments can reduce reactions. Several antagonistic drugs are used to block the action of allergens or to prevent activation of cells processes, including antihistamines, cortisone, adrenaline, etc.
Anaphylactic Shock	Widespread and very serious allergic reaction	Dizziness, loss of consciousness, labored breathing, swelling of the tongue and breathing tubes, blueness of the skin, low blood pressure, heart failure, and death.	Immediate emergency treatment is required for this type of shock, usually dose of epinephrine. Might be administration of antivenom in the case of bee or wasp stings.

(continued)

Condition	Disorder	Symptoms	Preventive Measures/ Treatment
Elephantiasis	Caused by a **parasitic** thread-like worm, common in tropical and subtropical regions of the world. The worm enters the body from a bite from a host, which is usually a mosquito or other type of insect.	Worm blocks the lymphatic vessels and causes edema and swelling.	Employing mosquito control is the most effective prevention. Treat following infection with medication.
Hodgkin's Disease: ■ Classical— 95% of cases ■ Nodular— 5% of cases	A malignant disorder characterized by painless, progressive enlargement of lymph nodes. The nodular lymphocyte is most common in young men.	Enlarged lymph nodes, weight loss, low-grade fever, night sweats, anemia, lekocytosis, and skin irritation.	Employing radiation and drug therapy treatments. Cause unknown.
Lymphadenitis	Inflammation of the lymph nodes, which may be caused from a variety sources.	Lymph nodes become enlarged, hard, smooth or irregular, red, and may feel hot to the touch.	Using drug therapy treatment.
Tonsillitis	Infection of the tonsils, frequently caused by streptococcus.	Severe sore throat, fever, headache, malaise, difficulty in swallowing, earache, and enlarged, tender lymph nodes in the neck.	Treating with antibiotics and surgery if infections frequently reoccur.

Medical Terminology

asplenia:	absence of a spleen	*splenectomy:*	surgical removal of the spleen
lymphadenectomy:	surgical removal of the lymph nodes	*splenitis:*	inflammation of the spleen
lymphadenopathy:	enlargement of the lymph nodes	*splenomegaly:*	abnormal enlargement of the spleen
lymphocytopenia:	an abnormally low number of lymphocytes in the blood	*splenorrhexis:*	rupture of the spleen
lymphocytosis:	abnormally high number of lymphocytes in the blood	*splenotomy:*	incision into the spleen
lymphoma:	tumor made up of lymphatic tissue	*thymectomy:*	surgical removal of the thymus gland
lymphosarcoma:	cancer in the lymphatic tissue	*thymitis:*	inflammation of the thymus gland

Jobs and Professions

Immunologist

An immunologist is someone who studies and/or treats the immune system. An immunologist may be a research scientist who works in a laboratory. The scientist investigates the components needed for a healthy immune system or the diseases that disrupt the immune system.

An immunologist can also be a doctor who treats people with immune system disorders including allergies or autoimmune disease. Some immunologists perform both duties and combine research with patient care.

Immunologists who conduct independent research usually have an advanced degree such as a Ph.D. or M.D., although some jobs only require a master's degree. Training must include a combination of coursework, laboratory research, and a thesis or dissertation, followed by two to four years in a postdoctoral training fellowship. Physicians who work as immunologists typically go to medical school, complete a residency in internal medicine, pediatrics, or a medicine-pediatrics program, and then spend more two years specializing in allergies/immunology.

Immunology Technologist

Immunology technologists study the human immune system and how it responds to foreign invaders. They strive to diagnose, treat, and prevent infections by studying the organisms that cause disease and how they attack the immune system. This work is done under the supervision of an immunologist or a physician. Because of the nature of their work, they often work with other scientists, including chemists, pathologists, geologists, and civil engineers.

Immunology technologists work in a variety of academic and health-related centers. Some work for hospitals; others are employed by research facilities or diagnostic laboratories. People can enter this profession with a B.S. degree in immunology or by completing an immunology technology program at a college or technical institute. Some states require immunology technologists to be licensed.

 Summary

The lymphatic system consists of organs and vessels that filter out or destroy antigens and drain excess fluids. In this section, you have learned about disorders of the lymphatic system. These disorders often result in swollen tissues or organs. Therapy with antibiotics or other drugs is often prescribed for lymphatic diseases.

SECTION	**13.5**	Review Questions

1. What is the difference between an antigen and an antibody?

2. Which lymph organ filters microorganisms and waste products from the blood?

3. How is the lymphatic system like the circulatory system?

4. What are the symptoms that signal an immune response?

5. What is the cause of AIDS?

6. What is lymphadenitis and what are its symptoms?

7. What does an immunologist do?

---

parasitic
(pare uh SIT ik)
Pertaining to an organism that lives in or on another organism, taking nourishment from it.

Immunity and Aging

As the body ages, the function of its immune cells decreases. The effect is decreased ability to fight off infection, so the risk of sickness is greater. Immunizations, such as flu shots, may not be as effective, and the protection that is received may not last as long as expected. There also is an increase in some types of cancers because the immune system gradually loses its ability to detect cell defects, as well as correct those defects.

Another area of immunity affected by aging is the body's tolerance of its own cells—an autoimmune disorder occurs when immune cells mistakenly attack organs or tissues when nothing is wrong with them. Often a sign of infection, inflammation can also be an autoimmune response.

Common immune-related problems in older people include: decreased ability to fight diseases; autoimmune disorders; cancer; and slow wound healing. Older adults should consult with their doctors about increasing their immunity by receiving immunizations for diseases such as tetanus, flu, hepatitis and pneumonia.

Learn By Doing: Section 13.5 Activity

1. Complete Worksheets 1 through 4 as assigned.

2. When you are confident that you can meet each objective for this section, ask your teacher for the section evaluation.

SECTION

13.6 The Respiratory System

Background

The respiratory system takes in the oxygen that cells need to remain alive. It also releases waste carbon dioxide and water vapor from the body into the atmosphere. The main organs of the respiratory system are the lungs. Lungs can be damaged by pollutants, such as soot and cigarette smoke. In this section, you will study structures within the lungs and how they function. You will also learn about lifestyle choices that can affect respiratory health.

Objectives

When you have completed this section, you will be able to do the following:

- Match key terms with their correct meanings.

- Label major organs of the respiratory system on a diagram.

- Describe the flow of oxygen through the body.

- Identify common disorders of the respiratory system.

- Describe how the respiratory system supports life.

- Explain why the health care worker's understanding of the respiratory system is important.

■ Introduction to the Respiratory System

Respiration is breathing. Breathing is necessary to supply life-giving oxygen to each cell in the body and to remove the waste products of each cell. The cell's gaseous waste product is called *carbon dioxide.*

Oxygen enters the body when air is pulled in through the mouth and nose. This process is called **inspiration/inhalation. Expiration/exhalation** occurs when the body forces air out of the lungs. This is the body's way of eliminating the cells' gaseous waste (carbon dioxide).

Structure of the Respiratory System

See **Figure 13.20** and **Table 13.8**.

inspiration/inhalation
(in spur AY shun)/
(in hull AY shun)
Process of breathing in air during respiration.

expiration/exhalation
(ex pur AY shun)/
(ex hull AY shun)
Process of forcing air out of the body during respiration.

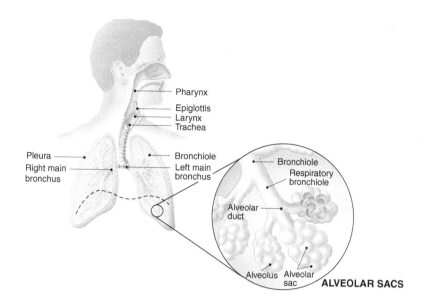

- The *nasal cavity* (nose) is where air enters the body. The nasal cavity is the preferred passage for air to enter the body. The nasal lining helps stop dust particles and pathogens. If dust and pathogens enter the lungs, the chance for infection is increased.

- *Paranasal sinuses* are mucus-lined cavities in the bones of the face, connected by passageways to the nose, which help to warm and moisten inhaled air. When drainage from the sinuses is blocked, as after a cold, they can become infected (a condition called sinusitis).

- The *oral cavity* (mouth) is where air enters the body when the nasal passage is blocked or when a person breathes through the mouth.

- The *pharynx* (throat) is the passageway that air enters after leaving the nose and mouth.

- The *epiglottis* is a flap that closes when food or water is swallowed. When it closes, it covers the opening of the trachea that leads to the lungs. This prevents food and water from entering the lungs.

- The *larynx* (voice box) is located just below the epiglottis. It is a **pouch** containing a cordlike framework that creates voice sounds.

- The *trachea* (windpipe) is the passageway between the pharynx and lungs.

- The *bronchi* are air passageways that connect to the trachea. The trachea divides into two main branches, the bronchial tubes that lead into the right and left lungs. The bronchial tubes are lined with hairlike objects called **cilia**. The cilia help move mucus, which catches dust and pathogens, up and out of the lungs.

- The *bronchioles* are the smallest subdivisions of the bronchi.

- The *alveoli* (air sacs) are at the end of each bronchiole. The alveoli are covered with capillaries that absorb oxygen into the blood. Carbon dioxide is forced out of the blood into the alveoli (carbon dioxide and oxygen exchange). Once the carbon dioxide has been released into the alveoli, it can be exhaled from the body.

- The *diaphragm* is the muscular wall that divides the chest cavity from the abdominal cavity. To begin inspiration, the diaphragm moves down, creating a vacuum that pulls air into the lungs. When the diaphragm relaxes and moves upward again, air is exhaled (forced out) from the lungs.

pouch
(POWCH)
Small bag or sac.

cilia
(SYL ee ah)
Hairlike projections that move rhythmically.

Table 13.8   Flow of Oxygen Through the Body

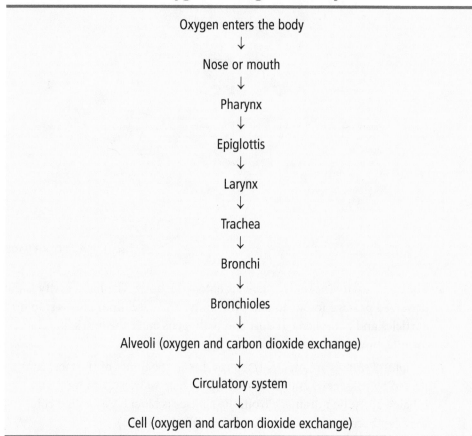

Oxygen enters the body
↓
Nose or mouth
↓
Pharynx
↓
Epiglottis
↓
Larynx
↓
Trachea
↓
Bronchi
↓
Bronchioles
↓
Alveoli (oxygen and carbon dioxide exchange)
↓
Circulatory system
↓
Cell (oxygen and carbon dioxide exchange)

pollutants
(puh LEW tents)
Things that contaminate
(e.g., smoke, smog).

malignant
(mah LIG nent)
Cancerous.

 ## Common Disorders of the Respiratory System

**Table 13.9   Common Disorders, Symptoms, and Preventive Measures/
Treatment of the Respiratory System**

Condition	Disorder	Symptoms	Preventive Measures/ Treatment
Asthma	The bronchial tube walls spasm, narrowing the passageways. With the passageways narrowed, it is difficult to exhale.	A suffocating feeling, breathing is difficult, anxiety can easily occur.	Treating with medication helps reduce the swelling in the bronchial tubes and allows air to move easily through the respiratory system. People with asthma should carry their medication with them at all times.
COPD (Chronic obstructive pulmonary disease)	Refers to any of several pulmonary diseases, especially emphysema, in which chronic airway obstruction causes respiratory abnormalities, including shortness of breath.	Shortness of breath, wheezing, decreased exercise tolerance, cough.	Stop smoking. Treatment includes use of inhalers, antibiotic drugs or steroids, and oxygen. Surgery to remove parts of the disease lung, lung rehabilitation programs or lung transplants.

(continued)

Table 13.9   Common Disorders, Symptoms, and Preventive Measures/ Treatment of the Respiratory System (continued)

Condition	Disorder	Symptoms	Preventive Measures/ Treatment
Common cold (also known as a viral respiratory tract infection)	A contagious illness that can be caused by a number of different types of viruses.	May feel tired and achy. Nasal stuffiness and drainage, sore throat, hoarseness, cough, and sometimes fever and headache.	Hand washing minimizes spread of colds. No cure. Treatments to minimize specific symptoms include antihistamines, decongestants, and acetaminophen or ibuprofen.
Emphysema	Progressive disease can result in disability, and in severe cases, heart or respiratory failure and death. The alveoli become stretched out and are not able to push the carbon dioxide and other **pollutants** out of the lungs. Can be caused from smoking, frequent, untreated respiratory infections, asthma, or abnormal stress on the lungs.	Anxiety, shortness of breath, difficulty breathing, cough, cyanosis, unequal chest expansion, rapid heartbeat, and elevated body temperature.	Achieving a balanced lifestyle that includes adequate rest, a balanced diet, and not smoking helps keep the lungs clean and able to function normally. Treatments include: use of medications, use of oxygen, possible lung transplant.
Lung cancer	**Malignant** tissue in the lungs that destroy tissue. Approximately 75% of cases are due to smoking.	Persistent cough, difficulty breathing, purulent or blood-streaked sputum, chest pain, frequent bronchitis and/or pneumonia.	Treating with radiation and chemical therapy. Surgery may also be an option.
Pneumonia	Inflammation of the lungs, usually caused by bacteria, viruses, or an irritation by chemicals.	Chills and fever, headache, cough, and chest pain.	Treating with antibiotic (if bacterial) and respiratory therapies.
Tuberculosis	Infectious disease caused by the tubercle bacillus. This bacillus is difficult to destroy. The tubercle bacillus can be carried on air currents and dust particles for a long time. When they are inhaled into the respiratory system, the bacillus may become active and destroy tissue.	Listlessness, vague chest pain, decreased appetite, fever, night sweats, and weight loss are early symptoms. Tubercle bacillus most ofteninfects the lungs, but it can also infect other organs of the body.	Treating the bacillus to become inactive keeps it from multiplying and from doing more damage to tissue. It is important for people with tuberculosis to always take their medication. If they stop taking it the bacillus may become active again. A major health risk today is a resistant strain of tuberculosis that does not become inactive with current treatments.
Upper respiratory infection (URI)	Infection of the trachea, larynx, throat, or nose.	Sore throat, congestion of the sinuses, nose, and eye with a fever and tiredness.	Getting adequate rest and eating a balanced diet help prevent infections. Handwashing and covering mouth with sleeved arm when coughing or sneezing can help prevent spread of infection. Infections caused by a virus usually improve after 10–12days. Bacterial infections may require antibiotics.

Personal Wellness

The Dangers of Smoking

One of the best ways to protect your health and prevent disease is not to smoke. According to the Centers for Disease Control, smoking causes harm to almost every organ in the body. One out of every five deaths in the U.S. each year is related to smoking. You might know that smoking causes lung cancer, emphysema, and other respiratory diseases.

You might not know that smoking can also cause many other cancers, including cancers of the mouth, larynx, pharynx, esophagus, bladder, kidney, pancreas, cervix, and stomach. Smoking also puts people at a higher risk for coronary heart disease and stroke.

Women who smoke when they are pregnant can damage the health of their fetus. Older women who smoke are more at risk for osteoporosis.

If you don't smoke, you should never start. Cigarettes are highly addictive, so it is difficult to quit smoking. If you smoke now, you should quit. Many health insurance companies have programs that can help smokers to quit. There are also many resources on the Internet to help smokers to become nonsmokers.

What diseases can be caused by smoking?

Medical Terminology

apnea: absence of breathing

bronchiectasis: dilation of the bronchi

bronchitis: inflammation of the bronchial tubes

dyspnea: difficult or painful breathing

EENT: abbreviation for "eyes, ears, nose, throat"

epistaxis: nosebleed

hypoxia: lack of oxygen

intercostal: between the ribs

laryngitis: inflammation of the larynx

nares: nostrils

pharyngospasm: spasmodic contraction of the pharynx

pleurocentesis: surgical puncture of the pleura

pneumonolysis: breakdown of lung tissue

pneumothoracic: pertaining to the lungs and chest

pulmonary edema: fluid, swelling of the lungs

rales: rattling or bubbling sounds in the chest

rhinoplasty: plastic repair of the nose

rhinorrhea: running nose

sublingual: beneath the tongue

tachypnea: rapid breathing

thoracotomy: incision into the chest

trachelosis: any condition of the neck

tracheostomy: opening into the trachea

URI: abbreviation for upper respiratory infection

Jobs and Professions

Pulmonologist

Pulmonologists are physicians who are specially trained to treat diseases and conditions of the chest. These conditions, which affect the lungs and bronchial tubes, include such things as pneumonia, asthma, tuberculosis, and emphysema. Pulmonologists do not perform major surgical procedures, but they do often obtain samples from the lining of a lung or the chest wall for diagnostic testing.

Pulmonology is a subspecialty of internal medicine. This means that in order to become a pulmonologist, you must first become certified in internal medicine. It takes at least seven years to accomplish this. Once this is completed, you must continue your studies for two or three more years focusing on conditions specifically related to the respiratory system.

Respiratory Therapist

Respiratory therapists work with patients who have breathing or other cardiopulmonary disorders. Working under the direction of a physician, these specialists evaluate, treat, and care for patients and are primarily responsible for all respiratory care therapeutic treatments and diagnostic procedures. They also supervise respiratory care technicians, who perform many of these same functions.

Respiratory therapists work with a variety of patients. They may work with premature babies whose lungs are not fully developed. They may also work with elderly patients whose lungs are diseased.

Many respiratory therapists work in hospitals. Some work for home health care agencies and travel to patients' homes. Many programs at colleges, universities, medical schools, and vocational/technical schools offer programs in respiratory therapy.

Some programs offer associate's degrees, which would prepare you for an entry-level position. Others offer bachelor's degrees, which would prepare you for an advanced position in this field. Graduates must then pass a test and become either a Registered Respiratory Therapist or a Certified Respiratory Therapist.

Thoracic Surgeon

A thoracic surgeon is a surgeon who specializes in conditions affecting organs in the chest. Some surgeons specialize in the lungs and esophagus. They are general thoracic surgeons. Others also care for the heart and major blood vessels. They are known as cardiothoracic surgeons.

Using minimally invasive procedures, thoracic surgeons perform heart bypass operations and heart and lung transplants. They also remove cancerous tumors. Thoracic surgeons treat patients during and after surgery, as well as while they are in critical care. Thoracic surgeons attend medical school and then complete five years in a general surgery residency and at least two years in a residency focusing on thoracic surgery.

Pulmonary Technician

Pulmonary technicians care for patients with lung-related problems. These technicians conduct pulmonary function tests, provide respiratory-related care, and treat patients as per a physician's orders. Specific duties include educating patients on medications and the use of oxygen, compiling test results and reviewing those results with physicians, helping physicians change tracheostomy tubing, and maintaining pulmonary function equipment and supplies.

Pulmonary technicians report to a nurse manager, physician, or other appropriate personnel. They typically work in a clinic, hospital or other facility. This position requires an associate's degree from an accredited respiratory therapy program and certification from the National Board for Respiratory Care.

Oxygen Technician

Oxygen technicians are responsible for understanding the use of the hyperbaric oxygen chamber, used in hyperbaric oxygen therapy (HBOT) programs. They have to check and control the chamber, pneumatic circuits, gas or compressed air reserves, air-compressors, and the rest of the technical parts of the facility. This is a specialized medical treatment in which the patient breathes 100 percent oxygen inside a pressurized chamber.

Commonly known for its use in treating scuba diving complications, modern hyperbaric therapy is also used to treat stubborn non-healing wounds. The therapy quickly delivers high concentrations of oxygen to the bloodstream, which assists in the healing process of wounds, and is effective in fighting certain types of infections. These technicians are high-level specialists, needing an official degree with a specialty in Pneumatic Systems, Hyperbaric Technology, or the like.

Otorhinolaryngologist

An otorhinolaryngologist is a physician/surgeon who specializes in head and neck surgery. Common ailments addressed include: head and neck cancer; tumors; sinus and allergic disease; thyroid and parathyroid problems; snoring and sleep apnea; and pediatric ear, nose and throat issues.

An otorhinolaryngologist might perform open surgery on the salivary or thyroid glands or reconstructive surgery of the head or neck. Other possibilities include microsurgery of the middle ear, sinus surgery, or surgery at the base of the skull. To become an otorhinolaryngologist, you must complete medical school, one year of general surgery residency, and four years of otorhinolaryngology training.

Otologist

An otologist, also known as a neurotologist, is a physician who specializes in conditions affecting the ears. These conditions include problems with balance and dizziness, all types of hearing loss, noises in the ear, facial nerve disorders, persistent infections, congenital malformations of the ear, and tumors of the ear. Trained as a surgeon, an otologist performs surgical procedures such as the repair of eardrum perforations, hearing reconstruction, and tumor removal.

To become an otologist, you must attend medical school and then become a trained otorhinolaryngologist. An otorhinolaryngologist, commonly known as an ENT, specializes in problems associated with the ear, nose, throat, and neck. To become an otorhinolaryngologist, you must complete medical school, one year of general surgery residency, and four years of otorhinolaryngology training. To specialize as an otologist, you must complete another residency in that area. All otologists must pass an exam in order to become board certified before practicing medicine.

Summary

In this section, you reviewed the structure and functions of the respiratory system. You learned that the lungs contain a system of branching tubes that get progressively smaller as they get farther away from the trachea. These tubes end in alveoli, or air sacs, that are covered with capillaries. As air flows into the alveoli, the capillaries absorb oxygen and release carbon dioxide.

Oxygen in the capillaries travels to the rest of the body in order to keep cells alive. Some disorders that affect the respiratory system make breathing difficult. This can reduce the amount of oxygen that gets to cells and may cause weakness or death. As a health care worker, you should be familiar with the causes and treatments of respiratory diseases. You should also be aware of the lifestyle choices that can prevent respiratory diseases.

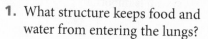

SECTION | **13.6** | **Review Questions**

1. What structure keeps food and water from entering the lungs?

2. Describe the path that air takes as it enters the body.

3. How does the diaphragm help you to breathe?

4. What is asthma and what are the treatments for asthma?

5. Which two respiratory disorders are often caused by smoking?

6. Why would health care professionals need to wear face masks or respirators when treating a patient who has tuberculosis?

7. What are the differences between an otologist and a trained otorhinolaryngologist?

Learn By Doing: Section 13.6 Activity

1. Complete Worksheets 1 through 5 as assigned.

2. When you are confident that you can meet each objective for this section, ask your teacher for the section evaluation.

The Digestive System

Background

The digestive system breaks down food into nutrients that can be absorbed by the body. It also passes solid wastes out of the body. In this section, you will learn the organs of the digestive system and the diseases that may affect those organs. You will also learn how lifestyle choices can affect digestive system function.

Objectives

When you have completed this section, you will be able to do the following:

- Match key terms with their correct meanings.
- Label a diagram of the digestive system and its accessory organs.
- Explain the functions of the digestive system.
- Recognize the function of organs associated with the digestive system.

- Match common disorders of the digestive system with their descriptions.
- Describe how the digestive system absorbs nutrients.
- Explain why the health care worker's understanding of the digestive system is important.

Introduction to the Digestive System

In this section, we discuss the body's processing of food. This process prepares nutrients so that they can be used by each cell. Body cells cannot absorb nutrients from food. Food must be changed into a substance that the body cells can use. This process of changing food into a usable substance is known as *digestion*. Once digestion occurs, nutrients move into the bloodstream and waste moves out. This transfer of nutrients into the blood is called **absorption**. Digestion and absorption are the two main functions of the digestive system.

Digestive Organs

The digestive system is a very long muscular tube that begins at the mouth and ends at the **anus**. This tube, called the **alimentary canal**, is made up of many parts (Figure 13.21):

- The *mouth* (oral cavity) is where food enters the body. The digestive process begins with the mechanical breakdown (the chewing, mashing, and grinding of food by the teeth).
- The *salivary glands* are located under the tongue, near the jawbone, and at the back of the throat. The purpose of the salivary glands is to produce a **secretion** that dissolves food and coats food with a mucus that allows it to pass through the esophagus more easily. **Amylase** from salivary glands also breaks down carbohydrates so that chemical digestion can start in the mouth. By the time food leaves the mouth, it is in the form of **bolus**.

---

absorption
(ab SAWRP shuhn)
Passage of a substance through a body surface into body fluids and tissues (e.g., nutrients from digested food pass through the wall of the small intestine into the blood).

anus
(EY nuhs)
Outlet from which the body expels solid waste.

alimentary canal
(al uh MEN tuh-ree kuh NAL)
Long muscular tube beginning at the mouth and ending at the anus.

secretion
(si KREE shuhn)
Producing and expelling a special substance (e.g., sebaceous glands secrete oil; salivary glands secrete saliva).

amylase
(AM me layz)
An enzyme in saliva and pancreatic juice that breaks down starch into simple sugars.

bolus
(BOW less)
A soft rounded ball, especially of chewed food.

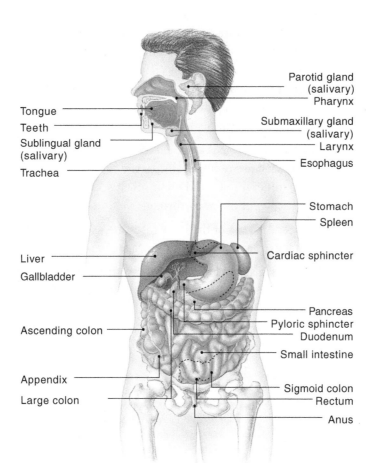

Labels in figure:
Parotid gland (salivary)
Pharynx
Tongue
Teeth
Sublingual gland (salivary)
Trachea
Submaxillary gland (salivary)
Larynx
Esophagus
Liver
Gallbladder
Stomach
Spleen
Cardiac sphincter
Ascending colon
Pancreas
Pyloric sphincter
Duodenum
Small intestine
Appendix
Large colon
Sigmoid colon
Rectum
Anus

- The *pharynx* (throat) is located at the back of the oral cavity and is a passageway for food.

- The *epiglottis* is a flap that covers the trachea when food or water is swallowed. By covering the trachea, the epiglottis keeps food and water out of the lungs.

- The *esophagus* receives food and water from the pharynx. Food is moved through the esophagus by a rhythmic wavelike motion called **peristalsis**.

- The *cardiac* **sphincter** is a ring of muscle fibers located where the esophagus and stomach join. This muscle keeps stomach contents from moving up into the esophagus.

- The *stomach* is an enlarged part of the alimentary canal that receives food and water from the esophagus. The stomach produces the enzyme, pepsin, which breaks down proteins. The stomach holds food until digestive juices have chemically broken down the food particles into **chyme**. Chyme is a creamy semifluid mixture of food and digestive juices.

- The *pyloric sphincter* is a ringlike muscle found at the far end of the stomach. Its main purpose is to keep food in the stomach long enough to become chyme.

- The *small intestine* is attached to the stomach at the pyloric sphincter. The small intestine is about 20 feet long. The first 10 to 12 inches of the small intestine are called the *duodenum.* The duodenum receives juices from the pancreas, liver, and gallbladder, which aid in further chemical breakdown of the chyme. This final chemical breakdown is the completion of digestion.

peristalsis
(pear is STALL sus)
Progressive, wavelike motion that occurs involuntarily in hollow tubes of the body.

sphincter
(SVING ter)
Circular muscle that allows the opening and closing of a body part (e.g., anus, pylorus).

chyme
(KIME)
Creamy semifluid mixture of food and digestive juices.

minute
(my NEWT)
Exceptionally small.

villi
(VIL eye)
Tiny projections.

feces
(FEE sees)
Solid waste that is evacuated from the body through the anus.

evacuated
(i VAK yoo yet)
Emptied out.

- The small intestine is the portion of the alimentary canal where most absorption takes place. The lining of the small intestine contains many **minute** projections called **villi**. Each villus contains capillaries that absorb nutrients from the food we eat. (**Figure 13.22**) Those food substances that are not absorbed are moved through the 20 feet of the small intestine by peristalsis to the large intestine.

- The *large intestine* is attached to the small intestine and receives food substances that are of little value to the body. The large intestine absorbs water, mineral salts, and vitamins. It secretes (discharges) mucus to aid in the movement of **feces** through the intestine.

- The *rectum*, part of the large intestine, is the last 6 to 8 inches of the alimentary canal. It serves as a storage area for feces.

- The *anus*, also part of the large intestine, is the end of the alimentary canal. It is where fecal material is **evacuated** from the body. Closure of the anus is controlled by the sphincter muscle, a circular muscle that normally maintains constriction of the orifice and which relaxes as required by normal body functioning.

FIGURE 13.22
Villi in the lining of the small intestine. What function do the capillaries serve in the villi of the small intestine?

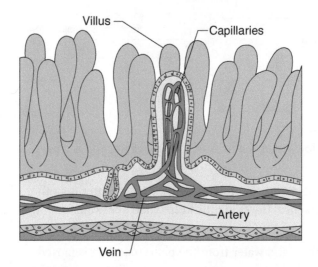

Villus — Capillaries
Artery
Vein

The Accessory Structures

The accessory structures of the digestive system assist in the process of digestion. These structures are the liver, the gallbladder, and the pancreas (**Table 13.10**):

- The *liver,* the largest gland in the body, has many functions. Some of these functions are:

  - Production of bile.
  - Removal of poisons that have been absorbed in the small intestines.
  - Storage of vitamins.
  - Production of heparin, which prevents blood from clotting.
  - Production of antibodies, which act against infection and foreign matter.

Apply It

Describe what happens after you eat your lunch.

You put food in your mouth. What happens to the food here? Is this chemical or mechanical digestion? Then, what happens in the esophagus? In the stomach? In the small intestine? In the large intestine? Work through each step in the digestive process.

- The *gallbladder*, a muscular sac, stores the bile that the liver produces. When chyme reaches the duodenum, the gallbladder squeezes bile into the duodenum to aid in chemical breakdown of the chyme.

- The *pancreas* produces pancreatic juices that also aid in the chemical breakdown of food. It also manufactures **insulin**, which regulates the amount of sugar used by the tissues.

insulin
(IN sel in)
Hormone secreted by the pancreas; essential for maintaining the correct blood sugar level.

Medical Terminology

anorexia:	lack of appetite	**enterocyst:**	cyst of the intestinal wall
antacid:	without acid	**enterohepatic:**	pertaining to the intestines and the liver
buccolingual:	pertaining to the cheek and tongue	**gastrointestinal:**	GI, pertaining to the stomach and intestines
cholecyst:	gallbladder	**gastrophrenic:**	pertaining to the stomach and diaphragm
cholelithotomy:	incision for the removal of a gallstone	**gastrosis:**	condition affecting the stomach
colitis:	inflammation of the colon	**hepatopathy:**	any disease of the liver
colostomy:	opening into the colon	**hepatoptosis:**	liver dropping downward
dysphagia:	difficult or painful swallowing	**metabolism:**	process by which food is changed into energy for the body's use
emesis:	vomiting		
emetic:	substance that induces vomiting		
enterocele:	hernia involving the intestine		

Common Disorders of the Digestive System

Table 13.10 shows common disorders, symptoms, and preventive measures/treatment of the digestive system and accessory structures.

flatulence
(FLA chu lens)
Excessive gas in the stomach and intestines that causes discomfort.

Table 13.10 Common Disorders, Symptoms, and Preventive Measures/Treatment of the Digestive System and Accessory Structures

Condition	Disorder	Symptoms	Preventive Measures/Treatment
Cholelithiasis *(Accessory Structure)*	Stones in the gallbladder.	Abdominal pain that may radiate toward the back, and heartburn especially after after eating.	Eating a low-fat diet. Surgical removal of stones and/or the gallbladder may be necessary.
Cirrhosis *(Accessory Structure)*	Liver cells become damaged, and scarring prevents the liver and other systems from functioning.	Nausea, **flatulence**, decreased appetite, weight loss, clay-colored stools, weakness, and abdominal pain.	Eating a balanced diet rich in protein and vitamins (especially folic acid), getting plenty of rest, and abstaining from alcohol. The liver does have the capacity to regenerate given time and the proper diet.

(continued)

Condition	Disorder	Symptoms	Preventive Measures/ Treatment
Colon cancer	Cancer that forms in the tissues of the colon (longest part of the large intestine). Most colon cancers begin in cells that make and release mucus and other fluids.	A change in bowel habits. Bleeding from the rectum, including bright red or dark blood in your stools or stools that look black. Constant or frequent diarrhea or constipation. Abdominal pain or problems with gas or bloating. Unexplained weight loss and fatigue.	Hard to detect. Use screening tests, such as stool analysis, fecal occult blood tests, or colonoscopy. Treatment includes surgery, chemotherapy, radiation or biotherapy. There are also clinical trials in which a patient can participate.
Constipation (*Digestive System*)	Infrequent, difficult **defecation** of fecal material.	Abdominal pain and cramping, inability to defecate.	Eating a balanced diet with adequate amounts of fruits and vegetables, exercising regularly, and drinking adequate amounts of water help to keep elimination of waste regular. When constipation occurs, medication and/or enemas may be necessary.
Diarrhea (*Digestive System*)	Abnormal frequent watery stool, usually the symptom of some underlying disorders.	Abdominal cramping that forces frequent defecation and generalized weakness.	Using medication and identifying the condition. It is important to carefully monitor people with diarrhea so they don't become dehydrated which may cause other serious conditions.
Diverticulitis	Small pouches that bulge outward through the colon, or large intestine, and become inflamed or infected.	Abdominal pain, usually on the left side. If infected, you may also have fever, nausea, vomiting, chills, cramping, and constipation. In serious cases, can lead to bleeding, tears, or blockages.	Treatment focuses on clearing up the infection with antibiotics, resting the colon and preventing future problems, by eating more fiber, drinking lots of fluids, and exercising. Serious cases may require a hospital stay.
Enteritis	Inflammation of the intestines.	Abdominal cramping and **diarrhea**.	See treatment under diarrhea.
Gastric reflux	The backward flow of stomach acid contents into the esophagus.	Heartburn, difficulty swallowing, chest pain.	Lifestyle changes, such as losing weight, elevating your head, dietary restrictions (avoiding coffee, alcohol, fatty foods, chocolate and acidy foods). Drug treatment includes antacids, H2 blockers (like Pepcid AC) or proton pump inhibitors (like Prilosec).
Gastric ulcer (*Digestive System*)	Open sore in the stomach.	Pain and sometimes internal bleeding.	Eating a soft bland diet, reducing stress, using medication. When symptoms are not relieved, surgery may be necessary.

(continued)

**Table 13.10   Common Disorders, Symptoms, and Preventive Measures/
Treatment of the Digestive System and Accessory Structures** (continued)

Condition	Disorder	Symptoms	Preventive Measures/ Treatment
Gastritis (Digestive System)	Inflammation of the stomach lining. If untreated, it could develop a gastric ulcer.	**Epigastric** pain, indigestion, and burning in the stomach area.	See treatment under gastric ulcer.
Gastroenteritis (Digestive System)	Inflammation of the stomach lining and intestines.	Vomiting, abdominal cramping, and diarrhea.	Taking lots of fluids (may be necessary to start an IV to administer fluids if vomiting is excessive) and medication.
Hepatitis (Accessory Structure)	Inflammation of the liver caused by a virus or a poison.	**Jaundice**, enlarged liver, decreased appetite, abdominal and gastric pain, clay-colored stools, and dark-colored urine.	Eating a balanced diet rich in protein and vitamins (especially folic acid), getting plenty of rest, and abstaining from alcohol. The liver does have the capacity to regenerate given time and the proper diet.
Pancreatitis (Accessory Structure)	Inflammation of the pancreas caused by an overproduction of its own pancreatic juices.	Severe abdominal pain radiating to the back, fever, loss of appetite, nausea, and vomiting.	Removing any stimulation of the pancreas by removing all stomach contents, IV medication and fluids. Surgery may be necessary.

 ## Jobs and Professions

Gastroenterologist

A gastroenterologist is a physician who specializes in the digestive system. A gastroenterologist treats diseases of the gastrointestinal tract, which includes the esophagus, stomach, small intestine, colon and rectum, pancreas, gallbladder, bile ducts, and liver. A gastroenterologist treats conditions including colon polyps, cancer, hepatitis, gastroesophageal reflux (heartburn), and Irritable Bowel Syndrome.

Gastroenterologists are trained in endoscopy, which is the use of narrow, lighted tubes with built-in cameras. By utilizing these instruments, one can see the inside of the intestinal tract.

To become a gastroenterologist, you must complete medical school followed by a three-year residency in internal medicine. Then you must complete additional specialized training in gastroenterology, which lasts two to three years.

Hepatologist

A hepatologist is a physician who specializes in treatment of the liver. As a hepatologist, you might deal with hepatitis, cirrhosis, genetic or metabolic liver diseases, liver cancer, liver transplants, or metabolic or immunologic issues related to the liver. To become a hepatologist, you must first be trained as a gastroenterologist.

To become a certified gastroenterologist, you must complete college, medical school, a three-year residency in internal medicine, and a two- to three-year fellowship in gastroenterology. To become a hepatologist, you must complete

defecation
(deaf uh KAY shun)
The pushing of solid material from the bowel.

metabolism
(muh TAB uh liz uhm)
Chemical interactions in the body that provide energy.

diarrhea
(dahy uh REE uh)
Passage of watery stool at frequent intervals.

epigastric
(ep uh GAS trik)
Pertaining to the area over the pit of the stomach.

jaundice
(JAWN dis)
Yellowing of the whites of the eyes, skin, and mucous membranes.

another one-year fellowship in which you will receive both clinical and research training specific to hepatology. Once this training is complete, you must pass an exam to become certified in this field.

Dietician

Dieticians plan food and nutrition programs that help treat or prevent disease. They are often part of a medical team in a hospital, private practice, or other health care facility. Dieticians promote healthy eating habits, evaluate clients' diets, and suggest modifications. Some dieticians specialize in the management of overweight or critically ill patients.

Because they help identify and treat health ailments, a detailed knowledge of growth and development, metabolism, and biochemistry of nutrients and food components is required.

To become a registered dietician, you must have at least a bachelor's degree in nutrition or dietetics and complete a 6- to 12-month internship at a health care facility, food service company, or nonprofit agency. You must also pass an exam given by the Commission on Dietetic Registration.

Dietary Aide

A dietary aide prepares and delivers food trays to patients in hospitals or facilities such as nursing homes. Duties may include: reading menu cards to determine which items to place on a tray; placing items on trays; helping the cook prepare food items; preparing foods for soft or liquid diets; pushing a food cart; serving meals to patients; collecting dirty dishes; washing dishes; and recording the amount and type of special foods served to patients. To become a dietary aide, you must have a high school diploma.

Summary

As food travels through the alimentary canal, mechanical and chemical digestion break down the food into nutrients. These nutrients are absorbed by the small intestine. Solid waste materials are excreted through the anus. In this section, you learned about the structure and function of the digestive system. You also learned ways to recognize and treat digestive system disorders. Digestive system disorders often cause abdominal pain. You can often treat these disorders with a low fat or balanced diet or medications.

SECTION **13.7** **Review Questions**

1. What is the alimentary canal?

2. What are five functions of the liver?

3. What are the differences in function between the small intestine and the large intestine?

4. What are the accessory structures of the digestive system?

5. What causes hepatitis and what are its symptoms?

6. What does a hepatologist do and what education/training is required?

Learn By Doing: Section 13.7 Activity

1. Complete Worksheets 1 through 5 as assigned.

2. When you are confident that you can meet each objective for this section, ask your teacher for the section evaluation.

SECTION

13.8 The Urinary System

Background

The urinary system maintains water balance and flushes liquid wastes out of the body. Urinary system disorders may cause inflammation or obstruction of the organs within the system. As a health care worker, it is important for you to understand the urinary system and to recognize symptoms of urinary system disorders in order to protect patients from organ damage.

Objectives

When you have completed this section, you will be able to do the following:

- Match key terms with their correct meanings.

- Label a diagram of the urinary system.

- Identify the function of organs in the urinary system.

- Match common disorders of the urinary system with their descriptions.

- Describe how the urinary system removes liquid waste and eliminates it from the body.

- Explain why the health care worker's understanding of the urinary system is important.

 Introduction to the Urinary System

The urinary system rids the body of liquid waste and assists in the regulation of water and chemical balance. Its functions include:

- The excretion of urine, a liquid waste produced in the body.

- The maintenance of water balance; water balance occurs when the intake of water equals the output of water.

- Regulation of the chemical balance or acid-base balance of the body; the body must maintain a balance of acids and bases in order to function properly.

These functions are accomplished by the organs of the urinary system. (**Figure 13.23**)

FIGURE 13.23

The urinary system removes liquid waste from the body. What are the tubes called that move waste from the kidneys to the urinary bladder?

nephron
(NEF rawn)
Functional part of the kidney that filters liquid waste.

mechanism
(MEK uh niz uhm)
Process or a series of steps that achieve a result.

obstruction
(ub STRUK shun)
Blockage or clogging.

dialysis
(die AL iss sus)
Process of removing waste from body fluids.

infuses
(in FYOO z)
Flows into the body by gravity (e.g., IV drips through a tube into the body).

peritoneal cavity
(pear it tun EEL kav it ee)
Area of the body containing the liver, stomach, intestines, kidneys, urinary bladder, and reproductive organs.

edema
(eh DEE muh)
Swelling; abnormal or excessive collection of fluid in the tissues. Usually, the swelling is in the hands, ankles, legs, or abdomen.

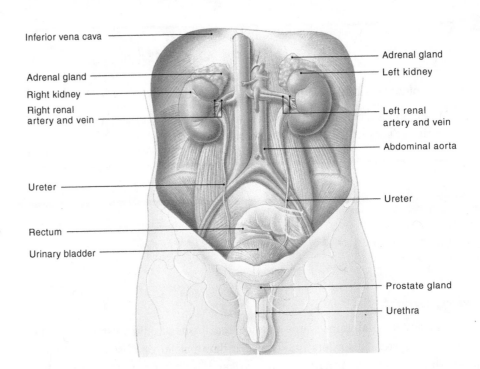

Inferior vena cava — Adrenal gland — Left kidney — Adrenal gland — Right kidney — Right renal artery and vein — Left renal artery and vein — Abdominal aorta — Ureter — Ureter — Rectum — Urinary bladder — Prostate gland — Urethra

Structure of the Urinary System

Two kidneys are located at the back of the upper abdomen. Their primary function is to filter (remove) waste products from the blood. Each kidney has the following structure (**Figure 13.24**):

- The *capsule* is the sac surrounding the kidney.
- The *cortex* is the outer part of the kidney.
- The *medulla* is the inner part of the kidney.
- The **nephron** is the chief filtering **mechanism** of the kidney. Part of the nephron is in the cortex, and part of it is in the medulla. The nephron is made up of:
  - A tiny twisted tube called the *convoluted tubule*.
  - A cuplike capsule called *Bowman's capsule*.
  - A cluster of capillaries in Bowman's capsule called the *glomerulus*.
- The *ureters* are tubes that carry urine (liquid waste) from the kidneys to the urinary bladder.
- The *urinary bladder* is a muscular sac that expands to hold urine received from the kidneys.
- The *urethra* is a tube extending from the urinary bladder to the outside of the body. This allows for the excretion of urine.

FIGURE 13.24

Cross section of a kidney. Where is the renal capsule located?

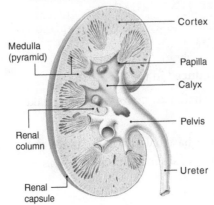

SECTIONED KIDNEY

Cortex — Medulla (pyramid) — Papilla — Calyx — Pelvis — Renal column — Ureter — Renal capsule

Common Disorders of the Urinary System

Table 13.11   Common Disorders, Symptoms, and Preventive Measures/ Treatment of the Urinary System

Condition	Disorder	Symptoms	Preventive Measures/ Treatment
Cystitis	Inflammation of the urinary bladder due to infection. The bladder is susceptible to infection because bacteria can easily travel up the urethra to infect the bladder.	Frequent, painful urination, possible blood in urine, fever and chills. More likely to occur in women because of their relatively shorter urethra—bacteria do not have to travel as far to enter the bladder.	Depending on the diagnosis, treating with antibiotics, increased fluid intake, bed rest, medication to control bladder wall spasms, and when necessary, surgery.
Hydronephrosis	Expanded renal pelvis. Normally caused by an **obstruction** (kidney stone or tumor) that keeps urine from flowing down the ureter.	May experience fever and pain on the side (flank), and, in some cases, urine may contain blood and/or pus.	Removing the obstruction surgically or placement of stints to provide for urinary excretion.
Kidney or renal failure	Nephron of the kidney is unable to filter liquid waste from the blood.	Early signs include fatigue and mental dullness. Later signs include absences of urination, convulsions, GI bleeding, malnutrition, and jaundiced (yellowed) skin that may be covered with a frostlike substance (uremic frost).	Treating with a renal diet and **dialysis**, which is a way to filter waste products from the blood. There are two methods of dialysis: ■ Hemodialysis, which circulates the body's blood through a machine that filters out the waste and returns the clean blood to the body. ■ Peritoneal dialysis, which **infuses** sterile fluids into the **peritoneal cavity** and then drains the fluid from the cavity. While the fluid is in the abdomen, waste products are chemically drawn out of tissues and into the fluid. When the fluid drains from the abdomen, the waste is also removed.
Nephritis	Inflammation of the kidney due to infection or arteriosclerosis.	**Edema**, a collection of fluid in the tissues that causes swelling.	Treating with medication or surgery to remove a kidney may be indicated, depending on the cause.
Renal calculi	Kidney stones that develop when the liquid waste from the blood becomes solid.	Sharp, severe pain in the lower back over the kidney, radiating into the groin.	Surgically removing the stones if they do not pass through the ureter and urethra normally.
Uremia	An accumulation of urine substances in the blood occurs when the nephron is unable to completely filter out waste from the blood.	Nausea, vomiting, headache, dizziness, coma, or convulsions; breath and perspiration may smell like urine.	Early diagnosis of kidney dysfunction. Treatment is dialysis.

Medical Terminology

calculi:	stones	**nephrostomy:**	artificial opening into the kidney
cystitis:	inflammation of the bladder	**pyelectasis:**	dilation of the renal pelvis
cystoscopy:	inspection of the bladder	**pyelitis:**	inflammation of the pelvis of the kidney of urine
diuresis:	passage of abnormally large amounts	**pyelolithotomy:**	removal of kidney stone
glycouria:	sugar in the urine	**pyelometry:**	measurement of the kidney's pelvis
hematuria:	blood in the urine	**renal:**	pertaining to the kidney
nephralgia:	renal pain	**renal colic:**	severe pain in the kidney
nephric:	pertaining to the kidney	**uremia:**	condition in which blood contains toxins usually excreted from the kidneys
nephroid:	resembling a kidney		
nephrolithotripsy:	crushing of kidney stones		
nephropexy:	surgical attachment of a floating kidney	**ureteropyelitis:**	inflammation of the kidney pelvis andthe ureter
nephrorrhagia:	renal hemorrhage	**urethrism:**	irritability or spasm of the urethra

Jobs and Professions

Urologist

Urologists specialize in issues related to the male and female urinary tracts and the male reproductive organs. People see urologists for issues ranging from discomfort while urinating to male infertility. Urologists look for such things as signs of infection, blood in the urine, or excess sugars or protein, which could indicate diabetes or other kidney problems.

Because urologists encounter such a wide variety of issues, they must have a broad knowledge of internal medicine, pediatrics, gynecology, and other specialties. Urologists must graduate from medical school and then complete an accredited urology residency program. This program can last up to five years and involves a combination of surgical and clinical training.

Urologists can specialize in a variety of areas, including urologic oncology, male infertility, female urology, or pediatric urology. To practice as a pediatric urologist, one more year of training is required. All urologists must also pass an exam to become certified in this field.

Nephrologist

A nephrologist, also called a renal physician, is someone who specializes in the treatment of patients with kidney diseases. This includes patients with diabetes, polycystic kidney disease, and chronic kidney failure. Many patients must receive dialysis therapy and some will require kidney transplants.

Nephrologists are trained in internal medicine. They do not perform surgery. However, they may do a kidney biopsy in order to obtain a sample of kidney tissue. Their goal is to find ways to preserve patients' remaining kidney function. To

---

Apply It

Form teams of four. Each team should create a model of a functioning urinary system from materials found in their homes (balloons, straws, etc.).

The system should show (1) kidneys that have produced urine, (2) ureters that transport the urine to the (3) bladder that can store the urine, to the (4) urethra which passes urine out of the body. Conduct an in-class science fair.

---

become a nephrologist, you must graduate from medical school, complete an internal medicine residency program, and complete a two- to three-year fellowship in nephrology. You must also take an exam to become certified in this field.

Dialysis Technician

A dialysis technician is the primary caregiver for patients who are undergoing dialysis, which is a process through which waste products are filtered from the blood when the kidneys are not functioning properly. Although the dialysis technician performs the actual dialysis treatment, a nurse is responsible for overall patient care.

The dialysis technician works under the supervision of that nurse. On-the-job duties include assembling supplies, preparing the machine for use, obtaining patient vital signs, administering local anesthetics and drugs under supervision, and closely monitoring the patient before, during, and after dialysis treatment.

Dialysis technicians work in hospitals, out-patient facilities, and home dialysis programs. To become a dialysis technician, you must have a high school diploma. A dialysis technician may be trained on the job, through an employer-sponsored training program, or at a vocational school or community college.

Summary

In this section, you learned that the kidneys are the main organs of the urinary system. Each kidney contains filtering mechanisms called nephrons. Nephrons filter the blood and move excess fluids (urine) into the kidney pelvis. Urine travels from the kidneys to the bladder through tubes called ureters, and out of the body through a tube called the urethra. Kidney diseases can cause fluid buildup or prevent adequate filtering of the blood. Patients may need dialysis or surgery if one or both kidneys stop functioning.

SECTION	13.8	Review Questions

1. What are the three functions of the urinary system?

2. What is dialysis and when is it used?

3. What is the purpose of the nephron?

4. What are the symptoms of renal calculi (kidney stones)?

5. Why is kidney failure dangerous to a patient's health?

6. A(n)_____, also called a renal physician, specializes in the treatment of patients with kidney diseases.

Learn By Doing: Section 13.8 Activity

1. Complete Worksheets 1 through 4 as assigned.

2. When you are confident that you can meet each objective for this section, ask your teacher for the section evaluation.

Background

Glands are small organs that are positioned throughout the body. Some glands release substances, such as tears and sweat, to the outside of the body. Other glands release substances directly into the bloodstream. Many glands produce hormones. Hormones help to regulate many body functions. As a health care worker, you should know the structure, functions, and disorders of the glandular system.

Objectives

When you have completed this section, you will be able to do the following:

- Match key terms with their correct meanings.

- Label endocrine glands on a diagram.

- Identify functions of the endocrine glands.

- Identify common disorders of the endocrine glands.

- Explain the difference between the endocrine and exocrine glands.

- Describe the effects of the endocrine glands on the body.

- Explain why the health care worker's understanding of the glandular systems is important.

Introduction to the Glandular Systems

The glands of the body (Figure 13.25) make substances that help regulate the body processes of growth, **metabolism**, muscle contraction, and many other processes. Glands are divided into two categories. These are the exocrine and endocrine glands:

- *Exocrine glands* have ducts that carry substances to organs, body parts, or the outside of the body. The substance made by the gland is **excreted** and is deposited in the organ or body part. *Examples:*

  - Digestive juices from the salivary glands, pancreas, and gallbladder.

  - Milk from the female mammary glands.

  - Moisture from the sweat glands.

  - Sebum (oil) from the **sebaceous** glands.

  - Tears from the **lacrimal** glands.

- *Endocrine glands* are glands without ducts. They secrete **hormones** directly into the bloodstream. The secretions from these glands are separated into two main groups:

  - *External secretions* (excretions) are fluids that are carried to a nearby organ or to the outside of the body.

  - *Internal secretions* are hormones that are carried to all parts of the body through the blood and lymph systems. The endocrine glands that secrete hormones are included in Table 13.12.

metabolism
(meh TAB uh liz um)
The body's process of using food to make energy and use nutrients.

excreted
(ex KREET ed)
Thrown off or eliminated as waste material.

sebaceous
(seh BAY shus)
Pertaining to fatty secretions.

lacrimal
(LAK rim uhl)
Pertaining to tears.

hormones
(HOR moans)
Protein substances secreted by an endocrine gland directly into the blood.

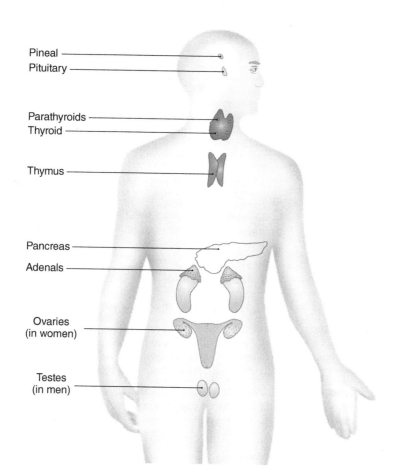

FIGURE 13.25

The glandular systems provide substances that help regulate body processes. Which glands are found in the head and the throat?

Pineal
Pituitary

Parathyroids
Thyroid

Thymus

Pancreas
Adenals

Ovaries
(in women)

Testes
(in men)

Table 13.12   Endocrine Glands, Hormones, and Their Functions

Gland	Hormone	Function
Pituitary	TSH (thyrotropic hormone), ACTH (adrenocorticotrophic hormone), FSH (follicle-stimulating hormone), LH (luteinizing hormone), ADH (antidiuretic hormone), oxytocin, oytocin, prolactin, and somatotropic hormone	Controls other glands; stimulates growth
Thyroid	Thyroxin	Controls rate of metabolism
Parathyroid	Parathyroid hormone	Regulates calcium and phosphorus metabolism
Pancreas	Insulin from islands of Langerhans	Enables utilization of glucose
Ovaries	Estrogen and progesterone	Develop and maintain female reproductive organs
Testes	Testosterone	Develop and maintain male reproductive organs
Adrenal medulla	Adrenalin	Prepares the body for fight or flight
Adrenal cortex	Corticoids	Aids body in coping with stress or infection
Pineal	Melatonin	May help modulate wake/sleep patterns

Common Disorders of the Glandular Systems

**Table 13.13   Common Disorders, Symptoms, and Preventive Measures/
Treatment of the Glandular System**

Condition	Disorder	Symptoms	Preventive Measures/ Treatment
Addison's disease	A life-threatening disease caused by insufficient amount of hormones from the adrenal glands.	Weakness, decreased endurance, increased **pigmentation** of the skin and mucous membranes, anorexia, dehydration, weight loss, GI disturbances, anxiety, depression, and decreased tolerance to cold.	Treating with medication, maintaining an adequate intake of fluids, eating a diet high in carbohydrates and protein and low in sodium and potassium.
Diabetes mellitus	Too much sugar (glucose) in the blood, usually the result of the pancreas failing to produce insulin. There are the following types of diabetes: ■ IDDM: insulin-dependent diabetes mellitus. ■ NIDDM: noninsulin-dependent diabetes mellitus. ■ GDM: gestational diabetes mellitus (during pregnancy). ■ Types of diabetes usually associated with pancreatic disease, hormonal changes, adverse effects of drugs, or genetic abnormalities. ■ IGT: impaired glucose tolerance.	Increased thirst (polydipsia) and urination (polyuria), and weight loss. Periods of excessive hunger (polyphagia), and low blood sugar levels (hypoglycemia). The eyes, kidneys, nervous system, skin, and circulatory system may be affected, and infections are common. Atherosclerosis often develops.	Maintaining insulin and glucose levels within normal values through diet, exercise, and medication.
Hyperthyroidism	Increased production of the thyroid secretion.	Excessive sweating, heat intolerance, increased bowel movements; tremors, nervousness, agitation, rapid heart rate. Weight loss, fatigue, decreased concentration. Irregular and scant menstrual flow. In older patients, irregular heart rhythms and heart failure can occur.	Treating the symptoms with antithyroid drugs; radioactive iodine. Surgery to partially remove thyroid gland.
Hypoglycemia	Too little sugar in the blood, usually caused by the excessive production of insulin in the pancreas.	Weakness, headache, hunger, visual disturbances, ataxia, anxiety, personality changes, and, if untreated, delirium, coma, and death.	Taking glucose in orange juice by mouth if the person is conscious, followed by protein, or administering intravenously if the person is unconscious.
Hypothyroidism	Decreased production of the thyroid secretion.	Fatigue, depression, modest weight gain, intolerance of cold, excessive sleepiness, dry or coarse hair, constipation, dry skin, muscle cramps, increased cholesterol levels, decreased concentration, aches and pains, swelling of legs.	Life-long treatment with T-4 form of thyroid hormone. Pill taken once a day, preferably in the morning.

Medical Terminology

acromegaly:	enlargement of bones of the extremities	*hyperthyroidism:*	increased production of the thyroid secretion
adenectomy:	removal of any gland	*hypothyroidism:*	decreased production of the thyroid secretion
adenoidectomy:	removal of the adenoids		
adrenogenic:	originating in the adrenals	*lymphocytopenia:*	deficiency of lymph cells
dwarfism:	condition of being abnormally small	*pancreatolysis:*	breakdown of the pancreas
		parathyrotoxicosis:	poisonous condition of the parathyroid
endocrine:	ductless; to secrete within		
endocrinotherapy:	treatment with endocrine preparation	*pinealoma:*	tumor of the pineal gland
		pituitarigenic:	originating in the pituitary
exocrine:	to secrete through a duct	*pituitarism:*	any disorder of the pituitary gland
goiter:	enlarged thyroid gland		
goitrogen:	any substance that causes a goiter	*thyroadenitis:*	inflammation of the thyroid gland

 Jobs and Professions

Endocrinologist

pigmentation
(pig men TAY shun
Natural color of the skin.

An endocrinologist is a physician who specializes in the endocrine system. These doctors treat conditions that affect your glands. This may include diabetes, thyroid diseases, metabolic disorders, osteoporosis, hypertension, lack of growth, infertility, or cancer.

Endocrinologists treat these hormone problems and try to restore a normal balance of hormones in their patients. Endocrinologists also do research to learn how glands work and to find the best treatments for patients with glandular problems.

Like many other specialties, to become an endocrinologist you must first complete medical school and then complete a two- to three-year residency to become certified in internal medicine. Following that, you must then spend two or three more years studying the endocrine system. It takes more than 10 years to become trained as an endocrinologist.

 Summary

In this section, you learned that glands produce hormones that help to regulate growth, metabolism, reproduction, and other body processes. Examples of glands include the thyroid, pancreas, ovaries, and testes. Disorders of the glandular system occur when a gland overproduces or underproduces hormones. These disorders may cause illness or death. Some glandular system disorders can be controlled by diet and medications.

1. What substance is produced by the adrenal cortex and what function does this substance have in the body?

2. What is the difference between endocrine and exocrine glands?

3. What do sebaceous glands produce?

4. What is diabetes mellitus and what causes this disorder?

5. Where are the adrenal glands located?

6. What are the symptoms and treatment for hypoglycemia?

7. A(n) _____ is a physician who specializes conditions that affect your glands.

Learn By Doing: Section 13.9 Activity

1. Complete Worksheets 1 through 4 as assigned.

2. When you are confident that you can meet each objective for this section, ask your teacher for the section evaluation.

SECTION

13.10 The Nervous System

Background

The nervous system receives, sends, and coordinates internal and external messages. This system helps us to sense and react to things that are happening outside of the body. It also controls automatic internal body functions, such as heartbeat and breathing. In this section, you will learn the structure and functions of the nervous system. You will also learn how diseases of the sensory organs or nerves can affect patients.

Objectives

When you have completed this section, you will be able to do the following:

- Match key terms with their correct meanings.

- Match and select the functions of various parts of the nervous system.

- Label diagrams of the eye and ear.

- Describe the influence of the nervous system on the body.

- Match common disorders of the nervous system with their correct names.

- Explain why the health care worker's understanding of the nervous system is important.

Introduction to the Nervous System

The nervous system is a delicate system of nerve cells (or neurons) (**Figure 13.26**) linked together to receive **stimuli** and to respond to stimuli.

Stimuli are anything that cause a reaction or response (e.g., when your hand touches a hot object or when something flies into your eye).

stimuli
(STIM you lie)
Elements in the external or internal environment that are strong enough to set up a nervous impulse.

FIGURE 13.26
Central and peripheral nervous systems; neuron (nerve cell). What does a motor neuron look like?

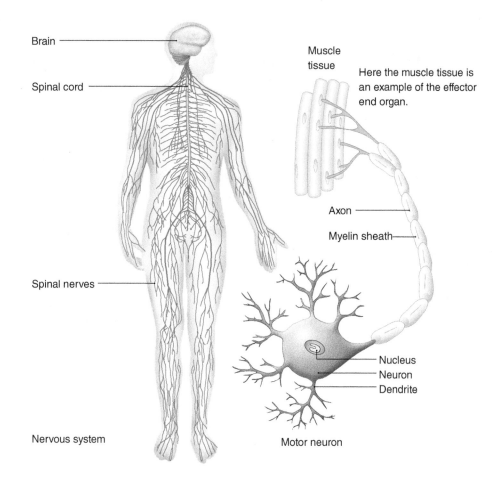

Brain

Spinal cord

Muscle tissue

Here the muscle tissue is an example of the effector end organ.

Axon

Myelin sheath

Spinal nerves

Nucleus
Neuron
Dendrite

Nervous system

Motor neuron

Response is the reaction to the stimuli (e.g., moving your hand when it touches something hot or tears in the eye when something flies into it).

The nervous system is divided into two parts: the central nervous system and the **peripheral** nervous system.

The *central nervous system (CNS)* includes the brain and the spinal cord. (**Figure 13.26**) Nerves of the spinal cord carry messages to and from the brain. The brain has three main parts:

- The *cerebrum* processes thought having to do with memory and learning. It controls voluntary movements and sense interpretation.

- The *cerebellum* coordinates muscle activity and balance so that muscles function smoothly.

- The *medulla*, a part of the brainstem, controls breathing, heartbeat, circulatory action, and digestive movements.

peripheral
(per IF er uhl)
Situated away from a central structure.

ganglia
(GANG glee ah)
Mass of nerve tissue composed of nerve cell bodies. Ganglia lie outside the brain and spinal cord.

neuron
(NUR awn)
Nerve; includes the cell and the long fiber coming from the cell.

The *peripheral nervous system* includes the nerves and **ganglia** outside the brain and spinal cord. There are:

- Twelve pairs of cranial nerves.
- Thirty-one pairs of spinal nerves.
- Various nerve branches in body organs.

All parts of the central and peripheral nervous systems work together to relay messages to the brain. Each message is carried to the correct area of the brain by its specialized **neuron** or nerve cell. (**Figure 13.26**)

Each specialized neuron leads into a passage that delivers the message or stimuli to the brain or the spinal cord. The areas in the spinal cord that can receive messages cause an action or response to stimuli that does not require interpretation. The stimuli that are received by the brain are interpreted and cause a response.

This response can occur anyplace in the body but is most easily recognized in the sense organs. For example, sound waves are received by the ears; light rays are received by the eyes; the nose and tongue respond to smell and taste; and the nerve endings throughout the body respond to pressure, heat, cold, pain, and touch.

The following are the sensory organs of the body.

The Eye

The eye provides vision. (**Figure 13.27**) It is a ball-shaped organ located in the eye orbit of the skull.

FIGURE 13.27

Cross section of the eye and external eye. Where is the cornea of the eye in relation to the lens and iris?

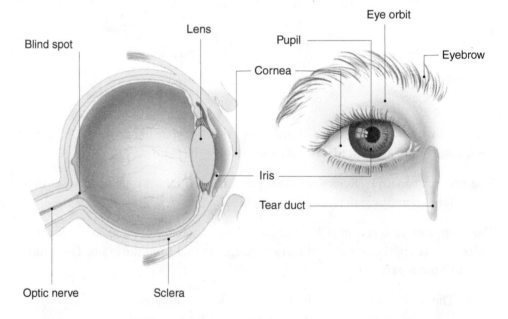

Blind spot — Lens — Pupil — Eye orbit — Eyebrow — Cornea — Iris — Tear duct — Optic nerve — Sclera

Protection for the Eye

duct
(DUHKT)
Narrow, round tube that carries secretions from a gland.

- The lids and eyelashes aid in protecting the eye.
- Tears from the lacrimal **duct** help wash away foreign matter.

Coats of the Eye

- The *sclera*, or the white of the eye, is the outer lining. The front portion of the sclera is clear and is called the *cornea*, or the "window of the eye".

- The *choroid*, the second coating, is heavily **pigmented** to keep light rays from **scattering**.

- The *retina*, the innermost coating of the eye, houses the mechanisms that sense vision.

- The *optic nerve*, located at the back of the eye, receives a picture and sends it to the brain for interpretation.

The Ear

The ear provides hearing and **equilibrium**. (Figure 13.28) The ear can be divided into three main parts:

- The *external ear* includes the following:
  - *Auricle*, or outside projection.
  - *External auditory canal.*
  - *Tympanic membrane* or eardrum, which separates the external and middle ear.
- The *middle ear* is an air space that contains three bones or **ossicles**. These bones **amplify** sound waves received by the tympanic membrane.
- The *inner ear* contains the semicircular canals, which transmit sound waves received from the middle ear to the nerves that allow us to **translate** sound. The inner ear is also responsible for equilibrium.

pigmented
(PIG men ted)
Colored; relating to various parts of the body (e.g., iris of the eye, lips, moles, freckles).

scattering
(SKAT e ring)
Spreading in many directions, dispersing.

equilibrium
(ee kwah LIB ree um)
State of balance.

ossicles
(OSS ik uhls)
Three small bones in the middle ear: incus, stapes, and malleus.

amplify
(AM pluh feye)
To increase or elevate a sound (e.g., the ossicles of the ear amplify sound waves).

translate
(trans LEYT)
To make understandable.

FIGURE 13.28
Cross section of the ear. Which part of the ear looks like a snail shell?

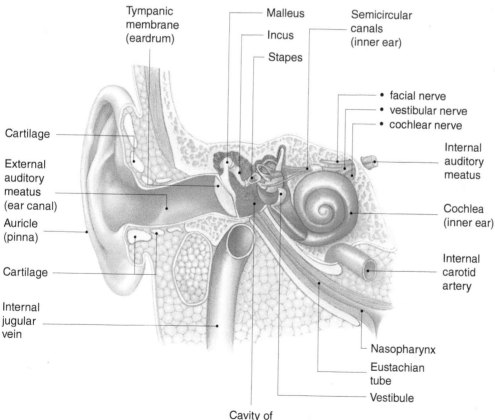

receptors
(ree SEP torz)
Nerves that respond to stimuli.

Organs of Taste and Smell
Sense of Taste

Taste is sensed by **receptors** in the tongue called *taste buds.* The taste buds sense four main tastes:

- Sweet.
- Salty.
- Sour.
- Bitter.

Sense of Smell

Receptors that receive smells are located high in the upper part of the nasal cavity called the *olfactory epithelium.* The *olfactory nerve* sends the smell to the brain for interpretation.

General Senses

General senses are found throughout the body. These general senses are different from the special senses of sight, hearing, taste, and smell; they are not limited to specific areas of the body. (**Figure 13.29**)

FIGURE 13.29
General senses: heat, cold, touch, pressure, pain. Which skin receptor detects cold?

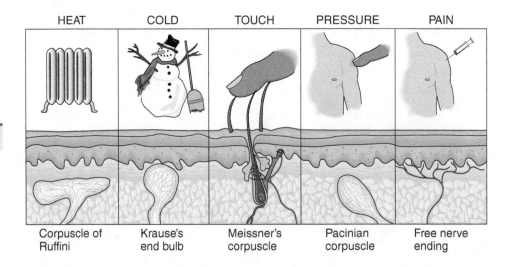

HEAT	COLD	TOUCH	PRESSURE	PAIN
Corpuscle of Ruffini	Krause's end bulb	Meissner's corpuscle	Pacinian corpuscle	Free nerve ending

Apply It

Play a game of Mystery Smells. List ten items belonging to a specific place/activity—a school, a ball game, the beach, a specific holiday, etc. that have an odor associated with them. List each item on one side of a 3 x 5 card.

On the opposite side, write a description of the smell. For instance, you might say "dessert" as the word, and "fruity" as the smell. Once the cards are made, try to have your fellow classmates guess the item by the smell and location.

Pressure Sense
Pressure is sensed by the pressure receptors in the **subcutaneous** tissue layer beneath the skin.

Temperature Sense
Heat and cold are sensed by receptors that respond only to heat or cold and send messages through nerves to the brain.

Sense of Touch
Touch is sensed by receptors called *tactile corpuscles.* These receptors are found in the dermis layer of skin. They are very close together in the fingertips and the toes and also in the tip of the tongue.

subcutaneous
(sub kyu TAIN ee us)
Beneath the skin.

Sense of Pain

Pain is the most important protective sense because it tells us that something is wrong in the body. Pain receptors are found in the:

- Skin.
- Muscles.
- Joints.
- Internal organs.

These receptors are nerve fibers that send messages of pain to the brain when parts of the body are injured.

 ## Common Disorders of the Nervous System

Table 13.14 Common Disorders, Symptoms, and Preventive Measures/ Treatment of the Nervous System

Condition	Disorder	Symptoms	Preventive Measures/ Treatment
Alzheimer's Disease	A progressive, degenerative disease of the brain that results in dementia.	Personality and behavior changes. Decline in memory. Reduced awareness of one's surroundings and of recent events. Repetitive behavior. Increased restlessness and agitation in late afternoon and evening; wandering. Bowel and bladder incontinence. Suspicion.	No current cure or way to stop the progression of the disease. Medications can improve symptom management; for example, cholinesterase inhibitors help memory and learning.
Cataract	Formation occurs when the lens of the eye loses its transparency. Light is less able to reach the inner eye. Cataracts are the most common cause of blindness and a very common ailment in the geriatric patient.	At first vision is blurred, then distortion and double vision may develop. If not treated, blindness can occur.	For cataracts that have developed through the aging process, treating with removal of the lens and then prescribing contacts or glasses.
Conjunctivitis or "Pink Eye"	Inflammation of the eyelid lining caused from bacteria or irritation from dirt in the eye. Highly contagious.	Red eyes, thick discharge, sticky eyelids in the morning, usually occurring without pain.	Wearing goggles to protect eyes from dirt and debris when possible. For example, when mowing the lawn, sawing wood, etc. Wash hands frequently to prevent transmission. Treatment for infected eyes is usually with antibiotics.

(continued)

Condition	Disorder	Symptoms	Preventive Measures/ Treatment
Glaucoma	Caused by increased intraocular pressure (IOP) resulting either from a malformation or malfunction of the eye's drainage structures. Pressure causes the optic nerve and retinal fibers to deteriorate resulting in a progressive, permanent loss of vision. Glaucoma appears frequently as a person ages.	*Acute glaucoma*—extreme pain, blurred vision, a red eye and dilated pupil. Nausea and vomiting may also occur. *Chronic glaucoma*—there may be no symptoms except a gradual loss of peripheral vision over time and perhaps a dull pain.	Treating with eye drops; surgery may also be helpful.
Neuritis	Inflammation of a nerve caused by injury, malnutrition, alcoholism, or toxic poison.	Pain, numbness, muscle atrophy, change in reflexes.	Eliminating the cause of irritation if possible. Treatment may consist of pain medication, nerve block procedure, and physical therapy to maintain muscle.
Otosclerosis	Hereditary condition in which the bones in the ear change and sounds are not transmitted properly.	Tinnitus (ringing in the ear), then loss of hearing.	No known prevention; treating surgically may be helpful.
Parkinson's	A degenerative disorder of the central nervous system that often impairs the sufferer's motor skills and speech.	Affects movement (tremors, rigidity, instability, shuffling walk), mood, behavior, thinking, and sensation.	No cure at this time. Patient and family education, support group services, general wellness maintenance, physiotherapy, exercise, and nutrition. Medications (most commonly L-dopa) or surgery can provide relief from the symptoms.
Prebyopia	A vision condition in which the crystalline lens of your eye loses its flexibility, which makes it difficult for you to focus on close objects.	Difficulty reading fine print, particularly in low light conditions, eyestrain when reading for long periods, momentarily blurred vision when transitioning between viewing distances.	Not curable, but can be treated with corrective eyeglasses or contacts. New surgical procedures may also provide solutions for those who do not want to wear glasses or contacts, including implanting accommodative intraocular lenses (IOLs).
Presbycusis	Loss of hearing that gradually occurs in most individuals as they grow older (usually greater for high-pitched sounds).	Sounds often seem less clear and lower in volume. The speech of others seems mumbled or slurred. High-pitched sounds such as "s" and "th" are difficult to hear and tell apart. Tinnitus (a ringing, roaring, or hissing sound in one or both ears) may occur.	Avoid damaging noises (firearms, lawnmowers, etc.) Use of earplugs or earmuffs can help prevent damage when using machinery. Hearing aids or assistive listening devices can provide further improvement. Training in speechreading can help.

(continued)

Table 13.14   Common Disorders, Symptoms, and Preventive Measures/Treatment of the Nervous System (continued)

Condition	Disorder	Symptoms	Preventive Measures/Treatment
Shingles or herpes zoster	Caused by a virus that can affect any sensory nerve but tends to invade nerves in the chest and head near the temple most often.	Many blisters appear on the skin over nerve routes and cause a great deal of pain. The blisters usually disappear in about a week, but the pain may recur for years afterward.	Treating with soothing creams to relieve itching, topical medications, and pain medications when necessary.

Medical Terminology

audiometer: instrument to measure hearing

blepharitis: inflammation of the eyelid

blepharorrhaphy: suturing the eyelid

cerebrocular: pertaining to the brain and eyes

dacryadenitis: inflammation of a tear duct

gustation: sense of taste

iridocele: hernia of the iris of the eye

iridoplegia: paralysis of the iris of the eye

lacrimal: pertaining to tear ducts

ophthalmologist: specialist in the study of the eye

otitismedia: inflammation of the middle ear

otoneurology: study of the ear and neural disorders

otoplasty: plastic repair of cartilage of the ear

otorrhea: purulent discharge from the ear

Jobs and Professions

Neurologist

A neurologist is a physician who specializes in nervous system disorders. This includes diseases of the brain, spinal cord, nerves, muscles, and the blood vessels that relate to these structures. Neurologists examine the nerves of the head or neck and test muscle strength and movement. They see how well you move and balance. They test your reflexes. They also examine your sense of sensation, your memory, speech, language, and other cognitive abilities. They do many tests to complete these assessments, including CAT scans, MRIs, and spinal taps.

To become a neurologist, you must complete medical school followed by a one-year internship. At least eight months of that internship must be spent in internal medicine. Then, you must complete a three-year residency in neurology and pass an exam to become a certified neurologist. If you choose to pursue a specialty area, such as child neurology, clinical neurophysiology, or pain medicine, you must complete one to three years of additional training.

Opthalmologist

An opthalmologist is a medical doctor who specializes in the eye and the visual system. Their job is to diagnose and treat eye disease. They also treat eye injuries.

Neurological Examination

More than imaging technology and laboratory tests are needed to determine whether nerves are, or are not, functioning. A neurological examination makes that determination. A neuro exam is a noninvasive series of questions and tests. The exam is divided into sections: mental status; cranial nerves; motor system; sensory system; deep tendon reflexes, coordination, and gait.

This may entail routine eye exams, diagnosis and treatment of eye disorders or diseases, prescribing eyeglasses or contact lenses, surgery, or managing problems caused by systemic illness.

To become an opthalmologist, you must complete college and medical school. That is followed by a one-year clinical internship and at least three years as a hospital resident in opthalmology. To specialize in a specific area, such as a disease, an eye part, or pediatrics, you must complete one or two years of additional training. Once training is complete, opthalmologists must pass an exam to become certified in this profession.

Otologist

An otologist, also known as a neurotologist, is a physician who specializes in conditions affecting the ears. These conditions include problems with balance and dizziness, all types of hearing loss, noises in the ear, facial nerve disorders, persistent infections, congenital malformations of the ear, and tumors of the ear. Trained as a surgeon, an otologist performs surgical procedures such as the repair of eardrum perforations, hearing reconstruction, and tumor removal.

To become an otologist, you must attend medical school and then become a trained otorhinolaryngologist. An otorhinolaryngologist, commonly known as an ENT, specializes in problems associated with the ear, nose, throat, and neck.

To become an otorhinolaryngologist, you must complete medical school, one year of general surgery residency, and four years of otorhinolaryngology training. To specialize as an otologist, you must complete another residency in that area. All otologists must pass an exam in order to become board certified before practicing medicine.

Otorhinolaryngologist

An otorhinolaryngologist is a physician/surgeon who specializes in head and neck surgery. Common ailments addressed include: head and neck cancer; tumors; sinus and allergic disease; thyroid and parathyroid problems; snoring and sleep apnea; and pediatric ear, nose, and throat issues.

An otorhinolaryngologist might perform open surgery on the salivary or thyroid glands or reconstructive surgery of the head or neck. Other possibilities include microsurgery of the middle ear, sinus surgery, or surgery at the base of the skull. To become an otorhinolaryngologist, you must complete medical school, one year of general surgery residency, and four years of otorhinolaryngology training.

 Summary

In this section, you learned that the nervous system consists of two parts: the central nervous system and the peripheral nervous system. The central nervous system includes the brain and the spinal cord. The peripheral nervous system is made up of nerves that are outside of the brain and spinal cord.

Sensory organs allow you to detect outside stimuli. Sensory organs include the eyes, ears, nose, and tongue. General sense receptors are found throughout the body. Nervous system disorders can damage nerves or sensory organs. These disorders often interfere with the patient's ability to sense and react to outside stimuli.

1. List and describe three disorders of the eye.

2. Which tactile corpuscles sense touch and pressure?

3. What four main tastes are detected by the taste buds?

4. Name the ossicles of the middle ear.

5. What structures are part of the peripheral nervous system?

6. Which part of the brain controls breathing and heartbeat?

7. What causes "Pink Eye" and how do you treat it?

8. What does a neurologist do and what education or training is required for this career?

Learn By Doing: Section 13.10 Activity

1. Complete Worksheets 1 through 6 as assigned.

2. When you are confident that you can meet each objective for this section, ask your teacher for the section evaluation.

SECTION

13.11 The Reproductive System

Background

The reproductive system allows humans to reproduce. This system produces sex cells that unite to form a fertilized egg that can develop into offspring. The reproductive system is controlled by hormones. This system usually becomes active during the teenage years. As a health care worker, you should be familiar with this system in order to monitor pregnant patients and prevent or treat reproductive disorders.

Objectives

When you have completed this section, you will be able to do the following:

- Match key terms with their correct meanings.

- Label a diagram of the male and female reproductive systems.

- Match the various organs in the reproductive systems with their functions.

- Match common disorders of the reproductive system with their descriptions.

- Describe how the reproductive system affects the body.

- Explain why the health care worker's understanding of the reproductive system is important.

sex cells
(SEX sel)
Cells that allow reproduction to occur.

fetus
(FEE tus)
Infant developing in the uterus after the first three months until birth.

estrogen
(ESS tro jen)
Female hormone.

matures
(me TCHOOR)
Becomes fully developed.

ovum
(OH vum)
Female reproductive cell that when fertilized by the male develops into a new organism.

Apply It

Divide into small groups. Each group will create a set of game cards that include answers to specific categories, such as female reproductive organs, male reproductive organs, diseases, etc. One student on each team will be the category giver and will read the category to their team. The team can answer as many questions as they can in an allotted time period (i.e., one minute). Teams will get one point for each correct answer. The team with the most points wins.

FIGURE 13.30

Cross section of the female reproductive system. Where are the female sex cells (ova) produced?

 # Introduction to the Reproductive System

Reproduction occurs in all species. Tiny one-celled organisms divide or separate by themselves to reproduce. Most animals require a male and female, each with their own special cells that unite to reproduce. The male and female reproductive systems have several characteristics in common. They are gonads, tubes that carry secretions, and exocrine glands.

- *Gonads* (endocrine glands) or sex glands in the male are called *testes,* and they produce sperm. In the female they are called *ovaries,* and they produce ova.
- The *tubes* form passageways for the **sex cells**, sperm and ova.

The Female Reproductive System

The main function of the female reproductive system is to produce the ovum for fertilization and to house a developing **fetus**. Reproduction occurs when the male and female sex cells unite within the female. After the union of these cells, the fertilized egg divides and grows for 9 months or 40 weeks and develops into a new individual. Look at **Figure 13.30** to identify parts of the female reproductive system.

- *Female gonads,* the ovaries, are small oval-shaped structures that produce the female sex cells or *ova* and the hormone called **estrogen**. Approximately every 28 days an ovum **matures** and is forced from the ovary and received by the fallopian tube.
- *Fallopian tubes* are muscular tubes about five inches long. The tubes do not connect to the ovaries. When the **ovum** is forced from the ovary into the peritoneal cavity, it floats in the peritoneal fluid. At the end of each fallopian tube, fingerlike projections called fimbriae create a current that sweeps the ovum into the tube.

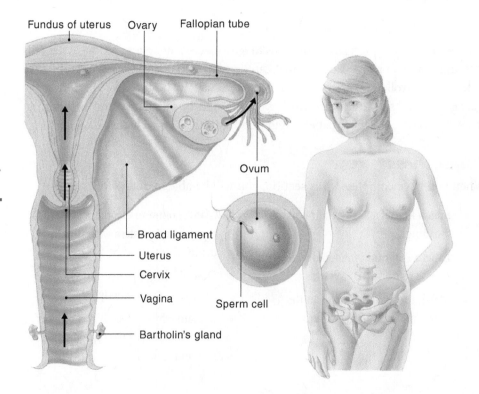

- Once inside the tube, the ovum is swept forward by small cilia and by peristalsis. The ovum takes about five days to move through the fallopian tube and is then deposited into the uterus.

- The *uterus*, a pear-shaped organ, is attached to the fallopian tubes. While the ovum is maturing, the uterus begins to build an interlining called the **endometrium**. If the ovum is not fertilized in the fallopian tube, it deteriorates shortly after entering the uterus. The endometrium then deteriorates, causing bleeding or **menstruation**. The main function of the uterus is to house and nourish the fertilized ovum until delivery of a fully developed fetus.

- The *vagina is* a muscular tube that houses the neck of the uterus or *cervix*. This tube extends approximately three inches to the outside of the body. The vagina is also known as the birth canal.

The Male Reproductive System

- *Male gonads* or *testes* are found outside the body, between the legs, in a sac called the *scrotum*. The testes produce the male sex cells or **spermatozoa** (or *sperm*) and the hormone **testosterone.** The *penis* is the primary male sex organ. It lies anterior to the testes. (**Figure 13.31**)

- The *epididymis* is a 20-foot-long tube that is coiled inside the scrotal sac. Sperm are stored here until they mature and are able to move by themselves. As the epididymis extends upward, it becomes the vas deferens.

- The *vas deferens*, the spermatic cord, extends through the abdominal wall and curves over and behind the urinary bladder. It functions as a passageway for sperm.

- *Seminal vesicles* are outpouchings at the end of the vas deferens. They produce a thick yellow secretion that adds to the volume of **semen** and nourishes the sperm.

endometrium
(en doh MEE tree um)
Interlining of the uterus.

menstruation
(men stroo AY shun)
Cyclic deterioration of the endometrium.

spermatozoa
(spur mat uh ZOH uh)
Male sex cells.

testosterone
(tess TOSS ter own)
Male hormone.

semen
(SEE mun)
Fluid from the testes, seminal vesicles, prostate gland, and bulbourethral glands. Contains water, mucin, proteins, salts, and sperm.

FIGURE 13.31
Cross section of the male reproductive system. Which tube connects to the epididymis and provides a passageway for sperm?

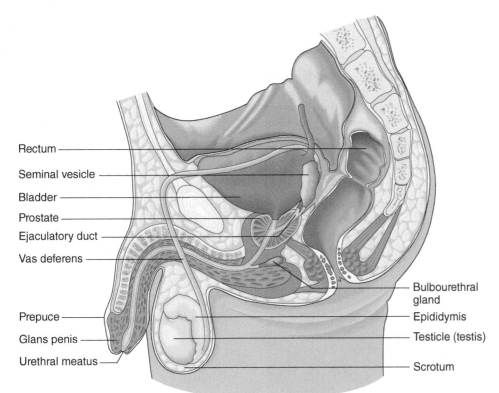

Rectum
Seminal vesicle
Bladder
Prostate
Ejaculatory duct
Vas deferens
Prepuce
Glans penis
Urethral meatus
Bulbourethral gland
Epididymis
Testicle (testis)
Scrotum

- The *prostate gland,* located just below the urinary bladder, produces a secretion that maintains mobility of sperm. The *ejaculatory duct* carries sperm from the junction of the vas deferens and the seminal vesicles through the prostate gland and connects to the urethra.

- The *urethra* is a small passage for urine and sperm, and leads from the urinary bladder through the prostate gland and the penis to the outside of the body.

monogamous
(mun OG ah mus)
Having a sexual relationship with only one partner during a period of time.

Common Disorders of the Reproductive System

Table 13.15   Common Disorders, Symptoms, and Preventive Measures/ Treatment of the Reproductive System

Condition	Disorder	Symptoms	Preventive Measures/ Treatment
Breast cancer	Cancer of the glandular breast tissue. Fifth most common cause of cancer death worldwide. Can occur in men (but rarely) as well as women.	Breast cancer symptoms vary widely—from lumps to swelling to skin changes. Many breast cancers have no obvious symptoms at all. Symptoms that are similar to those of breast cancer may be the result of non-cancerous conditions like infection or a cyst.	Monthly self exams and annual mammograms help early detection. Biopsies are used to confirm the diagnosis. Once detected, may be treated with surgery (lumpectomy), mastectomy, and lymph node dissection), then perhaps radiation, hormonal (anti-estrogen) therapy, and/or chemotherapy.
Cryptorchidism	Means "hidden testes." Also called undescended testes.	One or both testes fail to descend into the scrotum.	Administering hormone injections if the testicle does not descend into the scrotum by the age of one year. If this treatment is unsuccessful by the age of five years, surgery is performed to locate the testicle and place it in the scrotum or remove it.
Fibroid tumors	Common in women over the age of 50. They are usually benign.	There may be breakthrough bleeding between menstrual cycles and pressure from the tumor may cause frequent urination. There are often no symptoms.	Physician will monitor size and growth and determine if surgical removal is necessary.
Impotence (Erectile Dysfunction)	The consistent inability to obtain or maintain an erection of sufficient quality for satisfactory sexual intercourse.	Risk increases with age. Can range from a total inability to achieve an erection or ejaculation, an inconsistent ability to do so, or a tendency to sustain only very brief erections.	Healthier lifestyle, healthy diet, drink less and exercise more. Oral medications are available. In severe cases, patient may consider penile injections, or or implants.

(continued)

Table 13.15 Common Disorders, Symptoms, and Preventive Measures/ Treatment of the Reproductive System (continued)

Condition	Disorder	Symptoms	Preventive Measures/ Treatment
Prostate cancer	Cancer that forms in tissues of the prostate; usually occurs in older men.	May have little or no symptoms in early stages. Trouble passing urine; may gradually lose control of bladder function. A weak or interrupted stream of urine, an urgency to urinate, leaking or dribbling, and more often needing to urinate during the night. Difficulty in having an erection; painful ejaculation; blood in urine or semen.	Annual physical; physical (with attention to any enlargement of prostate); DRE and PSA tests can signal problems; biopsy to confirm. Slow growing so may watch and moniter at first. Treatment may include surgery, radiation therapy, hormone therapy, chemotherapy and other emerging treatments.
Sexually transmitted diseases (STDs)	Affect both male and female. The most common sexually transmitted diseases are acquired immune deficiency syndrome (AIDS), chlamydia, gonorrhea, and syphilis (see each below).	Symptoms vary as noted below.	For prevention, practice abstinence or use a protective barrier such as a condom during sex, and maintain **monogamous** relationships with uninfected partners. Some treatment options are listed below.
	Acquired immune deficiency syndrome (AIDS): AIDS is most commonly transmitted by sexual contact. It is a contagious disease that causes severe illness and often results in death. The AIDS virus enters the blood of a person from the blood or body fluids of a carrier.	Symptoms include swollen lymph glands, diarrhea, night sweats abnormal or unusual bleeding, fungal infection of the mouth and throat, loss of memory, fatigue, extreme weight loss, and constant cough. All or some of these symptoms may be present.	Although research is making great strides toward finding a cure, there is no successful treatment that cures AIDS. There are some medications and lifestyle changes that help individuals maintain a fairly healthy state for long periods.
	Chlamydia: A contagious bacterium, Chlamydia trachomatis, that lives in the conjunctiva of the eye and in the urethra and cervix of the uterus.	Purulent discharge from the urethra in the male or the vagina in the female.	Treating with antibiotics.
	Gonorrhea: A contagious bacterium, Neisseria gonorrhoeae, that affects the genitourinary tract and occasionally the pharynx, conjunctiva, or rectum.	Urethritis, dysuria, purulent greenish-yellow urethral or vaginal discharge, red or swollen urethral meatus, itching, burning or pain around the vaginal or urethral opening.	Treating with antibiotics.

(continued)

Table 13.15   Common Disorders, Symptoms, and Preventive Measures/ Treatment of the Reproductive System (continued)

Condition	Disorder	Symptoms	Preventive Measures/ Treatment
(STDs) *cont.*	*Syphilis:* Caused by a spirochete transmitted through sexual contact. It can affect any organ or system of the body. The spirochete is able to pass through the human placenta causing congenital syphilis in a newborn infant.	First stage—small, painless red pustule on the skin or mucous membrane (is contagious). Second stage—approximately two months later, generalized malaise, anorexia, nausea, fever, headache, loss of hair, bone and joint pain, skin rash that does not itch, sores in the mouth (remains contagious). Third stage—may not develop for many years. Appearance of soft, rubbery tumors that may cause a deep burrowing pain. Tumors may appear in any organ or system in the body.	Treating with antibiotics.
Testicular cancer	Cancer that occurs in the testes, located inside the scrotum. Compared with other cancers, relatively rare, but the most common cancer in younger males between the ages of 15 and 35.	There may be no symptoms. Discomfort or pain in the testicle or a feeling of heaviness in the scrotum. Enlargement of a testicle or a change in how it feels. Excess development of breast tissue (this may be a normal occurrence in adolescent boys who do not have testicular cancer). Lump or swelling in either testicle.	Monthly self exams (there is no known effective screening technique, so none is recommended). Once detected, may be treated with surgery to remove the testicle, radiation, or chemotherapy; one of the most treatable and curable cancers.

 Language Arts Link

Career Study

Many health care workers focus on one specific body system, such as the reproductive system, the respiratory system or the immune system. Select a specific career path and then learn more about the job opportunities for that position.

In paragraph form, describe the position, including job requirements and skills, and earning potential for health care workers in that field.

If you are able to speak with professionals in your selected fields, interview them about how they become interested in the area of study and what a typical day is like on the job.

Be sure to proofread your work to see if you can improve it by making it clearer, more concise, or more interesting to read. Check the spelling and grammar and correct any errors.

Exchange your report with a classmate. Provide feedback and corrections as necessary, and then exchange back. Read your classmate's comments and revise your document as necessary.

amenorrhea:	scant or no menstruation	**mammectomy:**	surgical removal of breast (or mastectomy) tissue
cervicitis:	inflammation of the cervix	**mastalgia:**	pain in the breast
colpectasis:	dilation of the vagina	**menorrhagia:**	excessive menstrual flow
colpoplasty:	plastic surgery on the vagina	**metrorrhexis:**	rupture of the uterus
dysmenorrhea:	painful or difficult menstruation	**oophorocystectomy:**	removal of an ovarian cyst
ectopic pregnancy:	pregnancy outside the uterus	**orchiopexy:**	fixation of the testes in the scrotum
gonorrhea:	flow from the genitals caused by infection	**orchioplasty:**	plastic surgery of the testes
gynecomastia:	abnormal enlargement of one or both breasts in men	**orchitis:**	inflammation of the testes
hysterectomy:	removal of uterus	**phimosis:**	refers to a tightness of the foreskin over the end of the penis
hystersalping oophorectomy:	removal of the uterus, fallopian tubes, and ovaries	**prenatal:**	occurring before birth
insemination:	injection of semen into the female reproductive system	**postnatal:**	occurring after birth
lactation:	secretion of milk from the breast	**sterile:**	unable to produce young
leukorrhea:	whitish vaginal discharge	**tubal ligation:**	procedure in which fallopian tubes are blocked
		vasectomy:	procedure for male sterilization

 ## Jobs and Professions

Embryologist

Embryologists study the early growth and formation of life. Clinical embryologists work with human embryos. They study the stages of pregnancy and watch how embryos grow and change day by day. Many embryologists work in infertility clinics They help infertile couples have children. To do this, they collect eggs and sperm from patients for examination and they check fertility levels. Sometimes, they prepare egg and sperm samples for in vitro fertilization.

Other times, an embryologist will combine the egg and sperm so that it grows into an embryo, which can be preserved and implanted at a later date. Embryologists may also study abnormalities in embryos. Their goal is discover why abnormalities occur and how they may be prevented.

Embryologists are highly trained in advanced laboratory techniques. They may work in hospitals, clinics, laboratories, or for a government agency, pharmaceutical company or biotechnology firm.

The minimum requirement for this position is a four-year bachelor's degree in embryology, microbiology or biochemistry. You must also have a background in genetics. This will qualify you to be a laboratory assistant or technician. To become a senior researcher, you must have a master's degree or a Ph.D.

Gynecologist

Gynecologists are physicians who specialize in the female organs and reproductive system. They manage hormonal disorders, treat infections, perform pap smears, diagnose cancers of the reproductive system, and perform operations such as hysterectomies. Much of a gynecologist's work is to perform routine check-ups so that serious problems do not occur. Some gynecologists specialize in a specific area such as critical care medicine, gynecologic oncology, or reproductive endocrinology.

To become a gynecologist, you must graduate from college and medical school. You must then complete a four-year gynecology residency and two years of clinical practice. One to three additional years of training is required if you decide to pursue a specialty area. All gynecologists must pass an exam to become certified before practicing medicine.

Obstetrician

An obstetrician is a physician who cares for women throughout childbirth. Some of their patients are women who are having complications during pregnancy. Obstetricians closely monitor the mother's health and diagnose any abnormalities or health issues in the developing fetus. If an issue does arise, the obstetrician may refer the mother to a specialist for treatment.

Many doctors who become obstetricians also train as gynecologists. To become an obstetrician, you must complete college and medical school. You must also complete a four-year residency specializing in obstetrics and gynecology and two more years of clinical practice. One to three more years of training is required for those who pursue an area of specialization. All obstetricians must also pass a national examination to become certified to practice in this field.

Midwife

Midwives are trained medical professionals who care for and support women throughout normal pregnancies. This care extends from the onset of pregnancy to just after delivery. Midwives stress communication with the mother and provide individualized health care information, emotional and social support, and continuous hands-on assistance during labor and delivery. If any problems arise, the midwife does not deliver the baby but calls for an obstetrician.

There are two types of midwives in the United States: direct-entry midwives and nurse-midwives. Direct-entry midwives are not nurses. However, they have at least a bachelor's degree, have completed specific health science courses, graduated from an accredited midwifery education program, and have passed a national exam to become certified. Nurse-midwives are registered nurses who have completed an accredited midwifery program and passed an exam to become certified.

▣ Summary

In this section, you learned that male and female reproductive systems have different structures and produce different hormones. However, both systems produce sex cells. You also learned about disorders of the reproductive system. These disorders include cryptorchidism, fibroid tumors, and sexually transmitted diseases, such as AIDS and syphilis. As a health care worker, you can help patients to avoid sexually transmitted diseases by suggesting lifestyle and behavioral changes.

1. How are the male testes similar to the female ovaries?

2. Describe how a mature egg gets to the uterus.

3. What do the seminal vesicles do?

4. Which sexually transmitted diseases can be treated with antibiotics?

5. What are the symptoms of fibroid tumors?

6. What two professions deal with childbirth and how do these professions differ?

Learn By Doing: Section 13.11 Activity

1. Complete Worksheets 1 through 5 as assigned.

2. When you are confident that you can meet each objective for this section, ask your teacher for the section evaluation.

SECTION

13.12 The Integumentary System

Background

In this section, you will learn about the integumentary system, which is commonly known as the skin. This system forms a protective barrier around the organs of the body. It keeps out pathogens and prevents injury to internal organs. It helps to regulate body temperature and eliminates wastes through sweat glands.

The integumentary system also senses stimuli, which allows the body to react to changing environmental conditions. As a health care worker, you should know the structure and functions of the integumentary system in order to treat disorders that may damage skin and make the body more vulnerable to injury or disease.

Objectives

When you have completed this section, you will be able to do the following:

- Match key terms with their correct meanings.

- Label a diagram of a cross section of skin.

- List the five main functions of skin.

- Identify three main layers of the skin.

- Match common disorders of the integumentary system with their descriptions.

- Describe how the integumentary system protects the body.

- Explain why the health care worker's understanding of the integumentary system is important.

◨ Introduction to the Integumentary System

The skin is the body's largest organ and is the first line of defense against infection. It contains several kinds of tissue, including epithelial, connective, and nerve tissues. This comprises skin, hair and nails. It also contains sweat and oil glands. The combination of these tissues and glands works together as the integumentary system. (**Figure 13.32**) The main functions of the skin are to:

- Protect the underlying body parts from injury and the invasion of pathogens.
- Regulate body temperature by controlling the loss of body heat.
- Eliminate wastes through perspiration.
- Store energy in the form of fat and vitamins.
- Sense touch, heat, cold, pain, and pressure through receptors.
- Produce vitamin D.

FIGURE 13.32
Cross section of the integumentary system (skin). What are the glands in the skin?

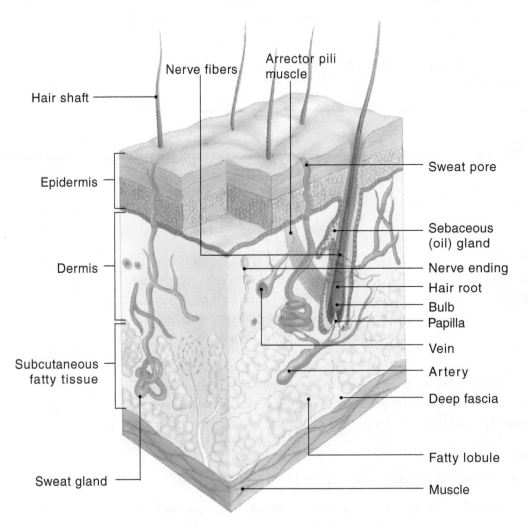

Structure of the Skin

Skin is made up of three main layers:

- The **epidermis** is the outermost layer and has no blood vessels. These cells are constantly **sloughed** off.

- The *dermis* is just beneath the epidermis and contains many blood vessels. New cells are continually forming to replace those lost from the epidermis. These cells come from the stratum germinativum layer of the epidermis.

- *Subcutaneous* means "under the skin," and this layer connects the skin to muscle.

As noted above, the integumentary system also includes hair, nails and cutaneous glands. Hair is an outgrowth of protein; it projects from the epidermis, though it grows from hair follicles deep in the dermis. Nails which are made of a tough protein called keratin, are produced from living skin cells in the fingers and toes. Cutaneous glands include:

- Sweat glands, that excrete sweat to regulate temperature.

- Sebaceous glands , oil-producing glands that keep skin and hair moist and soft.

- Ceruminous glands, located in the ear canal that produce earwax.

- Mammary glands, the milk-producing glands located in the breasts.

What's New?

Artificial Skin

Third-degree, or full-thickness, burns are the worst kinds of burns. They destroy the deepest layers of skin tissue and make patients vulnerable to infections. Not long ago, if a patient had third-degree burns over more than half of his or her body, that patient had a nearly no chance of survival.

Now, a new technology has significantly increased those odds to a 60 percent survival rate. The technology is a permanent, artificial skin. This skin has a dermal replacement layer composed of collagen derived from cow tendons and substances derived from shark cartilage. It also has a temporary epidermal replacement layer made of silicone. About a week after the artificial skin is implanted, blood vessels and proteins start to grow within the dermal layer.

After two or more weeks, the silicone epidermal layer can be removed and replaced with a small graft of the patient's own epidermis. After a month or more, the skin graft looks similar to normal skin.

Which part of the skin is permanently replaced by the artificial skin and which part is only temporarily replaced?

epidermis
(ep ih DER mus)
Outer layer of skin.

sloughed
(SLUFFED)
Discarded; separated from (e.g., to shed dead cells, as from the outer skin).

Career Connection

Research specialties in which the health care professional limits their expertise to the specific body systems, such as a Physical Therapist who works with the Skeletal and Muscular Systems.

Choose three different specialties and identify the professions that work in those fields. Which appeals to you and why?

Apply It

Each student should research a skin disease. You need to know the signs and symptoms for the disease. When you come to class, you must create that disease on a small part of your skin.

Each student will be assigned a patient number (five numbers). Students must interview and examine their patients (classmates) with those numbers. After writing down the signs and symptoms, students must come up with the diagnosis and correct treatment. Take a picture of the disease for a medical file.

Table 13.16 Common Disorders, Symptoms, and Preventive Measures/
Treatment of the Integumentary System

Condition	Disorder	Symptoms	Preventive Measures/ Treatment
Athlete's foot (tinea pedis)	Caused by a fungus. It usually involves the toes and the soles of the feet but is occasionally found on the hands.	Itching, scaling, and sometimes painful lesions.	For prevention, wearing shoes that do not constrict feet and allow good air circulation. Dry feet well after bathing and lightly apply powder between toes. Treating with (anti-fungal) medication may also be effective.
Atopic dermatitis or Eczema	Reddened areas on the surface of the skin.	Early stage—areas on the skin may be red, swollen, and weeping purulent fluid. Later stage—usually reddened, scaly, itchy areas on the skin.	Avoiding allergens. Topical applications and medication may be helpful as a treatment.
Boils (furuncle)	Skin abscess caused when bacteria enters the hair follicles or sebaceous glands.	Pain, redness, and swelling.	To prevent spreading of infection, it is important to avoid irritating or squeezing the lesion. Treatment may include antibiotics and local moist heat. Incision and drainage may be necessary.
Skin cancer	Rapid growth of cells on the skin that can invade blood vessels, lymph glands, and connecting ducts. The most common types of skin cancer are:	Raised, hard, reddish lesions with a pearly surface. Slightly elevated cells, tumors that may become sores that don't heal.	For prevention, applying sunscreen and avoiding excessive exposure to the sun. Skin cancers can be cured if treated early. Preferred treatment is removal with surgery and radiation. If skin cancer is left untreated, it may cause death.
	Basal cell carcinoma (BCC)	BCC looks like a raised, smooth, pearly bump, usuauly on the sun-exposed skin of the head, neck or shoulders. Crusting and bleeding in the center of the tumor frequently develops. It is often mistaken for a sore that does not heal.	Most basal cell carcinomas are removed by surgery.
	Squamous cell carcinoma (SCC)	Commonly a red, scaling, thickened patch on sun-exposed skin. Ulceration and bleeding may occur. When SCC is not treated, it may develop into a large mass.	Most squamous cell carcinomas are removed by surgery, followed by radiaiton.

(continued)

Table 13.16   Common Disorders, Symptoms, and Preventive Measures/ Treatment of the Integumentary System (continued)

Condition	Disorder	Symptoms	Preventive Measures/ Treatment
Skin cancer *(continued)*	Malignant melanoma	Most dangerous type and most likely to metastasize brown to black looking lesions. Signs include a change in size, shape, color or elevation of a mole. The appearance of a new mole during adulthood, or new pain, itching, ulceration or bleeding of an existing mole should be checked.	Most malignant melanomas are treated by surgery, followed by up to a year of radiation, and sometimes chemotherapy. Usually must check lymph nodes to make sure condition has not spread.

Medical Terminology

acne:	inflammation of the sebaceous gland	**desquamation:**	shedding skin in scales, sheets
alopecia:	baldness	**erythema:**	redness of the skin
burns:	damage to the skin or other body parts caused by extreme heat, flame, contact with heated objects, or chemicals. Burn depth is generally categorized as first, second, or third degree.	**keloid:**	excessive scarring, resembling a tumor
		keratoderma:	scaly skin
		keratogenesis:	formation of scaly skin
		pustule:	elevation of skin filled with pus
ceraceous:	waxlike in appearance	**scleroderma:**	hardened, thickened skin
ceroma:	tumor of waxy appearance	**sebaceous:**	pertaining to oily, fatty matter from the sebaceous gland
debridement:	removal of dead tissue	**sebolith:**	stone in a sebaceous gland
decubitus ulcers:	Also called bedsores; these are lesions caused by unrelieved pressure to any part of the body	**seborrhea:**	excessive discharge of sebum
		squamous:	platelike, scaly
dermatitis:	inflammation of the skin	**urticaria:**	itching wheals on the derma, hives

Jobs and Professions

Dermatologist

A dermatologist is a physician trained to treat conditions and diseases of the skin, hair, and nails. This may involve skin allergies, cancer, melanomas, moles, acne, or even some sexually transmitted diseases. Dermatologists must be able to perform various types of dermatologic surgery and be able to analyze and interpret cultures. They must also have a broad base of knowledge that includes things such as allergies and immunology, environmental and industrial medicine, radiology, microbiology, and surgery.

To become a dermatologist, you must complete college and medical school. Following medical school, all dermatologists must complete one year of clinical training. Next, they spend three to four years as a resident specializing in dermatology. Those who choose to specialize must train for one more year in that area.

Summary

In this section, you learned the importance of the integumentary system, or skin. The skin helps to protect the body's internal organs from injury or disease. It also helps the body to maintain homeostasis. You have learned that some skin disorders are mild and treatable. However, you have also learned that skin cancer is a life-threatening disorder that can cause death. Skin cancer can be prevented by limiting exposure to the sun and using sunscreen.

SECTION 13.12 | **Review Questions**

1. What are the five main functions of the skin?

2. What are the three main layers of tissue in skin?

3. Other than skin, what additional structures or tissues are associated with the integumentary system?

4. What is a boil and what causes it?

5. How can skin cancer be prevented?

6. What is acne?

7. A(n) _____ is a physician trained to treat conditions and diseases of the skin, hair, and nails.

Learn By Doing: Section 13.12 Activity

1. Complete Worksheets 1 and 2 as assigned.

2. When you are confident that you can meet each objective for this section, ask your teacher for the section evaluation.

Genetics

Background

DNA is the genetic material in the cell. It is passed from your father and mother to you through the process of sexual reproduction. DNA and environment influence your hair color, eye color, and other physical traits. DNA can also influence your health. Disorders such as muscular dystrophy and sickle cell anemia are examples of inherited diseases that cause health problems. As a health care worker, you should know how traits are inherited and how these traits may affect health.

Objectives

When you have completed this section, you will be able to do the following:

- Match key terms with their correct meanings.

- Describe the structure of DNA.

- Describe the role of DNA in human heredity.

- Match common genetic disorders with their descriptions.

- Explain why the health care worker's understanding of genetics is important.

Introduction to DNA

DNA, or **deoxyribonucleic acid**, is the genetic material that is present in all living cells. DNA is made of subunits called **nucleotides**. Each nucleotide has a sugar, a phosphate, and a base. The four bases in DNA are *adenine* (A), *thymine* (T), *guanine* (G), and *cytosine* (C). The DNA molecule has the form of a double helix. (**Figure 13.33**)

Shaped like a twisting ladder, the "rungs" of a double helix are made of bases that pair with each other. In DNA, adenine always pairs with thymine (A-T or T-A) and guanine always pairs with cytosine (G-C or C-G).

DNA is organized into **chromosomes**. Sections of DNA on each chromosome, called **genes**, code for different **traits**. A complete copy of the body's DNA, called the **genome**, is found in each body cell's nucleus. Gene splicing is achieved by using chemicals to "cut" DNA, in order to add genetic sequences into the broken chain. The chain is then repaired as a longer chain that now has additional DNA. The purpose of gene splicing is to help with medical conditions such as diabetes, where the gene splicing introduces insulin-producing genes.

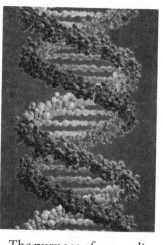

deoxyribonucleic acid
(dee AHKS ee rye bow new KLAY ik ASS id)
A molecule found in all living cells that contains information for building proteins and influencing traits.

nucleotides
(NEW klee oh tyde)
Subunits of DNA that each contain a phosphate, sugar, and base.

chromosomes
(KROM uh some)
Structures that contain coiled and condensed portions of the cell's DNA.

FIGURE 13.33
The double helix of DNA. What are the two sides of the DNA ladder made of?

genes
(JEENZ)
A portion of DNA that contains instructions for a trait.

traits
(TRAYTS)
Genetically determined characteristics or conditions.

genome
(JEE nohm)
The complete copy of the body's DNA.

Community Service

In a team of four, prepare a clinic on how smoking affects the different body systems and present the clinic to a class of middle school or 9th grade students.

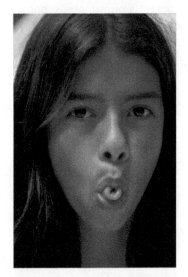

FIGURE 13.34
Tongue rolling is an inherited trait.

DNA and Heredity

The human genome is organized into 23 pairs of chromosomes for a total of 46 chromosomes in each cell of your body (excluding the sex cells). One chromosome from each pair comes from your mother and from your father. During sexual reproduction, chromosomes from your father's sperm cell combined with chromosomes from your mother's egg cell. Each gene on a chromosome codes for one trait or a set of traits. Because chromosomes come in pairs, you have two forms of the same gene, called **alleles**, coding for each trait. In some cases, both alleles influence a trait. For example, if you have a tall father and a short mother, you may be medium height.

In other cases, one allele has a **dominant** influence over the other, so that you show one trait instead of another. For example, tongue rolling is a dominant trait. The girl in the picture inherited the tongue-rolling allele from her father, who could also roll his tongue, and the non-tongue-rolling **recessive** allele from her mother, who could not. (Figure 13.34) Because she has one dominant allele, the girl shows the dominant trait and she can roll her tongue.

You inherited genes from both parents, so you are likely to have traits that resemble traits in each parent. For example, you and your father may both be able to roll your tongue. You and your mother may both have a similar nose.

Shared genetic traits can extend to your health. For example, if your mother had breast cancer, you may be more likely to get breast cancer. If your father lived a long life and always had a strong heart, you may be more likely to live long and avoid heart disease. If both parents have an allele for a disorder, such as sickle cell anemia, you might inherit that disorder.

Jobs and Professions

Geneticist

A geneticist is a scientist who is certified to work in medical and scientific areas related to genes. This work may involve experiments that explore and determine laws and environmental factors that affect the origin, transmission, and development of inherited traits. Geneticists may devise methods to alter traits or produce new traits. A geneticist may specialize in developing resistance methods to disease and disorders, understanding the relationship between heredity and fertility, or evaluating the genetic makeup that has caused a disorder or disability in order to help a patient manage a condition. To become a geneticist a doctoral degree and approximately two years of training in an accredited laboratory for certification are required.

Genetic Counselor

Genetic counselors work with families to fully understand risks of certain genetic disorders, such as neuromuscular diseases. A genetic counselor evaluates a family's history and provides information and insight into what that history means from a genetic point of view. The genetic counselor must patiently and thoroughly record details of each patient's medical history and then evaluate that data. This part of the job requires a scientific-based approach, but the job also requires caring support of patients as they go through the evaluation process and learn of risks and difficulties associated with their genetics. A genetic counselor must have a master's degree, preferably in the field of human genetics and/or counseling. Certification is recommended.

Common Inherited Disorders

Table 13.17 **Common Inherited Disorders, Symptoms, and Treatment**

Condition	Disorder	Symptoms/ Characteristics	Preventive Measures/ Treatment
Cystic Fibrosis	An illness causing serious lung problems that occurs when offspring inherit two recessive alleles for the disease.	Difficulty breathing, frequent respiratory infections, fever, cough, poor appetite.	Medications to reduce airway blockage and infection, bronchial drainage.
Duchene's Muscular Dystrophy	A genetic disorder linked to genes on the X-chromosome that causes muscle weakness and degeneration. Usually affects boys.	Muscle weakness, inability to walk.	Physical therapy, drug therapy. There is no cure for this disease. The patient's muscles may degenerate so that a ventilator or pacemaker is needed.
Down Syndrome	Delayed development and mental retardation caused by an extra copy of chromosome 21.	Low muscle tone and loose joints in infants, slow mental development, distinctive physical features, such as a flat face, enlarged tongue, and small ears.	Some children with Down Syndrome do not have health problems. Others may have heart defects or high blood pressure in the lungs which can be treated with medication or surgery. Many children with Down syndrome have treatable vision or hearing problems. Other treatable issues include thyroid problems, obesity, seizure disorders, and a higher risk for infection and childhood leukemia.
Sickle Cell Anemia	A blood disorder that creates deformed red blood cells that have trouble carrying oxygen. Caused when offspring inherit two recessive alleles for the disease.	Tiredness; severe pain in chest, stomach, arms, or legs; jaundice.	Folic acid, antibiotics, medications during episodes of pain, blood transfusions. There is no cure for sickle cell anemia.

Genetic Nurse

Genetic nurses specifically care for the genetic health of patients who have genetic issues, such as Huntington disease, hereditary breast cancer, and cystic fibrosis. Care may includes screening, early detection, risk identification, treatment, and testing. A genetic nurse usually has long-term relationships with patients and their families. The outcomes of patients with genetic problems are often negative, which a genetic nurse must be able to deal with and help families deal with, as well. Genetic nurses need additional training, education, and certification to work in the field.

 Summary

In this section, you learned that DNA is the molecule in cells that controls cell function and influences traits. DNA is composed of phosphates, sugars, and a backbone of paired bases. Your DNA was passed down to you by both your mother and your father. Because you inherited their DNA, you also inherited many of the traits that your parents have. Some of these traits may affect your health.

Medical Terminology

genetic amniocentesis:	procedure for prenatal diagnosis	**presymptomatic testing:**	laboratory testing to find out whether a condition will develop in the future, such as breast cancer
carrier:	person who does not have a disease, but has one non-functioning gene for a recessive disorder, and so may transmit the disease to offspring	**risk assessment:**	using laboratory tests and family history to determine the odds of a certain outcome
maternal serum screening:	blood testing done at 14–20 weeks to assess the risk of a fetus having a disorder	**X-linked:**	diseases whose genes are located on the X chromosomes, such as color-blindness, which most often affects males

 Science Link —————————————————————————

Human Genome Project

The U.S. Human Genome Project began in 1990. The project's main goals were to identify all of the genes in human DNA, to determine the sequence of base pairs that make up human DNA, to improve gene technologies and access to those technologies, and to address the social issues related to genetic research.

Researchers were able to create a draft sequence of the human genome by 2003. They continue to study it and correct errors in its sequence.

Researchers have found that humans have approximately 30,000 genes—not the 80,000 or 140,000 that had previously been estimated. They also found that everyone has the same order of nearly all nucleotide bases in their DNA.

Researchers have also been able to use the information from the Human Genome Project to understand disease. Genes have been found that are associated with breast cancer, deafness, blindness, and muscle disorders. Work continues on DNA sequences that may be associated with diabetes, arthritis, cardiovascular disease, and some cancers.

The information and technologies produced by the Human Genome Project have helped researchers to study how combinations of genes influence whole body systems. This expanded approach is likely to improve our understanding of the genetic connections to disease.

Why would it be useful to know whether a disease has a genetic component?

SECTION 13.13 | Review Questions

1. A child inherits a recessive allele for sickle cell anemia and a dominant allele for normal red blood cells. What kind of red blood cells will the child have? Why?

2. What is the cause of Down Syndrome?

3. How are genes, chromosomes, and DNA are related.

4. What is a nucleotide?

5. Why are there generally no cures for genetic disorders?

6. What is cystic fibrosis and how do we treat it?

 Learn By Doing: Section 13.13 Activity

1. Complete Worksheet 1.

2. Complete Worksheet/Activity 2 as assigned.

3. Complete Worksheet 3 and 4.

4. When you are confident that you can meet each objective for this section, ask your teacher for the section evaluation.

5. Prepare responses to each item listed in Chapter Review.

Chapter 13 Review

Chapter Review Questions

1. Describe the five types of tissue and their functions in the body. (13.1)

2. What is the appendicular skeleton? (13.2)

3. Describe all the structures that blood passes through as it travels between the aorta and the vena cava. (13.4)

4. How does the spleen keep the body healthy? (13.5)

5. The hairlike objects in the bronchial tubes that move mucus out of the lungs are called _____. (13.6)

6. What are the differences between gastritis, enteritis, and gastroenteritis? (13.7)

7. The _____ contains filtering mechanisms called nephrons. (13.8)

8. How is the function of the thyroid gland different from the function of the parathyroid glands? (13.9)

9. How does the ear help you to hear sound? (13.10)

10. How does muscular dystrophy affect a patient? (13.13)

Activities

1. As a health care worker, your alertness to symptoms and complications associated with the body systems is important for the well-being of your patients. Select and research a chronic disease and write an explanation of potential symptoms and complications.

2. Work with a partner to test how the skin senses different stimuli. With eyes closed, have your partner report the sensation he or she feels when you apply different stimuli to the skin of the arm. Use objects that are warm and cold. Also apply a light touch, pressure, and a light pinch. Write down your partner's sensations and the objects that caused these sensations. After applying all the stimuli, work together to write down the name of the tactile corpuscle that received each stimulus.

Case Studies

1. Ms. Wilson looks confused after her doctor has confirmed and explained her diagnosis of diabetes. You know from talking with her family that they usually call diabetes "sugar." How could you help Ms. Wilson better understand her condition? Brainstorm with classmates to think of other words people use for medical conditions or bodily functions that could cause confusion.

2. A patient complains of painful urination and blood in the urine. He says that he has had these symptoms for a few days. What other information should you get from the patient? What disorders would the symptoms indicate?

Chapter 13 Review

Thinking Critically

1. **Communication**—Explain how you think that your understanding of the body systems helps you communicate with patients/clients and co-workers. Your patient/client asks you to explain how the muscles in her upper arm cause the forearm to move. Write how you can communicate this information to a child under 6, an adult over 80, and a teenager.

2. **Patient Education**—Many patients have little knowledge of anatomy and or the correct terms for body parts. Try to find out if local health care facilities have policies that provide patients with illustrated brochures or diagrams to help explain medical conditions.

3. **Legal and Ethical**—A patient's doctor just told him that he has a serious problem in the gastrointestinal system. The doctor thinks that it is probably a malignant tumor. The patient asks you what you know about his condition. What is your responsibility in this case?

Media Connection

Use the Companion Web site for additional interactive learning activities: www.prenhall.com/badasch

Portfolio Connection

Employers look for health care workers who have knowledge of the body and body systems. Assistive personnel work in many different departments and must be able to recognize problems and report them correctly to a supervisor.

Complete the following exercise and put it in your portfolio for review in the future: Identify one body system disorder. Research the objective and subjective symptoms that result from this disorder. Explain your findings in a typed or neatly written paper.

PORTFOLIO TIP

Keep in mind that many cultures find it offensive to directly mention body parts: you may need to prompt your patients/clients as to where they feel discomfort.

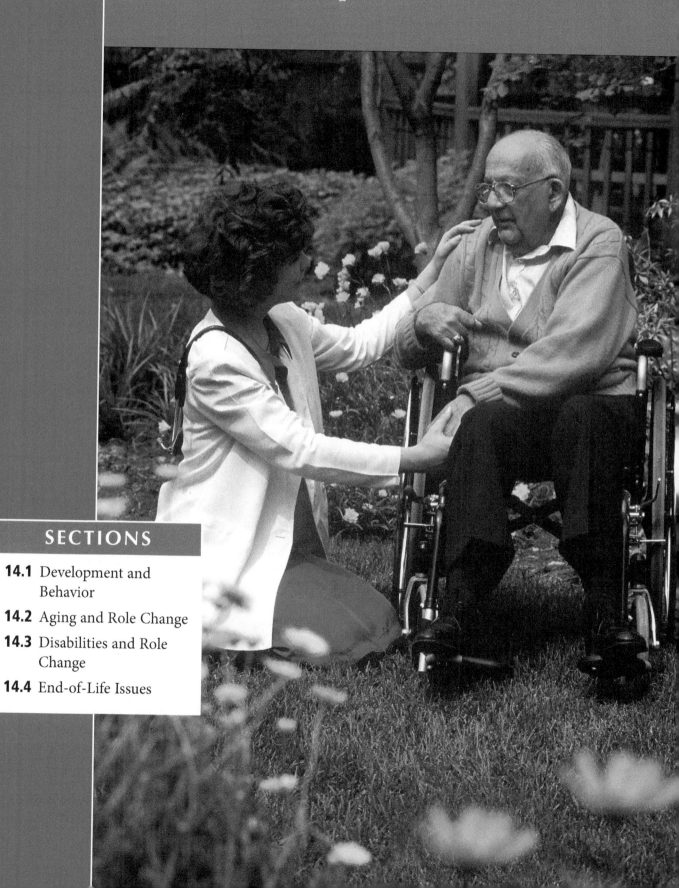

14 Human Growth and Development

Getting Started

Spend one school day with a "disabling condition" that may be experienced by an aged person. Select from the following: wheelchair bound, walk with a cane, cotton or other covering to restrict hearing capability, Vaseline covered eyeglasses, one arm bound to your side, or others you might consider. Determine the difficulty of normal daily activities and make suggestions as to how a local public area (shopping mall, restaurant, movie theatre) might improve access and support for those experiencing these conditions.

Development and Behavior

Background

Health care workers provide care for all age groups. It is important to understand the emotional and physical stages of the life continuum. This knowledge assists you in recognizing normal and abnormal development and behavior. This awareness of life's stages allows you to be an effective health care worker.

Objectives

When you have completed this section, you will be able to do the following:

- Match key terms with their correct meanings.

- Identify three stages of development between conception and birth.

- List four common developments of growth in the first year of life and the age at which they usually occur.

- Define and describe characteristics of adolescent development.

- Interview a person between the ages of 50 and 80.

- Compare your life experiences to each stage described in this chapter.

- Design a bulletin board representing one stage of growth and development, including age-specific communication requirements.

continuum
(kuhn TIN yoo uhm)
Progression from start (birth) to finish (death).

zygote
(ZAHY goht)
Any cell formed by the coming together of two reproductive (sex) cells.

coordination
(koh awr dn EY shuhn)
State of harmonized action, such as eye and hand coordination.

Development and Behavior

People experience many physical and emotional changes over a lifetime. These changes are part of the normal growth and development process. In this section, we discuss the stages of development and behavior from conception through the life **continuum**.

Conception, or fertilization, occurs when a male sperm and a female ovum combine. This combination causes the single-cell ovum to divide into many cells. This stage of development is called a **zygote**. Within five weeks, the rapidly multiplying cells duplicate into an embryo.

- Five weeks after conception, the embryo is about the size of a grain of rice.
- Six weeks after conception, the nervous system, eyes, and ears are visible.

- Twelve weeks, or 3 months after conception, the embryo has grown to about 2¹/₂ inches (6 cm) long and is now called a fetus.
- Babies are born 38 to 40 weeks after conception.

Understanding Different Stages of Life

As you work with people, it is helpful to know what to expect in terms of behavior and communication. Everybody is different, but there are stages of development that offer guidelines that you can use to better understand people. Tables 14.1–14.3 on the following pages provide information—by age and developmental stage—that will help you become aware of factors affecting behavior and communication, as well as techniques you can use to enhance communication.

Infancy Through Early Elementary School Age

From infancy through early elementary school, children develop dramatically. They progress from depending completely on others for care to having physical skills that allow them to run and play, along with mental skills that prompt them to look for reasons why things are the way they are in their lives. Use Table 14.1 to better understand infants and children up through the age of eight.

adolescent
(ad l ES uhnt)
Pertaining to the period of life between childhood and maturity.

decade
(DEK eyd)
Period of 10 years.

viable
(VAHY uh buhl)
Capable of living.

prone
(PROHN)
Lying on the stomach.

supine
(soo PAHYN)
Lying on the back.

Table 14.1 Infant Through Early Elementary School Age Stages

Age	Behavior	Age-Specific Communication Techniques	Effective Communication Techniques During Medical Care
6 Weeks	Baby first begins to smile.	Hold, cuddle, and softly speak frequently to infant.	When possible hold, cuddle, and softly speak frequently to infant.
10 weeks	Infant has the ability to roll from a **prone** to a **supine** position.	Hold, cuddle, and softly speak frequently to infant.	Comfort infants by speaking in a soothing tone and touch them gently to communicate your presence and reassurance.
4 to 6 months	Infant raises head and shoulders while in a supine position.	Talking to infants helps them recognize sounds and make associations. It is helpful to talk slowly and clearly when holding, feeding, or bathing infants at this age. Sudden, strange noise may cause fear.	Comfort infants by speaking in a soothing tone and touch them gently to communicate your presence and reassurance.
6 to 8 months	Infant sits without being supported; when placed on abdomen infant may scoot before mastering a crawl; eye color may change.	Distract or move infants when they are headed for trouble.	When possible perform procedures quickly and efficiently to minimize time the infant is exposed to discomfort. Take time to comfort infants by speaking in a soothing tone and touch them gently to communicate your presence and reassurance. Allow mom or other family members to be present when possible.

(continued)

Table 14.1   Infant Through Early Elementary School Age Stages (continued)

Age	Behavior	Age-Specific Communication Techniques	Effective Communication Techniques During Medical Care
8 to 12 months	Attempts to feed self and begins to crawl, stand, and take steps. As infant becomes toddler, expect frequent falls while learning to walk. Provide a safe environment free of sharp edges and, if possible, keep infant on carpeting instead of cement or tile flooring.	Use simple terms to warn them as they head toward trouble: "Hot!", "Hurt," or "Tastes bad." Always praise good behavior.	Perform procedures quickly and efficiently to minimize the infant's exposure to discomfort. Comfort infants by speaking in a soothing tone and touch them gently to communicate your presence and reassurance. Allow mom or other family to be present when possible.
1 year	Learning and experimenting absorbs most of infant's waking hours. Understands simple conversation or commands. Most toddlers at this age can say four or five words clearly.	Speak clearly and slowly, using simple words. Children who are spoken to with clear word pronunciation (not baby talk) develop clearer speech. Resist saying "No," constantly and be patient.	Speak in a calming voice tone. Allow mom or family to be available when possible.
18 months	Walks alone, feeds itself, and stacks objects. "Mine" becomes a favorite expression.	Communicate clear limits about acceptable and unacceptable behavior. Reinforce good behavior. Playing easy games and reading simple stories develops vocabulary. Time spent in this way provides positive, nurturing experiences.	*The following is appropriate for children 18 months through 8 years of age:* Refer to the child by his or her favorite name (name or nickname). Use the same words the family uses for toileting. Do not blame or scold if toileting accidents occur. Explain in simple terms what is happening to and around the child. Answer their questions honestly and in terms the child will understand. When possible spend time with the child, talking and playing simple games appropriate to their age. Taking time to communicate and enjoy activities with each child is important in creating a positive sense of well-being during medical care. When possible perform procedures quickly and efficiently to minimize time the child is exposed to discomfort. Following procedures that cause discomfort or emotional tension take time to comfort infants by speaking in a soothing tone and touch them gently to communicate your presence and reassurance.
20 to 24 months	Begins bowel and bladder control. Experiences exploration and a feeling of security. Vocabulary increases rapidly. Pronunciation may take time to develop.	Your patience fosters normal speech development. Resist trying to correct pronunciation too often. Listen carefully and confirm your understanding of the child's words.	
3 to 4 years	Talks in simple, complete sentences. Experiences a span of emotional growth.	Continue following techniques described above.	
4 to 5 years	Dresses and undresses with little assistance. Experiences a span of emotional growth.	*The following is appropriate for children 4 through 8 years of age:* Children at these ages require frequent reassurance and truthful, caring conversation. Keep discussions short and easy to understand, allowing time for the children to say everything they want to say. Positive acceptance of what the child says is important, and positive reflection back to them helps the child overcome shyness and withdrawal.	
5 to 6 years	Eye and body **coordination** improves. The child is able to hop, skip, and draw figures. Awareness of the ability to choose one action over another is present. Child begins to feel guilt and shame.	*(continued from above)*	*(continued from above)*

(continued)

Table 14.1   Infant Through Early Elementary School Age Stages (continued)

Age	Behavior	Age-Specific Communication Techniques	Effective Communication Techniques During Medical Care
6 to 8 years	Physical skills continue to improve. Children start school. They begin to look for reasons that explain why they believe certain things. They also compare themselves with others. At about age 7, they experience emotional withdrawal or shyness.		

Adolescence—Preteen Years Through Young Adult

Adolescence occurs from the ages of 11 to 21, or between childhood and adulthood. Development progresses through three stages: early (11–13), middle (14–18), and late (19–21). Each period has its own distinct characteristics of growth and development, but the exact time frame varies from person to person.

Puberty is the process of the body changing into the adult form that is capable of reproduction. Many factors can influence the timing, but the average age for the onset of puberty is 9–14 for girls, and 10–18 for boys.

Reasoning skills improve throughout adolescence. Emotional challenges are also encountered: need for separateness, disagreements with authority figures, changes in long-time friendships, stress from busy schedules, and sexual uncertainty. In later adolescent years, people typically start to become more independent. With maturity, they find that friends' approval is not as important as their own moral sense of right and wrong. Use Table 14.2 to better understand adolescents.

Table 14.2   Preteen Years Through Young Adult Stages

Age	Behavior	Age-Specific Communication Techniques	Effective Communication Techniques During Medical Care
9 to 12 years (preteen or preadolescent years)	Physical growth rate increases, and adult sexual characteristics become noticeable. Girls begin menstruation. Boys develop more hair on their faces and bodies, and voices deepen. Preteens look to their friends for acceptance and approval rather than to their parents. Children ages 8 to 12 experience emotional security; 13-year-olds feel insecure and shy.	Children 9 to 12 years old do best when you listen to them and give them a chance to express themselves. Use positive responses to indicate that you hear what they are saying. It is also important to explain clearly the differences between acceptable and unacceptable behavior. Acknowledge positive actions and discuss why other behaviors are not appropriate. Thirteen-year-olds often require increased words of reassurance and encouragement to overcome feelings of insecurity, shyness and fear.	When appropriate and possible, prior to a medical procedure offer to show them what will be done during procedures. Tell children what to expect concerning how they will physically feel and what they will see and hear. Reassure them by explaining how to get assistance if needed. Explain the importance of asking questions when they are unsure about the way they feel, or what they see or hear.

(continued)

Table 14.2   Preteen Years Through Young Adult Stages (continued)

Age	Behavior	Age-Specific Communication Techniques	Effective Communication Techniques During Medical Care
13 to 18 years (adolescent or teenage years)	The teenage years are the years between childhood and adulthood. Teenagers strive for independence. They also experience puberty, a dramatic sexual development caused by increased hormone production of certain glands. (Girls may start puberty by 11 years; boys usually start at 13 years.) Puberty is a time of both physical and emotional adjustment.	*The following is appropriate for 13 through 20 years of age:* **Adolescents** need others to listen and reflect their words back to them. This type of communication allows teenagers to hear what they are thinking and gain increased understanding of self. Respect their privacy. Quetion behavior only when pertinent to their health and well-being.	*The following is appropriate for 13 through 20 years of age:* When appropriate and possible, prior to a medical procedure offer to show them what will be done during procedures. Tell teenagers what to expect concerning how they will physically feel and what they will see and hear. Reassure them by explaining how to get assistance if needed.
18 to 20 years (young adulthood)	People become more independent. As they mature, they begin to seek ways of contributing to society.		

Adulthood

Adulthood occurs at the age of 21. Although adults' reasoning skills have developed, and they are basically fully grown from a physical standpoint, there are still stages through which adults pass: young adulthood (20s and 30s) middle age (40s and 50s), retirement age (60s and 70s), and old age (80s and beyond). Use Table 14.3 to better understand adults.

Table 14.3   Adulthood Ages 20 Through 70+ Years Stages

Age	Behavior	Communication Techniques with All Adults	Communication During Medical Care
20 to 30 years	This is the beginning of adulthood, when people attempt to build a firm, safe foundation for the future. There is a strong desire to do the right thing. Patterns of living are set during this decade, such as: helper patterns (rescuing others), leadership patterns (taking charge, organizing), passive patterns (acting without influence, not taking an active part in things). These are just a few patterns people may fall into; there are many others.	*The following is generally appropriate for ages 20 through the 60s:* Show positive interest in adults' conversation, and interpret and respond to their body language. Use words that are understandable and meaningful to each individual's level. Express your desire to protect privacy; resist questioning personal behaviors and habits unless they are pertinent to the person's health and well-being.	*The following is generally appropriate for ages 20 through the 60s:* Be aware of the impact medical care is having on each person. Be sensitive to fears; honestly explain procedures and expected outcomes. When speaking about a patient, always go to areas away from the patient's view and hearing. Your behavior must communicate respect for others—be aware of your body language and verbal tone; be aware of when words are helpful or silence is preferred.
30 to 40 years	In this decade, people often feel confined by the guidelines that they established for themselves in their 20s. This confined feeling often leads to restructuring of work, family, and social habits. Through this change, people develop more freedom and a new view of self.		

(continued)

Table 14.3   Adulthood Ages 20 Through 70+ Years Stages (continued)

Age	Behavior	Communication Techniques with All Adults	Communication During Medical Care
40 to 50 years	People often evaluate the first part of their life. They make decisions about future directions. Many find themselves adjusting basic values and their emphasis toward life. This time of adjustment is often referred to as "midlife crisis" or the "deadline decade." Women develop assertiveness. Men become more tender and make stronger commitments to ethical issues.	*(continued from above)*	*(continued from above)*
50 to 60 years	These are the years when people experience a sense of comfort, an acceptance of life, and a new warmth and mellowing. Privacy becomes important, and friends become more cherished. Truth and sincerity become more valued. Renewal of earlier hobbies and interests often sparks new energy and enthusiasm.		
60 to 70 years	These are the years in which people look forward to retirement. For some people there is a gradual change in their work lives. Others prefer full retirement. The additional hours away from work can now be filled with interests or hobbies. This newfound time often allows people to complete lifelong projects or desires. Sharing of oneself with others aids in maintaining a sense of self-worth.	*The following is appropriate for ages 60 and older:* Listening and sharing nterest in stories and experiences is a way for younger people to learn and to show gratitude for the mentorship of people of this age. When with a hearing impaired person use communication techniques that help promote their understanding. For example: go to a quiet area or eliminate unnecessary sounds, always look at the person when talking and speak clearly. Remember to make sure that the print in documents is large enough for an older person to read.	*The following is appropriate for ages 60 and older:* When appropriate and possible, prior to a medical procedure offer to show them what will be done during procedures. Tell what to expect concerning how they will physically feel and what they will see and hear. Reassure them by explaining how to get assistance if needed. When possible and if the patient requests, allow a significant other to stay with them.
70 and older	After the 70s, people continue their daily life in the same adult patterns. The effect of aging on the body is discussed in Section 14.2 of this chapter. If the body loses its resilience and functions become impaired, the individual's lifestyle may change. It is important to note that of the increasing geriatric population, only 5% require in-patient health care. The remaining 95% are **viable**, active seniors.		

Erik Erikson's Theory of Human Development

Erik Erikson was a psychologist and psycho-analyst who developed a theory of social development in humans that is widely accepted as accurately representing the stages that people go through as they grow and develop and age. Erikson's theory identifies and explains eight stages through which healthy humans pass.

For more on Erik Erikson's theory of development in humans, go to the Companion Web site at www.prenhall.com/badasch.

 Summary

In this section, you have learned about development from conception throughout the life continuum. You have also become aware of emotional and behavioral experiences and communication issues related to each decade of life. Communication techniques need to be adapted according to the age and development stage of people with whom you work.

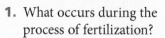

SECTION	**14.1**	Review Questions

1. What occurs during the process of fertilization?

2. Relate a zygote to an embryo.

3. How is a prone position different from a supine position

4. What period of life is described as adolescence?

5. Describe the behaviors pertinent to one stage (decade) in adulthood; for example, 30–40 years old or 60–70 years old.

6. What does it mean to say that a person is not a viable senior?

Learn By Doing: Section 14.1 Activity

1. Complete Worksheets 1 and 2.

2. Complete Worksheets/Activities 3 through 6 as assigned.

3. When you are confident that you can meet each objective for this section, ask your teacher for the section evaluation.

 Science Link

Life Cycles in Nature

The life cycle of an organism refers to its sequence of developmental stages between birth and death. Like humans, other mammals, as well as reptiles, amphibians, birds, fish, insects, and other invertebrates have life cycles.

There are two basic types of life cycles for insects. Complete metamorphosis has four stages: egg, larva, pupa, and adult. The female insect lays eggs that hatch into larvae. The larvae usually have a worm-like shape.

Caterpillars, maggots, and grubs are the larval stages of insects. At some point, larvae make a cocoon around themselves. While in the cocoon, larvae do not eat as their bodies develop into an adult shape with wings, legs, and internal organs. This change takes anywhere from several days to many months. When the larvae have

changed into adults, they break out of the cocoon. Mealworms, butterflies, and moths go through complete metamorphosis.

Incomplete metamorphosis has three stages: egg, nymph, and adult. In this life cycle, the female insect lays eggs in a protective covering. The eggs hatch into nymphs, which look like the adults but may not have wings.

Nymphs shed, or molt, their outer skeletons several times as they grow. When the nymph reaches its adult size, it stops molting. By this point, it has grown wings. Crickets, grasshoppers, and flower bugs go through incomplete metamorphosis.

What is one major way that complete metamorphosis differs from incomplete metamorphosis?

Aging and Role Change

Background

The population of people over the age of 65 is expanding. Most people over 65 are active, and they adapt well to change. They continue to enjoy physical activities such as tennis, biking, and skiing. Only five percent are in long-term care.

To care adequately for senior citizens with health problems, health care workers must be aware of the emotional and physical changes that occur during the aging process. Understanding these changes allows the health care worker to assist the aging person in adapting more easily to new roles and ability levels.

Objectives

When you have completed this section, you will be able to do the following:

- Match key terms with their correct meanings.

- Identify six body systems and the common physical changes that occur with aging.

- Identify basic human needs that are met through work, environment, socialization, and family relationships.

- Write an "action plan" to assist another person cope with changes caused by aging.

Physical Changes of Aging

The process of aging begins in every person at the moment of birth. Aging is a very natural process, and the health care worker needs to be aware of the physical changes that take place. Understanding these changes helps you be patient and less frustrated with others.

The older adult (age 70 and older) population is the most **heterogeneous** (different) of all age groups. People vary in how they age depending on their genetics, lifestyle (jobs, choices, habits) and environmental exposures. Health care decisions must be focused on the individual, not the group because of the wide variability of each person's cognitive and physical status. An easy rule to remember for the aging population is slower and stiffer for all systems.

heterogeneous
(ahet er uh JEE nee uhs)
Different in kind; unlike.

Career Connection

The teacher may invite a gerontologist or geriatric nurse to visit the class and describe the work that they do. Prepare at least one question you would like the visitor to answer regarding geriatric care.

Nervous System

- As the brain ages, a reduction in nerve cells and cerebral blood flow and metabolism are known to occur. These changes cause slower reflexes and delayed response to multiple stimuli. Elderly people may experience memory loss which can have several causative factors and can affect their problem solving capacity. Also, the older patient learns in a different way and may require repetitive explanations to enable understanding.

adaptation
(ad uhp TEY shuhn)
Changing to work better.

Community Service

Create an exercise program for a class of senior citizens. Some may be in wheelchairs; others may have walkers or canes. Consult with a physical therapist and keep in mind the type of restrictions their clients may have. Research the kind of music their clients would enjoy as part of the class. Then, teach this class at a community senior citizen center.

reflexes
(REE fleks ez)
Result when a nerve is stimulated and an involuntary action occurs (e.g., touch a hot stove, and the muscles react involuntarily to move the fingers away).

stamina
(STAM uh nuh)
Body's strength or energy.

- *Vision* begins to change with aging:
  - Small print, small items, and things at a distance are more difficult to see.
  - Twenty percent more light is needed to see things clearly.
  - Night driving may become difficult.
  - **Adaptation** to light is more difficult. The eyes take longer to adjust to changes from dark to light and from light to dark.
  - All patients over age 65 benefit from annual eye exams.
  - Diseases may occur:
    - *Cataract:* clouding of the normally transparent lenses of the eye.
    - *Glaucoma:* intraocular pressure causes damage to the optic disks and hardening of the eyeball.

- *Hearing* changes become noticeable in the 60s. When speaking to an elderly person with hearing loss remember to sit at eye level and speak clearly and in a lower tone of voice:
  - High-frequency sounds such as a telephone or doorbell may not be heard.
  - Loss of understanding of consonants and vowel sounds may result in a person complaining that others mumble or speak too softly.

- *Taste, smell,* and *touch* senses decline with age:
  - Elderly people may not smell gases, spoiled food, or body odor.
  - Taste buds decline 50 percent, and food enjoyment is reduced.
  - Elderly people may request extra salt and sugar because they cannot taste well.
  - Avoid using excessive heat or cold as the patient may have decreased awareness if an injury should occur.
  - Touch and **reflexes** change. The ability to respond to stimuli is decreased. Elderly people may burn themselves or hold an ice tray too long and damage tissue or take longer to respond to the directions you give.

Musculoskeletal System

- Osteoarthritis is an inflammation of the joints and causes pain and slowing down of movement.

- Osteoporosis is caused by a loss of calcium in the bone. This is found more in Caucasian women after menopause, when the bones may become very brittle. They may fracture with very little stress.

- Proper diet and exercise throughout the younger years can forestall or minimize osteoporosis symptoms. It is also important to encourage the older patient to remain active. The human body can build muscle up to the ninth decade and weight bearing will diminish bone loss.

- With reduced **stamina**, elderly people are often less active, which results in the muscles becoming smaller. They generally slow down, which may cause the health care worker to feel impatient.

Personal Wellness

Hearing Loss

The gradual hearing loss that occurs as you age (presbycusis) is a common condition. However, the number of people experiencing hearing loss at younger ages is gradually increasing.

Each day you are surrounded by a variety of sounds in your environment. Most sounds occur at safe levels that do not affect hearing. However, sounds that are too loud or last for a long time can damage sensitive structures called hair cells in the inner ear. The result is noise-induced hearing loss (NIHL).

Hair cells convert sound energy into electrical signals that travel to the brain. Once damaged, hair cells cannot grow back. Scientists once believed that the force of vibrations from loud sounds caused the damage to hair cells. Recent studies, however, have shown that exposure to harmful noise triggers the formation of molecules that can damage or kill hair cells.

NIHL can be caused by a single exposure to a quick, intense sound such as an explosion, or by long-term exposure to loud sounds over an extended period of time, such as noise generated in a woodworking shop. The loudness of sound is measured in decibels. Sources of noise that can cause NIHL range from 120 to 150 decibels. Examples include motorcycles, firecrackers, and small firearms.

Long or repeated exposure to sounds at or above 85 decibels can also cause hearing loss. The louder the sound, the shorter the time period before NIHL can occur. Sounds of less than 75 decibels, even after long exposure, are unlikely to cause hearing loss.

The good news is that NIHL is 100 percent preventable. In order to protect yourself, you must understand the hazards of noise and how to practice good hearing health in everyday life. To protect your hearing:

- Know which noises can cause damage.
- Wear earplugs or other hearing protective devices when involved in a loud activity.
- Be alert to hazardous noise in the environment.
- Protect the ears of children who are too young to protect their own.
- Make family, friends, and colleagues aware of the hazards of noise.
- If you suspect hearing loss, have a medical examination by an otolaryngologist, a physician who specializes in diseases of the ears, nose, throat, head, and neck. You may also have a hearing test by an audiologist, a health professional trained to measure and help individuals deal with hearing loss.

What are some sources of loud sounds to which you are exposed?

alveolar-capillary
(al VEE uh ler) -
(KAP uh ler ee)
Pertaining to air sacs in the
lungs.

Apply It

With a partner, research
age-specific diseases. Refer
to Chapter 13 and the
age-related changes to
body systems described in
this chapter to form the
basis of your research.
Some diseases are specific
to children or young
adults, while many are
specific to older adults.
Decide on one disease to
research further, and identify signs and symptoms of
the disease.

Prepare two to five pres-
entation slides that
describe and explain the
disease you researched.
Combine slides with those
of the rest of the class to
create a media presenta-
tion on age-specific
diseases.

constipation
(kon stuh PEY shuhn)
Infrequent or difficult
emptying of the bowel.

propensity
(pro PEN sit tee)
A natural inclination or
tendency.

retention
(ri TEN shuhn)
Keeping elements within
the body that are normally
eliminated (e.g., waste
products such as urine and
feces).

Respiratory and Circulatory System

- The lungs become less elastic, and the **alveolar-capillary** membrane thickens. This makes oxygen exchange more difficult.
- The rib cage does not expand as much.
- The heart becomes less efficient, and the arteries may become narrowed and clogged. The systolic pressure may rise and result in high blood pressure.
- The heart also becomes a less efficient pump. Heart disease is the number one cause of death in older people. Among these diseases are:
  - Congestive heart failure.
  - Cardiac arrhythmias.
  - Ischemic heart disease.
  - Hypertensive heart disease.

Gastrointestinal System

- Many elderly patients/clients experience **constipation**. This can occur because peristalsis of the intestine (the rhythmic contraction of smooth muscles to propel contents through the digestive tract) is often weakened in the elderly, hence they are more prone to constipation. In addition, elderly people may not be taking enough water and fiber in their diet, leading to hard feces.
- Loss of teeth may interfere with chewing and contribute to malnutrition.
- The liver is important in metabolism. With age, the liver loses up to 20 percent of its weight. This is not serious, because the liver can be effective at 50 percent capacity. However, the liver becomes less effective in metabolizing drugs.
- Older people must be monitored carefully and be alert to drug side effects. Encourage the older patient to "brown bag" all of their medications and bring them to their health care appointments at intervals. This would include both prescription and over the counter medications. The medications can be evaluated and with the patient's permission any inappropriate or discontinued medication can be discarded. Be alert to any medication which might affect the central nervous system and increase the **propensity** for falls.

Urinary System

- The bladder holds less urine as a person ages. This may cause an urgent and frequent need to urinate. In addition, an enlarged prostate may also contribute to urinary frequency in makes.
- Bladder infections may occur from **retention** of urine in the bladder. This results in urinary urgency and urinary discomfort. Be aware that the first sign of infection, such as a urinary tract infection or respiratory tract infection, may be an increase in confusion.

Integumentary System

- As people age, there is less adipose tissue (also called fat), and therefore, less padding for bones and much drier skin. The hair also thins. It may not be good for elderly patients to bathe every day, as this increases dryness.

- Your awareness of these changes helps you be patient and understanding. These physical changes often cause frustration in your patient and in you. Remember that these changes occur because the body is aging. Listen and reflect understanding. Explain procedures in understandable terms.

- Taking the time to understand your patient's baseline function and community support system will enhance your ability to effectively care for these patients. Understanding the process of aging and its complexities will help you to effectively evaluate needs and plan interventions.

Role Changes in People Who Are Aging

Aging persons are experiencing physical and cognitive changes. They want to continue being productive, and they need to feel respected. Understanding these changes will enable the health care worker to provide appropriate interventions to optimize their functional and cognitive status.

All people have basic needs that are met through the roles they have throughout their life span.

- **Work role.** The work a person does provides a sense of independence, security, and self-esteem. Successful aging is enhanced by a life style that provides a sense of accomplishment on a continuous basis.

- **Family relationships.** Being a member of a family meets our needs for emotional warmth, intimacy, and identity. When members of the family begin to leave or die, the person may be left without a means of filling these basic needs. To adapt to these losses, people need help in directing their interests and energies in other areas. Some of these may include social activities, volunteer work, or membership in organizations. When interviewing the older client be sure to inquire about their family situation and their role as a member of the community.

- **Social roles.** Social contacts fill a person's need for interaction with others. Through social contacts, the person feels respected and admired. As the years pass, friends move away or die, and personal relationships change. These losses may cause people to feel that they are no longer socially important. It is very important that the aging person take part in developing new social contacts. Senior centers, churches, and other organizations are available to help meet this need. Becoming involved helps fill the need for interaction with other human beings.

- **Environment.** The home a person lives in is a place where he or she can be in control, where he or she has a feeling of belonging. As aging occurs, it may become necessary to change environments. The home may become a financial burden, or it may be physically impossible to remain there.

- The older person may move into his or her children's home, a nursing home, or a room of his or her own. This change may be very frightening, and the need for control in their environment is threatened. Memory loss or cognitive impairment may worsen when the person's environment changes. Time and patience will be of utmost importance in helping them to make the best adjustment to their new situation.

environment
(en VAHY ruhn muhnt)
Surroundings we live in. Environmental disease can occur in any area around us (e.g., hospital, restaurants, public places, home, school).

As a health care worker, your understanding of these changes helps you develop the necessary skills to work with older clients. Human beings have a great ability to adjust to changes in their life roles. As people age, functional, cognitive, and social role changes occur. These changes affect most body systems. When these changes occur, older patients may experience frustration with their condition.

Summary

As people age, physical changes occur in the body. These changes affect many body systems. When these changes occur, older patients experience frustration with their conditions. The health care worker has an important role in helping the older patient understand and accept changes.

There are many role changes that occur in aging persons. They may no longer have the identity that their work gave them. They may lose a spouse or other important family members, leaving them lonely. Often, their social role changes as they are less involved in activities. They may find it difficult to develop new friendships. They may have to leave the home where they have their roots and move to a strange place. Awareness of these changes helps the health care worker work effectively with older patients.

SECTION 14.2 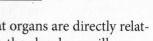 **Review Questions**

1. How does arteriosclerosis affect the thinking abilities of elderly people?

2. What is a cataract?

3. In what ways do a person's reflexes change with age?

4. What organs are directly related to the alveolar-capillary membrane?

5. Why does the need to urinate increase with age?

6. Describe the most common changes in hearing as people age.

 Learn By Doing: Section 14.2 Activity

1. Complete Worksheet/Activity 1.

2. Complete Worksheets 2 through 5 as assigned.

3. When you are confident that you can meet each objective for this section, ask your teacher for the section evaluation.

Disabilities and Role Change

Background

Physical disabilities can affect any age group. When a disability, injury, or illness changes a person's lifestyle, he or she must adapt to these changes. This is often difficult and causes frustration and depression. As a health care worker, you need to understand these changes. When you understand such changes, you are more effective, and you can be a positive influence as these patients/clients begin to adapt.

Objectives

When you have completed this section, you will be able to do the following:

- Match key terms with their correct meanings.
- Define *health*.
- List three examples of activities of daily living (ADL).
- Define assistive/adaptive devices.
- Identify ways to encourage independence.
- List eight birth defects.
- List ten debilitating illnesses.

- Identify seven common changes that occur following the loss of body functions.
- State the goal of rehabilitation.
- Select a disability and summarize your feelings and expectations concerning:
  - What you think it would be like to live with that disability
  - The type of care you would expect
  - The way others respond to the disability

Definition of Health

The *World Health Organization (WHO)* defines health as "a state of complete physical, mental, and social well-being and not merely the absence of disease or infirmity." As a health care worker, you strive to help patients/clients reach their highest potential.

Importance of Independence

When a person is ill or injured, they often have limitations. These limitations usually affect their activities of daily living. The activities include:

- Eating.
- Hygiene.
- Dressing.
- Toileting.
- Mobility.

Limitations can also affect what is known as **Instrumental Activities of Daily Living.** These activities require a higher level of function and cognition. These activities include:

- Shopping.
- Managing finances.
- Cooking.
- Transportation.
- Laundry.
- Telephone.

Some patients/clients can do these activities with little or no help. Others need a lot of help to **adapt.** The goal is to allow each person to be as independent as he or she possibly can be. Always encourage a patient to try an activity. (For example, the person may be able to put toothpaste on the brush but needs your help to brush the teeth.) You can encourage the client by being patient and positive and by letting him or her make choices. This helps the patient/client feel more independent and increases feelings of well-being and self-respect. There are many assistive/adaptive devices available. **(Figure 14.1)**

Computers are effective assistive/adaptive devices for children and adults with physical disabilities. People who cannot hold a pencil or speak can use computers with special enhancements to communicate. Individualized computer programs are created to guide learning.

Computers with e-mail and Internet capabilities provide opportunities for people with disabilities to interact with the outside world. The computer enables people with certain disabilities to communicate their needs, thoughts, desires, and intelligence to their parents and caregivers. These devices help the patient be more independent and self-sufficient. They help clients:

- Eat.
- Reach objects.
- Complete personal care.
- Dress and button clothing.
- Communicate.

Occupational Therapists specialize in assisting with adaptive devices for accomplishing activities of daily living and instrumental activities of daily living.

Physical Disabilities

Physical disabilities may be caused by a congenital condition, a debilitating illness, or an injury. Understanding disabilities helps you give better care to your patients.

Congenital Conditions

Babies who are born with a physical congenital condition, inherited **syndrome**, or other problems have a **congenital condition**. As a health care worker, you need to recognize these conditions in order to give good care and be supportive to family members. Common congenital defects are explained in Table 14.4.

Debilitating illness may occur at any age. Depending on the severity of the disease, physical changes may be minimal or very extensive. Common debilitating illnesses are explained in Table 14.5.

adapt
(uh dapt)
To change, to become suitable, to adjust.

Apply It

Divide yourselves into teams of at least four students. Each team will research a different kind of student disability serviced within your school system.

What support organizations exist for these disabilities? Where do they obtain their funding? Consider organizing a class fundraiser for one organization.

---

syndrome
(SIN drohm)
A number of symptoms occurring together.

congenital conditions
(kon JEN i tull kon DI shuns)
Existing at or before birth usually through heredity, as a disorder.

debilitating
(di BIL I teyt ing)
Causing weakness or impairment.

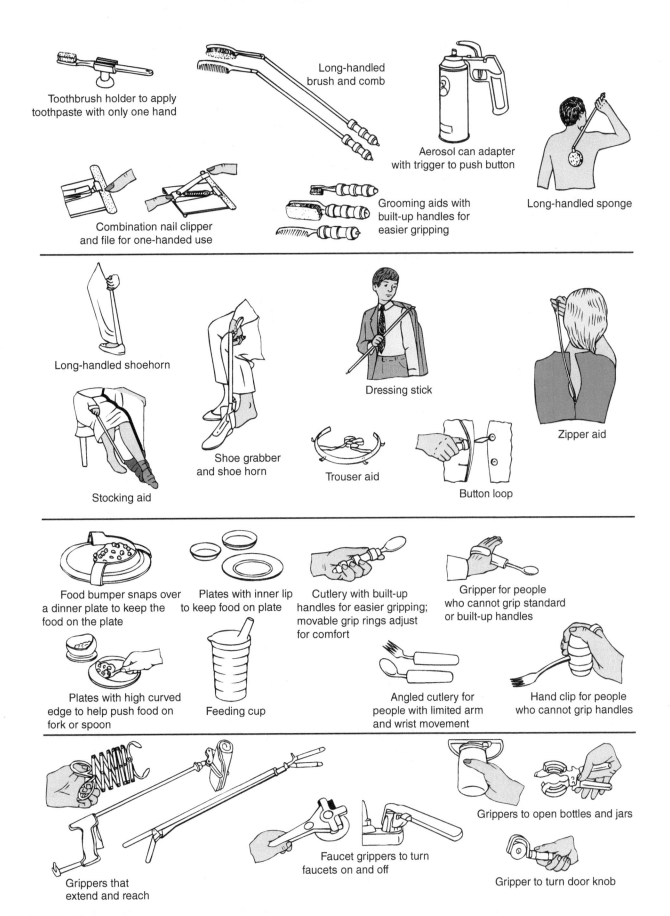

Toothbrush holder to apply toothpaste with only one hand

Long-handled brush and comb

Aerosol can adapter with trigger to push button

Long-handled sponge

Combination nail clipper and file for one-handed use

Grooming aids with built-up handles for easier gripping

Long-handled shoehorn

Stocking aid

Shoe grabber and shoe horn

Dressing stick

Trouser aid

Button loop

Zipper aid

Food bumper snaps over a dinner plate to keep the food on the plate

Plates with inner lip to keep food on plate

Cutlery with built-up handles for easier gripping; movable grip rings adjust for comfort

Gripper for people who cannot grip standard or built-up handles

Plates with high curved edge to help push food on fork or spoon

Feeding cup

Angled cutlery for people with limited arm and wrist movement

Hand clip for people who cannot grip handles

Grippers that extend and reach

Faucet grippers to turn faucets on and off

Grippers to open bottles and jars

Gripper to turn door knob

FIGURE 14.1

Assistive/adaptive devices. Which device might be most useful to a person confined in a wheelchair who wants to reach a box of cereal from a pantry shelf?

Table 14.4   Congenital Conditions

Condition at Birth	Condition	Identifying Characteristics
Autism	A brain development disorder that impairs social interaction and communication, and causes restricted and repetitive behavior, all starting before a child is three years old.	Makes little or no eye contact; does not speak as well as other children their age; does not use their imagination during play; shows no response when smiled at; can become unusually attached to objects; do not interact with other children; are prone to tantrums for no apparent reason.
Cerebral palsy	A motor function disorder that is caused by a brain defect or lesion present at birth or shortly after.	Spastic hemiplegia; seizures; some degree of mental retardation in some people; impaired vision, speech, and hearing; and stiff, awkward movements.
Cleft lip and/or cleft palate	Fusion of the palate and/or lip does not take place during **embryonic** development.	The cleft is often easily seen, but some display an inability to suck or nurse, crying when the child tries to nurse, with fluid coming out of the nose.
Cystic fibrosis	Inherited disorder of the exocrine glands that causes an excessive amount of thick mucus. Most affected are the pancreas, respiratory system, and sweat glands.	Usually diagnosed during infancy or in young children of Caucasian origin. Chronic cough, frequent foul-smelling stools, and persistent upper respiratory infections.
Down syndrome		Varying degrees of mental retardation and multiple defects; slanted eyes; depressed nasal bridge; low-set ears; large, protruding tongue; short, broad hands with a simian crease and stubby fingers; broad, stubby feet with wide spaces between the first and second toes; prone to respiratory infections, visual problems, and abnormalities in tooth development, and heart problems.
Epilepsy	**Neurological** disorders that may be birth defects but can occur later in life due to cerebral trauma, intracranial infection, brain tumor, **intoxication**, or chemical imbalance.	Recurrent **episodes** of convulsive seizures, sensory disturbances, abnormal behavior, loss of consciousness.
Hydrocephaly	Overproduction or underabsorption of cerebro-spinal fluid. May or may not cause increased pressure in the brain.	Globe-shaped head, flat nose bridge, eyes pushed downward and out, becoming widely spread; mild to severe retardation.
Sickle-cell anemia	A **hereditary** disease that is most common among African-American people. The red blood cell is crescent shaped (sickle shaped) and carries an abnormal **hemoglobin**.	Severe joint pain, thrombosis, fever, chronic anemia.
Spinal bifida	A developmental defect. A **hernial** sac containing the meninges, spinal cord, or both protrudes at the end of the vertebral column. This sac is easily ruptured, causing the characteristics at the right.	Leakage of spinal fluid, risk of **meningeal** cystica infection, severe neurological **dysfunction**, paralysis, muscle weakness, retardation.
Tay-Sachs syndrome	An inherited disease caused by an **enzyme deficiency**. It occurs primarily in families of Eastern European Jewish origin.	Difficult breathing and decreased exhange of oxygen and carbon dioxide.

What's New?

Identifying Congenital Conditions

While most babies are born healthy, the risk of having a baby with congenital conditions plagues many women throughout the early stages of pregnancy. Congenital conditions may be related to genetic material, organs, or body chemistry. Some congenital conditions have little impact on the child's life whereas others can be life threatening.

Advancements in technology continue to increase the ability of doctors to identify congenital conditions as early as possible. Just decades ago, doctors who had no forewarning of defects that would be present during delivery can now learn a tremendous amount of information as early as the first trimester of pregnancy (first three months).

Identifying conditions during pregnancy can be important because conditions, such as cleft lip, cleft palate, and some heart problems, can sometimes be surgically corrected shortly after birth or even during pregnancy. In addition, if an abnormality has been identified before birth, health care workers can be prepared to offer any special care needed upon birth.

Some tests performed during pregnancy are screening tests. These tests aim to identify the likelihood of a congenital condition. If the screening test is positive, which means that a problem is identified, a diagnostic test is performed to either confirm or rule out the problem. Keep in mind that no test is 100 percent accurate. In a false negative, test results do not identify congenital conditions when they are actually present. On the contrary, a false positive indicates a condition in a normal baby.

Two common screening tests, maternal serum triple or quad screening, check the pregnant mother's blood for specific substances related to different congenital conditions. These include some brain and spinal cord defects, related neural tube defects, and some chromosome defects. Ultrasound can be used to identify structural defects as well as signs of Down syndrome.

Common diagnostic tests include chorionic villus sampling (CVS) and amniocentesis, in which specific cells are obtained and analyzed for defects. Most recently, combinations of blood tests and ultrasound are being used to identify defects early on in the pregnancy.

How is identifying congenital conditions different today than it was 50 years ago?

---

embryonic
(em bree ON ik)
Pertaining to the embryo.

neurological
(noor uh LOG I kuhl)
Pertaining to the nervous system.

episodes
(EP i sod s)
Events in a series.

intoxication
(in tok si KEY shuhn)
State of poisoning or becoming poisoned.

hereditary
(huh RED i ter ee)
Passed from parent to child.

hemoglobin
(HEE muh gloh bin)
An iron-containing protein in red blood cells that combines reversibly with oxygen and transports it from the lungs to body tissues.

hernial
(HUR nee uh)
Pertaining to projection through an abnormal opening in the wall of a body cavity.

meninges
(mi NIN jeez)
Lining of the brain.

dysfunction
(dis FUHNGK shuhn)
Impaired or abnormal functioning.

enzyme
(EN zahym)
Substance that causes a change to occur in other substances.

deficiency
(di FISH uhn see)
Shortage (e.g., a deficient diet causes the body to function poorly because it is missing an important element).

Injury

Injuries may occur at any age and cause many different disabilities. Some of the most common are:

- Spinal cord injuries, which may cause paralysis.
- Stroke, which may cause paralysis, brain dysfunction, speech impairments, and/or loss of memory.
- Head injuries, which may cause **coma**, loss of memory, and/or paralysis.
- **Amputation** of a limb.

coma
(KOH muh)
Deep sleep; unconscious state for a long time.

amputation
(AM pyoo tey shuhn)
Removal of a body part.

Debilitating Illnesses

Elderly patients are more affected by a debilitating illness as they may not have sufficient physical, mental, or financial resources to accommodate recovery. An elderly person experiencing a fall or a hospitalization may experience a spiraling downward effect in their health status.

Table 14.5   Common Debilitating Illnesses

Debilitating Illness	Condition	Identifying Characteristics/Symptoms
Acquired immune deficiency syndrome (AIDS)	Caused by a virus that reduces the immune system's ability to respond to **opportunistic infections**.	Common opportunistic infections that result from AIDS include pneumocystis pneumonia, candidiasis, cryptococcus, and herpes. Cancers that may develop are Kaposi's sarcoma and lymphomas.
Alzheimer's disease	A degenerative disorder that affects the brain generally in later, middle life.	Confusion, memory failure, **disorientation**, restlessness, speech disturbances, inability to carry out purposeful movements, and hallucinations.
Arteriosclerosis	Hardening of the arteries, which reduces the elasticity of the arterial walls.	Elevated blood pressure.
Atherosclerosis	**Lipid**-containing material collects on the inside surfaces of the blood vessels causing thickening of the vessel walls and narrowing of the space that blood flows through, thus inhibiting blood flow. Through the space that blood flows through, thus inhibiting blood flow. Associated with obesity, hypertension, and diabetes.	Angina pectoris, myocardial infarction (MI), coronary heart disease, strokes.
Cancer	Uncontrolled growth of immature cells that invade normal tissue and travel to other tissues. More than 80 percent of cancers are caused by cigarette smoking, carcinogenic chemicals, radiation, and overexposure to the sun.	Signs of cancer vary, but it is wise to see a physician when the following occurs: change in bowel or bladder habits, a nonhealing sore, unusual bleeding or discharge, a thickening or lump anywhere, indigestion or trouble swallowing, an obvious change in a wart or mole, or a nagging cough or persistent hoarseness.
Cardiovascular disease	Any abnormal heart and/or circulatory condition. Cardiovascular disease remains a leading cause of death in the United States.	Dysfunction of the heart and blood vessels commonly causing angina, shortness of breath, weakness, and general fatigue.

(continued)

Table 14.5   Common Debilitating Illnesses (continued)

Debilitating Illness	Condition	Identifying Characteristics/Symptoms
Diabetes	Blood glucose, or sugar, levels are too high. With Type 1 diabetes, the body does not make insulin. With Type 2 diabetes, the more common type, the body does not make or use insulin well. Without enough insulin, the glucose stays in your blood. Being obese increases your risk of diabetes.	Excessive thirst and increased urination, flu-like feeling, weight gain or loss, increased fatigue, irritability, blurry vision.
Emphysema	The alveoli in the lungs are overextended and loose their elasticity. The lungs become less and less able to exchange oxygen and carbon dioxide.	Shortness of breath, cough, cyanosis, unequal chest expansion, rapid respiratory rate, elevated temperature. They may also experience, anxiety, restlessness, confusion, and weakness.
Leukemia	Rapid and abnormal growth of immature leukocytes in the blood-forming organs (bone marrow, spleen, and lymph nodes).	Males are affected twice as often as females. Symptoms include fatigue, pallor, weight loss, easy bruising, extreme weakness, bone or joint pain, repeated infections.
Multiple sclerosis	**Progressive** disease that affects the nerve fibers of the brain and spinal cord. It generally begins in young adulthood and continues throughout life.	Muscle weakness, visual disturbances, and dizziness. It affects the whole body, including emotional stability.
Parkinson's disease	Slowly progressive, degenerative, neurological disorder.	Tremors, shuffling gait, masklike face, forward flexion of the trunk, muscle rigidity, and weakness.

 ## Role Changes in People Who Are Physically or Mentally Challenged

When people experience a lengthy disability, they require understanding and patience. Disabled people need to remain a productive part of society and to maintain a sense of well-being. The health care worker can be a positive influence on patients/clients during the period of adjustment and rehabilitation.

People who lose a body part or a part of their body functions experience the same stages of loss as do people with a terminal illness. These are denial, rage and anger, bargaining, depression, and acceptance. Many people who suddenly find themselves disabled are dependent on others for many of their daily needs. Being dependent often leads to feelings of not being in control. Physical losses can cause various body functions to be impaired.

Loss of body function often means that changes may occur in the following:

- Communication skills.
- Sensory awareness.
- Ability to think and comprehend.
- Ability to move.
- Elimination of waste products.

opportunistic infections
(op er too NIS tik in FEK shen)
Infections that occur when the immune system is weakened. Common organisms that the body normally resists cause infection.

disorientation
(dis AWR ee uhn tey shuh n)
State of being confused about time, place, and identity of persons and objects.

arteriosclerosis
(ahr teer ee oh skluh ROH sis)
Condition of hardening of the arteries.

lipid
(LIP id)
Fat.

progressive
(pruh GRES iv)
Moving forward, following steps toward an end product.

- Eating.
- Sexual activity.

Loss of physical functions may cause emotional stability to change. The areas of emotional insecurity usually focus around the following:

- Self-esteem.
- Self-confidence.
- Self-image.

Physical impairments that lead to emotional changes may also create a sense of loss concerning the following:

- Ability to develop relationships with others.
- Ability to earn a living.
- Ability to be a useful member of society.

The health care worker helps patients/clients reach their goals by being understanding and knowledgeable about the process involved in acceptance of a disability and rehabilitation.

Rehabilitation

When physical changes occur, the goal of rehabilitation is to help the patient/client return to the highest level of functioning possible. Rehabilitation promotes a healthy return to a productive lifestyle. There are many rehabilitation areas involved in this process. The most common are as follows:

- Physical therapy restores the body to normal functioning when possible.
- Occupational therapy restores the ability to be involved in purposeful activity.
- Speech therapy restores the ability to communicate effectively.
- Psychotherapy changes inappropriate behavior patterns, improves interpersonal relationships, and resolves inner conflicts.

There are several groups available to aid the client and family during the recovery and rehabilitation period. These groups, called *support groups,* are organized to help patients and family members cope with changes during this period. Examples of groups are:

- Breast cancer support group.
- Ostomy support group.
- Vital Options—a support group for young adults with cancer.

You can locate groups in your area by contacting the social services department at hospitals, community centers, and organizations oriented to health care.

Community Service

Volunteer in a local rehabilitation center. Review a case history (without seeing the existing rehab plan), develop your own rehab plan and design an assistive device for the patient that will meet at least one of their needs. How does your plan match up with the plan created for the patient by licensed professional?

Summary

Physical disabilities, injury, and debilitating illness can occur from birth to old age. There are many different types of disabilities. Some of these are caused by accident, heredity, injury, or illness. When any of these are present, the patient may be frustrated or depressed. As a health care worker, you are responsible for the care and support of these patients. It is important to understand their illness and to be familiar with assistive/adaptive devices and support organizations that are available to help patients and their families.

SECTION **14.3** Review Questions

1. Give an example of a congenital condition that might limit a person's activities in some way.

2 How is a debilitating illness different from a birth defect?

3. What type of injury is most directly associated with a coma?

4. Which human body system is affected by neurological disorders?

5. What does it mean to say that sickle-cell anemia is a hereditary disease?

6. Give an example of a progressive disease.

 Learn By Doing: Section 14.3 Activity

1. Complete Worksheets 1 and 3 as assigned.

2. Complete Worksheets/Activities 2 and 4.

3. When you are confident that you can meet each objective for this section, ask your teacher for the section evaluation.

 Language Arts Link

Human Development and Aging

As people grow, develop and age, they experience many changes. For an aging person, some of the changes may be frightening or frustrating. Working with a partner, find a person who is willing to be interviewed on some of these changes. Ask your subject what they are experiencing and how they feel about some of these changes.

With your partner, write a detailed description of what you've learned about your subject. Include information on how you could help your subject manage some of these changes. Revise and edit your document by making it clearer, more concise, or more interesting to read. Try reading your writing aloud so that you and your partner can listen to the flow and clarity of what you've written. Check the spelling and grammar and correct any errors. Working with your partner, prepare a presentation on what you've learned and, if time allows, present your findings to the class.

End-of-Life Issues

Background

As a health care worker, you come in contact with clients who are nearing the end of their life. Your knowledge of the psychological stages experienced by those at the end of life gives you an understanding of their behavior.

Objectives

When you have completed this section, you will be able to do the following:

- Match key terms with their correct meanings.

- Match the psychological stages of a long terminal illness with their names.

- Identify and discuss your feelings about terminal illness.

- Explain the philosophy of hospice care.

Terminal Illness

Patients/clients who have an illness that cannot be cured are terminally ill. They are expected to die. When the patients learn of their illness, they usually pass through five different psychological stages. (**Figure 14.2**) Elisabeth Kübler-Ross, M.D. (1926–2004) was a Swiss-born psychiatrist, who first proposed these Five Stages of Grief as a pattern of phases, most or all of which people tend to go through, in sequence, after being faced with the tragedy of their own impending death.

Figure 14.2
Stages of dying. Which stage of dying follows denial?

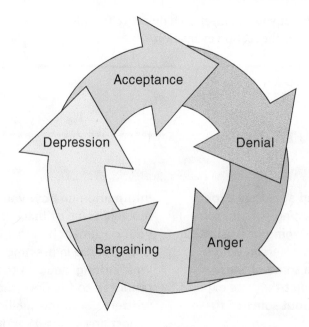

- **Stage one: Shock and denial.** People find it very difficult to believe that they are really going to die. "No, not me!" During this stage they feel very lonely and **isolated**. *Communication:* If they can discuss these feelings and talk about their **impending** death, they are able to move into the next stage. You may be the only health care worker available to listen to their feelings.

- **Stage two: Rage and anger.** No matter how much kindness you have shown, your client may become very insulting; there might be many complaints about everything you do. You may be tempted to leave them to their anger. *Communication:* If you realize it is not a personal attack, you will be able to listen and to understand that the anger is not directed at you. It is directed at the injustice of the situation. Be a good listener. When patients have exhausted their anger, they will move out of the anger stage.

- **Stage three: Bargaining.** Although they now admit to themselves that they are dying, the clients try to prolong their life with bargaining. For example, they might say, "Just let me live until my children are independent." *Communication:* Listen and reflect what is said, express your understanding, and be aware of your voice tone and body language. Be aware of times when your presence in silence is helpful and when words are not helpful.

- **Stage four: Depression.** Your patients may refuse to talk to you or even look at you. They are experiencing great sadness, for they are losing everyone and everything. *Communication:* Although they may not want to be bothered with friends or visitors, your touch is very important. Your understanding of their feelings of loss enables them to move into the last stage.

- **Stage five: Acceptance.** At last your clients can accept their death. This is a time when your presence lets them know you will not desert them. *Communication:* They may want to discuss their death. Your willingness to be available will help your patients in a very difficult time.

Of course, the patient can skip stages; in addition, he or she may regress back to a stage after they have passed through it. Friends and family often experience the same stages when someone they love and care about is terminally ill. As a health care worker, you need to be understanding. Family and friends may experience the following stages:

- **Shock and denial.** They may continue to make plans for the future that include the dying person.

- **Rage and anger.** They may be irritable and angry and say unkind things occasionally.

- **Bargaining.** They may ask the physician to keep the patient/client alive for a special occasion.

- **Depression.** They feel extreme sadness and even despair.

- **Acceptance.** They finally accept that death is going to occur. They may ask you to recommend someone for them to talk to.

isolated
(AHY suh leyt ed)
Limited in contact with others.

impending
(im PEN ding)
About to happen.

Decision Making at the End of Life

Decision making related to end-of-life issues must consider all aspects of care. It involves the patient's perception of death, psychological aspects of culture and spirituality, and all components of treatment and its expected outcome.

The patient and family's decision making must be supported in an ethical framework of respect for independence and dignity. Without the support of an individual's right to decision making, there is the risk that the patient will be treated as an object rather than as a person.

Health care decision making is built upon a relationship between patient and health care provider that requires mutual respect, trust, honesty, and confidentiality. Manipulation or intimidation must not hinder the resulting free exchange of information. Patients need to know and be informed of the following:

- Their condition.
- The proposed treatment.
- Expected results.
- Alternative treatment options.
- Potential risks, complications, and anticipated benefits.

Pain Management

When the terminally ill patient decides jointly with health care providers and the family that prolonging life with therapy is no longer possible, then comfort and pain relief becomes the treatment goal.

Most patients with a terminal illness fear physical pain much more than they fear death itself. Pain that is undertreated can have an extreme effect on the patient. It is important to work as a team with your co-workers to address the emotional, physical, spiritual, and psychological effects of pain and relieve discomfort as much as possible.

Relieving pain includes maintaining the patient's personal hygiene and body alignment, and speaking gently and clearly to the patient even if he or she is not able to respond to you. Reporting restlessness, excessive sweating, and rapid respirations to the charge nurse will provide information needed to determine if medication is appropriate.

Scales of 10 are commonly use in health care today for evaluating the level of discomfort. Teaching a patient to use a pain scale gives them a way of evaluating and communicating their pain to a caregiver.

 ## Hospice Care

In many communities, hospice care is available for terminally ill people. The hospice **philosophy** is to help patients/clients nearing the end of life live each day to the fullest. This care is provided in the home or in a hospice facility. Patients are kept comfortable and free from pain. When the time for death comes, they are allowed to die peacefully.

philosophy
(fi LOS uh fee)
Theory; a general principle used for a specific purpose.

An important service of hospice is family involvement. Families are counseled and helped to accept the impending death of a loved one. Following the death, the family has continuing support for at least a year. This support helps make the grieving period more tolerable.

You are an important member of the health care team. Your insight into the patient/client and his or her family and friends provides valuable information to decision makers concerning the care process. This knowledge of what your patients/clients may experience helps you meet their needs.

Euthanasia

Euthanasia, also referred to as a "mercy killing," is the act of ending the life of an individual suffering from a terminal illness or an incurable condition. The word "euthanasia" originated from the Greek language: "eu" means "good" and "thanatos" means "death"; so, it actually means a "good death." If death is not intended, then it is not an act of euthanasia. Euthanasia is carried out by lethal injection or by suspending extraordinary medical treatment. There are different types of euthanasia including:

- **Voluntary euthanasia.** When a person killed requested to be killed.
- **Non-voluntary euthanasia.** When the person killed gave no request or consent to be killed.
- **Involuntary euthanasia.** When the person killed made an expressed wish to the contrary.
- **Assisted suicide.** When someone provides an individual with the information, guidance, and means to take his or her own life with the intention that they will be used for this purpose. When a doctor who helps an individual to kill themselves it is called "physician assisted suicide."

The issue of euthanasia is very controversial. Some people argue that this is a case of freedom of choice—one that relieves an individual of extreme pain and suffering when their quality of life is low. Other believe that euthanasia devalues human life and can become a means of health care cost containment.

In April 2002, the Netherlands was the first country in the world to legalize euthanasia, soon followed by Belgium. Switzerland allows assisted suicide, under specific regulations, as does the state of Oregon. The U.S. government has tried to challenge this law, but has been unsuccessful so far.

Organ Procurement and Donation

Organ donation is the removal of tissues of the human body from an individual who has recently died or from a living donor. Organ procurement is the obtaining of organs for transplantation. It includes the transporting of donor organs, after surgical removal, to the hospital for processing and transplant.

The following organs can be procured: heart, intestines, kidneys, lungs, liver, pancreases, bones and skin. In addition, the following tissues can be procured for donation: tendons, corneas, heart valves, bone marrow, and veins.

Everyone is a potential organ and tissue donor. Age and medical history are not the determining factors; instead, the critical factor is the condition of your organs and tissues at the time of death.

If you are under age 18, a parent or guardian must give permission for you to become a donor. If you are 18 or older, you can agree to be a donor by signing a donor card. It is also important to let your family know your wishes.

Jobs and Professions

- Geriatrician—A doctor who specializes in the care for people 65 and older.

- Hospice worker—Provides terminally ill patients with services that range from companionship to personal care.

- Nurse assistant/orderly in long-term care facility—Works under the supervision of a nurse and provides assistance to patients with daily living tasks.

- Ambulatory care clinics.

- Assistive personnel—Includes certified nurse's aide, home health aide, and patient care technicians.

Summary

Most health care workers come in contact with terminally ill patients/clients and are involved in the care of a dying person. The terminally ill patient usually experiences five psychological stages: denial, anger, bargaining, depression, and acceptance. Patients who are terminally ill have an opportunity to choose a hospice for the final days of their illness.

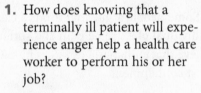

SECTION 14.4 **Review Questions**

1. How does knowing that a terminally ill patient will experience anger help a health care worker to perform his or her job?

2. What does a terminally ill patient do during the bargaining stage?

3. In what ways can a health care worker help a patient pass through the depression stage?

4. What is the fifth and final psychological stage experienced by terminally ill patients?

5. Describe the hospice philosophy.

6. Name three organs that can be procured.

Learn By Doing: Section 14.4 Activity

1. Complete Worksheets 1 and 2.

2. Complete Worksheet/Activity 3 as assigned.

3. Prepare responses to each item listed in Chapter Review.

4. When you are confident that you can meet each objective listed above, ask your teacher for the section evaluation.

Chapter Review Questions

1. List four common developments of growth that occur in the first year of life. (14.1)

2. What period of adjustment is sometimes described as a midlife crisis? (14.1)

3. What hearing changes often affect people in their 60s? (14.2)

4. Contrast osteoarthritis and osteoporosis and explain how they affect people. (14.2)

5. Why do people often experience a change in environment as they age? How might this affect the person's well being? (14.2)

6. How does a person's work role change throughout life? (14.2)

7. Why does arteriosclerosis result in elevated blood pressure? (14.2)

8. What does it mean for a person with a disability to adapt? (14.3)

9. What is euthanasia? (14.4)

10. How is pain management important to the care of a terminally ill patient? (14.4)

Activities

1. Community resources provide people who are critically or terminally ill with valuable information and assistance. As a health care worker you have the opportunity to share information about available community resources with your patients and their families. Identify community resources with the following basic information about each: services provided, name of the organization, address, telephone number, e-mail address, and all other pertinent information. Summarize your information in the chart and then create a card file for each resource.

Community Resource	Address	E-mail Address	Telephone Number	Services Provided/ Description

2. A 30-year-old woman suffered a head injury, which left her unable to speak. Her daily care provides a bath, clean clothes, and food. People around her rarely speak to her. She stays in her room and looks out the window most of the time. Compare and differentiate between her day and yours. Make specific recommendations that could assist in moving this person toward health as described by the World Health Organization. Explain how your recommendations would change this client's health status.

Case Studies

1. An elderly husband and wife decide to live in a long-term care facility so that their family won't worry about them. Upon admission, the wife is placed in room 125, and the husband is placed next door in room 126. They ask to share the same room, but the admitting clerk explains that the facility policy doesn't allow men and women to stay in the same room. Describe your remarks to the family and how you would respond to the admitting clerk or your supervisor.

2. Working in the pediatric ward, your team is proud of the progress made with a frightened, withdrawn four-year-old girl. But during visiting hours, her father becomes very angry, telling you that the hospital staff has made his daughter a bad girl because she is having tantrums. How would you handle this situation?

Chapter 14 Review

Thinking Critically

1. **Communication**—Following the medical plan, you are helping Mr. Green learn to use a walker after his stroke. The greatest challenge is that his wife and family tell him that he does not have to bother with learning to get around himself. Now that he is retired due to disability, they tell him that he can just sit in bed and watch television. How would you talk to Mr. Green and his family about the importance of staying mobile?

2. **Patient Education**—A 55-year-old male patient is recovering from a stroke. He is a high school principal and has always been able to take care of himself. His right hand and leg are paralyzed. Each day he is increasingly frustrated because he is unable to bathe or dress himself. Describe devices that could help reduce his frustration. Explain what you would say and do to educate him in the use of assistive/adaptive devices.

3. **Computers**—Patients/clients with disabilities are using computers to communicate and be productive citizens as they live with their disability. Do research on ways computers can be adapted to meet the needs of disabled individuals and write a report explaining what you have learned. Look for *assistive technology, alternative input mechanisms, alternative output mechanisms, and computer use with handicapped or disabled children.*

Media Connection

Use the Companion Web site for additional interactive learning activities: www.prenhall.com/badasch

Portfolio Connection

Working with people who are ill causes unfamiliar feelings and experiences. Your ability to identify your feelings and understand how you react to those feelings helps you carry on and continue to care for others.

Select a disability described in this chapter. Imagine that you are diagnosed with this disability. Identify your fears, feelings, and expectations. Explain what each day would be like, what type of care you would need, how others would respond to you, and how you would respond to others.

Your explanation must clearly identify your self-evaluation and new insights about disabilities and behaviors, and must show how you would approach others with disabilities. This assignment helps you investigate your feelings and identify possible behaviors of patients who live with disabilities. Including this assignment in your portfolio gives you easy access to it for review during your training. Comparing assignments throughout your training shows how your experiences have brought about change in your thinking.

PORTFOLIO TIP

Remember that aging means different things in different cultures.

15 | **Mental Health**

Getting Started

U nderstand that good mental health is as important to recovery from illness and injury as a patient's underlying physical condition. Recognize that there seems to be a prevalent number of incidents when poor mental health is causing people to become dysfunctional in current society.

Prepare a collage from articles in the newspaper or from the Internet that illustrate poor mental health. Consider entertainment figures, war veterans, families of children with disabling conditions such as autism, or those who suffer from obesity or anorexia to the point that it affects their daily habits of living.

SECTION

15.1 Mental Illness

Background

People react to the world around them in different ways. For most people, daily activities pose few problems. Although these people occasionally feel down or moody, they otherwise feel good about themselves and the people around them. For a small number of people, however, interactions with the world and other people are difficult. Their thoughts and emotions are hard to control, and they may withdraw from daily activities as a result.

Objectives

When you have completed this section, you will be able to do the following:

- Define mental illness.
- Identify seven types of mental illnesses.
- Identify three types of risk factors for mental illness.
- Describe four anxiety disorders.
- Describe two mood disorders.
- List three symptoms of attention deficit hyperactivity disorder.
- Describe two eating disorders.
- Relate substance abuse to mental illness.
- Describe Alzheimer's disease.

mental illness
(MEN tuhl IL nuhs)
Health condition that changes a person's thoughts, emotions, and behavior and that affects the person's ability to undertake daily functions.

Defining Mental Illness

Emotions and thoughts can be overwhelming. Sometimes, people have a hard time dealing with their emotions and the world around them. When this frequently happens, a person may be diagnosed with a **mental illness.** According to the National Institutes of Mental Health, as many as 26 percent of Americans suffer from a mental illness or know someone who does. A smaller percentage of Americans—about 6 percent—suffer from a serious mental illness.

Types of Mental Illness

Mental illnesses can be classified into various categories. These categories include the following:

- **Anxiety disorders:** include panic attacks, phobias, obsessive-compulsive disorder, and post-traumatic stress disorder.

- **Mood disorders:** include bipolar disorder and depression.

- **Personality disorders:** include schizophrenia.

- **Attention disorders:** include attention deficit hyperactivity disorder.

- **Eating disorders:** include anorexia nervosa and bulimia nervosa.

- **Drug abuse:** include alcoholism and abuse of performance enhancing drugs such as amphetamines, heroin, cocaine, and barbituates.

- **Alzheimer's disease:** most common form of dementia, it is a progressive and fatal disease.

Mental illness affects people of all ages, regardless of gender. Some diseases are more common in certain groups. For example, Alzheimer's disease usually affects older adults. Attention disorders are more common in children and young adults.

The Causes of Mental Illness

Scientists do not completely understand the causes of mental illness. Several risk factors can play a role in whether people develop mental illnesses. These risk factors include the following:

- **Biological factors:** Mental illnesses occur more often in some families than in others. This may be the result of *genetics,* or the traits passed from parent to child.

- **Environmental factors:** Head injuries, poor nutrition, and exposure to harmful or addictive chemicals can increase the risk of developing a mental illness.

- **Social factors:** Emotional trauma, abuse, exposure to violence, and other stressful events may affect whether someone develops a mental illness.

Anxiety Disorders

Each day, you probably feel some stress. It may be the stress of taking a test, or the stress of playing in an important game. One response to stress is **anxiety**. Because of anxiety, you may feel tense. You may sweat more. Anxiety can help you deal with a stressful situation. However, too much anxiety is unhealthy. People who frequently experience anxiety, often when facing everyday situations, may have an **anxiety disorder**.

Panic Disorder

Panic disorder is an anxiety disorder that is characterized by sudden attacks of terror. (Figure 15.1) People who experience one of these attacks may feel chilled. They may also feel nausea and as though they are being smothered. These panic attacks can occur at any time, even when a person is asleep. Some people have one

anxiety
(ang ZIE i tee)
A feeling of worry and fear that causes physical symptoms, such as sweating, and stress.

anxiety disorder
(ang ZIE i tee DIS ohr duhr)
A mental illness in which a person feels too much anxiety, often in response to everyday situations.

FIGURE 15.1

Panic attacks can happen at any time of day. Why do some sufferers of panic attacks refuse to leave their homes?

phobia
(FOH bee uh)
An irrational fear of an object or event that poses little or no actual risk.

obsessions
(ahb SESH uhns)
In obsessive-compulsive disorder, undesirable thoughts that occur constantly, causing anxiety.

compulsions
(cuhm PUHL shuhns)
In obsessive-compulsive disorder, behaviors or rituals that develop in response to the anxiety caused by obsessive thoughts.

panic attack and never develop a panic disorder. People who have a panic disorder live in fear of another attack. So, many of these people won't leave their homes or take part in normal activities.

Phobias

A phobia is a fear of something that poses little or no danger. People who suffer from a phobia may be afraid of wild animals (agrizoophobia), high places (acrophobia), open spaces (agoraphobia), or activities such as flying (aviophobia). Some people suffer from a *social phobia*, or a fear of social situations, such as talking to other people, giving speeches, and eating or drinking. Because of their fear, people who have a phobia often suffer from panic attacks. Both men and women are equally affected by phobias. Phobias usually begin during childhood or adolescence.

Obsessive-Compulsive Disorder

Obsessive-compulsive disorder (OCD) involves constant, disturbing thoughts, or **obsessions**, and repetitive behaviors, or **compulsions**, to control the anxiety caused by the thoughts. For example, someone who obsesses about germs and dirt may respond by compulsively washing his or her hands. A healthy person may also wash his or her hands, but people who have OCD cannot function properly. They

FIGURE 15.2

People who have OCD may spend too much time organizing things around their homes. What are the two parts of OCD?

may become locked into their compulsion, spending hours washing their hands or cleaning their homes. (**Figure 15.2**)

The effects of OCD may be mild, only partially affecting a person's ability to function. Or, the effects of OCD can be extreme, keeping people from leaving the house or even carrying out normal activities at home. OCD affects both men and women. It usually appears in childhood, adolescence, or early adulthood.

Post-Traumatic Stress Disorder

People develop **post-traumatic stress disorder (PTSD)** after an incident in which they are harmed or threatened with harm. For example, victims of a violent crime may develop PTSD. Soldiers who have been to war may develop PTSD. People who have PTSD startle easily and are emotionally numb. They lose interest in the things they once enjoyed and may respond aggressively or violently to other people. People suffering from PTSD may relive the incident that caused the PTSD in flashbacks. PTSD affects people of all ages, and affects women more often than it affects men.

Mood Disorders

Some mental illnesses affect the emotions in particular. *Mood disorders* cause people to have inappropriate emotional reactions. For example, people who have mood disorders may feel sad when they should feel happy. Mood disorders may cause an emotional reaction that does not fit the circumstances of an event. For example, a person may feel overly sad or angry about losing a pen. Bipolar disorder and depression are two examples of mood disorders.

Bipolar Disorder

Sometimes, you feel happy. A little while later, you might feel sad or upset. This mood swing is not unusual. Some people, however, suffer from severe mood swings. These people are often diagnosed with **bipolar disorder**. People who have bipolar disorder have periods of high energy and periods of low energy. These highs and lows are called *mania* and *depression*.

During mania, or a manic episode, a person has increased energy and is more active. He or she will experience racing thoughts and jump from one idea to the next. The person will get easily distracted and won't sleep much. He or she will show poor judgment and deny that anything is wrong.

During depression, a person will experience several negative emotions, including hopelessness, guilt, worthlessness, and helplessness. He or she will lose interest in activities that were once enjoyable. The person will feel tired, but he or she may not get enough sleep. Or the person will get too much sleep. He or she has difficulty concentrating and making decisions.

In severe cases of bipolar disorder, a person may experience **psychosis**. This person may have *hallucinations,* or hear or see something that doesn't exist. He or she will also have delusions, or false beliefs.

Bipolar disorder usually develops in adolescence or early adulthood. It affects both men and women.

Depression

People normally have periods during which they feel down. (**Figure 15.3**) Some people experience this for a long period of time or repeatedly as a result of a mental illness called **major depressive disorder**. In his or her lifetime, a person may experience only one episode of major depression, or he or she may experience it several times.

post-traumatic stress disorder (PTSD)
(POHST TRAW mat ik STRES DIS ohr duhr)
A mental illness that develops after a terrifying incident that involved physical harm or the threat of harm.

bipolar disorder
(BIE puhl uhr DIS ohr duhr)
A mental illness that causes unusual shifts in a person's mood, energy, and ability to function; also known as manic-depressive disorder.

psychosis
(SIE koh suhs)
Symptoms of mental illness in which a person experiences thoughts and ideas that are not based on reality; include hallucinations and delusions.

major depressive disorder
(MAY juhr DEE pres iv DIS ohr duhr)
Mental illness characterized by a combination of symptoms that include prolonged sadness and that interfere with a person's ability to undertake everyday activities.

Depression has several characteristics, including the following:

- Frequent sad feelings.

- Feelings of hopelessness.

- Irritability and restlessness.

- Loss of interest in activities and hobbies.

- Decreased energy.

- Difficulty sleeping or too much sleep.

- Change in eating habits.

- Thoughts of suicide.

- Body aches, headaches, and other physical problems.

Depression often occurs with other mental illnesses. It can affect people who suffer from anxiety disorders and who abuse drugs. Depression is also common among people who have serious illnesses, such as cancer, AIDS, and diabetes. Depression is more common among women than it is among men. It can affect people of all ages.

Schizophrenia

Schizophrenia is a personality disorder in which people lose contact with reality. Like bipolar disorder, a person who has schizophrenia experiences hallucinations and delusions. He or she may hear "voices" that other people cannot hear. These voices may comment on the person's behavior, talk to each other, or warn the person about danger that does not exist. Other symptoms of schizophrenia include the following:

- **Paranoia:** belief that other people want to harm someone.

- **Thought disorders:** unusual thought processes or difficulty organizing thoughts.

schizophrenia
(SKIT soh fren ee uh)
Mental illness in which a person loses touch with reality; often characterized by hallucinations, such as voices that other people cannot hear, and delusions.

paranoia
(PAIR ah noy uh)
Unfounded or irrational distrust of other people.

- **Movement disorders:** clumsiness or awkward movement.
- **Flat affect:** little facial expression and a flat voice.
- **Lack of activity:** difficulty starting and engaging in social activities.
- **Poor executive function:** difficulty understanding information and making decisions based on the information.
- **Poor working memory:** inability to remember something just learned.

Schizophrenia usually appears earlier in men than it does in women. Most men show symptoms in their late teens to early 20s. Women show symptoms in their 20s and 30s. Schizophrenia symptoms rarely begin to appear in children before the age of puberty and in adults after age 45.

 ## Attention Disorders

Children have a tendency to be very active and may be easily distracted. When children are frequently active at inappropriate times or have trouble paying attention, they may be diagnosed with an attention disorder such as **attention deficit hyperactivity disorder (ADHD)**. ADHD affects three to five percent of children in the United States. Even though ADHD is diagnosed mostly in children, it also occurs in adults. **(Figure 15.4)**

attention deficit hyperactivity disorder
(AH ten shuhn DEF uh sit HIE puhr ak tiv uh tee DIS ohr duhr)
A mental illness characterized by inattention, hyperactivity, and impulsiveness; diagnosed most often in children.

FIGURE 15.4
One sign of ADHD is excessive daydreaming. What are the three symptoms of ADHD?

ADHD is characterized by three symptoms:

- **Inattention:** A person cannot concentrate on what is going on around him or her. He or she may become easily bored with a task and not finish it. A person becomes easily distracted and often makes careless mistakes.
- **Hyperactivity:** A person is always in motion. He or she may squirm, fidget, or talk constantly. Older children and adults will feel internally restless and often try to do several things at once.
- **Impulsiveness:** A person lacks the ability to think things through before acting. He or she may say things suddenly and without evaluating the consequences. Adults who experience impulsiveness often do things that have instant results rather than working toward long-term results.

Individuals who have ADHD can be sorted into three general groups. The first group includes people who are primarily inattentive. The second group includes people who are primarily hyperactive and/or impulsive. The third group, or the combined group, is both inattentive and hyperactive and/or impulsive. Even though ADHD is diagnosed mostly in children, the effects of ADHD may continue into adulthood.

Personal Wellness

Diagnosing Mental Illness

The discussion of mental illness may make you worry about your own mental health or the health of the people around you. Keep in mind that mood swings and emotional outbursts can be a normal part of life, especially during adolescence. When these problems occur frequently and interfere with a person's ability to interact with the world around them, then that person should seek care.

While most cases of mental illness are not severe, the symptoms of mental illness should not be ignored. Only a medical professional can diagnose a mental illness. If you are concerned, visit your family doctor or a mental health specialist. The doctor will likely ask you about your family history. He or she may ask you to take a survey, or series of questions.

The doctor will examine you and take a blood sample to rule out physical illnesses. Depending on the results of the tests, the doctor will recommend treatment. Don't be afraid to visit the doctor; he or she will work to ensure your privacy.

Sometimes, the people affected by mental illness are your friends or family. You should encourage these people to get professional help, especially if they talk about suicide or other harmful behaviors. Be supportive, listen, and help the person understand that he or she can get help. If you have a friend or family member who won't get help, tell a trusted adult about your concerns.

When you work in health care, you may be exposed to people who have mental illnesses. Because people respond in different ways to an illness and its treatment, you may have to confront very stressful situations. Your facility will likely offer you mental health care to help you deal with these situations.

How should you deal with the symptoms of mental illness in a friend?

Eating Disorders

People need to eat to have energy for everyday activities. Sometimes, people eat too little food or too much food. When a person's eating habits have become severely disturbed, a person may be diagnosed with an eating disorder. Eating disorders are considered mental illnesses because they have a *psychological,* or mental, component. Eating disorders often happen to people who have another mental illness, such as depression, an anxiety disorder, or substance abuse. Eating disorders include the following:

- **Anorexia nervosa:** This eating disorder is characterized by an abnormal fear of gaining weight. People who have anorexia nervosa exercise and diet excessively, or they lose weight by vomiting and by using drugs, such as laxatives and diuretics, that cause their bodies to release more wastes. People who have anorexia have poor body image. They see themselves as overweight even when they are underweight.

- **Bulimia nervosa:** This eating disorder is characterized by cycles of *binging* and *purging.* During a binge, a person eats too much food and feels out of control of his or her eating habits. During a purge, the person gets rid of the food by vomiting or using laxatives and other drugs.

Eating disorders usually appear during adolescence. They affect women more often than they affect men, although there are increased incidences of these conditions in men.

 ## Drug Abuse

A **drug** is any chemical substance that alters the way a person thinks or acts and alters the person's body. Many drugs are helpful. For example, aspirin can be used to treat pain. Other drugs are harmful, and many of these drugs are illegal. These drugs include marijuana, cocaine, and methamphetamine, to name a few.

Tobacco and alcohol are drugs that are illegal for people under certain ages. Some prescription drugs although legitimately used for treating physical and mental illness can be addictive. The general public often does not recognize the dangers of misuse and overuse of prescription drugs.

Sometimes, people use harmful drugs and lose control of their drug use. At this point, the person is abusing the drug and has a **drug addiction.** Drug abuse is considered a mental illness because of the effect of drugs on the brain. Drug abuse changes the structure and function of the brain. (See the following Science Link.) Because of these changes, a person will have difficulty stopping the use of a drug.

Drug abuse is often related to other mental illnesses. For example, it can cause anxiety and depression. Or, it may be the result of a person's response to these diseases. For example, a person who feels depressed may decide to use drugs to try to feel better. Both men and women abuse drugs. Drug abuse usually starts in adolescence or early adulthood, but both children and older adults have been found to abuse drugs.

Apply It

Divide yourselves into sets of doctor/patient teams. The patient should describe a variety of specific symptoms and behaviors suggesting a mental disorder, such as OCD, PTSD, etc. The doctor needs to diagnose the disorder, describing why he or she has determined this to be the specific problem.

drug
(DRUHG)
Any chemical substance that changes a person's physical or psychological state.

drug addiction
(DRUHG AH dikt shuhn)
The uncontrolled use of a drug.

The Brain on Drugs

The brain is made up of cells called *neurons*. Neurons use both electrical signals and chemical messengers to transmit information. An electrical signal is transmitted along the length of a neuron. This signal causes the release of chemical messengers, called *neurotransmitters*, into the gap between one neuron and the next. Receptors on the next neuron respond to these neurotransmitters by producing an electrical signal and passing it on.

Some drugs, such as heroin and the drug in marijuana, are similar to neurotransmitters. When the drug is used, the neurons are fooled into firing by the drug.

Other drugs, such as cocaine or methamphetamine, cause nerve cells to release abnormally large amounts of neurotransmitters. Or, they prevent the recycling of neurotransmitters, a normal function that shuts off the signal between neurons.

In particular, drugs directly or indirectly affect a neurotransmitter called *dopamine*. Dopamine causes the euphoric feeling associated with drug use. Excess dopamine is released in response to drug use. As a person abuses a drug, the brain adapts to the excess dopamine. It reduces the amount of dopamine produced or reduces the number of dopamine receptors present. As a result, the drug abuser gets less enjoyment from the drug and uses more of it to get the same sensation.

What are three ways in which drugs affect chemical messengers in the brain?

Alzheimer's Disease

Dementia is a name used to describe a sustained loss of intellectual functions and memory severe enough to cause dysfunction in daily living activities. Although it can occur at any time during the adult years, it most frequently affects the elderly population. Some dementias can be reversed (about 20 percent). For this reason, all patients suffering from memory loss or reduced ability to solve life problems should be medically evaluated and would benefit from an evaluation by a geriatrician (a specialist in elder care).

Alzheimer's disease
(AWL sie muhrs DUH seez)
Type of dementia that causes the death of brain cells and subsequent impairment of thinking and memory.

Close to 66 percent of all dementias in the geriatric population can be attributed to **Alzheimer's disease**. Family history and increasing age are the primary risk factors for Alzheimer's disease. Research suggests a genetic linkage as a causal factor. Other possible risk factors include previous head injury, female sex, and lower educational level.

Alzheimer's disease is a mental illness that causes the death of cells in the brain. Because of this cell death, parts of the brain become disconnected. As a result, some messages cannot be sent from one part of the brain to another. This interferes with brain functions such as memory and impairs thinking.

Eventually people lose their ability to solve problems. For example, they may become lost while out driving in areas they are familiar with and cannot find their way back home. They may forget how to conduct activities of daily living, such as preparing a meal or even how to eat. Eventually, they may lose their ability to walk or communicate.

Some Alzheimer's patients may become paranoid and express anger and violence towards those around them. This is another expression of their inability to successfully evaluate and solve problems people deal with in their daily lives. The families and caregivers of these patients require an extensive support system. Eventually, many Alzheimer's patients need fulltime professional care.

Unlike many other mental illnesses, the effects of Alzheimer's disease are irreversible. At first, many people don't notice the symptoms of the disease. They think they are forgetful, but the forgetfulness gets worse as the disease progresses.

There are several main stages of Alzheimer's. Patients will progress form one stage to the next; for instance, the memory losses are not random, but reflective of each stage.

- **Early-stage Alzheimer's (Mild):** Memory loss or other cognitive deficits are noticeable, yet the person can compensate for them and continue to function independently. *Example:* Forgets names and words; might make up words; or quit talking to avoid mistakes.

- **Mid-stage Alzheimer's (Moderate):** Mental abilities decline, the personality changes, and physical problems develop so that the person becomes more and more dependent on caregivers. *Example:* Forgets recent events; forgets their own history; increasing difficulty in sorting out names and faces of family and friends.

- **Late-stage Alzheimer's (Severe):** Complete deterioration of the personality and loss of control over bodily functions requires total dependence on others for even the most basic activities of daily living. *Example:* Doesn't recognize familiar people, including their spouse and family members.

Some very rare forms of Alzheimer's disease will affect people as young as their 30s. Otherwise, Alzheimer's disease usually appears in people age 60 or older. Regardless, Alzheimer's disease is not a natural part of aging.

Summary

A mental illness is a health condition that changes a person's thoughts, emotions, and behavior. As a result of a mental illness, a person has difficulty participating in daily activities. Mental illnesses include anxiety disorders, mood disorders, personality disorders, attention disorders, eating disorders, substance abuse, and Alzheimer's disease.

The causes of mental illness are difficult to identify precisely. Biological factors, environmental factors, and social factors all play a role in the development of mental illness.

Community Service

As a member of a team, complete research to determine services and support available to assist those with mental health issues including the cost to the recipient of services. Put the information in a brochure that you can distribute to homeless shelters, at local mental health facilities and offices where care may be provided.

1. List seven types of mental illness.

2. What are three risk factors for mental illness?

3. Which mood disorder might result from a violent event, such as a mugging?

4. What are the two phases of bipolar disorder?

5. Describe the three symptoms of ADHD.

6. In which eating disorder does a person exercise or diet excessively?

7. Why is substance abuse classified as a mental illness?

 Learn By Doing: Section 15.1 Activity

1. Complete Worksheets 1 through 6.

2. When you are confident that you can meet each objective for this section, ask your teacher for the section evaluation.

SECTION

15.2 Techniques for Treating Mental Illness

Background

Because the symptoms of mental illness vary from mild to severe, the treatment for mental illness also varies. Treatment for mental illness is flexible and can be adapted as the patient's needs change. Some patients will need long-term care and may not be able to take care of themselves. So, the members of the health care team will need to meet their specific needs.

Objectives

When you have completed this section, you will be able to do the following:

- List three ways to treat mental illness.

- List consequences of not treating mental illness.

- Explain why mental illness patients may stop taking medications.

- Define *psychotherapy*.

- List four benefits of psychotherapy.

- Explain why treatment for drug abuse involves hospitalization.

- Describe why the treatment for Alzheimer's disease differs from the treatment for most other mental illnesses.

Mental Illnesses Are Treatable

Many people have the misconception that people who have mental illnesses are "crazy" or "nuts." This is simply not true. Most cases of mental illness are not severe. These cases can be treated, often with a combination of medication and regular meetings with a medical professional who specializes in treating mental illness.

When caught early, the symptoms of most mental illnesses can be reduced or even reversed. In very severe cases, a patient may be dangerous to himself or herself or to other people. So, he or she will need to be hospitalized.

The Consequences of Not Treating Mental Illness

Most people will go to the doctor for an illness such as the flu, asthma, diabetes, or heart disease. But many people hesitate to see a doctor about mental illnesses. Teenagers, especially, do not want to be labeled with a mental illness and have their peers or teachers find out.

Not seeking treatment may result in more advanced symptoms of the mental illness. Untreated mental illness can lead to increased physical illness. A person may think about or attempt suicide. Some mental illnesses cause violent thoughts or actions. In children, untreated mental illness has lead to learning problems and social problems.

Medication

Medicines are often used to treat mental illness. Medicines can be prescribed to treat anxiety disorders, mood disorders, attention disorders, and personality disorders. Medicines can also help some people overcome drug addictions and help treat eating disorders. Many of these medicines need to be taken for several days or weeks. Sometimes, people need the medicines for longer periods.

A doctor must carefully monitor mental illness medications. Some of these medicines have uncomfortable side effects. A doctor can adjust medications or dosages to make a patient more comfortable. Because of the uncomfortable side effects, some patients may decide to stop taking their medicines. As a member of health care team, you may need to assist with or monitor a patient's medicines. Review the procedures regarding medication in Chapter 20: Medical Assisting and Laboratory Skills.

Psychotherapy

During **psychotherapy**, a patient will meet with a medical professional such as a counselor, **psychiatrist**, or **psychologist** to discuss their feelings. Discussion helps patients understand their mental illness and work through their problems. Psychotherapy helps patients in the following ways:

- It can change thought patterns and behaviors.
- It can help patients recognize how past experiences affect their current behaviors.

psychotherapy
(SIE koh ther uh pee)
Treatment method in which a mental health professional and a patient discuss problems and feelings related to a mental illness.

psychiatrist
(SIE kie uh trist)
A medical professional who specializes in the prevention, diagnosis, and treatment of mental illness; has a medical degree (M.D.) and can prescribe medication as part of treatment.

psychologist
(SIE kahl uh jist)
A medical professional who specializes in the prevention, diagnosis, and treatment of mental illness; can only use talk therapy for treatment.

- It can help the patient learn skills to deal with their mental illness.
- It can help medical professionals monitor a patient's response to treatment and medication.

Psychotherapy (**Figure 15.5**) can occur individually or in a group setting. Usually, it involves talking, but it may involve activities such as art or music. Talking, art therapy, and music therapy help patients express themselves in healthy ways. Group therapy can help patients learn how to interact with other people.

Like medications, psychotherapy must occur over a period of time. Some people only need a few visits. Other people, who have more severe mental illnesses, will spend years in psychotherapy. When used with medication, psychotherapy has been shown to help patients more than medicines alone.

FIGURE 15.5
Psychotherapy gives patients a chance to discuss their problems and helps the therapist evaluate the patients' progress. What are four benefits of psychotherapy?

Language Arts Link

Mental Health and Social Services Career Paths

Mental health is all about how we think, feel, and interact with others as we manage the pressures of daily life. Everyone experiences some stress, sadness, or anxiety from time to time, but for a person with mental illness, these feelings do not go away.

Health care professionals help people with mental illnesses. There are many types of health care professionals including psychiatrists, psychologists, social workers, and counselors.

Working with a partner, research various mental-health careers. Using the Internet or a library, research the educational and skills needs to go into these areas of study. If you are able to speak with professionals in these fields, interview them about how they become interested in this subject, what the requirements were, and what their job responsibilities are.

After you've completed your research, create a document with several paragraphs on each career that you learned about. Be sure to proofread your work to see if you can improve it by making it clearer, more concise, or more interesting to read. Check the spelling and grammar and correct any errors.

Hospitalization

For very severe mental illnesses, patients may require constant care. As a result, they will be placed in a facility that specializes in the treatment of mental illnesses. In some cases, people only need a short hospitalization period and may never need to go back. In the most severe cases, some people cannot recover enough from their mental illness to leave a hospital.

Hospitalization for Drug Abuse

Hospitalization is often a treatment for drug abuse. Drug addiction creates a physical and psychological dependence on a drug. When a person stops taking the drug, he or she will experience **withdrawal**. The symptoms of withdrawal are often painful and uncomfortable and may even cause death. As a result, a drug addict should be monitored by medical professionals as he or she goes through withdrawal.

withdrawal
(with DRAW uhl)
Uncomfortable physical and psychological symptoms that arise when a drug addict stops using a drug.

 ## Treating Alzheimer's Disease

Unlike most other mental illnesses, the effects of Alzheimer's disease cannot be reversed. If caught early, the disease can be treated with medications that slow the progress of the disease. However, the symptoms will continue to worsen. In addition to memory problems, the patient will experience depression and anger. A patient may eventually forget basic skills, such as hygiene and the ability to read.

Eventually, an Alzheimer's patient will need fulltime care. He or she will need home care or will need to be placed in a care facility. As a health care worker, you may need to take care of the patient's basic needs, such as dressing, bathing, brushing teeth, or shaving. The procedures in Chapter 18: Measuring Vital Signs and Other Clinical Skills will help you understand these processes.

Many of the treatments for Alzheimer's disease are designed to stimulate the memory and to keep a patient engaged with the people around him or her. Activities, art therapy, and music therapy have been used to reinforce memories. Procedures 15.1, 15.2, and 15.3 describe these therapies.

Care for Alzheimer's patients requires a great deal of patience. On some days, a patient may seem completely normal. On other days, the patient will have difficulty remembering even simple things. As a member of the health care team, you will need to use listening skills and communication skills to help the patient deal with his or her day-to-day needs.

Career Connection

Research mental health professionals who have been in the news lately for evaluating or treating famous personalities. What is their training and background? Do they have a specialty?

PROCEDURE 15.1 Activities with Alzheimer's Patients

BACKGROUND: For people who have Alzheimer's disease, activities help structure the time. Activities also improve a patient's self-esteem.

ALERT: Follow Standard Precautions (see Section 17.2).

PREPROCEDURE

1. Wash hands.

2. Identify the patient and the activity in which he or she will be participating. Pay attention to:

   a. the patient's skills and abilities

   b. what the patient enjoys

   c. physical problems

   d. the physician's recommendations

3. Gather equipment for the activity (if needed).

4. Break the activity into small, measurable steps.

PROCEDURE

5. Greet the patient, and tell him or her what you are going to do today.

6. Help the patient get started with the activity.

7. Explain each step of the activity using simple terms. It may be necessary to repeat the explanation or to clarify in terms the patient understands.

8. Help the patient through difficult steps or if he or she appears frustrated. As much as possible, let the patient do most of the activity on his or her own.

9. Do not criticize or correct the patient.

POSTPROCEDURE

10. Put away equipment.

11. Wash hands.

12. Record the patient's response to the activity.

PROCEDURE 15.2 Music Therapy

BACKGROUND: Music helps Alzheimer's patients recall memories and emotions.

ALERT: Follow Standard Precautions (see Section 17.2).

PREPROCEDURE

1. Identify the patient.

2. Identify the type of music that the patient enjoys.

3. Provide a comfortable space in which the patient can listen to the music.

4. Gather and set up equipment. Choose music, something to play it on, pictures that mean something to the patient to help them recall memories.

5. Block other sources of sound. Close windows and doors, turn off televisions and other radios, and reduce background noise as much as possible.

PROCEDURE

6. Start the music.

7. Encourage the patient to clap or sing along with the music. When appropriate, encourage the patient to dance or move with the music.

8. While playing the music, show the patient pictures to help with memories.

POSTPROCEDURE

9. Put away equipment.

10. Record the patient's response to the activity.

PROCEDURE 15.3 Art Therapy

BACKGROUND: Like music, art can help an Alzheimer's patient reconnect with the world around him or her. Art provides a way for the patient to express himself or herself.

ALERT: Follow Standard Precautions (see Section 17.2).

PREPROCEDURE

1. Identify the patient.

2. Assemble materials. Avoid potentially harmful materials, such as sharp blades and tools. Materials may include the following:

   a. nontoxic acrylic paints or watercolor paints

   b. brushes and canvases or watercolor paper

   c. clay

3. Prepare a work area for the patient. Neatly arrange materials and cover surfaces to protect them from spillage.

PROCEDURE

4. Help the patient start the project.

5. Encourage the patient to talk about what he or she is doing. Ask the patient to remember events related to the project or to tell a story about the project.

6. Help the patient through difficult steps or if he or she appears frustrated. As much as possible, let the patient do most of the project on his or her own.

7. Do not criticize or correct the patient.

8. When the patient is finished with the project, help him or her clean up.

POSTPROCEDURE

9. Put away equipment.

10. Clean work space.

11. Record the patient's response to the activity.

Summary

Mental illness is treated with a combination of medication and psychotherapy. Medication will treat symptoms of mental illness, but uncomfortable side effects may cause some patients to stop taking their medicine. Psychotherapy gives patients a chance to talk about and understand their illness. In extreme cases, mental illness patients will be hospitalized. Unlike other most other mental illnesses, at this time, Alzheimer's disease cannot be cured. Eventually, an Alzheimer's patient may need home care or hospitalization.

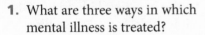

SECTION 15.2 Review Questions

1. What are three ways in which mental illness is treated?

2. What might happen if mental illness is not treated?

3. Define *psychotherapy*.

4. What are four benefits of psychotherapy?

5. Why do drug abuse patients need to be hospitalized during treatment?

6. How is Alzheimer's disease different from most other mental illnesses?

Learn By Doing: Section 15.2 Activity

1. Complete Worksheet 1.

2. Complete Worksheet/Activity 2 as assigned.

3. Prepare responses to reach item listed in Chapter Review.

4. When you are confident that you can meet each objective for this section, ask your teacher for the section evaluation.

What's New?

New Alzheimer's Disease Therapies

Once people develop Alzheimer's disease, the disease cannot be cured. Most of the drugs currently used to treat Alzheimer's slow the course of the disease, but they do not stop it.

According to the Mayo Clinic, the focus of future Alzheimer's treatments will be on preventing it in people who have a risk for the disease, but do not yet have it. Risk factors include age and genetics. Approximately 5 percent of Americans between the ages of 65 to 74, and almost half of those 85 years and older suffer from Alzheimer's disease. And, early-onset Alzheimer's has been clearly shown to be genetic in origin.

While mutations on chromosomes 9 and 19 have been linked with late-onset Alzheimer's (the most common form), not everyone with the mutations develops the disease. The relationship between genetics and late-onset Alzheimer's is not fully known.

Other possible factors *may* include prior traumatic head injury, lower education level, and female gender. Scientists are working on the following preventive measures:

■ Alzheimer's vaccine: A vaccine was developed and tested, but it caused dangerous side effects. Scientists continue to look for a vaccine that won't cause these side effects.

■ Secretase inhibitors: Secretase is an enzyme, or protein, that causes the formation of plaques in the brain. These plaques have been thought to be the cause of Alzheimer's disease. Secretase inhibitors will prevent the formation of secretase and, thus, plaques. Unfortunately, the inhibitors are large molecules that do not easily pass from the blood to the brain. Scientists are working to fix this problem. In addition, new research is indicating that the role of plaques is more complex than originally thought, which is prompting other ideas in the hunt for a drug treatment for Alzheimer's disease.

■ Cardiovascular therapies: The term *cardiovascular* refers to the heart and blood vessels. Cardiovascular diseases include high blood pressure and high cholesterol. These diseases often result from poor eating habits and lack of exercise. In some people, genetics plays a role in high blood pressure and high cholesterol. Some evidence indicates that controlling these diseases may also reduce the risk of Alzheimer's disease.

■ Anti-inflammatory drugs: Some drugs, such as ibuprofen, may reduce the risk of Alzheimer's disease. However, these drugs have caused stomach and intestinal problems.

For which of the above potential therapies might it be possible to use a treatment that does not involve drugs?

Chapter Review Questions

1. Which type of mental illness includes panic attacks and phobias? (15.1)

2. What is a focus of treatment for Alzheimer's disease? (15.1)

3. How does Alzheimer's disease cause memory problems? (15.1)

4. Compare anorexia nervosa and bulimia nervosa. (15.1)

5. _____ is a mental illness in which sufferers may hear voices that other people cannot hear. (15.1)

6. What are the three groups into which people who have ADHD may be classified? (15.1)

7. Obsessive-compulsive disorder is a mental illness characterized by _____ and _____

8. Why might some people stop taking medications for mental illness? (15.2)

9. Why might people who have a mental illness be hospitalized? (15.2)

10. A(n) _____ can prescribe medications when providing psychotherapy. (15.2)

Activities

1. Write a public service announcement about mental illness. Your public service announcement should inform people about the frequency of mental illness and how it is treated. It should also make people aware of the risks of avoiding treatment. Perform your public service announcement for the class.

2. Create a table that compiles mental health statistics for people in the United States. Your table should provide information about the illnesses discussed in the chapter. Use the table below as a sample upon which you can base your table.

Mental Illness	Percentage of Americans Affected	Suggested Treatments

Case Studies

1. Mr. Gomez seems to be forgetting things lately. He couldn't find his car keys and had trouble remembering his neighbor's name. His family thinks Mr. Gomez forgets things because of his age. Why should they be concerned? Should Mr. Gomez seek medical help? Why or why not? What might eventually happen to Mr. Gomez?

2. Sheila noticed lately that her friend Nan has stopped coming to social events. When she goes to Nan's house, Nan doesn't want to leave her bedroom and she seems sad. Additionally, Sheila noticed that Nan isn't eating much during lunch, and Nan told her that she hasn't been sleeping well. Based on this information, which mental illness might Nan have? What are some other symptoms of this illness? What kind of help does Nan need?

Chapter 15 Review

Thinking Critically

1. **Legal and Ethical**—As a health care provider, you will be asked to protect the privacy of your patients. Why is this especially important for people who suffer from mental illnesses?

2. **Cause and Effect**—Emanuel's mother has been treated for depression in the past. She received medication and psychotherapy. She responded well to the treatment and currently doesn't have any symptoms of depression. How might her mother's depression affect Emanuel's mental health?

3. **Identifying Relationships**—Art and music therapy are used to treat Alzheimer's patients. These activities often involve creativity and interaction. Describe how these activities likely benefit patients.

Media Connection

Use the Companion Web site or additional interactive learning activities: www.prenhall.com/badasch

Portfolio Connection

Volunteer with an organization that helps people who have mental illnesses. For example, some organizations will visit nursing homes to work with people who have Alzheimer's disease. Other organizations work with children who have ADHD or other behavioral disorders.

Keep a journal as you work with the organization. Describe the activities that you participate in. Ask the medical professionals with whom you work to identify how the activity helps the patient. Record your observations about the patient's response to the activity. (Note: Protect the patient's privacy by not using the patient's name in your journal.) Once you have finished your journal, write a short essay discussing how your thoughts about the care process and how the care benefits the patient.

PORTFOLIO TIP

Record keeping is one of the most important steps of patient care. Records must be accurate and private. When recording your observations, avoid adding personal comments that won't help a medical professional treat the patient. Be precise and informative, and avoid including judgmental statements or opinions.

16 | Nutrition

Getting Started

Health care workers must be healthy workers. It is well documented that those with good health habits miss fewer work days, are able to meet the required schedule more efficiently, and maintain a more rigorous work ethic. Eating right is a major factor in reaching and maintaining good health.

Keep a journal for one week of everything you eat. Analyze the strengths and weaknesses of your dietary habits, including potential diseases/disorders that might result from eating habits.

Keep a journal for the second week, eating a well-balanced diet; add a little exercise and then calculate your body mass index (BMI) chart to see if you are in the normal range (see What's New on p. 476). If you are not in the normal range, continue your well-balanced nutrition to maintain a healthy BMI, making a well-balanced diet part of your health habits.

Basic Nutrition

Background

vitality
(vahy TAL i tee)
The ability of an organism to go on living.

Health care workers must maintain good health in order to be efficient in their work. When you eat the proper foods, you have the energy and **vitality** to function effectively. Patients need a healthy diet to maintain or restore good health. Knowledge of nutrition helps you understand how to maintain good health for yourself and your patients/clients.

Objectives

When you have completed this section, you will be able to do the following:

- Match key terms with their correct meanings.
- Name the four functions of food.
- Name the five basic nutrients and explain how they maintain body function.
- Perform basic volume conversions.
- List five problems associated with obesity.
- Explain the USDA food pyramid.
- Compare your diet with the recommendations in the USDA food pyramid.

resistance
(ri ZIS tuhns)
The ability of the body to protect itself from disease.

Introduction to Basic Nutrition

Good nutrition promotes a healthier body and mind. It also aids in **resistance** to illness. When we eat a healthy diet, our energy and vitality are increased. The right foods speed the healing process and help a person feel better and sleep better.

Your patients/clients are all from different cultural and religious backgrounds. Each culture and religion has dietary differences. Appetites, food budgets, cultural food preferences, and religious restrictions influence some of these differences. You and your patients need the same basic nutrients provided by a balanced, healthy diet. The health care worker must understand about foods and their effect on the body in order to assess his or her own diet and the patient's diet.

The Function of Food

When food is taken into the body, it is used in many different ways. The right combination of nutrients work together in the body to:

- Provide heat.
- Promote growth.
- Repair tissue.
- **Regulate** body processes.

Basic Nutrients

Nutrients are chemical compounds found in food. When the food we eat enters the digestive tract, it is changed into a simple form and absorbed into the blood. The blood carries these nutrients to body cells, where they are used to maintain body functions. Table 16.1 lists the essential nutrients.

Water is **essential** to the body. Found in all body tissues, water makes up most of blood plasma. It carries nutrients to the body cells and carries waste products away from the body cells. It also lubricates the joints and helps regulate body temperature and body processes. The average person should drink 6–8 glasses of water daily.

Fiber

Fiber adds bulk to the diet and helps prevent bowel and colon diseases. **Cellulose** is often referred to as dietary fiber or roughage. It is not digestible by humans and acts as a bulking agent by absorbing water; this helps to prevent constipation.

The diet many people eat is high in protein, fats, and carbohydrates but very low in fiber. To keep the bowel healthy, a person should eat several servings of fiber each day. Fiber is found in greens, kale, cabbage, celery, vegetable salads, raw and cooked fruits, whole-grain food, and cereals.

Good nutrition enhances your appearance and increases your stamina. It is important to plan meals and snacks that include all of the basic nutrients each day. Poor nutrition can lead to **malnutrition**.

Calories

Food is the source of energy for our bodies. The body **metabolizes** food nutrients to create energy. As the body creates energy, it produces heat. Energy ensures that all of the body systems function. The amount of energy created by the food we eat is measured in **calories**. Calorie needs vary from person to person. A large, active person needs more calories than a smaller, inactive person does.

Basal metabolic rate (BMR) is the amount of energy, or calories, your body uses when it is at rest in a neutral environment. BMR is usually calculated after 12 hours of fasting so that the body is not even using energy to digest food. The temperature is set so that the environment is not hot or cold enough for the body to have to try and stay cool or warm.

regulate
(REG yuh leyt)
To control or adjust.

essential
(uh SEN shuhl)
Necessary (e.g., certain food elements are necessary for the body's functions).

cellulose
(SEL yo loz)
The primary component of plant cell walls which provides the fiber and bulk necessary for optimal functioning of the digestive tract.

malnutrition
(mal noo TRISH un)
Poor nutrition caused by an insufficient or poorly balanced diet or by a medical condition.

metabolize
(mi TAB e liz)
To break down substances in cells to obtain energy.

calorie
(KAL uh ree)
Unit of measurement of the fuel value of food.

protein

(PROH teen)
Complex compound found in plant and animal tissues, essential for heat, energy, and growth.

amino acids

(ah MEE no a sid)
Any of a large number of compounds found in living cells that contain carbon, oxygen, hydrogen, and nitrogen, and join together to form proteins.

Complementary Proteins

Complete proteins are found in animal and soy products; other plant-based sources of protein are incomplete. Many vegetarians combine foods containing complementary with incomplete proteins. For example, combining rice (which is limited in lysine) with red beans (which are high in lysine but deficient in tryptophan) results in a complete protein.

For more on complementary proteins, go to the Companion Web site at www.prenhall.com/badasch.

The number of calories we eat and the amount of exercise we do balance weight. If we eat more calories than we burn, we gain weight. If we burn more calories than we eat, we lose weight. The FDA food labeling standard adopts the Recommended Daily Allowances (RDAs) from the average USDA 2,000 calorie dietary guidelines.

When a patient is inactive and feels ill, she may not want to eat. It is your responsibility to encourage her to take in enough calories to produce the energy needed to heal the body.

Table 16.1 Essential Nutrients

Nutrient	What It Does
Proteins	<ul><li>Build and renew body tissues.</li><li>Provide heat energy.</li><li>Help produce antibodies.</li><li>Formed by organic compounds called **amino acids**.</li><li>Made up of 22 amino acids: 9 are essential, which means the body can not produce these amino acids and they must be supplemented through the diet. They are found in almost all animal sources.</li><li>Main sources/complete proteins: meat, fish, milk, cheese, and eggs.</li><li>Incomplete proteins: cereal/soybeans, dry beans, peas, and peanuts.</li><li>Complementary incomplete proteins can be combined to form complete proteins.</li><li>1 gram of protein = 4 calories</li></ul>
Carbohydrates	<ul><li>Provide the basic source of energy for body heat and body activities.</li><li>Starches or sugars.</li><li>Main sources: bread, cereal, pasta, crackers, potatoes, corn, peas, fruits, sugars, and syrups.</li><li>1 gram of carbohydrates = 4 calories</li><li>Simple carbohydrates are molecules made when one or two smaller sugar molecules (called saccharides) combine: found in raw and cooked fruits, some cooked vegetables, and refined sugar and its products (soda pop or candy).</li><li>Complex carbohydrates are long chains of glucose molecules bonded together. The chains may be straight, but usually branch and connect more than one chain together: found in grains, grain products (like bread or pasta), legumes, and some cooked vegetables and fruits.</li><li>Complex carbohydrates absorb slowly and provide a steady supply of energy; simple carbohydrates absorb so quickly, they are usually converted to fat.</li></ul>
Fats	<ul><li>Provide fatty acids for normal growth and development.</li><li>Provide energy.</li><li>Carry vitamins A and D to the cells.</li><li>Help maintain body temperature by providing insulation; helps cushion organs and bones; provides flavor to foods.</li><li>Essential component of every cell membrane.</li><li>Main sources: butter, margarine, oils, creams, fatty meats, cheeses, and egg yolk.</li><li>Classified as saturated (solid at room temperature) or polyunsaturated (liquid at room temperature).</li><li>Sometimes called **lipids**.</li><li>1 gram of lipid = 9 calories</li></ul>

(continued)

Table 16.1 Essential Nutrients (continued)

Nutrient	What It Does
Minerals	■ Regulate the activity of the heart, nerves, and muscles. ■ Build and renew teeth, bones, and other tissues. ■ Inorganic (nonliving) elements found in all body tissue. ■ More than 1/3 of the dietary nutrients needed each day are minerals. ■ Major dietary minerals: calcium, chloride, magnesium, phosphorus, potassium, sodium, sulfur. ■ Trace dietary minerals: chromium, copper, fluoride, iodine, iron, manganese, molybdenum, selenium, zinc. ■ See Figure 16.1.

Vitamins	■ Essential for normal metabolism, growth, and body development.
	■ Inorganic (non-living) elements found in all body tissues.
	■ Regulate body functions:
	  ● Metabolism; help release energy from other nutrients
	  ● Vital role in almost every chemical reaction within the body
	  ● Co-enzyme for normal health/growth (some behave like hormones)
	■ Only a small amount required—a well balanced diet provides required vitamins.
	■ Excess or deficiency can cause poor health.
	■ Water soluble or fat soluble (A, D, E, K).
	■ See Figure 16.2.

Water	■ All cells in the body must be bathed in water. ■ Water is active in most chemical reactions and is needed to carry other nutrients, to regulate body temperature, and to help eliminate wastes. Water makes up about 60% of an adult's body weight. ■ Lost through evaporation, urination, and respiration so it must be replaced every day. ■ Remove toxins and wastes from your body. ■ Dehydration, or under-hydration, is when the body loses more water than it takes in; may occur during hot weather when there is profuse sweating or as a result of prolonged exertion; older people may not recognize that they are becoming dehydrated because of their bodies not registering thirst, though thirst isn't the only sign. ■ Over-hydration is when the body takes in more water than it loses; may occur in people whose kidneys do not excrete urine normally or in athletes who drink more water than they need when trying to avoid dehydration.

Calcium

Milk and milk products, except butter; most dark green vegetables; canned salmon.

Iron

Eggs, meat, especially liver and kidney; deep yellow and dark green vegetables; potatoes, dried fruits, whole-grain products; enriched flour, bread, and breakfast cereals.

Iodine

Fish (obtained from the sea), some plant foods grown in soils containing iodine; table salt fortified with iodine (iodized).

lipids
(LIP id z)
Any of a group of organic compounds, including the fats, oils, triglycerides, etc. that—together with carbohydrates and proteins—constitute the principal structural material of living cells.

minerals
(MIN er uhl s)
Inorganic elements that occur in nature; essential to every cell.

vitamins
(VAHY tuh min s)
Group of substances necessary for normal functioning and maintenance of health.

Too Much or Too Little?

A *deficiency* is a disease caused by lack of a nutrient; *toxicity* is a disease caused by too much of a nutrient. There is a range between the two that is optimal for most humans. Vitamin intake, for instance, should fall within a range that assists the body in achieving optimal good health. There are Recommended Dietary Allowances (RDAs) for each nutrient to help you prevent diseases associated with getting too much or too little of a specific vitamin or nutrient.

For more on RDAs and diseases associated with getting too much or too little of nutrients, go to the Companion Web site at www.prenhall.com/ badasch.

FIGURE 16.1
Minerals are calcium, iron, and iodine. What are good dietary sources for calcium?

FIGURE 16.2

Vitamins include A, B complex, B1, B2, B12, C, D, and niacin. Why are vitamins an important part of our diet?

A

One form of vitamin A is yellow and one form is colorless. Apricots, cantaloupe, milk, cheese, eggs, meat organs (especially liver and kidney), fortified margarine, butter, fish-liver oils, dark green and deep yellow vegetables.

B Complex
B₁ (Thiamine)

Whole-grain and enriched grain products; meats (especially pork, liver, and kidney); dry beans and peas.

B₂ (Riboflavin)

Milk, cheese, eggs, meat (especially liver and kidney), whole-grain and enriched grain products, dark green vegetables.

B₁₂

Liver, other organ meats, cheese, eggs, milk.

C (Ascorbic Acid)

Fresh, raw citrus fruits and vegetables—oranges, grapefruit, cantaloupe, strawberries, tomatoes, raw onions, cabbage, green and sweet red peppers, dark green vegetables.

D

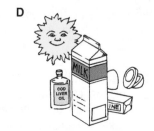

Provided by vitamin D fortification of certain foods, such as milk and margarine. Also fish-liver oils and eggs. Sunshine is also a source of vitamin D.

Niacin

Liver, meat, fish, poultry, eggs, peanuts; dark green vegetables, whole-grain and enriched cereal products.

digestion
(di JES chuh n)
The process of making food absorbable by dissolving it and breaking it down into simpler chemical compounds that occur in the living body chiefly through the action of enzymes secreted into the alimentary canal.

cholesterol
(kuh LES tuh rawl)
A type of lipid, or fat, found in the body; produced by the liver or eaten in food.

absorption
(ab SAWRP shuh)
To take up liquid or other matter.

excreted
(ik SKREE ted)
When waste matter is discharged from the blood, tissues, or organs.

Digestion and Absorption

Digestion is a complex process of turning the food we eat into the energy that we need to survive. Digestion begins before you even put food your mouth. Saliva forms in your mouth when you smell, see or think of food. Saliva helps to break down the chemicals, specifically carbohydrates, in food.

The tongue pushes food to the esophagus, which then carries the food to the stomach. The stomach acts as a mixer by grinding the food into smaller pieces and breaking down proteins which then go into the small intestine.

Cholesterol is often thought of only as a factor in heart disease. However, cholesterol is a component in digestion. It is a lipid made by the liver and, in addition to being involved in digestion, cholesterol is part of the transport process for nutrients. The job of the small intestine is to break the food down even more, so that our body can absorb all the vitamins, minerals, proteins, carbohydrates, and fats. This is the process of **absorption**. Although most nutrients are absorbed by the body, there is waste left. The waste travels through the colon, where any excess water is absorbed, and the waste becomes solid. The solid waste, stool, then is **excreted** from the body.

Our body gets the energy it needs from food through a process called **metabolism**. Metabolism is a constant process that occurs from the beginning of life to the end of life.

Estimated Energy Requirement (EER)

The EER is the average dietary energy intake that is predicted to maintain energy balance in a healthy adult. In other words, if the individual is currently a healthy weight, this amount of intake will cause him or her to maintain that healthy weight. EER deals with overall calorie intake; it does not specify which nutrients should comprise that total. The overall number of calories a person needs depends on their age, gender, weight, height, and physical activity level and health status. For many generic dietary calculations, such as the percentages of RDA met by a particular food as noted on the nutrition label, 2,000 calories is the usual "assumed" amount. However, in actual practice, this varies greatly from person to person.

The Food Pyramid

Good nutrition and a healthy diet help maintain good health. The U.S. Department of Agriculture (USDA) has provided the food pyramid (**Figure 16.3**) as a guideline. The "eating right" pyramid focuses on low-fat foods, such as grains, pasta, vegetables, fruits, nonfat dairy products, and lean meats.

The pyramid illustrates the recommended daily portions of each food group. Follow these guidelines for yourself and your patients/clients. The food choices of all cultures fit into these guidelines when you plan carefully.

metabolism
(mi TAH buh lih zum)
Collection of chemical reactions that takes place in the body's cells to convert the fuel in the food we eat into the energy needed to power everything we do.

Apply It

Factors that take into account a person's energy intake, energy expenditure, age, gender, weight, height, and physical activity level (PAL) are used to calculate EER. Research online for the information and equations appropriate for your personal factors, and compute your EER. In groups of 3–5, discuss your EER findings and whether you need to adjust your activity levels.

Activity
Activity is represented by the steps and the person climbing them, as a reminder of the importance of daily physical activity.

Moderation
Moderation is represented by the narrowing of each food group from bottom to top. The wider base stands for foods with little or no solid fats or added sugars. These should be selected more often. The narrower top area stands for foods containing more added sugars and solid fats. The more active you are, the more of these foods you can fit into your diet.

Personalization
Personalization is shown by the person on the steps, the slogan, and the URL. Find the kinds and amounts of food to eat each day at MyPyramid.gov.

Proportionality
Proportionality is shown by the different widths of the food group bands. The widths suggest how much food a person should choose from each group. The widths are just a general guide, not exact proportions. Check the website for how much is right for you.

Variety
Variety is symbolized by the 6 color bands representing the 5 food groups of the Pyramid and oils. This illustrates that foods from all groups are needed each day for good health.

Gradual Improvement
Gradual improvement is encouraged by the slogan. It suggests that individuals can benefit from taking small steps to improve their diet and lifestyle each day.

USDA U.S. Department of Agriculture Center for Nutrition Policy and Promotion April 2005 CNPP-16

USDA is an equal opportunity provider and employer.

GRAINS   VEGETABLES   FRUITS   OILS   MILK   MEAT & BEANS

FIGURE 16.3
The "eating right"
pyramid. What does the figure symbolize on the new MyPyramid?

The Department of Health and Humans Services (HHS) and the Department of Agriculture (USDA) jointly publish the Dietary Guidelines for Americans every five years. According to The Dietary Guidelines for Americans, 2005, a healthy diet emphasizes fruits, vegetables, whole grains, and fat-free or low-fat milk and milk products. It also includes lean meats, poultry, fish, beans, eggs, and nuts, and is low in saturated fats, and trans fats.

NOTE: Saturated fats are fats from animal products—a fat in which the carbon atoms are fully hydrogenated. A diet heavy in saturated fat is thought to raise cholesterol in the bloodstream. Trans fats are a specific type of fat formed when liquid fats are made into solid fats by the addition of hydrogen atoms, a process known as hydrogenation. They increase bad cholesterol and decrease good cholesterol.

What's New?

Food Pyramids

The U.S. government has been issuing dietary recommendations for more than 100 years. In 1992, the U.S. Department of Agriculture (USDA) released a nutrition guide known as the American food pyramid. This illustration suggested how much of each food category a person should eat each day.

Many nutritional experts, however, complained that the 1992 pyramid was not accurate based on the latest nutrition research. They believed it was heavy on beef and dairy and did not put enough emphasis on fruit and vegetables. For example, the food pyramid allowed some dietary choices that had been linked to heart disease, such as three cups of whole milk and an eight-ounce serving of hamburger every day.

In addition, the pyramid lumped all members of the protein-rich group ("Meat, Poultry, Fish, Dry Beans, Eggs, and Nuts") together and made no distinction between whole grains and refined products. Many people complained that the USDA was influenced by corporate interests such as the dairy, meat, and sugar industries and allowed lobbyists to change the wording.

As a result, in 2005, the USDA released a new nutritional guide known as MyPyramid. There were no foods pictured on the new MyPyramid image and no text. Instead, the new logo emphasized the importance of physical activity by showing a sort of stick figure climbing the stairs of the pyramid. MyPyramid was designed to be simple; colored vertical bands represent different food groups.

Six bands of color run from the top of MyPyramid to the base: orange for grains, green for vegetables, red for fruits, a teeny band of yellow for oils, blue for milk, and purple for meat and beans. Each stripe starts out as the same size, but doesn't end that way at the base. The widths suggest how much food a person should choose from each group.

MyPyramid does not recommend serving size. These amounts differ according to a person's age, weight, gender, and activity level. The MyPyramid Web site provides information to personalize daily food intake and exercise plans. You can access information about MyPyramid at http://www.mypyramid.gov/.

The Harvard School of Public Health has their own "Healthy Eating" pyramid as an alternative to the USDA's suggestions. Harvard's food pyramid includes calcium and multi-vitamin supplements as well as moderate amounts of alcohol. You can access Harvard's pyramid at http://www.hsph.harvard.edu/nutritionsource/pyramids.html.

Harvard's nutrition guide is not the only alternative to the USDA's MyPyramid. There are also special nutrition guides/pyramids based on Asian, Latin, Mediterranean, and vegetarian diets.

Why do you think the meat, dairy, and sugar industries would care about the USDA food pyramid?

π Math Link

Liquid Conversions

Even after the United States became independent, the people continued to use the English system of measurement. This system had grown naturally for hundreds of years. People used familiar objects and parts of the body, such as "feet," as measuring devices. They measured liquid volume with common household items such as tea spoons, cups, and pails (the word "gallon" comes from an old name for a pail). Although this system could be quite confusing, it is still used in the United States today.

The metric system was developed in France during the French Revolution in the 1790s. The metric system has several advantages over the English system. The metric system was based on a decimal system, which made it much easier to do calculations. The scientific community adopted the metric system almost from its inception. It came to be used by most other nations of the world.

The dual systems create problems for Americans. Liquid measurement seems to be an incomprehensible whirl of drams, milliliters, cups, and tablespoons. The situation is not helped by the fact that one cubic centimeter (cc) equals one milliliter (ml); they are the same. Here's a conversion chart to help you out on the trickier volume conversions:

> one teaspoon = 5 cc = 5 ml
>
> one tablespoon (tbl) = three teaspoons
>
> one tablespoon = 15 cc = 15 ml
>
> one fluid ounce (U.S. liquid) = 30 cc = 30 ml = 2 tablespoons = 6 teaspoons
>
> one cup = eight fluid ounces = 16 tablespoons
>
> one pint = 2 cups = 16 fluid ounces

Actually, one teaspoon equals 4.928921594 milliliters, but the chart has rounded it off to make things easier. Similarly, one fluid ounce (U.S.) equals 29.573529562 milliliters. Believe it or not, it actually makes a difference. At some point, "rounding off" errors would become serious. However, for the problems below, you can use the easier equivalents.

What is the volume in cc of 500 ml?

The answer is 500 ml—they are equivalent amounts.

There are two bottles of electrolyte supplement on the shelf at the pharmacy. One contains 9.5 oz and the other has 300 cc. Which has the larger volume?

1 fl. oz = 30 cc

9.5 fl. oz = 285 cc

The 300 cc bottle contains more liquid than the 9.5 oz. bottle.

Example 1

Billy must drink 2,250 cc of water each day. How many pints of water will he drink? Round to the nearest tenth of a pint.

1 pint = 16 oz.

1 oz = 30 cc

16 oz × 30 cc = 480 cc

2,250 cc divided by 480 cc = 4.688 pints

4.7 pints

Example 2

Convert 55 tbsp into an equal volume of cups. Round to the nearest tenth of a cup.

1 cup = 6 tbs

55 divided by 6 = 9.167 cups

9.2 cups

1. A dose of a specific medicine is 1 tbs. How many doses does an 8 oz bottle contain?

2. A bottle of juice contains 2 liters. If 1 liter equals 33.8 fl. oz, how many cc of juice are there in the 2-liter bottle?

3. The humidifier for the nursing station holds 14 pints of water.

   a. How many ounces will completely fill the reservoir?

   b. How many 8-oz bottles will be needed to fill the reservoir?

4. U.S. fluid ounces and British fluid ounces are not the same volume. One British fluid ounce equals only 28.41 milliliters. Why is this evidence that the metric system is easier to use than the English system of measurement?

Apply It

Form nutrition teams of five or six students. Create a profile of a person, including how tall he or she is, weight, activity level, and so forth. Use MyPyramid to plan a day's menus, including meals, snacks, and beverages, for the person you profiled. Before planning, you may find it helpful to calculate the person's BMI, their daily calorie needs and/or their EER. Be sure to consult nutrition labels for information about the nutrients found in the foods you are including in the menus. When the day's menus are complete, present them to the class.

hemoglobin
(HEE muh gloh bin)
Complex chemical in the blood; carries oxygen and carbon dioxide.

bingeing
(binj ing)
Eating excessively.

purging
(perg ing)
Causing oneself to vomit.

obesity
(oh BEE sih tee)
Extreme fatness; abnormal amount of fat on the body.

Community Service

Help a food distribution agency such as Meals on Wheels or the Salvation Army or another group plan and serve a well-balanced nutritious menu for one day.

A nutrition label provides information about how much, and what type of, fats you are eating in a food. Nutrition labels also alert you to how much cholesterol is in foods. *For more on your body and cholesterol and saturated and unsaturated fats, go to the Companion Web site at www.prenhall.com/www.prenhall.com/badasch.*

Good food habits are learned and should be taught to children. To ensure children have good food habits:

- Give children enough time at the table, don't rush the meal.
- Be a good role model and practice what you preach.
- Don't reward, punish, or appease children with food so you can avoid food problems later on in life.

How Poor Nutrition Affects the Body

When we do not supply our bodies with the proper nutrients, many things can go wrong. We lose stamina and vitality. An unhealthy diet often results in illness and disease. Not having the proper nutrients for good health may come from either excessive or inadequate intake of essential nutrients. The following are a few of the problems that poor nutrition can cause:

- *Anemia*, a decreased number of red blood cells or a decreased amount of **hemoglobin**, results in:
  - Fatigue.
  - Paleness.
  - Rapid heartbeat.
  - Dyspnea (shortness of breath) on exertion.
  - Headache.
  - Indigestion.
  - Insomnia (inability to sleep).

- *Anorexia nervosa* occurs when a person refuses to eat or drastically reduces his or her intake of food. This is related to an emotional disturbance about image (e.g., a person who is very underweight sees herself or himself as overweight). Anorexia nervosa is seen primarily in teenage girls. It results in:
  - Amenorrhea.
  - Skeletonlike appearance.
  - Loose teeth and hair.
  - Muscle spasms.

- *Bulimia* occurs when a person experiences intervals of food craving and **bingeing** and then **purging**. The side effects are the same as those of anorexia and result in depression.

- *Constipation* is infrequent, difficult defecation. It is commonly caused by lack of activity and by not eating enough vegetables, fruit, or water.

- *Dull hair and eyes* are symptoms of poor diet.

- *Mental slowdown* can occur when nutrition is poor.

- **Obesity** occurs when a person takes in more calories than the body uses. This results in increasing amounts of fatty tissue.

- *Osteoporosis* occurs when bones become porous, causing them to break easily. This is caused by inadequate calcium intake or absorption.

- *Rickets* is a softening of the bones in children, potentially leading to fractures and deformity. This occurs from a lack of vitamin D.

- *Dehydration* occurs when more water is lost than taken in. This can be caused by not drinking enough liquids, diarrhea, vomiting, excessive sweating, and some diseases such as diabetes.

- *Poor skin condition* results from poor nutrition.

Malnutrition in the Elderly Population

Due to a variety of factors malnutrition is prominent among the elderly population. As people age they experience sensory loss, especially in taste and smell leading to decreased appetite. Poor dentition also may put the patient at risk because the patient will select foods high in carbohydrates and sugars which are easier to chew.

Another factor can be an alteration in functional status which prevents the patient from obtaining food (grocery shopping) or preparing food (cooking). These patients will require assistance in obtaining and preparing food. They may benefit from the home delivery of prepared meals or the purchase of pre-packaged meals which can be easily prepared in a microwave.

The presence of disease in the elderly can affect their dietary intake. In many cases liberalization of diet is called for in order to achieve adequate nutritional intake.

Personal Wellness

Obesity in the U.S.

Americans, especially young people, are getting fatter. In the past 25 years, there has been a dramatic increase in obesity in the United States. In 1980, 25 percent of adults in the United States were overweight. By 1991, this figure had risen to 33 percent. In 2001, about two-thirds of the adult population, more than 120 million people, was classified as overweight.

In a way, the numbers are even bleaker for children. The number of overweight children between the ages of 6 and 19 tripled between 1980 and 2004. An estimated 9 million children over the age of six (about 15 percent) are currently obese. About four out of every five of these obese children will remain overweight into adulthood.

So what is so bad about being overweight? The answer is quite simple. Overweight and obese people have an increased risk for many diseases and health conditions such as the following:

- Hypertension (high blood pressure)
- Coronary heart disease
- Gallbladder disease
- Some cancers (endometrial, breast, and colon)
- Osteoarthritis (a degeneration of cartilage and its underlying bone within a joint)
- Diabetes
- Stroke
- Sleep apnea and respiratory problems

The U.S. government estimates that the cost of obesity in the United States in 2000 was more than $117 billion ($61 billion direct and $56 billion indirect). Obesity is now considered one of the major health crises affecting the United States.

The solution to the problem is simple, but instituting it is not. People have to eat less, eat smarter, and exercise more. Fatty, sugary diets have contributed to growing waistlines. Fast food and junk food are not nutritionally sound.

More than half of all Americans do not get the recommended amount of physical activity—thirty minutes daily for adults; sixty minutes daily for children. Kids spend more time staring at television and computer screens than they do in physical play; nearly one quarter of American children eight or older spend more than five hours a day watching television or playing computer/video games.

Both children and adults have to limit their time in front of the television or computer and follow the recommendations of the new food pyramid.

▣ Summary

A balanced, healthy diet is essential for maintaining health and stamina. Everyone needs certain basic nutrients in his or her diet. When you plan your daily meals using the guidelines in the "eating right" pyramid, you meet your body's nutritional needs and help maintain good health. All individuals must eat a healthy diet that provides balanced nutrients and meets cultural and religious needs.

What's New?

Body Mass Index

Looking at height and bone structure is one way of assessing appropriate body weight. Another method that is gaining wide acceptance with many health practitioners is the body mass index (BMI).

BMI is a number based on a person's weight and height that provides an indication of the percent of the body that is made up of fat. Because the percentage of body fat is a truer indication of health that weight alone, BMI is a useful diagnostic tool that can be used to determine if a person is overweight and by how much. BMI is an estimate of body fat. It may not be accurate for older people or for athletes that have a great amount of muscle. However, it closely tracks the amount of fat the normal person has.

BMI can be calculated with this formula:

$$\text{weight} \div \text{height}^2 \times 703 = \text{BMI}$$

For example, you would calculate the BMI for a person who weighs 150 pounds and is 5 feet 5 inches (65 inches total) tall like this:

$$150 \div 65^2 \times 703 = 24.96$$

Next, you find the BMI on this chart:

BMI	Weight Status
Below 18.5	Underweight
18.5–24.9	Normal
25.0–29.9	Overweight
30.0 and above	Obese

How can BMI be used to help people understand when they need to change their lifestyle?

SECTION **16.1** Review Questions

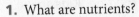

1. What are nutrients?

2. What foods are good to eat in order to get a large supply of fiber?

3. What is anorexia nervosa?

4. What are the problems associated with obesity?

5. How many teaspoons are there in two fluid ounces?

6. What is the food pyramid?

Learn By Doing: Section 16.1 Activity

1. Complete Worksheet 1.

2. Complete Worksheet/Activity 2.

3. Complete Worksheets 3 through 5 after your teacher discusses this chapter in class.

4. Complete Worksheets/Activities 6 and 7.

5. Complete Worksheet 8.

6. When you are confident that you can meet each objective for this section, ask your teacher for the section evaluation.

SECTION

16.2 | Therapeutic Diets

Background

Some patients/clients have illnesses that require special diets. Therapeutic diets are diets that modify a patient's normal diet in order to treat an illness. Understanding why the diet has been changed helps you to encourage clients to eat the food prepared for them. When you are knowledgeable about their diet, you are able to explain how important it is to their recovery.

Objectives

When you have completed this section, you will be able to do the following:

- Match key terms with their correct meaning.

- List three factors that influence food habits.

- Select a correct therapeutic diet for physical disorders.

- Discuss characteristics and treatment of common eating disorders

- List four commonly abused substances and their negative impacts on the human body.

 Introduction to Therapeutic Diets

It is especially important to remember the factors that influence food habits for patients who are on a therapeutic diet. Always respect the patient's personal attitudes and preferences, nationality, race, and religious needs.

metabolic

(met uh BOL ik)
Pertaining to the total of all the physical and chemical changes that take place in living organisms and cells.

deficient

(di FISH uhnt)
Lacking something (e.g., a deficient diet causes the body to function poorly because it is missing an important element).

gastrointestinal

(gas troh in TES tuh nuhl)
Pertaining to the stomach and intestine.

colitis

(kuh lahy tis)
Inflammation of the colon.

ileitis

(il ee AHY tis)
Inflammation of the ileum (the lower three-fifths of the small intestine).

diabetes mellitus

(dahy uh BEE teez mel uh thus)
Condition that develops when the body cannot change sugar into energy; there is an insufficient amount of insulin, leading to an increased amount of sugar in the blood.

soluble

(SOL yuh buhl)
Able to break down or dissolve in liquid.

atherosclerosis

(ath uh roh skluh ROH sis)
Condition of hardening of the arteries due to fat deposits that narrow the space blood flows through.

A therapeutic diet is often very different from the foods the patient normally eats. Your understanding of the reason for the diet and your patients' special needs helps ease their concerns. The dietitian will talk with the patient and try to adapt a therapeutic diet to meet a patient's nutritional and personal needs. An example of a special or personal need is religious restrictions.

Many religions of the world follow specific dietary laws. These guidelines are very important to clients. The stress caused by breaking the law when clients are on a therapeutic diet may cause added worry. Always be respectful of the dietary requests that your clients make, and report their requests to your supervisor. Ask your clients what diet they normally follow. If there is a problem with the diet, report it to your supervisor, who will talk with the dietitian. Table 16.2 lists a few of the restrictions that you may observe.

Purposes of Therapeutic Diets

Therapeutic diets are given to:

- Regulate the amount of food in **metabolic** disorders.
- Prevent or restrict edema by restricting sodium intake.
- Assist body organs to regain and/or maintain normal function.
- Aid in digestion by avoiding foods that irritate the digestive tract.
- Increase or decrease body weight by adding or eliminating calories.

Table 16.2 Religious Dietary Restrictions

Religion	Restriction
Christian Science	Avoid alcohol, coffee, tea.
Church of Latter-Day Saints (Mormons)	Avoid alcohol, coffee, tea.
Conservative Protestants	Avoid alcohol, coffee, tea.
Greek Orthodox	No meat or dairy products on fast days.
Muslim (Moslem)	No alcohol, pork, or pork products.
Orthodox Jewish	No shellfish, pork, or non-kosher meats. No serving milk and milk products with meat. No eating leavened bread during Passover. Abstain from eating on specific fast days.
Roman Catholic	No food one hour before communion and no meat on Ash Wednesday, Good Friday, and all the Fridays during Lent.
Buddhist	Generally vegetarian.
Hindu	Generally vegetarian.

Types of Therapeutic Diets

Table 16.3 describes the various types of therapeutic diets and their purposes.

The physician may order other diets. Always check the diet that has been ordered for the patient/client. If you have any question about it, ask the person in charge. Correct diets are essential in maintaining good health, and only those foods allowed should be served.

Table 16.3   Some Therapeutic Diets and Their Purposes

Type of Diet	Purpose of Diet	Description
Clear liquid Nutritionally inadequate	Replaces fluids lost from vomiting, diarrhea, surgery	Plain gelatin, ginger ale, tea, coffee (no cream), fruit or apple juice (no pulp), fat-free broth
Full liquid May be **deficient** in iron	Trouble chewing or swallowing, **gastrointestinal** disturbances	All clear liquids, fruit or vegetable juices, strained soup, custard, ice cream, sherbet, milk, cream, eggs, buttermilk, carbonated beverages, eggs, cocoa, eggnog
Soft Nutritionally inadequate	For patients who have trouble chewing, postsurgically	Foods that are soft in consistency, such as fish, ground beef, broth, pureed vegetables, strained cream soup, tender cooked vegetables, fruit juices, cooked fruit, refined cereals, pasta, sherbet, ices, ice cream, custard, plain cookies, angel food cake, tea, coffee, cocoa, carbonated beverages, cheese, cottage cheese
Bland Nutritionally adequate	Soothes gastrointestinal tract, avoids irritation in ulcers, **colitis**	Foods low in fiber and connective tissue that are mild flavored and easy to digest, such as bananas, prune juice, applesauce, custard, pudding, ice cream, plain cookies, sponge cake, decaffeinated coffee, milk, cheese, yogurt
Restricted residue Nutritionally adequate	Reduces normal work of the intestine, in cases of rectal diseases, colitis, **ileitis**	Foods low in fiber and low in bulk, such as milk, buttermilk, cottage cheese, butter, margarine, eggs (not fried), tender poultry, fish, lamb, ground beef (broiled, boiled, baked), broth, refined bread, cereals, pasta, gelatin, angel food or sponge cake, mild-flavored cooked vegetables, lettuce, vegetable and fruit juice, applesauce, canned fruit, citrus fruit without membranes
Low carbohydrate (diabetic) Nutritionally adequate	Matches food intake with insulin uptake and nutritional requirements, used for patients with hyperinsulism and **diabetes mellitus**	Foods that supply enough protein, fat, and carbohydrate to maintain health and activities; requires a balance of carbohydrates, protein, and fat to meet the individual need of the patient; restricts sugar, cookies, pies, candies, etc.
Low fat Deficient in fat **soluble** vitamins	For patients with gallbladder and liver disease, obesity, and heart conditions	Foods high in carbohydrates and proteins; all fats are limited; skim milk, buttermilk, cottage cheese, lean fish, poultry, meats, fat-free soup broths, cooked vegetables, lettuce, fruit juice, bananas, citrus fruits, gelatin, angel food cake, coffee, tea, carbonated beverages, jelly, honey as desired

(continued)

Table 16.3 Some Therapeutic Diets and Their Purposes (continued)

Type of Diet	Purpose of Diet	Description
Low cholesterol Nutritionally adequate	Regulates amount of cholesterol in the blood for patients with coronary disease and **atherosclerosis**	Foods low in fat, such as lean muscle meat, fish, poultry without skin or fat, skim milk, vegetables, fruits
Low calorie Nutritionally adequate (800–2,000 cal)	Reduces number of calories for overweight patients and for clients with arthritis or cardiac conditions	Foods low in fats and calories: skim milk, buttermilk, lean meats, clear soup, vegetables, fresh fruit, coffee, tea, herbs, onions, garlic
High calorie (2,000+ cal) Nutritionally adequate	For persons 10 percent or more below desired weight; for patients with **anorexia nervosa** and hyperthyroidism	All foods with nutritionally balanced proteins, carbohydrates, fats, vitamins, minerals
Low sodium Nutritionally adequate	Reduces salt intake for patients with kidney disease, cardiovascular disorders, edema, and **hypertension**	Natural foods prepared without salt, such as fresh fruits, fresh vegetables, foods without salt added
High protein Nutritionally adequate	For children and adolescents needing additional protein for growth; during pregnancy, **lactation**; postsurgically; during illnesses resulting from protein loss	Foods high in protein, such as milk, cheese, eggs, lean meats, fish, and poultry; fruit, cereals, vegetables

anorexia nervosa
(an uh REK see uh
nur VOH suh)
Loss of appetite with serious weight loss. It is considered a mental disorder.

hypertension
(hahy per TEN shuhn)
High blood pressure.

lactation
(lak TEY shuhn)
Body's process of producing milk to feed newborns.

Career Connection

Participate in a job shadow of a Dietician in either an acute care or long-term care facility and learn about the therapeutic diets required for specific conditions such as diabetes, high blood pressure, or hypoglycemia.

 ## Eating Disorders

Eating disorders are not due to a failure of will. They are real and treatable medical illnesses. The three main types of eating disorders are anorexia nervosa, bulimia, and binge-eating. All three can affect a person's health including causing serious heart conditions, kidney failure, and electrolyte imbalance. The cause of eating disorders is not entirely clear. They seem to have a basis in biology but they are also affected by emotions, genes, and culture.

Eating is controlled by many factors including a person's appetite, the availability of food, family, peer, and cultural practices, and attempts at voluntary control. An eating disorder involves a serious disturbance in eating behavior, such as extreme reduction of food intake, severe overeating, or intentional vomiting. Eating disorders frequently develop during adolescence or early adulthood and can often be found with other problems such as depression, substance abuse, and anxiety disorders.

Women are much more likely than men to develop an eating disorder. Women's magazines, fashion trends, and some activities and professions promote dieting to achieve the "perfect" lean body. This can lead to pressure on women to be thin. Eating disorders are sometimes triggered by the stress of being unable to reach an unattainable goal. Males make up only about 10 percent of people with anorexia or bulimia.

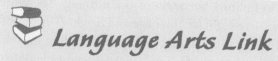

Language Arts Link

Dietary Careers

Proper nutrition is vital for both health care workers—so that they maintain the stamina and health required for the job—and patients—so that they grow stronger or stay healthy. Eating a balanced diet is important for both the brain and the body. As many Americans do not follow a healthy diet, the role of the dietary worker is becoming more and more important to the populations' health. There are different types of dietary careers, including Registered Dietitians, Dietetic Technicians, and Food Service Workers.

Working with a partner, research various dietary careers. Using the Internet or a library, research the educational and skills needs to go into this area of study. If you are able to speak with professionals in these fields, interview them about how they become interested in this subject, what the requirements were, and what their job responsibilities are.

After you've completed your research, create a document with several paragraphs on each dietary career that you learned about. Be sure to proofread your work to see if you can improve it by making it clearer, more concise, or more interesting to read. Check the spelling and grammar and correct any errors.

Anorexia Nervosa

People with *anorexia nervosa* see themselves as overweight and have an immense fear of becoming fat even though they are dangerously thin. In addition, many athletes have eating disorders. For them, eating becomes an obsession. They develop unusual eating habits such as avoiding meals, eating only a few foods in small quantities, or carefully weighing food. People with anorexia may repeatedly check their body weight or exercise compulsively.

People with anorexia are often perfectionists. They are driven to succeed but cannot achieve the unattainable standards they set for themselves. When they fail to meet these standards, they often look for a part of their lives they can control such as food or weight.

Bulimia Nervosa and Binge-Eating Disorder

Bingeing means eating an excessive amount of food within a short period of time. Bulimia sufferers have recurring episodes of binge eating. They usually feel unable to control their appetite during a bingeing episode.

Afterwards, they try desperately to compensate in order to avoid gaining weight. A person with bulimia might engage in inappropriate behavior known as "*purging*," brought on by self-induced vomiting, or misuse of laxatives, diuretics, or other medications.

Because purging follows the binge-eating episodes, people with bulimia usually have a "normal" weight for their age and height. However, like people with anorexia, people with bulimia often feel extremely dissatisfied with their bodies. They might also feel disgusted and ashamed when they binge and perform both bingeing and purging behavior in secret.

Apply It

Working in pairs, choose a therapeutic diet and pretend you have been put on it. Go to several different grocery stores and collect the sale papers for the week.

Create a menu for one week, based on this diet. Make sure you keep track of grocery cost and compare your menu to the food guide pyramid recommendations to see if it is nutritious.

Binge-eating disorder is similar to bulimia but without the purging. Therefore, many people with the disorder are overweight for their age and height. The out-of-control eating may be associated with eating rapidly, eating until feeling uncomfortably full, or eating large amounts when not feeling hungry. Binge-eaters often feel embarrassed, depressed, or guilty after overeating. This can lead to overeating again, creating a cycle of binge eating.

Treatment

People with eating disorders often do not recognize or admit that they are ill. They may strongly resist getting and staying in treatment. Family members or friends can be helpful in making sure that a person with an eating disorder receives the necessary care. Eating disorders can be treated and a healthy weight restored. The sooner a doctor diagnoses and treats these disorders, the better the outcomes are likely to be.

Eating disorders often have multiple causes and require a complex treatment plan. This may include medical care, psychological treatment, nutritional counseling, and medication. Ongoing research by scientists continues to advance the understanding and treatment of eating disorders.

Personal Wellness

Substance Abuse

Substance abuse refers to the use of legal or illegal substances that cause harm to a person's health or life. Abused substances usually produce some form of intoxication that alters judgment, perception, or physical control.

Substance abuse in the United States is widespread. In 2007, there were an estimated 16.4 million Americans using illicit drugs and about 15 million heavy alcohol users. About one out of five Americans smokes cigarettes.

People use alcohol and other drugs because they like the way these substances make them feel. However, substance abuse may lead to addiction. Addiction is a compulsion to continue using a substance even though it has negative consequences. People can become addicted to illegal drugs, drugs that doctors prescribe, or to things they may not think of as drugs, such as alcohol and the nicotine in cigarettes.

Many abused substances can produce a phenomenon known as *tolerance*. This means a person would have to use a larger amount of the drug to produce the same level of intoxication. Once a person is addicted to a drug, it becomes almost impossible to stop using it. Sometimes, when people stop using a drug, they experience withdrawal. Withdrawal can range from mild anxiety to seizures and hallucinations.

Alcohol

Despite the focus on illegal drugs, alcohol remains the main drug problem in the United States. Alcohol lessens a person's inhibitions, slurs speech, and decreases coordination. Many people use alcohol without any negative consequences. However, there are approximately 15 million people in the country addicted to alcohol; more than 4.5 million of them are women.

Alcohol is the most common cause of liver failure in the U.S. The drug can also cause heart enlargement and cancer of the pancreas, esophagus, and stomach. Alcohol abuse is associated with nearly half of all fatal motor vehicle accidents. Every year in the United States, alcohol abuse also causes 500,000 injuries, 600,000 assaults, and 70,000 sexual assaults.

Personal Wellness (continued)

Tobacco

Cigarettes kill more Americans than alcohol, car accidents, suicide, AIDS, homicide, and illegal drugs combined. Yet, amazingly, people continue to smoke. Cigarettes and other forms of tobacco contain nicotine, one of the most addictive of all drugs. Despite the rising cost of cigarettes, more than 40 million U.S. adults were smokers in 2004. This is 21 percent of all American adults.

About half of all Americans who continue to smoke will die because of the habit. Each year about 440,000 people die in the United States from illnesses related to cigarette smoking such as heart disease, lung cancer, emphysema, and stroke.

Although 70 percent of smokers want to quit and 35 percent attempt to quit each year, fewer than 5 percent succeed. This is because smokers not only become physically addicted to nicotine but they also become psychologically addicted. Nicotine withdrawal symptoms of smoking include anxiety, hunger, sleep disturbances, and depression. All these factors make it very difficult for a person to stop smoking once he or she starts.

Illegal Drugs

Marijuana comes from the plant Cannabis sativa and is the most commonly used illegal drug in the United States. Marijuana is a popular drug because it produces a feeling of pleasure and relaxation without a high risk of addiction. More than 83 million Americans have tried marijuana. However, there are dangers associated with it. Like anything that is smoked, it can irritate a person's lungs.

Smoking marijuana also impairs coordination and memory. Perhaps most importantly, possession of even small amounts of marijuana in the United States remains a crime. In 2005, 42 percent (787,000) of all drug arrests were for marijuana.

Americans in large numbers use many other types of illegal drugs. Cocaine, derived from the coca plant of South America, is the most abused major stimulant in America. More than 2 million Americans use heroin despite the very real danger of death through overdose.

Methamphetamines are a powerful stimulant that increases alertness and decreases appetite. An assortment of so-called "club drugs" have also become popular in the last two decades, including Ecstasy, PCP, GHB, Rohypnol, Ketamine, and LSD.

Most of these drugs deliver a feeling of happiness, excitement, and energy. However, most of them are physically and/or psychologically addictive. Withdrawal symptoms can be particularly harrowing for some drugs such as heroin. In addition, prolonged use of any of them can lead to serious health problems including coronary problems, dangerously high blood pressure, and stroke.

Steroids

Anabolic steroids are artificial versions of the hormone testosterone. Testosterone brings out male sexual traits. Steroids are often used to treat delayed puberty and the wasting of the body caused by diseases. However, anabolic steroids also help the growth of skeletal muscle. For this reason, these compounds have been abused by bodybuilders, weightlifters, and athletes in many other sports.

By the 2000s, the use of steroids was becoming epidemic among college and high school athletes. In 2006, 1.6 percent of eighth graders and 2.7 percent of twelfth graders reported using steroids without a prescription at least once in their lifetimes.

Anabolic steroids can be injected, taken by mouth, or rubbed on the skin when in gels or creams. Anabolic steroid abuse has been associated with a wide range of adverse side effects such as irritability, aggression, acne, breast development in men, liver cancer, and heart attacks. Most of the effects are reversible if the abuser stops taking the drug, but some can be permanent.

Summary

There are many factors that influence food habits. Some of these factors are personal attitudes, nationality, race, and religious restrictions. A health care worker must be aware of these factors in order to help the patient/client adapt to therapeutic diets.

The therapeutic diet is prescribed for various ailments. It is important to understand why the diet was prescribed and how it helps in regaining a healthier state. The health care worker should be aware of the foods allowed and not allowed in therapeutic diets and serve only proper foods to his or her patients.

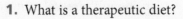

SECTION **16.2** **Review Questions**

1. What is a therapeutic diet?

2. What is a common dietary restriction for Muslims?

3. What is the purpose of a clear liquid diet?

4. If a patient has ulcer problems, what kind of therapeutic diet would be most helpful?

5. What foods are high in protein?

6. What types of care might be included in a treatment program for eating disorders?

 Learn By Doing: Section 16.2 Activity

1. Complete Worksheets 1 and 2 as assigned.

2. Complete Worksheet/Activity 3.

3. Complete Worksheets 4 and 5.

4. Prepare responses to each item listed in Chapter Review.

5. When you are confident that you can meet each objective for this section, ask your teacher for the section evaluation.

Chapter 16 Review

Chapter Review Questions

1. Why is water important to the human body? (16.1)

2. If a person consumes 2,000 calories a day, will he or she gain weight or lose weight? What factors play a role beside calorie intake? (16.1)

3. How do vitamins affect the human body? (16.1)

4. What were some of the complaints about the 1992 USDA food pyramid? (16.1)

5. Where and when was the metric system invented? (16.1)

6. What are three purposes of a therapeutic diet? (16.2)

7. Why would a low carbohydrate (diabetic) diet work best for a patient with diabetes? (16.2)

8. What kinds of food can be found in a low cholesterol diet? (16.2)

9. What is the difference between bulimia and binge-eating disorder? (16.2)

10. What are some problems associated with the use of anabolic steroids? (16.2)

Activities

1. Research a religious group listed on Table 16.2: Religious Dietary Restrictions. You can use an encyclopedia or the Internet. Discuss the religion's dietary laws in more detail than the chart provides. Make sure you quote directly from the religion's scriptures or holy book that regulates diet.

2. Make a list of five questions you would ask a psychologist about eating disorders. Then look up "psychologist" in the phone book or the Internet. Find someone who specializes in eating disorders and ask or e-mail your questions. When you get your responses, create a newspaper article on eating disorders. Work the quotations directly into the article. Don't forget to include citations.

Case Studies

1. Mrs. Cohen, an Orthodox Jew, has been in St. Andrews Nursing Home for several years. This evening the staff in the kitchen sent her a dinner with mashed potatoes, pork roast, green beans, and custard. She is very upset and is crying: She is hungry, but does not want to eat because of her dietary restrictions. You know that the staff in the kitchen is new. What steps can you take to remedy this problem?

2. Richard is your patient. He is on a low-fat diet because of coronary difficulties. Richard is feeling disgruntled and is complaining about everything on his tray. He says the "food here stinks," and keeps asking family members to sneak him donuts. How can you help Richard understand the reason for the diet?

Chapter 16 Review

Thinking Critically

1. **Communication**—As you are distributing meal trays, you notice that one of your patients is trying to exchange food with the patient next to him. This patient is supposed to be on a bland diet because he has ulcers. Instead of raising your voice and asking, "What do you think you are doing?," how would you explain to the patient about the importance of following the diet prescribed for him?

2. **Cultural Competency**—An Orthodox Jewish patient is upset because the hospital keeps bringing her kosher chicken and milk for her dinner. She is supposed to be on a bland diet, but refuses to eat. Why is the patient upset? How would you calm her down? What steps would you take?

3. **Cause and Effect**—Each year about 440,000 people die in the United States from illnesses related to cigarette smoking. Cigarettes kill more Americans than alcohol, car accidents, suicide, AIDS, homicide, and illegal drugs combined. Yet smoking cigarettes is legal in the United States while smoking marijuana is illegal. Why do you think this is?

Media Connection

Use the Companion Web site for additional interactive learning activities: www.prenhall.com/badasch

Portfolio Connection

When you care for patients, it is important to know if they are eating a healthy diet. Therapeutic diets do not always meet the standards of a healthy diet.

Choose an illness that requires a therapeutic diet. Write a paragraph about the illness. Explain the symptoms, how the body is affected, and the treatment. Use the food pyramid as a guide to evaluating the therapeutic diet required. Describe in what ways the diet is nutritionally healthy or deficient.

Place this exercise in your portfolio to help you review the food pyramid, healthy diets, and therapeutic diets.

PORTFOLIO TIP

Food preferences and diet can be more of a source of distress and conflict for patients than the actual illness. Make a large photocopy of the food pyramid and keep it in your portfolio.

Write notes for yourself demonstrating how you would explain to patients the importance of a varied diet.

17 Controlling Infection

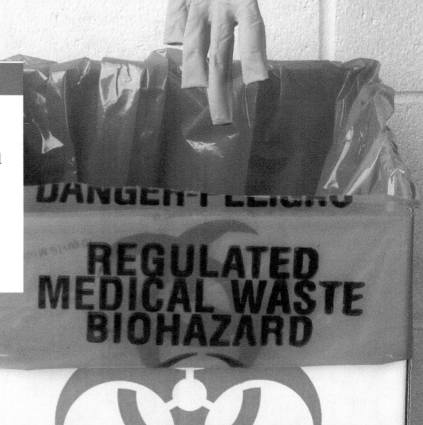

Getting Started

Wash your hands with different products: soap, betadine, alcohol, and hand sanitizer. Then, make finger impressions in different agar plates for each product used. After 24 hours, check to see which product worked best to kill the microorganisms.

The Nature of Microorganisms

Background

Microorganisms are all around us, but we cannot see them. There are both good and bad microorganisms. To help prevent the spread of infection and disease, you must be aware of microorganisms and how they are spread.

Objectives

When you have completed this section, you will be able to do the following:

- Match key terms with their correct meanings.

- Define *pathogenic* and *nonpathogenic*.

- List conditions affecting the growth of bacteria.

- List ways that microorganisms and viruses cause illness.

- List ways that microorganisms and viruses spread.

- List five ways to prevent the spread of microorganisms and viruses.

- Describe generalized and localized infections.

- Explain the difference in signs and symptoms of generalized and localized infections.

microorganisms
(mie kroh ORG uhn izms)
Tiny organism, such as a fungi, protists, or bacteria, that can only be seen under a microscope.

viruses
(VAHY ruhs es)
Genetic material that is surrounded by a protective coat and that can only reproduce inside a host cell; can only be seen under a microscope.

Introduction to Microorganisms

We are surrounded by tiny **microorganisms** and **viruses**. They are in the air we breathe, on our skin, in our food, and on everything we touch. You cannot see these organisms and viruses without a microscope because they are so small. (**Figure 17.1**) Viruses are much smaller than microorganisms. So, stronger microscopes are used to look at viruses.

Some microorganisms and viruses cause illness, infection, or disease and are called *pathogenic*. Some microorganisms help keep a balance in the environment and in the body. These microorganisms are called *nonpathogenic*.

Viruses do not have all of the characteristics of living organisms. For example, viruses do not eat. They also cannot reproduce on their own. So, viruses are not considered living as microorganisms are. For microorganisms to live, they must

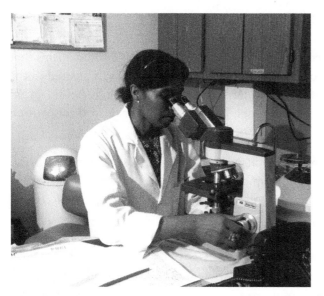

Figure 17.1
A microscope is needed to see microorganisms. Stronger microscopes are needed to see viruses, which are much smaller than microorganisms are. List a step you might need to take to ensure that a microscope works properly.

anaerobic
(an uh ROH bik)
Able to grow and function without oxygen.

saprophytes
(SAP ruh fahyts)
Organisms that live on dead organic matter.

parasites
(PARE uh sahyts)
Organisms obtaining nourishment from other organisms they are living in or on.

have certain elements in their environment. Some organisms require oxygen in order to survive. These are called *aerobic*. Other microorganisms live in an environment without oxygen. These are called **anaerobic**.

Most microorganisms that cause illness thrive in warm temperatures—about the temperature of the body. All organisms need moisture, and most microorganisms prefer a dark area to grow in. (**Figure 17.2**) Microorganisms also need food to survive. Some of these organisms live on dead matter or tissues and are called **saprophytes**. Other organisms that live on living matter or tissues are called **parasites**. (**Figure 17.2**)

Figure 17.2
Conditions affecting the growth of bacteria. What are three things that you can do to help prevent the growth of bacteria in patient's room?

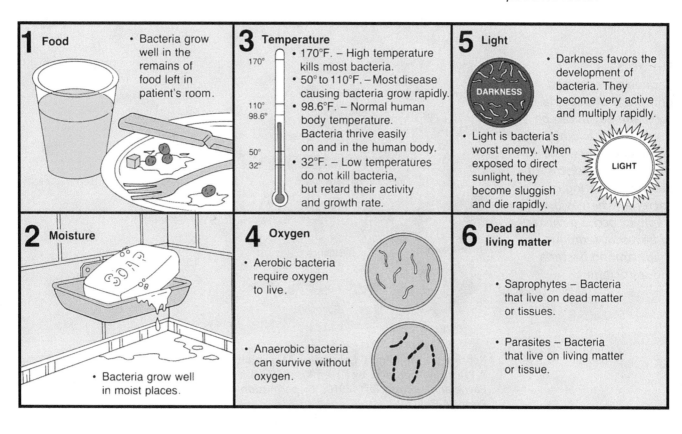

1 Food
- Bacteria grow well in the remains of food left in patient's room.

2 Moisture
- Bacteria grow well in moist places.

3 Temperature
- 170°F. – High temperature kills most bacteria.
- 50° to 110°F. – Most disease causing bacteria grow rapidly.
- 98.6°F. – Normal human body temperature. Bacteria thrive easily on and in the human body.
- 32°F. – Low temperatures do not kill bacteria, but retard their activity and growth rate.

4 Oxygen
- Aerobic bacteria require oxygen to live.
- Anaerobic bacteria can survive without oxygen.

5 Light
- Darkness favors the development of bacteria. They become very active and multiply rapidly.
- Light is bacteria's worst enemy. When exposed to direct sunlight, they become sluggish and die rapidly.

6 Dead and living matter
- Saprophytes – Bacteria that live on dead matter or tissues.
- Parasites – Bacteria that live on living matter or tissue.

Nonpathogenic Microorganisms

pathogenic
(path oh JEN ik)
Disease-causing.

nonpathogenic
(nahn path oh JEN ik)
Not disease causing.

decompose
(dee kuhm POES)
To decay, to break down.

There are many microorganisms that are not disease causing, or **pathogenic**. These microorganisms, called **nonpathogenic**, are "good" microorganisms that are used in different ways. For example, these microorganisms can be used in the following ways: to make buttermilk, to ferment grain for alcoholic beverages, to make bread rise, and so on. Many nonpathogenic organisms also **decompose** organic materials in nature.

In the body, nonpathogenic microorganisms work in the digestive system to break down food elements that the body cannot use. This broken down food is eventually eliminated as a part of feces. Nonpathogenic microorganisms also help control the growth of pathogenic organisms.

Pathogenic Microorganisms and Viruses

rickettsiae
(rih KET see ee)
Parasitic microorganisms that live on another living organism and cause disease.

spirochetes
(SPAHY ruh keets)
Slender, coil-shaped organisms.

Health care workers must be aware of the different kinds of pathogens that cause disease. There are several kinds of disease-causing microorganisms: bacteria, protozoa, fungi, and **rickettsiae**. Viruses are also pathogens.

- **Bacteria**—Bacteria are responsible for many diseases (**Figure 17.3**). For example, strep throat is caused by streptococci, staph infection is caused by staphylococci, and syphilis is caused by **spirochetes.** These are only a few of the diseases that bacteria cause.

  Staphylococcus and streptococcus are organisms that are always present in health care environments. Staphylococcus (staph) infections can have a serious impact on patients, caregivers, and families. An uncontrolled or untreated staph infection in a newborn nursery, for example, can cause infants to die. People who have a stressed immune system have trouble fighting a staph infection and may die.

Figure 17.3

Common shapes and groupings of bacteria. The cocci and bacilli can be single, pairs, and higher-order assemblies. The streptococci and strepto-bacilli are a string of bacteria, whereas the staphylococci is a cluster of bacteria. A unique shape among bacteria is the spirochete

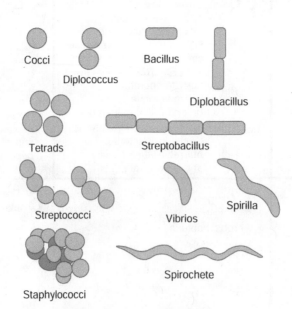

Reprinted from Clinical Laboratory Microbiology: A Practical Approach, by Karen Kiser, William Payne and Theresa Taff (2010), by permission of Prentice-Hall, Inc.

Hospital stays are prolonged because of staph infections. Staph is usually the cause of pimples or boils found on the skin. All drainage from a pimple or boil should be handled according to Standard Precautions to prevent the spread of infection. Patients who have staph infections are always treated with Standard Precautions.

- **Protozoa**—Protozoa are larger than viruses but also grow within a **host** cell. They cause trichomoniasis, amebic dysentery, and malaria. Most protozoa are too small to be seen with the naked eye, but can easily be found under a microscope. Protozoa are found in water and soil environments and play an important role in their ecology.

- **Fungi**—Microscopic fungi include molds and yeasts. Some fungi can cause disease, such as athlete's foot, thrush, vaginitis, and serious lung diseases.

- **Rickettsiae**—Rickettsiae are parasites that live in lice, fleas, ticks, and mites. When one of these organisms is infected with rickettsiae, the disease is transferred to a person after he or she is bitten. Rickettsiae are responsible for many of the world's worst epidemics, including various types of typhus and spotted fever. Rodent and insect control helps prevent rickettsiae infection.

- **Viruses**—Viruses are much smaller than bacteria. They cannot reproduce until they have taken over a living cell. Viruses cause the common cold and many upper respiratory infections. They also cause smallpox, chickenpox, measles, mumps, influenza, and fever blisters. One of the most serious viruses is human immunodeficiency virus (HIV), which causes acquired immunodeficiency syndrome (AIDS). These are only a few of the illnesses caused by viruses.

When nonpathogenic microorganisms leave their normal environment in the body and move into other areas, they become pathogens. Some common examples are:

- **Escherichia coli** or E. coli—E. coli is a normally nonpathogenic bacterium found in the intestine of many animals and humans. E. coli from the colon can come in contact with other parts of the beef, thus contaminating the meat. E. coli infections may cause food poisoning and even death. E. coli infections can be prevented by cooking meat until it reaches a temperature of about 160°F (71.1°C).

  Poor personal hygiene can allow E. coli to spread from the human colon to the urethra causing urinary tract infections known as **urethritis** and **cystitis**. Health care workers who have dirty hands—especially hands that are not washed after using the toilet—can spread E. coli to patients' food or onto equipment used to provide care.

- **Salmonella**—Salmonella infections are caused by bacteria. Salmonella infections may cause food poisoning or death. Salmonella infections can be caused by eating chicken that is undercooked or from eating foods that contain raw eggs. Salmonella can also be spread to food when food service workers do not wash their hands. Salmonella is also spread when cooking utensils or surfaces are not cleaned properly after preparing raw meat, chicken, or egg dishes in particular.

host
(ho st)
The organism from which a microorganism takes nourishment. The microorganism gives nothing in return and causes disease or illness.

Chronic vs. Acute

Acute infections occur suddenly or last a short time. Chronic infections happen slowly over a long period of time and may last months, or even years.

For more on chronic and acute infections and diseases, go to the Companion Web site at www.prenhall.com/badasch.

urethritis
(yoor uh THRAHY tihs)
Inflammation of the urethra.

cystitis
(sis TAHY tihs)
Inflammation of the urinary bladder.

salmonella
(sal muh NEL uh)
A rod-shaped bacterium found in the intestine that can cause food poisoning, gastroenteritis, and typhoid fever.

We know that infections are caused by pathogens. Infections fall into two groups: *endogenous* and *exogenous*. An endogenous infection grows or develops from within an organism, tissue, or cell when an individual is in an already weakened state. An endogenous infection is caused by an infectious agent already present in the body, with the previous infection having been dormant or non-apparent.

An exogenous infection originates from outside the body. Examples of exogenous infections include salmonella poisoning after eating an uncooked egg or poultry, catching a cold after eating off of someone else's fork, or contracting rabies after getting bit by a dog.

An opportunistic infection occurs when there is weakness or compromise in the immune defenses of an individual. Opportunistic infections may be caused by bacteria, fungi, viruses, or parasites. These infections can be fought off by people with strong immune systems; however, they can be fatal for AIDS patients.

toxins
(TAHKS ihns)
Poisonous substances.

enterotoxin
(ehn tuhr oh TAHKS uhn)
Poisonous substance that is produced in, or originates in, the contents of the intestine.

 ## How Microorganisms Affect the Body

Pathogens cause disease in several different ways. Some microorganisms produce **toxins** that affect the body. For instance, staphylococcus produces an **enterotoxin** that is the cause of food poisoning. The toxin causes fatigue, diarrhea, and vomiting. The tetanus bacilli produce a toxin that enters the bloodstream and attacks the central nervous system, causing severe damage and frequently death.

 ## Science Link

Prions

Unlike bacteria, protists, and fungi, viruses are not living organisms. Another type of nonliving pathogen is called a *prion*. Prions are infectious protein molecules. Prions are a defective version of a protein found in normal brain cells. They cause several brain diseases, including Creutzfeld-Jakob disease and mad cow disease.

Unlike viruses and microorganisms, prions do not replicate themselves. So, how do they infect people and animals? According to one theory, the prion is taken into the body. In the case of mad cow disease, humans eat infected beef. The prions enter brain cells, and the cells begin producing the prion instead of the normal protein. This happens because the prion comes in contact with normal proteins. The normal proteins become prions, which in turn spread to other cells.

Prions cause the death of the brain cells that send signals to and from the body. Over time, the cell death keeps the body from sending signals to and from the brain. So, the body stops functioning properly, eventually leading to death.

Prion infections are rare. In the case of mad cow disease, they can be prevented by avoiding raw meat, especially meat that has been or may have been contaminated with the prion. Other prion diseases are transmitted by contaminated equipment used during medical procedures. Proper cleaning and sterilization of equipment prevents the spread of prions. Some prion diseases are inherited, so little action can be taken to prevent the disease.

Proteins are denatured, or inactivated, by heat. How does this reaction to heat apply to the prevention of prion infection?

Some microorganisms and all viruses invade living cells and destroy them; this is called *cell invasion*. For example, there is a **protist** that invades the red blood cells of the host. As the protists grow, the cells rupture and cause chills and fever.

The presence of some microorganisms causes a violent *allergic reaction* in the body. A runny nose, watery eyes, and sneezing can be caused by the presence of a microorganism to which the host is allergic.

How Microorganisms and Viruses Spread

Now that you know something about microorganisms and viruses, you need to know how they are spread and how they enter the body. This helps you protect yourself and your patients/clients from infection.

For microorganisms or viruses to cause disease or infection, they must have a **susceptible** host. This host is unable to fight off infection because its resistance to the pathogen is low. Low resistance may be caused by poor diet, fatigue, inadequate rest, stress, or poor health. Table 17.1 shows five primary ways by which microorganisms and viruses are spread.

A model used to understand the infection process is the **chain of infection**. This model represents each component in the cycle. Each component must be present and in sequential order: infectious agent, reservoir, portal of exit from the reservoir, mode of transmission, portal of entry into the susceptible host.

Understanding the characteristics of each link provides the health care professional with methods to support vulnerable patients, prevent the spread of infection and protect themselves.

protist
(PRO tis t)
An organism belonging to the kingdom that includes protozoans, bacteria, and single-celled algae and fungi.

susceptible
(suh SEHP tuh buhl)
Capable of being affected or infected (e.g., body can be attacked by microorganisms and become ill).

chain of infection
(CHAY in ove in FEC shun)
A chain of events all interconnected is required for an infection to spread.

Career Connection

Your teacher will invite an Infection Control Nurse to visit the class and discuss the Chain of Infection as related to appropriate hand washing and other preventive techniques.

Table 17.1   Five Ways Microorganisms and Viruses Are Spread

Method	Information	Examples	Prevention Guidelines
Direct contact	Occurs when organisms or viruses are transmitted directly from one person to another.	■ Physical contact by touch on open or closed skin or a body opening ■ Sexual contact ■ Breathing in pathogens directly from an infected person	■ Abstain from sex. ■ Do not drink or eat from dishes or utensils used by another person. ■ Stay an appropriate distance away from individuals who are coughing or sneezing. ■ Do not, without proper protection, touch objects used by someone who has an infection.
Indirect contact	Occurs when organisms or viruses are transferred from one object to another.	■ Contaminated substances and objects, such as food, air, soil, feces, clothing, and equipment	■ Do not, without proper protection, touch objects used by someone who has an infection. ■ Hold contaminated linen, belongings, or other items away from your uniform.

(continued)

Table 17.1   Five Ways Microorganisms and Viruses Are Spread (continued)

Method	Information	Examples	Prevention Guidelines
Airborne	Some microorganisms and viruses are carried in the air. Coughing and sneezing project droplets into the air, and these droplets are carried on air currents until they find a place to land. The droplets cling to hair, uniforms, and medical equipment, or they fall on the floor. As you move from place to place, you may spread these pathogens.	■ Influenza ■ Chickenpox ■ Wound infections	■ Keep your hair short or tied back so that it does not swing around, spreading microorganisms. ■ Cover your mouth and nose with your sleeve, when you sneeze or cough, then wash your hands. ■ Change out of your uniform after working and before going anywhere other than home. ■ Consider anything dropped on the floor as contaminated, DO NOT USE IT. ■ Stay home when you are sick with an acute respiratory infection.
Oral route	Microorganisms or viruses enter the body through the mouth by way of **contaminated** water and food, dirty hands, and from other contaminated objects.	■ Food poisoning ■ Polio ■ Hepatitis ■ Salmonellosis ■ Typhoid fever	■ Wash your hands: – before eating or handling food – after using the toilet – before/after helping patients ■ Refrigerate food properly to prevent contamination and microorganism growth. ■ Dispose of wound drainage promptly and according to policy.
Insects and pests	Organisms or viruses are picked up by insects and other pests from contaminated areas and carried to water, food, and people.	■ Bubonic plague ■ Malaria ■ Amoebic dysentery	■ Keep all flies and insects out of the environment. ■ Report insects or pests immediately.

contaminated
(kuhn TAM uh nayt uhd)
Soiled, unclean, not suitable for use.

Fallacies of Disease Transmission

In the nineteenth and twentieth centuries, developments such as the culture plate method of identifying disease-causing organisms, pasteurization, vaccines, antiseptics, and asepsis dramatically lowered the incidence of disease. A common fallacy, however, is to think that an infectious disease is completely controlled—in the early 1990s, a resurgence of measles in the Unites States was a reminder that effective immunization requires diligence. Another example of a fallacy related to disease transmission is the assumption that bats carry rabies—bats are mammals and can contract rabies, but that does not make them specific carriers of the disease. There are also many fallacies and misunderstandings concerning the transmission of bloodborne diseases, but standard precautions have been developed to effectively address realistic risks.

Protection from Microorganisms

Standard Precautions and Transmission-Based Precautions were created to provide guidelines that prevent the spread of microorganisms. These guidelines are described in Sections 17.2 and 17.3 of this chapter. Section 17.4 provides guidelines regarding bloodborne diseases. Read the guidelines carefully and follow them whenever infectious microorganisms are present.

Signs and Symptoms of Infection

An infection may be **generalized**, or it may be **localized**. If the infection is generalized, there is usually headache, fatigue, fever, and increased pulse and respiration. There may also be vomiting and/or diarrhea. If the infection is localized, you can see and feel one or more of the following: redness, swelling, heat, and/or drainage. There is usually pain at the site of the infection.

 ## Summary

We are surrounded by microorganisms and viruses. They are in the air we breathe, on our skin, in our food, and on everything we touch. Some microorganisms and viruses are pathogens; other microorganisms are nonpathogens. Pathogens include some bacteria, some protists, some fungi, rickettsiae, and viruses. Since pathogens cause illness, it is important to understand how they are spread and how they can be controlled. Learning the signs and symptoms of infection will help you provide better patient care.

It is the responsibility of every health care worker to help prevent the spread of infection. Every year thousands of patients have extended stays in the hospital because they have acquired a nosocomial infection while hospitalized. It is vital that all health care workers practice good techniques to prevent the spread of infection.

generalized
(JEN uhr uhl ahyzd)
Affecting all of the body.

localized
(LOH kuhl ahyzd)
Affecting one area of the body.

Apply It

Play medical charades in class. Take turns acting out a specific pathogen or a different way in which viruses are spread.

SECTION 17.1 | **Review Questions**

1. Define the terms *pathogenic* and *nonpathogenic*.

2. A microorganism that doesn't need oxygen is called what?

3. List five disease-causing pathogens.

4. What are five ways by which microorganisms and viruses spread?

5. Compare generalized and localized infections.

6. What conditions affect the growth of bacteria?

 ## Learn By Doing: Section 17.1 Activity

1. Complete Worksheet 1.

2. Complete Worksheet 2 as assigned.

3. Ask your instructor for directions to complete Worksheets/Activities 3 and 4.

4. When you are confident that you can meet each objective for this section, ask your teacher for the section evaluation.

Asepsis and Standard Precautions

Background

The environment of the health care worker contains larger numbers of microorganisms than do most other environments. The health care worker must acquire the knowledge and skills required to restrict the spread of pathogenic microorganisms. The health care worker who practices good aseptic technique and follows Standard Precautions protects patients, co-workers, and the community from infection.

Objectives

When you have completed this section, you will be able to do the following:

- Match key terms with their meanings.
- Define *medical asepsis*.
- Match terms related to medical asepsis with their correct meanings.
- List five aseptic techniques.
- List some of the Standard Precaution guidelines concerning the use of protective equipment.

- Demonstrate appropriate handwashing techniques.
- Explain the difference between *bactericidal* and *bacteriostatic*.
- List reasons why asepsis is important.

Introduction to Asepsis

Health care facilities are filled with people who are ill. Some of their illnesses are caused by body dysfunctions; other illnesses are caused by infections or injury. Thus, health care environments are constantly contaminated with the pathogens carried by patients, visitors, and staff.

This constant presence of pathogens requires the staff to wage an all-out battle against these microorganisms and viruses. This battle is waged by the continual use of medical asepsis, or the destruction of the environment that allows pathogens to live, breed, and spread. Medical asepsis is accomplished by using **aseptic technique**. Aseptic technique is very important when you are working with patients/clients. The practice of aseptic technique helps to prevent:

- Cross infection, which is caused by infecting the patient with a new microorganism or virus from another patient or health care worker (**nosocomial infection**).
- Reinfection with the same microorganism or virus that caused the original illness.

aseptic technique
(ay SEP tihk tek NEEK)
Method used to make the environment, the worker, and the patient as germ-free as possible.

nosocomial infection
(nohs uh KOH mee uhl ihn FEHKT shuhn)
An infection acquired while in a health care setting, such as a hospital.

- Self-inoculation by the patient's own organisms, such as *E. coli* from the intestines entering the urethra.

- An illness passing from the patient to the health care worker or from the health care worker to the patient.

Aseptic technique includes:

- Proper handwashing.

- Employees being clean and neat.

- Proper handling of all equipment.

- Using sterile procedure when necessary.

- Using proper cleaning solutions: *bacteriostatic* solutions, which slow or stop the growth of bacteria, or *bactericidal* solutions, which kill bacteria

- Following **Standard Precautions**.

The health care team must strive toward achieving an aseptic environment to reduce the infection rate in the health care setting.

Standard Precautions

Transmission of infectious agents requires three elements: 1) a source of infectious agents; 2) a susceptible host with a source of entry receptive to the agent; and 3) a mode of transmission for the agent. All blood, body fluids, secretions, excretions—except sweat—nonintact skin, and mucous membranes may contain contagious infectious agents.

Because of the risk of **transmitting** these infections agents, a set of standard precautions were developed. In 1985, health care isolation practices in the United States changed to defend against the increased risk of exposure to hepatitis B virus (HBV) and human immunodeficiency virus (HIV). For the first time, all blood and body fluids were treated as infected substances.

The Occupational Safety and Health Administration (OSHA) of the U.S. Department of Labor established mandatory guidelines published in the *Occupational Exposure to Bloodborne Pathogens: Final Rule.* These guidelines ensure that all employers provide personal protective equipment to employees at risk of exposure to body fluids. In 1992, OSHA increased its mandate to employers, insisting that training and immunization be provided to all employees within 10 days of hire. This means that employees at risk for exposure to body fluids must:

- Be offered hepatitis B vaccine (HBV) at no charge.

- Be trained to use the appropriate protective equipment to prevent exposure to body fluids.

- Receive an annual update and review.

In 1996, the Centers for Disease Control and Prevention (CDC) expanded the bloodborne pathogen guidelines to assist in the prevention of nosocomial infections. These expanded guidelines are known as Standard Precautions. The CDC updated these Standard Precautions in 2007 to include a new section on

Standard Precautions
(STAN derd prih KAW shuhn) Guidelines designed to reduce the risk of transmission of microorganisms from recognized and unrecognized sources of infection in the hospital.

transmitting
(trahnz MIHT ihng) Causing to go from one person to another person.

State Board of Health

In addition to national agencies that deal with safety guidelines in regard to transmission of infectious agents, each state has a board of health. A state board of health licenses health care facilities and requires compliance with OSHA and CDC guidelines.

Locate your state board of health online and learn what the expectations are for preventing the transmission of infectious agents.

Respiratory Hygiene/Cough Etiquette, primarily in response to the SARS virus outbreak in 2003. A complete summary of the updated 2007 CDC Standard Precautions is included for reference in Appendix A.

Standard Precautions are appropriate for all patients receiving care or service in a health care environment regardless of their diagnosis. Standard Precautions provide protection from contact with blood, mucous membranes, nonintact skin, and all body fluids. Body fluids include the following:

- Blood.
- Vaginal secretions.
- Pericardial fluid.
- Body fluids containing visible blood.
- **Amniotic fluid.**
- **Peritoneal fluid.**
- Tissue specimens.
- **Cerebrospinal fluid.**
- **Interstitial fluid.**
- **Semen.**
- **Pleural fluid.**

Infection with HBV and HIV occur through:

- Direct injection of infected blood or a contaminated needle that punctures the skin.
- Contact of infected body fluids with mucous membranes such as the eye or inside of the mouth.
- Sexual contact.
- Pregnancy—when the mother is infected, the infection is transferred to the newborn infant.

The risk of being infected in the health care setting is high. It is important for you to treat all patients as though they were infected. If you provide hands-on care to patients, you must follow all Standard Precaution guidelines (Table 17.2) to protect yourself and others. Make it a habit to follow each step in the Standard Precaution guidelines.

These include practices that apply to all health care providers, patients, visitors, and family members. Hand hygiene is the single-most effective way to prevent the spread of infections. Other safe practices may involve the use of gloves, goggles, face shield, and/or a gown when there is a risk of splashing or spray of blood or body fluids. Safe handling of soiled linens also reduces the risks of spreading infectious agents. Listed below are procedures to follow to minimize the risk of spreading infectious agents.

Surgical Asepsis
Medical asepsis includes all practices used to limit the number of microorganisms, their growth, and their transmission and to confine them to a specific area. Surgical asepsis, or sterile technique, includes all practices that keep an area completely free of microorganisms.

amniotic fluid
(am nee AH tihk FLOO ihd)
Liquid that surrounds the fetus during pregnancy.

peritoneal fluid
(per ih toh NEE uhl FLOO ihd)
Liquid in the peritoneal cavity.

cerebrospinal fluid
(suh ree broh SPAHYN uhl FLOO id)
Liquid that flows through and around brain tissue.

interstitial fluid
(ihnt uhr STIHSH uhl FLOO id)
Liquid that fills the space between most of the cells of the body.

semen
(SEE muhn)
Fluid from the testes, seminal vesicles, prostate gland, and bulbourethral glands.

pleural fluid
(PLOOR uhl FLOO id)
Liquid that surrounds the lungs.

Table 17.2   Standard Precaution Guidelines

Protective Equipment	When to Use Personal Protective Equipment (PPE)

Gloves (see procedure for removing gloves on page 514)	■ Wear when in contact with:
	  – Any body fluid
	  – Nonintact skin and mucous membrane, or potentially contaminated intact skin (e.g., of a patient incontinent of stool or urine)
	■ Wear when your hands are chapped, when a rash is present, or when you have open sores.

Nonpermeable gowns or aprons (see procedure for removing and discarding gowns on page 503)	■ Wear during procedures that are likely to expose you to:
	  – Any body fluid
	  – Nonintact skin and mucous membrane

Mask and protective eyewear or face shield	■ Wear when:
	  – Body fluid droplets or splashes are likely
	  – Patients are coughing continuously

Special masks and eyewear that seal against face	■ Wear when assisting with procedures that cause body tissues to be aerosolized (e.g., laser treatments).
Handwashing (see procedure on page 502)	■ Wash hands before putting on and after removing gloves and before and after working with each patient, with his or her equipment, or both.
Shared equipment/multiple-use patient care equipment (e.g., blood pressure cuff, stethoscope, aural thermometer)	■ Remove all shared equipment for cleaning after use on each patient. ■ Need to clean shared equipment between every patient—not just when exposed to body fluids or non-intact skin.

Controlling the Spread of Infection

Skin and hair cannot be **sterilized** because any solutions or procedures that kill microorganisms are harmful to skin. You use a bacteriostatic solution for cleaning skin. Bacteriocidal solutions are used on equipment. This method of controlling the spread of infection is called **disinfection**.

There are a variety of methods of disinfection. You can use boiling water to kill germs. You can add a 10% solution of household bleach to disinfect items that tolerate exposure to mild bleach solution. You can use stronger disinfection for cleaning inanimate items, such as floors, walls, tables, and patient care equipment.

There are also ultrasonic cleaners, which offer a fast, consistent, and inexpensive way to remove contaminants from all kinds of surfaces. Ultrasonic cleaners are especially useful for precision cleaning of small parts that contain contamination in small hard-to-reach crevices. These machines mean you use less cleaning solution.

CAUTION: Never use bleach on any item that will be put into the body or with any other product (e.g., cleansers, sprays).

sterilized
(STEHR uhl ahyzd)
Made free from all living microorganisms.

disinfection
(dis ihn FEHKT shuhn)
Process of freeing from microorganisms by physical or chemical means.

Community Service

In a team of three or four students, prepare a presentation for elementary or middle school students on proper hand washing. Design a poster on how germs are transmitted and how proper hand washing techniques limit transmission of germs.

exposed
(eks POEZD)
Left unprotected.

autoclaves
(AH toh klayvz)
Sterilizers that use steam under pressure to kill all forms of bacteria on fomites (objects that pathogens live on and can transfer infection).

Sterilization is the process of killing all microorganisms, even spores (bacteria that have a protective shell around them). Spores are killed when they are **exposed** to steam under pressure at high temperatures. **Autoclaves** are used to produce steam. Gas autoclaves and chemical baths are used to sterilize equipment that would be damaged by steam, such as plastic and rubber devices and fiber optics. Items needing sterilization are those that are put into the body or around an open wound.

Handwashing

Handwashing is the process of removing microorganisms from contaminated hands. Proper handwashing is the most effective way to prevent infecting yourself or others. See Table 17.3 for proper handwashing guidelines.

Table 17.3 Handwashing Guidelines

Directions	Information
Always wash your hands: – Before and after contact with a patient and/or patient's belongings – Before and after eating – After using the bathroom – After handling any contaminated fluid or object – After touching body fluids, even if wearing gloves	Handwashing is the most effective way to reduce the spread of microorganisms.
Use enough soap from dispenser to make a good lather.	A bar of soap is considered contaminated after it is opened.
Interlace your fingers together and rub all sides of fingers and hands to produce friction for **10 seconds**. Be sure to clean beneath fingernails and around knuckles. If no nail brush is available rub fingernails on palms of hands.	Lather and friction help remove microorganisms.
Hold hands lower than elbows and rinse thoroughly to remove pathogens.	This prevents lather and water from running over arms and causing contamination.
Turn on and off faucets with dry paper towel.	Faucets and sink are considered contaminated.
Rewash your hands if you touch the sink or faucet.	Touching a contaminated area recontaminates your hands.
Dry hands completely from tips of fingers to wrist.	Reddened and chapped hands easily leave open areas that can become infected.

Hand Cleansing

If hands are not visibly soiled, a facility's procedures may allow the use of an alcohol-based hand rub for cleansing hands instead of washing them. According to CDC guidelines, situations where hand cleansing, instead of washing, may be appropriate include:

- Before having direct contact with patients.
- After contact with a patient's intact skin, for example after taking a pulse or blood pressure, or after lifting a patient.
- After removing gloves.

- After contact with inanimate objects, including medical equipment, when near a patient.

A facility-approved hand lotion should be used to prevent irritation and chapping from frequent hand washing or cleansing because repeatedly using an alcohol-based hand-rub can irritate the skin; irritated skin poses a risk of an individual becoming infected or infecting others.

What's New?

Antibiotic Resistant Bacteria

Bacterial diseases are treated with drugs called antibiotics. Antibiotics can be highly effective in treating bacterial infections, but many bacteria have developed a resistance to antibiotics. As a result, these infections are more difficult to treat.

Why does antibiotic resistance occur? Some bacteria are naturally resistant to antibiotics or mutate to develop a resistance. Sometimes, these bacteria survive to produce more antibiotic resistant bacteria. Resistant bacteria arise when antibiotics are used incorrectly:

- A prescription for antibiotics is not completed. Some people stop taking their antibiotics after they feel better. Doing so increases the chance that resistant bacteria will survive. Often, these patients become ill again.

- Antibiotics are taken when a patient does not need them; for example, a patient who has the flu. The antibiotics will not help the patient get over the flu because the flu is caused by a virus, which is not affected by antibiotics. As a result, resistant bacteria may arise. Doctors often avoid prescribing antibiotics such a case.

- The widespread use of antibiotics in cleaning products has been linked to antibiotic resistance. Repeated exposure to an antibiotic can result in strains of bacteria that are resistant to the drug.

Several bacteria that were once easily controlled by antibiotics are now major health threats. Examples of these bacteria include:

- Tuberculosis: Tuberculosis is a contagious disease that affects the lungs. About one percent of tuberculosis cases involve a strain of bacteria that is resistant to multiple antibiotics. These cases need almost four times more recovery time than nonresistant strains of tuberculosis. Treatment of resistant strains is also more expensive and has more uncomfortable and dangerous side effects.

- Methicillin-resistant staphylococcus aureus (MRSA): Resistant forms of S. aureus were first noted in the 1960s. Since, it has become one of the most common antibiotic resistant bacteria found in hospitals. Infection by S. aureus has been linked to longer hospital stays and increased risk of death from secondary infections. In addition to the ongoing incidence of MRSA in hospitals, there also have been school-based outbreaks of the infection. Although not considered a super-bug by public health officials, MRSA is a threat that should be respected.

- Streptococcus: Various species of streptococci are resistant to antibiotics. These bacteria cause diseases such as pneumonia, meningitis, and arthritis.

While some antibiotics have little effect on bacteria, some substances, such as alcohol and bleach are effective. Additionally, some equipment can be autoclaved to destroy bacteria. Regardless, careful monitoring of antibiotic use and proper equipment care are needed to prevent the development of resistance and the spread of resistant bacteria.

One of your patients is refusing to finish his antibiotic prescription. What would you tell him to make sure that he finishes his medicine?

BACKGROUND: Contaminated hands are the most common cause of infection. Proper handwashing technique is the most effective way to prevent the spread of infection.

PREPROCEDURE

1. Wash your hands between patient contacts.

2. Wash your hands after removing protective gloves.

3. Wash your hands after contact with body fluids, even if gloves have been worn.

PROCEDURE

4. Stand at sink. Avoid contact of your uniform with the sink. Roll a paper towel out to have ready to use after washing your hands.

5. Turn on water and adjust water temperature.

6. Wet the hands and wrist area. Keep hands lower than elbows.

7. Using soap from dispenser lather thoroughly.

8. Using soap and friction, wash the palms, backs of the hands, fingers, between the fingers, knuckles, wrists and forearms. Clean nails. If no nail brush is available, rub nails across palms of hands.

9. Continue washing for at least 15 seconds.

10. Rinse thoroughly with fingertips downward.

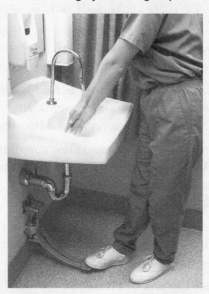

11. Dry hands.

12. Use a paper towel to turn off faucets and open door if necessary.

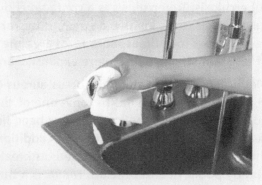

13. Use lotion on hands to prevent chapping, if needed.

BACKGROUND: Personal protective equipment (PPE) are a variety of barriers and respirators used alone or in combination to protect mucous membranes, airways, skin, and clothing from contact with infectious agents.

PREPROCEDURE

1. Determine the expected level of exposure.

2. Refer to the CDC guidelines for the use of Personal Protective Equipment to determine the appropriate PPE equipment to use.

3. Always practice safe work practices, which includes:

   a. Keep hands away from face.

   b. Work from clean to dirty.

   c. Limit surfaces touched.

   d. Change when torn or heavily contaminated.

   e. Perform hand hygiene.

PROCEDURE

NOTE: When using Personal Protective Equipment, don in the order the procedures are given. Prior to donning protective equipment:

   a. Remove your watch or push it well up your arm.

   b. Wash your hands.

Gown

1. Untie the gown's waist strings; then put the gown on and wrap it around the back of your uniform.

2. Tie or snap the gown at the neck and at the waist making sure your uniform is completely covered.

Mask

Surgical type masks are used to cover the nose and mouth and provide protection from contact with large infectious droplets (over 5 mm in size). For protection from inhalation of small particles or droplet nuclei particulate respirators are recommended. The health care worker must be fitted for these masks prior to use in order to maintain appropriate seal and protection. The infection control department staff will do fit testing for the employee during the employees orientation period.

1. Determine the appropriate type of face mask to be used.

2. Place the mask snugly over your nose and mouth. Secure the mask by tying the strings behind your head or placing the loops around your ears.

3. If the mask has a metal strip, squeeze it to fit your nose firmly.

4. If you wear eyeglasses, tuck the mask under their lower edge.

Goggles/Face Shield

Goggles or face shield should be worn when there is a risk of contaminating the mucous membranes of the eyes.

Mouthpieces, Resuscitation Bags, and Other Ventilation Devices

Use a ventilation device, which provides protection for the caregiver from oral contact and secretions, as alternative to mouth to mouth resuscitation.

Gloves

Gloves should be worn when there is risk of touching blood or body fluids. Gloves are worn only once and are discarded according to agency policy. Some care activities for an individual patient may require changing gloves more than once. Hands should be thoroughly washed after gloves are removed.

1. Use clean, disposable gloves.

2. Select a glove that provides appropriate fit.

3. Place the gloves on the hands so that they extend to cover the wrist of the isolation gown.

(continued)

Removing Personal Protective Equipment

Remember that the outside surfaces of your Personal Protective Equipment are contaminated.

1. While wearing gloves, untie the gowns waist strings.

2. With your gloved left hand, remove the right glove by pulling on the cuff, turning the glove inside out as you pull.

3. Remove the left glove by placing two fingers in the glove and pulling it off, turning it inside out as you remove it. Discard. Wash your hands.

4. Untie the neck strings of your gown. Grasp the outside of the gown at the back of the shoulders and pull the gown down over your arms, turning it inside out as you remove it.

5. Holding the gown well away from your uniform, fold it inside out. Discard it in the laundry hamper.

6. Wash your hands. Turn off the faucet using a paper towel and discard the towel in trash container.

7. Remove the mask/goggles to avoid contaminating your face or hair in the process. Untie your mask and/or remove your goggles by holding only the strings/strap. Discard.

8. Wash your hands and forearms with soap or antiseptic after leaving the room.

PROCEDURE **17.3** **Caring for Soiled Linens**

BACKGROUND: The hospital laundry uses water temperature and cleaning products capable of destroying any pathogens that might be present in patient's bed linens.

ALERT: Follow Standard Precautions.

PREPROCEDURE

1. Wash hands.

2. Don disposable gloves.

PROCEDURE

3. Fold the soiled bed linens inward upon themselves when removing them from the bed.

4. Hold the linens away from your uniform when removing from room.

5. Place in the nearest hamper.

6. Should the outside surface of the linen hamper bag become soiled it should be placed in a clean outer bag prior to pickup by the laundry staff.

PROCEDURE 17.4 Disposing of Sharps

BACKGROUND: Because of the danger inherent in handling sharp objects or contaminated needles the health care industry has moved towards needleless systems whenever possible. When a needleless system cannot be provided, needles with have a protective sheath used to cover before and after use. There is no longer any need to recap used needles.

ALERT: Follow Standard Precautions.

PREPROCEDURE

1. Select the safest method of using sharps, using a needleless system whenever possible.

2. Wash hands.

3. Don disposable gloves.

4. Locate the closest sharps container to the area you will be working in.

NOTE: Gloves are not meant to protect the care giver from needle stick or sharps injuries.

PROCEDURE

5. After the use of any needle place the protective sheath before leaving the patient area.

6. If sharps are used during a procedure, carefully separate them from other items on the tray and cover them with the procedure tray cover.

7. Place any disposable sharps items in the closest sharps container.

8. For non-disposable sharps items place them in the designated area of the closest dirty utility room.

9. Remove and discard disposable gloves.

10. Wash hands.

PROCEDURE 17.5 Wrapping Instruments for Autoclave

BACKGROUND: Reusable items used for providing patient care must be cleaned and sterilized before re-use. This requires that the item be cleaned and appropriately wrapped prior to being sterilized. This will include instruments, basins, glassware, patient care equipment, and any other items deemed necessary. The facility will provide an area, known as the Decontamination Room, for this activity.

ALERT: Follow Standard Precautions.

PREPROCEDURE

1. Retrieve/receive instruments and equipment to be decontaminated.

2. Don appropriate attire:

   a. scrub uniform

   b. head cover

   c. cover gown

   d. gloves

   e. goggles and/or face mask

PROCEDURE

3. Sort grossly soiled instruments from those less soiled.

4. Soak instruments that have gross soil in approved enzymatic hospital cleaner. If manual scrubbing is necessary, a soft bristled brush will be used below the water line to decrease the possibility of aerosol contamination.

(continued)

5. Place instruments with moving parts or hard to reach areas in Sonic Cleaner in open position for cycle. All large surface instruments, retractors and elevators will be cleaned manually.

6. Rinse all instruments, washed mechanically or manually, in standing tap water, and running tap water.

7. Immerse instruments with moving parts in instrument lubricant for 45 seconds.

8. Wash instrument trays, washbasins, and rubber items in warm water.

9. Rinse items in standing tap water and running tap water, and dry before wrapping.

10. Wash glassware, such as syringes, in warm water and appropriate cleaner. Rinse in standing, running tap water, and distilled water.

11 Air-dry syringes before preparing for sterilization.

12. After the cleaning process, move all instruments to the assembly table in the clean processing room.

13. Assemble, using the appropriate item list for each tray. Note any shortages and try to locate any missing instruments.

14. Make note of any sets with missing instruments.

15. Place tray with items onto designated wrapper. Fold each side of the wrapper in towards the middle. Secure the wrapper with autoclave tape.

(a)

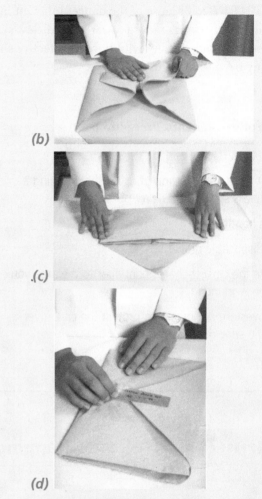

(b)

.(c)

(d)

16. Notify autoclave personnel of trays, items when readied for sterilizing.

POSTPROCEDURE

17. Personnel are responsible for maintaining a clean area.

18. Hand washing is mandatory prior to leaving the area.

🖳 Summary

Infection control is critical in health care environments. Asepsis is the method used to destroy the environment that allows pathogens to live, breed, and spread. Major factors in the control of microorganisms are handwashing, disinfection, sterilization, and following Standard Precautions. The effective health care worker always strives to provide an aseptic environment by following aseptic technique procedures and Standard Precautions.

SECTION 17.2 Review Questions

1. Define the term *asepsis*.

2. What are five aseptic techniques?

3. List five body fluids that should be handled using Standard Precautions.

4. What is the difference between bactericidal and bacteriostatic substances?

5. Why is it important to maintain asepsis?

6. What are the guidelines for handwashing?

Learn By Doing: Section 17.2 Activity

1. Complete Worksheets 1 and 2.

2. Complete Worksheet/Activity 3 as assigned.

3. When you are confident that you can meet each objective for this section, ask your teacher for the section evaluation.

SECTION 17.3 Transmission-Based Precautions

Background

As a health care worker, you are exposed to patients, equipment, and supplies that are contaminated with pathogens. An estimated 2.4 million hospital-acquired infections occur in the United States each year. These infections may cause as many as 30,000 deaths annually. Use the techniques taught in this chapter to protect yourself and other people and to help prevent the spread of infection to patients, co-workers, and the community.

Objectives

When you have completed this section, you will be able to do the following:

- Match key terms with their meanings.
- Name primary levels of precautions identified in the guidelines developed by the Centers for Disease Control and Prevention (CDC).
- Identify three types of Transmission-Based Precautions.
- Demonstrate the correct procedure for entering and leaving an area where Transmission-Based Precautions are followed.
- Differentiate between Standard Precautions and Transmission-Based Precautions.

 ### Introduction to Standard and Transmission-Based Precautions

The 2007 guidelines from the CDC established the need for two levels of protection. Standard Precautions are the primary strategy for successful hospital-acquired (nosocomial) infection control. Standard Precautions are appropriate for all patients receiving care or service in a health care environment, regardless of their diagnosis.

As stated in Section 17.2, these precautions provide protection from contact with blood, mucous membranes, nonintact skin, and all body fluids. Transmission-Based Precautions are designed for patients suspected to be infected with pathogens spread by **airborne** or **droplet** transmission, contact with dry skin, or contact with contaminated surfaces.

Sterile technique is first and foremost about minimizing possible sources of infection. *Sterile* means free of bugs that can infect people. Sterility will apply to surfaces of objects or to substances that will be introduced into a patient's body. Some objects, like hands or surgical masks, can be clean, but not sterile. Only specific prepared surfaces or substances, like surgical tools, are considered sterile.

Transmission-Based Precautions are used in addition to Standard Precautions when some contagious diseases are present. There are three types of Transmission-Based Precautions:

- Airborne Precautions.
- Droplet Precautions.
- Contact Precautions.

Follow the guidelines in Table 17.4 when working with patients in Transmission-Based Precaution environments.

Communicable Diseases

The AIDS Patient

AIDS (Autoimmune deficiency syndrome) is a chronic, life threatening condition caused by the human immunodeficiency virus (HIV). HIV destroys the cells of the immune system which affects the body's ability to fight bacteria, fungi, and viruses. This makes the body more susceptible to certain types of cancers and opportunistic infections that the body would normally resist, such as pneumonias, Kaposi's sarcoma, and tuberculosis.

The first cases of this disease were reported in the 1980s. When first discovered, there was rampant fear of anyone with HIV or AIDS. People avoided contact with infected people. Even some health care workers devoted to the care of the ill refused to care for them. The homosexual population was particularly affected by this isolation, and even those that were not infected were sometimes treated as outcasts.

AIDS has become a global epidemic—38.6 million people are living with HIV. In 2005, more than 4 million people were newly infected with HIV; 25 million have died of AIDS since the epidemic began. Progress has been made in the treatment of and improved access to care. However, our best hope for stemming the spread of the virus lies in prevention, treatment and education.

On a positive note, the recognition of this disease was instrumental in the creation of Standard Precautions and the continuing revision of precautions for Occupational Health and Bloodborne Pathogens. Education about the causes and treatment of the disease has progressed to the point that health care workers and the general public are more accepting and much less fearful of those infected. Famous people who have become infected with this virus have done much to quell the fear and isolation of this population.

Table 17.4 Transmission-Based Precautions

Common Communicable Diseases Requiring Special Precautions	Type of Precautions	Precaution Guidelines

Chickenpox (Varicella zoster)
Tuberculosis
Herpes zoster (Shingles, Varicella zoster)
	Airborne: Reduces the spread of airborne droplet nuclei (5 **microns** or smaller in size) or dust particles containing the pathogen	■ Standard Precautions
		■ Private room with specific ventilation criteria
		■ Keep the room door closed
		■ Wear respiratory protection
		■ Wash hands:
		  – before entering the room
		  – before leaving the room
		  – after leaving the room

Haemophilus influenzae
Some forms of meningitis
Diphtheria
Pertussis
Adenovirus
Mumps
Some forms of pneumonia
Severe viral infections
	Droplet: Reduces the risk of transmission by contact of the mucous membranes of the eye, nose, or mouth with large particle droplets	■ Standard Precautions
		■ Private room or room with another patient with same pathogen
		■ Wear a mask when working within three feet of the patient
		■ Wash hands
		  – before entering the room
		  – before leaving the room
		  – after leaving the room

Multidrug-resistant infections of:
Gastrointestinal system
Respiratory system
Integumentary system (skin) such as gloves and gowns
	Contact: Reduces the risk of of transmission through direct or indirect contact	■ Standard Precautions
		■ Private room or room with another patient with same pathogen
		■ Use personal protective equipment (PPE)
		■ Wash hands:
		  – before entering the room
		  – before leaving the room
		  – after leaving the room

Use the following precautions against HIV and AIDS:

- Education about safe sex practices.
- Use clean needles. Dispose of used needles appropriately in designated sharps boxes. Never re-cap needles.
- Report and receive follow-up care for any needle sticks or exposures to bloodborne pathogens.
- Remember the importance of following the procedure for Standard Precautions.
- Don't become complacent.

When treating HIV positive or AIDS patients, be sure to:

- Educate yourself and the patient.
- Help the patient understand options for treatment.
- Be supportive.
- Promote the patient's role as an individual and a member of the community.

microns
(MAHY krohns)
Units equaling one millionth of a meter.

When treating HIV positive or AIDS patients, do NOT:

- Avoid personal contact.
- Isolate patient from human contact.
- Exhibit personal prejudices.

NOTE: There is no need to wear protective gloves when directly interacting with these patients. Only use gloves when there is a danger of contact with blood or body fluids, mucous membrane or non-intact skin. As with any other patient practicing good hand washing techniques is always appropriate and in the caregiver and patient's best interest.

Patients with Communicable Diseases

Patients who can contaminate the area with known communicable diseases should be in a private room or isolated from other patients. There will be a list of diseases which are communicable and the cautions which should be taken available on the patient unit. The infection control department will monitor all admissions and advise staff of any additional precautions that need to be taken.

Before you start to measure vital signs or work with patients, you must remember to follow the basic Standard Precautions necessary to protect yourself when contact with blood or body fluids is possible. Make sure you review Tables 17.5 and 17.6.

Table 17.5 Standard Precautions with Risk Categorization

Infection-control guidelines exist to protect employees and patients against infectious viruses and bacteria. The Standard Precautions you take depend on the (1) potential for contact with blood, (2) potential for contact with any body fluids, and (3) tasks (procedures) that you perform. This table tells you what to wear when you are doing various tasks. Follow these guidelines to protect yourself and others from infection.

Category	Task Requires	Protect Yourself By	Have Available

I: High risk	Direct contact with blood or other body fluids	■ Washing hands:
		  – If you touch blood/body fluids
		  – After removing gloves
		■ Wearing:
		  – Apron or gown
		  – Eye protection
		  – Face mask
		■ Never recapping needles or bending/breaking them
		■ Placing used needles in a sharps container
		■ Cleaning off blood/body fluids immediately
		■ Disposing of waste materials in biohazard container
		■ Being vaccinated for hepatitis B
			Gloves
			Apron
			Eye protection
			Face mask

II: Low risk	When you have close contact with patients but are not likely to come in contact with blood/body fluids	Washing hands	Mask Eye protection Gloves
III: No risk	Your routine work requires no contact with blood/body fluid	Washing hands, as a general rule	

Table 17.6   Standard Precautions: Examples of Tasks and Use of Protective Equipment

Task	Gloves	Gown	Mask	Protective Eyewear
Controlling spurting blood	Yes	Yes	Yes	Yes
Controlling minimal bleeding	Yes	No	No	No
Blood drawing	Yes	Yes	Yes	Yes
Oral or nasal suction	Yes	No	Yes	Yes
Handling/cleaning contaminated instruments	Yes	Yes	Yes	Yes
Measuring blood pressure	No	No	No	No

Transmission-Based Precaution Rooms

Figures 17.5 and 17.6 illustrate precautions that should be taken within the room when contagious diseases are present. When entering or leaving a Transmission-Based Precaution room, follow the specific directions on the precaution card at the door.

There is also another type of isolation: reverse or protective isolation. This is the type of isolation used for patients who are not contagious, but whose immune system is so weak that they must be protected from other people that might be carrying disease. Some examples of these are patients on chemotherapy, leukemia, burn patients, etc.

Figure 17.4
Protective clothing and gear includes gloves, masks, aprons, and goggles.

The procedures titled *Applying Personal Protective Equipment* and *Removing Personal Protective Equipment* guide you through the steps in applying and removing personal protective equipment. Each medical environment determines the specific order in which to apply each item. Always follow your organization's policies and procedures.

Psychosocial Issues During Special Precautions

Transmission-Based Precautions may be difficult for patients. The patients are alone most of the time. Visitors must wear personal protective wear. Hugs or touching may not be allowed. The health care worker cannot stay and visit because there is other work to do. This may cause the patient to feel angry, depressed, and frustrated.

Take as much time as you can to listen to the patient's feelings and concerns. Encourage communication, and be supportive. If the patient seems unusually upset, report it to your supervisor.

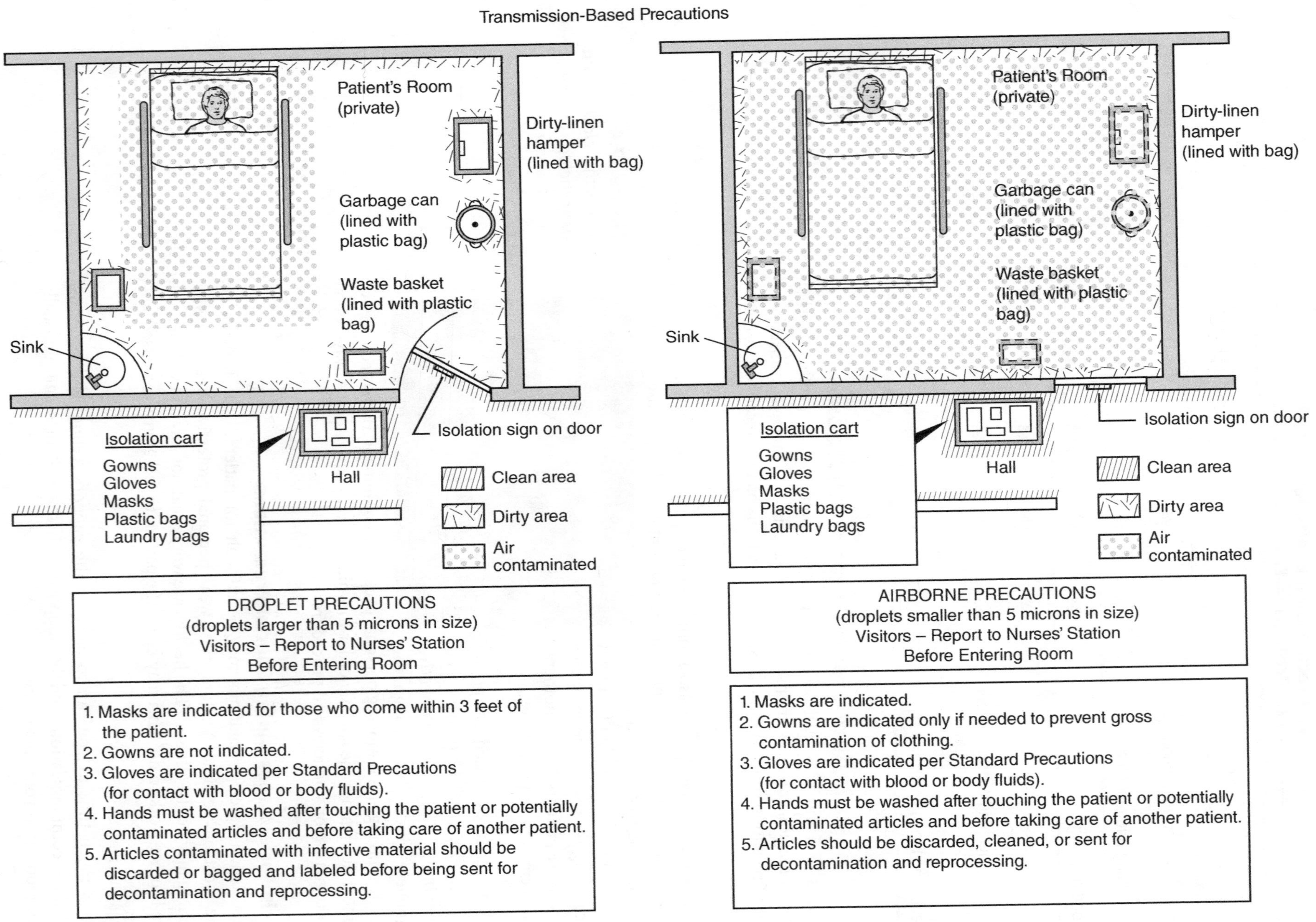

Transmission-Based Precautions

Dirty-linen hamper (lined with bag)

Patient's Room (private)

Garbage can (lined with plastic bag)

Waste basket (lined with plastic bag)

Sink

Isolation sign on door

Hall

Isolation cart
Gowns
Gloves
Masks
Plastic bags
Laundry bags

Clean area

Dirty area

Air contaminated

AIRBORNE PRECAUTIONS
(droplets smaller than 5 microns in size)
Visitors – Report to Nurses' Station
Before Entering Room

1. Masks are indicated.
2. Gowns are indicated only if needed to prevent gross contamination of clothing.
3. Gloves are indicated per Standard Precautions (for contact with blood or body fluids).
4. Hands must be washed after touching the patient or potentially contaminated articles and before taking care of another patient.
5. Articles should be discarded, cleaned, or sent for decontamination and reprocessing.

Dirty-linen hamper (lined with bag)

Patient's Room (private)

Garbage can (lined with plastic bag)

Waste basket (lined with plastic bag)

Sink

Isolation sign on door

Hall

Isolation cart
Gowns
Gloves
Masks
Plastic bags
Laundry bags

Clean area

Dirty area

Air contaminated

DROPLET PRECAUTIONS
(droplets larger than 5 microns in size)
Visitors – Report to Nurses' Station
Before Entering Room

1. Masks are indicated for those who come within 3 feet of the patient.
2. Gowns are not indicated.
3. Gloves are indicated per Standard Precautions (for contact with blood or body fluids).
4. Hands must be washed after touching the patient or potentially contaminated articles and before taking care of another patient.
5. Articles contaminated with infective material should be discarded or bagged and labeled before being sent for decontamination and reprocessing.

Figure 17.5
Transmission-Based Precautions. How do precautions for airborne and droplet transmission differ?

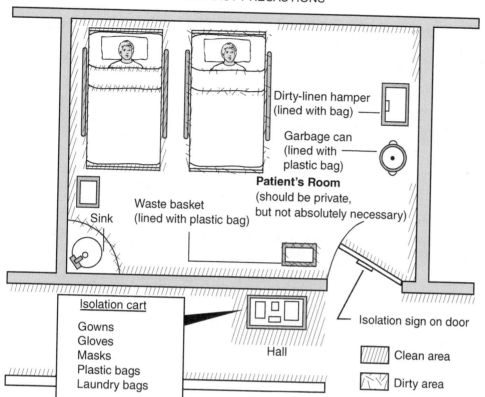

CONTACT PRECAUTIONS

Figure 17.6
Contact precautions. When do you need to use gloves, gowns, and masks for a patient undergoing contact precautions?

Dirty-linen hamper (lined with bag)

Garbage can (lined with plastic bag)

Patient's Room (should be private, but not absolutely necessary)

Waste basket (lined with plastic bag)

Sink

Isolation sign on door

Isolation cart

Gowns
Gloves
Masks
Plastic bags
Laundry bags

Hall

///// Clean area

Dirty area

CONTACT PRECAUTIONS
Visitors – Report to Nurses' Station
Before Entering Room

---

1. **Masks** are not indicated.
2. **Gowns** are indicated if soiling is likely.
3. **Gloves** are indicated for touching infective material.
4. **Hands must be washed after touching the patient or potentially contaminated articles and before taking care of another patient.**
5. **Articles** contaminated with infective material should be discarded or bagged and labeled before being sent for decontamination and reprocessing.

A private room is indicated for Contact Precautions if patient hygiene is poor. A patient with poor hygiene does not wash hands after touching infective material, contaminates the environment with infective material, or shares contaminated articles with other patients. In general, patients infected with the same organism may share a room.

Taking steps to educate patients and their families on procedures during special precaution situations can help reduce anxiety for everyone involved. You can make a difference by staying attuned and responding to patients' feelings and moods, always treating each person with dignity, and by providing the very best care. Some age-specific considerations for patients/clients requiring Transmission-Based Precautions are listed in Table 17.7.

Table 17.7   Age-Specific Considerations

Isolation is difficult for patients of any age. Understanding the special needs of each group gives the patient a sense of security and improves the healing process.

Age	Communication	Comfort	Safety
Birth–5 years	Explain the reason for isolation to the parents and family members.	Keep child with parent or family member to increase feeling of security.	Teach family the procedures that must be followed in an isolation area.
5–12 years	Explain the reason for isolation and the importance of staying in the isolation unit.	Keep child with parent or family member to increase feeling of security.	Teach patient, parent, or family member the procedures.
12+ years	Explain the reason for isolation and the importance of staying in the isolation unit.	Encourage peer, parent, or family member to stay as much as possible.	Teach patient, peer, and family members the procedures for isolation.

PROCEDURE 17.6

Putting on Sterile Gloves and Removing Gloves

BACKGROUND: Sterile gloves cover the hands and allow treatment of open skin areas. Following the procedure is essential to prevent contamination of the gloves. Contamination allows bacteria to enter the treatment area and may cause infection.

PREPROCEDURE

1. Assemble equipment.

2. Wash hands.

PROCEDURE

3. Pick up wrapped gloves.

4. Check to be certain that they are sterile.

    a. Package intact

    b. Seal of sterility

5. Place on clean, flat surface.

6. Open wrapper by handling only the outside. (Figures a and b).

7. Maintain sterility of wrap and gloves.

8. Position with cuff end toward self.

9. Use your left hand to pick up the right-handed glove at folded cuff edge, touching only the inside of glove (Figure c).

(a)

10. Grasp inside of glove with thumb and forefinger.

11. Lift glove out and insert other hand.

12. Put on glove while maintaining sterility.

13. Put glove on right hand (Figure d).

(continued)

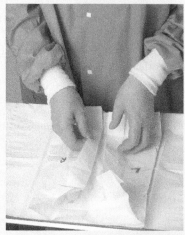

(b)

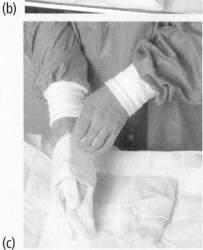

(c)

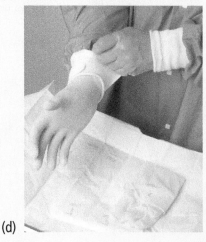

(d)

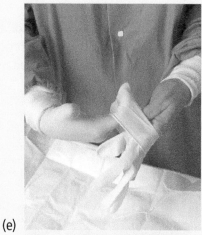

(e)

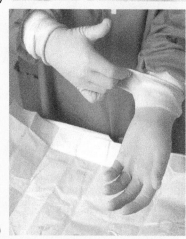

(f)

14. Use gloved right hand to pick up left-handed glove (Figures e–f).

15. Place finger of gloved right hand under cuff of left-handed glove.

16. Lift glove up and away from wrapper to pull onto left hand.

17. Continue pulling left glove under wrist. (Be certain that gloved right thumb does not touch skin or clothing.)

18. Place fingers under cuff of right glove and pull cuff up over right wrist with gloved left hand.

19. Adjust fingers of gloves as necessary.

20. Keep hands in view and above waist one sterile gloves are on.

21. If either glove tears, remove and discard. Begin with new gloves!

POSTPROCEDURE

22. Turn gloves inside out as you remove them.

17.7

Transmission-Based Precautions: Applying Personal Protective Equipment

BACKGROUND: A primary responsibility of all health care workers is to prevent the spread of pathogenic microorganisms. Wearing appropriate protective equipment is one way health care workers can protect themselves and others from being infected by pathogenic microorganisms.

ALERT: Follow Standard Precautions

PREPROCEDURE

1. Assemble equipment.

2. Wash hands.

PROCEDURE

3. Cover all hair on head with a paper cap.

4. Put on a mask by:

   a. Unfolding mask if appropriate.

   b. Cover mouth and nose with mask.

   c. Secure mask by:

      (1) Pulling elastic on each side of mask over ear, or

      (2) Tying top string at sides of mask at back of head and tie lower string at back of neck.

5. Put on gown with opening at back. Slip arms into sleeves of gown.

   a. Tie bow at back of neck.

   b. Overlap gown edges.

   c. Tie at waist with bow or fasten with Velcro strip.

   d. Make sure that uniform is completely covered.

BACKGROUND: A primary responsibility of all health care workers is to prevent the spread of pathogenic microorganisms. Removing and disposing of protective equipment appropriately is one way health care workers prevent the spread of pathogenic microorganisms.

ALERT: Follow Standard Precautions

PREPROCEDURE

1. Untie waist tie of gown.

PROCEDURE

2. Remove gloves by:

   a. With dominant hand, remove other glove by grasping it just below wrist.

   b. Pulling the first glove inside out as you remove it from hand.

   c. With first two fingers of ungloved hand, reach inside glove without touching outside of glove —pull glove off hand covering the first glove. (The second glove removed surrounds the first and both are inside out.) Discard.

3. Wash hands.

4. Untie gown at neck.

5. Remove gown by:

   a. Crossing arms and grasping shoulder of gown with each hand.

   b. Pull gown forward causing it to fold inside out.

   c. Roll gown so that all contaminated portions are inside of roll, and place in dirty hamper marked *Toxic Waste* or *Hazardous Waste* inside room.

6. Wash hands.

7. Remove cap and mask, and discard.

POSTPROCEDURE

8. Use paper towel to open door.

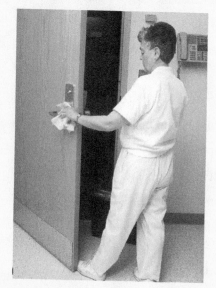

9. Discard towel inside room.

10. Wash hands immediately after leaving the room.

BACKGROUND: Proper technique in changing a sterile dressing prevents wound infection and contamination to the health care worker.

ALERT: Follow Standard Precautions.

PREPROCEDURE

1. Wash hands.
2. Assemble supplies.
   a. Pair of nonsterile examination gloves
   b. Pair of sterile examination gloves
   c. Sterile dressing material
   d. Tape
   e. Biohazardous waste container
3. Explain procedure to patient.
4. Position patient/client.

PROCEDURE

5. Put on nonsterile gloves.
6. Remove soiled dressing and examination gloves. Note appearance of wound (size, color, drainage).
7. Discard in biohazardous waste container.
8. Wash hands.
9. Designate a site to be used as a sterile field.
   a. Place sterile drape on site.
   b. Open and place all sterile dressing supplies on sterile field.
   c. Pour wound-cleaning solution or antiseptic into sterile container.
10. Put on sterile gloves.
11. Medicate wound as directed by physician.
12. Apply a double layer of gauze to wound or incision.

NOTE: If moderate to heavy drainage is expected, reinforce dressing. If drainage seeps through to outer layer, wound will be contaminated.

POSTPROCEDURE

13. Remove gloves and place in biohazardous waste container.
14. Wash hands.
15. Secure dressing with tape.
16. Document the following:
    a. Date
    b. Time
    c. Type of dressing applied
    d. Appearance of wound
    e. Your name and certification

Summary

In this section you learned about Transmission-Based Precautions, which are designed for patients suspected to be infected with pathogens. In the preceding section you learned about Standard Precautions, which are required for the care of all patients. Your careful use of these precautions prevents transmission of infectious agents that cause disease and illness in yourself and other people.

SECTION **17.3** **Review Questions**

1. List three types of Transmission-Based Precautions.

2. Describe the procedure for entering and leaving an area where Transmission-Based Precautions are followed.

3. Compare Standard Precautions and Transmission-Based Precautions.

4. How might a patient respond to Transmission-Based Precautions?

5. Describe an age-related concern for Transmission-Based Precautions.

6. What is the meaning of *sterile*?

Learn By Doing: Section 17.3 Activity

1. Complete Worksheet 1.

2. Complete Worksheet/Activity 2.

3. Complete the Chapter Review.

4. When you are confident that you can meet each objective for this section, ask your teacher for the section evaluation.

Bloodborne Diseases and Precautions

Background

Bloodborne diseases are a potential risk in the health care setting. A caregiver must understand how to protect him- or herself from blood and body fluids that are contaminated with blood. Additional precautions are required to prevent the spread of bloodborne pathogens.

Objectives

When you have completed this section, you will be able to do the following:

- Describe three bloodborne diseases.
- Define the term *vaccine*.
- List three ways by which bloodborne diseases are accidentally passed.
- List two behaviors that increase the risk of contracting bloodborne diseases.

- Describe Universal Precautions.
- List six pieces of equipment used in Universal Precautions.
- Discuss ethical and legal issues related to bloodborne diseases.

bloodborne
(BLUHD born)
Carried in the blood.

hepatitis B (HBV)
(hep uh TAHY tuhs BEE)
Bloodborne viral disease that affects the liver; transmitted by blood exposure, sexual contact, sharing needles, or from infected mother to infant.

vaccine
(vak SEEN)
Harmless form of a pathogen that helps the body develop immunity to a disease.

hepatitis C (HVC)
(hep uh TAHY tuhs SEE)
Bloodborne viral disease that affects the liver; transmitted by blood exposure, sharing needles, or from infected mother to infant; rarely transmitted by sexual contact.

Types of Bloodborne Illnesses

Sometimes, pathogens are transmitted through contact with blood, body fluids contaminated with blood, semen, or vaginal secretions. These pathogens are called **bloodborne** pathogens. In the health care setting, you may be exposed to the following three bloodborne pathogens:

- **Hepatitis B (HBV):** Hepatitis B is a viral disease that attacks the liver. It causes scarring of the liver and liver cancer and can eventually lead to death. There is no cure for HBV, but health care personnel should receive a **vaccine** (Figure 17.7) against the disease.

- **Hepatitis C (HCV):** Like HBV, HCV is a virus that attacks the liver, causing many of the same problems as HBV does. The HBV vaccine may help prevent HCV infection, but there is not vaccine for HCV.

- **Human immunodeficiency virus (HIV):** HIV is a viral disease that attacks the immune system. It breaks down the body's immune defenses, making it easier for other infections to occur. HIV does not kill a patient, but it weakens the immune system so much that the patient may die from an opportunistic infection. HIV causes **acquired immunodeficiency syndrome** (AIDS).

Transmission of Bloodborne Diseases

In the health care setting, bloodborne diseases are rarely passed between caregiver and patient. However, the risk is still present, so precautions should be taken. Direct contact with infected blood and blood-contaminated body fluids can introduce a bloodborne disease. The following accidents may result in bloodborne disease infection:

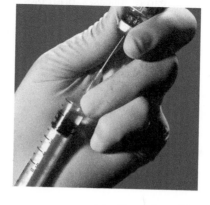

Figure 17.7
Vaccines prevent diseases such as HBV. Who should be vaccinated against HBV?

- Accidental needlesticks: Puncture wounds from needles contaminated with diseased blood.

- Cuts from sharp instruments: Cuts from sharp instruments that have been in contact with infected blood.

- Direct contact with infected blood: Infected blood comes in contact with the eyes, nose, mouth, or skin.

Bloodborne diseases are sometimes passed from an infected mother to her infant. In the past, these diseases were transmitted to people through blood transfusions and organ donations from infected donors. New testing methods have made this mode of infection rare.

Bloodborne diseases are **not** spread through casual contact, hugging, or kissing. Additionally, they cannot be spread by food or water, sharing utensils and dishes, coughing, or sneezing.

At-Risk Behaviors

Some behaviors put people at greater risk of contracting a bloodborne disease. Those behaviors include the following:

- Unprotected sex, including oral sex.
- Sharing needles to inject illegal drugs.

Each of these behaviors puts people in contact with blood, semen, or vaginal fluids, all of which can carry bloodborne pathogens. (A notable exception is HCV, which is rarely spread through sexual contact. Instead, HCV is spread by transmitted by blood-to-blood contact, such as unsterilized injection equipment or infusion of inadequately screened blood and blood products.)

Universal Precautions

As a health care worker, you should follow Standard Precautions in dealing with patients. Additionally, you should use **Universal Precautions** to prevent the transmission of bloodborne diseases. Universal Precautions are similar to Standard Precautions. You should avoid direct contact with blood, vaginal secretions, semen, pericardial fluid, amniotic fluid, peritoneal fluid, interstitial fluid, and pleural fluid. You do not need to take Universal Precautions for feces, nasal secretions, sputum, sweat, tears, urine, vomit, or saliva unless it is contaminated with blood.

human immunodeficiency virus (HIV)
(HYOO man i MYOO noe dih FIHSH uhn see VAHY ruhs)
Virus that infects cells of the immune system, reducing the immune system's ability to fight disease; transmitted by blood exposure, sexual contact, sharing needles, or from infected mother to infant.

acquired immunodeficiency syndrome (AIDS)
(uh KWAHY uhrd i myoo noh dih FIHSH uhn see SIHN droem)
Late stages of HIV infection; characterized by secondary infections.

Universal Precautions
(yoo nuh VER suhl pree KAHW shuhns)
A set of precautions that prevents the transmission of HIV, HBV, HCV, and other bloodborne pathogens when providing health care.

CAUTION: You should always wear gloves when handling body fluids to prevent the spread of diseases, both bloodborne and not.

Universal Precautions require the use of the following protective equipment:

- Gloves.
- Gowns.
- Aprons.
- Masks.
- Protective eyewear. (Figure 17.8)
- Resuscitation equipment that prevents the spread of pathogens.

Figure 17.8
Gloves protect your hands from infected blood. Goggles protect your eyes from infected blood. Does the protective eyewear in the photo completely protect the eyes? Explain your reasoning.

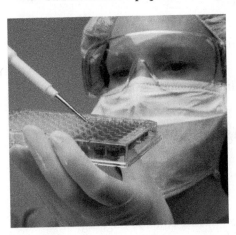

Under Universal Precautions, you should also take steps to avoid injuries caused by contaminated scalpels, needles, and other sharp instruments. Surfaces and equipment that come in contact with infected blood should be sterilized using a bleach solution or as dictated by facility guidelines.

Testing for Bloodborne Diseases

There are some external symptoms of HBV and HCV infections, such as jaundiced (yellowed) skin. However, HIV infection may not have external symptoms. A blood test can confirm the presence of any of these three diseases. A false positive is possible, so multiple tests are required to verify infection.

As a health care worker, your facility likely has a routine blood testing procedure in place. You will need to undergo regular blood testing. If you are exposed to infected blood, you likely will need to be tested more often.

Ethical and Legal Issues

As a health care worker, your employer has certain obligations to keep you safe. The employer should provide protective equipment at all times. Your employer should also have practices in place that reduce your risk of exposure. You should also be vaccinated with the HBV vaccine.

If you are exposed to a bloodborne disease, your employer should also offer management and treatment for the disease. Exposure, whether you contract the disease or not, will be recorded in your confidential medical records. It may be reported to government agencies for disease tracking and research purposes. Regardless, your personal information will remain private.

Personal Wellness

What to Do After Exposure to Bloodborne Pathogens

Imagine that you are exposed to blood during work. Do you know what to do? You should first take theses steps:

Wash accidental needlesticks and cuts with soap and water.

- If your nose, mouth, or skin is exposed, flush the affected area with water.

- If your eyes are exposed, flush with water, saline, or other sterile solutions as mandated by your facility.

- Always report the exposure to your manager. You will need to discuss the exposure with your facility's exposure management department to evaluate your risks and postexposure treatment.

Postexposure treatment depends on the type of exposure. Because health care workers are given the HBV vaccine, the risk of infection is low. Workers should be tested within a couple months of vaccination to make sure immunity is complete. Hepatitis B immune globulin and/or the HBV vaccine can be given after exposure to prevent infection. Treatment should start within 24 hours of exposure. Because postexposure treatment is usually effective, routine follow-up is not recommended unless there are symptoms.

For HCV, there is no vaccine. Also, there is no postexposure medical treatment. So, preventative measures are important in the case of HCV. However, the incidence of HCV infection after exposure is relatively low when compared to HBV. A person who is exposed to HCV should be tested immediately after exposure and 4 to 6 months after exposure to see if he or she is infected.

As with HCV, there is no vaccine for HIV. The use of antiretroviral drugs after exposure has been shown to reduce the transmission of HIV. However, these drugs have serious side effects, so they are not used unless exposure is significant. Treatment should start as soon as possible. A person exposed to HIV should be tested for the virus as soon as possible after exposure. Testing should be repeated at 6 months and then again at one year. Compare the postexposure treatments for HBV, HCV, and HIV.

People who have a bloodborne disease, including health care workers, have certain legal rights. A health care facility must maintain a patient's confidentiality. Participation in any treatment and testing must be voluntary. A facility should also offer adequate information, support, and referrals to help an infected individual and his or her family understand the disease and its treatment. Depending on state and federal laws, a health care facility must report bloodborne diseases and make an effort to warn other people who are at risk in a confidential manner.

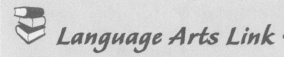

Language Arts Link

Employers and Safety Standards

Pretend that you work for a company that disposes of medical waste. You are concerned that your employer is not taking proper precautions for the safety of the employees.

Write a letter to the manager in charge of safety standards. Include specific examples of your concerns with suggestions for improvements. Be sure to proofread your work to see if you can improve it by making it clearer, more concise, or more interesting to read.

Check the spelling and grammar and correct any errors. When you've completed your letter, exchange it with a classmate. Provide feedback on your classmate's letter, and then exchange back. Read your classmate's comments and revise your letter as necessary.

Summary

Bloodborne diseases include HBV, HCV, and HIV. These diseases are rarely passed between a patient and caregiver, but they still pose a significant risk. A caregiver must follow not only Standard Precautions, but also Universal Precautions. Universal Precautions reduce exposure to blood and blood-contaminated fluids, thus reducing exposure to bloodborne diseases. Additionally, a health care facility is obligated to provide protection and confidentiality to both its patients and its employees.

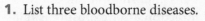

SECTION | **17.4** | **Review Questions**

1. List three bloodborne diseases.

2. What is a vaccine?

3. In the health care setting, how are bloodborne diseases passed from one person to another?

4. What two risky behaviors increase the risk of contracting a bloodborne disease?

5. What are six pieces of equipment used in Universal Precautions?

6. What legal rights are afforded to health care workers who have a bloodborne disease?

Learn By Doing: Section 17.4 Activity

1. Please complete the appropriate worksheets, as directed by your teacher.

2. Prepare responses to each item listed in Chapter Review.

3. When you are confident that you can meet each objective for this section, ask your teacher for the section evaluation.

Chapter Review Questions

1. What is the difference between generalized and localized infections? (17.1)

2. As a health care worker, what preventative measures can you take to avoid contracting microorganisms that are airborne? (17.1)

3. What does the practice of aseptic techniques prevent? (17.2)

4. List some examples of items that require sterilization. (17.2)

5. Why is it important to dry your hands completely after washing them? (17.2)

6. What transmission-based guidelines should a health care worker take when working with a patient that has tuberculosis? (17.3)

7. Why is important for health care workers to provide time and frequent communication to patients that are placed in special precaution rooms or separated from other patients and staff? (17.3)

8. List three types of accidents that could result in bloodborne disease infection. (17.4)

9. Explain Universal Precautions. (17.4)

10. What are an employer's obligations to keep employees safe? (17.4)

Activities

1. Create a table similar to the one below. In the table, describe three bloodborne diseases, their effects, how they are treated, what personal protective equipment the health care worker should use and how a health care worker should respond to exposure. Use this table to create a pamphlet to educate health care workers about bloodborne diseases.

2. Imagine that you are writing questions for a quiz show. Write ten questions that relate to Standard Precautions, Transmission-Based Precautions and Universal Precautions. After writing your questions, test them out on your classmates to see how well they work.

Pathogen	Description of Infection	Treatment	Appropriate PPE	Postexposure response
1.				
2.				
3.				

Case Studies

1. Patients in restricted Transmission-Based Precautions feel isolated and locked away from everyday life. They are often avoided by health care workers and family because of the additional, time-consuming procedures required for their care. Mrs. Grey was just admitted for a tuberculosis infection. Her condition requires her to be in Transmission-Based Airborne Precautions. Write a plan describing how you will comfort Mrs. Grey. Include details about how you will identify and satisfy her special needs.

2. One of your coworkers accidentally cuts her hand with a scalpel after treating a patient who has HCV. How should your coworker respond to the cut?

Chapter 17 Review

Thinking Critically

1. **Communication**—Write a half-page scenario describing how you would explain to a patient the precautionary measures taken daily to control infection in the health care environment. Think in simple terms, such as replacing handkerchiefs with disposable tissues.

2. **Patient Education**—A patient in a Transmission-Based Precaution room requests fresh water immediately after you have cleaned her wound. After you wash your hands and return to get the water jug it becomes clear from her distressed silence that she is offended. Think of ways to talk to her about asepsis and passing on infection so that she understands that this is not a personal matter.

3. **Computers**—Advances in medicine are continually changing the way health care workers protect themselves and treat infections. Explain how computers help keep the medical community informed about the latest medical progress. Describe ways you can access this information if you do not own a computer.

4. **Patient Satisfaction**—Patients in restricted Transmission-Based Precautions feel isolated and locked away from everyday life. They are often avoided by health care workers and family because of the additional, time-consuming procedures required for their care. Mrs. Grey was just admitted for a respiratory tubercle bacillus (tuberculosis—T/B) infection. Her condition requires her to be in Transmission-Based, Airborne Precautions. Write a plan telling how you will provide a sense of comfort and satisfaction while she is in the hospital. Include details about how you will identify and satisfy her special needs.

Media Connection

Use the Companion Web site for additional interactive learning activities: www.prenhall.com/badasch

Portfolio Connection

The medical community is constantly finding new information about how microorganisms affect our lives. This constant flow of new information makes it necessary to research how new findings affect us. Conduct your own research and write a paper about a microorganism. Select a microorganism from those mentioned in this chapter or from another source. Explain how the microorganism affects society and describe its shape, size, color, and pattern of growth. Describe its nature (aerobic or anaerobic), its effect on the body, and the physical symptoms it causes.

Contact a local hospital or the County Health Department infection control manager and ask them to come to class. Develop questions to ask during the class interview that will provide insight into the greatest infectious health risks in the hospital or community and find out why the risk is so high. Write a report and place it in the section of your portfolio labeled "Written Reports and Assignments."

PORTFOLIO TIP

Health care levels of cleanliness may be more demanding than some households. Patients are not necessarily dirty when noncompliant and must not be shamed. It is important to show patients and their families respect in all situations.

Role-play with a classmate and record for your portfolio the rationales you would give two patients. One patient wants to bathe morning and night while the other patient prefers bathing only once a week. Without quoting facility policy, how would you explain to each patient what the acceptable levels of hygiene are and the reasons for them?

18 Measuring Vital Signs and Other Clinical Skills

Getting Started

With a partner, take and record each others' pulse at the beginning of class. Next, as a class, lie still for 5 minutes and obtain a resting pulse. Then, take and record each others' pulse rate again to determine any change. Next, complete 20 jumping jacks or a similar exercise, and then take and record each other's pulse. At the end of the class, take and record the final pulse to compare how the different activities impacted your pulse rate.

NOTE: The restricted breathing exercise results in a comparable physical discomfort to one who has an asthmatic condition or is a long-time smoker.

SECTION 18.1

Temperature, Pulse, and Respiration

Background

Vital signs are important indicators of your patient's health status. Vital signs give you information about breathing, body temperature, and the heart. They indicate how well the body systems are functioning. As a health care worker, you need to observe patients whenever you are near them. Your knowledge of vital signs and how to measure them helps you know when to report that a patient is having problems.

Objectives

When you have completed this section, you will be able to do the following:

- List the vital signs.
- List fourteen factors that influence body temperature.
- Name the sites where temperature can be measured.
- Tell how normal temperature differs depending on the site.
- Describe how to measure oral, rectal, and axillary temperature.

- Describe a common method for measuring a pulse.
- List six factors that influence the pulse rate.
- Demonstrate counting and recording a radial pulse.
- Recognize the two parts of a respiration.
- List eight factors that affect respiration.

Introduction to Vital Signs

Homeostatic mechanisms regulate a person's cardinal vital signs. These vital signs consist of a person's temperature, pulse, **respiration**, and **blood pressure** (BP). The measurement of these cardinal signs indicates the physiologic status of the person and should be compared to norms for the person's developmental level and baseline measurements.

Vital signs are monitored at prescribed times for the hospitalized patient. The frequency of these measurements is increased with any change in the patient's physical condition or whenever an invasive procedure is performed. It is the nurse's responsibility to be able to interpret these vital signs and to know when an intervention is necessary—such as notifying the physician, medicating the patient, or altering any physical activity prescribed for the patient.

Another important indicator of body functioning is the oxygen concentration in the hemoglobin of the arterial blood. This can be measured through a noninvasive technique called **pulse oximetry**.

Pain is considered the fifth cardinal sign. Because it is sometimes difficult to relate to the patient's report of pain, it is best to teach the patient how to use a valid and reliable scale for objectively measuring and reporting pain. This is most frequently a scale of 1–10 with 10 being the patient's highest level of discomfort.

For children or others unable to relate to a numerical scale, the use of differing degrees of the happy face from very happy to very sad is used. For the cognitively impaired patient, it is important that we use our observation skills to determine level of comfort. Look for crying, moaning, grimacing, restlessness. Most importantly, we must allow the patient to rate and report their own pain and not use our subjective views to determine their need for pain relief.

It is extremely important that vital signs be measured and recorded accurately. Be sure to verbally report to the nurse in charge of the patient's care any alteration from norms in vital signs, reports or displays of discomfort, or perceived alterations in the patient's physical or mental status. The nurse will rely on the assistant's ability to communicate this information.

Remember that other health care workers depend on this information when making decisions about the patient's treatment. In this section, you will learn how to measure body temperature and count the pulse rate and respiratory rate. Together, these measurements are referred to as **TPR**. Section 18.2 teaches you to measure blood pressure.

 ## Temperature

Temperature is the measure of body heat. Heat is produced in the body by the muscles and glands and by the **oxidation** of food. Heat is lost from the body by respiration, perspiration, and **excretion**. The balance between the heat produced and the heat lost is the body temperature.

homeostasis
(hoh mee uh STEY sis)
A state of balance, when vital signs are within normal limits.

respiration
(res puh REY shuhn)
Taking oxygen into the body and expelling carbon dioxide (CO_2) from the body.

blood pressure (BP)
(bluhd PRESH er)
Highest and lowest pressure of the blood pushing against the walls of the arteries.

pulse oximetry
(puhls ok SIM I tree)
Procedure used to determine the oxygen concentration in the hemoglobin of the arterial blood.

TPR
(TEE PEE R)
An abbreviation that stands for "temperature, pulse, respiration."

oxidation
(ok si DAY-shun)
The mixing of oxygen and another element

excretion
(ex SKREE-shun)
The process of eliminating waste material

afebrile
(ey FEE bruhl)
Referring to temperature within a normal range.

febrile
(FEE bruhl)
Referring to elevated temperature.

hypothermia
(hahy puh THUR mee uh)
Below-normal temperature.

pyrexia
(pahy REK see uh)
Above-normal temperature.

pyrogenic
(pahy ruh JEN ik)
Producing fever.

If body temperature is within a normal range, it is **afebrile**. Normal body temperature will vary among individuals from .5 to 1 degree Fahrenheit. Using a chart for recording temperatures will allow you to reference the current temperature against past readings to determine the status of the patient. If temperature is elevated, usually considered one degree over the patient's norm, it is **febrile**. Temperature below normal, usually below 95°F, is called **hypothermia**. Temperature above normal is called **pyrexia** (this is another word for fever). Any substance that produces fever is called **pyrogenic**. Table 18.1 shows the factors that influence temperature.

Abnormal Conditions

Fever is not an illness. Actually, it is an important part of the body's defense against infection. Many infants and children develop high fevers with minor viral illnesses. The older adult loses some thermoregulatory control and an elevated temperature will not be the first presenting symptom of infection. While a fever signals that a battle might be going on in the body, the fever is fighting **for** the person, not against.

Most bacteria and viruses that cause infections in people thrive best at 98.6°F. Raising the temperature a few degrees can give your body the winning edge. In addition, a fever activates the body's immune system to make more white blood cells, antibodies, and other infection-fighting agents.

Although infections are the most common causes of elevated body temperature, fevers have a long list of other causes, including toxins, cancers, and autoimmune diseases. Unexplained fevers that continue for days or weeks are called fevers of undetermined origin (FUO).

The most common causes of fevers are "abnormal" conditions, such as:

- Viral and bacterial infections.
- Colds or flu-like illnesses.
- Sore throats and strep throats.
- Ear infections.
- Viral gastroenteritis or bacterial gastroenteritis.
- Acute bronchitis.
- Infectious mononucleosis ("mono").
- Urinary tract infections (UTIs).
- Upper respiratory infections, such as tonsillitis or laryngitis.

Occasionally, fevers indicate more serious problems, such as pneumonia, appendicitis, tuberculosis, and meningitis; or rheumatoid diseases and autoimmune disorders, AIDS, ulcerative colitis, and cancer.

Thermometers

A thermometer is an instrument used to measure temperature. There are several types of thermometers: glass thermometers, aural thermometers, temporal artery thermometers, chemically treated paper or plastic thermometers, and electronic/digital thermometers.

Table 18.1 Factors That Influence Temperature

Increase Temperature	Decrease Temperature
Exercise	Sleep
Digestion of food	Fasting
Increased environmental temperature	Exposure to cold
Illness	Certain illnesses
Infection	Decreased muscle activity
Excitement	Mouth breathing
Anxiety	Depression

Glass Thermometers (Clinical)

A glass thermometer is used mainly for home care. It is a hollow glass tube with **calibration** lines on it. The liquid in the glass thermometer is heat sensitive and rises up the hollow tube when exposed to heat. This enables you to read the patient's temperature. The two most common types of glass thermometers are the **oral** thermometer and the **rectal** thermometer. (Figure 18.1) The oral thermometer has a long, slender tip, and the rectal thermometer has a shorter, stubby, and rounded tip.

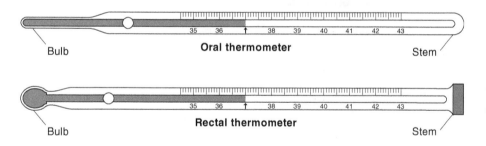

Although still available, mercury thermometers are rarely used because of the risks of mercury poisoning if they should break. Mercury-free glass thermometers and digital thermometers are replacing glass mercury thermometers. Exposure to high levels of mercury can cause respiratory and digestive problems and renal (kidney) damage. Even exposure to low levels of mercury can cause chest pains, chills, nausea, and diarrhea.

To read a glass thermometer, follow these four steps:

1. Hold the thermometer by the stem at eye level. Rotate the thermometer until you can see the line indicating the temperature reading.

2. Look at the lines on the scale at the upper side of the liquid. Each line represents a whole degree. There are four short lines between each of the long lines. The short lines represent $2/10$ (0.2) of a degree. Only even numbers are shown on a Fahrenheit clinical thermometer, for example 96°, 98°, 100° (Figure 18.2).

calibration
(KAL i bray-shun)
Standard measure (e.g., each line on a thermometer or a ruler is a calibration).

oral
(AWR uhl)
Referring to the mouth.

rectal
(REK tl)
Referring to the far end of the large intestine just above the anus.

Figure 18.1
Two types of glass thermometers. The rectal thermometer has a rounded bulb that helps prevent perforation of tissue. How do these thermometers work?

3. If the liquid ends at one of the short lines, look to see which long line is just before it. This tells you the degree of temperature. Then add two-tenths of a degree for each short line.

4. Read a **Celsius** thermometer the same way. Each long line represents a degree. Each short line represents 1/10 (0.1) of a degree. (**Figure 18.2**)

Figure 18.2

Average normal temperatures on Fahrenheit and Celsius thermometers. Are Fahrenheit and Celsius thermometers read in the same way?

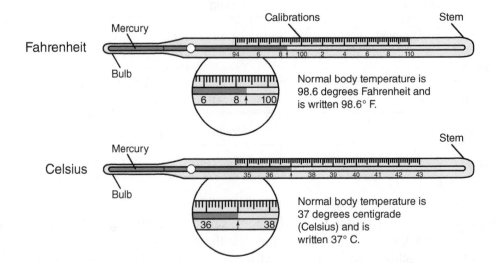

Celsius

(SEHL see uhs)
Measure of heat; in medicine a Celsius thermometer is sometimes used to measure body heat. Also called centigrade.

Fahrenheit

(FEHR uhn hite)
Measure of heat; in medicine a Fahrenheit thermometer is often used to measure body heat.

You may be asked to change a temperature from Celsius to **Fahrenheit** or from Fahrenheit to Celsius. If you need to make these changes, use the information in Table 18.2.

Table 18.2   Fahrenheit and Celsius Comparison

Fahrenheit	Celsius/Centigrade	Fahrenheit	Celsius/Centigrade
32	0	100.4	38
95	35	101.2	38.4
96	35.5	102.2	39
96.8	36	103	39.4
97.8	36.5	104	40
98.6	37	105	40.5
99.6	37.5	105.8	41
		106.8	41.5

Aural Thermometers (Ear)

The aural thermometer is commonly used because it is accurate, fast, easy to use, and safe. It is especially effective for babies and children. The probe from the aural thermometer is positioned in the aural canal of the ear. Some aural thermometers can take a temperature in just one second. (**Figure 18.3**) Although aural temperatures are commonly used in children, there is some question about the accuracy of the reading, especially in children younger than 6 years of age.

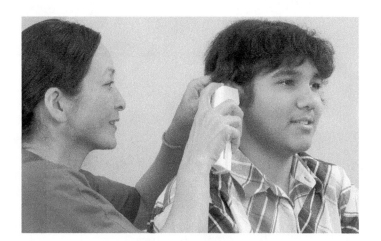

Figure 18.3
Aural, or ear, thermometer. What are the advantages of an aural thermometer?

Liquid Crystal Thermometer (Forehead)

This type of thermometer uses heat-sensitive liquid crystals in a plastic strip that is applied to the forehead. Temperature changes affect the color of the crystals. The color change indicates the patient's temperature based on the heat emitted from the surface of the skin. A liquid crystal thermometer can be used on children and babies. The strip can be left on the forehead for a continuous update on temperature changes. (**Figure 18.4**)

Courtesy of Dorling Kindersley.

Figure 18.4
Temporal artery thermometer. What technology does this type of thermometer use?

Chemically Treated Paper or Plastic Thermometers

This type of thermometer is read by noting its change in color. It is discarded after one use.

Electronic/Digital Thermometers

This thermometer has a probe that is covered with a protective, disposable shield. (**Figure 18.5**) The temperature is measured and displayed digitally on a screen. Electronic thermometers are quick and easy to use. There are various types of electronic equipment available and different probes for oral and rectal temperatures. Always follow the manufacturer's instructions.

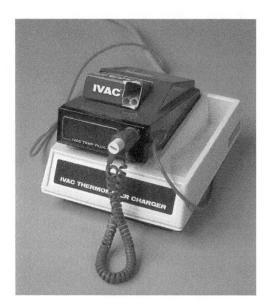

Figure 18.5
Electronic/digital thermometer. What is the main advantage of this type of thermometer?

π Math Link

Converting between Celsius and Fahrenheit

If you do not have a reference like Table 18.2, you will need to know how to convert a Celsius (C) reading to a Fahrenheit (F) and a Fahrenheit reading to a Celsius. You may sometimes hear the word "centigrade." It is just another word for "Celsius."

Fahrenheit is based on 32 degrees at the freezing point of water and 212 degrees at the boiling point of water. Celsius, on the other hand, is based on 0 degrees at the freezing point of water and 100 degrees at the boiling point. Here are the formulas for converting from one to another.

To convert Celsius to Fahrenheit:

$F = (C \times 1.8) + 32$

To convert Fahrenheit to Celsius:

$C = (F - 32) \div 1.8$

Example 1

Convert 35° C to degrees Fahrenheit:

$F = (35 \times 1.8) + 32$

$F = (63) + 32$

$F = 95°$

Example 2

Convert 104°F to degrees Celsius:

$C = (104 - 32) \times 1.8$

$C = 72 \div 1.8$

$C = 40°$

What are the conversions for the following temperatures?

a. 37.2°C

b. 101.6°F

c. 96°F

d. 41°C

Why is it very important for you to double-check your results when you make temperature conversions?

Sites to Take Body Temperature

Oral

The simplest and most common, convenient, and comfortable site to take a temperature is the oral (referring to the mouth) cavity. The average normal oral temperature is 98.6°F or 37°C. The normal range is 97.6°F to 99.6°F, or 36°C to 37.5°C. Use the oral cavity whenever possible and when the patient has:

- Diarrhea.
- Rectal surgery.
- Fecal impaction.

Rectal

Rectal temperature is the most accurate way to measure body temperature. When measuring a rectal temperature of an infant or small child, always have a second person assist you by holding the child in an appropriate position to prevent the child from being injured. A normal rectal temperature is 99.6°F or 37.5°C.

NOTE: Normal range can be 98.6–100.6°.

Rectal temperature is taken when patients:

- Are less than six years of age.
- Have difficulty breathing.
- Are extremely weak.
- Are confused, unconscious, or senile.
- Are being given oxygen.
- Are mouth breathers.
- Are experiencing partial paralysis of the face caused by a stroke or accident.

Aural

The aural (referring to the ear) site, like the oral cavity, is also accurate and easy to use. The aural site can be used in place of the oral cavity and for the same types of patients. To measure an aural temperature, an aural probe is positioned in the ear canal. A normal aural temperature is 98.6°F or 37°C

Axillary

The least accurate temperature is taken in the armpit. The normal temperature for this site is 97.6°F or 36.4°C. The normal range is 96.6°F to 98.6°F or 35.9°C to 37°C. Use the **axillary** technique only when the temperature cannot be taken orally, aurally, or rectally. Figure 18.6 shows a thermometer that can be used for measuring axillary or oral temperature. Always report a temperature that is above normal to your supervisor.

axillary
(AK suh lair ee)
Referring to the armpit.

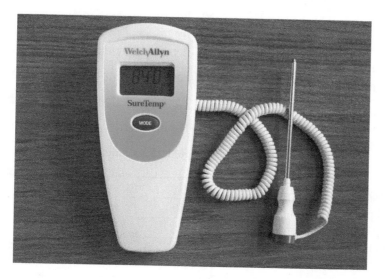

Figure 18.6
Axillary or oral thermometer. When is an axillary thermometer used to take a patient's temperature?

BACKGROUND: There are many different kinds of thermometers. The electronic thermometer is the most commonly used in the hospital setting. If another kind of thermometer is used please refer to the procedure manual provided by the facility. This procedure explains how to use an electronic thermometer to measure body temperature. When you use an electronic thermometer, it is very important to check to see that the batteries are charged. A low battery can cause an inaccurate temperature reading.

ALERT: Follow Standard Precautions. Also, for this and all Procedures involving patient movement, see Section 21.4 for information on proper body mechanics.

PREPROCEDURE

1. Wash hand (follow hand-washing guidelines).

2. Assemble equipment:*

   a. Plastic thermometer cover/sheath

   b. Electronic thermometer with appropriate probe (blue for oral and axillary; red for rectal)

3. Identify patient. Pull privacy curtain or close the door to provide for the patient's privacy.

4. Explain procedure to patient.

5. Need to ask the patient if they have had anything to eat, drink or smoke in the last 15 minutes. If they have, you need to wait 15 minutes to take an oral temperature.

PROCEDURE

6. Place plastic thermometer cover over probe to prevent contamination.

7. Insert probe in proper position to measure body temperature (blue-tipped probe under tongue or in axilla; red-tipped probe in rectum). If taking axillary temperature, need to hold arm down.

8. Hold probe in place until thermometer indicates reading is complete.

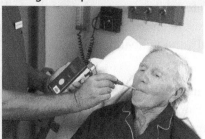

9. Remove plastic sheath and discard it into a biohazardous waste container.

POSTPROCEDURE

10. Record temperature. Health care professionals will record a patient's temperature on their chart. Report elevated temperature to a supervisor.

11. Position patient for comfort. Open curtain or door.

12. Wash hands (follow hand-washing guidelines).

13. Return electronic thermometer to its storage place.

14. Report any unusual observation immediately.

> 12/15/11   1900
>
>   T– 97.4°F Ⓡ
>
>   S. Jones CNA

* Wear gloves when measuring rectal temperatures. Follow facility policy for measuring oral temperature.

BACKGROUND: This procedure explains how to measure temperature with an oral probe.

ALERT: Follow Standard Precautions.

PREPROCEDURE

1. Wash hands (follow hand-washing guidelines).

2. Assemble equipment:*

   a. Clean oral (reusable or disposable) thermometer

   b. Alcohol wipes

   c. Watch with second hand

   d. Disposable thermometer cover

3. Identify patient and preferred route to be used. Pull privacy curtain or close door.

4. Explain procedure to patient.

PROCEDURE

5. Apply disposable probe cover.

6. Ask patient whether he or she has been smoking, eating, or drinking. If the answer is yes, wait 15 minutes before taking temperature.

7. Place thermometer under tongue and to the side of the mouth.

8. Instruct patient to hold thermometer with closed lips. You might need to help the patient hold the thermometer.

9. Leave in mouth until thermometer indicates reading is complete.

10. Remove from mouth.

11. Remove and discard disposable cover in a biohazardus waste container.

12. Note thermometer reading correctly.

13. Open curtain or door.

* **Follow facility policy for wearing gloves.**

POSTPROCEDURE

14. Wash thermometer in cool water and dry. Discard thermometer if it is disposable.

15. Wash hands (follow hand-washing guidelines).

16. Record temperature correctly on pad.

17. Report any unusual observation immediately.

A Insert the thermometer gently into the client's mouth under the tongue.

B Position the thermometer to the side of the mouth.

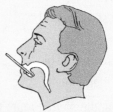
C Instruct the client to keep the thermometer under the tongue by gently closing the lips around the thermometer.

12/03/11   1600

T– 99.6°F Ⓡ

_____ S. Jones CNA

BACKGROUND: This procedure explains how to measure a temperature using a rectal thermometer probe.

CAUTION: Do not take a rectal temperature if a patient has had recent rectal surgery, rectal injury, or has had recent treatment that causes body tissues to become thin and fragile. For example, do not take a rectal temperature on a patient who has been undergoing chemotherapy or radiation or has been taking steroids. Rectal temperatures can also be dangerous for people with heart disease because the thermometer can stimulate the vagus nerve in the rectum which can slow down the heart rate.

ALERT: Follow Standard Precautions.

PREPROCEDURE

1. Wash hands (follow hand-washing guidelines).

2. Assemble equipment:

   a. Clean rectal (reusable or disposable) thermometer

   b. Alcohol wipes

   c. Watch with second hand

   d. Lubricant

   e. Disposable nonsterile gloves

   f. Disposable thermometer cover

3. Identify patient and preferred route to be used.

4. Explain procedure to patient. Pull privacy curtain or close the door.

5. Put on disposable gloves.

PROCEDURE

6. Remove thermometer from container and apply disposable cover.

7. Lower backrest on bed. Have patient lie on their left side with right leg bent at the knees.

8. Apply lubricant to probe end.

9. Separate buttocks by pulling up on upper buttock.

10. Insert thermometer 1.5 inches into rectum, or 1 to 1.2 inch for an infant. Do not force thermometer.

11. Hold in place until thermometer indicates reading is complete.

12. Remove thermometer. Wipe anal area to remove excess lubricant and any feces. Cover the patient.

13. Remove and discard disposable cover in a biohazardous waste container.

14. Read thermometer correctly. Open curtain or door.

POSTPROCEDURE

15. Clean equipment and return to appropriate storage place.

16. Remove and discard disposable gloves.

17. Wash hands.

18. Record temperature correctly. Remember to indicate that it is a rectal temperature with an R.

19. Report any unusual observation immediately.

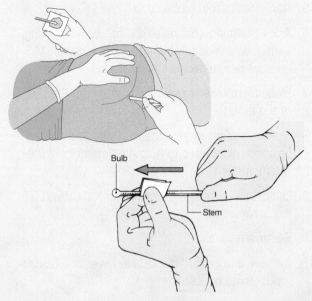

Bulb

Stem

12/14/11   1500

T– 99.2°F Ⓡ

_____ J. Gonzalez CNA

PROCEDURE 18.4 | Measuring an Axillary Temperature

BACKGROUND: This procedure explains how to measure a temperature using an axillary probe.

ALERT: Follow Standard Precautions.

PREPROCEDURE

1. Wash hands (follow hand-washing procedure).

2. Assemble equipment:

   a. Clean reusable or disposable thermometer

   b. Alcohol wipes

   c. Watch with second hand

   d. Disposable thermometer cover

3. Identify patient and preferred route to be used. Pull privacy curtain or close the door.

4. Explain procedure to patient.

PROCEDURE

5. Remove thermometer from container and apply disposable cover.

6. Dry the axilla with a towel.

7. Place the thermometer in axilla. Hold the arm close to the body. Leave in place until thermometer indicates reading is complete.

8. Remove thermometer.

9. Remove and discard disposable cover in biohazardous waste container.

10. Read thermometer correctly. Open curtain or door.

POSTPROCEDURE

11. Clean equipment and return to appropriate storage space.

12. Wash hands (follow hand-washing guidelines).

13. Record temperature correctly. You must indicate it was an axillary temperature.

14. Report any unusual observation immediately.

6/14/12   0400

T– 97°F AX

_____   H. Ferguson RMA

PROCEDURE 18.5 Measuring an Aural (or Tympanic) Temperature

BACKGROUND: The human body has a homeostatic mechanism that regulates all systems and maintains normal function. One of the body's homeostatic mechanisms is the control of body temperature. Body temperature is the balance between heat production and heat loss.

The hypothalamus is the main regulator of body temperature. Factors such as loss of skin integrity with an extensive burn, exposure to extreme weather conditions, disease states such as tumors or strokes involving the hypothalamus can affect our ability to maintain normal body temperature. An elevated temperature, pyrexia, is a protective mechanism for the body, believed to aid the body in fighting disease.

The elderly patient may have difficulty maintaining homeostasis. For that reason an elevated temperature may not be their first sign of infection. The pediatric patient has greater variation in temperature control and may respond to a disease state with a more elevated degree of pyrexia.

ALERT: Follow Standard Precautions.

PREPROCEDURE

1. Determine the device to be used for measuring the patient's temperature. Special devices are available for use in the outer ear canal.

Note: While the use of an aural (tympanic) thermometer has proven easiest for use in the pediatric patient, research is still in progress to determine its reliability.

2. Review the patient's graphic record to determine baseline temperature and any recent alterations from baseline.

PROCEDURE

3. Wash hands.

4. Explain procedure to patient.

5. Gently pull the ear straight back for children under age 1, or up and back for age 1 or older. Insert the covered probe gently but firmly into the external ear.

6. Activate the device.

7. Note the temperature reading.

8. Remove the device and discard the probe cover in a biohazardous waste container.

POSTPROCEDURE

9. Assure that the patient is comfortable and has no further needs before leaving the area.

10. Record the reading on the designated form. Remember to indicate that this was an aural route.

11. Note if the temperature is elevated. Compare the reading with previous temperature readings.

12. If temperature is elevated, communicate that information to the nurse in charge of the patient's care.

Pulse

The pulse is caused by the pressure of the blood pushing against the wall of an artery as the heart contracts and relaxes. (Figure 18.7) It is the throbbing of an artery as the human heart beats. The pulse rate is an important vital sign because it indicates how well the blood is circulating through the body. When you check the pulse rate, you count the number of beats (heartbeats) in 1 minute. This is called beats per minute (bpm).

Location of Pulse Points

When you count the pulse, place your fingers over an artery and squeeze gently against the bone. **Figure 18.8** shows the locations on the body where the pulse may be taken. The pulse rate should be the same at all pulse sites. **Table 18.3** shows the factors that affect pulse rate.

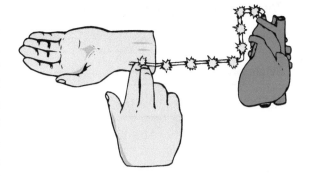

Figure 18.7
The pulse rate is a measure of the heartbeat. A pulse is usually taken for how long a period of time?

Pulse Characteristics

Just counting the beats is not enough. It is important to observe the characteristics of the pulse. This means that you must also note the:

- **Rate.** Number of pulse beats per minute. **Table 18.4** lists normal pulse rates for different ages.

- **Rhythm.** Regularity of the beats. Is the rhythm steady or irregular, slow or fast? Sometimes there are uneven intervals between the beats. It is also important to identify if the uneven intervals are regular or irregular. If the uneven interval is irregular, it is called an irregular rhythm. This condition is called **arrhythmia**. Always report a heartbeat below 60 or over 100 beats per minute (bpm).

- **Volume.** Strength or pressure felt with each beat. Note a gentle normal pulse, or a **bounding** forceful pulse. You might also feel a weak pulse that may feel like a thin thread. This is called a **thready** pulse.

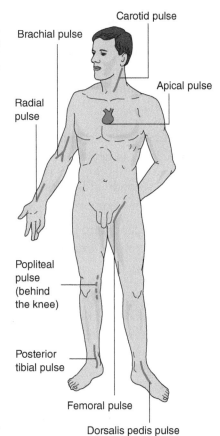

Carotid pulse
Brachial pulse
Apical pulse
Radial pulse
Popliteal pulse (behind the knee)
Posterior tibial pulse
Femoral pulse
Dorsalis pedis pulse

Figure 18.8
Pulse points of the body. Which site is used most often?

arrhythmia
(uh RITH mee uh)
An irregular pulse rate.

bounding
(BAUND ing)
Leaping, strong, or forceful pulse.

thready
(THRED ee)
Weak, barely felt pulse; thin, like a thread.

Table 18.3 Factors That Affect Pulse Rate

Increase Pulse Rate	Decrease Pulse Rate
Exercise	High level of aerobic fitness
Illness	Depression
Anxiety	Medication
Medication	Cardiac dysfunction
Shock	Sleep

Table 18.4 Normal Pulse Rates

Age	Rate
Before birth	140–150
At birth	90–160
First year of life	115–130
Childhood years	80–115
Adult	60–80

hemorrhage
(HEM er rij or HEM-rij)
Large amount of bleeding.

tachycardia
(tak i KAHR dee uh)
Pulse rate over 100 beats per minute (for adults).

bradycardia
(brad i KAHR dee uH)
Pulse rate below 60 beats per minute.

apex
(AY peks)
Pointed end of something (for example, the pointed end of the heart is called the apex of the heart).

stethoscope
(STETH uh skohp)
Instrument used to amplify sound.

Pulse Rate

Pulse rate generally increases with exercise, emotional excitement, **hemorrhage**, or elevated temperature. Drugs can increase or decrease the heart rate. When the rate is over 100 beats per minute, it is called **tachycardia**. When the rate is below 60 beats per minute, it is called **bradycardia**. When the rate is irregular, it is called arrhythmia.

The pulse rate is determined by counting the number of times you feel a pulse in 1 minute. You can determine the rate by counting the pulse for:

- 15 seconds and multiply by 4 (there are four 15-second periods in 1 minute). For example, 22 beats (in 15 seconds) × 4 = 88 beats per minute.
- 30 seconds and multiply by 2 (there are two 30-second periods in 1 minute). For example, 44 beats (in 30 seconds) × 2 = 88 beats per minute.

If you count the pulse for 60 seconds, this will give you the beats per minute (bpm). When the pulse rate is irregular, it is important to count the pulse for a full 60 seconds to be sure that the count is accurate. Be sure to follow up your facility's policy on how long to count the pulse.

ALERT: When you record the pulse rate, always report to your supervisor anything that is abnormal. This includes rate (Table 18.4), rhythm, and force.

Radial Pulse

The radial pulse is the most common site for counting the pulse rate. This pulse is counted on the thumb side of the wrist. Do not use your thumb to count a pulse because you have a pulse in your thumb.

Apical Pulse

You may be asked to count an apical pulse. This is the pulse counted at the **apex** (pointed end) of the heart. Count the apical heartbeat by placing the **stethoscope** 2 to 3 inches to the left of the sternum, just below the nipple on the chest.

BACKGROUND: It is important for health care workers to monitor the patient's physical status. One way to determine this status is by counting the patient's pulse rate. This procedure explains how to count a radial pulse.

ALERT: Follow Standard Precautions.

PREPROCEDURE

1. Wash hands (follow hand-washing guidelines).

2. Assemble equipment:

    a. Watch with second hand

    b. Pad and pencil

3. Identify patient. Pull privacy curtain or close the door.

4. Explain procedure to patient.

PROCEDURE

5. Place three fingers on the radial artery—do not use thumb.

6. Count pulse (number of beats or pulsations) for 1 minute.

7. Record pulse rate on pad immediately. Open curtain or door.

POSTPROCEDURE

8. Wash hands (follow hand-washing guidelines).

9. Record pulse rate on chart.

10. Immediately report any unusual observation. Examples include an irregular pulse, a bounding or weak pulse, or a pulse rate less than 60 bpm or more than 100 bpm.

NOTE: If the pulse is difficult to assess, irregular, weak, or rapid, the apical rate should be assessed.

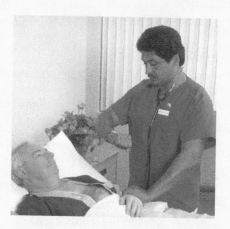

| 2/14/11 | 1300 |
| Pulse = 72 |
| Regular and strong |
| ———— T. Morales CNA |

BACKGROUND: The apical pulse is assessed upon admission, when the peripheral pulse is difficult to assess, and also when giving medications that alter heart rate and rhythm, such as digoxin.

ALERT: Follow Standard Precautions.

PREPROCEDURE

1. Assemble equipment.

   a. Stethoscope

   b. Alcohol swabs

2. Wash hands (follow hand-washing guidelines).

3. Identify patient. Pull privacy curtain or close door.

4. Explain procedure to patient.

PROCEDURE

5. Uncover left side of patient's chest.

6. Locate the apex of the heart between the fifth and the sixth rib, about 3 inches to the left of the median line and slightly below the nipple.

7. Place stethoscope over apical region and listen for heart sounds. The apical rate of an infant is easily palpated with the fingertips.

8. Count the beats for 1 minute; note rate, rhythm, and strength of beat.

9. Cover patient. Open the curtain or door.

10. Record pulse rate on pad.

POSTPROCEDURE

11. Wash hands (follow hand-washing guidelines).

12. Record apical pulse rate on chart. Remember to indicate that it was an apical pulse.

13. Report any unusual observation immediately.

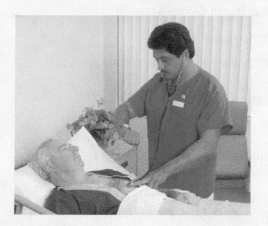

12/14/11	1000
	82 / 78 AP
	Pulse deficit = 4
	Quality of beat strong
	——— S. Padlewski RMA

 Respiration

Respiration is the process of taking oxygen (O_2) into the body and expelling carbon dioxide (CO_2) from the body. One inspiration (breathing in) and one expiration (breathing out) are considered as one respiration. (**Figure 18.9**)

When you count a patient's respiration, you do not want the patient to be aware of what you are doing. If the patient realizes that you are counting respirations, he or she may not breathe normally. Count the respiration rate after you finish counting the pulse. **Table 18.5** shows the factors that affect respiration.

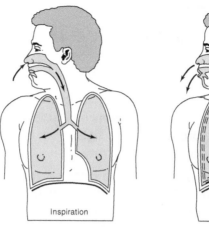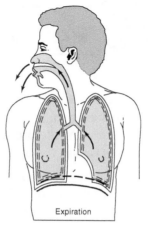

Inspiration

Expiration

Table 18.5 Factors That Affect Respiration

Increase Respiration	Decrease Respiration
Exercise	Relaxation
Anxiety	Depression
Respiratory disease	Head injury
Medication	Medication
Pain	
Heart disease (e.g., congestive heart failure)	

 ## Pulse Oximetry

Pulse oximetry is a procedure used to determine the oxygen (O_2) saturation of arterial blood. Pulse oximetry is useful for monitoring patients at risk for hypoxia, and postoperative patients. The device that measures the oxygen in the blood is called a pulse oximeter. (**Figure 18.10**)

Blood O_2 content is an important indicator of a patient's respiratory and cardiac condition. The oximeter sends red and infrared light through a pulsating arterial vascular bed through a sensor attached to the fingertip, ear lobe, bridge of the nose or toe. This measures the O_2 content of the blood and the pulse rate and displays the reading on a monitor.

Low readings cause an alarm to sound. The normal range is considered to be between 95 and 100 percent. Any reading below 90 percent may indicate that oxygenation to the tissues is inadequate. Interventions such as increasing oxygen therapy, providing nebulizer treatments or changing the mode of oxygen delivery may be necessary.

Personal Wellness

Asthma

Asthma is a chronic condition that occurs when the main air passages of the lungs, known as the bronchial tubes, become inflamed. The muscles of the bronchial walls tighten and extra mucus is produced. This causes the airways to narrow.

In the United States, asthma sufferers number about 50 million. According to the Mayo Clinic, about 4,000 Americans die each year from asthma, and another 500,000 people are hospitalized.

Symptoms of asthma include:

■ Shortness of breath or wheezing.

■ Disturbed sleep caused by shortness of breath, coughing, or wheezing.

■ Chest tightness or pain.

Asthma is a very treatable disease. However, if left untreated, asthma can result in reduced lung function and possibly permanent lung damage. Therefore, if you have symptoms of asthma, the first step is a visit to your doctor.

The doctor will develop a treatment plan. If you have persistent asthma, the doctor may prescribe an inhaled anti-inflammatory medication. A doctor may also prescribe a quick-relief inhaler to be used only when you have asthma symptoms. Remember to keep your inhaler with you.

What can you do to help a friend or relative who has asthma?

Figure 18.10
Digital pulse oximeter. When would you not use a digital pulse oximeter?

BACKGROUND: It is important for health care workers to monitor the patient's physical status. One way to determine this status is by counting the patient's respiratory rate. This procedure explains how to count the number of times a patient breathes in a minute.

ALERT: Follow Standard Precautions.

PREPROCEDURE

1. Wash hands (follow hand-washing guidelines).

2. Assemble equipment.

   a. Watch with second hand.

   b. Pad and pencil.

3. Identify patient. Pull privacy curtain or close door.

4. Explain to the patient that you are going to take their pulse.

PROCEDURE

5. Relax fingers on pulse point.

6. Observe rise and fall of chest.

7. Count respirations and calculate rate.

8. Note rate, rhythm, and quality of respirations.

POSTPROCEDURE

9. Open curtain or close door.

10. Wash hands (follow hand-washing guidelines).

11. Record the respiratory rate accurately. Make sure you take it for 30 seconds and multiply times two. If respirations are irregular, take for one full minute.

12. Report any unusual observation immediately. This could include irregular respiration, noisy breathing, and pain with or difficulty breathing.

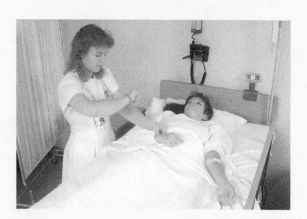

5/22/12   0930

Resp. 20 and regular

M. Taylor CNA

Respiratory Characteristics

Age influences respiration. The rate of newborns may be 40 respirations per minute. The suggested normal adult rate is 12 to 20 respirations per minute. When you measure respiration, always note the following:

- **Rate.** The number of respirations per minute.
- **Rhythm.** The regularity, or irregularity, of breathing.
- **Quality.** The amount of air exchanged and the effort it takes to breathe.
- **Dyspnea.** Shortness of breath. Is breathing difficult?
- **Tachypnea.** Abnormally fast respirations.

rate of respirations
(reyt of resp puh REY shuhn)
The number of respirations per minute

rhythm of respirations
(RITH uh m of res puh REY shuhn)
The regularity, or irregularity, of breathing.

quality of respirations
(KWOL i tee of
res puh REY shuhn)
The amount of air taken into
the body and expelled from
the body and the effort it
takes to do this.

- **Apnea.** Has breathing stopped?
- **Cheyne-Stokes.** Are there periods of labored respirations followed by apnea?
- **Rales.** Can you hear bubbling or rattling sounds caused by mucus in the air passages?

ALERT! Always report any unusual or abnormal respirations to your supervisor.

 ## Recording Vital Signs

Always write the temperature, pulse, and respiration (TPR) in the same order:

T	P	R
98.6	72	16

Since all health care workers write vital signs in the same way, you do not need to put *T P R* above the figures. Write 98.6/72/16 for an oral temperature, or write 98.6°. Put an ® next to a rectal temperature (for example, 99.6®) and an *AX* next to an axillary temperature (for example 97.6AX).

Some facilities may have a policy requiring that a *T* be placed next to the aural temperature (for example, 98.6T). These symbols tell other health care workers where you measured the temperature, and this helps ensure accuracy. Some health care workers include BP (blood pressure) after TPR. *Always report abnormal or unusual vital signs to your supervisor.*

Taking vital signs may seem routine, but the information is important to the well-being of the patient. Careful recording of vital signs is essential for the protection of the patient.

Always compare most recent reading to those in the recent past. Look for patterns in the readings, such as temperature always elevated at a particular time of day, or blood pressure elevated during an episode of acute discomfort. Reporting the patterns, as well as the current reading, will help the nurse determine the significance of the current data.

What's New?

Obtaining and Recording Temperatures with Accuracy

Caregivers monitor a patient's temperature at intervals and use the readings to determine health status of their patients. An elevated temperature may be the first indication of a change in health status. An elevated temperature is one of the body's protective mechanisms used to fight infection or to indicate that an inflammatory process is present.

There have been some recent concerns regarding the accuracy of tympanic thermometers. In some instances, facilities are replacing tympanic thermometers with newer versions of the electronic oral and rectal thermometers. Because of the importance of accurately determining the temperature of your patients, it is very important to use appropriate technique and the most accurate instruments available for measurement.

Summary

Vital signs are important indicators of the body's condition. Three of these vital signs are temperature, pulse, and respiration (TPR). Many factors influence TPR in the human body, and it is important to be aware of them. You have learned the steps for taking temperature, pulse, and respiration, and you know how to recognize a normal TPR and an abnormal TPR.

You may also be responsible for accurately measuring oxygen (O_2) in the blood. You also know that pain is an important sign in how the body is functioning. All this information is essential in giving good patient care and in recognizing problems with your own personal health.

SECTION 18.1 Review Questions

1. Name four different types of thermometers.

2. Identify four sites on the body where temperature may be taken.

3. When would you not take an oral temperature?

4. What vital sign indicates how well the blood is circulating through the body?

5. Where is the most common site on the body for counting the pulse rate?

6. What are the two components, or parts, of one respiration?

7. What does TPR stand for?

 Learn By Doing: Section 18.1 Activity
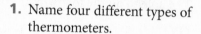

1. Complete Worksheets 1 through 5.

2. Complete Worksheet/Activity 6 as assigned..

3. When you are confident that you can meet each objective for this section, ask your teacher for the section evaluation.

Background

You have learned that temperature, pulse, and respiration are signs that indicate whether the body is functioning within normal limits. Blood pressure is the fourth vital sign. Measuring the patient's blood pressure gives you a complete picture of his or her vital signs. A complete record of all vital signs helps in the diagnosis and treatment of the patient.

Objectives

When you have completed this section, you will be able to do the following:

- Match key terms with their correct meanings.

- Define *blood pressure*.

- Match descriptions of systolic and diastolic blood pressure.

- List four factors that increase blood pressure.

- List four factors that can reduce blood pressure.

- State the normal range of blood pressure.

- Demonstrate how to measure and record a blood pressure accurately.

- Explain how vital signs provide information about the patient's health.

Blood Pressure

systolic pressure
(sis TAHL ic)
Highest pressure against blood vessels. It is represented by first heart sound or beat heard when taking a blood pressure.

diastolic pressure
(DIE es tahl ic)
Lowest pressure against the blood vessels of the body. It is measured between contractions.

Blood pressure is the force of the blood pushing against the walls of the blood vessels. The **systolic pressure** is the greatest force exerted on the walls of the arteries by the heart. This pressure is exerted when the heart is contracting. You hear the first beat when contraction occurs. The **diastolic pressure** is the least force exerted on the walls of the arteries by the heart. This pressure occurs as the heart relaxes between contractions. When the heart relaxes, there is no sound (beat). The normal systolic blood pressure is below 135. For the diastolic pressure, it is below 85.

Blood pressure depends on the volume of blood in the circulating system, the force of the heartbeat, and the condition of the arteries. When arteries lose their elasticity, they give more resistance, and the blood pressure increases.

When the blood pressure is below the normal range, it is called hypotension. A very low blood pressure can indicate decreased perfusion which can cause a decrease in organ function such as to the brain. When this occurs the patient may lose consciousness. Table 18.6 shows the factors that affect blood pressure.

Table 18.6   Factors That Affect Blood Pressure

Increase Blood Pressure	Decrease Blood Pressure
Loss of elasticity in the arteries (arteriosclerosis)	Hemorrhage
Exercise	Inactivity
Eating	Fasting
Stimulants (e.g., medication, coffee)	Suppressants (e.g., medications that cause blood pressure to lower)
Anxiety	Depression
	Shock

Normal Blood Pressure

The normal blood pressure range is between 90 and 140 **millimeters** (mm) mercury for the *systolic pressure*. For the *diastolic pressure*, it is between 60 and 90 millimeters (mm) of mercury. When you record a blood pressure, it is written

$$120/80 = \frac{120 \text{ systolic}}{80 \text{ diastolic}}$$

In addition, the normal pulse pressure range is 30–40 mm of Mg. You find this by subtracting diastolic from systolic.

When the blood pressure is above the normal range, it is called hypertension, or high blood pressure. **Hypertension** is called the silent killer. It is a disease that is **asymptomatic** in most cases. This condition is discovered only when a patient's blood pressure is measured.

Heredity plays a major role in patients who develop hypertension. Some of the effects are stroke, kidney problems, changes in the retina, and heart disease. When the blood pressure is below the normal range, it is called **hypotension**.

Blood Pressure Apparatus

Blood pressure is measured with an instrument called a **sphygmomanometer**. In the word *sphygmomanometer*:

- **Sphygmo** refers to pulse.
- **Mano** refers to pressure.
- **Meter** refers to measure.

Most health care workers refer to the sphygmomanometer as a BP cuff or blood pressure cuff. There are different kinds of blood pressure **apparatus**:

- Aneroid.
- Electronic/digital.

millimeters
(MILL ih mee tehr)
Measure of length.

hypertension
(hahy per TEN shuh n)
High blood pressure.

asymptomatic
(ey simp tuh MAT ik)
Without visible symptoms.

hypotension
(hahy puh TEN shuhn)
Low blood pressure.

Sphygmomanometer
(sfig moh muh NOM i ter)
A device used to measure the pressure against the arteries of the body.

apparatus
(ap uh RAT uhs)
Equipment needed to perform a task. For example, blood pressure apparatus includes a blood pressure cuff and a stethoscope.

gauge
(GAYJ)
Standard scale for measurement.

inflated
(in FLEY tid)
To swell or fill up with air.

The aneroid apparatuses have a **gauge**, which is marked with a series of long and short lines. The long lines are at 10-mm (millimeter) intervals. The short lines are between the long lines and indicate 2 mm (millimeters) each. When you measure a blood pressure, you must do two things at one time. You listen to the heartbeat as it pulses through the artery. You also watch the gauge in order to take a reading.

The blood pressure cuff is a cloth-covered rubber bladder that fills with air as the bulb is squeezed. When the cuff is **inflated** around the arm, it stops the flow of blood. As the pressure is relieved, the flow returns and you hear a beat. This is the systolic pressure. As the cuff continues to deflate, you hear a last beat and then silence. The last beat you hear is the diastolic pressure.

Stethoscope

When you listen to pulse sounds, you use a stethoscope. A stethoscope picks up sound when it is placed against the body. The stethoscope has earpieces, a spring to help keep the earpieces in the ears, flexible rubber tubing that carries sound, a bell and a diaphragm that magnifies sound.

 ## Palpating Blood Pressure

You may be asked to take a blood pressure by first palpating (feeling) the radial pulse. This allows you to determine the correct inflation pressure when inflating the cuff.

 # What's New?

Holter Monitors

A Holter monitor is a machine that continuously records the heart's rhythms. The monitor is usually worn for 24 hours during normal activity. It may also be called an ambulatory electrocardiography.

One of the problems with Holter monitors is the refusal of many patients to wear them. Traditional Holter monitors were bulky and had to be worn and attached for 24 to 48 hours at a time. These requirements reduced the willingness to wear this important device.

New technology has now been developed to increase patient compliance by making the Holter monitor more user-friendly. Some newer monitors weigh only 1 ounce (28g) and are no bigger than a single AAA battery. This monitor is so small and lightweight that it may be worn comfortably underneath clothing and patients hardly notice they are wearing the device. Another company has experimented with a wireless monitor that eliminates the need for electrodes.

Modern monitors record onto digital flash memory devices. The data is then uploaded into a computer through a secure USB connection. The computer analyzes the input and calculates summary statistics such as average heart rate, and minimum and maximum heart rate.

The new technology in Holter monitors makes sure doctors get the quick results they need. The report can be returned to the referring physician within 24 hours to help them diagnose the nature of their patient's potential heart problem.

BACKGROUND: As a health care worker, it is important to monitor the patient's physical status. One way to determine this status is by measuring the patient's blood pressure. This procedure explains how to palpate a blood pressure so you will know how high to inflate the blood pressure cuff.

ALERT: Follow Standard Precautions.

PREPROCEDURE

1. Wash hands (follow hand-washing guidelines).

2. Explain procedure to patient. Pull privacy curtain or close door.

PROCEDURE

3. Select the appropriate cuff for your patient. A cuff that is too small may cause a false-high reading and a cuff that is too large may cause a false-low reading.

4. Support patient's arm, palm side up, on a firm surface.

5. Roll up patient's sleeve above elbow, being careful that it is not too tight.

6. Wrap wide part of cuff around patient's arm directly over brachial artery. Most cuffs have an arrow to position over the brachial artery. The lower edge of cuff should be 1 or 2 inches above bend of elbow.

7. Find radial pulse with your fingertips.

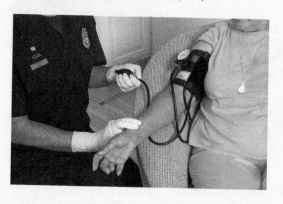

8. Inflate cuff until you can no longer feel radial pulse. Continue to inflate another 30 mm of mercury.

9. Open valve and slowly deflate cuff until you feel the first beat of radial pulse again.

10. Observe mercury or dial reading. This is the placatory systolic pressure. It is recorded, for example, as B/P 130 (P).

11. Deflate cuff rapidly and squeeze out all the air.

12. Using your first and second fingers, locate brachial artery. You will feel it pulsating. Place bell or diaphragm of stethoscope directly over artery. You will not hear the pulsation. Do not hold the stethoscope in place with your thumb.

13. Tighten thumbscrew of valve to close it. Turn to the left.

14. Hold stethoscope in place and inflate cuff until the dial points to about 30 mm above the palpated B/P.

15. Open valve counterclockwise. Let air out slowly until you hear first beat.

16. At this first sound, note reading on sphygmomanometer. This is the systolic pressure.

17. Continue to release air slowly. Note number on the indicator at which you hear last beat or the sound changes to a dull beat. This is the diastolic pressure.

18. Open valve and release all the air.

19. Remove cuff. Open curtain or door.

POSTPROCEDURE

20. Record time and blood pressure.

21. Clean stethoscope—earpieces and diaphragm.

22. Wash hands.

23. Report any unusual observation immediately.

BACKGROUND: As a health care worker, it is important to monitor the patient's physical status. One way to determine this status is by measuring the patient's blood pressure. This procedure explains how to determine the patient's systolic (highest pressure) and diastolic (lowest pressure) blood pressure.

ALERT: Follow Standard Precautions.

PREPROCEDURE

1. Wash hands (follow hand-washing guidelines).
2. Assemble equipment:
   a. Alcohol wipes
   b. Sphygmomanometer
   c. Stethoscope
   d. Pad and pencil
3. Identify patient. Pull privacy curtain or close the door.
4. Explain procedure to patient.

PROCEDURE

5. Delay obtaining the blood pressure if the patient is in acute pain, has just exercised, or is emotionally upset, unless there is an urgent reason to obtain a blood pressure reading.
6. Select the appropriate arm for application of the cuff. Limbs that have an intravenous infusion, breast or axillary surgery on that side, arteriovenous shunt, or are injured or diseased should not be used.
7. Apply cuff correctly. This should be about one inch above the anticubital space. (Refer to steps 4 and 5 in Procedure 18.9 "Palpating a Blood Pressure".)
8. Clean earpieces on stethoscope.
9. Place earpieces in ears.
10. Locate brachial artery. Place stethoscope over it.
11. Tighten thumbscrew on valve. (Remember the two clues: righty tighty and lefty loosey.)
12. Hold stethoscope in place. Do not use your thumb.
13. Inflate cuff to 170 mm.
14. Open valve. If systolic sound is heard immediately, reinflate cuff to 30 mm mercury above systolic sound.

15. Note systolic at first beat.
16. Note diastolic.
17. Open valve and release air.
18. Record time and blood pressure reading correctly on pad. Open curtain or door.

POSTPROCEDURE

19. Wash hands.
20. Wash earpieces on stethoscope.
21. Put away equipment.
22. Record blood pressure in chart.
23. Report any unusual observation immediately.

Step 7

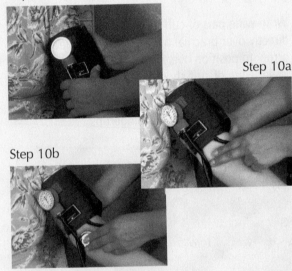

Step 10a

Step 10b

7/29/11	0900
	B/P 134/88
left arm, sitting	
_____	R. Martin CNA

π Math Link

EKG Graph Paper Speed

ECG/EKG graph paper can be run through the EKG machine at different speeds. The standard speed is 25 mm per second. However, faster speeds are sometimes used.

Each small block of EKG paper equals 1 square mm. At a standard paper speed of 25 mm per second, one small block of EKG paper equals $\frac{1}{25}$th of a second or 0.04.

If five small blocks equal one large block, how many seconds are represented by one large block?

5 blocks × 0.04 seconds = 0.20 seconds

If one large block equals 0.20 seconds, how many large blocks equal one second?

1 large block = 0.20 seconds

1 second divided by 0.20 seconds = 5

5 × 1 large block = 5 large blocks

Example 1

A sample EKG reading takes $5\frac{1}{2}$ minutes. How many large blocks of graph paper would that take up 25 mm per second? How many small blocks?

5.5 minutes = 330 seconds

330 seconds × 5 blocks/second = 1,650 large blocks

1 large block = 5 small blocks

1,650 large blocks = 8,250 small blocks

Example 2

A sample EKG reading at 25 mm per second takes up 427 large blocks. How long did the EKG procedure take?

1 large block = 0.20 seconds

427 × 0.20 = 85.4 seconds

85.4 seconds = 1 minute and 25.4 seconds

How many small blocks would be used in an EKG procedure at 25 mm per second for the following times?

a. 50 seconds

b. 1.5 minutes

If an EKG reads at 25 mm per second, how long were the following procedures?

c. 998 large blocks

d. 50,000 small blocks

Why would it matter if the EKG paper speed were 25mm per second or 50 mm per second?

Personal Wellness

Warning Signs of Heart Attacks

An EKG (electrocardiogram) is a graphic produced by an electrocardiograph, which records the electrical activity of the heart over time. An EKG can determine if there is narrowing in an artery leading to the heart muscle. This narrowing is a warning sign of a possible heart attack.

Cardiovascular disease affects more than 50 million Americans and coronary heart disease is the main cause of death in the United States. Stroke is the third leading cause of death and a major cause of serious disability.

Unfortunately, all the EKGs in the world won't help you if you ignore the warning signs of heart attacks. Some heart attacks are very sudden and there is no doubt about what is happening. However, most heart attacks begin slowly with only mild discomfort.

(continued)

Personal Wellness (continued)

People who experience these symptoms often are not sure what's wrong and wait too long before getting help. Sometimes they don't want to "bother" the doctor, or they don't want to appear "weak," or they have too many "important things" to do. These can be fatal mistakes.

Here are some of the indications that a heart attack is occurring:

- **Chest discomfort.** Most heart attacks involve pain in the center of the chest that lasts more than a few minutes. Sometimes the discomfort goes away and comes back again. It can feel like uncomfortable pressure, squeezing, fullness, or pain.

- **Discomfort in other areas of the upper body.** Symptoms can include pain or discomfort in one or both arms, the back, neck, jaw, or stomach.

- **Shortness of breath.** Sudden difficulty breathing may occur with or without chest discomfort.

- **Breaking out in a cold sweat.**

- **Nausea.**

- **Lightheadedness.**

- **Extreme fatigue.** This is particularly important for women who may not have other symptoms.

Even if you are not sure if it is a heart attack, have it checked out. In the event of any these symptoms the appropriate action is to keep the patient still and call 911. Every minute, and even every second, matters during a heart attack. Fast action can save lives—maybe even your own.

Community Service

Have a blood pressure clinic at lunch for students and faculty. Make and display posters that list the blood pressure risk factors and the dangers of hypertension.

 Summary

Blood pressure is the fourth vital sign. Many factors influence blood pressure, and an abnormal blood pressure may indicate a serious condition. It is important to be accurate in following the step-by-step instructions for taking a blood pressure, recording the blood pressure of your patient, and reporting any abnormalities immediately.

SECTION **18.2** **Review Questions**

1. What is blood pressure?

2. What is the difference between systolic and diastolic pressure?

3. What factors lead to increased blood pressure?

4. What is the normal range of blood pressure?

5. How is blood pressure written?

6. Why is hypertension called "the silent killer?"

Learn By Doing: Section 18.2 Activity

1. Complete Worksheets 1 through 3.

2. When you are confident that you can meet each objective for this section, ask your teacher for the section evaluation.

Nursing Skills and Assistive and Therapeutic Techniques

Background

Each day, you do many things to get ready for the day, such as taking a shower and brushing your teeth. You likely also have nighttime habits. Patients in the hospital also have daily habits and other needs. As a nurse assistant, you will need to know how to help patients undertake these activities. Also, you will be responsible for their safety and comfort.

Objectives

When you have completed this section, you will be able to do the following:

- Complete all objectives in Part One of this book.

- Match key terms with their correct meanings.

- Identify the following:
  - Responsibilities of the nurse or nurse assistant.
  - Four skin conditions requiring special attention.
  - Areas on the body where pressure sores usually develop.
  - Antipressure aids.
  - Occupied bed, closed bed, and open bed.
  - Causes and symptoms of dehydration.
  - Common types of specimens collected for analysis.
  - Six common prosthetic devices.

- List the following:
  - Four types of bathing.
  - Two body areas requiring special attention during the bathing process.
  - Four changes in the skin that may indicate the beginning of a pressure sore.
  - Four techniques for positioning patients.
  - Seven reasons why ambulation is important.
  - Nine steps to preparing a patient for a meal.
  - Six ways to prevent pressure sores.
  - Causes and symptoms of edema.
  - Five conditions that may develop when using postural supports.
  - Five things you must do when using postural supports.

- Explain the following:
  - Four reasons to give mouth care.
  - Six reasons for routine bathing.
  - Why patients who have diabetes must have their toenails cut by a podiatrist.
  - Why a urinary drainage bag is not raised above the level of insertion.
  - Six causes of incontinence.
  - Procedures for bowel and/or bladder training.
  - Important observations about urine.
  - Important observations about stool.

- Define the following terms:
  - *AM* and *PM care.*
  - *Good body alignment.*
  - *Postural supports.*
- Match range-of-motion vocabulary words with their meanings.
- Calculate in cc's and record fluid intake properly.
- Evaluate and determine appropriate action for a given situation.
- Demonstrate each procedure in this chapter.

Nursing Responsibilities

Nurses and nurse assistants are important members of the health care team. They are responsible for giving personal care to the patient. They spend more time with the patient than the other members of the team. This gives them an opportunity to give extra support and understanding to the patient. They may work in an acute care hospital or in long-term care.

As a nurse or nurse assistant you will:

- Provide AM and PM care.
- Provide oral hygiene.
- Offer the bedpan and urinal.
- Monitor the patient's elimination functions.
- Assist with dressing and undressing.
- Bathe patients.
- Provide effective skin care.
- Follow the patient care plan. (Figure 18.11)
- Perform range of motion.
- Provide body alignment and positioning.
- Care for hair and nails.
- Shave the patient.
- Apply hot and cold applications.

- Make the bed.
- Assist patients to move and ambulate.
- Apply prosthetic devices and supports.
- Assist with feeding the patient.
- Record intake and output.
- Care for the **incontinent** patient.
- Understand tubes and **catheters.**
- Collect specimens.
- Measure height and weight.
- Take seizure precautions.
- Give **stoma** care.
- Do **postmortem** care.

incontinent
(in KAHNT uh nuhnt)
Unable to control the bowel or bladder.

catheters
(KAHTH uh tuhrs)
Tubes inserted into body opening or cavity.

stoma
(STOH muh)
Opening, e.g., opening in abdomen in an ostomy.

postmortem
(POHST mor tuhm)
After death.

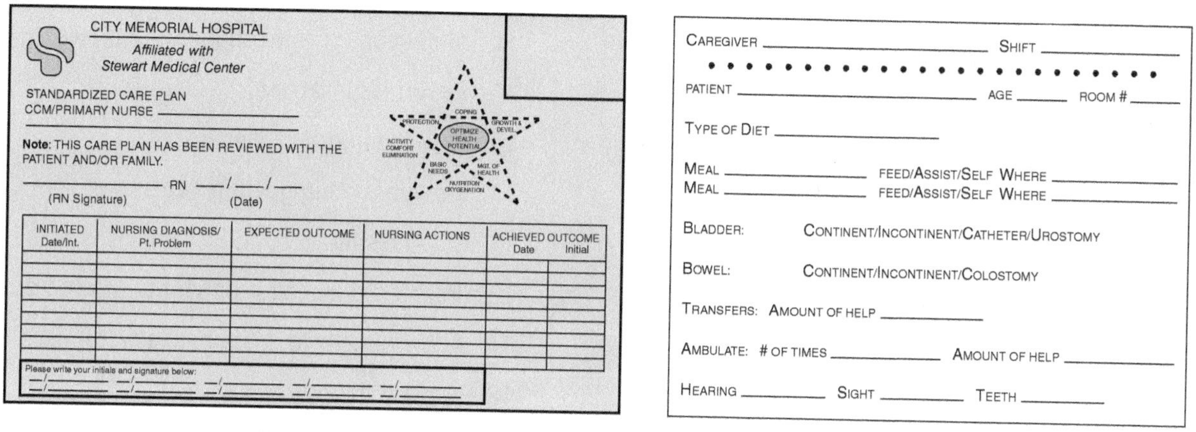
CITY MEMORIAL HOSPITAL
Affiliated with
Stewart Medical Center

STANDARDIZED CARE PLAN
CCM/PRIMARY NURSE ____________

Note: THIS CARE PLAN HAS BEEN REVIEWED WITH THE PATIENT AND/OR FAMILY.

____________ RN ___/___/___
(RN Signature) (Date)

INITIATED Date/Int.	NURSING DIAGNOSIS/ Pt. Problem	EXPECTED OUTCOME	NURSING ACTIONS	ACHIEVED OUTCOME Date	Initial

Please write your initials and signature below:

CAREGIVER ____________ SHIFT ________

PATIENT ____________ AGE ____ ROOM # ____

TYPE OF DIET ____________

MEAL ________ FEED/ASSIST/SELF WHERE ________
MEAL ________ FEED/ASSIST/SELF WHERE ________

BLADDER: CONTINENT/INCONTINENT/CATHETER/UROSTOMY

BOWEL: CONTINENT/INCONTINENT/COLOSTOMY

TRANSFERS: AMOUNT OF HELP ________

AMBULATE: # OF TIMES ________ AMOUNT OF HELP ________

HEARING ________ SIGHT ________ TEETH ________

Figure 18.11
Components of the patient care plan. Why is a patient care plan important?

Standard Precautions

Always follow Standard Precautions when caring for a patient (see Chapter 17). You must evaluate the situation before you start a procedure to determine when you must wear protective gear. The following procedures indicate when to put on gloves and when to discard them. However, you are responsible for determining when to wear gloves. There are times when you need gloves to protect yourself from body fluids that may not be addressed in a procedure. Carefully think through the care you are giving and protect yourself and others.

Morning and Evening Care (AM and PM Care)

The beginning of the day is very important. How you care for the patient when he or she first awakens sets the tone for the entire day. This care is called AM care and is given before breakfast.

Awaken the patient quietly; never be loud or abrupt. Do not shake the person by the shoulder. Touch him or her on the arm and say the person's name. After the person is awake, there are several steps in the care you give. Follow the AM care procedures.

The PM care given to patients just before sleep is also important. Use this time to make patients comfortable for the night. Unhurried care allows the patients to feel relaxed, and they sleep better. If you take care of all their needs before you leave the room, it gives you time to finish your other duties. If you do not make them comfortable (e.g., see if they need to go to the bathroom), you have to return frequently to their rooms. Follow the PM care procedures.

PROCEDURE 18.11 AM Care

BACKGROUND: AM care refreshes the patient. Clean teeth, clean hands, morning elimination, and other comfort measures help improve appetite and enjoyment of breakfast.

ALERT: Follow Standard Precautions.

PREPROCEDURE

1. Wash hands.

2. Gently awaken patient.

3. Assemble equipment:

   a. Washcloth and towel

   b. Toothbrush and toothpaste

   c. Emesis basin

   d. Glass of water

   e. Denture cup if needed

   f. Clean gown if necessary

   g. Clean linen if necessary

   h. Comb and brush

   i. Disposable gloves (two pair)

4. Explain what you plan to do.

5. Provide privacy by pulling privacy curtain.

6. Elevate head of the bed if allowed.

7. Put on disposable gloves.

PROCEDURE

8. Provide a bedpan or urinal if needed, or escort patient to bathroom.

9. Empty bedpan or urinal, rinse it, and dispose of gloves.

10. Put bedpan or urinal out of sight.

11. Allow patient to wash hands and face.

12. Put on disposable gloves.

13. Assist with oral hygiene.

14. Provide a clean gown if necessary.

15. Smooth sheets if patient remains in bed.

16. Transfer to a chair if patient is allowed out of bed.

17. Allow patient to comb hair; assist if necessary.

18. Prepare the overbed table.

    a. Clear tabletop.

    b. Wipe off.

19. Position overbed table and make sure call bell is within reach if patient is to remain in the room, or transport patient to dining room.

POSTPROCEDURE

20. Remove and discard gloves.

21. Wash hands.

10/06/11	0630
	AM care given
	Patient looking forward to breakfast
	No complaints
	S. Gomez CNA

BACKGROUND: PM care refreshes, relaxes, and comforts a patient, providing a quiet time before sleep.

ALERT: Follow Standard Precautions.

PREPROCEDURE

1. Wash hands.

2. Tell patient what you are going to do.

3. Provide privacy.

4. Assemble equipment:

   a. Washcloth and towel

   b. Toothpaste and toothbrush

   c. Glass of water

   d. Emesis basin

   e. Denture cup, if necessary

   f. Night clothes

   g. Lotion

   h. Linen as needed

   i. Disposable gloves

PROCEDURE

5. Encourage patient to do his or her own care if capable.

6. Assist if unable to do his or her own care.

7. Put on disposable gloves.

8. Provide bedpan or urinal if necessary, or escort to bathroom.

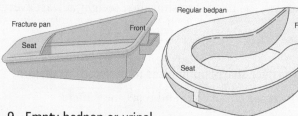

9. Empty bedpan or urinal.

10. Rinse and place in a convenient place for night-time use.

11. Remove and dispose of gloves.

12. Wash patient's hands and face.

13. Put on gloves.

14. Provide for oral hygiene.

15. Change gown, if soiled.

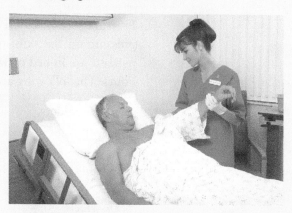

16. Transfer patient from chair or wheelchair into bed, if out of bed.

17. Give back rub with lotion.

18. Observe skin for irritations or breakdown.

19. Smooth the sheets.

20. Change draw sheets if necessary.

21. Provide extra blankets if necessary.

22. Position side rails as ordered after patient is in bed.

POSTPROCEDURE

23. Remove and discard gloves.

24. Wash hands.

25. Provide fresh drinking water.

26. Place bedside table within patient's reach.

27. Secure call light within patient's reach.

8/30/11	2045
	PM care given
	No complaints
	————— *S. Gomez CNA*

Skin Management

Skin is the first defense against infection. When you bathe your patients, you have an opportunity to observe their skin. You should look for:

- Dryness.
- Bruising.
- Any unusual condition.
- Broken area (pressure sore/decubitus).

Pressure sores/*decubiti* are very serious. Patients must be moved to help remove pressure on the skin, or pressure sores develop. This pressure can occur when patients are in bed or when they are sitting. They must be moved at least every 2 hours. The following areas are very sensitive to pressure:

- Shoulders.
- Elbows.
- Hips.
- Sacrum.
- Heels.
- Ankles.
- Ears.
- Toes.

Watch these areas carefully (**Figures 18.12** and **18.13**) The bones press against the skin and stop circulation of blood. This causes the skin and tissue to break down. Pressure sores/decubiti are very painful and are difficult to heal. They can become quite deep and require a surgical procedure to help them heal. They can be prevented! Report any changes, such as redness, heat, tenderness, or broken skin, to the charge nurse.

To help prevent pressure sores/decubiti:

- Change the patient's position at least every 2 hours.
- If patient is up in chair, ask the patient to shift their weight at least every two hours.
- Keep skin clean.
- Massage reddened areas over sharp, bony areas to increase circulation.
- Provide back rubs to increase circulation and relax the patient.
- Keep linen dry and free of wrinkles.
- Consider the use of specialized beds or gel-filled pads for the patient at high risk of a break in skin integrity.

If a patient should develop a break in skin integrity, the area should be documented as to: 1) stage of breakdown; 2) size of breakdown in centimeters; and 3) steps taken to care for breakdown.

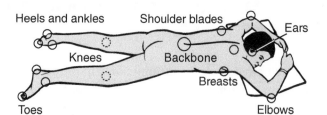

Places to Check for Signs of Bedsores

Heels and ankles — Shoulder blades — Ears — Knees — Backbone — Toes — Breasts — Elbows

Figure 18.12
Places to check for signs of pressure sores. Why are these areas prone to pressure sores?

Patients who are stationary for long periods of time can easily develop pressure sores. In the past, egg crate mattresses were thought to provide protection. We now know that the at-risk patient will need other therapeutic measures to help in avoiding skin integrity problems. These include:

- **Low-Air-Loss Beds:** Composed of segmented cushions covered by a low friction fabric. The cushions inflate reducing pressure on skin surfaces and diminish sheering forces when patients are turned. Low-air-loss beds circulate cool air which helps to evaporate moisture and reduce temperature, thereby excess skin moisture and preventing additional breakdown. These beds are indicated for patients with skin grafts, pressure ulcers, edema and advanced arthritis.

- **Rotation Beds:** These beds rotate from side to side in a cradle like motion. They are especially useful for patients with spinal cord injury, multiple trauma, or severe burns.

- **Air-Fluidized Beds:** This bed allows for minimal contact between the bed and the patient. They sometimes have a low-air-loss component as well. The fluid-like surface reduces pressure on the skin helping to prevent pressure ulcers and to promote wound healing.

- **Gel Pads:** These specialized pads are useful for patients who sit in chairs for prolonged periods of time and have difficulty shifting their body positions. They reduce the pressure placed on the sacral area.

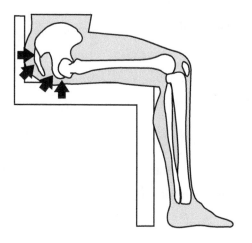

Figure 18.13
Pressure from the ischial bones and sacrum with the patient in the sitting position. How can health care workers help alleviate pressure from the ischial bones and sacrum?

BACKGROUND: Giving a back rub provides an opportunity to help the patient relax and to check for any skin changes. It is also a good time to listen to any complaints or concerns the patient might have.

CAUTION: Check with team leader for permission to give a back rub.

ALERT: Follow Standard Precautions.

PREPROCEDURE

1. Wash hands.

2. Assemble equipment:

    a. Lotion

    b. Powder

    c. Towel

    d. Washcloth

    e. Soap

    f. Water (105°F)

    g. Disposable gloves

3. Tell patient what you are going to do.

4. Provide privacy by pulling privacy curtains.

PROCEDURE

5. Place lotion container in warm water to help warm it.

6. Raise bed to a comfortable working height.

7. Lower side rail on the side you are working on.

8. Put on disposable gloves.

9. Position patient on side or in prone position.

10. Place a towel along back to protect linen if patient is in a side-lying position.

11. Wash back thoroughly.

12. Rub a small amount of lotion into your hands.

13. Begin at base of spine and apply lotion over entire back.

14. Use firm, long strokes, beginning at buttocks and moving upward to neck and shoulders.

15. Use firm pressure as you stroke upward, and light circular strokes returning to buttocks.

NOTE: Pay special attention to bony prominences.

16. Use a circular motion over each area (shoulder blades, backbone).

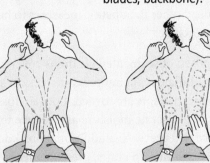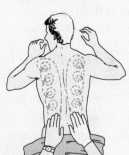

17. Observe skin for irritation or breakdown.

NOTE: Do not rub or apply lotion to any open area on the skin.

18. Repeat several times (3 to 5 minutes).

19. Dry back.

20. Adjust gown for comfort.

21. Remove towel.

22. Position patient comfortably.

23. Return bed to lowest height.

24. Put up side rail if required.

25. Secure call light in reach of patient.

POSTPROCEDURE

26. Remove and discard gloves.

27. Wash hands.

28. Record procedure and any observations (e.g., redness, broken areas, dry skin).

7/15/12	1350
	Back rub given
	No shin change noted
	Rails up
	——— *R. Johnson CNA*

Oral Hygiene

Good mouth care should be provided at least three times a day: before breakfast when you give AM care, after lunch, and after dinner. It is important because it:

- Reduces odor.
- Helps prevent tooth decay.
- Is refreshing.
- Relieves dry lips and mouth, especially if the patient has an elevated temperature or breathes through the mouth.

PROCEDURE | **18.14** | **Giving Special Mouth Care to the Unconscious Patient**

BACKGROUND: The mouth must be cared for during illness. If the patient is helpless, the nurse needs to make certain the patient receives the care necessary to keep the mouth clean and moist, every 1 to 2 hours as necessary.

PREPROCEDURE

1. Wash hands prior to and after administering care.

2. Put on disposable gloves.

PROCEDURE

3. Assemble equipment within reach—toothbrush, toothpaste, emesis basin, normal saline solution, cup with cool water, towel, mouthwash, sponge toothette, padded tongue blade, irrigating syringe with rubber tip, petroleum jelly, suction catheter with suction apparatus.

4. Provide privacy for the patient. Adjust the height of the bed to a comfortable position for the nurse. Lower the side rail next to the nurse and position the patient on their side with the head of the bed lowered. Place the towel across the patient's chest and emesis basin in position under the chin.

5. Open the patient's mouth and gently insert a padded tongue blade between the back molars if necessary.

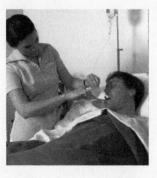

6. If teeth are present, brush carefully with toothbrush and paste. If dentures are present, remove gently and cleanse before replacing. Use a toothette moistened with normal saline to gently cleanse gums, mucous membranes, and tongue.

7. If necessary, use the irrigating syringe with rubber tip and rinse mouth gently with a small amount of water. Position the patient's head to allow for the return of water or use suction apparatus to remove the water from the oral cavity.

8. Apply petroleum jelly to the patient's lips.

9. Remove equipment and return the patient to a comfortable position. Raise the siderail and lower the bed.

POSTPROCEDURE

10. Document the nursing assistant's oral assessment and any unusual findings.

Some patients may have **dentures**. Often patients are sensitive about removing their dentures. Provide privacy and encouragement for oral care. Learn the correct method of handling dentures so that you do not break them.

BACKGROUND: A clean mouth and clean teeth help prevent oral problems, freshen the breath, and give an overall feeling of well-being.

ALERT: Follow Standard Precautions.

PREPROCEDURE

1. Wash hands.

2. Assemble equipment:

   a. Toothbrush

   b. Toothpaste

   c. Mouthwash

   d. Cup of water with straw, if needed

   e. Emesis basin

   f. Bath towel

   g. Tissues

3. Identify patient and explain what you are going to do.

4. Screen patient by pulling privacy curtain around bed.

PROCEDURE

5. Raise head of the bed if patient is allowed to sit up.

6. Place towel over blanket and patient's gown.

7. Place toothbrush, toothpaste, mouthwash, emesis basin, and glass of water on overbed table.

8. Remove overbed table when patient has completed brushing.

9. Put away towel and make patient comfortable.

10. Put up side rails if required.

11. Secure call bell within patient's reach.

12. Put away all equipment and tidy unit.

POSTPROCEDURE

13. Wash hands.

14. Chart procedure.

6/14/11	0640
	Set up equipment on overbed table
	Brushed teeth without assistance
	_____ S. Gomez CNA

BACKGROUND: A clean mouth and clean teeth help prevent oral problems, freshen the breath, and give an overall feeling of well-being.

ALERT: Follow Standard Precautions.

PREPROCEDURE

1. Wash hands.

2. Assemble equipment:

   a. Toothbrush

   b. Toothpaste

   c. Mouthwash

   d. Cup of water with straw, if needed

   e. Emesis basin

   f. Bath towel

   g. Tissues

   h. Disposable nonsterile gloves

3. Identify patient and explain what you are going to do.

4. Screen patient by pulling privacy curtain around bed.

PROCEDURE

5. Raise head of bed if patient is allowed to sit up.

6. Place a towel over blanket and patient's gown.

7. Put on gloves.

8. Pour water over toothbrush; put toothpaste on brush.

9. Insert brush into the mouth carefully.

10. Place brush at an angle on upper teeth and brush in an up-and-down motion starting at rear of mouth.

11. Repeat on lower teeth

12. Give patient water to rinse mouth. If necessary, use a straw.

13. Hold emesis basin under chin. Have patient expectorate (spit) water into the basin.

14. Offer tissues to patient to wipe mouth and chin. Discard tissues.

15. Provide mouthwash if available. Use emesis basin and tissues as above.

16. Put up side rails before turning away from patient.

17. Return all equipment.

18. Remove gloves and put in hazardous waste.

POSTPROCEDURE

19. Wash hands.

20. Tidy up unit.

21. Secure call bell within patient's reach.

22. Make patient comfortable before leaving the room.

23. Chart procedure and how patient tolerated it.

5/14/12	0825
Brushed teeth, provided oral hygiene	
Tolerated well	
No oral problems noted	
_____	R. Johnson CNA

PROCEDURE 18.17 Oral Hygiene—Ambulatory Patient

BACKGROUND: A clean mouth and clean teeth help prevent oral problems, freshen the breath, and give an overall feeling of well-being.

ALERT: Follow Standard Precautions.

PREPROCEDURE

1. Wash hands.

2. Tell patient what you are going to do.

PROCEDURE

3. Set up equipment at sink.

   a. Toothbrush

   b. Toothpaste

   c. Tablets or powder to soak dentures in

   d. Towel

   e. Glass

POSTPROCEDURE

4. Rinse equipment and put away.

5. Wash hands.

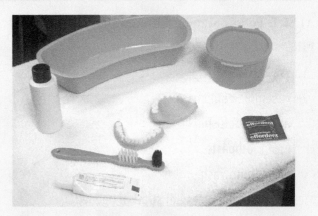

5/24/11   0745

Brushed teeth without assistance

_____ *S. Gomez CNA*

PROCEDURE 18.18 Oral Hygiene—Denture Care

BACKGROUND: Food and bacteria collect under dentures causing discomfort due to tissue breakdown and mouth odor. Clean dentures protect against oral problems and refresh the mouth.

ALERT: Follow Standard Precautions.

PREPROCEDURE

1. Wash hands.

2. Assemble equipment:

   a. Tissues

   b. Paper towel or gauze squares

   c. Mouthwash

   d. Disposable denture cup

   e. Toothbrush or denture brush

   f. Denture paste or toothpowder

   g. Towel

   h. Disposable nonsterile gloves

   i. Emesis basin

3. Identify patient.

4. Explain what you are going to do.

(continued)

PROCEDURE

5. Pull privacy curtain.

6. Lower side rails.

7. Raise head of bed if allowed.

8. Place towel across patient's chest.

9. Prepare emesis basin by placing tissue, paper towel or washcloth in bottom of basin.

10. Put on gloves.

11. Have patient remove his or her dentures.

12. Remove dentures if patient cannot.

   Upper Denture

   a. Explain what you are going to do.

   b. Use a gauze square to grip upper denture.

   c. Place your index finger between top ridge of denture and cheek.

   d. Gently pull on denture to release suction.

   e. Remove upper denture.

   Lower Denture

   a. Use a gauze square to grip lower denture.

   b. Place your index finger between lower ridge and cheek.

   c. Gently pull on denture to release suction.

   d. Remove lower denture.

13. Place dentures in lined emesis basin and take to sink or utility room.

14. Remember to pull side rails up if you walk away from the bed.

15. Hold dentures firmly in palm of hand.

16. Put toothpowder or toothpaste on toothbrush.

17. Rinse dentures in cool water.

18. Hold dentures under cold running water and brush dentures on all surfaces until clean.

19. Rinse dentures under cold running water.

20. Remember to rinse denture cup with cold water before placing clean dentures in the cup.

21. Place in denture cup.

22. Place some mouthwash and cool water in cup.

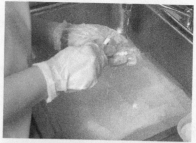

23. Help patient rinse mouth with mouthwash; if food particles are between cheek and gumline, gently swab away with gauze. Clean gums with toothette.

24. Have patient replace dentures.

25. Place dentures in labeled denture cup next to bed, if dentures are to be left out.

26. Rinse equipment and put away.

POSTPROCEDURE

27. Remove gloves; dispose of in hazardous waste.

28. Wash hands.

29. Position patient.

30. Secure call bell within patient's reach.

31. Chart procedure and how it was tolerated.

NOTE: The patient may want to soak dentures overnight after PM care has been given. Place dentures in a solution in a denture cup and store in a safe place.

7/07/11	0725
	Set out equipment for denture care
	Able to clean dentures
	Or: Removed dentures, cleaned,
	and freshened
	Provided oral hygiene
	No oral problems noted
	_____ R. Johnson CNA

BACKGROUND: The unconscious patient often mouth breathes causing very dry lips and mucous membrane. Careful care and observation help prevent oral problems.

ALERT: Follow Standard Precautions.

PREPROCEDURE

1. Wash hands.

2. Tell patient what you are going to do. When patient is unconscious he or she may hear even if he or she cannot respond.

3. Provide privacy.

4. Assemble equipment:

   a. Emesis basin

   b. Towel

   c. Lemon glycerin swabs

   d. Tongue blades

   e. 4 × 4 gauze

   f. Lip moisturizer

   g. Disposable nonsterile gloves

5. Position bed at a comfortable working height.

6. Put on gloves.

PROCEDURE

7. Position patient's head to side and place towel on bed under patient's cheek and chin.

8. Secure emesis basin under patient's chin.

9. Wrap a tongue blade with 4 × 4 gauze and slightly moisten. Swab mouth being certain to clean gums, teeth, tongue, and roof of mouth.

10. Apply lip moisturizer to lips and swab mouth with lemon and glycerin if available.

11. Remove towel and reposition patient.

12. Make sure side rails are up and bed is in low position.

13. Discard disposable equipment in hazardous waste.

14. Clean basin and put away.

15. Remove gloves and put in hazardous waste.

POSTPROCEDURE

16. Wash hands.

17. Report and document patient's tolerance of procedure.

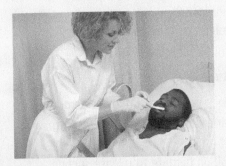

6/16/11	1040
Cleaned teeth, moistened lips,	
provided oral hygiene	
Noted small canker sore on palate	
Reported to team leader	
	S. Gomez CNA

Offering the Urinal and/or Bedpan

Eliminating waste products from the body is necessary for good health. When patients are confined to bed, they must use a bedpan or urinal. Male patients use urinals to empty the bladder. Women use the bedpan for both urine and the elimination of solid waste (bowel movement). Men also use a bedpan for the elimination of solid waste. Solid waste is called *feces* or *stool*. When patients eliminate liquid waste, we call it *urinating* or *voiding*. Liquid bowel movements, such as diarrhea, may also be referred to as liquid waste.

If your patient does not eliminate liquid waste from the bladder, he or she may develop a urinary tract infection. This is very painful and serious. Small amounts of liquid elimination may indicate infection, dehydration, or fluid retention in the body.

If solid waste is not eliminated, large amounts of stool may cause an impaction. When a large amount of stool stays in the bowel it causes discomfort, and the patient experiences nausea and sometimes vomiting. This can be prevented by carefully recording bowel movements and letting the charge nurse know if a patient has not had a bowel movement. The charge nurse will give the patient a **laxative**, **suppository**, or enema (**Figure 18.14**), which is discussed later in this chapter.

laxative
(LAK suh tiv)
A medicine for relieving constipation.

suppository
(suh POZ i tawr ee)
A solid, conical mass of medicinal substance that melts upon insertion into the rectum.

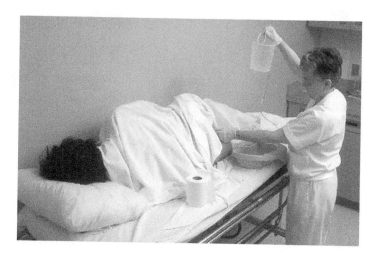

Figure 18.14
Cleansing enema. Under what conditions might it be necessary to give a patient an enema?

BACKGROUND: Carefully placing the bedpan prevents discomfort. This procedure allows observations for skin breakdown and elimination.

ALERT: Follow Standard Precautions.

PREPROCEDURE

1. Wash hands.

2. Assemble equipment:

   a. Bedpan with cover

   b. Toilet tissue

   c. Soap and water

   d. Towel and washcloth

   e. Disposable nonsterile gloves (two pairs)

3. Ask visitors to wait outside room.

4. Provide privacy for patient with curtain, screen, or door.

5. Put on clean gloves before handling the bedpan.

6. Remove bedpan from storage space.

7. Warm metal bedpans by running warm water over them and drying.

PROCEDURE

8. Lower head of bed if it is elevated.

9. Fold top covers back enough to see where to place the pan. Do not expose patient.

10. Ask patient to raise hips off bed. Help support patient by placing your hand at patient's midback.

    a. Roll the patient onto his or her side if the patient is unable to lift the hips.

    b. Place bedpan on buttocks. For a standard bedpan: Position bedpan so wider end of pan is aligned with patient's buttock; for a fracture pan: position bedpan with handle toward the foot of the bed.

    c. Hold in place with one hand and help patient roll back onto bedpan.

11. Slide bedpan into place.

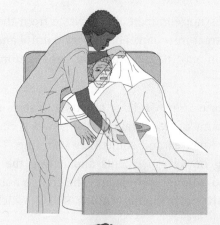

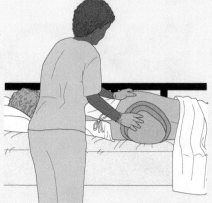

12. Cover patient again.

13. Raise head of bed for comfort.

14. Put toilet tissue within patient's reach.

(continued)

15. Remove gloves.

16. Wash your hands.

17. Leave call light with patient and ask patient to signal when finished.

18. Leave room to provide privacy.

19. Watch for call light to signal patient's readiness to be removed from bedpan.

20. Put on gloves.

21. Assist patient as necessary to ensure cleanliness.

22. Lower head of bed before removing bedpan.

23. Remove bedpan and empty, rinse bedpan and pours rinse into the toilet.

24. Use a paper towel to flush the toilet and the faucet, since still have gloves on.

25. Measure urine if on I & O.

26. Remove gloves and dispose of in biohazardous container.

POSTPROCEDURE

27. Wash hands.

28. Put on clean gloves.

29. Provide washcloth, water, and soap for patient to wash hands.

30. Dispose of soiled washcloth or wipes in proper container.

31. Provide comfort measures for patient.

32. Secure call light in patient's reach, make sure side rails are up and bed is in lowest position.

33. Remove and dispose of gloves in biohazardous container.

34. Wash hands.

35. Open privacy curtain.

36. Chart the following:

    a. Bowel movement amount, color, consistency

    b. Amount voided if on I & O

4/10/12	0830
Small, light brown, dry bowel	
Complained of discomfort when eliminating	
Noted small amount bright red blood	
Reported to team leader	
	R. Johnson CNA

BACKGROUND: Offering a urinal at the time of elimination allows the patient who is not able to go into the bathroom, a way to stay in bed or in a chair and eliminate liquid waste. Remember to provide privacy to maintain the patient's dignity.

ALERT: Follow Standard Precautions.

PREPROCEDURE

1. Wash hands.

2. Assemble equipment:

   a. Urinal with cover

   b. Soap and water

   c. Towel and washcloth

   d. Disposable nonsterile gloves

3. Ask visitors to wait outside room.

4. Provide privacy for patient.

PROCEDURE

5. Hand urinal to patient.

   a. Place call light at patient's side.

   b. Wash your hands.

   c. Leave room until patient signals with the call light.

(If the patient is unable to place urinal, place penis in urinal. If necessary, stand and hold urinal until patient has finished voiding.) Wear gloves for this step.

6. Return to room when patient has finished voiding.

7. Put on gloves.

8. Offer washcloth for patient to wash their hands.

9. Place cover over urinal and carry it into bathroom.

10. Check to see if patient is on I & O or if a urine specimen is needed. (See I & O and specimen collection in this chapter.)

11. Observe urine color, consistency, and odor.

12. Empty into toilet.

13. Use a paper towel to turn on the faucet and flush the toilet, since still have gloves on. Rinse urinal with cold water.

POSTPROCEDURE

14. Cover and place in a convenient location for the patient.

15. Remove gloves and place in biohazard container.

16. Wash hands.

17. Secure call light in reach of patient.

18. Report and document unusual color, odor, or consistency of urine.

19. Record amount if on I & O.

4/10/12	1030
	Voided 250 cc.
	Recorded on I & O sheet
	—————— R. Johnson CNA

PROCEDURE 18.22 Elimination—Bedside Commode

BACKGROUND: A bedside commode allows patients who cannot ambulate to the toilet to eliminate body waste by sitting on a chairlike device at the bedside. Patients generally have less difficulty eliminating waste when they use a commode instead of a bedpan.

ALERT: Follow Standard Precautions.

PREPROCEDURE

1. Wash hands.

2. Assemble equipment:
   a. Bedside commode
   b. Toilet tissue
   c. Washcloth
   d. Warm water
   e. Soap
   f. Towel
   g. Disposable nonsterile gloves

3. Identify patient.

4. Explain what you are going to do.

PROCEDURE

5. Place commode chair next to bed facing head of bed. *Lock wheels!*

6. Check to see if receptacle is in place under seat.

7. Provide privacy by pulling privacy curtains.

8. Lower bed to lowest position.

9. Lower side rail.

10. Help patient to sitting position.

11. Help patient swing legs over side of bed.

12. Put on patient's slippers and assist to stand.

13. Have patient place hands on your shoulders.

14. Support under patient's arms, pivot patient to right, and lower to commode. (See the procedure "Transferring—Pivot Transfer from Bed to Wheelchair.")

15. Place call bell within reach.

16. Place toilet tissue within reach.

17. Remain nearby if patient seems weak.

18. Return immediately when patient signals.

19. Put on gloves.

20. Assist patient to stand.

21. Clean anus or perineum if patient is unable to help self.

22. Remove gloves and put in hazardous waste.

23. Help patient wash hands. Remember to do this before you stand the patient up.

24. Assist back to bed and position comfortably.

25. Put up side rail if required.

26. Put on gloves.

27. Put down cover on commode chair and remove receptacle.

28. Empty contents, measuring if on I & O.

29. Empty and clean per hospital policy.

30. Remove gloves and put in hazardous waste.

(continued)

POSTPROCEDURE

31. Wash hands.

32. Replace equipment and tidy unit.

33. Record the following:

    a. Bowel movement

        (1) Amount

        (2) Consistency

        (3) Color

    b. Any unusual observations, such as

        (1) Weakness

        (2) Discomfort

11/24/11	1030
	Eliminated moderate amount of brown,
	formed stool and 200 cc of urine Returned
	to bed, positioned for comfort; Tolerated
	activity well
	S. Gomez CNA

PROCEDURE **18.23** Assisting to Bathroom

BACKGROUND: It is the nurse's responsibility to obtain an assessment of the patient's baseline functional status at the time that care for the patient is assumed. Understanding the baseline functional status of the patient enables the nurse to establish goals for activities of daily living. The goal must always be to maintain or improve the baseline function of the patient.

Institutionalization where staff may take over these activities promotes decreased self mobility and may contribute to the future dependency of the patient. Assisting the patient with toileting activities can maintain continence as well as provide opportunities for the patient to ambulate and build strength.

ALERT: Follow Standard Precautions.

PREPROCEDURE

1. Establish the baseline function of the patient. Determine the amount of assistance required (one nurse, two nurses).

2. Establish the need for assertive devices such as cane, walker, gait belt.

    NOTE: The use of a gait belt for any patient that is not fully independent is highly recommended. This a protective device for both the patient and the nurse.

3. Assure that the path to be used is clear of obstruction.

4. Explain to the patient what is to be done. Instruct the patient to alert the nurse of any lightheadedness or discomfort.

PROCEDURE

5. Assist the patient to an erect position at the edge of the bed.

6. Pause at the edge of the bed (and again after the patient arises) to ensure that the patient feels steady. You should stand in front of and face the patient. Brace the patient's lower extremities. Place belt around the patient's waist.

7. Elevate the bed to a height that allows the patient's legs to rest firmly on the ground but not to have to lift his body from a low position as the patient rises.

8. With your hands under the gait belt assist the patient to rise.

(continued)

9. Patients who are fearful of walking may tend to bend forward and look at their feet. They will need to be reminded to stand erect and hold their head high.

10. Guide the patient to the bathroom with one hand under the gait belt at the patient's back and the other hand guiding the patient's free arm. Walk slightly behind and to one side of the patient for the full distance, while holding on to the belt. Assist with lowering the patient onto the toilet seat. For those patients who have functional disabilities it is advisable to obtain and use an elevated toilet seat. This will enable the patient to sit and rise with the least amount of energy use and the greatest degree of safety.

11. Instruct the patient on using the nurse call light to call for assistance after toileting is complete.

12. After toileting is complete assist the patient with completing personal hygiene as necessary.

13. Return the patient to the bedside and assist as necessary with positioning the patient back into bed.

POSTPROCEDURE

14. Assure that all needs are met and that the patient is comfortable prior to leaving the area.

15. Document in the medical record the patient's level of activity, any problems with independent function, and the level of assistance required.

Movement and Ambulation of the Patient

You are responsible for moving your patient in many different ways:

- Into a chair or wheelchair.
- Into bed from a chair or wheelchair.
- From bed to gurney.
- From gurney to bed.
- Transferring into a wheelchair.
- Transporting by gurney.
- Using a mechanical lift. (**Figure 18.15**)

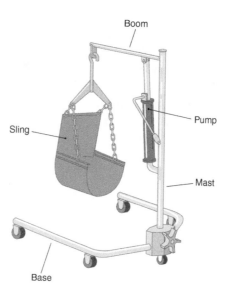

Figure 18.15
Mechanical lift. Under what circumstances would you use a mechanical lift for a patient?

BACKGROUND: Patients that have been immobile for a period of time may need assistance from the nurse to sit, stand, and walk. Determining what the patient's baseline activity level has been, any recent changes in mobility, and goals of care are the first steps to improving the patient's functional level.

The goal must always be to maintain or improve baseline function. A patient who has not been walking at all may have a goal of taking one independent step. One who has diminished tolerance of activity may have a goal of increasing the number of feet walked without an increase in fatigue. The goal should always be individualized to the particular patient.

ALERT: Follow Standard Precautions.

PREPROCEDURE

1. Assess the functional level of the patient. Include the patient when determining the plan of care and goals.

2. Explain the procedure to the patient.

3. Provide privacy for the patient.

4. Ensure a clear path for ambulation.

5. Place a chair midway of the distance to be traveled to facilitate a rest spot if necessary.

PROCEDURE

6. Assist the patient to an erect position on the side of the bed. Pause to determine the patient's tolerance of the activity.

7. Place a gait belt around the patient's waist to ensure safety for the patient and the nurse.

8. Stand the patient at the bedside. Pause to determine the patient's tolerance of the activity.

9. With the nurses nearest hand placed under the gait belt at the patient's back and the other hand grasping the patient's nearest elbow: (a) Guide the patient forward. (b) Assess the patient's gait and tolerance of activity as the patient progresses forward.

10. If the patient should faint or begin to fall the nurse can use the gait belt to pull the patient towards the nurse and ease the patient to the ground.

11. Return the patient to the bedside and assist the patient into a chair or back into the bed. Assure that the patient is comfortable and has no further needs.

12. Reassure and encourage the patient to continue the mobility program for increasing functional status.

POSTPROCEDURE

13. Wash hands.

14. Document in observation note patient's gait, feet walked and tolerance of activity.

NOTE: If the patient has numerous tethers and ambulation is problematic an alternative activity can be marching in place at the bedside.

Be careful not to injure the patients or yourself when you move them. Review the section on body mechanics in Chapter 21. Always remember to evaluate whether you need help before you start to move the patient, and do not hesitate to ask someone to give you a hand.

When patients first try to get out of bed, they may feel dizzy. Help them sit on the side of the bed. Encourage the patient to swing his or her legs slightly back and forth until you determine that he or she is strong enough to stand and walk.

When your patients are able to walk, encourage them to do as much as they are capable of. They may seem slow, and it may take you a little extra time, but it is important for them. Walking (**ambulation**):

- Helps maintain stamina.
- Increases joint mobility.
- Improves muscle tone.
- Helps prevent lung congestion.
- Improves circulation.
- Helps prevent blood clots.
- Helps maintain independence.
- Provides a sense of accomplishment.

ambulation
(AM byoo lay shuhn)
Walking.

Your patients may need a device such as a cane, crutches, or walker. They may need a wheelchair much of the time but still be able to ambulate in a limited way.

Before patients are moved, check to see if there are tubes or catheters in place. You must be careful not to pull them out, crimp them, or put a strain on them. If patients have drainage equipment (e.g., Foley bag), do not raise the tubing above the level of insertion into the body. If they have an IV, do not allow the tubing to drop below the bed level.

Never let any tubing touch the floor. If you have any question about moving patients, *ask your teacher or the charge nurse before moving them.*

BACKGROUND: Pivot transfer allows you to move the patient in one easy, safe motion into or out of a wheelchair. Use good body mechanics, explain each step, and reassure the patient of his/her safety.

ALERT: Follow Standard Precautions.

PREPROCEDURE

1. Wash hands.

2. Explain procedure to patient, speaking clearly, slowly and directly, maintaining face-to-face contact whenever possible.

3. Provide for patient's privacy during the procedure, using a curtain, screen or door.

4. Make sure that wheels on bed are locked.

5. Lift foot rests or swing leg supports out of way.

6. Position wheelchair alongside bed. (See teacher for directions in working with stroke patients.) *Lock wheels.*

PROCEDURE

7. Place bed at a safe and appropriate level for the patient. Support patient's back and hips and assist patient to sitting position with feet flat on the floor.

8. Move patient to edge of bed, with legs over side (see top right).

9. Before transferring patient, put non-skid footwear on patient and securely fasten.

10. Have patient dangle legs for a few minutes and take slow, deep breaths. Observe for dizziness.

11. Remember to use a gait belt. Stand in front of patient, positioning yourself to ensure your safety and that of your patient during transfer (e.g., knees bent, feet apart, back straight), place belt around patient's waist, and grasp belt.

12. Brace patient's lowest extremities to prevent slipping.

13. Count to three (or say other prearranged signal) to alert patient to begin transfer.

14. Support him or her at midriff and ask patient to stand, if patient is not dizzy.

15. Once standing, have patient pivot (turn) and hold onto armrest of wheelchair with both arms or one strong arm (see bottom right).

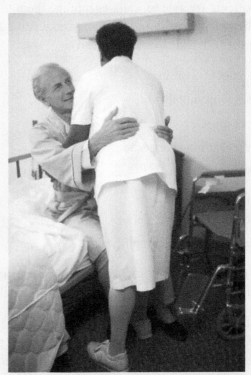

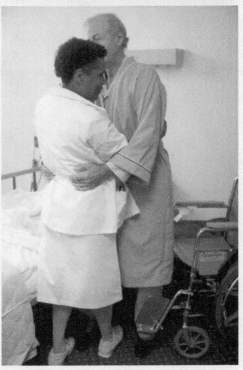

(continued)

16. Gently ease patient into a sitting position, as shown in the following two pictures.

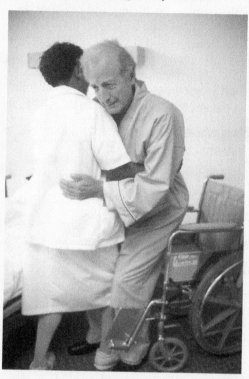 

17. Position yourself at back of wheelchair. Ask patient to push on the floor with feet as you lift gently under each arm to ease patient into a comfortable position against backrest. Make sure patient's hips are touching the back of the wheelchair and then remove the transfer belt, if used.

18. Return foot rests to normal position and place feet and legs in a comfortable position on rests. Make sure the signaling device is within the patient's reach.

19. Do not leave a patient who requires a postural support until it is in place.

20. Reverse above procedure to return patient to bed.

POSTPROCEDURE

21. Wash hands

BACKGROUND: Sliding transfer allows you to assist the patient who is paralyzed from the waist down to easily move in and out of a wheelchair. Use good body mechanics, explain each step, and reassure the patient of his or her safety.

ALERT: Follow Standard Precautions.

PREPROCEDURE

1. Wash hands.

2. Assemble equipment: wheelchair with removable arms.

3. Explain the procedure to the patient.

4. Provide privacy for the patient.

PROCEDURE

5. Position wheelchair at bedside with back parallel to head of bed. *Lock* wheels. Move foot rests out of the way.

6. Remove wheelchair arm nearest to bedside.

7. Place bed level to chair seat height if possible. *Lock* bed wheels.

8. Raise head of bed so that patient is in sitting position.

9. Position yourself beside wheelchair and carefully assist patient to slide from bed to wheelchair.

10. Replace wheelchair arm and return foot rests to their normal position.

11. Position patient for comfort and apply postural supports.

POSTPROCEDURE

12. Make sure call bell is within reach.

13. Wash hands.

5/30/11	0945
	Transferred from bed into
	wheelchair
	Tolerated sliding transfer well
	R. Johnson CNA

Transferring—Two-Person Lift from Bed to Chair and Back

BACKGROUND: A person who is unable to bear his or her weight during a pivot transfer can be lifted by two people. Use good body mechanics, explain each step, and reassure the patient of his or her safety.

ALERT: Follow Standard Precautions.

PREPROCEDURE

1. Wash hands.

2. Assemble equipment: chair.

3. Ask one other person to help.

4. Tell patient what you are going to do.

5. Provide privacy for the patient.

PROCEDURE

6. Position chair next to bed with back of chair parallel with head of bed. *Lock wheels.*

7. Position patient near edge of bed. Lock wheels of bed.

8. Position co-worker on side of bed near feet.

9. Position yourself behind chair at head of bed.

10. Place your arms under patient's axillae and clasp your hands together at patient's midchest.

11. Co-worker places hands under patient's upper legs.

12. Count to three. On the count of three, lift patient into chair.

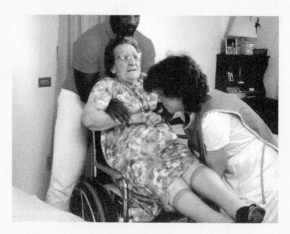

13. Position for comfort and secure postural supports PRN.

POSTPROCEDURE

14. Put call bell within reach of patient.

15. Wash hands.

11/20/11	2100
	Transferred per two-person lift from
	chair into bed, positioned for HS
	comfort
	Tolerated transfer well
	A. Chaplin, CNA

BACKGROUND: A sliding transfer of a patient on and off a gurney is easily and safely accomplished with two people using a pull sheet. Use good body mechanics, explain each step, and reassure the patient of his or her safety.

ALERT: Follow Standard Precautions.

PREPROCEDURE

1. Wash hands.

2. Assemble equipment:

   a. Gurney

   b. Cover sheet

3. Ask a co-worker to help.

4. Explain what you are going to do and lock wheels on bed.

5. Provide privacy for the patient.

PROCEDURE

6. Cover patient with sheet and remove bed covers.

7. Raise bed to gurney height: lower side rail and move patient to side of bed.

8. Loosen draw sheet on both sides so it can be used as a pull sheet.

9. Position gurney next to bed and *lock* wheels on gurney.

10. Position yourself on outside of gurney—one arm at the head, the other at the hips. Co-worker is on other side of bed.

11. Reach across gurney and securely hold edge of draw sheet. Pull patient onto gurney and cover. (If patient is large, a third person on the opposite side of bed may be necessary.)

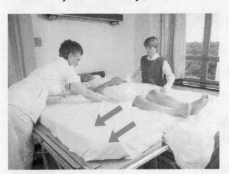

12. Position patient for comfort.

13. Secure with safety straps or raise side rails.

POSTPROCEDURE

14. Wash hands.

9/10/11	0900
	Transferred to radiology via gurney
	following a sliding transfer from bed
	Tolerated transfer well
	_____ *A. Chaplin CNA*

BACKGROUND: Patients who are paralyzed can be easily transferred with a mechanical lift. Mechanical lifts allow patients who would otherwise be bedridden to be placed into a bathtub or chair.

Your ability to use the lift safely will provide important environmental and physical stimulation for the patient. Remember to ask a co-worker to double-check all connections and positions before moving the patient to ensure their safety.

ALERT: Follow Standard Precautions.

PREPROCEDURE

1. Wash hands.

2. Gather equipment:

   a. Mechanical lift

   b. Sheet or blanket for patient comfort

   c. Sling

3. Check all equipment to be sure it is in good working order and that the sling is not damaged or torn.

4. Ask one other person to help.

5. Prepare patient's destination.

   a. Chair

   b. Gurney

   c. Bathtub

   d. Shower

6. *Lock* wheels on bed and explain what you are going to do.

7. Provide privacy for the patient.

PROCEDURE

8. Roll patient toward you.

9. Place sling on bed behind patient.

   a. Position top of sling at shoulders.

   b. Position bottom of sling under buttocks.

   c. Leave enough of sling to support body when the body is rolled back. Fan-fold remaining sling next to body. It will be pulled through when patient is rolled back.

10. Roll patient to other side of bed and pull fan-folded portion of sling flat. Remove all wrinkles and allow patient to lie flat on back.

11. Position lift over patient, being sure to broaden base of lift. This stabilizes the lift while raising patient.

12. Raise head of bed to a semi-Fowler's position.

13. Attach straps on lift to sling loops. Shorter straps must be attached to shoulder loops. Longer straps are attached to loops at hips. *(Important: If you reverse the strap attachment, the patient's head will be lower than his or her hips.)*

14. Reassure patient. Let patient know you will keep him or her from falling. Gently raise patient from bed with hand crank or pump handle.

15. Keep patient centered over base of lift as you move lift and patient to his or her destination. (It is helpful to have a helper stand by and steady patient while moving so that patient doesn't swing.)

16. Position patient over chair, commode, bathtub, shower chair, etc. Ask a co-worker to steady chair.

17. Slowly lower patient into chair using foot-pedal positioning.

18. Unhook sling from lift straps and carefully move lift away from patient.

19. Provide all comfort measures for patient.

20. Secure postural supports if necessary.

21. Return lift to storage area.

(continued)

POSTPROCEDURE

22. Wash hands.

23. Reverse procedure when returning patient to bed.

NOTE: The mechanical lift is an expensive item. Depending on the size of the facility you are in, there may be a limited number available. Always return the lift to its storage area so that it will be available for others to use.

4/20/12	0830
	Transferred via mechanical lift to bathtub
	Tolerated bath well
	Positioned in day chair and taken to patio
_____	*S. Gomez CNA*

PROCEDURE **18.30**

Transferring—Moving a Patient on a Gurney or Stretcher

BACKGROUND: Patients who are medicated or must stay in a reclined position can be moved throughout a facility on a gurney or stretcher. It is important to secure safety rails and wheel them in a safe manner.

ALERT: Follow Standard Precautions.

PREPROCEDURE

1. Wash hands.

2. Position bed to gurney height.

3. *Lock* all the brakes on gurney and bed.

4. Follow the procedure for transferring to and from a gurney.

PROCEDURE

5. Stand at the patient's head and push the gurney with patient's feet moving first down the hallway.

6. Slow down when turning a corner. Always check the intersection mirrors for traffic.

7. Enter an elevator by standing at patient's head and pulling gurney into elevator. The feet will be the last to enter elevator.

8. Leave elevator by carefully pushing the gurney out of elevator into corridor.

9. Position yourself at patient's feet, and back a patient on a gurney down a hill.

10. Never leave a patient unattended on a gurney.

11. Raise side rails and secure a safety strap.

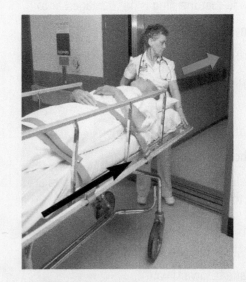

POSTPROCEDURE

13. Wash hands.

12/14/11	1320
	Transferred via gurney to surgery
_____	*R. Johnson CNA*

Positioning and Body Alignment

Always position your patients with the head in a straight line with the spine and the body in a comfortable, normal **alignment**. If a patient is bent in an unnatural position (slumped forward, rolled in a ball) the patient may experience:

- Breathing problems.
- Added pressure to the bony areas, causing skin breakdown (decubiti).
- Strain on the lumbar spine.
- Contractures, chronic loss of joint motion due to structural changes in non-bony tissue. These non-bony tissues include muscles, ligaments, and tendons.
- Decreased circulation.
- Discomfort and pain.
- Edema.
- Foot drop.

Confining a patient to a bed should be avoided whenever possible. The hydraulic lift can be used to move the paralyzed patient out of the bed. This lift should only be used when there is no possibility of the patient ever becoming independently mobile. Otherwise, the patient should be encouraged to function at the highest possible level.

If a patient must be maintained on bed rest, all systems of the body will be affected. Respiratory, GI, Renal, skeletal-muscular function as well as skin integrity will all be diminished by absolute bed rest. The patient will need the support of the caregiver for passive range of motion and positional changes. Specialty beds may be necessary.

The nurse must monitor the patient's functions frequently. These patients will be more prone to the development of pneumonia, urinary tract infections and diminished renal function, fecal impaction, decubiti, etc. The following nursing actions can promote optimal well being of the bedridden patient:

- Pillow support at back for side lying.
- Pillow support from the knee to ankle to support upper leg.
- **Trochanter** support to prevent outward rotation.
- Footboard and padded splints to prevent foot drop.

Good body alignment is important at all times. This includes when the patient is lying in bed, sitting in a chair, and sitting in a wheelchair. When your patients are positioned in good body alignment, they look comfortable.

alignment
(uh LINE muhnt)
Keeping a patient in proper position.

Trochanter
(TROW kan ter)
One of the bony prominences toward the near end of the thigh bone (the femur).

18.31 Transferring—Moving a Patient in a Wheelchair

BACKGROUND: Patients can easily be transferred from place to place in a wheelchair. It is important to move them safely and secure their transfer in and out of the wheelchair.

ALERT: Follow Standard Precautions.

PREPROCEDURE

1. Wash hands.

2. Position wheelchair.

3. *Lock* all brakes on wheelchair and bed.

PROCEDURE

4. Follow procedure for transferring patient to and from a wheelchair.

5. Push wheelchair carefully into hallway, watching for others who may be near doorway.

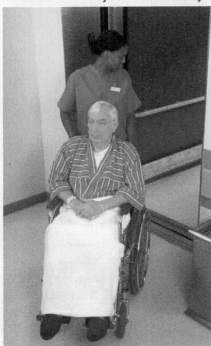

6. Move cautiously down hallway, being especially careful at intersections.

7. Always back a patient in a wheelchair over bumps, doorways, and into or out of elevators.

8. Always back a patient in a wheelchair down a hill.

9. Check patient for comfort measures before leaving.

10. Always notify appropriate person that patient has arrived.

POSTPROCEDURE

11. Wash hands.

10/10/12	1730
	Transferred via wheelchair to radiology
	S. Gomez CNA

BACKGROUND: Keeping patients in good alignment helps prevent a decubitus, respiratory problems, and general discomfort. Following correct procedures when lifting and moving the patient prevents injury to the patient and the nurse assistant(s).

ALERT: Follow Standard Precautions.

PREPROCEDURE

1. Wash hands.

2. Ask a co-worker to help move patient. (Co-worker will work on opposite side of bed.)

3. Identify patient and explain what you are going to do. (Even if the patient seems unresponsive, he or she may be able to hear.) Provide privacy for the patient.

PROCEDURE

4. Lock wheels of bed. Raise bed to comfortable working position, and lower side rails.

5. Remove pillow and place it at head of bed or on a chair.

6. Loosen both sides of draw sheet.

7. Roll edges toward side of patient's body.

8. Face head of bed and grasp rolled sheet edge with hand closest to patient.

9. Place your feet 12 inches apart with foot farthest from the edge of bed in a forward position.

10. Place your free hand and arm under patient's neck and shoulders, supporting head.

11. Bend your hips slightly.

12. On the count of three, you and your co-worker will raise patient's hips and back with draw sheet, supporting head and shoulders, and move patient smoothly to head of bed.

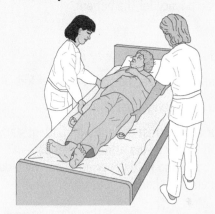

13. Replace pillow under patient's head and check for good body alignment.

14. Tighten and tuck in draw sheet and smooth bedding.

15. Raise side rails and lower bed.

POSTPROCEDURE

16. Wash hands.

BACKGROUND: Some patients are too weak to adjust themselves in bed. Sitting up comfortably helps prevent fatigue and poor body alignment. Using correct procedure prevents injury to the patient and the nurse assistant(s).

ALERT: Follow Standard Precautions.

PREPROCEDURE

1. Wash hands.

2. Identify patient and explain what you are going to do. Provide privacy for the patient.

PROCEDURE

3. Lock bed and lower all the way down.

4. Face head of bed, keeping your outer leg forward.

5. Turn your head away from patient's face.

6. Lock your arm nearest patient with patient's arm. To lock arms, place your arm between patient's arm and body, and hold upper arm near shoulder. Have patient hold back of your upper arm.

7. Support patient's head and shoulder with your other arm.

8. Raise patient to sitting position. Adjust head of bed and pillows.

POSTPROCEDURE

9. Wash hands.

5/10/11	0850
	Helped to sitting position
	No complaints of discomfort
	———— R. Johnson CNA

BACKGROUND: Maintaining alignment is essential to prevent injury. Logrolling helps prevent movement of the back following surgery.

ALERT: Follow Standard Precautions.

PREPROCEDURE

1. Wash hands.

2. Identify patient and explain what you are going to do.

3. Provide privacy by pulling privacy curtain.

PROCEDURE

4. Lock wheels of bed. Raise bed to a comfortable working position.

5. Lower side rail on side you are working on.

6. Be certain that side rail on opposite side of bed is in up position.

7. Leave pillow under head.

(continued)

8. Place a pillow lengthwise between patient's legs.

9. Fold patient's arms across chest.

10. Roll patient onto his or her side like a log, turning body as a whole unit, without bending joints.

11. Check for good body alignment.

12. Tighten and tuck in draw sheet and smooth bedding.

13. Tuck pillow behind back for support.

14. Raise side rails and lower bed.

15. Secure call light in patient's reach.

POSTPROCEDURE

16. Wash hands.

17. Chart position of patient and how procedure was tolerated.

10/24/11	1145
	Logrolled to left side
	Moved every 2 hours
	Skin in good condition
	Complained of slight pain in left leg
	when moved
	Pillows placed behind back to maintain
	alignment
	Made comfortable with rails up
	A. Chaplin CNA

PROCEDURE **18.35** **Moving—Turning Patient Away from You**

BACKGROUND: Following correct procedure for turning patients away from you when bed changing, bathing, and positioning provides good alignment and prevents injury.

ALERT: Follow Standard Precautions.

PREPROCEDURE

1. Wash hands.

2. Identify patient and explain what you are going to do. Provide privacy for the patient.

PROCEDURE

3. Lock bed and elevate to a comfortable working height.

4. Lower side rail on side you are working from.

5. Have patient bend knees. Cross arms on chest.

6. Place arm nearest head of bed under patient's shoulders and head. Place other hand and forearm under small of the patient's back. Bend your body at hips and knees, keeping your back straight. Pull patient toward you.

7. Place forearms under patient's hips and pull patient toward you.

8. Place one hand under ankles and one hand under knees and move ankles and knees toward you.

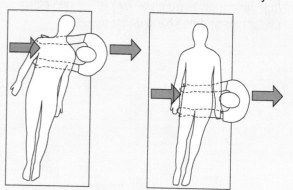

As a safety measure, this procedure must be done before turning a patient onto his side. It ensures that the patient, when turned, is located in the center of the mattress.

(continued)

9. Cross patient's leg closest to you over other leg at ankles.

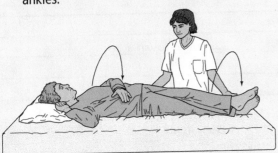

A Bend the resident's farthest arm next to her head and place the other arm across her chest. Cross her near leg over the other leg.

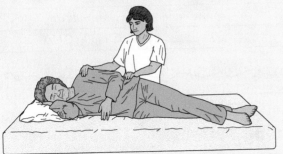

B Place one hand on the resident's shoulder and the other on her hip. Turn her away from you onto her side.

C Place pillows under her upper arm and leg for support.

10. Roll patient away from you by placing one hand under hips and one hand under shoulders.

11. Place one hand under patient's shoulders and one hand under patient's head. Draw patient back toward center of bed.

12. Place both hands under patient's hips and move hips toward center of bed.

13. Put a pillow behind patient's back to give support and keep patient from falling onto his or her back.

14. Be certain patient is in good alignment.

15. Place upper leg on a pillow for support.

16. Replace side rail on near side of bed and return bed to lowest height.

17. You may place a turning sheet under a helpless or heavy patient to help with turning. Use a folded large sheet or half sheet and place it so that it extends just above shoulders and below hips.

POSTPROCEDURE

18. Wash hands.

8/04/11	1145
	Turned to left side
	Pillows placed behind back to
	maintain good body alignment
	Resting comfortably
	Side rails up
	A. Chaplin CNA

BACKGROUND: The nurse's responsibility is to determine baseline function of the patient and to strive to maintain and/or improve function. Prolonged periods of bedrest are harmful to the overall status of the patient and must be avoided whenever possible. However, when a patient cannot turn in bed without assistance nurses need to use their knowledge of correct body mechanics and correct alignment to change the patient from one position to another.

ALERT: Follow Standard Precautions.

PREPROCEDURE

1. Wash hands.

2. Explain procedure to patient.

3. Provide privacy for the patient with curtain, screen, or door.

PROCEDURE

4. Raise the bed to a height that allows the nurse to remain in an erect posture while moving patient. Adjust the bed to a flat position or as low as the patient can tolerate. Make sure side rails on side to which patient's body will be turned are raised. Lower the side rail nearest to nurse.

5. Use a pull sheet or pad for moving the patient in order to avoid the effects of friction on the patient's skin integrity.

6. Place the patient's arms across the chest and cross the patient's far leg over the near one. Grasping the pull sheet on the far side of the patient pull the patient towards the nurse.

7. Slowly roll patient onto side toward raised side rail while supporting patient's body.

8. Place a pillow under the head and the neck to prevent lateral flexion of the neck.

9. Place a pillow behind the patient's back to promote the side lying position. Ensure that the shoulders are aligned with the hips.

10. Place a pillow under the upper arm. The lower arm should be flexed and positioned comfortably. Make sure patient is not lying on their arm.

11. Use one or two pillows as needed to support the leg from the groin to the foot. Avoid having bony prominences resting against hard surfaces.

12. Assure that the two shoulders are aligned with the two hips.

13. For the completely immobile patient it is important that passive range of motion exercises by provided during the time used to reposition the patient.

14. Readjust the bed height and position and raise the side rail if appropriate. Put the bed in the lowest position.

15. Assure that the patient is comfortable and has no further needs before leaving the bedside.

16. Put the call signal within the patient's reach.

POSTPROCEDURE

17. Wash your hands.

BACKGROUND: Following correct procedure for turning patients toward you when bed changing, bathing, and positioning provides good alignment and prevents injury.

ALERT: Follow Standard Precautions.

PREPROCEDURE

1. Wash hands.

2. Identify patient and explain what you are going to do. Provide privacy for the patient.

PROCEDURE

3. Lock bed and elevate to a comfortable working height.

4. Lower side rail on side you are working from.

5. Cross patient's far leg over leg that is closest to you.

6. Place one hand on patient's far shoulder. Place your other hand on the hip.

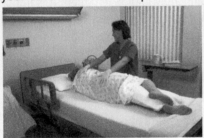

7. Brace yourself against side of bed. Roll patient toward you in a slow, gentle, smooth movement.

8. Help patient bring upper leg toward you and bend comfortably (Sims position).

9. Put up side rail. Be certain it is secure.

10. Go to other side of bed and lower side rail.

11. Place hands under patient's shoulders and hips. Pull toward center of bed. This helps maintain side-lying position.

12. Be certain to align patient's body properly.

13. Use pillows to position and support legs if patient is unable to move self.

14. *Check tubing to make certain that it is not caught between legs or pulling in any way if patient has an indwelling catheter.*

15. Tuck a pillow behind patient's back. This forms a roll and prevents patient from rolling backward onto back.

16. Return bed to low position.

17. Secure call light in patient's reach.

POSTPROCEDURE

18. Wash hands.

5/05/11	1000
	Repositioned on right side
	Skin care given
	Skin is clean and dry
	S. Gomez CNA

🖥 Principles of Applying Restraints

The Omnibus Budget Reconciliation Act 1987 (OBRA) set forth regulations regarding the use of restraints in nursing homes. According to these guidelines, restraints cannot be used for convenience or discipline.

Before restraints are used on a patient, the nurse must make an assessment and get a physician to agree that restraints are necessary and that all other alternatives have failed. The patient cannot be restrained until a health care professional explains to the patient, family member, or legal representative about the restraining device and that it will be used for a specified period of time. Every time a patient is restrained, they must be assessed and all methods must be documented.

Nurses must reassess a restrained person every 30 minutes and assess circulation to the hands, feet, and toes, skin for bruising, and activities for daily living such as eating, drinking, and toileting. All of this must be documented in the patient's chart.

Restraints can be beneficial to patients by preventing a patient from getting out of bed, moving arms or legs excessively, or preventing patient from hurting themselves or others. For example, restraints are often used to keep a patient from inflicting self-harm or injury, (usually with suicidal patients), to prevent patients from removing medically necessary tubes, intravenous lines, and dressing, and to keep a child still during a surgical procedures, such as receiving stitches. In health care, the use of restraints should be a last resort.

restraints
(ri STREYNT)
A piece of equipment or device that restricts a patient's ability to move.

The most commonly used physical restraints include:

- Soft wrist and ankle restraints.
- Strap fastening vest (posey jacket).
- Seat belt with buckle (restraint belt).
- Mittens (restraint mitts).
- Leather wrist and ankle restraints.

For a patient's safety, restraints should be tied/locked to the bed frame, not the bed rails. A quick-release knot should be used to allow for immediate release.

Restraints can cause complications to a patient, including injury to the restrained extremity (fracture, muscle strain, dislocation, or contusion) or numbness and tingling.

Postural Supports

Soft postural supports (soft cloth ties used on arms and legs, or vests) are used to protect elderly or disoriented patients from hurting themselves or someone else (Figure 18.16). It is much better if you do not have to use them. They can be used only if they are ordered by the doctor. Precautions must be taken when they are used as they may create the following conditions:

- Increased agitation.
- Immobilized patient.
- Increased risk of pneumonia.
- Skin breakdown.
- Decreased circulation.

When postural supports are used, you must:

- Anticipate elimination needs.
- Check for swelling above, below, and at the site of supports.
- Release the supports periodically.
- Provide for hydration by offering fluids.
- Change position frequently.

There are times when postural support must be used:

- To prevent patient from pulling out tubes and catheters.
- To prevent patient from scratching or injuring self and others.
- To keep patient from falling out of bed or chair.

However, there must be a valid reason for using the supports. Do not use them just because you are annoyed that the patient takes too much of your time.

Figure 18.16
Soft protective devices:
(a) limb, (b) vest,
(c) mitten, (d) body.
Under what circumstances
might these be necessary?

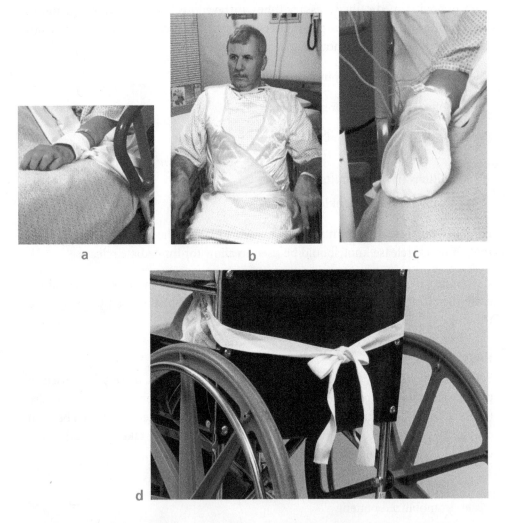

a   b   c

d

Postoperative Care Supportive Devices and Equipment

Fractures and joint replacement are two major areas in sub-acute postoperative care. Keeping the patient in good *alignment* is very important. Poor alignment can cause a new hip joint to move out of the socket and cause improper healing of fractures. The following are some of the common supportive devices:

- **Trochanter roll:** A towel or small blanket is rolled and put next to the greater trochanter (femur). It keeps the hip from rotating outward and prevents permanent disability or difficulties with walking.
- **Abduction splint:** This is a device that keeps the thighs apart and keeps the hip joints in proper alignment.

- **Abductor wedge:** A wedge-shaped, spongy material is placed between the legs. The wedge is used to keep the hip that has been replaced or fractured away from the center of the body. This prevents excessive strain on the hip and prevents a dislocation of the repair.

- **Footboard:** A padded board is placed at the feet when the patient is in a prone or supine position. The feet naturally extend when lying in this position. If the feet are not aligned correctly, contractures occur and cause problems with walking.

- **Pillows:** Pillows of different sizes and shapes are placed to support joints and provide support for proper body alignment.

PROCEDURE 18.38 Applying Restraints

BACKGROUND: Restraints should be used only as a last resort when alternative measures have failed, and the patient is at an increased risk for harming himself or others. Alternative measures might include: assuring that basic patient needs have been met; providing a sitter; providing distraction.

CAUTION: Physically restraining a patient can escalate the patient's confusion and their level of agitation.

ALERT: Follow Standard Precautions.

PREPROCEDURE

1. Determine the need for restraints and that alternative measures have been attempted.

2. Assess patient's physical condition, behavior and mental status.

PROCEDURE

3. Determine the agency's policy for application of restraints. Secure a physician's order.

4. Explain the reason for use to patient and family. Clarify how the patient's needs will be met and that the use of restraints is only temporary.

5. Wash your hands.

6. Apply restraints according to manufacturer's directions (each type of restraint may require a different type of application).

   a. Choose the least restrictive type of device that allows the greatest degree of mobility.

   b. Pad bony prominences. Ensure that two fingers can be inserted between the restraint and the patient's wrist or ankle.

   c. Maintain restrained extremity in normal anatomical position.

   d. Use a quick release tie for all restraints.

   e. Fasten restraint to bed not side rail.

   f. Remove restraint every two hours or according to agency policy and patient need.

   g. While removed check for signs of decreased circulation, impaired function of limb, or impaired skin integrity.

   h. Perform range-of-motion exercises before reapplying.

   i. Reevaluate the need for use of physical restraints, alternative measures attempted before reapplying.

   j. Document procedure and rationale.

   k. Obtain a new physician's order for restraint every 24 hours if continued need.

POSTPROCEDURE

7. Assure that patient safety and comfort has been maintained throughout the period that restraints are in place.

Ambulatory Devices

There are many different ambulatory devices, such as walkers, crutches, and canes. These are discussed in Chapter 19.

PROCEDURE 18.39 How to Tie Postural Supports

BACKGROUND: Postural supports must be secured with a quick-release knot that allows the patient to be moved quickly in the event of an emergency.

ALERT: Follow Standard Precautions.

PREPROCEDURE

1. Wash hands.

PROCEDURE

2. Assemble equipment: a postural support that has been ordered.

3. Tie a half-bow knot or quick-release knot. Tie the same way you tie a bow on a shoe. Once bow is in place, grasp one loop and pull end of tie through knot.

4. Knot can be easily released pulling end of loop.

NOTE: Half-bow knot/quick-release knot is always used when a restraint is attached to wheelchair or mattress support. This allows quick release if it is necessary to move patient in a hurry.

POSTPROCEDURE

5. Wash hands.

9/09/11	0930
	Transferred to wheelchair
	Vest postural support applied and
	secured with a quick-release knot
	at back of chair
	_____ S. Gomez CNA

BACKGROUND: Postural supports for the limbs are necessary to prevent some patients from causing injury to themselves or others.

ALERT: Follow Standard Precautions.

PREPROCEDURE

1. Check for physician's order.

2. Wash hands.

3. Assemble equipment: a limb support.

4. Identify patient. Provide privacy for the patient by curtain, screen, or door.

PROCEDURE

5. Explain what you are going to do, even if the patient is confused.

6. Place soft side of limb support against skin. Check to make sure the wrinkles are out.

7. Wrap around limb and put one tie through opening on other end of support (see Figure 18.16a).

8. Gently pull until it fits snugly around limb.

9. Buckle or tie in place so that support stays on limb.

10. Tie out of patient's reach. (See the procedure "How to Tie Postural Supports.")

    a. Tie to bed frame *(not side rails)*.

    b. Tie to wheelchair *(not to stationary chair)*.

11. Check for proper alignment and comfort of patient.

12. Check to be certain that knots or wrinkles are not causing pressure.

13. Check to be certain that support is snug but does not bind. *(You should be able to put two fingers under edges.)*

14. Place call light where it can be easily reached.

POSTPROCEDURE

15. Wash hands.

16. Circulation under restraint should be checked every 15–30 minutes and documented.

17. Check patient frequently and move at least every 2 hours. Restraints should be removed every 2 hours for at least 5–10 minutes.

18. Chart the following:

    a. Reason for use of support

    b. Type of support used

    c. When it was applied

    d. When it was released

    e. Times of repositioning

    f. How patient tolerated it

    g. Condition of skin

10/14/11	0200

Resident disoriented; swinging arms and legs against side rails
Limb postural supports applied and secured with a quick-release knot to legs and arms, to prevent injury per physician's order

_____ R. Johnson CNA

BACKGROUND: Mitten postural supports prevent the hands from grasping objects.

ALERT: Follow Standard Precautions.

PREPROCEDURE

1. Check for physician's order.

2. Wash hands.

3. Assemble equipment: a soft cloth mitten.

4. Identify patient.

5. Explain what you are going to do.

PROCEDURE

6. Slip mitten on hand with padded side against palm and net on top of hand.

7. Lace mitten (see **Figure 18.16c**).

8. Gently pull until it fits snugly around wrist.

9. Tie with a double bow knot so that support stays on hand.

NOTE: Double bow knot helps secure the restraint to the patient. Use only a half-bow/quick-release knot to tie a postural support to a bed, wheelchair, or other furniture.

10. Check for proper alignment and comfort of patient.

11. Check to be certain knots or wrinkles are not causing pressure.

12. Check to be certain support is snug but does not bind. *(You should be able to put two fingers under edges.)*

13. Place call light where it can be easily reached.

POSTPROCEDURE

14. Wash hands.

15. Check circulation and document every 15–30 minutes.

16. Remove mitten restraint every 2 hours for at least 5–10 minutes.

17. Check patient frequently and move at least every 2 hours.

18. Chart the following:

   a. Reason for use of support

   b. Type of support used

   c. When it was applied

   d. When it was released

   e. Times of repositioning

   f. How patient tolerated it

   g. Condition of skin

11/07/11	1400
	Bilateral mitten postural supports applied
	and secured with a quick-release knot to
	prevent the resident from removing
	abdominal dressing and IV per physician's
	order
	_____ *S. Gomez CNA*

BACKGROUND: Vest postural support is necessary to prevent some patients from injuring themselves.

ALERT: Follow Standard Precautions.

PREPROCEDURE

1. Check for physician's order.

2. Wash hands.

3. Assemble equipment: a vest support.

4. Identify patient.

5. Explain what you are going to do.

PROCEDURE

6. Put arms through armholes of vest with opening to back (see **Figure 18.16b**).

7. Cross back panels by bringing tie on left side over to right and right tie to left.

8. Carefully smooth material so that there are no wrinkles.

9. Tie where patient cannot reach. (See the procedure "How to Tie Postural Supports.")

    a. Tie to bed frame *(not side rails)*.

    b. Tie to wheelchair *(not stationary chair)*.

10. Check for proper alignment and comfort of patient.

11. Check to be certain that knots or wrinkles are not causing pressure.

12. Check to be certain that support is snug but does not bind. *(You should be able to put two fingers under edges.)*

13. Place call light where it can be easily reached.

POSTPROCEDURE

14. Wash your hands.

15. Check skin condition and circulation every 15–30 minutes.

16. Remove restraint every 2 hours for 5–10 minutes.

17. Check patient frequently and move at least every 2 hours.

18. Chart the following:

    a. Reason for use of support

    b. Type of support used

    c. When it was applied

    d. When it was released

    e. Times of repositioning

    f. How patient tolerated it

    g. Condition of skin

9/14/11	1700
Vest postural support applied to
protect resident from getting out of
bed and falling, per physician's order
A. Chaplin CNA

Bathing the Patient

Providing for your patients' cleanliness is an important responsibility. Bathing is important because it:

- Removes perspiration and dirt.
- Removes odor.
- Increases circulation.
- Allows for some exercise.
- Gives you an opportunity to observe the patients' skin.
- Provides relaxation.

You may be asked to give several different types of baths. This depends on the patient's condition. Always check the chart to see what type of bath is ordered. The following are types of baths:

- Bed bath.
- Tub bath.
- Whirlpool bath.
- Shower.

Patients may not have a complete bath every day. Sometimes they are bathed only twice a week. This is especially true of elderly patients, who have drier skin, less subcutaneous fat, and more fragile tissues.

Always wash the perineum (pericare) and the underarms every day. These areas tend to develop an odor because they have more bacteria and are not open to the air. Good pericare is especially important when there is a urinary catheter in place. Good pericare helps prevent infection. Back care should be provided as a part of the daily hygiene process. Even if the patient does not receive a complete bath, the provision of back care will promote the patient's comfort level.

BACKGROUND: Providing a bed bath improves circulation, relaxes the patient, provides an opportunity to examine the skin, and enables you to interact with the patient.

ALERT: Follow Standard Precautions.

PREPROCEDURE

1. Wash hands.

2. Assemble equipment:

   a. Soap and soap dish

   b. Face towel

   c. Bath towel. Will need at least 2.

   d. Washcloth. Will need at least 2.

   e. Hospital gown or patient's sleepwear

   f. Lotion or powder

   g. Nailbrush and emery board

   h. Comb and brush

   i. Bedpan or urinal and cover

   j. Bed linen

   k. Bath blanket

   l. Bath basin, water at 105° F

   m. Disposable nonsterile gloves

3. Place linens on chair in order of use and place towels on overbed table.

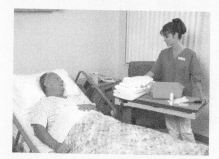

4. Identify patient.

5. Explain what you are going to do.

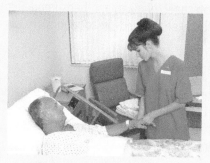

6. Provide for privacy by pulling the privacy screen curtain, or door.

PROCEDURE

7. Raise bed to a comfortable working height.

8. Offer bedpan or urinal. Empty and rinse before starting bath. Wash your hands. (Remember to wear gloves when handling urine.)

(continued)

9. Lower headrest and knee gatch (raised knee area/bed) so that bed is flat.

10. Lower the side rail only on side where you are working.

11. Put on gloves.

12. Loosen top sheet, blanket, and bedspread. Remove and fold blanket and bedspread, and place over back of chair.

13. Cover patient with a bath blanket.

14. Ask patient to hold bath blanket in place. Remove top sheet by sliding it to foot of bed. *Do not expose patient.* (Place soiled linen in laundry container.)

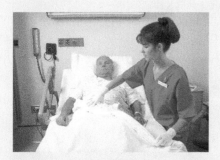

15. Leave a pillow under patient's head for comfort.

16. Remove patient's gown and place in laundry container. If nightwear belongs to patient, follow hospital policy (i.e., send home with family or to hospital laundry).

17. To remove gown when the patient has an IV:

NOTE: Most facilities provide gowns with snaps for easy removal around existing intravenous tubing.

   a. Loosen gown from neck.

   b. Slip gown from free arm.

   c. Be certain that patient is covered with a bath blanket.

   d. Slip gown away from body toward arm with IV.

   e. Gather gown at arm and slip downward over arm and tubing. *Be careful not to pull on tubing.*

   f. Gather material of gown in one hand and slowly draw gown over tip of fingers.

   g. Lift IV free of stand with free hand and slip gown over bottle.

   h. *Do not lower bottle! Raise gown.*

18. Fill bath basin two-thirds full with warm water. Test water temperature and ensure it is safe and comfortable before bathing patients and adjust if necessary.

19. Help patient move to side of bed nearest you.

20. Fold face towel over upper edge of bath blanket. This will keep it dry.

21. Form a mitten by folding washcloth around your hand.

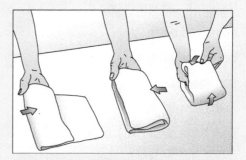

22. Wash patient's eyes from nose to outside of face. Use different corners of washcloth.

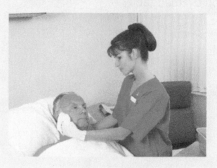

(continued)

23. Ask patient if he or she wants soap used on the face. Gently wash and rinse face, ears, and neck. Be careful not to get soap in eyes. Dry face with towel, using a blotting motion.

24. To wash patient's arms, shoulders, axilla:

    a. Uncover patient's far arm (one farthest from you).

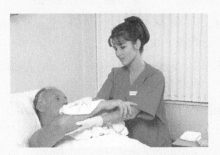

    b. Protect bed from becoming wet with a bath towel placed under arm. Wash with long, firm, circular strokes, rinse, and dry.

    c. Wash and dry armpits (axillae). Apply deodorant and powder.

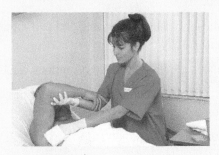

25. To wash hand:

    a. Place basin of water on towel.

    b. Put patient's hand into basin.

    c. Wash, rinse, and dry and push back cuticle gently.

26. Repeat on other arm.

27. To wash chest:

    a. Place towel lengthwise across patient's chest.

    b. Fold bath blanket down to patient's abdomen.

    c. Wash chest. Be especially careful to dry skin under female breasts to prevent irritation. Dry area thoroughly.

28. To wash abdomen:

    a. Fold down bath blanket to pubic area.

    b. Wash, rinse, and dry abdomen.

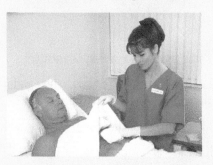

    c. Pull up bath blanket to keep patient warm.

    d. Slide towel out from under bath blanket.

29. To wash thigh, leg, and foot:

    a. Ask patient to flex knee if possible.

    b. Fold bath blanket to uncover thigh, leg, and foot of leg farthest from you.

    c. Place bath towel under leg to keep bed from getting wet.

    d. Place basin on towel and put foot into basin.

    e. Wash and rinse thigh, leg, and foot.

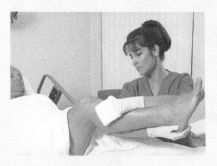

(continued)

f. Dry well between toes. Be careful to support the leg when lifting it.

30. Follow same procedure for leg nearest you.

31. Change water. You may need to change water before this time if it is dirty or cold.

32. Raise side rail on opposite side if it is down.

33. To wash back and buttocks:

    a. Help patient turn on side away from you.

    b. Have patient move toward center of bed.

    c. Place a bath towel lengthwise on bed, under patient's back.

    d. Wash, rinse, and dry neck, back, and buttocks.

    e. Give patient a back rub. Help patient turn back on their back and make sure they are still covered with a bath blanket. Massage back for at least a minute and a half, giving special attention to shoulder blades, hip bones, and spine. *Observe for reddened areas.* (See the procedure "Skin Care—Giving a Back Rub.")

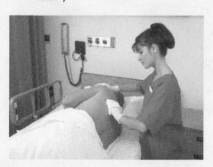

34. To wash genital area:

    a. Offer patient a clean, soapy washcloth to wash genital area.

    b. Give the person a clean, wet washcloth to rinse with and a dry towel to dry with.

35. Clean the genital area thoroughly if patient is unable to help. To clean the genital area:

    a. Put a towel or disposable pad under the patient's buttock.

    b. When washing a female patient always wipe from front to back.

    c. Separate the labia and use a clean area of the wash cloth for each side of the perineal area.

    d. When washing a male patient, be sure to wash and dry penis, scrotum, and groin area carefully. Clean the tip of the penis using a circular motion and clean the shaft of the penis from top to bottom. Remember to pull back the foreskin if the patient is not circumcised.

    e. Remove towel or disposable pad and discard appropriately.

    f. Remove gloves and put in hazardous waste.

36. If range of motion is ordered, complete at this time. (See the procedure "Range of Motion.")

37. Put a clean gown on patient.

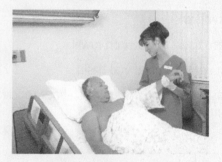

(continued)

38. If patient has an IV:

    a. Gather the sleeve on IV side in one hand.

    b. Lift bottle free of stand. Do not lower bottle.

    c. Slip bottle through sleeve from inside and rehang.

    d. Guide gown along the IV tubing to bed.

    e. Slip gown over the patient's hand. Be careful not to pull or crimp tubing.

    f. Put gown on arm with IV, then on opposite arm.

39. Comb or brush hair.

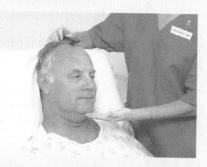

40. Follow hospital policy for towels and washcloths. Some have you hang them for later use; others have you place them in the laundry containers immediately.

41. Leave patient in a comfortable position and in good body alignment.

42. Place call bell within reach. Replace furniture and tidy unit.

POSTPROCEDURE

43. Wash hands.

44. Chart procedure and how patient tolerated it. Note any unusual skin changes or patient complaints.

10/24/11	0945
	Completed bed bath
	Dime-sized red area on sacrum
	Reported to charge nurse
	No complaints of discomfort
	Resting quietly with rails up
	_____ A. Chaplin CNA

BACKGROUND: Providing a partial bath relaxes the patient and prevents odors. The interaction with the patient is important through communication and touch.

ALERT: Follow Standard Precautions.

PREPROCEDURE

1. Wash hands.

2. Assemble equipment:

   a. Soap and soap dish

   b. Face towel

   c. Bath towel

   d. Washcloth

   e. Hospital gown or patient's sleepwear

   f. Lotion or powder

   g. Nail brush and emery board

   h. Comb and brush

   i. Bedpan or urinal and cover

   j. Bath blanket

   k. Bath basin, water at 105°F

   l. Clean linen, as needed

   m. Disposable gloves

3. Identify patient.

4. Explain what you are going to do.

5. Provide privacy by pulling privacy screen, curtain, or door.

6. Offer bedpan or urinal. Empty and rinse before starting bath. (Wear gloves if handling body fluid.)

7. Raise headrest to a comfortable position, if permitted.

8. Lower side rails if permitted. If they are to remain up, lower only side rail on side where you are working.

PROCEDURE

10. Loosen top sheet, blanket, and bedspread. Remove and fold blanket and bedspread and place over back of chair.

11. Cover patient with a bath blanket.

12. Ask patient to hold bath blanket in place. Remove top sheet by sliding it to the foot of bed: *Do not expose patient.* (Place soiled linen in laundry container.)

13. Leave a pillow under the patient's head for comfort.

14. Remove patient's gown and place in laundry container. If nightwear belongs to patient, follow hospital policy (i.e., send home with family or to hospital

15. To remove gown when patient has an IV, see the procedure "Giving a Bed Bath."

16. Fill bath basin two-thirds full with warm water and place on overbed table. Test water temperature and ensure it is safe and comfortable before bathing patients; adjust if necessary.

17. Put overbed table where patient can reach it comfortably.

18. Place towel, washcloth, and soap on overbed table.

19. Ask patient to wash as much as he or she is able to and tell the person that you will return to complete bath.

20. Place call bell where patient can reach it easily. Ask patient to signal when ready.

21. Remove glove, wash your hands, and leave unit.

22. When patient signals, return to unit, wash your hands, and put on gloves.

(continued)

23. Change water. Test water temperature and ensure it is safe and comfortable before bathing patients and adjust if necessary.

24. Complete bathing areas the patient was unable to reach. Make sure that face, hands, axillae, genitals, and buttocks are dry. To wash the genital area:

    a. Offer the patient a clean, soapy washcloth to wash genital area. Provide a clean, wet washcloth to rinse with and a dry towel to dry with. If patient is unable to help, you will need to clean the genital area thoroughly.

    b. When washing a female patient, always wipe from front to back.

    c. Separate the labia and use a clean area of the wash cloth for each side of the perineal area.

    d. When washing a male patient, be sure to wash and dry penis, scrotum, and groin area carefully. Clean the tip of the penis using a circular motion and clean the shaft of the penis from top to bottom. Remember to pull back the foreskin if the patient is not circumcised.

    e. Remove gloves and put in hazardous waste. If range of motion is ordered, complete it at this time. (See the procedure "Range of Motion.")

25. Give a back rub. (See the procedure "Skin Care—Giving a Back Rub.")

26. Put a clean gown on patient.

27. If patient has an IV, see the procedure "Giving a Bed Bath."

28. Assist patient in applying deodorant and putting on a clean gown.

29. Change bed according to hospital policy. Not all facilities change linen every day.

30. Put up side rails if required.

31. Leave patient in a comfortable position and in good body alignment.

POSTPROCEDURE

32. Remove and discard gloves.

33. Wash hands.

34. Place call bell within reach. Replace furniture and tidy unit.

35. Chart procedure and how it was tolerated.

9/23/11	0730
	Partial bath
	No skin breakdown noted
	Complained of headache
	Reported to charge nurse
	_____ S. Gomez CNA

BACKGROUND: Providing a relaxing tub/shower bath gives one-on-one time to the patient. It is an opportunity to check for skin and other problems. Careful observation is essential.

ALERT: Follow Standard Precautions.

PREPROCEDURE

1. Wash hands.

2. Assemble equipment on a chair near the tub. Be certain the tub is clean.

   a. Bath towels

   b. Washcloths

   c. Soap

   d. Bath thermometer

   e. Wash basin

   f. Clean gown

   g. Bathmat

   h. Disinfectant solution

   i. Shower chair if necessary

3. Identify patient and explain what you are going to do.

4. Provide privacy by pulling privacy curtain, screen, or door.

PROCEDURE

5. Help patient out of bed.

6. Help with robe and slippers.

7. Check with head nurse to see if the patient can ambulate or if a wheelchair or shower chair is needed. If a shower chair is used, always do the following:

   a. Cover patient with a bath blanket or sheet so that patient is not exposed in any way.

   b. Provide adequate clothing for patient, such as a robe or extra cover.

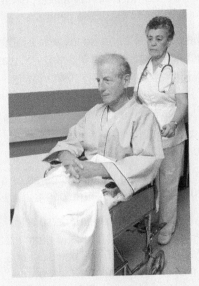

8. Take patient to shower or tub room.

9. For tub bath, place a towel in bottom of tub to help prevent falling.

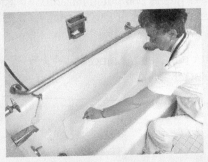

10. Fill tub with water or adjust shower flow (95–105°F).

11. Help patient undress. Give a male patient a towel to wrap around his midriff.

12. Assist patient into tub or shower. If shower, leave weak patient in shower chair.

NOTE: Remember to put on gloves.

(continued)

13. Wash patient's back. Observe carefully for reddened areas or breaks in skin.

14. Patient may be left alone to complete genitalia area if feeling strong.

NOTE: If patient shows signs of weakness, remove plug from tub and drain water, or turn off shower. Allow patient to rest until feeling better.

15. Assist patient from tub or shower.

16. Wrap bath towel around patient to prevent chilling.

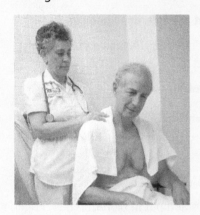

17. Remove gloves and put in biohazardous container.

18. Assist in drying and dressing.

19. Return to unit and make comfortable. Make sure call bell is within patient's reach.

20. Put away equipment.

21. Clean bathtub with disinfectant solution.

POSTPROCEDURE

22. Wash hands.

23. Chart procedure and how patient tolerated it.

NOTE: Use gloves if you are in contact with body fluids.

7/07/11	0900
	Assisted with shower
	Taken to shower on shower chair
	No skin problems noted
	Tolerated well
	_____ A. Chaplin CNA

PROCEDURE 18.46 Patient Gown Change

BACKGROUND: Changing a patient's gown makes the patient feel clean and refreshed. It also allows you to visually examine the skin.

ALERT: Follow Standard Precautions.

PREPROCEDURE

1. Wash hands.

2. Assemble equipment: clean patient gown.

3. Tell patient what you are going to do.

4. Provide privacy by pulling privacy curtain.

5. Put on gloves in case you come in contact with bodily fluids.

PROCEDURE

6. Untie strings of gown at neck and midback. (It may be necessary to assist patient onto side.)

7. Pull soiled gown out from sides of patient.

8. Unfold clean gown and position over patient.

9. Remove soiled gown one sleeve at a time.

10. Leave soiled gown laying over patient's chest; insert one arm into sleeve of clean gown.

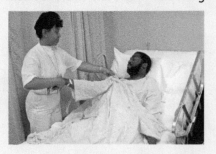

11. Fold soiled gown to one side as clean gown is placed over patient's chest.

12. Insert other arm in empty sleeve of gown.

13. Tie neck string on side of neck.

14. Tie midback tie if patient desires.

15. Remove soiled gown to linen hamper.

16. Slip gown under covers, being careful not to expose patient.

17. Position patient for comfort.

18. Raise side rails when necessary.

19. Place bedside stand and call light in patient's reach.

POSTPROCEDURE

20. Remove gloves and put in biohazardous container.

21. Wash hands.

BACKGROUND: Perineal care provides cleansing around areas where body waste is eliminated. The perineal area is dark, warm, and moist, providing an environment for bacterial growth. Keeping the perineum free of drainage and bacteria is an important preventive health measure and helps patients feel more comfortable.

ALERT: Follow Standard Precautions.

PREPROCEDURE

1. Wash hands.

2. Assemble equipment.

    a.   Bath blanket

    b.   Bedpan and cover

    c.   Basin

    d.   Solution, water, or other if ordered

    e.   Cotton balls

    f.   Waterproof protector for bed

    g.   Disposable gloves

    h.   Perineal pad and belt if needed

3. Identify patient.

4. Explain what you are going to do.

5. Provide privacy by pulling privacy curtain.

PROCEDURE

6. Put warm water in basin.

7. Raise bed to a comfortable working height.

8. Lower side rail.

9. Put on disposable gloves.

10. Remove spread and blanket.

11. Cover patient with bath blanket.

12. Have patient hold top of bath blanket, and fold top sheet to bottom of bed.

13. Place waterproof protector under patient's buttocks.

14. Pull up bath blanket to expose perineal area.

15. Provide male and female pericare.

a.   Circumcised male: Wipe away from urinary meatus as you wash with soap and water, rinse, and dry in a circular motion. Clean the shaft of the penis from top to bottom.

Urethra (start here and wipe downward)

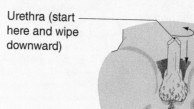

b.   Uncircumcised male: Gently move foreskin back away from tip of penis. Wash as directed in step a. After drying, gently move foreskin back over tip of penis.

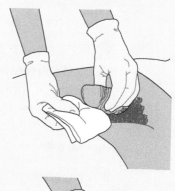

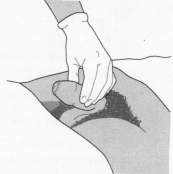

(continued)

c. Female:

(1) Instruct patient to bend knees with feet flat on bed.

(2) Separate patient's knees.

(3) Separate the labia and wipe from front to back away from the urethra as you wash with soap and water, rinse, and dry. Use a clear part of the washcloth for each stroke.

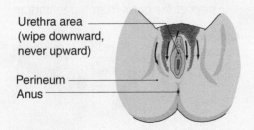

Urethra area (wipe downward, never upward)

Perineum

Anus

16. Remove waterproof protector from bed and dispose of gloves.

17. Cover patient with sheet and remove bath blanket.

18. Return top covers.

19. Return bed to lowest position and put up side rails if required.

20. Secure call bell within patient's reach.

POSTPROCEDURE

21. Clean equipment; dispose of disposable material according to hospital policy.

22. Discard gloves and put in biohazardous container.

23. Wash hands.

4/14/12	1045
	Perineal care provided
	Observed a dime-sized reddened area
	on the interior left thigh approximately
	2 inches below the groin
	R. Johnson CNA

Care of Hair and Nails

Hair and nail care helps patients feel good about themselves. Good grooming adds to a feeling of well-being. Hair is always kept clean and neatly arranged. Style hair appropriately for the age of the patient. For example, ponytails are not a hairstyle that an elderly person would normally select. If patients can have a tub bath or shower, shampoo their hair at bath time.

It is important to keep your patients' hair clean even when they are on bed rest. Today there are chemical shampoos that remove oil and refresh the scalp. You will need a physician's order together with a facility policy that says you can use a chemical shampoo. To use a packaged chemical on the hair, always follow the directions on the package. To wash hair in bed with water and shampoo, carefully follow the steps below.

Keep nails trimmed and clean. Long nails may scratch the patient or someone else. They break more easily and are more difficult to clean when they are not kept short. Toenails may become very thick and hard. Often it is necessary to have a podiatrist (foot doctor) cut them.

If the patient has diabetes, *do not cut the nails.* Diabetic patients tend to have poor circulation and do not heal well. This results in severe **ulcerations** if their skin is knicked or broken. Whenever you cut fingernails or toenails, check first with the charge nurse.

ulcerations
(UHL suhr ay shuhns)
Open areas, or sores.

BACKGROUND: Clean hair makes a patient feel fresh and provides a sense of well-being. Your careful attention to the steps below will make this a pleasant experience for the patient and yourself.

ALERT: Follow Standard Precautions.

PREPROCEDURE

1. Wash hands.

2. Assemble equipment:

    a. Chair

    b. Basin of water (105°F)

    c. Pitcher of water (115°F)

    d. Paper or Styrofoam cup

    e. Large basin

    f. Shampoo tray or plastic sheet

    g. Waterproof bed protector

    h. Pillow with waterproof cover

    i. Bath towels

    j. Small towel

    k. Cotton balls

3. Identify patient.

4. Explain what you are going to do.

5. Provide privacy by pulling privacy curtain.

PROCEDURE

6. Raise bed to a comfortable working position.

7. Place a chair at side of bed near patient's head.

8. Place small towel on chair.

9. Place large basin on chair to catch water.

10. Put cotton in patient's ears to keep water out of ears.

11. Have patient move to side of bed with head close to where you are standing.

12. Remove pillow from under head. Lower head of bed and remove pillows. Cover pillow with waterproof case.

13. Place pillow under patient's back so that when he or she lies down the head will be tilted back.

14. Place bath blanket on bed.

15. Have patient hold top of bath blanket, and pull top covers to foot.

16. Place waterproof protector under head.

17. Put shampoo tray under patient's head (i.e., plastic bag with both ends open).

18. Place end of plastic in large basin.

19. Have patient hold washcloth over eyes.

20. Put basin of water on bedside table with paper cup. Have pitcher of water for extra water. Test water temperature to ensure it is safe and comfortable before wetting patient's hair. Adjust if needed.

21. Brush patient's hair thoroughly.

22. Fill cup with water from basin.

23. Pour water over hair; repeat until completely wet.

24. Apply small amount of shampoo; use both hands to massage the patient's scalp with your fingertips. Be careful not to scratch the scalp with your fingernails.

25. Rinse soap off hair by pouring water from cup over hair. Have patient turn head from side to side. Repeat until completely rinsed.

26. Dry patient's forehead and ears.

27. Remove cotton from ears.

28. Lift patient's head gently and wrap with bath towel.

29. Remove equipment from bed.

30. Change patient's gown and be certain patient is dry.

31. Gently dry patient's hair with towel. (Use a hair dryer if allowed by your facility.)

(continued)

32. Comb or brush hair and arrange neatly.

33. Remove bath blanket and cover patient with top covers.

34. Make patient comfortable.

35. Lower bed to its lowest position.

36. Put up side rail if required.

POSTPROCEDURE

37. Return equipment.

38. Tidy unit.

39. Wash hands.

40. Record procedure.

9/06/11	1130
	Hair washed while in bed
	There is a dime-sized red scaly area
	on scalp directly above left ear
	Resident denies pain or itching at site
	Notified charge nurse
	Hair dried with hair dryer and styled
	to suit resident
	———— *R. Johnson CNA*

PROCEDURE **18.49** | **Shampooing in Shower or Tub**

BACKGROUND: Clean hair makes a patient feel fresh and provides a sense of well-being. Your careful attention to the steps below will make this a pleasant experience for the patient and yourself.

ALERT: Follow Standard Precautions.

PREPROCEDURE

1. Wash hands.

2. Assemble equipment:

   a. Shampoo

   b. Washcloth

   c. Towel

   d. Cream rinse, if desired

3. Provide privacy by pulling curtain or door.

4. Explain what you are going to do.

PROCEDURE

5. Instruct patient to tip head back.

6. Wet hair with water, being careful not to get eyes wet.

7. Give patient a washcloth to wipe his or her face as needed.

8. Apply a moderate amount of shampoo to hair. Massage head and hair until a lather develops. (Be careful not to use fingernails.)

9. Rinse hair with clean, clear water until shampoo has disappeared.

10. Repeat shampooing procedure a second time. When rinsing, be sure to remove all shampoo.

11. If a cream rinse is used, apply a small amount to hair, paying special attention to ends of hair.

12. Allow rinse to remain on hair for a few seconds before rinsing.

(continued)

13. Rinse thoroughly with clean, clear water.

14. Towel dry.

15. Gently comb or brush hair to remove tangles.

16. Use a hair dryer to dry hair.

17. Arrange in an appropriate hairstyle for the patient's age and manner. (Remember that ponytails, pigtails, etc. are not appropriate for a 70-year-old patient.)

POSTPROCEDURE

18. Return equipment.

19. Wash hands.

20. Record procedure.

> 10/13/11   0830
>
> *Hair washed while in shower*
> *Scalp is clean and there is no*
> *evidence of sores or scratches present*
> *Upon return to room, hair styled*
> *according to resident's preference*
> ———————   *A. Chaplin CNA*

PROCEDURE **18.50** **Arranging the Hair**

BACKGROUND: A patient's outward appearance plays a significant role in his or her self-image. Arranging the hair is a key part of the daily grooming routine for every patient. It is important to arrange your patient's hair according to their preferences.

ALERT: Follow Standard Precautions.

PREPROCEDURE

1. Wash hands.

2. Assemble equipment.
   a. Comb and/or brush
   b. Towel

3. Identify patient.

4. Explain what you are going to do.

5. Provide privacy by pulling privacy curtain.

6. Raise bed to a comfortable working height.

PROCEDURE

7. Assist as needed.

8. If total assistance is needed:
   a. Section the hair, starting at one side, working around to other side.
   b. Comb or brush hair thoroughly, being careful not to pull it.
   c. Arrange hair neatly.

9. Lower bed to lowest position.

10. Put up side rail if required.

11. Secure call light in patient's reach.

POSTPROCEDURE

12. Clean and replace all equipment.

13. Wash hands.

14. Report procedure and observations (e.g., dry scalp, reddened areas).

Shaving the Patient

Men usually shave every day when they are able to care for themselves. Encourage them to shave themselves when possible. They will feel much better about themselves. If they are unable to shave themselves, take time to shave them.

Women tend to have facial hair when they age. This can be very distressing to the patient. Follow the procedures that your facility has to remove the facial hair. In some facilities it is plucked; in others it is shaved. Be certain to look in the procedure book.

PROCEDURE 18.51 Nail Care

BACKGROUND: A patient's outward appearance plays a significant role in his or her self-image. Nail care is a key part of the daily grooming routine for every patient. Keeping nails clean and trimmed prevents sores from developing around the nail beds and eliminates unintentional scratches that could become infected.

ALERT: Follow Standard Precautions.

PREPROCEDURE

1. Wash hands.

2. Assemble equipment.
   a. Warm water
   b. Orange sticks
   c. Emery board
   d. Nail clippers

NOTE: Do not clip a diabetic patient's nails.

3. Identify the patient and explain the procedure.

4. Provide privacy for the patient by pulling a curtain or closing the door.

5. Test water temperature and ensure it is safe and comfortable before immersing patient's fingers in water; adjust if needed.

6. Place basin of water at a comfortable level for patients. Cleanse nails by soaking in water.

7. Put on gloves.

PROCEDURE

8. Use slanted edge of orange stick to clean dirt out from under nails. Wipe orangewood stick on towel after each nail and dry patient's hand/fingers, including between fingers.

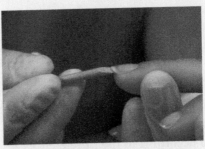

9. File nails with emery board to shorten. (Clip if permitted by your facility.)

10. Use smooth edge of emery board to smooth.

11. Apply lotion to help condition cuticle.

12. Massage hands and feet with lotion.

13. Make patient comfortable.

14. Raise side rail if required. Make sure call bell is within reach.

POSTPROCEDURE

15. Empty, rinse and wipe basin

16. Return equipment.

17. Remove and dispose of gloves in biohazardous container.

18. Wash hands.

19. Record procedure and any unusual conditions (e.g., hangnails, broken nails).

BACKGROUND: Providing and assisting with foot care is an important part of total patient care. For elderly patients and the diabetic patient improper foot care can lead to decreased mobility and even loss of mobility.

Both the elderly and the diabetic may experience decreased circulation and decreased sensation to the lower extremities. This makes it even more imperative that the condition of the feet are checked frequently for any change in status or acute problems.

ALERT: Follow Standard Precautions.

PREPROCEDURE

1. Wash hands.

2. Put on disposable gloves.

3. Explain procedure to patient and provide for patient privacy with curtain, screen, or door.

PROCEDURE

4. Inspect the feet for any problems/change in skin integrity. Check for the presence of pulses and note their strengths. Assess for any patient complaints.

5. Test water temperature and ensure it is safe and comfortable before placing patient's foot in water and adjust if needed.

6. Place basin at a comfortable position on protective barrier.

7. Completely submerge and soak foot in water

8. Bathe the feet thoroughly in tepid water with a mild soap. Be sure to clean the interdigital areas.

9. Dry the feet thoroughly, paying particular attention to the interdigital areas. Apply lotion to feet but avoid leaving lotion in the interdigital areas as it could provide a moist environment for bacteria and fungal growth. Support foot and ankle throughout the procedure.

10. If nails are overgrown use a file instead of scissors or clippers. If the patient is a diabetic and a file is not sufficient refer the patient to a Podiatrist for further nail care.

11. Empty, rinse and wipe bath basin and return to proper storage.

12. Dispose of soiled linens in proper container. Remove glove and place in biohazardous container.

13. Make sure the patient is comfortable and the call bell is within reach.

14. Discourage the patient from going barefoot. Decreased sensation may allow an injury to occur without the patient noting it.

15. Encourage the patient to use appropriate footwear. Ill fitting shoes may contribute to skin breakdown. All new footwear should be broken in gradually over time. All shoes that are rough or worn or do not provide adequate foot support should be discarded.

16. Clean, dry socks that provide warmth, absorb perspiration and protect the feet should be worn.

POSTPROCEDURE

17. Return equipment.

18. Remove and dispose of gloves in biohazardous container.

19. Wash hands.

20. Report any signs of foot problems to the physician. Early interventions will diminish the magnitude of any problems noted.

NOTE: It is always the caregiver's responsibility to provide education to the patient during the process of providing care.

BACKGROUND: A patient's outward appearance plays a significant role in his or her self-image. Shaving facial hair is a key part of the daily grooming routine for many patients. Carefully follow the steps below as you groom your patient each day.

ALERT: Follow Standard Precautions.

PRETPROCEDURE

1. Wash hands.

2. Assemble equipment:

   a. Electric shaver or safety razor

   b. Shaving lather or an electric preshave lotion

   c. Basin of warm water

   d. Face towel

   e. Mirror

   f. Aftershave

   g. Disposable gloves

3. Identify patient and explain what you are going to do.

4. Provide privacy by pulling privacy curtains.

PROCEDURE

5. Raise head of bed if permitted.

6. Place equipment on overbed table.

7. Place a towel over patient's chest.

8. Adjust light so that it shines on patient's face.

9. Shave patient.

   a. If you are using a safety razor:

      (1) Put on gloves.

      (2) Moisten face and apply lather.

      (3) Start in front of ear; hold skin taut and bring razor down over cheek toward chin. Use short firm strokes. Repeat until lather on cheek is removed and skin is smooth.

      (4) Repeat on other cheek.

      (5) Wash face and neck. Dry thoroughly.

      (6) Apply aftershave lotion or powder if desired.

      (7) Discard gloves according to facility policy.

   b. If you are using an electric shaver:

      (1) Put on gloves.

      (2) Apply preshave lotion.

      (3) Gently shave until beard is removed.

      (4) Wash face and neck. Dry thoroughly.

      (5) Apply aftershave lotion or powder if desired.

      (6) Remove gloves.

10. Lower bed if you raised it and make sure side rails are up.

11. Make sure patient is comfortable and call bell is within reach.

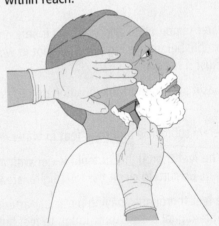

POSTPROCEDURE

12. Wash hands.

13. Chart procedure and how procedure was tolerated.

12/10/11	0730
	Face shaved with a safety razor
	Skin is clear and free of irritation
	R. Johnson CNA

Dressing and Undressing the Patient

It is very important for the patient to be up and dressed. Patients must not remain in bed unless the doctor orders bedrest. Being up and dressed creates an attitude of wellness. Staying in bedclothes presents an attitude of "being sick." Be certain that patients are dressed nicely and that their clothes are in good repair. Match the clothing rather than just throwing on "anything that's handy."

For patients who have a handicap, take special care in how you put on their clothes. This is also true of patients who have an IV. The following are some rules to follow:

- Always dress the weak or most involved side first. A **limb** that does not function well slides into a sleeve or pant leg if you start on that side.

- Always undress the weak or most involved side last.

- If the patient has an IV, be very careful not to disturb or dislodge it. Ask your teacher how to do this.

limb
(LIM)
Arm, leg.

 ## Terminal and Postmortem Care

You might be called upon to provide care for someone who is dying. Refer to Chapter 14, Section 14.4, "End-of-Life Issues." This helps you understand the stages that the patient goes through. Always be gentle and respectful both before and after death. Before death occurs, gently wash away discharges that have accumulated.

As death approaches, the muscles lose their tone and the body openings drain. Gently straighten the limbs and make the patient as comfortable as possible. After death occurs, you may be asked to prepare the body. Check the procedures of the facility you work in and follow the steps your facility provides.

The loss of a family member is a very significant time for loved ones. It is important that we provide as much time as necessary for the family to be with the patient preceding and immediately after death. Cleaning the deceased patient and placing the patient in a comfortable position for the family to view is an important part of a nurse's care.

Career Connection

Dealing with terminal care situations can be an extremely rewarding experience, but it is not for everyone. Volunteer at a hospice and shadow one of the health care professionals working there as they deal with terminal patients, the death of a patient and the families left behind.

Apply It

As a class, discuss how to appropriately interact with family members of a recently deceased patient. Once you are aware of the type of behavior you should exhibit and the kinds of things you should say, divide into groups and role play the scenario.

BACKGROUND: Provides direction for the preparation of the body following death.

ALERT: Follow Standard Precautions.

PREPROCEDURE

1. Wash hands.

2. Assemble equipment.

   a. Wash basin with warm water

   b. Washcloth and towel

   c. Shroud/postmortem set:

      (1) Sheet or plastic container

      (2) Identification tags

      (3) Large container for personal belongings

      (4) Plastic pad

   d. Gurney or morgue cart

   e. Nonsterile disposable gloves

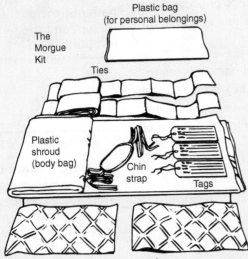

The Morgue Kit

Plastic bag (for personal belongings)

Ties

Plastic shroud (body bag)

Chin strap

Tags

Cellu-cotton pads

3. Close privacy curtains.

4. Put on gloves.

PROCEDURE

5. Position body in good alignment in supine position.

6. Keep one pillow under head.

7. Straighten arms and legs.

8. Gently close each eye. Do not apply pressure to eyelids.

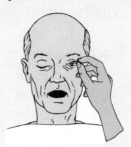

9. Put dentures in mouth or in a denture cup. If placed in a denture cup, put cup inside shroud so that mortician can find.

10. Remove all soiled dressings or clothing.

11. Bathe body thoroughly.

12. Apply clean dressings where needed.

13. Attach identification tags to wrists and ankles. Tag is usually placed on the right great toe and also on the outside of the shroud. Fill in tags with:

   a. Name

   b. Sex

   c. Hospital ID number

   d. Age

(continued)

14. Place body in a shroud, sheet, or other appropriate container. Do this in the following way:

    a. Ask for assistance from a co-worker.

    b. Logroll body to one side. Place shroud behind body leaving enough material to support body when rolled back. Fan-fold remaining shroud next to body.

    c. Place a plastic protection pad under buttocks.

    d. Roll body on its back and then to the other side.

    e. Pull fan-folded portion of shroud until flat.

    f. Roll body on its back.

    g. Cover entire body with shroud.

    h. Tuck in all loose edges of cover.

    i. Position a tie above elbows and below knees and secure around body.

    j. Attach ID tag to tie just above elbows.

15. Remove gloves and discard according to facility policy and procedure.

16. Wash hands.

17. Place all personal belongings in a large container. Label container with:

    a. Patient's name

    b. Age

    c. Room number

18. Place list of belongings in container and on patient's chart.

19. Follow your facility's procedure for transporting body and belongings through hallways.

20. Remove all linen and other supplies from room.

POSTPOCEDURE

21. Wash hands.

22. Report procedure completed to charge nurse.

> 12/07/11   0430
>
> *Postmortem care completed*
>
> *Belongings listed and placed in bag,*
>
> *given to family*
>
> *Charge nurse notified*
>
>   *R. Johnson CNA*

 ## Prosthetic Devices

A prosthesis or prosthetic device replaces or aids a body part that is injured, lost, or not working correctly. These include:

- Dentures.
- Glasses/contact lenses.
- Hearing aids.
- Artificial limbs.
- Artificial eyes.
- Artificial breasts (after mastectomy).

These devices are very important to the well-being of the patient and are treated carefully. You need to learn the correct way to put them on. Your patient is an excellent source of information on how they fit. Always put them in the same place when the patient is not using them, so that they are not lost and the patient can find them.

🗐 Bedmaking

When bedding is wrinkled or wet, it causes irritation to the skin and is very uncomfortable. Keeping the bed smooth and dry prevents a decubitus, a severe breakdown of the skin (see the section "Skin Management").

The number of times that you change the bed depends on whether or not the patient is continent. When the patient is in bed, check to be sure that the wrinkles are smoothed out and that the bed is dry.

The hospital bed has a small sheet, called a draw sheet that is placed in the midsection of the bed between the patient's knees and shoulders. This provides protection to the bottom sheet and can be changed easily without having to change the entire bottom sheet.

Often, a plastic cover is placed over the bottom sheet and under the draw sheet to prevent soiling. Be certain that the plastic sheet is always smooth.

There are several ways that hospital beds are made. If the patient is up and about, you make a closed bed. If the patient must remain in bed, you have to make an occupied bed. When the patient is in and out of bed during the day, you make an open bed.

PROCEDURE 18.55 Making a Closed Bed

BACKGROUND: Clean linens help prevent the spread of bacteria in the health care environment. A closed bed is made ready for new admissions or when a patient is not expected to return to bed until evening. Neatly made beds create a sense of order.

ALERT: Follow Standard Precautions.

PREPROCEDURE

1. Wash hands.
2. Assemble equipment:
   a. Fitted bottom sheet and one large sheet
   b. Draw sheet or large pad
   c. Blankets as needed
   d. Spread
   e. Pillow
   f. Pillowcase
3. Raise bed to a comfortable working height. Lock wheels on bed.
4. Place a chair at the side of bed.

5. Put linen on chair in the order in which you will use it. (First things you will use go on top.)

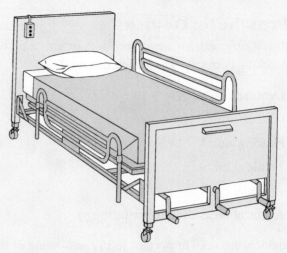

(continued)

PROCEDURE

6. Position mattress at head of bed until it is against head board.

7. Work on one side of bed until that side is completed. Then go to other side of bed. This saves you time and energy.

8. Tuck edges of fitted bottom sheet under bed.

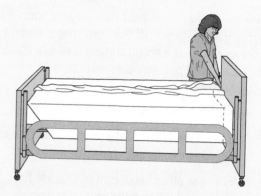

Tuck the entire side of the sheet under the mattress.

9. Place pad midway on bed or tuck in draw sheet.

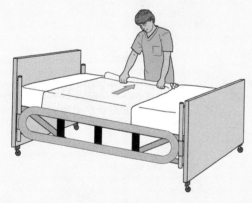

10. Top sheet is folded lengthwise. Place on bed.

   a. Place the center fold at center of bed from head to foot.

   b. Put large hem at head of bed, even with top of mattress.

   c. Open the sheet. Be certain rough edge of hem is facing up.

   d. Tightly tuck the sheet under at foot of bed.

   e. Make a mitered corner at foot of bed.

   f. Do not tuck in sheet at side of bed.

11. Blanket is folded lengthwise. Place it on bed.

   a. Place center fold of blanket on center of bed from head to foot.

   b. Place upper hem 6 inches from top of mattress.

   c. Open blanket and tuck it under foot tightly.

   d. Make a mitered corner at foot of bed.

   e. Do not tuck in at sides of bed.

12. Bedspread is folded lengthwise. Place it on bed.

   a. Place center fold in center of bed from head to foot.

   b. Place upper hem even with upper edge of mattress.

   c. Have rough edge down.

   d. Open spread and tuck it under at foot of bed.

   e. Make a mitered corner.

   f. Do not tuck in at sides.

13. Go to other side of bed. Start with bottom sheet.

   a. Pull sheet tight and smooth out all wrinkles.

   b. Make a mitered corner at top of bed.

   c. Pull draw sheet tight and tuck it in.

   d. Straighten out top sheet. Make a mitered corner at foot of bed.

   e. Miter foot corners of blanket and bedspread.

14. Fold top hem of spread over top hem of blanket.

(continued)

15. Fold top hem of sheet back over edge of spread and blanket to form cuff. The hem should be on the underside so that a rough surface does not come in contact with patient's skin and cause irritation.

16. Put pillowcase on pillow.

   a. Hold pillowcase at center of end seam. Do not tuck pillow under the chin.

   b. With your other hand, turn pillowcase back over hand holding end seam.

   c. Grasp pillow through case at center of end of pillow.

Grasp the pillow at the center of one end with the hand that is inside the pillowcase.

   d. Bring case down over pillow and fit pillow into corners of case.

   e. Fold extra material over open end of pillow and place it on bed with open end away from door.

With one hand, hold the pillowcase at the center of the seamed end.

Pull the pillowcase down over the pillow with your free hand.

Turn the pillowcase back over that hand with your free hand.

Straighten the pillowcase.

17. Put bed in lowest position.

POSTPROCEDURE

18. Wash hands.

BACKGROUND: Clean linens help prevent the spread of bacteria in the health care environment. Making an occupied bed with fresh linen will provide cleanliness, comfort, and will help the patient maintain a healthy skin condition.

ALERT: Follow Standard Precautions.

PREPROCEDURE

1. Wash hands.

2. Assemble equipment:

   a. Draw sheet or large pad

   b. Two large sheets or fitted bottom sheet and one large sheet

   c. Two pillowcases

   d. Blankets as needed

   e. Bedspread (if clean one is needed)

   f. Pillow

   g. Disposable gloves if needed

3. Identify patient and explain what you are going to do.

4. Raise bed to comfortable working height. Lock wheels on bed.

5. Place chair at side of bed.

6. Put linen on chair in the order in which you will use it. (First things you will use go on top.)

7. Provide for privacy by pulling privacy curtain.

PROCEDURE

8. Lower headrest and kneerest until bed is flat, if allowed.

9. Loosen linens on all sides by lifting edge of mattress with one hand and pulling out bedclothes with the other. *Never shake linen: This spreads microorganisms.*

10. Push mattress to top of bed. Ask for assistance if you need it.

11. Remove bedspread and blanket by folding them to the bottom, one at a time. Lift them from center and place over back of chair.

12. Place bath blanket or plain sheet over top sheet. Ask patient to hold top edge of clean cover if he or she is able to do so. If patient cannot hold the sheet, tuck it under patient's shoulders.

13. Slide soiled sheet from top to bottom and put in dirty linen container. Be careful not to expose patient.

14. Ask patient to turn toward the opposite side of bed. Have patient hold onto the side rail. Assist patient if he or she needs help. Patient should now be on far side of bed from you.

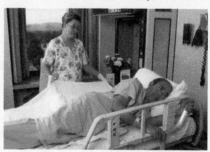

15. Adjust pillow for patient to make him or her comfortable.

16. Fan-fold soiled draw sheet and bottom sheet close to patient and tuck against patient's back. This leaves mattress stripped of linen.

17. Work on one side of bed until that side is completed. Then go to other side of bed. This saves you time and energy.

18. Take fitted bottom and fold it lengthwise. Be careful not to let it touch floor.

19. Place sheet on bed, still folded, with fold on middle of mattress.

(continued)

20. Fold top half of sheet toward patient. Tuck folds against patient's back.

21. Miter corner at head of mattress. Tuck bottom sheet under mattress on your side from head to foot of mattress.

22. Place clean bottom draw sheet or large pad that has been folded in half with fold along middle of mattress. Fold top half of sheet toward patient. Tuck folds against patient's back.

23. Raise side rail and lock in place.

24. Lower side rail on opposite side.

25. Ask patient to roll away from you to other side of bed and onto clean linen. Tell patient that there will be a bump in the middle. (Be careful not to let patient become wrapped up in bath blanket.)

26. Remove old bottom sheet and draw sheet from bed and put into laundry container.

27. Pull fresh linen toward edge of mattress. Tuck it under mattress at head of bed.

28. Tuck bottom sheet under mattress from head to foot of mattress. Pull firmly to remove wrinkles.

29. Pull draw sheet very tight and tuck under mattress. If pad used, pull from patient and straighten.

30. Have patient roll on back, or turn patient yourself. Loosen bath blanket as patient turns.

31. Change pillowcase.

    a. Hold pillowcase at center of end seam.

    b. With your other hand turn pillowcase back over hand, holding end seam.

    c. Grasp pillow through case at center of end of pillow.

    d. Bring case down over pillow and fit pillow into corners of case.

    e. Fold extra material over open end of pillow and place pillow under patient's head.

32. Spread clean top sheet over bath blanket with wide hem at the top. Middle of sheet should run along middle of bed with wide hem even with top edge of mattress. Ask patient to hold hem of clean sheet. Remove bath blanket by moving it toward foot of bed. Be careful not to expose patient.

33. Tuck clean top sheet under mattress at foot of bed. Make to epleat in top sheet so that patient's feet can move freely. To make a toepleat, make 3-inch fold toward foot of bed in topsheet before tucking in sheet. Tuck in and miter corner.

34. Place blanket over patient, being sure that it covers the shoulders.

35. Place bedspread on bed in same way. Tuck blanket and bedspread under bottom of mattress and miter corners.

36. Make cuff.

    a. Fold top hem edge of spread over blanket.

    b. Fold top hem of top sheet back over edge of bedspread and blanket, being certain that rough hem is turned down.

37. Position patient and make comfortable.

38. Put bed in lowest position.

39. Open privacy curtains.

40. Raise side rails, if required.

41. Place call light where patient can reach it.

POSTPROCEDURE

42. Tidy unit.

43. Wash hands.

44. Chart linen change and how the patient tolerated procedure.

BACKGROUND: Clean linens help prevent the spread of bacteria in the health care environment. An open bed provides easy access for patients returning to bed within a short period.

ALERT: Follow Standard Precautions.

PREPROCEDURE

1. Wash hands.

PROCEDURE

2. Grasp cuff of bedding in both hands and pull to foot of bed.

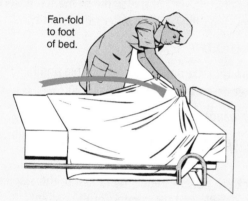

Fan-fold to foot of bed.

3. Fold bedding back on itself toward head of bed. The edge of cuff must meet fold. (This is called fan-folding.)

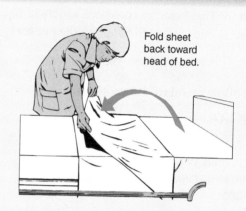

Fold sheet back toward head of bed.

4. Smooth the hanging sheets on each side into folds.

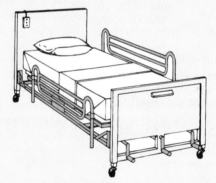

POSTPROCEDURE

5. Wash hands.

PROCEDURE 18.58 Placing a Bed Cradle

BACKGROUND: There can be situations where having the top bed linens touching the patient's lower extremities could be harmful to the patient. In this case, an apparatus called a bed cradle can be used.

A cradle is usually a metal frame that supports the bed linens away from the patient while providing privacy and warmth. These cradles come in a variety of sizes and shapes. If used, the cradle should be fastened to the bed so that it does not slide or fall on the patient.

ALERT: Follow Standard Precautions.

PREPROCEDURE

1. Identify the patient requiring a bed cradle. Assess the extremity to be protected. Note any special requirements necessitated by the patient's condition.

2. Wash hands.

3. Explain the procedure to the patient.

PROCEDURE

4. Address any needs for repositioning prior to placing the cradle.

5. Fold down the top covers off of the patient.

6. Place cradle over the patient's lower extremities.

7. Secure the cradle to the bed frame so that it will not collapse on to the patient.

8. Replace the top covers over the top of the cradle

9. Assure that no part of the cradle or the top covers are touching the patient's affected extremity.

POSTPROCEDURE

10. Assure that the patient is comfortable and has no further needs before leaving the area.

11. Wash hands.

12. Document the procedure noting any special findings or needs of the patient.

13. Check the patient frequently to assure the stability of the cradle and the comfort of the patient.

Feeding the Patient

Mealtime is a pleasant time for patients. It is often the most pleasurable event of the day. This should be an unhurried, enjoyable experience. Be certain that the patient is prepared for meals before the food arrives. The elderly patient may tolerate more small meals better than fewer large meals. Providing extra nourishments between meals may increase overall intake.

The preparation for the meal includes the following:

- Assisting patients or reminding them to wash their hands.

- Removing any unpleasant items from the area, such as **emesis** basins and bedpans.

- Offering the opportunity to use the bedpan or the bathroom.

- Providing for the patient's comfort:
  - Raise the head of the bed.
  - Position the patient in a chair.
  - Transport the patient to the dining area.

emesis
(eh MUH suhs)
Vomit.

- Checking to be certain that you have the right tray for the patient and that it is the correct diet.
- Always placing the food within reach.
- Checking the tray to be certain that everything is there.
- Preparing any item that the patient cannot manage.
- Telling the patient where each item is according to the face of a clock if the patient is blind.

PROCEDURE 18.59 Preparing the Patient to Eat

BACKGROUND: Meals are an important part of every culture. Preparing patients for a meal by providing clean, neat surroundings and encouraging toileting and washing hands before eating can help patients enjoy their meal and promote their appetites.

ALERT: Follow Standard Precautions.

PREPROCEDURE

1. Wash hands.
2. Assemble equipment:
   a. Bedpan or urinal
   b. Toilet tissue
   c. Washcloth
   d. Hand towel
3. Assist patient as needed to empty bladder and wash hands and face.
4. Explain that you are getting ready to give patient a meal.

PROCEDURE

5. Clear bedside table.
6. Position patient for comfort and a convenient eating position.
7. Wash your hands.
8. Identify patient and check name on food tray to ensure that you are delivering the correct diet to patient.

9. Place tray in a convenient position in front of patient.

10. Open containers if patient cannot.
11. If patient is unable to prepare food, do it for patient.
    a. Butter the bread
    b. Cut meat
    c. Season food as necessary
12. Follow the procedure for feeding a patient if patient needs to be fed.

POSTPROCEDURE

13. Wash hands.

Preparing the Patient to Eat in the Dining Room

BACKGROUND: Eating in the dining room provides a more normal environment for patients, creating an opportunity to visit with others during the meal.

ALERT: Follow Standard Precautions.

PREPROCEDURE

1. Wash hands.

PROCEDURE

2. Help patient take care of toileting needs.

3. Assist with handwashing.

4. Take patient to dining room.

5. Position patient in wheelchair at table that is proper height for wheelchair.

6. Be certain patient is sitting in a comfortable position in wheelchair.

7. Provide adaptive feeding equipment if needed.

8. Bring patient tray.

9. Identify patient.

10. Serve tray and remove plate covers.

11. Provide assistance as needed (e.g., cut meat, butter bread, open containers).

12. Remove tray when finished, noting what patient ate.

13. Assist with handwashing and take patient to area of choice.

POSTPROCEDURE

14. Wash hands.

15. Record what patient ate.

16. Record I & O if necessary. (See the section "Measuring Intake and Output" later in the section.)

8/10/11	0800
	Taken by wheelchair to dining room
	80% of breakfast eaten, and
	tolerated well
	_____ S. Gomez CNA

BACKGROUND: Food is essential to maintain health. As a health care worker you are responsible to encourage patients to maintain their health by eating routine meals. Your attitude and willingness to assist patients who require your attention during meals can encourage their intake of a balanced diet.

ALERT: Follow Standard Precautions.

PREPROCEDURE

1. Wash hands.

2. Check patient's ID band with name on food tray to ensure that you will be feeding correct diet to patient.

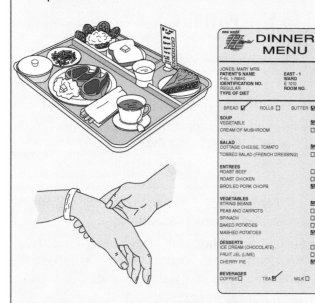

PROCEDURE

3. Tell patient what food is being served.

4. Ask patient how he or she prefers food to be prepared (e.g., salt, pepper, cream or sugar in coffee).

5. Position patient in a sitting position, as allowed by physician. If ordered to lie flat, turn patient on side.

6. Position yourself in a comfortable manner, facing the patient, so that you won't be rushing patient because you are uncomfortable. (Do not sit on bed.)

7. Cut food into small bite-sized pieces.

8. Place a napkin or small hand towel under patient's chin.

9. Put a flex straw in cold drinks. Hot drinks tend to burn mouth if taken through a straw.

10. Use a spoon to feed patient small to average-sized bites of food. (Encourage patient to help self as much as possible.)

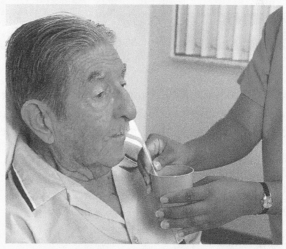

11. Always feed patient at a slow pace. It may take more time for him or her to chew and swallow than you think is necessary.

12. Always be sure that one bite has been swallowed before you give another spoonful to patient.

13. Tell patient what is being served and ask which item he or she prefers first, if patient cannot see food.

14. Offer beverages to patient throughout the meal.

15. Talk with patient during meal.

16. Encourage patient to finish eating, but do not force.

17. Assist patient in wiping face as necessary and when patient is finished eating.

(continued)

18. Observe amount of food eaten.

POSTPROCEDURE

19. Remove tray from room.

20. Position patient for comfort and safety.

21. Place call light in a convenient place.

22. Wash hands.

23. Record amount of food eaten (half, three-fourths, one-fourth, etc.) on chart, and indicate if food was tolerated well or not.

10/10/11	1800
	50% of meal taken with assistance and tolerated well.
	Resident stated that he doesn't like beef
	Dietitian notified of resident's request for meat other than beef.
	_____ R. Johnson CNA

PROCEDURE **18.62** **Serving Food to the Patient in Bed (Self-Help)**

BACKGROUND: As a health care worker you are required to identify the right diet for each patient and recognize what they need assistance with. Your opening packages and cartons or cutting food into bite-sized pieces may make the difference between a patient eating or refusing his or her food.

ALERT: Follow Standard Precautions.

PREPROCEDURE

1. Wash hands.

2. Assemble equipment:

   a. Food tray with diet card

   b. Flex straws

   c. Towel

PROCEDURE

3. Assist patient with bedpan or urinal.

4. Place in a sitting position if possible.

5. Help patient wash hands and face.

6. Remove unsightly or odor-causing articles.

7. Clean overbed table.

8. Check tray with diet card for

   a. Patient's name

   b. Type of diet

   c. Correct foods according to diet (e.g., diabetic, puréed, chopped, regular)

9. Set up tray and help with foods if needed (e.g., cut meat, butter bread, open containers). *Do not add foods to the tray until you check on diet.*

10. Encourage patient to eat all foods on tray.

11. Remove tray when finished and note what patient ate.

12. Help patient wash hands and face.

13. Position patient comfortably and make sure call bell is within reach.

(continued)

POSTPROCEDURE

14. Remove tray.
15. Be certain that water is within reach.
16. Wash hands.
17. Record I & O if required.
18. Record amount eaten.

11/03/11	1230
	Lunch served with meat and vegetables
	cut into bite-sized pieces.
	Mr. Axel struggled to butter the bread
	without assistance. He said, "I knew
	I could butter it without help." 90% of
	lunch eaten, tolerated well.
	S. Gomez CNA

PROCEDURE **18.63** **Providing Fresh Drinking Water**

BACKGROUND: Providing fluids for the patient is an integral part of the process of returning the patient to an optimal health status. The elderly patient may experience a diminished sense of thirst and may require additional encouragement and assistance to maintain adequate oral intake. Recording the volume of oral intake is the responsibility of the nurse assigned to the patient's care.

ALERT: Follow Standard Precautions.

PREPROCEDURE

1. Identify any patients whose fluids may be restricted as a medical necessity.
2. Wash hands.
3. Assemble equipment: the container to be used for patient's water supply.

PROCEDURE

4. Collect and discard any of the containers previously used for the patient's water supply.

5. Establish the temperature of water preferred by the patient, i.e., iced, tepid, etc.
6. Provide a clean container and fresh water for the patient.
7. Establish that the patient has no further needs before leaving the bedside.

POSTPROCEDURE

8. Wash hands.

BACKGROUND: Patients must routinely eat a balanced diet. You are required to feed patients who are not able to feed themselves. Your patience and willingness to feed them in a gentle, caring, compassionate manner could make the difference in their eating or not eating.

ALERT: Follow Standard Precautions.

PREPROCEDURE

1. Wash hands.

2. Bring patient's tray.

3. Check name on card with patient ID band.

4. Explain to patient what you are going to do.

PROCEDURE

5. Sit comfortably, facing patient.

6. Tuck a napkin under patient's chin.

7. Season food the way patient likes it.

8. Use a spoon and fill only half full.

9. Give food from tip, not side of spoon.

10. Name each food as you offer it, if patient cannot see food.

11. Describe position of food on plate (e.g., hot liquids in right corner, peas at the position of 3 o'clock on a clock) if patient cannot see but can feed self.

12. Tell patient if you are offering something that is hot or cold.

13. Use a straw for giving liquids.

14. Feed patient slowly and allow time to chew and swallow. Offer beverages throughout the meal.

15. Note amount eaten and remove tray when finished.

16. Help with washing hands and face.

17. Position patient comfortably and place call bell within reach.

POSTPROCEDURE

18. Wash hands.

19. Record amount eaten and I & O if required. See following pages for directions on recording I & O.

INTAKE AND OUTPUT SHEET

Hospital #_____ Patient Name _____
Date _____ Room #_____

Time 7-3	BY MOUTH	TUBE	PARENTERAL	VOIDED	CATHETER	EMESIS	SUCTION
TOTAL							
Time 3-11							
TOTAL							
Time 11-7							
TOTAL							
24 HOUR TOTAL							
24 Hour Grand Total • Intake				24 Hour Grand Total • Output			

INTAKE — OUTPUT (URINE / GASTRIC)

12/12/11   1830

Ate 60% of food and drank
240cc of tea
Chokes easily when drinking liquids
Reported choking incidents to team
leader

_____   A. Chaplin CNA

BACKGROUND: Between-meal nourishments are served to people who need additional nutrients to maintain or improve their health. People with diabetes need nourishments to maintain balanced glucose levels. Some may need protein to build and repair body tissue and others may need specific vitamins.

ALERT: Follow Standard Precautions.

POSTPROCEDURE

1. Wash hands.

2. Assemble equipment:

   a. Nourishment

   b. Cup, dish, straw, spoon

   c. Napkin

3. Identify patient.

PROCEDURE

4. Take nourishment to patient.

5. Help if needed.

6. After patient is finished, collect dirty utensils.

POSTPROCEDURE

7. Return utensils to dietary cart or kitchen.

8. Record intake on I & O sheet if required.

9. Wash hands.

10. Record nourishment taken.

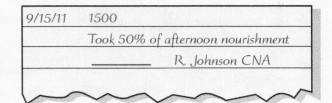

9/15/11   1500

Took 50% of afternoon nourishment

_____   R. Johnson CNA

Additional Nourishments

Nourishments are usually served to patients who require additional nutrition. You are required to identify the right nourishment for patients and to recognize what they need assistance with. Telling the patient that the nourishment is served, making it ready to drink or eat, or feeding him or her if necessary makes it possible for the patient to receive the needed nourishment.

You may have a patient with a nasogastric (N/G) tube. The nasogastric tube is used when the patient has difficulty swallowing or has no swallow reflex. It is a soft, plastic tube that is inserted in the nostril and goes down the back of the throat through the esophagus to the stomach. The tube is taped to the patient's nose.

Fluids such as liquid food and medication are put into the tube. Another type of tube is the gastric tube. This tube enters the stomach through the abdominal wall. It is left in place and capped after each feeding. Be very careful not to pull out these tubes.

🖳 Measuring Intake and Output

One of your most important responsibilities is helping the patient with fluid balance. Normally, our bodies maintain this balance without our thinking about it. We take in fluids in our foods and liquids. About the same amount is eliminated by the kidneys (urine), respiration, and perspiration. However, in some patients, fluid balance becomes a very serious problem. Fluid imbalance occurs when fluid stays in the tissues, causing edema, or when there is excessive loss of fluid (dehydration).

dehydration
(dee HIE dray shuhn)
Severe loss of fluid from tissue and cells.

Dehydration is caused by:

- Diarrhea.
- Vomiting.
- Bleeding.
- Excessive perspiration (diaphoresis).
- Poor fluid intake.

If you notice any of the following symptoms of dehydration, report them immediately:

- Fever is present.
- There is a decrease in urine.
- Urine is concentrated.
- Weight loss occurs.
- Membranes are dry, and patient has difficulty swallowing.
- Tongue is coated and thickened.
- Skin becomes hard and cracks and is dry and warm.

Edema is serious; it is caused by:

- High salt intake.
- Infections.
- Injuries or burns.
- Certain kidney diseases.
- Certain heart diseases or heart inefficiencies.
- Sitting too long in one position.
- Infiltration of IV fluid.

If you notice any of the symptoms of edema, report them immediately:

- Decrease in urine output.
- Gain in weight.
- Puffiness or swelling.
- Sometimes shortness of breath.

When any of these situations occur, the doctor writes an order to record intake and output (I & O). You record any fluid taken in and any fluid that is eliminated. To measure intake, record the amount of fluid consumed by mouth. (Figure 18.17) Be sure to include the following:

- All liquid taken by mouth.

- Any food item that turns to liquid at room temperature (e.g., gelatin, ice cream) All fluid taken by IV or tube feeding.

Your facility has a charting method for you to use. Record the amount of liquid taken at the time it is taken. This way, you do not forget this important task. You are probably most familiar with measuring liquid in ounces.

When you record liquid intake, you record it in cubic centimeters (cc's). This is a metric measure and is used in medical facilities. Most facilities have a chart that helps you determine how many cubic centimeters are in a serving. (Table 18.7) If you need to change ounces to cubic centimeters, use the formula below.

$$30 \times (\text{number of ounces}) = \text{number of cc}$$

For example:

$$30 \times 8 \text{ ounces} = 240 \text{ cc}$$

To measure patient output, measure all of the following:

- Urine.

- Liquid stool.

- Emesis (vomit).

- Suctioned secretion.

- Drainage.

- Excessive perspiration.

Suctioned secretion (Figure 18.18) and perspiration are estimated. It is a good idea to have an experienced person help you determine the amount. When you have measured input and output, record them on the chart provided. You may be asked to empty a urinary bag and measure the urine at the end of your shift. The totals are taken each 24 hours. If you notice any unusual recordings, be absolutely certain that you report it.

Table 18.7 Customary Liquid Measures and Their Equivalents*

Liquid Measurment	Equivalents
1 cc/1 mL	15 drops
1 cc/1 mL	1/4 teaspoon
5 cc/mL	1 teaspoon
15 cc/mL	1 tablespoon
30 cc/mL	1 oz
60 cc/mL	2 oz
120 cc/mL	4 oz
180 cc/mL	6 oz
240 cc/mL	8 oz (1 cup)
500 cc/mL	16 oz (1 pint)
1,000 cc/mL	32 oz (1 quart)
4,000 cc/mL	64 oz (1 gallon)

*cc, cubic centimeter; mL, milliliter; oz, ounce.

Figure 18.18
Nasogastric suction. Why is important to measure all secretions?

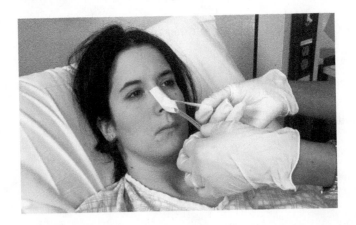

🔲 Special Procedures

Enemas

You may have the responsibility of giving the patient an enema. Fluid is run into the rectum to remove feces and gas from the bowel. The solution in the bowel causes the patient to feel uncomfortable and want to force the fluid out. Encourage him or her to retain the fluid as long as possible. This gives better results.

An enema is given only when there is a doctor's order. There are several different kinds of enemas. These include tap water, soap suds, saline, and prepackaged enemas. An oil retention enema is held in the bowel longer than the cleansing enema. Encourage the patient to retain the oil solution for 20 to 30 minutes.

BACKGROUND: All body systems rely on fluid balance to maintain normal functioning. By measuring urinary output, you can determine the body's ability to maintain fluid balance and observe characteristics of urine that indicate normalcy or potential abnormalities.

ALERT: Follow Standard Precautions.

PREPROCEDURE

1. Wash hands.

2. Assemble equipment:

   a. Bedpan, urinal, or special container

   b. Graduate or measuring cup

   c. Disposable nonsterile gloves

3. Put on gloves.

PROCEDURE

4. Pour urine into measuring graduate.

5. Place graduate on flat surface and read amount of urine.

6. Observe urine for:

   a. Unusual color

   b. Blood

   c. Dark color

   d. Large amounts of mucus

   e. Sediment

7. Save the specimen and report to nurse immediately if you notice any unusual appearance.

8. Discard in toilet if urine is normal. Use a paper towel to flush toilet and turn on faucet.

9. Rinse graduate or pitcher and put away.

POSTPROCEDURE

10. Remove gloves and discard according to facility policy.

11. Wash hands.

12. Record amount of urine in cc's on I & O sheet.

11/23/12	1600
	Voided 100 cc pink-tinged urine
	Complained of pain upon urination
	Team leader notified
	_____ *S. Gomez CNA*

11/23/12	1200
	Voided 300 cc dark,
	amber-colored urine
	_____ *S. Gomez CNA*

BACKGROUND: Oil retention enema solutions stimulate the bowl and lubricate the colon and rectum, which facilitates the release of stool from the colon.

ALERT: Follow Standard Precautions.

PREPROCEDURE

1. Wash your hands.

2. Assemble equipment:

   a. Prepackaged oil retention enema

   b. Bedpan and cover

   c. Waterproof bed protector

   d. Toilet tissue

   e. Towel, basin of water, and soap

   f. Disposable gloves

3. Identify patient.

4. Ask visitors to leave the room. Provide privacy with curtain, screen, or door.

5. Explain what you are going to do.

6. Put on gloves.

PROCEDURE

7. Cover patient with a bath blanket, and fan-fold linen to foot of bed.

8. Put bedpan on foot of bed.

9. Elevate the bed to a comfortable working height and lower the side rail on the side you are working on.

10. Place bed protector under buttocks.

11. Help patient into the Sims' position.

NOTE: The Sim's position is a position in which the patient lies on one side with the under arm behind the back and the upper thigh flexed.

12. Tell patient to retain enema as long as possible.

13. Open a prepackaged oil retention enema.

14. Fold the bath blanket back to expose the buttock.

15. Lift patient's upper buttock and expose anus.

16. Tell patient when you are going to insert prelubricated tip into anus. (Instruct patient to take deep breaths and try to relax.) Insert tip 2–4 inches into the rectum.

17. Squeeze container slowly and steady until all solution has entered rectum.

18. Remove container; place in original package to be disposed of in contaminated waste according to facility policy and procedure.

19. Instruct patient to remain on side and retain the solution for at least 30 minutes.

20. Lower the bed and pull the side rail up. Leave the call bell in place.

21. Remove gloves and discard according to facility policy.

22. Check patient every 5 minutes until fluid has been retained for at least 20 minutes. Usually it is at least 30 minutes.

23. Position patient on bedpan or assist to bathroom. Instruct patient not to flush toilet.

24. Raise head of bed, if permitted, if using a bedpan.

25. Place toilet tissue and call bell within easy reach.

26. Stay nearby if patient is in bathroom.

27. Put on gloves.

28. Remove bedpan or assist patient to return to bed. Observe contents of toilet or bedpan for

    a. Color, consistency, unusual materials, odor

    b. Amount of return

29. Cover bedpan and dispose of contents. Use paper towel to flush toilet and turn on faucet.

30. Remove gloves and discard in biohazardous container.

(continued)

31. Replace top sheet and remove bath blanket and plastic bed protector.

32. Give patient soap, water, and towel for hands and face.

POSTPROCEDURE

33. Wash your hands.

34. Chart the following:

    a. Type of enema given

    b. Consistency and amount of bowel movement

    c. How the procedure was tolerated

5/13/12	1930
	16 oz oil retention enema administered
	and retained 12 minutes
	Passed large amount of dark brown
	formed stool
	_____ R. Johnson CNA
6/07/12	0800
	Tolerated enema well
	Resting quietly
	_____ S. Gomez CNA

PROCEDURE 18.68 Prepackaged Enemas

BACKGROUND: Prepackaged enema solutions stimulate the bowel and facilitate the release of stool from the colon.

ALERT: Follow Standard Precautions.

PREPROCEDURE

1. Wash your hands.

2. Assemble equipment.

    a. Prepackaged enema

    b. Bedpan and cover

    c. Waterproof bed protector

    d. Toilet tissue

    e. Towel, basin of water, and soap

    f. Disposable gloves

3. Identify patient.

4. Ask visitors to leave room.

5. Explain what you are going to do and provide privacy with curtain, screen, or door.

PROCEDURE

6. Cover patient with a bath blanket, and fan-fold linen to foot of bed.

7. Put on gloves.

8. Raise bed to comfortable working height and lower side rail.

9. Place bed protector under buttocks.

10. Put bedpan on foot of bed.

11. Help patient into the Sims' position.

12. Fold back blanket and expose buttock.

13. Tell patient to retain enema as long as possible.

14. Open a prepackaged enema.

(continued)

15. Lift patient's upper buttock and expose anus.

16. Tell patient when you are going to insert prelubricated tip into anus. (Have patient take deep breaths and try to relax.)

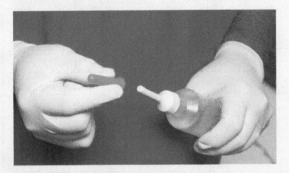

17. Squeeze container until all the solution has entered the rectum.

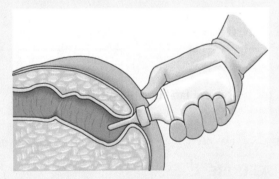

18. Remove container; place in original package to be disposed of according to facility policy.

19. Remove gloves and dispose of in biohazardous container.

20. Instruct patient to remain on side and to hold solution as long as possible. Have call bell in reach.

21. Put on gloves.

22. Position patient on bedpan or assist to bathroom. Instruct patient not to flush toilet.

23. Raise head of bed if permitted if patient is using a bedpan.

24. Place toilet tissue and call bell within easy reach.

25. Stay nearby if patient is in bathroom.

26. Remove bedpan or assist patient to return to bed.

27. Observe contents of toilet or bedpan for

    a. Color, consistency, unusual materials, odor

    b. Amount of return

28. Cover bedpan and dispose of contents. Use paper towels to flush toilet and turn on facet.

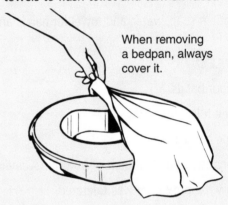

When removing a bedpan, always cover it.

POSTPROCEDURE

29. Remove gloves and dispose of according to facility policy.

30. Replace top sheet and remove bath blanket and plastic bed protector.

31. Give the patient soap, water, and towel for hands and face.

32. Wash hands.

33. Chart the following:

    a. Type of enema given

    b. Consistency and amount of bowel movement

    c. How the procedure was tolerated

9/10/12	1430
	12 oz prepackaged enema
	administered and retained 5 minutes
	Complained of severe abdominal cramps.
	Passed 12 oz watery, tan-colored fluid.
	Reported to team leader
	_____ A. Chaplin CNA
9/10/12	1515
	Restless
	Continues to complain about abdominal
	cramps
	Team leader notified
	_____ A. Chaplin CNA

Tap Water, Soap Suds, Saline Enemas

BACKGROUND: Tap water, soap suds, and saline solutions stimulate the bowel and facilitate the release of stool from the colon.

ALERT: Follow Standard Precautions.

PREPROCEDURE

1. Wash your hands.

2. Assemble equipment.

   a. Disposable gloves

   b. Disposable enema equipment

     (1) Plastic container

     (2) Tubing

     (3) Clamp

     (4) Lubricant

   c. Enema solution as instructed by the head nurse, e.g.:

     (1) Tap water, 700–1,000 cc water (105°F)

     (2) Soap suds, 700–1,000 cc (105°F), one package enema soap

     (3) Saline, 700–1,000 cc water (105°F), 2 teaspoons salt

   d. Bedpan and cover

   e. Urinal, if necessary

   f. Toilet tissue

   g. Waterproof disposable bed protector

   h. Paper towel

   i. Bath blanket

3. Identify patient.

PROCEDURE

4. Ask visitors to leave room

5. Tell patient what you are going to do.

6. Attach tubing to irrigation container. Adjust clamp to a position where you can easily open and close it. Close clamp.

7. Fill container with warm water (105° F).

   a. Add one package enema soap for soap suds enema.

   b. Add 2 teaspoons salt for saline enema.

   c. For tap water enema, do not add anything.

8. Provide privacy by pulling privacy curtain.

9. Raise bed to working level and put down side rail on the side you are working on.

10. Cover patient with a bath blanket. Remove upper sheet by fan-folding to foot of bed. *Be careful not to expose patient.*

11. Put on gloves.

12. Put waterproof protector under patient's buttocks.

13. Place bedpan on foot of bed.

14. Place patient in the Sims position.

15. Open clamp on enema tubing and let a small amount of solution run into bedpan. (This eliminates air in tubing and warms tube.) Close clamp.

16. Put a small amount of lubricating jelly on tissue. Lubricate enema tip. Check to be certain that the opening is not plugged.

17. Expose buttocks by folding back bath blanket.

18. Lift the upper buttock to expose anus.

19. Tell patient when you are going to insert lubricated tip into anus.

20. Hold rectal tube about 5 inches from tip and insert slowly into rectum.

(continued)

21. Tell patient to breathe deeply through mouth and to try to relax.

22. Raise container 12 to 18 inches above patient's hip.

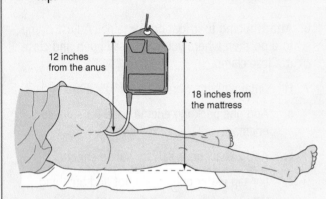

12 inches from the anus

18 inches from the mattress

23. Open clamp and let solution run in slowly. If patient complains of cramps, clamp tubing for a minute and lower bag slightly.

24. When most of solution has flowed into rectum, close clamp. Gently withdraw rectal tube. Wrap tubing with paper towel and place into enema can.

25. Ask patient to hold solution as long as possible.

26. Assist patient to bathroom and stay nearby if patient can go to bathroom. Ask patient not to flush toilet.

27. Help patient onto bedpan and raise head of bed if permitted.

28. Place call light within reach and check patient every few minutes.

29. Dispose of enema equipment while you are waiting for patient to expel enema. *Follow hospital policy.*

30. Remove bedpan or assist patient back to bed.

31. Observe contents for

    a. Color, consistency, unusual materials

    b. Note amount (i.e., large or small)

32. Cover bedpan and remove bed protector.

33. Remove gloves and dispose of according to facility policy. Wash hands.

34. Replace top sheet and remove bath blanket.

35. Give patient soap, water, and a towel to wash hands.

36. Secure call light in patient's reach.

POSTPROCEDURE

37. Clean and replace all equipment used and wash your hands.

38. Chart the following:

    a. Date and time

    b. Type of enema given

    c. Results (amount, color, consistency) of bowel movement

    d. How the procedure was tolerated

4/14/12	1800
	1,000 cc soap suds enema
	administered and retained 15 minutes
	Complained about severe abdominal
	cramps
	Passed large amount of brown, formed
	stool, brown-colored liquid, and loose
	brown stool particles
	_____ S. Gomez CNA
4/14/12	1845
	Resting quietly in bed, no pain
	_____ S. Gomez CNA

Incontinent Patient

When a patient is incontinent, he or she loses the ability to control the bowel or bladder or both. This is embarrassing to most patients. They are often irritable and depressed. You can help them by having a positive attitude and by being patient and kind. Some of the causes of incontinence are:

- Infections.
- Surgical problems (e.g., prostate surgery).
- Spinal cord injuries.
- Loss of sphincter control (muscle control).
- Some diseases, such as multiple sclerosis and central nervous system damage.
- Disorientation.

Bladder training is one method that is used to help relieve incontinence. This requires the cooperation of the health care workers and the patient. Your part in helping with the retraining of the bladder is to follow instructions carefully. They include the following:

- Keeping a careful intake and output record.
- Giving fluids at specific times.
- Taking the patient to void at specific intervals.
- Watching for symptoms of bladder distension:
    - Restlessness.
    - Dribbling.
    - Distended lower abdomen.
    - Sensation of pressure.
    - **Residual** urine.

residual
(REE sid yoo uhl)
Left over.

Staying on a schedule is the only way that bladder training can be successful. Everyone who cares for the patient must cooperate.

Indwelling foley catheters are a source of nosocomial infections and their use should be avoided whenever possible. If an indwelling catheter must be used it should be monitored and removed as soon as medically feasible.

When caring for the patient with an indwelling catheter, assess the urinary output in the collection bag. It should be:

- Clear, not cloudy.
- Straw-colored, pale yellow (not deep in color).
- 1,200 to 1,500 cc per day; if less than 30 cc per hour, notify the charge nurse.

If you notice anything unusual about the urine, report it immediately. This includes blood, mucus, or deep color.

NOTE: Never allow the urinary drainage bag to be higher than the hips of the patient. Keeping the bag lower provides drainage away from the urinary bladder. If the drainage bag were higher, urine could flow back into the bladder and cause an infection.

Figure 18.19
Urinary catheter. What symptoms might signal a potential problem?

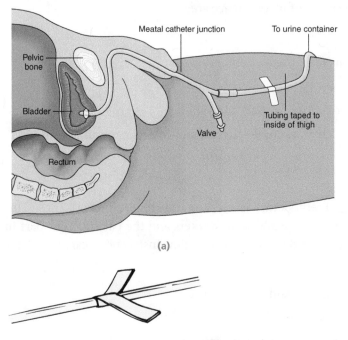

(a)

How to Loosely Tape Tubing in Place

(b)

Specimen Collection

Specimens that you collect from your patients are sent to the laboratory and tested. These tests give the physician information that helps him or her treat the patient. It is important that specimens be collected carefully and properly. They must also be labeled correctly.

Urine specimens are collected in different ways. The following are five common urine specimen collection procedures:

- Routine urine specimen.
- Clean-catch urine specimen.
- Fresh fractional urine.
- 24-hour urine specimen.
- Strained urine.

When obtaining urine specimens, always observe and record:

- **Color:** may range from light straw color to dark amber.
- **Clearness, cloudiness, or particles**.
- **Odor:** normal, strong, or unusual.

BACKGROUND: Disconnecting an indwelling catheter from the drainage bag and plugging the catheter keeps urine from draining out of the body. This procedure is commonly followed when the physician wants to remove the catheter and bladder retraining is necessary; or to allow the patient to participate in activities without the urinary drainage bag

ALERT: Follow Standard Precautions.

PREPROCEDURE

1. Wash hands.

2. Assemble equipment.

   a. Disinfectant (Can use an alcohol or Betadine swab.)

   b. Sterile gauze sponges

   c. Sterile cap or plug

   d. Disposable gloves

3. Identify patient and provide privacy with curtain, screen, or door.

4. Explain what you are going to do.

5. Put on gloves.

PROCEDURE

6. Place a towel under the tubing where it connects to the catheter.

7. Disinfect connection between catheter and drainage tubing where it is to be disconnected by applying disinfectant with cotton or gauze.

8. Disconnect catheter and drainage tubing. *Do not allow catheter ends to touch anything!*

9. Insert a sterile plug in end of catheter. Place sterile cap over exposed end of drainage tube.

10. Carefully secure drainage tube to bed.

POSTPROCEDURE

11. Remove gloves and discard according to facility policy.

12. Wash hands.

13. Record procedure. *Reverse procedure to reconnect.*

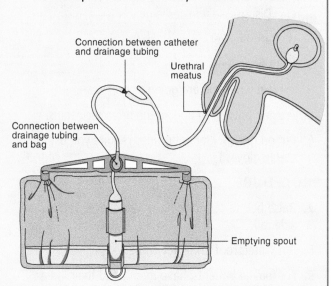

Connection between catheter and drainage tubing

Urethral meatus

Connection between drainage tubing and bag

Emptying spout

5/11/12	1000
	Urinary catheter disconnected and
	plugged with a sterile plug
	_____ S. Gomez CNA
5/11/12	1130
	Lower abdominal pain
	Catheter drained 400 cc of urine
	Plug reinserted
	_____ S. Gomez CNA

BACKGROUND: Giving indwelling catheter care helps to prevent infection and provides an opportunity to observe the insertion site for irritation and to adjust catheter position to maximize efficient drainage.

ALERT: Follow Standard Precautions.

PREPROCEDURE

1. Wash hands.

2. Assemble equipment:

   a. Antiseptic solution or catheter care kits.

   b. Waterproof bed protector

   c. Disposable nonsterile gloves

   d. Bath Blanket

3. Identify patient.

4. Explain what you are going to do.

5. Provide privacy by pulling the privacy curtains.

6. Put on gloves. (Some facilities require you use sterile gloves.)

PROCEDURE

7. Raise bed to comfortable working level and lower side rail.

8. Put waterproof protector on bed.

9. For female patients, have them bend their knee and drape them with the bath blanket, so that only the perineum is exposed. For males, pull covers back to knee and cover top half of body with bath blanket.

10. Carefully clean perineum.

11. Observe around catheter for sores, leakage, bleeding, or crusting. Report any unusual observation to nurse.

12. For females, separate labia with forefinger and thumb. Apply antiseptic solution around area where catheter enters the urethra. Wipe from front to back and place used applicator or gauze pad in biohazardous container. Use a clean applicator or gauze with antiseptic solution each time you wipe from back to front.

13. For males, pull back foreskin on uncircumcised patient and apply antiseptic to entire area. Wipe from the meatus down the shaft of the penis. Use a clean applicator or gauze with every stroke.

14. Apply antiseptic ointment (if allowed in your facility).

15. Position patient so catheter does not have kinks and is not pulling. *Be sure the tubing is free of kinks and is draining!*

16. Remove waterproof protector.

15. Cover patient.

17. Dispose of supplies according to facility policy.

18. Remove gloves and dispose of according to facility policy.

19. Position patient comfortably. Lower bed and raise side rail.

20. Secure call light within patient's reach.

POSTPROCEDURE

21. Wash hands.

22. Record procedure.

11/02/12	0920
	Perineal care complete
	Catheter insertion site clean and free
	from irritation
	Catheter secured to left inner thigh to
	allow drainage
	_____ R. Johnson CNA

BACKGROUND: An incontinent patient may use an external urinary catheter to control the flow of urine into a drainage bag in place of wearing a diaper. This is sometimes known as a condom catheter, because the device fits over the penis like a condom.

ALERT: Follow Standard Precautions.

PREPROCEDURE

1. Wash hands.

2. Assemble equipment:

   a. Basin warm water

   b. Washcloth

   c. Towel

   d. Waterproof bed protector

   e. Gloves

   f. Plastic bag

   g. Condom with drainage tip

   h. Paper towels

3. Identify patient.

4. Explain what you are going to do.

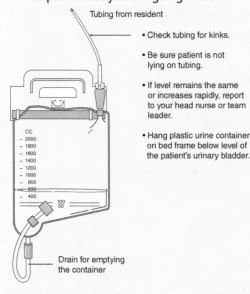

Tubing from resident

• Check tubing for kinks.

• Be sure patient is not lying on tubing.

• If level remains the same or increases rapidly, report to your head nurse or team leader.

• Hang plastic urine container on bed frame below level of the patient's urinary bladder.

CC
- 2000
- 1800
- 1600
- 1400
- 1200
- 1000
- 800
- 600
- 400

100
50

Drain for emptying the container

PROCEDURE

5. Provide privacy by pulling privacy curtain.

6. Raise bed to comfortable working height.

7. Cover patient with bath blanket. Have patient hold top of blanket, and fold cover to bottom of bed.

8. Put on gloves.

9. Place waterproof protector under patient's buttocks.

10. Pull up bath blanket to expose genitals only.

11. Remove condom by rolling gently toward tip of penis.

12. Wash and dry penis.

13. Observe for irritation, open areas, bleeding.

14. Report any unusual observations.

15. Check condom for "ready stick" surface. If there is none, apply a thin spray of tincture of benzoin. *Do not spray on head of penis.*

16. Apply new condom and drainage tip to penis by rolling toward base of penis.

17. Reconnect drainage system.

18. Remove and dispose of gloves in biohazardous container.

19. Pull up top bedding and remove bath blanket.

20. Replace equipment.

21. Lower bed to lowest position.

22. Put up side rail if required.

23. Secure call light within patient's reach.

POSTPROCEDURE

24. Tidy unit.

25. Wash hands.

26. Record procedure.

4/10/12	0730
Shower taken and tolerated well	
Urinary condom drainage system	
applied and drains well	
	A. Chaplin CNA

BACKGROUND: Emptying the urinary drainage bag provides an opportunity to:

1. Measure urinary output for a specific period of time
2. Observe characteristics of urine

ALERT: Follow Standard Precautions.

PREPROCEDURE

1. Wash hands.

2. Identify patient and explain procedure

3. Provide privacy with curtain, screen, or door.

4. Assemble equipment.

 a. Graduate or measuring cup

 b. Disposable gloves

 c. Paper towel

 d. An alcohol swab

5. Put on disposable gloves.

PROCEDURE

6. Place towel on floor and set graduate cylinder on top of the towel.

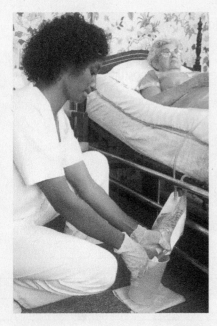

7. Carefully open drain outlet on urinary bag. *Do not allow container outlet to touch floor!* This will introduce microorganisms into bag and can cause infection.

8. Drain bag into graduate and clean drain outlet with alcohol swab. Then reattach drainage outlet securely.

9. Observe urine for:

 a. Dark color

 b. Blood

 c. Unusual odor

 d. Large amount of mucus

 e. Sediment

10. Report any unusual observations to nurse immediately (do not discard urine).

11. Hold graduate at eye level and read amount of urine on measuring scale.

12. Discard urine if normal. Flush toilet and turn on faucet with paper towel.

13. Rinse graduate and put away.

POSTPROCEDURE

14. Remove gloves and discard in hazardous waste.

15. Wash hands.

16. Record amount of urine in cc's on the I & O record.

10/10/11   0700
     15.00 Urinary drainage, 1,290 cc
_____   A. Chaplin CNA

Use the urine specimen collection procedures to guide you in the correct way to collect useful specimens.

Other specimens commonly collected for testing include stool and sputum. (Figure 18.20) The stool samples are examined for occult (hidden) blood and for microorganisms. Sputum samples help the physician determine what is causing an illness of the respiratory system.

When obtaining these specimens always observe and record:

- Color.
- Consistency.
- Odor.

Use the correct specimen collection procedures to guide you when obtaining these specimens.

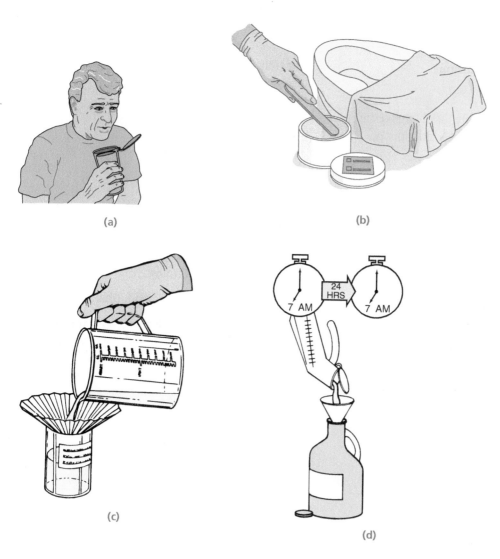

(a)

(b)

(c)

(d)

Figure 18.20
(a) Collecting the sputum specimen; *(b)* collecting a stool specimen; *(c)* straining the urine; *(d)* collecting a 24-hour specimen. What should a health care professional observe and record?

Collect Specimen Under Transmission-Based Precautions

BACKGROUND: Concerns about the transmission of blood borne diseases, such as AIDS and the hepatitis B virus, and the increasing incidence of hospital acquired infections has caused a change in the focus of infection control programs. Since 1987 the CDC (Centers for Disease Control) has promoted the use of *universal precautions.*

It is recommended that health-care workers use gloves, gowns, masks, and protective eyewear when exposure to blood or body fluids is likely and that all patients be considered potentially infected. Universal precautions are used along with category-specific isolation systems when indicated.

Efforts have also been made to remove all sharps, such as needles, from the health-care system whenever possible, thus diminishing contamination from needle sticks. Collecting specimens requires some contact with body fluids so the prudent use of universal precautions becomes a critical part of the process.

ALERT: Follow Standard Precautions.

PREPROCEDURE

1. Collect the equipment necessary for obtaining the specimen (specimen cup, lab tubes, tourniquets, etc.).

2. Wash hands.

3. Put on disposable gloves, gowns, mask, and protective eyewear as may be required depending on the specimen to be collected.

PROCEDURE

4. Provide an explanation to the patient regarding the specimen to be collected. Answer any questions the patient may have.

5. Collect the specimen using aseptic or sterile technique as required.

6. Label the specimen with the patient's name, date, and time of collection.

7. Place the specimen in a protective package as prescribed by the institution.

8. Assure that the patient has no further needs.

9. Dispose of any used supplies and any protective items used in the collection of the specimen in the appropriate manner, as determined by your institution.

POSTPROCEDURE

10. Wash hands.

11. Send the specimen to the laboratory.

BACKGROUND: To evaluate the chemical structure of urine and determine the need for further testing.

ALERT: Follow Standard Precautions.

PREPROCEDURE

1. Wash hands.

2. Assemble equipment:

   a. Graduate (pitcher)

   b. Bedpan or urinal

   c. Urine specimen container

   d. Label

   e. Paper bag

   f. Disposable nonsterile gloves

3. Identify patient.

4. Explain what you are going to do.

PROCEDURE

5. Label specimen carefully:

   a. Patient's name

   b. Date

   c. Time

   d. Room number

6. Provide privacy by pulling privacy curtain.

7. Put on gloves.

8. Have patient void (urinate) into clean bedpan or urinal.

9. Ask patient to put toilet tissue into paper bag.

10. Pour specimen into graduate.

11. Pour from graduate into specimen container until about three-quarters full.

12. Place lid on container.

13. Discard leftover urine.

14. Clean and rinse graduate, bedpan, or urinal, and put away.

15. Remove gloves.

16. Position patient comfortably.

17. Assist patient to wash hands.

POSTPROCEDURE

18. Wash hands.

19. Store specimen according to direction for lab pickup.

20. Report and record procedure and observation of specimen.

PROCEDURE 18.76 Midstream Clean-Catch Urine, Female

BACKGROUND: A midstream clean-catch urine procedure provides a way to collect urine free of bacteria present at the urethral meatus at the beginning of urination, and in sediment in the urinary bladder which drains at the end of urination.

ALERT: Follow Standard Precautions.

PREPROCEDURE

1. Wash hands.

2. Assemble equipment:

   a. Antiseptic solution or soap and water or towelettes

   b. Sterile specimen container

   c. Tissues

   d. Nonsterile gloves

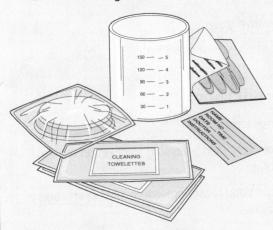

3. Identify patient.

4. Explain what you are going to do.

PROCEDURE

5. Label specimen:

   a. Patient's name

   b. Time obtained

   c. Date

6. If patient is on bedrest:

   a. Put on gloves.

   b. Lower side rail.

   c. Position bedpan under patient.

7. Have patient carefully clean perineal area if able; if not, you will be responsible for cleaning perineum:

   a. Wipe with towelette or gauze with antiseptic solution from front to back.

   b. Wipe one side and throw away wipe.

   c. Use a clean wipe for other side.

   d. Use another wipe down center.

   e. Then proceed with collecting midstream urine.

8. Explain procedure if patient can obtain own specimen.

   a. Have patient start to urinate into bedpan/toilet.

   b. Allow stream to begin.

   c. Stop stream and place specimen container to collect midstream.

   d. Remove container before bladder is empty.

9. Wipe perineum, if on bedpan.

10. Remove bedpan.

11. Rinse bedpan and put away.

12. Remove gloves and discard according to facility policy and procedure.

13. Raise side rail.

14. Secure call light in patient's reach.

15. Dispose of equipment. Never handle contaminated equipment without gloves.

POSTPROCEDURE

16. Wash hands.

17. Record specimen collection.

18. Report any unusual

    a. Color

    b. Consistency

    c. Odor

7/14/12	1300
	Clean-catch urine collected
	Urine was straw colored
	Labeled and sent to the laboratory
	R. Johnson CNA

BACKGROUND: A midstream clean-catch urine procedure provides a way to collect urine free of bacteria present at the urethral meatus at the beginning of urination, and in sediment in the urinary bladder which drains at the end of urination.

ALERT: Follow Standard Precautions.

PREPROCEDURE

1. Wash hands.

2. Assemble equipment:

   a. Antiseptic solution or soap and water or towelettes

   b. Sterile specimen container

   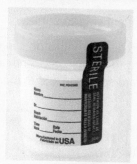

   Courtesy of ShutterStock.

   c. Tissues

   d. Disposable gloves

3. Identify patient.

PROCEDURE

4. Label specimen:

   a. Patient's name

   b. Date

   c. Time obtained

5. Explain procedure (if possible allow patient to obtain his own specimen).

   a. Put on gloves.

   b. Cleanse head of penis in a circular motion with towelette or gauze and antiseptic. (If patient is uncircumcised, have him pull back foreskin before cleaning.)

   c. Have patient start to urinate into clean bedpan, urinal, or toilet. (If he is uncircumcised, have patient pull back foreskin before urinating.)

   d. Allow stream to begin.

   e. Stop stream and place specimen container to collect midstream.

   f. Remove container before bladder is empty.

6. Dispose of equipment according to facility policy.

POSTPROCEDURE

7. Remove and discard gloves according to facility policy and procedure.

8. Make patient comfortable and put call bell within reach.

9. Wash hands.

10. Record specimen collection.

5/16/12   1300
Clean-catch urine collected
Urine was dark amber in color with
white sediment
Labeled and sent to the laboratory
———   A. Chaplin CNA

BACKGROUND: HemaCombistix detects the presence of blood in urine.

ALERT: Follow Standard Precautions.

PREPROCEDURE

1. Wash hands.

2. Assemble equipment.

   a. Bottle of HemaCombistix

   b. Nonsterile gloves

3. Identify patient.

4. Explain what you are going to do.

5. Put on gloves.

PROCEDURE

6. Secure fresh urine sample from patient.

7. Take urine and reagent to bathroom.

8. Remove cap and place on flat surface. Be sure top side of cap is down.

9. Remove strip from bottle by shaking bottle gently. *Do not touch areas of strip with fingers.*

10. Dip reagent stick in urine. Remove immediately.

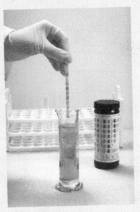

11. Tap edge of strip on container to remove excess urine.

12. Compare reagent side of test areas with color chart on bottle. Use time intervals that are given on bottle.

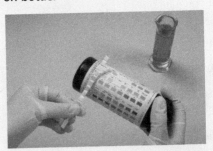

NOTE: Do not touch reagent strip to bottle.

13. Remove gloves and discard both strip and urine specimen according to facility policy and procedure. Need to discard specimen and then take off gloves.

POSTPROCEDURE

14. Replace equipment.

15. Wash hands.

16. Record results.

    a. Date and time

    b. Name of procedure used

    c. Results

10/04/11	1800
	Urine specimen tested with a
	hemacombistix
	Results negative for blood
	R. Johnson CNA

BACKGROUND: Pouring urine through a strainer allows calculi (kidney stones) to be collected.

ALERT: Follow Standard Precautions.

PREPROCEDURE

1. Wash hands.

2. Assemble equipment:

   a. Paper strainers or gauze

   b. Specimen container and label

   c. Bedpan or urinal and cover

   d. Laboratory request for analysis of specimen

   e. Sign for patient's room or bathroom explaining that all urine must be strained

   f. Nonsterile gloves

3. Identify patient.

PROCEDURE

4. Tell the patient to urinate into a urinal or bedpan and that the nurse assistant must be called to filter each specimen. Tell patient not to put paper in specimen.

5. Put on gloves.

6. Pour voided specimen through a paper strainer or gauze into a measuring container.

7. Place paper or gauze strainer into a dry specimen container if stones or particles are present after pouring urine through.

NOTE: Do not attempt to remove the particles from strainer.

8. Measure the amount voided and record on intake and output record.

9. Discard urine and container according to facility policy and procedure.

10. Clean urinal or bedpan and put away. Flush toilet and turn faucet on with a paper towel.

11. Remove gloves and discard according to facility policy and procedure.

12. Wash hands.

13. Label specimen:

    a. Patient's name

    b. Date

    c. Room number

    d. Time

14. Return patient to comfortable position.

15. Place call button within reach of patient.

16. Provide for patient safety by raising side rails when indicated or using postural supports as ordered.

POSTPROCEDURE

17. Wash hands.

18. Report collection of specimen to supervisor immediately.

19. Record specimen collection.

6/20/12	1400
	300 cc strained
	Two small stones collected
	Given to team leader
	_____ S. Gomez CNA

BACKGROUND: Stool specimens are collected most frequently to determine if blood or parasites are present in the stool.

ALERT: Follow Standard Precautions.

PREPROCEDURE

1. Wash hands.

2. Assemble equipment:

   a. Stool specimen container with label

   b. Wooden tongue depressor

   c. Disposable gloves

   d. Bedpan and cover

3. Identify patient.

4. Explain what you are going to do.

PROCEDURE

5. Be certain container is properly labeled with

   a. Patient's name

   b. Time

   c. Date

   d. Room number

6. Provide privacy by pulling privacy curtains.

7. Put on gloves.

8. Take bedpan into bathroom after patient has had bowel movement.

9. Use tongue depressor to remove about 1 to 2 tablespoons of feces from bedpan.

10. Place specimen in specimen container.

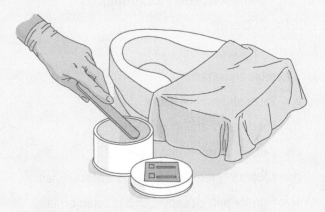

11. Cover container immediately.

12. Wrap tongue depressor in paper towel and discard as per facility rules.

13. Remove gloves and dispose of according to facility policy.

POSTPROCEDURE

14. Wash hands.

15. Follow instruction for storage of specimen for collection by lab.

16. Position patient comfortably with call bell in place.

17. Report and record procedure.

12/14/11 1000
Soft, brown stool collected,
labeled, and sent to laboratory
R. Johnson CNA

BACKGROUND: Occult blood Hematest reveals the presence of blood in a stool specimen.

ALERT: Follow Standard Precautions.

PREPROCEDURE

1. Wash hands.

2. Assemble equipment:

    a. Hematest Reagent filter paper

    b. Hematest Reagent tablet

    c. Distilled water

    d. Tongue blade

    e. Disposable gloves

3. Identify patient.

4. Explain what you are going to do.

5. Put on gloves.

PROCEDURE

6. Secure stool specimen from patient.

7. Place filter paper on glass or porcelain plate.

8. Use tongue blade to smear a thin streak of fecal material on filter paper.

9. Place Hematest Reagent tablet on smear.

10. Place 1 drop distilled water on tablet.

11. Allow 5 to 10 seconds for water to penetrate tablet.

12. Add second drop, allowing water to run down side of tablet onto filter paper and specimen.

13. Gently tap side of plate to knock water droplets from top of tablet.

14. Observe filter paper for color change (2 minutes). Positive is indicated by blue halo on paper.

15. Dispose of specimen and equipment according to your facility's policy.

16. Remove gloves and dispose of according to your facility's policy.

POSTPROCEDURE

17. Wash hands.

18. Report and record results (e.g., date, time, procedure, and results).

PROCEDURE 18.82 24-Hour Urine Test

BACKGROUND: Routine urine tests were performed as early at 1821. Analysis of the patient's urine is useful for diagnosing renal disease or metabolic disease not related to the kidneys. For some laboratory studies, 24-hour urine specimens are required.

ALERT: Follow Standard Precautions.

PREPROCEDURE

1. Determine the laboratory test and any special requirements associated with the test.

   This could include altering the dietary intake, special collection containers, adding preservatives to the designated container, icing the container, etc.

2. The nurse should determine if any drugs affect the results of this test. Obtain a history of any drugs the patient is currently taking and advise the laboratory as necessary.

3. Obtain the appropriate container to be used for urine collection. Label the container with the patient's name, hospital number, date, and time of the urine collection.

PROCEDURE

4. Explain the procedure to the patient. Provide a means for the patient to collect their urinary output, if the patient is able to participate in the procedure.

5. Post a sign that all urine is to be collected for a specified time. Assure that all staff providing care for this patient during this period of time are aware of the need to save all urine output.

6. When initiating the collection the patient will empty his bladder, and this specimen will be discarded. All urine produced after this time will be saved. At the end of the time period, the patient will again empty his bladder and this last specimen will be added to the specimen container.

7. If any urine is inadvertently discarded during the 24-hour collection, the test must be restarted.

POSTPROCEDURE

8. At the end of the test period, transport the labeled specimen to the laboratory.

Language Arts Link

Portrayal of Health Care Workers on TV

The number of TV shows about hospitals and health care professionals has increased significantly over the last several years. Many of the health care workers shown on TV appear as glamorous, hard working, and dedicated professionals.

How do you feel the depiction of health care workers on TV effects how people expect health care workers to actually be? Do the TV shows help or hurt the image of the health care professional?

Create a new document on the computer, or get a blank sheet of paper. In paragraph form, write how you feel about the portrayal of health care workers on TV. Include a title for your report and a thesis statement (a sentence stating your main ideas) in the opening paragraph.

Check the spelling and grammar and correct any errors. Be sure to cite any sources that you use in the format required by your teacher. Exchange reports with a classmate. Provide feedback and corrections as necessary, and then exchange back. Read your classmate's comments and revise your report as necessary.

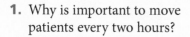

SECTION 18.3   Review Questions

1. Why is important to move patients every two hours?

2. List five ways to prevent pressure sores/decubiti.

3. Why is bathing a patient important?

4. Why is hair and nail care important?

5. List the five common urine specimen collection procedures.

6. What is the formula for converting ounces to cubic centimeters?

7. Under what conditions might you use restraints on a patient?

Community Service

At the completion of the chapter, assist at a health care clinic or assist the school nurse with taking and recording vital signs under direct supervision of a health care professional.

 ## *Learn By Doing: Section 18.3 Activity*

1. Complete Worksheets 1 and 2.

2. Complete Worksheets/Activities 3 through 5.

3. Complete Worksheets 6 through 8 and 12 through 15 as assigned.

4. Complete Worksheets/Activities 9 through 11 as assigned.

5. Prepare response to each item listed in Chapter Review.

6. When you are confident that you can meet each objective for this section, ask your teacher for the section evaluation.

Chapter 18 Review

Chapter Review Questions

1. List three factors that may increase body temperature and three factors that may decrease body temperature. (18.1)

2. Where on the body is the most accurate temperature reading taken? Under what conditions is a patient's temperature taken at this site? (18.1)

3. At what site on the body is the apical pulse counted? What instrument is used to count an apical pulse? (18.1)

4. Name three factors that may cause a decreased pulse rate. (18.1)

5. What does a pulse oximeter measure? (18.1)

6. Vital signs are recorded in this order: TPR. Why is it important that you record vital signs in this order? (18.1)

7. Blood pressure depends on three factors. Name these three factors. (18.2)

8. Name five factors that can decrease blood pressure. (18.2)

9. What is a sphygmomanometer? (18.2)

10. What is hypotension? (18.2)

11. List ten responsibilities of a nurse or nurse assistant. (18.3)

12. Why is it important to encourage patients to walk? (18.3)

13. List three examples of when postural supports or restraints should be used. (18.3)

14. List the steps for preparing a patient for a meal. (18.3)

15. Compare the symptoms of dehydration and edema. (18.3)

16. List three causes of incontinence. (18.3)

Activities

1. Find your radial pulse on both arms. Record the number of beats per minute (bpm). Then do the same for two other sites, such as the carotid, brachial, or popliteal sites. Are the results the same in all locations?

2. Ask five people of various ages if you can practice counting their pulse and respiration. Prepare a chart similar to the one shown here. Fill in the information and submit the completed chart to your teacher.

Person	Age	Pulse	Pulse Characteristics	Respiratory Rate	Respiration Characteristics
1					
2					
3					
4					
5					

Case Studies

1. You are assigned a patient and you need to take vital signs. Mr. Marks is an elderly man and seems very agitated and upset. You know that his agitation affects his vital signs. What verbal and nonverbal communication skills can you use to reduce his anxiety? Write a brief description of how to help Mr. Marks relax so that you can take accurate vital signs.

2. Mr. Ames is on oxygen and cannot breathe comfortably when you remove his oxygen mask. It is time to take his vital signs. He has a severe infection, and an accurate temperature reading is extremely important. What is the correct location for taking his temperature? Explain why. What information is appropriate to give Mr. Ames before you take his temperature?

Thinking Critically

1. **Medical Terminology**—Define the following medical terms and explain why they are important when taking vital signs: arrhythmia, aural, axillary, Celsius, diastolic pressure, homeostasis, hypertension, pyrexia, systolic pressure, thready.

2. **Safety Alert**—Never forget the safety aspects of procedures. For example, when using a glass thermometer, caution the patient not to bite down. Brainstorm with classmates on other safety alerts you should give.

3. **Patient Education**—Write a short script for what you would say to a patient as you begin a blood pressure reading. Remember that many patients become frightened of the mounting pressure on their arm.

Media Connection

Use the Companion Web site for additional interactive learning activities: www.prenhall.com/badasch

Portfolio Connection

As a health care worker, you are expected to observe patients for their state of health. You are obligated to report any unusual or abnormal signs or symptoms. Answer the following questions in report form. This report will demonstrate your evaluating, observing, and reporting skills.

Your patient has an elevated blood pressure of 210/140. Does this blood pressure cause concern? What is the medical term for this blood pressure? What are the possible causes of an elevated blood pressure? What can you observe about the patient that is important in your report to your supervisor? Should you report this blood pressure immediately or wait until you report at the end of your day? What are the key things that you must report? Follow your teacher's instructions on saving this report in your portfolio.

PORTFOLIO TIP

Taking a temperature is a vital procedure, but to many patients it seems a nuisance. Try to explain to the patient as you start the process what a change in temperature will tell the health care staff and how checking it will keep recovery on track.

19 Therapeutic Techniques and Sports Medicine

SECTIONS

19.1 Therapeutic Techniques and Sports Medicine

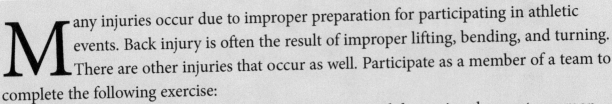

Many injuries occur due to improper preparation for participating in athletic events. Back injury is often the result of improper lifting, bending, and turning. There are other injuries that occur as well. Participate as a member of a team to complete the following exercise:

- Select three different individual or team sports and determine the most common injuries for each and the percentage of athletes that sustain each injury.
- Prepare a comparison chart or graph that displays your findings.
- Display your completed chart/graph in the classroom.

SECTION

19.1 Therapeutic Techniques and Sports Medicine

Background

Physical therapy, sometimes known as physiotherapy, is a medical treatment of injuries or disorders using methods such as exercise, massage, or the application of water, light, or heat. Physical therapy helps condition muscles. It also restores strength and movement when people are injured, recovering from surgery, or have a physical disability such as cerebral palsy. That way, they can learn or relearn to do normal things such as walk, get out of bed, or throw a ball. A physical therapist also can prescribe splints, canes, special shoes, and other assistive devices.

Objectives

When you have completed this section, you will be able to do the following:

- Describe the responsibilities of a physical therapy aide.
- Describe the responsibilities of a sports medicine aide.
- Define ultraviolet light and name four conditions treated with ultraviolet light.
- Describe four conditions treated with diathermy.
- List three conditions commonly treated by ultrasound.

- Document the most important question to ask a patient when preparing for an ultrasound treatment.
- Identify two kinds of thermotherapy and the conditions they treat.
- Identify two ways to give cryotherapy and conditions they treat.
- Define *hydrotherapy* and list three reasons hydrotherapy is used.
- Explain the purpose of range of motion.

- Define *guarding technique* and *guarding belt*.
- List five commonly used ambulation devices.
- List two transporting devices commonly used.
- Demonstrate range of motion.
- Demonstrate each procedure in this chapter.

The Physical Therapy Department

The physical therapy department is made up of a number of trained people who work as a team to assist and direct patients in the rehabilitation process. Their main goal is to reduce pain, prevent deformity, and promote healing. They also attempt to restore function or assist patients by teaching them new ways to adjust to their disabilities.

The entry-level job title for this department is "physical therapy aide." A "sports medicine aide" is a physical therapy aide who specializes in treating athletes and participants in sports. Physical therapy workers may be employed in the following facilities and agencies:

- Acute care facilities.
- Long-term care facilities.
- Rehabilitation centers.
- Schools that educate disabled persons.
- Public health agencies.
- Home health-care agencies.
- Sports medicine centers.
- Professional or school sports teams.

Responsibilities of a Physical Therapy Aide

As a physical therapy aide, you are required to do the following tasks:

- Prepare equipment (e.g., **hydrotherapy** pools).
- Assist patients:
  - With walking and gait training.
  - To dress and undress.
  - To position themselves.
  - To remove and replace braces, splints, and slings.
- Change linens on beds and tables.
- Fold linens.
- Clean equipment and work area.
- May inventory materials and supplies.

hydrotherapy
(hahy druh THER uh pee)
The use of water (hot, cold, steam, or ice) to relieve discomfort and promote physical well-being.

Sports Medicine Aide/Athletic Trainer

One subspecialty of working as a physical therapy aide is working as a sports medicine aide. Sports medicine is one of the fastest growing fields in medicine. It includes working with professional sports teams, high school and college athletes, and individuals with sports-related injuries. Sports medicine aides perform the duties of physical therapy aides but deal with the practical aspects of sports injury prevention, recognition, and treatment of sports-related injuries.

Responsibilities of a Sports Medicine Aide/Athletic Trainer

As a sports medicine aide, you may be required to do the following tasks:

- Perform all the duties of a physical therapy aide.
- Prepare equipment (e.g., massage tables).
- Assist in injury treatments, evaluations, and rehabilitation of athletes.
- Assist or perform taping, wrapping, protective bracing, and equipment fitting.
- Help out in pre-practice preparations and post-practice follow-up.
- Be on hand to assist in event coverage.

Massage Therapy Techniques in Sports Medicine

Massage therapy plays an important role in sports medicine. Massage is the practice of manipulating the soft tissues of the human body in order to prevent injury, or aid in the recovery from injury. There are more than two hundred varieties of massage.

Some practitioners use several different techniques such as stroking, kneading, tapping, compression, friction, and pressure. Oils, lotions, and powders may also be included to reduce friction on the skin. In professional settings, the patient is treated while lying on a massage table, lying on a pad on the floor, or sitting upright in a massage chair.

The benefits of massage are an accepted part of many physical rehabilitation programs, especially in sports medicine. Massage therapy is helpful for several chronic conditions including lower back pain, arthritis, bursitis, and fatigue. In sports medicine, massage helps prevent injury and restores mobility to injured muscle tissue.

Massage therapists can only massage. They are not allowed to diagnose, prescribe, manipulate, or adjust the human skeletal structure. You need a specific state license in order to practice branches of medicine such as orthopedics, physical therapy, podiatry, chiropractic, osteopathy, psychotherapy, or acupuncture.

Preparing Patients for Therapy

As an aide in the physical therapy department, you assist the therapist and prepare:

- The patient.
- Supplies.
- Equipment.

There are various types of therapy, and each requires a slightly different preparation. Some of the most common types of therapy are discussed next.

Personal Wellness

Overuse Injuries

One of the leading problems requiring physical therapy is overuse injuries, also known as cumulative trauma disorders. These are particularly common among participants in sports. Certain ailments are simply known as "tennis elbow," "golfer's elbow," and "runner's knee." However, overuse injuries are common in many fields; musicians get tendonitis, dancers sustain stress fractures, and people who work with computers develop carpal tunnel syndrome.

The term "overuse injury" refers to many different diagnoses, and there is no clear medical definition. Nonetheless, a sports medicine aide certainly will see numerous examples of the disorder.

An overuse injury occurs when any biological tissue, such as muscle, bone, ligament, or tendon, is stressed beyond its physical limit. Tissues are able to adapt to the stresses placed on them over time.

However, overuse injuries develop when repeated physical challenges are followed by insufficient recovery time. As the tissues attempt to adapt to the demands placed on them, they can become injured unless they have enough time to heal. These injuries are usually microscopic tears that lead to small amounts of bleeding and swelling in the injured area.

Overuse injuries can occur suddenly from one hard training session or become progressively worse over a long period. It is impossible to estimate the precise number of overuse injuries in the United States. However, one study showed that about two-thirds of runners develop injuries every year.

Athletes with repetitive stress injuries do not always seek medical attention because they are afraid the doctor will advise them to give up their sport temporarily or permanently. Instead, they try to avoid pain in training by changing their body mechanics. This usually does even more damage. Eventually, the injury gets so bad that the pain is unavoidable. By the time the athlete does seek help, there are usually multiple problems that need rehabilitation.

The simplest way to avoid an overuse injury is to allow for sufficient recovery time between workouts or stress. This is not always easy. Data entry clerks cannot simply decide to skip work. Psychological factors might keep athletes from scheduling rest days in their workout schedule. However, it is important to remind patients of something that they have probably already learned—overuse injuries are much easier to prevent than to cure.

ultraviolet light
(uhl truh VAHY uh lit lahyt)
An invisible band of radiation at the upper end of the visible light spectrum.

Ultraviolet-light therapy is used to treat various diseases, especially those of the skin. It is used to treat the following:

- Acne.
- Pressure sores.
- Psoriasis.
- Wound infections.

This treatment can cause severe burning. For this reason, the patient cannot be left unobserved in the room during a treatment.

CAUTION: Do not turn on the light before the therapist is ready to start the treatment.

diathermy
(DAHY uh thur mee)
The use of electric currents to produce heat in body tissues, usually as an aid to healing.

Diathermy is a heat-inducing treatment that increases the circulation in the treated area. It is often used to treat the following:

- Muscle problems.
- Arthritis.
- Bursitis.
- Tendonitis.

Metal attracts heat during this procedure, so it is your responsibility to do the following:

- Have the patient remove all metal jewelry, belts, hairpins, and so on.
- Ask the patient if they have any metal implants in joints or in other parts of the body. If they do, report it to the therapist right away.

ultrasound
(UHL truh sound)
Medical therapy that uses sound frequencies (above 20 kHz) beyond the limits of human hearing to treat hard-to-reach body areas.

Ultrasound uses high-frequency sound waves to penetrate deep tissues. It is most commonly used to treat:

- Pain.
- Muscle spasms.
- Problems in circulation.

Ultrasound is also used to diagnose specific conditions. However, physical therapy uses ultrasounds only in a therapeutic mode. Because ultrasound vibrates tissues, caution has to be taken with patients with joint implants. Always ask patients during the preparation if they have any joint implants. If so, report it to the therapist.

thermotherapy
(thur moh THER uh pee)
Medical therapy involving the application of heat.

Thermotherapy refers to heat treatments. Heat is used to speed up the healing process. Heat causes the blood vessels to expand (dilate). This allows more blood to circulate to the area and helps the healing process. The blood brings oxygen and food needed for healing. If the area is swollen and/or inflamed, the blood helps absorb and carry away the extra fluid. This type of treatment is used to do the following:

- Relieve pain.
- Promote muscle relaxation.
- Reduce muscle spasms.

- Reduce inflammation.
- Treat skin ulcers.
- Treat perineal lacerations.
- Reduce swelling.
- Promote drainage.

There are two kinds of thermotherapy. One type is *moist heat*. The other type is *dry heat*. Moist heat is applied with the following:

- Hot soaks.
- Hot compresses.
- Hot packs.

Dry heat is applied with:

- Heat lamps.
- Infrared lights.
- Standard electric bulbs.
- Heating pads.

 ## Science Link

Ultraviolet Light

Ultraviolet (UV) light is an invisible band of radiation at the upper end of the visible light spectrum. The name means "beyond violet" (from the Latin word *ultra* meaning "beyond") because violet has the shortest wavelengths of visible light. UV rays were first identified in 1801 by Johann Wilhelm Ritter, a German physicist. UV rays have wavelengths from 10 to 400 nm. In the light spectrum, they begin at the end of visible light and end at the beginning of x-rays.

The main source of ultraviolet light is the sun. Sunlight contains two main types of ultraviolet light: UVA and UVB. UVA rays have longer wavelengths that penetrate deep into the skin. Limited exposure to UVA rays causes the skin to tan. The wavelengths of UVB rays are much shorter and affect the outermost layers of skin. UVB rays cause sunburn and are sometimes known as the "burning rays."

Ultraviolet light has been used as a medical treatment since the early 1900s. A so-called "sunlamp" can produce UV rays artificially. The rays can be used to help people generate vitamin D in their bodies. Vitamin D helps prevent rickets and various bone disorder conditions.

Ultraviolet light is also useful as a disinfectant. UV rays can kill bacteria and so they are sometimes used to sterilize the air in operating rooms. They can also be used to treat skin disease, such as psoriasis, and seasonal affective disorder (SAD).

CAUTION: Prolonged exposure to UV radiation can result in acute and chronic health effects on the eyes, skin, and immune system.

Example 1

What is a suntan? What does sunscreen do? What is an SPF number? Use an encyclopedia or the Internet and write a brief report on the nature of tanning and skin protection. Make sure you discuss ultraviolet rays in your report.

Example 2

Use the Internet to examine the use of ultraviolet light in tanning beds and sun lamps. List two arguments supporting and two arguments disputing the safety of artificial tanning. Cite your sources so the reader can judge if they are reliable.

Explain the difference between UVA and UVB. Which do you think is more dangerous?

BACKGROUND: You can prevent injury by using the correct temperature for the hot moist pads. Make sure you carefully observe the treated area to watch for irritation or excessive redness.

ALERT: Follow Standard Precautions.

PREPROCEDURE

1. Check physician's orders.

2. Wash hands.

3. Assemble equipment:

   a. **Hydroculator pad**

   b. Towel

4. Identify patient.

5. Explain what you will be doing and reassure patient that procedure is painless.

6. Provide privacy.

7. Cover warm hydroculator pad with towel.

8. Expose site to be treated.

9. Position patient for comfort.

PROCEDURE

10. Apply covered warm hydroculator pad to appropriate site. (Never put warm hydroculator pad directly on the skin, unless it is covered.)

11. Make sure call bell is in reach.

12. Wash hands.

13. Recheck patient frequently—every 5 minutes when heating device is on skin. Look for:

    a. Severely reddened areas

    b. Irritated areas

    c. Painful areas

14. Remove soaks as ordered.

POSTPROCEDURE

15. Position patient for comfort and make sure call bell is in reach.

16. Wash hands.

17. Report and record patient's tolerance of treatment and any changes in condition you observed.

hydroculator pad
(HI droc u la tor pad)
A moist heat pack treatment.

You need to prepare hot packs so that they are ready when needed. Always check the skin for signs of extreme redness or burning. If a patient complains of discomfort, remove the packs immediately.

Cryotherapy means cold therapy. Cold therapy causes the blood vessels to get smaller (contract). This slows the flow of blood to the area. This reduces the amount of fluid and helps reduce pain. Cold application is used to:

- Relieve pain.
- Reduce body temperature.
- Control bleeding.
- Reduce inflammation.
- Prevent edema.

Cryotherapy can be given in two ways: dry cold and moist cold. *Dry cold* includes the use of:

- Ice bags.
- Ice collars.

Moist cold includes the use of:

- Cold compresses.
- Cold packs.
- Ice massage.

Prepare cold packs for cryotherapy (cold, moist, or dry treatments) so that they are ready when needed. Always check the skin for signs of whiteness (blanching) or bluishness. If these occur, stop the treatment immediately.

What's New?

Acupuncture

Acupuncture certainly is not new. The practice of inserting needles in the human body to ease pain and aid recovery is at least 2,500 years old. What is new is acupuncture's increasing acceptance in mainstream medicine.

Not so long ago, Americans viewed acupuncture as a strange therapy, not unlike voodoo. Now, it is increasingly recognized as an effective treatment for some disorders and a common accompaniment to physical therapy, a massage, or a trip to the orthopedist.

The World Health Organization (WHO) recommends acupuncture as an effective treatment for more than 40 medical problems. In the United States, more than 2 million people use acupuncture each year, and an estimated 8.2 million adults have used it as a therapy.

Acupuncture involves the insertion and manipulation of sharp, thin needles in the body at very specific points. This process is believed to adjust and alter the body's energy flow (which the Chinese call "chi") into healthier patterns. Scientists are still studying how effective acupuncture is and why it works.

However, the U.S. National Institutes of Health now states that, "promising results have emerged, showing efficacy of acupuncture, for example, in adult postoperative and chemotherapy nausea and vomiting . . . . There are other situations—such as . . . stroke rehabilitation . . . tennis elbow . . . osteoarthritis, low-back pain, carpal tunnel syndrome, and asthma—in which acupuncture may be useful as an adjunct treatment or an acceptable alternative . . . . "

For example, knee osteoarthritis is a common condition seen by physical therapists in which changes in the knee joints lead to pain. Treatments include physical therapy, exercise, and drugs to decrease pain and inflammation.

Recently, a study showed that acupuncture provided pain relief for people with knee osteoarthritis and would serve as an effective complement to standard care. As a physical therapy aide, you might soon find yourself making sure acupuncture needles are sterile and setting up disinfectants for acupuncture treatments.

Why do you think the U.S. medical establishment was reluctant to recognize acupuncture as a possible medical treatment therapy?

BACKGROUND: You can prevent injury by using the correct temperature for moist cryotherapy. Make sure you carefully observe the treated area to watch for any pain or irregularities. Using correct temperature for moist cryotherapy and careful observation of the treated area prevents injury.

ALERT: Follow Standard Precautions.

PREPROCEDURE

1. Check doctor's orders.

2. Wash hands.

3. Assemble equipment:

   a. Cool, wet cloth

   b. Plastic cover

   c. Dry towel

PROCEDURE

4. Explain procedure to client/patient.

5. Apply cool, wet cloth to patient as ordered.*

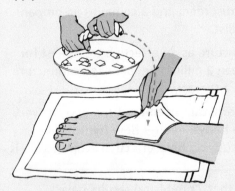

6. Cover wet area with plastic cover.

7. Cover plastic with dry towel.

* Wear gloves if there are broken areas on the skin.

8. Wash hands.

9. Recheck frequently for:

   a. Coolness of cloth

   b. Position

   c. Patient's comfort needs (reapply PRN)

10. Remove as ordered.

POSTPROCEDURE

11. Dry skin.

12. Dispose of supplies and clean area.

13. Wash hands.

14. Report and document effects of treatment.

11/20/11	1100
	No skin reddened or irritated areas
	Moist, cold towels applied times 15
	minutes
	Recheck skin at site
	No reddened or irritated areas
	Patient states: Pain is better
	after treatment but returns in
	about an hour
	_____ A. Cantina student

BACKGROUND: Using the correct temperature for dry cryotherapy and careful observation of the treated area prevents injury.

ALERT: Follow Standard Precautions.

PREPROCEDURE

1. Check physician's orders.

2. Wash hands.

3. Assemble equipment:

   a. Ice bag or commercial cold compress

   b. Ice

   c. Cover for ice bag

4. Fill bag with ice. (Run water over cubes to soften sharp edges.)

5. Remove air from bag by pressing sides together.

6. Close end and check for leaks.

7. Cover bag with cloth or towel. (Never apply bag directly to skin; it may stick, burn, and tear skin when removed.)

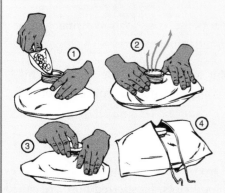

8. Identify patient by checking order and name with patient's armband or patient chart.

PROCEDURE

9. Explain procedure to patient.

10. Gently position ice bag as ordered. (The metal cap cannot touch the skin.)*

* Wear gloves if there are broken areas on the skin.

11. Secure bag so that it does not move away from affected area.

12. Provide needed comfort measures for patient. Make sure call bell is in reach.

13. Wash hands.

14. Return frequently to check for:

    a. Coolness of ice bag

    b. Position of ice bag

    c. Color of skin (remove ice if skin is white or bluish in color or if patient reports numbness and report)

15. Remove ice bag at ordered time.

16. Make sure patient is comfortable and call bell is in reach.

POSTPROCEDURE

17. Wash hands.

18. Recheck skin, and report and document effects of treatment.

19. Wash hands.

20. Empty bag, dry, and return to appropriate area for cleaning.

11/20/11	1100
	No skin reddened or irritated areas Dry
	cold compress applied times 15 minutes
	Recheck skin at site
	No reddened or irritated areas
	Patient states: Pain is better after
	treatment but returns in about an hour
	_____ *A. Cantina student*

Hydrotherapy is water therapy. Hydrotherapy is usually given in a whirlpool. The whole body may be treated or just a limb. This treatment is used to:

- Apply soothing medication
- Promote relaxation
- Improve circulation and mobility of an injured limb
- Loosen and remove dead skin

This treatment is accomplished in various-sized tubs ranging from small basins to a swimming pool. Your responsibility is to:

- Assist the patient in disrobing or exposing the area to be treated.
- Ensure that the water temperature is correct (95° F to 105° F).
- Secure the patient to ensure there is no danger of injury.
- Disinfect and clean the equipment.
- Assist the patient when large areas of the body are to be submerged.
- Clean the tub after each treatment.

Range of Motion

Range-of-motion (ROM) exercises are very important for the resident who has limited movement. ROM exercises are given to:

- Stimulate circulation to decrease chance of blood clots or decubitus ulcers.
- Encourage **flexibility** and mobility of the joints.
- Prevent contractures (permanent **contraction** of the muscle).
- Prevent mineral loss.
- Prevent other problems such as poor appetite, constipation, urinary infections, respiratory problems, and hypostatic pneumonia.

Residents are encouraged to move each joint to the best of their ability. This is active ROM. When you do passive ROM for your residents, you move the joints for them.

Antiembolism Hose

Antiembolism hose are used to prevent blood from pooling in the legs. This reduces the possibility of developing phlebitis and blood clots. Elasticized hose are called TEDS or antiembolism hose. Sometimes elastic bandages are used. These extend from the ankle or foot to calf or midthigh. They are applied after surgery and when there is danger of a clot forming and causing thrombophlebitis. They must be applied so that they are smooth and even and do not cut off the circulation. Be certain to remove them and reapply them at least once every 8 hours.

range-of-motion (ROM)
(reynj uhv MOH shuhn)
Measurement of the achievable distance between the flexed position and the extended position of a particular joint or muscle group.

flexibility
(FLEK suh buhl itee)
The ability to easily bend.

contraction
(kuh n TRAK shuhn)
One that occurs when a muscle fiber lengthens or shortens.

BACKGROUND: Correct ROM provides exercise to the joints and muscles, preventing contractures and immobility.

NOTE: The use of passive and active range of motion (ROM) is related to resident's ability level.

- **Active ROM**—Resident is able to perform all movements without assistance.
- **Passive ROM**—Health care worker moves body parts for resident.

ALERT: Follow Standard Precautions.

PREPROCEDURE

1. Wash hands.
2. Assemble equipment:
   a. Sheet or bath blanket
   b. Treatment table or bed
   c. Good lighting
3. Identify resident.
4. Explain what you are going to do.
5. Ask visitors to wait outside, and provide privacy.

PROCEDURE

6. Place resident in a supine position on bed or treatment table and cover with sheet or bath blanket. Only expose affected area. Instruct resident to do the following movements at least five times each or to tolerance.

Head Flexion and Extension

7. Bend head until chin touches chest (flexion), then gently bend backward (extension).

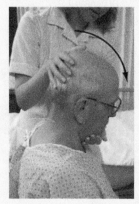 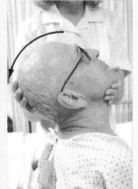

Right/Left Rotation

8. Turn head to right (right rotation), then turn head to left (left rotation).

Right/Left Lateral Flexion

9. Move head so that right ear moves toward right shoulder (right lateral flexion), then move head to central position and continue moving head so that left ear moves toward left shoulder (left lateral flexion).

(continued)

Hyperextension and Extension

10. Place the pillow under the shoulders and gently support the head in a backward tilt and return to straight position. Readjust pillow under head when finished.

Shoulder Flexion and Extension

11. Raise one arm overhead keeping elbow straight. Return to side position. Repeat with other arm.

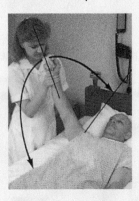

12. With the shoulder in abduction, flex the elbow and raise the entire arm over the head.

Shoulder Abduction and Adduction

13. Raise arm overhead, then lower, keep arm out to side. Repeat with other arm.

14. With the shoulder in abduction, flex the elbow and raise the arm over the head.

Internal and External Rotation of Shoulder

15. Roll entire arm toward body and away.

Elbow Flexion and Extension

16. Bend one hand and forearm toward shoulder (flexion) and straighten (extension). Repeat with other arm.

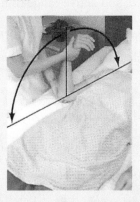

Forearm Pronation and Supination

17. Bend arm at elbow and rotate hand toward body (pronation), then rotate away from body (supination). Repeat with other arm.

Wrist Flexion and Extension

18. Bend hand at wrist toward shoulder (flex), then gently force backward past a level position with arm (extension) to below arm level (hyperextension). Repeat with other hand.

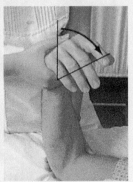

(continued)

Ulnar and Radial Deviation

19. Holding hand straight, move toward thumb (radial deviation), then move hand toward little finger (ulnar deviation). Repeat with other hand.

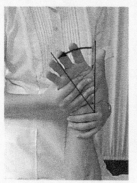 

Finger Flexion and Extension

20. Bend thumb and fingers into hand making a fist (flexion), then open hand by straightening fingers and thumb (extension). Repeat with other hand.

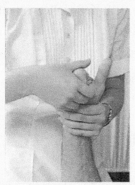 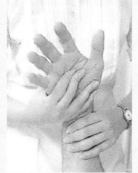

21. Move thumb away from hand (abduct), then toward hand (adduct). Repeat with other hand.

Finger/Thumb Opposition

22. Move thumb toward little finger, touch tips. Touch tip of thumb to each finger. Open hand each time. Repeat with other hand.

Finger Adduction and Abduction

23. Keeping fingers straight, separate them (abduction), then bring them together (adduction). Repeat with other hand.

 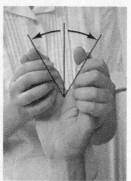

Hip/Knee Flexion and Extension

24. Raise leg, bend knee, then return to bed straightening knee. Repeat with other leg.

Straight Leg Raising

25. Keep knee straight. Slowly raise and lower leg. Repeat with other leg.

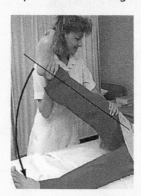

(continued)

Hip Abduction and Adduction

26. Supporting the knee and ankle, separate legs (abduction), then bring back together (adduction). Then turn both legs so knees face outward. Turn legs so knees face inward.

Lateral and Medial Hip Rotation

27. Roll leg in a circular fashion away from body and then toward body.

28. Rotate one foot toward other foot (internal rotation), then rotate away from other foot (external rotation). Repeat with other foot.

Ankle Dorsiflexion and Plantar Flexion

29. Grasp toes while supporting ankle. Move foot so that toes move toward knee (dorsi flexion), then move foot so that toes point away from head (plantar flexion). Repeat with other foot.

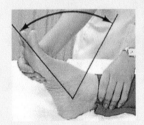

Toe Flexion and Extension

30. Spread toes apart (abduction) on one foot, then bring toes together (adduction). Repeat on other foot.

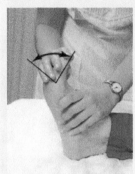 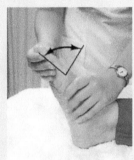

31. Turn resident in a prone position.

Arm Abduction and Adduction

32. Move arm toward ceiling; do not bend elbows (hyperextension), then return to bed. Repeat with other arm.

Leg Flexion and Extension

33. Bend leg so that foot moves toward resident's back (flexion), then straighten leg (extension). Repeat with other leg.

34. Position resident for comfort.

POSTPROCEDURE

35. Place bath blanket or sheet in laundry basket.

36. Wash your hands.

37. Report and document resident's tolerance of procedure.

12/06/11	1510
	Passive ROM to all joints
	Complained of some discomfort
	in left elbow
	Noted some increased stiffness
	in fingers of the right hand
	Reported to charge nurse
	ROM tolerated well
	_____ S. Gomez CNA

BACKGROUND: Tape and elastic bandages are used to provide support and strength for a joint such as the ankle, elbow, wrist, or shoulder. Tape may be used for support in an athletic setting but caution must be used to avoid constriction of the circulatory system or worsening of any swelling that might be present in an injured joint.

The bandage is a continuous strip of elasticized material that is wound on itself to form a cylinder or roll. The common name used for these bandages is **Ace**. These bandages vary in width from 1 to 6 inches.

ALERT: Follow Standard Precautions.

PREPROCEDURE

1. Identify the patient and joint which requires the use of a supportive bandage. Check the physician's order for any special instructions. Gather the appropriate bandage.

2. Wash hands. Put on gloves.

3. Explain the procedure to the patient. Assist the patient to a comfortable position that provides easy access to the affected joint.

PROCEDURE

4. Remove any old bandage and discard. If the bandage is to be reused, it may be unwound by keeping the loose end together and passing it as a ball from one hand to the other while unwinding it. Assess the joint for mobility and pain.

5. Clean the area before reapplying bandage. Make sure skin is dry before re-wrapping.

6. To begin, the free end of the bandage roll is held in place with one hand while the other hand passes the roll around the top middle of the ankle and then around the back of the Achilles tendon. After the bandage is anchored, the roll is passed or tolled around the ankle.

7. After the bandage is anchored, the roll is passed or rolled under the foot and back up the outside of the ankle, taking care to exert equal tension in all turns. There should be even overlapping of one-half to two-thirds the width of each bandage, except for the circular turn.

8. The figure-of-eight turn is most effective for use around joints such as the ankle. The figure-of-eight turns consists of making oblique overlapping turns that ascend and descend alternatively.

POSTPROCEDURE

9. Assure that the patient is comfortable and has no other needs before leaving the area.

10. Wash hands.

11. Document the appearance of the joint, any discomfort present and the application of the new bandage.

BACKGROUND: Elastic hose help prevent blood from pooling in the legs, thus reducing the possibility of developing phlebitis.

ALERT: Follow Standard Precautions as needed.

PREPROCEDURE

1. Wash hands.

2. Select elastic hose. Check to be sure that they are the correct size and length.

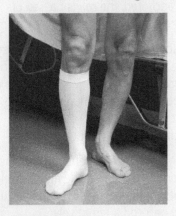

3. Identify resident and explain procedure to patient.

4. Provide for patient's privacy.

5. Have resident lie down; expose one leg at a time.

PROCEDURE

6. Hold the hose with both hands at top and roll toward toe end. Turn stockings inside-out, at least to heel area.

7. Place hose over toes, positioning opening at base of toes unless toes are to be covered. The raised seams should be on outside.

8. Pull top of stocking over foot, heel, and leg. Move patient's foot and leg gently and naturally. Avoid forcing and overextending limbs and joints.

9. Check to be sure that the stocking is applied evenly and smoothly. There must be no wrinkles.

10. Repeat on opposite leg.

POSTPROCEDURE

11. Make patient comfortable, lower bed and raise side rails. Make sure call bell is within reach of patient.

12. Wash hands.

13. Record the following in the medical record:

    a. Date and time applied

    b. Any skin changes, temperature change, or swelling

14. Remove and reapply at least once every 8 hours, or more often if necessary.

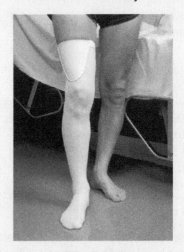

Guarding Techniques

Use **guarding techniques** when moving patients from place to place. These techniques protect the patient while transferring a patient from the bed to a **gurney** or chair, chair to a chair, chair to a toilet, or commode and back again. You use a variety of techniques to transfer the patient:

- **Pivot technique.** (**Figure 19.1**) You generally use this technique when moving a patient who can bear weight on at least one foot. It works best when moving from a bed or chair to a chair, toilet, or commode and back again. Normally this technique involves one person, using a transfer belt to help the patient.

- **Sliding technique.** You use sliding when a patient needs to be moved and cannot get up or bear weight on either foot. It works best when moving from bed to gurney, chair, commode, or toilet and back again. Paraplegic and quadriplegic patients may use a flat boardlike device to slide on. This provides security and decreases the chance of separation between chairs and bed and so on.

  Slide boards/transfer boards should be used when transferring between equal height surfaces. Slide boards should also be used to facilitate transfer to a wheelchair and for a patient with excessive weakness in their lower limbs.

- **Lifting technique.** (**Figure 19.2**) Use this technique when there is ample help and strength to support the patient fully while moving him or her from one support to another. Make sure you keep your back straight, avoid twisting, stay close to the patient and keep a smooth flow of action (no jerking motions).

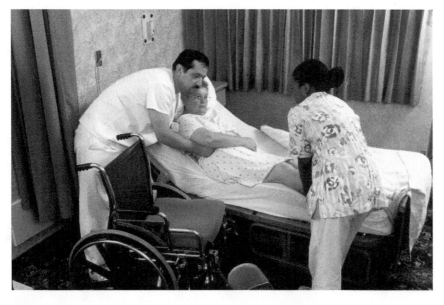

Figure 19.1
Transferring a patient from a bed to a wheelchair using the pivot technique. Why would you use the pivot technique?

You also use guarding techniques when the patient is ambulating. All patients who can support themselves are encouraged to walk alone or with the assistance of another person. Patients who are uncomfortable usually resist having to move. Your encouragement is needed to keep their body functions as normal as possible. There are a variety of techniques you may use:

Figure 19.2
Lifting technique. When would you use the lifting technique?

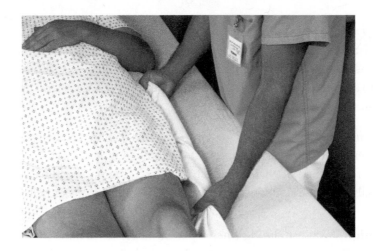

Apply It

Set up a "team" of health care advisors to work with a "mock" soccer team. As each soccer player complains of a specific problem, develop a potential diagnosis and treatment plan.

- A guarding belt (walking or gait belt) (**Figure 19.3**) supports and helps the patient feel secure. You may support the patient by placing one hand on the side of the gait belt and the other hand behind the patient holding onto the belt.

- Some patients may need to hold on to you. Just your hand may be enough to steady them in those first few steps after a lengthy stay in bed.

- Some patients may require two people to assist them. One person on each side of the patient should hold each arm and hold the person securely around the waist.

- Walking next to a rail is helpful. Patients often feel insecure when they are dependent on another person for support. A solid railing provides the extra security they need.

Safety is very important at all times. The patient may lose his or her balance, feel faint, or the legs can collapse. If the patient falls, prevent injury by helping the resident to the floor. Protect yourself from injury by using good body mechanics. Stay with the patient and call for help. A licensed nurse should evaluate the patient before moving him or her. Ask for help when lifting a patient from the floor.

Figure 19.3
Health care worker using a gait belt on a patient to ease a fall. What is the proper way to use a gait belt?

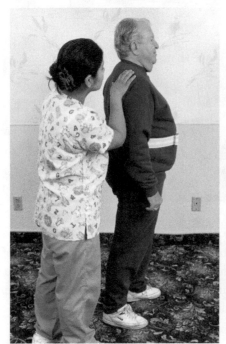
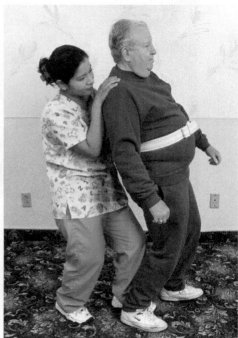

PROCEDURE 19.7 — Ambulating with a Gait Belt

BACKGROUND: Using a **gait belt** protects the patient from falling when ambulating. It ensures the safety and security of the patient. Gait belts also decrease caregiver injuries and enable the caregiver to assist heavy patients they would not be able to assist otherwise.

NOTE: Caregivers are sometimes seen assisting a patient by holding them at the axillary area and without a gait belt. This type of assistance could result in the subluxation of the shoulder joint. If a patient cannot ambulate independently a gait belt should always be used.

ALERT: Follow Standard Precautions.

PREPROCEDURE

1. Wash hands.

2. Assemble equipment:

   a. Gait belt/walking belt (correct size)

   b. Patient's robe

   c. Patient's footwear

3. Identify patient.

4. Explain what you are going to do.

5. Provide for privacy and lower side rail.

6. Assist patient to sitting position on side of bed.

7. Encourage patient to take a few deep breaths and ask if he or she feels dizzy. (If dizziness is present, let the patient sit a while before walking.)

8. Assist patient with robe and slippers.

9. Secure gait belt around patient's waist over clothing.

10. Tighten belt and buckle securely. Position buckle/clasp slightly off center. Check to see if patient can breathe easily and that breasts are above the belt.*

PROCEDURE

11. Stand in front of patient with broad base of support.

12. Instruct patient to put hands on your shoulder. Position yourself to ensure the safety of both yourself and the patient during transfer (e.g., knees bent, feet apart, back straight). Place hands under side of belt. Give signal for patient to stand.

13. Ease patient to a standing position and hold handgrip securely at back of belt.

14. Keep your back straight /straighten knees as patient stands. Move to position behind patient. Keep one hand on side of belt and other hand should grasp the back of the belt.

TIP: If patient is confused, grip the gait belt from underneath in the back, holding the patient's arm nearest the caregiver, and pointing the patient's arm in the direction you want to move. This helps the patient move with you instead of against you.

15. Ambulate patient as ordered.

16. Observe patient for weakness or discomfort.

17. Return patient to room and make comfortable.

18. Remove belt, help take off robe and slippers, position patient in bed, raise siderails, and make sure call bell is in place.

POSTPROCEDURE

19. Document and report patient's tolerance of procedure.

20. Return gait belt to storage area so that it will be available for the next procedure.

21. Wash hands.

* Belt is too tight if you cannot put two fingers under it.

gait belt
(geyt belt)
A safety device used to move a patient from one place to another; also used to help hold up a weak person while they walk.

Exercising

Physical therapy department personnel work with patients to maintain normal functions of all parts of the body. They use range-of-motion exercises to move all joints in the body. This is accomplished through:

- **Active ROM**—The patient moves the body part without help.
- **Passive ROM**—Someone else moves the body part for the patient. (See the procedure "Range of Motion.") The physical therapist directs an exercise program that improves strength and mobility. These exercises may use complicated machines or simple items, such as a rubber ball that can be routinely squeezed. Regardless of the technique you use, it is essential that you are secure with the procedure before you attempt to assist a patient.

Rehabilitation Equipment

Ambulation Devices

Ambulation devices assist patients to walk. (**Figure 19.4**) Some of the most common devices are described in the next paragraphs.

ambulation
(AM byuh lay shun)
The ability to walk and move around freely.

Figure 19.4
Ambulation devices:
(a) short leg brace,
(b) cane, (c) quad cane,
(d) wheeled walker,
(e, f) crutches. What is one advantage and one disadvantage to having a walker with wheels?

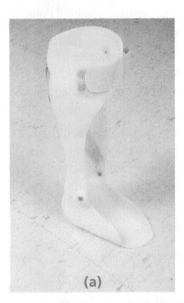

(a)

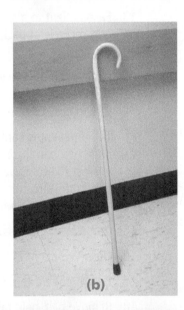

(b)

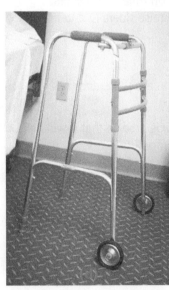

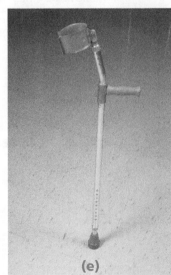

(e)

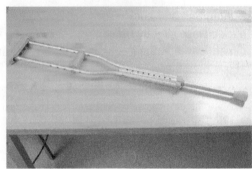

Canes provide a third base of support for patients who are slightly unstable on their feet. Use a cane when patients are:

- Slightly weaker on one side.
- Easily thrown off balance.
- Insecure walking alone.

Special considerations to keep in mind when preparing a cane for use include the following:

- The patient's height.
- Use of a single-foot cane or multifoot cane.
- Condition of rubber tips.
- Weight and appearance of the cane.

Crutches provide support and stability by promoting use of the hands and arms more than the legs. Use them when patients are able to bear weight:

- On one foot or leg.
- Only partially on one leg or on both feet and legs.

Special considerations when preparing crutches for use include the following:

- Adjusting their height for the patient. Keep in mind:
  - Axillary pressure—too much pressure causes injury.
  - Hand level—position the handgrips to allow a slight bend of the elbows, like they are when you walk normally.
- The patient's footwear (slippery soles, open toes, etc.).
- Condition of rubber tips, hand pads, and axillary pads.
- Securing all joints on the crutches.

crutch
(kruhch)
A support used by physically disabled people as an aid in walking. It usually fits under the armpit and is often used in pairs.

Walkers provide support and stability. Use them when patients are:

- Relearning to walk.
- On limited weight-bearing.
- Unstable on their feet.

Special considerations to keep in mind when preparing walkers for patient use include the following:

- Adjusting the walker to the patient's height.
- Assuring that the patient wears supportive shoes.
- Securing all joints on walker.
- Condition of rubber tips.

walker
(WAH ker)
A waist-high four-legged framework of lightweight metal, for use by a weak or disabled person as a support while walking.

19.8 **Walking with a Cane**

BACKGROUND: Safe canes, if correctly sized, and careful safety instruction protect the patient from falls or injuries.

ALERT: Follow Standard Precautions.

PREPROCEDURE

1. Wash hands.

2. Assemble equipment:

   a. Cane in good repair and with rubber tip

   b. Patient's/client's footwear

   c. Patient's/client's robe

3. Identify patient.

4. Assist patient with shoes and robe.

5. Explain what you are going to do.

6. Provide privacy as appropriate.

7. Assist to sitting position, feet resting on floor. Secure gait belt snug enough to provide support and loose enough to provide comfort. Place cane in reach.

8. Position patient in a standing position (have a co-worker help you if necessary).

9. Check height of cane. Top of cane should be at the patient's hip joint.

PROCEDURE

10. Check arm position at side of body and hold top of cane. Arm should be bent at a 25 to 30° angle.

11. Have patient hold cane in hand on strongest side of body (unaffected side). Walk mostly beside, but slightly to the rear of the patient, while grasping gait belt to provide support. Observe for discomfort or weakness.

12. Assist patient as needed while ambulating. Most physicians order a standard gait procedure.

    a. With cane in hand on strongest side, move cane and weakest foot forward.

    b. Place body weight forward on cane and move strongest foot forward. (Patient will have cane's maximum support when this procedure is used when walking on flat surface, hill, or stairs. Remember: Weak leg and cane move together.)

13. When you have completed ordered ambulation, return patient to the starting place.

POSTPROCEDURE

14. Provide for patient's comfort.

15. Place cane in proper location. If patient is capable and physician permits ambulation without assistance, leave cane in a convenient place for patient.

16. Wash hands.

17. Report/document patient's tolerance of procedure.

    a. Date

    b. Time

    c. Ambulated with cane (e.g., 15 minutes in hall)

    d. How tolerated

    e. Signature and classification

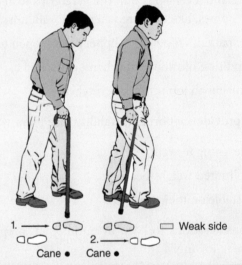

1. → Weak side
Cane ●   2. → Cane ●

11/03/11   2100

Height of cane correct

Checked for safety

Instructions given with emphasis

on using the cane on the

affected side

Ambulated without difficulty 15

minutes in hall

Tolerated well

_____   J. Munoz student

BACKGROUND: Measuring crutches to fit properly and careful instruction in how to use crutches safely prevents injury.

ALERT: Follow Standard Precautions.

PREPROCEDURE

1. Wash hands.

2. Assemble equipment:

   a. Crutches in good repair with rubber tips

   b. Patient's footwear

   c. Patient's robe, if necessary

3. Identify patient.

4. Explain what you are going to do.

5. Help patient with shoes and robe. Provide privacy if needed.

PROCEDURE

6. Check fit of crutches to patient.

   a. Have patient stand with crutches in place. (Ask a co-worker to assist if necessary.)

   b. Position foot of crutches about 4 inches to side of patient's foot and slightly forward of foot.

   c. Check distance between underarm and crutch underarm rest. It should be about 2 inches.

   d. Check angle of patient's arm. When hand is on hand rest bar and crutches are in walking position, arms should be at a 30° angle.

7. Remind patient that the hands support most of the body weight, not the underarms (axilla).

8. Assist patient to ambulate following gait method ordered. There are a variety of crutch walking gaits. The following will provide guidelines to the most commonly used:

   a. Three-point gait (beginners):

      (1) One leg is weight-bearing.

   (2) Place both crutches forward along with non-weight-bearing foot. Weight will be supported primarily by weight-bearing foot.

   (3) Shift weight to hands on crutches and move weight-bearing foot forward.

   b. Four-point gait (beginners) (see figure below):

      (1) Both legs are weight-bearing.

      (2) Place one crutch forward.

      (3) Move foot on opposite side of body forward, parallel with forward crutch.

      (4) Place other crutch forward and parallel with first crutch.

      (5) Move other foot forward so that it rests next to first foot.

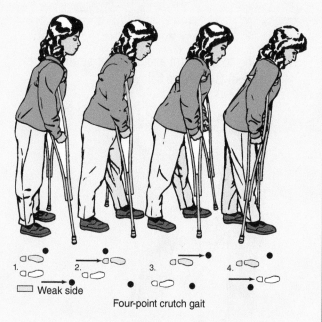

Four-point crutch gait

(continued)

c. Two-point gait (advanced) (see figure below):

(1) Both legs are weight-bearing.

(2) Place one crutch forward and move opposite foot forward with it.

(3) Place other crutch forward and parallel with first crutch. Then move opposite foot forward so that it is even with other foot.

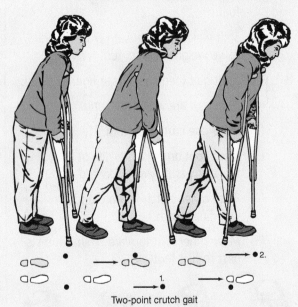

Two-point crutch gait

d. Swing-to gait (arm and shoulder strength are needed) (see figure below):

Swing-to gait

(1) One or both legs are weight-bearing.

(2) Balance weight on weight-bearing limb.

(3) Place both crutches forward.

(4) Shift weight to hands on crutches.

(5) Swing both feet forward until parallel with crutches.

CAUTION: Placing crutches too far forward can result in a fall!

e. Swing-through gait (advanced: arm and shoulder strength are needed) (see figure below):

(1) One or both legs are weight-bearing.

(2) Balance weight on weight-bearing limb(s).

(3) Place both crutches forward.

(4) Shift weight to hands on crutches.

(5) Swing both feet forward just ahead of crutches.

Swing-through gait

9. Return to room.

(continued)

POSTPROCEDURE

10. Ensure that patient is comfortable.

11. Wash hands.

12. Record the following:

  a. Date
  b. Time
  c. Distance ambulated
  d. How tolerated
  e. Signature and classification

NOTE: Patients with memory loss (dementia) are not good candidates for education in the use of canes, crutches, or walkers as they can not retain information and may be endangered using this type of equipment.

12/10/11	2000
	Measured crutches for
	correct size and safety
	Instructed patient in safe
	use to prevent additional injury
	Ambulated for 15 minutes in hallway
	Tolerated well
	_____ J. Munoz student

To use a walker, the patient must be able to use their hands and arms to adapt properly to these devices. However, if the patient has paralysis of one side of their body (hemi paralysis) there are hemiwalkers made specifically for their use. Some additional devices that aid in ambulation include the following:

Braces provide specific support for weakened muscle joints or immobilize an injured joint. Patients use them when they have:

- Weakened joints or muscles.
- Injuries that need to be stabilized.

Special considerations to keep in mind when preparing braces for a patient include the following:

- They are custom-made for each patient; they are not meant to be shared.
- They may require padding to protect the skin.
- There is only one way to apply a brace; be sure you know the correct way.

A **prosthesis** is an artificial body part or an aid to a part of the body that minimizes a disability. When a body part is missing, the prosthesis gives a natural appearance and provides maximum usability for the person. The prosthesis most commonly dealt with in physical therapy is the artificial arm or leg. Special considerations to keep in mind when preparing a prosthesis for a patient include the following:

- You must have the right device.
- The end resting against the patient is padded.
- All straps must be in good condition.
- It is clean and the overall appearance is natural.
- Report tender areas at attachment site.

prosthesis
(pros thee sis)
An artificial body part such as a limb, tooth, or eye, used to replace a natural body part and minimize a disability.

Personal Wellness

Back Injuries

As a medical assistant, you will be called upon to support and to lift patients. It is very important that you take the time to:

1. Check the physician's orders regarding activity privileges.

2. Check with the patient's nurse regarding baseline and current functional status.

3. Use a gait belt if there are any doubts as to the patient's ability to function independently.

You can often assist patients by yourself. Many times standby assistance for safety is all that is required. If you are unsure of patient status it is always best to ask another assistant to stand by to help if necessary when moving the patient.

Always use a gait belt if there are any doubts as to the patient's ability to ambulate independently. Explain to the patient that you are protecting the patient and yourself through this action. Be aware, that occasionally patients may unexpectedly fall or collapse, requiring you to support their entire weight. If a gait belt is in place you can gently lower the patient to the floor using good body mechanics:

- Take a wide stance to give yourself as much stability as possible. Use your legs, not your back, when lifting. Bend your knees and let your knees do the lifting.

- Try to avoid bending, leaning, stooping, and reaching. These positions make you vulnerable to injury.

- Keep your back straight. Don't twist it. If you need to turn the patient, swivel your hips or, better still, turn your feet.

- If you are lifting someone to or from a bed or wheelchair, make sure the wheels are locked before attempting the lift.

When you must lift a patient to assist the person in moving or in an emergency when the patient falls, think safety first. If something happens and you drop a patient, the person can be badly injured. If you attempt a lift and the weight is too much for you, you can seriously injure yourself.

What should you do if you know a patient is weak and unsteady and is too heavy for you to safely lift by yourself?

BACKGROUND: It is important to measure a walker to fit properly and give the patient careful safety instruction in order to prevent injury.

ALERT: Follow Standard Precautions.

PREPROCEDURE

1. Wash hands.

2. Assemble equipment:

    a. Walker in good condition

    b. Patient's footwear

    c. Patient's robe if necessary

3. Identify patient.

4. Tell patient what you are going to do.

5. Check walker for safety.

6. Help put on proper and safe footwear and robe if necessary.

7. Assist to sitting position with feet resting on the floor.

8. Secure gait belt snug enough to provide support and loose enough to provide comfort. Place walker within reach.

PROCEDURE

9. Stand patient up with walker. (Ask a co-worker to help if necessary.) Remind patient to stand as straight as possible.

10. Check to see if walker fits patient properly.

    a. Walker's handgrips should be at top of patient's leg or bend of leg at hip joint.

    b. Arm should be at a 25 to 30° angle.

11. Gripping gait belt from behind, assist patient to ambulate as ordered. Basic guidelines for walking with a walker are as follows:

    a. Patient begins by standing inside walker frame.

    b. Patient lifts walker (never slides) and places back legs of walker parallel with toes (never ahead of toes).

    c. Patient shifts weight onto hands and walker (for balance and support).

    d. Patient then walks into walker.

    e. Place yourself just to side and slightly behind patient. This position will allow you to observe and be close enough to assist if necessary.

    f. Ambulate as ordered, observing for correct use of walker.

12. When you have completed the ordered ambulation, return patient to his or her starting place.

POSTPROCEDURE

13. Provide for patient's comfort with call signal in reach.

14. Place walker in proper location. If patient is capable and physician permits ambulation without assistance, leave walker in a convenient place for patient.

15. Wash hands.

16. Report/document patient's tolerance of procedure.

17. Record the following:

    a. Date

    b. Time

    c. Distance and amount of time ambulated

    d. How tolerated

    e. Signature and classification

12/04/11   0800

Checked walker for safety measures

Instructed patient in correct use

of walker

Ambulated in hallway for 10 minutes

Patient complained of dizziness

initially

Dangled from bed until dizziness subsided

Tolerated with some difficulty with fatigue

Patient stated "I feel really tired

after using the walker."

_____ J. Munoz P.T. Aide

Transporting Devices

Transport devices include equipment to move patients from one place to another. The most common transporting devices are wheelchairs and gurneys. Gurneys and wheelchairs make it easy to move patients who are unable to walk. You are responsible for a variety of procedures as a physical therapy aide. Be sure that you are knowledgeable and confident about each procedure before working with patients.

Adaptive-Assistive Devices

Adaptive-assistive devices (Figure 19.5) include equipment that helps a person perform daily activities. These devices range from special holders for silverware to devices that help people put on socks or button clothing.

Figure 19.5
Adaptive devices:
(a) reaching stick,
(b) long-handled shoe-horn, and
(c) adaptive silverware,
What other daily activities might patients need adaptive devices for?

Community Service

With a team of three others visit an elementary or middle school class and show the students how to properly lift, bend, and turn to help reduce back injuries.

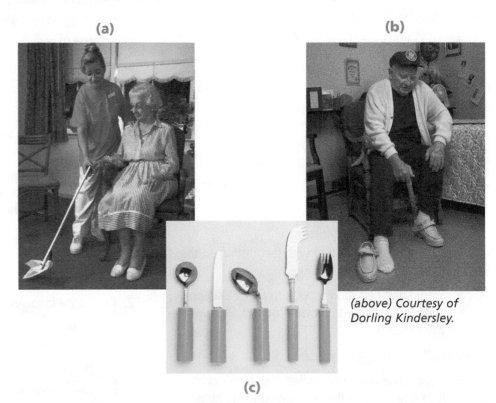

(a)   **(b)**

(c)

(above) Courtesy of Dorling Kindersley.

Language Arts Link

Sports Medicine Careers

Sports medicine is the diagnosis and treatment of injuries caused by exercise or sports. The injuries are often to the joints and muscles. A whole team of specialists deal with these types of injuries. They include surgeons, physical therapists, doctors, acupuncturists, and even nutritionists.

Working with a partner, research various sports medicine careers. Using the Internet or a library, research the educational and skills needs to go into these areas of study. If you are able to speak with professionals in these fields, interview them

about how they became interested in this subject, what the requirements were, and what their job responsibilities are.

After you've completed your research, create a document with several paragraphs on each career that you learned about. Be sure to proofread your work to see if you can improve it by making it clearer, more concise, or more interesting to read. Check the spelling and grammar and correct any errors.

Oxygen Therapy

Some residents require oxygen to help them breathe. Concentrated oxygen helps these residents breathe more easily. The following are common ways to give oxygen therapy:

- **Nasal cannula**—a two-pronged tube that fits into the nostrils and is secured with an elastic strap that stretches around the back of the head.

- **Mask**—a plastic see-through mask that fits over the nose and mouth and is secured with an elastic strap that stretches around the back of the head.

PROCEDURE 19.11 Respiratory Therapy

BACKGROUND: Respiratory therapy is the provision of care dedicated to improving the pulmonary function of the patient. The provision of respiratory therapy has developed into a stand-alone discipline because of the specialized learning required to provide this care.

A respiratory therapist is trained in techniques that improve pulmonary function and oxygenation. Respiratory therapists may also be responsible for administering a variety of tests that measure lung function and for educating the patient about the use of various devices and machines prescribed by the physician.

The health care professional must have knowledge of respiratory physiology, the variables, and diseases that affect respiratory function. In some cases, the health care professional will be responsible for using specific equipment and protocols necessary to diagnose and treat respiratory problems.

ALERT: Follow Standard Precautions.

PREPROCEDURE

1. Determine the baseline function of the patient's respiratory system.

2. Consult the physician's orders to determine any specific respiratory treatment prescribed for the patient.

3. Determine the health care professional's responsibility for administering/supporting the treatment.

PROCEDURE

4. Assess the patient's current respiratory status.

5. Review available documentation to determine when specific respiratory treatments were last delivered, and when they will be due again.

6. Determine what the health care professional's role is to be in assisting/promoting respiratory therapy.

7. Consult with the respiratory therapist for any necessary instructions on the use of equipment or procedures.

8. Encourage the patient to use good pulmonary toileting techniques such as deep breathing, coughing, incentive spirometry.

   NOTE: Incentive spirometry works to mimic natural sighing or yawning by encouraging the patient to take long, slow, deep breaths.

9. Provide continuous monitoring of the patient's respiratory status so that any decline in function can be addressed early and successfully.

POSTPROCEDURE

10. Collaborate with the physician and the respiratory therapist if there is a decline in the patient's respiratory status.

11. Document the respiratory assessment and any ongoing problems and their resolution in the medical chart.

You have specific responsibilities when you care for a resident on oxygen therapy, including the following:

- Ensuring that all oxygen safety rules are followed. Review Chapter 18.
- Checking the face and behind the ears to see if the strap is chafing and is a firm fit.
- Cleaning the cannula, catheter, or mask and checking the skin for irritation.
- Providing oral hygiene by moistening the lips and mouth frequently. Encourage fluid intake if allowed.
- Keeping tubing free of kinks or blockage.
- Checking flow rate and oxygen humidifier frequently.
- Immediately reporting to supervisor any changes or problems, e.g., cyanosis, dyspnea, shortness of breath.

 Summary

Physical therapy is a health-care profession that deals with prevention and management of movement disorders arising from conditions and diseases occurring throughout the lifespan. Physical therapists provide services that restore function, improve mobility, relieve pain, and prevent or limit permanent physical disabilities. They restore, maintain, and promote overall fitness and health.

SECTION 19.1 Review Questions

1. What tasks are required of physical therapy aides?

2. Compare moist heat and dry heat.

3. What is the purpose of range-of-motion (ROM) exercises?

4. When would antiembolism hose be used on a patient?

5. Explain the pivot, sliding, and lifting techniques.

6. When preparing a prosthesis for a patient, what considerations should you keep in mind?

 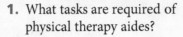 *Learn By Doing: Section 19.1 Activity*

1. Complete Worksheet 2. Ask your teacher for directions to complete activities.

2. Complete Worksheets/Activity 3.

3. Prepare responses to each item listed in Chapter Review.

4. When you are confident that you can meet each objective for this section, ask your teacher for the section evaluation.

Chapter Review Questions

1. List four types of therapy you might encounter as a physical therapy aide? (19.1)

2. What is one of the problems associated with UV therapy? (19.1)

3. What are the steps to fit crutches for a patient? (19.1)

4. What is thermotherapy and for what is it primarily used? (19.1)

5. Why are overuse injuries difficult to prevent? (19.1)

6. What is the standard temperature for water in hydrotherapy treatment? (19.1)

7. According to its supporters, what is the main principle behind acupuncture? (19.1)

8. Which guarding technique is best for paraplegics? (19.1)

9. What is the standard gait procedure for walking with a cane? (19.1)

10. What is a prosthesis? (19.1)

Activities

1. Review and expand your personal plans for exercise and good body mechanics. You cannot help patients if you are not in fit condition yourself. What do you need to change? What interim steps will you take?

2. Use the Internet to make a list of three common running injuries. Then suggest one or two possible physical therapy options that might prove useful to alleviate pain and restore mobility.

Case Studies

1. Mr. Watkins has an exercise program designed by his physical therapist to restore full ROM after his complex leg fracture. The exercises cause some discomfort and he wants to stop exercising, insisting that a limited, shuffling gait is good enough. How would you explain to him the importance of her ROM exercises and the restoration of normal functioning? Find a partner and role-play how you would overcome his objections.

2. Ms. Starr has very bad arthritis that keeps her from doing some of the things she loves such as gardening and playing bridge. The physical therapist has decided to try diathermy to see if it can alleviate her pain. Before the treatment, you notice Ms. Starr has a wedding ring on. When you ask her to remove it, she refuses, telling you that "she never takes the ring off because it reminds her of her dear departed husband." What would you do?

Thinking Critically

1. **Communication**—Describe what you would say to a patient who was going to have his first hydrotherapy treatment. What special precautions would you take? What would you tell the patient about the possible outcome of his treatment?

2. **Legal**—Explain what it means to "know your limitations" as a physical therapy aide working in the physical therapy department.

3. **Ethical**—Use the Internet to look up the "Guide for Conduct of the Physical Therapist Assistant" issued by the American Physical Therapy Association (APTA). Take any standard or substandard in the guide and invent a hypothetical ethical dilemma that pertains to that standard. Make sure you give your solution to the problem quoting from the guide.

Chapter 19 Review

Media Connection

Use the Companion Web site for additional interactive learning activities: www.prenhall.com/badasch

Portfolio Connection

When you are competent as a physical therapy aide, ask for permission to copy your documentation of treatment for a patient. (Remove all patient identifiers.) Place this copy in your portfolio to document your skills. Place a copy of your on-site trainer's evaluation in your portfolio.

Write a paper describing your doubts and realizations and the barriers that you were able to overcome during your physical therapy experiences. For example, were you concerned about helping care for patients who are experiencing a lot of pain? Describe the ways you plan to use the skills, information, and insights that you gained about people and about this job. This assignment must be in standard report format.

PORTFOLIO TIP

Encourage all patients to keep a list of their questions and concerns for the medical staff. This both saves time for the staff and helps patients bring their concerns to the attention of the medical staff.

20 Medical Assisting and Laboratory Skills

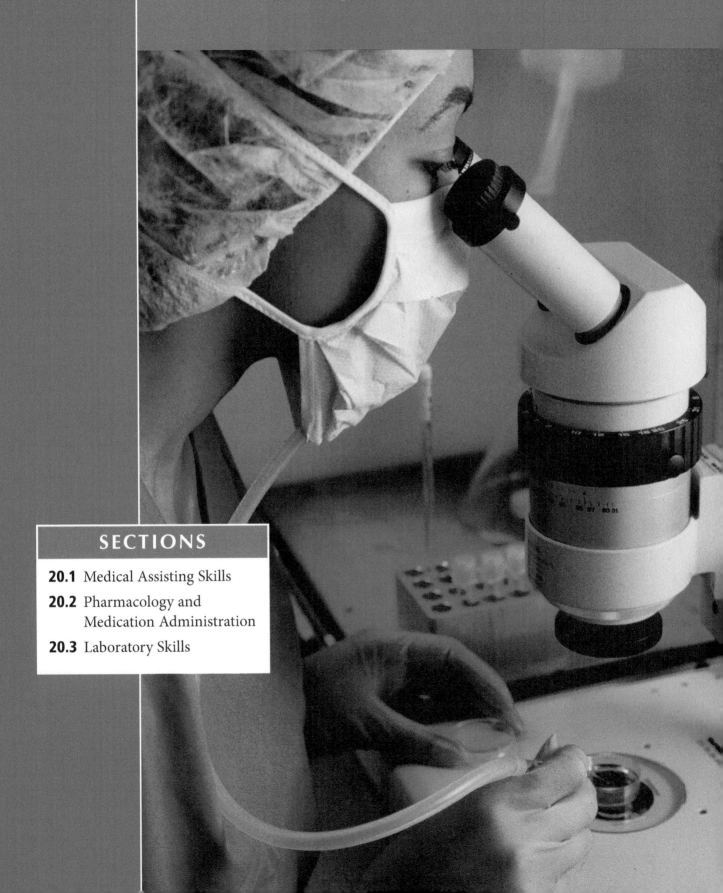

Getting Started

At home, "Brown Bag" all of the medications you can find in your home. You should include all over the counter medicines, herbal, and vitamin supplements. Inspect the medicines. Can you find any outdated medications? Any medications that are no longer prescribed? Any two medications that treat the same problem, but have a different name? If you are not sure what they are used for, look the medications up in the PDR.

NOTE: Everyone should inspect their medicine cabinets annually. Older patients should be encouraged to "brown bag" their medicines, including any over the counter medicines and bring them to their physician's office once a year to assure appropriateness and patient safety. Older patients are usually on more than five medications.

SECTION 20.1

Medical Assisting Skills

Background

The medical assisting skills of admitting, registering, transferring, and discharging a patient are important processes in a patient's health. As a health care worker admitting and discharging a patient, you are the first and last person with whom the patient will interact and making a patient feel at ease is key. In addition, you need to be able to perform the basic tasks of measuring height and weight as well as understand the examination positions and techniques.

Objectives

When you have completed this section, you will be able to do the following:

- Match key terms with their correct meanings.

- Explain the process of admitting, registering, transferring, and discharging a patient.

- Measure and record height and weight of an adult, child, and infant.

- Explain how to read a visual acuity test and the importance of the results.

- Summarize the important of measuring the circumference of an infant's head.

- Compare and identify examination positions by name.

- List four basic examination techniques and explain their purposes.

Admission

Since you are one of the first people to interact with the patient, it is very important to establish that the patient is not in any kind of acute distress. Inquire about their comfort level; quickly assess their general appearance for any kind of acute distress. If the patient appears to be in any kind of distress, quickly excuse yourself and notify the licensed nurse in charge of the patient's care. (Figure 20.1)

Be pleasant and try to put everyone at ease. The facility where you work has a procedure for you to follow when you admit the

Courtesy of ShutterStock.

Figure 20.1
Admitting a patient. Why should you follow set procedures when admitting a patient?

patient. Do not rush the patient. Give the person time to adjust to the new environment. When a patient is admitted to the hospital, there are some basic procedures that are followed. (Figure 20.2 for a sample of an admission checklist.) These include the following:

- Making a clothing list.
- Making a list of personal items.
- Requesting that the family take home valuables or see that they are put in a safe place.
- Taking vital signs.
- Weighing the patient.
- Explaining the call light and routine.
- Collecting urine specimens if required.

NOTE: All medical records must be written in black ink. Always remember to record date, time, personal care or treatment given, any complaints, problems reported to the team leader/head nurse, and any other required information. Complaints or patient statements should be put in quotes. Always sign with your name and certification.

Charting Flow Sheet

Many facilities provide a printed flow sheet for charting. The sheet includes activities of daily living (ADL), vital signs, diet, liquids, and type of care given. This checkoff list (Figure 20.3) helps the charter provide all of the necessary information about patient care. If your facility doesn't have a flow sheet, use the charting examples.

Figure 20.2

Sample admission check-list. Why is it important to use an admission checklist when admitting a patient?

A SAMPLE ADMISSION CHECK LIST
(Fill in every statement and check every appropriate item)

Resident's name _____   Room number _____

Time of admission _____ a.m./p.m.   Date of admission _____
Unit ready to receive resident? Yes ☐ No ☐ Equipment ready? Yes ☐ No ☐
Admitted by stretcher _____ wheelchair _____ walking _____
Check identification bracelet? Yes ☐ No ☐ Bed tag in place? Yes ☐ No ☐
Did the resident need help to get undressed? Yes ☐ No ☐
Is the resident in bed at this time? Yes ☐ No ☐ Time _____ a.m./p.m.
Siderails up? Yes ☐ No ☐
Bruises, marks, rashes, or broken skin noted? Yes ☐ No ☐ _____
    If yes, describe _____
Weight _____ Height _____ Scale Used? Yes ☐ No ☐
Temperature _____ Pulse _____ Respirations _____ Blood Pressure _____
Admission urine specimen collected? Yes ☐ No ☐ Sent to lab? Yes ☐ No ☐
Unusual behavior noted? Yes ☐ No ☐ Unusual appearance noted? Yes ☐ No ☐
    If yes, describe _____
Does the resident have any difficulty with the English language? Yes ☐ No ☐
Is the resident allergic to food? Yes ☐ No ☐ Allergic to drugs? Yes ☐ No ☐
Reason for admission _____
Complaints _____
Dentures? Yes ☐ No ☐ Partial? Yes ☐ No ☐ Full? Yes ☐ No ☐ Denture cup? Yes ☐ No ☐
Vision problems? Yes ☐ No ☐ Does the resident wear glasses? Yes ☐ No ☐ Contact lenses? ☐
Valuables: Money? Yes ☐ No ☐ Describe _____
    Jewelry? Yes ☐ No ☐ Describe _____
Is the resident hard of hearing? Yes ☐ No ☐ Hearing aid? Yes ☐ No ☐ Contact lenses? Yes ☐ No ☐
    Artificial limb? Yes ☐ No ☐ Brace? Yes ☐ No ☐
Is the resident calm? Yes ☐ No ☐ Is the resident very anxious? Yes ☐ No ☐
    Angry? Yes ☐ No ☐ Is the resident agitated or very excited? Yes ☐ No ☐
Has the resident been admitted to this hospital before? Yes ☐ No ☐
Is the clothing list completed? Yes ☐ No ☐ Signed by _____
Is the signal cord attached to the bed? Yes ☐ No ☐
Have drugs brought into the hospital by the resident been given to the charge nurse? Yes ☐ No ☐
Name of the nurse drugs were given to _____
Additional comments _____
Admitted by _____

Figure 20.3

Example of a flow chart. How and when should a flow chart be used?

ACTIVITIES OF DAILY LIVING CHECKLIST

SELF —Done by patient
ASSIST —Patient assisted by nursing staff
TOTAL —Done by nursing staff
✔ —Check procedure performed. Include time if appropriate.

DATE															
DIET	B'fast	Dinner	Supper	B'fast	Dinner	Supper	B'fast	Dinner	Supper	B'fast	Dinner	Supper	B'fast	Dinner	Supper
Ate all food served															
Ate approx. ½ food served															
Refused to eat															
PROCEDURE	11-7	7-3	3-11	11-7	7-3	3-11	11-7	7-3	3-11	11-7	7-3	3-11	11-7	7-3	3-11
A.M. or H.S. Care															
Oral Hygiene															
Bath–Bed bath complete															
Bed bath partial															
Shower															
Tub															
Self Care															
Back Care															
Bed Made															
ELIMINATION															
Bowel movement															
Involuntary B.M.															
Voided															
Incontinent															
Foley cath.															
Sitz Bath ⓦ															
ACTIVITY															
Bed rest complete															
Dangle															
Bed rest–B.R.P.															
Up in chair															
Up in room															
Walk in hall															
Ambulatory															
POSITION CHANGED															
Flat in bed															
Semi–Fowler's															
Deep breathe, cough															
Range of motion															
Turn from side to side															
Side Rails–Up															
Down															
Fresh Water ⓦ															
SIGNATURE & TITLE															

BACKGROUND: Carefully following the admitting procedure gives the patient a sense of well-being and security. It also protects the facility from errors in identification and loss of patients' belongings.

ALERT: Follow Standard Precautions.

PREPROCEDURE

1. Wash hands.

2. Assemble equipment.

   a. Admission checklist

   b. Admission pack (may be all disposable depending on facility)

     (1) Bedpan

     (2) Urinal

     (3) Emesis basin

     (4) Wash basin

     (5) Tissues

   c. Gown or pajamas

   d. Portable scale

   e. Thermometer

   f. Blood pressure cuff

   g. Stethoscope

   h. Clothing list

   i. Envelope for valuables

PROCEDURE

3. Fan-fold bed covers to foot of bed. (See the procedure "Making an Open Bed.")

4. Put away patient's equipment.

5. Put gown or pajamas on foot of bed.

6. Greet patient and introduce yourself.

7. Identify patient by looking at arm band and asking name (see figure at top right). Ask what they like to be called.

8. Introduce patient to roommates, if appropriate.

9. Explain:

   a. How call signal works

   b. How bed controls work (see figure below)

   c. Hospital regulations

   d. What you will be doing to admit him or her

   e. How telephone and television work

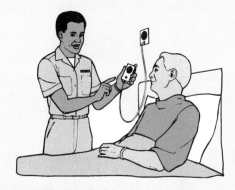

10. Provide privacy by pulling privacy curtains.

11. Ask patient to put on gown or pajamas.

12. Check weight and height. (You will find this skill later in this chapter.)

13. Help to bed if ordered. (Check with nurse.)

14. Put up side rails if required.

(continued)

15. If patient has valuables:

    a. Make a list of jewelry, money, wallet, etc.

    b. Have patient sign list

    c. Have relative sign list

    d. Either have relative take home valuables or send to cashier's office in valuables envelope

16. Take and record the following:

    a. Temperature, pulse, respiration

    b. Blood pressure

    c. Urine specimen, if required

17. Complete admission checklist noting:

    a. Allergies

    b. Medications being taken

    c. Food preferences and dislikes

    d. Any prosthesis

    e. Skin condition

    f. Handicaps (e.g., deafness, sight, movement)

NOTE: This is usually done by a registered nurse.

18. Orient patient to meal times, visiting hours, use of television and telephone.

19. Ask if patient has any questions regarding the information given.

POSTPROCEDURE

20. Wash hands.

21. Record information according to your facility's policy.

10/04/12	1500
	VS 98=76=18 120/80
	Admitted and oriented to facility.
	Admission checklist completed.
	Sitting in chair.
	States "Wish I could stay at home."
	_____ S. Gomez CNA

 Registration

New patients must complete two basic forms when registering:

1. Patient information forms.

2. Medical history forms.

Patient Information Forms

The patient information form gives the following information:

- Patient's name, address, and phone number.

- Birth date, sex, marital status, Social Security number.

- Patient's employer name, address, and phone number.

- Insurance company's name, address, and phone number.

- Insured's employer name, address, and phone number.

- If the patient is a minor, name of the responsible party.

Medical History Forms

The medical history form, usually filled out by an RN or other licensed personnel, gives the provider the necessary information to evaluate the physical condition of the patient. The patient must give you the following information (Figure 20.4):

- Previous surgeries.
- Allergies.
- Chronic illness.
- Medications taken.
- General medical history.
- Childhood diseases.
- Persons to contact in case of medical emergency.
- Nutritional status and any problems related to nutritional intake.
- Activities of daily living and instrumental activities of daily living.
- Family related medical history.
- Any substance abuse history.
- Mental health history.
- Notation of any alterations in skin integrity (bruising, open areas, abnormal growths, etc).

If a health care professional is taking or reviewing a patient's medical history, he/she might want to ask a series of questions about things that cannot be observed, such as:

- In general, how are you feeling?
- What is your biggest concern?
- Do you have any pains?

These types of questions should be asked in a non-leading way; for example: "How does your stomach feel?" rather than "Are you nauseous?" In addition to medications, health care professionals need to determine if the person is on any over the counter medications or supplements, such as herbs. Finally, they need to visually assess the overall physical and mental state of the patient—are they particularly stressed, nervous, out of breath, etc.

Both the patient information form and the medical history form must be completed accurately and fully to serve the needs of both the patient and the provider. Do not leave any blanks on these forms. If it does not apply to the patient, you should write N/A or not applicable.

GREEN VALLEY MEDICAL GROUP, INC.
MEDICAL HISTORY

NAME _____ DATE OF BIRTH _____

OCCUPATION _____ MARITAL STATUS: S   M   D   W

ALLERGIES:

Are you allergic to:

Penicillin	Yes _____	No _____
Sulfa	Yes _____	No _____
Aspirin	Yes _____	No _____
Codeine	Yes _____	No _____
Tetanus Injections	Yes _____	No _____
Iodine	Yes _____	No _____
Foods	Yes _____	No _____
Tape	Yes _____	No _____

Other _____

_____

MEDICATIONS:

List all medications, including over the counter, you are currently taking:

_____

_____

_____

_____

_____

HABITS:

Do you:

Smoke?   Yes _____ No _____ How Much _____

Drink Alcohol? Yes _____ No _____ How Much _____

Drink Beverages That Contain Caffeine?

           Yes _____ No _____ How Much _____

Limit Cholesterol   Yes _____ No _____

Use Other Substances   Yes _____ No _____

         What? _____

EXERCISE:

Do you on a regular basis:

Walk	Yes _____	No _____
Run	Yes _____	No _____
Bike	Yes _____	No _____
Swim	Yes _____	No _____
Aerobic Exercise	Yes _____	No _____
Other	Yes _____	No _____

MENSTRUAL HISTORY (FEMALES):

Date of last PAP & results _____

Date of last normal period _____

Date of last mammogram & results _____

Length of cycle (days) _____

Usual duration (days) _____

Number of pregnancies _____

Number of children _____

PRESENT COMPLAINTS:

Do you have:

Headaches	Yes _____	No _____
Fever	Yes _____	No _____
Cough	Yes _____	No _____
Chest Pains	Yes _____	No _____
Nausea	Yes _____	No _____
Vomiting	Yes _____	No _____
Diarrhea	Yes _____	No _____
Constipation	Yes _____	No _____
Black Stools	Yes _____	No _____
Bloody Stools	Yes _____	No _____
Painful Urination	Yes _____	No _____
Recent Weight Gain or Loss ...	Yes _____	No _____

Other Complaints _____

_____

PAST ILLNESS:

Have you ever had:

High Blood Pressure	Yes _____	No _____
Heart Trouble	Yes _____	No _____
Pneumonia	Yes _____	No _____
Hepatitis	Yes _____	No _____
Cancer	Yes _____	No _____
Diabetes	Yes _____	No _____
Tuberculosis	Yes _____	No _____
Asthma	Yes _____	No _____
Ulcers	Yes _____	No _____
Seizures	Yes _____	No _____
Sexually Transmitted Disease ..	Yes _____	No _____
Blood Disorder	Yes _____	No _____

Other _____

_____

OPERATIONS:

Have you had any surgery:

Appendix	Yes _____	No _____
Tonsils	Yes _____	No _____
Gallbladder	Yes _____	No _____
Stomach	Yes _____	No _____
Hemorrhoids	Yes _____	No _____
Female Organs	Yes _____	No _____
Thyroid	Yes _____	No _____
Hernia	Yes _____	No _____
Heart	Yes _____	No _____

Other _____

_____

Figure 20.4

Medical history form. Why are medical history forms important?

Height and Weight

Patients are weighed and measured for height when they are admitted. These measurements provide a baseline during the patient's stay. (Table 20.1) Measurements must be accurate, as they are important to the well-being of the patient. Accurate heights and weights are very important to the physician and the pharmacist for accurate dosing of any medications to be given. The patient's weight is important because it indicates:

- Nutritional status.
- Any change (weight loss or gain) in condition, which **might** indicate potential physical or emotional problems, or other issues.

There are several different types of scales and most are available digitally. Digital scales can measure with precision accuracy. Each type of scale is designed for ease in weighing patients with varying problems. Types of scales include:

- Standing scale.
- Bed scale.
- Infant scale.
- Scale with mechanical lift.
- Wheelchair scale. (**Figure 20.5**)

Patients who are wheelchair-bound can be left in the wheelchair and weighed. Allowance is made for the weight of the wheelchair and platform by subtracting a certain amount from the weight or by having the scale adjusted to allow for the extra weight. You can also use a mechanical lift that has a scale. It is operated by using a hydraulic pump to raise and lower the patient.

Most facilities have in-bed scales available. The bed must be balanced prior to taking the patient's weight and the amount of bedding used should be consistent. This method makes weighing the patient much easier for both the patient and the nurse.

Height is used as an indicator of the ideal weight of the patient. You may have to measure the patient with a measuring tape if the person is unable to stand. If the patient can stand, use the measure on the standing scale.

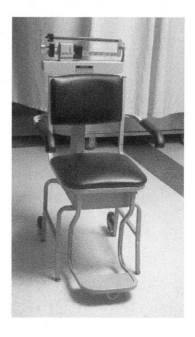

Figure 20.5
Chair scale. In what situations would a chair scale be used to weigh a patient?

Table 20.1 Height and Weight Table for Adults

Men					Women				
Height		Bone Structure (lbs)			Height		Bone Structure (lbs)		
ft. & in.	in. only	Small	Medium	Large	ft. & in.	in. only	Small	Medium	Large
5'2"	62	128–134	131–141	138–150	4'10"	58	102–111	109–121	118–131
5'3"	63	130–136	133–143	140–153	4'11"	59	103–113	111–123	120–134
5'4"	64	132–138	135–145	142–156	5'0"	60	104–115	113–126	122–137
5'5"	65	134–140	137–148	144–160	5'1"	61	106–118	115–129	125–140
5'6"	66	136–142	139–151	146–164	5'2"	62	108–121	118–132	128–143
5'7"	67	138–146	142–154	149–168	5'3"	63	111–124	121–135	131–147
5'8"	68	140–148	145–157	152–172	5'4"	64	114–127	124–138	134–151
5'9"	69	142–151	148–160	155–176	5'5"	65	117–130	127–141	137–155
5'10"	70	144–154	151–163	158–180	5'6"	66	120–133	130–144	140–159
5'11"	71	146–157	154–166	161–184	5'7"	67	123–136	133–147	143–163
6'0"	72	149–160	157–170	164–188	5'8"	68	126–139	136–150	146–167
6'1"	73	152–164	160–174	168–192	5'9"	69	129–142	139–153	149–170
6'2"	74	155–168	164–178	172–197	5'10"	70	132–146	142–156	152–173
6'3"	75	158–172	167–182	176–202	5'11"	71	135–148	145–159	155–176
6'4"	76	162–176	171–187	181–207	6'0"	72	138–151	148–162	158–179

BACKGROUND: Weighing the patient provides a weight baseline. This baseline is used to compare decreases or increases in the patient's weight. Changes in body weight may indicate a change in the patient's health.

ALERT: Follow Standard Precautions.

PREPROCEDURE

1. Wash hands.
2. Assemble equipment.
   a. Portable balance or digital scale
   b. Paper towel
   c. Paper and pencil/pen
   d. Knock before entering the patient's room
3. Identify patient.
4. Explain what you are going to do and ask patient if they need to void before you weigh them.
5. Provide privacy with curtain, screen, or door.

PROCEDURE

6. Take patient to scale or bring scale to patient's room.
7. Place paper towel on platform of scale (with standing scale).
8. Put both weights to the very left on zero.

   When using a digital scale, turn the scale on and wait for the display to show a reading; make sure the display reads "zero" before you begin weighing the patient.

9. Balance beam pointer must stay steady in middle of balance area. (If pointer does not center, turn balance screw until it remains centered.)

   The manufacturer's instructions for a digital scale will provide instructions on how to calibrate the scale, or bring the display to zero. There usually is a button to push for calibration.

10. Have patient remove shoes and assist to stand on scale.

NOTE: The balance bar raises to top of bar guide and pointer is not centered.

11. While keeping one hand near the patient's back, use other hand to move large weight to estimated weight of patient.
12. Move small weight to right until balance bar hangs free halfway between upper and lower bar guide.
13. The largest (lower) weight is marked in increments of 50 pounds; the smaller (upper weight) is marked in single pounds. The even-numbered pounds are marked with numbers (e.g., 2, 4, 6). The uneven pounds are unmarked long lines and the short line is one-fourth of a pound.
14. Write down weight on a notepad. Record weight displayed on a digital scale.
15. Help patient with shoes and make him or her comfortable.

POSTPROCEDURE

16. Discard towel.
17. Replace scale. With a digital scale, make sure the power is off.
18. Wash hands.
19. Chart weight. Report any unusual increases or decreases in weight.

| 10/05/12 | 0900 |
| Standing scale weight 125; 10 |
| pounds less than last weight. |
| No complaints of loss of appetite, |
| pain, or other problems. Weight |
| change reported to head nurse. |
| _____ S. Gomez CNA |

PROCEDURE 20.3 Measuring Weight on a Chair Scale

BACKGROUND: The chair scale provides a safe way to weigh a nonambulatory patient. Weighing the patient provides a weight baseline. This baseline is used to compare decreases or increases in the patient's weight. Changes in body weight may indicate a change in the patient's health.

ALERT: Follow Standard Precautions.

PREPROCEDURE

1. Wash hands.

2. Assemble equipment.

   a. Balance scale

   b. Paper towel

   c. Paper and pencil/pen

   d. Knock before entering the patient's room

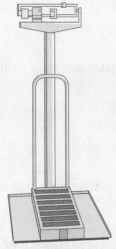

Wheelchair scale

3. Identify patient.

4. Explain what you are going to do and ask patient if they need to void before you weigh them.

5. Provide privacy with curtain, screen, or door.

PROCEDURE

6. Take patient to scale or bring scale to patient's room.

7. Put both weights to the very left on zero. If you are using a digital scale, make sure the display reads zero.

8. Balance beam pointer must stay steady in middle of balance area. (If pointer does not center, turn balance screw until it remains centered.) Calibrate a digital scale according to the manufacturer's instructions.

9. Have patient remove shoes and move patient to chair at the side of the scale. .

10. Place wheelchair on scale and weigh it.

11. Assist patient back into wheelchair. Weigh wheelchair with patient in it.

NOTE: To determine weights, see previous procedure: "Measuring Weight on a Standing Balance or Digital Scale."

12. Determine patient weight by subtracting the weight in #10 above from the weight in #11.

13. Write down weight on a notepad. Record weight displayed on a digital scale.

14. Help patient with shoes and make him or her comfortable.

POSTPROCEDURE

15. Replace scale. With a digital scale, make sure the power is off before replacing it.

16. Wash hands.

17. Chart weight. Report any unusual increases or decreases in weight.

05/03/11	0800
	Chair scale weight 125;
	no weight change.
	_____ S. Gomez CNA

BACKGROUND: The mechanical lift provides a safe method for weighing a bedridden patient. Weighing the patient provides a weight baseline. This baseline is used to compare decreases or increases in the patient's weight. Changes in body weight may indicate a change in the patient's health.

ALERT: Follow Standard Precautions.

PREPROCEDURE

1. Wash hands.

2. Assemble equipment.

   a. Mechanical lift

   b. Sling

   c. Clean sheet

3. Identify patient.

4. Explain what you are going to do.

5. Pull privacy curtain.

Scale with mechanical lift

PROCEDURE

6. Lower side rail on side you are working on.

7. Cover sling with clean sheet.

8. Help patient roll on side and place sling with top at shoulders and bottom at knees.

9. Fan-fold remaining sling.

10. Help patient roll to other side onto one half of sling and pull other half of sling through.

11. Broaden base of lift.

12. Wheel lift to side of bed with base beneath bed.

13. Position lift over patient.

14. Attach sling using chains and hooks provided. *Keep open end of hook away from patient to avoid injury.*

15. Use hand crank or pump handle to raise patient from bed. Make certain that buttocks are not touching bed.

16. Check to be certain that patient is in center of sling and is safely suspended.

17. To weigh patient:

   a. Swing feet and legs over edge of bed; move lift away from bed so that no body part contacts bed.

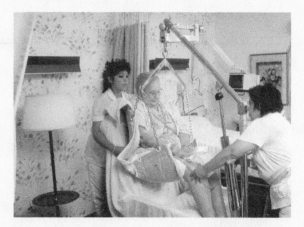

   b. If bed is low enough, raise patient above bed so that no body part contacts bed.

(continued)

18. Adjust weights until scale is balanced. (See the procedure "Measuring Weight on a Standing Balance Scale.") Remember, that most mechanical lift scales these days are electric. You just make sure it is on zero before you weigh them.

19. Return patient to bed by reversing steps.

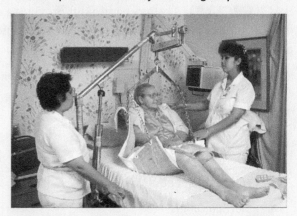

POSTPROCEDURE

20. Replace mechanical lift.

21. Wash hands.

22. Note weight.

02/26/12	1000
	Chair scale weight 250
	No changes since last weighing
	Tolerated well.
	Noted reddened area on left
	shoulder. Reported to head nurse
	_____ S. Gomez CNA

BACKGROUND: Accurately measuring height provides a baseline to help determine the patient's ideal weight. A loss in height over a period of time may indicate osteoporosis.

ALERT: Follow Standard Precautions.

PREPROCEDURE

1. Wash hands.

2. Assemble equipment.

   a. Balance scale with height rod

   b. Paper towels

3. Identify patient and explain procedure.

4. Put paper towel on platform of scale.

5. Explain what you are going to do.

6. Have patient remove shoes.

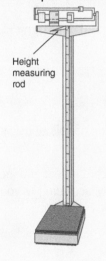

Height measuring rod

PROCEDURE

7. Raise measuring rod above head.

8. Assist patient onto the scale. Have patient stand with back against measuring rod.

9. Instruct patient to stand straight, with heels touching measuring rod.

10. Lower measuring rod to rest on patient's head.

11. Check number of inches indicated on rod. This number is found where the sliding rod enters the hollow post.

12. Assist patient off of the scale.

13. Record in meters, centimeters, or feet and inches according to hospital policy.

POSTPROCEDURE

14. Help patient with shoes.

15. Chart height.

16. Discard paper towel and wash hands.

02/09/11	0700	
	Height 55 inches on admission.	
	_____	S. Gomez CNA

Measuring Height, Weight, and Head Circumference: Infants and Toddlers (Under 3 Years of Age)

Infant and toddler growth is rapid and requires frequent monitoring. Infants are usually seen every 2 months to monitor growth and development patterns. Careful measuring and graphing of these patterns can help detect early changes that are important.

Measuring Head Circumference

Measuring head circumference screens infants and toddlers for abnormal head size. Watching head size can alert the provider if a problem such as **hydroencephaly** is present. Always place the measuring tape over the occipital bone on the back of the head and wrap forward just above the ears to center of forehead.

Measuring Infant and Toddler Height

Infant and toddler heights indicate normal or abnormal growth patterns. Always use the same technique to measure their height and weight. Never estimate height. Use a tape measure or the ruler on the scale or tabletop.

hydroencephaly
(hi DROW n sef awl ee)
Excessive accumulation of cerebrospinal fluid in the brain, often leading to increased brain size and other brain trauma.

PROCEDURE | **20.6** | ## Measuring Height of Adult/Child (Over 3 Years of Age)

BACKGROUND: Height measurement is an indicator of normal or abnormal growth and development. Accurate measurement helps determine whether the child is developing normally.

ALERT: Follow Standard Precautions.

PREPROCEDURE

1. Wash hands.

2. Put paper towel on platform of scale.

3. Explain procedure and provide privacy.

PROCEDURE

4. Raise height-measuring rod on back of scale so that tip of height-measuring rod is above patient's head.

5. Instruct patient to remove shoes.

6. Ask patient to step onto scale and turn around to face away from balance bar.

7. Instruct patient to place heels against back of scale and stand straight.

8. Lift up measuring rod so that it points out above patient's head.

9. Lower rod gently until it rests on patient's head.

10. Assist patient in stepping off scales.

11. Read numbers just above edge of hollow bar of rod at back of scale.

12. Record height on medical record in feet and inches, centimeters, or inches only, according to your provider's policy.

POSTPROCEDURE

13. Discard paper towel.

14. Wash hands.

12/09/11	1500	
	Height 33 in.	
		M. Gonzales CMA
	or	
04/02/11	1500	
	Height 82.5 cm.	
		M. Gonzales CMA

20.7 **Measuring the Head Circumference of an Infant/Toddler (Under 3 Years of Age)**

BACKGROUND: Head circumference is an indicator of normal or abnormal growth development. Accurate measurement helps determine whether the infant/toddler is developing normally.

ALERT: Follow Standard Precautions.

PREPROCEDURE

1. Wash hands.

2. Obtain measuring tape.

3. Identify the patient.

4. Explain procedure to parent.

PROCEDURE

5. Place infant in supine position.

6. Position measuring tape over occipital bone and wrap toward forehead. Bring tape just above ears to the center of the forehead.

7. Record measurement.

POSTPROCEDURE

8. Wash hands.

04/02/11	1000
	Head circumference measures 15 in.
	_____ M. Gonzales CMA
	or
04/26/12	1000
	Head circumference measures 37.5 cm
	_____ M. Gonzales CMA

PROCEDURE **20.8** **Measuring the Height of an Infant/Toddler**

BACKGROUND: Height is an indicator of normal or abnormal growth development. Accurate measurement helps determine whether the infant/toddler is developing normally.

ALERT: Follow Standard Precautions.

PREPROCEDURE

1. Wash hands.

2. Obtain tape measure or measuring bar.

PROCEDURE

3. Place infant on flat surface.

4. Place zero mark of tape or measuring bar level with top of infant's head.

5. Ask parent or co-worker to hold top of head gently at zero mark.

6. Gently straighten legs.

7. Read measurement that is level with infant's heel.

NOTE: An alternative is to lay the infant on exam paper or sheet. Draw a line at the top of the infant's head.

Have the parent hold on to the infant and stretch out the infant's leg. Draw another line at the infant's heel. Have parent pick up the infant, and then measure between the two lines.

POSTPROCEDURE

8. Wash hands.

02/23/11	1000
	Height 21 in.
	_____ M. Gonzales CMA
	or
03/30/12	1000
	Height 52.5 cm
	_____ M. Gonzales CMA

Measuring Weight: Infant/Toddler

Infant and toddler weights are an important measure of growth patterns. Weight in an infant can change very quickly during an illness. Weight loss is an important indicator of dehydration. *Do not* change from weighing with clothes during one visit to weighing without clothes the next visit. Be consistent.

A large difference in the expected growth pattern may indicate a problem (for example, glandular imbalance or nutritional deficiency).

PROCEDURE **20.9** **Measuring the Weight of an Infant/Toddler**

BACKGROUND: Infant weight is an indicator of normal or abnormal growth development. Accurate measurement helps determine whether the infant/toddler is developing normally.

ALERT: Follow Standard Precautions.

PREPROCEDURE

1. Wash hands.

2. Assemble equipment.

   a. Infant scale, either balance or digital

   b. Towel

   c. Growth chart

3. Ask parent to remove infant's clothing.

4. Place clean towel on scale cradle to decrease shock of cold metal against infant or to prevent friction on a plastic cradle.

5. Balance the scale at zero with towel in place. Calibrate a digital scale to zero with towel in place.

PROCEDURE

6. Place infant face up on scale. Keep diaper or towel over infant's genital area in case of elimination.

7. Place one hand over infant (almost touching) to give a sense of security.

8. Slide weight easily until scale balances or take measurement from digital reading.

9. Read scale in pounds and ounces or in kilograms.

10. Return infant to parent.

POSTPROCEDURE

11. Balance the scale at zero mark or power off a digital scale.

12. Discard towel.

13. Wash hands.

14. Record weight on growth chart and in patient's chart.

04/29/12	0800
	Measured on balance scale, wt. 25 lb.
	_____ M. Gonzales CMA
	or
04/29/12	0800
	Weighed mother and then mother
	and child to determine weight
	Infant too distressed to weigh
	on infant balance scale
	Wt. 25 lb.
	_____ M. Gonzales CMA

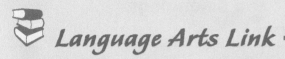

Language Arts Link

Working with Infants and Toddlers

Dealing with infants and toddlers can be very challenging. During the first two years of a child's life, most parents feel uncomfortable in determining if their toddler is unwell or simply fearful of the doctor's office. And, of course, the toddler cannot explain what is bothering them. So, you have to make both the child and parent comfortable.

Working with a partner, research the basic practices used in a pediatric office if a toddler comes in for a routine checkup and starts to cry hysterically. You still must measure the infant's height and weight, and conduct normal procedures.

If you are able to speak with professionals in these fields, interview them about how they deal with infants and with distraught parents. What tips can they offer to someone considering that field?

After you've completed your research, create a checklist that can be used by a medical assistant in a pediatric office to calm a parent and deal with a crying toddler.

Be sure to proofread your work to see if you can improve it by making it clearer, more concise, or more accurate. Check the spelling and grammar and correct any errors.

Transfer

When you assist in transferring the patient to another area, the patient may be unhappy about the move. Be calm and pleasant, and explain that you will make the move as easy as possible. Be certain that all of the patient's belongings are transferred to the new area and that the nurse assistant who is responsible for the patient knows that the patient has arrived. Follow the policies and procedures of your facility for transferring patients.

Discharge

A patient cannot be discharged without an order from his or her physician. If your patient plans to leave when it has not been ordered, report it to the head nurse immediately. Each facility has a policy and procedure for discharging the patient. Know what you are expected to do if you are asked to assist in discharging the patient. Be sure that the patient has all of his or her personal belongings. If the patient has valuables that were put away for safekeeping, remind the person to take them home. This is usually a happy time for the patient.

Moving Patient and Belongings to Another Room

BACKGROUND: Following the transfer procedure provides a sense of security for the patient and ensures that personal belongings are not lost. Introduction to the new area, roommate, and caregiver reduces the stress and provides continuing care.

ALERT: Follow Standard Precautions.

PREPROCEDURE

1. Wash hands.

2. Assemble equipment.

   a. Patient's chart

   b. Nursing care plan

   c. Medications (Remember: Nursing assistants cannot transfer medications.)

   d. Paper bag

3. Identify patient.

4. Explain what you are going to do.

PROCEDURE

5. Determine location to which patient is being transferred and see if new room is ready.

6. Gather patient belongings. (Check admission list.)

7. Determine how patient is to be transported.

   a. Wheelchair

   b. Stretcher

   c. Entire bed

   d. Ambulation

8. Transport patient to new unit.

9. Introduce to staff on new unit.

10. Introduce to new roommate.

11. Make patient comfortable.

12. Put away belongings.

13. Notify family members listed on patient's admission record of the move.

POSTPROCEDURE

14. Wash hands.

15. Give transferred medications, care plan, and chart to nurse. (Remember: Nursing assistants cannot transfer medication.)

16. Before leaving unit, record the following:

    a. Date and time of transfer

    b. How transported (e.g., wheelchair)

    c. How transfer was tolerated by patient.

17. Return to original unit and report completion of transfer.

> 07/14/11   1430
> Transferred in bed to room 20
> Introduced to roommate and
> caregiver. Resting quietly in bed.
> _____   S. Gomez CNA

BACKGROUND: Carefully following the discharge procedure ensures that the patient takes all medications and personal belongings and that final arrangements are completed.

ALERT: Follow Standard Precautions.

PREPROCEDURE

1. Check chart for discharge order.

2. Wash hands.

3. Identify patient.

4. Explain what you are going to do.

5. Provide privacy by pulling the privacy curtain.

PROCEDURE

6. Check with the patient's nurse regarding discharge status prior to continuing process. The nurse will need to:

   a. Remove any tethers such as IV lines or indwelling catheters.

   b. Review the patient's medication list, especially new medications and their use.

   c. Notify the patient of any follow up appointments to be scheduled or already scheduled with the physician, or for follow up lab or diagnostics.

   d. Inform the patient of any restriction of activity or diet.

7. Help patient dress.

8. Collect patient's belongings. Check room carefully. Remember to check for hearing aids and dentures.

9. Check belongings against admission list.

10. Secure and return valuables.

    a. Verify with patient that all valuables are there.

    b. Have patient sign for them.

11. Check to see if patient has prescriptions and/or medications and discharge instructions to take home.

12. Check to see if any equipment is to be taken home.

13. Help patient into wheelchair.

NOTE: Patients may have to go by the financial office before leaving.

14. Help patient into car.

POSTPROCEDURE

15. Return to unit.

    a. Remove all items left in unit (e.g., basins, disposable items).

    b. Clean unit according to your facility's policy.

16. Wash hands.

17. Record discharge.

    a. Date and time

    b. Method of transport

    c. Whom patient left with

08/31/12	1100
	Discharged by wheelchair with son,
	personal belongings,
	medications, and instructions
	———— *S. Gomez CNA*

Assisting with Examinations

Patients need reassurance during a physical examination. The patien may not know what to expect and may feel anxious. To help put him or her at ease, be friendly and efficient.

Equipment

Set up equipment according to the provider's request and check all equipment to be sure it works properly. Equipment varies depending on the body areas to be examined. Learn to anticipate each provider's needs and have equipment and supplies ready before he or she asks for them. Basic equipment includes the following:

- Pen light.
- Blood pressure cuff and sphygmomanometer.
- Stethoscope.
- Opthalmoscope. (**Figure 20.6**)
- Otoscope. (**Figure 20.7**)
- Percussion hammer. (**Figure 20.8**)
- Disposable gloves.
- Basin/pan.
- Tape measure. (**Figure 20.9**)
- Tongue blade. (**Figure 20.10**)
- Speculums.

You may need to set up additional equipment. The type of examination determines which equipment the provider will need.

Courtesy of ShutterStock.

Courtesy of ShutterStock.

Figure 20.6
Ophthalmoscope. When would an ophthalmoscope be used?

Figure 20.7
Otoscope. Who would use an otoscope and why?

Figure 20.8
Percussion hammer. Why would a percussion hammer be used?

Figure 20.9
Tape measure. When would you use a tape measure with a patient?

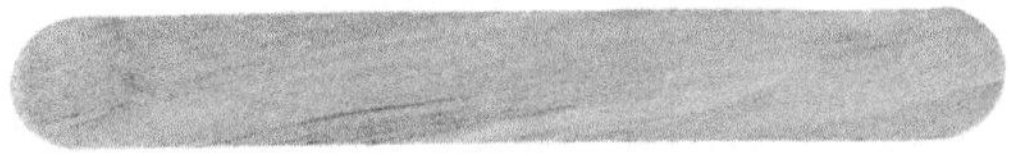

Figure 20.10
Tongue blade. What is the purpose of a tongue blade?

Examination Positions

There are specific positions for each procedure. Putting the patient in the correct position makes the examination easier. Always protect the patient's privacy by positioning and draping according to the directions in each procedure.

- **Horizontal recumbent (supine) position.** Use this position for examination, treatment, and surgical procedures of the ventral (anterior) part of the body (for example, for abdominal pain, removal of stitches in chest).

- **Fowler's position.** This position relieves patients who are having trouble breathing (for example, asthma, chest pain). This position allows examination of the anterior and posterior chest (for example, listening to heart and lung sounds).

- **Trendelenburg position.** This position helps restore blood flow to the brain when the body experiences shock. This position also helps promote drainage of congested lungs.

- **Dorsal lithotomy position.** Use this position to examine or perform surgical procedures on the peritoneal and rectal areas (for example, vaginal exam, cystoscopy).

- **Prone position.** Use this position for examination, treatment, or surgical procedures of the dorsal (back) part of the body.

- **Left lateral position and left Sims' position.** Use this position for minor rectal examinations, enemas, and treatments.
- **Knee-chest position.** Use this position for rectal examinations and surgical procedures. Some examination tables adjust to support the patient's abdomen and chest.
- **Jackknife.** Use this position for inserting a tube into the urethra.
- **Dorsal recumbent.** Use this position for the examination and treatment of the abdominal area and for vaginal or rectal exams.

PROCEDURE 20.12 Horizontal Recumbent (Supine) Position

BACKGROUND: Placing the patient in the correct position for treatment, examinations, and for comfort measures is essential for safe and accurate care of the patient.

ALERT: Follow Standard Precautions.

PREPROCEDURE

1. Wash hands.
2. Explain to patient what you are going to do.

PROCEDURE

3. Assist patient with gown.
4. Determine any problems associated with placing the patient in this position, such as increased respiratory distress, etc..

5. Assist patient to a position lying flat on his or her back with arms at side in good alignment, with a small pillow under the head.
6. Drape cover so that he or she is not exposed, leaving all edges of drape loose.

POSTPROCEDURE

7. After exam, assist patient off the table and with dressing if needed.
8. Wash hands.

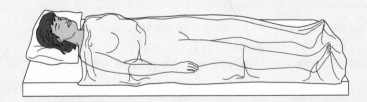

PROCEDURE 20.13 Fowler's Position

BACKGROUND: Placing the patient in the correct position for treatment, examinations, and for comfort measures is essential for safe and accurate care of the patient.

ALERT: Follow Standard Precautions.

PREPROCEDURE

1. Wash hands.

2. Explain to patient what you are going to do.

3. Assist patient with gown.

PROCEDURE

4. Determine any problems associated with placing the patient in this position, such as increase in back pain, etc.

5. Assist patient to a position lying flat on his or her back in good alignment with small pillow under their head.

6. Keep patient covered so that he or she is not exposed.

7. Flex knees slightly and support them with a pillow.

8. Adjust backrest to one of the following positions according to patient's or physician's needs: Low Fowlers 25°; Semi-Fowlers 45°; High Fowlers 90°. (See figure at top right.)

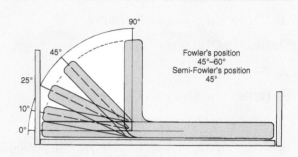

9. Drape cover so that patient is not exposed, leaving all edges of drape free.

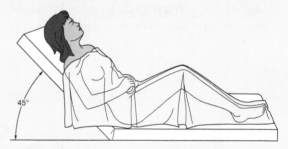

POSTPROCEDURE

10. After exam, assist patient off and table and with dressing.

11. Wash hands.

BACKGROUND: Placing the patient in the correct position for treatment, examinations, and for comfort measures is essential for safe and accurate care of the patient.

ALERT: Follow Standard Precautions.

PREPROCEDURE

1. Wash hands.

2. Explain to patient what you are going to do.

3. Assist patient with gown.

4. Determine any problems associated with placing patient in this position, such as increased respiratory distress, etc.

5. Assist patient to a position lying flat on his or her back in good alignment.

PROCEDURE

6. Drape cover so that he or she is not exposed, leaving all edges of drape loose.

7. Lower the head of the table until the body is at a 45° angle. Legs may be bent or extended.

8. Reassure patient that he or she will not slide off table. Remain with patient at all times.

POSTPROCEDURE

9. After exam, assist patient off the table and with dressing.

10. Wash hands.

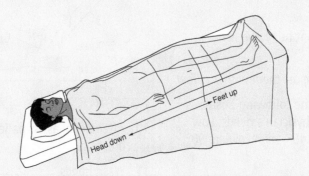

PROCEDURE 20.15 Dorsal Lithotomy Position

BACKGROUND: Placing the patient in the correct position for treatment, examinations, and for comfort measures is essential for safe and accurate care of the patient.

ALERT: Follow Standard Precautions.

PREPROCEDURE

1. Wash hands.

2. Explain to patient what you are going to do

3. Assist patient with gown.

PROCEDURE

4. Determine any problems associated with placing patient in this position, such as increased pain, etc.

5. Assist patient to a position lying flat on his or her back with arms at side.

6. Place pillow under head.

7. Cover patient so that he or she is not exposed.

8. Gently assist patient to bend knees.

9. Separate legs by placing each foot flat on bed about 2 feet apart or in stirrups attached to examination table.

10. Move patient's hips to edge of end of table when stirrups are available.

11. Drape with half-size sheet positioned with one corner toward head and opposite corners between legs. Secure side corner around legs.

12. Remain with the patient.

POSTPROCEDURE

13. After exam, assist patient off the table and with dressing.

14. Wash hands.

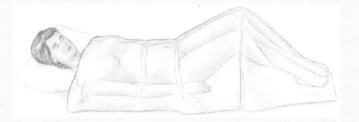

20.16 **Prone Position**

BACKGROUND: Placing the patient in the correct position for treatment, examinations, and for comfort measures is essential for safe and accurate care of the patient.

ALERT: Follow Standard Precautions.

PREPROCEDURE

1. Wash hands.

2. Explain to patient what you are going to do.

3. Assist patient with gown.

PROCEDURE

4. Determine any problems associated with placing patient in this position, such as increased pain or respiratory distress.

5. Turn patient toward self.

6. Position patient on the abdomen with arms flexed by head.

7. Position head to side on small pillow.

8. Cover patient so that he or she is not exposed and let drape hang loosely.

POSTPROCEDURE

9. After exam, assist patient off the table and with dressing.

10. Wash hands.

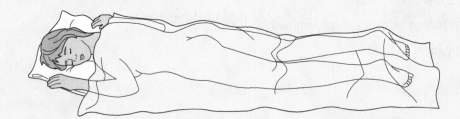

BACKGROUND: Placing the patient in the correct position for treatment, examinations, and for comfort measures is essential for safe and accurate care of the patient.

ALERT: Follow Standard Precautions.

PREPROCEDURE

1. Wash hands.

2. Explain to patient what you are going to do.

3. Assist patient with gown.

PROCEDURE

4. Determine any problems associated with placing patient in this position, such as increased pain, respiratory distress, etc.

5. Assist patient to a position lying flat on his or her back.

6. Cover patient so that he or she is not exposed.

7. Assist patient to turn onto left side.

8. Position patient's left arm slightly behind him or her on bed and bend right arm in front of the body.

9. Turn head to side on small pillow.

10. Gently bend both knees.

11. Place right leg slightly forward of left leg for lateral position.

12. Bend right knee toward chest for Sims' position.

13. Drape with one sheet; make sure drape is hung loosely.

POSTPROCEDURE

14. After exam, assist patient off table and with dressing.

15. Wash hands.

PROCEDURE 20.18 Knee-Chest Position

BACKGROUND: Placing the patient in the correct position for treatment, examinations, and for comfort measures is essential for safe and accurate care of the patient.

ALERT: Follow Standard Precautions.

PREPROCEDURE

1. Wash hands.

2. Explain to patient what you are going to do.

3. Determine any problems associated with placing patient in this position such as increased pain, etc.

4. Assist patient to a position lying flat on his or her back.

PROCEDURE

5. Cover patient so that he or she is not exposed.

6. Assist patient to turn onto his or her stomach, keeping patient covered.

7. Instruct patient to raise hips upward by kneeling on both knees.

NOTE: It is hard for the patient to stay in this position, so put them in it immediately prior to the procedure and stay with them.

8. Rest patient's head and shoulders on a pillow.

9. Flex arms slightly and have them at the side of their head.

10. Drape with a large sheet, allowing edges to hang free.

POSTPROCEDURE

11. After exam, assist patient off table and with dressing.

12. Wash hands.

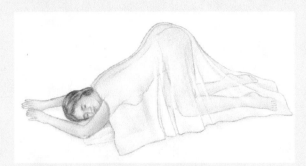

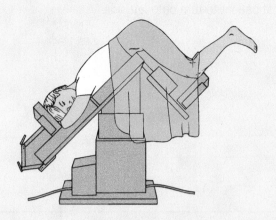

Examination and Diagnostic Techniques

Examinations require four basic techniques:

1. **Observation/Inspection.** Here the provider looks at the patient for normal and abnormal appearance. Skin, eyes, hair, nails, movements, or actions that look unusual may be important in determining an illness. (Figure 20.11a)

2. **Palpation.** In this procedure, the provider feels parts of the body for unusual or abnormal conditions. Feeling and applying pressure also allow the provider to locate tender or painful areas. (Figure 20.11b)

3. **Percussion.** Providers use their fingers to tap over areas of the body. The sounds the provider hears during percussion indicate the fullness, emptiness, and size of internal organs. (Figure 20.11c)

4. **Auscultation.** The provider listens to body sounds through a stethoscope. Sounds of the heart and lungs, bowel sounds, and even the flow of blood through arteries can be heard. (**Figure 20.11d**)

These four techniques give a provider clues about how the body is working. For example, if a patient complains of a chest cold, the provider listens to the chest with a stethoscope. Gurgling sounds or very little airflow in the lungs tell the provider that the lungs are congested with fluid. A chest x-ray confirms what **auscultation** indicated.

auscultation
(aw skuhl TEY shuh n)
The act of listening, either directly or through a stethoscope or other instrument, to sounds within the body as a method of diagnosis.

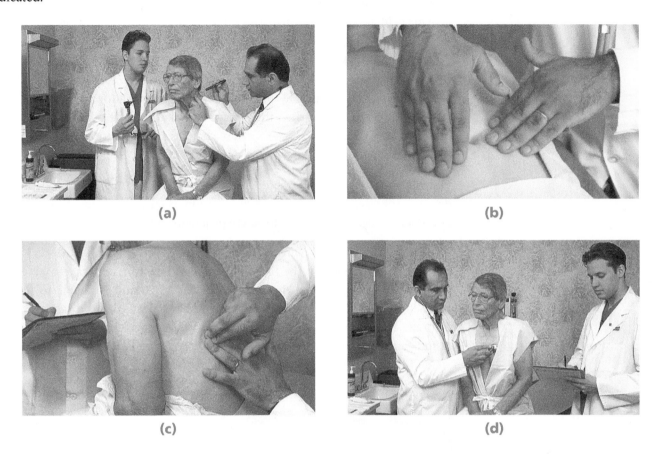

(a)

(b)

(c)

(d)

When a patient complains of pain or other problems, the provider uses the four basic examination techniques. Prepare each patient for observation, palpation, percussion, and auscultation. Tell patients what you want them to do. Remember that patients are often nervous. Show patience and understanding.

To determine a final **diagnosis** the physician looks for clues from the following sources:

- Patient history.
- Physical examination findings.
- Vital signs.
- Laboratory results.
- Diagnostic test results.
- Symptoms described by the patient.

figure 20.11
Methods of physical examinations:
(a) inspection,
(b) palpation,
(c) percussion,
(d) auscultation.

diagnosis
(dahy uh g NOH sis)
Identification of a disease or condition.

baseline
(BEYS lahyn)
A number, graph, or indication to use as a guideline. A measurement taken at a later time may differ from the baseline, indicating a possible cause for concern.

If there is more than one possible diagnosis, the provider needs to rule out each possible condition before determining a final diagnosis. For example, a patient complaining of abdominal pain may need additional tests to:

- Rule out (R/O) appendicitis.
- Rule out (R/O) gastroenteritis.
- Rule out (R/O) pelvic inflammatory disease (PID).

The provider makes a final diagnosis when tests rule out possible conditions and provide evidence of a specific disease.

Testing Visual Acuity

Vision acuity (clearness) testing helps the provider detect eye disease or injury. Vision acuity tests are usually part of a physical examination. A provider always does a vision acuity test when the patient complains of eye pain, itching, tenderness, or injury. The provider can identify changes and evaluate the treatment more effectively when there is a **baseline** acuity test.

Patients over age 65 should be encouraged to obtain annual eye exams for early diagnosis of disease and correction of common problems associated with the aging eye. Poor eyesight contributes to safety problems in the aged.

To read the result of the visual acuity test on a Snellen chart (**Figure 20.12**), find the fraction to the left of the line the patient is able to read. For example, if the patient reads all the letters in the line marked 20/20 and is unable to read line 20/15, the patient's vision is 20/20. The top number means that the patient is 20 feet from the chart. The bottom number is the distance at which a patient with normal vision can read that row of letters. If line 20/50 is the last line read, the patient's vision is 20/50. This means that the patient is able to read at 20 feet what a person with normal vision sees at 50 feet.

Figure 20.12
Shellen eye chart for English readers. Using the Shellen eye chart, what is your vision?

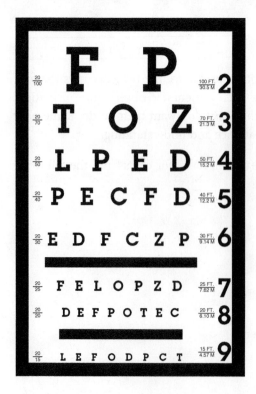

PROCEDURE 20.19 Testing Visual Acuity: Snellen Chart

BACKGROUND: Vision affects all activities of daily living. Correct measurement of visual acuity is essential to determine whether patient has normal or abnormal eyesight.

ALERT: Follow Standard Precautions.

PREPROCEDURE

1. Wash hands.

2. Assure that the Snellen Chart is at patient's eye level and that the tape for them to stand on is 20 feet from the chart.

3. Identify patient.

4. Explain procedure to patient.

PROCEDURE

5. Position patient 20 feet (6 meters) from Snellen chart. Have patient stand with heel on 20 foot mark.

6. Instruct patient to keep both eyes open during testing. Ask them to remove corrective lenses.

7. Ask patient to cover left eye with an occluder and read smallest line of letters that he or she can see.

8. Use a pointer and point to letters in the row in random order. Do not cover the letter or symbol with the pointer.

9. Record the distance patient is from the chart compared to the size of letters patient can see clearly (e.g., 20/20, 20/30, 20/40).

10. Repeat test with right eye covered.

11. Repeat test, allowing patient to use both eyes.

12. Repeat each test with patient wearing glasses (if he or she has prescription lenses).

POSTPROCEDURE

13. Wash hands.

Summary

The medical assisting skills of admitting, registering, transferring, and discharging a patient are important processes in a patient's health. You must interact with and make the patient feel at ease, as well as perform some basic tasks (such as measuring height and weight.)

SECTION 20.1 — Review Questions

1. When admitting a patient, what are the basic procedures?

2. What two forms must be completed by new patients when registering?

3. How would you measure an infant's head circumference?

4. List the five basic pieces of equipment used during examinations.

5. Why is it important to use a consistent method in weighing an infant?

6. Name and explain the purpose of three examination and diagnostic techniques.

Learn By Doing: Section 20.1 Activity

1. Complete Worksheets 1 and 2.

2. Complete Worksheets 3, 4, and 5 as assigned.

3. Complete Worksheet/Activity 6 as assigned.

4. When you are confident that you can meet each objective for this section, ask your teacher for the section evaluation.

SECTION 20.2

Pharmacology and Medication Administration

Background

Medical assistants are responsible for understanding the guidelines for preparing and administering medications. There are a variety of resources commonly available to help answer their questions. In addition, medical assistants must be aware of the legal ramifications of controlling, using, and distributing various drugs.

Objectives

When you have completed this section, you will be able to do the following:

- Match key terms with their correct meanings.

- Match common prescription abbreviations with their meanings.

- Match controlled substances with their assigned schedule level.

- Name four drug reference books.

- Describe methods to ensure safekeeping of medication.

- Write a formula for calculating medication dosage.

- Name six rights of medication administration.

- Recognize the guidelines for preparing and administering medications.

- Demonstrate all procedures in this chapter.

Pharmacology and Medication Administration

Working with medication and administering medication are serious responsibilities. As a medical assistant you are responsible for the following:

- Administering medication.

- Being aware of side effects.

- Interpreting prescriptions.

- Reinforcing the provider's instructions.
- Recognizing adverse effects of medications.
- Reporting accurate observations.
- Using references to obtain directions.

Common Prescription Abbreviations

Special abbreviations and symbols are used when working with medication. Abbreviations are commonly used when delivering medical care. Some of these are listed below. However, each facility may use a different set of accepted abbreviations. It is very important that you follow your facilities accepted list. Using abbreviations that are not considered acceptable in your facility can lead to errors in treatment that could be serious.

cap(s)	capsule(s)
Dil.	dilute
Dr	dram
D/W	dextrose in water
fl or fld	fluid
Gal	gallon
gt or gtt	drop
IM	intramuscular
IU	international units
IV	intravenous
Kg	kilogram
L	liter
Liq	liquid
m or min	minim
Mcg.	microgram
mEq	milliequivalent
Mg	milligram
Ml	milliliter
NS	normal saline
OD	right eye
Oint	ointment
OS	left eye
OU	both eyes
Oz	ounce
Pt	pint or patient
Pulv	powder
sc or subc or subq	subcutaneous
tinc or tr or tinct	tincture

Legal Issues

There are federal guidelines and legislation regulating the manufacture, distribution, dispensing, and sale of medication. Federal regulations are monitored by the Drug Enforcement Agency (DEA) of the Department of Justice. State regulations are monitored by the State Department of Health and Human Services.

The medical assistant supports the provider by:

- Monitoring expiration dates of the physician's DEA registration.
- Keeping records and inventory that are legally acceptable.
- Controlling access to all drugs, controlled substances, and prescription pads.
- Destroying medication when expired. Disposal of controlled substances must be witnessed.

Drugs that can cause addiction and abuse are divided into five groups, called schedules. Each schedule names the drugs and explains their ability to become addicting and/or abused. (Table 20.2)

Prescriptions

Prescription drugs are medications that require monitoring by a licensed physician. The Federal Drug Administration determines which drugs must be prescribed by a physician. Prescriptions are instructions to a pharmacist to supply the patient with medication in a specified amount. The prescription also provides directions for taking medication. The prescription is a legal document. There are six parts to complete in a prescription:

1. Patient information and superscription:
   - Date.
   - Patient's name.
   - Patient's address.
   - Age, if child.
   - Rx, meaning "recipe" or "take."
2. Inscription:
   - Name of medication.
   - Amount of medication.
3. Subscription:
   - Directions to pharmacist.
4. Sig or signa:
   - Directions to patient.
5. Physician's signature and address, registry number, and controlled substances approval number (BNDD).
6. Number of times, if any, the prescription can be refilled.

Table 20.2   Schedule of Controlled Substances

The drugs and drug products that come under the jurisdiction of the Controlled Substances Act are divided into five schedules. Some examples from each schedule are outlined below. For a complete listing of all of the controlled substances, contact any office of the Drug Enforcement Administration or log on to www.DEA.GOV and click on "Drug Scheduling."

Category	Description	Examples	
Schedule I	The substances in this schedule are those that have no accepted medical use in the United States and have a high abuse potential.	acetylmethadol dihydromorphine fenethylline heroin LSD marijuana MDMA (Ecstasy)	mescaline methaqualone N-ethylamphetamine peyote psilocybin tilidine
Schedule II	The substances in this schedule have a high abuse potential with severe psychic or physical dependence liability. Schedule II controlled substances consist of certain narcotic, stimulant, and depressant drugs.	amobarbital amphetamine (Dexedrine) cocaine codeine dronabinol etorphine hydrochloride fentanyl (Sublimaze) hydromorphone (Dilaudid) meperidine (Demerol) methadone methamphetamine (Desoxyn) methylphenidate (Ritalin) morphine	nabilone opium oxycodone (Percodan) oxymorphone (Numorphan) pantopon pentobarbital phenmetrazine (Preludin) phenylacetone secobarbital sufentanil
Schedule III	The substances in this schedule have an abuse potential less than those in Schedules I and II, and include compounds containing limited quantities of certain narcotic drugs and non-narcotic drugs.	amobarbital compounds benphetamine chlorphentermine clortermine derivatives of barbituric acid nalorphine	paregoric pentobarbital compounds phendimetrazine secobarbital compounds Tylenol with Codeine
Schedule IV	The substances in this schedule have an abuse potential less than those listed in Schedule III.	alprazolam (Xanax) Barbital chloral hydrate chlordiazepoxide (Librium) clonazepam (Clonapin) clorazepate (Tranxene) detropropoxyphene (Darvon) diazepam (Valium) diethylpropion ethclorovynol (Placidyl) ethinamate (Valmid) fenfluramine flurazepam (Dalmane) halazepam (Paxipam) lorazepam (Ativan) mebutamate meprobamate (Equanil, Miltown) methohexital methylphenobarbital	midazolam (Versed) oxazepam (Serax) pentazocine (Talwin-NX) phenobarbital phentermine prazepam (Verstran) quazepam (Dormalin) temazepam (Restoril) triazolam (Halcion) paraldehyde

(continued)

Table 20.2   Schedule of Controlled Substances (continued)

Category	Description	Examples
Schedule V	The substances in this schedule have an abuse potential less than those listed in Schedule IV and consist primarily of preparations containing limited quantities of certain narcotic and stimulant drugs generally for antitussive, antidiarrheal, and analgesic purposes.	buprenorphine propylhexedrine

Medication/drugs are described in three ways:

1. A brand name is assigned to a drug by the manufacturer. The brand name is commonly used in advertising a medication.

2. A generic name often describes the chemical makeup or classification of a drug. Generic names are adopted by the U.S. Adopted Name Council (USAN); Pharmacopia (USP), *a database catalog;* or the United States National Formulary (NF), *the dictionary of drug names.*

3. The chemical name reflects the chemicals in the drug and its structure.

The cost of generic medication is usually less than that of brand-name medication. Patients save money if the doctor prescribes the generic form or tells the patient that a generic medication is acceptable.

Drug Reference Books

There are so many medications available that it is difficult to remember all the important information. To determine the best medication for a patient, doctors often refer to reference books. Nurses must have knowledge of the use, common dosages, and side effects of every medication they administer.

Your facility will provide an up to date nurse reference book for use on the unit. No medication should be given until the nurse feels comfortable with her knowledge of the medication.

Whenever possible, the patient should be advised of the medication being delivered. If the patient questions the medication, the nurse should check the physician's order and the medication to assure that it is correct and then reassure the patient. Patients have the right to refuse medication as well as any other treatment being provided to them.

The following paragraphs briefly describe the most frequently used reference books.

The *United States Pharmacopia* (USP)–*National Formulary* (NF) is published every five years. The publication lists only official drugs, and it identifies drug standards. The NF chapter explains the ingredients of each drug. Drug information includes the following:

- Description of drug.

- Standards for purity.

- Strength and composition.

- Storage.
- Use.
- Dosage.

American Medical Association Drug Evaluations is a periodically revised book of officially established and recognized drug names and standards.

American Hospital Formulary Services (AHFS) provides periodic supplements that maintain current information. This publication gives unbiased drug information. Drugs are listed by generic names according to their therapeutic or pharmacological class.

The *Physicians' Desk Reference (PDR)* is not an official drug reference book but it is the most commonly used (**Figure 20.13**). It is published annually; periodic (twice yearly) supplements provide information on newest medications. PDR information is also available at PDR.net, for which the health care facility where you work may have an online membership. Access to PDR.net is free to many health care professionals, so you will be able to obtain the information on a computer or smartphone. The PDR contains the following information:

- Partial list of drug manufacturers, including their addresses.
- Emergency telephone number.
- Brand-name drugs (Section 2, pink pages).
- Drugs listed by category or classification (Section 3, blue pages).
- Drugs listed by generic and chemical names (Section 4, yellow pages).
- Locations of poison control centers (following Section 4) (Section 5).
- Pictures of drugs with their manufacturers.
- Each drug's composition, uses and action, administration, dosage, precautions, contraindications, and side effects, and its common, generic, and chemical names (Section 6, the largest section of white pages).
- List of manufacturers of diagnostic drugs and the uses of those drugs (Section 7, green pages).

It is important for MAs to understand how to use reference books. MAs are responsible for giving medication correctly. Drug reference books provide guidelines for responsible administration of prescribed medication. The *Physicians' Desk Reference* is the most available reference.

Using the Physicians' Desk Reference (PDR)

The PDR can be used in a variety of ways. To demonstrate this we will use the example of a patient who hands you an oval-shaped pill with "Wallace 200" stamped on it. You can take that pill to the PDR and compare it with the pictures in Section 5. An exact comparison indicates that Wallace is the manufacturer and 200 is the dose. To become more familiar with the PDR, follow the steps in Procedure 20.20.

Physicians' Desk Reference (PDR)
A commonly used reference book that provides information about drugs, drug manufacturers, emergency phone numbers, and more.

Figure 20.13
The PDR is a frequently used reference in medical settings (see Procedure 20.20).

BACKGROUND: It is important for the health care worker to know details about medications. The PDR is an essential tool that provides information about medications the health care worker gives. Understanding how to use the PDR helps in finding information in a timely manner.

PROCEDURE

1. Identify the name of the manufacturer by going to Section 5; compare the tablet with pictures to identify the medication.

   a. Wallace is the manufacturer.

   b. Turn to the page where Wallace pills are displayed.

   c. Match the pill with pictures of pills displayed.

   d. A yellow oval pill marked "Wallace 200" matches "Soma Compound with Codeine 200 mg" in the display.

2. Turn to Section 2, the pink pages. Find "Soma Compound with Codeine 200 mg." Two page numbers are listed.

   a. The first page number refers to Section 5, the picture of the medication.

   b. The second page number refers to Section 6 and provides product information.

3. Turn to the page number indicated in Section 6 to find specific drug information.

   a. Description of drug

   b. Clinical pharmacology

   c. Indications and usage (describes the reasons for using the drug)

   d. Contraindications (reasons not to give this drug)

   e. Warnings

   f. Precautions

   g. Dosage and administration

   h. How supplied

   i. Storage recommendations

4. Go to Section 1 for more information about a drug. Find the manufacturer:

   a. Wallace Laboratories is listed with the W's in the alphabetical list.

   b. Write requests for information using the address supplied.

   c. Call for assistance using the professional services telephone number or night and weekend emergency number if available.

Storage and Handling of Drugs

Medication requires special handling. To ensure the safekeeping of medications, always:

- Keep medications in a locked area away from other supplies.
- Keep medications in original containers.
- Refrigerate medications that require storage at lower than room temperatures.
- Rotate medications so that the oldest are used before expiration dates.
- Destroy expired medications. (Follow office policy when destroying medication.)

- Keep medications requiring darkness out of the light (in a dark cupboard or container).
- Be aware of medications that react with other materials (for example, some medications react with plastic so must be stored in glass).

To organize the storage of drugs, use a simple, logical system. One example of a system is alphabetic arrangement by classification—for example, all **antibiotics** together, **contraceptives** together, **diuretics** together. Within each classification, separate oral, **parenteral**, **topical**, and other medications. Federal law requires that you place all controlled substances (see Table 20.2) in a locked cabinet safely separated from other medications. Any controlled substances that are lost or stolen must be reported by the physician to the Drug Enforcement Agency.

Drug Dosage

Pharmacy calculations are an essential function of the Pharmacy Technician. In order to read, write and fill out prescriptions, the health care professional must understand Roman Numerals. They are commonly used in pharmacology, especially in the directions (or Sig) on prescriptions. For instance, 3 tablets three times a day is often written as lll tabs t.i.d. It is expected that pharmacy technicians will understand the primary Roman Numerals and the rules for adding and subtracting them.

A basic list of the Roman Numerals is included below:

II or ii for 2	VIII or viii for 8
III or iii for 3	IX or ix for 9
IV or iv for 4	X for 10
V or v for 5	XI or xi for 11
VI or vi for 6	XXXII or xxxii for 32
VII or vii for 7	XLV or xlv for 45

Giving the right medication dosage is an important part of administering medication. Many medications are prepackaged and ready to give. Some medications require dosage calculation. A simple **formula** for calculating dosage is:

$$\frac{\text{dosage you want}}{\text{dosage you have}} = \text{dosage you give}$$

Example: The physician orders 200 mg (milligrams) of a medication. You have 100-mg tablets of the medication.

$$\frac{\text{dosage you want}}{\text{dosage you have}} = \frac{200 \text{ mg}}{100\text{-mg tablets}} = \text{dosage you give}$$

Divide 200 mg by 100 mg:

$$100 \overline{)200} \\ 200 \\ ^{2}$$

The patient needs to take two tablets to receive 200 mg of the ordered medicine.

antibiotics
(anti bi ot ik)
Substances that slow growth of or destroy microorganisms.

contraceptives
(kon tre sept tivs)
Items that serve to prevent pregnancy.

diuretics
(die ret ik)
Drugs that increase urine output.

parenteral
(pa REN ter uhl)
Not in the digestive system (e.g., injections are parenterally administered.

topical
(TOP i kuhl)
Surface of the body.

formula
(FAWR myuh luh)
Accepted rule (e.g., a math formula and a baby formula are both guidelines or rules).

The medication that the doctor orders must be measured in the same terms as the medication you have on hand. For example, if the physician orders a medication in milligrams and you have doses measured in grams, you must convert milligrams to grams. To convert measures, see Table 20.3 or use the following easy steps:

- To convert grams to grains or grains to grams, you must learn that 1 g = 15 gr.

- To convert grams to grains, multiply the number of grams × 15. *Example:* 30 g × 15 = 450 gr

- To convert grains to grams, divide the number of grains by 15. *Example:* 450 gr ÷ 15 = 30 g

- To convert grams to milligrams, move the decimal three places to the right. *Example:* 1 g = 1,000 mg (1 g = 1,000. mg)

- To convert milligrams to grams, move the decimal three places to the left. *Example:* 1,000 mg = 1 g (1,000. mg = 1.000 g)

Table 20.3   Metric Dosage and Apothecary Equivalents

Liquid Measure		Weight	
Metric	Approximate Apothecary Equivalents	Metric	Approximate Apothecary Equivalents
1,000 mL	1 quart = 1 L	30 g	1 ounce
750 mL	$1^1/_2$ pints	15 g	4 drams
500 mL	1 pint	10 g	$2^1/_2$ drams
240 mL	8 fluidounces	7.5 g	2 drams
200 mL	7 fluidounces	6 g	90 grains
100 mL	$3^1/_2$ fluidounces	5 g	75 grains
50 mL	$1^3/_4$ fluidounces	3 g	45 grains
30 mL	1 fluidounce	2 g	30 grains ($^1/_2$ dram)
15 mL	4 fluidrams	1.5 g	22 grains
10 mL	$2^1/_2$ fluidrams	1 g	15 grains
8 mL	2 fluidrams	0.75 g	12 grains
5 mL	$1^1/_4$ fluidrams	0.6 g	10 grains
4 mL	1 fluidram	0.5 g	$7^1/_2$ grains
3 mL	45 minims	0.4 g	6 grains
2 mL	30 minims	0.3 g	5 grains
1 mL	15 minims	0.25 g	4 grains
0.75 mL	12 minims	0.2 g	3 grains
0.6 mL	10 minims	0.15 g	$2^1/_2$ grains
0.5 mL	8 minims	0.12 g	2 grains
0.3 mL	5 minims	0.1 g	$1^1/_2$ grains
0.25 mL	4 minims	75 mg	$1^1/_4$ grains
0.2 mL	3 minims	60 mg	1 grain
0.1 mL	$1^1/_2$ minims	50 mg	$^3/_4$ grain
0.06 mL	1 minim	40 mg	$^2/_3$ grain
0.05 mL	$^3/_4$ minim	30 mg	$^1/_2$ grain
0.03 mL	$^1/_2$ minim	25 mg	$^3/_8$ grain
		20 mg	$^1/_3$ grain
		15 mg	$^1/_4$ grain
		12 mg	$^1/_5$ grain
		10 mg	$^1/_6$ grain

(continued)

Table 20.3   Metric Dosage and Apothecary Equivalents (continued)

Liquid Measure		Weight	
Metric	**Approximate Apothecary Equivalents**	**Metric**	**Approximate Apothecary Equivalents**
		8 mg	$1/8$ grain
		6 mg	$1/10$ grain
		5 mg	$1/12$ grain
		4 mg	$1/15$ grain
		3 mg	$1/20$ grain
		2 mg	$1/30$ grain
		1.5 mg	$1/40$ grain
		1.2 mg	$1/50$ grain
		1 mg	$1/60$ grain
		0.8 mg	$1/80$ grain
		0.6 mg	$1/100$ grain
		0.5 mg	$1/120$ grain
		0.4 mg	$1/150$ grain
		0.3 mg	$1/200$ grain
		0.25 mg	$1/250$ grain
		0.2 mg	$1/300$ grain
		0.15 mg	$1/400$ grain
		0.12 mg	$1/500$ grain
		0.1 mg	$1/600$ grain

Some measurements and equivalents* for pouring medicines (to be memorized):

04 mL (4–5 mL)	=	1 teaspoon	or	1 dram	or	60 drops (gtt)
01 mL	=	$1/4$ teaspoon	or	$1/4$ dram	or	15–16 drops (gtt)
02 mL	=	$1/2$ teaspoon	or	$1/2$ dram	or	30–32 drops (gtt)
15 mL	=	3 teaspoons	or	4 drams	or	$1/2$ ounce (oz)
30 mL	=	6 teaspoons	or	8 drams	or	1 ounce (oz)
1 tablespoon	=	3 teaspoons	or	15 mL	or	$1/2$ ounce (oz)
2 tablespoons	=	6 teaspoons	or	30 mL	or	1 ounce (oz)
6 fluidounces	=	1 teacupful	or	150–180 mL		
8 fluidounces	=	1 glassful	or	240–250 mL		
2 pints	=	1 quart	or	1,000 mL		
4 quarts	=	1 gallon	or	4,000 mL		

* These equivalents are approximate only. In practice, the cubic centimeter and the milliliter are equal. Actually, the cubic centimeter is less than the milliliter by 0.000028 cc.

Review Chapter 11, Section 11.2. This review will help you remember common medical weights and measures. Use the formula in Chapter 11 to review and practice changing or converting the following:

- Ounces (oz) to cubic centimeters (cc) or milliliters.
- Milliliters (mL) to ounces (oz).
- Pounds (lb) to kilograms (kg).
- Kilograms (kg) to pounds (lb).

Community Service

Volunteer to create a poster for a senior citizen's center that describes the parts of a prescription label. Part of the poster should be an enlargement of a standard prescription label from a local pharmacy, with each line identified and described.

(a)

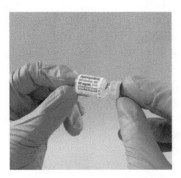

(b)

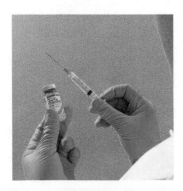

(c)

Figure 20.14
The safety and proper care of patients depends on your correct and careful handling of medications. Always confirm the six "rights" of medication administration.

Administering Medications

To prevent mistakes and injury to the patient, always follow carefully the six "rights" of medication administration:

1. Right drug (Figure 20.14a).
2. Right dose (Figure 20.14b).
3. Right route of administration (Figure 20.14c).
4. Right time.
5. Right patient.
6. Right documentation.

Guidelines for Preparing and Administering Medications

1. Wash hands.
2. Follow only written medication orders.
3. Do not allow yourself to be distracted while preparing medication.
4. Always read the medication label three times:
   a. When taking it from the shelf (do not use medication that is not clearly labeled).
   b. Before measuring the ordered amount.
   c. When returning the container to the shelf or discarding it.
5. Know the drug you are giving. Look it up in one of the reference books to confirm the expected action, dosage, and route of administration. You need to know the side effects. For example, if the patient will have dry mouth, you might want to have hard candy available for them or make sure they had plenty of water to drink. If the medicine will turn their urine blue or orange, might want to warm them about this, so that they don't get upset.
6. Calculate the ordered dosage if necessary. Verify calculations with a co-worker.
7. Measure medications.
   a. Measure solid medications such as pills, tablets, or capsules by dropping the medication from the package into a medicine cup.
   b. Observe liquid medications for:
      ■ Color change.
      ■ Cloudiness.
      ■ Sedimentation.

NOTE: If these conditions exist, discard the medication.

   c. Always have a second nurse verify order, dose, and measured medication in syringe when giving:
      ■ Insulin.
      ■ Heparin.

   d. Gently shake emulsions and suspensions to mix ingredients completely. Shaking distributes all of the ingredients equally. This allows you to give accurate amounts of all ingredients.

e. When pouring liquids, place the label of the bottle in the palm of your hand to keep liquid from dripping on label.

f. Pour the liquid into a medicine cup; hold at eye level to achieve an accurate measure.

g. Clean the neck of the medication bottle before capping.

h. Never mix two or more medications unless ordered (check compatibility).

ALERT: Follow Standard Precautions.

8. Apply topical medications to the skin, mucous membrane (including vaginal creams and suppositories), or the cornea of the eye. Always follow the specific directions on the medication. Use aseptic technique to prevent contamination of medication.

9. Never leave medication unattended. Prepare medication and administer immediately. Watch the patient swallow oral medication.

10. Never administer medication prepared by another person.

11. Always verify the patient's name and the order on the chart to ensure that the right medication is given to the right patient.

12. Check patient allergies before administering medication. Look at allergies listed on patient's chart and ask patient if he or she is allergic to the medication.

Table 20.4   Medication Administration Procedures

Administration Route	Type of Medication	Administration Procedure
Buccal	Tablets	Tablet placed between the gums and cheek of the mouth; absorbed as tablet dissolves
Inhalation	Medicated aerosols, mists, sprays, streams	Liquid medication inhaled through nebulizer, respirator, or inhalation device
Irrigation	Solutions	Solution washed through a body cavity or over a membrane
Installation	Solutions	Medication dropped into area requiring treatment, such as ear or eye
Injunction or topical	Liniments, lotions, ointments, powders, solutions, sprays, tinctures	Medication applied to skin (use gloves to apply)
Oral	Capsules, pills, solutions, spansules, tablets	Medication taken by mouth and swallowed
Parenteral	Sterile solutions	Medicated solution injected into body tissue and absorbed
Rectal	Suppositories, solutions	Medicated solution or suppository inserted into rectum
Sublingual	Tablets	Tablet placed under the tongue to dissolve
Vaginal	Creams, foams, liquids, ointments, solutions, suppositories	Medication applied, inserted, or irrigated (douche)

Personal Wellness

Health Risks

As a health information technician, your contact with patients will be casual. You will be talking to them, getting and giving information, but you will have little if any more physical contact. Nonetheless, anyone working in a health care environment is at some risk of infection. So how much at risk of infection are you and what can you do to reduce your risk?

Hepatitis B Virus (HBV) is one of the most serious infections. It is typically spread through sexual contact, by sharing needles among drug users, and by accidental needle sticks, which represent the greatest risk to health care workers. HBV cannot be contracted by casual contact with infected patients. Check with your supervisor. You may be entitled to an inoculation against HBV at no cost.

Human immunodeficiency virus (HIV) is primarily transmitted by sexual contact and intravenous drug use. It is not transmitted by casual contact, through contaminated food or water, or through the air.

Influenza is a common illness that often brings patients into the medical facility. To protect yourself from infection and to avoid spreading the flu to other patients, you should consider getting an annual flu vaccination. Check with your supervisor about the provider's policy.

The health information technician may be exposed to other microorganisms that can be spread through casual contact in the medical facility. The best precaution against infection is to regularly and frequently wash your hands. Keep your hands away from your mouth. If you develop any signs or symptoms of illness, report them immediately.

How does your health affect the health of patients? How can you protect them?

 Summary

Medical assistants are responsible for working and administering medicines, so they must be knowledgeable about the legal issues associated with dispensing and administering medicines. In addition, medical assistants need to know how to handle and store prescriptions and convert dosages.

1. Which agency monitors the federal guidelines for regulating the manufacturing, distribution, dispensing, and sales of medications?

2. What do the following prescription abbreviations mean: IV, dil, OU, OS, OD?

3. List two controlled substances in each of the five schedules (groups).

4. What types of information does the Physician's Desk Reference (PDR) contain?

5. List five ways to ensure the safekeeping of medications.

6. Why are health care workers at risk for contracting the Hepatitis B Virus (HBV)?

Learn By Doing: Section 20.2 Activity

1. Complete Worksheets 1 and 2.

2. Complete Worksheet 3 as assigned.

3. Complete Worksheet/Activity 4 as assigned.

4. Complete Worksheet 5.

5. When you are confident that you can meet each objective for this section, ask your teacher for the section evaluation.

SECTION

20.3 Laboratory Skills

Background

Laboratory assistants are responsible for understanding laboratory guidelines and safety procedures. They also need to gather and test specimens, such as blood and urine, and ensure that appropriate quality controls are in place in the laboratory.

Objectives

When you have completed this section, you will be able to do the following:

- Match key terms with their correct meanings.

- Follow 12 general laboratory guidelines.

- Practice laboratory safety.

- Demonstrate loading and operating an autoclave.

- List eight types of specimen studies.

- Identify general rules for testing specimen.

- Discuss quality control in the laboratory.

- Label a diagram of a microscope.

- Identify steps to acquire a midstream clean-catch urine specimen for male and female.

- Identify seven items learned from a CBC.

- Explain why a hematocrit and hemoglobin test are important.

- Explain the importance of counting WBCs and RBCs.

Responsibilities of a Laboratory Assistant/Medical Assistant

Some of the tests performed by laboratory assistants/medical assistants are highly technical: laboratory assistants/medical assistants run tests that assist in diagnosing an illness or disease. Their duties include the following:

- Cleaning laboratory equipment.

- Preparing cleaning solutions.

- Drying glassware and instruments using a cloth, hot air dryer, or acetone bath.

- Examining clean equipment for cracks or chips.

- Operating an autoclave to sterilize equipment.

- Preparing stains, solutions, and culture media.

- Counting blood cells.

- Separating plasma from whole blood using a centrifuge.

- Incubating cultures.

- Using computerized test equipment to test blood specimens.

- Performing venipuncture with a Vacutainer™ and/or a needle and syringe.

- Monitoring control tests.

- Performing laboratory tests on stool, urine, blood, and sputum.

- Preparing specimens for processing.

- Giving patients instructions for specimen collection or self-testing.

Importance of Laboratory Tests

Laboratory tests are important because they are:

- A valuable diagnostic tool.

- Used to monitor the amount of medication a patient has in his or her system (therapeutic drug level).

- A measure of the body's chemical balance that compares blood and urine samples with normal test values.

- A way to use blood and urine tests to diagnose a certain disease or condition.

CLIA (see below) periodically sends tests to labs for reading. Tests are returned to CLIA to confirm the laboratory's readings. This is CLIA's quality control on laboratories.

Laboratory Standards

Medical laboratories and medical offices that perform lab tests on human specimens are regulated by a federal amendment called the Clinical Laboratory Improvement Amendment of 1988 (or CLIA). CLIA sets standards and regulates all laboratories, physicians' offices, and other labs that use human specimens to diagnose, prevent, or treat disease.

As a laboratory assistant/medical assistant you can perform simple tests allowed by CLIA. The lab or medical office must have a CLIA waiver certificate before you perform these tests. The tests include the following:

- Dipstick or tablet reagent urinalysis for bilirubin, glucose, hemoglobin, ketone, leukocytes, nitrite, pH, protein, urobilinogen, specific gravity.

- Ovulation tests: visual color test to tell if human luteinizing hormone is present.

- Urine pregnancy tests: visual color comparison test.

- Erythrocyte sedimentation rate (nonautomated).

- Hemoglobin copper sulfate (nonautomated).

- Fecal occult blood.

- Spun microhematocrit.

- Blood glucose by glucose monitoring devices cleared by the Food and Drug Administration for home use.

Do not perform these tests unless you know that there is a waiver certificate and you have been trained properly.

Operating a laboratory with **uniformity** and maintaining standards of measure quality are important. People who work in the laboratory must follow the same guidelines that all laboratory workers follow. These guidelines are as follows:

uniformity
(yoo nuh FAWR mi tee)
A state of being all the same; does not vary.

- Clean and cover microscope daily according to manufacturer's guidelines.

- Maintain all infection control logs.

- Report all defective equipment immediately to your supervisor.

- Maintain and observe quality control logs.
- Follow all directions to ensure accurate results from each test.
  - Refrigerate promptly.
  - Transport specimens in racks.
  - Follow instructions when watching for serum separation.
  - Instruct patients in proper collection of all specimens.
  - Use appropriate technique with all specimen collections.
- Check temperatures of appliances daily.
- Learn new techniques for testing new material or equipment changes.
- Check expiration dates of all reagents and testing kits weekly.
- Do quality control checks on all testing materials and equipment following manufacturer's directions and CLIA standards.
- Ask the supervisor for help when in doubt regarding any procedure or result.
- Recognize the importance of correct and accurate test results for doctors.
- Report all "stats" immediately.

hazardous
(HAZ er duhs)
Dangerous.

The medical laboratory is an environment with hazards. The laboratory assistant/medical assistant or anyone working with laboratory tests must be aware of possible dangers. In the laboratory, you work with patient specimens that must be treated as **hazardous** materials. You also work with various chemicals that can react when mixed together. Some of these chemicals are harmful to the skin, eyes, and/or the respiratory system. To be safe in the laboratory:

- Learn safety measures and follow them carefully.
- Always follow Standard Precautions as listed in the Chapter 17 tables.

General Safety Practice Guidelines: Personal Safety
The protective equipment you wear includes the following:

- A nonpermeable lab coat to protect your clothes.
- Safety eye goggles/glasses to guard your eyes from splashes.
- Gloves to keep you from being contaminated by infectious material.
- A rubber apron to protect you from **acids** that can spill or splash.
- Metal tongs when working with hot objects.

acids
(as ids)
Substances that cause the urine to have an acid pH.

Other safety considerations are as follows:

- Never use your mouth to pipette.
- Do not eat, drink, or apply makeup in the laboratory area.
- Flush eyes first, then report eye contamination immediately to supervisor for eye treatment.
- Dispose of all broken glass, needles, or other sharp objects in a sharps container.
- Do not bend, break, or recap needles.

- Follow Standard Precautions and consider all specimens as highly infectious.
- Disinfect counters, surfaces, and equipment daily.

Fire Prevention
- Locate the fire extinguisher.
- Participate in fire drills.
- Report all potential electrical hazards to the supervisor immediately.
- Use grounded plugs for equipment.

 *Science Link*

Acids and Bases

Some substances break up into parts called ions when added to water. An ion is an atom that has lost or gained negatively charged electrons. If the ions produced by a compound in solution are hydrogen ions ($H+$), the compound is an acid. If the ions are hydroxide ions, ($OH-$), the compound is a base.

The pH scale is used to measure the concentration of $H+$ ions in solution. The pH scale spans from 0 to 14. If there is a high concentration of $H+$ ions, the solution is very acidic and the pH value is low. Solutions with pH values lower than 7.0 are acids.

If there is a high concentration of $OH-$ ions, the concentration of $H+$ ions must be low and the pH value is high. Solutions with pH values higher than 7.0 are bases. A solution with a pH value of 7.0 is neither an acid nor a base: It is a neutral solution.

How can you describe human blood plasma with a pH of 7.4 in terms of acids and bases?

Additional Safety Practice Guidelines
- Clearly label and date all **reagents**.
- Label all waste containers with a biohazard symbol.
- Complete incident reports. These are used to report any unusual or dangerous occurrences—for example, an accident, an injury, a hazardous spill or fire—to supervising personnel.
  - Incident or injury to patients or self.
  - Chemical spills.
  - Electrical or fire hazards.
- Keep trash from building up in any area.
- Keep all posters and decorations away from lights and vents.
- Inspect areas where heating elements are used for possible fire hazards.
- Keep spills wiped up and use a disinfectant when necessary.
- Discard any rag with a flammable substance on it in a metal container with a self-closing lid.

reagents
(re a jents)
Chemical substances that react to the presence of other substances in the blood and urine.

Sterilization

You must sterilize all items in the laboratory that have contact with body tissue or fluids. The most effective way to sterilize equipment is in an autoclave. (**Figure 17.5** and Chapter 17) The autoclave produces steam under pressure. The high heat of the steam kills organisms that cause disease. Keep items that you are sterilizing in the autoclave for the specified length of time to ensure that all microorganisms are killed. (See Chapter 17 for additional information on sterilization.)

Figure 20.15
Autoclave. Why is an autoclave used in a laboratory?

CAUTION: The autoclave is a heavy piece of equipment with a chamber that withstands high degrees of temperature and a great deal of pressure. Steam under pressure can burn skin, hair, and eyes. Always follow these basic rules when operating an autoclave:

1. Read the directions for the autoclave you are using.
2. Use protective gloves when placing articles in an autoclave or taking them out.
3. In order to maintain sterility of surgical instruments, use sterilization wraps. Most commonly, current popular wrapping products use a layered design consisting of three thermally bonded layers, which provide strength and a barrier to microbial contaminations. To further minimize contamination, many hospitals double wrap instruments.
4. Protect yourself if the autoclave is hot from recent use.
5. Do not overload. If you pack material into the autoclave too tightly, the steam cannot circulate and the items will not be sterilized.
6. Allow the temperature and pressure to return to normal before opening the autoclave when sterilization is complete.
7. Clean the autoclave according to the manufacturer's directions.

Items that you cannot reuse are not sterilized. Never put body tissue, body fluid, or any article that has been in contact with blood, body fluids, or tissues in the regular trash. Dispose of them in a biohazard container following your facility's policies. All health care workers have the responsibility to protect themselves and others.

The increased concerns over hazardous and/or toxic materials in all areas of work create the need for strict guidelines to protect people. The federal Occupational Safety and Health Administration (OSHA) provides guidelines to help ensure safety. Your laboratory supervisor has these guidelines in a notebook with material safety data sheets The MSDS forms follow OSHA guidelines by explaining how to dispose of and handle hazardous materials safely. The sheets also describe possible physical symptoms of overexposure and proper first-aid treatment if exposed. Ingredients of the hazardous product are also identified on MSDS forms. It is important to follow the general guidelines above and check the MSDS for specific information on each substance.

Contaminated/Hazardous Material

Specimens being analyzed in the laboratory come from patients. The physician often does not know what is causing a patient's illness, so you must treat every specimen as though it is contaminated and potentially hazardous. *Always follow Standard Precautions.*

When you work in a laboratory or medical office, you must practice good aseptic technique at all times. The most important steps include washing your hands before and after each procedure. Always wear gloves when working with specimens.

Biohazardous Waste Containers

In the medical setting, you must dispose of all contaminated biohazardous materials in biohazardous waste containers. The laboratory containers are lined with red plastic. Put all discarded contaminated/biohazardous materials in the red-lined containers marked "Biohazardous."

Empty all containers at the end of each shift or when full. Carefully tie the bag and be certain that it will stay closed. Mark the tied bag "Biohazardous." Reline the container with a new red bag. Place the marked bag in a red sealed container for pickup. Handle all contaminated/hazardous materials according to OSHA guidelines (Figure 20.16). Never mix them with ordinary trash.

 **Laboratory Tests**

Laboratory workers are responsible for testing specimens. The most common specimens include urine, blood, sputum, and stool. The results of these tests provide information about the patient's health. This information helps:

- Diagnose the illness.
- Determine the cause of the illness.
- Confirm a diagnosis.
- Evaluate progress.
- Regulate treatment.
- Establish a baseline for future tests.

Guidelines for Laboratory Tests

When you receive a laboratory request, check it for all information. This information includes:

- Patient's name and address.
- Patient's age and sex.
- Name of test requested.

(a)

(b)

(c)

Figure 20.16
Handle all contaminated/ hazardous materials according to OSHA guidelines.

- Time and date of collection.
- Physician's name and address.
- Method of collection.
- Possible diagnosis.
- Type and source of specimen.
- Medications the patient is taking.
- Stat or routine tests.

Preparation of Patients

There are many different kinds of laboratory tests. Some of the tests require very specific preparation. The results of some tests are affected by medication, food, time of day, and type of activity. Know the advance preparation for each test. If you are not certain about preparation, look it up in the procedures manual. Instruct the patient to follow the preparation orders exactly. Advance preparation may include

- **Fasting.** Eating before some tests changes the results of the test (e.g., fasting blood sugar [FBS], glucose tolerance test [GTT], SMA-12 profile). During fasting, patients must not eat or drink fluid (except water). They usually fast for 12 to 14 hours before the test.
- **Medication restriction.** Many medications can change the chemical and physical qualities of the specimen. The patient needs special instruction if taking medications that can change test results. Medication affects urine specimens more than it affects blood. If the patient can be off the medication without causing injury, the medication is stopped 48 to 72 hours before the tests. The physician makes this decision.

Analyzing Specimens

There are many different studies that help identify and diagnose physical problems.

- **Urinalysis.** Examines urine chemically, physically, and microscopically.
- **Hematology.** Examines blood for disease conditions.
- **Microbiology.** Identifies pathogens in the body.
- **Histology.** Studies body tissues microscopically to detect diseased tissues.
- **Cytology.** Examines cells microscopically to discover abnormal cells.
- **Clinical chemistry.** Examines substances in body fluids, feces, tissues.
- **Serology and blood banking.** Studies antigen-antibody reactions to discover presence of foreign substance or disease.
- **Parasitology.** Determines parasite that is causing illness.

General Rules for Testing the Specimen

There are basic steps to follow for testing all specimens.

1. Measure the amount of specimen required for the test carefully. This is very specific.
2. Combine the correct chemical reagent for the test with the specimen.

3. Process the specimen correctly (e.g., centrifuge, heat in a water bath, incubate, heat fix, etc.).

4. Assess the sample by manual or automatic method.

5. Calculate results by hand or machine.

6. Record all the information on the lab report sheet, including:

   a. Patient's name.

   b. Age and sex.

   c. Time and date.

   d. Source of specimen.

   e. Name of test completed.

   f. Results of test.

Always follow the approved procedure in your facility.

Methods of Testing Specimens

The *manual method* requires carefully following a series of steps. Some small labs and physicians' offices use manual methods for simple tests (e.g., urinalysis).

Semiautomated analysis is a combination of manual and automated testing (e.g., glucose monitor). To perform a glucose test, you stick the finger to get blood. The glucose monitor measures the glucose in the blood. *Automatic analyzers* can do more than one specimen at a time. These analyzers measure the specimen, add reagent, process the specimen, and give the results.

Quality Control for Specimen Testing

There must be a method for quality control when performing laboratory tests. Performing these test controls tells you that the test is accurate. Quality control helps ensure that the test result is a true picture of the patient's condition. Some tests have the control built in. When the information is reliable, the physician can make a diagnosis. Quality control methods include:

- Discarding outdated reagents.
- Following the procedure for exact testing.
- Routinely verifying that laboratory equipment is reading specimens accurately.
- Maintaining equipment by having it serviced routinely.

Quality control includes keeping accurate logs. The log includes important information about the test (e.g., expiration date, lot number, date tested, and pass/fail of control). You must initial each test in the log.

Laboratory Equipment

There are many kinds of laboratory equipment. The simple microscope and centrifuge are found in all laboratories. Some equipment is more complicated than others; for example, very advanced computers and analyzers.

Microscope

The microscope is an important tool that magnifies and enlarges objects. (**Figure 20.17**) You use it to see microorganisms and other components that are too small to see without magnification. The ability to see these components helps find the cause of illnesses. Learning to use the microscope is necessary for laboratory workers.

FIGURE 20.17
Microscope. What is the purpose of using a microscope in the laboratory?

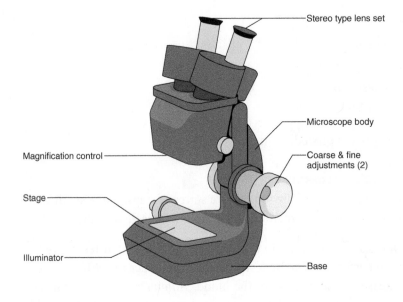

Stereo type lens set

Microscope body

Coarse & fine adjustments (2)

Magnification control

Stage

Illuminator

Base

How to Use a Microscope

There are different types of microscopes. Some microscopes have one eyepiece. These are **monocular** microscopes. Microscopes with two eyepieces are **biocular**.

Basic Parts of the Microscope

- **Base.** Supports the microscope; it keeps the microscope from falling over.
- **Arm.** Supports the eyepiece and is used to carry the microscope.
- **Stage.** Holds slides that are put on the stage after you prepare them.
- **Slide clips.** Hold the prepared slide in place.
- **Iris diaphragm.** Adjusts the amount of light that enters the microscope through the opening in the stage.
- **Mirror or illumination light.** Provides light so that you can see the object on the slide. You control the amount of light with the iris diaphragm. When you use a mirror, you turn the mirror to pick up a light source and *reflect* it into the microscope.
- **Eyepiece.** Lets you see the object on the slide. Some microscopes have eyepieces that magnify to 10 times (10×), others to 20 times (20×).
- **Objectives.** Magnify what you have on the slide. Most microscopes have three objectives. The most common objectives are
  - High-power objectives that magnify the objects 40 times (40×).
  - Medium-power objectives that magnify the object 10 times (10×).
  - Low-power objectives that magnify 4 times (4×).

monocular
(muh NOK yuh ler)
Having one eyepiece.

binocular
(buh NOK yuh ler)
Having two eyepieces.

- Oil immersion: the oil immersion objective magnifies 95× to 100×. You put a drop of oil on a specimen that is dark and hard to see. The oil concentrates the light and makes the specimen easier to see.
- **Body tube.** Connects the eyepiece to the objectives, which are on the revolving nosepiece.
- **Revolving nosepiece.** The objectives are attached to the revolving nosepiece. You turn it to place the objective over the specimen.

PROCEDURE | 20.21 | Using a Microscope

BACKGROUND: Proper care and use of the microscope prevents errors.

ALERT: Follow Standard Precautions.

PREPROCEDURE

1. Assemble equipment.
   a. Microscope
   b. Lens paper
   c. Slides and slide cover
   d. Specimen
   e. Oil if using oil immersion
   f. Gloves if specimens have been contaminated by blood or body fluids.
2. Wash hands.
3. Place specimen (e.g., hair, scraping from under nails, scraping from tooth) on clean slide (one drop only if liquid specimen).
4. Add required solution.
5. Drop clean slide cover over specimen. Hold cover at an angle and let it drop. Make sure there are no air bubbles between the slide and cover slip. If there are bubbles, must do again.
6. Clean eyepiece with lens paper.
7. Clean objectives with lens paper.
8. Turn on illuminating light.
9. Open iris diaphragm.
10. Turn revolving nosepiece to low-power objective.

PROCEDURE

11. Place slide on stage under slide clips. Avoid getting finger prints on the slide.
12. Turn coarse adjustment knob to move objective close to slide. Do not look into eyepieces while doing this, as you could crack the slide.
13. Look into eyepiece and slowly turn coarse adjustment to move tube upward until you focus specimen.
14. Turn fine-adjustment knob until specimen is clear and focused.
15. Continue steps 12 through 14 using higher objectives until you have best possible focus for specimen.
16. Observe specimen. If setup is for technician or physician, tell that person that slide is ready.

POSTPROCEDURE

17. Remove slide after it is read.
18. Discard slide according to procedure in your facility.
19. Clean lens and objective with lens paper.
20. Turn off illuminating light.
21. Put cover back on microscope
22. Wash hands
21. Fill out lab slips according to your facility's policies.

How to Determine Total Magnification of the Specimen

Specimens are very small samples. It is important to know how many times the specimen is magnified. To determine how many times the specimen is magnified, multiply the power of the eyepiece by the power of the objective. For example:

Power of eyepiece 10×
Power of objective 4×
10 × 4 = 40

This means that the specimen is enlarged 40 times its actual size.

NOTE: Always remember to record patient's name, account number, date, time, physician's name, type of test, results of test. Always sign with your name and certification.

There are both a coarse adjustment and a fine adjustment on the microscope:

- **Coarse adjustment.** Upper knob on the arm, which moves the objectives up and down. This helps you put the specimen in rough focus.
- **Fine adjustment.** Lower, smaller knob, which moves the objective more slowly. This helps you have a clear image of the specimen.

CAUTION: Turning the adjustments too quickly can cause the glass slide to break. Turn each knob slowly. Begin with the coarse adjustment and then focus the image with the fine adjustment.

The microscope must be taken care of. Remember to:

- Use special lens paper to clean the eyepiece, or you will scratch the lens.
- Watch the objectives when you move them up and down. This prevents damaging the objectives or breaking the slide.
- Cover the microscope when you are not using it. This keeps out dust.
- Keep the microscope in a safe place where it cannot be knocked to the floor (see the procedure "Using a Microscope").

Urinalysis

A routine urinalysis provides information about the patient. The urinalysis gives the physician information about the physical, chemical, and microscopic characteristics of the urine. This information tells many different things about the patient's health: Is a woman pregnant? Is a urinary tract infection present? Does the urine show high levels of protein which could be an indicator of kidney disease?

Urine Collection

Proper urine collection is important. The way you collect the urine affects the test. The following are some general guidelines for urine collection:

- Use a clean, dry container.
- A specimen over 32 hours old may give inaccurate test results.
- Refrigerate it and write the collection time on the label if it is necessary to keep a specimen over two hours.
- If possible, collect on-site for immediate testing.

Reagent Strips

Your facility may use reagent strips and/or other individual tests. Always follow the procedures of your facility.

Reagent strips have small pads that react to a specific substance. When you dip the strip in a fresh urine sample, there is a chemical reaction. Carefully match the reagent strip with the color chart on the container label. The procedure for using all reagent strips is similar.

Guidelines for Using Reagent Strips

- Check the bottle for an expiration date.
- Keep the bottle in a cool, dry area with the top tightly closed. (Do not refrigerate.)
- Check the strips for a change in color. A tan-to-brown color change indicates deterioration. Do not use the strips.
- Keep the specimen container clean.
- Use freshly voided urine. Urine over 2 hours old gives poor results. Refrigerate if it stands more than 2 hours.
- A clean-catch urine is best for determining leukocytes.
- First urine in the morning is best for determining nitrates.
- Match colors on strips to the color chart on the label. Follow the times on the label carefully.
- Write the type of strips used when recording the type of test.

Microscopic Examination of the Urine

Urinary sediment contains the solid materials in the urine. There are many components in the sediment that help the **provider** confirm or determine a diagnosis. The sediment may contain renal or kidney cells, casts, crystals, bacteria, parasites, mucus, or other substances. The sediment settles to the bottom of a centrifuged urine specimen. A small sample of the sediment is placed on a slide for the provider to look at. The provider looks for a cause of illness (e.g., bacteria causing a bladder infection, renal cells indicating renal damage, or red blood cells from irritation). Spinning urine (centrifuging) will be one of your duties.

provider
(pruh VAHY der)
Physician, physician assistant, nurse practitioner.

BACKGROUND: Careful testing with reagent strips and accurate reporting of information are essential to reach a correct diagnosis. Always use the proper techniques to prevent contamination of the specimen.

ALERT: Follow Standard Precautions.

PREPROCEDURE

1. Wash hands.

2. Assemble equipment.

   a. Reagent strips and bottle

   b. Laboratory report slip

   c. Watch

   d. Urine specimen

   e. Disposable nonsterile gloves

3. Complete laboratory slip.

   a. Name

   b. Sex

   c. Age

   d. Physician

   e. Date

   f. Type of test

4. Put on gloves.

PROCEDURE

5. Hold specimen to light and observe:

   a. Color (colorless, yellow, light yellow, brown, orange, etc.)

   b. Clarity (clear, hazy, cloudy)

6. Write color and clarity on lab slip.

7. Open reagent jar and remove one strip .

   a. Note expiration date. *Do not use if expired.*

   b. Replace jar cover immediately.

8. Hold strip by clear end and immerse in urine (see figure top right).

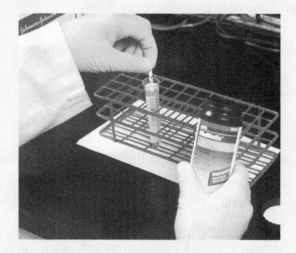

9. Remove strip immediately by pulling gently over lip of tube to remove excess urine.

10. Hold strip in horizontal position to prevent mixing of chemicals.

11. Hold strip close to color blocks on bottle label and match carefully. Note time.

12. Read strip at time indicated and record results.

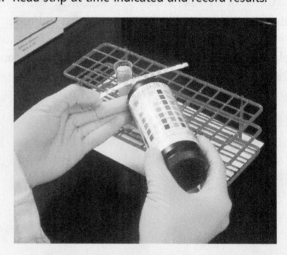

13. Discard reagent strip in biohazard waste.

(continued)

POSTPROCEDURE

14. Clean and replace equipment.

15. Remove gloves.

16. Wash hands.

17. Record required information.

18. Report any abnormal results to supervisor immediately.

1/03/12	0700
	Reagent strip test, pH 7,
	Protein: Pos., Glucose: 1%, Ketones: Tr.,
	Blood: Neg. Positive protein and
	trace blood reported to health care
	provider
	_____ G. Jones Lab Asst.

Special Urine Tests

Measuring Specific Gravity

You can measure specific gravity on a reagent stick. The urinometer is another simple way to check specific gravity. Specific gravity gives the dilution of urine. The normal range for specific gravity of urine is 1.010 to 1.025. An abnormal reading that is not within the range indicates possible problems. High specific gravity is above 1.025. Concentrated (heavy) urine may be caused by dehydration, sugar in the urine from diabetes mellitus, and too many substances in the urine due to kidney disease. Low specific gravity is below 1.010. Diluted urine may be caused by diabetes insipidus, diuretic medications, and kidney disease when unable to concentrate the urine. Specific gravity can also be measured with a refractometer.

Pregnancy Tests

The physician may request a pregnancy test for several reasons, including the following:

- To begin prenatal care early in pregnancy.

- To make certain that medication that causes fetal damage is not given.

- To prevent the use of procedures that may cause injury to the fetus.

A common test for determining pregnancy is a simple urine test. The test is performed on a concentrated urine specimen. The urine is tested for a hormone called human chorionic gonadotropin (HCG). This hormone is produced by the developing fertilized egg. Some of the hormone is secreted into the urine and blood. It is very important to read the manufacturer's instructions carefully before completing a pregnancy test.

To perform an accurate pregnancy test, follow these guidelines:

- Use clean urine containers to collect urine.

- Use the first voided morning specimen for the highest accumulation of HCG.

- Check the specific gravity. If it is less than 1.010, the urine is too dilute.

- Have the urine specimen at room temperature.
- Follow the manufacturer's instructions for storing the reagents.
- Do not use reagents after the expiration date.
- Do not contaminate the specimen.

PROCEDURE 20.23 Measuring Specific Gravity with Urinometer

BACKGROUND: Careful testing of specific gravity and accurate reporting of information are essential to reach a correct diagnosis. Always use proper techniques to prevent contamination of the specimen.

ALERT: Follow Standard Precautions.

PREPROCEDURE

1. Wash hands.

2. Assemble equipment.

   a. Disposable gloves

   b. Glass cylinder (5 inches high)

   c. Urinometer (This is a float with a stem that is calibrated in thousands: 1.000, 1.001, 1.002, etc.)

   d. Fresh urine specimen. Do not refrigerate.

3. Put on gloves.

PROCEDURE

4. Pour urine into cylinder to about one inch from the top.

5. Place urinometer in urine.

6. Spin urinometer gently. You must not touch side or bottom.

7. Place cylinder with lower line of meniscus at eye level.

NOTE: In glass containers, which curve at the edges, the curvature is called the meniscus. You measure the level at the horizontal center or inside part of the meniscus.

With water in glass, the meniscus will curve up at the edges and down in the center so we say you read the bottom of the meniscus.

8. Read specific gravity:

   a. Look at point where lowest part of meniscus crosses urinometer scale.

   b. Read gauge on nearest line.

9. Record reading to enter in computer or on lab slip.

10. Discard urine according to facility's contaminated waste policy.

11. Rinse urinometer with water and dry.

12. Rinse cylinder with water and dry.

13. Remove gloves and discard in contaminated waste.

POSTPROCEDURE

14. Wash hands.

15. Record specific gravity in computer or on lab list.

16. Document according to facility procedure.

1/01/12	0800
	Sp Gr 1.011
————	S. Jones MA

Measuring Specific Gravity with Refractometer

BACKGROUND: Careful testing of specific gravity and accurate reporting of information are essential to reach a correct diagnosis. Always use proper techniques to prevent contamination of the specimen.

ALERT: Follow Standard Precautions.

PREPROCEDURE

1. Wash hands.

2. Assemble equipment

    a. Disposable gloves

    b. Refractometer

    c. Distilled water

    d. Fresh urine sample Do not refrigerate.

    e. Will need eye dropper or pipette to get drop of water and/or urine

3. Put on gloves.

PROCEDURE

4. Place one drop of distilled water on the glass plate.

5. Close lid.

6. Look through eyepiece to read specific gravity.

NOTE: Make sure it reads 1.000. If reading is not 1.000, follow manufacturer's directions to recalibrate refractometer.

7. Transfer one drop of well-mixed urine onto glass plate of refractometer.

8. Close lid.

9. Look through eyepiece to read specific gravity.

10. Record reading to enter in computer or on lab slip.

11. Discard urine according to facility's contaminated waste policy.

POSTPROCEDURE

12. Clean refractometer according to manufacturer's directions.

13. Remove gloves and discard in contaminated waste.

14. Wash hands.

15. Record specific gravity in computer or on lab list.

10/10/11   0800

Sp. gravity 1.040, reported to lab tech

S. Jones Lab Asst.

Testing Urine for Drugs

The collection of urine to determine drug use is becoming more and more common. Some reasons for drug testing:

- Employer requests a preemployment test.
- Department of Transportation requires testing of pilots, truck drivers, and others.
- Employer requests test for employee suspected of using drugs.

There are many strict rules that you *must* adhere to when you collect urine for drug testing. Follow the instructions and proceed step by step. *Be very exact.*

Clean-Catch Collection

Clean-catch midstream urine collection has a specific procedure. The physician may order a clean-catch urine when he or she suspects that a urinary infection is present or for any urine test. The clean-catch method reduces possible contamination of the specimen. Clean the area around the meatus carefully to remove microorganisms.

Collect the urine in a sterile cup using medical aseptic techniques. Pour off part of the specimen for the dipstick test and for spinning down when you collect a clean-catch urine. This leaves the urine in the specimen container uncontaminated. If necessary, you can use it for culture and sensitivity testing.

There are other urine specimen tests that may be ordered. Your facility has a procedure manual with instructions for each test that your lab performs. Follow the instructions for collection carefully.

PROCEDURE **20.25** **Centrifuging a Urine Specimen**

BACKGROUND: Careful centrifuging ensures that urine is properly concentrated for testing. Specimens must be properly prepared in order to achieve accurate results.

ALERT: Follow Standard Precautions.

PREPROCEDURE

1. Wash hands.
2. Assemble equipment.
   a. Centrifuge
   b. Two centrifuge tubes
   c. Microscope slide (number slide)
   d. Coverslip
   e. Pipette
   f. Disposable nonsterile gloves
   g. Urine specimen. It's best to use the first voiding in AM , as it is more concentrated.
3. Fill in lab slip:
   a. Name
   b. Date
   c. Time
4. Put on gloves.

(continued)

PROCEDURE

5. Mix urine to suspend sediment by rolling specimen container gently between your hands.

6. Pour 10 mL of urine into centrifuge tube.

7. Put tube with urine into centrifuge.

8. Pour 10 mL of water into second centrifuge tube.

9. Place in centrifuge opposite the tube with urine. This is very important for balance.

10. Secure centrifuge lid.

11. Set centrifuge timer for 4 to 5 minutes. (Allow it to stop on its own.)

12. Remove tube with urine.

13. Carefully invert urine centrifuge tube quickly over sink to pour 9 mL of urine into sink.

14. Turn tube right side up immediately. (About 1.0 cc will remain in tube.)

15. Mix sediment by snapping end of centrifuge tube with finger or gently shaking.

16. Pipette 1 drop of urine on numbered slide. A pipette works by creating a vacuum above the liquid-holding chamber and then selectively releasing this vacuum to draw up and dispense liquid.

17. Put on coverslip. (Redo if air bubbles appear under coverslip.)

18. Put slide on microscope stage.

19. Use 10× objective with coarse adjustment to focus on slide. Watch while moving course adjustment, so that slide does not break.

20. Adjust light source.

21. Follow your facility's policy for reading slide. (If setup is for technician, tell him or her that slide is ready.)

22. Remove slide after it is read.

23. Discard slide according to facility procedure.

24. Clean lens and objective with lens paper.

25. Cover microscope.

POSTPROCEDURE

26. Clean equipment and replace equipment.

27. Remove gloves, and dispose of according to facility policy.

28. Wash hands.

29. Record results if you read the specimen.

30. Document according to facility procedure.

1/20/12   0745

Microscopic Exam: epithelial:

few/1pf, WBCs: 2-3, /hpf,

RBCs: few/hpf, casts: neg.,

crystals: few/hpf

B Smith MA

BACKGROUND: Careful instruction of the patient helps prevent contaminating the specimen. A clean-catch specimen is essential to accurately diagnose and treat the patient.

ALERT: Follow Standard Precautions.

PREPROCEDURE

1. Wash hands.

2. Assemble equipment.

   a. Sterile urine container for clean catch

   b. Label

   c. Disposable antiseptic towelettes

   d. Disposable nonsterile gloves: wear if you handle cup with specimen.

PROCEDURE

3. Label container.

4. Instruct patient to:

   a. Wash hands.

   b. Remove container lid and place on counter with inside of lid facing up.

   c. Separate labia to expose meatus.

   d. Take towelette and wipe on side of urinary meatus from front to back.

   e. Dispose of towelette.

   f. Repeat with new towelette on other side.

   g. Wipe directly over meatus with new towelette.

   h. Continue to hold labia open.

   i. Urinate small amount into toilet.

   j. Stop stream.

   k. Place sterile container under meatus and void into container (60 cc).

   l. Stop stream.

   m. Remove container carefully.

   n. Empty bladder.

   o. Carefully replace lid.

   p. Wipe outside of container with paper towel.

   q. Transport the specimen to the laboratory within 30 minutes of collection or else refrigerate.

5. Put on gloves.

6. Finish testing as ordered (e.g., dipstick, set up microscopic exam, drug test).

POSTPROCEDURE

7. Document procedure according to facility procedure.

8. Wash hands.

03/26/12   0800

Instructed in correct procedure

for collecting clean catch

S. Jones CNA

BACKGROUND: Careful instruction of the patient helps prevent contaminating the specimen. A clean-catch specimen is essential to accurately diagnose and treat the patient.

ALERT: Follow Standard Precautions.

PREPROCEDURE

1. Wash hands.

2. Assemble equipment.

   a. Sterile container for clean catch

   b. Label

   c. Disposable antiseptic towelettes

   d. Disposable nonsterile gloves: wear if handling container with specimen

PROCEDURE

3. Label container.

4. Instruct patient to:

   a. Wash hands.

   b. Remove container lid and place on counter with inside of lid facing up.

   c. Cleanse head of penis in a circular motion with towelette. (If uncircumcised, pull back foreskin before cleaning.)

   d. Urinate into toilet. (If uncircumcised, pull back foreskin while urinating.)

   e. Allow stream to begin.

   f. Stop stream and place specimen container to collect midstream. (Fill about half way full or 60 mL.)

   g. Remove container before bladder is empty.

   h. Empty bladder into toilet.

   i. Carefully replace lid.

   j. Wipe outside of container with paper towel.

   k. Transport the specimen to the laboratory within 30 minutes of collection or else refrigerate.

5. Put on gloves.

6. Finish testing as ordered (e.g., dip stick, set up microscopic exam, drug test).

POSTPROCEDURE

7. Document procedure according to facility procedure.

8. Wash hands.

06/17/12 0800
Instructed in correct procedure
for collecting clean catch
S. Jones CNA

BACKGROUND: Using the proper technique prevents leakage around the bag and thus prevents contamination of the specimen.

ALERT: Follow Standard Precautions.

PREPROCEDURE

1. Wash hands.

2. Assemble equipment.

   a. Specimen container

   b. Disposable urine collector (small plastic bag with opening and sticky area)

   c. Disposable nonsterile gloves

3. Identify patient.

4. Explain to parents what you are going to do.

5. Tell child what you are going to do even if you think that he or she is too young to understand. Children often understand.

PROCEDURE

6. Put on gloves.

7. Remove diaper.

8. Make certain that skin is clean and dry in genital area.

9. Remove outside cover that is around opening of bag. This has a sticky area that is applied to vulva or around penis. Place over vulva or penis (see figures at top right).

10. Replace diaper.

11. Remove gloves and dispose of according to facility procedure.

12. Check every half hour to see if bag has urine in it.

13. Remove bag when specimen is collected.

14. Rinse, clean, and dry genital area.

15. Replace diaper.

16. Put specimen in specimen container for lab.

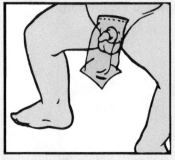

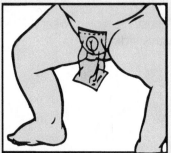

POSTPROCEDURE

17. Label with:

    a. Patient's name

    b. Time of collection

    c. Date

    d. Room number

18. Record collection of specimen.

19. Wash hands.

10/25/11	1030
	Urine bag applied
	Specimen successfully collected
	for testing
	Sent to lab
	H. Martinez CNA

Laboratory Cultures

Physicians need a culture of the microorganism that is causing an illness. Knowing what organism is causing the problem helps with the diagnosis and the treatment. Microorganisms that cause strep throat, staph infections, and other illnesses can be treated when they are identified. You need to know how to:

- Obtain a specimen.
- Place the specimen on the medium, where it can grow and reproduce.
- Stain a sample of the culture.

Take a specimen for the culture from the affected body sites. These sites include any skin lesion, such as an open, draining sore. Cultures are also taken from any body opening, such as eyes, ears, nose, throat, and vagina. You must be careful when you take a specimen for culturing. Poor technique causes a false test result. You must use a sterile swab to secure the specimen and be careful not to contaminate the sample.

A specimen may be placed on a slide immediately. This is a direct smear. When the technician or doctor reads the smear, he or she can identify the organism. Prepare a direct smear slide following the procedure for using a microscope.

The physician may also request that the microorganism be grown on an *agar plate*. The agar in the plate provides food and moisture. The organisms grow and multiply when you place the agar plate in a warm incubator, at 36 to 37° Celsius (97 to 99° Fahrenheit) for 24 to 36 hours.

A common test is called a culture and sensitivity test. This test identifies the antibiotic that kills the organism. It also identifies the antibiotics to which the organisms are **resistant**. This information helps the physician decide which medication to prescribe. To do a culture and sensitivity test, place paper disks coated with antibiotic on an agar plate streaked with a specimen. If the organism is resistant to the antibiotic, it continues to grow around the disk. If the specimen is sensitive to the antibiotic, the colony around the disk dies. The physician then knows which antibiotic to prescribe for the patient.

resistant
(ri ZIS tuh nt)
Able to protect itself.

Gram Stain

Gram staining is a process that dyes and fixes microorganisms (**Figure 20.18**). The stain helps make the organism more visible in the microscope. It also helps in identifying the microorganism. The slide can be kept and reviewed if necessary. To prepare a slide from colonies grown in an agar plate for staining, a small colony of organisms is taken from the agar plate. These organisms are placed on a slide and stained.

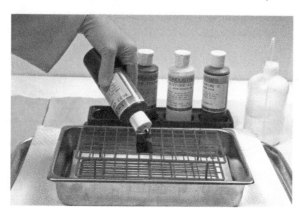

Figure 20.18
Gram staining is a diagnostic tool used in clinical and research settings.

What's New?

Rapid Medical Tests

Years ago, it took days or even longer to obtain the results from common medical tests. Now, results are often produced within minutes. One of the most commonly used tests is the rapid strep test. This test is used to determine whether a patient has pharyngitis that is due to a group A streptococcal infection. A *streptococci* cause pharyngitis in 5–15 percent of adults and 15–30 percent of children.

It is important that strep infections be identified as quickly as possible and treated with antibiotics. Strep throat is contagious and can spread to close contacts, especially among children. In addition, if the infection is not treated, secondary complications including rheumatic fever (which can damage the heart) and glomerulonephritis (which affects the kidneys) can develop. At the same time, it is essential that patients are not prescribed antibiotics to treat the common viruses that can also cause sore throats.

A rapid strep test produces results in just 5–10 minutes. If the results are positive, further testing is not needed. The person carries the infection and a health care provider will most likely prescribe antibiotic therapy. However, if the rapid strep test is negative, a culture to grow the bacteria should be done to confirm the results. Up to one-third of negative rapid strep test results are false. This means that in up to one-third of the cases in which a rapid strep test produces negative results, the person actually has a strep throat infection. A throat culture is more accurate than the rapid strep test, but takes several days to produce results.

Because sensitivity reports can take several days to provide results, the patient will probably be on a broad based antibiotic already. If the patient is receiving an antibiotic and the sensitivity report indicates that the identified bacteria is not sensitive to this particular antibiotic, the physician must be notified. The physician will want to prescribe an antibiotic to which the bacteria is sensitive.

Other rapid tests are becoming equally as common, and many of them are being sold for use in the home. These include pregnancy tests, ovulation kits, drug tests as well as tests to identify certain medical conditions such as tuberculosis. As with the rapid strep tests, results are not always 100 percent reliable and should not only be repeated, but also interpreted by a qualified health care provider.

What is one advantage and one disadvantage of a rapid strep test over a throat culture?

Blood, Blood Composition, and Blood Testing

Components of Blood

Whole blood has many formed elements that are suspended in a clear yellow liquid called *plasma*. Plasma makes up 55 percent of the whole blood. The other 45 percent has the formed elements. These elements are:

- **Erythrocytes.** RBC (carry O_2 to cells, carry away CO_2).
- **Leukocytes.** WBC (protect against infection and disease).
- **Thrombocytes.** Platelets (start the clotting process).

The average adult has six to eight quarts of blood.

 ## Personal Wellness

Triglycerides

It is important to understand the chemistry of blood. One important commonly measured quantity is the level of triglycerides, which are the chemical form of animal and vegetable fats. In the human body, these are carried through the blood plasma, and unused molecules are stored in the body as fat. Triglycerides are later released from fat tissue to meet the body's needs for energy between meals.

An excess of triglycerides in plasma is called hypertriglyceridemia. This condition is directly linked to coronary artery disease in some people. Like cholesterol, increases in triglyceride levels can be detected by plasma measurements. These measurements should be made after an overnight food and alcohol fast.

What can you do if you have high triglycerides? Changes in lifestyle habits may be the answer. You should consider the following:

- Cut down on calories to reach your ideal body weight.
- Reduce your dietary intake of saturated fat, trans fat, and cholesterol.
- Consume more fruits and vegetables.
- Reduce your intake of alcohol.
- Stop smoking if you do so.
- Get at least 30 minutes of physical activity each day.
- Substitute fish high in omega-3 fatty acids for high-fat meats.

Keep in mind that triglycerides do not only result from the consumption of fats, but also from the consumption of carbohydrates. Most carbohydrates are naturally turned into triglycerides by the body. Therefore, even if you follow a diet that is low in fat, but high in carbohydrates, you may still be increasing your triglyceride level.

In some cases, drugs may be required in addition to dietary management and exercise. People with high triglycerides should follow the specific plans prescribed by their health care providers.

Why shouldn't foods that result in the production of triglycerides be completely eliminated from the diet?

Blood Tests

Physicians order blood tests for routine checkups and to help diagnose an illness. There are many blood tests available. This chapter covers the blood tests that the physician orders frequently. (See Table 20.5, which gives you the important reasons for the tests you are doing.) Refer back to the table before you practice a blood test procedure.

The laboratory most often uses capillary/peripheral blood and venous blood. You usually obtain capillary blood from the finger and sometimes from the earlobe. You use a heel stick for infants. The amount of blood is limited to a few drops. This is enough blood to do the following:

- Complete blood count (CBC).
- Hematocrit/microhematocrit.
- Some bleeding and coagulation times.
- Some chemical and **agglutination** tests.

When you need a larger amount of blood, you draw venous blood from the veins with a Vacutainer™ or syringe and needle. Some states and schools do not allow students to perform blood tests. Your teacher will tell you what you can do. *Never practice these tests without training.*

Complete Blood Count

The laboratory worker performs many different types of blood tests. The most frequently ordered test is a complete blood count. The complete blood count (CBC) gives a lot of information about the patient's condition. It includes the following:

- RBC (red blood cell) count.
- WBC (white blood cell) count.
- Hemoglobin determination.
- Hematocrit determination.
- Differential white blood cell count.
- Estimate of the number of platelets.
- RBC morphology (size and shape).

Hematocrit/Microhematocrit

A hematocrit measures the volume of packed red blood cells in the blood. When you do this test you separate cell elements from the plasma. You perform this test with a few drops of capillary blood. Collect the blood in a **heparinized** capillary tube from a finger or earlobe stick for adults. In infants collect the blood from a heel stick. Centrifuge the blood to pack the cells. Low hematocrit readings tell the physician that there is a problem (e.g., anemia). High hematocrit readings provide important information (e.g., **polycythemia**). (Table 20.5)

agglutination
(uh gloot n EY shuhn)
Clumping together (e.g., red blood cells clump together).

heparinized
(HEP uh rin eyesd)
Containing heparin, an anticoagulant.

polycythemia
(pol e si theme a)
Condition of having too much blood.

Table 20.5　Common Blood Tests

Test	Abbreviation	Normal Range	Examples of Possible Diagnosis	
			Increase	Decrease
White blood cell count	WBC	5000–10,000 mm3	Acute infection, leukemia, mononucleosis	Viral infections, bone marrow depression
Red blood cell count	RBC	Female: 4–5 million/mm^3 Male: 5–6 million/mm^3	Polycythemia, poisoning, pulmonary fibrosis	Anemia, multiple myeloma, lupus erythemia
Differential white blood cell count	Diff	Neutrophils 50–70%	*Neutrophilia:* acute bacterial infections, parasitic infections, liver disease	*Neutropenia:* acute viral infections, blood diseases, hormone diseases
		Eosinophils 1–4%	*Eosinophilia:* allergic conditions, parasitic infections, lung and bone cancer	*Eosinopenia:* infectious mononucleosis, congestive heart failure, aplastic and pernicious anemia
		Basophils 0–1%	*Basophilia:* leukemia, hemolytic anemia, Hodgkin's disease	*Basopenia:* acute allergic reactions, hyperthyroidism, steroid therapy
		Lymphocytes 20–35%	*Lymphocytosis:* acute and chronic infections, carcinoma, hyper-thyroidism	*Lymphopenia:* cardiac failure, Cushing's disease, Hodgkin's disease
		Monocytes 3–8%	*Monocytosis:* viral infections, bacterial and parasitic infections, collagen diseases, cirrhosis	*Monocytopenia:* prednisolone treatment, hairy cell leukemia
Hemoglobin	Hgb	Female: 12–16 g/100 mL Male: 14–18 g/100 mL	Congestive heart failure (CHF), chronic obstructive pulmonary disease(COPD), severe burn	Hodgkin's disease, hyperthyroidism, cirrhosis
Hematocrit/ microhematocrit	Hct, HCT	Female: 40–54% Male: 37–47%	Shock, dehydration, burns	Anemia, leukemia, acute blood loss
Prothrombin time	PT	11–16 sec	Anticoagulant therapy, liver disease, biliary obstruction	Diuretics, pulmonary embolism, multiple myeloma
Erythrocyte sedimentation rate	ESR	(According to method used)	Collagen disease, inflammatory disease, rheumatoid arthritis	Sickle cell anemia, CHF, polycythemia
Platelet count		200,000–400,000/mm^3	Cancer, leukemia, splenectomy	Bone-marrow-depressant drug, pneumonia infection

Hemoglobin

Hemoglobin (Hgb) tests measure the oxygen-carrying capacity of the blood. Hemoglobin has the *heme,* which carries iron, and *globin,* which is the protein in the red blood cell. Hemoglobin picks up oxygen in the lungs and transports it to the cells. It also helps carry waste product, CO_2, from the body cells back to the lungs. One way to measure hemoglobin is with a hemoglobinometer.

 ## Summary

Laboratory assistants are responsible for understanding what laboratory tests are important and why, following laboratory guidelines, knowing how to test specimens, knowing how to use a microscope, and understanding blood and blood tests.

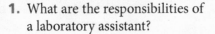

SECTION 20.3 Review Questions

1. What are the responsibilities of a laboratory assistant?

2. As a lab assistant, what kinds of protective equipment would you wear in a laboratory?

3. What are laboratory tests important?

4. What are the four methods of quality control when testing specimens?

5. Describe the basic parts of the microscope?

6. What types of information does a complete blood count (CBC) provide?

 Learn By Doing: Section 20.3 Activity

1. Complete Worksheets 1 and 2.

2. Follow your teacher's directions to complete Worksheet/Activity 3.

3. Complete Worksheets 4 through 7 as assigned.

4. Prepare responses to each item listed in Chapter Review.

5. When you are confident that you can meet each objective for this section, ask your teacher for the section evaluation.

Chapter Review Questions

1. List four basic diagnostic techniques and their purpose. (20.1)

2. What type of information is gathered when completing a patient's medical history form? (20.1)

3. List the three factors that determine which Standard Precautions employees should take to avoid infection? (20.1)

4. Describe the seven examination positions. (20.1)

5. As a medical assistant, what would your responsibilities be in working with and administering medications? (20.2)

6. Explain each of the five schedules of controlled substances? (20.2)

7. What is the formula for dosage calculation? (20.2)

8. What are the six "rights" of medication administration? (20.2)

9. Which tests require a laboratory or medical office to have a CLIA waiver certificate before a lab assistant can perform he test? (20.3)

10. Why is it important to follow the rules when operating an autoclave? (20.3)

11. List the six general rules for testing specimens. (20.3)

12. How much blood does the average adult have in their body? (20.3)

Activities

1. Imagine that you are writing questions for a quiz show. Write ten questions that relate to Standard Precautions. After writing your questions, exchange them with your classmates to see how well you do.

2. Use the Internet or visit a local Biotechnology Lab and prepare a display citing the steps in preparing a new drug for marketing including number and types of trials.

Case Studies

1. Mr. Grey needs to be admitted to a hospital for a routine procedure and is a little nervous. He asks you to explain exactly what will occur when he is admitted and registered. What do you tell him?

2. A new coworker is a little nervous about collecting blood and urine specimens. What general safety practice guidelines can you tell her to follow?

Thinking Critically

1. **Communication**—Create a poster explaining the "Safey First" procedures that health care professionals need to follow in the laboratory setting; for example, why your must wash your hands and use gloves.

2. **Patient Education**—A patient is complaining of a variety of flu-like symptoms. She is unhappy that the doctor isn't prescribing a series of medications to address each of the symptoms.

Describe how you would explain to her about drug interactions.

3. **Computers**—Advances in medicine are continually changing the way health care workers protect themselves and treat infections. Explain how computers help keep the medical community informed about the latest medical progress. Describe ways you can access this information if you do not own a computer.

Chapter 20 Review

Media Connection

Use the Companion Web site for additional interactive learning activities: www.prenhall.com/badasch

Portfolio Connection

The medical community is constantly finding new information about how microorganisms and viruses affect our lives. This constant flow of new information makes it necessary to research how new findings affect us. Conduct your own research and write a research paper about a microorganism or virus. Select a microorganism or virus from those mentioned in this chapter or from another source. Describe the microorganism's or virus's shape, size, color, and pattern of growth. Describe its nature (aerobic or anaerobic), its effect on the body, and the physical symptoms it causes.

Contact a local hospital or the County Health Department infection control manager, and ask for an infection health care professional to come and visit the class. Conduct a "class interview," using one student as a moderator. Develop questions to ask during the interview that will provide insight into the greatest infectious health risks in the hospital or community, and find out why the risk is so high. Write a report and place it in the section of your portfolio labeled "Written Reports and Assignments."

PORTFOLIO TIP

Health care levels of cleanliness may be more demanding than those in some households. Patients are not necessarily dirty when noncompliant and must not be shamed. It is important to show patients and their families respect in all situations. Role-play with a classmate and record for your portfolio the rationales you would give the following two patients: One patient wants to bathe morning and night while the other patient prefers bathing only once a week.

21 Patient and Employee Safety

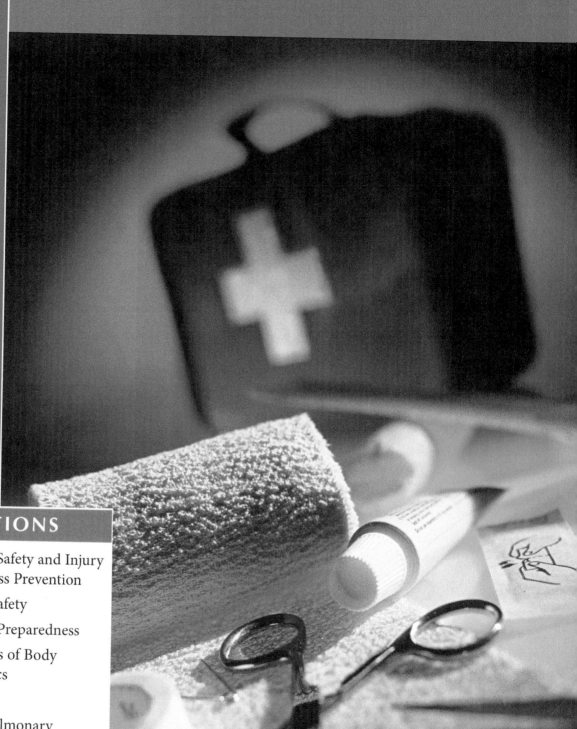

Getting Started

Your teacher will present information on several conditions that requires immediate and temporary care. At the end of the lesson, the teacher will divide the class into teams of eight students.

Each team will prepare a set of 3 × 5 cards of the alphabet; five cards for each vowel (five of letter A, five of letter E, etc.) and three cards for each consonant (three of letter B, three of letter C, three of letter D, etc.).

The teacher will begin reading signs and symptoms that may require immediate and temporary care. As each team identifies the condition being described, they use the cards to correctly spell the condition. So, if a student thinks they know the answer, they would pick the first letter. Once the team agrees that they've guessed the correct answer, they complete the word and raise their hands. The teacher keeps score for the first team to identify and correctly spell the condition being described.

General Safety and Injury and Illness Prevention

Background

A health care worker is responsible for maintaining a safe environment. You must know your employer's policies and procedures and be able to respond quickly to prevent injury. Your employer is also obligated to provide a safe environment by supplying equipment that protects against injury.

The Occupational Safety and Health Administration (OSHA) of the U.S. Department of Labor determines, develops, and monitors safe practices for each industry. If you or your employer fails to provide appropriate safety for all, OSHA will penalize your employer with a large fine or lock the doors of the facility until the safety violation is corrected. If you are at fault for not providing safe conditions, you could lose your job.

Objectives

When you have completed this section, you will be able to do the following:

- Match key terms to their correct meanings.

- Define *OSHA* and explain the agency's role in safety.

- Differentiate between IIPP, hazard communication, and exposure control.

- Name places to find information about hazards in a facility.

- Explain the health care worker's role in maintaining a safe workplace.

- Discuss the employer's role in maintaining a safe workplace.

- Identify 14 general safety rules.

- Summarize the importance of safety in a health care environment.

OSHA Standards

The Occupational Safety and Health Administration (OSHA) is part of the U.S. Department of Labor. OSHA establishes the guidelines for a safe work environment for all employers and their employees. The OSHA standards say that employees have the "right to know" what hazards are present in their environment.

OSHA regulations require employers to train and offer immunizations to high-risk employees in the first 10 days of a new job. A committed partnership between the employer and employee is necessary to provide a safe environment for everyone. This section explains the areas with which health care agencies and facilities must **comply**. They are the:

- Ergonomic Program.
- Injury and Illness Prevention Program.
- Hazard Communication Program.
- Exposure Control Plan.

Ergonomic Program

Employers are changing the work environment to meet the expected OSHA **ergonomic** standards. You spend a large portion of your day in the work environment. You should be comfortable, use good posture, and learn exercises to prevent getting stiff and sore.

The safety officer where you work will help you adjust your environment to accomplish this. If you sit in a workstation during the day, your chair, desk, and computer must be adjusted to fit your needs. If patients need to be lifted and moved in your workplace, there should be procedures and equipment in place to facilitate lifts and movements.

Guidelines in your Student Activity Guide will help you evaluate your work environment to ensure that you are in good alignment as you work. This prevents physical problems caused by improper working conditions.

comply
(kum PLAHY)
To follow directions, do what you are asked to do.

ergonomic
(erg uh NOM ik)
An object or practice designed to reduce injury.

You should get into the routine of stretching frequently during the day if you sit at a work station. Stretching and other simple exercises can reduce the risk of injury due to repetitive activities. The following exercises can reduce eyestrain, headaches, and tension in your back, neck, shoulders, and wrists:

1. **Deep Breathing:** Close your eyes. Inhale deeply and slowly through your nose. Exhale slowly through your mouth. Repeat at least four times.

2. **Changing Focus:** Look up from your computer screen and focus your eyes on a distant object. Look back at an object that is close and allow your eyes to focus on it. Repeat this exercise four times.

3. **Arm and Hand Shake:** Drop your arms and hands to your side and let them relax. Shake your relaxed hands for a few seconds. Then shake your hands and arms.

4. **Finger Stretch:** Grab the edge of your desk with your palms down and your thumb below the edge. Press down for a few seconds. Then press up for a few seconds. Turn your hands upside-down, so palms are facing up and your four fingers are below the edge. Repeat the exercise.

5. **Ankle Stretch:** Sit upright in your chair. Rotate both feet to the right, so that your ankles are stretched. Then rotate both feet to the left.

6. **Body Stretch:** Lock your hands behind your head. Lean back in your chair and arch your back.

7. **Shoulder Shrug:** Bring your shoulders up to your ears and try to press your shoulders and ears together. Hold for a few seconds. Let go of your shoulders and allow them to drop. Repeat four times.

Injury and Illness Prevention Program

The Injury and Illness Prevention Program (IIPP) **mandates** that every employer establish, **implement**, and maintain an effective IIPP.

As a student or employee, you are responsible for:

- Knowing who is responsible in the facility for the IIPP.
- Practicing policies and procedures that ensure safe and healthy work practices.
- Understanding the communication system used to keep you informed of hazards.
- Knowing what hazards are present and how to prevent injury from them.
- Knowing to whom to report an injury or illness during work hours and what documentation to complete.
- Knowing where the safety bulletin board (or communication book) is in your facility. You are responsible for reading all items posted each month.

Your school or employer will test you for signs of tuberculosis (TB). Exposure to tuberculosis is determined by a TB skin test. If your TB test indicates exposure, additional tests will be necessary. You will also be offered hepatitis B vaccine. This vaccine protects you from getting hepatitis B while working in the health care environment.

mandates
(MAN dayts)
Orders or commands.

implement
(IM pluh ment)
To carry out a rule or procedure.

Hazard Communication Program

The Hazard Communication Program mandates that employers inform employees of:

- Chemicals or hazards in the environment.

- Where chemicals or hazards are stored and used.

- How to interpret chemical labels and hazard signs.

- Methods and equipment for cleaning chemical spills.

- Personal protection equipment and its storage location.

- The hazard communication system.

As a student or employee, you are responsible for knowing:

- What chemicals or hazards are in your work area.

- Where the chemicals or hazards are stored or used.

- How to read and interpret container signs and labels.

- What to do when a chemical or **biohazard** spills.

- What personal protective equipment (PPE) to wear when working with or around chemicals and biohazards.

- Your facility's system for informing you of hazards in the work area.

biohazard
(BAYH o haz uhrd)
Biological materials or infectious agents that may cause harm to human, animal, or environmental health.

 ## Science Link

Biohazardous Material

Biohazardous materials are defined as biological materials or infectious agents that may cause harm to human, animal, or environmental health. Viruses that cause disease (such as the human immunodeficiency virus, or HIV) are biohazards. So are disease-causing bacteria (such as *E. coli*).

Plant toxins, allergens (such as pollen), and snake venom are biological agents that may cause disease, so they may be classified as biohazards. Certain types of recombinant DNA may also be classified as biohazards. This is DNA that has the potential to harm plants or animals if it escapes into the environment.

Viruses, bacteria, and other biohazardous material can be spread by blood or other body fluids. Therefore, care must be taken to minimize patient and health care worker exposure to body fluids. Any equipment that is used on a patient must be sterilized before it is used on any other

patient. Health care professionals must wear gloves, protective clothing, and (in some cases) masks when working with patients. Needles must be used carefully and discarded in a designated container after use.

Any clothes or linens exposed to blood or other body fluids must be stored in properly labeled biohazard containers until they can be washed. Drawn blood must be transported carefully and stored in labeled safety cabinets or containers.

OSHA has developed procedures for the proper handling and disposal of biohazardous materials. These procedures must be followed in every health care facility, for the safety of patients, visitors, and staff.

What is the difference between a biohazard and a chemical hazard?

Hazard Categories

The way that harm is caused determines the hazard category.

- *Chemical hazards* cause harm when a chemical is mixed with another chemical, causing a reaction. When a chemical reacts with another substance or because of temperature change, it creates a new chemical. For example: Chlorine bleach mixed with ammonia creates a harmful (even deadly) gas called chloramines.

- *Health hazards* have the potential to harm a healthy body. For example, acid burns and destroys skin.

Material Safety Data Sheets (MSDSs)

Product manufacturers prepare material safety data sheet (MSDS) forms to provide the information needed to handle chemicals safely. Employers must make the MSDSs available to employees. Figure 21.1 identifies the type of information discussed on the MSDS.

The Hazard Communication Program explains how the employer plans to keep people safe when chemicals are present. The communication system must explain:

- What hazards are present and where they are stored and used.
- What precautions to take when hazardous products are present. These precautions include:
  - Wearing appropriate personal protective equipment (PPE).
  - Proper room ventilation.
  - Keeping flammable products away from flames or other heat sources.
- How to use potentially hazardous products safely.
- Proper cleanup and disposal of hazardous products.
- First aid if exposure occurs.
- How to label containers with a chemical, by always including:
  - Product name.
  - Chemicals in the product.
  - Precautions for use of the product.

As a student or employee you are responsible for knowing where hazard communications are kept and how to access them. You find hazard information on manufacturer's literature. You may receive memorandums from your employer alerting you to new hazards in the environment. Most facilities keep hazard communications:

- In safety policy and procedure manuals.
- In material safety data sheet (MSDS) books.
- On the safety bulletin board.
- On product labels.
- On signs.

MATERIAL SAFETY DATA SHEET

I Product Identification

COMPANY NAME: Calgon Vestal Laboratories
ADDRESS: 5035 Manchester Avenue
St. Louis, Missouri 63110   Nights: 314-802-2000
CHEMTREC: (800) 424-9300
PRODUCT NAME: Klenzyme   Product No.:   1103
SYNONYMS: Medical Apparatus and Instrument Presoak

II Hazardous Ingredients of Mixtures

Material	(CAS#)	% by Wt.	TLV	PEL
Subtilisins (Proteolytic enzymes)	(9014-01-1)	< 5	.06ppb	N/A
Sodium tetraborate, decahydrate	(1303-96-4)	< 5	5mg/m3	10mg/m3

III Physical Data

Vapor Pressure, mmHg: N/A
Evaporation Rate (ether = 1): N/A
Solubility in H_2O: Complete
Freezing Point F: N/A
Boiling Point F: > 212F
Specific Gravity H_2O = 1 @ 25C: 1.08

Vapor Density (Air = 1) 60–90 F: Undeterm.
% Volatile by wt: N/A
pH @ Undiluted Solution: N/A
pH as Distributed: 7.5–8.0
Appearance: Amber liquid
Odor: Typical, mild odor

IV Fire and Explosion

Flash Point F: N/A   Flammable Limits: N/A
Extinguishing Media: Not flammable. In event of fire, use water fog, CO_2, and dry chemical.
Special Fire Fighting Procedures: No special requirements given. As with any chemical fire, proper cautions should be taken, such as wearing a self-contained breathing apparatus.
Unusual Fire and Explosion Hazards: None known

V Reactivity Data

Stability-Conditions to avoid: Stable
Incompatibility: None known
Hazardous Decomposition Products: Propionaldehyde, CO, CO_2 in fire situations
Conditions Contributing to Hazardous Polymerization: Will not occur

VI Health Hazard Data

Effects of Overexposure (Medical Conditions Aggravated/Target Organ Effects)
A. Acute (Primary Route of Exposure)
Eyes & Skin: Upon contact, mildly irritating to eyes. Prolonged or repeated contact may irritate skin.
Inhalation: Spray mists or dusts from dried residues may result in respiratory irritation, coughing and/or difficulty in breathing.
Ingestion: May cause upset to gastrointestinal tract.
B. Subchronic, Chronic, Other: Subtilisins chronic exposure to dusts showed allergic sensitization with respiratory allergic reactions within minutes or delayed up to 24 hours.

VII Emergency and First Aid Procedures

Eyes: Immediately flush eyes with plenty of water for at least 15 minutes. See a physician.
Skin: Immediately wash with soap and plenty of water for at least 15 minutes while removing contaminated clothing. If irritation develops, seek medical aid.
Inhalation: Remove to fresh air. If not breathing, give artificial respiration. If breathing difficult, give oxygen if available. Seek medical aid and report all inhalation exposures to health and safety personnel.
Ingestion: Do not induce vomiting. Give water to dilute. Call a physician. Never give anything by mouth to an unconscious person.

VIII Spill or Leak Procedures

Spill Management: Contain spill and absorb material with an inert substance. Collect waste in suitable container.
Waste Disposal Methods: Dispose of in accordance with local, state, and federal regulations.

IX Protection Information/Control Measures

Respiratory: Not required under normal use
Eye: Safety glasses
Glove: Rubber
Other Clothing and Equipment: Clothes sufficient to avoid contact
Ventilation: Local exhaust

X Special Precautions

Precautions to be taken in Handling and Storing: Avoid exposure to high temperature or humidity. Wash hands thoroughly after use. Keep container closed when not in use.
Additional Information: Read and observe all labeled precautions.

Prepared by: R. C. Jente
Revision Date: 08/24/96
Seller makes no warranty, expressed or implied, concerning the use of this product other than indicated on the label. Buyer assumes all risks of use and/or handling of this material when such use and/or handling is contrary to label instructions.
While Seller believes that the information contained herein is accurate, such information is offered solely for its customers' consideration and verification under their specific use conditions. This information is not to be deemed a warranty or representation of any kind for which Seller assumes legal responsibility.

FIGURE 21.1
Example of an MSDS form. Which portions of the MSDS form may be most useful for health professionals?

What's New?

Green Cleaning

Most traditional cleaning supplies, even the mildest of them, come with warnings. They may cause blindness, vomiting, or even death if swallowed. Although they are effective cleaners, they seem to be an odd choice to use around extremely sick people. At least that's the thinking that has inspired some institutions to search for green cleaning supplies and other eco-friendly products. These products, which are made from natural products, are often far safer for use around people and have a lower impact on the environment.

Green cleaning goes beyond just using natural products. It sometimes also means using less of the chemicals that have always been used. Frequently, we simply use more cleaners than we need for a particular job. For instance, new ways of cleaning using microfibers can reduce the need for chemicals. Microfiber mops require less water, and less chemical cleaners, than do traditional cotton mops.

In the past, many facilities have stayed away from green products because they thought they would be more costly. Green products do not have to be more expensive, particularly when all costs are taken into account. Government agencies closely regulate many toxic chemicals. With green products, there are fewer toxic chemicals to track, which cuts regulatory costs and results in fewer injuries due to chemical accidents.

While green cleaning is not yet widespread, more and more institutions are beginning to see its advantages. Look for even more hospitals and environmental services departments to begin considering green cleaning in the future.

What additional benefits can you see in the use of eco-friendly products?

Exposure Control Program

An exposure control plan provides steps to reduce employee or student exposure to bloodborne pathogens. The plan includes the following:

- Determining the possibility of exposure under each position description.
- Developing a schedule and method for ensuring that the plan is enforced.
- Postexposure evaluation.

See the Occupational Exposure to Bloodborne Pathogens: Final Rule and Standard Precautions in Section 17.4 of Chapter 17 for more specific protective guidelines under the Exposure Control Program.

What's New?

Safety Equipment

Some health care institutions are providing new safety equipment designed to keep health professionals safe. Respirators filter air to keep health care workers safe from SARS, influenza, and other contagious diseases that are spread when infected patients cough or sneeze.

Needle safety devices and personal protective gear help to reduce the risk of being stuck by a needle. A needle stick doesn't just hurt. It can spread bloodborne pathogens, such as HIV, from infected patients.

Needle safety devices either provide built-in needle shields or containers that separate the needle from the syringe right after blood is drawn. Puncture-resistant finger or arm guards also help to eliminate needle sticks.

Most facilities are now using needleless systems. Although it may be impossible to remove all use of needles from health care facilities, the use of needleless systems for intravenous fluid systems and covered needle systems for any necessary needle use has decreased the incidence of needle stick injuries. There is no longer any need to recap needles.

Why is it important to handle needles safely?

Community Service

Create a poster that provides safety information pertinent to a local after-school center or program. Review the safety tips with the program participants. Ask if they have any other suggestions and add them to the poster with credit to person who suggested the idea.

General Safety

Safety is everyone's responsibility. There are rules that are important to all health care workers. To be a safe worker and to protect yourself, co-workers, and patients, learn the rules listed here.

- **Walk! Never run in hallways.** If you run, you may fall and injure yourself. You can collide with another person or object. You can injure someone else, or you might create panic.

- **Walk on the right-hand side of the hall not more than two abreast**. It is important to leave hallways open so that there are no traffic jams. In an emergency, a traffic jam can cause a delay and mean the difference between life and death.

- **Use handrails when using the stairs.** This prevents falling and injuring yourself.

- **Watch out for swinging doors.** Be certain that someone is not on the other side of a swinging door. You might injure yourself or someone else. (Figure 21.2)

- **Horseplay** is not tolerated. It is disturbing to others, may lead to accidents, causes confusion, and shows a lack of respect for patients and personnel.

abreast
(a BREST)
Side by side.

horseplay
(HAWS play)
Rowdy behavior; acting inappropriately in a work environment.

- **Always check labels.** Never use anything from containers that are not labeled. Using the wrong contents can cause injury or death to a patient. Using the wrong contents may also damage or ruin equipment.
- **Wipe up spills and place litter in containers.** A wet floor can cause someone to slip and fall. If there is litter on the floor, someone may trip and be seriously injured.
- **Dispose of sharps in designated containers.** Used needles, broken glass, and other sharp objects should be deposited in specially marked safety containers, to minimize injury.
- **Follow instructions carefully.** If you do not understand instructions or do not know how to do a task, always ask for instructions. If you do something incorrectly, you may cause a serious problem.
- **Report any injury to yourself or others to your supervisor immediately.** Reporting an injury ensures treatment for the injured without delay and correction of the potential hazard.
- **Do not use electrical cords that are frayed or damaged.** Frayed or damaged cords can cause **shocks**, burns, or fire.
- **Report a shock you receive from electrical equipment to your supervisor.** This prevents fire or a shock to someone else.
- **Do not use malfunctioning equipment.** It is dangerous and may cause serious injury to you or someone else.
- **Make sure all medical supplies and equipment are secure.** Sharp instruments, drugs, and chemicals may cause harm if taken by patients or other visitors to the health care facility. Keep these and other supplies in locked drawers or closets, if possible.
- **Report unsafe conditions to your supervisor immediately.** Safety is everyone's business. Be aware of your environment. Watch for unsafe conditions.
- Follow Standard Precaution guidelines.

frayed
(frayd)
Worn or tattered (e.g., electrical cords may be worn, causing wires to be exposed).

shock
(SHAHK)
Convulsion of muscles and extreme stimulation of nerves when an electric current passes through the body.

malfunctioning
(mal fungk shen ing)
Not working as it is supposed to.

FIGURE 21.2
Watch for swinging doors! What should you do when you approach a swinging door?

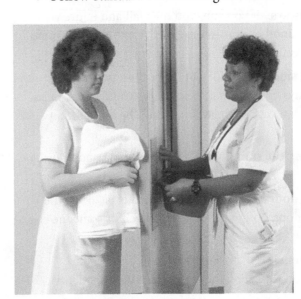

Personal Wellness

Slips, Trips, and Falls

Slipping on wet surfaces, falling, and tripping over obstacles are among the most common injuries suffered by workers. The Occupational Safety and Health Administration (OSHA), a U.S. Department of Labor agency, provides guidelines to help workers avoid some of these accidents. The following are some OSHA recommendations:

- Clean only one half of a hallway or staircase at a time so that staff, visitors, and patients have a dry surface to walk on. Use warning signs to alert people to slippery floors.

- Clean all spills immediately and thoroughly.

- Keep floors dry and clean. This can be especially important in entry ways when people walk in out of the rain. Put down mats to help reduce slipping.

- Do not leave buckets, mops, or other supplies sitting in hallways when they are not in use.

- Use appropriate ladders or step stools to reach hard-to-reach places or to perform maintenance, such as when cleaning light fixtures.

- Use non-skid waxes in toilets and shower areas to reduce slipping.

  Immediately report damaged surfaces, poor or ineffective lighting in halls, stairways, or other areas, and other conditions that can lead to injury.

- Areas that are frequently wet or moist—such as an outside walkway with poor drainage—can become especially slippery due the growth of mold and fungi. Report such areas to your supervisor. Additionally, keep these areas clean. Use appropriate cleaners to reduce the growth of molds and fungi.

- Wear functional shoes with good grip.

Why are EVS (Environmental Services Technician)/housekeeping workers especially at risk for slipping, tripping, and falling?

🖼 Summary

Safety is the responsibility of all health care workers. Employers must inform employees of workplace risks and take steps to minimize those risks. Employees must follow rules and practice safe behavior to minimize risks of injury to themselves, coworkers, and patients. OSHA is very strict about enforcement of regulations that keep the work environment safe.

Apply It

Pretend you are a school "hall monitor." Make a list of all of the dangerous actions/activities/situations you see during a day at school. Then, go to the local elementary school and conduct the same activity with an elementary school partner. Can the younger students identify potentially dangerous situations?

Emergency Codes

There are emergency terms that are common to all health care facilities, such as "no code" or "DNR." However, each facility has its own emergency terminology with which employees must be familiar. Many health care facilities combine the word *code* with other words or numbers to communicate particular kinds of emergencies when calling emergency medical teams to an area of the hospital (e.g., *code zero*, *code blue*, or *code 99*).

Learn By Doing: Section 21.1 Activity

1. Complete Worksheets 1 through 3 as assigned.

2. Complete Worksheets/Activities 4 through 6 as assigned.

3. Complete Worksheets 7 and 8 as assigned.

4. When you are confident that you can meet each objective for this section, ask your teacher for the section evaluation.

SECTION 21.2   Patient Safety

Background

Health care workers are responsible for the safety of patients. If you do not follow Standard Precautions and basic safety precautions, patients can be seriously injured. Accidents involving patients are reduced if simple safety measures are followed. In this section, we explain rules to follow when using ambulation devices, transporting devices, postural supports, and side rails.

Objectives

When you have completed this section, you will be able to do the following:

- Match key terms with their correct meaning.

- Explain how to use ambulation devices, transporting devices, postural supports, and side rails safely.

- Match descriptions and principles associated with ambulation devices, transporting devices, postural supports, and side rails.

- Explain the importance of safety measures.

- Follow safe practice guidelines when caring for patients.

Identifying the Patient

When you work directly with a patient, you must identify him or her to avoid a mistake. Errors are avoided if you follow these *important* steps:

- Check with the nurse's station for the right room number.

- Check the requisition or physician's order, which has the patient's name on it, against the patient's identification band.

- In ambulatory care, confirm chart name and information with each patient.

Ambulation Devices

Ambulation devices are devices used to assist in walking. The most common devices in the health care setting are canes, crutches, and walkers. (**Figure 19.4**) These devices give the patient additional support and aid in balancing while walking or standing.

ambulation devices
(am byoo LAY shun duh VYS iz)
Canes, crutches, walkers, or other equipment that help a patient to walk.

Safe Practice Guidelines When Using Ambulation Devices

It is essential that all devices be in good condition, because patients depend on these items.

- Devices must always be structurally safe, without dents or cracks. For example, wood crutches are unsafe if the wood is split or cracked. A loose joint in a walker allows it to wobble or break, and the patient can fall.

- Areas touching the ground must be covered with rubber tips to prevent slipping.

- The devices must always be clean and free of blood or body fluids.

Transporting Devices

Transporting devices include equipment used to move patients from one place to another. The most common transporting devices are wheelchairs and **gurneys**. Gurneys and wheelchairs make it easy to move patients who are unable to walk. Follow these basic principles to ensure the patient's safety. (**Figure 21.3**)

gurney
(GUR nee)
A stretcher on wheels.

Safe Practice Guidelines When Using Gurneys and Wheelchairs
- Always lock the brakes except when you are moving.

- Back a wheelchair over indented or raised doorways, such as an elevator or any ridges on the floor.

- Always back a patient in a wheelchair or a gurney down a hill.

- Always secure straps or put side rails up on a gurney.

- Lock brakes when moving the patient on or off a gurney.

- Always back the patient on a gurney headfirst into an elevator.

- Never leave a patient on a gurney unattended.

- Always keep the gurney free of blood and body fluids.

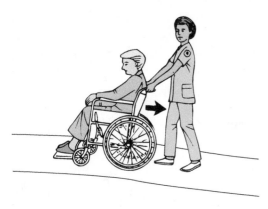

Back a wheelchair over indented or raised doorways, such as an elevator or any ridges on the floor.

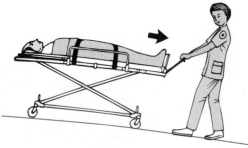

Always back a patient in a wheelchair or a gurney down a hill.

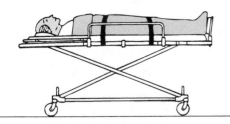

Never leave a patient on a gurney unattended.

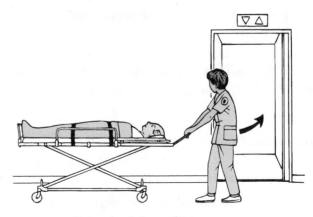

Always back the patient on a gurney headfirst into an elevator.

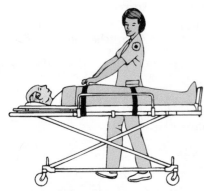

Always secure straps or put side rails up on a gurney.

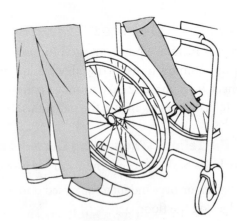

Always lock the brakes except when you are moving.
Lock brakes when moving the patient on or off a gurney.

FIGURE 21.3
Principles in the use of gurneys and wheelchairs. How should you move a patient in a gurney or wheelchair down a hill?

Postural Supports

Postural supports are devices that **restrict** a patient's movement. This type of restriction is necessary only when the patient's safety is in jeopardy. Occasionally, patients become disoriented due to a change of environment or as a response to medication. When this occurs, postural supports are used to keep patients safe.

Postural supports are more common in long-term care facilities. *Example:* A confused patient may not realize that he is too weak to walk to the bathroom without falling. Use a postural support to remind patients to call for assistance when they need to get out of bed. There are many types of supports. The most common are vest supports, wrist supports, and ankle supports. When you use postural supports, certain **principles** must be observed. (See Chapter 18.)

Safe Practice Guidelines When Using Postural Supports

- A physician's order is required by law.

- Never use a postural support on a patient in a chair or bed without wheels.

- Patients requiring postural supports must be checked frequently. The support must be released or loosened every two hours.

- Use a half-bow knot to secure the support.

- Leave at least two fingers' ease between the patient's skin and the support so his or her circulation is not restricted.

- Never secure supports to side rails; always attach to the framework of a bed or gurney.

- Secure the half-bow knot out of the patient's reach.

- Discard supports that have touched blood or body fluids, following Standard Precautions.

- Always try alternative methods of supporting patients before applying physical restraints.

- Postural supports are of valid use when a patient is at high risk of injuring self or others, such as in the procedure or operating room, while undergoing conscious or unconscious sedation, when moving could cause significant injury.

- Follow the guidelines under your facilities restraint policy and procedure.

 Side Rails

Side rails are not to be used as a restraint. Research has shown that the use of side rails as a restraint device can actually increase falls and the injury from falls. Placing a side rail up with the intent of securing a confused patient will only increase the probability of a patient becoming caught in a side rail or falling from an even greater height.

There have been incidents where a patient has become caught and severely injured from the use of side rails with the intent to restrain. Half side rails may be used to facilitate the use of bed controls or turning by the patient.

postural supports
(POS chuh ruhl suh PORTS)
Soft restraints used to protect residents.

restrict
(ree STRIKT)
To keep within limits; to confine.

principles
(PRIN suh puhl)
Codes of behavior.

Safe Practice Guidelines When Using Side Rails

- A form releasing the facility of responsibility must be completed if a patient and/or family requests the use of full side rails.

- Side rails must be locked securely if used. Patients may lean on the rail for support and fall, if not secured.

- Precautions must be taken when side rails are put up or down. Tubing and the patient's legs and arms must be away from the rail.

- Side rails should always be clean and free of body fluids.

Summary

By following each of the simple principles discussed in this section, you provide safe conditions for your patients. You have learned to identify the patient to prevent errors and to keep your patients safe when using ambulation devices, transporting devices, postural supports, and side rails.

SECTION **21.2** 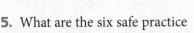 **Review Questions**

1. What are transporting devices?

2. What does *ambulation* mean?

3. Under what circumstances might postural supports be used?

4. How would you move a patient in a transporting device onto an elevator?

5. What are the six safe practice guidelines for using side rails?

6. What are the safe practice guidelines when using gurneys and wheelchairs?

Learn By Doing: Section 21.2 Activity

1. Complete Worksheet 1.

2. When you are confident that you can meet each objective for this section, ask your teacher for the section evaluation.

Disaster Preparedness

Background

Disasters can occur anywhere and at any moment. As a health care worker, you are expected to respond quickly according to your agency disaster plan. You must be familiar with the practices that are detailed in that plan and be able to follow them if a disaster occurs.

A disaster is anything that causes damage and injury to a group of people. Examples are flood, earthquake, tornado, explosion, fire, and bioterrorism. Be alert to emergency equipment, exits, and the disaster plan. They provide the essentials necessary to respond effectively to a disaster.

Be particularly aware of instructions in the disaster plan telling you how to cooperate with first responders, police and fire personnel, and disaster-specific instructions from local, state, and federal officials.

Objectives

When you have completed this section, you will be able to do the following:

- Match key terms with their correct meaning.

- Identify what you are responsible for knowing and doing when a disaster occurs.

- List the three elements required to start a fire.

- Explain four ways to prevent fires.

- Summarize all safety requirements that protect the employee/student, patient, and employer.

Disaster Plan

Your facility is required to have a disaster plan. You are responsible for knowing the plan and responding when a disaster occurs. To be prepared for any type of disaster you need to know the following:

- The floor plan of your facility.
- The nearest exit route.
- The location of alarms and fire extinguishers.
- How to use alarms and fire extinguishers.
- Your role as a health care worker when a disaster occurs.

The following are some basic rules to remember when a disaster strikes:

- Assess the situation; count to 10 to calm yourself.
- Be sure that you are not in danger. (Placing yourself in danger only makes the situation worse.)

- Remove those who are in immediate danger, if it is safe to do so.
- Notify others of the emergency according to facility policy.
- Use stairs, *not* the elevator.

Fire is often the result of a disaster. It is your responsibility to be alert to causes of fire and act to prevent fire when possible.

Fire Causes and Prevention

There are three elements that must be present before a fire can start (Figure 21.4a):

- Oxygen.
- Heat.
- Fuel.

Most fires can be prevented if everyone is **observant** and careful. The following are some ways you can help prevent fires:

- Smoking is restricted to **designated** outdoor areas. Monitor garbage containers.
- Check electrical equipment for proper functioning and frayed electrical cord. If there is any problem, report it immediately. (Figure 21.4b)
- When using **flammable** liquids, take only the amount needed to complete the task. You would spill only the amount you poured, not the whole container. Keep flammable liquids in a container approved by the Underwriters' Laboratories.

observant
(ob ZUR vent)
Quick to see and understand.

designated
(DEZ ig nay ted)
Chosen for a specific purpose.

flammable
(FLAM uh buhl)
Catches fire easily or burns quickly.

FIGURE 21.4
(a) The three elements needed to start a fire. What is needed to cause flammable materials to begin to burn?
(b) Misuses of electricity. What does a frayed electrical cord look like?

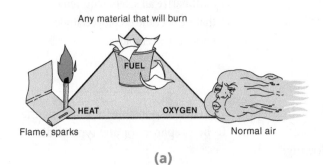

Any material that will burn

FUEL

HEAT   OXYGEN

Flame, sparks   Normal air

(a)

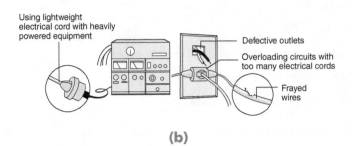

Using lightweight electrical cord with heavily powered equipment

Defective outlets

Overloading circuits with too many electrical cords

Frayed wires

(b)

BACKGROUND: Health care facilities are required by law to establish safety boards and to inspect the facility regularly for any type of potential fire hazard. Equipment must be checked regularly and escape routes must be kept open.

Fire drills are performed at specific intervals to assure that the facility and its staff are equipped to handle any fire emergency. Nurses are educated and tested annually on their knowledge of the procedures for response to a fire and how to remove patients from danger. Fire extinguishers can be used for types A, B, or C fires.

A Trash, wood, or paper
B Liquids
C Electrical equipment
ABC Use on all fires

ALERT: Follow Standard Precautions.

PREPROCEDURE

1. First Response: **RACE**

   Rescue

   Alert appropriate facility officials

   Contain Fire

   Extinguish Fire

PROCEDURE

2. Locate fire extinguisher and check type.

NOTE: Every nurse should know the location of the closest fire extinguisher to his/her work station.

3. Hold fire extinguisher upright. Pull ring pin.

4. Stand back six to ten feet and direct flow towards base of the fire.

5. Squeeze lever, sweeping side to side.

POSTPROCEDURE

6. Replace or have extinguisher recharged after use.

Classes of Fire Extinguishers

There are four classes of fire extinguishers. Each type extinguishes a different type of fire.

Class A extinguishers are the most common and put out fires in ordinary combustibles, such as wood, paper, cloth, and many plastics. These extinguishers contain pressurized water. Class A extinguishers have a green triangle marking of an "A" and depict a garbage can and wood pile burning.

Class B extinguishers should be used on fires involving flammable liquids, such as grease, gasoline, and oil. These extinguishers contain carbon dioxide. Class B extinguishers have a red square marking of a "B" and depict a gasoline can with a burning puddle.

Apply It

Partner with a classmate and review the disaster relief plans in local buildings—schools, government offices, libraries, museums, etc.

Compare your results. What are the best features of each plan? Has your school's plan been updated recently? Is there anything you think should change?

Class C extinguishers should be used on energized electrical equipment or wiring where the electric non-conductivity of the extinguishing agent is important. These extinguishers contain potassium bicarbonate or potassium chloride. Class C extinguishers have a blue circle marking a "C" and depict an electric plug with burning outlet.

Class D extinguishers are designed for use on combustible metals such as sodium, titanium, and magnesium. These extinguishers contains either sodium chloride or copper powder and are pressurized with nitrogen. Class D extinguishers have a yellow star marking of a "D." There is no picture designator for Class D extinguishers and they are not given a multi-purpose rating for use on other types of fires.

In addition, there is a **Class ABC** extinguisher that can be used on wood, cloth, paper, flammable liquids, gasoline, grease and electrical equipment. A Class ABC fire extinguisher is designed to extinguish Class A, B, and C fires. It contains a graphite type chemical that is irritating to the skin.

Bioterrorism

Everyone must be aware of the dangers of chemical or biological disasters. Facilities have plans to provide for the safety of patients, physicians, staff, and visitors. These plans include shelter-in during a possible exposure.

Shelter-in is a nationally accepted term indicating the need to remain inside of the facility during a potential exposure to chemical and biological hazards. These plans include securing entrances and exits to the building and securing outside air sources. Your responsibility is to learn what your facility plan is and to follow the procedures that are in place.

Summary

Disaster preparedness is everyone's responsibility. Each person is responsible for responding to a disaster and being alert to **potential** hazards.

There are three elements required to start a fire: oxygen, heat, and fuel. There are at least three ways to help prevent fires. These include checking for frayed electrical cords and malfunctioning equipment, careful handling of flammable liquids, and following proper oxygen procedures.

Know the disaster plan of your agency or facility. Move patients to safety if they are in danger. Know where to find the fire extinguishers and which exits to use. Do not use an elevator. Be calm. Do not panic!

potential
(puh TEN chul)
Possible.

1. Why would you want to be observant during a disaster?

2. What are three ways that you can prevent fires in a health care facility?

3. What should the staff of a health care facility do to ensure their safety and the safety of patients during a possible bioterrorism attack?

4. What are six basic rules to follow during a disaster?

5. When you are working in a health care facility, what do you need to know in order to be prepared for a disaster?

6. What is the generally accepted term indicating the need to remain inside of the facility during a potential exposure to chemical and biological hazards?

Learn By Doing: Section 21.3 Activity

1. Complete Worksheet 1 as assigned.

2. When you are confident that you can meet each objective for this section, ask your teacher for the section evaluation.

Language Arts Link

Job Safety

Whether you work in a hospital or on an office, safety is important workplace issue. The Occupational Safety & Health Administration (OSHA) is a branch of the U.S. Department of Labor, responsible for assuring the safety and health of America's workers.

OSHA sets the standards for on the job safety that every business in the United States is required to follow. In addition, many health care facilities have their own safety standards, and provide education for employees on proper behavior and precautions. They also institute plans and procedures to follow in case of an emergency.

Create a document that lists primary causes of work-related accidents and injuries in hospitals or other health care facilities. You may be able to locate statistics on the Internet or in your library, or you can try to imagine possibilities, such as falls, repetitive stress injuries, or back strain.

You may also be able to locate information about the costs of such accidents, in terms of lost productivity, worker's compensation, or insurance claims.

When the list is complete, write a report that a human resources department could distribute to employees explaining ways to prevent accidents. Also provide instructions for the company's emergency plan.

Principles of Body Mechanics

Background

As a health care worker, you lift, move, and carry many different objects and patients. It is important to use ergonomic practices and proper body mechanics when you are lifting or moving anything. Ergonomic practices prevent both fatigue and injury. If you injure yourself, you then become ineffective in your job. Worker injuries can cost a large facility thousands of dollars each year.

Objectives

When you have completed this section, you will be able to do the following:

- Match key terms with their correct meanings.
- Define *body mechanics.*
- List six rules of correct body mechanics.
- List six principles of body mechanics.
- Demonstrate correct lifting and moving of objects.

Body Mechanics

Health care workers move, lift, and carry all types of equipment and supplies. They also help position or move patients. Moving patients can be particularly hazardous to your back, as the patient may struggle or twist during movement.

Ergonomic practices suggest the use of specialized equipment for moving patients. Special equipment could include wheelchairs, walkers, canes, hydraulic lifts, or gait belts.

Of these items, the simplest and possibly most effective item for decreasing injuries to both the patient and the health care worker is the gait belt. Every facility should have gait belts available for use in all patient areas. Gait belts combined with good body mechanics allow the health care worker to safely lift, transfer, and ambulate the heavier and disabled patients with less personal strain or danger of injury.

efficiency
(ee FISH uhn see)
Ability to accomplish a job with the least possible difficulty.

When equipment is unavailable, ergonomic practices emphasize proper body mechanics during movement. When you use proper body mechanics, you save energy, prevent muscle strain, and increase your **efficiency.** Body mechanics is the coordination of body alignment, balance, and movement. When you use your body and your muscles properly, you are practicing good body mechanics.

Principles of Body Mechanics

Good body mechanics require you to keep your body in a neutral, upright position. You should keep your back straight at all times. You should let your leg muscles do most of the work. You should never twist your body. You should never strain as you perform work.

It is essential to practice good body mechanics when you are lifting or moving patients, in order to prevent strain and injury. You should also practice good body mechanics when you are performing simple tasks, such as checking blood pressure or entering data into a computer. Injuries from these simple tasks can develop over time if you use poor body mechanics. The following principles will help you to maintain good body mechanics.

1. Stoop. Do not bend.

   - Stand close to the object. Create a base of support by placing your feet wide apart.
   - Place one foot slightly forward.
   - Bend at your hips and knees with your back straight, lower your body, and bring your hands down to the object. (**Figure 21.5a**)
   - Use the large muscles in your legs to return to a standing position. (**Figure 21.5b**)

2. Lift firmly and smoothly after you size up the load.

   - If you cannot easily pull the object to you (i.e., the **load** is too heavy), *get help!*
   - Grasp the load firmly.
   - Lift by using the large muscles of your legs. (**Figure 21.6a**)
   - Keep the load close to your body. (**Figure 21.6b**)
   - Do not twist your body.
   - To change direction, shift your feet in the direction you want to go.

load
(LOHD)
Weight of an object or person that is to be moved.

FIGURE 21.5
Use large muscles of legs when lifting (a), and keep your back straight (b). Why should you use the large muscles of your legs instead of your back muscles to lift?

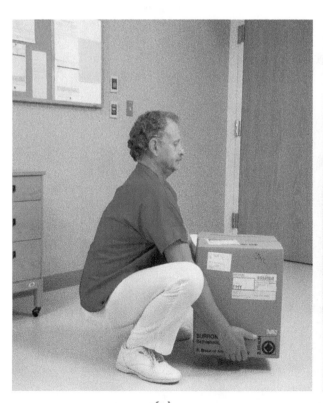

(a)

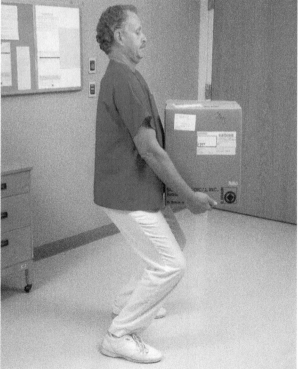

(b)

FIGURE 21.6
(a) A health care worker safely lifts a bag. Why is it important to use safe lifting techniques?
(b) One of the factors that contributes to safe lifting is to make sure you bend at the knees. Why is this important?

(a)

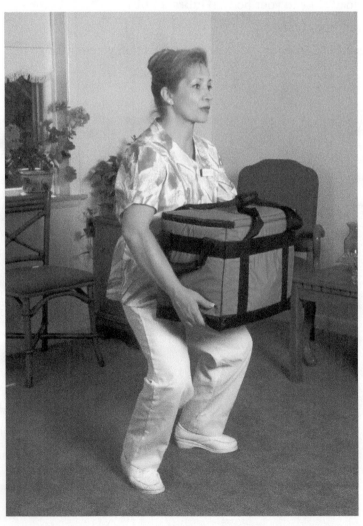

(b)

3. Always use the center of **gravity** when carrying a load.

- Keep your back as straight as possible.

- Keep the weight of the load close to the body and centered over your hips. (**Figure 21.7**)

- Put down the load by bending at the hips and knees. Keep your back straight and the load close to your body.

- If the load is too heavy, *get help!*

- When two or more people carry the load, assign one person as the leader so that he or she can give commands.

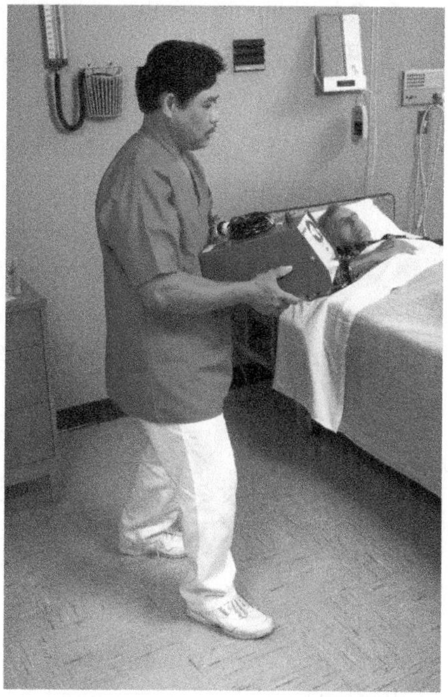

4. Pulling: Push or pull rather than lift the load.

- Place your feet apart with one foot slightly forward. Keep close to the object you are moving.

- Grasp the object firmly, close to its center of gravity.

- **Crouch**; lean away from the object.

- Pull by straightening your legs. Keep your back straight.

- Walk backwards. Your leg muscles should do all the work.

5. Pushing: Push or pull rather than lift the load.

- Stand close to the object to be moved.

- Crouch down with your feet apart.

- Bend your elbows and put your hands on the load at chest level.

- Lean forward with your chest and shoulders near the object. (**Figure 21.8**)

- Keep your back straight.

- Push with your legs.

FIGURE 21.7
As you carry a load, keep its weight close to your body and centered over your hips. Why should you keep your joints slightly bent when carrying heavy objects?

gravity
(GRAV i tee)
Natural force or pull toward the earth. In the body, the center of gravity is usually the center of the body.

crouch
(KROWCH)
To stoop, using the large muscles of the legs to help maintain balance.

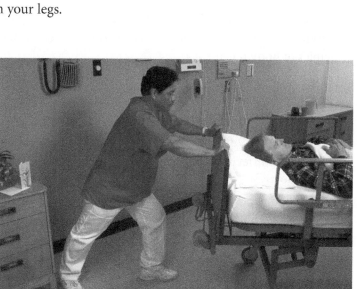

FIGURE 21.8
To push an object, such as a moveable hospital bed, lean forward with your chest and shoulders near the bed as you push forward.

6. Reaching: Carefully evaluate the distance.

   ■ Always use a stool or a ladder to reach objects that are too high.

   ■ Stand close to the object.

   ■ If you are standing on the floor, place your feet wide apart, one foot slightly forward.

   ■ Maintain good body **alignment**. Move close to the object. Do not reach to the point of straining.

   ■ When reaching for an object that is above your head, grip it with your palms up, and lower it. Keep it close to your body on the way down.

Evaluating Ergonomics to Avoid Injury

Using the principles of body mechanics can help you to avoid injury. As you are working, however, it is sometimes hard to determine whether your body is in the proper position. One aspect of ergonomics is self-evaluation or evaluation by supervisors or coworkers.

Evaluation can help you and your coworkers to correct bad habits and avoid injury. Evaluation can also help to identify problems in the workplace that may lead to poor body mechanics. You can do the following to evaluate ergonomic practices:

1. **Watch each other:** Tell your coworkers if they are twisting their bodies or bending their backs when working with patients. Ask coworkers to watch your body mechanics as well.

2. **Check equipment:** Equipment that is faulty or hard to operate can cause you to strain muscles. Make sure brakes on wheelchairs are working, so that you do not hurt your back while moving a patient. Make sure other equipment is at the correct height (between the waist and the shoulders), so you do not have to bend to use it.

3. **Discuss Procedures:** In some situations, good body mechanics alone may not be enough to prevent injury. Discuss whether you need to create lifting teams instead of having staff move patients by themselves. Also discuss how you can use equipment to help move patients.

Summary

In this section, you learned that by following basic principles, you prevent fatigue and injury. There are six important rules to remember when following the basic principles of body mechanics.

Six Rules to Remember:

1. Keep your back straight.

2. Bend at the hips and knees.

3. Keep your feet approximately 6 to 8 inches apart to provide a wide base of support.

4. Use the strongest muscles of your legs.

5. Do not twist your body.

6. Use the weight of your body to help push or pull.

When you learn to lift and move correctly, you protect yourself and others from injury.

1. What does the term *body mechanics* mean?

2. What are the six principles of body mechanics?

3. Where is your center of gravity?

4. Describe how you would safely pull a load.

5. How can using proper body mechanics help you to stay healthy and perform well in a health care position?

6. How can you evaluate ergonomic practices?

Learn By Doing: Section 21.4 Activity

1. Complete Worksheet 1.

2. Complete Worksheet/Activity 2 as assigned.

3. When you are confident that you can meet each objective for this section, ask your teacher for the section evaluation.

Personal Wellness

Staying Fit

Maintaining fitness is important when you are a health care professional. A fit body is strong and flexible and can help you to move patients and equipment without fatigue or injury. A fit mind can help you to handle the stresses of caring for people. Exercise can help you to maintain both a fit body and a fit mind.

Lifting weights can help you to build strength in your arm, leg and back muscles. Pilates, yoga, or dance can help you to strengthen muscles, improve balance, and focus your mind. Running or biking can help to increase your endurance. Any exercise can help you to work off stress.

Choose an exercise that appeals to you. Make sure you exercise at least three times per week. Incorporate a variety of exercises into your weekly routine for different physical and mental benefits.

How can an exercise program help a health care worker to avoid injury on the job?

Background

In or out of the clinical setting, the health care worker is expected to respond quickly and effectively when there is a sudden illness or injury. As a health care worker you are responsible for seeking information and becoming competent in first-aid skills. This knowledge enables you to be a well-prepared and effective health care worker.

Objectives

When you have completed this section, you will be able to do the following:

- Match key terms with their correct meanings.
- Demonstrate the procedures for:
  - Mouth-to-mouth breathing
  - Obstructed airway
  - Serious wounds
  - Preventing shock
  - Splints
  - Slings
  - Bandaging

Introduction to First Aid

This section is an overview of commonly used first-aid techniques. The authors of this book strongly advise that everyone attend a basic first-aid class and a heart saver or **cardiopulmonary** resuscitation (CPR) class in order to become proficient. These classes are given by the American Red Cross and the American Heart Association.

Appropriate first aid can save a life and prevent a permanent disability. Most situations requiring first aid need prompt, **definitive** action. To gain understanding and a high skill level, you need supervised practice for each of the procedures listed.

First aid is the emergency care given to a victim of an accident or a sudden illness. This treatment is required immediately and continues as needed until advanced medical care is available.

General Principles of First Aid

1. Never panic; always remain calm. Unfortunately, this statement is easier said than done. Here are some basic rules that help you remain calm:
   - Take a few slow, deep breaths.
   - Survey the surrounding area and ensure that it is safe before approaching.
   - Determine what resources are available and what is needed.

cardiopulmonary
(kahr dee oh PUHL muh ner ee)
Having to do with the heart and lungs.

definitive
(di FIN i tiv)
Clear, without question, exacting (e.g., when giving emergency care, each treatment should be done in a definitive manner).

2. Evaluate the situation by:
   - Checking the victim's level of consciousness.
   - Opening the victim's airway.
   - Checking for breathing.
   - Checking circulation, including pulse and bleeding.
3. Determine if the victim is in a safe environment, free from danger.
4. Determine **priorities** of treatment (i.e., decide which condition requires the most immediate care).
   - Urgent care is required in life-threatening situations, such as stopped breathing, heart attack, shock, serious wounds, poisoning, and burns.
   - A victim may need first aid, but the situation may not be life threatening. Nonlife-threatening conditions include **fracture** of an arm or leg and a minor **contusion** or **laceration**.
5. Decide how to provide the care that is needed and begin providing any care you are trained or permitted to give.
6. Call or send for help as soon as possible. If an adult patient is conscious, you must get their permission to help them. If the patient is a child and a parent is available, you must get a parent's permission to help the child.

CAUTION: Carry disposable gloves. Also carry a pocket mask for delivering rescue breaths. Use these items to prevent exposure to body fluids. Always follow Standard Precautions.

Life-Threatening Situations

Most cities have an emergency medical system (EMS) that responds immediately with emergency care providers. The most common number used to alert the EMS system is 911. If this is not in place, dial 0 and ask local operator to connect you the Emergency Medical System. The following situations are considered life threatening and require emergency medical care.

Oxygen is necessary for brain cells to live. Permanent brain damage can occur if oxygen is not present for four to six minutes. You have only a few minutes to save the life of a person who has stopped breathing.

Obstructed Airway (Closed Airway, Stopped or Not Breathing)

An obstructed airway occurs when an object blocks the airway leading to the lungs. This occurs when a piece of food or other object lodges in the back of the throat or in the windpipe. Early detection of an airway obstruction is important in determining your plan of action. There are two types of obstructions:

- *Partial obstruction* occurs when some air can be exchanged. There may be *good air exchange* when the victim coughs forcefully or wheezes between coughs. *Do not* interfere with the victim's attempt to cough the object out. If there is *poor air exchange* and the victim:
  - Becomes weak.
  - Has an ineffective cough.

priorities
(prah AWR i tee)
Those things that are most important.

fracture
(FRAK cher)
Broken bone.

contusion
(cuhn TOO shuhn)
Condition in which the skin is bruised, swollen, and painful, but is not broken.

laceration
(las uh RAY shuhn)
Wound or tear of the skin.
Treat the victim for complete airway obstruction (conscious victim).

- Has a crowing or high-pitched noise during inhalation.
- Has increased difficulty breathing.
- Turns bluish around the mouth and fingernails.

- *Complete obstruction* occurs when there is no air exchange or there is poor air exchange. The signs of complete obstruction are present when the victim:

  - Is suddenly unable to breathe, cough, or speak.
  - Clutches neck or throat—this is the universal choking sign and a way of telling people around you that you are choking (see photograph in Procedure 21.3).
  - Is struggling to breathe.

When you observe these signs, follow the procedure for obstructed airway.

PROCEDURE | 21.2 | Rescue Breathing—Adult

BACKGROUND: Rescue breathing is used when a victim is no longer breathing on his or her own. Rescue breathing delivers essential oxygen to the brain cells of the victim. This procedure explains how to administer rescue breathing to an adult.

ALERT: Follow Standard Precautions.

PREPROCEDURE

1. Put on disposable gloves.

2. Check for consciousness by shaking victim's shoulder gently and asking if he or she is OK. If there is no response, activate EMS system.

PROCEDURE

3. Open airway by placing one hand at victim's chin and the other hand on victim's forehead; gently lift chin by supporting jawbone with fingertips and lifting upward to open mouth. (Do not put pressure on throat; this may block airway.) This is called the *head tilt/chin lift.*

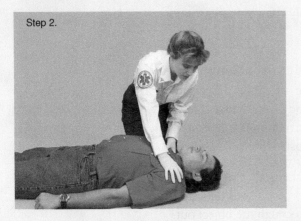

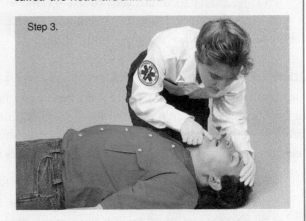

(continued)

4. Check for breathing by placing your ear near victim's mouth and nose. Turn your head so that you can see his or her chest. Look to see if chest is rising or falling. Listen for breathing. Feel for air from victim's mouth or nose on your cheek. If breathing is *not* present go to step 5.

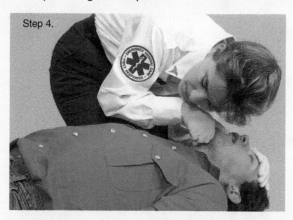

Step 4.

5. Ventilate. Place a pocket mask over mouth and nose. Put apex (point) over bridge of nose and base between lip and chin. Give two breaths ($1^1/2$ to 2 seconds per breath) through the one-way valve. Allow lungs to empty between each breath. (If dentures obstruct the airway, remove them.) If air does *not* inflate lungs: retilt head to ensure an open airway and repeat the two breaths. Watch for chest to rise, allow for exhalation between breaths. (If lungs still do not inflate, treat victim for an obstructed airway; see the Obstructed Airway procedures.)

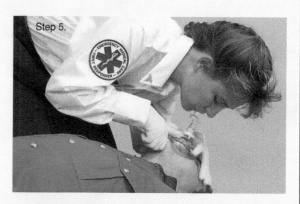

Step 5.

6. Check carotid pulse.

7. If breathing is absent and pulse is present, keep the airway open and give one breath to victim every 5 seconds. If there is no pulse, cardiopulmonary resuscitation (CPR) is needed to circulate oxygenated blood through body.

See Section 21.6 for CPR procedures. CPR should be learned by taking a course given by a qualified instructor approved by the American Heart Association or American Red Cross.

POSTPROCEDURE

8. Ensure that victim has follow-up treatment or assessment by Emergency Medical Technicians or hospital personnel.

9. Discard gloves and wash hands (follow handwashing guidelines).

Obstructed Airway in a Conscious Victim—Adult

BACKGROUND: An obstructed airway may occur if a victim inhales food or drink. This procedure explains how to apply pressure from an abdominal thrust (also called the Heimlich maneuver) to force an obstruction out of an adult victim's airway.

ALERT: Follow Standard Precautions.

PREPROCEDURE

When signs of choking are present:

1. Ask "Are you choking?" Observe victim for coughing or wheezing. Do *not interfere* if good air exchange is present.

PROCEDURE

2. Give **abdominal thrust**, sometimes called the **Heimlich maneuver**. Stand in back of victim; put your arms around victim's waist. Make a fist with one hand and put the thumb side of the fist slightly above the navel and well below the breast bone.

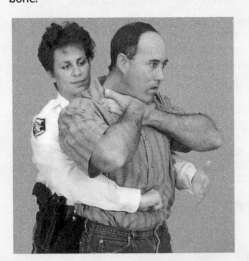

Take your other hand and grasp fist; pull into victim's abdomen with quick upward thrust. Repeat separate, rapid inward and upward thrusts until airway is cleared or patient becomes unconscious. (Use chest thrusts for a pregnant or obese victim.)

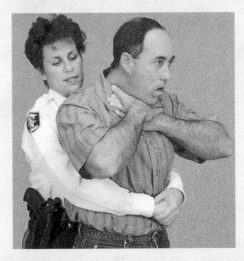

POSTPROCEDURE

3. Ensure that victim has follow-up treatment or assessment by Emergency Medical Technicians or hospital personnel, if needed.

4. Wash hands (follow hand-washing guidelines).

abdominal thrust or Heimlich maneuver
(HYM lik muh noo ver)
Forceful thrust on the abdomen, between the sternum and the navel, in an upward motion toward the head.

Obstructed Airway in an Unconscious Victim—Adult

BACKGROUND: An airway obstruction can cause the victim to become unconscious due to lack of oxygen. This procedure explains how to clear an obstructed airway in an adult.

ALERT: Follow Standard Precautions.

PREPROCEDURE

If the victim becomes unconscious:

1. Activate the EMS system.

2. Put on disposable gloves.

PROCEDURE

3. Open airway. Place one hand at victim's chin and the other hand on victim's forehead; gently tip head back. Lift chin in head tilt/chin lift position.

4. Attempt to ventilate. Open the airway and ventilate through a pocket face mask with a one-way valve. If no air enters, retilt head and try to ventilate again. Every time you give a breath, open mouth wide and look for object. If you see an object, remove it with fingers. If you do not see an object, proceed with CPR.

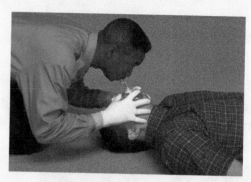

POSTPROCEDURE

5. Ensure that victim has follow-up treatment or assessment by Emergency Medical Technicians or hospital personnel.

6. Discard gloves and wash hands (follow handwashing guidelines).

PROCEDURE 21.5 Stopped Breathing in an Infant

BACKGROUND: It is important to quickly deliver oxygen to an infant who has stopped breathing. An infant's brain is actively developing and may become damaged if it lacks oxygen. This procedure explains how to deliver rescue breaths to an infant who has stopped breathing.

ALERT: Follow Standard Precautions.

PREPROCEDURE

1. Put on disposable gloves.

2. **Check for consciousness.** Shake baby's shoulders gently and speak baby's name. If no response, shout for help.

PROCEDURE

3. **Open airway.** Use head tilt/chin lift method. Do not overtilt head or neck.

4. **Check for breathing.** Look, listen, and feel.

If not breathing:

5. Place an infant-sized barrier device on the infant's face.* Ventilate through the one-way valve and give rescue breathing. Give two slow breaths using only air in your cheeks. (Too much air may overinflate an infant's lungs.)

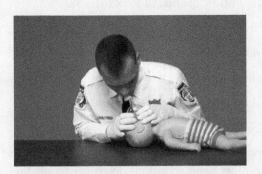

Watch for chest to rise and allow chest to fall or deflate between each breath. If air does not inflate lungs:

6. Retilt head to ensure open airway. Repeat the two breaths. If lungs still do not inflate, treat infant for an obstructed airway.

If lungs do inflate:

7. **Keep airway open**, and give one breath to infant every 3 seconds. After 1 minute activate EMS.

8. **Check pulse.** Place three fingers over brachial artery/pulse. The baby's heart may have stopped. In this event, only cardiopulmonary resuscitation (CPR) will help to circulate oxygenated blood throughout the body. See Procedures 21.22, 21.23 and 21.24 for CPR procedures. CPR should be learned by taking a course offered by an instructor who is certified by the American Heart Association or the American Red Cross. We strongly recommend you complete such a program.

POSTPROCEDURE

9. Ensure that victim has follow-up treatment or assessment by Emergency Medical Technicians or hospital personnel.

10. Discard gloves and wash hands (follow handwashing guidelines).

---

* Adult-sized pocket face masks can be adapted by inverting (reversing) them. See manufacturer's guidelines.

21.6 Obstructed Airway in a Conscious Infant

BACKGROUND: The procedures for clearing an obstructed airway in an infant are different from the procedures for an adult. Care must be taken to protect the smaller, more delicate organs and bones of the infant. This procedure explains how to clear an obstructed airway in a conscious infant.

ALERT: Follow Standard Precautions.

PREPROCEDURE

1. Put on disposable gloves

2. Observe to determine infant's ability to cry, cough, or breathe. If there is no evidence of air exchange, shout for help.

PROCEDURE

3. Give five back blows. Place infant face down, supporting head and neck and tilting infant so that the head is lower than rest of body. Give five firm hits with heel of your hand over backbone and between shoulder blades.

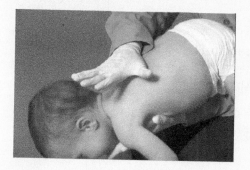

4. Give five chest thrusts by turning infant on its back with head lower than rest of body. Using two to three fingers, push five times on midsternum, which is about one finger's width below nipple line at midchest at a rate of about one per second.

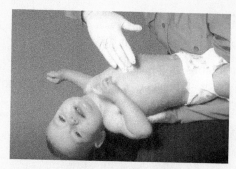

5. Continue procedure until obstruction is clear or infant becomes unconscious. If infant becomes unconscious, stop giving black blows and start CPR.

POSTPROCEDURE

6. Ensure that victim has follow-up treatment or assessment by Emergency Medical Technicians or hospital personnel.

7. Discard gloves and wash hands (follow handwashing guidelines).

BACKGROUND: It is important to deliver oxygen to an infant who is not breathing as soon as possible to prevent brain damage. This procedure explains how to clear an obstructed airway in an unconscious infant.

ALERT: Follow Standard Precautions.

PREPROCEDURE

1. Put on disposable gloves

2. Observe to determine infant's ability to cry, cough, or breathe. If there is no evidence of air exchange, shout for help.

PROCEDURE

3. Place infant on a firm flat surface.

4. Open infant's airway and look for an object in the pharynx. If an object is visible, remove it. Do not perform a blind finger sweep.

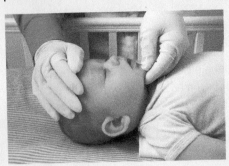

5. Begin CPR with one extra step—each time you open the airway, look for the obstructing object in the back of the throat. If you see an object, remove it. After about 2 minutes, activate the EMS.

6. Once the airway is clear, ventilate once every 3 seconds.

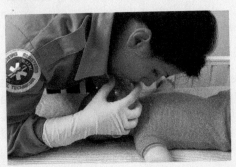

POSTPROCEDURE

7. Ensure that victim has follow-up treatment or assessment by Emergency Medical Technicians or hospital personnel.

8. Discard gloves and wash hands (follow hand-washing guidelines).

Heart Attack

The first two hours after the onset of a heart attack are the highest-risk period. Recognition of early warning signs alerts you to an impending heart attack. Early warning signs are:

- Squeezing feeling in the chest ("feels like a band is around my chest"), pressure, or tightness ("feels like an elephant is sitting on my chest").

- Persistent discomfort that spreads to shoulders, arms, neck, jaw, or across the chest.

- Sweating, nausea, vomiting, shortness of breath, or feeling faint.

When one or all of these signs are present, call for advanced life support systems (doctor or paramedics depending upon the health care setting). If signs continue, the heart and breathing may stop, and it will be necessary to start CPR.

Table 21.1 Common Cardiovascular Conditions, Possible Treatments, and Patient Education

Condition	Possible Treatments	Patient Education
Coronary artery disease; also called arteriosclerosis (narrowing of arteries of the heart).	Medication Surgery Diet	1. Explain importance of low-salt, low-fat diet; weight control; prescribed exercise program. 2. Reduce stress factors. 3. Stress importance of taking prescribed medication. 4. Provide written information on condition.
Myocardial infarction (MI, heart attack)	Medication Rehabilitation	1. Encourage patient to follow prescribed diet, medication program, and exercise program. 2. Provide written instructions and information about condition.
Congestive heart failure (CHF), (tissues of heart and lungs are edematous)	Medication Rest Diet Antiembolism stocking	1. Encourage patient to follow prescribed diet and medication program. 2. Provide written instructions and information about condition.
Hypertension (blood pressure above 140/90)	Medication Diet therapy Exercise program	1. Warn patient not to stop medication without seeing physician. 2. Stress importance of diet and exercise. 3. Explain why blood pressure increases with weight gain and poor dietary habits.
Varicose veins (veins that allow blood to pool and not return to the heart)	TED (thromboembolic devices) Warm soaks Surgery	1. Explain importance of changing position frequently (sitting, standing). 2. Explain application of elastic stockings and their purpose. 3. Stress importance of elevating legs. 4. Stress importance of loose clothing so that circulation is not impaired.
Thrombophlebitis	Medication Surgery Warm compresses	1. Instruct in application of warm compresses. 2. Instruct in elevation of legs. 3. Teach to watch for danger signs.
Cerebral vascular accident (CVA, stroke)	Hospitalization Physical therapy Occupational therapy Speech therapy Medication	1. Encourage patient to reach highest potential. 2. Teach awareness of adaptive devices and assist in selection.

 ## Wound Care and Observation

Patients who have suffered a trauma or surgery have very specific needs. Their wounds may be life threatening and must be cared for properly. As a nurse assistant, your primary responsibility in caring for wounds includes careful, specific observations and reporting.

You must understand wounds in order to make good observations and reports. Always observe and report the location, size, appearance, and odor of the wound; the condition of the surrounding skin; and the type and amount of drainage.

Wounds often have drainage, and there are other complications to watch for. Refer to Section 9.4 for help with observation and charting.

Wounds may be described by color:

- **Red wounds:** Red is the color of healthy tissue and indicates normal healing.
- **Yellow wounds:** Yellow is the color of exudates produced by microorganisms. Too many organisms in accumulated exudates causes the wound to have drainage and appear yellow.
- **Black wounds:** Black wounds signify necrosis or dead tissue.
- **Multicolored wounds:** There may be more than one color present in a wound. In this case describe it by the least healthy color. An example of this would be a wound that is both yellow and black should be described as a black wound.

Types of Wounds

Wounds are described as being either *open* or *closed* (Figure 21.9):

- **Closed wounds:** Tissue is injured, but the skin is not broken. These wounds can be caused by bruising, sprains, and twists.
- **Open wounds:** The skin or mucous membrane is broken. These wounds can be caused by bites, cuts, and incisions. Whenever there is an open wound there is a chance of infection. Open wounds can be either partial thickness or full thickness wounds:
  - **Partial thickness wounds:** The dermis and epidermis are broken.
  - **Full thickness wounds:** The dermis, epidermis, and subcutaneous tissue are penetrated. Muscle and bone may be involved.

FIGURE 21.9
Closed wound on the arm and open, clotted wound on the neck. Which type of wound carries the most risk for infection?

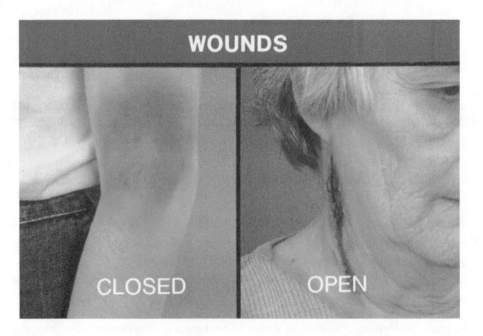

The following are some common types of wounds:

- **Abrasion:** partial thickness wound caused by scraping the skin away.
- **Amputation:** removal of all or part of a limb or digit of the body, as by surgery.
- **Contusion:** closed wound caused by a blow to the body.
- **Incision:** intentional wound made with a scalpel.
- **Laceration:** open wound with jagged edges and torn tissue.
- **Penetrating wound:** open wound caused by piercing the underlying tissues of the skin.
- **Puncture wound:** open wound caused by a sharp object entering the skin and underlying tissues.

How Wounds Heal

Types of Healing

Wounds are allowed to heal in different ways:

- **Primary (first) intention:** The wound is pulled together by suturing, stapling, taping, clipping, or gluing. This is a clean wound that usually heals quickly.
- **Secondary (second) intention:** The wound edges are not brought together. The wound is cleaned, and dead tissue is removed. This method is often used in infected and contaminated wounds. The closure of the wound with granulations means that there is formation in wounds of small, rounded masses of tissue during healing.
- **Third intention:** The wound is left open and may be closed at a later time. Poor circulation and infection are common reasons for using this method. In this case, we choose to treat the grossly contaminated wound by delaying closure until after contamination has been markedly reduced and inflammation has subsided.

Medical Emergencies in Wound Healing

Wound healing is dependent on many factors, including the type of wound and the patient's age, nutrition, and lifestyle. The patient's medical history is also very important. Poor circulation, diabetes, some medications, and a weakened immune system can cause complications. The following are major complications:

- **Dehiscence:** The skin layer and/or the underlying tissues separate, reopening the wound. Stress to the wound from coughing, vomiting, and abdominal distension is usually the cause of dehiscence. This is a surgical emergency. Notify your supervisor immediately.
- **Evisceration:** The skin layer is separated by the **protrusion** of an internal organ through the wound. The causes are the same as in dehiscence. This is also a surgical emergency. Notify your supervisor immediately.

protrusion
(proh TROO shuhn)
Pushing through.

- **Hemorrhage:** Excessive bleeding that is life threatening. *Hemorrhage is a medical emergency and must be reported to your supervisor immediately.* The patient is in immediate danger.
  - *External hemorrhage* is easily seen. Dressings soak with blood and blood may flow under the body. Always check under the patient for pooling blood when you see saturated dressings.
  - *Internal hemorrhage* cannot be seen. The bleeding is in the tissue of the body and in the body cavities. Signs of internal bleeding include the patient's vomiting blood or coughing up blood, shock, and loss of consciousness. A hematoma may form (i.e., blood collects under the skin, causing swelling and discoloration).

Types of Drainage

Wound drainage occurs during the inflammatory stage of healing when healing fluid and cells escape from the surrounding tissues. The overlying skin heals, but the underlying tissue does not. Drainage that is trapped in the wound and underlying tissue causes swelling and pain and may cause infection. The doctor puts in a drainage tube when large amounts of drainage are expected.

There are several different types of drainage, including the following:

- **Purulent drainage:** thick green, yellow, or brown drainage.
- **Sanguineous drainage:** bloody drainage. Large amounts may indicate hemorrhage.
- **Serous drainage:** watery, clear drainage.
- **Serosanguineous drainage:** thin, watery, blood-tinged drainage.

Remember always to follow Standard Precautions when in contact with any type of drainage.

Severe Wounds

Serious wounds, or severe wounds, are life threatening because heavy bleeding is frequently present. Bleeding that pulsates or **spurts** with each heartbeat is from an artery. The victim will bleed to death if the bleeding is not controlled. Venous bleeding is also serious and must be controlled. An open wound allowing a constant flow of blood from a vein can also cause death. The open area is also susceptible to infection and needs to be covered.

To stop bleeding and minimize infection, apply direct pressure with your gloved hand and some type of dressing or pad. Sterile gauze pads/gauze **dressings** are very effective. If gauze dressings are not available, use a piece of clean cloth, a handkerchief, or toweling. Even though the cloth is not sterile, it aids in controlling the bleeding.

Wound Infection

Wounds often get infected because they become contaminated with dirt and bacteria. Deep scrapes and puncture wounds are the most likely wounds to become infected. The following are signs that a wound has become infected:

- Pus or cloudy fluid draining from the wound.
- Pimple or yellow crust appears.

spurts
(SPURTZ)
Forces out in a burst; squirts.

dressings
(DRES ing)
Gauze pads that are used to cover a wound.

- Increased scab size.
- Red streak spreading beyond the wound.
- Increased tenderness.
- Increased pain or swelling.
- Wound becomes blistered.
- Appearance of black dead tissue around the wound.
- Fever.

Review Chapter 17, Controlling Infection.

How to Treat Serious Wounds

1. Follow the Procedure 21.8.

2. Apply direct pressure over the wound with gauze or clean materal and your gloved hand. Apply a pressure dressing and secure with a roll bandage. Hold for 5–10 minutes. If blood soaks through, apply second dressing on top of original dressing.

3. Elevate the wounded area if you do not think there are broken bones and continue to apply pressure. (Figure 21.10)

4. Check pulse below pressure bandage to check for circulation

5. If direct pressure and elevation do not control bleeding:

   a. Apply pressure to the appropriate pressure point above the wound. (Figure 21.11) The pressure point must be on the same limb or the same side of the body.

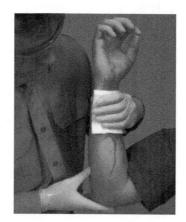

FIGURE 21.10
Combine elevation and direct pressure to treat serious wounds. What should you do when a person has a serious leg wound but no broken bones?

   b. Continue to apply direct pressure and maintain elevation to the wound. Do not remove the dressings and bandages when they are **saturated**. Apply dry dressings over the saturated bandage.

   c. When bleeding is under control, gradually release pressure at the pressure point. Keep applying direct pressure over the pressure dressing.

6. Remove gloves and wash hands thoroughly.

7. Call or send for help as soon as possible.

saturated
(SACH uh reyt id)
Soaked; filled to capacity.

Shock

Shock is life threatening. Shock is usually caused by major loss of body fluids or blood: it can be caused by vomiting and diarrhea. If it is due to major blood loss, body cells and organs are deprived of oxygen, which is carried by the blood. Shock slows body functions and keeps the major organs from functioning normally.

Anyone with a serious injury should seek advanced medical care immediately. A victim can be treated appropriately for an injury, yet die from shock because of the fluid or blood and oxygen loss. Treat every victim for a life-threatening injury until the victim is stabilized and emergency care providers or doctors arrive. Follow the procedure to prevent shock.

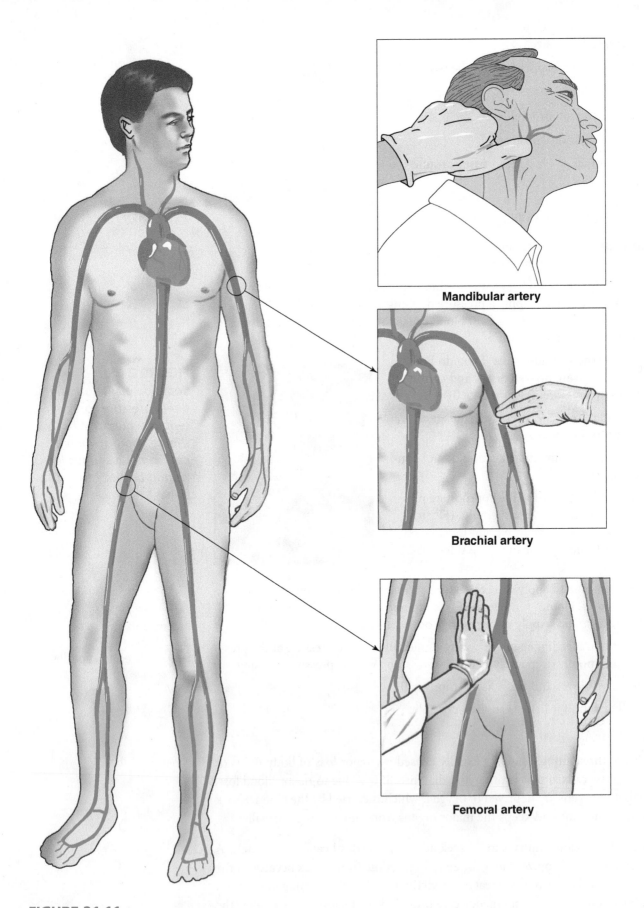

Mandibular artery

Brachial artery

Femoral artery

FIGURE 21.11

Use of pressure points to control profuse bleeding from the upper extremity, lower extremity, and neck. Where is the pressure point to stop bleeding in the leg?

Poisoning

Poisoning often causes sudden collapse, vomiting, and difficult breathing. Poisoning can occur in various ways—for example, **ingestion**, inhalation (which is breathing in a poisonous substance), absorption through the skin, or injection, insect stings or animal bites, or from needles that puncture the skin. Look for items near the victim that may be the source of poisoning, such as an empty container or a needle. To care for a poisoning victim follow the procedure for a *conscious* victim.

An *unconscious victim* who is suffering from poisoning may be convulsing and vomiting. Follow the procedure for an unconscious poison victim.

ingestion
(in JES chuhn)
Take in by mouth.

PROCEDURE | **21.8** | **Preventing Shock**

BACKGROUND: Shock is a life-threatening condition that must be treated immediately. A victim who remains in shock could die. The most common symptoms of shock include an extremely low blood pressure; fast but weak pulse; dizziness, faintness or light-headedness; feeling weak or nauseous ; moist, clammy skin; profuse sweating; unconsciousness; rapid, shallow breathing; feeling anxious, agitated or confused; chest pain; and/or blue lips and fingernails. This procedure explains how to stabilize a victim and prevent shock.

ALERT: Follow Standard Precautions.

PREPROCEDURE

1. If patient is located in the field (not in a health care facility), contact EMS.

PROCEDURE

2. Provide comfort, quiet, and warmth.

3. Maintain normal body temperature by covering with blanket.

4. Keep victim calm.

5. Keep victim lying down on back if possible. Elevate feet and arms. Do not elevate an unsplinted arm or leg that is fractured.

6. If victim is vomiting, bleeding from mouth, or feels like vomiting, position victim on side. Do not move the victim if there is any possibility of a spinal injury or if the victim complains of numbness, tingling, lack of sensation, or inability to move limbs.

7. If person has a head injury, neck injury, or breathing problem, feet should not be elevated and the victim should not be turned on his or her side.

8. Do not give the victim anything to eat or drink.

9. Provide oxygen as soon as possible if you have the training and equipment to do so; otherwise, call immediately for someone who does.

POSTPROCEDURE

10. Discard gloves and wash hands (follow hand-washing guidelines).

PROCEDURE 21.9 Treating a Conscious Poison Victim

BACKGROUND: A poison victim should get emergency treatment as soon as possible. A person who has ingested poison may experience organ damage, shock, or death. This procedure explains how to treat a conscious poison victim.

ALERT: Follow Standard Precautions.

PREPROCEDURE

1. Put on disposable gloves.

2. Try to locate poison container (try to identify source of poisoning); do not waste time. Check victim's body and clothes for signs of poisoning.

3. Position victim on his side to let mouth drain.

PROCEDURE

4. Call 911 to get an ambulance as soon as possible; then call the nearest poison center, hospital, or physician.* (Directions on poison containers and for ingested substances are *not* always correct.) When you call, state that you have a poisoning emergency. If you have the container, be prepared to read ingredients. Follow the directions from the poison center.

5. If poison on skin, wash with water.

6. If poison is from a snakebite: Cover and wrap the affected snakebite area. Continue wrapping the entire affected limb and apply a splint. This is called the pressure immobilization technique.

Remember to make sure the wound does not swell enough to make the splint a tourniquet, cutting off the blood flow. Get person to an emergency care center as soon as possible.

7. If poison is from an insect bite: Apply cold compresses. A doctor may prescribe calcium gluconate for muscle pain and an anti-anxiety drug for spasms. For any poisonous insect bite, be sure your tetanus immunization is current.

8. Be alert for breathing problems. If breathing stops, you will perform mouth-to-mask (rescue breathing) resuscitation as discussed at beginning of section.

9. Follow procedure for preventing shock.

POSTPROCEDURE

10. Ensure that victim has follow-up treatment or assessment by Emergency Medical Technicians or hospital personnel.

11. Discard gloves and wash hands (follow hand-washing guidelines).

* Ambulance personnel can communicate directly with the hospital and the poison control center. They can start lifesaving procedures with special equipment and poison treatment medications.

Burns

The seriousness of a burn is determined by the degree or depth of the burn (**Figure 21.12**):

Severity of Burns

- Superficial or *first-degree burns* are surface burns.

- Partial thickness or *second-degree burns* are deeper or just below the surface of the skin, and blistering occurs.

- Full thickness or *third-degree burns* are even deeper, destroying both surface and underlying tissue.

BACKGROUND: An unconscious poison victim must receive emergency medical treatment as quickly as possible, to prevent damage to organs, shock, or death. This procedure explains how to treat an unconscious poison victim.

ALERT: Follow Standard Precautions.

PREPROCEDURE

1. Put on disposable gloves.

2. Do *not* give any fluids.

PROCEDURE

3. Position victim on his or her side in a safe place.

4. Try to identify the poison source; do not waste time.

5. Call 911 to get an ambulance as soon as possible; then call the nearest poison center, hospital, or physician. Follow their directions.*

6. If chemicals have gotten on skin, wash with water. Remove clothes and jewelry that are contaminated.

7. Be alert for breathing problems.

8. Follow procedure for preventing shock.

POSTPROCEDURE

9. Ensure that victim has follow-up treatment or assessment by Emergency Medical Technicians or hospital personnel.

10. Discard gloves and wash hands (follow hand-washing guidelines).

* Ambulance personnel can communicate directly with the hospital and the poison control center. They can start lifesaving procedures with special equipment and poison treatment medications.

Burns around the mouth or nose may indicate that the airway is burned. This can cause swelling that may obstruct the airway. If breathing stops, follow the procedure for rescue breathing as discussed at the beginning of this section. However, if the airway is swollen causing breathing to stop, rescue breathing may be ineffective. Call emergency care providers immediately. Blistering and swelling may not appear until later.

A full thickness burn destroys nerve endings, so a burn victim may not feel pain in that area, but surrounding areas may be painful. The absence of pain *does not* indicate a mild burn. Do the following for a burn victim as described in the following procedure:

- Relieve pain.
- Minimize the chance of infection.
- Prevent shock (Procedure 21.8).

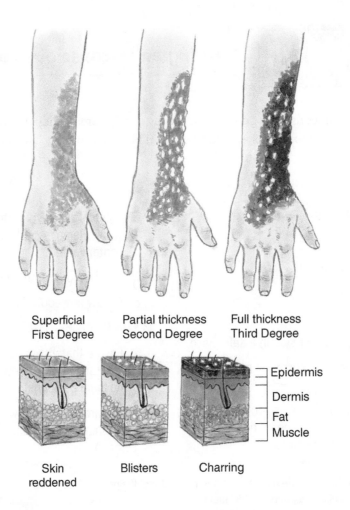

FIGURE 21.12
Severity of burns. What is a third-degree burn?

Superficial
First Degree

Partial thickness
Second Degree

Full thickness
Third Degree

Epidermis

Dermis

Fat

Muscle

Skin reddened

Blisters

Charring

Non-Life-Threatening Situations

The bone fractures described below are examples of non-life-threatening conditions. Such conditions require first aid or medical care but not urgent care.

Bone Fractures

There are two main types of fractures: closed and open:

- A *closed fracture* is difficult to determine. The following are signs and symptoms of closed fractures:
  - Swelling.
  - Pain.
  - Change in the color of the skin.
  - Deformity.
- An *open fracture* is present when the skin over the fracture site is broken or open and/or the broken bone protrudes through the skin.

Call or send for advanced medical help if you believe a fracture is present. If medical help is not available or the victim must be taken to a medical facility, splint the fracture (**Figure 21.13** for a leg or hip fracture).

BACKGROUND: A burn destroys tissue and may send a victim into shock. This procedure explains how to treat victims of first-degree, second-degree, or third-degree burns. You must identify the degree of the burn:

- *First-Degree Burn* (superficial partial-thickness burn): Appears pink or red; sensitive to touch
- *Second-Degree Burn* (deep partial-thickness burn): Appears pink or red with a mottled appearance; blisters and edema; touching causes severe pain
- *Third-Degree Burn* (full-thickness burn): Appears red, waxy white, brown or black; insensitive to touch; loss of hair in area

ALERT: Follow Standard Precautions.

PREPROCEDURE

1. Put on disposable gloves.

PROCEDURE

First-Degree Burn

2. Apply cool water to burn area, submerge burn site in cool water, or cover the are with cool damp cloths; this will reduce pain.

3. Large surface burns should never be wet as this causes shock. Large burns may be dried with sterile dressing. Apply a cold pack over dressing to reduce discomfort. Partial thickness or deeper burns (full thickness) require the following procedure.

PROCEDURE

Second- and Third-Degree Burns

1. Stop the burning process by smothering or dousing with water and removing smoldering or hot clothing. Remove any sources of heat such as metal jewelry, belts, etc.

2. Cover burned area with dry, sterile, nonstick dressing to help prevent infection. Do not pull away clothing that is stuck to burn site.

3. Check the patient's:

   Airway
   Breathing
   Circulation

   Perform CPR if necessary

4. Contact emergency medical service.

5. Cover with a dry sterile dressing if available. A non-fuzzy clean sheet or tablecloth could be substituted if sterile dressing is not available.

6. If you can elevate the burned area to decrease swelling, especially if head is involved and victim is having trouble breathing.

7. Follow procedure to prevent shock.

POSTPROCEDURE

8. Ensure that victim has follow-up treatment or assessment by Emergency Medical Technicians or hospital personnel.

9. Discard gloves and wash hands (follow hand-washing guidelines).

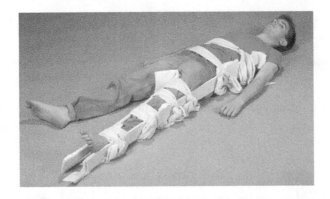

A fracture of the arm usually requires a sling. Apply a triangle sling so that the victim's hand and forearm are slightly higher than the elbow. This helps to minimize the swelling. A sling is a triangular bandage used to support the arm. Once the patient's arm is placed in a sling, a **swathe** (Figure 21.14) can be used to hold the patient's arm against the side of the chest.

swathe
(SWOTH)
Bandage.

FIGURE 21.14
An EMT ties a swathe around a patient with his arm in a sling. Why would you use a swathe on a patient?

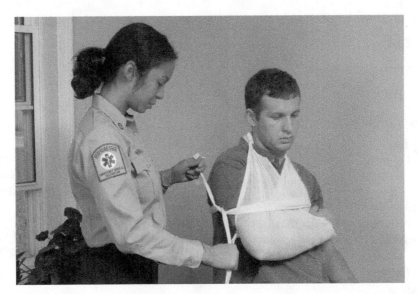

Commercial slings are available. Roller bandage can be used to form a sling and swathe. Velcro straps can be used to form a swathe. Use whatever materials you have on hand, provided that they will not cut into the patient as will narrow cords or wire. Remember: Shirts, ties, and wide belts can be used to make both sling and swathe.

Dislocations

A dislocation is when there is the separation of two bones where they meet a joint. Dislocations temporarily deform and immobilize joints and may cause ligament or nerve damage. They may occur from a fall, sports injury, or other trauma such as a motor vehicle accident. The hip, shoulder, knee, fingers, and toes are the most common places to have a dislocation. You have to immobilize the joint and seek immediate medical attention. DO NOT try to pop the bones back in place.

The following are symptoms of a dislocation:

- Visibly out of place.
- Limited movement.

- Swollen or discolored.
- Intense pain.
- Tingling or numbness.

To diagnose a dislocation, an x-ray or MRI might be necessary.

Strains and Sprains

A strain is when a muscle or tendon is stretched or torn. This is also known as a pulled muscle. Strains are caused by overuse or misuse of a muscle. The most common strains occur in the hamstring or back. The symptoms of a strain include pain, stiffness, swelling, and bruising.

A sprain is when a ligament is stretched or torn. Sprains are caused when a joint is forced into an unnatural position. The most common sprains occur in the ankles and knees. The symptoms of a sprain include rapid swelling, joint and muscle pain, and bruising.

Dressings and Bandages

Dressings cover wounds and help prevent infectious bacteria from entering a wound. Also use dressing to apply direct pressure over a wound to control bleeding. There are many types of dressings used for various body locations. Bandages hold dressings in place.

Principles of Bandaging

- Always wear disposable gloves and follow Standard Precautions.
- Never encircle a wound with a non-elastic bandage. If swelling occurs a restrictive bandage may cause undue pressure and circulatory impairment.
- The bandage needs to be snug enough to hold the dressing in place but not tight enough to stop the circulation.
- When applying dressings and bandages to wounds on arms or legs, leave fingers and toes exposed so that you can watch for discoloration of the skin or swelling.
- Check pulse below bandage.
- Check the skin temperature. Cold skin may indicate poor circulation caused by a bandage that is too tight. Check the bandage to be certain it is not too tight. You should be able to insert a finger under the bandage.
- Loosen bandages if the patient complains of numbness or a tingling feeling.
- Do not remove a dressing once it has been applied. If blood soaks through, add another layer of dressings and secure with a bandage.

BACKGROUND: A splint helps to stabilize a broken bone and prevent further injury to tissues. This procedure explains how to make a splint out of a variety of materials.

ALERT: Follow Standard Precautions.

PREPROCEDURE

1. Put on disposable gloves.

2. Move fractured area as little as possible.

PROCEDURE

3. Splint area with a firm object, such as newspapers, magazines folded flat, wood, or a commercially made **splint**. The splint should extend from the fingertips to the elbow. Need to immobilize joints above and below injury. Pad splint with clothing or towels if possible. Place padding or roller gauze in the hand for support and comfort.

4. Secure splint in place using roller gauze, wrapping it snugly and overlapping about two-thirds each wrap, or secure splint to extremity with strips of cloth at distal and proximal ends of the arm. You can wrap roller gauze over the fracture site. Do not exert any pressure over the injury.

5. If it is an open fracture, apply dressing over wound and secure in place with tape or with roller gauze that holds splint in place.

POSTPROCEDURE

7. Ensure that victim has follow-up treatment or assessment by Emergency Medical Technicians or hospital personnel.

8. Discard gloves and wash hands (follow hand-washing guidelines).

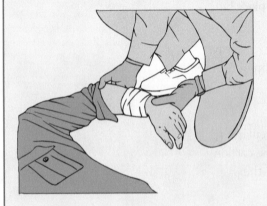

splint
(SPLINT)
Firm object used to support
an unstable body part.

BACKGROUND: A sling is a bandage that holds up and stabilizes an injured arm. This procedure explains how to make a sling out of any long piece of cloth.

ALERT: Follow Standard Precautions.

PREPROCEDURE

1. Put on disposable gloves.

2. Make a sling from a piece of cloth, clothing, towel, or sheet; fold or cut this material into shape of a triangle. The ideal sling is about 50 to 60 inches long at its base and 36 to 40 inches long on each side.

PROCEDURE

3. Position triangular material over top of patient's chest opposite the injured arm, as shown in Figure A. Fold patient's arm across chest. If patient cannot hold his or her own arm, have someone assist you, or provide support for patient's arm until you are ready to tie sling. Note that one point of triangle should extend beyond patient's elbow on injured side.

4. Take bottom point of triangle and bring this end up over patient's arm. When you are finished, take this bottom point over top of patient's shoulder on the side of injured arm. (See Figure B.)

5. Draw up on ends of sling so that patient's hand is about 4 inches above elbow. Tie the two ends of the sling together, making sure that the knot does not press against back of patient's neck. Place a flat pad of dressing or a handkerchief under the knot. (Figure C.) Leave patient's fingertips exposed so that you can see any color changes that indicate lack of circulation. Check for radial pulse. If pulse is absent, take off sling and attempt to reposition arm to regain pulse, then repeat procedure.

6. Take point of material at patient's elbow and fold it forward. Pin it to front of sling. This forms a pocket for the elbow. If you do not have pin, twist excess material and tie knot in point. This will provide a shallow pocket for patient's elbow. (Figure D.)

A

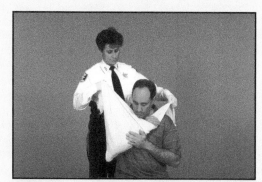

B

C

D

(continued)

7. Create a swathe by folding a triangular bandage in half and then folding it to a 4-inch width. This swathe is tied around chest and injured arm, over sling. Do not place this swathe over patient's arm on uninjured side. (See Figure E.)

POSTPROCEDURE

8. Ensure that victim has follow-up treatment or assessment by Emergency Medical Technicians or hospital personnel.

9. Discard gloves and wash hands (follow hand-washing guidelines).

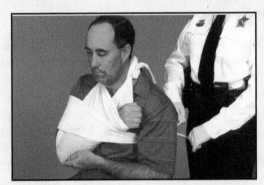

E

21.14 Triangular Bandaging of an Open Head Wound

BACKGROUND: A triangular bandage can be used to hold a dressing on a wound. This procedure explains how to fold a triangular bandage to bandage an open head wound.

ALERT: Follow Standard Precautions.

PREPROCEDURE

1. Put on disposable gloves.

2. Fold triangular bandage to make 2-inch hem along base.

PROCEDURE

3. Apply gauze pad over wound. With folded edge face out, position bandage on patient's forehead, just above eyes. Make certain that point of bandage hangs down behind patient's head.

4. Draw ends of bandage behind patient's head and tie them.

5. Next, pull ends to front of patient's head and tie them together.

6. Tuck in the tail at back.

POSTPROCEDURE

7. Ensure that victim has follow-up treatment or assessment by Emergency Medical Technicians or hospital personnel.

8. Discard gloves and wash hands (follow hand-washing guidelines).

Step 3

Step 4

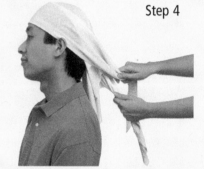

Step 2

Courtesy of Dorling Kindersley.

Courtesy of Dorling Kindersley.

Step 5

Step 6

Courtesy of Dorling Kindersley.

Courtesy of Dorling Kindersley.

BACKGROUND: Circular bandaging holds a dressing in place over a wound and applies pressure to the wound. This procedure explains how to apply a circular bandage to a small leg or arm wound.

ALERT: Follow Standard Precautions.

PREPROCEDURE

1. Put on disposable gloves.

PROCEDURE

2. Apply dressing to wound and elevate extremity.

3. Place end of gauze roll (1 to 2 inches wide) on dressing. Anchor end of gauze roll over dressing with two initial wraps. (Place end of gauze over the dressing. Wrap gauze around the area once. Fold angled corner of gauze back over wrapped gauze.) Continue to wrap from distal (far) end of extremity to proximal (near the torso) end until entire dressing is covered. Bandage will overlap dressing on both sides. Pull bandage snug as you wrap. Overlap each wrap by about two-thirds. Cut gauze and tape end or tie gauze to secure in place.

POSTPROCEDURE

4. Ensure that victim has follow-up treatment or assessment by Emergency Medical Technicians or hospital personnel.

5. Discard gloves and wash hands (follow hand-washing guidelines).

BACKGROUND: Spiral bandaging can be used to hold on a dressing and apply pressure to a large

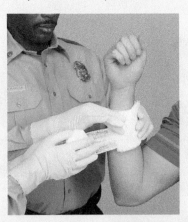

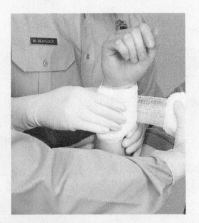

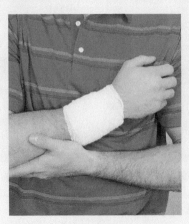

PROCEDURE 21.16 — Spiral Bandaging of a Large Wound

wound of the arm or leg. This procedure explains how to use spiral bandaging on a large wound.

ALERT: Follow Standard Precautions.

PREPROCEDURE

1. Put on disposable gloves.

PROCEDURE

2. Apply dressing to wound.

3. Place end of gauze roll (3 to 6 inches wide) on lower edge of dressing.

4. Anchor end.

5. Wrap gauze around arm or leg at an angle and overlap the edges.

6. If you use up the gauze, continue the wrap with another roll.

7. Secure end by taping or tying off.

POSTPROCEDURE

8. Ensure that victim has follow-up treatment or assessment by Emergency Medical Technicians or hospital personnel.

9. Discard gloves and wash hands (follow hand-washing guidelines).

PROCEDURE 21.17 — Bandaging of an Ankle or Foot Wound

BACKGROUND: A bandage can be wrapped around the ankle or foot, to secure a dressing and apply pressure to a wound. This procedure explains how to bandage an ankle or foot wound.

ALERT: Follow Standard Precautions.

PREPROCEDURE

1. Put on disposable gloves.

PROCEDURE

2. Apply dressing to wound.

3. Place end of gauze roll (1 to 2 inches wide) on top of foot just above toes, and anchor ends.

4. On second wrap around foot, bring gauze around back of ankle and over top of foot. Bring gauze under foot and over top of foot again. Wrap around ankle and over top of foot, then under foot. Continue these steps until dressing is covered, and secure gauze by tying off or taping.

POSTPROCEDURE

5. Ensure that victim has follow-up treatment or assessment by Emergency Medical Technicians or hospital personnel.

6. Discard gloves and wash hands (follow hand-washing guidelines).

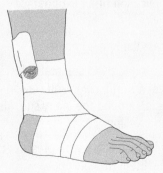

BACKGROUND: A dislocation occurs when excessive stress in an abnormal direction on one or more bones near a joint disrupts the continuity of joint configuration and articulation. When this occurs the bones' articulating surfaces no longer contact each other. Most dislocations result from trauma. Damage to ligaments and soft tissue may complicate these injuries.

ALERT: Follow Standard Precautions.

PREPROCEDURE

Expect the patient to complain of pain and decreased range of motion around the affected joint. Dislocations generally occur during a traumatic event so expect that the patient may have other injuries which could include a fracture of the joint. Depending on the nature of the injury the patient may require closed reduction of the injured joint or a surgical intervention to properly realign the affected joint. Expect that an x-ray of the affected joint will be necessary.

1. Determine the traumatic event leading to the injury.

2. Inspect the patient's affected joint for swelling, bruising, odd configuration of joint anatomy, and altered mobility.

3. Gently palpate the joint noting any tenderness. Palpate nearby pulses to assess the circulatory status. Obtain medical assistance right away.

PROCEDURE

Closed Reduction

NOTE: Closed Reduction and Surgical Correction will occur in a hospital or other care facility and will be done by physicians.

4. Provide support for the patient during the examination and any procedure that may be indicated.

5. Assist with the application of an external immobilization device.

6. Apply ice for at least the first 24 hours.

7. Monitor the patient's neurovascular status by checking for pulses, warmth, color, and sensory function of the region around the injury site. Also note any increased swelling.

NOTE: The patient will be medicated with prescribed pain medication only by licensed individuals.

8. Use a pain rating scale, such as a scale of 1 to 10, to evaluate the effectiveness of the pain medication.

9. Provide education to the patient/family regarding any ongoing care necessary and any rehabilitative exercise program prescribed for after the immobilizing device is removed.

Surgical Correction

10. Monitor the patient closely in the immediate post-operative period for:

   ■ neurovascular status
   ■ pain
   ■ alteration in vital signs

11. Expect the patient to have either a cast or an external immobilizer.

12. Provide pain medication as directed by the physician.

13. Apply ice as directed by the physician.

14. Use a pain rating scale, such as a scale of 1 to 10, to evaluate the effectiveness of the pain medication and other interventions provided to relieve discomfort.

15. Prepare the patient for the rehabilitation period.

Note: Possible complications of a joint dislocation and its treatment include:

   ■ vascular impairment
   ■ nerve injury
   ■ residual joint laxity with chronic joint instability.
   ■ degenerative arthritis
   ■ thromboembolic complications
   ■ neurovascular compromise
   ■ skin breakdown from extended wearing of an immobilization device

BACKGROUND: A strain occurs when partial, microscopic muscle tears result from overuse or over-stretching of a single muscle, muscle group, or tendon. A strain can be acute or chronic. An acute strain arises from a sudden forced movement that overstretches a muscle; a chronic strain results from the cumulative effects of repeated muscle overuse.

Strains commonly result from injury suffered while playing active sports or from poor body mechanics, such as improper lifting and carrying techniques. Strains are classified into three grades of injury:

- *Grade I* (mild): microscopic muscle and/or tendon tear with no strength loss.

- *Grade II* (moderate): incomplete muscle and/or tendon tear with bleeding into muscle tissue and some strength loss.

- *Grade III* (severe): complete muscle and/or tendon tear usually resulting from separation of muscle from muscle, muscle from tendon, or tendon from bone.

It is worth remembering RICE when it comes to the treatment of uncomplicated soft tissue, such as strains and sprains. This stand for:

R (rest)
I (ice)
C (compression)
E (elevate)

ALERT: Follow Standard Precautions.

PREPROCEDURE

Expect the patient to complain of pain, decreased mobility, and strength loss at the site of injury. Important points to remember when assessing the patient are:

1. Ask how the injury occurred.

2. Ask about prior joint injuries.

3. Inspect the injured joint for swelling, bruising.

4. Palpate the joint, noting any tenderness. Palpate nearby pulses to assess the circulatory status.

5. To rule out a fracture, the physician will order x-rays.

PROCEDURE

6. Consult with the physician for any specific instructions related to the injury.

7. Apply a compression bandage as ordered by the physician.

8. Elevate the affected joint.

9. Check with the physician. Apply ice or heat as directed. If injury is several days old the physician may order heat rather than ice to reduce pain.

10. Elevate the affected extremity.

11. Monitor the patient's neurovascular status by checking for pulses, warmth, color, and sensory function of the region around the injury site. Also note any increased swelling.

12. Medicate as directed by the physician. In most cases, analgesics, anti-inflammatory drugs, or a muscle relaxant will be prescribed. These should be dispensed by licensed heath care professionals.

13. Use a pain rating scale, such as a scale of 1 to 10, to evaluate the effectiveness of the Pain medication and other interventions.

14. Advise the patient to rest and avoid using the strained muscle.

15. Educate the patient on prescribed exercises to follow after healing has begun.

16. Advise the patient to resume activities gradually.

PROCEDURE 21.20 How to Care for a Sprain

BACKGROUND: A sprain occurs when a ligament or the capsule surrounding a joint becomes stretched or torn. A moderate or severe sprain can cause joint instability and loss of function. Sprains are classified into three grades of injury:

- *Grade I* (mild): minor or partial ligament tear with normal joint stability and function
- *Grade II* (moderate): partial ligament tear with mild joint laxity and function loss.
- *Grade III* (severe): complete ligament tear or complete separation of ligament from bone, causing total joint laxity and function loss.

ALERT: Follow Standard Precautions.

PREPROCEDURE

Expect the patient to complain of pain around the affected joint. The patient may also complain of diminished function of the joint. Important points when assessing this patient are:

1. Ask how the injury occurred.
2. Ask about prior joint injuries.
3. Observe the patient as he stands, walks, and sits, noting abnormalities such as change in gait or inability to bear weight on joint.
4. Inspect the injured joint for swelling and bruising.
5. Palpate the joint, noting any tenderness. Palpate nearby pulses to assess the circulatory status.

NOTE: Be sure to compare extremities on both sides of the body when assessing musculoskeletal injuries. The patient needs to be seen by a physician and have x-rays to rule out fracture.

PROCEDURE

6. Consult with the physician for any specific instructions related to the injury.
7. Immobilize the joint, using a splint or aircast.
8. Monitor the patient's neurovascular status by checking for pulses, warmth, color, mobility and sensory function of the region around the injury site. Also note any increased swelling.
9. Elevate the injured extremity to reduce swelling and pain.
10. Apply ice to the injury.
11. Medicate the patient with prescribed pain medication. Remember: Only licensed people can give medication.
12. Use a pain rating scale, such as a scale of 1 to 10, to evaluate the effectiveness of the pain medication and other interventions.
13. Provide education to the patient/family regarding any ongoing care necessary.

BACKGROUND: A cast is a hard mold that encases a body part, usually an extremity, to provide immobilization without discomfort. It can be used to treat injuries such as fractures, correct orthopedic conditions such as deformities, or promote healing after general or plastic surgery, amputation, or nerve and vascular repair.

Casts may be constructed of plaster, fiberglass or other synthetic materials. Typically, a physician applies a cast and a nurse prepares the patient and the equipment and assists during the procedure. The orthopedic technician, after special training, may apply or change a standard cast but the orthopedist must reduce and set the fracture.

ALERT: Follow Standard Precautions.

PREPROCEDURE

Prior to the application of the cast the nurse should establish a baseline assessment of the area to be casted. This would include:

- Palpation of the distal pulses
- Assessment of the color, temperature, and capillary refill of the skin.
- Neurologic function, including sensation and motion in the affected area.

Special Considerations: A fiberglass cast dries immediately after application. A plaster cast dries in approximately 24 to 48 hours. During this drying period, the cast must be properly positioned to prevent a surface depression that could cause pressure areas or dependent anemia

PROCEDURE

1. Assess your patient frequently.

2. Check the casted area for drainage stains.

3. Elevate the extremity above patient's heart level.

4. Place absorptive pads between the moist cast and any bedding to absorb moisture.

5. Periodically check the cast for flat spots or dents. These may cause pressure areas, resulting in skin breakdown.

6. Reposition the patient every 2 hours to ensure even cast drying. Use the palm of the hand, not the fingers for repositioning in order to avoid denting the cast. Make sure bony prominences, such as heels, ankles, and elbows are pressure free.

7. Routinely assess your patient's neurovascular status. Check for swelling, pallor, numbness, tingling, loss of pulses, and cool skin areas around the cast. Notify the doctor immediately for any of these signs.

8. Notify the doctor for:

   - drainage from the wound on the cast
   - malodor from the cast

9. Protect the cast from getting wet.

10. Provide skin care

Diabetes Mellitus

Diabetes Mellitus is an endocrine disorder which manifests as a carbohydrate intolerance. This disease is caused when the islets (islands) of Langerhans in the pancreas do not produce enough insulin. When there is an insulin imbalance, you must watch the resident carefully for signs of diabetic coma or **insulin shock**. Diabetic coma occurs when the diabetic resident does not have enough insulin, when there is an infection, or if there is increased stress. The following are symptoms of diabetic coma:

- Loss of appetite.

- Abdominal discomfort or pain.

- Dry skin.

- Flushed skin.

- Sweet or fruity odor of the breath.

- Soft eyeballs (also known as sunken eyeballs, caused by excessive dehydration.

- Generalized aches.

- Increased urination.

- Air hunger, increased respiration, labored breathing.

- Nausea and/or vomiting.

- Dulled senses.

- Weakness.

- Excessive thirst.

Diabetes is classified as:

1. Diabetes Mellitus.

   a. Insulin-Dependent Type I (DM): Usually genetically determined abnormality.

   b. Non-Insulin Dependent (NIDDM) Type II: Adult onset—altered production and use of insulin.

2. Impaired Glucose Tolerance (IGT).

3. Gestational Diabetes (GDM): Onset during pregnancy due to altered secretion of hormones.

When there is an endocrine disorder such as diabetes the patient must monitor their blood glucose levels. A blood glucose level over 115 is called hyperglycemia. A glucose level under 80 is called hypoglycemia. Hyperglycemia is caused by lack of adequate insulin, infection and increased stress. The symptoms of hyperglycemia include:

- Altered mental state.

- Excessive thirst.

- Flushed skin.

- Sweet or fruity breath.

- Increased urination.

insulin shock
(IN suh lin shok)
Condition caused by too much insulin.

- Blurred vision.
- Weakness.
- Abdominal discomfort.
- Loss of appetite.
- Labored breathing.

Hypoglycemia is caused by excessive insulin, decreased nutritional intake and excessive exercise. The symptoms of hypoglycemia include:

- Hunger.
- Blurred vision.
- Irritability.
- Weakness.
- Headache.
- Tremors.

One of your responsibilities in caring for the diabetic patient is monitoring blood sugars with a glucose monitor at designated intervals, usually before meals and at bedtime. Documenting these results accurately and notifying the nurse about too high or too low blood sugars is very important.

These patients should also be monitored for physical and cognitive signs of hypo- or hyperglycemia. If these symptoms are present, the patient should be immediately tested with the blood glucose monitor.

Patients with higher than normal blood sugar levels may need additional insulin. Patients with lower than normal blood sugar levels may need additional oral nutrition or glucose.

A blood glucose of 40 or less is a medical emergency. The patient with severe hypoglycemia must receive instant glucose either by mouth or through their intravenous site if present. You may find this patient unconscious. If so, seek immediate medical assistance.

ALERT: Blood sugars that are either too high or too low can cause irreversible loss of system functions. These injuries are cumulative over time and may cause such problems as diabetic retinopathy, renal failure, or failure to heal with loss of limbs.

Blood Glucose Testing
Diabetic Patient

Diabetes is a disease that affects many people. The diabetic patient does not produce enough insulin. This causes glucose to remain in the blood. Too much glucose in the blood can cause:

- Circulatory problems.
- Poor healing of lesions on legs and feet.
- Changes in the retina (which can lead to blindness).
- Nerve disorders.

Some patients with diabetes can successfully control sugar levels in the blood with diet and exercise. Others need medication to control their sugar levels.

The diabetic patient controls the disease with diet, exercise, and medication. A clinical study conducted between 1983 and 1993 called the Diabetes Control and Complications Trial (DCCT) showed that controlling glucose levels reduces the risk of eye, kidney, nerve, and cardiovascular disease. New studies confirm the DCCT findings.

A laboratory test called Glycosolated Hemoglobin (HbA_1C) provides indications of glucose control. Each number above 7 grams HbA_1C means an increase in the risk of disease for patients with diabetes. Patients who need insulin must check the level of glucose in their blood. The level of glucose tells them how much insulin they need. Patients use a glucose meter to measure the sugar level in their blood before taking insulin.

General Guidelines for Testing Blood for Glucose

1. Complete quality control checks at prescribed times.
2. Store reagent strips according to instructions.
3. Keep the lid on the reagent bottle tightly closed.
4. *Do not touch* the pad on the reagent strip.
5. Use careful technique in obtaining blood specimen.

There are many different glucose meters. Each one is a little different from the others. Learn the steps for the meter that is used in your facility.

Convulsions

Convulsions are when a person's body shakes rapidly and uncontrollably. This is caused by the muscles contracting and relaxing repeatedly. Most convulsions are harmless and last anywhere from 30 seconds to two minutes.

The symptoms of convulsions include blacking out, confusion, loss of bladder or bowel control, clenching teeth, uncontrollable muscle spasms, drooling, and grunting.

When a person experiences a convulsion, it is important to protect the person from injury. To do this, clear the area around the person, lay the person on the ground, cushion the person's head, loosen any tight clothing, turn the person on their side, and call for medical help. A person experiencing low blood glucose is susceptible to have convulsions, If this occurs, seek medical treatment immediately.

Summary

In this section, you learned very basic first-aid skills. You were introduced to the general principles of handling both life-threatening and non–life-threatening situations. You learned about rescue breathing, obstructed airway, and heart attack.

We discussed the treatment for shock, poisoning, serious wounds, and burns. It is very important for you to become proficient in first aid. To do this, you should attend a class given by a qualified American Red Cross instructor.

NOTE: Your teacher can provide information on the most current American Heart Association CPR guidelines from the *Health Science Fundamentals* Companion Web site.

1. What word describes the condition in which the skin is bruised, swollen, and painful, but is not broken?

2. A person in a restaurant starts coughing and wheezing after eating some chicken. What should you do?

3. What are the early warning signs of a heart attack?

4. How would you clear an obstruction from the airway of a conscious infant?

5. What are three pressure points that can be used to stop bleeding?

6. What causes shock?

7. How is a second-degree burn different from a first-degree burn?

8. What kind of bandaging would you use to cover a small wound on the leg?

Learn By Doing: Section 21.5 Activity

1. Complete Worksheets 1 through 8 as assigned.

2. Complete Worksheet/Activity 9 as assigned.

3. Prepare responses to each item listed in chapter review.

4. When you are confident that you can meet each objective for this section, ask your teacher for the section evaluation.

SECTION

21.6 Cardiopulmonary Resuscitation (CPR)

Background

With each heart beat, blood is pumped throughout the body. Red blood cells deliver oxygen to body cells. The blood removes cell waste products, such as carbon dioxide. If the heart stops beating due to cardiac arrest, cells cannot get oxygen, and they begin to die.

Cardiopulmonary resuscitation (CPR) is a procedure that can keep blood moving through the body after cardiac arrest. CPR is performed until the heart can be shocked back into a normal rhythm, using a defibrillator. As a health care professional, you should know how to perform CPR.

cardiac
(KAR dee ack)
Relating to the heart.

resuscitation
(ri suhs i TAY shuhn)
Bringing back to life, reviving.

oxygenated
(OK si juh nayt ed)
Containing oxygen.

defibrillator
(dee FIB ruh lay ter)
A device that administers an electric shock to restore normal heartbeat.

FIGURE 21.15
CPR pumps the heart to keep oxygenated blood flowing to organs after cardiac arrest. Why is it important to keep oxygen flowing to organs?

Objectives

When you have completed this section, you will be able to do the following:

- Match key terms with their correct meanings.
- Demonstrate the procedures for cardiopulmonary resuscitation (CPR).
- Explain the role of a defibrillator in restoring normal heart beat.

Cardiac Arrest and CPR

Cardiac arrest, or heart attack, can cause the heart to change rhythm and ultimately stop beating. During sudden cardiac arrest, a normal beat changes to ventricular fibrillation (VF). The rhythm of a heart in VF is fluttery and irregular. The heart needs a shock to bring it back into a normal rhythm.

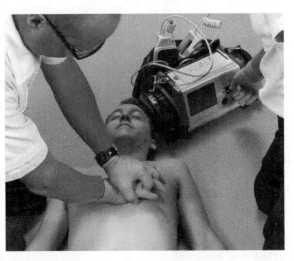

Cardiopulmonary **resuscitation** (CPR) provides body cells with **oxygenated** blood, in order to keep the cells alive. (Figure 21.15) CPR does not cause the heart to start beating again with a normal beat. It buys time until the heart can be shocked back into a normal rhythm, by a device called a **defibrillator**.

Cardiopulmonary Resuscitation for Children

The child victim is identified as about one year of age to the onset of puberty (about 12 to 14 years of age, and defined by the presence of secondary sex characteristics).

Asphyxial (pulmonary) arrest is more common than sudden cardiac arrest in children. Because of this difference, compressions are emphasized for adult CPR and ventilation is emphasized in CPR for children.

When ventilating the child, a pocket mask may be placed over the mouth and nose if available. However, if a pocket mask is not available, give direct mouth-to-mouth breathing. Studies do not support a decrease in infection transmission with the use of a barrier.

Perform five cycles (2 minutes—30 compressions to 2 breaths), and then call for Emergency Medical Services.

When determining the depth of compression appropriate for the child victim, the guideline should be one-third to one-half the depth of the chest.

Remember to provide adequate ventilation and push hard, push fast when delivering compressions.

PROCEDURE 21.22 | Cardiopulmonary Resuscitation—Adult

BACKGROUND: CPR allows you to circulate blood and oxygen to the organs when a patient's heart has stopped. This procedure explains how to perform CPR on an adult victim. NOTE: Your teacher can provide information on the most current American Heart Association CPR guidelines from the *Health Science Fundamentals* Companion Web site

ALERT: Follow Standard Precautions.

PREPROCEDURE

1. Put on disposable gloves.

2. Check for consciousness by shaking victim's shoulder gently and asking if he or she is OK. If there is no response, activate EMS system.

PROCEDURE

3. Check for breathing by placing your ear near victim's mouth and nose. Turn your head so that you can see his or her chest. Look to see if chest is rising or falling. Listen for breathing. Feel for air from victim's mouth or nose on your cheek. If breathing is *not* present:

4. Open airway by placing one hand at victim's chin and the other hand on victim's forehead; gently lift chin by supporting jawbone with fingertips and lifting upward to open mouth. (Do not put pressure on throat; this may block airway.) This is called the *head tilt/chin lift.*

5. Ventilate. Place a pocket mask over mouth and nose. Put apex (point) over bridge of nose and base between lip and chin. Give two breaths (1^1/$_2$ to 2 seconds per breath) through the one-way valve. Allow lungs to empty between each breath. (If dentures obstruct the airway, remove them.) If air does *not* inflate lungs: retilt head to ensure an open airway and repeat the two breaths. Watch for chest to rise, allow for exhalation between breaths.

6. Check carotid pulse for 5–10 seconds.

7. If pulse is absent, begin chest compressions. Kneel on one side of the victim. Draw an imaginary line between the nipples. Place two fingers on the breast bone just below this line. Place the **heel** of one hand at this location. Place the other hand on top and **interlace** fingers. Push straight down on the chest for 30 compressions. The chest should be pushed down about 1^1/$_2$ to 2 inches during each compression. Compressions should be faster than one per second, so that blood is pumped through the body at a rate of 100 pumps per minute.

8. Give two breaths.

9. Continue to deliver 30 **compressions** for every two breaths until help arrives. Recheck pulse every two minutes.

POSTPROCEDURE

10. Ensure that victim has follow-up treatment or assessment by Emergency Medical Technicians or hospital personnel.

11. Discard gloves and wash hands (follow hand-washing guidelines).

 Defibrillator

CPR alone rarely ever revives a person whose heart has failed. CPR keeps the person alive until their heart can be shocked with a defibrillator. Automated external defibrillators (AEDs) are becoming more available in public places, such as airports and shopping malls.

These devices can be used by anyone who has received proper training. To learn how to operate an AED, you should attend a class given by a qualified American Heart Association or American Red Cross instructor.

heel
(HEEL)
Part of the hand between the palm and the wrist.

interlace
(in tur las)
Put between.

compressions
(kuhm PRESH uhns)
Pumps.

BACKGROUND: Sudden cardiac arrest is a leading cause of death in the United States. The provision of cardiopulmonary resuscitation can improve a victim's chance of survival.

ALERT: Follow Standard Precautions.

PREPROCEDURE

The provider should understand that the critical concepts of quality CPR include:

- Push hard, push fast: compress at a rate of 100 compressions per minute.

- Allow full chest recoil after each compression.

- Minimize interruptions in chest compressions.

- Avoid hyperventilation

PROCEDURE

When a second rescuer is available to help, that second rescuer should activate the emergency response system and get the AED if available. The first rescuer should remain with the victim to begin CPR immediately.

After the second rescuer returns, the rescuers should take turns doing chest compressions, switching after every 5 cycles of CPR. Follow the procedure for one person cardiopulmonary resuscitation assigning tasks as follows:

Rescuer	Location	Actions
Rescuer 1	At the victim's side	<ul><li>Performs chest compressions.</li><li>Counts out loud.</li><li>Switches duties with rescuer 2 every 5 cycles, taking less than 5 seconds to switch.</li></ul>
Rescuer 2	At the victim's head	<ul><li>Maintains an open airway.</li><li>Gives breaths, watching for chest rise.</li><li>Encourages rescuer 1 to perform compressions that are fast and deep enough to allow full chest recoil between compressions.</li><li>Switches duties with rescuer 1 every 5 cycles taking less than 5 seconds to switch.</li></ul>

BACKGROUND: An infant may go into respiratory arrest during a severe asthma attack. CPR can keep oxygen flowing to organs until help arrives. This procedure explains how to perform CPR on an infant.

ALERT: Follow Standard Precautions.

PREPROCEDURE

1. Put on disposable gloves.

2. Check for consciousness. Shake the infant's foot for reflex action gently and speak baby's name. If no response, shout for help.

PROCEDURE

3. Open airway. Use head tilt/chin lift method. Do not overtilt head or neck.

4. Check for breathing. Look, listen, and feel.

If not breathing:

5. Place an infant-sized barrier device on the infant's face.* Ventilate through the one-way valve and give rescue breathing. Give two slow breaths using only air in your cheeks. (Too much air may overinflate an infant's lungs.) Watch for chest to rise and allow chest to fall or deflate between each breath. If air does not inflate lungs:

6. Retilt head to ensure open airway. Repeat the two breaths. If lungs still do not inflate, treat infant for an obstructed airway.

If lungs do inflate:

7. Check pulse. Place three fingers over brachial artery/pulse. The baby's heart may have stopped.

8. If pulse is absent, begin chest compressions. Place two or three fingers near the center of the chest, just below the nipples. Push down gently on the chest for 30 compressions. The chest should be pushed down about 1/3 of its depth during each compression. Compressions should be faster than one per second, so that blood is pumped through the body at a rate of 100 pumps per minute.

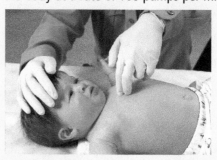

9. Give two breaths and deliver 30 more compressions.

10. After two minutes of breaths and compressions, activate EMS system.

11. Continue cycle of breaths and compressions until help arrives.

POSTPROCEDURE

10. Ensure that victim has follow-up treatment or assessment by Emergency Medical Technicians or hospital personnel.

11. Discard gloves and wash hands (follow hand-washing guidelines).

*Adult-sized pocket face masks can be adapted by inverting (reversing) them. See manufacturer's guidelines.

BACKGROUND: The interval from collapse to defibrillation is one of the most important determinants of survival from cardiac arrest.

AEDS are computerized devices that are attached to a pulseless victim with adhesive pads. They will recommend shock delivery only if the victim's heart rhythm is one that a shock can treat. AEDS give rescuers visual and voice prompts to guide rescuer actions.

AEDs are reliable and simple to operate, allowing laypersons and health care providers to attempt defibrillation safely. More and more often this tool has become available in the community setting and its availability has improved the overall outcomes of cardiopulmonary resuscitation.

Use AEDs only when victims have the following three clinical findings:

- No response
- No breathing
- No pulse

ALERT: Follow Standard Precautions.

PROCEDURE

Once the AED arrives, put it at the victim's side, next to the rescuer who will operate it. This will allow a second rescuer to perform CPR from the opposite side of the victim without interfering with AED operation. The following are four universal steps for operating an AED:

1. Power on the AED:

   - Open the carrying case.
   - Turn the power on.

2. **ATTACH** electrode pads to the victim's bare chest:

   - Choose correct pads for size/age of victim. Child pads will be used for children less than 8 years of age. Adult pads are used for the victim who is over 8 years of age.
   - Peel the backing away from the electrode pads.
   - Quickly wipe the victim's chest dry if covered with sweat or water. If the chest is covered with hair and electrode pads will not stick, pull the pad away from chest. This should take the hair with it. If still will not stick, shave area with razor included in the AED Kit.

   - Attach the adhesive electrode pads to the victim's bare chest.

     — Place one electrode pad on the upper-right side of the bare chest to the right of the breastbone, directly below the collarbone.

     — Place the other pad to the left of the nipple, a few inches below the left arm pit.

   - Attach the AED connecting cables to the AED box (some are preconnected).

3. "Clear" the victim and **ANALYZE** the rhythm.

   - Always clear the victim during the analysis. Be sure that no one is touching the victim, not even the person in charge of giving breaths.

   - Some AEDS will tell you to push a button to allow the AED to begin analyzing the heart rhythm; others will do that automatically. The AED may take about 5 to 15 seconds to analyze.

   - The AED then tells you if a shock is needed. Remember if the victim has an unshockable rhythm there will be no advice to shock.

(continued)

4. If the AED advises a shock, it will tell you to be sure to clear the victim.

   ■ Clear the victim before delivering the shock; be sure no one is touching the victim to avoid injury to rescuers.

     — Loudly state a "clear the patient" message, such as "I'm clear, you're clear, everybody's clear."

     — Perform a visual check to ensure that no one is in contact with the victim.

■ Press the **SHOCK** button.

■ The shock will produce a sudden contraction of the victim's muscles.

5. As soon as the AED gives the shock, begin CPR starting with chest compressions.

6. After 2 minutes of CPR, the AED will prompt you to repeat steps 3 and 4.

Summary

CPR is an important technique that can keep organs alive until the heart can be shocked with a defibrillator. All health professionals must become proficient in CPR. To do this, you should attend a class given by a qualified American Heart Association or American Red Cross teacher.

NOTE: Your teacher can provide information on the most current American Heart Association CPR guidelines from the *Health Science Fundamentals* Companion Web site.

Career Connection

Participate in either a ride-along with a first responder, paramedic, police officer, or fire service professional or job shadow an emergency dispatcher to determine the response for different emergency situations.

As an alternative opportunity, consider joining an EMT Explorer Post, or invite one of these professionals to speak to your class.

SECTION **21.6** **Review Questions**

1. What does a defibrillator do?

2. How many compressions should be given per minute during CPR?

3. Describe the position of your hands when performing CPR on an adult.

4. What are the basic steps for performing CPR on an adult?

5. How do you deliver a chest compression to an infant who has no heartbeat?

Learn By Doing: Section 21.6 Activity

1. Complete the appropriate worksheets, as directed by your teacher.

2. Prepare responses to each item listed in Chapter Review.

3. When you are confident that you can meet each objective for this section, ask your teacher for the section evaluation.

Chapter 21 Review

Chapter Review Questions

1. Why is it important to clean up litter and wipe up spills on the floor? (21.1)

2. What is the purpose of MSDS forms? (21.1)

3. Under what circumstances should side rails be used on a bed? (21.2)

4. Devices that restrict a patient's movement are called _____. (21.2)

5. What are four ways that electricity can be used incorrectly? (21.3)

6. What are four ways to prevent a fire? (21.3)

7. Describe the correct way to pick up a load, using the principles of body mechanics. (21.4)

8. What kind of bandaging procedure would you perform for a large leg wound? (21.5)

9. Why is it important to treat seriously injured patients for shock? (21.5)

10. When performing CPR on an infant, the ratio of chest compressions to rescue breaths is _____. (21.6)

Activities

1. Have a classmate pretend to have three different types of wounds. Perform the correct bandaging procedure for each type of wound.

2. Work with a classmate to practice the correct procedures for moving patients using a wheelchair. If a wheelchair is not available, carefully use an office chair with wheels.

Case Studies

1. Your facility is being evacuated due to a bomb threat. You are in charge of moving a patient who is unable to sit up or walk. What kinds of precautions should you take to make sure the patient is safe as she is being moved?

2. Mr. Benton is a patient who is in the hospital after suffering a heart attack. He is hooked up to a heart monitor and has an IV in his arm that delivers fluids and medications. He has also been prescribed a medication in pill form. You are assigned to give Mr. Benton his pill and check his vital signs. You enter his room and see that he is in bed with the side rails up. How do you make sure that Mr. Benton safely receives his medicine and remains safe after you leave the room?

Thinking Critically

1. **Medical Terminology**—Use the following medical terms in two or three sentences related to first aid: cardiopulmonary, priorities, laceration, dressings.

2. **Customer Service**—In a home care environment you notice that your patient is very careless with the kitchen stove. Describe how you could demonstrate safer stove use while assisting the patient with meal preparation.

3. **Patient Education**—Mrs. Green is the most cheerful patient in the facility and a pleasure to work with. She is fond of telling everyone that whatever is in the cards will happen, whatever you do. How will you get her to cooperate with the facility's safety policies and procedures, such as fire drills? Describe how you would talk to her about safety requirements and what is necessary for patients to understand and to do.

Media Connection

Use the Companion Web site for additional interactive learning activities: www.prenhall.com/badasch

Portfolio Connection

Reading product labels correctly is a key component of many of our daily projects. We need to know if products will do what we want them to do. We need to know if there is a risk in using a product.

In this chapter, we discussed MSDS (material safety data sheet) forms. You learned that MSDSs provide all the primary information needed for any product in the work environment. If you become a home health aide, you work in patients' homes. There will not be an MSDS book to refer to. You will have to read the labels on products for the information you need.

Choose three household products from home—for example, toothpaste, a cleaning product, Wite-Out®, a synthetic food product—and create your own MSDS form for each of these three products. Use the following headings in your forms:

1. Product Identification
2. Hazardous Ingredients of Mixture
3. Physical Data
4. Fire and Explosion
5. Reactivity Data
6. Health Hazard Data
7. Emergency and First-Aid Procedures
8. Spill or Leak Procedures
9. Protection Information/Control Measures
10. Special Precautions

Completion of this assignment for your portfolio shows your ability to assimilate information and transfer your knowledge into a usable format for your daily use. When you appropriately apply each step of your learning, you show others that you are capable of taking responsibility in a work environment. Place these three forms in the section of your portfolio labeled "Written Reports and Assignments."

PORTFOLIO TIP

Always keep good body mechanics in mind as you work so that you stay strong and limber. Make notes for your portfolio identifying the most enjoyable ways of staying in shape. Interview family and friends and keep the emphasis on fun and relaxation: how many types of dancing could you learn? Line dancing, tap, ballroom?

22 | Responsibilities of a Dental Assistant

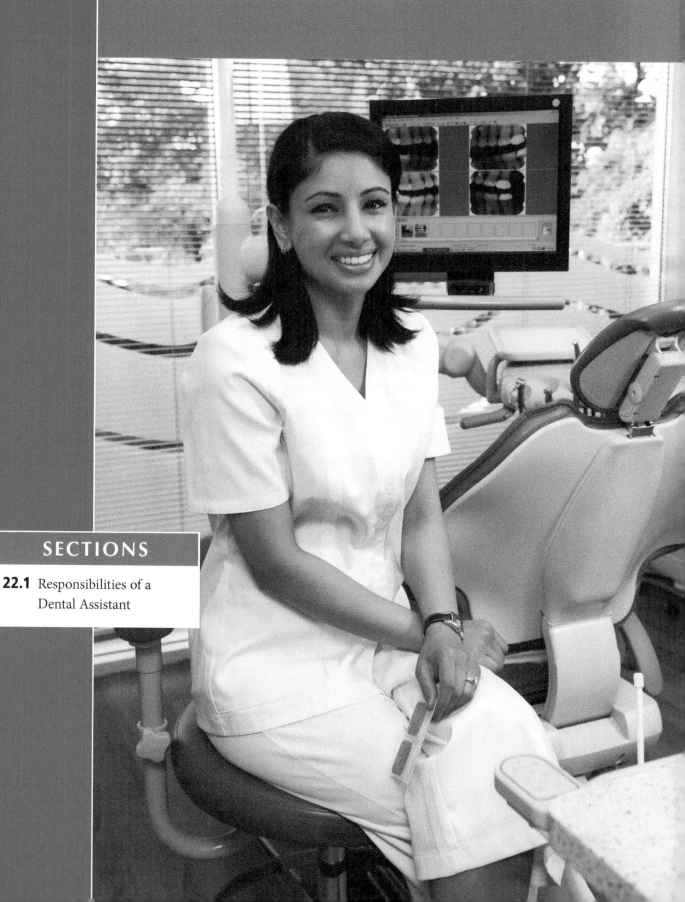

Getting Started

U nder the guidance of a health care professional, you will practice correct brushing and flossing to promote good oral health. Test your process with a disclosing tablet that highlights any area that retains bacteria or any other substance.

22.1 Responsibilities of a Dental Assistant

Background

Dental assistants work closely and under the direction of a dentist. Dental assistants provide different types of patient care, office duties, and laboratory duties. They do not perform the same duties as a dental hygienist, but they need to be skilled in patient care, preparing and cleaning dental rooms, and setting up and sterilizing equipment and instruments. They need to be knowledgeable about the tooth: function, placement, identification, and anatomy.

Objectives

When you have completed this section, you will be able to do the following:

- Match key terms with their correct meanings.

- Describe the responsibilities of dental assistants.

- Differentiate between posterior and anterior teeth and their functions.

- Identify the following:

  — Deciduous and permanent teeth by name on a diagram.

  — Surfaces of a tooth.

  — Dental office equipment and instruments by name.

- Label the following:

  — Parts of the oral cavity on a diagram.

  — Teeth on a diagram using the universal method.

  — Anatomical structure of a tooth on a diagram.

- Teach the following:

  — How to use disclosing tablets/ solutions.

  — The Bass toothbrushing technique.

  — Dental flossing techniques.

Duties of a Dental Assistant

Dental assistants are valued members of the dental health care team. Their primary duty is chairside assisting during oral care procedures. Their basic duty is to maintain **visibility** in the mouth. They also provide instruments and materials as the dentist needs them to complete the dental treatment. Constant observance and

visibility
(vis uh BIL it tee)
Ability to see.

consideration of the patient's/client's comfort level and health status are important in the role of a dental assistant. The responsibilities of a dental assistant include the following:

- Working directly with the dentist in the treatment room.
- Preparing and cleaning dental treatment rooms following infection control guidelines.
- Preparing necessary equipment and instrumentation for dental procedures
- Processing and mounting dental x-rays.
- Caring for and maintaining dental equipment.
- Teaching patients oral hygiene methods.
- Taking and pouring study models (may be an expanded role in your state).
- Possibly performing some front office duties.
- Exposing x-rays (radiographs) (requires completion of a state-approved radiology course or examination).

What's New?

Teeth Whitening

In recent years, teeth whitening has become a popular practice. Consumers can now buy toothpaste that whitens teeth as well as at-home bleaching kits. Dental offices also provide patients with the opportunity to whiten their teeth. Dental assistants may likely assist with such procedures.

Teeth whitening that is done in a dentist's office may require more than one office visit. Each visit may take 30 minutes to one hour. First, a dentist applies either a gel to the gums or a rubber shield to protect the oral soft tissues. Then a bleaching agent is applied to the teeth. A special light may be used to enhance the action of the agent.

Many in-office bleaching agents have the ADA Seal of Acceptance. That means that these agents have met the standards of safety and effectiveness. Sometimes lasers are used during the whitening process to enhance the action of the whitening agent. However, these whitening products that use lasers have not been accepted by the ADA.

Dentists may also provide patients with a teeth-whitening agent to take home. These whiteners contain peroxide and often come in a gel. The patient places the gel in a mouth guard that the dentist custom fits to the patient's teeth. Some products are used twice a day for two weeks, and others are used overnight for one to two weeks.

How might a dental assistant assist a dentist with the teeth-whitening procedure?

Glossary

accessory
(ak SES uh ree)
Helping.

masticate
(MAS ti keyt)
Chew.

primary
(PRAHY mere e)
First.

deciduous
(di SIJ oo uhs)
Falling out (e.g., primary teeth fall out to make room for permanent teeth).

erupt
(I RUHPT)
Push through.

dentition
(den TISH uhn)
Natural teeth in the dental arch.

restorative
(ri STAWY uh tiv)
To return to as close to normal conditions as possible.

Odontology

Odontology is the study of teeth. Teeth are **accessory** organs that help **masticate** food. There are two sets of teeth. They are the **primary** or **deciduous** (baby) teeth and the permanent teeth. When a baby is born it has 44 tooth buds. The tooth buds begin to **erupt** when the baby is about 6 months old. Deciduous teeth are the 20 baby teeth (primary teeth). Each tooth has a specific function in processing food and acting as a guide for a permanent tooth.

When the child is between 5 and 12 years old, the deciduous teeth begin to fall out and the permanent teeth erupt through the gingiva/gums. Permanent teeth are the 32 adult teeth. The child who has some deciduous teeth and some permanent teeth has mixed **dentition**.

Introduction to the Teeth and Oral Cavity

Teeth are identified by name, number, and the function they perform in the digestion of food. The following information teaches you how to identify teeth, where the teeth are located, and the anatomy of a tooth.

Face and Oral Cavity

When dentists examine patients they look at the face first. Dentists ask themselves:

- Is the bone structure normal and balanced?
- Do the skin and lips (labia) look healthy?

Next, the dentist does an oral examination. (**Figure 22.1**) This examination tells the dentist things about the patient's health and habits (for example, whether he or she practices good oral care). Often, a nondental disease shows up in the oral cavity first and is identified during the examination. For example, signs of periodontal disease or bacteria may indicate a previously undiagnosed heart condition or diabetes. A routine oral health exam also can uncover signs and symptoms of osteoporosis and low bone mass; eating disorders, such as anorexia nervosa and bulimia, which can be detected by thin tooth enamel and a red mouth; and HIV, which often shows signs in the mouth first.

The complete oral examination is one of the most important procedures that a dentist performs. As a dental assistant, you help the dentist during this examination and during **restorative** care. To assist the dentist, you need to know the following:

- Simple anatomy of the face and oral cavity
- Tooth numbers, parts, surfaces, and structures

Maxillary and Mandibular Arches

Refer to **Figure 22.2**, an illustration of the skull.

- **Maxilla**—the arched bone in the face where the roots of the upper teeth fit into the sockets (alveolus).
- **Mandible**—the arched lower bone (jawbone), where the roots of the lower teeth fit into the alveolus.
- **Median line or midline**—divides the teeth into left and right sides.

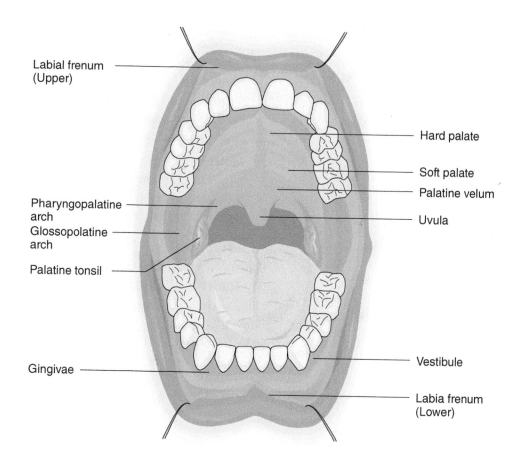

Labial frenum (Upper)

Hard palate

Soft palate

Palatine velum

Pharyngopalatine arch

Uvula

Glossopolatine arch

Palatine tonsil

Gingivae

Vestibule

Labia frenum (Lower)

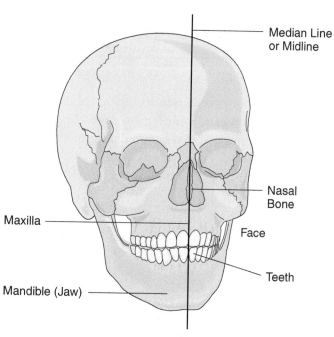

FIGURE 22.2
Skull. What does the median line or midline do?

Median Line or Midline

Nasal Bone

Maxilla

Face

Teeth

Mandible (Jaw)

Placement and Function of Teeth

The following are the anterior teeth (**Figure 22.3**):

- **Incisors**—located in the very front of the mouth. Their thin cutting edge cuts food by biting pieces. They include the central and lateral incisors.

- **Cuspids/canines**—located next to the lateral incisors. Their sharp points/cusps tear food that is too tough for the incisors to cut. Cuspids have the longest roots of all teeth.

FIGURE 22.3

cusps
(kusps)
Pointed or rounded raised areas on the surface of the tooth.

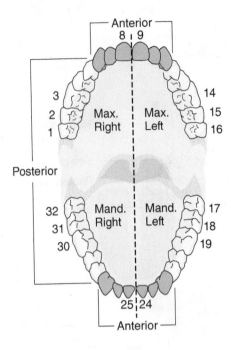

ala
(ey luh)
Outer side of the nostril.

FIGURE 22.4
Universal method of identifying permanent teeth. How many permanent teeth are in the dentition?

The following are the posterior teeth (Figure 22.3):

- **Premolars**—located next to the cuspids/canines. They are also called *bicuspids* because they have two **cusps** for tearing and grinding.

- **Molars**—located next to the bicuspids. These are the largest teeth in the mouth. They have broad grinding surfaces that grind down large chunks of food.

Identification of Teeth by Name and Location

There are 32 permanent teeth (also known as secondary teeth) in the dentition. (Figure 22.4) The following are the maxillary teeth:

- 2 central incisors in the center next to the midline.
- 2 lateral incisors next to the central incisors.
- 2 cuspids under the **ala** next to the lateral incisors.
- 2 first premolar/bicuspids next to the cuspids.
- 2 second premolar/bicuspids next to the first bicuspids.
- 2 first molars next to the second bicuspid.
- 2 second molars next to the first molar.
- 2 third molars or "wisdom teeth" in the back of the mouth. Not everyone has these molars. Some remain under the gingiva/gums line or in the alveolar bone and are often removed if the mouth does not have room for them.

The mandibular teeth:

- 2 central incisors in the center next to the midline.
- 2 lateral incisors next to the central incisors.
- 2 cuspids under the corner of the nose next to the lateral incisors.
- 2 first premolar/bicuspids next to the cuspids.
- 2 second premolar/bicuspids next to the first bicuspids.
- 2 first molars next to the second bicuspid.

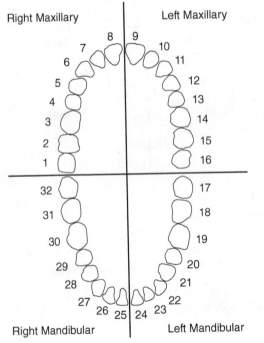

- 2 second molars next to the first molar.
- 2 third molars or "wisdom teeth" in the back of the mouth. Not everyone has these molars. Some molars remain under the gingiva/gums line and are often removed if the mouth does not have room for them.

There are 20 deciduous teeth in the dentition (**Figure 22.5**):

- 2 central incisors in the center next to midline.
- 2 lateral incisors next to the central incisors.
- 2 cuspids just under the ala wing of the nose.
- 0 THERE ARE NO BICUSPIDS IN THE DECIDUOUS DENTITION.
- 2 primary first molars.
- 2 primary second molars.

The mandibular arch:

- 2 central incisors in the center next to midline.
- 2 lateral incisors next to the central incisors.
- 2 cuspids just under the ala wing of the nose.
- 0 THERE ARE NO BICUSPIDS IN THE DECIDUOUS DENTITION.
- 2 primary first molars.
- 2 primary second molars.

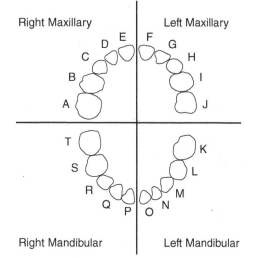

FIGURE 22.5
Universal method of identifying deciduous teeth. How does the method of identifying deciduous teeth differ from the method of identifying permanent teeth?

Apply It

With your classmates, play a game of "tooth fairy." Using a tooth chart, identify the 32 permanent teeth. Define the name, number, and the function they perform in the digestion of food.

Identification of Teeth by Letter and Number

One method of identifying teeth is the *universal method.* In this method, deciduous/primary teeth are identified by letter, and permanent teeth are identified by number.

When identifying deciduous teeth, begin lettering with the right second molar in the maxillary arch. (**Figure 22.5**) It is labeled A. Continue lettering from upper right to upper left, then lower left to lower right. The last molar on the right mandibular arch is labeled T.

When identifying permanent teeth, begin numbering with the right third molar in the maxillary arch. (**Figure 22.4**) It is numbered 1. Continue numbering from upper right to upper left, then lower left to lower right. The last third molar on the mandibular arch is numbered 32. A tooth that has not erupted or is missing is still counted.

Anatomy of the Tooth

The dental assistant works directly with the dentist. It is important to communicate with the dentist during **intraoral** procedures. You must know the anatomy of the tooth to communicate effectively with the dentist.

intraoral
(in tra or el)
Within the oral cavity.

Sections of the Tooth

A tooth is divided into three main sections (Figure 22.6):

- **Crown**—covered with enamel. The enamel is the white part of the tooth that we can see in our mouth.
- **Cervix**—neck of the tooth. It begins where the enamel stops and the **cementum** begins. Dentists call this the CEJ (cemento-enamel junction).
- **Root**—covered with cementum, lies below the gingiva/gums. It holds the tooth in the bony sockets of the jaw. A tooth may have more than one root, depending on where it is in the mouth.
  - Mandibular molars have two roots.
  - Maxillary molars have three roots.

cementum
(si MEN tuh m)
Hard, thin covering or shell covering root of tooth.

FIGURE 22.6
Sections of a tooth. Which part of the tooth can people see in their mouths?

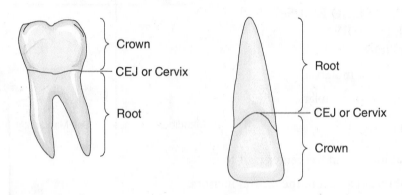

Parts of the Tooth

Each tooth has several parts (Figure 22.7):

- **Enamel**—the hardest tissue in the body. It covers the crown section of the tooth. Enamel is a protective sheet made of calcium and phosphorus that protects the dentin of the tooth.
- **Dentin**—harder than bone but softer than enamel. Dentin makes up the bulk of a tooth. It does not have nerves but it senses pain caused by **decay**, temperature, and chemical changes. Dentin may grow a second layer or wall of defense to try to keep decay from entering the pulp or nerve of the tooth.
- **Cementum**—the hard, thin covering or shell that covers the root.
- **Periodontal ligaments/periodontal membranes**—small fibers that are anchored in the cementum and attached to the bone socket. They act as a shock absorber for the tooth and help the tooth withstand **functional stress**.
- **Pulp**—the soft tissue inside the hard wall of enamel and dentin. It has veins, arteries, and nerve tissue that nourish the tooth and sense pain.
- **Apex**—the very tip of each root. The blood vessels and nerves of the tooth enter through the **apical foramen** in the apex of the tooth.

decay
(di KEY)
Breaking down; rot.

functional stress
(FUHNGK shuh nl stress)
Stress to tooth caused by its normal function (e.g., force of pressure when biting something hard).

apical foramen
(EY pi kuhl fuh REY muhn)
Opening in the apex.

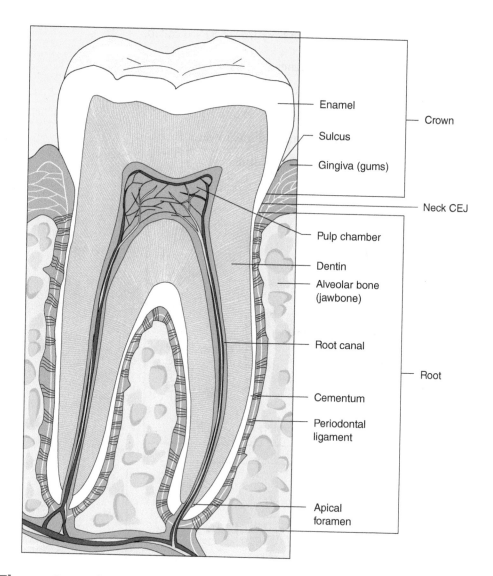

FIGURE 22.7
Parts of the tooth. Which part makes up the bulk of the tooth?

Enamel
Sulcus
Gingiva (gums)
Crown
Neck CEJ
Pulp chamber
Dentin
Alveolar bone (jawbone)
Root canal
Root
Cementum
Periodontal ligament
Apical foramen

Tissues Around the Teeth

The structures that surround the teeth are also important. They are as follows:

- **Alveolar processes (bone)**—form the sockets that hold and support teeth in their position.
- **Gingiva/gums**—cover the alveolar bone, protecting the tooth and deeper tissues from injury or infection.
- **Gingival sulcus**—the open space between gingiva/gums and a tooth. This is the area where dental floss is applied to remove bacteria and food particles.

Surfaces of the Teeth

Dentists use terms that specify surfaces (sides of the tooth) to record information about the condition of each tooth. To chart conditions of the teeth, the dental assistant must know the crown surfaces. Each tooth has a crown and root. Each tooth also has four sides and a biting or chewing surface (**Figure 22.8**):

- **Anterior teeth**—central and lateral incisors and the cuspids.
- **Posterior teeth**—bicuspids and molars.

sulcus
(SUHL kuhs)
Depression, groove, area where gingival tip meets tooth enamel.

The surfaces of the anterior teeth (**Figure 22.8**) are called:

- **Labial**—surface that touches the lips.
- **Lingual**—surface facing toward the tongue.
- **Incisal**—edge of the tooth that we bite with.
- **Distal**—surface away from midline, toward the back.
- **Mesial**—surface toward the midline.

FIGURE 22.8
Surfaces of the anterior and posterior teeth. Which surfaces are found on both anterior and posterior teeth?

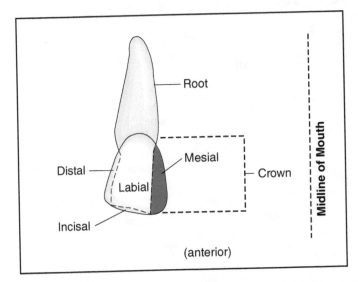

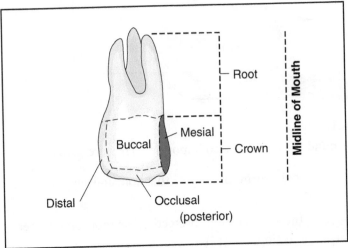

The surfaces of the posterior teeth (**Figure 22.8**) are called:

- **Buccal**—surface that touches the cheeks.
- **Lingual**—surface facing toward the tongue.
- **Occlusal**—large chewing surface where food is ground.
- **Distal**—surface away from midline.
- **Mesial**—surface toward the midline.

proximal
(PROK suh muhl)
Nearest or next to.

All teeth have mesial and distal sides that touch each other. The mesial side of one tooth touches the distal side of the tooth next to it. These sides are **proximal** to each other and are called proximal surfaces.

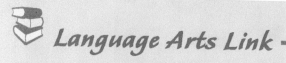

Dental Equipment

A dental treatment (operatory) room is designed and organized to ensure that the dentist and assistant perform procedures in a safe and time-efficient manner. Treatment room equipment includes the following:

- Dental chair.
- Dental unit.
- Operational light.
- Mobile carts or cabinets.
- Operatory stools.
- X-ray machine and view box.

The type of equipment varies depending on the office. As a dental assistant, you are responsible for learning how to use the various types of equipment. Dental equipment is costly and requires special care. It is important that you follow the manufacturers' cleaning and operating instructions.

Dental Chair

Parts of a dental chair are as follows. (**Figure 22.9b**) The body of the chair includes the backrest, seat, and leg support.

- The armrest is usually movable.
- The headrest supports the patient's head and is movable.
- The control panel is on the side or back of the chair. Foot pedals are attached to base of chair or rest on the floor. These are used to move the chair into either a sitting or reclining (supine) position.
- The swivel lever is at the base of the chair, which allows the chair to rotate.

FIGURE 22.9
(a) Dental unit,
(b) Chair,
(c) Air/water syringe,
(d) Dental unit,
(e) Eye protection,
(f, g) Operatory stools.
*What are the basic parts
of a dental unit?*

Courtesy of A-dec, Inc.

Courtesy of A-dec, Inc.

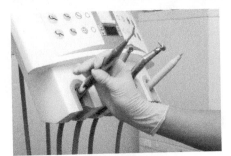

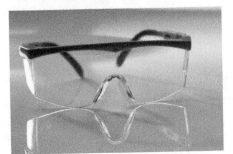

Courtesy of ShutterStock.

Courtesy of ShutterStock.

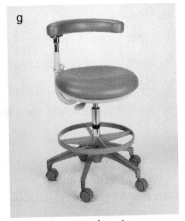

Courtesy of A-dec, Inc.

Courtesy of A-dec, Inc.

Courtesy of A-dec, Inc.

Dental Unit

A dental unit is attached to the dental chair (**Figure 22.9b**) or to a separate movable cart. (**Figure 22.9a**)

The basic parts of a dental unit are as follows:

- Master switch/control for:
  - Water and air.
  - Handpiece.
- Dental handpiece with burs or drills:
  - High speed.
  - Slow speed.
- Foot control (**rheostat**), which provides power to the handpiece.

rheostat
(REE uh stat)
Control for flow of electric
current.

- Air/water syringe to rinse and dry teeth (**Figure 22.9c**).
- Oral **evacuation** system to **aspirate** saliva and drainage from the mouth. This system has two hoses attached to:
  - A suction tip.
  - A small saliva ejector.
- Cuspidor, the bowl that patients spit into (modern offices use suction in place of a cuspidor).

evacuation
(i vak yoo EY shuhn)
Removal.

aspirate
(AS puh reyt)
Remove substances.

Dental Tools

Some common tools used by dental assistants include the following:

- **Mouth mirror**—to reflect light to see the surfaces of the teeth to inspect teeth, tongue, gingival, and oral cavity; and for retraction (hold the check back).
- **Explorer**—to feel teeth for decay or other problems. Explorers are sharp, pointed metallic instruments.
- **Non-locking cotton pliers**—to pick up gauze/cotton to dry areas of mouth/teeth. Cotton pliers are tong-like and metallic.
- **Scalers**—locate and remove plaque especially between the teeth. When a scaler is used, a patent may experience pain.
- **Excavators**—remove small amounts of decay close to the nerve. There are two types: spoons and hoes.
- **Carvers**—used to carve amalgam filling to the shape of the tooth. A cleoid carver is a claw-shaped dental instrument used to remove carious material from a cavity. A discoid carver does the same but is flat and circular.
- **Root elevator**—a screwdriver-shaped instrument with a grooved and beveled blade, used to break the periodontal membrane and elevate and remove the root.
- **Surgical forceps**—a two-bladed instrument with a handle for compressing or grasping tissues in surgical operations, and for handling sterile dressings, etc.

Operational Light

The operational light is attached to the chair or the ceiling. It has handles to move the light. The light must focus on the site where the dentist is working.

Personal Protective Equipment

Standard precautions should be followed for work in a dental office. Dental workers should use appropriate personal protective equipment including gloves, gowns, masks, and eye protection. (**Figure 22.9d**)

Dental Mobile Carts or Cabinets

The dental cart/cabinet provides storage for a small number of sterile instruments, treatment trays, dental materials, and supplies. (**Figure 22.9e**) Large amounts of supplies are stored in areas away from the patient treatment room.

Operatory Stools

Operatory stools vary in design. (**Figure 22.9f**, **22.9g**) There may be a footrest ring near the base on some stools, but all include the following:

- Padded seat.
- Five casters at the base to prevent tipping.
- Height-adjustment lever to position:
    - Dental assistant four to six inches above the dentist.
    - Dentist stabilized below the assistant, with thighs parallel to floor when feet are flat on the floor.
- Adjustable back support.

Radiology Machine

A radiology machine uses radiation to take x-rays. All radiology machines must operate according to state regulations to ensure safety. State regulations tell how to prevent **overexposure** to radiation and provide safety guidelines for machine operations. These regulations require the following:

- Registration of each radiology machine.
- **Periodic** inspection of equipment to ensure safe operation.
- A licensed person to operate a radiology machine.

Oral Hygiene

Human teeth are meant to last a lifetime. Remember that enamel is the hardest tissue in the body. Why, then, do we lose teeth? The bacteria that live in everyone's mouth cause disease. There are two main reasons why we lose teeth:

- Disease of the gingiva/gums, periodontal tissues, and/or the alveolar process (bony socket).
- Holes in the enamel and/or dentin (cavities).

Proper toothbrushing and flossing plus good nutrition can help prevent disease and destruction (review Chapter 16).

Dental assistants explain and demonstrate proper toothbrushing and flossing techniques to their patients. The instruction must be clear and meet each patient's needs (for example, working around a bridge). Correct flossing and brushing helps:

- Remove **plaque**.
- Prevent bad breath (halitosis).
- Prevent periodontal infection.
- Prevent bleeding gingiva/gums.

---

overexposure
(OH ver ik SPOH zher)
Too much contact with radiation.

periodic
(peer ee OD ik)
Occurring at regular intervals.

plaque
(plak)
Soft deposit of bacteria and bacterial products on teeth.

Personal Wellness

Oral Hygiene and Your Overall Health

Your mouth can be a clue about your body's overall health. Ingesting, chewing, and swallowing food is the first step of the process of digestion and nutrition. Poor dentition puts the patient at risk for malnutrition because the patient will select soft foods often high in sugars and carbohydrates and low in nutrients.

Also, patients with loss of dentition or ill fitting dentures will suffer diminished caloric intake due to the effort necessary to properly chew food. They frequently tire before adequate calorie intake is achieved.

The first sign of a disease may shows up in your mouth. In addition, infections in your mouth such as gum disease can cause problems in other areas of your body.

Many times, symptoms of a disease will first appear in your mouth. A person with diabetes has an increased risk of gum disease, cavities, tooth loss, or dry mouth. Also, people with AIDS may experience severe gum infections or unusual white spots or lesions on their tongues. While taking routine dental x-rays, a dentist may first notice osteoporosis. Certain cancers, eating disorders, syphilis, gonorrhea, and substance abuse can also show early symptoms in the mouth.

Not only can diseases first show themselves in your mouth, but diseases in your mouth can cause problems in other parts of your body. Your mouth is full of bacteria. However, good oral hygiene helps to control the bacteria. Your saliva also has enzymes that play an important role against bacteria and viruses. Sometimes harmful bacteria grow out of control and lead to serious gum infections. This gum disease provides bacteria a place to enter your bloodstream.

Some researchers believe that these bacteria in your bloodstream can lead to cardiovascular disease, premature birth, or difficulty with controlling diabetes. Bacteria from gum disease enter your bloodstream and travel to the arteries in your heart. This can affect the overall health of the cardiovascular system. In addition, research shows that these bacteria can end up in the placenta or amniotic fluid, possibly causing premature birth. These infections cause your blood sugar to rise, requiring diabetic patients to use more insulin to keep their levels under control.

What can you do daily to improve your health and prevent disease?

Teaching Oral Hygiene

Your dentist may ask you to use disclosing tablets or solution to show the patient that there is plaque in the mouth. The disclosing tablets are usually red and stain the plaque to help the patient see the areas where plaque has formed. Patients can see that even when they think plaque is removed, it may not be. This is a very good way to help patients understand that correct brushing and flossing are important.

There are several types of brushing techniques. Use the technique your dentist prefers. The Bass technique is a common one.

Common abbreviations for charting patient education:

- **OHI**—oral hygiene instruction, complete cleansing of oral cavity
- **TBI**—toothbrushing instruction
- **DFI**—dental floss instruction

interproximal surfaces
(in ter prok semal SUR fis)
Sides between teeth.

Flossing removes the plaque from the **interproximal surfaces** (between teeth). It removes plaque and food. Flossing cleans areas where brushing cannot reach. Correct flossing is very important because tooth decay often begins on the interproximal surfaces.

PROCEDURE | **22.1** | **Bass Toothbrushing Technique**

BACKGROUND: Correct brushing is essential for healthy teeth and gums. Explain the importance of correct brushing and show a patient good technique help protect against dental problems.

ALERT: Follow Standard Precautions.

PREPROCEDURE

1. Wash hands.
2. Assemble equipment:
   a. Tooth model (if using a model for teaching)
   b. Protective wear (if brushing patient's teeth or if there is contact with saliva), including gloves, mask, and goggles
   c. Toothbrush

PROCEDURE

3. Explain importance of toothbrushing.
4. Demonstrate correct brushing using model or on patient.

   NOTE: Put on gloves if demonstrating on patient.

   a. Place soft brush on upper right molars (maxillary).
   b. Position brush at 45° angle to teeth.
   c. Gently move bristles into gingival sulcus.

   d. Move brush in short strokes at least 10 to 20 times, keeping brush in place (wiggle-jiggle motion).
   e. Move brush to next two or three teeth and repeat until all buccal/labial surfaces are brushed.

   NOTE: Place brush in vertical or horizontal position for anterior teeth.

   f. Repeat technique beginning at upper right molars until all maxillary teeth are brushed.
   g. Use short, vibrating motion to scrub occlusal surfaces.
   h. Repeat this procedure for lower teeth (mandibular).

5. Ask client if he or she has any questions.

POSTPROCEDURE

6. Remove and clean equipment.
7. Remove protective wear.
8. Wash hands.
9. Chart TBI (toothbrushing instruction).

PROCEDURE 22.2   Dental Flossing

BACKGROUND: Correct dental flossing is essential for healthy teeth and gums. Explaining the importance of correct flossing and showing a patient good technique help protect against dental problems.

ALERT: Follow Standard Precautions.

PREPROCEDURE

1. Wash hands.

2. Assemble equipment:

   a. Tooth model (if using a model for teaching)

   b. Gloves, mask, and goggles (if flossing patient's teeth or if there is contact with saliva)

   c. Dental floss (waxed or unwaxed according to policy)

PROCEDURE

3. Explain importance of flossing.

4. Demonstrate correct flossing technique using model or patient.

   NOTE: Put on protective wear if demonstrating on patient.

   a. Cut floss 18 inches (measure from finger to elbow).

   b. Wrap floss around middle or index finger of both hands, leaving 1 to 2 inches between fingers.

   c. Stretch floss between fingers and gently guide floss in between teeth. Do not snap floss; it can damage gingiva/gums.

   d. Pass floss through contacts (where teeth touch) and wrap it around tooth in a C shape.

   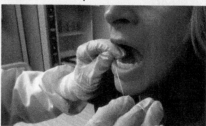

   e. Move floss up and down several times on sides of each tooth.

   NOTE: Make sure that floss goes beneath gingiva/gums into the sulcus.

   f. Unroll new floss from one hand and wrap used floss around middle finger of other hand.

   g. Repeat for each tooth until all teeth in maxilla and mandible are completed.

5. Explain that there may be some bleeding of the gingiva/gums the first few times the patient does this procedure.

6. Ask patient if he or she has any questions.

POSTPROCEDURE

7. Remove protective wear.

8. Remove and clean equipment.

9. Wash hands.

10. Chart DFI (dental flossing instruction).

Dental Radiographs

Dental assistants must have special training before they can take radiographs of the mouth. (Check with your state dental board or association for information.) As an entry-level dental assistant, you may mount dental radiographs after they are developed. To mount radiographs correctly, you need some basic information.

Dental radiographs are photographs of the teeth. The radiographs allow the dentist to see between the teeth, the pulp of each tooth, and the bone (for example, caries, metallic restorations, poorly fitted crowns, root end infection, **resorption** of alveolar bone). Radiographs allow the dentist to identify problems and make repairs before the problems cause further damage.

resorption
(ri SAWP shuhn)
Loss of substance or bone.

Radiography Terminology

- *Radiopaque* structures do not allow radiation to pass through. Enamel, metallic restorations, and dentin are radiopaque. They are very white on the film.

- *Radiolucent* structures allow rays to penetrate through them. Pulp and caries are radiolucent. They are dark areas on the film.

- *Periapical* films (PA) show two or three teeth and their surrounding bone structure. (**Figure 22.10**)

- *Bite wings* (BWX) show the crowns of the maxillary and mandibular teeth. These are often called the cavity detector films.

- *Occlusal* (OCC) is a large film that shows the whole arch from the occlusal view. (**Figure 22.11**)

- *Panographic* (PANX) is a long film taken from outside the mouth (extra oral) by a special machine. It shows all structures and teeth.

FIGURE 22.10
Full set of dental x-rays. In what situation would a dentist want a full set of x-rays?

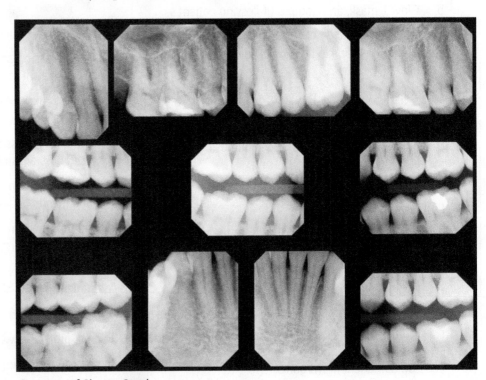

Courtesy of ShutterStock.

FIGURE 22.11
Panoramic survey. In what situation would a dentist want a panoramic survey?

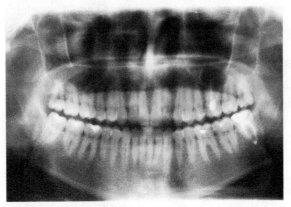

Courtesy of ShutterStock.

BACKGROUND: Correct mounting of dental films helps the dentist assess whether the patient needs treatment.

ALERT: Follow Standard Precautions.

PREPROCEDURE

1. Wash hands.

2. Assemble equipment:

    a. Developed x-rays

    b. X-ray mounts

    c. View box

PROCEDURE

3. Turn on view box.

4. Lay out x-rays. (Make certain that raised dot is facing upward.)

5. Arrange film on view box before placing into mount.

6. Mount the two or four bite-wing films.

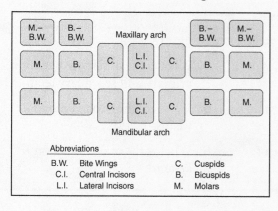

Abbreviations			
B.W.	Bite Wings	C.	Cuspids
C.I.	Central Incisors	B.	Bicuspids
L.I.	Lateral Incisors	M.	Molars

NOTE: Bicuspid views are closest to the center of the mount.

7. Mount two central (CI) and lateral (LI) incisor films. Place mandibular films with roots downward and maxillary films with roots upward.

8. Mount the four cuspid (C) films. The two longest cuspids are maxillary teeth.

9. Mount the four bicuspid (BC) films.

10. Mount the four molars (M) films. The molars with three roots are the maxillary molars.

11. Review the anatomical charts to check mount for accuracy.

12. Turn off view box.

POSTPROCEDURE

13. Clean and replace equipment.

14. Wash hands.

15. Record the following on patient chart and dental x-ray mount:

    a. Patient's name

    b. Date x-rays were taken

    c. Name of person who took x-rays

    d. Dentist's name and address

The radiographs serve as a guide that helps determine the treatment plan. After the radiograph is taken, it must be developed and mounted. Mounting film may be one of your duties.

Types of Mounts

Mounts come in different sizes. They may have 1, 2, 4, 7, 14, 16, 18, 20, and 28 windows. Bite-wing mounts have 2 or 4 windows. Common periapical mounts have 16 or 18 windows. When mounting films, you must remember the following:

- Periapical films show the crown and roots.

- Maxillary molars have three roots.

convex
(kon VEKS)
Raised.

- Maxillary cuspids are the longest teeth in the mouth.
- Maxillary lateral incisors are larger than mandibular lateral incisors.
- Maxillary central incisors are larger than mandibular central incisors.
- Mandibular molars have two roots.
- Mandibular lateral incisors are wider than mandibular central incisors.
- The center of the mount is the median line.
- If the distal portion is on the right margin, it is the left-hand side of the dental arch.
- If the distal portion is on the left margin, it is the right-hand side of the dental arch.
- Dental film has a raised dot on a corner of the film.
- Place all films with the dot facing upward, which is a convex view.
- **Convex** is a facial surface view.
- Concave is a lingual surface view.
- A full-mouth series usually includes 14 periapical films plus two or four bite wings.

 ## Summary

Dental assistants help dentists provide efficient dental care. Dental assistants have a responsibility to be considerate of the patent and make the patient feel comfortable. It is important for dental assistants to be familiar with standard concepts, practices, and procedures related to the field of the dentistry.

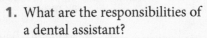

SECTION **22.1** Review Questions

1. What are the responsibilities of a dental assistant?

2. How many permanent teeth do adults have?

3. Explain the Bass technique of toothbrushing.

4. What is the difference between primary and secondary teeth?

5. What are the two main reasons we lose teeth?

6. What is the oral evacuation system?

 Learn By Doing: Section 22.1

1. Complete Worksheets 1 through 5.

2. Complete Worksheets/Activities 6 through 8.

3. Prepare responses to each item listed in Chapter Review.

4. When you are confident that you can meet each objective, ask your teacher for the section evaluation.

Chapter Review Questions

1. List the anterior and posterior teeth and their functions. (22.1)

2. Explain the universal method for identifying teeth. (22.1)

3. What are the three sections of a tooth? (22.1)

4. Describe the six parts of a tooth. (22.1)

5. Identify the surfaces of anterior and posterior teeth. (22.1)

6. What equipment would you find in a dental treatment room? (22.1)

7. Why is important to use proper flossing and brushing techniques? (22.1)

8. What are the structures that surround the teeth? (22.1)

9. Describe the following dental instruments: mouth mirror, scalers, spoon excavator, and cleoid and discoid carvers. (22.1)

10. Explain the dental flossing technique. (22.1)

Activities

1. Imagine that you are writing questions for a quiz show. Write ten questions that relate to the duties of a Dental Assistant. After writing your questions, exchange them with your classmates to see how well you do.

2. Use the Internet or visit a local dental group and prepare a display on oral hygiene that can be used in elementary schools.

Case Studies

1. You are preparing the room for a patient who is coming in for a routine cleaning. As a dental assistant, what are your responsibilities before, during and after the procedure?

2. A patient needs dental x-rays. He wants to understand why they are necessary, what you look for and who does what during the process. How do you answer his questions?

Thinking Critically

1. **Communication**—The dental assistant may work directly with the dentist during routine procedures. Mrs. Smith, a new client, is upset by the precautions taken in the dental office—masks, gloves, etc. How do you explain to her why this is necessary?

2. **Medical Terminology**—An 8-year-old boy fell off of his bike and knocked his top two front teeth out. Using appropriate terminology and identifiers, write a description for a dental record of the dentition on this boy.

3. **Patient Education**—Describe what you would tell a patient about the need for and benefits of brushing and flossing. How would you show a patient where plaque is building up?

4. **Computers**—Describe ways computers are used in dental care.

Chapter 22 Review

Media Connection

Use the Companion Web site for additional interactive learning activities: www.prenhall.com/badasch

Portfolio Connection

Once you attain competence as a dental assistant, ask for permission to copy an example of your charting. (Remove all patient identifiers.) Place this copy in your portfolio as evidence of your skills. Place a copy of your on-site trainer's evaluation in your portfolio.

Write a paper describing your doubts and realizations and the barriers that you were able to overcome during the dental assistant experience. For example, were you afraid that you couldn't learn to use the equipment? Describe the ways you plan to use the skills, information, and insights that you gained about people and about this job. This assignment must be in standard report format.

PORTFOLIO TIP

Keep a pocket notebook with you at all times to jot down any tips for your personal portfolio section and any other helpful observations.

CDC Recommendations for Standard Precautions

In 2007, the Centers for Disease Control updated and expanded the 1996 Guidelines for Isolation Precautions in Hospitals. This Appendix provides a summary of the New Elements in the 2007 CDC Standard Precautions.

Go to `http://www.cdc.gov/hicpac/2007IP/2007isolationPrecautions.html` for the complete text of the 2007 CDC Standard Precautions as well as any updates to the guidelines.

III.A.1. New Elements of Standard Precautions Infection control problems that are identified in the course of outbreak investigations often indicate the need for new recommendations or reinforcement of existing infection control recommendations to protect patients. Because such recommendations are considered a standard of care and may not be included in other guidelines, they are added here to Standard Precautions.

Three such areas of practice that have been added are: Respiratory hygiene/Cough Etiquette, safe injection practices, and use of masks for insertion of catheters or injection of material into spinal or epidural spaces via lumbar puncture procedures (e.g., myelogram, spinal or epidural anesthesia). While most elements of Standard Precautions evolved from Universal Precautions that were developed for protection of health care personnel, these new elements of Standard Precautions focus on protection of patients.

III.A.1.a. Respiratory Hygiene/Cough Etiquette The transmission of SARSCoV in emergency departments by patients and their family members during the widespread SARS outbreaks in 2003 highlighted the need for vigilance and prompt implementation of infection control measures at the first point of encounter within a health care setting (e.g., reception and triage areas in emergency departments, outpatient clinics, and physician offices). The strategy proposed has been termed Respiratory Hygiene/Cough Etiquette and is intended to be incorporated into infection control practices as a new component of Standard Precautions.

The strategy is targeted at patients and accompanying family members and friends with undiagnosed transmissible respiratory infections, and applies to any person with signs of illness including cough, congestion, rhinorrhea, or increased production of respiratory secretions when entering a health care facility. The term cough etiquette is derived from recommended source control measures for M. tuberculosis. The elements of Respiratory Hygiene/Cough Etiquette include:

1) education of health care facility staff, patients, and visitors;
2) posted signs, in language(s) appropriate to the population served, with instructions to patients and accompanying family members or friends;
3) source control measures (e.g., covering the mouth/nose with a tissue when coughing and prompt disposal of used tissues, using surgical masks on the coughing person when tolerated and appropriate);

4) hand hygiene after contact with respiratory secretions; and

5) spatial separation, ideally >3 feet, of persons with respiratory infections in common waiting areas when possible.

Covering sneezes and coughs and placing masks on coughing patients are proven means of source containment that prevent infected persons from dispersing respiratory secretions into the air. Masking may be difficult in some settings (e.g., pediatrics), in which case, the emphasis by necessity may be on cough etiquette.

Physical proximity of <3 feet has been associated with an increased risk for transmission of infections via the droplet route (e.g., N. meningitidis and group A streptococcus) and therefore supports the practice of distancing infected persons from others who are not infected. The effectiveness of good hygiene practices, especially hand hygiene, in preventing transmission of viruses and reducing the incidence of respiratory infections both within and outside health care settings is summarized in several reviews.

These measures should be effective in decreasing the risk of transmission of pathogens contained in large respiratory droplets (e.g., influenza virus, adenovirus, B. pertussis and Mycoplasma pneumoniae). Although fever will be present in many respiratory infections, patients with pertussis and mild upper respiratory tract infections are often afebrile. Therefore, the absence of fever does not always exclude a respiratory infection.

Patients who have asthma, allergic rhinitis, or chronic obstructive lung disease also may be coughing and sneezing. While these patients often are not infectious, cough etiquette measures are prudent. Health care personnel are advised to observe Droplet Precautions (i.e., wear a mask) and hand hygiene when examining and caring for patients with signs and symptoms of a respiratory infection. Health care personnel who have a respiratory infection are advised to avoid direct patient contact, especially with high risk patients. If this is not possible, then a mask should be worn while providing patient care.

III.A.1.b. Safe Injection Practices   The investigation of four large outbreaks of HBV and HCV among patients in ambulatory care facilities in the United States identified a need to define and reinforce safe injection practices. The four outbreaks occurred in a private medical practice, a pain clinic, an endoscopy clinic, and a hematology/oncology clinic. The primary breaches in infection control practice that contributed to these outbreaks were 1) reinsertion of used needles into a multiple-dose vial or solution container (e.g., saline bag) and 2) use of a single needle/syringe to administer intravenous medication to multiple patients. In one of these outbreaks, preparation of medications in the same workspace where used needle/syringes were dismantled also may have been a contributing factor.

These and other outbreaks of viral hepatitis could have been prevented by adherence to basic principles of aseptic technique for the preparation and administration of parenteral medications. These include the use of a sterile, single-use, disposable needle and syringe for each injection given and prevention of contamination of injection equipment and medication.

Whenever possible, use of single-dose vials is preferred over multiple-dose vials, especially when medications will be administered to multiple patients. Outbreaks related to unsafe injection practices indicate that some health care personnel are unaware of, do not understand, or do not adhere to basic principles of infection control and aseptic technique. A survey of U.S. health care workers who provide medication through injection found that 1% to 3% reused the same needle and/or syringe on multiple patients.

Among the deficiencies identified in recent outbreaks were a lack of oversight of personnel and failure to follow-up on reported breaches in infection control practices in ambulatory settings. Therefore, to ensure that all health care workers understand and adhere to recommended practices, principles of infection control and aseptic technique need to be reinforced in training programs and incorporated into institutional polices that are monitored for adherence.

III.A.1.c. Infection Control Practices for Special Lumbar Puncture Procedues In 2004, CDC investigated eight cases of post-myelography meningitis that either were reported to CDC or identified through a survey of the Emerging Infections Network of the Infectious Disease Society of America. Blood and/or cerebrospinal fluid of all eight cases yielded streptococcal species consistent with oropharyngeal flora and there were changes in the CSF indices and clinical status indicative of bacterial meningitis.

Equipment and products used during these procedures (e.g., contrast media) were excluded as probable sources of contamination. Procedural details available for seven cases determined that antiseptic skin preparations and sterile gloves had been used. However, none of the clinicians wore a face mask, giving rise to the speculation that droplet transmission of oralpharyngeal flora was the most likely explanation for these infections.

Bacterial meningitis following myelogram and other spinal procedures (e.g., lumbar puncture, spinal and epidural anesthesia, intrathecal chemotherapy) has been reported previously. As a result, the question of whether face masks should be worn to prevent droplet spread of oral flora during spinal procedures (e.g., myelogram, lumbar puncture, spinal anesthesia) has been debated. Face masks are effective in limiting the dispersal of oropharyngeal droplets and are recommended for the placement of central venous catheters.

In October 2005, the Health Care Infection Control Practices Advisory Committee (HICPAC) reviewed the evidence and concluded that there is sufficient experience to warrant the additional protection of a face mask for the individual placing a catheter or injecting material into the spinal or epidural space.

Source: Centers for Disease Control.

Clinical Internship   Appendix B

Whether you are participating in a clinical rotation, internship, or mentorship, your attitude and performance will determine whether it is a positive experience for you.

It is your responsibility to ensure that learning takes place. You must communicate to the health care staff what knowledge and skills you bring to the clinical opportunity. Ask questions of health care staff and seek out learning opportunities. When you show initiative, your clinical rotation will be more meaningful to you.

Getting Ready for the Clinical Experience

1. Research the facility and/or particular unit where you will be working during the rotation.
2. Investigate what type of uniform or professional clothing is required and purchase them. Remember to include footwear.
3. Obtain a name tag. (Many health care facilities require a picture ID.)
4. Read and complete any orientation materials the facility requires.
5. Gather immunization records and have a Tuberculosis Test. (Some facilities also require a physical within the past year.)
6. Arrange transportation to the facility.

Dress Code for the Clinical Experience

1. Uniform or professional clothing should be neat, clean, and pressed.
2. Shoes should be clean, comfortable leather shoes with socks or stockings.
3. Hair should be clean and cut in a conservative style. If long, it should be pulled away from the face.
4. Jewelry should be limited to a watch with a second hand, one small pair of stud earrings, and no more than one ring.
5. Fingernails should be trimmed with no artificial nails and clear nail polish only.
6. Cosmetics should be minimal and used to enhance appearance. Avoid wearing perfumes, colognes, or aftershaves.
7. While in your clinical uniform, you should avoid chewing gum and being around cigarette smoke.

Having a Positive Clinical Experience

1. Be on time each day. (Getting there 10 minutes early is even more impressive.) If you will not be able to attend that day or you are running late, notify the clinical site AND your instructor.

2. Bring a black pen and small notepad to make notes about your experiences.

3. Turn cell phones off and do not make personal phone calls or send text messages during your clinical experience.

4. Never leave your assigned area without notifying the health professional you are working with.

5. Perform only the skills you have learned to perform in your classroom.

6. Show initiative and seek out learning opportunities. Be self directed and ask questions.

7. Use critical thinking skills and practice infection control and standard precaution concepts appropriately.

8. Respect the property of others and care for the equipment and supplies in the health care facility.

9. Obey all safety rules of the facility.

10. Report ANY accidents or incidents that occur in the clinical area to your mentor and instructor. Complete appropriate reports if needed.

11. Behave professionally toward employees, patients, and fellow students. Discuss problems in an appropriate manner.

12. Avoid discussing your personal life in the clinical area.

13. Respect the Patient's Bill of Rights and patient confidentiality.

14. Be flexible and positive. Things are always changing in the health care environment. Embrace the unexpected as a learning opportunity.

The Post-Clinical Experience

1. Complete assignments and/or journal as assigned by your instructor. Continue to respect patient confidentiality when writing about your experiences.

2. Send a thank you note to your mentor or the clinical facility.

3. Reflect on the clinical experience.
   - What did you learn?
   - What did you do well?
   - What could you improve?
   - What do you want to learn more about?

◨ Completing a Clinical Journal

Print out and complete the following Journal worksheet while you are working as a clinical intern.

Name: _____   Date: _____

Clinical Site: _____   Area: _____

Summary of clinical experience: _____
_____
_____
_____
_____

Describe two things you learned today and explain how you will be able to use them in the future.

   1. _____
_____
_____

   2. _____
_____
_____

Describe one procedure or treatment you saw today and the patient's response: _____
_____
_____
_____

List one new medical term you learned today and explain what it means:

   1. _____

I performed these hands-on-skills today: _____
_____
_____
_____

Name one positive and one negative experience you had in your clinical rotation today: _____
_____
_____
_____
_____

Feelings, Smells, Sounds:

   I felt _____
   I smelled _____
   I heard _____

Glossary

numbers

24-hour time/military time   Method of telling time by counting each hour consecutively for 24 hours (i.e., . . . 11, 12, 13, . . .).

A

abbreviations   Words that have been shortened.

abdominal thrust or Heimlich maneuver   Forceful thrust on the abdomen, between the sternum and the navel, in an upward motion toward the head.

ability   Something a person does well.

abrasive   Compound used to rub away or scrape away another substance.

abreast   Side by side.

abscesses   Pockets of pus in a limited area.

absorption   Passage of a substance through a body surface into body fluids and tissues (e.g., nutrients from digested food pass through the wall of the small intestine into the blood).

accessible   Available to obtain.

accessory   Helping.

accredited   Attested and approved as meeting prescribed standards.

accuracy   How close a measurement is to the actual value.

accurate   Exact, correct, or precise.

acids   Substances that cause the urine to have an acid pH.

acquired immunodeficiency syndrome (AIDS)   Late stages of HIV infection; characterized by secondary infections.

acquired   Refers to a condition, disease, or characteristic that began after birth.

actin   A protein present in all cells and in muscle tissue; plays a role in contraction.

active immunity   Protection that occurs when a body produces its own antibodies.

ADA   American Dental Association.

adapt   To change, to become suitable, to adjust.

adaptation   Changing to work better.

adequate Enough, sufficient.

administrative Pertaining to processing, such as handling of paperwork, that assists in patient care and supports the physician.

admit To let someone in, take in.

adolescent Pertaining to the period of life between childhood and maturity.

aerobic Requiring oxygen.

afebrile Referring to temperature within a normal range.

agency An administrative division of a government or international organization.

agent A person or business authorized to act on another's behalf.

agglutination Clumping together (e.g., red blood cells clump together).

aggressiveness Tendency to start fights and quarrels or to attack without reason.

airborne Articles that float in the air.

ala Outer side of the nostril.

alginate Material for making impressions.

alignment Keeping the body in proper position—in a straight line without twisting.

alimentary canal Long muscular tube beginning at the mouth and ending at the anus.

alleles Forms of a gene that influence a trait or set of traits.

alveolar-capillary Pertaining to air sacs in the lungs.

Alzheimer's disease Type of dementia that causes the death of brain cells and subsequent impairment of thinking and memory.

ambulation devices Canes, crutches, walkers, or other equipment that help a patient to walk.

ambulation Walking.

ambulatory Serving patients who are able to walk.

amino acids Any of a large number of compounds found in living cells that contain carbon, oxygen, hydrogen, and nitrogen, and join together to form proteins.

amniotic fluid Liquid that surrounds the fetus during pregnancy.

amplify To increase or elevate a sound (e.g., the ossicles of the ear amplify sound waves).

amputation Removal of a body part.

amylase An enzyme in saliva and pancreatic juice that breaks down starch into simple sugars.

anaerobic Able to grow and function without oxygen.

anatomical position The position with the body erect with the arms at the sides and the palms forward.

anatomy The science dealing with the structure of animals and plants.

anesthesia Loss of feeling or sensation.

annoyance Irritation (e.g., to feel irritated with a co-worker or patient).

anorexia nervosa Loss of appetite with serious weight loss. It is considered a mental disorder.

antagonist Something that works against.

anterior Located in the front; opposite of posterior (e.g., the abdominal wall is anterior to the back).

antibiotics Substances that slow growth of or destroy microorganisms.

antigen Foreign matter that causes the body to produce antibodies.

antiseptic Substance that slows or stops the growth of microorganisms.

antitoxin Substance that provides immunity to a toxin.

anus Outlet from which the body expels solid waste.

anxiety A feeling of worry and fear that causes physical symptoms, such as sweating, and stress.

apex Pointed end of something (for example, the pointed end of the heart is called the apex of the heart).

apical foramen Opening in the apex.

apparatus Equipment needed to perform a task. For example, blood pressure apparatus includes a blood pressure cuff and a stethoscope.

appearance The way someone or something looks.

appendicular Pertaining to any body part added to the axis (e.g., arms and legs are attached to the axis of the body).

applicant A person applying for a job.

apprenticeship The act of learning a trade or occupation through experience.

appropriate Suitable, correct.

arrhythmia An irregular pulse rate.

arteriosclerosis Condition of hardening of the arteries.

artifacts Unwanted marks on an electrocardiogram.

asepsis Sterile condition, free from all germs.

aseptic Free from the living germs of disease.

aseptic technique Method used to make the environment, the worker, and the patient as germ-free as possible.

aspirate Remove substances.

aspiration Withdrawal of a fluid.

asymptomatic Without visible symptoms.

atherosclerosis Condition of hardening of the arteries due to fat deposits that narrow the space blood flows through.

attachment A file linked to an e-mail message.

attention deficit hyperactivity disorder A mental illness characterized by inattention, hyperactivity, and impulsiveness; diagnosed most often in children.

audiology The study of hearing disorders.

auditing Formal checking for correctness.

augmented Increased (e.g., augmented voltage leads show an increase in graph size).

auscultation The act of listening, either directly or through a stethoscope or other instrument, to sounds within the body as a method of diagnosis.

autoclaves Sterilizers that use steam under pressure to kill all forms of bacteria on fomites (objects that pathogens live on and can transfer infection).

automated Method of lab testing that uses equipment to perform a series of steps, as compared to a manual method.

autopsy Medical procedure after death to determine the cause of death.

axes Reference lines that mark the borders of a graph; graphs may have two or more axes (singular, axis).

axial Pertaining to the central structures of the body (e.g., vertebrae, skull, ribs, and sternum).

axillary Referring to the armpit.

axis A center point that can be rotated around.

B

barriers Items that prevent infectious material from contacting surface.

baseline A number, graph, or indication to use as a guideline. A measurement taken at a later time may differ from the baseline, indicating a possible cause for concern.

benefits Payment and assistance based on an agreement.

biases Tendencies; prejudices.

biconcave Having a depressed surface on both sides.

bingeing Eating excessively.

binocular Having two eyepieces.

biohazard Biological materials or infectious agents that may cause harm to human, animal, or environmental health.

bipolar disorder   A mental illness that causes unusual shifts in a person's mood, energy, and ability to function; also known as manic-depressive disorder.

birth defects   Defects present at birth.

blind carbon copy   An e-mail feature that allows a person to send an e-mail to multiple people without them seeing the other receivers' e-mail addresses.

blood pressure (BP)   Highest and lowest pressure of the blood pushing against the walls of the arteries.

bloodborne   Carried in the blood.

bolus   A soft rounded ball, especially of chewed food.

boundaries   Legal limits (e.g., you may know how to perform a task, but you may not do it because you are limited by your license, certification, registration, or rules and regulations).

bounding   Leaping, strong, or forceful (e.g., a very strong pulse is a bounding pulse).

bradycardia   Pulse rate below 60 beats per minute.

brittle   Fragile, easy to break.

budget   An amount of money allocated for a particular purpose.

bulk   A greater amount.

C

calcify   To harden by forming calcium deposits.

calculated   Figured out.

calibration   Standard measure (e.g., each line on a thermometer or a ruler is a calibration).

calorie   Unit of measurement of the fuel value of food.

capitation   Payment to provide care for a set number of people.

carbon copy   An e-mail feature that allows a person to send a copy of an e-mail to another person.

carbon dioxide   A gas, heavier than air; a waste product from the body.

cardiac   Relating to the heart.

cardiopulmonary   Having to do with the heart and lungs.

career   A profession; a person's life work.

career plan   A strategy for a person's growth as a professional.

caries   Decay.

cartilage   Tough connective tissue; forms pads at end of bones, is found in the nasal septum and external ear, and forms the major portion of the embryonic skeleton.

catheters   Tubes inserted into body opening or cavity.

cell membrane   Thin, soft layer that surrounds the cell and holds it together.

cell   Smallest structural section in the body that is capable of independent functioning.

cellulose   The primary component of plant cell walls which provides the fiber and bulk necessary for optimal functioning of the digestive tract.

Celsius   Measure of heat; in medicine a Celsius thermometer is sometimes used to measure body heat. Also called centigrade.

cementum   Hard, thin covering or shell covering root of tooth.

central processing unit   The part of a computer that interprets and carries out instructions.

cerebrospinal fluid   Liquid that flows through and around brain tissue.

cerebrovascular accidents (CVA)   Complete or partial loss of blood flow to brain tissue caused by blood vessel spasms, intracranial bleeding, and/or obstruction of the blood vessels in the brain.

certification   A process by which a person is made able to do a job, and recognized as such.

certified   A person who has received a certificate that shows he or she demonstrates understanding.

cervix   Neck (e.g., the cervix of the uterus is the neck of the uterus).

chain of infection   A chain of events all interconnected is required for an infection to spread.

characterized   Distinguished by; refers to a trait or quality.

chart   To write observations or records of patient care.

chiropractic   The method of adjusting the segments of the spinal column.

cholesterol   A type of lipid, or fat, found in the body; produced by the liver or eaten in food.

chromosomes   Structures that contain coiled and condensed portions of the cell's DNA.

chronic   Continuing over many years or for a long time (e.g., chronic illness).

chyme   Creamy semifluid mixture of food and digestive juices.

cilia   Hairlike projections that move rhythmically.

circulation   Continuous one-way movement of blood through the heart and blood vessels to all parts of the body.

civil law   The body of law governing certain relationships between people, such as marriage, contracts, and torts (injuries).

clammy   Moist, cold skin.

classify   To put like items together.

clerical   Of or pertaining to keeping records, filing, typing, or other general office tasks.

clumped   Stuck together.

coding   Identifying items to be filed according to particular categories, such as surgical or laboratory.

cohesiveness   State of being well-integrated or unified.

co-insurance   A percentage the subscriber is required to pay of every medical bill.

colitis   Inflammation of the colon.

collaborate   To work together.

coma   Deep sleep; unconscious state for a long period of time.

commitment   A pledge or promise.

communicable   Capable of passing directly or indirectly from one person or thing to another.

communication   Act of exchanging information.

compensation   Payment.

competent   Capable or able to perform a skill or task.

complex   Having two or more related parts.

comply   To follow directions, do what you are asked to do.

components   Parts or elements of a whole; an ingredient.

composed   Formed by putting many parts together.

compressions   Pumps.

compromise   A settlement of differences between parties by each party agreeing to give up something that it wants.

compromising   Giving up something important.

compulsions   In obsessive-compulsive disorder, behaviors or rituals that develop in response to the anxiety caused by obsessive thoughts.

concave   Curved inward, depressed; dented.

concentrated   Increased strength, strong solution.

conception Occurs when the male sperm fertilizes the female ovum and a new organism begins to develop.

concisely   In a brief manner; to express in a few words.

confidential   Private; personal; restricted; secret

conflict   A contradiction, fight, or disagreement.

congenital   conditions Existing at or before birth usually through heredity, as a disorder.

connective tissue   Tissue specialized to bind together and support other tissues.

consecutive   Following one after the other.

consistency   Thickness.

constipation   Infrequent or difficult emptying of the bowel.

consultant   A person who gives professional or expert advice.

contacts   Place where surface of teeth touch.

contaminated   Soiled, unclean, not suitable for use.

contingency   Event that may occur but is not intended or likely to happen.

continuity of care   Assurance that an updated, relevant "snapshot" of the patient's health information is available to any and all clinicians at time of encounter.

continuum   Progression from start (birth) to finish (death).

contraceptives   Items that serve to prevent pregnancy.

contract   To shorten, to draw together; muscles shorten when you flex a body part.

contraction   One that occurs when a muscle fiber lengthens or shortens.

contracts   A legally binding exchange of promises or an agreement between parties that the law will enforce.

controlled experiments   Experiments in which only one factor, or variable, is changed.

contusion   Condition in which the skin is bruised, swollen, and painful, but is not broken.

convalescence   The gradual recovery of health and strength after illness.

convents   Establishments of nuns.

converse   Talk, have a conversation.

convex   Raised.

convey   To say, tell, or express.

coordination   State of harmonized action, such as eye and hand coordination.

co-payment   A set amount the subscriber pays for each medical service.

coping   Handling difficult situations.

corporal   Bodily. For example, corporal punishment involves hitting or harming the body.

courteous   Polite; considerate toward others.

cover letter   A letter that introduces you to a potential employer.

cover page   The first page of a fax.

credible   Worthy of belief or confidence; trustworthy.

criminal law   The body of law that defines criminal offenses, deals with the apprehension, charging, and trial of suspected persons, and fixes penalties applicable to convicted offenders.

crouch   To stoop, using the large muscles of the legs to help maintain balance.

crutch   A support used by physically disabled people as an aid in walking. It usually fits under the armpit and is often used in pairs.

cusps   Pointed or rounded raised areas on the surface of the tooth.

custodial   Marked by watching and protecting rather than seeking to cure.

cycle   Repeating steps (e.g., a wash cycle).

cylinder   Long, narrow, circular container.

cystitis   Inflammation of the urinary bladder.

cytoplasm   The liquid within the cell that surrounds the nucleus and other parts of the cell.

D

data   Information.

debilitating   Causing weakness or impairment.

decade   Period of 10 years.

decay   Breaking down; rot.

deciduous Falling out (e.g., primary teeth fall out to make room for permanent teeth).

decimal A number containing a decimal point.

decompose To decay; to break down.

decontamination Removal of unclean matter and living organisms.

deductible An amount the subscriber must pay before the insurance begins to pay.

defamatory Statement that causes injury to another's reputation.

defecation The pushing of solid material from the bowel.

defibrillator A device that administers an electric shock to restore normal heartbeat.

deficiency Shortage (e.g., a deficient diet causes the body to function poorly because it is missing an important element).

deficient Lacking something (e.g., a deficient diet causes the body to function poorly because it is missing an important element).

definitive Clear, without question, exacting (e.g., when giving emergency care, each treatment should be done in a definitive manner).

dehydration Severe loss of fluid from tissue and cells.

delegation To give another person responsibility for doing specific task.

delinquent Late.

denominators The bottom numbers of fractions.

dentition Natural teeth in the dental arch.

dentures False teeth.

deoxyribonucleic acid A molecule found in all living cells that contains information for building proteins and influencing traits.

designate To appoint or determine.

designated Chosen for a specific purpose.

deteriorate Break down.

deviations Departures from a standard or norm.

diabetes mellitus Condition that develops when the body cannot change sugar into energy; there is an insufficient amount of insulin, leading to an increased amount of sugar in the blood.

diagnosis Identification of a disease or condition.

diagnostic Pertaining to the determination of the nature of a disease or injury by examining (e.g., using x-ray and laboratory tests).

dialysis Process of removing waste from body fluids.

diarrhea Passage of watery stool at frequent intervals.

diastolic pressure Lowest pressure against the blood vessels of the body. It is measured between contractions.

diathermy The use of electric currents to produce heat in body tissues, usually as an aid to healing.

digestion The process of making food absorbable by dissolving it and breaking it down into simpler chemical compounds that occurs in the living body chiefly through the action of enzymes secreted into the alimentary canal.

dignity The quality of value and worth.

Diluent (dilutant) Liquid added to powder that dissolves the powder.

directive Something that serves to guide or impel towards an action or goal.

disbursement Payment.

discharging The act of releasing or allowing to leave.

discipline A branch of instruction or learning, such as cardiology.

disease Any change in the normal structure or function of the body.

disinfection Process of freeing from microorganisms by physical or chemical means.

dismantles Takes apart.

disorientation State of being confused about time, place, and identity of persons and objects.

disoriented Being confused about time, place, or identity of persons and objects.

dispense To distribute or pass out.

disposition Act of disposing of (e.g., a person desires that his or her monies be given to an organization after his or her death).

dissection Act or process of dividing, taking apart.

distal Farthest from the point of attachment.

distension Stretched out; bloated.

distress Great pain or suffering.

distribute To deliver.

diuretics Drugs that increase urine output.

diverticulitis Inflammation of the small sacs in the wall of the colon.

division The process of separating into parts; the operation opposite of multiplication.

document Written record.

documentation A record of something, such as a patient's progress.

dominant Shows influence or control.

dressings Gauze pads that are used to cover a wound.

droplet A small drop of fluid.

drug addiction The uncontrolled use of a drug.

drug Any chemical substance that changes a person's physical or psychological state.

duct Narrow, round tube that carries secretions from a gland.

durable power of attorney A type of advance medical directive in which legal documents provide the power of attorney (the authorization to act on someone else's behalf in a legal or business matter) to another person in the case of an incapacitating medical condition.

dynamics Motivating or driving forces.

dysfunction Impaired or abnormal functioning.

E

edema Swelling; abnormal or excessive collection of fluid in the tissues. Usually, the swelling is in the hands, ankles, legs, or abdomen.

efficiency Ability to accomplish a job with the least possible difficulty.

EKG/ECG Graphic record of the electrical currents produced by the heart.

elastic Easily stretched.

electrocardiograph Instrument that records electric currents produced by the heart.

elements The basic assumptions or principles of a subject.

eligibility The quality or state of being qualified.

elimination Process of expelling or removing, especially of waste products from the body.

embryo Living human being during the first 8 weeks of development in the uterus.

embryonic Pertaining to the embryo.

emesis Vomit.

encephalitis Inflammation of the brain.

endometrium Interlining of the uterus.

endowments Gifts of property or money given to a group or organization.

enemas Solution introduced into the rectum.

ensure To make certain.

enterotoxin Poisonous substance that is produced in, or originates in, the contents of the intestine.

entrepreneur A person who organizes and manages a business.

environment Surroundings we live in. Environmental disease can occur in any area around us (e.g., hospital, restaurants, public places, home, school).

environmental sanitation   Methods used to keep the environment clean and to promote health.

enzyme   Substance that causes a change to occur in other substances.

epidemics   Diseases affecting many people at the same time.

epidermis   Outer layer of skin.

epigastric   Pertaining to the area over the pit of the stomach.

epilepsy   Chronic disease of the nervous system.

episodes   Events in a series.

epithelial   Pertaining to covering of the internal and external organs of the body.

equilibrium   State of balance.

equipment   Instruments, machines, or items used to perform a task.

ergonomic   Related to the study of the work environment.

erupt   Push through.

essential   Necessary (e.g., certain food elements are necessary for the body's functions).

estimate   Determine approximate value of a number.

estrogen   Female hormone.

ethics   Social values; conduct; description of what is right and wrong

ethylene oxide   Gas that kills living microorganisms.

euthanize   To painlessly end the life or permit the death of a hopelessly sick or injured animal or individual for reasons of mercy.

evacuated   Emptied out.

evacuation Removal.

excellence   The quality of having outstanding qualities.

excreted   Thrown off or eliminated as waste material.

excretion   Process of eliminating waste material.

exorcise   To force out evil spirits.

expiration/exhalation   Process of forcing air out of the body during respiration.

exploitation   To use another person for profit or enjoyment.

exposed   Left unprotected.

expressed contracts   Contracts in which terms are written out in the document.

extemporaneous   Completed with little preparation.

extract   Identify and take out or emphasize.

extremities   Arms, legs, hands, and feet.

F

facilitator   A person responsible for leading or coordinating a group.

facilities   Places designed or built to serve a special function (e.g., hospital, clinic, doctor's office).

facsimile/fax machine   A device that sends and receives printed pages or images as electronic signals over telephone lines.

Fahrenheit   Measure of heat; in medicine a Fahrenheit thermometer is often used to measure body heat.

fairness   Applying good rules equally to all people.

familiar   Known.

faulty   Defective or imperfect.

febrile   Referring to elevated temperature.

feces   Solid waste that is evacuated from the body through the anus.

feedback   Information received as a result of something done or said.

fetus   Infant developing in the uterus after the first three months until birth.

FICA   Federal Insurance Contribution Act.

fixation   Repair or fix.

flammable   Catches fire easily or burns quickly.

flatulence   Excessive gas in the stomach and intestines that causes discomfort.

flexibility   The ability to easily bend.

flushed   Showing reddening of the skin.

formula   Accepted rule (e.g., a math formula and a baby formula are both guidelines or rules).

foster   To develop; to promote; to stimulate.

fracture   Broken bone.

frayed   Worn or tattered (e.g., electrical cords may be worn, causing wires to be exposed).

friction   Disagreement because of a difference of opinion.

full time   Describes a job requiring between 32 and 40 hours per week.

function   Action or work of tissues, organs, or body parts (e.g., the heart's function is to pump blood).

functional stress   Stress to tooth caused by its normal function (e.g., force of pressure when biting something hard).

functions   Action or work of tissues, organs, or body parts (e.g., the heart's function is to pump blood).

G

gait belt   A safety device used to move a patient from one place to another; also used to help hold up a weak person while they walk.

gamma globulin   Substance that acts as an antibody to increase immunity.

ganglia   Mass of nerve tissue composed of nerve cell bodies. Ganglia lie outside the brain and spinal cord.

gastrointestinal   Pertaining to the stomach and intestine.

gauge   Standard scale for measurement.

generalized   Affecting all of the body.

generic   Major group (e.g., heart disease or skin disease).

genes   A portion of DNA that contains instructions for a trait.

genome   The complete copy of the body's DNA.

geriatric   Pertaining to old age.

germicidals   Solutions that kill most bacteria.

gestures   Motions of a part of the body to express feelings or emotions (e.g., nodding the head yes or no).

goals   Aims, purposes, or intentions.

graphic chart   A visual record of data in graphic or tabular form.

gravity   Natural force or pull toward the earth. In the body, the center of gravity is usually the center of the body.

Greenwich time   Standard time, a 12-hour clock.

gross pay   Money earned before deductions are removed.

guarding techniques   Ways to protect a patient when he or she is being moved.

gurney   A stretcher on wheels.

H

harass   To behave in an offensively annoying or manipulative way.

hazardous   Dangerous.

heart block   Interference with the conduction of the electrical impulses of the heart that is either partial or complete.

HEDIS   Health Plan Employer Data and Information System; an organization that provides quality care guidelines.

heel   The part of the hand between the palm and the wrist.

Heimlich maneuver   Forceful upward thrust on the abdomen, between the sternum and the navel.

hematoma   Collection of blood beneath the skin.

hemoglobin   An iron-containing protein in red blood cells that combines reversibly with oxygen and transports it from the lungs to body tissues.

hemorrhage   Large amount of bleeding.

heparinized   Containing heparin, an anticoagulant.

hepatitis C (HVC)   Bloodborne viral disease that affects the liver; transmitted by blood exposure, sharing needles, or from infected mother to infant; rarely transmitted by sexual contact.

hereditary   Passed from parent to child.

heredity   Characteristics passed from parent to child.

hernia   Pertaining to projection through an abnormal opening in the wall of a body cavity.

heterogeneous   Different in kind; unlike.

holistic   Pertaining to the whole; considering all factors.

homeostasis   A state of balance, when vital signs are within normal limits.

hormones   Protein substances secreted by an endocrine gland directly into the blood.

horseplay   Rowdy behavior; acting inappropriately in a work environment.

HOSA (formerly Health Occupations Students of America)   The student organization for health occupation students at the secondary, postsecondary, adult, and college level.

host   The organism from which a microorganism takes nourishment. The microorganism gives nothing in return and causes disease or illness.

hostility   Unfriendliness; ill will toward another.

Human immunodeficiency virus (HIV)   Virus that infects cells of the immune system, reducing the immune system's ability to fight disease; transmitted by blood exposure, sexual contact, sharing needles, or from infected mother to infant.

humidity   Wetness, or moisture.

hydroculator pad   A moist heat pack treatment.

hydroencephaly   Excessive accumulation of cerebrospinal fluid in the brain, often leading to increased brain size and other brain trauma.

hydrotherapy   The use of water (hot, cold, steam, or ice) to relieve discomfort and promote physical well-being.

hygiene   The practice of keeping clean.

hypertension   High blood pressure.

hypotension   Low blood pressure.

hypothermia   Below-normal temperature.

hypothesis   An explanation for an observation that is based on scientific research and that can be tested.

I

idolizing   Loving to excess.

ileitis   Inflammation of the ileum (the lower three-fifths of the small intestine).

immunizations   Substances given to make disease organisms harmless to the patient; may be given orally or by injection (e.g., tetanus, polio).

impaction   Any tooth that does not erupt when it should (e.g., tooth blocked by bone and/or tissue, keeping it under the surface of the gum). Also, being tightly wedged into a part (e.g., fecal material wedged into the bowel that requires mechanical means to remove).

impatience   Unwillingness to tolerate.

impending   About to happen.

implement   To accomplish; make it work.

implied contracts   Contracts in which some terms are not specifically stated, but are understood by the parties based on the nature of the transaction.

impulses   Measures of electrical activity to the heart tissue recorded on a graph.

incontinent   Unable to control the bowel or bladder.

indexing   Organizing items in the order they are to be filed.

inferior   Lower (e.g., one product is inferior in quality to another product).

infirmity   Unsound or unhealthy state of being.

inflated   To swell or fill up with air.

informed consent   The legal condition in which a person agrees to something, after he or she understands all the facts and implications of an action or event.

infuses   Flows into the body by gravity (e.g., IV drips through a tube into the body).

ingestion   Take in by mouth.

initial   First.

injectable   Medication given by needle.

inoculation   Instill, to put into the body.

input   To enter data into a computer for processing.

inspiration/inhalation   Process of breathing in air during respiration.

instruments   Tools and measuring devices.

insulin   Hormone secreted by the pancreas; essential for maintaining the correct blood sugar level.

insulin shock   Condition caused by too much insulin.

interdependent   Depending on each other.

interdisciplinary   Involving two or more disciplines.

interests   Something that concerns, draws the attention of, or arouses the curiosity of a person.

interlace   Put between.

Internet   A worldwide computer network with information on many subjects.

interproximal surfaces   Sides between teeth.

interstitial fluid   Liquid that fills the space between most of the cells of the body.

intervention   The act of interfering to modify an outcome.

intoxication   State of poisoning or becoming poisoned.

intracranial   Inside the skull.

intraoral   Within the oral cavity.

intravenously   Directly into a vein.

invasive   Entering the body.

involuntary   Not under control (e.g., muscle twitching).

irregularities   Different than normal.

irreversible   Cannot be changed; condition will remain the same.

isolated   Limited in contact with others.

J

jaundice   Yellowing of the whites of the eyes, skin, and mucous membranes.

job outlook   The expectation or prospect of a particular job in the future.

K

keywords   Significant or descriptive words.

kick buckets   Metal buckets on wheels that can be kicked out of the way.

L

labeling   Describing a person with a word that limits them (e.g., lazy, stupid).

laceration   Wound or tear of the skin.

lacrimal   Pertaining to tears.

lactation   Body's process of producing milk to feed newborns.

lateral   Relating to the sides or side of.

law   A rule of conduct or procedure recognized by a community as binding or enforceable by authority.

lawsuits   A legal action started by one person against another based on a complaint that the person failed to perform a legal duty.

laxative   Liquid or pill that causes evacuation of the bowel.

leadership   Ability to influence or lead.

legal disability   A person has a disability for legal purposes if he has a physical or mental impairment which has a substantial and long-term adverse effect on his ability to carry out normal day-to-day activities.

legal record   Record that can be used in a law suit (e.g., the patient chart).

legible   Capable of being read easily.

legislation   A law or body of laws.

leisure   Time free from the demands of work.

length   The measure of something from end to end.

liable   Legally responsible.

licensure   A process by which a governmental authority gives permission to a person or health care organization to operate or to work in a profession.

limb   Arm, leg.

lipid   Fat.

listlessness   A state of being without energy.

living will   A will in which the signer requests not to be kept alive by medical life-support systems in the event of a terminal illness.

load   Weight of an object or person that is to be moved.

localized   Affecting one area of the body.

lumen   Opening (e.g., opening in a tube or needle).

lymphocytes   Type of white cell.

M

magnify   Enlarge.

maintain   Keep up.

major depressive disorder   Mental illness characterized by a combination of symptoms that include prolonged sadness and that interfere with a person's ability to undertake everyday activities.

malaise   Weakness or discomfort.

malfunctioning   Not working as it is supposed to.

malignant   Cancerous.

malnutrition   Poor nutrition caused by an insufficient or poorly balanced diet or by a medical condition.

malpractice   Failure of a professional person, as a physician, to render proper services through reprehensible ignorance or negligence or through criminal intent, especially. when injury or loss follows.

managed care   A health care plan or system that seeks to control medical costs by contracting with a network of providers and by requiring preauthorization for visits to specialists.

mandates   Commands, orders.

manual   Book with guidelines.

mass   The amount of matter in an object.

masticate   Chew.

maternal   Relating to the mother or from the mother.

matures   Becomes fully developed.

mechanism   Process or a series of steps that achieve a result.

memorandum   A short note written to help a person remember something or to remind a person to do something.

meninges   Lining of the brain.

meningitis   Inflammation of the membrane covering the brain.

menstruation   Cyclic deterioration of the endometrium.

mental illness   Health condition that changes a person's thoughts, emotions, and behavior and that affects the person's ability to undertake daily functions.

mentor   An experienced person who can offer advice and guidance.

metabolic   Pertaining to the total of all the physical and chemical changes that take place in living organisms and cells.

metabolism   The body's process of using food to make energy and use nutrients.

metabolize   To break down substances in cells to obtain energy.

meterstick   A measuring stick one meter long that is marked off in centimeters and usually millimeters.

microbiology   The branch of biology dealing with the structure, function, uses, and modes of existence of microscopic organisms.

microns   Units equaling one millionth of a meter.

microorganisms   Tiny organism, such as a fungi, protists, or bacteria, that can only be seen under a microscope.

microscopic   Too small to be seen by the eye but large enough to be seen through a microscope.

millimeters   Measure of length.

minerals   Inorganic elements that occur in nature; essential to every cell.

minor   Underage the legal age of full responsibility.

minute   Exceptionally small.

misrepresentations   Untruths; lies.

mission statement   A summary describing the aims, values, and overall plan of an organization or individual.

mixed numbers   Numbers with whole numbers and a fraction (e.g., $6\frac{1}{4}$, $7\frac{2}{3}$).

monasteries   Homes for men following religious standards.

monocular   Having one eyepiece.

monocytes   Large single-nucleus white cells.

monogamous   Having a sexual relationship with only one partner during a period of time.

mucosa   Thin lining on the inside of the intestines.

Multiplication   Finding the product of two numbers.

myosin   A protein in muscles that helps them contract.

N

narrative   A story or account of events.

neglect   To ignore or not provide for.

nephron   Functional part of the kidney that filters liquid waste.

net pay   Money earned after deductions are removed.

neurological   Pertaining to the nervous system.

neurologist   A physician specializing in the nerves and nervous system.

neuron   Nerve; includes the cell and the long fiber coming from the cell.

nondominant hand   Hand that is not used for writing or other tasks.

noninvasive   Not involving penetration of the skin.

nonpathogenic   Not disease causing.

nonwhole numbers   Numbers with decimals (e.g., 6.25, 9.85).

nosocomial infection   An infection acquired while in a health care setting, such as a hospital.

notation   The act of noting, marking, or setting down in writing.

nucleotides   Subunits of DNA that each contain a phosphate, sugar, and base.

nucleus   The part of a cell that is vital for its growth, metabolism, reproduction, and transmitted characteristics.

numerators   The top numbers of fractions.

nutrients   Substances that the cell needs in order to function.

O

obesity   Extreme fatness; abnormal amount of fat on the body.

objective   Relating to a symptom or condition perceived by someone other than the person affected.

obligation   Moral responsibility.

observant   Quick to see and understand.

Observation(s)   Act of watching; using the senses and other means to get information about surroundings.

obsessions   In obsessive-compulsive disorder, undesirable thoughts that occur constantly, causing anxiety.

obsolete   Out of date.

obstetrics   The branch of medical science concerned with childbirth.

obstruction   Blockage or clogging.

occult   Hidden, unseen.

ombudsman   A social worker, nurse, or trained volunteer who ensures that patients are properly cared for and respected.

omission   Neglect of duty.

opportunistic infections   Infections that occur when the immune system is weakened. Common organisms that the body normally resists cause infection.

oral   Referring to the mouth.

orthopedics   The medical specialty concerned with correcting problems with the skeletal system.

osseous   Bonelike.

ossicles   Three small bones in the middle ear: incus, stapes, and malleus.

outpatients   Patients/clients who do not require hospitalization but are under a physician's care.

output   To produce information; turn out

overexposure   Too much contact with radiation.

ovum   Female reproductive cell that when fertilized by the male develops into a new organism.

oxidation   The mixing together of oxygen and another element.

oxygen   Element in the atmosphere that is essential for maintaining life.

oxygenated   Containing oxygen.

P

palpation   Examine by feeling for unusual or abnormal conditions.

parallel   Same direction and a distance, so that two points do not touch.

paralysis   Loss of sensation and muscle function.

paranoia   Unfounded or irrational distrust of other people.

parasites   Organisms obtaining nourishment from other organisms they are living in or on.

parasitic   Pertaining to an organism that lives in or on another organism, taking nourishment from it.

parenteral   Not in the digestive system (e.g., injections are parenterally administered).

part time   Describes a job requiring fewer than 32 hours per week.

passive immunity   Protection that occurs when a body receives antibodies from another source.

pasteurization   To heat food for a period of time to destroy certain microorganisms.

pathogenic   Disease causing.

Patient's/Client's Bill of Rights   Document written by the American Hospital Association outlining expected patient/client rights while in a hospital.

payroll   A list of employees to be paid a specific amount.

penetrates   Enters or passes through (e.g., a fractured bone passes through the skin).

percentages   Portions in relation to a whole (e.g., 65%, 22%).

periapical   Around the apex (e.g., of the tooth).

pericardial fluid   Liquid that surrounds the heart.

perineal   Region between the vulva and anus in a female, or between the scrotum and anus in a male.

periodic   Occurring at regular intervals.

peripheral   Situated away from a central structure.

peristalsis   Progressive, wavelike motion that occurs involuntarily in hollow tubes of the body.

peritoneal cavity   Area of the body containing the liver, stomach, intestines, kidneys, urinary bladder, and reproductive organs.

peritoneal fluid   Liquid in the peritoneal cavity.

personnel   People who work in an establishment; a personnel office is where a worker goes to apply for a job.

pertinent   Relating directly to the matter at hand; relevant.

phagocytes   Cells that surround, eat, and digest microorganisms and cellular waste.

philosophy   Theory; a general principle used for a specific purpose.

phlebotomy   Practice of opening a vein by incision or puncture to remove blood.

phobia   An irrational fear of an object or event that poses little or no actual risk.

Physicians' Desk Reference (PDR)   A commonly used reference book that provides information about drugs, drug manufacturers, emergency phone numbers, and more.

physiological   Pertaining to normal body functions.

physiology   The branch of biology dealing with the functions and activities of living organisms and their parts.

pigmentation   Natural color of the skin.

pigmented   Colored; relating to various parts of the body (e.g., iris of the eye, lips, moles, freckles).

plane   A flat surface determined by the position of three points in space.

plaque   Soft deposit of bacteria and bacterial products on teeth.

plasma   Watery, colorless fluid containing leukocytes, erythrocytes, and platelets.

pleural fluid   Liquid that surrounds the lungs.

pneumonia   Inflammation of the lungs.

podiatry   The diagnosis and treatment of foot disorders.

pollutants   Things that contaminate the air (e.g., smoke, smog).

polycythemia   Condition of having too much blood.

polyps   Small tumorlike growths.

porous   Filled with tiny holes.

portfolio   A collection of materials that show you knowledge, abilities, skills, and insights.

posterior   Behind, to the rear, toward the back (e.g., the heel is posterior to the toes).

postmortem   After death.

post-traumatic stress disorder (PTSD)   A mental illness that develops after a terrifying incident that involved physical harm or the threat of harm.

postural supports   Soft restraints used to protect resident.

potential   Possible.

pouch   Small bag or sac.

precision   For multiple measurements of the same thing, how close the values of the measurements are to each other.

predators   Organisms or beings that destroy.

prehistoric   Ancient or prehistoric.

prejudge   To decide or make a decision before having the facts.

prejudices   Judgments or opinions formed before the facts are known.

premium   The periodic payment to Medicare, an insurance company, or a health care plan for health care or prescription drug coverage.

prepaid   Paid ahead of time.

prestige   Influence obtained through success, wealth, or some other source.

preventable   Able to be kept from happening.

primarily   For the most part; chiefly.

primary   First.

primitive   Ancient or prehistoric

principal   First or among the first in importance or rank.

principles   Codes of behavior.

priorities   Those things that are most important.

prioritize   To arrange or deal with in the order of importance.

productivity   The power to reach goals and get results.

professional development   Education for people who have already begun their careers to help them continue to grow.

professional   One who is paid for their work.

progressive   Moving forward, following steps toward an end product.

prohibit   To not allow.

project   To show or reflect

prone   Lying on the stomach.

propensity   A natural inclination or tendency.

proportions   Parts of a whole.

prosthesis   An artificial body part such as a limb, tooth, or eye, used to replace a natural body part and minimize a disability.

protein   Complex compound found in plant and animal tissues, essential for heat, energy, and growth.

protest   An organism belonging to the kingdom that includes protozoans, bacteria, and single-celled algae and fungi.

protrusion   Pushing through.

provider   Physician, physician assistant, nurse practitioner.

proximal   Nearest or next to.

prudent   Careful or cautious.

psychiatric   Pertaining to the mind.

psychiatrist   A medical professional who specializes in the prevention, diagnosis, and treatment of mental illness; has a medical degree (M.D.) and can prescribe medication as part of treatment.

psychiatry   The practice or science of diagnosing and treating mental disorders.

psychological   Pertaining to the mind.

psychologist   A medical professional who specializes in the prevention, diagnosis, and treatment of mental illness; can only use talk therapy for treatment.

psychology   The science of the mind or of mental states and processes.

psychosis   Symptoms of mental illness in which a person experiences thoughts and ideas that are not based on reality; include hallucinations and delusions.

psychotherapy   Treatment method in which a mental health professional and a patient discuss problems and feelings related to a mental illness.

pulse oximetry   Procedure used to determine the oxygen concentration in the hemoglobin of the arterial blood.

purging   Causing oneself to vomit.

pyrexia   Above-normal temperature.

pyrogenic   Producing fever.

Q

quackery   Practice of pretending to cure diseases.

quality of respirations   The amount of air taken into the body and expelled from the body and the effort it takes to do this.

R

radiology   The science dealing with x-rays or nuclear radiation.

radiopaque   Shows as a white material when a fluoroscope x-ray is taken.

range-of-motion (ROM) Measurement of the achievable distance between the flexed position and the extended position of a particular joint or muscle group.

rapport Harmony; a close relationship with another.

rate of respirations The number of respirations per minute

reagents Chemical substances that react to the presence of other substances in the blood and urine.

receptors Nerves that respond to stimuli.

recessive Passive or hidden.

recipient One who receives.

recognition Acknowledgment as being worthy of approval.

recommendations Suggestions.

reconstituting Adding water to a powdered drug.

rectal Referring to the far end of the large intestine just above the anus.

refer To send to.

reflexes Result when a nerve is stimulated and an involuntary action occurs (e.g., touch a hot stove, and the muscles react involuntarily to move the fingers away).

registration A list of individuals on an official record who meet the qualifications for an occupation.

regulate To control or adjust.

rehabilitation Process that helps people who have been disabled by sickness or injury to recover as many of their original abilities for activities of daily living as possible.

reimburse To pay back for something given or spent.

relevant Pertaining to, or having to do with, the patient/client.

reliable Dependable, accurate, honest.

remainder The amount left over after division that is less than a whole number.

rendered Given or provided.

replenish Refill or build up again.

reprimanded Punished.

reproduction Process that takes place in animals to create offspring.

requisitions A formal written request for something needed.

resident Able to protect itself.

residual Left over.

resistance Ability of the body to protect itself from disease.

resorption Loss of a substance or bone.

respiration The inhalation and exhalation of air, or breathing.

respiratory Pertaining to or serving for breathing.

responsibility One's answerability to an employer in areas such as dependability and honesty.

restorative To return to as close to normal conditions as possible.

restraints A piece of equipment or device that restricts a patient's ability to move.

restrict To keep within limits; to confine.

resultant Resulting from an action.

resuscitation Bringing back to life, reviving.

retention Keeping elements within the body that are normally eliminated (e.g., waste products such as urine and feces).

rheostat Control for flow of electric current.

rhythm of respirations The regularity, or irregularity, of breathing.

rickettsiae Parasitic microorganisms that live on another living organism and cause disease.

roles A position, responsibility, or duty.

rotary Move in a circular fashion.

S

sacral region The area where the sacrum is located; forms the tail end of the spinal column.

salmonella A rod-shaped bacterium found in the intestine that can cause food poisoning, gastroenteritis, and typhoid fever.

salutation A greeting (e.g., Dear Sir).

saprophytes Organisms that live on dead organic matter.

saturated Soaked; filled to capacity.

saturating Soak.

scales Instruments with marks that help to determine weight or mass.

scattering Spreading in many directions, dispersing.

schizophrenia Mental illness in which a person loses touch with reality; often characterized by hallucinations, such as voices that other people cannot hear, and delusions.

scientific methods Processes scientists use to answer questions.

scope of practice A legal set of directives developed by a state board that governs practice for a health care professional.

seating Putting firmly in place to prevent moving.

sebaceous Pertaining to fatty secretions.

secretion Producing and expelling a special substance (e.g., sebaceous glands secrete oil; salivary glands secrete saliva).

sedate Calm.

sedentary Immobilized; does not move around very much.

seizure Involuntary muscle contraction and relaxation.

self-esteem Belief in oneself.

semen Fluid from the testes, seminal vesicles, prostate gland, and bulbourethral glands.

septic arthritis Bacterial inflammation of the joint caused by bloodborne bacteria carried from another place in the body.

serrated Sawlike notches.

service Caring for others.

sex cells Cells that allow reproduction to occur.

shock Convulsion of muscles and extreme stimulation of nerves when an electric current passes through the body.

sloughed Discarded; separated from (e.g., to shed dead cells, as from the outer skin).

soluble Able to break down or dissolve in liquid.

solutions Two or more liquids mixed together.

sorting Separating items to be filed according to the filing system being used, such as alphabetical, numerical, color, chronological, and geographical.

specialties Fields of study or professional work (e.g., pediatrics, orthopedics, obstetrics).

specifications Exact way something should be done.

spermatozoa Male sex cells.

sphincter Circular muscle that allows the opening and closing of a body part (e.g., anus, pylorus).

sphygmomanometer Measuring device used to measure the pressure against the arteries of the body.

spirochetes Slender, coil-shaped organisms.

splints Firm object used to support an unstable body part.

spontaneous Occurring naturally without apparent cause.

spurts To force out in a burst; to squirt.

stability Ability to maintain a balance, both mentally and physically.

stamina Body's strength or energy.

stance The way you stand.

Standard Precautions Guidelines designed to reduce the risk of transmission of microorganisms from recognized and unrecognized sources of infection in the hospital.

sterility Absence of living organism or inability to produce offspring.

sterilized Made free from all living microorganisms.

stethoscope Instrument used to hear sound in the body (e.g., heartbeat, lung sounds, bowel sounds).

stimuli Elements in the external or internal environment that are strong enough to set up a nervous impulse.

stoma Opening; e.g., opening in abdomen in an ostomy.

structure The way that parts of the body are put together.

subcutaneous Beneath the skin.

subjective Relating to a symptom or condition perceived by the patient and not by the examiner.

sufficient Enough.

sulcus Depression, groove, area where gingival tip meets tooth enamel.

superstitious Trusting in magic or chance.

supine Lying on the back.

suppository A solid, conical mass of medicinal substance that melts upon insertion into the rectum.

surgical Repairing or removing a body part by cutting.

susceptible Capable of being affected or infected (e.g., body can be attacked by microorganisms and become ill).

swathe Bandage.

syncope Fainting.

syndrome A number of symptoms occurring together.

systems Coordinated bodies of methods or plans of procedure.

systolic pressure Highest pressure against blood vessels. It is represented by first heart sound or beat heard when taking a blood pressure.

T

tachycardia Pulse rate over 100 beats per minute (for adults).

tasks A function to be performed; job.

teamwork Cooperative effort from a group of people working together for a common purpose.

telemedicine Using electronic communications to exchange medical information from one site to another.

terminal Last or ending.

terminology Specialized terms used in any occupation.

testicles Site of production of the male sex cell.

testosterone Male hormone.

The Health Insurance Portability and Accountability Act (HIPAA) A law that includes regulations ensuring the privacy of patient information.

therapeutic Pertaining to the treatment of disease or injury (e.g., physical therapy, radiology, diet, nursing).

thermotherapy Medical therapy involving the application of heat.

thready Weak, barely felt pulse; thin, like a thread.

tickler file Special file kept to remind you of tasks that need to be done at a certain time.

tissues Group of cells of the same type that act together to perform a specific function.

tomography X-ray technique that produces film of detailed cross sections of tissue.

tone Firmness or tightness.

topical Surface of the body.

tort Under civil law, a wrong committed by one person against another.

toxins   Poisonous substances.

TPR   Stands for "temperature, pulse, respiration."

traditional   Customary beliefs passed from generation to generation.

traits   Genetically determined characteristics or conditions.

transcribe   To make a written copy.

translate   To make understandable.

transmitting   Causing to go from one person to another person.

transversely   In a cross direction.

trauma   Damage to the body caused by an injury, wound, or shock; mental trauma occurs from emotional shock.

trend   General direction or movement.

trochanter   One of the bony prominences toward the near end of the thigh bone (the femur).

tuberculosis   Disease caused by tubercle bacilli; may cause death if untreated.

U

ulcerations   Open areas, or sores.

ultrasound   Medical therapy that uses sound frequencies (above 20 kHz) beyond the limits of human hearing to treat hard-to-reach body areas.

ultraviolet light   An invisible band of radiation at the upper end of the visible light spectrum.

uniformity   A state of being all the same; does not vary.

Universal Precautions   A set of precautions that prevents the transmission of HIV, HBV, HCV, and other bloodborne pathogens when providing health care.

unoxygenated   Lacking oxygen.

urethritis   Inflammation of the urethra.

urology   The study of the urine and urinary organs in health and disease.

username   A unique identifier composed of alphanumeric characters, used as a means of initial identification to gain access to a computer system or Internet Service Provider.

V

vaccines   A weakened bacteria or virus given to a person to build immunity against a disease.

value   Importance, worth.

variables   Any factor that can change or be present in varying amounts.

venipuncture   Puncture of a vein.

vessels   Tubes that carry fluid in the body.

viable   Capable of living.

villi   Tiny projections.

viruses   Genetic material that is surrounded by a protective coat and that can only reproduce inside a host cell; can only be seen under a microscope.

visibility   Ability to see.

vital   A must, essential.

vitality   Ability of an organism to go on living.

vitamins   Group of substances necessary for normal functioning and maintenance of health.

vocational   Pertaining to a particular occupation, business, or profession.

volume   The amount of space that an object or liquid takes up.

voluntary   Under the control of the person (e.g., you voluntarily raise your arm; it does not rise automatically).

W

wages   Money that is paid or received for work or services.

walker   A waist-high four-legged framework of lightweight metal, for use by a weak or disabled person as a support while walking.

waste products   Elements that are unfit for the body's use and are eliminated from the body.

Web site   A group of pages on the Internet developed by a person or organization about a topic.

weight   Measures the force of gravity on an object; varies due to distance between objects and mass.

whole numbers   Numbers that do not contain decimals or fractions (e.g., 1,2 3).

withdrawal   Uncomfortable physical and psychological symptoms that arise when a drug addict stops using a drug.

written consent   Legal document, signed by the patient or his designee, stating that the patient understands any potential medical risks in surgery, experimental treatment, etc.

Z

zygote   Any cell formed by the coming together of two reproductive (sex) cells.

Index

treatment by, 457–458
Psychosis, 449
Psychotherapy, 457–458
PTSD (post traumatic stress disorder), 449
Public Health Department, 29
Puerperal fever, 8
Pulling the load, 801
Pulmonary artery, 349–350
Pulmonary semilunar valve, 352
Pulmonary technicians, 368
Pulmonologists, 367
Pulp of tooth, 856–857
Pulse, 540–544
    apical pulse, 542, 544
    characteristics of, 541
    factors affecting, 541
    location of pulse points, 541
    normal pulse rates, 542
    radial pulse, 542, 543
    rate of pulse, 541, 542
    recording procedure, 548
Pulse oximeters, 545–546
Pulse oximetry, 529, 545–546
Puncture wounds, 815
Purging, 474, 481–482
Purulent drainage, 816
Pushing the load, 801
Pyloric sphincter, 371
Pyrexia, 530
Pyrogenic, 530

Q

Qigong, 170
Quackery, 7
Quad canes, 688
Quality
    of respirations, 547–548
    specimen testing, control for, 755
Quality control, 33
Quinine, 5

R

Rabies, 9
Race, 188–189
    and prejudice, 187
Radial pulse, 542, 543
Radiographs of teeth, 865–868
    mounting dental films, 867–868
Radiologists, 32, 77
Radiology machine, dental, 862
Radiology workers, 76–77
Radiolucent structures, 866
Radiopaque structures, 866
Rales, 548
Range of motion, 678–684
    active ROM, 688
    passive ROM, 688
    procedures for exercises, 679–682
Rapid medical tests, 770
Rapport with co-workers, 183

Rate
    of pulse, 541, 542
    of respirations, 547–548
Rationalization, 183
Reaching, mechanics of, 802
Reaching sticks, 696
Reagents
    labeling of, 751
    urinalysis, strips for, 759–761
Reasonable care, 144
Receiver of communication, 220
Receptionists, 81
Receptors, defined, 390
Recessive alleles, 410
Recipients, 11
    of faxes, 227
Recognition, certification for, 135
Recommendations, 17–18
Recreation therapists, 94
Rectal temperature, 534–535
    procedure for measuring, 538
    thermometers, 531
Rectum, 372
    medications, rectal, 745
Red blood cells (RBCs), 771
    sedimentation rate test, 773
Red Cross, 12–13, 30
Red wounds, 814
Referrals, 31
Reflexes, 424
Refractometers, measuring specific gravity with, 761, 763
Registered medical records administrator (RRA), 84
Registered Nurses (RNs). *See* Nurses
Registration, defined, 134–135
Registration procedures, 248–256, 706–708
    digital paperwork, 250
    filing systems, 251–256
Regulatory agencies, 33, 49
Rehabilitation, 436
    centers, 28
    equipment, 688–696
    senior day care providing, 29
Relevant, defined, 136
Religion
    cultural issues and, 198
    dietary restrictions, 478
    ethics and, 151
    and prejudice, 188
Remainders, 288
Renaissance, medicine in, 7
Renal calculi, 379
Repetitive stress injuries, 671
    computers and, 235
Replication of DNA, 10
Reportable incidents, recognizing, 157–158
Reporting
    injuries, 786
    medical reporting, 238
Reprimands, 20
Reproduction of cells, 321

Photo Credits